What's New in This Edition

■ Expanded coverage of ANSI and Access SQL queries via Visual C++ 4 code.

■ Additional techniques for OLE automation.

■ Information on programming with the new OLE containers.

■ Coverage of OLE Custom Controls, which let you add new features to Visual C++ applications with minimal programming effort.

■ Information on OLE Custom Controls for 32-bit environments.

■ Techniques for using the new data access objects that Microsoft added to Visual C++ to position the product as a direct competitor to Visual Basic. These new techniques make Visual C++'s support of Access, FoxPro, and Paradox for Windows in the desktop database market even more complete.

■ Detailed information on the redistributable 32-bit Microsoft Jet 3.0 database engine, which offers substantially improved performance compared to the 16-bit jet engine.

■ Coverage of Visual C++'s built-in MFC classes, along with AppWizard, to let you quickly create a form to display database information with little or no Visual C++ code. Included is a sample program that actually has no programmer-written code at all.

■ Information on the Microsoft ODBC Administrator application, included with Visual C++, which lets you connect to the Microsoft and Sybase versions of SQL Server and to Oracle client-server relational database management systems.

■ Extensive coverage of building Visual C++ 4 front ends to interface with client-server RDBMSs.

■ Clear examples that illustrate significant development topics, such as crosstab queries, action queries, transaction processing, and record locking.

■ Programming examples and techniques for using Sockets and MAPI services.

Database Developer's Guide

with VISUAL C++™ 4

Second Edition

Peter Hipson
Roger Jennings

SAMS
PUBLISHING

201 West 103rd Street
Indianapolis, Indiana 46290

This book is dedicated to Kathareeya "Katie" Tonyai, a brand new granddaughter. —Peter Hipson

This book is dedicated to the memory of my father, George H. Jennings, Structural Engineer. —Roger Jennings

Copyright © 1996 by Sams Publishing

SECOND EDITION

International Standard Book Number: 0-672-30913-0

Library of Congress Catalog Card Number: 95-72921

99 98 97 96   4 3 2 1

Interpretation of the printing code: the rightmost double-digit number is the year of the book's printing; the rightmost single-digit, the number of the book's printing. For example, a printing code of 96-1 shows that the first printing of the book occurred in 1996.

Composed in AGaramond, Optima, Helvetica, and MCPdigital by Macmillan Computer Publishing

Printed in the United States of America

Publisher and President	*Richard K. Swadley*
Acquisitions Manager	*Greg Wiegand*
Development Manager	*Dean Miller*
Managing Editor	*Cindy Morrow*
Marketing Manager	*John Pierce*
Assistant Marketing Manager	*Kristina Perry*

Acquisitions Editor
Grace Buechlein

Development Editor
Michael Watson

Software Development Specialist
Steve Straiger

Production Editor
Gayle L. Johnson

Copy Editor
Anne Owen

Technical Reviewers
Robert Bogue
Jeff Perkins

Editorial Coordinator
Bill Whitmer

Technical Edit Coordinator
Lynette Quinn

Formatter
Frank Sinclair

Editorial Assistants
Carol Ackerman
Andi Richter
Rhonda Tinch-Mize

Cover Designer
Tim Amrhein

Book Designer
Alyssa Yesh

Production Team Supervisor
Brad Chinn

Production
Steve Adams, Charlotte Clapp, Mike Dietsch, Terri Edwards, Jason Hand, Sonja Hart, Kevin Laseau, Clint Lahnen, Casey Price, Laura Robbins, Bobbi Satterfield, Andrew Stone, Mark Walchle, Todd Wente, Colleen Williams

Indexers
Gina Brown
Tom Dinse

Overview

Contents

II Database and Query Design Concepts

III An Introduction to Database Front-End Design

IV Advanced Programming with Visual C++

V Multiuser Database Applications

Acknowledgments

The authors are indebted to Neil Black of Microsoft's Jet Program Management Group and Stephen Hecht of Microsoft's Jet Development Group for their "Jet Database Engine 2.0 ODBC Connectivity" white paper. This white paper made a substantial contribution to the writing of Chapter 7, "Using the Open Database Connectivity API." You can find this white paper and a number of other works by these authors on the Microsoft Development Library CD. Search for the authors' names.

Special thanks to Microsoft and Steve Serdy at Microsoft Developer Support for their excellent assistance. Steve's help with the Win32 Common Controls was most valuable.

Thanks are also due to Robert Bogue and Jeff Perkins, the technical editors for this book. Jeff's help in getting our references to Microsoft SQL Server 6 up-to-date was most valuable. Thanks also to Grace Buechlein, our acquisitions editor. Grace's professionalism was most valuable when we had problems, and we hope to work with her again. Thanks to Michael Watson, our development editor, for his extra work in making sure that the book presented the very latest information available. Thanks also to Gayle Johnson, our production editor, and to Anne Owen, our copy editor.

About the Authors

Peter Hipson is a developer, consultant, and author. His work is mostly in the Windows arena, but he also pursues work in ODBC, database, and GIS applications. He was a member of the Microsoft beta-test team for QuickC for Windows; Visual C++ 1.0, 1.5, 2.0, and 4.0; Windows 3.0 and 3.1; Windows 95; Windows for Workgroups 3.1 and 3.11; and Windows NT. Peter is the author of Sams Publishing's *Advanced C, What Every Visual C++ 2 Programmer Should Know,* and *Visual C++ Developer's Guide,* as well as Que's *Using QuickC for Windows.* He was a coauthor of *Database Developer's Guide with Visual C++* and *Programming Windows 95 Unleashed,* both from Sams Publishing. He also occasionally writes for the *Windows Technical Journal.* He will be writing a column on database programming in *The Win'95 Magazine,* which will publish its first issue in mid-1996. He also has a column in an Asian magazine on the Internet. Peter has been working with microcomputers since the mid-1970s. He also has many years of experience with IBM mainframes. He is the author of STARmanager, a GIS-type application that assists sales and marketing managers in managing their resources. You may contact Peter via CompuServe (`70444,52`) or the Internet (`phipson@darkstar.mv.com`).

Roger Jennings is a consultant specializing in Windows database, multimedia, and video applications. He was a member of the Microsoft beta-test team for Visual C++ 2.0; Visual Basic 2.0, 3.0, and 4.0; the Professional Extensions for Visual Basic 1.0; Visual Basic for DOS; Microsoft Access 1.0, 1.1, 2.0, and 7; Word for Windows 2.0; the 32-bit versions of Word and Excel; Microsoft Project 4.0 and 4.1; Windows 3.1 and Windows 95; Windows for Workgroups 3.1 and 3.11; Windows NT 3.5, 3.51, and 4.0 Workgroup and Server; the Microsoft ODBC 2.0 and 2.5 drivers; Video for Windows 1.1; and Multimedia Viewer 2.0. Roger is the author of Sams Publishing's *Database Developer's Guide with Visual Basic 4,* upon which much of this book is based. He also wrote *Access 2 Developer's Guide* and *Access 95 Developer's Guide,* both from Sams Publishing, and two other books on Microsoft Access, as well as books devoted to Windows 95, Windows NT, and desktop video production with Windows 95 and Windows NT 3.5x. He also is a contributing editor for Fawcette Technical Publications' *Visual Basic Programmer's Journal.* Roger has more than 25 years of computer-related experience, beginning with his work on the Wang 700 desktop calculator/computer. He has presented technical papers on computer hardware and software to the Academy of Sciences of the former USSR, the Society of Automotive Engineers, the American Chemical Society, and a wide range of other scientific and technical organizations. He is a principal of OakLeaf Systems, a Northern California software consulting firm. You may contact him via CompuServe (`70233,2161`), the Internet (`70233.2161@compuserve.com`), or the Microsoft Network (`Roger_Jennings`).

Introduction

The release of Visual C++ clearly shows that Microsoft is taking the lead in creating C++ development platforms. Visual C++ 4 continues to build on the development platform that the C/C++ program has established. MFC, with versions 2.0, 2.5, 3.0, and 4, offers the C++ programmer an advanced object-oriented methodology to develop applications that are easy to develop and maintain.

Microsoft's OLE and the Common Object Model (COM) are now firmly entrenched as the new compound document standard for Windows, and OLE Automation replaces DDE as the primary means of interapplication communication. Huge system resource consumption by OLE megaservers, typified by Excel and Word, limited the adoption of OLE Automation in commercial database front ends. Windows 95 and Windows NT 3.51 have overcome most resource limitations when running 32-bit OLE applications. Thus, 32-bit Visual C++ programs are likely to be the glue that binds industrial-strength solutions orchestrating members of 32-bit Microsoft Office with OLE Automation. Out-of-process OLE Automation servers, especially the big ones, are not renowned for their speed. Fortunately, there's a trend toward a Pentium on every power-user's desktop, so faster hardware comes to the rescue again. OLE Custom Controls (OLE controls), which are in-process OLE Automation servers, don't suffer from the performance hit associated with the Lightweight Remote Procedure Calls (LRPCs) required by out-of-process servers. Thus, OLE controls typically are as quick as VBXs, which OLE controls replace in the 32-bit versions of Windows.

Microsoft's addition of the Microsoft Jet database engine's DAO interface to MFC makes Visual C++ a strong competitor to the principal players in the desktop database market: Access, Visual Basic, FoxPro for Windows, Lotus Approach, and Borland International's dBASE and Paradox for Windows. The Open Database Connectivity (ODBC) application programming interface (API), introduced in Visual C++, made Visual C++ a major factor in client-server front-end development throughout the world. DAO promises to lead Visual C++ 4 into areas that in the past have been the private domain of Visual Basic. Using 32-bit ODBC resolves the controversy in the computer press regarding the relative performance of DBLib and ODBC with Microsoft SQL Server. Tests show that 32-bit ODBC is as fast as or faster than equivalent calls to DBLib functions. The three major sections of this Introduction describe the new database connectivity features of Visual C++ and show how Visual C++ fits into the database front-end and back-end market.

What's New in Visual C++ for Database Developers

Visual C++'s new features fall into two basic categories:

- Features that are of interest only to database developers
- Features that affect all Visual C++ developers, regardless of whether they use Visual C++'s Data Access Objects

First, it is very important to realize that programmers today use many different versions of Visual C++.

- The first version of Visual C++, 1.0, was available in both a 16-bit and a 32-bit edition. Both of these products are now out-of-date and aren't used much by professional programmers.

- The next major release of Visual C++, 1.5, was made available only in a 16-bit version. This version included MFC 2.5 and other improvements.

- The 16-bit versions of Visual C++ that followed Visual C++ 1.5 include 1.51 through 1.52. Version 1.52c is distributed with Visual C++ 4. Microsoft distributes both versions together to give developers of 32-bit applications access to the 16-bit development tools. The 1.5x versions of the 16-bit Visual C++ products incorporate minor changes and additions, such as the inclusion of the OLE controls development platform.

- The second major release of the 32-bit version of Visual C++ was Visual C++ 2. This product, released in the fall of 1994, supports only 32-bit applications. A redesigned development environment, MFC 3, and other features made Visual C++ 2 a major player in the 32-bit C/C++ development arena.

- The next release of the 32-bit version of Visual C++ was Visual C++ 4. This product, released in the fall of 1995, supports only 32-bit applications. MFC 4, DAO, numerous improvements to the developer environment, and other features make Visual C++ 4 a must-have for any serious Windows developer.

- A subscription program was offered to Visual C++ programmers who needed regular updates to Visual C++. Originally slated to be delivered every quarter, releases have been coming out about twice a year. The current subscription program promises the "next two releases," which would represent about a year in time. Microsoft has announced that Visual C++ 4.1 should be available in the spring of 1996. The subscription version of Visual C++ is available from Microsoft directly and from most resellers.

There will be more releases of Visual C++ as the years go by. However, it is beyond the scope of this book to speculate what the future holds for Visual C++. The following sections describe the categories of Visual C++ features.

New Features of Visual C++

The most apparent change in Visual C++ 4 for database programmers is the adoption of MFC 4 and the addition of the MFC Data Access Object (DAO) classes. Additionally, Windows 95's Rich Text common control has been integrated into MFC. The following list briefly describes the most important differences between Visual C++ 4 and earlier versions of Visual C++:

- Visual C++ 1.5x develops 16-bit applications, whereas Visual C++ 4 is a 32-bit (only) development platform.

- Visual C++ 4 uses a much more advanced development environment. The integration of Visual C++ 4's components is much tighter than it was with Visual C++ 2. There have been major improvements to Visual C++ 4's ClassWizard, too. This lets the programmer have docked windows, more flexible toolbars, and other ease-of-use features.

- Visual C++ 4 offers MFC 4 and supports 32-bit OLE.

- Visual C++ 4 has integrated the functionality of the AppStudio program (which is used to edit program resources) into Visual C++'s development environment. There are improved toolbar editing and design tools, and the graphics editor is much better. For programmers who are just moving up to the 32-bit version of Visual C++, there is no need to switch between Visual C++ and AppStudio while developing applications.

- Visual C++ 4 can edit resources in applications. You can use this functionality, missing from Visual C++ 2, when running Visual C++ 4 under Windows NT.

- Visual C++ applications support toolbars, status bars, dialog bars, and floating palettes. Toolbars are dockable and have optional tooltip support built-in.

- Visual C++ supports 32-bit OLE Custom Controls, more commonly called OLE controls in this book. Because VBX controls can't be used in 32-bit environments, OLE controls are your only custom control choice when creating 32-bit Visual C++ 4 applications. Third-party VBX publishers have created a wide array of OLE controls, with functionality similar to their most popular VBX controls.

- Visual C++ 4 comes with a number of useful OLE controls, including the ever-popular Grid control, and a number of sample controls that can be rewritten if you like.

- Customization lets you alter Visual C++'s user interface by adding menu choices, modifying toolbars, and manipulating other elements of the design environment. Visual C++ 4 lets you configure the editor to emulate either the Brief or Epsilon editors.

- Visual C++ 4 supports remote debugging using either a network connection or serial ports. However, there is still no support for dual-monitor debugging.

- You can create out-of-process OLE miniservers (OLE applets, typified by Microsoft Graph 5.0) that you can use with any application that can act as an OLE Automation client, including Visual C++. Microsoft calls these miniservers *LOBjects* (line-of-business objects). You can run multiple instances of Visual C++ in order to test your newly created OLE applet.

A Database Developer's View of Visual C++

Making the choice between Access, Visual Basic, Visual FoxPro, Paradox for Windows, dBASE for Windows, Delphi, or Visual C++ as your primary database development platform is not a simple matter, especially for seasoned developers of character-based applications. Most programmers don't consider Visual C++ to be a database development tool, so they adopt one or more of the popular Windows desktop database systems or Visual Basic.

FoxPro for Windows offers xBase language compatibility and, without question, is the fastest of all the Windows desktop databases. Access has a unique user interface that lets you run simple to moderately complex database applications with a minimum of effort, and it also supports OLE controls (OCXs). Visual Basic offers more programming flexibility than Access, and you can incorporate a variety of commercial and shareware OLE controls to simplify database front-end development. The Paradox for Windows desktop RDBMS has a wider variety of field data types than any RDBMS, Windows or DOS, including client-server database systems. Each of these products has its own feature set, together with limitations that might not become apparent until you're embroiled in your first large-scale client-server database front-end application. Chapter 1, "Positioning Visual C++ in the Desktop Database Market," compares Visual C++ to your alternatives among the major combatants in the Windows database wars.

If you've invested several years in developing xBase or PAL programming skills and are reluctant to abandon xBase RDBMSs or Paradox for a new object-oriented, event-driven Windows programming language, welcome to the crowd. COBOL programmers have the same problem when their employers downsize from mainframe "legacy" databases to client-server systems running on PCs. Unfortunately for PAL programmers, the ObjectPAL programming language of Paradox for Windows bears little resemblance to the character-based PAL of Paradox. xBase and PAL, however, all have their roots in the original Dartmouth BASIC. The C programming language has a structure similar to PL/I or PASCAL. Thus, you might find the structure of Visual C++ applications similar to the xBase or PAL programs you're now writing.

If only C++ were as simple as C! C is, for the most part, easy to use, but when many programmers are exposed to C++ for the first time, they find it to be totally different than C. Nothing could be further from the truth, however. C++ is easy to learn and adapt to if you remember that the original C language is a subset of C++. The quickest conversion from C to C++ is to simply rename the file.

Simply choosing Visual FoxPro, dBASE for Windows, or Paradox for Windows because you're accustomed to writing xBase or PAL code isn't likely to be a viable long-term solution to your Windows database development platform dilemma (notwithstanding John Maynard Keynes' observation that "in the long term, we are all dead"). If you create Windows applications for a living, either as an in-house or independent developer, you're expected to provide your firm or client with applications that incorporate today's new technologies. You need to prepare now for OLE, with its in-place activation and OLE Automation (OA), and Visual C++ OLE controls. Windows is where the action is. More than 60 million copies of Windows (a mixture of Windows 3.x, Windows 95, and Windows NT) give Microsoft the marketing clout to make OLE, ODBC, and OLE controls the "standards" of the desktop computers of the world (whether the "industry" agrees or not). The alternative vaporware standards proposed by groups of software vendors organized to combat the Microsoft behemoth are very unlikely to replace OLE, ODBC, and OLE controls in the foreseeable future.

Windows desktop database applications present a challenge to developers accustomed to writing a thousand or more lines of code to create character-based RDBMS applications in Visual Basic, xBase, PAL, C, or other programming languages. You can create a very simple but usable Visual C++ database application with AppWizard and very little Visual C++ code. One example in this book contains no programmer-written code at all. Microsoft Access offers code-free capabilities—if you don't consider Access macros to be code. You'll need to write substantial amounts of code to create a usable database application with dBASE, Visual FoxPro's xBase, or Paradox's ObjectPAL. However, the reality is that you have to write a substantial amount of code to create a commercial-quality production database application with any of these products. The issue isn't how much code you have to write, but in which language you will write the code. Here are some of the language issues that will affect your career opportunities or the size of the numbers on your 1099s:

- xBase and PAL are yesterday's most prevalent desktop database programming languages. Will xBase and ObjectPAL ultimately survive the onslaught of Microsoft's present Object Basic dialects, such as Visual Basic and the Visual Basic for Applications (VBA) variants of Microsoft Word 7, Access 7, and Excel 7?

- Visual C++ lets you write incrementally compiled database applications that don't require helper libraries such as VBRUN300.DLL. Borland's Delphi offers fully compiled .EXEs but uses a variation of Pascal as its programming language. Does Delphi's Pascal really stand a chance of replacing C++ as the preferred language for writing commercial Windows applications or of making Object Basic/VBA extinct as an application programming (macro) language?

- Visual C++ 4, Access 7, and Visual Basic 4 act as containers for OLE Custom Controls. Excel, Word, and Project also support OLE controls. Will many of the new applications systems that will be released in the next few years also support OLE controls?

■ Visual C++ 4 allows cross-platform development for a number of different platforms, including applications for Macintosh computers. Microsoft now has a Macintosh version of Visual C++ that enables Windows developers to easily port their Windows applications to the Macintosh. Most development done under Windows NT can be directly ported to Windows 95 with minimum modifications.

This book doesn't purport to answer these questions directly, but you're likely to reach your own conclusions before you finish reading it.

At the time this book was written, Visual C++, Visual Basic 4, and Access were the major database development platforms to fully support OLE, OLE Automation, and OLE controls. Visual C++ is the only development platform, other than Visual Basic, that lets you create your own OLE Automation miniservers. Chapter 16, "Creating OLE Controls with Visual C++ 4," and Chapter 17, "Using OLE Controls and Automation with Visual C++ Applications," describe how OLE, OLE Automation, and OLE controls fit into your decision-support database front ends.

NOTE

Access 2 was released before the OLE Custom Control specification was finalized and many months before the retail release of Microsoft Visual C++ 2.0's Control Development Kit (CDK), which developers need in order to implement OLE controls. Access 2's OC1016.DLL isn't compatible with the final version of commercial OLE controls designed for use with Visual C++, which use OC25.DLL. The Access 2 Service Pack updates Access 2.0 to accommodate 16-bit OLE controls based on Visual C++ 1.5's OC25.DLL. If you find that you need to work with Access 2, you should keep these restrictions in mind. Access 7 doesn't present these problems.

Whatever language you ultimately choose, you must adapt to the event-driven approach to application design, inherited from the Windows graphical user interface (GUI). You also need to face the fact that Windows applications won't perform with the blazing speed of your Clipper or FoxPro applications running directly under DOS. Few, if any, Windows applications can match their DOS counterparts in a speed contest, but this situation is likely to change when you run your 32-bit database front end under Windows NT on a high-powered RISC workstation. Fortunately, most Windows users have grown accustomed to the sometimes sluggish response of Windows. It's possible, however, to design Visual C++ client-server front ends that rival the performance of their character-based counterparts. Chapter 15, "Designing Online Transaction-Processing Applications," and Chapter 20, "Creating Front Ends for Client-Server Databases," provide examples of "plain vanilla" front ends that deliver excellent performance.

Visual C++ and Microsoft BackOffice

When this book was written, Microsoft Office (both 4.2x and Office 95) had garnered more than 80 percent of the Windows productivity application suite (front-end) market. Microsoft Office 4.2 includes Excel 5.0, Word 6.0, PowerPoint 4.0, and a Microsoft Mail 3.2 client license. Microsoft Office 95 includes Excel 7, Word 7, and PowerPoint 7, all in 32-bit versions that run under both Windows 95 and Windows NT. The Professional Versions of Microsoft Office also include Microsoft Access (Office 4.3 contains Access 2.0, while Office 95 includes Access 7). Encouraged by the success of Office, Microsoft introduced its server (back-end) suite, BackOffice, in the fall of 1994. Microsoft BackOffice comprises a bundle of the following server products:

- Microsoft Windows NT 3.51 Server, the operating system on which the other components of BackOffice run as processes.
- Microsoft SQL Server 6, a client-server RDBMS. Will be upgraded to Microsoft SQL Server 6.5 in the spring of 1996.
- Microsoft SNA Server 2.11, which provides connectivity to IBM mainframes and AS/400 series minicomputers via IBM's System Network Architecture.
- Microsoft Systems Management Server (SMS) 1.1, which helps you distribute software and track client hardware and software. Version 1.2 is scheduled to be released to beta sites sometime in 1996.
- Microsoft Exchange Server, which integrates e-mail, group scheduling, electronic forms, and groupware applications on a single platform that can be managed with a centralized, easy-to-use administration program. It's designed to make messaging easier, more reliable, and more scalable for businesses of all sizes.
- Microsoft Mail Server 3.5, a file-sharing e-mail system. Will be upgraded to Microsoft Exchange Server when it becomes available in the spring of 1996.

Like Microsoft Office, you get a substantial discount (of about 40 percent) from the individual server license prices when you purchase the BackOffice bundle. Unlike earlier versions of Windows NT Server and SQL Server, which were available in "Enterprise" versions with unlimited client licenses, BackOffice doesn't include client licenses. The commercial success of BackOffice is by no means assured. It's not likely that large numbers of major corporations, the target market for BackOffice, will adopt this bundle until final versions of all of its promised components are delivered, which might not happen until 1997.

Microsoft SQL 6.0 and Exchange Server use OLE and OLE Automation pervasively. The Messaging API 1.0 (Extended MAPI), on which Exchange is based, uses Messaging OLE objects, and Schedule+ 7.0 has its OLE/Schedule+ object collections. The development tools for Microsoft SQL Server 6.0 RDBMS and Exchange e-mail system use VBA. (Exchange Server is a nonrelational database optimized for messaging services.) Ultimately, all of the members of the BackOffice suite are likely to offer VBA extensions for customization. Microsoft has positioned Visual C++ as a development platform for "building solutions" based on BackOffice servers. Visual C++ developers stand to gain a huge new revenue base writing database applications for Microsoft Exchange and SQL Server 6.0.

Who Should Read This Book

This book is intended primarily, but not exclusively, for the following categories of readers:

- Visual C++ developers who want to take maximum advantage of Visual C++'s database connectivity to create high-speed, production-grade graphic front ends for a variety of desktop and client-server databases.

- Access developers who have found that they need more control over their data display and editing forms than is afforded by the present version of Microsoft Access. Visual C++ database applications also consume far fewer Windows resources than equivalent Access applications.

- Visual Basic developers who want to take advantage of Visual C++'s automated access to the Windows APIs, gain function callback capability, and manipulate pointers.

- Developers of character-based DOS database applications whose clients or organizational superiors have decided to migrate from DOS to Windows applications.

- Users of xBase or Paradox products who need to create industrial-strength, 32-bit database front ends running under Windows 95 or Windows NT 3.51. (Windows NT 3.51 might not yet be a major player in the operating systems numbers game, but firms that adopt Windows NT 3.51 are major employers of database consultants.)

- Programmers who would like to develop database applications by expending less than 25 percent of the time and effort required to create equivalent applications with C and C++. Those addicted to C++ can quickly create prototype database applications with Visual C++. (It's amazing how many prototype Visual C++ applications become production database front ends.)

- Victims of the corporate downsizing revolution, principally COBOL, PL/I, or FORTRAN programmers who need to acquire C, C++, and Windows database development skills to remain gainfully employed.

- Users of proprietary GUI front-end development applications for client-server databases who are tired of forking over substantial per-seat licensing fees for each client workstation that is attached to the server.

- Chief information officers (CIOs) or management information services (MIS) executives who need to make an informed decision as to which Windows front-end generator their organization will adopt as a standard.

- Others who are interested in seeing examples of commercially useful Visual C++ database applications that earn developers a comfortable or better-than-comfortable living.

This book assumes that you have experience with Visual C++ or one of the traditional PC programming languages for Windows, such as Microsoft or Borland C or C++, Turbo Pascal for Windows, or the Windows version of SmallTalk. This book doesn't contain an introduction to C/C++ programming techniques; many excellent tutorial and reference books are available to fill this need. (The bibliography that appears later in this Introduction lists some of the better books and other sources of information for beginning-to-intermediate-level C/C++ programmers.) Instead, this book begins with an overview of how Visual C++ fits into the desktop and client-server database market and proceeds directly to dealing with data sources in Visual C++. The entire content of this book is devoted to creating useful Visual C++ database applications, and most of the examples of Visual C++ code involve one or more connections to database(s).

All the code examples in this book, except for minor code fragments, are included on the accompanying CD. Sample databases in each of the formats supported by the Access 7 database engine are provided. Some of the sample databases are quite large, so you can use their tables for performance comparisons. Tips and notes based on the experience of database developers with Visual C++ and Access appear with regularity.

What You Need to Use This Book Effectively

You need Visual C++ 4 (or later) to re-create or modify the sample applications that appear in this book. Although you can use Visual C++ 2.x , Visual C++ 4 (or later) is a necessity for serious database development using the 32-bit environment provided by Windows 95 and Windows NT, mostly due to the fact that Visual C++ 4 supports DAO. Executable versions of selected sample applications are included on the accompanying CD, as are a number of programs, demos, and other items.

I strongly recommend that you purchase a copy of Microsoft Access if you intend to use Access .MDB database files in commercial applications. You can't really create new databases and add tables using the ODBC drivers that are supplied with Visual C++; however, DAO does allow the creation of Access databases. You can use Access's query design window to create a query graphically, test the result, and then copy the Access SQL statement underlying the query to your Visual C++ code. Using Access's Relationships window to establish rules for enforcing referential integrity and creating business rules that maintain domain integrity is much simpler than Visual C++'s code-centric approach. An additional benefit of acquiring Access is the availability of database design and documentation tools for Access that are not yet available to Visual C++ database developers. Some of the new design and documentation tools for Access databases are described in Chapter 4, "Optimizing the Design of Relational Databases," and in Chapter 22, "Documenting Your Database Applications." If you develop Visual C++ database applications for a living, you'll save many times your investment if you buy a copy of Access.

> **NOTE**
>
> If you don't have Excel or Word for Windows, it might be well worth the investment to get the Microsoft Office Professional Edition, which includes Word for Windows, Excel, Access, and PowerPoint.

Developers of commercial database applications with Visual C++ are likely to want the additional features offered by third-party, data-aware custom controls. As these controls become available (WinWidgets/32 is an example), they can save the programmer substantial effort in developing applications. Although Microsoft has co-opted the data-aware grid, combo box, and list box OLE control market by providing 16- and 32-bit OLE control versions of these controls with Visual C++ 4, many third-party publishers offer quite useful enhancements to Microsoft's set. Several third-party custom controls are used to create the sample applications in this book. Sources of these OLE controls are provided in Appendix A, "Resources for Developing Visual C++ Database Applications."

Most Visual C++ database applications for Windows 3.1+ and Windows 95 will perform satisfactorily on 80386DX/33 or faster computers with 8M or more of RAM. If you plan to use Access, you should have a minimum of 16M of RAM. If you plan to take full advantage of OLE and OLE Automation, 12M to 16M of RAM is recommended, regardless of which applications you will be running. All of the 32-bit versions of the sample applications in this book run satisfactorily under Windows NT Workstation 3.51 with 16M of RAM, and on a Windows 95 80386DX/33 with 8M of RAM. All development work was done on a Pentium 90 with 32M of RAM, a machine of acceptable performance. The authors recommend running Visual C++ 4 with at least 16M of RAM on a fast 486 (or better) processor.

How This Book Is Organized

This book is divided into six parts that contain 24 chapters. Each part deals with related database application design subjects. The parts are ordered in a way that parallels a typical database application development program. The contents of each part and chapter are described in the sections that follow.

Part I

Part I, "Visual C++ Data Access," introduces you to Visual C++'s capabilities as a Windows database application development environment. Chapter 1, "Positioning Visual C++ in the Desktop Database Market," analyzes the features that Visual C++ offers database developers and shows how the language fits into Microsoft's strategy to dominate the desktop and client-server database development markets. Chapter 2, "Understanding MFC's ODBC Database Classes," provides a detailed description of how you create and manipulate Visual C++ MFC classes and collections using Access .MDB databases. Chapter 3, "Using Visual C++ Database Functions," covers the ODBC API-level SQL...() functions and presents some functions that use the ODBC API and that can be called from both C and C++ programs.

Part II

Part II, "Database and Query Design Concepts," deals with relational database design and shows you how to use SQL to create SELECT and action queries that employ the Access database engine and the ODBC API to process the queries. Chapter 4, "Optimizing the Design of Relational Databases," shows you how to normalize data in order to eliminate data redundancy in your application. Chapter 5, "Learning Structured Query Language," discusses ANSI SQL-89 and SQL-92 and tells how Access SQL differs from the "standard" SQL used by client-server and mainframe databases. Chapter 6, "The Microsoft Jet Database Engine," provides insight on the use of the Jet ODBC drivers with xBase, Paradox, and Btrieve tables. It also introduces you to Microsoft's Data Access Objects (DAO), a technology newly incorporated into Visual C++ 4.0. Chapter 7, "Using the Open Database Connectivity API," shows how Visual C++ applications interface with ODBC drivers. Chapter 8, "Running Crosstab and Action Queries," advances beyond simple SQL SELECT queries and shows you how to write queries that include TRANSFORM, PIVOT, INTO, and other less commonly used SQL reserved words that modify the data in your tables.

Part III

Part III, "An Introduction to Database Front-End Design," is devoted to creating commercial-quality decision-support front ends for databases. Chapter 9, "Designing a Decision-Support Application," describes the principles of converting raw data into easily comprehensible information that can be displayed on Visual C++ forms. Chapter 10, "Creating Your Own Data Access Controls," shows you how to take advantage of OLE Custom Controls. Chapter 11, "Using the New Win32 Common Controls," gives examples of using Visual C++ with the new Win32 Common Controls in programs that will work in both Windows 95 and Windows NT. Chapter 12, "Printing Reports with Report Generators," shows you how to design reports and how to seamlessly integrate report generation with your database applications.

Part IV

Part IV, "Advanced Programming with Visual C++," takes you deeper into the realm of commercial database application development. Chapter 13, "Understanding MFC's DAO Classes," shows you the new MFC 4 implementation of the Data Access Object interface to the Microsoft Jet database engine, providing a reference to the DAO classes. Chapter 14, "Using MFC's DAO Classes," presents a practical tutorial dealing with the DAO classes. Chapter 15, "Designing Online Transaction-Processing Applications," describes how to design forms for heads-down, high-speed data entry and how to use Visual C++'s transaction-processing reserved words to speed bulk updates to tables. Chapter 16, "Creating OLE Controls with Visual C++ 4," explains how to develop practical OLE controls. Chapter 17, "Using OLE Controls and Automation with Visual C++ Applications," describes how to add OLE controls to your applications using Visual C++ 4. Part IV concludes with Chapter 18, "Translating Visual Basic for Applications Code to Visual C++," for Access developers who are porting Access applications to Visual C++.

Part V

Up until Part V, "Multiuser Database Applications," this book is devoted to self-contained applications designed for a single user. Part V provides the background and examples you need to add networking and client-server database capabilities to your Visual C++ database applications. Examples employ Windows 95, Windows NT Server 3.51, and SQL Server 6 for Windows NT. Chapter 19, "Running Visual C++ Database Applications on a Network," describes how to use peer-to-peer and network servers to share databases among members of a workgroup or throughout an entire organization. Chapter 20, "Creating Front Ends for Client-Server Databases," describes how to use the ODBC API to set up and connect to client-server and mainframe data sources with your Visual C++ applications. Decision-support and online transaction processing examples that connect Microsoft SQL Server for Windows NT are included. Chapter 21, "Interacting with Microsoft Mail, MAPI, and TAPI," details the use of the MAPI custom control, the Schedule+ Access Library (SAL), and TAPI. Examples of using Microsoft's Electronic Forms Designer (EFD) to create mail-enabled Visual C++ applications are provided as well. Chapter 21 also gives you a brief glimpse of what you can expect when you begin to develop applications for Microsoft Exchange.

Part VI

Part VI, "Distributing Production Database Applications," shows you that no production database application is complete without full documentation and an online help system for users. Chapter 22, "Documenting Your Database Applications," shows you how to use Visual C++'s database object collections to create a data dictionary in the form of a text file that you can import into other applications, such as Word for Windows 7 or Excel 7. Chapter 23, "Creating Help Files for Database Applications," describes how to use Word for Windows and commercial WinHelp assistants, such as Doc-To-Help and RoboHelp, to speed the addition of context-sensitive help to your Visual C++ applications. Chapter 24, "Creating Distribution Disks for Visual C++ Applications," shows you how to create a professional installation application that uses either the Microsoft Setup application for Visual C++ or other mainstream Windows setup applications.

Appendixes

The appendixes provide useful reference data. Appendix A, "Resources for Developing Visual C++ Database Applications," lists add-in products that offer new features to your database applications. It also lists publishers of periodicals devoted to Visual C++ and databases in general. Suppliers and publishers are categorized by subject, and entries include addresses, telephone numbers, and fax numbers, as well as brief descriptions of the products listed. Appendix B, "Naming and Formatting Conventions for Visual C++ Objects and Variables," describes the prefix tags used in this book to identify the object or data type of variables. These naming conventions are based on a slightly modified form of Hungarian Notation that is commonly used in C and C++ programming. This notation was invented by Charles Simonyi, who worked on the development of Access 1.0 at Microsoft. Appendix C, "Using the CD-ROM," describes the files included on the CD that comes with this book.

Conventions Used in This Book

This book uses several typesetting styles to distinguish between explanatory material, the entries you make in Windows dialog boxes, components of initialization (.INI) files, and the code you enter in Visual C++'s code editing window. The sections that follow describe the typographic conventions used in this book.

Key Combinations and Menu Options

Accelerator key combinations (Alt-*key*) and shortcut key combinations (Ctrl-*key*) that you use to substitute for mouse operations are designated by joining the key with a hyphen (-). Ctrl-C, for example, is the shortcut key for copying a selection to the Windows clipboard. Alt-H is a common accelerator key combination that takes the place of clicking the Help button in dialog boxes. Some applications, such as Microsoft Word 6, use multiple-key shortcuts, such as Ctrl-Shift-*key,* to activate macros.

Menu options are separated by a vertical bar. For example, "File | Open" means "Choose the File menu and select the Open option."

Visual C++ Code, SQL Statements, and Source Code in Other Languages

Visual C++ code, Visual C++ reserved words, keywords (such as the names of collections), SQL statements, and source code fragments in other programming languages appear in monospace type. Reserved words and keywords in ANSI SQL and xBase programming languages appear in uppercase monospace. Here is an example of the formatting of an SQL statement:

```
SELECT Name, Address, City, Zip_Code FROM Customers WHERE Zip_Code >= 90000
```

The equivalent of the preceding statement in xBase is formatted as

```
USE customers LIST name, address, city zip_code WHERE zip_code >= 90000
```

The code line continuation character (➥) is used when the length of a code line exceeds the margins of this book. For example:

```
EXF=3.0;File;&Export Folder...;11;IMPEXP.DLL;0;;Exports folders to a
➥backup file;MSMAIL.HLP;2860
```

Note that this separator character isn't a valid character when embedded in an SQL statement `String` variable, nor is it valid in C/C++ source code. Wherever possible, C/C++ code is broken so that the ➥ character isn't needed. Some listings created by Visual C++'s AppWizard contain lines that are too long to fit on one line of this book. These lines are printed on two lines. When you look at the code in an editor, however, you will see these lines as one long line.

Special implementations of SQL that don't conform to ANSI SQL-92 standards, such as the {ts *DateVariable*} syntax that Microsoft Query uses to indicate the timestamp data type, appear as in the SQL dialog box of the application. The PIVOT and TRANSFORM statements of Access SQL that (unfortunately) weren't included in SQL-92, however, retain uppercase status.

Entries in Initialization and Registration Database Files

Entries in Windows, Visual C++, and Microsoft Access 2 initialization (.INI) files appear in monospace type. Sections of .INI files are identified by square brackets surrounding the section identifier, as in

```
[Options]
SystemDB=c:\vbapps\system.mda
```

Entries that you make in Windows 3.1+'s registration database using the registration database editor application, REGEDIT.EXE, in verbose mode also appear in monospace to preserve indentation that indicates the level of the entry in the tree (file-directory-like) structure of registration database entries. The full path to HKEY_CLASSES_ROOT and other entries in the Registry of Windows 95 and Windows NT is provided unless otherwise indicated in the accompanying text.

Visual C++ Code Examples and Code Fragments

As mentioned earlier, all examples of Visual C++ code, as well as code examples, appear in monospace. Monospace type also is used for code fragments. Styles and weights are applied to code examples and fragments according to the following rules:

- Names of symbolic constants, including the constants TRUE, FALSE, and NULL, appear in uppercase.

- Additions to Visual C++ AppWizard-produced programs typically appear in **bold monospace**. This lets you see what has been added to create the application's functionality.

- Replaceable variable names, arguments, and parameters, also known as *placeholders,* appear in *italic monospace.* Data type identification tag prefixes that identify the data type of variables of Visual C++'s fundamental data types and the type of object for variables of object data types don't appear in italic, as in int *nObjectVar.*

- French braces ({}) indicate that you must select one of the optional elements separated by the pipe character (¦) and enclosed in the braces. This doesn't apply to the unusual employment of French braces by Microsoft Query in SQL statements.

- An ellipsis (...) indicates that the remaining or intervening code required to complete a statement or code structure is assumed and doesn't appear in the example.

Prefix Tags for Data or Object Type Identification

The code examples in this book use two- or three-letter prefix tags to identify the data type of variables and symbolic constants of the fundamental data types of Visual C++ and other Object Basic dialects, as well as object variables.

Examples of Hungarian variable names of the fundamental data types are sz*StringVar,* n*IntegerVar,* l*LongVar,* d*Double,* and p*Pointer.* Microsoft and this book use the term *fundamental data type* to distinguish conventional variables, which have names that are Visual C++ reserved words, from variables of object data types, which might have names that are either reserved or keywords.

Prefix tags also are used to identify the type of object when you declare variables of the various object data types supported by Visual C++. The most common object prefix tags in this book are ws*WorkSpace,* db*Database,* and qdf*QueryDef.*

Appendix B provides detailed information on the derivation and use of type identifier prefix tags.

A Visual C++ and Database Bibliography

As I mentioned earlier, this book is intended for readers who are familiar with writing Visual C++, Visual Basic for Applications, and/or Access Basic code. If your first Visual C++ application is a full-fledged database front end, you might want to acquire one or more tutorial or reference books on introductory or intermediate-level Visual C++ programming. Access Basic programmers who are porting Access 2 or Access 7 applications to Visual C++ will benefit from developer-level Visual C++ guides. You also might want more details on the 1992 version of ANSI SQL, SQL-92, and the background of the ODBC API. The following sections provide recommendations of up-to-date books that fulfill these needs.

Introductions to Visual C++ Programming

The following books are designed to introduce you to Visual C++'s event-driven graphical programming environment:

Essential Visual C++, by Mickey Williams (Indianapolis: Sams Publishing, 1995, ISBN: 0-672-30787-1)

Teach Yourself Visual C++ 4 in 21 Days, by Nathan and Ori Gurewich (Indianapolis: Sams Publishing, 1994, ISBN: 0-672-30795-2)

Visual C++ in 12 Easy Lessons, by Greg Perry and Ian Spencer (Indianapolis: Sams Publishing, 1995, 0-672-30637-9)

What Every Visual C++ 2 Programmer Should Know, by Peter Hipson (Indianapolis: Sams Publishing, 1994, ISBN: 0-672-30493-7)

Visual C++ Books for Developers

The following books cover intermediate-to-advanced Visual C++ programming topics:

Develop a Professional Visual C++ Application in 21 Days, by Mickey Williams (Indianapolis: Sams Publishing, 1995, ISBN: 0-672-30593-3)

Master Visual C++, Third Edition, by Nathan and Ori Gurewich (Indianapolis: Sams Publishing, 1995, ISBN: 0-672-30790-1)

Visual C++ 2 Developer's Guide, Second Edition, by Nabajyoti Barkakati (Indianapolis: Sams Publishing, 1995, ISBN: 0-672-30663-8)

Visual C++ 4 Unleashed, by Viktor Toth (Indianapolis: Sams Publishing, 1996, ISBN: 0-672-30874-6)

A Book on the Microsoft Jet Database Engine

The following book offers an excellent reference to the Microsoft Jet database engine:

Microsoft Jet Database Engine Programmer's Guide, by Dan Haught and Jim Ferguson (Redmond: Microsoft Press, 1996, ISBN: 1-55615-877-7)

The Primary Guide to SQL-92

If you want to fully understand the history and implementation of the American National Standards Institute's X3.135.1-1992 standard for SQL-92, you need a copy of Jim Melton and Alan R. Simpson's *Understanding the New SQL: A Complete Guide* (San Mateo: Morgan Kaufmann Publishers, 1993, ISBN: 1-55860-245-3). Jim Melton of Digital Equipment Corp. was the editor of the ANSI SQL-92 standard, which comprises more than 500 pages of fine print.

Publishers of Database Standards

The syntax of SQL is the subject of a standard published by the American National Standards Institute (ANSI). At the time this book was written, the current standard, X3.135.1-1992 or SQL-92, was available from

> The American National Standards Institute
> 11 West 42nd Street
> New York, NY 10036
> (212) 642-4900 (Sales Department)

The SQL Access Group (SAG) consists of users and vendors of SQL database management systems. SAG publishes standards that supplement ANSI X3.135.1-1989, such as the Call-Level Interface (CLI) standard used by Microsoft's ODBC API. You can obtain SAG documents from

> The SQL Access Group
> 1010 El Camino Real, Suite 380
> Menlo Park, CA 94025
> (415) 323-7992 (extension 221)

Keeping Up to Date on Visual C++

A variety of sources of up-to-date information are available to Visual C++ developers in print and electronic formats. Both print periodicals and online sources address management and development issues that are applicable to database development as a whole. Several forums on CompuServe offer product support services for Access and Windows. The sections that follow describe some of the sources you can use to expand your Visual C++ horizons.

Periodicals

The following are a few magazines and newsletters that cover Visual C++ or Access, or in which articles on either appear on a regular basis:

- *Data Based Advisor* is published by Data Based Solutions, Inc., a firm related to the publishers of *Access Advisor*. *Data Based Advisor* covers the gamut of desktop databases, with emphasis on xBase products, but Visual C++ receives its share of coverage, too.

- *DBMS* magazine, published by M&T, a Miller-Freeman company, is devoted to database technology as a whole, but it concentrates on the growing field of client-server RDBMSs. *DBMS* covers subjects, such as SQL and relational database design, that are of interest to all developers, not just those who use Visual C++.

- *Smart Access* is a monthly newsletter from Pinnacle Publishing, Inc., which publishes other database-related newsletters and monographs. *Smart Access* is directed primarily at developers and Access power users. This newsletter tends toward advanced topics, such as creating libraries and using the Windows API with Access and Visual C++. A diskette is included with each issue.

- *Windows Watcher*, Jesse Berst's (now Ziff-Davis') monthly newsletter, analyzes the market for Windows applications, reviews new products for Windows, and provides valuable insight into Microsoft's future plans for Windows 95, Windows NT, and Windows applications, including Visual C++.

The majority of these magazines are available from newsstands and bookstores. Names and addresses of the publishers are listed in Appendix A.

The MSDN Support Product

Microsoft sells three sets of subscription services available on CD-ROM called MSDN (Microsoft Developer Network) Level I, MSDN Level II, and MSDN Level III. Level I support consists of quarterly disks that contain a vast amount of information and documentation. These CDs are very valuable to all programmers.

Level II support consists of Level I and all the development tools (excluding compilers) such as SDKs and platforms (including versions of Windows, Windows 95, and Windows NT) that Microsoft offers, excluding the BackOffice suite. These CDs (the count varies from quarter to quarter, but usually there are about 20 CDs per release) provide a firm foundation for all professional developers at a very affordable price.

Level III support includes Level II plus the Microsoft BackOffice development system.

Microsoft Internet Services

Microsoft and other firms sponsor services on the Internet. Some of the best support can be obtained, without charge, by using the Microsoft Knowledge Base product, which can be accessed from the Internet. This allows you to query the database that the Program Support Services (PSS) people use and obtain answers to technical questions.

I

Visual C++ Data Access

1

Positioning Visual C++ in the Desktop Database Market

Between November 1992 and the end of 1995, Microsoft introduced a number of new Windows relational database products: Access 7, Visual FoxPro 3.0 for Windows, and Visual C++ 4.0. Microsoft heralded Access as "the database that anyone can use" and sold 750,000 bargain-priced copies in 90 days when Access 1.x was first released. FoxPro for Windows targeted existing FoxPro developers and prospective users of Borland's long-promised dBASE for Windows. Both Access and FoxPro targeted the market for Borland's Paradox for Windows, which emerged shortly after the retail release of Access 1.0. Access (upgraded to version 7.0 with the introduction of Windows 95), Visual FoxPro, and Paradox for Windows are categorized as desktop databases.

Since its introduction, Visual Basic has had better support for database interface than Visual C++. Only with Visual C++ 4 has the C/C++ programmer had a real interface with the Microsoft Jet database engine. *Desktop databases* are applications that employ a proprietary (native) database file or index structure (or both) and that can be run on a PC of moderate performance (for example, an 80486 with 8M of RAM). Desktop databases also include an application programming language that is designed specifically for use with the native database structure.

When the first edition of this book was written, Microsoft had sold more than four million copies of Access versions 1.0, 1.1, and 2.0. Between mid-June and mid-November of 1995, Microsoft released Windows 95 and 32-bit "designed for Windows 95" versions of Access (7.0), Visual FoxPro (3.0), Visual Basic (4.0), and Visual C++ (4.0), together with the 32-bit Microsoft Office 95. Microsoft wanted to make sure that early adopters of Windows 95 would have 32-bit applications to run.

> **NOTE**
>
> Access 7 for Windows 95 started shipping near the end of 1995, much later than Word 7 and Office 95.

Visual C++ is Microsoft's most extensive and powerful programming language. Microsoft's original objective for Visual C++ was to provide a powerful and flexible platform that programmers could use to create their own Windows applications while running under Windows. Microsoft achieved this goal with Visual C++ 1.0. Many experienced programmers abandoned DOS-based C, C++, and Pascal in favor of Visual C++ because they could develop Windows applications faster than with traditional programming languages while working with Windows' graphical interface. Microsoft enriched Visual C++ 1.5 with improvements in the interface and extensions to the MFC C++ libraries, while Visual C++ 2.x moved programmers into the 32-bit application world. Visual C++ 4.0 moves the programmer interface, class library, and feature set to a new high. With the introduction of Visual C++ 4.0, a new set of database features has been added. Visual C++ 4.0 supports DAO (Data Access Objects) in addition to ODBC and also greatly extends other support, such as the addition of container support for OLE Custom Controls. Independent firms have created a variety of utilities, libraries, and add-on features for Visual C++, the majority of which addressed database applications. There will be, in the very near future, a plethora of new OLE Custom Controls for database programmers.

By early 1993, a Microsoft market study showed that more than 70 percent of Windows applications involved databases in one form or another. In October of 1995, Microsoft's Visual C++ product manager noted in a speech in Boston that between 40 and 60 percent of all Visual C++ applications were database oriented. Visual C++ can be expected to also be a popular database applications development tool. Even before the introduction of Visual C++ 4.0, with its data access objects (CRecordset, CDatabase, and CRecordView) that greatly enhance database functionality, C and C++ were major but unrecognized players in the Windows database market. The introduction of Visual C++ 4.0 has now pushed Visual C++ to be a strong competitor of Visual Basic in the database development platform arena. The failure of market research firms to place Visual C++ in the Windows database category caused significant distortion of the desktop database market statistics for 1993 and later.

This chapter describes Visual C++'s role in database application development and shows how Visual C++, OLE (Object Linking and Embedding) automation, ODBC (Open Database Connectivity), DAO, and MFC fit into Microsoft's strategy to maintain its domination of the Windows application marketplace. This chapter also discusses the advantages and drawbacks of using Visual C++ for database applications and gives you a preview of many of the subjects that are covered in detail in the remaining chapters of this book.

It's becoming a 32-bit, "Designed for Windows 95" world out there, so this book concentrates on 32-bit application development with Visual C++ 4.0.

Choosing Visual C++ as Your Database Development Platform

Visual C++ now includes the database connectivity and data handling features that qualify the language as a full-fledged database application development environment. The new data access features that Microsoft added to Visual C++ position the product as a direct competitor to Visual Basic and make Visual C++'s support of Access, FoxPro, and Paradox for Windows in the desktop database market even more complete. Visual C++'s primary advantages over its database competitors are simplicity, flexibility, and extensibility:

■ The 32-bit Microsoft Jet 3.0 database engine offers substantially improved performance compared to 16-bit Jet 2+. Jet 3.0 is multithreaded, with a minimum of three threads of execution. (You can increase the number of available threads by an entry in the Windows 95 or Windows NT Registry.) Overall optimization and code tuning also contribute to faster execution of Jet 3.0 queries.

- Visual C++'s built-in MFC classes, along with AppWizard, let you quickly create a form to display database information with little or no Visual C++ code. Chapter 2, "Understanding MFC's ODBC Database Classes," contains a sample program that actually has no programmer-written code at all.

- Visual C++ is flexible because it doesn't lock you into a particular application structure, as is the case with Access's multiple document interface (MDI). Nor do you have to use DoCmd instructions to manipulate the currently open database.

- Visual C++ 4.0 database front ends require substantially fewer resources than their Access counterparts. Most 32-bit Visual C++ 4.0 database applications run fine under Windows 95 with PCs having 8M of RAM and under Windows NT 3.51+ in the 16M range. Microsoft says Access 95 requires 12M of RAM under Windows 95, but you need 16M to achieve adequate performance of all but trivial Access 95 applications. A typical Visual C++ database front-end program would probably run with satisfactory performance on a system with as little as 12M of RAM under Windows 95. This same program would run well under the same amount of RAM in future versions of Windows NT.

- OLE Custom Controls, not yet available in all other database development platforms, let you add new features to Visual C++ applications with minimal programming effort. Third-party developers can create custom control add-ins to expand Visual C++'s repertoire of data access controls. Custom controls can take the form of OLE Custom Controls for the 32-bit environments.

The most important benefit of selecting Visual C++ as your primary database development platform, however, isn't evident in Microsoft's feature list. There is a vast array of tools and support for ODBC and database development with Visual C++ today. Examples of the use of Visual C++ are found throughout this book.

Another reason for choosing Visual C++ for database application development is its OLE compatibility. At the time this book was written, Visual C++ was the best database development environment that incorporated OLE.

OLE automation is likely to be the most significant OLE feature for the majority of Visual C++ database developers. OLE automation lets you control the operation of other OLE-compliant server applications from within your Visual C++ database application. Applications need not include Visual Basic for Applications to act as OLE automation source applications (servers); Word for Windows 6 and later supports OLE automation using the conventional Word Basic macro language syntax.

The Windows database war wasn't over at the time this book was written (heck, it may never be over), but Microsoft's multipronged attack with Visual Basic, Access, Visual FoxPro, SQL Server, and Visual C++ is forcing competing publishers of desktop database managers into their defensive trenches. As a group, Microsoft's database applications for Windows, together with ancillary products such as ODBC, DAO, and the Access Jet database engine, have a breadth and depth that no other software publisher presently can match.

Using Visual C++ as a Database Front End

All of Microsoft's 32-bit mainstream Windows productivity applications and programming languages presently support or soon will accommodate the 32-bit Microsoft Jet 3.0 database engine. The Jet database engine is a software component that adheres to Microsoft's Component Object Model (COM) architecture. COM is Microsoft's infrastructure for creating code modules (called *objects*) that are independent of programming languages and computer platforms. COM defines a set of *interfaces* that applications must support; OLE 2+ is a high-level implementation of COM designed for sharing objects between Windows applications and for application programming. OLE 2+ defines its own set of interfaces to permit use of one program's objects by another program. As an example, applications that support VBA, such as Visual Basic 4.0, Access 95, Excel 95, and Project 95, communicate with the Jet 3.0 database engine (MSJT3032.DLL) through the Microsoft Jet 3.0 Data Access Object (DAO), DAO3032.DLL, an in-process OLE Automation server. (Access 95 also directly calls functions in MSJT3032.DLL.) Thus, only a single copy of the Jet 3.0 DLLs is required in your \Windows\System folder; each application creates its own instance of Jet as needed. A similar approach is used to share other components, such as DAO, spell-checking, graphing, and VBA 2.0; the component files are located in subfolders of your \Windows\Program Files\Common Files\Microsoft Shared folder if you're running Windows 95.

Visual C++ is the wildcard in the desktop database deck. Visual C++ doesn't really have a native database structure. All four of the basic database types supported by Visual C++ are treated the same. Microsoft Access is simply the default database type. Visual C++ and its Access database engine, combined with Microsoft or third-party ODBC drivers, presently can connect to the relational database management systems (RDBMS) listed in Table 1.1.

Table 1.1. Visual C++-compatible databases and file drivers.

Access Database Engine Drivers	*Microsoft ODBC Drivers*	*Third-Party ODBC Drivers*
Access (.MDB)	Microsoft SQL Server	Digital Rdb
Btrieve (.DAT)	Oracle 6	Gupta SQLBase
dBASE III+ (.DBF, .NDX)	Sybase SQL Server	HP AllBase/SQL
dBASE IV (.DBF, .MDX)	Excel (.XLS)*	HP Image/SQL
FoxPro (.DBF, .CDX, .IDX)	Text (.TXT)*	IBM DB2, DB2/2
Paradox (.DB, .PX)	Access*	IBM OS/2 DBM
	Btrieve*	IBM SQL/DS
	dBASE III+*	Informix
	dBASE IV*	Ingres

continues

Table 1.1. continued

Access Database Engine Drivers	Microsoft ODBC Drivers	Third-Party ODBC Drivers
	FoxPro 2.x*	NCR Teradata
	Paradox*	NetWare SQL
		Progress
		Tandem Nonstop SQL
		Watcom SQL
		XDB

NOTE

Databases and files in the Microsoft ODBC Drivers column that are marked with an asterisk (*) are included in the Microsoft ODBC Desktop Database Drivers kit (16-bit) and Microsoft Query. With the exception of the ODBC driver for Rdb supplied by Digital Equipment Corporation and the Watcom SQL driver, the third-party drivers listed in the third column of Table 1.1 are products of Intersolv Software. Intersolv Software offers the same collection of ODBC drivers as Microsoft, except for the Access ODBC driver. Other database suppliers and third-party developers supply ODBC database drivers that you can use with Visual C++. A list of suppliers of ODBC database drivers appears in Appendix A, "Resources for Developing Visual C++ Database Applications."

Windows 95 currently is being shipped with no ODBC drivers. Drivers are released from time to time by Microsoft, and Visual C++ 4.0 includes a full set of redistributable 32-bit ODBC drivers (for both Windows 95 and for Windows NT). Some of the original Windows NT ODBC drivers don't work well under Windows 95, so programmers might be well advised to test their applications under both platforms and with as many ODBC drivers as possible.

The Access database engine that is included with ODBC lets you use dBASE III+, dBASE IV, FoxPro, Paradox, Btrieve, and Access databases with equal facility. Microsoft's ODBC Administrator application and the ODBC drivers created by Microsoft and third-party developers add at least 20 additional databases and file types to the list of those with which a Visual C++ database application can be connected. Only Access can rival Visual C++'s universal database connectivity. Details of the two methods of adding database functionality to Visual C++ applications are given in Chapter 6, "The Microsoft Jet Database Engine."

> **NOTE**
>
> To use Btrieve databases with Visual Basic 4.0, you need a Windows dynamic link library (DLL) that is included with the Btrieve for Windows application and other Btrieve products. Appendix A of this book, "Resources for Developing Visual C++ Database Applications," provides information on how to obtain the required Btrieve DLLs.

Borland's Paradox 7 for Windows 95 takes a tentative step in the multidatabase direction by letting you use Paradox or dBASE files interchangeably. If you want to, you can create a FoxPro or Paradox application that doesn't involve a single database file. However, you need to open an .MDB file to use Access; only a few Access database utility functions are available before you open a new or existing .MDB file.

Included with Microsoft Office and the 16-bit versions of Visual C++ is an add-in application, MS Query, that lets you create new Access databases as well as add, delete, and modify tables in new or existing Access, dBASE, FoxPro, and Paradox databases. Figure 1.1 shows MS Query's Table window for the Orders table of NorthWind.MDB, the sample Access database supplied with Access.

FIGURE 1.1.

Visual C++'s data manager application, MS Query.

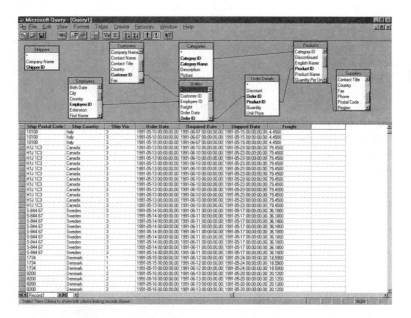

> **NOTE**
>
> Visual C++ 1.5x includes the MS Query product and a second NWIND database; however, this example is a dBASE format database, not an Access format. If you need a sample dBASE database, you can use this one. Since dBASE database files aren't specific to 16-bit or 32-bit applications, this database will work with any of the dBASE ODBC drivers.

The Table window displays the structure of the existing fields of a table and lets you add new fields and indexes to a table. MS Query is an example of a Visual C++ database application that uses MDI forms. MDI lets you create database applications with several windows (called MDI *child* windows or forms) that are contained within a conventional window (called the *parent* window or form).

The Microsoft ODBC Administrator application, included with Visual C++, lets you connect to the Microsoft and Sybase versions of SQL Server and to Oracle client-server relational database management systems. Client-server RDBMSs are discussed later in this chapter. You can even treat text files and Excel worksheets as database tables by using the Microsoft ODBC Desktop Database Drivers kit. Independent software development firms, such as Intersolv Software, provide a variety of ODBC drivers for client-server and desktop databases, as well as for worksheet and text files. Some of Intersolv's ODBC drivers provide features that aren't available when you use the Access database engine; an example is Intersolv's capability to employ transactions with dBASE III+, IV, and 5.0 files. Figure 1.2 shows the ODBC Setup window for the Pubs sample database of Microsoft SQL Server 4.2 running on LAN Manager 2.2. Using ODBC drivers with Visual C++ is the subject of later sections in this chapter and, in fact, the entire book. The Intersolv DataDirect ODBC pack supports ALLBASE, Btrieve, CA-Ingres, Clipper, DB2, DB2/2, DB2/6000, dBASE, Excel, FoxBase, FoxPro, Gupta SQLBase, IMAGE/SQL, INFORMIX, InterBase, Microsoft SQL Server, Oracle, Paradox, PROGRESS, Scalable SQL (formerly Netware SQL), SQL/400, SQL/DS, SYBASE System 10, SYBASE SQL Server 4, Teradata, text files, and XDB.

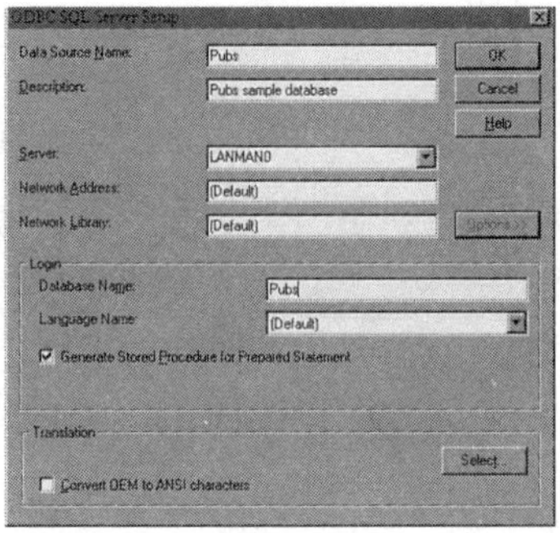

FIGURE 1.2.

The ODBC Setup window for the Microsoft SQL Server.

> **NOTE**
>
> If you have Visual C++ 4.0, you can distribute the Microsoft ODBC Administrator application and the Microsoft/Sybase SQL Server or Oracle ODBC drivers with your Visual C++ applications. The Microsoft ODBC Desktop Database Drivers kit and Intersolv Software ODBC drivers require payment of a license fee for distribution. Contact Microsoft Corporation or Intersolv for the terms, conditions, and costs of distribution licenses.
>
> The file \MSDEV\REDIST\MSVC15\REDIST\REDISTRB.WRI contains details on distribution of the ODBC drivers. These drivers can be used with applications under both Windows 95 and Windows NT. The 16-bit ODBC can be used with legacy 16-bit ODBC applications under Windows 95, but these drivers can't be used under Windows NT, nor can they be used with 32-bit applications under Windows 95. For 32-bit applications, Intersolv ODBC drivers look like the best alternative when it is necessary to use non-Microsoft-supplied ODBC drivers.

Visual C++'s broad spectrum of database connectivity makes Visual C++ an excellent candidate for developing database front-end applications. The term *database front end* is used to describe a computer application that can select items of data contained in a database and display the chosen data items as information that is meaningful to the user. The database system itself is called the *back end*. The back-end database is, at the minimum, a collection of related tables. Traditional desktop database managers store these related tables as individual files in a single directory, together with index files that are used to speed the data-gathering process. Access and client-server RDBMS store all related tables and indexes in a single database file.

Microsoft has achieved dramatic success in making the Windows graphical user interface (GUI) a worldwide standard for use on corporate PCs. At the time this book was written, Microsoft claimed to have sold more than 25 million copies of Windows 3.x. Windows 95 earned Microsoft more than $260 million in the quarter when it was released and more than $180 million in the following quarter.

Windows 95 was released in August of 1995. Even in early 1995, Windows 95 had garnered enormous attention. Thus, it's no surprise that virtually all of today's database front ends are being created to run under Windows 95, or Windows NT. With Visual C++ and Access, Microsoft also has the upper hand in creating Windows database applications that employ a variety of database structures. Wide-ranging database connectivity is one of the major elements of Microsoft's strategy to obtain a major share of the enterprise-wide computing market.

Database Front-End Generators

This book uses the term *front-end generator* to describe a Windows application with which you can quickly create a database front-end application for a wide variety of desktop and client-server RDBMSs. Theoretically, any programming language that can create executable files for

Windows can qualify as a front-end generator. You can write a Windows front end by using Visual Basic, C, C++, or Pascal compilers; and many large-scale MIS applications are written in C or C++. Writing even a simple Windows database front end in Visual Basic, however, requires a major programming effort that fails the "quickly" test. Visual Basic isn't as easy to use as it is sometimes purported to be. Thus, this book restricts the classification of front-end generators to the following two types of products:

■ User-definable query processors let users create queries against a variety of RDBMSs by point-and-click or drag-and-drop techniques. A *query* is an SQL statement that you use to select records for display or updating. (SQL is discussed in more detail later in this book.) Query processors don't include a programming language per se, but many of these products provide a scripting or macro language to automate repetitive tasks. Some query processors include a graphical forms designer so that users can determine the appearance of the information returned by the query. Asymetrix InfoAssistant is a new 32-bit user-definable query processor that can deal with a variety of desktop and client-server databases. Channel Computing's Forest and Trees application is one of the more popular Windows query processors. Microsoft Query, which replaces the Intersolv add-in application included with earlier versions of Excel, offers drag-and-drop query generation based on the methods employed by Access's query design window.

■ Front-end development tools include, at the minimum, a graphical-forms designer and an application programming language. Queries are created by using graphical QBE (query by example) or by embedding SQL statements in a program. One of the tests of a front-end development tool is the product's capability to create a user-definable query processor. Microsoft Visual C++, Access, and FoxPro qualify in this category, as does PowerSoft Corporation's PowerBuilder. FoxPro qualifies because FoxPro can use ODBC to connect to a variety of database back ends.

More than 200 commercial Windows front-end generators were available at the time this book was written, about evenly divided between the two preceding categories. Most of these products also include a report generator to print formatted data. The retail version of Access uniquely qualifies in both categories of front-end generators because Access's user interface (UI) is simple enough that nonprogrammers can create their own database applications. Presently, Access is one of Visual C++'s most viable competitors in the front-end development tool market, as is Visual Basic.

A critical requirement of any front-end generator is the capability to transfer data to other Windows applications easily. Copying database information to the Windows Clipboard and pasting the Clipboard data into a compatible application, such as Excel, provides basic interapplication or interprocess communication (IPC) capability. Windows DDE (dynamic data exchange) is the most universal method of automatically transferring data to and from database front ends; however, DDE implementations, other than pasted dynamic links, seldom meet the "easily" part of the requirement. Visual C++ currently offers a combination of database connectivity and OLE compatibility.

Visual C++ and SQL

If you aren't proficient in SQL, you probably will need to learn yet another programming language to create database front ends with Visual C++. To select the data you want from a database attached to a Visual C++ application, write the necessary SQL statement and then send the statement as a string variable to the Access database engine or an ODBC driver. SQL (properly pronounced "S-Q-L," not the more common "sequel" or "seekel") is the *lingua franca* of relational database systems. SQL has its roots in a language called SEQUEL (Structured English Query Language), which IBM developed at its San Jose Research Laboratory in the mid-1970s. SEQUEL later became SEQUEL/2 and ultimately was renamed SQL. The first two relational databases to use SQL were Oracle, developed by Relational Software, Inc. (now Oracle Corporation), and IBM's SQL/DS.

The purpose of SEQUEL and its successors was to provide a relatively simple, nonprocedural programming language to manipulate relational database systems. Visual C++ is a procedural language: You write a series of statements, such as if...else, to instruct the Visual C++ compiler to generate a series of instructions in a sequence you define. You control how the program executes to achieve the result you want. A nonprocedural language, on the other hand, expects you to write a series of statements that describes what you want to happen, such as SELECT * FROM TableName. The application that processes the statement determines how the statement is executed and simply returns the result—in this case, all the records contained in TableName.

One of the advantages of using SQL to manipulate relational databases is that the language has been standardized by a committee (X3.135) of the American National Standards Institute (ANSI). The first standardization effort began in the mid-1980s; ANSI X3.135-86 (SQL-86) specified the first standardized version of SQL. The 1986 standard was updated in 1989 (SQL-89) and in 1992 (SQL-92). Developers of RDBMSs that use SQL are free to extend the language in any way they see fit; however, SQL-reserved words that are included in the ANSI standard must return the result specified by the standard. Extended SQL languages—such as Transact-SQL, which is used by the Microsoft and Sybase SQL Server RDBMS—offer useful extensions to SQL. Some implementations of SQL, such as IBM's version for DB2, don't comply with the latest ANSI standards; for instance, you can't use the AS keyword to assign a derived column name to a DB2 column that contains a value expression, such as SUM(Expr).

NOTE

Database programmers and many users usually use the term *xBase* to refer to database back ends that use dBASE-compatible files. With a dBASE database, each table and index is contained in a separate file.

Users of xBase RDBMSs, such as dBASE and FoxPro, will find the structure of SQL statements to be quite similar to the interactive xBase statements that you enter at the dot prompt.

In this book, *xBase* refers to any desktop relational database management system that uses the dBASE file structure and supports, at a minimum, all the commands and functions of the dBASE III+ programming language. The two xBase statements executed at the dot prompt are

```
USE customer LIST name, address, city, state, zip_code FOR zip_code >= 90000
```

and the single SQL statement contained in a Visual C++ string variable:

```
SELECT name, address, city, state, zip_code FROM customer WHERE zip_code >= 90000
```

Both return the same result: a list of the names, addresses, cities, states, and zip codes of all customers whose zip codes are equal to or greater than 90000.

Most of the recent implementations of desktop RDBMSs include SQL implementations that have varying degrees of conformance to the ANSI SQL-89 specification. Access's dialect of SQL conforms quite closely to ANSI-89 syntax, but it's missing the Data Definition Language (DDL) elements of SQL that you need to create databases and tables with conventional SQL statements. Access SQL also omits the Data Control Language (DCL) that lets you GRANT or REVOKE privileges for users to gain access to the database or the tables it contains. Access SQL compensates for this omission, at least in part, by providing the TRANSFORM and PIVOT keywords that let you create very useful crosstab queries (which are described in a moment). Chapter 5, "Learning Structured Query Language," describes the structure of SQL statements and how to implement SQL in your Visual C++ code.

Classifying Database Front-End Applications

Database front-end applications that you create with front-end generators fall into two broad categories:

- Decision-support applications that only let you display and print information culled from the database by predefined (hard-coded) or user-defined queries
- Transaction-processing front-end applications that include the capability to edit data or add data to the database

The following sections describe the basic characteristics of these two categories of database front ends.

Database Front Ends for Decision Support

Decision-support applications represent the most common type of database front-end application. Single-purpose decision-support front ends typically display sales information for selected customers or products. At the other end of the decision-support spectrum, complex management information systems (MIS) provide summarized information concerning virtually all of the quantifiable aspects of large organizations' operations. Decision-support applications usually involve read-only access to the data in the underlying database. Chapter 9,

"Designing a Decision-Support Application," is devoted to writing Visual C++ code to display information gleaned from relational databases.

Many decision-support front-end development tools include the capability to create graphs and charts based on summary data. Grouping and totaling data to create summary information often is called *rolling up* the data. The Access database engine lets Visual C++ decision-support applications perform crosstab rollups. Crosstab methods let you display summary data in worksheet format, usually as a time series. Using a crosstab query, you can display sales of products (in rows) by month or by quarter (in columns) directly from tables that contain only raw invoicing data. Crosstab queries is one of the subjects of Chapter 8, "Running Crosstab and Action Queries." Drill-down methods let you show the detailed data that underlies your summary information.

In-house and independent database-application developers use Visual C++ to create a wide variety of single-purpose and MIS decision-support front ends. Here are the principal advantages of Visual C++ over competing front-end development tools for creating decision-support applications:

■ You can distribute unlimited numbers of your compiled Visual C++ front-end applications without paying royalties. Most other front-end generators require that you pay a license fee for each copy of the compiled front-end applications you install. (License fees for applications you create are called *per-seat* charges.) However, you might need to pay a per-seat license fee for the ODBC drivers you use with your Visual C++ application if you need to use drivers other than those supplied with Visual C++.

■ The purchase price of Visual C++ is substantially less than the prices charged for other front-end generators with comparable or inferior feature sets.

■ Few front-end generators support the Access SQL TRANSFORM and PIVOT statements, which let you quickly create crosstab queries when you use the Microsoft Jet database engine.

■ Visual C++ applications can embed OLE graphic objects from applications such as Microsoft Graph.

■ Visual C++ is OLE-compliant (as a destination or client application and as a server application) and includes OLE Automation capability. You can use *in-situ editing* (also called *in-place editing*) and exercise control over other Windows applications that share OLE Automation capability.

■ You don't need to learn a new and arcane programming language to develop Visual C++ database front ends. The structure and syntax of Visual C++ is closely related to traditional database programming languages such as xBase and the Paradox Application Language (PAL).

■ Visual C++ is flexible. Often, constructs that are difficult or impossible using other development platforms can easily be created using Visual C++.

■ Visual C++ is an object-oriented language. Visual C++ qualifies as a full-scale, object-oriented programming (OOP) language. It's likely that future versions will include an even more extensive implementation of MFC. Competing front-end development tools that claim to be object-oriented seldom reach Visual C++'s level of compliance with the object programming model.

Many of the advantages in the preceding list apply equally to decision-support and transaction-processing front ends. This list is by no means comprehensive. Many other advantages that derive from choosing Visual C++ as your database front-end development tool will become apparent as you progress through this book.

Here are the principal drawbacks to using Visual C++ as a decision-support front end:

■ Visual C++ has limited support for graphics formats in image and picture boxes. Visual C++ supports only Windows bitmaps (.BMP and .DIB), icons (.ICO), and Windows metafile (.WMF) vector images. However, a variety of third-party add-ins and custom controls are available that dynamically convert .PCX, .TIF, .JPG, .GIF, and other common graphics file formats to one of Visual C++'s supported formats. It can be expected that there will be many OLE Custom Controls for graphics available to Visual C++ programmers in the next few years.

■ With ODBC, Visual C++ lacks the direct capability to establish rules that enforce referential integrity at the database level with Access .MDB files, and ODBC can't add validation rules to enforce domain integrity at the Access table level. You need to write Visual C++ code to enforce referential and domain integrity in all supported databases when using ODBC. Visual C++ enforces referential and domain integrity rules that you establish when you create the database with Access. Many Visual C++ 4 front-end applications will use DAO for accessing Access databases.

■ Visual C++ can't directly implement the security features inherent in Access .MDB databases when using ODBC. By default, Visual C++ doesn't use Access's SYSTEM.MDA file (or Access 7's SYSTEM.MDW file), which contains user names, passwords, and other security information for .MDB files created by Access. If your front-end application is used by members of only one workgroup, you can specify the name and location of the workgroup's SYSTEM.MDA/MDW file in Visual C++'s VB.INI file or the Visual C++ *APPNAME*.INI file associated with the *APPNAME*.EXE file for your application. (Visual C++ expects the filename of the .EXE and .INI files to be the same.) If you have implemented or need to implement security features, such as adding new users to your Access database, you can use the Access ODBC driver (RED110.DLL). This lets you attach a SYSTEM.MDA/MDW file to implement database security instead of using a Visual C++ database object to connect directly to the Access database engine. Use the GRANT and REVOKE SQL reserved words to manage database- and table-level security. These limits don't apply to applications developed using the MFC DAO classes, however.

The limitations of Visual C++ are likely to affect only a small portion of the decision-support front ends you create for production-database applications. Future versions of Visual C++ probably will include an equivalent to Access's OLE object frame controls.

> **NOTE**
>
> Unlike earlier versions of Visual C++, the Visual C++ 4.0 product includes a redistributable copy of the Access Jet database engine. The Jet engine is used by the DAO functionality of Visual C++ 4.0. This version of the Microsoft Jet database engine is 32-bit only and doesn't support 16-bit applications. There is no 16-bit version of the Microsoft Jet database engine for Visual C++.

Transaction-Processing Applications

Front ends for transaction processing let users update the tables of databases. Transaction processing involves editing or deleting existing records in the database tables or adding new records to the tables. Thus, users of transaction-processing applications need read-write access to the tables they want to modify. Transaction-processing applications require that either the database itself or your Visual C++ code preserve the integrity (related to accuracy) of the data. Enforcing domain (data value) integrity and referential (record) integrity in databases that users can update is covered in Chapter 4, "Optimizing the Design of Relational Databases."

Transaction processing implies the capability of using the SQL reserved words COMMIT and ROLLBACK to execute or cancel pending changes to the tables, respectively. All modern client-server databases support COMMIT and ROLLBACK transaction processing, but only a few desktop databases incorporate native transaction-processing capabilities. Access databases, for example, support transaction processing internally, whereas dBASE databases do not. Visual C++ supports transaction processing with the functions SQLPrepare(), SQLTransact(), and the keywords SQL COMMIT and SQL ROLLBACK. Chapter 15, "Designing Online Transaction-Processing Applications," shows you how to use Visual C++'s transaction-processing keywords to speed updates to RDBMS tables.

> **NOTE**
>
> ODBC drivers can provide transaction-processing capability for databases that don't ordinarily support SQL COMMIT/ SQL ROLLBACK transaction processing. Intersolv's dBASE ODBC driver, for example, lets you use SQL COMMIT or SQL ROLLBACK in your call to SQLTransact() that operates on dBASE tables.

In a multiuser environment, transaction-processing front ends must maintain database consistency and concurrency. Simplified descriptions of these two terms follow:

■ *Consistency* problems occur when the first user executes a transaction that updates a set of records and a second user attempts to view the records while the transaction is in process. Depending on the level of localization provided by the database management system, the second user might see the wrong data (called a *dirty read*), the wrong data followed by the right data (a *nonrepeatable read*), or erroneous data that results from the first user's transactions, which alter the rows that are included in the result of the second user's query (called *phantom data*).

■ *Concurrency* problems result when two or more users attempt to update the same record simultaneously. Unless a method is provided of locking the values of data in a record until the first user's transaction completes, you can't predict which user's update will prevail. Database, table, page, and/or record locking are provided by most database management systems to overcome concurrency problems. Locking the entire database or one or more tables during a transaction is seldom a satisfactory method in a multiuser environment because of the lock's affect on other users. Page or record locking, however, can result in a condition called *deadlock,* in which two users attempt to execute transactions on the same records in a set of two or more tables. Client-server database management systems use a variety of methods to detect and overcome deadlock conditions. If you're using a desktop RDBMS, you usually need to write your own anti-deadlock code in Visual C++.

Both consistency and concurrency issues can be controlled by the locking methods employed in multiuser environments. Visual C++ supports the following locking methods:

■ Database-level locking for client-server and Access .MDB databases, in which your application opens the database for exclusive rather than shared use. Database-level locking ordinarily is used only when you alter the structure of a database or when you compact or repair an Access database.

■ Table-level locking is available for all database types. A table lock opens a dBASE, Paradox, or Btrieve file for exclusive use. You open Access and client-server databases for shared use and then open the table for exclusive use. You can prevent consistency problems by setting the value of the Options property of the table to deny other users the capability to read the values in the table while it's locked.

■ Dynaset-level locking locks all of the tables that are used by the Dynaset object. A dynaset, a unique feature of Visual C++ and Access, is an updatable view of a database. Dynaset-level locking is available for all database types. To resolve consistency problems at the expense of concurrency, you can deny others the capability to read data with the Dynaset object's Options property.

■ Record-level locking is used for databases whose tables have fixed-length records, such as dBASE, FoxPro, and Paradox. Record-level locking provides the highest level of concurrency. You open the table file for shared use to employ record-level locking.

■ Page-level locking is used for Access and most client-server databases that use variable-length records. Access databases, for example, lock 2,048-byte pages. Thus, locking a single page also can lock many contiguous records if each record contains only a small amount of data. Page-level locking usually results in a lower level of concurrency than record locking.

> **NOTE**
>
> If you write a database program that appears unable to access a record because it's locked, but your application doesn't have that record locked, it's possible that the database page is locked by another application and that your program is actually functioning correctly.

■ Pessimistic locking applies only to record-level and page-level locking. Pessimistic locking locks the page(s) or record(s) as soon as a user employs the Edit or BeginTrans method and doesn't release the lock until the Update or CommitTrans method completes the edit, or until the edit is canceled with the Rollback method. Pessimistic locking is Visual C++'s default locking method that guarantees that your edit will succeed.

■ Optimistic locking also is restricted to record-level and page-level locking. Optimistic locking places locks on the record or page only during the time that it takes for the Update or CommitTrans method to execute. Optimistic locking offers a greater degree of concurrency, but you can't be assured which of two simultaneous edits will prevail.

When you use a client-server RDBMS, the server back end usually handles the page-level locking process for you. The majority of client-server RDBMSs let you specify the level of locking and the page-level locking method to be employed through SQL keywords such as SQL Server's HOLDLOCK instruction. You need to use the SQL pass-through option when you want to use SQL reserved words that aren't included in Access SQL. SQL pass-through is discussed in the section "Client-Server RDBMSs" later in this chapter.

The Access database engine can create and maintain indexes for each database type that the engine supports. You need a primary key index in order to update data contained in Paradox and client-server database tables. (Visual C++ doesn't use or maintain Paradox secondary or query speed-up indexes that are created on more than one column or that are designated as unique.) It's good database-programming practice to create indexes on the primary key field(s) of all of the tables in your database. (Visual C++, however, doesn't recognize indexes on primary key fields of dBASE or Btrieve tables as PrimaryKey indexes.) Adding indexes on the foreign key fields of related tables speeds queries that involve more than one table.

> **NOTE**
>
> Visual C++'s ODBC drivers can neither read nor maintain the .NTX index files created for .DBF files by CA-Clipper applications. Intersolv Software offers an ODBC driver that can read and update CA-Clipper .NTX indexes. If you want to use Visual C++ front ends concurrently with CA-Clipper DOS applications, you need to use the Intersolv ODBC driver to convert all the database indexes to dBASE-compatible index file formats.

As you add more indexes to your tables, the speed of transaction processing operations decreases when you update the data values contained in the indexed fields. Thus, the number of indexes you create for a table depends on whether the table is used primarily for decision-support or transaction-processing applications. Choosing the right index structure is discussed in Chapter 4.

> **NOTE**
>
> Multiple indexes drastically slow the importation of data from unsupported file types, such as delimited text files, to your existing tables.
>
> When you import data, you might find it much faster to create a new table to hold the imported data, then index the new table and append the data from the new table to the existing table.

Categorizing Database Management Systems for Visual C++

You can write Visual C++ front ends for a variety of types of database management systems. In fact, if you use the ODBC drivers and write SQL statements that use reserved words included in the ODBC Core-level SQL grammar, it's likely that you can create a single application that will perform satisfactorily with virtually any of the more commonly used relational database management systems. The ODBC Core-level SQL grammar is a subset of ANSI SQL-89 and is specified in Microsoft's Programmer's Reference for the Microsoft Open Database Connectivity Software Development Kit (ODBC SDK). The Microsoft ODBC Desktop Database Drivers Kit supports Core-level SQL grammar, as do the SQL Server and Oracle ODBC drivers supplied with Visual C++, and the ODBC drivers supplied by Intersolv Software. Chapter 5 includes a list of the SQL reserved words included in the Basic-level, Core-level, and Extended-level SQL grammars of ODBC.

> **NOTE**
>
> The 32-bit ODBC driver for Microsoft SQL Server also can be used with Sybase SQL Server and Sybase System 10, but the driver isn't supported by Microsoft for use with Sybase RDBMSs. When used with Sybase products, some features of Sybase System 10 aren't available when using the Microsoft driver.

The following sections describe the four basic categories of database management systems you can use with your Visual C++ database applications.

Traditional Desktop RDBMSs

Traditional desktop RDBMSs, typified by dBASE and Paradox, use separate files for each table and index, or collection of indexes for a single table in the case of dBASE IV and later .MDX and FoxPro .CDX indexes. dBASE and Paradox tables use fixed-width (also called fixed-length) records. You specify the maximum size of each field of the Character data type. Data values shorter than the maximum size automatically are padded with blanks (spaces) to the maximum size of the field. Btrieve tables provide for variable-length character fields. Variable-length character fields can save a substantial amount of disk space if the length of data values in character fields varies greatly.

The Visual C++ documentation defines a database comprising traditional desktop RDBMS table and index files as an *external database*. This book doesn't use the term *external database* because no complementary internal database is defined in Visual C++. The dBASE, FoxPro, Paradox, or Btrieve database is specified as the *well-formed path* to the directory that contains the table and index files that you need for your application. A well-formed path, also called a *fully-qualified path*, consists of the drive designator and the path to the folder that contains the table and index files, such as C:\VBDBS\DBASE. If your tables are stored on a file server (such as Windows NT or Windows 95) that uses the Uniform Naming Convention (UNC), you substitute the server name for the drive identifier, as in \\SERVER\VBDBS\DBASE.

You specify the indexes to be used with each of the tables in individual .INF files located in the same directory. The filename of the .INF file is the same as the table file. Thus, the information file for CUSTOMER.DBF is named CUSTOMER.INF. If you use dBASE IV multiple-index files, only one entry is required: NDX1=CUSTOMER.MDX. For dBASE III+ indexes, the index files are identified by sequentially numbered entries, such as NDX1=CUSTNAME.NDX, NDX2=CUSTZIP.NDX, and so on, with each entry on a separate line. You need .INF files for dBASE III+, dBASE IV, and FoxPro files, but not for Paradox or Btrieve fields. When you create a dBASE or FoxPro table and specify an index, Visual C++ automatically creates the .INF files for you. To use existing .MDX or .NDX index files with your .DBF file, you need to use Windows Notepad or another text editor to create the .INF file.

Btrieve's data definition file, FILES.DDF, serves the same purpose as the .INF file. Access can't create the FILES.DDF file for Btrieve databases. You need Xtrieve or a third-party Btrieve utility program to create the necessary Btrieve data definition file. Other requirements for the creation of Btrieve files are discussed in Chapter 6.

> **NOTE**
>
> The Access database engine doesn't have the capability to remove deleted records from dBASE and FoxPro table files. You need an application that supports the xBase PACK statement to eliminate deleted records and recover the fixed disk space that the deleted records consume.

FoxPro and dBASE III+/IV memo files that are associated with database tables must be stored in the same directory as the table that contains a Memo field data type. If the associated memo file is missing or corrupted, you receive an error message from Visual C++ when you attempt to open the table file. With dBASE 5/Visual dBASE databases, you also have OLEOBJECT data types, which are stored externally from the main database file(s).

> **NOTE**
>
> It's good database-programming practice to place all the table, memo, and index files you need for your application in a single database directory. Some xBase applications, such as accounting products, require that groups of files be stored in different directories. Visual C++ lets you open more than one database at a time; thus, you can deal with table, memo, and index files that are located in more than one directory.

The manipulation of data in the table files and the maintenance of the indexes of traditional desktop databases are the responsibility of the database application. The application translates high-level statements, such as SQL's SELECT or dBASE's LIST expressions, into low-level instructions that deal directly with records in the table files. If you run queries from a workstation against large table files that are located on a network file server, a very large number of low-level instructions are sent across the network to the file server. When a large number of users attempt to run queries simultaneously, to the same or other tables on the server, performance can suffer dramatically because of network congestion.

> **NOTE**
>
> There is no equivalent in Visual C++ to the record number associated with traditional RDBMS tables. Microsoft makes the valid point that record numbers are meaningless

in SQL databases. (However, Access assigns record numbers to tables and query results that Access displays in datasheet mode.)

Client-Server RDBMSs

The term *front end* originally appeared in conjunction with client-server RDBMS applications. *Front end* refers to the client application that runs on a workstation connected to the server (back end) on a local area network (LAN) or wide area network (WAN). The rapid growth of the client-server database market in the 1990s is because users of mainframe and minicomputer database management systems want to downsize their information systems. *Downsizing* means substituting relatively low-cost file servers, most often based on PC architecture, for expensive mainframe and minicomputer hardware and database software products that are costly to maintain. Today's trend is toward distributed client-server systems. In *distributed* database systems, tables that contain the data to satisfy a query might be located on several different servers in widely varying locations that are connected by a WAN.

The operating system for the server portion of the client-server RDBMS need not be (and often is not) the same as the operating system used by the client workstations. For example, Microsoft SQL Server 6 runs under Windows NT Server, and Sybase SQL Server runs under UNIX on minicomputers or as a NetWare Loadable Module (NLM) on Novell PC file servers. However, it's likely that the majority of both Microsoft and Sybase SQL server clients now run under the Windows graphical environment.

Client-server systems differ greatly from desktop database management systems. The primary distinction is that all SQL statements issued by the front-end application are executed by the server. When a workstation sends a conventional SELECT query to the server, only the rows that meet the query's specifications are returned to the workstation. The server is responsible for executing all SQL statements sent to the server by workstations. The server also handles all concurrency and consistency issues, such as locking. If a query issued by a workstation can't be completed by the server, the server returns an error message to the workstation. Combining high-level and low-level instruction processing at the server solves most network congestion issues.

The majority of client-server RDBMSs store all databases in a single, very large file. Where necessary, the file can be divided between server computers, but the divided file is treated as a single file by the server's operating system. Client-server RDBMSs include other sophisticated features, such as the maintenance of transaction logs that let databases be re-created in the event of corruption by a major hardware or software failure. Most client-server products now can use fixed disk arrays and mirrored fixed disks that reduce the likelihood that a failure of part or all of a single fixed disk drive will bring client services to a halt.

The easiest method of connecting your Visual C++ database application to a client-server database is to use the appropriate ODBC driver. This book refers to a client-server database connected through an ODBC driver as a *datasource*. To open a connection to a datasource, you need to have previously defined the datasource with the ODBC Administrator application that is supplied with the Professional Edition of Visual C++ or another Microsoft application, such as Microsoft Query, that uses ODBC. You need the datasource name (DSN), a valid user login identifier (UID), and a valid password (PWD) to open a client-server datasource as a Visual C++ CDatabase object or to attach tables from the datasource to an open Access database.

NOTE

Often, programs will have references to the MFC database objects (CDatabase, CRecordset, and CRecordView). The programmer who is writing only in C can get the same functionality using the SQL...() functions, which are supported by the ODBC connectivity libraries.

Although you can use the Access database engine to process queries against client-server databases that you open as Visual C++ database objects or that you attach to an Access database, using the SQL pass-through option takes better advantage of the client-server environment. When you specify the use of SQL pass-through, the server processes the query and returns a recordset structure that contains the rows returned by the query (if any). The term *recordset* refers to any database object that contains data in the form of records. You also can use SQL pass-through to execute action queries that append, update, or delete records but don't return a query result set. SQL pass-through lets you execute *stored procedures* if your client-server database supports stored procedures. (The Microsoft and Sybase versions of SQL Server support stored procedures.) A *stored procedure* is a compiled version of a standard SQL query that your application uses repeatedly. Stored procedures execute much faster than conventional SQL queries, especially when the query is complex.

Client-server RDBMSs vary widely in purchase price. As a rule, the price of the server software depends on the number of simultaneous workstation connections that the server supports. As with runtime versions of traditional RDBMSs, you purchase copies of the workstation software that are necessary to connect to the server. Microsoft SQL Server is currently the lowest-cost commercial client-server RDBMS available from a major software publisher. You can run Microsoft SQL Server as a service of the Microsoft LAN Manager 2.2 network operating system (NOS), under Novell NetWare, or under Windows NT. Chapter 20, "Creating Front Ends for Client-Server Databases," describes how to use these Microsoft RDBMSs with Visual C++ front ends.

Access: A Nontraditional Desktop RDBMS

Access deserves its own category because Access databases bear little resemblance to traditional desktop database structures. The Microsoft documentation for Visual C++ refers to both "Access databases" and "Visual C++ databases." It's likely that Microsoft intended these two terms to mean "databases created with Access" (which requires a SYSTEM.MDA file for versions of Access prior to 7 and SYSTEM.MDW for Access 7 and later) and "databases created with Visual C++" (which doesn't require SYSTEM.MDA or SYSTEM.MDW), respectively. For consistency, this book uses the term *Access database* no matter what application is used to create the .MDB file (which contains the actual data).

> **NOTE**
>
> Access 95 replaces Access 1.x and 2.0 SYSTEM.MDA files with SYSTEM.MDW, called a *workgroup* file, which fulfills similar security functions. The .MDA file extension is now reserved for Access library files. Visual C++ 4.0 doesn't require SYSTEM.MDW or SYSTEM.MDA, but a workgroup file is needed if you want to take advantage of the Groups and Users collections to manipulate permissions for secure multiuser .MDB files.

As mentioned at the beginning of this chapter, Access is the default database type for Visual C++. Microsoft's choice for the default database type is understandable because Access .MDB files have a structure that is proprietary to Microsoft Corporation. Thus, you need to purchase a Microsoft product to use Access database files. All the Microsoft applications that can handle Access database files are Windows applications. It is highly unlikely that Microsoft will publish the intimate details of the Access .MDB file structure as an "open standard," at least in the foreseeable future. Despite the proprietary nature of Access database files, you're likely to find that Access is the database type to select when the choice is yours to make.

Access database files include many of the features of the client-server databases described in the preceding section. Much of the architecture of Access .MDB files is based on the structure of Microsoft SQL Server database files. Here are some similarities between Access and client-server databases:

■ All the tables and indexes for a database are stored in a single .MDB file. Fields of the Text, Memo, and OLE Object field data types are variable-width. Access tables adjust the sizes of numeric fields to accommodate the fundamental data type used in the field.

■ Date fields include time information. The Date field data type corresponds to the timestamp data type of SQL-92 but isn't stored in timestamp format.

■ Access tables support null values. The null value, indicated by the keyword SQL_NULL_DATA, is different from the NULL identifier word in Visual C++ and indicates that no data has been entered in the data cell of a table. The null value isn't the same as an empty string (" "). All client-server databases support null values, but few other desktop databases do.

■ You can store *query definitions*, which are SQL statements saved as named objects, in Access databases. A QueryDef object is similar to an SQL SELECT statement compiled as an SQL Server stored procedure.

■ Access Memo fields behave as if the field data type were Text and could hold up to 32,000 characters.

■ The size of OLE Object (LargeBinary or BLOB, an acronym for *binary large object*) fields is limited only by the size of the database, which in turn is likely to be limited by your fixed-disk capacity, not by the Access .MDB file structure. You can store data of any type in an Access table's BLOB field using the Get Chunk and Append Chunk methods to read and write data to BLOB fields. BLOBs are usually used for graphics images.

■ You can enforce referential integrity between tables and enforce domain integrity at the table level in Access databases. (Enforcement of domain integrity occurs only when you attempt to change the value of a field.)

■ Access databases include built-in security features and might be encrypted. You need a second table, usually named SYSTEM.MDW, to implement the security features of Access databases.

Other advantages of using Access databases include the capability to attach tables of other supported database types. The Microsoft documentation contains ambiguous references to *external tables* and *attached tables*. As I mentioned earlier in this chapter, this book doesn't use the term *external tables*. You can gain a significant speed advantage if you attach tables from client-server databases to an Access database rather than opening the client-server data source as a Visual C++ CDatabase object.

> **NOTE**
>
> You usually gain an even greater speed advantage when you use the SQL pass-through option to cause your SQL query statements to be executed by the database server rather than by the Access database engine.

Mainframe and Minicomputer Database Management Systems

If you have the appropriate software and hardware (called a *gateway* or *MiddleWare*), you can connect to several popular mainframe and minicomputer RDBMSs, such as IBM's DB2 or

Digital Equipment Corporation's Rdb. Suppliers of gateways to DB2 databases that are compatible with ODBC include Micro Decisionware, Inc. (now part of Sybase); Information Builders, Inc.; Sybase; TechGnosis, Inc.; and IBM Corporation. (Additional information on these gateways is included in Appendix A.) In addition to the gateway, you need the appropriate ODBC driver for the mainframe or minicomputer database to which you want to connect. One of the principal commercial uses of Visual C++ is to create front ends for IBM DB2 databases.

> **NOTE**
>
> IBM now offers DB2/2 for use under OS/2 version 2.x in both a single-user and a multiuser version, and it is readying another DB2 variant for use under Windows NT. DB2/2 is the replacement for the OS/2 Database Manager (DBM) for OS/2 version 1.3. You can use the Intersolv DB2/2 ODBC driver with either the single-user or multiuser version of DB2/2 to emulate mainframe DB2 databases during development of your front-end application. Having a desktop version of DB2 can save many hours of negotiation with your DB2 database administrator when you need to restructure or reload your test database.

You can even use SQL statements to query nonrelational databases such as CODASYL network databases or hierarchical databases typified by IBM's IMS. Products such as Information Builder's EDA/Link for Windows and the IBI EDA/SQL database engine make network and hierarchical databases behave like client-server applications.

Abandoning Traditional Database Programming Languages

This book's Introduction states that this book is intended for readers who are familiar with Visual C++ programming techniques. Some readers have a tendency to skip Introductions and proceed to the first chapters in a book of this type. The following sections are designed for database developers who haven't yet fully mastered Visual C++ programming or for whom creating a database application will be their first experience with Visual C++ programming. Developers evaluating Visual C++ as an alternative to Access or Visual Basic also might benefit from the brief description of Visual C++ programming that follows. Visual C++ pros undoubtedly will want to skip the following two sections.

Adapting to the Windows Event-Method Environment

Creating database applications for the character-based environment of DOS traditionally has involved top-down programming techniques. Using xBase as an example, you start at the "top" with a main program, such as APPNAME.PRG, in which you declare your PUBLIC (Global) variables and constants, and then you add the code you need to create the DO WHILE .T....ENDDO main menu loop for your application. Next, you add the procedures that include more menu loops for the next level of submenus. Then you write the procedures that contain the @...SAY and @...GET statements to create the screens that constitute the core of your DOS application. Finally, you add the accouterments, such as data validation procedures and report printing operations. As an experienced database developer, you write modular source code. You've written your own libraries of standard procedures and user-defined functions that you reuse in a variety of applications. You also might employ add-in libraries created by other developers. If you use CA-Clipper, you spend a substantial amount of time recompiling and linking your application during the development cycle.

To use Visual C++, you'll need to abandon most of the programming techniques to which you've grown accustomed and adopt Windows' object-oriented, event-driven, method-centered programming style. The first major difference you'll discover when you switch to Visual C++ as your database development platform is that you don't create a "main" program. The "main" program is Microsoft Windows. There is a hidden WinMain function in every Visual C++ program, but Windows itself has the final say on how your application executes. Your application can't execute any code until an event occurs because Visual C++ procedures begin as event handlers. *Event handlers* are methods that your application executes in response to events.

NOTE

The preceding paragraph describes all Visual C++ functions as being event handlers. Even though a C program might not seem to be written by using event handlers, it actually is. With C++ programs created by using AppWizard, the event/function relationship is very visible through the ClassWizard interface.

You can't generate or respond to an event without creating an application because

- Events originate from user-initiated actions, such as mouse clicks or keystrokes, that occur when a Visual C++ form is the active window. The active window is said to *have the focus*. During the time that your application is quiescent (when no events are being processed), Windows is in an idle loop, waiting for the next event. A Windows idle loop replaces the traditional for() {...} menu loops of character-based DOS applications.

- Your Visual C++ event-handling code is contained in modules that are matched to each dialog box and menu in your application. You can create modules and declare variables with global scope.

Dealing with Programming Objects

Visual C++ makes extensive use of object-oriented programming terminology to describe the components of applications. Visual C++ classifies dialog boxes, controls on dialog boxes, databases, and tables as *objects*. An object possesses characteristics and behavior. The characteristics of an object are the object's *properties* (data), and the behavior of the object is determined by its *methods* (incorporated in event-handling code). An object is a container for data and code. Objects can contain other objects; dialog boxes, for example, contain control objects. Each Visual C++ object has its own predetermined set of properties to which Visual C++ assigns default values. The methods that are applicable to a programming object are a set of Visual C++ reserved words that are pertinent to the class of the object. The set of methods that is applicable to dialog boxes differs greatly from the set of methods that is used with recordset objects.

Visual C++ lets you create object variables that refer to objects with the `CObject * ObjectPointer` and `ObjectPointer = &Object` statements. After these two statements are executed, `ObjectPointer` is a reference (pointer) to the original object. You can assign as many different variables to the same object as you want. If you add the reserved word `new` to the assignment statement, as in `NewObject = new ObjectName`, you can create a new instance of the original object. An instance of an object is a copy of the object that you can manipulate independently of the object you have copied. Object variables are an essential element of database application programming with Visual C++.

The Data Types of Visual C++

Variables declared with the xBase reserved words `PUBLIC` and `PRIVATE` default to the Logical data type and are assigned a new data type when they are initialized with a value other than `.T.` or `.F.`. Because xBase has only the four fundamental field data types used in dBASE III+ .DBF files (Character, Numeric, Date, and Logical), it's a simple matter for an xBase interpreter to determine the data type from the assigned value and to treat the variable according to its content. xBase is said to have weak data typing. In contrast, compiled languages such as Pascal and C have strong data typing. You must explicitly declare the data type when you name the variable.

Early versions of the C language took the middle road to data typing: All variables were explicitly declared, but assignments between differing types were only weakly controlled. As the sophistication of C increased (actually, with the introduction of C++), C/C++ compilers began to more strictly enforce the usage of data types. You can still cast a variable of one type and assign the result to a variable of a differing type, but using explicit casts is no longer considered an acceptable programming technique.

There are three problems with strong data typing when you're dealing with objects and databases:

- You might not know in advance what data type(s) will be returned by an object when that object is created by another Windows application. For example, an object consisting of a range of cells in an Excel worksheet is likely to contain dates, strings, and numbers. The capability to accommodate indeterminate data types is an important consideration when you use OLE and its OLE Automation features.

- You can't concatenate variables of different fundamental data types without using data-type conversion functions. The need for data-type conversion complicates operations such as creating a composite index on table fields of different Field data types (such as Text and Date). This eliminates the need for indexing constructs, such as xBase's INDEX ON *CharField* + DTOS(*DateField*) TO *IndexFile*.

- Many database types now support null values. Conventional data types don't support the null value directly. The work-around, using SQL_NULL_DATA to specify a null value, is often cumbersome.

Visual C++ uses the SQLBindCol() function, which solves all the preceding problems of matching the SQL datatypes with Visual C++ variable types. An added benefit of the SQLBindCol() function is that you can use a number of different type conversions. Table 1.2 shows the acceptable conversions between C/C++ variable types and SQL data types. A D signifies a default conversion, a dot is a possible alternative conversion, and an empty space signifies that there is no conversion between these types. The types SQL_C_TINYINT and SQL_C_SHORT don't have default conversions.

Table 1.2. SQL-datatype-to-C-datatype conversions.

SQL Data Type / C/C++ Data Type	SQL_C_CHAR	SQL_C_BIT	SQL_C_STINYINT	SQL_C_UTINYINT	SQL_C_TINYINT	SQL_C_SSHORT	SQL_C_USHORT	SQL_C_SHORT	SQL_C_SLONG	SQL_C_ULONG	SQL_C_LONG	SQL_C_FLOAT	SQL_C_DOUBLE	SQL_C_BINARY	SQL_C_DATE	SQL_C_TIME	SQL_C_TIMESTAMP
SQL_CHAR	D	•	•	•	•	•	•	•	•	•	•	•	•	•	•	•	•
SQL_VARCHAR	D	•	•	•	•	•	•	•	•	•	•	•	•	•	•	•	•
SQL_LONGVARCHAR	D	•	•	•	•	•	•	•	•	•	•	•	•	•	•	•	•
SQL_DECIMAL	D	•	•	•	•	•	•	•	•	•	•	•	•	•			
SQL_NUMERIC	D	•	•	•	•	•	•	•	•	•	•	•	•	•			
SQL_BIT	•	D	•	•	•	•	•	•	•	•	•	•	•	•			
SQL_TINYINT (signed)	•	•	D	•	•	•	•	•	•	•	•	•	•	•			
SQL_TINYINT (unsigned)	•	•	•	D	•	•	•	•	•	•	•	•	•	•			
SQL_SMALLINT (signed)	•	•	•	•	•	D	•	•	•	•	•	•	•	•			
SQL_SMALLINT (unsigned)	•	•	•	•	•	•	D	•	•	•	•	•	•	•			
SQL_INTEGER (signed)	•	•	•	•	•	•	•	•	D	•	•	•	•	•			
SQL_INTEGER (unsigned)	•	•	•	•	•	•	•	•	•	D	•	•	•	•			
SQL_BIGINT	D	•	•	•	•	•	•	•	•	•	•	•	•	•			
SQL_REAL	•	•	•	•	•	•	•	•	•	•	•	D	•	•			
SQL_FLOAT	•	•	•	•	•	•	•	•	•	•	•	•	D	•			
SQL_DOUBLE	•	•	•	•	•	•	•	•	•	•	•	•	D	•			
SQL_BINARY	•													D			
SQL_VARBINARY	•													D			
SQL_LONGVARBINARY	•													D			
SQL_DATE	•													•	D		•
SQL_TIME	•													•		D	•
SQL_TIMESTAMP	•													•	•	•	D

Table 1.3 contains the SQL C types (shown in Table 1.2) matched to native C/C++ types. The DATE_STRUCT, TIME_STRUCT, and TIMESTAMP_STRUCT structures are defined in the SQLEXT.H header file. They make date and time manipulation easier.

Table 1.3. SQL C types matched to native C/C++ types.

SQL C Type Identifier	ODBC C Type	C/C++ Type
SQL_C_BINARY	UCHAR FAR *	unsigned char far *
SQL_C_BIT	UCHAR	unsigned char
SQL_C_CHAR	UCHAR FAR *	unsigned char far *
SQL_C_DATE	DATE_STRUCT	struct DATE_STRUCT

continues

Table 1.3. continued

SQL C Type Identifier	ODBC C Type	C/C++ Type
SQL_C_DOUBLE	SDOUBLE	double
SQL_C_FLOAT	SFLOAT	float
SQL_C_SLONG	SDWORD	long int
SQL_C_SSHORT	SWORD	short int
SQL_C_STINYINT	SCHAR	signed char
SQL_C_TIME	TIME_STRUCT	struct TIME_STRUCT
SQL_C_TIMESTAMP	TIMESTAMP_STRUCT	struct TIMESTAMP_STRUCT
SQL_C_ULONG	LDWORD	unsigned long int
SQL_C_USHORT	UWORD	unsigned short int
SQL_C_UTINYINT	UCHAR	unsigned char

The three date and time structures are shown in Listing 1.1. These structures are defined in SQLEXT.H so that you don't have to define them in your application.

Listing 1.1. SQL time and date transfer structures.

```
typedef struct tagDATE_STRUCT
{
        SWORD year;        // 0 to 9999
        UWORD month;       // 1 to 12
        UWORD day;         // 1 to valid number of days in the month
} DATE_STRUCT;

typedef struct tagTIME_STRUCT
{
        UWORD hour;        // 0 to 23
        UWORD minute;      // 0 to 59
        UWORD second;      // 0 to 59
} TIME_STRUCT;

typedef struct tagTIMESTAMP_STRUCT
{
        SWORD year;        // 0 to 9999
        UWORD month;       // 1 to 12
        UWORD day;         // 1 to valid number of days in the month
        UWORD hour;        // 0 to 23
        UWORD minute;      // 0 to 59
        UWORD second;      // 0 to 59
        UDWORD fraction;   // Nanoseconds
} TIMESTAMP_STRUCT;
```

The Data Access Objects of Visual C++

Database objects have existed in MFC and Visual C++, and these database objects are applicable to databases connected through the ODBC drivers. Visual C++'s Microsoft Jet database engine, combined with newly added database functions and methods incorporated in the Visual C++ data access object, lets you create database objects using tables native to any of the more common desktop and client-server RDBMSs. In addition, Visual C++ lets you define and create new databases for the majority of the supported database types, assuming that the ODBC driver supports this type of operation.

Following are the objects that are contained in MFC and Visual C++:

- CDatabase objects function as the linkage between the application and the actual dataset. In C programs, the functionality of the CDatabase object is available using the SQL...() functions. You can open and use as many simultaneous CDatabase objects as you want.

- CRecordset objects represent the results, or set of records, obtained from a dataset. The CRecordset object contains CDatabase tables contained in the CDatabase object.

- CRecordView objects are based on the CFormView class. With CFormView, your application functions much like any other dialog-based application. When you use App-Wizard to create a Visual C++ application, the default is to use the CFormView class to display your records.

In the preceding list, the examples of the syntax of statements that create the database objects represent the simplest form of these statements. CDatabase and CRecordset objects have optional arguments or required calls to initialization functions to open and define the actual dataset. You set the value of the optional arguments based on the database type you choose and the type of locking you want.

Object Collections

A *collection* is a set of references to related objects, similar to but not identical to an array. The specification for creating and naming collections is included in the Microsoft OLE publication *Creating Programmable Applications.* The references (pointers) to objects in a collection are called *members* of the collection. Each member of a collection has a unique name and index value. Unlike arrays, however, the index number of a member may change, and index numbers need not be contiguous. It's possible for a collection to contain no members at all. Most collections have a property, Count, that returns the number of members of the collection. The index to a collection need not be an integer, but it usually is. Some objects use string indexes. The safest approach is to always specify the unique name of the member of a collection you want to use.

The name of a collection is the English plural of the class of object in the collection. In Visual C++, collections might include dialog boxes (all dialog boxes that have been loaded by the application), controls (each control on a loaded dialog box), the data access object collections in the following list, and collections of objects exposed by OLE applications that support OLE Automation. This discussion is limited to data access objects that incorporate the following three object class collections:

■ `TableDefs` is the collection of `TableDef` objects that contain a description of each table contained in the database.

■ `Fields` is the collection of `Field` objects for a `TableDef` object. `Field` objects contain a description of each field of a table.

■ `Indexes` is the collection of `Index` objects for a `TableDef` object. `Index` objects describe each index on one or more fields of the table.

The Data Control Object

Visual C++ provides a `CRecordView` object that lets you add controls to a Visual C++ dialog box that may be used to display records from a dataset. Controls may be used to display and update data in the current record of a specified `CRecordset` object. Figure 1.3 illustrates a Visual C++ application's use of the `CRecordView` dialog box and controls to display and update information contained in the Customers table of NorthWind.MDB (supplied with Access).

FIGURE 1.3.

A `CRecordView`*-based application.*

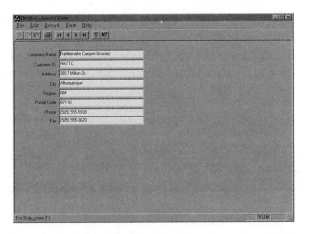

The advantage of using the `CRecordView` object is that you can create a form to browse through the records in a `CRecordset` object without writing any Visual C++ code at all. The source for this program is in the CHAPTR02\Record View folder on the CD that comes with this book.

The sample program shown in Figure 1.3 has no code added by me (the author). I did add the controls to display the data in the dialog box and bind (existing) variables to these controls. I didn't modify any source files by hand to create this project. All the modifications were done by using the resources editor and ClassWizard working on an application generated by using AppWizard. Perhaps the day of programmerless programming has arrived to C++ programming!

One feature of the program that AppWizard creates is the toolbar with its VCR-style buttons, similar to the record selector buttons of Access's datasheet view. Many database developers prefer to use command buttons with Alt-*key* combinations for record selection. The majority of the sample applications in this book use Visual C++ code generated by using AppWizard rather than trying to code the database access by hand.

Visual C++ provides the following dialog box control objects that you can use in conjunction with dialog boxes:

■ *Text box controls* are the basic control element for data control objects. You can display and edit data of any field data type, not just text, in a bound text box control.

■ *Label controls* display the data in a field but don't allow editing of the data. Bound label controls can't receive Windows focus; thus, label controls are useful in decision-support applications in which read-only access to the database is the norm.

■ *Check box controls* display or update data in fields of the Boolean field data type (called yes/no fields in Access 1.x and logical fields in xBase). The null value is represented by making the check box gray.

Chapter 3, "Using Visual C++ Database Functions," provides examples of simple decision-support and transaction-processing applications that you can create with the data control and bound control objects.

Access developers will regret the absence of a Visual C++ equivalent of the drop-down combo box in Access. You need to write a substantial amount of Visual C++ code to duplicate the features of Access's built-in bound combo box. Visual C++ also lacks an equivalent of Access's subforms.

OLE and Visual C++

Visual C++ applications can be data-aware applications that support OLE and OLE Automation. A *data-aware* application is one that includes the built-in capability to extract data from a variety of databases, with the Access database engine using ODBC or DAO. OLE extends the capabilities of OLE 1.0 by adding the following features:

■ In-place activation of OLE server (source) applications: When you double-click to activate an embedded OLE object in your container (OLE client) application, the server application takes over the window created by your form and substitutes the server application's menus for the menus of your form. (You can activate an OLE object when the OLE control receives the focus by setting the AutoActivate property of the OLE control to 1.) OLE applications create their own editing window when activated. Visual C++ supports in-place activation only with embedded objects.

■ Persistent OLE objects: The data associated with an OLE object ordinarily isn't *persistent*—that is, the data is no longer accessible after you close a form. The OLE control lets you save the OLE object's data as a persistent object and restore the persistent OLE object from a binary file. (The standard file extension for an OLE object file is, not surprisingly, .OLE.)

■ OLE Automation: OLE Automation gives your OLE controls access to application programming objects by OLE server applications that support OLE Automation. Microsoft Excel, Project, and Word for Windows include OLE Automation capabilities. OLE Automation lets you manipulate data in an OLE object with Visual C++ code; thus, you can place data from a Visual C++ database application into an Excel worksheet directly rather than by using DDE.

The first commercial product to support OLE was CorelDRAW! 4.0, which Corel Systems released after the first version of Visual C++ appeared.

The lack of OLE-compliant applications caused the description of OLE features in the Visual C++ documentation to be sketchy at best. The OLE sample applications provide you with little assistance when you want to add OLE features to your Visual C++ applications. To fill this gap, the following sections provide an introduction to OLE Automation. Chapter 17, "Using OLE Controls and Automation with Visual C++ Applications," includes sample applications that demonstrate OLE features that are especially useful for database applications.

> **NOTE**
>
> One of the best books on OLE is Kraig Brockschmidt's *Inside OLE 2,* Second Edition (Microsoft Press, 1995). This book is universally considered to be the bible of OLE programmers. Microsoft Press also publishes a two-volume reference on OLE called

the *OLE Programmer's Reference* (1994). These books were published electronically on the MSDN CD in early 1995; however, they are no longer available on CD.

NOTE

When using OLE under Windows 3.1, you need to use the DOS TSR application SHARE.EXE prior to loading Windows. Specify at least 500 available locks with a `SHARE /l:500` statement in your AUTOEXEC.BAT file.

Windows 95 and the enhanced mode of Windows for Workgroups 3.1 and later install a driver, VSHARE.386, that substitutes for and disables SHARE.EXE. Thus, if you need SHARE.EXE only for applications that you run under Windows for Workgroups 3.1+, you don't need to (and therefore shouldn't) load SHARE.EXE.

OLE Automation

Visual C++ lets you create applications that orchestrate interprocess communication among Windows applications without requiring that you suffer through the coding and testing of DDE operations. In the language of OLE, Visual C++ is called an *external programming tool.* OLE Automation programming tools let you do the following:

- Create new objects of the object classes supported by OLE Automation source applications.

- Manipulate existing objects in OLE Automation source and container applications.

- Obtain and set the values of properties of objects.

- Invoke methods that act on the objects.

Prior to Visual C++ and OLE Automation, you could link or embed source documents in a destination document created by the OLE control, but you couldn't use Visual C++ code to edit the source document. DDE was the only practical method of programmatically altering data in an object created by another application. (*Programmatically* is an adverb recently added to computerese by Microsoft. It refers to the capability of manipulating an object with program code.)

The following list explains the principal advantages of the use of OLE Automation to replace DDE for applications that require IPC (interprocess communication):

- OLE places an object-oriented shell around IPC applications. You can manipulate objects in OLE Automation applications as if they were objects of your Visual C++ application. You also can manipulate an OLE object that is embedded in or linked to an OLE control object contained in a Visual C++ form.

■ You create a new object in an OLE source application by declaring an object.

■ After you've created an object variable, you can change the value of each object property that isn't read-only and apply any of the methods that are applicable to the object with statements in your Visual C++ code. Methods usually include all of the application's menu choices, plus the equivalents of other statements or functions in the application's macro language. Thus, OLE Automation lets you substitute an Excel worksheet for a Visual C++ grid control in your database applications.

■ As mentioned earlier in this chapter, you can create a persistent copy of an OLE object by saving the value of the object's Data property to an .OLE file. Later, you can retrieve the object by reading the data from the .OLE file into an OLE control.

OLE Automation offers the most significant opportunity for the improvement of Windows applications since Microsoft introduced OLE 1.0 with Windows 3.1. The majority of the major software publishers have announced their intention to support OLE, but few firms other than Microsoft have committed to dates when such products will reach the shelves of software retailers. OLE 1.0 proved difficult to implement, and creating OLE applications is an even more challenging task. At the time this book was written, Symantec's C++ product and Borland's C++ 4.5 were a few of the programming tools to compete with Visual C++. At the present, only Microsoft's Windows applications offer you the sizable benefits of OLE Automation. OLE Automation is expected to be a feature of future versions of other popular Microsoft applications, such as Access and PowerPoint. By the end of 1995, virtually all mainstream Windows applications implemented OLE Automation. Much of the adoption of OLE has been forced by Microsoft, which requires all certified Windows 95 applications to be fully OLE-compliant, if applicable.

Visual Basic for Applications

Why am I mentioning Visual Basic in a book on Visual C++? Mostly for background. It's likely that you have some background in Visual Basic or that you're interested in Visual Basic's relationship to Microsoft products. Also, Visual Basic for Applications is the OLE automation language.

Bill Gates, chairman and chief executive officer of Microsoft, decreed in 1991 that all of Microsoft's mainstream applications for Windows would share a common macro language (CML) derived from BASIC. His pronouncement wasn't surprising because Microsoft's first product was a BASIC interpreter for the original personal computers that used the Intel 8080 as their CPU. Microsoft's QuickBASIC and QBasic products ultimately became the most widely used flavors of structured BASIC of the world's IBM-compatible PCs. Word for Windows 1.0's Word BASIC was the first macro language for a Microsoft application that used a dialect of BASIC.

No other Microsoft application adopted BASIC as its macro language until Microsoft released Access 1.0 in November 1992. Access, however, had its own macro language that wasn't derived from BASIC, so Microsoft called Access Basic an *application programming language*. Access Basic is a direct descendant of Visual Basic 2.0 that introduced object variables to the Visual Basic language. Access Basic was originally called "Embedded Basic." You see occasional references to "EB" and "Cirrus Basic" in Access 1.0 help files and add-in library code. Cirrus was the code name for Access during its beta-testing period.

Visual Basic for Applications is an OLE Automation programming tool classified as an embedded macro language. Visual Basic for Applications is based on Visual Basic and offers many of Visual Basic's capabilities. The structure and syntax of Visual Basic for Applications code is very similar to that of Visual Basic. Following are some of the most significant differences you'll find between Visual C++ and Visual Basic for Applications:

- All Visual Basic for Applications code is contained in one or more modules stored within the application. Excel stores code modules in a workbook. You create an Excel 7 module by choosing Insert | Macro | Module.

- Like Word Basic macros, all the functions and procedures in a module appear consecutively rather than in the individual windows employed by the Visual Basic and Visual Basic for Applications code editors. Most applications execute the entry point by selecting the macro from a list box of the dialog box that appears when you choose Tools | Macros. To prevent subprocedures from appearing in the macro list box, you preface `Sub ProcName` with the `Private` reserved word.

- There is no Declarations section in a Visual Basic for Applications module. You declare `Global` and module-level variables and constants at the beginning of a module, before the first function or procedure you write.

- After you open a module, you can use the Object Browser to display the objects that are exposed by an OLE Automation application and thus are available to your application. Figure 1.4 shows the Object Browser dialog box for Visual Basic for Applications opened over an Excel module containing demonstration code. Object Browsers are another class of OLE Automation programming tools.

- You can use Visual Basic for Applications to reconstruct the menu choices of applications and to create custom toolbars. The smiley-face button that appears at the left of the top toolbar in Figure 1.4 is added with a Visual Basic for Applications procedure.

- Windows DLLs that incorporate OLE Automation code expose functions that appear in the Object Browser dialog. You don't need to use the `Declare Function` or `Declare Sub` statements to use OLE Automation functions in OLE-compliant DLLs.

- Visual Basic for Applications supports no visual objects of its own, such as forms. The only exceptions are Windows message boxes and input boxes. The OLE Automation application itself must provide a window to display other control objects, such as text boxes and command buttons. Excel, for example, provides a Dialogs collection of `Dialog` objects that constitute Excel's built-in dialog boxes, and it provides a `DialogSheet` object that can contain a custom-designed dialog box that includes default OK and Cancel buttons. Each Workbook object can contain a `DialogSheets` collection. You create an Excel dialog sheet by choosing Insert | Macro | Dialog. Figure 1.5 shows the design-mode and run-mode appearance of an Excel 5 dialog box with typical control objects.

FIGURE 1.4.

Excel 5's module editing window displaying the Object Browser dialog.

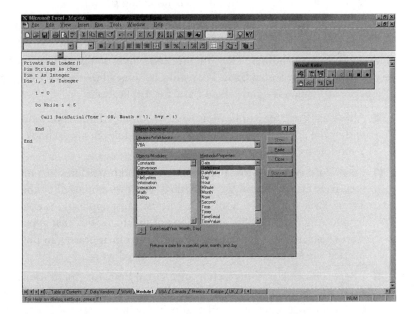

FIGURE 1.5.

The design-mode and run-mode versions of an Excel dialog sheet.

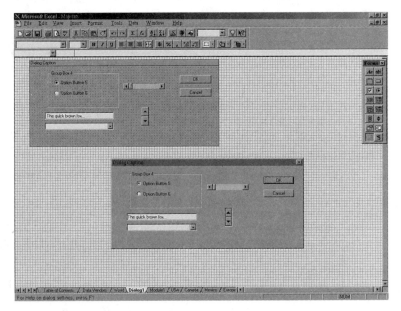

■ You can declare any object that is exposed by an OLE Automation application as an object variable of the appropriate class. For example, you can declare an Excel worksheet as an object of the class Worksheets. Other Excel object classes are Application and Range.

■ You have access to each of the properties and can apply any of the methods of the application object. You can apply the Cells method to any of the Excel object classes to return a collection of cells contained in the object.

■ `Property Let ProcName...End Property` procedures assign the values of properties of objects, and `Property Get FunctionName...End Property` functions return the values of properties of objects. The structure of `Property` procedures and functions is identical to conventional `Function FunctionName...End Function` and `Sub ProcName...End Sub` procedures.

■ Visual Basic for Applications runs on both Intel 80x86 and Macintosh computers. You need to make only minor changes to your code to port a Visual Basic for Applications program from the PC to the Mac. You declare and use functions in Macintosh code resources and Windows dynamic link libraries with the same Visual Basic syntax.

During the development of Visual Basic for Applications (when its code name was Object Basic), Microsoft reportedly was willing to license Visual Basic for Applications to other software publishers for incorporation in their applications. Subsequently, Microsoft announced that Visual Basic for Applications would remain a proprietary Microsoft product and would be available only as a component of Microsoft applications for Windows.

Lotus now provides a common programming interface to its products. Lotus also is committed to supporting OLE in its products. Lotus Notes will prove to be a formidable competitor in the next few years.

Lotus is working to become compatible with standard languages, which will allow database programmers to leverage their existing programming skills.

Summary

This chapter covered the process of choosing Visual C++ as a database development tool, using Visual C++ as a database front-end generator, migrating from the more traditional database programming languages, the MFC ODBC and DAO classes, and OLE. This chapter also gave you an overview of Visual C++'s capabilities as a database development platform and how Microsoft plans to use Visual C++, OLE Automation, and Visual Basic for Applications to cement the firm's leadership position in the Windows desktop database market. You don't need to be clairvoyant to conclude that the Macintosh version of Visual C++ (actually a cross compiler) will emerge as a major player in the Macintosh world in the future, together with an Access database engine designed to run as a Macintosh code resource. No matter what your opinions are relating to Microsoft's predominance in the Windows and Macintosh applications markets and the methods Microsoft has used to achieve their present market share, the Microsoft desktop database juggernaut is a fact. Developers of traditional character-based database applications in xBase or PAL who don't face this fact will find a rapidly diminishing market for their services in the mid- to late 1990s.

The remaining two chapters in Part I of this book give you the basic details you need to use Visual C++'s data access objects, the CFormView object, and bound control objects to create simple Visual C++ database applications that display and edit data contained in Access databases. Even accomplished Visual C++ developers should scan the next two chapters, because Visual C++'s data access objects differ somewhat from the other Visual C++ MFC objects when used in an AppWizard-generated application.

2

Understanding MFC's ODBC Database Classes

The MFC data access classes are Visual C++'s object-oriented method of interacting with datasources. MFC's implementation of ODBC supports three major objects: CDatabase, CRecordView, and CRecordset. Supporting classes include CDBException, CFieldExchange, and CLongBinary. Most commonly, programmers use these objects when working with applications created with Visual C++'s AppWizard program. Any database application created by using AppWizard will incorporate these classes.

Chapter 1, "Positioning Visual C++ in the Desktop Database Market," introduced Visual C++ and accessing databases. This chapter describes the structure of the MFC data access classes in detail because the member functions of these classes constitute the foundation on which all of your Visual C++ MFC database applications are built. This chapter features examples that use the member functions to create Visual C++ code. By the time you complete this rather lengthy chapter, it's very likely that you will have learned more than you ever wanted to know about data-related objects and classes!

Programmers who want to "roll their own" and use the database classes will have few (if any) problems incorporating them into their applications. However, for a simple front-end application in which data access and updating are the main functions of the program, using AppWizard is the simplest choice. The sample program shown in Figure 2.1 took only about 10 minutes to write and required no manual source code modification to create. The source code for this program is on the CD that comes with this book (see the directory CHAPTR02\Record View). Take a look at the program to see how simple it is to create a quick ODBC application.

FIGURE 2.1.

A CRecordView-based application.

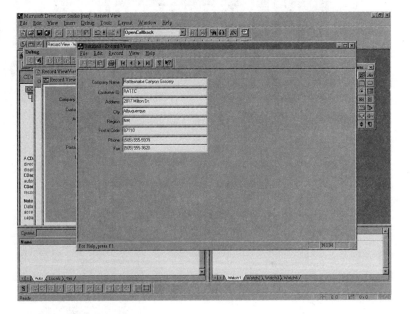

NOTE

Also found on the CD is a 16-bit MFC 2.5 version of the same program, which is in the directory CHAPTR02\RECVIEW. The RECVIEW program should be built only by using Visual C++ 1.5x.

Defining the Characteristics of Data-Related Objects and Classes

In the object-oriented terminology of OLE, *objects* are containers for properties, methods, and other objects. Methods are called *member functions* of an object. They perform an action on the object, such as changing its color, size, or shape. *Properties* are member function pairs of a *programmable* object. You can set or return information about the state of a programmable object, such as the value of a data item in the field of a table. One member function sets the data, and another member function returns the data—thus the term *pair*. All of the member functions are said to be *encapsulated* in the object.

NOTE

Technically, you should be able to alter any property of a programmable object by assigning an appropriate value to the "set" member of the function pair. The ability to set property values under specific conditions depends on the type of object and the application in which the object is used. Access 1.x, for example, has many objects whose properties can be set only in design mode.

The MFC Database Classes

The MFC database classes may be implemented by the programmer or by AppWizard when it creates an application; in either case, these classes are easy to use.

There are differences between MFC 2.5 (the 16-bit version, used with Visual C++ 1.5x), MFC 3.0 (a 32-bit version, used with Visual C++ 2.x), and MFC 4, which is supplied with Visual C++ 4.0. Where significant differences exist, I describe both. Most differences are between the 16-bit MFC 2.5 and the later 32-bit versions. In keeping with the concept of compatibility, generally an application written for MFC 2.5 will run without error when recompiled by using one of the 32-bit versions of Visual C++. However, after you've implemented any of the enhancements from MFC 3.0 (or MFC 4) in a 16-bit MFC 2.5 application (and converted it to 32-bit), you won't be able to build that application using Visual C++ 1.5!

CDatabase

The CDatabase class object is used to encapsulate a connection to a database. The CDatabase object may then be used to operate on the database and is derived from the CObject base class. Figure 2.2 shows the class hierarchy for the CDatabase class.

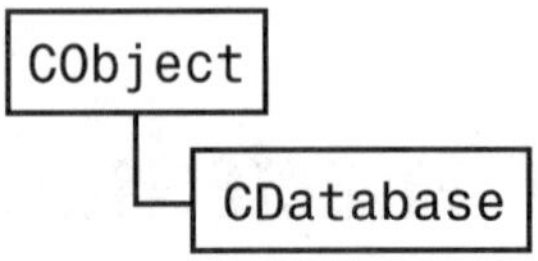

FIGURE 2.2.
The CDatabase class hierarchy.

The CDatabase class object has a number of member functions. These functions are divided into the following five categories:

- Data members: The data members of the CDatabase class hold information that is used when you're working directly with the database that the CDatabase object has been attached to.
- Construction: The constructor and a set of database open/close functions form the construction members.
- Database attributes: Nine functions are used to obtain information about the database that the CDatabase object has been attached to.
- Database operations: The five database operation functions allow for transaction processing and the execution of direct SQL commands.
- Database overrides: Two overridable functions are provided to let the programmer customize the functionality of the CDatabase object.

The following sections take a closer look at the members of this class. The members of the CObject class (which CDatabase is derived from) aren't covered in this book. Refer to the Visual C++ documentation (either the manuals or the online help system) for full information about the CObject class.

Data Members

The CDatabase object contains only one data member.

The m_hdbc member variable contains the ODBC connection handle to the database that is currently open. If no database is currently open, this member variable doesn't contain useful data.

The m_hdbc member variable is of type HDBC. It can be used wherever an HDBC type variable is needed (for example, in one of the SQL...() functions).

Here's an example of the usage of m_hdbc:

```
nReturnCode = ::SQLGetInfo(cdb.m_hdbc, SQL_ODBC_SQL_CONFORMANCE,
    &nReturn, sizeof(nReturn), &cbValue);
```

In this example, a call to a function that isn't a member function of CDatabase is made by using the m_hdbc member data variable.

Construction

Three member functions deal directly with CDatabase construction: CDatabase(), Open(), and Close(). There also is a default destructor, which I don't document here because it's never called by an application. The following paragraphs describe each construction member function and, where applicable, give examples of usage.

The CDatabase() function is used to construct the CDatabase object. This function isn't called directly and has no parameters. The process of calling the constructor is taken care of during the initialization of the CDatabase object when it's created. Here is a typical creation of a CDatabase object (this code is usually in the header file for the document class):

```
CDatabase m_dbCustomerDB;   // No parameters
```

When creating a CDatabase object, your application must make sure that the CDatabase object is connected to a database. This is accomplished in a member function in the containing class, often called GetDatabase() (if the containing class is based on a CDocument type object).

If you call CDatabase::Open(), passing a NULL as the *lpszDSN* parameter, the user will be presented with an open datasource dialog box. The Record View sample program for this chapter shows this dialog box (see Figure 2.1).

```
CDatabase* CMyDoc::GetDatabase()
{// Returns NULL in the event of a failure!
// m_dbCustomerDB is a member of CMyDoc!

    // Connect the object to a database
    if(!m_dbCustomerDB.IsOpen() && !m_dbCustomerDB.Open(NULL))
    (// The database cannot be opened; we've failed!
        return(NULL);
    }
    else
    {// We already had a database, or opened one:
        return(&m_dbCustomerDB);
    }
}
```

The Open() member function is used to establish a connection to a database. This connection is established through an ODBC driver. The Open() function takes a number of parameters. Here's the prototype of the MFC 2.5 version of the Open() function:

```
BOOL Open( LPCSTR lpszDSN,           // The name of the dataset
    BOOL bExclusive = FALSE,         // If the dataset is to be exclusive
    BOOL bReadOnly = FALSE,          // If the dataset is read-only
    LPCSTR lpszConnect = "ODBC;");   // The method of connection
```

The prototype of the MFC 3.0 (and later) versions of the Open() function adds a new final parameter to the function:

```
BOOL Open( LPCSTR lpszDSN,           // The name of the dataset
    BOOL bExclusive = FALSE,         // If the dataset is to be exclusive
    BOOL bReadOnly = FALSE,          // If the dataset is read-only
    LPCSTR lpszConnect = "ODBC;",    // The method of connection
    BOOL bUseCursorLib = TRUE);      // Use ODBC cursor library
```

The return value will be nonzero if the function is successful and zero if the user clicks the Cancel button in the Connection Information dialog box (if displayed). All other failures will cause the Open() function to throw an exception of type CDBException or CMemoryException.

The Close() function is used to close the connection that was established with the Open() function. The Close() function takes no parameters and has no return value. If no connection is currently open, this function does nothing. A call to Close() will cancel any pending AddNew() or Edit() statements and will roll back (discard) any pending transactions.

Database Attributes

The database attribute functions are used to provide information to the application about the connection, driver, and datasource. These functions are often used in front-end applications. Other functions in this group set options for the datasource for the application. The following list shows the database attribute functions. The functions in the first column are supported by all datasources, and those in the second column might not be supported by all datasources.

Supported by All Datasources	*Not Supported by All Datasources*
GetConnect()	SetLoginTimeout()
IsOpen()	SetQueryTimeout()
GetDatabaseName()	SetSynchronousMode()
CanUpdate()	
CanTransact()	
InWaitForDataSource()	

The GetConnect() function is used to return the ODBC connect string that was used to connect the CDatabase object to a datasource. There are no parameters to the GetConnect() function, and it returns a CString object reference. The GetConnect() function's prototype is

```
const CString& GetConnect();
```

If there is no current connection, the returned CString object will be empty.

The IsOpen() function is used to determine whether a datasource is currently connected to the CDatabase object. This function returns a nonzero value if there is currently a connection and a zero value if no connection is currently open. For an example of IsOpen(), see the earlier discussion of the Open() function.

The `GetDatabaseName()` function returns the name of the database currently in use. `GetDatabaseName()` returns a `CString` object. Its prototype is

```
CString GetDatabaseName();
```

The `GetDatabaseName()` function returns the database name if there is one. Otherwise, it returns an empty `CString` object.

The `CanUpdate()` function returns a nonzero value if the database can be updated (by either modifying records or adding new records). If the database can't be modified, the `CanUpdate()` function returns a zero value. `CanUpdate()` takes no parameters and has the following prototype:

```
BOOL CanUpdate();
```

The ability to update a database is based both on how it was opened (how you set the read-only parameter in `Open()`) and on the capabilities of the ODBC driver. Not all ODBC drivers support the updating of databases.

The `CanTransact()` function returns a nonzero value if the datasource supports transactions. (See the section "Database Operations" for more information about transactions with the `CDatabase` object.) The `CanTransact()` function takes no parameters and has the following prototype:

```
BOOL CanTransact();
```

The ability to support transactions is based on ODBC driver support.

The `InWaitForDataSource()` function returns a nonzero value if the application is waiting for the database server to complete an operation. If the application isn't waiting for the server, the `InWaitForDataSource()` function returns a zero. `InWaitForDataSource()` takes no parameters and has the following prototype:

```
static BOOL PASCAL InWaitForDataSource();
```

This function is often called in the framework to disable the user interface while waiting for the server to respond. This is done to prevent the user from stacking unwanted commands or operations while the application waits for the server.

The `SetLoginTimeout()` function is used to set the amount of time that the system will wait before timing out the connection. This option must be set before a call to `Open()` is made; it will have no effect if it's called after a database has been opened. This function has no return value. `SetLoginTimeout()` takes one parameter—the number of seconds after which a datasource connection attempt will time out. `SetLoginTimeout()` has the following prototype:

```
void SetLoginTimeout(DWORD dwSeconds);
```

The default login timeout is 15 seconds, an acceptable value for most applications. For applications that might be running on slow systems (perhaps where there are many other connections), the login timeout value might need to be set to a larger value.

The SetQueryTimeout() function is used to set the amount of time that the system will wait before timing out the query. This option must be set before you open the recordset. It will have no effect if it's called after the recordset has been opened. This function has no return value. SetQueryTimeout() takes one parameter—the number of seconds after which a datasource connection attempt will time out. SetQueryTimeout() has the following prototype:

```
void SetQueryTimeout(DWORD dwSeconds);
```

The default query timeout is 15 seconds, an acceptable value for most applications. For applications that might be running on slow systems (perhaps where there are many other connections), the query timeout value might need to be set to a larger value.

> **WARNING**
>
> Setting the query timeout value to zero results in no time-outs and might cause the application to hang if a connection can't be made.

The SetQueryTimeout() function affects all subsequent Open(), AddNew(), Edit(), and Delete() calls.

The SetSynchronousMode() function is used to either enable or disable synchronous processing for all recordsets and SQL statements associated with this CDatabase object. SetSynchronousMode() takes one parameter and has no return value. SetSynchronousMode() has the following prototype:

```
void SetSynchronousMode(BOOL bSynchronousMode);
```

The default operation is asynchronous processing.

Database Operations

Database operation functions are used to work with the database. The transaction processing functions (used to update the database) and the function used to issue an SQL command are all database operation functions. The database operation functions are

```
BeginTrans()
CommitTrans()
Rollback()
Cancel()
ExecuteSQL()
```

With the exception of ExecuteSQL(), these functions might not be implemented by all datasources. The BeginTrans() function is used to start a *transaction* on a database. Transactions are calls to AddNew(), Edit(), Delete(), or Update(). After the application has completed the transaction calls, either CommitTrans() or Rollback() must be called.

The `BeginTrans()` function takes no parameters and returns a nonzero value if the call is successful. `BeginTrans()` has the following prototype:

```
void BeginTrans(BOOL bSynchronousMode);
```

`BeginTrans()` should never be called prior to opening a recordset; otherwise, there might be problems when calling `Rollback()`. Each `BeginTrans()` call must be matched to a `CommitTrans()` or `Rollback()` prior to a subsequent call to `BeginTrans()`, or an error will occur. If there are pending transactions when the datasource is closed, they are discarded, much as if there had been a call to `Rollback()` prior to closing the datasource.

The `CommitTrans()` function is used to complete a transaction set begun with a call to `BeginTrans()`. `CommitTrans()` tells the datasource to accept the changes that were specified. `CommitTrans()` takes no parameters and returns a nonzero value if the call is successful. `CommitTrans()` has the following prototype:

```
BOOL CommitTrans();
```

You can discard the transaction by calling `Rollback()`.

The `Rollback()` function is used to end a transaction processing operation, discarding the transaction. `Rollback()` takes no parameters and returns a nonzero value if the call was successful. `Rollback()` has the following prototype:

```
void Rollback();
```

You can accept the transaction by using the `CommitTrans()` function.

The `Cancel()` function is used to terminate an asynchronous operation that is currently pending. This function causes the `OnWaitForDataSource()` function to be called until it returns a value other than `SQL_STILL_EXECUTING`. `Cancel()` takes no parameters and has no return value. `Cancel()` has the following prototype:

```
void Cancel();
```

If no asynchronous operation is pending, this function simply returns.

The `ExecuteSQL()` function is used to execute an SQL command. The SQL command is contained in a `NULL`-terminated string. A `CString` object may also be passed to the `ExecuteSQL()` function if desired. `ExecuteSQL()` takes one parameter and has no return value. `ExecuteSQL()` has the following prototype:

```
void ExecuteSQL(LPCSTR szSQLCommand);
```

The `ExecuteSQL()` function throws a `CDBException` if there is an error in the SQL statement. `ExecuteSQL()` won't return any data records to the application. Use the `CRecordset` object to obtain records instead.

Database Overridables

The overridable functions OnSetOptions() and OnWaitForDataSource() are used to allow the framework to set options and control the operation of the application. Neither of these functions is mandatory. If the programmer elects not to code these functions, a default operation will take place.

The OnSetOptions() function is called when the ExecuteSQL() function is being used to execute an SQL statement. OnSetOptions() takes one parameter and has no return value. OnSetOptions() has the following prototype:

```
void OnSetOptions(HSTMT hstmt);
```

The default OnSetOptions() function is shown in the following code fragment. You could use this code in your handler as an example of how to code an OnSetOptions() function. The default implementation sets the query timeout value and the processing mode to either asynchronous or synchronous. Your application can set these options prior to the ExecuteSQL() function call by calling SetQueryTimeout() and SetSynchronousMode(). Microsoft uses the calls to AFX_SQL_SYNC() in its database code.

```
void CDatabase::OnSetOptions(HSTMT hstmt)
{
    RETCODE nRetCode;
    ASSERT_VALID(this);
    ASSERT(m_hdbc != SQL_NULL_HDBC);

    if (m_dwQueryTimeout != -1)
    {
        // Attempt to set query timeout.  Ignore failure
        AFX_SQL_SYNC(::SQLSetStmtOption(hstmt, SQL_QUERY_TIMEOUT,
            m_dwQueryTimeout));
        if (!Check(nRetCode))
            // don't attempt it again
            m_dwQueryTimeout = (DWORD)-1;
    }

    // Attempt to set AFX_SQL_ASYNC.  Ignore failure
    if (m_bAsync)
    {
        AFX_SQL_SYNC(::SQLSetStmtOption(hstmt, SQL_ASYNC_ENABLE, m_bAsync));
        if (!Check(nRetCode))
            m_bAsync = FALSE;
    }

}
```

The OnWaitForDataSource() function is called to allow the application to yield time to other applications while waiting for asynchronous operations. OnWaitForDataSource() takes one parameter and has no return value. OnWaitForDataSource() has the following prototype:

```
void OnWaitForDataSource(BOOL bStillExecuting);
```

The bStillExecuting parameter is set to TRUE for the first call to OnWaitForDataSource() when it's called prior to an asynchronous operation.

The following code fragment shows the default OnWaitForDataSource() function. You could use this code in your handler as an example of how to code an OnWaitForDataSource() function if your application requires one.

```
void CDatabase::OnWaitForDataSource(BOOL bStillExecuting)
{
    ASSERT_VALID(this);
    ASSERT(m_hdbc != SQL_NULL_HDBC);

    _AFX_THREAD_STATE* pThreadState = AfxGetThreadState();
    CWinApp* pApp = AfxGetApp();

    if (!bStillExecuting)
    {
        // If never actually waited...
        if (m_dwWait == 0)
            return;

        if (m_dwWait == m_dwMaxWaitForDataSource)
            pApp->DoWaitCursor(-1);        // EndWaitCursor
        m_dwWait = 0;
        pThreadState->m_bWaitForDataSource--;
#ifdef _DEBUG
        if (afxTraceFlags & traceDatabase)
            TRACE0("DONE WAITING for datasource.\n");
#endif
        return;
    }

    if (m_dwWait == 0)
    {
        pThreadState->m_bWaitForDataSource++;
        // 1st call; wait for min amount of time
        m_dwWait = m_dwMinWaitForDataSource;
#ifdef _DEBUG
        if (afxTraceFlags & traceDatabase)
            TRACE0("WAITING for datasource.\n");
#endif
    }
    else
    {
        if (m_dwWait == m_dwMinWaitForDataSource)
        {
            // 2nd call; wait max time; put up wait cursor
            m_dwWait = m_dwMaxWaitForDataSource;
            pApp->DoWaitCursor(1);        // BeginWaitCursor
        }
    }

    CWinThread* pThread = AfxGetThread();
    DWORD clockFirst = GetTickCount();
    while (GetTickCount() - clockFirst < m_dwWait)
    {
        MSG msg;
```

```
        if (::PeekMessage(&msg, NULL, NULL, NULL, PM_NOREMOVE))
        {
            TRY
            {
                pThread->PumpMessage();
            }
            CATCH_ALL(e)
            {
                TRACE0("Error: exception in OnWaitForDataSource - continuing.\n");
                DELETE_EXCEPTION(e);
            }
            END_CATCH_ALL
        }
        else
            pThread->OnIdle(-1);
    }
}
```

CRecordset

The CRecordset object is used to manage recordsets. This object is often used with the CDatabase and CRecordView objects. The member functions in the CRecordset object offer a powerful set of database record manipulation tools.

The CRecordset object is derived from the CObject base class. Figure 2.3 shows the class hierarchy for the CRecordset class.

FIGURE 2.3.
The CRecordset *class hierarchy.*

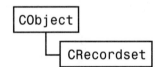

The CRecordset class object has a number of member functions. These functions are divided into the following seven categories:

- Data members: The data members of the CRecordset class hold information that is used when you're working directly with the database that the CRecordset object has been attached to.
- Construction: The constructor and a set of database open/close functions form the construction members.
- Recordset attributes: Thirteen functions are used to obtain information about the recordset that the CRecordset object has been attached to.
- Recordset update operations: The four CRecordset update operation members allow for transaction processing.
- Recordset navigation operations: The five CRecordset navigation operation functions allow for moving throughout the records contained within the recordset.

■ Other recordset operations: The eight other CRecordset operation functions provide miscellaneous functionality.

■ Recordset overrides: Five overridable functions are provided to let the programmer customize the functionality of the CRecordset object.

The following sections take a closer look at the members of this class. I don't cover the members of the CObject class (which CRecordset is derived from) in this book. Refer to the Visual C++ documentation (either the manuals or the online help system) for full information about the CObject class.

Data Members

There are a number of data members in the CRecordset object:

■ The m_hstmt member variable contains the ODBC statement handle for the recordset. This variable has a type of HSTMT.

■ The m_nFields member variable contains the number of field data members (the number of columns retrieved from) in the recordset. This variable has a type of UINT.

■ The m_nParams member variable contains the number of parameter data members in the recordset. This variable has a type of UINT.

■ The m_strFilter variable contains a CString that contains an SQL WHERE clause. This CString will be used as a filter to select only records that meet the specified search criteria.

■ The m_strSort variable contains a CString that contains an SQL ORDER BY clause. This CString will be used to control the sorting of the retrieved records.

Construction/Destruction

Three member functions deal directly with CRecordset construction: CRecordset(), Open(), and Close(). There also is the default destructor, which I won't document here because it's never called by an application. The following paragraphs describe each construction member function and, where applicable, give examples of usage.

The CRecordset() function is the constructor for the CRecordset class object. CRecordset() takes one parameter, and, because it's a constructor, it has no specified return value. CRecordset() has the following prototype:

```
void CRecordset(CDatabase * pDatabase = NULL);
```

The default operation is to create and initialize the CRecordset object. If pDatabase is specified, this CDatabase object will be used with the CRecordset object. If the pDatabase pointer is NULL, the constructor will create a default CDatabase member class.

If you create a derived class, the derived class must have its own constructor. Your constructor will then call the CRecordset::CRecordset() constructor, passing the appropriate parameter.

The Open() function is used to run a query that will return a recordset to the application. Open() takes three parameters and has no return value. Open() has the following prototype:

```
virtual BOOL Open(
    UINT nOpenType = snapshot,   // Either dynaset, snapshot, or forwardOnly
    LPCSTR lpszSql = NULL,       // NULL, table name, SELECT, or CALL statement
    DWORD dwOptions = none);     // None, appendOnly, or readOnly
```

The default operation for Open() is to open a datasource. Open() will throw a CDBException, CMemoryException, or CFileException if there are errors.

The Close() function is used to close the currently open recordset. If no recordset is open, this function simply returns. After calling Close(), it's possible to then re-call Open() to reopen the recordset, thereby reusing the CRecordset object. The Close() function takes no parameters and has no return value. Close() has the following prototype:

```
void Close();
```

The default operation for Close() is to close the recordset and the ODBC HSTMT that was associated with the recordset.

Recordset Attributes

Thirteen member functions deal directly with CRecordset attributes. These member functions are listed here:

```
CanAppend()
CanRestart()
CanScroll()
CanTransact()
CanUpdate()
GetRecordCount()
GetStatus()
GetTableName()
GetSQL()
IsOpen()
IsBOF()
IsEOF()
IsDeleted()
```

With these member functions, applications can obtain information about the recordset.

The CanAppend() function is used to determine whether or not new records can be appended to the end of the recordset. Records are added by using the AddNew() function. CanAppend() takes no parameters and returns a nonzero value if the recordset can have records appended. CanAppend() has the following prototype:

```
BOOL CanAppend();
```

Typically, `CanAppend()` is called to enable or disable the user interface's record append commands and tools.

The `CanRestart()` function is used to determine whether the query can be restarted. `CanRestart()` takes no parameters and returns a nonzero value if the query can be restarted. `CanRestart()` has the following prototype:

```
BOOL CanRestart();
```

The `CanRestart()` function is usually called prior to calling the `Requery()` member function.

The `CanScroll()` function is used to determine whether the recordset allows scrolling. `CanScroll()` takes no parameters and returns a nonzero value if the recordset allows scrolling. `CanScroll()` has the following prototype:

```
BOOL CanScroll();
```

> **NOTE**
>
> Not all recordsets allow scrolling.

The `CanTransact()` function is used to determine whether the recordset supports transactions. `CanTransact()` takes no parameters and returns a nonzero value if transactions are supported. `CanTransact()` has the following prototype:

```
BOOL CanTransact();
```

> **NOTE**
>
> Many, but not all, ODBC drivers support transactions.

The `CanUpdate()` function is used to determine whether the recordset supports updating. Updating would typically fail if the underlying database were opened in read-only mode. `CanUpdate()` takes no parameters and returns a nonzero value if the recordset supports updating. `CanUpdate()` has the following prototype:

```
BOOL CanUpdate();
```

The most common reason that a recordset can't be updated when the ODBC driver supports updating is that it has been opened in read-only mode. Read-only mode offers faster access (there is no need to perform record locking) at the expense of being able to update the recordset.

The `GetRecordCount()` function is used to determine the number of records in the current recordset. `GetRecordCount()` takes no parameters and returns the number of records in the recordset—a −1 value if the number of records can't be determined and a zero value if there are no records in the recordset. GetRecordCount() has the following prototype:

```
long GetRecordCount();
```

The number of records in a recordset can be determined only if the application scrolls through the entire recordset. The count of records is maintained as a counter that is incremented with each forward read. The true total number of records is known only after the application has scrolled past the last record. Using MoveLast() won't affect the record counter.

The GetStatus() function is used to obtain status information about the current recordset. GetStatus() takes one parameter, a reference to the CRecordsetStatus structure, and has no return value. GetStatus() has the following prototype:

```
void GetStatus(CRecordsetStatus & rsStatus);
```

The members of the CRecordsetStatus class are shown in the following code fragment:

```
struct CRecordsetStatus
{
    long    m_lCurrentRecord;     // Zero-based index of current record
                                  // if the current record is known, or
                                  // AFX_CURRENT_RECORD_UNDEFINED if the
                                  // current record is undefined.
    BOOL    m_bRecordCountFinal;  // Nonzero if the total number of records
                                  // in the recordset has been determined.
};
```

The GetTableName() function is used to fetch the name of the recordset table. GetTableName() takes no parameters and returns a CString reference. GetTableName() has the following prototype:

```
CString & GetTableName();
```

The CString returned won't contain a name if the recordset was based on a join or if the recordset was created by a call to a stored procedure.

The GetSQL() function is used to return a CString reference that contains the current SQL statement. The SQL statement is the SELECT statement used to generate the recordset. GetSQL() takes no parameters and returns a CString reference. GetSQL() has the following prototype:

```
CString & GetSQL();
```

The returned SQL string usually will have been modified by the system to include any filtering (a WHERE clause) and sorting (an ORDER BY clause).

The IsOpen() function is used to determine whether the CRecordset Open() or Requery() functions have been called and whether the recordset has been closed. IsOpen() takes no parameters and returns a nonzero value if there has been a call to Open() or Requery() without an intervening call to Close(). IsOpen() has the following prototype:

```
BOOL IsOpen();
```

Your application should check the IsOpen() function prior to calling Open().

The IsBOF() function is used to check whether the current record is the first record in the dataset. IsBOF() takes no parameters and returns a nonzero value if the recordset is empty or if the application has scrolled to before the first record in the recordset. IsBOF() has the following prototype:

```
BOOL IsBOF();
```

> **CAUTION**
>
> The IsBOF() function should be called prior to scrolling backward in a recordset. Scrolling backward when there are no records in the recordset or when the current record pointer is before the first record in the recordset causes an error.

The IsEOF() function is used to determine whether the current record is the last record in the dataset. IsEOF() takes no parameters and returns a nonzero value if the recordset is empty or if the application has scrolled to after the last record in the recordset. IsEOF() has the following prototype:

```
BOOL IsEOF();
```

> **CAUTION**
>
> The IsEOF() function should be called prior to scrolling forward in a recordset. Scrolling forward when there are no records in the recordset or when the current record pointer is after the last record in the recordset causes an error.

The IsDeleted() function is used to determine whether the current record in the recordset has been deleted. IsDeleted() takes no parameters and returns a nonzero value if the current record has been marked as deleted. IsDeleted() has the following prototype:

```
BOOL IsDeleted();
```

> **CAUTION**
>
> It's considered an error to update or delete a record that has been marked as deleted.

Recordset Update Operations

Four member functions deal directly with CRecordset updating:

```
AddNew()
Delete()
Edit()
Update()
```

With these member functions, applications can add, delete, and edit records in the recordset.

The AddNew() function is used to prepare a new record to be added to the recordset. This record's contents must then be filled in by the application. After the new record's contents are filled in, Update() should be called to write the record. AddNew() takes no parameters and has no return value. AddNew() has the following prototype:

```
void AddNew();
```

The AddNew() function throws a CDBException or a CFileException if an error occurs (such as trying to add records to a dataset that is read-only). AddNew() can be used as part of a transaction if the dataset supports transactions.

The Delete() function is used to delete the current record from the recordset. After calling Delete(), you must explicitly scroll to another record. Delete() takes no parameters and has no return value. Delete() has the following prototype:

```
void Delete();
```

The Delete() function will throw a CDBException if an error occurs (such as trying to delete records in a dataset that is read-only). Delete() can be used as part of a transaction if the dataset supports transactions.

The Edit() function is used to prepare the current record for editing. The Edit() function will save the current record's current values. If you call Edit(), make changes, and then call Edit() a second time (without a call to Update()), the changes will be lost, and the record will be restored to the original values. Edit() takes no parameters and has no return value. Edit() has the following prototype:

```
void Edit();
```

The Edit() function throws a CDBException if an error occurs. Edit() can be used as part of a transaction if the dataset supports transactions.

The Update() function is used to write the record that has been added to or edited by other recordset update operations. Update() takes no parameters and returns a nonzero value if a record was actually updated or a zero if no records were updated. Update() has the following prototype:

```
BOOL Update();
```

The Update() function throws a CDBException if an error occurs. Update() can be used as part of a transaction if the dataset supports transactions.

Recordset Navigation Operations

Five member functions deal directly with CRecordset record navigation:

```
Move()
MoveFirst()
MoveLast()
MoveNext()
MovePrev()
```

You should also refer to the IsBOF() and IsEOF() functions, described in the section "Recordset Attributes." With these member functions, applications can move forward, backward, to a specific record, to the beginning of a recordset, and to the end of a recordset.

The Move() function is used to move to a specific record in the recordset, relative to the current record. This function allows random movement in the recordset. Move() takes one parameter and has no return value. Move() has the following prototype:

```
void Move(long lRows);
```

Use a negative parameter value to move backward from the current record. The Move() function throws a CDBException, CFileException, or CMemoryException if it fails.

> **WARNING**
>
> Don't call any move function for a recordset that doesn't have any records (if both IsEOF() and IsBOF() return nonzero, the recordset is empty).

The MoveFirst() function is used to move to the first record in the recordset. MoveFirst() takes no parameters and has no return value. MoveFirst() has the following prototype:

```
void MoveFirst();
```

The MoveFirst() function throws a CDBException, CFileException, or CMemoryException if it fails.

The MoveLast() function is used to move to the last record in the recordset. MoveLast() takes no parameters and has no return value. MoveLast() has the following prototype:

```
void MoveLast();
```

The MoveLast() function throws a CDBException, CFileException, or CMemoryException if it fails.

The MoveNext() function is used to move to the next record in the recordset. If you're positioned after the last record in the recordset, don't call MoveNext(). MoveNext() takes no parameters and has no return value. MoveNext() has the following prototype:

```
void MoveNext();
```

The MoveNext() function throws a CDBException, CFileException, or CMemoryException if it fails.

The MovePrev() function is used to move to the previous record in the recordset. If you're positioned before the first record in the recordset, don't call MovePrev(). MovePrev() takes no parameters and has no return value. MovePrev() has the following prototype:

```
void MovePrev();
```

The MovePrev() function throws a CDBException, CFileException, or CMemoryException if it fails.

Other Recordset Operations

Eight member functions deal directly with CRecordset operations:

```
Cancel()
IsFieldDirty()
IsFieldNull()
IsFieldNullable()
Requery()
SetFieldDirty()
SetFieldNull()
SetLockingMode()
```

With these member functions, applications can perform miscellaneous operations on recordsets.

The Cancel() function is used to cancel a pending asynchronous operation. Cancel() takes no parameters and has no return value. Cancel() has the following prototype:

```
void Cancel();
```

The default operation, should there be no pending asynchronous operation, is simply to return.

The IsFieldDirty() function is used to determine whether a specified field has been changed. IsFieldDirty() takes one parameter—a pointer to a field data member—and returns a nonzero value if the field has, in fact, been modified. IsFieldDirty() has the following prototype:

```
BOOL IsFieldDirty(void * pField);
```

If the pField pointer parameter is NULL, all fields in the record are checked.

The IsFieldNull() function is used to determine whether a specified field is currently null (contains no value). IsFieldNull() takes one parameter—a pointer to a field data member—and returns a nonzero value if the field is, in fact, null. IsFieldNull() has the following prototype:

```
BOOL IsFieldNull(void * pField);
```

If the pField pointer parameter is NULL, all fields in the record are checked. Note that the C/C++ NULL is different from the SQL null.

The IsFieldNullable() function is used to determine whether a specified field can be set to null (containing no value). IsFieldNullable() takes one parameter—a pointer to a field data member—and returns a nonzero value if the field can be set to null. IsFieldNullable() has the following prototype:

```
BOOL IsFieldNullable(void * pField);
```

If the pField pointer parameter is NULL, all fields in the record are checked. Note that the C/C++ NULL is different from the SQL null.

The Requery() function is used to refresh the recordset. A call to the function CanRestart() should be made prior to calling Requery(). Requery() takes no parameters and returns a nonzero value if the refresh was successful. Requery() has the following prototype:

```
BOOL Requery();
```

The Requery() function throws a CDBException, CFileException, or CMemoryException if it fails.

The SetFieldDirty() function is used to modify the dirty flag for a specified field. SetFieldDirty() takes two parameters—a pointer to a field data member and a Boolean value specifying the new value for the dirty flag. SetFieldDirty() has no return value and has the following prototype:

```
void SetFieldDirty(void * pField, BOOL bDirty = TRUE);
```

If the pField pointer parameter is NULL, all fields in the record are marked with the value of the bDirty parameter. Note that the C/C++ NULL is different from the SQL null.

The SetFieldNull() function is used to modify the null flag for a specified field. SetFieldNull() takes two parameters—a pointer to a field data member and a Boolean value specifying the new value for the dirty flag. SetFieldNull() has no return value and has the following prototype:

```
void SetFieldNull(void * pField, BOOL bDirty = TRUE);
```

If the pField pointer parameter is NULL, all fields in the record are marked with the value of the bDirty parameter. Note that the C/C++ NULL is different from the SQL null.

The `SetLockingMode()` function is used to change the record locking mode. `SetLockingMode()` takes one parameter—nMode, which must be either optimistic or pessimistic. `SetLockingMode()` has no return value and has the following prototype:

```
void SetLockingMode(UINT nMode);
```

Pessimistic mode is more cautious than optimistic mode. Both pessimistic and optimistic are defined in `CRecordset`. Pessimistic mode locks the record as soon as `Edit()` is called, and optimistic mode locks the record only while the update is being performed.

Recordset Overridables

Applications may override five members to allow control over the recordset:

```
DoFieldExchange()
GetDefaultConnect()
GetDefaultSQL()
OnSetOptions()
OnWaitForDataSource()
```

The `DoFieldExchange()` function is used to transfer data to and from the field variables and records in the recordset. If your application is built with AppWizard, a default `DoFieldExchange()` function will be created. Also, modifications to the AppWizard-created `DoFieldExchange()` will be done by ClassWizard. `DoFieldExchange()` takes one parameter and has no return value. `DoFieldExchange()` has the following prototype:

```
void DoFieldExchange(CFieldExchange * pFX);
```

The `CFieldExchange` class object definition is shown in the following code fragment. The actual definition can be found in the AFXDB.H header file.

```
// CFieldExchange - for field exchange
class CFieldExchange
{
// Attributes
public:
    enum RFX_Operation
    {
        BindParam, // Register user's parameters with ODBC SQLBindParameter
        RebindParam, // Migrate param values to proxy array before requery
        BindFieldToColumn, // Register user's fields with ODBC SQLBindCol
        BindFieldForUpdate, // Temporarily bind columns before
                            // update (via SQLSetPos)
        UnbindFieldForUpdate, // Unbind columns after update (via SQLSetPos)
        Fixup, // Set string lengths and clear status bits
        MarkForAddNew,
        MarkForUpdate,  // Prepare fields and flags for update operation
        Name, // Append dirty field name
        NameValue, // Append dirty name=value
        Value, // Append dirty value or parameter marker
        SetFieldDirty, // Set status bit for changed status
        SetFieldNull,  // Set status bit for null value
```

```
            IsFieldDirty, // Return TRUE if field is dirty
            IsFieldNull, // Return TRUE if field is marked NULL
            IsFieldNullable, // Return TRUE if field can hold NULL values
            StoreField, // Archive values of current record
            LoadField,  // Reload archived values into current record
            GetFieldInfoValue,  // General info on a field via pv for field
            GetFieldInfoOrdinal,  // General info on a field via field ordinal
#ifdef _DEBUG
            DumpField,  // Dump bound field name and value
#endif
    };
    UINT m_nOperation;  // Type of exchange operation
    CRecordset* m_prs;  // Recordset handle

// Operations
    enum FieldType
    {
        noFieldType,
        outputColumn,
        param,
    };

// Operations (for implementors of RFX procs)
    BOOL IsFieldType(UINT* pnField);

    // Indicate purpose of subsequent RFX calls
    void SetFieldType(UINT nFieldType);

// Implementation
    CFieldExchange(UINT nOperation, CRecordset* prs, void* pvField = NULL);

    void Default(LPCTSTR szName,
        void* pv, LONG* plLength, int nCType, UINT cbValue, UINT cbPrecision);

    int GetColumnType(int nColumn, UINT* pcbLength = NULL,
        int* pnScale = NULL, int* pnNullable = NULL);

    // Long binary helpers
    long GetLongBinarySize(int nField);
    void GetLongBinaryData(int nField, CLongBinary& lb, long* plSize);
    BYTE* ReallocLongBinary(CLongBinary& lb, long lSizeRequired,
        long lReallocSize);

    // Current type of field
    UINT m_nFieldType;

    // For GetFieldInfo
    CFieldInfo* m_pfi;  // GetFieldInfo return struct
    BOOL m_bFieldFound; // GetFieldInfo search successful

    // For returning status info for a field
    BOOL m_bNull;       // Return result of IsFieldNull(able)/Dirty operation
    BOOL m_bDirty;      // Return result of IsFieldNull(able)/Dirty operation

    CString* m_pstr;    // Field name or destination for building various SQL
                        // clauses
    BOOL m_bField;      // Value to set for SetField operation
    void* m_pvField;    // For indicating an operation on a specific field
```

```
    CArchive* m_par;     // For storing/loading copy buffer
    LPCTSTR m_lpszSeparator; // Append after field names
    UINT m_nFields;      // Count of fields for various operations
    UINT m_nParams;      // Count of fields for various operations
    UINT m_nParamFields;    // Count of fields for various operations
    HSTMT m_hstmt;       // For SQLBindParameter on update statement
    long m_lDefaultLBFetchSize;     // For fetching CLongBinary data of
                                    // unknown length
    long m_lDefaultLBReallocSize;   // For fetching CLongBinary data of
                                    // unknown length

#ifdef _DEBUG
    CDumpContext* m_pdcDump;
#endif //_DEBUG

};
```

A typical AppWizard-created `DoFieldExchange()` function is shown in the following code fragment. This example is from the sample program shown in Figure 2.1.

```
void CRecordViewSet::DoFieldExchange(CFieldExchange* pFX)
{
    //{{AFX_FIELD_MAP(CRecordViewSet)
    pFX->SetFieldType(CFieldExchange::outputColumn);
    RFX_Text(pFX, _T("[CustomerID]"), m_CustomerID);
    RFX_Text(pFX, _T("[CompanyName]"), m_CompanyName);
    RFX_Text(pFX, _T("[ContactName]"), m_ContactName);
    RFX_Text(pFX, _T("[ContactTitle]"), m_ContactTitle);
    RFX_Text(pFX, _T("[Address]"), m_Address);
    RFX_Text(pFX, _T("[City]"), m_City);
    RFX_Text(pFX, _T("[Region]"), m_Region);
    RFX_Text(pFX, _T("[PostalCode]"), m_PostalCode);
    RFX_Text(pFX, _T("[Country]"), m_Country);
    RFX_Text(pFX, _T("[Phone]"), m_Phone);
    RFX_Text(pFX, _T("[Fax]"), m_Fax);
    //}}AFX_FIELD_MAP
}
```

The `GetDefaultConnect()` function is used to return the default SQL connect string. `GetDefaultConnect()` takes no parameters and returns a `CString` reference. `GetDefaultConnect()` has the following prototype:

```
CString & GetDefaultConnect();
```

The default `GetDefaultConnect()` function created by AppWizard is shown in the following code fragment. This example is from the sample program shown later in this chapter (see the section called "An AppWizard-Generated Program"). It causes ODBC to display an open database dialog box.

```
CString CRecordViewSet::GetDefaultConnect()
{
    return _T("ODBC;DSN=Access 95 Northwind");
}
```

The `GetDefaultSQL()` function is used to return the default SQL string used to select records from the datasource to be placed in the recordset. `GetDefaultSQL()` takes no parameters and returns a `CString` reference. `GetDefaultSQL()` has the following prototype:

```
CString & GetDefaultSQL();
```

The default `GetDefaultSQL()` function created by AppWizard is shown in the following code fragment. This example is from the sample program shown later in this chapter.

```
CString CRecordViewSet::GetDefaultSQL()
{
    return _T("[Customers]");
}
```

The `OnSetOptions()` function is used to set options for the specified `HSTMT`. `OnSetOptions()` takes no parameters and has no return value. `OnSetOptions()` has the following prototype:

```
void OnSetOptions(HSTMT hstmt);
```

An AppWizard-created application doesn't have a default `OnSetOptions()` function. If you need one, you must write it yourself.

The `OnWaitForDataSource()` function is used to allow the application to perhaps ask the user (or simply query a control) whether there is a need to cancel the current asynchronous operation. If the user really wants to cancel, your `OnWaitForDataSource()` function should call the `Cancel()` function to end the asynchronous operation. `OnWaitForDataSource()` takes one parameter—a Boolean value that will be nonzero if the datasource is still waiting for an asynchronous operation—and has no return value. `OnWaitForDataSource()` has the following prototype:

```
void OnWaitForDataSource(BOOL bStillWaiting);
```

An AppWizard-created application doesn't have a default `OnWaitForDataSource()` function. If you need one, you must write it yourself. ClassWizard will add the shell of the `OnWaitForDataSource()` handler for you, which you then can fill in as needed.

CRecordView

The `CRecordView` object is used to manage recordsets. This object is usually used with the `CDatabase` and `CRecordset` objects. The member functions in the `CRecordView` object offer a powerful set of database record manipulation tools.

The `CRecordView` object is derived from the `CFormView` base class. Figure 2.4 shows the class hierarchy for the `CRecordView` class.

The `CRecordView` class object has a number of member functions. These functions are divided into three categories:

- ■ Construction: The constructor is the only construction member.
- ■ Attributes: Three functions are used to obtain information about the recordset that the `CRecordView` object has been attached to.
- ■ Operations: A single function, `OnMove()`, is provided to let the programmer change the `CRecordView` current record pointer.

FIGURE 2.4.
The CRecordView
class hierarchy.

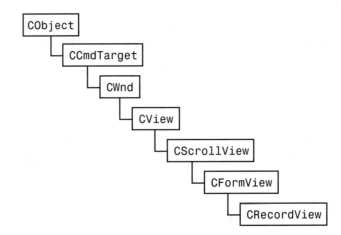

The following sections take a closer look at the members of this class. This book doesn't cover the members of the other classes on which CRecordView is based. Refer to the Visual C++ documentation (either the manuals or the online help system) for full information about these classes.

Construction

There is one construction member function: CRecordView(). There also is the default destructor, which I won't document here because it's never called by an application. The following list describes the construction member function and gives an example of its use.

The CRecordView() function is used to initialize the CRecordView object. CRecordView() takes one parameter: an identifier for the dialog box template. Because CRecordView() is a constructor, it has no defined return value. CRecordView() has the following prototype(s):

```
CRecordView(LPCSTR lpTemplateName);
```

or

```
CRecordView(UINT nTemplateID);
```

The following code fragment shows the default override constructor provided by AppWizard when a database application is created. This example is from the sample program shown later in this chapter.

```
CRecordViewView::CRecordViewView()
    : CRecordView(CRecordViewView::IDD)
{
    //{{AFX_DATA_INIT(CRecordViewView)
    m_pSet = NULL;
    //}}AFX_DATA_INIT
    // TODO: add construction code here

}
```

Attributes

Three member functions deal directly with CRecordView attributes: OnGetRecordset(), IsOnFirstRecord(), and IsOnLastRecord(). With these member functions, applications can obtain information about the record view.

The OnGetRecordset() function is used to get the pointer to the default CRecordset object that is attached to this CRecordView. OnGetRecordset() takes no parameters and returns a CRecordset pointer. OnGetRecordset() has the following prototype:

```
CRecordset * OnGetRecordset();
```

The following code fragment shows the default OnGetRecordset() provided by AppWizard when a database application is created. In this example, m_pSet was initialized in the constructor. This example is from the sample program shown later in this chapter.

```
CRecordset* CRecordViewView::OnGetRecordset()
{
        return m_pSet;
}
```

The IsOnFirstRecord() function is used to tell the view that the current record is the first record. This is necessary to allow the user interface to enable/disable the interface for moving to previous records. IsOnFirstRecord() takes no parameters and returns a nonzero value when the current record is the first record. IsOnFirstRecord() has the following prototype:

```
BOOL IsOnFirstRecord();
```

An AppWizard-created application doesn't have a default IsOnFirstRecord() function. If you want to provide special processing in your IsOnFirstRecord() handler, you must write it yourself. ClassWizard won't create a shell IsOnFirstRecord() handler for you. The default IsOnFirstRecord() function is shown in the following code fragment:

```
BOOL CRecordView::IsOnFirstRecord()
{
        ASSERT_VALID(this);
        CRecordsetStatus status;
        OnGetRecordset()->GetStatus(status);
        return status.m_lCurrentRecord == 0;
}
```

The IsOnLastRecord() function is used to tell the view that the current record is the last record. This is necessary to allow the user interface to enable/disable the interface for moving to later records. IsOnLastRecord() takes no parameters and returns a nonzero value when the current record is the last record. If IsOnLastRecord() is unable to determine whether the current record is the last record, it returns zero. IsOnLastRecord() has the following prototype:

```
BOOL IsOnLastRecord();
```

An AppWizard-created application doesn't have a default IsOnLastRecord() function. If you want to provide special processing in your IsOnLastRecord() handler, you must write it yourself. ClassWizard won't create a shell `IsOnLastRecord()` handler for you. The default `IsOnLastRecord()` function is shown in the following code fragment:

```
BOOL CRecordView::IsOnLastRecord()
{
        ASSERT_VALID(this);
        CRecordset* pRecordset = OnGetRecordset();
        CRecordsetStatus status;
        pRecordset->GetStatus(status);
        if (!status.m_bRecordCountFinal)
                return FALSE;
        return ((status.m_lCurrentRecord+1 == pRecordset->GetRecordCount()));
}
```

Operations

One member function deals directly with `CRecordView` operations. With this member function, applications can control which actions take place when the current record pointer is changed.

The `OnMove()` function is used to let the programmer change the current record pointer. Despite the name of this function, it's not normally overridden by an application. `OnMove()` takes one parameter and returns a nonzero value if the record pointer was successfully moved and a zero value if the call failed. `OnMove()` has the following prototype:

```
BOOL OnMove(UINT nMoveCommand);
```

The `nMoveCommand` parameter must be one of the manifest values shown in Table 2.1.

Table 2.1. `OnMove()` `nMoveCommand` values.

Value	Description
ID_RECORD_FIRST	Moves to the first record in the recordset.
ID_RECORD_NEXT	Moves to the next record in the recordset, provided that the current record isn't the last record in the recordset.
ID_RECORD_LAST	Moves to the last record in the recordset.
ID_RECORD_PREV	Moves the previous record in the recordset, provided that the current record isn't the first record in the recordset.

WARNING

Be careful not to call `OnMove()` on a recordset that has no records.

CFieldExchange

The CFieldExchange class is used to support the record field exchange used by the other data-base classes. The DoFieldExchange() function has a CFieldExchange pointer passed to it. The CFieldExchange class object is used to encapsulate the exchange of data between records in a recordset and variables in the application that hold the column data. The CFieldExchange object is a base class that isn't derived from any other MFC class. Figure 2.5 shows the class hierarchy for the CFieldExchange class.

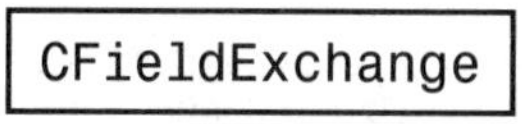

FIGURE 2.5.
The CFieldExchange
class hierarchy.

```
CFieldExchange
```

The CFieldExchange class object has two public member functions: IsFieldType() and SetFieldType(). These functions aren't divided into categories.

The IsFieldType() function is used to determine if the current operation (transfer) can be performed on the current field. IsFieldType() takes one parameter—pnField, a pointer to an index to the field—and returns a nonzero value if the operation can be performed. IsFieldType() has the following prototype:

```
BOOL IsFieldType(UINT * pnField);
```

The IsFieldType() function is useful when you write your own RFX functions. An example of an RFX function is shown in the following code fragment. This code is from the DBRFX.CPP file. The call to IsFieldType() appears in bold.

```
void AFXAPI RFX_Int(CFieldExchange* pFX, LPCTSTR szName, int& value)
{
    ASSERT(AfxIsValidAddress(pFX, sizeof(CFieldExchange)));
    ASSERT(AfxIsValidString(szName));

    UINT nField;
    if (!pFX->IsFieldType(&nField))
        return;

    LONG* plLength = pFX->m_prs->GetFieldLength(pFX);
    switch (pFX->m_nOperation)
    {
    case CFieldExchange::BindFieldToColumn:
        {
#ifdef _DEBUG
            int nSqlType = pFX->GetColumnType(nField);
            if (nSqlType != SQL_C_SHORT)
            {
                // Warn of possible field schema mismatch
                if (afxTraceFlags & traceDatabase)
                    TRACE1("Warning: int converted from SQL type %ld.\n",
                        nSqlType);
            }
```

```
#endif
        }
        // fall through

    default:
LDefault:
        pFX->Default(szName, &value, plLength, SQL_C_LONG,
            sizeof(value), 5);
        return;

    case CFieldExchange::Fixup:
        if (*plLength == SQL_NULL_DATA)
        {
            pFX->m_prs->SetFieldFlags(nField,
                AFX_SQL_FIELD_FLAG_NULL, pFX->m_nFieldType);
            value = AFX_RFX_INT_PSEUDO_NULL;
        }
        return;

    case CFieldExchange::SetFieldNull:
        if ((pFX->m_pvField == NULL &&
            pFX->m_nFieldType == CFieldExchange::outputColumn) ||
            pFX->m_pvField == &value)
        {
            if (pFX->m_bField)
            {
                // Mark fields null
                pFX->m_prs->SetFieldFlags(nField,
                    AFX_SQL_FIELD_FLAG_NULL, pFX->m_nFieldType);
                value = AFX_RFX_INT_PSEUDO_NULL;
                *plLength = SQL_NULL_DATA;
            }
            else
            {
                pFX->m_prs->ClearFieldFlags(nField,
                    AFX_SQL_FIELD_FLAG_NULL, pFX->m_nFieldType);
                *plLength = sizeof(value);
            }
#ifdef _DEBUG
            pFX->m_bFieldFound = TRUE;
#endif
        }
        return;

    case CFieldExchange::MarkForAddNew:
        // Can force writing of psuedo-null value (as a non-null) by
        // setting field dirty
        if (!pFX->m_prs->IsFieldFlagDirty(nField, pFX->m_nFieldType))
        {
            if (value != AFX_RFX_INT_PSEUDO_NULL)
            {
                pFX->m_prs->SetFieldFlags(nField,
                    AFX_SQL_FIELD_FLAG_DIRTY, pFX->m_nFieldType);
                pFX->m_prs->ClearFieldFlags(nField,
                    AFX_SQL_FIELD_FLAG_NULL, pFX->m_nFieldType);
            }
        }
```

```
            return;

    case CFieldExchange::MarkForUpdate:
        if (value != AFX_RFX_INT_PSEUDO_NULL)
            pFX->m_prs->ClearFieldFlags(nField,
                AFX_SQL_FIELD_FLAG_NULL, pFX->m_nFieldType);
        goto LDefault;

    case CFieldExchange::GetFieldInfoValue:
        if (pFX->m_pfi->pv == &value)
        {
            pFX->m_pfi->nField = nField-1;
            goto LFieldFound;
        }
        return;

    case CFieldExchange::GetFieldInfoOrdinal:
        if (nField-1 == pFX->m_pfi->nField)
        {
LFieldFound:
            pFX->m_pfi->nDataType = AFX_RFX_INT;
            pFX->m_pfi->strName = szName;
            pFX->m_pfi->pv = &value;
            pFX->m_pfi->dwSize = sizeof(value);
            // Make sure field found only once
            ASSERT(pFX->m_bFieldFound == FALSE);
            pFX->m_bFieldFound = TRUE;
        }
        return;

#ifdef _DEBUG
    case CFieldExchange::DumpField:
        *pFX->m_pdcDump << "\n" << szName << " = " << value;
        return;
#endif //_DEBUG

    }
}
```

The `SetFieldType()` function is used to set the field types prior to calls to the RFX functions. `SetFieldType()` takes one parameter—nFieldType, an enum that is declared in `CFieldExchange` (see Table 2.2). `SetFieldType()` has no return value and has the following prototype:

```
void SetFieldType(UINT nFieldType);
```

The valid nFieldTypes are listed in Table 2.2.

Table 2.2. Valid `nFieldType` enum values.

enum	Description
CFieldExchange::outputColumn	The field is an output column.
CFieldExchange::param	The field is a parameter.

For example, the default `DoFieldExchange()` function that AppWizard includes in a database application calls `SetFieldType()` as its first function call, with a parameter of `CFieldExchange::outputColumn`:

```
void CRecordViewSet::DoFieldExchange(CFieldExchange* pFX)
{
    //{{AFX_FIELD_MAP(CRecordViewSet)
    pFX->SetFieldType(CFieldExchange::outputColumn);
    RFX_Text(pFX, _T("[CustomerID]"), m_CustomerID);
    RFX_Text(pFX, _T("[CompanyName]"), m_CompanyName);
    RFX_Text(pFX, _T("[ContactName]"), m_ContactName);
    RFX_Text(pFX, _T("[ContactTitle]"), m_ContactTitle);
    RFX_Text(pFX, _T("[Address]"), m_Address);
    RFX_Text(pFX, _T("[City]"), m_City);
    RFX_Text(pFX, _T("[Region]"), m_Region);
    RFX_Text(pFX, _T("[PostalCode]"), m_PostalCode);
    RFX_Text(pFX, _T("[Country]"), m_Country);
    RFX_Text(pFX, _T("[Phone]"), m_Phone);
    RFX_Text(pFX, _T("[Fax]"), m_Fax);
    //}}AFX_FIELD_MAP
}
```

CDBException

The `CDBException` class is used to handle error conditions that occur when a number of the database class's member functions encounter problems. The `CDBException` class object is used to encapsulate the error condition. The `CDBException` object is derived from the `CException` class, which in turn is derived from the `CObject` class. Figure 2.6 shows the class hierarchy for the `CDBException` class.

FIGURE 2.6.
The CDBException
class hierarchy.

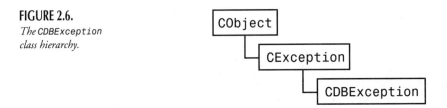

The `CDBException` class object has three public member functions, which are all in the data members category.

The following sections take a closer look at the members of this class. This book doesn't cover the members of the other classes on which `CDBException` is based. You should refer to the Visual C++ documentation (either the manuals or the online help system) for full information about these classes.

Data Members

There are three data members in the CDBException object class: m_nRetCode, m_strError, and m_strStateNativeOrigin.

The m_nRetCode member variable is used to hold the return code that has the error code. Valid return codes are shown in Table 2.3. The file \MSDEV\MFC\include\AFXDB.RC documents these values using string resource definitions.

Table 2.3. m_nRetCode values.

Identifier	Description
All Versions of MFC	
AFX_SQL_ERROR_API_CONFORMANCE	A CDatabase::Open() call was made, and the driver doesn't conform to the required ODBC API conformance level.
AFX_SQL_ERROR_CONNECT_FAIL	The datasource connection failed. A NULL CDatabase pointer was passed to the CRecordset constructor, and a subsequent attempt to create a connection based on a call to GetDefaultConnect() failed.
AFX_SQL_ERROR_DATA_TRUNCATED	More data was requested than would fit in the storage you provided. See the nMaxLength argument for the RFX_Text() and RFX_Binary() functions for information on expanding the space available.
AFX_SQL_ERROR_DYNASET_NOT_SUPPORTED	The call to CRecordset::Open() that requested a dynaset failed. This was due to the fact that dynasets weren't supported by this ODBC driver.
AFX_SQL_ERROR_EMPTY_COLUMN_LIST	An attempt was made to open a table. However, no columns were identified in record field exchange (RFX) function calls in your DoFieldExchange() function.

continues

Table 2.3. continued

Identifier	*Description*
All Versions of MFC	
AFX_SQL_ERROR_FIELD_SCHEMA_MISMATCH	Your call to an RFX function in your DoFieldExchange() function wasn't compatible with the column data type in the recordset.
AFX_SQL_ERROR_ILLEGAL_MODE	A call was made to CRecordset::Update() without having previously called CRecordset::AddNew() or CRecordset::Edit().
AFX_SQL_ERROR_LOCK_MODE_NOT_SUPPORTED	A request to lock records for update couldn't be fulfilled because the ODBC driver being used doesn't support locking.
AFX_SQL_ERROR_MULTIPLE_ROWS_AFFECTED	A call was made to CRecordset::Update() or CRecordset::Delete() for a table with no unique key, and multiple records were changed.
AFX_SQL_ERROR_NO_CURRENT_RECORD	Your application has attempted to edit or delete a previously deleted record. The application must scroll to a different (nondeleted) record after deleting the current record.
AFX_SQL_ERROR_NO_POSITIONED_UPDATES	The application's request for a dynaset couldn't be fulfilled because the ODBC driver doesn't support positioned updates.
AFX_SQL_ERROR_NO_ROWS_AFFECTED	A call was made to CRecordset::Update() or CRecordset::Delete(), but when the operation began, the record couldn't be found anymore.
AFX_SQL_ERROR_ODBC_LOAD_FAILED	The attempt to load ODBC.DLL failed. Windows couldn't find or couldn't load the ODBC.DLL. This error is fatal, and your program must end.

Identifier	Description
AFX_SQL_ERROR_ODBC_V2_REQUIRED	The application's request for a dynaset couldn't be fulfilled because a Level 2-compliant ODBC driver is required, and the current ODBC driver isn't Level 2-compliant.
AFX_SQL_ERROR_RECORDSET_FORWARD_ONLY	The attempt to scroll was unsuccessful because the datasource doesn't support backward scrolling.
AFX_SQL_ERROR_SNAPSHOT_NOT_SUPPORTED	The application made a call to `CRecordset::Open()` requesting a snapshot, but the call failed. Snapshots aren't supported by the driver. This will occur only when the ODBC cursor library, ODBCCURS.DLL, can't be found.
AFX_SQL_ERROR_SQL_CONFORMANCE	A call to `CDatabase::Open()` was made, and the driver doesn't conform to the required minimum ODBC SQL conformance level.
AFX_SQL_ERROR_SQL_NO_TOTAL	It wasn't possible to specify the total size of a `CLongBinary` data value. This most likely happened because a global memory block couldn't be preallocated.
AFX_SQL_ERROR_RECORDSET_READONLY	An attempt was made to update a recordset that was opened in read-only mode, or the datasource is read-only.
SQL_ERROR	The function failed. The error message returned by `::SQLError()` is stored in the `m_strError` data member.
SQL_INVALID_HANDLE	A handle (either environment, connection, or statement) was invalid. This was caused by a programmer error. This error isn't reported in MFC version 4.

continues

Table 2.3. continued

Identifier	Description
MFC Version 4 Only	
AFX_SQL_ERROR_INCORRECT_ODBC	An incorrect version of ODBC was reported.
AFX_SQL_ERROR_DYNAMIC_CURSOR_NOT_SUPPORTED	This ODBC driver doesn't support dynamic cursors.
AFX_SQL_ERROR_NO_DATA_FOUND	The application attempted to move before the first record, after the last record.
AFX_SQL_ERROR_ROW_FETCH	There was an attempt to fetch a row from the server during an Open or Requery operation.
AFX_SQL_ERROR_ROW_UPDATE_NOT_SUPPORTED	The ODBC driver doesn't support dynasets.
AFX_SQL_ERROR_UPDATE_DELETE_FAILED	A call to SQLSetPos() returned SQL_SUCCESS_WITH_INFO explaining why the function call to CRecordset::ExecuteSetPosUpdate() failed.

When you're writing an application, it's important that all error trapping be implemented. It's unacceptable for an application to fail because of an unhandled exception condition.

The m_strError member variable is used to hold a string that contains the text of the error message. The string is in the format *State* %s, *Native* %ld, *Origin* %s. The *State* value is a five-character string containing the SQL error code. The *Native* error code is specific to the datasource. The *Origin* string is error message text returned by the ODBC component generating the error condition.

The m_strStateNativeOrigin member variable contains the error condition formatted as *State* %s, *Native* %ld, *Origin* %s. The *State* value is a five-character string containing the SQL error code. The *Native* error code is specific to the datasource. The *Origin* string is error message text returned by the ODBC component generating the error condition.

CLongBinary

The CLongBinary class is used to hold large binary objects contained in databases. These objects are often referred to as *BLOBs* (*binary large objects*). Typical BLOBs are bitmap images, audio or video tracks, and specialized binary data. The CLongBinary class object is used to encapsulate the error condition. The CLongBinary object is derived from the CObject class. Figure 2.7 shows the class hierarchy for the CLongBinary class.

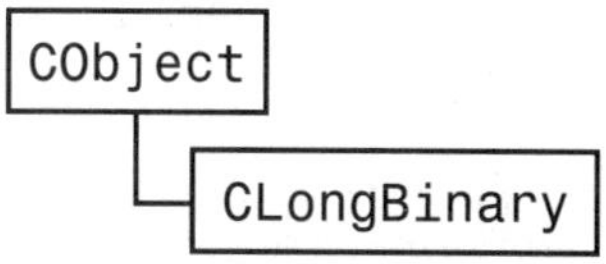

FIGURE 2.7.
*The CLongBinary
class hierarchy.*

```
┌─────────┐
│ CObject │
└─────────┘
     └──┐
        │ ┌─────────────┐
        └─│ CLongBinary │
          └─────────────┘
```

The CLongBinary class object has three public member functions that can be divided into two categories:

- Data members: The data members of the CLongBinary class hold both a handle to the object and the object's length in bytes.
- Construction: The constructor for the CLongBinary class.

The following sections take a closer look at the members of this class. This book doesn't cover the members of the other classes on which CLongBinary is based. Refer to the Visual C++ documentation (either the manuals or the online help system) for full information about these classes.

Data Members

There are two data members in the CLongBinary object class: m_dwDataLength and m_hData.

- The m_dwDataLength member variable contains the real size of the object that is stored in the block of memory specified by the m_hData handle. The actual amount of storage allocated may exceed this value.
- The m_hData member variable holds the Windows handle to the memory block that will contain the BLOB. You can determine the size of this memory block (which must be larger than the BLOB) by using a call to ::GlobalSize().

Construction Member

The CLongBinary object class has a single constructor.

The CLongBinary() function is used to construct the CLongBinary object. CLongBinary() takes no parameters. Because it's a constructor, no return value is specified. CLongBinary() has the following prototype:

```
CLongBinary();
```

The CLongBinary class is used with the RFX_LongBinary() field exchange function.

RFX Functions

RFX functions transfer data to and from the application's variables to a record's column. These functions are placed in a DoFieldExchange() function. The following code fragment shows an example of a DoFieldExchange() function:

```
void CRecordViewSet::DoFieldExchange(CFieldExchange* pFX)
{
    //{{AFX_FIELD_MAP(CRecordViewSet)
    pFX->SetFieldType(CFieldExchange::outputColumn);
    RFX_Text(pFX, _T("[CustomerID]"), m_CustomerID);
    RFX_Text(pFX, _T("[CompanyName]"), m_CompanyName);
    RFX_Text(pFX, _T("[ContactName]"), m_ContactName);
    RFX_Text(pFX, _T("[ContactTitle]"), m_ContactTitle);
    RFX_Text(pFX, _T("[Address]"), m_Address);
    RFX_Text(pFX, _T("[City]"), m_City);
    RFX_Text(pFX, _T("[Region]"), m_Region);
    RFX_Text(pFX, _T("[PostalCode]"), m_PostalCode);
    RFX_Text(pFX, _T("[Country]"), m_Country);
    RFX_Text(pFX, _T("[Phone]"), m_Phone);
    RFX_Text(pFX, _T("[Fax]"), m_Fax);
    //}}AFX_FIELD_MAP
}
```

Each of the RFX_...() functions allows transfer of a different type of data to and from the record's columns. Table 2.4 lists each RFX_...() function and describes its data types.

Table 2.4. The RFX_...() functions.

Function	Data Type	Description
RFX_Bool()	BOOL	Transfers a Boolean (TRUE/FALSE) value.
RFX_Byte()	BYTE	Transfers a byte (unsigned character) value.
RFX_Binary()	CByteArray	Transfers an array of byte values to the specified CByteArray object.
RFX_Double()	double	Transfers a floating-point (double) value.
RFX_Single()	float	Transfers a floating-point (float) value.
RFX_Int()	int	Transfers an integer (unsigned) value.
RFX_Long()	long	Transfers a long integer (unsigned long) value.
RFX_LongBinary()	CLongBinary	Transfers an array of byte values to the specified CLongBinary object.
RFX_Text()	CString	Transfers a character string (CString) value.
RFX_Date()	CTime	Transfers a time value to a CTime object.

If there is no RFX...() function to transfer the type of data you need, you can create your own RFX...() functions. You can use the existing RFX...() functions in the DBRFX.CPP file as starting points.

An AppWizard-Generated Program

This chapter's example is an AppWizard (Visual C++ 4) database program that uses ODBC. The final functionality (the dialog box controls for the main window, as well as connections between the controls in the dialog box and the program's variables) was done with the Visual C++ 4 IDE and ClassWizard. The actual time it took to develop this application was only a few minutes.

> **NOTE**
>
> Windows 95, Windows NT, and Visual C++ 4 all now support long filenames. This lets the names of the class implementation files have meaningful names. You should give your projects meaningful names because you're no longer limited to project names that had to be only a few characters to fit into DOS's 8.3 filename structure.

This program uses the CDatabase class, the CRecordset class, and the CRecordView class. This final part of the chapter takes a look at the files that support the CRecordView class (the Record ViewView.cpp file) and the CRecordset class (the Record ViewSet.cpp file).

CRecordView Support

The CRecordView class is supported in the RecordView View.cpp file. The minimal support is sufficient to create a working application that can be easily turned into a working record browser with editing capabilities. The default implementation of the AppWizard-produced program doesn't support adding records to the recordset, but you can add this functionality easily.

First, the RecordView View.cpp file, shown in Listing 2.1, contains the constructor and destructor for our CRecordView object, which is called CRecordViewView.

The next function is DoDataExchange(), which transfers the fields in the recordset to the application's data variables. This is the first time I've mentioned the DoDataExchange() function. Its purpose is to transfer data to and from the application's variables to the main window's dialog box controls.

> **NOTE**
>
> Don't confuse the DoDataExchange() function, which transfers data between an application's variables and dialog box controls, with DoFieldExchange(), which transfers data from the same variables and the current record in the recordset.

The Record ViewView.cpp file also contains functions to assist the programmer in implementing printer support (including print preview) and diagnostic support.

Listing 2.1. The CRecordView handler: Record ViewView.cpp.

```cpp
// Record ViewView.cpp : implementation of the CRecordViewView class
//

#include "stdafx.h"
#include "Record View.h"

#include "Record ViewSet.h"
#include "Record ViewDoc.h"
#include "Record ViewView.h"

#ifdef _DEBUG
#define new DEBUG_NEW
#undef THIS_FILE
static char THIS_FILE[] = __FILE__;
#endif


/////////////////////////////////////////////////////////////////////////////
// CRecordViewView

IMPLEMENT_DYNCREATE(CRecordViewView, CRecordView)

BEGIN_MESSAGE_MAP(CRecordViewView, CRecordView)
    //{{AFX_MSG_MAP(CRecordViewView)
        // NOTE - the ClassWizard will add and remove mapping macros here.
        //     DO NOT EDIT what you see in these blocks of generated code!
    //}}AFX_MSG_MAP
    // Standard printing commands
    ON_COMMAND(ID_FILE_PRINT, CRecordView::OnFilePrint)
    ON_COMMAND(ID_FILE_PRINT_DIRECT, CRecordView::OnFilePrint)
    ON_COMMAND(ID_FILE_PRINT_PREVIEW, CRecordView::OnFilePrintPreview)
END_MESSAGE_MAP()

/////////////////////////////////////////////////////////////////////////////
// CRecordViewView construction/destruction

CRecordViewView::CRecordViewView()
    : CRecordView(CRecordViewView::IDD)
{
    //{{AFX_DATA_INIT(CRecordViewView)
    m_pSet = NULL;
    //}}AFX_DATA_INIT
    // TODO: add construction code here

}

CRecordViewView::~CRecordViewView()
{
}

void CRecordViewView::DoDataExchange(CDataExchange* pDX)
{
    CRecordView::DoDataExchange(pDX);
    //{{AFX_DATA_MAP(CRecordViewView)
    DDX_FieldText(pDX, IDC_ADDRESS, m_pSet->m_Address, m_pSet);
    DDX_FieldText(pDX, IDC_CITY, m_pSet->m_City, m_pSet);
    DDX_FieldText(pDX, IDC_COMPANY_NAME, m_pSet->m_CompanyName, m_pSet);
```

```
    DDX_FieldText(pDX, IDC_CUSTOMER_ID, m_pSet->m_CustomerID, m_pSet);
    DDX_FieldText(pDX, IDC_FAX, m_pSet->m_Fax, m_pSet);
    DDX_FieldText(pDX, IDC_PHONE, m_pSet->m_Phone, m_pSet);
    DDX_FieldText(pDX, IDC_POSTAL_CODE, m_pSet->m_PostalCode, m_pSet);
    DDX_FieldText(pDX, IDC_REGION, m_pSet->m_Region, m_pSet);
    //}}AFX_DATA_MAP
}

BOOL CRecordViewView::PreCreateWindow(CREATESTRUCT& cs)
{
    // TODO: Modify the Window class or styles here by modifying
    // the CREATESTRUCT cs

    return CRecordView::PreCreateWindow(cs);
}

void CRecordViewView::OnInitialUpdate()
{
    m_pSet = &GetDocument()->m_recordViewSet;
    CRecordView::OnInitialUpdate();
}

/////////////////////////////////////////////////////////////////////////////
// CRecordViewView printing

BOOL CRecordViewView::OnPreparePrinting(CPrintInfo* pInfo)
{
    // Default preparation
    return DoPreparePrinting(pInfo);
}

void CRecordViewView::OnBeginPrinting(CDC* /*pDC*/, CPrintInfo* /*pInfo*/)
{
    // TODO: add extra initialization before printing
}

void CRecordViewView::OnEndPrinting(CDC* /*pDC*/, CPrintInfo* /*pInfo*/)
{
    // TODO: add cleanup after printing
}

/////////////////////////////////////////////////////////////////////////////
// CRecordViewView diagnostics

#ifdef _DEBUG
void CRecordViewView::AssertValid() const
{
    CRecordView::AssertValid();
}

void CRecordViewView::Dump(CDumpContext& dc) const
{
    CRecordView::Dump(dc);
}

CRecordViewDoc* CRecordViewView::GetDocument() // Nondebug version is inline
{
```

continues

Listing 2.1. continued

```
    ASSERT(m_pDocument->IsKindOf(RUNTIME_CLASS(CRecordViewDoc)));
    return (CRecordViewDoc*)m_pDocument;
}
#endif //_DEBUG

/////////////////////////////////////////////////////////////////////////
// CRecordViewView database support
CRecordset* CRecordViewView::OnGetRecordset()
{
    return m_pSet;
}


/////////////////////////////////////////////////////////////////////////
// CRecordViewView message handlers
```

When you use ClassWizard to add message handlers, these functions will be added to the end of the RecordView View.cpp file.

CRecordset Support

The `CRecordset` class is supported in the Record ViewSet.cpp file. The minimal support is sufficient to create a working application that easily can be turned into a working record browser with edit capabilities.

First in the Record ViewSet.cpp file, shown in Listing 2.2, is the constructor for the `CRecordset` object. There is no default destructor, but you could provide one if it were needed.

After the constructor are the `GetDefaultConnect()` and `GetDefaultSQL()` functions.

The final function in the Record ViewSet.cpp file is the `DoFieldExchange()` function. This function manages the transfer of data to and from the application's variables and the recordset's current record.

Listing 2.2. The `CRecordset` support file Record ViewSet.cpp.

```
// Record ViewSet.cpp : implementation of the CRecordViewSet class
//

#include "stdafx.h"
#include "Record View.h"
#include "Record ViewSet.h"

#ifdef _DEBUG
#define new DEBUG_NEW
#undef THIS_FILE
static char THIS_FILE[] = __FILE__;
#endif
```

```
/////////////////////////////////////////////////////////////////////////
// CRecordViewSet implementation

IMPLEMENT_DYNAMIC(CRecordViewSet, CRecordset)

CRecordViewSet::CRecordViewSet(CDatabase* pdb)
    : CRecordset(pdb)
{
    //{{AFX_FIELD_INIT(CRecordViewSet)
    m_CustomerID = _T("");
    m_CompanyName = _T("");
    m_ContactName = _T("");
    m_ContactTitle = _T("");
    m_Address = _T("");
    m_City = _T("");
    m_Region = _T("");
    m_PostalCode = _T("");
    m_Country = _T("");
    m_Phone = _T("");
    m_Fax = _T("");
    m_nFields = 11;
    //}}AFX_FIELD_INIT
    m_nDefaultType = snapshot;
}

CString CRecordViewSet::GetDefaultConnect()
{
    return _T("ODBC;DSN=Access 95 Northwind");
}

CString CRecordViewSet::GetDefaultSQL()
{
    return _T("[Customers]");
}

void CRecordViewSet::DoFieldExchange(CFieldExchange* pFX)
{
    //{{AFX_FIELD_MAP(CRecordViewSet)
    pFX->SetFieldType(CFieldExchange::outputColumn);
    RFX_Text(pFX, _T("[CustomerID]"), m_CustomerID);
    RFX_Text(pFX, _T("[CompanyName]"), m_CompanyName);
    RFX_Text(pFX, _T("[ContactName]"), m_ContactName);
    RFX_Text(pFX, _T("[ContactTitle]"), m_ContactTitle);
    RFX_Text(pFX, _T("[Address]"), m_Address);
    RFX_Text(pFX, _T("[City]"), m_City);
    RFX_Text(pFX, _T("[Region]"), m_Region);
    RFX_Text(pFX, _T("[PostalCode]"), m_PostalCode);
    RFX_Text(pFX, _T("[Country]"), m_Country);
    RFX_Text(pFX, _T("[Phone]"), m_Phone);
    RFX_Text(pFX, _T("[Fax]"), m_Fax);
    //}}AFX_FIELD_MAP
}

/////////////////////////////////////////////////////////////////////////
// CRecordViewSet diagnostics
```

continues

Listing 2.2. continued

```
#ifdef _DEBUG
void CRecordViewSet::AssertValid() const
{
    CRecordset::AssertValid();
}

void CRecordViewSet::Dump(CDumpContext& dc) const
{
    CRecordset::Dump(dc);
}
#endif //_DEBUG
}
```

Summary

You need a thorough understanding of the member objects that constitute Visual C++'s data access object class to develop commercial-quality Visual C++ database applications. This chapter began by showing each of the data access object classes, with a detailed explanation of the member functions of each data-related member object. The Record View sample application introduced you to the code that AppWizard creates when you use AppWizard to create a basic database application. This chapter also can serve as a reference for the functions and member variables of the data access classes.

Chapter 3, "Using Visual C++ Database Functions," completes Part I of this book by showing you how to use Visual C++'s native C database SQL...() functions. The SQL...() functions can be used both with the MFC data access classes or alone, without any of the data access classes. These functions are useful when your application must have greater control over the process of database access.

3

Using Visual C++
Database Functions

In Chapter 2, "Understanding MFC's ODBC Database Classes," you learned about the MFC data access objects. These C++ classes were built on the data access functions that are part of the SQL library that interfaces with ODBC. These functions offer a powerful interface to ODBC.

The first part of this chapter is a reference to the SQL...() functions that make up the ODBC SDK 2.x interface. Those functions that were present in the ODBC SDK 1.0 version (such as SQLSetParam()) and that have been deleted in more recent versions of ODBC aren't covered in this chapter. The second part of this chapter presents a set of functions that you can use to access datasets. It generally is more difficult to use the SQL...() functions than to use the MFC database classes described in Chapter 2. However, these functions do offer more flexibility to the programmer who is writing an application that must access many different types of datasources, with differing tables and schema (layout and definitions).

Notwithstanding the existing functionality found in the MFC ODBC classes, there is no reason why you can't use both the MFC classes and the SQL...() functions in the same code. The MFC ODBC classes have all the necessary handles to allow usage of the SQL...() functions; in fact, the MFC ODBC classes use the SQL...() functions to perform most of their database manipulation tasks.

The *SQL...()* Functions

This reference to the SQL...() functions will show virtually everything you need to know in order to use most of these functions. However, some functions are complex and return a substantial amount of information. If you need more information, you can refer to the various help files available (including the MSDN CD set, the ODBC SDK, and Visual C++'s help facility).

> **NOTE**
>
> The SQL...() functions haven't changed substantially since their introduction. Minor changes to accommodate 32-bit programming (the original SQL...() functions were 16-bit) account for virtually all the changes found.

When you use the SQL...() functions, remember that there is a fixed order of usage. The sample code in the second part of this chapter provides more information about how to use the functions.

Each function is presented with a prototype, function arguments (if any), an explanation of the return value (if any), a description of what the function should do, and an explanation of possible failures that might occur when you use the function. Some functions will fail for a number of reasons. When you encounter a failure, use SQLError() to determine the cause of the failure.

> **NOTE**
>
> Using the SQL logging facility is often very useful in determining why an SQL function failed during development. Of course, you shouldn't expect your application's users to have SQL logging turned on.
>
> Don't forget that SQL logging will significantly affect ODBC performance because detailed information is written to the logging file for each and every SQL operation. Don't turn on SQL logging indiscriminately; use it when you need it and then turn it off.

In all cases where the return value is shown as type RETCODE, you should create a variable defined as this type to hold the return code. You can then use either an if() or a switch() statement to check the return code for errors.

> **NOTE**
>
> There are two versions of the ODBC SDK 2.1: 2.10a and 2.10b. You should use 2.10b, which was released in August of 1995, if you're using Visual C++ 2.x. The version of ODBC that is included with Visual C++ 4.0 is 2.5. Version 2.5 is intended for use on both Windows 95 and on Windows NT versions 3.5 and 3.51.

> **NOTE**
>
> The current version of the ODBC SDK is 2.5, which is included with both Visual C++ 4 and Visual C++ 1.5x. Microsoft hasn't announced whether (or when) further updates to the ODBC SDK will occur. It can be assumed that new versions of Visual C++ may well include new versions of ODBC.

SQLAllocConnect()

Prototype:

```
RETCODE SQLAllocConnect(HENV henv, HDBC FAR * phdbc)
```

Parameters:

HENV *henv*	The environment handle from the call to SQLAllocEnv().
HDBC FAR * *phdbc*	A pointer to the storage for the connection handle.

Return Value:

This function will return one of the following values:

SQL_SUCCESS	The function was successful.
SQL_SUCCESS_WITH_INFO	The function was successful, and more information is available.
SQL_ERROR	The function failed. Call SQLError() to get more information about the specific failure.
SLQ_INVALID_HANDLE	The function failed. The handle that was passed wasn't a valid handle. Possibly, the function that created the handle had failed and didn't return a valid handle.

If this function fails, your SQL function should end or the error should be corrected; the function should then be re-executed.

Usage:

The SQLAllocConnect() function is used to allocate the connection between the application and the datasource. It's called after a call to SQLAllocEnv(), and SQLAllocStmt() is called after a call to SQLAllocEnv().

You must call the SQLAllocConnect() function after getting an HENV handle from SQLAllocEnv(). Without a valid HENV handle, this function won't succeed. Always check the return code from this function for errors.

Notes:

The function's results are placed in the handle pointed to by the *phdbc* parameter. If the SQLAllocConnect() function fails, the *phdbc* handle will be set to SQL_NULL_HDBC.

SQLAllocEnv()

Prototype:

```
RETCODE SQLAllocEnv(HENV FAR * phenv)
```

Parameter:

    HENV FAR * *phenv*   A pointer to an environment handle.

Return Value:

This function will return one of the following values:

SQL_SUCCESS	The function was successful.
SQL_ERROR	The function failed. Call SQLError() to get more information about the specific failure.

If this function fails, your SQL function should end or the error should be corrected; the function should then be re-executed. Often, this function is the first SQL...() function that is called. If it fails, there may be no recovery.

Usage:

Call the SQLAllocEnv() function to initialize the SQL environment. You should make a matching SQLFreeEnv() call when your calling function has finished accessing the datasource. Always check the return code from these functions for errors.

Notes:

This function places the HENV in the supplied handle. If SQLAllocEnv() fails, the resultant *phenv* parameter is set to SQL_NULL_HENV.

SQLAllocStmt()

Prototype:

RETCODE SQLAllocStmt(HDBC *hdbc*, HSTMT FAR * *hstmt*)

Parameters:

HDBC *hdbc*	A handle to an HDBC as returned by the call to the SQLAllocConnect() function.
HSTMT FAR * *hstmt*	A pointer to a statement handle that will be filled in by this function.

Return Value:

This function will return one of the following values:

SQL_SUCCESS	The function was successful.
SQL_SUCCESS_WITH_INFO	The function was successful, and more information is available.
SQL_ERROR	The function failed. Call SQLError() to get more information about the specific failure.
SLQ_INVALID_HANDLE	The function failed. The handle that was passed wasn't a valid handle. Possibly, the function that created the handle had failed and didn't return a valid handle.

If this function fails, your SQL function should end or the error should be corrected; the function should then be re-executed.

Usage:

The SQLAllocStmt() function is used to allocate a statement handle. This statement handle is associated with the datasource to which the HDBC handle was connected.

Notes:

If this function fails, the returned HSTMT handle will be set to SQL_NULL_HSTMT.

SQLBindCol()

Prototype:

```
RETCODE SQLBindCol(HSTMT hstmt, UWORD icol, SWORD fCType,
PTR rbgValue, SDWORD cbValueMax, SDWORD FAR * pcbValue)
```

Parameters:

HSTMT *hstmt*	A statement handle returned by the call to SQLAllocStmt().
UWORD *icol*	The index to the column in the table to which the variable is being bound.
SWORD *fCType*	The data type of the data variable that is being bound to column *icol*.
PTR *rgbValue*	A pointer to the location in the application where the column's data is to be stored. The data type of *rgbValue* should be defined by *fCType*.
SDWORD *cbValueMax*	The number of bytes in the storage location pointed to by *rgbValue*. Usually, the C sizeof() operator can be used for this parameter.
SDWORD FAR * *pcbValue*	A pointer to an SDWORD variable that will receive the count of how many bytes in *rgbValue* were used.

Return Value:

This function will return one of the following values:

SQL_SUCCESS	The function was successful.
SQL_SUCCESS_WITH_INFO	The function was successful, and more information is available.
SQL_ERROR	The function failed. Call SQLError() to get more information about the specific failure.
SLQ_INVALID_HANDLE	The function failed. The handle that was passed wasn't a valid handle. Possibly, the function that created the handle had failed and didn't return a valid handle.

If this function fails, your SQL function should end or the error should be corrected; the function should then be re-executed.

Usage:

Call the SQLBindCol() function only for the columns in a table that you need. You don't have to bind to every column in a table. Columns that don't have a variable bound to them will be discarded without error.

You make a call—usually in a loop—to SQLFetch() or SQLExtendedFetch() to actually get the data from a record.

Always check the return code from this function for errors.

Notes:

If this function fails, use the SQLError() function to find out why. When a column hasn't been bound and later must be accessed, use SQLGetData().

SQLBindParameter()

Prototype:

```
RETCODE SQLBindParameter(HSTMT hstmt, UWORD ipar, SWORD fParamType,
SWORD fCType, SWORD fSqlType, UDWORD cbColDef,
SWORD ibScale, PTR rgbValue, SDWORD cbValueMax, SDWORD pcbValue)
```

Parameters:

HSTMT *hstmt*	A statement handle returned by the call to SQLAllocStmt().
UWORD *ipar*	The parameter number, which is one-based (not zero-based) from left to right.
SWORD *fParamType*	Parameter *ipar*'s type.
SWORD *fCType*	The C data type of the parameter.
SWORD *fSqlType*	The SQL data type of the parameter.
UDWORD *cbColDef*	The column's precision.
SWORD *ibScale*	The column's scale.
PTR *rgbValue*	A pointer to the location in the application where the column's data is to be stored. The data type of *rgbValue* should be defined by *fCType*.
SDWORD *cbValueMax*	The number of bytes in the storage location pointed to by *rgbValue*. Usually the C sizeof() operator can be used for this parameter.
SDWORD FAR * *pcbValue*	A pointer to an SDWORD variable that will receive the count of how many bytes in *rgbValue* were used.

Return Value:

This function will return one of the following values:

SQL_SUCCESS	The function was successful.
SQL_SUCCESS_WITH_INFO	The function was successful, and more information is available.
SQL_ERROR	The function failed. Call SQLError() to get more information about the specific failure.
SLQ_INVALID_HANDLE	The function failed. The handle that was passed wasn't a valid handle. Possibly, the function that created the handle had failed and didn't return a valid handle.

If this function fails, your SQL function should end or the error should be corrected; the function should then be re-executed.

Usage:

Call the SQLBindParameter() function to bind a buffer to a parameter marker in an SQL statement. Always check the return code from this function for errors.

Notes:

If this function fails, use the SQLError() function to find out why. This function replaces the SQLSetParam() function found in ODBC version 1.x.

SQLBrowseConnect()

Prototype:

```
RETCODE SQLBrowseConnect(HDBC hdbc, UCHAR FAR * szConnStrIn, SWORD cbConnStrIn,
UCHAR FAR * szConnStrOut, SWORD cbConnStrOutMax, SWORD FAR * pcbConnStrOut)
```

Parameters:

HDBC hdbc	A handle to an HDBC as returned by the call to the SQLAllocConnect() function.
UCHAR FAR * szConnStrIn	The input connection string.
SWORD cbConnStrIn	The number of bytes in szConnStrIn.
UCHAR FAR * szConnStrOut	The output connection string.
SWORD cbConnStrOutMax	The number of bytes available in szConnStrOut.
SWORD FAR * pcbConnStrOut	The count of the number of bytes actually used in szConnStrOut.

Return Value:

This function will return one of the following values:

SQL_SUCCESS	The function was successful.
SQL_SUCCESS_WITH_INFO	The function was successful, and more information is available.
SQL_NEED_DATA	The function failed. More information in the input connect string was required than was supplied. Call SQLError() to get more information about the specific failure.
SQL_ERROR	The function failed. Call SQLError() to get more information about the specific failure.
SLQ_INVALID_HANDLE	The function failed. The handle that was passed wasn't a valid handle. Possibly, the function that created the handle had failed and didn't return a valid handle.

If this function fails, your SQL function should end or the error should be corrected; the function should then be re-executed.

Usage:

Call the SQLBrowseConnect() function to enumerate the attributes of a specific datasource. Always check the return code from this function for errors, making additional calls as necessary to gather the desired information to establish the connection.

Notes:

When a return code of either SQL_SUCCESS or SQL_SUCCESS_WITH_INFO is returned, your application will know that the enumeration process has completed and the application is connected to the datasource.

SQLCancel()

Prototype:

RETCODE SQLCancel (HSTMT *hstmt*)

Parameter:

HSTMT *hstmt*	A statement handle returned by the call to SQLAllocStmt().

Return Value:

This function will return one of the following values:

SQL_SUCCESS	The function was successful.
SQL_SUCCESS_WITH_INFO	The function was successful, and more information is available.
SQL_ERROR	The function failed. Call `SQLError()` to get more information about the specific failure.
SLQ_INVALID_HANDLE	The function failed. The handle that was passed wasn't a valid handle. Possibly, the function that created the handle had failed and didn't return a valid handle.

If this function fails, your SQL function should end or the error should be corrected; the function should then be re-executed.

Usage:

Call the `SQLCancel()` function to cancel an asynchronous operation pending on the parameter statement indicated by *hstmt*. Always check the return code from this function for errors.

Notes:

You can cancel functions running on *hstmt* that are running on other threads. You also can cancel functions on *hstmt* that require more data.

SQLColAttributes()

Prototype:

```
RETCODE SQLColAttributes (HSTMT hstmt, UWORD icol, UWORD fDescType,
PTR rgbDesc, SWORD cbDescMax, SWORD FAR * pcbDesc, SWORD FAR * pfDesc)
```

Parameters:

HSTMT *hstmt*	A statement handle returned by the call to `SQLAllocStmt()`.
UWORD *icol*	The index to the column in the table that the variable is being bound to.
UWORD *fDescType*	A valid descriptor.
PTR *rgbDesc*	A pointer to the location in the application where the column's data is to be stored. The data type of *rgbValue* should be defined by *fCDescType*.
SWORD *cbDescMax*	The number of bytes in the storage location pointed to by *rgbDesc*. Usually, the C `sizeof()` operator can be passed for this parameter.
SWORD FAR * *pcbDesc*	A pointer to an SDWORD variable that will receive the count of how many bytes in *rgbDesc* were used.
SWORD FAR * *pfDesc*	A pointer to an integer variable that will receive the results of a query which returns a numeric result.

Return Value:

This function will return one of the following values:

`SQL_SUCCESS`	The function was successful.
`SQL_SUCCESS_WITH_INFO`	The function was successful, and more information is available.
`SQL_ERROR`	The function failed. Call `SQLError()` to get more information about the specific failure.
`SLQ_INVALID_HANDLE`	The function failed. The handle that was passed wasn't a valid handle. Possibly, the function that created the handle had failed and didn't return a valid handle.

If this function fails, your SQL function should end or the error should be corrected; the function should then be re-executed.

Usage:

Call the `SQLColAttributes()` function to gather information about a column in a table. Always check the return code from this function for errors.

Notes:

Table 3.1 shows the information that will be returned for columns.

Table 3.1. Column attributes returned by `SQLColAttributes()`.

Identifier	*Minimum ODBC Version*	*Where Returned*	*Description*
`SQL_COLUMN_AUTO_INCREMENT`	1.0	*pfDesc*	Returns TRUE if the column is an auto-increment column and FALSE if it isn't. Only numeric columns can be auto-increment. Values may be inserted into an auto-increment column, but the auto-increment column can't be updated.

continues

Table 3.1. continued

Identifier	Minimum ODBC Version	Where Returned	Description
SQL_COLUMN_CASE_SENSITIVE	1.0	*pfDesc*	Returns TRUE if the column will be considered case-sensitive for sorts and comparisons. Columns that aren't character-based will return FALSE.
SQL_COLUMN_COUNT	1.0	*pfDesc*	Number of columns that are in the result set. The *icol* argument will be ignored.
SQL_COLUMN_DISPLAY_SIZE	1.0	*pfDesc*	Returns the maximum number of characters positions that will be necessary to display data from the column.
SQL_COLUMN_LABEL	2.0	*rgbDesc*	The column's label or title. As an example, an Access database may have a column called ZipCodes that could be labeled (or titled) "5-Digit Zip Code." The column name is returned for columns that don't have specified labels or titles. For unnamed columns (such as those found in a text file datasource), an empty string is returned.
SQL_COLUMN_LENGTH	1.0	*pfDesc*	The number of bytes of data that will be transferred on an SQLGetData() or

Identifier	Minimum ODBC Version	Where Returned	Description
			SQLFetch() operation when the SQL_C_DEFAULT parameter is specified.
SQL_COLUMN_MONEY	1.0	*pfDesc*	Returns TRUE if the column is a money data type.
SQL_COLUMN_NAME	1.0	*rgbDesc*	Returns the column name. If the column is unnamed, an empty string is returned. See SQL_COLUMN_LABEL earlier in this table.
SQL_COLUMN_NULLABLE	1.0	*pfDesc*	Returns SQL_NO_NULLS if the column doesn't accept null values, or returns SQL_NULLABLE if the column accepts null values. Returns SQL_NULLABLE_UNKNOWN if it can't be determined whether the column accepts null values.
SQL_COLUMN_OWNER_NAME	2.0	*rgbDesc*	Returns the name of the owner of the table that contains the specified column. When the datasource doesn't support owners (such as for xBase files) or the owner name can't be determined, an empty string will be returned.

continues

Table 3.1. continued

Identifier	Minimum ODBC Version	Where Returned	Description
SQL_COLUMN_PRECISION	1.0	*pfDesc*	Returns the precision of the column on the datasource.
SQL_COLUMN_QUALIFIER_NAME	2.0	*rgbDesc*	Returns the table qualifier for the column. For datasources that don't support qualifiers or where the qualifier name can't be determined, an empty string will be returned.
SQL_COLUMN_SCALE	1.0	*pfDesc*	Returns the scale of the column on the datasource.
SQL_COLUMN_SEARCHABLE	1.0	*pfDesc*	Returns SQL_UNSEARCHABLE when the column can't be used in a WHERE clause.
			Returns SQL_LIKE_ONLY if the column can be used in a WHERE clause only with the LIKE predicate. When the column is a type SQL_LONGVARCHAR or SQL_LONGVARBINARY this is the usual return.
			Returns SQL_ALL_EXCEPT_LIKE if the column can be used in a WHERE clause with all comparison operators except LIKE.

Identifier	Minimum ODBC Version	Where Returned	Description
			Returns SQL_SEARCHABLE if the column can be used in a WHERE clause with any comparison operator.
SQL_COLUMN_TABLE_NAME	2.0	*rgbDesc*	Returns the table name for the table that contains the column. When the table name can't be determined, an empty string is returned.
SQL_COLUMN_TYPE	1.0	*pfDesc*	Returns the SQL data type for the column.
SQL_COLUMN_TYPE_NAME	1.0	*rgbDesc*	A character string indicating the data type of the column: CHAR, VARCHAR, MONEY, LONG VARBINARY, or CHAR() for bit data. When the data type is unknown, an empty string is returned.
SQL_COLUMN_UNSIGNED	1.0	*pfDesc*	Returns TRUE if the column is either nonnumeric or is an unsigned numeric value.
SQL_COLUMN_UPDATABLE	1.0	*pfDesc*	The column will be described with one of the following constants: SQL_ATTR_READONLY, SQL_ATTR_WRITE, SQL_ATTR_READWRITE_UNKNOWN, SQL_COLUMN_UPDATABLE,

continues

Table 3.1. continued

Identifier	Minimum ODBC Version	Where Returned	Description
			which describe how the column may be updated. When it can't be determined whether the column may be updatable, SQL_ATTR_READWRITE_UNKNOWN is typically returned.

SQLColumnPrivileges()

Prototype:

```
RETCODE SQLColumnPrivileges(HSTMT hstmt, UCHAR FAR * szTableQualifier,
SWORD cbTableQualifier, UCHAR FAR * szTableOwner, SWORD cbTableOwner,
UCHAR FAR * szTableName, SWORD cbTableName, UCHAR FAR * szColumnName,
SWORD cbColumnName)
```

Parameters:

HSTMT *hstmt*	A statement handle returned by the call to SQLAllocStmt().
UCHAR FAR * *szTableQualifier*	The table qualifier. Use an empty string for tables that don't support table qualifiers.
SWORD *cbTableQualifier*	The length of *szTableQualifier*.
UCHAR FAR * *szTableOwner*	The table owner name. Use an empty string for tables that don't support table owners.
SWORD *cbTableOwner*	The length of *szTableOwner*.
UCHAR FAR * *szTableName*	The table name.
SWORD *cbTableName*	The length of *szTableName*.
UCHAR FAR * *szColumnName*	The search pattern string (used for column names).
SWORD *cbColumnName*	The length of *szColumnName*.

Return Value:

This function will return one of the following values:

SQL_SUCCESS	The function was successful.
SQL_SUCCESS_WITH_INFO	The function was successful, and more information is available.
SQL_STILL_EXECUTING	An asynchronous event is still pending.
SQL_ERROR	The function failed. Call SQLError() to get more information about the specific failure.
SLQ_INVALID_HANDLE	The function failed. The handle that was passed wasn't a valid handle. Possibly, the function that created the handle had failed and didn't return a valid handle.

If this function fails, your SQL function should end or the error should be corrected; the function should then be re-executed.

Usage:

Call the SQLColumnPrivileges() function to obtain a list of columns and privileges for the specified table. Always check the return code from this function for errors.

Notes:

The information is returned as a result set.

SQLColumns()

Prototype:

```
RETCODE SQLColumns(HSTMT hstmt, UCHAR FAR * szTableQualifier,
SWORD cbTableQualifier, UCHAR FAR * szTableOwner,
SWORD cbTableOwner, UCHAR FAR * szTableName, SWORD cbTableName,
UCHAR FAR * szColumnName, SWORD cbColumnName)
```

Parameters:

HSTMT *hstmt*	A statement handle returned by the call to SQLAllocStmt().
UCHAR FAR * *szTableQualifier*	The table qualifier. Use an empty string for tables that don't support table qualifiers.
SWORD *cbTableQualifier*	The length of *szTableQualifier*.
UCHAR FAR * *szTableOwner*	The table owner name. Use an empty string for tables that don't support table owners.
SWORD *cbTableOwner*	The length of *szTableOwner*.
UCHAR FAR * *szTableName*	The table name.

SWORD *cbTableName*	The length of *szTableName*.
UCHAR FAR * *szColumnName*	The search pattern string (used for column names).
SWORD *cbColumnName*	The length of *szColumnName*.

Return Value:

This function will return one of the following values:

SQL_SUCCESS	The function was successful.
SQL_SUCCESS_WITH_INFO	The function was successful, and more information is available.
SQL_ERROR	The function failed. Call SQLError() to get more information about the specific failure.
SLQ_INVALID_HANDLE	The function failed. The handle that was passed wasn't a valid handle. Possibly, the function that created the handle had failed and didn't return a valid handle.

If this function fails, your SQL function should end or the error should be corrected; the function should then be re-executed.

Usage:

Call the SQLColumns() function to obtain a list of the columns in a specified table. Always check the return code from this function for errors.

Notes:

The results are returned as a result set. The columns returned in the result set are shown in Table 3.2.

Table 3.2. Columns in the SQLColumns() result set.

Column Number	Data Type	Description
1	SQL_C_CHAR	Qualifier
2	SQL_C_CHAR	Owner
3	SQL_C_CHAR	Table Name
4	SQL_C_CHAR	Column Name
5	SQL_C_SSHORT	Data Type
6	SQL_C_CHAR	Type Name
7	SQL_C_SLONG	Precision
8	SQL_C_SLONG	Length
9	SQL_C_SSHORT	Scale

Column Number	Data Type	Description
10	SQL_C_SSHORT	Radix
11	SQL_C_SSHORT	Nullable
12	SQL_C_CHAR	Remarks

SQLConnect()

Prototype:

```
RETCODE SQLConnect(HDBC hdbc, UCHAR FAR * szDSN, SWORD cbDSN,
UCHAR FAR * szUID, SWORD cbUID, UCHAR FAR * szAuthStr, SWORD cbAuthStr)
```

Parameters:

HDBC hdbc	A handle to an HDBC as returned by the call to the SQLAllocConnect() function.
UCHAR FAR * szDSN	A pointer to a string containing the datasource name.
SWORD cbDSN	The length of szDSN.
UCHAR FAR * szUID	A pointer to the string that contains the user's identifier.
SWORD cbUID	The length of szUID.
UCHAR FAR * szAuthStr	The password or authentication string.
SWORD cbAuthStr	The length of szAuthStr.

Return Value:

This function will return one of the following values:

SQL_SUCCESS	The function was successful.
SQL_SUCCESS_WITH_INFO	The function was successful, and more information is available.
SQL_ERROR	The function failed. Call SQLError() to get more information about the specific failure.
SLQ_INVALID_HANDLE	The function failed. The handle that was passed wasn't a valid handle. Possibly, the function that created the handle had failed and didn't return a valid handle.

If this function fails, your SQL function should end or the error should be corrected; the function should then be re-executed.

Usage:

Call the SQLConnect() function to establish a connection between the application and a specific datasource. Always check the return code from this function for errors.

Notes:

The SQLConnect() function tells ODBC to load the driver in preparation for using the datasource.

SQLDataSources()

Prototype:

```
RETCODE SQL (HENV henv, UWORD fDirection, UCHAR FAR * szDSN,
SWORD cbDSNMax, SWORD FAR * pcbDSN, UCHAR FAR * szDescription,
SWORD cbDescriptionMax, SWORD FAR * pcbDescription)
```

Parameters:

HENV *henv*	Environment handle.
UWORD *fDirection*	This parameter is used to determine whether the driver manager will fetch the next datasource name in the list (use the SQL_FETCH_NEXT identifier) or whether the search starts from the beginning of the list (use the SQL_FETCH_FIRST identifier).
UCHAR FAR * *szDSN*	A pointer to a storage buffer for the datasource name.
SWORD *cbDSNMax*	Maximum length of the *szDSN* buffer. The maximum length supported by ODBC is SQL_MAX_DSN_LENGTH + 1.
SWORD FAR * *pcbDSN*	The total number of bytes returned in *szDSN*. If the returned string won't fit in *szDSN*, the datasource name is truncated to cbDSNMax − 1 bytes.
UCHAR FAR * *szDescription*	A pointer to storage buffer for the description string of the driver associated with the datasource. The *szDescription* buffer should be at least 255 bytes long. Driver descriptions might be dBASE or SQL Server.
SWORD *cbDescriptionMax*	Maximum length of *szDescription*.
SWORD FAR * *pcbDescription*	The total number of bytes returned in *szDSN*. If the returned string won't fit in *szDescription*, the description is truncated to *cbDescriptionMax* − 1 bytes.

Return Value:

This function will return one of the following values:

SQL_SUCCESS	The function was successful.
SQL_SUCCESS_WITH_INFO	The function was successful, and more information is available.

SQL_NO_DATA_FOUND	There were no datasources remaining.
SQL_ERROR	The function failed. Call `SQLError()` to get more information about the specific failure.
SLQ_INVALID_HANDLE	The function failed. The handle that was passed wasn't a valid handle. Possibly, the function that created the handle had failed and didn't return a valid handle.

If this function fails, your SQL function should end or the error should be corrected; the function should then be re-executed.

Usage:

Call the `SQLDataSources()` function to enumerate a list of the currently installed datasources. Always check the return code from this function for errors.

Notes:

You should call the `SQLDataSources()` function in a loop while the application checks the return code. When the return code is `SQL_NO_DATA_FOUND`, then all the datasources have been enumerated.

SQLDescribeCol()

Prototype:

```
RETCODE SQL (HSTMT hstmt, UWORD icol, UCHAR FAR * szColName,
SWORD cbColNameMax, SWORD FAR * pcbColName,
SWORD FAR * pfSqlType, UDWORD FAR * pcbColDef,
SWORD FAR * pibScale, SWORD FAR * pfNullable)
```

Parameters:

HSTMT *hstmt*	A statement handle returned by the call to `SQLAllocStmt()`.
UWORD *icol*	The index to the column in the table to which the variable is being bound.
UCHAR FAR * *szColName*	A pointer to a string that will contain the column name. For columns that have no name, or when the name can't be determined, an empty string will be returned.
SWORD *cbColNameMax*	The size of the *szColName*.
SWORD FAR * *pcbColName*	The number of bytes returned in *szColName*. If the column name won't fit in *szColName*, the column name is truncated to *cbColNameMax* − 1 bytes.
SWORD FAR * *pfSqlType*	The column's SQL data type. Use one of the constants shown in Table 3.3 for this parameter.
UDWORD FAR * *pcbColDef*	The column's precision, or zero if the precision can't be determined.

| SWORD FAR * *pibScale* | The column's scale, or zero if the scale can't be determined. |
| SWORD FAR * *pfNullable* | A constant that indicates whether this column supports null data values. Will be either SQL_NO_NULLS, SQL_NULLABLE, or SQL_NULLABLE_UNKNOWN. |

Table 3.3. Column types.

Identifier	*Description*
SQL_BIGINT	Integer data
SQL_BINARY	Binary data
SQL_BIT	Bit-field data
SQL_CHAR	Character data
SQL_DATE	Date field
SQL_DECIMAL	Decimal data
SQL_DOUBLE	Double data
SQL_FLOAT	Floating-point data
SQL_INTEGER	Integer data
SQL_LONGVARBINARY	Binary data
SQL_LONGVARCHAR	Variable-length character data
SQL_NUMERIC	Numeric data
SQL_REAL	Floating-point data
SQL_SMALLINT	Integer data
SQL_TIME	Time data
SQL_TIMESTAMP	Timestamp data
SQL_TINYINT	Integer data
SQL_VARBINARY	Variable-length binary data
SQL_VARCHAR	Variable-length character data
Other	Driver-specific data

Return Value:

This function will return one of the following values:

| SQL_SUCCESS | The function was successful. |
| SQL_SUCCESS_WITH_INFO | The function was successful, and more information is available. |

SQL_STILL_EXECUTING	An asynchronous operation is still pending.
SQL_ERROR	The function failed. Call SQLError() to get more information about the specific failure.
SLQ_INVALID_HANDLE	The function failed. The handle that was passed wasn't a valid handle. Possibly, the function that created the handle had failed and didn't return a valid handle.

If this function fails, your SQL function should end or the error should be corrected; the function should then be re-executed.

Usage:

Call the SQLDescribeCol() function to get information about a specific column in a datasource. Always check the return code from this function for errors.

Notes:

If this function fails, use the SQLError() function to find out why.

SQLDescribeParam()

Prototype:

```
RETCODE SQLDescribeParam(HSTMT hstmt, UWORD ipar,
SWORD FAR * pfSqlType, UWORD FAR * pcbColDef,
SWORD FAR * pibScale, SWORD FAR * pfNullable)
```

Parameters:

HSTMT *hstmt*	A statement handle returned by the call to SQLAllocStmt().
UWORD *ipar*	The parameter marker index, ordered sequentially left to right. This index is one-based, not zero-based.
SWORD FAR * *pfSqlType*	A pointer to a variable that will be used to return the SQL type of the parameter. Valid SQL types are listed in Table 3.4.
UDWORD FAR * *pcbColDef*	The column's precision.
SWORD FAR * *pibScale*	The column's scale.
SWORD FAR * *pfNullable*	A constant that indicates whether this column supports null data values. Will be either SQL_NO_NULLS, SQL_NULLABLE, or SQL_NULLABLE_UNKNOWN.

Table 3.4. Column return types.

Identifier	Description
SQL_BIGINT	Integer data
SQL_BINARY	Binary data
SQL_BIT	Bit-field data
SQL_CHAR	Character data
SQL_DATE	Date field
SQL_DECIMAL	Decimal data
SQL_DOUBLE	Double data
SQL_FLOAT	Floating-point data
SQL_INTEGER	Integer data
SQL_LONGVARBINARY	Binary data
SQL_LONGVARCHAR	Variable-length character data
SQL_NUMERIC	Numeric data
SQL_REAL	Floating-point data
SQL_SMALLINT	Integer data
SQL_TIME	Time data
SQL_TIMESTAMP	Timestamp data
SQL_TINYINT	Integer data
SQL_VARBINARY	Variable-length binary data
SQL_VARCHAR	Variable-length character data
Other	Driver-specific data

Return Value:

This function will return one of the following values:

SQL_SUCCESS	The function was successful.
SQL_SUCCESS_WITH_INFO	The function was successful, and more information is available.
SQL_STILL_EXECUTING	An asynchronous operation is still pending.
SQL_ERROR	The function failed. Call SQLError() to get more information about the specific failure.
SLQ_INVALID_HANDLE	The function failed. The handle that was passed wasn't a valid handle. Possibly, the function that created the handle had failed and didn't return a valid handle.

If this function fails, your SQL function should end or the error should be corrected; the function should then be re-executed.

Usage:

Call the `SQLDescribeParam()` function to obtain a description of the parameter marker in an SQL statement. Always check the return code from this function for errors.

Notes:

If this function fails, use the `SQLError()` function to find out why.

SQLDisconnect()

Prototype:

```
RETCODE SQLDisconnect(HDBC hdbc)
```

Parameter:

> HDBC *hdbc*   A handle to an HDBC as returned by the call to the `SQLAllocConnect()` function.

Return Value:

This function will return one of the following values:

SQL_SUCCESS	The function was successful.
SQL_SUCCESS_WITH_INFO	The function was successful, and more information is available.
SQL_ERROR	The function failed. Call `SQLError()` to get more information about the specific failure.
SLQ_INVALID_HANDLE	The function failed. The handle that was passed wasn't a valid handle. Possibly, the function that created the handle had failed and didn't return a valid handle.

If this function fails, your SQL function should end or the error should be corrected; the function should then be re-executed.

Usage:

Call the `SQLDisconnect()` function to disconnect from the currently connected datasource. Always check the return code from this function for errors.

Notes:

If this function fails, use the `SQLError()` function to find out why.

SQLDriverConnect()

Prototype:

```
RETCODE SQLDriverConnect(HDBC hdbc, HWND hwnd, UCHAR FAR * szConnStrIn,
SWORD cbConnStrIn, UCHAR FAR * szConnStrOut, SWORD cbConnStrOutMax,
SWORD FAR * pcbConnStrOut, UWORD fDriverCompletion)
```

Parameters:

HDBC *hdbc*	A handle to an HDBC as returned by the call to the SQLAllocConnect() function.
HWND *hwnd*	The window handle of the parent window. This is used if the SQLDriverConnect() function must display any dialog boxes to prompt the user for information (such as user ID or passwords). If a NULL pointer is specified, SQLDriverConnect() won't present any dialog boxes.
UCHAR FAR * *szConnStrIn*	A pointer to a full connection string, a partial connection string, or an empty string. Don't pass a NULL pointer.
SWORD *cbConnStrIn*	The length of *szConnStrIn*.
UCHAR FAR * *szConnStrOut*	A pointer to a buffer that will receive the resulting string that is used to connect to the datasource. This buffer should be at least 255 bytes or longer.
SWORD *cbConnStrOutMax*	The size of the *szConnStrOut* buffer.
SWORD FAR * *pcbConnStrOut*	A pointer to the variable that will receive the number of bytes that have been stored in *szConnStrOut*. If the buffer was too small to contain the connect string, the connect string in *szConnStrOut* is truncated to *cbConnStrOutMax* − 1 bytes.
UWORD *fDriverCompletion*	Contains a flag that tells whether the driver manager or driver must prompt for more connection information. See Table 3.5 for valid values for this string.

Table 3.5. Driver completion values.

Value	*Description*
SQL_DRIVER_PROMPT	The driver manager will display the datasources dialog box for the user to select the datasource.
SQL_DRIVER_COMPLETE	The driver will use the connection string specified by the application if the connection string contains the DSN keyword; otherwise, the same action as SQL_DRIVER_PROMPT is taken.

Value	Description
SQL_DRIVER_COMPLETE_REQUIRED	The driver will use the connection string specified by the application if the connection string contains the DSN keyword; otherwise, the same action as SQL_DRIVER_PROMPT is taken.
SQL_DRIVER_NOPROMPT	The driver manager uses the connection string specified by the application.

Return Value:

This function will return one of the following values:

SQL_SUCCESS	The function was successful.
SQL_SUCCESS_WITH_INFO	The function was successful, and more information is available.
SQL_NO_DATA_FOUND	The command didn't find the driver to connect to.
SQL_ERROR	The function failed. Call SQLError() to get more information about the specific failure.
SLQ_INVALID_HANDLE	The function failed. The handle that was passed wasn't a valid handle. Possibly, the function that created the handle had failed and didn't return a valid handle.

If this function fails, your SQL function should end or the error should be corrected; the function should then be re-executed.

Usage:

Call the SQLDriverConnect() function to connect to a specific driver. Always check the return code from this function for errors.

Notes:

If this function fails, use the SQLError() function to find out why.

SQLDrivers()

Prototype:

```
RETCODE SQLDrivers(HENV henv, UWORD fDirection, UCHAR FAR * szDriverDesc,
SWORD cbDriverDescMax, SWORD FAR * pcbDriverDesc,
UCHAR fAR * szDriverAttributes, SWORD cbDrvrAttrMax, SWORD FAR * pcbDrvrAttr)
```

Parameters:

HENV *henv*	An environment handle, as returned by a call to SQLAllocEnv().
UWORD *fDirection*	This parameter is used to determine whether the driver manager fetches the next, or first, driver description in the list. Use SQL_FETCH_NEXT or SQL_FETCH_FIRST.
UCHAR FAR * *szDriverDesc*	A pointer to a buffer for the driver description.
SWORD *cbDriverDescMax*	The size of the *szDriverDesc* buffer.
SWORD FAR * *pcbDriverDesc*	A pointer to a variable that will hold the number of bytes returned in *szDriverDesc*. If the size of the string returned is too large for *szDriverDesc*, the driver description in *szDriverDesc* will be truncated to *cbDriverDescMax* − 1 bytes.
UCHAR FAR * *szDriverAttributes*	A pointer to a buffer that will hold the list of driver attribute value pairs.
SWORD *cbDrvrAttrMax*	The size of the *szDriverAttributes* buffer.
SWORD FAR * *pcbDrvrAttr*	A pointer to a variable that will hold the number of bytes placed in *szDriverAttributes*. If the size of the string returned is too large for *szDriverAttributes*, the list of attribute value pairs in *szDriverAttributes* will be truncated to *cbDrvrAttrMax* − 1 bytes.

Return Value:

This function will return one of the following values:

SQL_SUCCESS	The function was successful.
SQL_SUCCESS_WITH_INFO	The function was successful, and more information is available.
SQL_ERROR	The function failed. Call SQLError() to get more information about the specific failure.
SLQ_INVALID_HANDLE	The function failed. The handle that was passed wasn't a valid handle. Possibly, the function that created the handle had failed and didn't return a valid handle.

If this function fails, your SQL function should end or the error should be corrected; the function should then be re-executed.

Usage:

Call the SQLDrivers() function to list the drivers and driver attributes. Always check the return code from this function for errors.

Notes:

If this function fails, use the SQLError() function to find out why.

SQLError()

Prototype:

```
RETCODE SQLError(HENV henv, HDBC hdbc, HSTMT hstmt,
UCHAR FAR * szSqlState, SDWORD FAR * pfNativeError,
UCHAR FAR * szErrorMsg, SWORD cbErrorMsgMax, SWORD FAR * pcbErrorMsg)
```

Parameters:

HENV *henv*	A handle to an HENV as returned by the call to the SQLAllocEnv() function, or SQL_NULL_HENV to query all open environments.
HDBC *hdbc*	A handle to an HDBC as returned by the call to the SQLAllocConnect() function, or SQL_NULL_HDBC to query all open database connections.
HSTMT *hstmt*	A handle to an HSTMT as returned by the call to the SQLAllocStmt() function, or SQL_NULL_HSTMT to query all open statements.
UCHAR FAR * *szSqlState*	A buffer containing the SQLSTATE, formatted as a null-terminated string, will be returned.
SDWORD FAR * *pfNativeError*	The returned native error code.
UCHAR FAR * *szErrorMsg*	A buffer that will point to the error message text.
SWORD *cbErrorMsgMax*	A variable that specifies the maximum length of the *szErrorMsg* buffer. This buffer's size must be less than or equal to SQL_MAX_MESSAGE_LENGTH − 1.
SWORD FAR * *pcbErrorMsg*	A pointer to a variable that will contain the number of bytes in *szErrorMsg*. If the string is too large for *szErrorMsg*, the text in *szErrorMsg* will be truncated to *cbErrorMsgMax* − 1 bytes.

Return Value:

This function will return one of the following values:

SQL_SUCCESS	The function was successful.
SQL_SUCCESS_WITH_INFO	The function was successful, and more information is available.
SQL_NO_DATA_FOUND	The command didn't find any error conditions on which to report.
SQL_ERROR	The function failed. Call SQLError() to get more information about the specific failure.
SLQ_INVALID_HANDLE	The function failed. The handle that was passed wasn't a valid handle. Possibly, the function that created the handle had failed and didn't return a valid handle.

If this function fails, your SQL function should try to recover—displaying or saving whatever diagnostic information is appropriate—or the error should be corrected and the function should be re-executed.

Usage:

Call the SQLError() function to obtain more information about the error condition. Always check the return code from this function for errors.

Notes:

If this function fails, use the SQLError() function to find out why.

SQLExecDirect()

Prototype:

RETCODE SQLExecDirect(HSTMT *hstmt*, UCHAR FAR * *szSqlStr*, SDWORD *cbSqlStr*)

Parameters:

HSTMT *hstmt*	A statement handle returned by the call to SQLAllocStmt().
UCHAR FAR * *szSqlStr*	A pointer to an SQL statement to be executed.
SDWORD *cbSqlStr*	The length of the string in *szSqlStr*.

Return Value:

This function will return one of the following values:

SQL_SUCCESS	The function was successful.
SQL_SUCCESS_WITH_INFO	The function was successful, and more information is available.

SQL_NEED_DATA	The function needs more information to process the request.
SQL_ERROR	The function failed. Call SQLError() to get more information about the specific failure.
SLQ_INVALID_HANDLE	The function failed. The handle that was passed wasn't a valid handle. Possibly, the function that created the handle had failed and didn't return a valid handle.

If this function fails, your SQL function should end or the error should be corrected; the function should then be re-executed.

Usage:

Call the SQLExecDirect() function to execute (usually once) a preparable SQL statement. Always check the return code from this function for errors.

Notes:

This function is probably the fastest way to execute SQL statements when the statement needs to be executed only one time. If this function fails, use the SQLError() function to find out why.

SQLExecute()

Prototype:

RETCODE SQLExecute(HSTMT *hstmt*)

Parameter:

HSTMT *hstmt*   A statement handle returned by the call to SQLAllocStmt().

Return Value:

This function will return one of the following values:

SQL_SUCCESS	The function was successful.
SQL_SUCCESS_WITH_INFO	The function was successful, and more information is available.
SQL_NEED_DATA	The function needs more information to process the request.
SQL_STILL_EXECUTING	An asynchronous operation is still pending.
SQL_ERROR	The function failed. Call SQLError() to get more information about the specific failure.
SLQ_INVALID_HANDLE	The function failed. The handle that was passed wasn't a valid handle. Possibly, the function that created the handle had failed and didn't return a valid handle.

If this function fails, your SQL function should end or the error should be corrected; the function should then be re-executed.

Usage:

Call the `SQLExecute()` function to execute a prepared statement using the parameter values contained in marker variables, if there are any. Always check the return code from this function for errors.

Notes:

If this function fails, use the `SQLError()` function to find out why.

SQLExtendedFetch()

Prototype:

```
RETCODE SQLExtenedeFetch(HSTMT hstmt, UWORD fFetchType,
SDWORD irow, UDWORD FAR * pcrow, UWORD FAR * rgfRowStatus)
```

Parameters:

HSTMT *hstmt*	A statement handle returned by the call to `SQLAllocStmt()`.
UWORD *fFetchType*	Specifies the type of fetch desired. Table 3.6 describes valid values for this parameter.
SDWORD *irow*	Specifies the number of the row to be fetched.
UDWORD FAR * *pcrow*	Returns the count of the number of rows that were actually fetched.
UWORD FAR * *rgfRowStatus*	A pointer to an array of status values.

Table 3.6. Valid fetch values.

Identifier	*Description*
SQL_FETCH_NEXT	Fetch the next row.
SQL_FETCH_FIRST	Fetch the first row.
SQL_FETCH_LAST	Fetch the last row.
SQL_FETCH_PRIOR	Fetch the previous row.
SQL_FETCH_ABSOLUTE	Fetch the row specified absolutely.
SQL_FETCH_RELATIVE	Fetch the row specified relative to the current row.
SQL_FETCH_BOOKMARK	Fetch the marked row.

Return Value:

This function will return one of the following values:

SQL_SUCCESS	The function was successful.
SQL_SUCCESS_WITH_INFO	The function was successful, and more information is available.
SQL_NO_DATA_FOUND	The command didn't find the driver to connect to.
SQL_STILL_EXECUTING	An asynchronous operation is still pending.
SQL_ERROR	The function failed. Call SQLError() to get more information about the specific failure.
SLQ_INVALID_HANDLE	The function failed. The handle that was passed wasn't a valid handle. Possibly, the function that created the handle had failed and didn't return a valid handle.

If this function fails, your SQL function should end or the error should be corrected; the function should then be re-executed.

Usage:

Call the SQLExtendedFetch() function to fetch one or more rows from a result set. Always check the return code from this function for errors.

Notes:

If this function fails, use the SQLError() function to find out why.

SQLFetch()

Prototype:

```
RETCODE SQLFetch(HSTMT hstmt)
```

Parameter:

HSTMT *hstmt*	A statement handle returned by the call to SQLAllocStmt().

Return Value:

This function will return one of the following values:

SQL_SUCCESS	The function was successful.
SQL_SUCCESS_WITH_INFO	The function was successful, and more information is available.
SQL_NO_DATA_FOUND	The command didn't find the driver to connect to.

SQL_STILL_EXECUTING	An asynchronous operation is still pending.
SQL_ERROR	The function failed. Call SQLError() to get more information about the specific failure.
SLQ_INVALID_HANDLE	The function failed. The handle that was passed wasn't a valid handle. Possibly, the function that created the handle had failed and didn't return a valid handle.

If this function fails, your SQL function should end or the error should be corrected; the function should then be re-executed.

Usage:

Call the SQLFetch() function to fetch a single row of data from the result set. Always check the return code from this function for errors.

Notes:

If this function fails, use the SQLError() function to find out why.

SQLForeignKeys()

Prototype:

```
RETCODE SQLForeignKeys(HSTMT hstmt,
UCHAR FAR * szPkTableQualifier, SWORD cbPkTableQualifier,
UCHAR FAR * szPkTableOwner, SWORD cbPkTableOwner,
UCHAR FAR * szPkTableName, SWORD cbPkTableName,
UCHAR FAR * szFkTableQualifier, SWORD cbFkTableQualifier,
UCHAR FAR * szFkTableOwner, SWORD cbFkTableOwner,
UCHAR FAR * szFkTableName, SWORD cbFkTableName)
```

Parameters:

HSTMT hstmt	A statement handle returned by the call to SQLAllocStmt().
UCHAR FAR * szPkTableQualifier	A pointer to the primary key table qualifier.
SWORD cbPkTableQualifier	The length of szPkTableQualifier.
UCHAR FAR * szPkTableOwner	A pointer to the primary key owner name.
SWORD cbPkTableOwner	The length of szPkTableOwner.
UCHAR FAR * szPkTableName	A pointer to the primary key table name.
SWORD cbPkTableName	The length of szPkTableName.
UCHAR FAR * szFkTableQualifier	A pointer to the foreign key table qualifier.
SWORD cbFkTableQualifier	The length of szFkTableQualifier.
UCHAR FAR * szFkTableOwner	A pointer to the foreign key owner name.
SWORD cbFkTableOwner	The length of szFkTableOwner.

| UCHAR FAR * szFkTableName | A pointer to the foreign key table name. |
| SWORD cbFkTableName | The length of szFkTableName. |

Return Value:

This function will return one of the following values:

SQL_SUCCESS	The function was successful.
SQL_SUCCESS_WITH_INFO	The function was successful, and more information is available.
SQL_STILL_EXECUTING	An asynchronous operation is still pending.
SQL_ERROR	The function failed. Call SQLError() to get more information about the specific failure.
SLQ_INVALID_HANDLE	The function failed. The handle that was passed wasn't a valid handle. Possibly, the function that created the handle had failed and didn't return a valid handle.

If this function fails, your SQL function should end or the error should be corrected; the function should then be re-executed.

Usage:

Call the SQLForeignKeys() function to return either a list of foreign keys in the specified table or a list of foreign keys in other tables that refer to the primary key in the specified table. Always check the return code from this function for errors.

Notes:

If this function fails, use the SQLError() function to find out why.

SQLFreeConnect()

Prototype:

```
RETCODE SQLFreeConnect(HDBC hdbc)
```

Parameter:

HDBC hdbc   A handle to an HDBC as returned by the call to the SQLAllocConnect() function.

Return Value:

This function will return one of the following values:

| SQL_SUCCESS | The function was successful. |
| SQL_SUCCESS_WITH_INFO | The function was successful, and more information is available. |

SQL_ERROR	The function failed. Call sqlError() to get more information about the specific failure.
SLQ_INVALID_HANDLE	The function failed. The handle that was passed wasn't a valid handle. Possibly, the function that created the handle had failed and didn't return a valid handle.

If this function fails, your SQL function should end or the error should be corrected; the function should then be re-executed.

Usage:

Call the sqlFreeConnect() function to release the connection established with the sqlAllocConnect() function. Always check the return code from this function for errors.

Notes:

If this function fails, use the sqlError() function to find out why.

SQLFreeEnv()

Prototype:

```
RETCODE SQL (HENV henv)
```

Parameter:

HENV *henv* A handle to an HENV as returned by the call to the SQLAllocEnv() function.

Return Value:

This function will return one of the following values:

SQL_SUCCESS	The function was successful.
SQL_SUCCESS_WITH_INFO	The function was successful, and more information is available.
SQL_ERROR	The function failed. Call sqlError() to get more information about the specific failure.
SLQ_INVALID_HANDLE	The function failed. The handle that was passed wasn't a valid handle. Possibly, the function that created the handle had failed and didn't return a valid handle.

If this function fails, your SQL function should end or the error should be corrected; the function should then be re-executed.

Usage:

Call the sqlFreeEnv() function to free the environment established by the sqlAllocEnv() function. Always check the return code from this function for errors.

Notes:

If this function fails, use the SQLError() function to find out why.

SQLFreeStmt()

Prototype:

```
RETCODE SQLFreeStmt(HSTMT hstmt, UWORD fOption)
```

Parameters:

HSTMT *hstmt*	A statement handle returned by the call to SQLAllocStmt().
UWORD *fOption*	An option from the list shown in Table 3.7.

Table 3.7. fOption values from SQLFreeStmt().

Identifier	Description
SQL_ CLOSE	Used to close the cursor associated with *hstmt* (if one was defined) and discard any pending results. Later, the application will be able to reopen the cursor by executing a SELECT statement again with the same or different parameter values.
SQL_DROP	Used to release the *hstmt*, free all resources associated with it, close the cursor, and discard any rows that are pending. This option terminates all access to the *hstmt*. The *hstmt* may not be reused.
SQL_UNBIND	Used to release any column buffers bound by SQLBindCol() for the given *hstmt*.
SQL_RESET_PARAMS	Used to release all parameter buffers set by SQLBindParameter() for the given *hstmt*.

Return Value:

This function will return one of the following values:

SQL_SUCCESS	The function was successful.
SQL_SUCCESS_WITH_INFO	The function was successful, and more information is available.
SQL_ERROR	The function failed. Call SQLError() to get more information about the specific failure.
SLQ_INVALID_HANDLE	The function failed. The handle that was passed wasn't a valid handle. Possibly, the function that created the handle had failed and didn't return a valid handle.

If this function fails, your SQL function should end or the error should be corrected; the function should then be re-executed.

Usage:

Call the `SQLFreeStmt()` function to free the statement handle allocated by the `SQLAllocStmt()` function. Always check the return code from this function for errors.

Notes:

If this function fails, use the `SQLError()` function to find out why.

SQLGetConnectOption()

Prototype:

```
RETCODE SQL (HDBC hdbc, UWORD fOption, PTR pvParam)
```

Parameters:

HDBC *hdbc*	A handle to an HDBC as returned by the call to the `SQLAllocConnect()` function.
UWORD *fOption*	Specifies the option to retrieve.
PTR *pvParam*	The buffer where the value associated with *fOption* will be placed. This variable will be either a 32-bit integer value or a pointer to a null-terminated character string.

Return Value:

This function will return one of the following values:

SQL_SUCCESS	The function was successful.
SQL_SUCCESS_WITH_INFO	The function was successful, and more information is available.
SQL_NO_DATA_FOUND	The command didn't find the driver to connect to.
SQL_ERROR	The function failed. Call `SQLError()` to get more information about the specific failure.
SLQ_INVALID_HANDLE	The function failed. The handle that was passed wasn't a valid handle. Possibly, the function that created the handle had failed and didn't return a valid handle.

If this function fails, your SQL function should end or the error should be corrected; the function should then be re-executed.

Usage:

Call the `SQLGetConnectOption()` function to get the settings for the current connection. Always check the return code from this function for errors.

Notes:

If this function fails, use the `SQLError()` function to find out why.

SQLGetCursorName()

Prototype:

```
RETCODE SQLCursorName(HSTMT hstmt, UCHAR FAR * szCursor,
SWORD cbCursorMax, SWORD FAR * pcbCursor)
```

Parameters:

HSTMT *hstmt*	A statement handle returned by the call to `SQLAllocStmt()`.
UCHAR FAR * *szCursor*	A pointer to a buffer that will receive the cursor name.
SWORD *cbCursorMax*	The length of *szCursor*.
SWORD FAR * *pcbCursor*	A pointer to a variable that will have the length of *szCursor* stored in it. If the cursor name is too large for *szCursor*, the cursor name in *szCursor* is truncated to *cbCursorMax* − 1 bytes.

Return Value:

This function will return one of the following values:

SQL_SUCCESS	The function was successful.
SQL_SUCCESS_WITH_INFO	The function was successful, and more information is available.
SQL_ERROR	The function failed. Call `SQLError()` to get more information about the specific failure.
SLQ_INVALID_HANDLE	The function failed. The handle that was passed wasn't a valid handle. Possibly, the function that created the handle had failed and didn't return a valid handle.

If this function fails, your SQL function should end or the error should be corrected; the function should then be re-executed.

Usage:

Call the `SQLGetCursorName()` function to get the name for the cursor specified by the *hstmt* parameter. Always check the return code from this function for errors.

Notes:

If this function fails, use the `SQLError()` function to find out why.

SQLGetData()

Prototype:

```
RETCODE SQLGetData(HSTMT hstmt, UWORD icol, SWORD fCType,
PTR rgbValue, SDWORD cbValueMax, SDWORD FAR * pcbValue)
```

Parameters:

HSTMT *hstmt*	A statement handle returned by the call to `SQLAllocStmt()`.
UWORD *icol*	The column number starting at column 1. Specifying a column number of 0 will retrieve a bookmark for the row. Neither ODBC 1.0 drivers nor `SQLFetch()` support bookmarks.
SWORD *fCType*	A constant that specifies the column's resultant C data type values. See Table 3.8 for valid values.
PTR *rgbValue*	A pointer to location used to store the data.
SDWORD *cbValueMax*	Specifies the length of the buffer *rgbValue*.
SDWORD FAR * *pcbValue*	One of the values specified in Table 3.9.

Table 3.8. SQL C data types for `SQLGetData()`.

Identifier	*Description*
SQL_C_BINARY	Binary data.
SQL_C_BIT	Bitmapped data.
SQL_C_BOOKMARK	Bookmark data.
SQL_C_CHAR	Character string data.
SQL_C_DATE	Date data.
SQL_C_DOUBLE	Floating-point data.
SQL_C_FLOAT	Floating-point data.
SQL_C_SLONG	Integer data.
SQL_C_SSHORT	Integer data.
SQL_C_STINYINT	Integer data.
SQL_C_TIME	Time-formatted data.
SQL_C_TIMESTAMP	Timestamp formatted data.
SQL_C_ULONG	Integer data.
SQL_C_USHORT	Integer data.
SQL_C_UTINYINT	Integer data.
SQL_C_DEFAULT	This identifier specifies that data be converted to its default C data type.

Identifier	Description
SQL_C_LONG	Integer data.
SQL_C_SHORT	Integer data.
SQL_C_TINYINT	Integer data.

Drivers must support the final three C data type values listed in Table 3.8 from ODBC 1.0. Applications must use these values, rather than the ODBC 2.0 values, when calling an ODBC 1.0 driver.

Table 3.9. Values for the `pcbValue` parameter.

Identifier	Description
SQL_NULL_DATA	Specifies that the total number of bytes (excluding the null termination byte for character data) that was returned in the *rgbValue* parameter.
SQL_NO_TOTAL	For character data, if *pcbValue* is greater than or equal to *cbValueMax*, the data in *rgbValue* is truncated to *cbValueMax* − 1 bytes and is null-terminated by the driver.
SQL_NO_TOTAL	For binary data, if *pcbValue* is equal to or greater than *cbValueMax*, the data in *rgbValue* is truncated to *cbValueMax* bytes.

Return Value:

This function will return one of the following values:

SQL_SUCCESS	The function was successful.
SQL_SUCCESS_WITH_INFO	The function was successful, and more information is available.
SQL_NO_DATA_FOUND	The command didn't find the requested data.
SQL_STILL_EXECUTING	An asynchronous operation is still pending.
SQL_ERROR	The function failed. Call `SQLError()` to get more information about the specific failure.
SLQ_INVALID_HANDLE	The function failed. The handle that was passed wasn't a valid handle. Possibly, the function that created the handle had failed and didn't return a valid handle.

If this function fails, your SQL function should end or the error should be corrected; the function should then be re-executed.

Usage:

Call the SQLGetData() function to obtain information about a specific column in a datasource. Always check the return code from this function for errors.

Notes:

If this function fails, use the SQLError() function to find out why.

SQLGetFunctions()

Prototype:

RETCODE SQLGetFunctions(HDBC *hdbc*, UWORD *fFunction*, UWORD FAR * *pfExists*)

Parameters:

HDBC *hdbc*	A handle to an HDBC as returned by the call to the SQLAllocConnect() function.
UWORD *fFunction*	Either the constant SQL_API_ALL_FUNCTIONS or a #defined value that will identify the ODBC function for which information is desired.
UWORD FAR * *pfExists*	A pointer to a variable that will contain either a pointer to an array (if *fFunction* is SQL_API_ALL_FUNCTIONS) or the information returned for a specific function.

Return Value:

This function will return one of the following values:

SQL_SUCCESS	The function was successful.
SQL_SUCCESS_WITH_INFO	The function was successful, and more information is available.
SQL_ERROR	The function failed. Call SQLError() to get more information about the specific failure.
SLQ_INVALID_HANDLE	The function failed. The handle that was passed wasn't a valid handle. Possibly, the function that created the handle had failed and didn't return a valid handle.

If this function fails, your SQL function should end or the error should be corrected; the function should then be re-executed.

Usage:

Call the SQLGetFunctions() function to obtain information about other SQL...() functions. Always check the return code from this function for errors.

Notes:

If this function fails, use the SQLError() function to find out why. The functions supported are shown in Table 3.10.

Table 3.10. SQLGetFunctions() **function index.**

Function	Notes
SQLGetFunctions	Implemented in the driver manager.
SQLDataSources	Implemented in the driver manager.
SQLDrivers	Implemented in the driver manager.
SQL_API_SQLALLOCCONNECT	ODBC core function.
SQL_API_SQLFETCH	ODBC core function.
SQL_API_SQLALLOCENV	ODBC core function.
SQL_API_SQLFREECONNECT	ODBC core function.
SQL_API_SQLALLOCSTMT	ODBC core function.
SQL_API_SQLFREEENV	ODBC core function.
SQL_API_SQLBINDCOL	ODBC core function.
SQL_API_SQLFREESTMT	ODBC core function.
SQL_API_SQLCANCEL	ODBC core function.
SQL_API_SQLGETCURSORNAME	ODBC core function.
SQL_API_SQLCOLATTRIBUTES	ODBC core function.
SQL_API_SQLNUMRESULTCOLS	ODBC core function.
SQL_API_SQLCONNECT	ODBC core function.
SQL_API_SQLPREPARE	ODBC core function.
SQL_API_SQLDESCRIBECOL	ODBC core function.
SQL_API_SQLROWCOUNT	ODBC core function.
SQL_API_SQLDISCONNECT	ODBC core function.
SQL_API_SQLSETCURSORNAME	ODBC core function.
SQL_API_SQLERROR	ODBC core function.
SQL_API_SQLSETPARAM	ODBC core function.
SQL_API_SQLEXECDIRECT	ODBC core function.
SQL_API_SQLTRANSACT	ODBC core function.
SQL_API_SQLEXECUTE	ODBC core function.
SQL_API_SQLBINDPARAMETER	For ODBC 1.0 drivers, SQLGetFunctions() will return TRUE if the driver supports SQLSetParam().

continues

Table 3.10. continued

Function	Notes
`SQL_API_SQLSETPARAM`	For ODBC 1.0 drivers, `SQLGetFunctions()` will return TRUE if the driver supports `SQLSetParam()`.
`SQL_API_SQLSETPARAM`	For ODBC 2.0 drivers, `SQLGetFunctions()` will return TRUE if the driver supports `SQLBindParameter()`.
`SQL_API_SQLBINDPARAMETER`	For ODBC 2.0 drivers, `SQLGetFunctions()` will return TRUE if the driver supports `SQLBindParameter()`.
`SQL_API_SQLBINDPARAMETER`	ODBC extension level 1 function.
`SQL_API_SQLGETTYPEINFO`	ODBC extension level 1 function.
`SQL_API_SQLCOLUMNS`	ODBC extension level 1 function.
`SQL_API_SQLPARAMDATA`	ODBC extension level 1 function.
`SQL_API_SQLDRIVERCONNECT`	ODBC extension level 1 function.
`SQL_API_SQLPUTDATA`	ODBC extension level 1 function.
`SQL_API_SQLGETCONNECTOPTION`	ODBC extension level 1 function.
`SQL_API_SQLSETCONNECTOPTION`	ODBC extension level 1 function.
`SQL_API_SQLGETDATA`	ODBC extension level 1 function.
`SQL_API_SQLSETSTMTOPTION`	ODBC extension level 1 function.
`SQL_API_SQLGETFUNCTIONS`	ODBC extension level 1 function.
`SQL_API_SQLSPECIALCOLUMNS`	ODBC extension level 1 function.
`SQL_API_SQLGETINFO`	ODBC extension level 1 function.
`SQL_API_SQLSTATISTICS`	ODBC extension level 1 function.
`SQL_API_SQLGETSTMTOPTION`	ODBC extension level 1 function.
`SQL_API_SQLTABLES`	ODBC extension level 1 function.
`SQL_API_SQLBROWSECONNECT`	ODBC extension level 2 function.
`SQL_API_SQLNUMPARAMS`	ODBC extension level 2 function.
`SQL_API_SQLCOLUMNPRIVILEGES`	ODBC extension level 2 function.
`SQL_API_SQLPARAMOPTIONS`	ODBC extension level 2 function.
`SQL_API_SQLDATASOURCES`	ODBC extension level 2 function.
`SQL_API_SQLPRIMARYKEYS`	ODBC extension level 2 function.
`SQL_API_SQLDESCRIBEPARAM`	ODBC extension level 2 function.
`SQL_API_SQLPROCEDURECOLUMNS`	ODBC extension level 2 function.
`SQL_API_SQLDRIVERS`	ODBC extension level 2 function.

Function	Notes
SQL_API_SQLPROCEDURES	ODBC extension level 2 function.
SQL_API_SQLEXTENDEDFETCH	ODBC extension level 2 function.
SQL_API_SQLSETPOS	ODBC extension level 2 function.
SQL_API_SQLFOREIGNKEYS	ODBC extension level 2 function.
SQL_API_SQLSETSCROLLOPTIONS	ODBC extension level 2 function.
SQL_API_SQLMORERESULTS	ODBC extension level 2 function.
SQL_API_SQLTABLEPRIVILEGES	ODBC extension level 2 function.
SQL_API_SQLNATIVESQL	ODBC extension level 2 function.

SQLGetInfo()

Prototype:

```
RETCODE SQLGetInfo(HDBC hdbc, UWORD fInfoType, PTR rgbInfoValue,
SWORD cbInfoValueMax, SWORD FAR * pcbInfoValue)
```

Parameters:

HDBC *hdbc*	A handle to an HDBC as returned by the call to the SQLAllocConnect() function.
UWORD *fInfoType*	The type of information that is desired. See the ODBC documentation for more information about this parameter.
PTR *rgbInfoValue*	A pointer to a buffer used to store the information.
SWORD *cbInfoValueMax*	The size of the buffer *rgbInfoValue*.
SWORD FAR * *pcbInfoValue*	A pointer to a variable that will receive the count of the number of bytes stored in *rgbInfoValue*.

Return Value:

This function will return one of the following values:

SQL_SUCCESS	The function was successful.
SQL_SUCCESS_WITH_INFO	The function was successful, and more information is available.
SQL_ERROR	The function failed. Call SQLError() to get more information about the specific failure.
SLQ_INVALID_HANDLE	The function failed. The handle that was passed wasn't a valid handle. Possibly, the function that created the handle had failed and didn't return a valid handle.

If this function fails, your SQL function should end or the error should be corrected; the function should then be re-executed.

Usage:

The `SQLGetInfo()` function returns a vast array of information about ODBC. Always check the return code from this function for errors.

Notes:

Refer to the documentation supplied with ODBC and Visual C++ for more information about this function. If this function fails, use the `SQLError()` function to find out why.

SQLGetStmtOption()

Prototype:

RETCODE SQLGetStmtOption(HSTMT *hstmt*, UWORD *fOption*, PTR *pvParam*)

Parameters:

HSTMT *hstmt*	A statement handle returned by the call to `SQLAllocStmt()`.
UWORD *fOption*	Value that indicates which option to retrieve.
PTR *pvParam*	A pointer to a buffer that will receive the option's value.

Return Value:

This function will return one of the following values:

SQL_SUCCESS	The function was successful.
SQL_SUCCESS_WITH_INFO	The function was successful, and more information is available.
SQL_ERROR	The function failed. Call `SQLError()` to get more information about the specific failure.
SLQ_INVALID_HANDLE	The function failed. The handle that was passed wasn't a valid handle. Possibly, the function that created the handle had failed and didn't return a valid handle.

If this function fails, your SQL function should end or the error should be corrected; the function should then be re-executed.

Usage:

Call the `SQLGetStmtOption()` function to retrieve information about the specified statement. Always check the return code from this function for errors.

Notes:

If this function fails, use the `SQLError()` function to find out why.

SQLGetTypeInfo()

Prototype:

```
RETCODE SQLGetTypeInfo(HSTMT hstmt, SWORD fSqlType)
```

Parameters:

HSTMT *hstmt*	Statement handle for the result set.
SWORD *fSqlType*	The SQL data type. This must be one of the identifiers from Table 3.11.

Table 3.11. Valid values for `fSqlType` parameter.

Identifier	Description
SQL_BIGINT	Integer data
SQL_BINARY	Binary data
SQL_BIT	Bit-field data
SQL_CHAR	Character data
SQL_DATE	Date field
SQL_DECIMAL	Decimal data
SQL_DOUBLE	Double data
SQL_FLOAT	Floating-point data
SQL_INTEGER	Integer data
SQL_LONGVARBINARY	Binary data
SQL_LONGVARCHAR	Variable-length character data
SQL_NUMERIC	Numeric data
SQL_REAL	Floating-point data
SQL_SMALLINT	Integer data
SQL_TIME	Time data
SQL_TIMESTAMP	Timestamp data
SQL_TINYINT	Integer data
SQL_VARBINARY	Variable-length binary data
SQL_VARCHAR	Variable-length character data
SQL_ALL_TYPES	Returns information about all types
Other	Driver-specific data

Return Value:

This function will return one of the following values:

SQL_SUCCESS	The function was successful.
SQL_SUCCESS_WITH_INFO	The function was successful, and more information is available.
SQL_STILL_EXECUTING	An asynchronous operation is still pending.
SQL_ERROR	The function failed. Call SQLError() to get more information about the specific failure.
SLQ_INVALID_HANDLE	The function failed. The handle that was passed wasn't a valid handle. Possibly, the function that created the handle had failed and didn't return a valid handle.

If this function fails, your SQL function should end or the error should be corrected; the function should then be re-executed.

Usage:

Call the SQLGetTypeInfo() function to return information about a specific data type. Always check the return code from this function for errors.

Notes:

This functions returns the results as a result set. If this function fails, use the SQLError() function to find out why.

SQLMoreResults()

Prototype:

```
RETCODE SQLMoreResults(HSTMT hstmt)
```

Parameter:

HSTMT *hstmt*   A statement handle returned by the call to SQLAllocStmt().

Return Value:

This function will return one of the following values:

SQL_SUCCESS	The function was successful.
SQL_SUCCESS_WITH_INFO	The function was successful, and more information is available.
SQL_NO_DATA_FOUND	The command didn't find the driver to connect to.
SQL_STILL_EXECUTING	An asynchronous operation is still pending.

SQL_ERROR	The function failed. Call `SQLError()` to get more information about the specific failure.
SLQ_INVALID_HANDLE	The function failed. The handle that was passed wasn't a valid handle. Possibly, the function that created the handle had failed and didn't return a valid handle.

If this function fails, your SQL function should end or the error should be corrected; the function should then be re-executed.

Usage:

Call the `SQLMoreResults()` function to determine whether there are more results available from the SELECT, UPDATE, INSERT, or DELETE SQL statements. If there are more results, `SQLMoreResults()` will initiate processing for the additional results. Always check the return code from this function for errors.

Notes:

If this function fails, use the `SQLError()` function to find out why.

SQLNativeSql()

Prototype:

```
RETCODE SQLNativeSql(HDBC hdbc, UCHAR FAR * szSqlStrIn,
SDWORD cbSqlStrIn, UCHAR FAR * szSqlStr, SDWORD cbSqlStrMax,
SDWORD FAR * pcbSqlStr)
```

Parameters:

HDBC *hdbc*	A handle to an HDBC as returned by the `SQLAllocConnect()` function.
UCHAR FAR * *szSqlStrIn*	A pointer to the buffer holding the SQL statement that is to be translated.
SDWORD *cbSqlStrIn*	The length of the *szSqlStrIn* text string.
UCHAR FAR * *szSqlStr*	A pointer to a buffer that will hold the translated SQL string.
SDWORD *cbSqlStrMax*	The size of the *szSqlStr* buffer.
SDWORD FAR * *pcbSqlStr*	The number of bytes stored in *szSqlStr*. If the translated SQL string is too long to fit in *szSqlStr*, the translated SQL string in *szSqlStr* is truncated to *cbSqlStrMax* − 1 bytes.

Return Value:

This function will return one of the following values:

SQL_SUCCESS	The function was successful.
SQL_SUCCESS_WITH_INFO	The function was successful, and more information is available.
SQL_ERROR	The function failed. Call SQLError() to get more information about the specific failure.
SLQ_INVALID_HANDLE	The function failed. The handle that was passed wasn't a valid handle. Possibly, the function that created the handle had failed and didn't return a valid handle.

If this function fails, your SQL function should end or the error should be corrected; the function should then be re-executed.

Usage:

Call the SQLNativeSql() function to translate an SQL string for a native ODBC driver. Always check the return code from this function for errors.

Notes:

If this function fails, use the SQLError() function to find out why.

SQLNumParams()

Prototype:

```
RETCODE SQLNumParams(HSTMT hstmt, SWORD FAR * pcpar)
```

Parameters:

| HSTMT *hstmt* | A statement handle returned by the call to SQLAllocStmt(). |
| SWORD FAR * *pcpar* | A pointer to a variable that will hold the number of parameters in the statement. |

Return Value:

This function will return one of the following values:

SQL_SUCCESS	The function was successful.
SQL_SUCCESS_WITH_INFO	The function was successful, and more information is available.
SQL_STILL_EXECUTING	An asynchronous operation is still pending.
SQL_ERROR	The function failed. Call SQLError() to get more information about the specific failure.
SLQ_INVALID_HANDLE	The function failed. The handle that was passed wasn't a valid handle. Possibly, the function that created the handle had failed and didn't return a valid handle.

If this function fails, your SQL function should end or the error should be corrected; the function should then be re-executed.

Usage:

Call the SQLNumParams() function to get the number of parameters in the SQL statement. Always check the return code from this function for errors.

Notes:

If this function fails, use the SQLError() function to find out why.

SQLNumResultCols()

Prototype:

```
RETCODE SQLNumResultCols(HSTMT hstmt, SWORD FAR * pccol)
```

Parameters:

HSTMT *hstmt*	A statement handle returned by the call to SQLAllocStmt().
SWORD FAR * *pccol*	A pointer to a variable that will hold the number of columns in the result set.

Return Value:

This function will return one of the following values:

SQL_SUCCESS	The function was successful.
SQL_SUCCESS_WITH_INFO	The function was successful, and more information is available.
SQL_STILL_EXECUTING	An asynchronous operation is still pending.
SQL_ERROR	The function failed. Call SQLError() to get more information about the specific failure.
SLQ_INVALID_HANDLE	The function failed. The handle that was passed wasn't a valid handle. Possibly, the function that created the handle had failed and didn't return a valid handle.

If this function fails, your SQL function should end or the error should be corrected; the function should then be re-executed.

Usage:

Call the SQLNumResultCols() function to find out how many columns are in the result set. Always check the return code from this function for errors.

Notes:

If this function fails, use the SQLError() function to find out why.

SQLParamData()

Prototype:

RETCODE SQLParamData(HSTMT *hstmt*, PTR FAR * *prgbValue*)

Parameters:

HSTMT *hstmt*	A statement handle returned by the call to SQLAllocStmt().
PTR FAR * *prgbValue*	A pointer to a buffer used to store the results returned by the SQLParamData() function.

Return Value:

This function will return one of the following values:

SQL_SUCCESS	The function was successful.
SQL_SUCCESS_WITH_INFO	The function was successful, and more information is available.
SQL_NEED_DATA	The function needs more information to process the request.
SQL_STILL_EXECUTING	An asynchronous operation is still pending.
SQL_ERROR	The function failed. Call SQLError() to get more information about the specific failure.
SLQ_INVALID_HANDLE	The function failed. The handle that was passed wasn't a valid handle. Possibly, the function that created the handle had failed and didn't return a valid handle.

If this function fails, your SQL function should end or the error should be corrected; the function should then be re-executed.

Usage:

Call the SQLParamData() function with SQLPutData() to supply parameter data at statement execution time. Always check the return code from this function for errors.

Notes:

If this function fails, use the SQLError() function to find out why.

SQLParamOptions()

Prototype:

RETCODE SQLParamOptions(HSTMT *hstmt*, UWORD *crow*, UWORD FAR * *pirow*)

Parameters:

HSTMT *hstmt*	A statement handle returned by the call to SQLAllocStmt().
UDWORD *crow*	The number of values for the parameter. If *crow* is greater than 1, the *rgbValue* argument in SQLBindParameter() points to an array of parameter values, and *pcbValue* points to an array of lengths.
UDWORD FAR * *pirow*	A pointer to a buffer used to store the current row number.

Return Value:

This function will return one of the following values:

SQL_SUCCESS	The function was successful.
SQL_SUCCESS_WITH_INFO	The function was successful, and more information is available.
SQL_ERROR	The function failed. Call SQLError() to get more information about the specific failure.
SLQ_INVALID_HANDLE	The function failed. The handle that was passed wasn't a valid handle. Possibly, the function that created the handle had failed and didn't return a valid handle.

If this function fails, your SQL function should end or the error should be corrected; the function should then be re-executed.

Usage:

Call the SQLParamOptions() function to specify values for parameters created with SQLBindParameter(). Always check the return code from this function for errors.

Notes:

If this function fails, use the SQLError() function to find out why.

SQLPrepare()

Prototype:

```
RETCODE SQLPrepare(HSTMT hstmt, UCHAR FAR * szSqlStr, SDWORD cbSqlStr)
```

Parameters:

HSTMT *hstmt*	A statement handle returned by the call to SQLAllocStmt().
UCHAR FAR * *szSqlStr*	A pointer to the buffer containing the SQL text string.
SDWORD *cbSqlStr*	The length of the string in *szSqlStr*.

Return Value:

This function will return one of the following values:

SQL_SUCCESS	The function was successful.
SQL_SUCCESS_WITH_INFO	The function was successful, and more information is available.
SQL_STILL_EXECUTING	An asynchronous operation is still pending.
SQL_ERROR	The function failed. Call SQLError() to get more information about the specific failure.
SLQ_INVALID_HANDLE	The function failed. The handle that was passed wasn't a valid handle. Possibly, the function that created the handle had failed and didn't return a valid handle.

If this function fails, your SQL function should end or the error should be corrected; the function should then be re-executed.

Usage:

Call the SQLPrepare() function to prepare an SQL string for execution. Always check the return code from this function for errors.

Notes:

If this function fails, use the SQLError() function to find out why.

SQLPrimaryKeys()

Prototype:

```
RETCODE SQLPrimaryKeys(HSTMT hstmt, UCHAR FAR * szTableQualifier,
SWORD cbTableQualifier, UCHAR FAR * szTableOwner, SWORD cbTableOwner,
UCHAR FAR * szTableName, SWORD cbTableName)
```

Parameters:

HSTMT *hstmt*	A statement handle returned by the call to SQLAllocStmt().
UCHAR FAR * *szTableQualifier*	A pointer to a buffer containing the qualifier name.
SWORD *cbTableQualifier*	The length of the string in *szTableQualifier*.
UCHAR FAR * *szTableOwner*	A pointer to a buffer containing the table owner.
SWORD *cbTableOwner*	The length of the string in *szTableOwner*.
UCHAR FAR * *szTableName*	A pointer to a buffer containing the table name.
SWORD *cbTableName*	The length of the string in *szTableName*.

Return Value:

This function will return one of the following values:

SQL_SUCCESS	The function was successful.
SQL_SUCCESS_WITH_INFO	The function was successful, and more information is available.
SQL_STILL_EXECUTING	An asynchronous operation is still pending.
SQL_ERROR	The function failed. Call SQLError() to get more information about the specific failure.
SLQ_INVALID_HANDLE	The function failed. The handle that was passed wasn't a valid handle. Possibly, the function that created the handle had failed and didn't return a valid handle.

If this function fails, your SQL function should end or the error should be corrected; the function should then be re-executed.

Usage:

Call the SQLPrimaryKeys() function to retrieve the column names that comprise the primary key for the specified table. Always check the return code from this function for errors.

Notes:

If this function fails, use the SQLError() function to find out why.

SQLProcedureColumns()

Prototype:

```
RETCODE SQLProcedureColumns(HSTMT hstmt, UCHAR FAR * szProcQualifier,
SWORD cbProcQualifier, UCHAR FAR * szProcOwner, SWORD cbProcOwner,
UCHAR FAR * szProcName, SWORD cbProcName, UCHAR FAR * szColumnName,
SWORD cbColumnName)
```

Parameters:

HSTMT *hstmt*	A statement handle returned by the call to SQLAllocStmt().
UCHAR FAR * *szProcQualifier*	A pointer to a buffer containing the procedure qualifier name.
SWORD *cbProcQualifier*	The length of the string contained in *szProcQualifier*.
UCHAR FAR * *szProcOwner*	A pointer to a buffer containing the string search pattern for procedure owner names.
SWORD *cbProcOwner*	The length of the string contained in *szProcOwner*.

`UCHAR FAR * szProcName`	A pointer to a buffer containing the string search pattern for procedure names.
`SWORD cbProcName`	The length of the string in `szProcName`.
`UCHAR FAR * szColumnName`	A pointer to a buffer containing the string search pattern for column names.
`SWORD cbColumnName`	The length of the string in `szColumnName`.

Return Value:

This function will return one of the following values:

`SQL_SUCCESS`	The function was successful.
`SQL_SUCCESS_WITH_INFO`	The function was successful, and more information is available.
`SQL_STILL_EXECUTING`	An asynchronous operation is still pending.
`SQL_ERROR`	The function failed. Call `SQLError()` to get more information about the specific failure.
`SLQ_INVALID_HANDLE`	The function failed. The handle that was passed wasn't a valid handle. Possibly, the function that created the handle had failed and didn't return a valid handle.

If this function fails, your SQL function should end or the error should be corrected; the function should then be re-executed.

Usage:

Call the `SQLProcedureColumns()` function to obtain a list of input and output parameters for the specified procedure. This function will also retrieve the columns that make up the result set for this procedure. Always check the return code from this function for errors.

Notes:

If this function fails, use the `SQLError()` function to find out why.

SQLProcedures()

Prototype:

```
RETCODE SQLProcedures(HSTMT hstmt, UCHAR FAR * szProcQualifier,
SWORD cbProcQualifier, UCHAR FAR * szProcOwner, SWORD cbProcOwner,
UCHAR FAR * szProcName, SWORD cbProcName)
```

Parameters:

| `HSTMT hstmt` | A statement handle returned by the call to `SQLAllocStmt()`. |

UCHAR FAR * *szProcQualifier*	A pointer to the buffer that contains the procedure qualifier.
SWORD *cbProcQualifier*	The length of the string in *szProcQualifier*.
UCHAR FAR * *szProcOwner*	A pointer to the buffer containing the string search pattern for procedure owner names.
SWORD *cbProcOwner*	The length of the string in *szProcOwner*.
UCHAR FAR * *szProcName*	A pointer to the buffer containing the string search pattern for procedure names.
SWORD *cbProcName*	The length of the string in *szProcName*.

Return Value:

This function will return one of the following values:

SQL_SUCCESS	The function was successful.
SQL_SUCCESS_WITH_INFO	The function was successful, and more information is available.
SQL_STILL_EXECUTING	An asynchronous operation is still pending.
SQL_ERROR	The function failed. Call SQLError() to get more information about the specific failure.
SLQ_INVALID_HANDLE	The function failed. The handle that was passed wasn't a valid handle. Possibly, the function that created the handle had failed and didn't return a valid handle.

If this function fails, your SQL function should end or the error should be corrected; the function should then be re-executed.

Usage:

Call the SQLProcedures() function to retrieve a list of all the procedure names stored in the specified datasource. Always check the return code from this function for errors.

Notes:

If this function fails, use the SQLError() function to find out why.

SQLPutData()

Prototype:

```
RETCODE SQLPutData(HSTMT hstmt, PTR rgbValue, SDWORD cbValue)
```

Parameters:

HSTMT *hstmt*	A statement handle returned by the call to SQLAllocStmt().
PTR *rgbValue*	A pointer to a buffer used to store the actual data for the parameter or column. The data's type must be a C data type as specified in the SQLBindParameter() or SQLBindCol().
SDWORD *cbValue*	The length of the data in *rgbValue*.

Return Value:

This function will return one of the following values:

SQL_SUCCESS	The function was successful.
SQL_SUCCESS_WITH_INFO	The function was successful, and more information is available.
SQL_STILL_EXECUTING	An asynchronous operation is still pending.
SQL_ERROR	The function failed. Call SQLError() to get more information about the specific failure.
SLQ_INVALID_HANDLE	The function failed. The handle that was passed wasn't a valid handle. Possibly, the function that created the handle had failed and didn't return a valid handle.

If this function fails, your SQL function should end or the error should be corrected; the function should then be re-executed.

Usage:

Call the SQLPutData() function to send data for a parameter or column to the driver at execution time. Always check the return code from this function for errors.

Notes:

If this function fails, use the SQLError() function to find out why.

SQLRowCount()

Prototype:

RETCODE SQLRowCount(HSTMT *hstmt*, SDWORD FAR * *pcrow*)

Parameters:

HSTMT *hstmt*	A statement handle returned by the call to SQLAllocStmt().
SDWORD FAR * *pcrow*	A pointer to a variable that will typically hold the number of rows affected by the request, or − 1 if the number of affected rows isn't available.

Return Value:

This function will return one of the following values:

SQL_SUCCESS	The function was successful.
SQL_SUCCESS_WITH_INFO	The function was successful, and more information is available.
SQL_ERROR	The function failed. Call SQLError() to get more information about the specific failure.
SLQ_INVALID_HANDLE	The function failed. The handle that was passed wasn't a valid handle. Possibly, the function that created the handle had failed and didn't return a valid handle.

If this function fails, your SQL function should end or the error should be corrected; the function should then be re-executed.

Usage:

Call the SQLRowCount() function to determine how many rows were affected by an UPDATE, DELETE, or INSERT, or by an SQL_UPDATE, SQL_DELETE, or SQL_ADD operation. Always check the return code from this function for errors.

Notes:

If this function fails, use the SQLError() function to find out why.

SQLSetConnectOption()

Prototype:

```
RETCODE SQLSetConnectOption(HDBC hdbc, UWORD fOption, UDWORD vParam)
```

Parameters:

HDBC *hdbc*	A handle to an HDBC as returned by the call to the SQLAllocConnect() function.
UWORD *fOption*	The option to set. See the ODBC documentation for more details.
UDWORD *vParam*	The value to be associated with the option specified in *foption*.

Return Value:

This function will return one of the following values:

SQL_SUCCESS	The function was successful.
SQL_SUCCESS_WITH_INFO	The function was successful, and more information is available.

| SQL_ERROR | The function failed. Call SQLError() to get more information about the specific failure. |
| SLQ_INVALID_HANDLE | The function failed. The handle that was passed wasn't a valid handle. Possibly, the function that created the handle had failed and didn't return a valid handle. |

If this function fails, your SQL function should end or the error should be corrected; the function should then be re-executed.

Usage:

Call the SQLSetConnectOption() function to set connection options. Always check the return code from this function for errors.

Notes:

The SQLSetConnectOption() has many valid parameter values, which are detailed in the ODBC documentation. If this function fails, use the SQLError() function to find out why.

SQLSetCursorName()

Prototype:

RETCODE SQLSetCursorName(HSTMT *hstmt*, UCHAR FAR * *szCursor*, SWORD *cbCursor*)

Parameters:

HSTMT *hstmt*	A statement handle returned by the call to SQLAllocStmt().
UCHAR FAR * *szCursor*	A pointer to a buffer containing the cursor name.
SWORD *cbCursor*	The length of the string contained in *szCursor*.

Return Value:

This function will return one of the following values:

SQL_SUCCESS	The function was successful.
SQL_SUCCESS_WITH_INFO	The function was successful, and more information is available.
SQL_ERROR	The function failed. Call SQLError() to get more information about the specific failure.
SLQ_INVALID_HANDLE	The function failed. The handle that was passed wasn't a valid handle. Possibly, the function that created the handle had failed and didn't return a valid handle.

If this function fails, your SQL function should end or the error should be corrected; the function should then be re-executed.

Usage:

Call the `SQLSetCursorName()` function to associate a name with the specified *hstmt*. Always check the return code from this function for errors.

Notes:

If your application doesn't set cursor names, the driver will automatically generate default cursor names. If this function fails, use the `SQLError()` function to find out why.

SQLSetPos()

Prototype:

```
RETCODE SQLSetPos(HSTMT hstmt, UWORD irow, UWORD fOption, UWORD fLock)
```

Parameters:

HSTMT *hstmt*	A statement handle returned by the call to `SQLAllocStmt()`.
UWORD *irow*	Indicates the position of the row in the rowset on which to perform the operation specified. If 0, the operation is applied to every row in the rowset.
UWORD *fOption*	The operation to perform: `SQL_POSITION`, `SQL_REFRESH`, `SQL_UPDATE`, `SQL_DELETE`, or `SQL_ADD`.
UWORD *fLock*	Tells how the row is to be locked after the operation has been performed. Values include `SQL_LOCK_NO_CHANGE`, `SQL_LOCK_EXCLUSIVE`, and `SQL_LOCK_UNLOCK`.

Return Value:

This function will return one of the following values:

SQL_SUCCESS	The function was successful.
SQL_SUCCESS_WITH_INFO	The function was successful, and more information is available.
SQL_NEED_DATA	The function needs more information to process the request.
SQL_STILL_EXECUTING	An asynchronous operation is still pending.
SQL_ERROR	The function failed. Call `SQLError()` to get more information about the specific failure.
SLQ_INVALID_HANDLE	The function failed. The handle that was passed wasn't a valid handle. Possibly, the function that created the handle had failed and didn't return a valid handle.

If this function fails, your SQL function should end or the error should be corrected; the function should then be re-executed.

Usage:

Call the `SQLSetPos()` function to set the cursor position in a result set. Always check the return code from this function for errors.

Notes:

If this function fails, use the `SQLError()` function to find out why.

SQLSetScrollOptions()

Prototype:

```
RETCODE SQLSetScrollOptions(HSTMT hstmt, UWORD fConcurrency,
UWORD crowKeyset, UWORD crowRowset)
```

Parameters:

HSTMT *hstmt*	A statement handle returned by the call to `SQLAllocStmt()`.
UWORD *fConcurrency*	Parameter to specify the cursor's concurrence. Valid values are listed in Table 3.12.
UWORD *crowKeyset*	Specifies the number of rows for which to buffer keys. Either greater than or equal to *crowRowset,* or must be one of the following: `SQL_SCROLL_FORWARD_ONLY`, `SQL_SCROLL_STATIC`, `SQL_SCROLL_KEYSET_DRIVEN`, or `SQL_SCROLL_DYNAMIC`.
UWORD *crowRowset*	Specifies the number of rows in a rowset. The *crowRowset* parameter defines the number of rows that will be fetched by each call to `SQLExtendedFetch()` and the number of rows that the application buffers.

Table 3.12. `fConcurrency` values.

Identifier	*Description*
SQL_CONCUR_READ_ONLY	The cursor is read-only.
SQL_CONCUR_LOCK	The cursor uses the lowest level of locking sufficient to ensure that the row can be updated.
SQL_CONCUR_ROWVER	The cursor uses optimistic concurrency control.
SQL_CONCUR_VALUES	The cursor uses optimistic concurrency control.

Return Value:

This function will return one of the following values:

SQL_SUCCESS	The function was successful.
SQL_SUCCESS_WITH_INFO	The function was successful, and more information is available.
SQL_ERROR	The function failed. Call SQLError() to get more information about the specific failure.
SLQ_INVALID_HANDLE	The function failed. The handle that was passed wasn't a valid handle. Possibly, the function that created the handle had failed and didn't return a valid handle.

If this function fails, your SQL function should end or the error should be corrected; the function should then be re-executed.

Usage:

The SQLSetScrollOptions() function should be used only with ODBC 1.x drivers. For ODBC 2, use SQLSetStmtOption(). Always check the return code from this function for errors.

Notes:

If this function fails, use the SQLError() function to find out why.

SQLSetStmtOption()

Prototype:

```
RETCODE SQLSetStmtOption(HSTMT hstmt, UWORD fOption, UDWORD vParam)
```

Parameters:

HSTMT *hstmt*	A statement handle returned by the call to SQLAllocStmt().
UWORD *fOption*	Specifies the option that is to be set. Valid options include SQL_ASYNC_ENABLE, SQL_BIND_TYPE, SQL_CONCURENCY, SQL_CURSOR_TYPE, SQL_KEYSET_SIZE, SQL_MAX_LENGTH, SQL_MAX_ROWS, SQL_NOSCAN, SQL_QUERY_TIMEOUT, SQL_RETRIEVE_DATA, SQL_ROWSET_SIZE, SQL_SIMULATE_CURSOR, and SQL_USE_BOOKMARKS.
UDWORD *vParam*	The value to which the option is to be set.

Return Value:

This function will return one of the following values:

SQL_SUCCESS	The function was successful.
SQL_SUCCESS_WITH_INFO	The function was successful, and more information is available.

`SQL_ERROR`	The function failed. Call `SQLError()` to get more information about the specific failure.
`SLQ_INVALID_HANDLE`	The function failed. The handle that was passed wasn't a valid handle. Possibly, the function that created the handle had failed and didn't return a valid handle.

If this function fails, your SQL function should end or the error should be corrected; the function should then be re-executed.

Usage:

Call the `SQLSetStmtOption()` function to set statement options. Always check the return code from this function for errors.

Notes:

If this function fails, use the `SQLError()` function to find out why.

SQLSpecialColumns()

Prototype:

```
RETCODE SQLSpecialColumns(HSTMT hstmt, UWORD fColType,
UCHAR FAR * szTableQualifier, SWORD cbTableQualifier,
UCHAR FAR * szTableOwner, SWORD cbTableOwner,
UCHAR FAR * szTableName, SWORD cbTableName,
UWORD fScope, UWORD fNullable)
```

Parameters:

HSTMT *hstmt*	A statement handle returned by the call to `SQLAllocStmt()`.
UWORD *fColType*	Specifies the type of column to return. Must be either `SQL_BEST_ROWID` or `SQL_ROWVER`.
UCHAR FAR * *szTableQualifier*	A pointer to a buffer containing the qualifier name for the table.
SWORD *cbTableQualifier*	The length of the string in *szTableQualifier*.
UCHAR FAR * *szTableOwner*	A pointer to a buffer containing the owner name for the table.
SWORD *cbTableOwner*	The length of the string in *szTableOwner*.
UCHAR FAR * *szTableName*	A pointer to a buffer containing the table name.
SWORD *cbTableName*	The length of the string in *szTableName*.
UWORD *fScope*	The minimum required scope of the row ID.
UWORD *fNullable*	Specifies when to return special columns that can have a NULL value.

Return Value:

This function will return one of the following values:

SQL_SUCCESS	The function was successful.
SQL_SUCCESS_WITH_INFO	The function was successful, and more information is available.
SQL_STILL_EXECUTING	An asynchronous operation is still pending.
SQL_ERROR	The function failed. Call SQLError() to get more information about the specific failure.
SLQ_INVALID_HANDLE	The function failed. The handle that was passed wasn't a valid handle. Possibly, the function that created the handle had failed and didn't return a valid handle.

If this function fails, your SQL function should end or the error should be corrected; the function should then be re-executed.

Usage:

Call the SQLSpecialColumns() function to retrieve information about the optimal set of columns that will uniquely identify a row in a table, or columns that are automatically updated when a value in the row has been updated by transactions. Always check the return code from this function for errors.

Notes:

If this function fails, use the SQLError() function to find out why.

SQLStatistics()

Prototype:

```
RETCODE SQLStatistics(HSTMT hstmt, UCHAR FAR * szTableQualifier,
SWORD cbTableQualifier, UCHAR FAR * szTableOwner, SWORD cbTableOwner,
UCHAR FAR * szTableName, SWORD cbTableName, UWORD fUnique, UWORD fAccuracy)
```

Parameters:

HSTMT hstmt	A statement handle returned by the call to SQLAllocStmt().
UCHAR FAR * szTableQualifier	A pointer to a buffer containing the qualifier name.
SWORD cbTableQualifier	The length of the string in szTableQualifier.
UCHAR FAR * szTableOwner	A pointer to a buffer containing the owner name.
SWORD cbTableOwner	The length of the string in szTableOwner.

UCHAR FAR * *szTableName*	A pointer to a buffer containing the table name.
SWORD *cbTableName*	The length of the string in *szTableName*.
UWORD *fUnique*	Indicates the index type; either SQL_INDEX_UNIQUE or SQL_INDEX_ALL.
UWORD *fAccuracy*	Specifies the importance of the CARDINALITY and PAGES columns in the result set. Use SQL_ENSURE to request that the driver retrieve the statistics unconditionally. Use SQL_QUICK to request that the driver retrieve results only if they are readily available from the server.

Return Value:

This function will return one of the following values:

SQL_SUCCESS	The function was successful.
SQL_SUCCESS_WITH_INFO	The function was successful, and more information is available.
SQL_STILL_EXECUTING	An asynchronous operation is still pending.
SQL_ERROR	The function failed. Call SQLError() to get more information about the specific failure.
SLQ_INVALID_HANDLE	The function failed. The handle that was passed wasn't a valid handle. Possibly, the function that created the handle had failed and didn't return a valid handle.

If this function fails, your SQL function should end or the error should be corrected; the function should then be re-executed.

Usage:

Call the SQLStatistics() function to retrieve a list of statistics regarding a specified single table. Always check the return code from this function for errors.

Notes:

If this function fails, use the SQLError() function to find out why.

SQLTablePrivileges()

Prototype:

```
RETCODE SQLTablePrivileges(HSTMT hstmt,
UCHAR FAR * szTableQualifier, SWORD cbTableQualifier,
UCHAR FAR * szTableOwner, SWORD cbTableOwner,
UCHAR FAR * szTableName, SWORD cbTableName)
```

Parameters:

HSTMT *hstmt*	A statement handle returned by the call to SQLAllocStmt().
UCHAR FAR * *szTableQualifier*	A pointer to a buffer containing the table qualifier.
SWORD *cbTableQualifier*	The length of the string in *szTableQualifier*.
UCHAR FAR * *szTableOwner*	A pointer to a buffer containing the string search pattern for owner names.
SWORD *cbTableOwner*	The length of the string in *szTableOwner*.
UCHAR FAR * *szTableName*	A pointer to a string search pattern for table names.
SWORD *cbTableName*	The length of the string in *szTableName*.

Return Value:

This function will return one of the following values:

SQL_SUCCESS	The function was successful.
SQL_SUCCESS_WITH_INFO	The function was successful, and more information is available.
SQL_STILL_EXECUTING	An asynchronous operation is still pending.
SQL_ERROR	The function failed. Call SQLError() to get more information about the specific failure.
SLQ_INVALID_HANDLE	The function failed. The handle that was passed wasn't a valid handle. Possibly, the function that created the handle had failed and didn't return a valid handle.

If this function fails, your SQL function should end or the error should be corrected; the function should then be re-executed.

Usage:

Call the SQLTablePrivileges() function to return a list of tables and privileges for each table in the list. Always check the return code from this function for errors.

Notes:

The SQLTablePrivileges() function returns the results in the form of a result set. If this function fails, use the SQLError() function to find out why.

SQLTables()

Prototype:

```
RETCODE SQLTables(HSTMT hstmt,
UCHAR FAR * szTableQualifier, SWORD cbTableQualifier,
```

```
UCHAR FAR * szTableOwner, SWORD cbTableOwner,
UCHAR FAR * szTableName, SWORD cbTableName,
UCHAR FAR * szTableType, SWORD cbTableType)
```

Parameters:

HSTMT *hstmt*	A statement handle returned by the call to SQLAllocStmt().
UCHAR FAR * *szTableQualifier*	A pointer to a buffer containing the qualifier name.
SWORD *cbTableQualifier*	The length of the string in *szTableQualifier*.
UCHAR FAR * *szTableOwner*	A pointer to a buffer containing the string search pattern for owner names.
SWORD *cbTableOwner*	The length of the string in *szTableOwner*.
UCHAR FAR * *szTableName*	A pointer to a buffer containing the string search pattern for table names.
SWORD *cbTableName*	The length of the string in *szTableName*.
UCHAR FAR * *szTableType*	A pointer to a buffer containing a list of table types to match.
SWORD *cbTableType*	The length of the string in *szTableType*.

Return Value:

This function will return one of the following values:

SQL_SUCCESS	The function was successful.
SQL_SUCCESS_WITH_INFO	The function was successful, and more information is available.
SQL_STILL_EXECUTING	An asynchronous operation is still pending.
SQL_ERROR	The function failed. Call SQLError() to get more information about the specific failure.
SLQ_INVALID_HANDLE	The function failed. The handle that was passed wasn't a valid handle. Possibly, the function that created the handle had failed and didn't return a valid handle.

If this function fails, your SQL function should end or the error should be corrected; the function should then be re-executed.

Usage:

Call the SQLTables() function to obtain a list of tables in the datasource. Always check the return code from this function for errors.

Notes:

If this function fails, use the SQLError() function to find out why.

SQLTransact()

Prototype:

```
RETCODE SQLTransact(HENV henv, HDBC hdbc, UWORD fType)
```

Parameters:

HENV *henv*	A handle to an HENV as returned by the call to the SQLAllocEnv() function.
HDBC *hdbc*	A handle to an HDBC as returned by the call to the SQLAllocConnect() function.
UWORD *fType*	Either SQL_COMMIT or SQL_ROLLBACK.

Return Value:

This function will return one of the following values:

SQL_SUCCESS	The function was successful.
SQL_SUCCESS_WITH_INFO	The function was successful, and more information is available.
SQL_ERROR	The function failed. Call SQLError() to get more information about the specific failure.
SLQ_INVALID_HANDLE	The function failed. The handle that was passed wasn't a valid handle. Possibly, the function that created the handle had failed and didn't return a valid handle.

If this function fails, your SQL function should end or the error should be corrected; the function should then be re-executed.

Usage:

Call the SQLTransact() function to commit or rollback the transaction. Always check the return code from this function for errors.

Notes:

If this function fails, use the SQLError() function to find out why.

Using the *SQL...()* Functions

In the first part of this chapter, you learned about the library of SQL...() functions. These functions are usable in both C and C++ applications. However, it's possible to write a set of wrapper functions around some of the more commonly used sets of SQL...() commands.

The second part of this chapter shows how to use the SQL...() functions and presents a few useful functions (which can be called from both C and C++ programs) that use these functions.

Using a Datasource

The first example is a simple function that accesses a table, determines what columns are in the accessed table, and then fetches data from the datasource. Although this routine is a simple implementation, it can form the basis of a number of useful applications.

First, look at the sequence of operation in accessing an SQL datasource. Unlike most other statements, the SQL...() statements require a rather fixed sequence of execution. You simply can't call the SQLExecute() function without first setting up the SQL environment. The most basic part of any data access application is the initialization of the SQL environment.

Listing 3.1 shows a simple function that initializes the ODBC SQL environment. This function gets the names of the columns in the datasource that the user selects and then fetches the first four columns in this datasource. The routine would be better if it were to check to make sure that there were more than four columns in the datasource. I also have coded checks for errors, but I didn't call error handlers in this example. A later example shows a simple error handler routine that can be used by most ODBC functions to display information to the developer and the user.

> **NOTE**
>
> Listings 3.1 through 3.6 are on the CD that comes with this book. These listings don't compile into stand-alone components; they're meant to provide helper functions for your ODBC programs. Chapter 22, "Documenting Your Database Applications," has a sample program, DOCDB (also on the CD), that uses these functions.

Listing 3.1. INITODBC.C: A simple function that initializes the ODBC SQL environment.

```
//   INITODBC.C

#include "windows.h"

#include "odbcmisc.h"

#include "sql.h"
#include "sqlext.h"
#include <stdio.h>
#include <stdlib.h>
#include <string.h>
#include <ctype.h>
```

```
/*******************************************************************************
**
**       TITLE: ODBC1.c
**
**    FUNCTION: Open DataBase Connectivity interface code
**
**      INPUTS: VARIOUS
**
**     OUTPUTS: VARIOUS
**
**     RETURNS: YES
**
**       CALLS: ODBC routines: SQL...()
**
**      AUTHOR: Peter D. Hipson
**
**    COPYRIGHT 1995 BY PETER D. HIPSON, All rights reserved.
**
*******************************************************************************/

// Static, for this module only:


// Routines:

void SimpleODBC(HWND hWnd)
{

#define STR_LEN 128+1
#define REM_LEN 254+1

/* Declare storage locations for result set data */

UCHAR  szQualifier[STR_LEN], szOwner[STR_LEN];
UCHAR  szTableName[STR_LEN], szColName[STR_LEN];
UCHAR  szTypeName[STR_LEN], szRemarks[REM_LEN];
SDWORD Precision, Length;
SWORD  DataType, Scale, Radix, Nullable;

/* Declare storage locations for bytes available to return */

SDWORD cbQualifier, cbOwner, cbTableName, cbColName;
SDWORD cbTypeName, cbRemarks, cbDataType, cbPrecision;
SDWORD cbLength, cbScale, cbRadix, cbNullable;


char    szSource[60];
char    szDirectory[132];
char    szTable[60];
//      Keep above, delete below...
char    szDSN[256];
char    szConStrOut[256];
char    szBuffer[513];
char    szColumn1[128];
char    szColumn2[128];
char    szColumn3[128];
char    szColumn4[128];
```

continues

Listing 3.1. continued

```
int             i;
int          j;

HENV      henv;
HDBC      hdbc;
HSTMT      hstmt = SQL_NULL_HSTMT;
RETCODE RC;

int             nConStrOut;

SDWORD  sdReturn;
SWORD    swReturn;

//  Keep this line:
szSource[0] = '\0';
szTable[0] = '\0';
szDirectory[0] = '\0';

//  The GetODBC() function returns the ODBC source
//  table and directory that the user selects.

GetODBC(
     szSource, sizeof(szSource),
     szTable, sizeof(szTable),
     szDirectory, sizeof(szDirectory));

SQLAllocEnv(&henv);
SQLAllocConnect(henv, &hdbc);

RC = SQLDriverConnect(hdbc, hWnd,
     (unsigned char far *)szDSN, SQL_NTS,
     (unsigned char far *)szConStrOut, sizeof(szConStrOut),
     (short far *)&nConStrOut, SQL_DRIVER_COMPLETE);

  if (RC != SQL_SUCCESS && RC != SQL_SUCCESS_WITH_INFO)
  {// Call whatever error handler your application uses
  }
  else
  {// Connect was successful. Just continue in most cases
  }

RC = SQLAllocStmt(hdbc, &hstmt);

  if (RC != SQL_SUCCESS && RC != SQL_SUCCESS_WITH_INFO)
  {// Could not allocate the statement! Call an error handler:
  }

//  Get the DBMS version string. Just for our information, it is not used.

  SQLGetInfo(hdbc, SQL_DBMS_VER, szConStrOut,
       sizeof(szConStrOut), &swReturn);

//  Get the columns in the specified table:

  RC = SQLColumns(hstmt,
       NULL, 0,     // All qualifiers
```

```
            NULL, 0,     // All owners
            szTable, SQL_NTS,        // The table!
            NULL, 0);         // All columns

    if (RC != SQL_SUCCESS && RC != SQL_SUCCESS_WITH_INFO)
    {// Could not determine columns! Call an error handler:
    }

//    Now bind variables to columns!

    SQLBindCol(hstmt, 1,  SQL_C_CHAR,   szQualifier, STR_LEN,&cbQualifier);
    SQLBindCol(hstmt, 2,  SQL_C_CHAR,   szOwner, STR_LEN, &cbOwner);
    SQLBindCol(hstmt, 3,  SQL_C_CHAR,   szTableName, STR_LEN,&cbTableName);
    SQLBindCol(hstmt, 4,  SQL_C_CHAR,   szColName, STR_LEN, &cbColName);
    SQLBindCol(hstmt, 5,  SQL_C_SSHORT, &DataType, 0, &cbDataType);
    SQLBindCol(hstmt, 6,  SQL_C_CHAR,   szTypeName, STR_LEN, &cbTypeName);
    SQLBindCol(hstmt, 7,  SQL_C_SLONG,  &Precision, 0, &cbPrecision);
    SQLBindCol(hstmt, 8,  SQL_C_SLONG,  &Length, 0, &cbLength);
    SQLBindCol(hstmt, 9,  SQL_C_SSHORT, &Scale, 0, &cbScale);
    SQLBindCol(hstmt, 10, SQL_C_SSHORT, &Radix, 0, &cbRadix);
    SQLBindCol(hstmt, 11, SQL_C_SSHORT, &Nullable, 0, &cbNullable);
    SQLBindCol(hstmt, 12, SQL_C_CHAR,   szRemarks, REM_LEN, &cbRemarks);


// Then get the column names:

    while(TRUE)
    {// Do till we break out:
        RC = SQLFetch(hstmt);

        if (RC == SQL_NO_DATA_FOUND)
        {// Fetch done; got last column...
                break;
        }

        if (RC != SQL_SUCCESS && RC != SQL_SUCCESS_WITH_INFO)
        {// Fetch failed; may (or may not) be fatal!
                break;
        }

        if (RC == SQL_SUCCESS ¦¦ RC == SQL_SUCCESS_WITH_INFO)
        {// Fetch was OK; display the results:
            sprintf(szBuffer,
                "%20.20s %10.10s %15.15s %15.15s %10.10s %10.10s \n",
                szQualifier,
                szOwner,
                szColName,
                szTableName,
                szTypeName,
                szRemarks);

            OutputDebugString(szBuffer);
        }
    }

    SQLFreeStmt(hstmt, SQL_CLOSE);
    SQLFreeStmt(hstmt, SQL_UNBIND);
```

continues

Listing 3.1. continued

```
//   END: Get the columns in the specified table:

//   Get data from the table:

    strcpy(szConStrOut,
        "SELECT * FROM \"");
    strcat(szConStrOut, szTable);
    strcat(szConStrOut, "\" ");

    RC = SQLExecDirect(hstmt, (unsigned char far *)szConStrOut, SQL_NTS);

    if (RC != SQL_SUCCESS && RC != SQL_SUCCESS_WITH_INFO)
    {// Something is wrong; error message, and then DIE!
    }
    else
    {// Bind to whichever columns in result set are needed:

        SQLBindCol(hstmt, 1, SQL_C_CHAR, (unsigned char far *)szColumn1,
            sizeof(szColumn1), &sdReturn);

        SQLBindCol(hstmt, 2, SQL_C_CHAR, (unsigned char far *)szColumn2,
            sizeof(szColumn2), &sdReturn);

        SQLBindCol(hstmt, 3, SQL_C_CHAR, (unsigned char far *)szColumn3,
            sizeof(szColumn3), &sdReturn);

        SQLBindCol(hstmt, 4, SQL_C_CHAR, (unsigned char far *)szColumn4,
            sizeof(szColumn4), &sdReturn);

//      In our example, we will simply get up to 100 rows from the dataset:

        i = 0;
        j = 0;

        while(++j < 100)
        {// j is the number of rows

            RC = SQLFetch(hstmt);

            if (RC == SQL_ERROR ¦¦ RC == SQL_SUCCESS_WITH_INFO)
            {// There was a problem!
            }

            if (RC == SQL_SUCCESS ¦¦ RC == SQL_SUCCESS_WITH_INFO)
            {// Now we have our row's data! Use it (like write a report?)
                sprintf(szBuffer, "1 '%15.15s' 2 '%15.15s' "
                    "3 '%15.15s' 4 '%15.15s' 5 '%d' \n",
                    szQualifier, szOwner, szColName, szTypeName, i);

                OutputDebugString(szBuffer);
            }
            else
            {// That's all, folks... No more data here!
                break;
            }
        }
```

```
    }

    SQLFreeStmt(hstmt, SQL_DROP);

    SQLDisconnect(hdbc);
    SQLFreeConnect(hdbc);
    SQLFreeEnv(henv);
}
```

Take a look at the `SimpleODBC()` function. First, the following code fragment shows what is necessary to initialize the ODBC system.

```
    SQLAllocEnv(&henv);
    SQLAllocConnect(henv, &hdbc);

    RC = SQLDriverConnect(hdbc, hWnd,
        (unsigned char far *)szDSN, SQL_NTS,
        (unsigned char far *)szConStrOut, sizeof(szConStrOut),
        (short far *)&nConStrOut, SQL_DRIVER_COMPLETE);

    if (RC != SQL_SUCCESS && RC != SQL_SUCCESS_WITH_INFO)
    {// Call whatever error handler your application uses
    }
    else
    {// Connect was successful. Just continue in most cases
    }

    RC = SQLAllocStmt(hdbc, &hstmt);
```

Notice how a call is made to `SQLAllocEnv()` and then a call is made to `SQLAllocConnect()`. These two calls (which must be made in the order shown) initialize the ODBC environment and allocate the memory necessary for the connection handle.

After this setup is performed, it's then possible to connect the actual database to the application. This is done with a call to the `SQLDriverConnect()` function. This function takes, as arguments, information to let ODBC locate the datasource and the `HDBC` handle to connect to.

After the database has been connected, you need to open a statement handle. This statement handle is used to let the application issue SQL commands to the datasource.

At this point, the datasource is truly connected to the application, and the application is able to obtain both information about the datasource and information from the datasource.

In the sample program, the next step performed is to obtain information about the table that was opened. `SQLColumns()` is called to obtain information about each column in the datasource. `SQLColumns()` returned results are part of a result set. A result set is simply a set of "records" that the application is able to retrieve, either one at a time or in blocks.

```
    RC = SQLColumns(hstmt,
        NULL, 0,    // All qualifiers
        NULL, 0,    // All owners
        szTable, SQL_NTS,    // The table!
        NULL, 0);    // All columns
```

```
if (RC != SQL_SUCCESS && RC != SQL_SUCCESS_WITH_INFO)
{// Could not determine columns! Call an error handler:
}

//    Now bind variables to columns!

SQLBindCol(hstmt, 1,  SQL_C_CHAR,   szQualifier, STR_LEN,&cbQualifier);
SQLBindCol(hstmt, 2,  SQL_C_CHAR,   szOwner, STR_LEN, &cbOwner);
SQLBindCol(hstmt, 3,  SQL_C_CHAR,   szTableName, STR_LEN,&cbTableName);
SQLBindCol(hstmt, 4,  SQL_C_CHAR,   szColName, STR_LEN, &cbColName);
SQLBindCol(hstmt, 5,  SQL_C_SSHORT, &DataType, 0, &cbDataType);
SQLBindCol(hstmt, 6,  SQL_C_CHAR,   szTypeName, STR_LEN, &cbTypeName);
SQLBindCol(hstmt, 7,  SQL_C_SLONG,  &Precision, 0, &cbPrecision);
SQLBindCol(hstmt, 8,  SQL_C_SLONG,  &Length, 0, &cbLength);
SQLBindCol(hstmt, 9,  SQL_C_SSHORT, &Scale, 0, &cbScale);
SQLBindCol(hstmt, 10, SQL_C_SSHORT, &Radix, 0, &cbRadix);
SQLBindCol(hstmt, 11, SQL_C_SSHORT, &Nullable, 0, &cbNullable);
SQLBindCol(hstmt, 12, SQL_C_CHAR,   szRemarks, REM_LEN, &cbRemarks);
```

In the preceding code fragment, first the `SQLColumns()` function is called. Then you must bind variables in the application to the columns in the result set that `SQLColumns()` returns. In this example, you will look at all the columns; however, many applications may need to use only a few of the result set columns (such as getting the name of the column and the column's data type).

```
// Then get the column names:

while(TRUE)
{// Do till we break out:
    RC = SQLFetch(hstmt);

    if (RC == SQL_SUCCESS || RC == SQL_SUCCESS_WITH_INFO)
    {// Fetch was OK; display the results:
        sprintf(szBuffer,
            "%20.20s %10.10s %15.15s %15.15s %10.10s %10.10s \n",
            szQualifier,
            szOwner,
            szColName,
            szTableName,
            szTypeName,
            szRemarks);

        OutputDebugString(szBuffer);
    }
}

SQLFreeStmt(hstmt, SQL_CLOSE);
SQLFreeStmt(hstmt, SQL_UNBIND);
```

This code fragment shows how to get the actual records from the result set. The process, done in a `while()` loop, is simple and easy to program. A call to `SQLFetch()` at the beginning of the loop is followed by whatever code is necessary to process the information that `SQLFetch()` returns. The column names could be added to a list box to let the user select a specific column.

After the records from the result set have been processed, you need to discard the result set. You do this by using calls to SQLFreeStmt(), as the following code fragment shows. Notice that you needed to call SQLFreeStmt() two times with different arguments:

```
SQLFreeStmt(hstmt, SQL_CLOSE);
SQLFreeStmt(hstmt, SQL_UNBIND);
```

The first call to SQLFreeStmt() closed the statement handle. The second call was used to actually tell ODBC to discard the result set's contents and release the memory that the result set occupied.

To obtain information from a table in a datasource, you must actually issue an SQL command to fetch the desired records. This chapter won't try to detail SQL commands; SQL commands are covered in Chapter 5, "Learning Structured Query Language."

```
//  Get data from the table:

    strcpy(szConStrOut,
        "SELECT * FROM \"");
    strcat(szConStrOut, szTable);
    strcat(szConStrOut, "\" ");

    RC = SQLExecDirect(hstmt, (unsigned char far *)szConStrOut, SQL_NTS);
```

This example simply creates an SQL statement SELECT * FROM and appends the table name. You need to make sure that the table name is quoted in this example; however, the rules on quoting a name are based on whether the name contains embedded spaces or not. Later in this chapter, you will see an example of a function that quotes names when quotes are needed.

Like SQLColumns(), SQLExecDirect() returns the results of the SQL statement as a result set. This result set contains the records from the datasource that the SQL statement has selected (usually limited using a WHERE clause). Because the example simply gets all columns in the datasource, you must either know in advance (perhaps a database was created) or determine (using a call to SQLColumns()) what columns have been included in the result set.

Whenever a result set has been returned by an SQL...() function, you must bind variables in your application to the columns in the result set. The SQLFetch() function will place in these variables the data from the current row.

```
SQLBindCol(hstmt, 1, SQL_C_CHAR, (unsigned char far *)szColumn1,
    sizeof(szColumn1), &sdReturn);

SQLBindCol(hstmt, 2, SQL_C_CHAR, (unsigned char far *)szColumn2,
    sizeof(szColumn2), &sdReturn);

SQLBindCol(hstmt, 3, SQL_C_CHAR, (unsigned char far *)szColumn3,
    sizeof(szColumn3), &sdReturn);

SQLBindCol(hstmt, 4, SQL_C_CHAR, (unsigned char far *)szColumn4,
    sizeof(szColumn4), &sdReturn);
```

In this example, four columns are bound in the result set. If there are columns in the result set that your application doesn't need, you don't have to bind variables to any columns that you don't want.

You can always bind a character variable to a column, and the SQL...() routines will convert the column's data to a character-based format. However, the default conversion for numeric data might not be formatted the way you want.

After variables have been bound to columns, the next step is to actually fetch the rows from the result set. These rows are fetched with either SQLFetch() or SQLExtendedFetch(). In the following example, SQLFetch() is called to get the data from the result set.

```
while(TRUE)
{
    RC = SQLFetch(hstmt);

    if (RC == SQL_ERROR ¦¦ RC == SQL_SUCCESS_WITH_INFO)
    {// There was a problem!
    }

    if (RC == SQL_SUCCESS ¦¦ RC == SQL_SUCCESS_WITH_INFO)
    {// Now we have our row's data! Use it (like write a report?)
    }
    else
    {// That's all, folks... No more data here!
    break;
    }
}
}
```

The preceding code shows a simple while() loop; the first line in the loop is a call to SQLFetch(). After SQLFetch() completes successfully, you can use the data (which in this example is stored in the variables szBuffer1, szBuffer2, szBuffer3, and szBuffer4).

After the results of the result set have been processed by the application and the application is finished with the entire datasource, the statement handle should be discarded, as shown next. It's also necessary to disconnect from the datasource, free the connection handle, and then free the environment handle. These calls are done in the opposite order than when they were created, at the beginning of the sample function.

```
SQLFreeStmt(hstmt, SQL_DROP);

SQLDisconnect(hdbc);
SQLFreeConnect(hdbc);
SQLFreeEnv(henv);
```

Handling Errors in *SQL...()* Statements

When calls to SQL...() statements are made, the function will return a return code that should always be examined by the application to determine whether the function was successful or not. When a function fails, the application must determine what failed and, if possible, correct this failure with a minimum amount of interruption to the user's workflow. Except for the most disastrous failures, the application should try to recover without user interaction if possible. When the error problem is so serious that recovery is impossible, the application must notify the user and explain the problem.

Don't put a message like Error 0x1003 occurred, program ending in your application. This type of message went out with the 8088. Make sure that the error message provides as much information as possible to assist the user in correcting the problem. For example, Could not open database C:\MSOffice\Access\Samples\NorthWind.MDB, please check and make sure that the database is in this directory is a better message to give to the user.

Regardless of how your application "talks" to the user, the SQLError() function will let your application obtain information about the failure. The function shown in Listing 3.2 is an error function that will use the SQLError() function's return values to format an error message.

Listing 3.2. SQLERROR.C: An error handler.

```
//   SQLError.C

#include "windows.h"

#include "resource.h"

#include "odbcmisc.h"

#include "sql.h"
#include "sqlext.h"
#include <stdio.h>
#include <stdlib.h>
#include <string.h>
#include <ctype.h>

/*****************************************************************************
**
**       TITLE: SQLError.c
**
**    FUNCTION: Open DataBase Connectivity interface code
**
**      INPUTS: VARIOUS
**
**     OUTPUTS: VARIOUS
**
**     RETURNS: YES
**
**       CALLS: ODBC routines: SQL...()
**
**      AUTHOR: Peter D. Hipson
**
**   COPYRIGHT 1995 BY PETER D. HIPSON, All rights reserved.
**
*****************************************************************************/

// Static, for this module only:
```

continues

Listing 3.2. continued

```
// Routines:

// A typical SQL type query:


void    SQLPrintError(HENV henv, HDBC hdbc, HSTMT hstmt)
{
RETCODE RC;
char    szSqlState[256];
char    szErrorMsg[256];
char    szMessage[256];

SDWORD     pfNativeError;
SWORD    pcbErrorMsg;

RC = SQLError(henv, hdbc, hstmt,
        szSqlState,
        &pfNativeError,
        szErrorMsg,
        sizeof(szErrorMsg),
        &pcbErrorMsg);

    if (RC == SQL_SUCCESS ¦¦ RC == SQL_SUCCESS_WITH_INFO)
    {
        sprintf(szMessage, "SQL State = '%s', \nMessage = '%s'",
            szSqlState, szErrorMsg);
        MessageBox(NULL, szMessage, "ODBC Error...", MB_OK);
    }
    else
    {
        MessageBox(NULL, "SQLError() returned an error!!!",
            "ODBC Error...", MB_OK);
    }
}
```

The SQLPrintError() function shown in Listing 3.2 really isn't that user-friendly. It displays a cryptic message about SQL states and messages without telling the user exactly what went wrong and what to do about the failure.

A better example of an SQLPrintError() function would be a function that actually parsed the error condition returned by SQLError() and then offered both the reason and possible corrective actions. A hot link to WinHelp with a help file that contained more detailed information about both the failure and possible corrective action wouldn't be out of order. Of course, adding a help button would require writing a custom replacement for MessageBox(); however, that wouldn't be too difficult if you used the Visual C++ resource editor.

Quoting Names

When an SQL statement is built in a string, it's necessary to quote some names. Any name that contains embedded blanks must be quoted (column names often have embedded blanks, as in 'Zip Code').

The function QuoteName() shown in Listing 3.3 is a function that will quote a string if the string contains a character that isn't a letter, number, or an underscore. This function takes two parameters: a pointer to a buffer containing the string and the size of the buffer. This size parameter isn't the length of the string but the size of the memory allocated to the buffer. The size is needed so that the function can determine whether there is enough room to add the two quote characters to the string.

Listing 3.3. QUOTES.C: Puts quotes around a string.

```
//  QUOTES.C

#include "windows.h"

#include "resource.h"

#include "odbcmisc.h"

#include "sql.h"
#include "sqlext.h"
#include <stdio.h>
#include <stdlib.h>
#include <string.h>
#include <ctype.h>

/******************************************************************************
**
**        TITLE: Quotes.c
**
**    FUNCTION: Open DataBase Connectivity interface code
**
**      INPUTS: VARIOUS
**
**     OUTPUTS: VARIOUS
**
**     RETURNS: YES
**
**       CALLS: ODBC routines: SQL...()
**
**      AUTHOR: Peter D. Hipson
**
**    COPYRIGHT 1995 BY PETER D. HIPSON, All rights reserved.
**
******************************************************************************/
```

continues

Listing 3.3. continued

```
// Static, for this module only:


// Routines:


BOOL QuoteName(
 char * szName,
 int    nMaxLength)
{
// This function will enclose, in quotes, an SQL name if it contains
// a character that is not alphabetic, numeric, or an underscore

int i;
BOOL bMustQuote = FALSE;

    for (i = 0; i < (int)strlen(szName); i++)
    {
        if(!__iscsym(szName[i]))
        {
            bMustQuote = TRUE;
        }
    }

    if (bMustQuote)
    {//      Had a special character!
        if((int)strlen(szName) + 2 > nMaxLength)
        {//       Error: No room for quotes!
            bMustQuote = FALSE;
        }
        else
        {//      Quote this string...
            memmove(&szName[1], &szName[0], strlen(szName) + 1);
            szName[0] = '"';
            strcat(szName, "\"");
        }
    }
    return(bMustQuote);
}
```

Calling QuoteName() makes it easy to pass correct SQL commands because if a name that must be quoted doesn't have quotes, the SQL command will fail.

Getting the Datasource from the User

It's necessary to get the datasource name from the user. You can do this by using a simple set of C++ functions (which are callable from C code). The final part of this section shows the GetODBC() function that is called to get the datasource and table names.

This code is written in two parts. The first part is the main calling routine, GetODBC(), which is in the file GETODBC.CPP. This file is shown in Listing 3.4.

Listing 3.4. GETODBC.CPP: The `GetODBC()` function.

```cpp
//   GETODBC.CPP

#include "stdafx.h"
#include <afxdb.h>

// Include *YOUR* application header here (instead of application.h):
#include "application.h"

#include "odbcmisc.h"

#include "sql.h"
#include "sqlext.h"
#include <stdio.h>
#include <stdlib.h>
#include <string.h>
#include <commdlg.h>
#include "odbctabl.h"
#include "odbcinfo.h"

/*****************************************************************************
**
**      TITLE: GETODBC.CPP - Database Developer's Guide with Visual C++
**
**   FUNCTION: Open DataBase Connectivity interface code
**
**     INPUTS: VARIOUS
**
**    OUTPUTS: VARIOUS
**
**    RETURNS: YES
**
**    WRITTEN: 1 February 1995
**
**      CALLS: ODBC routines: SQL...()
**
**  CALLED BY: Things that need data from databases
**
**     AUTHOR: Peter D. Hipson
**
**   COPYRIGHT 1995 BY PETER D. HIPSON, All rights reserved.
**
*****************************************************************************/

// Static, for this module only:

// Functions (may be shared):

// Shared data objects, not otherwise allocated:

// Routines:

BOOL GetODBC(
    char * szDataSource,
    int    nDataSourceSize,
    char * szDataTable,
```

continues

Listing 3.4. continued

```
    int     nDataTableSize,
    char *  szDataDir,
    int     nDataDirSize)
{
BOOL        bReturnCode = TRUE;

    ODBCInfo    COdbcInfo;

    if (szDataSource)
        szDataSource[0] = '\0';
    if (szDataTable)
        szDataTable[0] = '\0';
    if (szDataDir)
        szDataDir[0] = '\0';

    bReturnCode = COdbcInfo.GetInfo();

//    A little debugging output for the programmer!

    TRACE("At the GetODBC() end: return %d Datasource "
    "'%s' table '%s' datadir '%s'\n",
        bReturnCode,
        (const char *)COdbcInfo.m_DataSourceName,
        (const char *)COdbcInfo.m_DataTableName,
        (const char *)COdbcInfo.m_DataTableDir);

    if (bReturnCode && szDataSource != NULL)
    {// User wants the datasource name
        if (COdbcInfo.m_DataSourceName.GetLength() < nDataSourceSize)
        {
            strcpy(szDataSource, COdbcInfo.m_DataSourceName);
        }
        else
        {
            szDataSource[0] = '\0';
            bReturnCode = FALSE;
        }
    }

    if (bReturnCode && szDataTable != NULL)
    {// User wants the datatable name
        if (COdbcInfo.m_DataTableName.GetLength() < nDataTableSize)
        {
            strcpy(szDataTable, COdbcInfo.m_DataTableName);
        }
        else
        {
            szDataTable[0] = '\0';
            bReturnCode = FALSE;
        }
    }

    if (bReturnCode && szDataDir != NULL)
    {// User wants the datatable directory name
        if (COdbcInfo.m_DataTableDir.GetLength() < nDataTableSize)
```

```
        {
            strcpy(szDataDir, COdbcInfo.m_DataTableDir);
        }
        else
        {
            szDataDir[0] = '\0';
            bReturnCode = FALSE;
        }
    }
// Finally, return either success or failure.
    return(bReturnCode);
}
```

The `GetODBC()` function creates an object of class `ODBCInfo`. This class is in the file ODBCINFO.CPP, which is shown in Listing 3.5. Notice that even though a C++ class is used, the `CDatabase` class is used in this function. This is because `CDatabase` offers integrated functionality to the program. This functionality could also have been incorporated by using the `SQL...()` functions if desired.

Listing 3.5. ODBCINFO.CPP: Get ODBC datasource information.

```
//   ODBCINFO.CPP

#include "stdafx.h"

// After stdafx.h, include the application's main .H file.
// The application's resources must have the IDD_SELECT_ODBC_TABLE dialog
// defined! (save ODBC.RC, and copy using the resource editor and clipboard)

#include "APPLICATION.h"

#include <afxdb.h>

#include "sql.h"
#include "sqlext.h"
#include "odbcinfo.h"
#include <stdio.h>
#include <stdlib.h>
#include <string.h>
#include <commdlg.h>
#include "odbctabl.h"


/****************************************************************************
**
**      TITLE: ODBCINFO.CPP
**
**   FUNCTION: Open DataBase Connectivity interface code
**
**     INPUTS: VARIOUS
**
**    OUTPUTS: VARIOUS
**
```

continues

Listing 3.5. continued

```
**      RETURNS: YES
**
**      WRITTEN: 1 February 1995
**
**       CALLS: ODBC routines: SQL...()
**
**   CALLED BY: Things that need data from databases
**
**      AUTHOR: Peter D. Hipson
**
**       NOTES: Win 3.11 & later.
**
**    COPYRIGHT 1995 BY PETER D. HIPSON, All rights reserved.
**
***************************************************************************/

// Static, for this module only:


// Shared data objects, not otherwise allocated:


// Routines:

// Construction

ODBCInfo::ODBCInfo()
{// Initialize variables, etc.
//  This sets the default table types that
//  will be displayed. To not display a table type at
//  startup time, change the appropriate variable to FALSE.

    m_Synonyms = TRUE;
    m_SystemTables = TRUE;
    m_Tables = TRUE;
    m_Views = TRUE;
}

BOOL ODBCInfo::GetInfo()
{
HSTMT        hstmt = SQL_NULL_HSTMT;
char         szConStrOut[256];
SWORD        swReturn;
CString        CDBType;
RETCODE        RC;
int            nReturnCode = TRUE;


    TRY
    {
        if (!m_CDodbc.Open(m_TableInfo))
        {//    User selected Cancel. Go home. No more playing for 'im.
            return(FALSE);
        }
    }
    CATCH(CDBException, e)
```

```
    {// User probably hit Return w/o selecting datasource! Msg and return!
        return FALSE;
    }
    END_CATCH

    m_DatabaseName = m_CDodbc.GetDatabaseName();
    m_Connect = m_CDodbc.GetConnect();

    m_CanUpdate = m_CDodbc.CanUpdate();
    m_CanTransact = m_CDodbc.CanTransact();

//    C++'s MFC CRecordSet() class is a bit too unflexible to
//        really work well with an undefined database.
//        Therefore, we simply break into the older API (SQL...()) calls

    RC = SQLGetInfo(m_CDodbc.m_hdbc, SQL_DATA_SOURCE_NAME, szConStrOut,
        sizeof(szConStrOut), &swReturn);

    m_DataSourceName = szConStrOut;

// Lines below are simply for debugging (nice to see what happened):
//
//        TRACE("Datasoure: '%s'\n", m_DataSourceName);
//
//        SQLGetInfo(m_CDodbc.m_hdbc, SQL_DRIVER_NAME, szConStrOut,
//                sizeof(szConStrOut), &swReturn);
//        TRACE("Driver Name %s\n", szConStrOut);
//
//        SQLGetInfo(m_CDodbc.m_hdbc, SQL_DRIVER_VER, szConStrOut,
//                sizeof(szConStrOut), &swReturn);
//        TRACE("Driver Version %s\n", szConStrOut);
//
//        SQLGetInfo(m_CDodbc.m_hdbc, SQL_ODBC_VER, szConStrOut,
//                sizeof(szConStrOut), &swReturn);
//        TRACE("ODBC Version %s\n", szConStrOut);
//
//        SQLGetInfo(m_CDodbc.m_hdbc, SQL_SERVER_NAME, szConStrOut,
//                sizeof(szConStrOut), &swReturn);
//        TRACE("Server Name %s\n", szConStrOut);
//
//        SQLGetInfo(m_CDodbc.m_hdbc, SQL_DATABASE_NAME, szConStrOut,
//                sizeof(szConStrOut), &swReturn);
//        TRACE("Database Name %s\n", szConStrOut);
//
//        SQLGetInfo(m_CDodbc.m_hdbc, SQL_DBMS_VER, szConStrOut,
//            sizeof(szConStrOut), &swReturn);
//        TRACE("DBMS Version %s\n", szConStrOut);

//    Once a datasource is provided, we need to get the TABLE that
//    the user will want. If the datasource is a text file,
//    we use a CFileDialog object (with modifications...)

    SQLGetInfo(m_CDodbc.m_hdbc, SQL_DBMS_NAME, szConStrOut,
        sizeof(szConStrOut), &swReturn);

    CDBType = szConStrOut;
```

continues

Listing 3.5. continued

```
if (CDBType == "TEXT")
{// Data type is text. Use common dialog support to open file.
 // This code will break under Windows 95's new Explorer system,
 // which does not support common dialog template modifications
 // in the same manner as Windows 3.x and Windows NT! It forces
 // usage of "old style" dialog box!

    CString Filter;
    Filter =
        "CSV Files (*.csv)|*.csv|"
        "TAB Files (*.tab)|*.tab|"
        "Text Files (*.txt)|*.txt|"
        "Data Files (*.dat)|*.dat||";

    CFileDialog dlg(TRUE, "txt", NULL, OFN_FILEMUSTEXIST | OFN_HIDEREADONLY,
        (const char *)Filter);

//      Patch to use our dialog box template:
    dlg.m_ofn.hInstance = AfxGetInstanceHandle();
    dlg.m_ofn.lpTemplateName = MAKEINTRESOURCE(TABLESELECT);
    dlg.m_ofn.Flags |= OFN_ENABLETEMPLATE;

    if (dlg.DoModal() == IDOK)
    {
        m_DataTableName = dlg.GetPathName();
        int nPosition = m_DataTableName.ReverseFind('\\');
        if (nPosition > 0)
        {
            m_DataTableDir = m_DataTableName.Left(nPosition);
            m_DataTableName = m_DataTableName.Mid(nPosition + 1);
        }
    }
    else
    {
        nReturnCode = FALSE;
    }
}
else
{// Data type is not text; possibly Access, dBASE, or FoxPro
 // (but could be others)

    OdbcTabl OTDlg;

    OTDlg.m_Synonyms = m_Synonyms;
    OTDlg.m_SystemTables = m_SystemTables;
    OTDlg.m_Tables = m_Tables;
    OTDlg.m_Views = m_Views;
    OTDlg.m_CDB = &m_CDodbc;

    if (OTDlg.DoModal() == IDOK)
    {
        m_DataTableName = OTDlg.m_TableName;
    }
    else
    {
        nReturnCode = FALSE;
```

```
        }
    }
//    Finally, a successful return
    return(nReturnCode);
}


void    ODBCInfo::PrintError(HENV henv, HDBC hdbc, HSTMT hstmt)
{// Private, programmer's error handler. Outputs to the debugging
//   terminal and doesn't use a message box!

RETCODE RC;
char    szSqlState[256];
char    szErrorMsg[256];
SDWORD     pfNativeError;
SWORD   pcbErrorMsg;

    RC = SQLError(
        henv,
        hdbc,
        hstmt,
        (UCHAR FAR*)szSqlState,
        &pfNativeError,
        (UCHAR FAR*)szErrorMsg,
        sizeof(szErrorMsg),
        &pcbErrorMsg);

    TRACE("SQL ERROR:\n");
    if (RC == SQL_SUCCESS ¦¦ RC == SQL_SUCCESS_WITH_INFO)
    {
        TRACE("%s\n", szSqlState);
        TRACE("%s\n", szErrorMsg);
    }
    else
    {
        TRACE("%s\n", "SQLError() returned an error!!!");
    }
}
```

The ODBCInfo class shows a number of features. First, there is a call to the CDatabase::Open()
function to open a datasource. Then you must prompt the user to select a table in the datasource.
The call to the CDatabase::Open() function is followed by a number of other CDatabase member function calls, as the following edited code fragment shows:

```
    m_CDodbc.Open(m_TableInfo

    m_DatabaseName = m_CDodbc.GetDatabaseName();
    m_Connect = m_CDodbc.GetConnect();

    m_CanUpdate = m_CDodbc.CanUpdate();
    m_CanTransact = m_CDodbc.CanTransact();

    RC = SQLGetInfo(m_CDodbc.m_hdbc, SQL_DATA_SOURCE_NAME, szConStrOut,
        sizeof(szConStrOut), &swReturn);

    m_DataSourceName = szConStrOut
```

```
SQLGetInfo(m_CDodbc.m_hdbc, SQL_DBMS_NAME, szConStrOut,
    sizeof(szConStrOut), &swReturn);
```

;

This example shows the call to Open() and then calls to get the database name and the connect string and finds out whether the database can be updated (not all datasources are updatable) and whether the database supports transactions. You also get the datasource name and the DBMS name.

After you have the database, you must determine which table in the database the user is working with. Again, this type of information is individual to each application: perhaps there will be a number of predefined tables that will be used, or perhaps the user may have to be prompted to supply information about the table.

In my example, I present either a custom dialog box of class OdbcTabl (for databases that aren't text-based) or I use the CFileDialog MFC class, with a custom template, to select which text file the user will be using for the table.

The sample function actually has two dialog box templates (see ODBC.RC, included on this book's CD, and Figure 3.1). The ODBCTABL.CPP file is shown in Listing 3.6. This class uses calls to the SQL...() functions to manage the gathering of information about tables in the specified datasource.

FIGURE 3.1.

Dialog boxes for ODBCTABL.

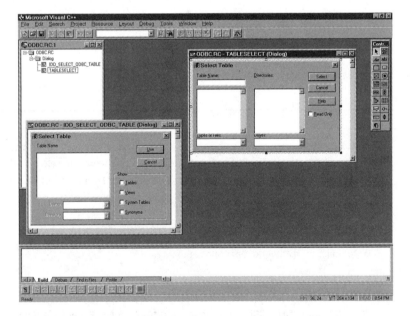

Listing 3.6. ODBCTABL.CPP: Dialog box allowing users to select a table.

```
// odbctabl.cpp : implementation file
//

#include "stdafx.h"
#include <afxdb.h>

// After stdafx.h, include the application's main .H file.
// The application's resources must have the IDD_SELECT_ODBC_TABLE dialog
// defined! (save ODBC.RC, and copy using the editor)


#include "sql.h"
#include "sqlext.h"
#include "odbctabl.h"

#ifdef _DEBUG
#undef THIS_FILE
static char BASED_CODE THIS_FILE[] = __FILE__;
#endif


/////////////////////////////////////////////////////////////////////////////
// OdbcTabl dialog


OdbcTabl::OdbcTabl(CWnd* pParent /*=NULL*/)
    : CDialog(OdbcTabl::IDD, pParent)
{
    //{{AFX_DATA_INIT(OdbcTabl)
    m_Synonyms = FALSE;
    m_SystemTables = FALSE;
    m_Tables = FALSE;
    m_Views = FALSE;
    //}}AFX_DATA_INIT
}

void OdbcTabl::DoDataExchange(CDataExchange* pDX)
{
    CDialog::DoDataExchange(pDX);
    //{{AFX_DATA_MAP(OdbcTabl)
    DDX_Control(pDX, IDC_SYNONYMS, m_CSynonyms);
    DDX_Control(pDX, IDC_VIEWS, m_CViews);
    DDX_Control(pDX, IDC_TABLES, m_CTables);
    DDX_Control(pDX, IDC_SYSTEM_TABLES, m_CSystemTables);
    DDX_Control(pDX, IDC_LIST1, m_TableList);
    DDX_Check(pDX, IDC_SYNONYMS, m_Synonyms);
    DDX_Check(pDX, IDC_SYSTEM_TABLES, m_SystemTables);
    DDX_Check(pDX, IDC_TABLES, m_Tables);
    DDX_Check(pDX, IDC_VIEWS, m_Views);
    //}}AFX_DATA_MAP
}

BEGIN_MESSAGE_MAP(OdbcTabl, CDialog)
    //{{AFX_MSG_MAP(OdbcTabl)
    ON_BN_CLICKED(IDC_SYNONYMS, OnSynonyms)
```

continues

Listing 3.6. continued

```
    ON_BN_CLICKED(IDC_SYSTEM_TABLES, OnSystemTables)
    ON_BN_CLICKED(IDC_TABLES, OnTables)
    ON_BN_CLICKED(IDC_VIEWS, OnViews)
    //}}AFX_MSG_MAP
END_MESSAGE_MAP()


/////////////////////////////////////////////////////////////////////////////
// OdbcTabl message handlers

BOOL OdbcTabl::OnInitDialog()
{
    CDialog::OnInitDialog();

    m_TableList.SetTabStops(75);
     LoadTableList();
    return TRUE;  // Return TRUE  unless you set the focus to a control
}

void OdbcTabl::LoadTableList()
{
HSTMT     hstmt = SQL_NULL_HSTMT;
long      lReturnLength;
int       i;
SWORD     swReturn;
RETCODE    RC;
char      szQualifier[128];
char      szOwner[128];
char      szName[128];
char      szType[128];
char      szConStrOut[256];
char      szRemarks[254];

    RC = SQLAllocStmt(m_CDB->m_hdbc, &hstmt);

    if (RC != SQL_SUCCESS && RC != SQL_SUCCESS_WITH_INFO)
    {
        TRACE("SQLAllocStmt() FAILED!!!!\n");
        PrintError(SQL_NULL_HENV, m_CDB->m_hdbc, hstmt);
    }

    RC = SQLTables (hstmt,
        (unsigned char far *)"%", SQL_NTS, (unsigned char far *)"", 0,
        (unsigned char far *)"", 0, (unsigned char far *)"", 0);

    SQLFreeStmt(hstmt, SQL_CLOSE);
    SQLFreeStmt(hstmt, SQL_UNBIND);

    SQLGetInfo(m_CDB->m_hdbc, SQL_MAX_OWNER_NAME_LEN,
        &i, sizeof(int), &swReturn);


    szRemarks[0] = '\0';
    if (m_CTables.GetCheck() == 1)
    {
        strcat(szRemarks, "'TABLE'");
```

```
    }
    if (m_CSystemTables.GetCheck() == 1)
    {
        if (strlen(szRemarks) > 0)
            strcat(szRemarks, ", ");

        strcat(szRemarks, "'SYSTEM TABLE'");
    }
    if (m_CViews.GetCheck() == 1)
    {
        if (strlen(szRemarks) > 0)
            strcat(szRemarks, ", ");

        strcat(szRemarks, "'VIEW'");
    }
    if (m_CSynonyms.GetCheck() == 1)
    {
        if (strlen(szRemarks) > 0)
            strcat(szRemarks, ", ");

        strcat(szRemarks, "'SYNONYM'");
    }

    RC = SQLTables(hstmt,
        NULL, SQL_NTS,    // Table qualifier
        NULL, SQL_NTS,    // Table owner
        NULL, SQL_NTS,    // Table name
        (unsigned char far *)szRemarks, strlen(szRemarks));

    if (RC != SQL_SUCCESS && RC != SQL_SUCCESS_WITH_INFO)
    {
        PrintError(SQL_NULL_HENV, m_CDB->m_hdbc, hstmt);
    }

    SQLGetInfo(m_CDB->m_hdbc, SQL_DBMS_VER, szConStrOut,
        sizeof(szConStrOut), &swReturn);
    TRACE("%s\n", szConStrOut);

//    Now bind variables to columns!

    RC = SQLBindCol(hstmt, 1, SQL_C_CHAR,
        szQualifier, sizeof(szQualifier), &lReturnLength);
    RC = SQLBindCol(hstmt, 2, SQL_C_CHAR,
        szOwner, sizeof(szOwner), &lReturnLength);
    RC = SQLBindCol(hstmt, 3, SQL_C_CHAR,
        szName, sizeof(szName), &lReturnLength);
    RC = SQLBindCol(hstmt, 4, SQL_C_CHAR,
        szType, sizeof(szType), &lReturnLength);
    RC = SQLBindCol(hstmt, 5, SQL_C_CHAR,
        szRemarks, sizeof(szRemarks), &lReturnLength);

// Then get the table names:
    m_TableList.ResetContent();

    while(TRUE)
    {
        RC = SQLFetch(hstmt);
```

continues

Listing 3.6. continued

```
            if (RC == SQL_ERROR ¦¦ RC == SQL_SUCCESS_WITH_INFO)
            {
                TRACE("SQLFetch() FAILED!!!!\n");
                PrintError(SQL_NULL_HENV, m_CDB->m_hdbc, hstmt);
            }
            if (RC == SQL_SUCCESS ¦¦ RC == SQL_SUCCESS_WITH_INFO)
            {
//              Must set tab stops for this list to look good!
                sprintf(szRemarks, "%s\t%s", szType, szName);
                m_TableList.AddString(szRemarks);
            }
             else
            {// That's all, folks...
                break;
            }
        }

    m_TableList.SetCurSel(0);

     SQLFreeStmt(hstmt, SQL_CLOSE);
    SQLFreeStmt(hstmt, SQL_UNBIND);
    SQLFreeStmt(hstmt, SQL_DROP);
}


void OdbcTabl::OnSynonyms()
{
    // TODO: Add your control notification handler code here
    LoadTableList();
}

void OdbcTabl::OnSystemTables()
{
    // TODO: Add your control notification handler code here
    LoadTableList();
}

void OdbcTabl::OnTables()
{
    // TODO: Add your control notification handler code here
    LoadTableList();
}

void OdbcTabl::OnViews()
{
    // TODO: Add your control notification handler code here
    LoadTableList();
}

void OdbcTabl::OnOK()
{
CString       TempString;
    // TODO: Add extra validation here
    m_TableList.GetText(m_TableList.GetCurSel(), TempString);
```

```
//    Get everything after the tab...
    m_TableName    = TempString.Mid(TempString.Find('\t') + 1);


    CDialog::OnOK();
}

void    OdbcTabl::PrintError(HENV henv, HDBC hdbc, HSTMT hstmt)
{// Private, programmer's error handler. Outputs to the debugging
//      terminal and doesn't use a message box!
RETCODE RC;
char    szSqlState[256];
char    szErrorMsg[256];
SDWORD    pfNativeError;
SWORD    pcbErrorMsg;

    RC = SQLError(henv, hdbc, hstmt,
        (UCHAR FAR*)szSqlState,
        &pfNativeError,
        (UCHAR FAR*)szErrorMsg,
        sizeof(szErrorMsg),
        &pcbErrorMsg);

    TRACE("SQL ERROR:\n");
    if (RC == SQL_SUCCESS ¦¦ RC == SQL_SUCCESS_WITH_INFO)
    {
        TRACE("%s\n", szSqlState);
        TRACE("%s\n", szErrorMsg);
    }
    else
    {
        TRACE("%s\n", "SQLError() returned an error!!!");
    }
}
```

Summary

This chapter introduced you to the ODBC SQL...() functions and provided a reference section. A set of sample routines provided practical examples of how to use the SQL...() functions and also showed examples of how to use the MFC database objects that were covered in Chapter 2.

This chapter completes Part I of this book. You will create more sophisticated examples of decision support and transaction processing applications when you reach Part III, "An Introduction to Database Front-End Design," and Part IV, "Advanced Programming with Visual C++." The next chapter, "Optimizing the Design of Relational Databases," introduces you to database design methodology and shows you some of the CASE design tools that are available for Access and client-server databases.

II

Database and Query Design Concepts

4

Optimizing the Design of Relational Databases

This chapter describes the theoretical and practical sides of relational database management systems (RDBMSs), including how to design a relational database system or a set of relational tables to achieve optimum performance with Visual C++ 4.0 database applications. This book distinguishes between a client-server RDBMS such as Microsoft SQL Server 6.0, a desktop RDBMS such as Access 2.0/95, and a set of relational tables such as a database created from a collection of dBASE table and index files. This chapter also covers indexing methods that improve the speed of searching for a specific record in a table and increase the performance when two or more related tables are joined.

This book is aimed at Visual C++ programmers who want to extend their programming skills to 32-bit Windows database applications and at database developers who are making the transition from the character-based world of DOS to Windows' graphical environment.

Visual C++ 4.0 is an ideal tool for use with client-server RDBMSs (also called SQL databases), so a substantial part of this book is devoted to creating front ends for displaying and updating data in networked client-server environments. This chapter is intended for readers with limited database design experience. If you're an accomplished relational database developer, you might want to skip this chapter for now and proceed to Chapter 5, "Learning Structured Query Language."

Classifying Database Systems

The history of digital computers is inexorably tied to the concurrent development of database methodology. It's probably a safe estimate that at least 80 percent of worldwide computer resources and programming activity are devoted to database applications.

The first military and commercial applications for tabulating machines and digital computers were devoted to retrieving, calculating, and reporting on data stored in the form of punched cards. For example, a deck of cards containing the names and addresses of customers constituted a database table. Another deck of punched cards, containing information on the invoices issued to customers for a given period, represented another table. Using a collating device, you could shuffle the two decks so that a new deck was created wherein each customer card was followed by the cards detailing the orders for that customer. You could then use the cards to print a report in which the customer's card provided a report subheading and all of the orders for that customer were printed under the subheading. Cards from other decks could be collated into the two-level deck to create more detailed reports. Early tabulating machines could create customer subtotals and order grand totals. Figure 4.1 shows the effect of collating two decks of cards to print a report of invoices.

The obvious problem with the punched-card collation technique was that every time you wanted a different report, you had to separate (decollate) the cards back into their original decks, then manually run a different set of collation processes. Replacing tabulating machines with computers equipped with nine-track magnetic tape drives solved many of the problems associated with moving decks of cards back and forth between collators. You transferred the data from a sorted deck of cards to a magnetic tape and then mounted the tapes you needed on tape drives and let the computer combine (merge) the data from the "table" tapes onto a new tape whose data was identical to that of a collated deck of punched cards. Now you could print a report from the data on the newly recorded tape.

FIGURE 4.1.

Collating punched cards for customers and invoices in order to print a report.

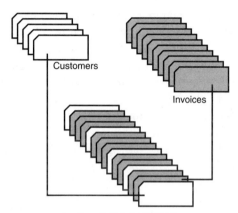

Customers

Invoices

Invoices Collated with Customers

Punched-card decks and magnetic tapes are sequential devices. Finding a particular record requires that you begin searching from the first card of the deck or the first record of a tape and read each card or record until you find a match (or determine that no matching record exists). When high-capacity random-access data storage devices (such as disk drives) became available, searching for a particular record became much faster, even if you had to read each record in the table. To speed the process, sorting and indexing methods were developed to minimize the number of records that the computer had to read until it found the matching data. The seminal work in this field was Volume 3 of Stanford University Professor Donald E. Knuth's *Art of Computer Programming* series, *Sorting and Searching* (Addison-Wesley, 1973). It's still in print today.

Advances in computer technology after the advent of the random-access disk drive have occurred primarily in the form of architectural, rather than conceptual, changes to both hardware and software. The pace of improvement in the operating speed and the rate of cost reduction of computer hardware has far out-distanced the rate of progress in software engineering, especially in database design and programming methodology. You can substantially improve the performance of an ill-conceived and poorly implemented database design simply by acquiring a faster computer. The price of a new computer is usually much less than the cost of re-engineering the organization's legacy database structure. Ultimately, however, poor database designs and implementations result in a severe case of organizational inefficiency. One of the purposes of this chapter is to provide a sufficient background in database design to make sure that the database structures you create don't fall into this category.

The following sections discuss elementary database terminology in the object-oriented language to which you were introduced in Chapter 2, "Understanding MFC's ODBC Database Classes." Then you will learn about the different types of computer database structures used today.

Database Terminology

Whatever data storage and retrieval mechanism is used, the fundamental element of a database is a *table*. A table is a database object that consists of a collection of *rows* (*records*) that have an identical collection of properties. The values associated with the properties of a table appear in *columns* (*fields*). Row-column (spreadsheet) terminology is most commonly used in databases that employ SQL statements to manipulate table data; desktop databases commonly use record-field terminology. This book uses the terms *record* and *field* when referring to persistent database objects (Tabledef objects) and *row* and *column* when referring to virtual tables (Recordset objects) created from Tabledef and Querydef objects. The distinction between the two forms of terminology, however, isn't very significant. Figure 4.2 illustrates the generalized structure of a database table.

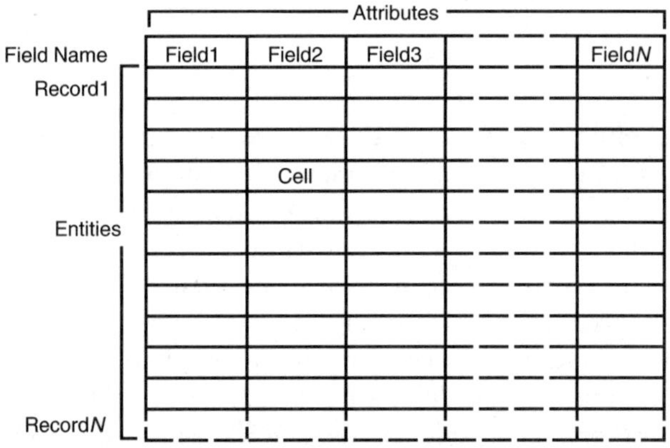

FIGURE 4.2.

The generalized structure of a database table.

> **NOTE**
>
> The object hierarchy of the Microsoft Jet 1.x database engine supplied with Visual Basic 3.0 and Access 1.x included a Table object, a member of the Tables collection. The Table object and Tables collections don't appear in the Microsoft DAO 3.0 Object library or the Microsoft DAO 2.5/3.0 Compatibility library. Visual C++ 4.0 supports operations on Table objects, such as the OpenTable method, for backward compatibility with Jet 1.x code.

The following list describes the most important properties of database table objects. These property descriptions and rules apply to tables of conventional databases that use only fundamental data types: character strings and numerical values.

- A *record* is a representation of a real-world object, such as a person, a firm, an invoice, or one side of a transaction involving money. A record of a table is the equivalent of one punched card in a deck. In formal database terminology, a row or record is an *entity*. Synonyms for *entity* include *data entity, data object, data instance,* and *instance.* Tables are the *collection* (set) of all entities of a single entity class; statisticians call a table a *homogeneous universe.*

- A *field* describes one of the characteristics of the objects represented by records. A field corresponds to a column of spreadsheets.

- The intersection between a row and a column is called an *attribute* and represents the value of a significant property of a real-world object. Attributes are also called *cells* and *data cells*—terms derived from spreadsheet applications. All the attributes contained in a single column of a table are called an *attribute class.*

- The fundamental rule of all table objects is that each field is devoted to one and only one property. (This rule is implied by the terms *attribute* and *attribute class.*) Attribute values are said to be *atomic,* used here as a synonym for *indivisible.* Each field is assigned a field name that is unique within the table. A Name field that contains entries such as "Dr. John R. Jones, Jr." isn't atomic; the field actually consists of five attributes: title, first name, middle initial, last name, and suffix. You can sacrifice the atomicity of fields to a limited degree without incurring serious problems. It's common practice to combine first name and middle initial, and sometimes the suffix, into a single field.

- It's desirable, but not essential, for each record in a table to have a set of attributes by which you can uniquely distinguish one record in the table from any other record. This set is called the *entity identifier* or *identifier.* In some cases, such as tables that contain the line items of invoices, records need not have a unique identifier. It's good database design practice, however, to provide such an identifier, even if you have to add an item number attribute class to establish the uniqueness.

- The fields that include the identifier attributes are called the *primary key* or *primary key fields* of the table. By definition, the set of attribute values that make up the primary key must be unique for each record. Records in related tables are joined by values of the primary key in one table and by equal values in the primary key or the foreign keys of the other table. A *foreign key* is one or more attributes that don't constitute the primary key of the table. These attributes connect the record with another record in the same table or a different table.

■ Tables that contain records identifying objects that are inherently unique, such as human beings, are called *primary* or *base* tables. Each of the records of a primary table must have one or more attributes that uniquely identify the entity. Theoretically, all U.S. citizens (except newborns) have a unique Social Security number that is used for identification purposes. Thus, an employee table in the U.S. should be able to use a single attribute—Social Security number—to serve as an entity identifier. A duplicate Social Security number usually indicates either a data entry error or a counterfeit Social Security card.

■ Tables are logical constructs; that is, they don't need to be stored on a disk drive in tabular format. Traditional desktop database managers, such as dBASE and Paradox, have a file structure that duplicates the appearance of the table. However, most mainframe and client-server database management systems store many tables (and even more than one database) within a single database file. Microsoft Access 1.0 was the first widely accepted desktop RDBMS to store all the tables that constitute a single database in one Jet .MDB file. There is no easily discernible relationship between the physical and logical structures of tables of mainframe, client-server, and Jet database types.

■ dBASE II introduced the concept of a *record number* to the world of PC databases. The record number, returned by xBase's RECNO() function, is an artificial construct that refers to the relative physical position (called the *offset*) of a record in a table file. Record numbers change when you physically reorder (sort) the table file. Record number isn't an attribute of a table unless you create a field and add record number values (often called a *record ID* field). Record numbers that appear in Access 95's equivalent of the Data control (navigation buttons) are generated by Access, not by the Jet database engine.

> **NOTE**
>
> Online help defines a base table as "a table in a Microsoft Jet database." This is a Jet-centric definition of base table, not the definition commonly used in RDBMS circles.

A database consists of one or more tables; if more than one table is included in a database, the entities described in the tables must be related by at least one attribute class (field) that is common to two of the tables. The formal statistical name for a database is *heterogeneous universe;* a recently coined alternative term is *universe of discourse*. This book adheres to the term *database*. Object-oriented databases (OODBs) don't conform strictly to the atomicity rules for attributes. Similarly, the OLE Object field data type of Jet databases isn't atomic, because the data in fields of the OLE Object field data type contains both the object's data and a reference to the application that created the object. The object type of the contents of Jet OLE Object fields may vary from record to record.

A *query* is a method by which you obtain access to a subset of records from one or more tables that have attribute values satisfying one or more criteria. There are a variety of ways to process queries against databases. Processing queries against databases with the Jet database engine is the subject of Chapter 5. You also can use queries to modify the data in tables. This type of query is described in Chapter 8, "Running Crosstab and Action Queries."

Flat-File Databases

The simplest database form consists of one table with records having enough columns to contain all the data you need in order to describe the entity class. The term *flat file* is derived from the fact that the database itself is two-dimensional. The number of table fields determines the database's width, and the quantity of table records specifies its height. There are no related tables in the database, so the concept of data depth, the third dimension, doesn't apply. Any database that contains only one table is, by definition, a flat-file database, if the database requires that the tables be flat. (Relational databases, for example, require flat tables.)

Flat-file databases are suitable for simple telephone and mailing lists. Windows 3.x's Cardfile is an example of a simple flat-file database designed as a telephone list. Ranges of cells, which are designated as "databases" by spreadsheet applications, also are flat files. A mailing list database, for example, has designated fields for names, addresses, and telephone numbers. Data files used in Microsoft Word's print merge operations constitute flat-file databases.

You run into problems with flat-file databases when you attempt to expand the use of a mailing list database to include, for example, sales contacts. If you develop more than one sales contact at a firm, there are only two ways to add the data for the new contact:

- Add a new record with duplicate data in all fields except the contact and, perhaps, the telephone number field.
- Add new fields so that you can have more than one contact name and telephone number field per record. In this case, you must add enough contact field pairs to accommodate the maximum number of contacts you expect to add for a single firm. The added fields are called *repeating groups*.

Neither of these choices is attractive, because both choices are inefficient. Both methods can waste a considerable amount of disk space, depending on the database file structure you use. Adding extra records duplicates data, and adding new fields results in many records that have no values (nulls) for multiple contact and telephone number fields. Adding new fields causes trouble when you want to print reports. It's especially difficult to format printed reports that have repeating groups.

Regardless of the deficiencies of flat-file databases, many of the early mainframe computers offered only flat-file database structures. All spreadsheet applications offer "database" cell ranges that you can sort using a variety of methods. Although spreadsheet "databases" appear to be flat, this is seldom truly the case. One of the particular problems with spreadsheet databases is that the spreadsheet data model naturally leads to inconsistencies in attribute values and repeating groups. Time-series data contained in worksheets is a classic example of a repeating group. The section "Organizing Entity Classes" shows you how to deal with inconsistent entity classes that occur in worksheet "databases," and the section "Normalizing Table Data" describes how to eliminate repeating groups.

The Network and Hierarchical Database Models

The inability of flat-file databases to efficiently deal with data that involved repeating groups of data led to the development of a variety of different database structures (called *models*) for mainframe computers. The first standardized and widely accepted model for mainframe databases was the *network model,* developed by the Committee for Data System Languages (CODASYL), which also developed Common Business-Oriented Language (COBOL) to write applications that manipulate the data in CODASYL network databases. Although the CODASYL database model has its drawbacks, an extraordinary number of mainframe CODASYL databases remain in use today. There are billions of lines of COBOL code in everyday use in North America.

CODASYL databases substitute the term *record type* for *table,* but the characteristics of a CODASYL record type are fundamentally no different from the properties of a table. CODASYL record types contain *pointers* to records of other record types. A pointer is a value that specifies the location of a record in a file or in memory. For example, a customer record contains a pointer to an invoice for the customer, which in turn contains a pointer to another invoice record for the customer, and so on. The general term used to describe pointer-based record types is *linked list;* the pointers link the records into an organized structure called a *network.* Network databases offer excellent performance when you're seeking a set of records that pertain to a specific object, because the relations between records (pointers) are a permanent part of the database. However, the speed of network databases degrades when you want to browse the database for records that match specific criteria, such as all customers in California who purchased more than $5,000 worth of product "A" in August 1995.

The problem with CODASYL databases is that database applications (primarily COBOL programs) need to update the data values and the pointers of records that have been added, deleted, or edited. The need to sequentially update both data and pointers adds a great deal of complexity to transaction-processing applications for CODASYL databases.

IBM developed the *hierarchical model* for its IMS mainframe database product line, which uses the DL/1 language. The hierarchical model deals with repeating groups by using a data structure that resembles an upside-down tree: Data in primary records constitutes the branches, and data in repeating groups makes up the leaves. The advantage of the hierarchical model is that the methods required to find related records are simpler than the techniques needed by the network model. As with the CODASYL model, a large number of hierarchical databases are running on mainframe computers today.

The Relational Database Model

The *relational database model* revolutionized the database world and allowed PCs to replace expensive minicomputers and mainframes for many database applications. The relational database model was developed in 1970 by Dr. E. F. Codd of IBM's San Jose Research Laboratories. The primary advantage of the relational model is that there is no need to mix pointers and data in tables. Instead, records are linked by *relations* between attribute values. A relation consists of a linkage between records in two tables that have identical attribute values. Figure 4.3 illustrates relations between attribute values of relational tables that constitute part of a sales database.

FIGURE 4.3.

Relationships between tables in a sales database.

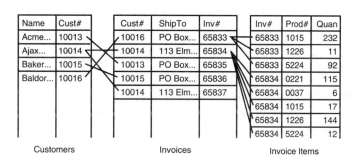

Name	Cust#
Acme...	10013
Ajax...	10014
Baker...	10015
Baldor...	10016

Customers

Cust#	ShipTo	Inv#
10016	PO Box...	65833
10014	113 Elm...	65834
10013	PO Box...	65835
10015	PO Box...	65836
10014	113 Elm...	65837

Invoices

Inv#	Prod#	Quan
65833	1015	232
65833	1226	11
65833	5224	92
65834	0221	115
65834	0037	6
65834	1015	17
65834	1226	144
65834	5224	12

Invoice Items

Because relational tables don't contain pointers, the data in relational tables is independent of the methods used by the database management system to manipulate the records. A relational database management system is an executable application that can store data in and retrieve data from sets of related tables in a database. The RDBMS creates transitory *virtual pointers* to records of relational tables in memory. Virtual pointers appear when they are needed to relate (*join*) tables and are disposed of when the database application no longer requires the relation. The "joins" between tables are shown in Figure 4.3. Joins are created between primary key fields and foreign key fields of relational tables. The primary and foreign key fields of the tables in Figure 4.3 are listed in Table 4.1.

Table 4.1. The primary and foreign keys of the tables shown in Figure 4.3.

Table	Primary Key	Foreign Key
Customers	Cust#	None
Invoices	Inv#	Cust#
Invoice Items	Inv# and Prod#	Inv#

Relational databases require duplicate data among tables but don't permit duplication of data within tables. You must duplicate the values of the primary key of one table as the foreign key of dependent tables. A *dependent table* requires a relationship with another table to identify its entities fully. Dependent tables often are called *secondary* or *related tables*. For example, the

Invoices table is dependent on the Customers table to supply the real-world name and address of the customer represented by values in the Cust# field. Similarly, the Invoice Items table is dependent on the Invoices table to identify the real-world object, in this case an invoice, to which records are related.

Three types of relations are defined by the relational database models:

■ *One-to-one* relations require that one and only one record in a dependent table relate to a record in a primary table. One-to-one relations are relatively uncommon in relational databases.

■ *One-to-many* relations let more than one dependent table relate to a record in a primary table. The term *many-to-one* is also used to describe one-to-many relations. One-to-many relations constitute the relational database model's answer to the repeating-groups problem. Repeating groups are converted to individual records in the table on the "many" side of the relation. One-to-many relations are the most common kind of relations.

■ *Many-to-many* relations aren't true relations, because many-to-many relations between two tables require an intervening table, called a *relation table,* to hold the values of the foreign keys. (Relational-database theory only defines relations between two tables.) If Figure 4.3 had included a Products table to describe the products represented by the Prod# field of the Invoice Items table, the Invoice Items table would serve as a relation table between the Invoices and Products tables. Some relation tables include only foreign key fields.

TIP

One situation in which a one-to-one relationship is useful is for an employees table in which the employees' names, addresses, and telephone numbers need to be available to many database users, but information about salaries, benefits, and other personal information needs to be restricted on a need-to-know basis. Databases such as Jet don't provide column-level permissions, so you create a one-to-one relationship between the table that contains the nonconfidential data and the one that contains confidential information. Then, you grant read-only permission to everyone (the users group) for the nonconfidential table and grant permission to only a limited number of users for the confidential table.

The proper definition of the relations between entity classes and the correct designation of primary and foreign keys constitute the foundation of effective relational database design methods. The relational database model is built on formal mathematical concepts embedded in relational algebra. Fortunately, you don't need to be a mathematician to design a relational database structure. A set of five rules, discussed in the section "Normalizing Table Data," defines the process of creating tables that conform to the relational model.

Types of Relational Database Managers

The preceding description of the relational database model made the important point that the properties of (such as the data in) a relational table object are independent of the methods used to manipulate the data. This means that you can use any relational database management application to process the data contained in a set of relational tables. For example, you can export the data in the tables of an IBM DB2 mainframe database as a set of text files that preserve the tables' structure. You can then import the text files into tables created by another database management system. Alternatively, you can use Jet, an ODBC driver for DB2, and a network gateway to the DB2 database to access the data directly. The independence of data and implementation in relational databases also lets you attach tables from one database type to another. You can join the attached tables to the native tables in your Jet database without going through the export-import exercise. Thus, you can design a relational database that can be implemented with any relational database manager.

TIP

Relational database managers differ in the types of data that you can store in tables and in how you name the fields of tables. Many RDBMSs, such as SQL Server, include the `long varbinary` field data type, which lets you store image data in tables; others, including the most commonly used versions of IBM's DB2, don't support `long varbinary` fields or their equivalent. You can embed spaces and other punctuation symbols in Jet table and field names, but you can't in most other RDBMS tables. If you're designing a database that may be ported from the original RDBMS to another relational database implementation, make sure you use only the fundamental field data types and conform to the table- and field-naming conventions of the least versatile of the RDBMSs.

There are, to be sure, substantial differences in how relational database systems are implemented. These differences are often overlooked by people new to database management or people converting from a mainframe database system to a desktop database manager. The following sections discuss how mainframe, minicomputer, and client-server databases differ from traditional desktop database managers.

Relational SQL Database Management Systems

Full-featured client-server relational database management systems separate the database management application (server or back end) from the individual (client) applications that display, print, and update the information in the database. Client-server RDBMSs, such as Microsoft SQL Server 6.0, run as a process on the server computer. Most client-server systems in use today run under one or more flavors of the UNIX operating system, but Windows NT 3.5+ rapidly is gaining ground on UNIX as an application server operating system. The client-server RDBMS is responsible for the following activities:

- Creating new databases and one or more files to contain the databases. (Several databases may reside in a single fixed-disk file.)

- Implementing database security to prevent unauthorized people from gaining access to the database and the information it contains.

- Maintaining a catalog of the objects in the database, including information on the owner (creator) of the database and the tables it contains.

- Generating a log of all modifications made to the database so that the database can be reconstructed from a backup copy combined with the information contained in the log (in the event of a hardware failure).

- Usually preserving referential integrity, maintaining consistency, and enforcing domain integrity rules to prevent corruption of the data contained in the tables. Most client-server RDBMSs use preprogrammed triggers that create an error when an application attempts to execute a query that violates the rules.

- Managing concurrency issues so that multiple users can access the data without encountering significant delays in displaying or updating data.

- Interpreting queries transmitted to the database by user applications and returning or updating records that correspond to the criteria embedded in the query statement. Virtually all client-server RDBMSs use statements written in SQL to process queries—thus the generic name "SQL RDBMS."

- Often executing *stored procedures,* which are precompiled queries that you execute by name in an SQL statement. Stored procedures speed the execution of commonly used queries by eliminating the necessity of the server to optimize and compile the query.

Separate database applications (front ends) are responsible for creating the query statements sent to the database management system and for processing the rows of data returned by the query. Front ends, as mentioned in Chapter 1, "Positioning Visual C++ in the Desktop Database Market," handle all of the data formatting, display, and report-printing chores. One of the primary advantages of using an SQL RDBMS is that the features in the preceding list, such as security and integrity, are implemented by the RDBMS itself. Thus, the code to implement these features doesn't need to be added to each different front-end application. Chapter 20, "Creating Front Ends for Client-Server Databases," describes the features of client-server RDBMSs in greater detail.

Three-Tier Client-Server Architecture and LOBjects

The stored procedures of client-server databases used to execute predefined queries and maintain database integrity use SQL, plus proprietary SQL language extensions such as Transact-SQL, used by Microsoft and Sybase SQL Server, and Sybase System 10+. SQL is a set-oriented, not procedural, programming language. Thus, dialects of SQL aren't well suited to writing programs for validating data in accordance with complex business rules. Here's an example of a complex business rule: "The current credit limit of a customer is equal to the customer's maximum credit limit, less uncontested open invoices and orders in process, unless the customer has outstanding, uncontested invoices beyond terms plus 10 days, or if the total amount of contested invoices exceeds 50 percent of the total amount of open invoices. If a pending order exceeds the customer's calculated credit limit or any customer payment behind terms plus 10 days, approval must be obtained from the credit manager before accepting the order." Such a test is quite difficult to program as an SQL stored procedure, because obtaining the credit manager's approval would be difficult for the SQL stored procedure.

Three-tier client-server architecture adds a processing layer between the front-end client and the back-end server. This processing layer, often called a *line-of-business object* (LOBject), processes requests from client applications, tests the requests for conformance with programmed business rules, and sends conforming requests to the back-end RDBMS, which updates the affected tables. Each client application using the LOBject creates its own instance of the RAO (Remote Automation Object). Figure 4.4 illustrates the architecture of a three-tier client-server application that uses Microsoft Mail 3.5 to process credit approvals (or rejections) for the scenario described in the preceding paragraph.

FIGURE 4.4.

A three-tier client-server database system for implementing a credit management LOBject.

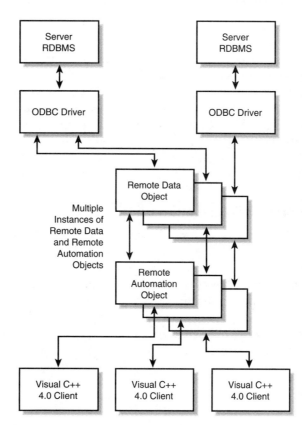

Traditional Desktop Relational Database Managers

Traditional desktop database managers, such as dBASE and Paradox, combine their database management features with the interpreter or compiler that executes the application's source code. The early versions of these products let you create quite sophisticated database applications that would run on PCs with only 256K of RAM. The constraints of available RAM in the early days of the PC required that the database management portion of the desktop DBM's code include only features that were absolutely necessary to make the product operable. Thus, products of this type, which also include early versions of FoxPro and Clipper for DOS, don't truly qualify as full-fledged relational database management systems; they are more properly termed *database file managers*. You implement the "relational" and the "management" features through the application source code you write.

The components of the dBASE and Paradox DBMs that manipulate the data contained in individual tables don't provide the built-in features of true relational database management systems listed in the preceding section. (The exception is the desktop products' capability to create a file that contains one table.) You need to write application code to enforce referential and domain integrity (however, Paradox for Windows will enforce referential integrity), and a one-DOS-file-per-table system doesn't lend itself to establishing secure databases.

The commercial success of dBASE (especially dBASE III+) and Paradox for DOS created a user base of perhaps six million people. (Borland claims there are four million dBASE users worldwide, about the same number of copies of Microsoft Access that had been sold when this book was written.) Thus, dBASE and Paradox product upgrades need to be backwardly compatible with tens of millions of .DBF and .DB files and billions of lines of dBASE and PAL code. New features, such as file and record locking for multiuser applications and the capability to use SQL to create queries, are add-ins (or tack-ons) to the original DBM. Thus, both dBASE and Paradox are currently losing market share to relatively low-cost client-server RDBMSs such as Microsoft SQL Server, Microsoft Access, a hybrid of the desktop DBM and the full-featured RDBMS, and Visual C++.

Microsoft Access: A Hybrid RDBMS

Microsoft Access is a cross between a conventional desktop DBM and a complete, full-featured RDBMS. Access uses a single database file that includes all the tables that are native to the database. Access's Jet database engine enforces referential integrity for native tables at the database level, so you don't need to write Access Basic (Access 1+) or VBA (Access 95) code to do so. Jet enforces domain integrity at the field and table level when you alter the value of a constrained field. Jet databases include system tables that catalog the objects in the database, and the database drivers handle concurrency issues.

Access lets you break the back end/front end barrier that separates RDBMSs from desktop DBMs. Application code and objects, such as forms and reports, can be included in the same database file as the tables. Microsoft used Access's ability to include both front-end and back-end components in a single .MDB file as a strong selling point. It soon became apparent to Access developers that separating application and database objects into individual .MDB files was a better design. You create a Jet database that contains only tables and attach the tables to an Access .MDB file that provides the front-end functionality. User names and passwords are stored in a separate .MDW workgroup library file. This is necessary because a Jet .MDB file contains only one database. Here again, you can put sets of unrelated tables in a single .MDB file. Jet's flavor of SQL (which is proprietary, as are most other implementations of SQL) is the native method of manipulating data in tables, not an afterthought. The Jet DLLs that implement the database functionality are independent of the MSACCESS.EXE file, which includes the code you use to create forms and reports. Jet databases are about as close as you can get to an RDBMS in a low-cost, mass-distributed software product.

Using Jet .MDB database files with Visual C++ front ends approximates the capabilities and performance of client-server RDBMSs at a substantially lower cost for both hardware and software. If you're currently using one-file-per-table DBMs, consider attaching the tables to a Jet database during the transition stage while both your new Windows front ends and your present DBM or old character-based DOS applications need to simultaneously access the tables. Once the transition to Visual C++ front ends is complete, you can import the data to a Jet database and take full advantage of the additional features that .MDB files offer. If you outgrow the Jet database structure, it's a quick and easy port to SQL Server 6.0 for Windows NT 3.5 using the Microsoft SQL Server ODBC driver.

> **NOTE**
>
> You no longer need a copy of Access in order to take advantage of Access's built-in enforcement of referential integrity and the security features of Jet databases. Visual C++ 4.0 and the Jet 3.0 Data Access Object now provide programmatic implementation of referential integrity and security. The Jet database engine and the 32-bit Jet ODBC 2.0 driver now support the SQL FOREIGN KEY and REFERENCES reserved words to define relationships during table creation. However, don't yet implement the SQL-92 CHECK reserved word, which lets you enforce domain integrity with ranges or lists of values that constrain attribute values. If you're seriously into database development with Jet 3.0 databases, purchasing a copy of Access for Windows 95 (sometimes called Access 7 or Access 95) quickly repays your investment, because Access lets you establish relationships in a graphic relationships window, supplies a simple method of adding field-level and table-level constraints, provides a graphic query-by-design window, and generates Jet SQL statements for you.

Modeling Data

The first step in designing a relational (or any other) database is to determine what objects need to be represented by database entities and what properties of each of these objects require inclusion as attribute classes. The process of identifying the tables required in the database and the fields that each table needs is called *data modeling*. You can take two approaches when data modeling:

■ *Application-oriented* design techniques start with a description of the type of application(s) required by the potential users of the database. From the description of the application, you design a database that provides the necessary data. This is called the *bottom-up* approach, because applications are ordinarily at the bottom of the database hierarchy.

■ *Subject-oriented* design methodology begins by defining the objects that relate to the subject matter of the database as a whole. This approach is called *top-down* database design. The content of the database determines what information front-end applications can present to the user.

Even though application-oriented design might let you quickly create an *ad hoc* database structure and the applications to accomplish a specific goal, bottom-up design is seldom a satisfactory long-term solution to an organization's information needs. It's common to find several application-oriented databases within an organization that have duplicate data, such as independent customer lists. When the firm acquires a new customer, each of the customer tables needs to be updated. This is an inefficient and error-prone process.

Subject-oriented database design is a far more satisfactory method. You might want to divide the design process into department-level or workgroup-related databases, such as those in the following list:

■ A *sales* database that has tables that are based on customer, order and line item, invoice and line item, and product entity classes.

■ A *production* database with tables for parts, suppliers, bills of material, and cost accounting information. The product and invoice tables of the sales department's database would be attached to the production database.

■ A *personnel* database with tables for employees, payroll data, benefits, training, and other subjects relating to human-resources management. The production and sales databases would attach to the employees table—production for the purposes of cost accounting purposes, and sales for commissions.

■ An *accounting* database with tables comprising the general ledger and subsidiary ledgers. The accounting database would attach to the majority of the tables in the other databases to obtain access to current finance-related information. Accounting databases often are broken into individual orders, accounts receivable, accounts payable, and general ledger databases.

There is no fixed set of rules to determine which shared tables should be located in what database. Often, these decisions are arbitrary or are based on political, rather than logical, reasoning. Department-level databases are especially suited for multiuser Jet databases running on peer-to-peer networks with 30 or fewer users. Each department can have its own part-time database administrator (DBA) who handles backing up the database, granting and revoking the rights of users to share individual tables in the database, and periodically compacting the database to regain the space occupied by deleted records.

Database Diagrams

Diagramming relations between tables can help you visualize database design. *Entity-relation* (E-R) *diagrams,* also called *entity-attribute-relation* (EAR) *diagrams,* are one of the most widely used methods of depicting the relations between database tables. The E-R diagramming method was introduced by Peter Chen in 1976. An E-R diagram consists of rectangles that represent the entity classes (tables). Ellipses above table rectangles show the attribute class (field) involved in the relation. Pairs of table rectangles and field ellipses are connected by parallelograms to represent the relation between the fields. Figure 4.5 is an E-R diagram for the Customers and Invoices tables of the database described in Figure 4.3 and Table 4.1. The "1" and "m" adjacent to the table rectangles indicate a one-to-many relationship between the two tables.

FIGURE 4.5.

An entity-relationship diagram showing the relationship between the Customers and Invoices tables.

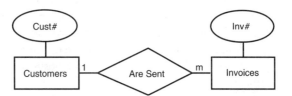

E-R diagrams describe relations by predicates. One of the dictionary definitions of the noun "predicate" is "a term designating a property or relation." If you remember parsing sentences in English class, you'll observe that "Customers" is the subject, "Are Sent" is the predicate, and "Invoices" is the predicate object of a complete sentence. E-R diagrams can describe virtually any type of allowable relation between two tables if you add more symbols to the basic diagram shown in Figure 4.5. A large number of E-R diagrams are required to define relationships between the numerous entities in enterprise-wide databases.

Using Modeling Tools for Database Design

Designing databases to accommodate the information requirements of an entire firm is a major undertaking. Thus, computer-aided software engineering (CASE) tools often are used to design complex database systems. CASE tools for database design usually include the following capabilities:

- Business model generation: The first step in the use of a high-end CASE tool is to create an operational model of an enterprise, which consists of defining virtually every activity involved in operating the organization. Accurately modeling the operations of a large firm as they relate to information requirements is an extraordinarily difficult and time-consuming process.

- Schema development: A database schema is a diagram that describes the entire information system pictorially, usually with less detail than that offered by E-R diagrams. The schema for a large information system with a multiplicity of databases might cover an entire wall of a large office or conference room.

- Relation diagramming: Some CASE tools support several methods of diagramming relations between tables. Most, but not all, CASE tools support E-R diagrams, as well as other pictorial methods, such as Bachman diagrams.

- Data dictionary development: A data dictionary is a full description of each table in the database and each field of every table. Other properties of tables and fields, such as primary keys, foreign keys, indexes, field data types, and constraints on field values, are included. Creating data dictionaries is one of the subjects of Chapter 22, "Documenting Your Database Applications."

- Repository creation: A repository is a database that is part of the CASE tool. It contains all the details of the structure and composition of the database. Data in the repository is used to create schema, relation diagrams, and data dictionaries. The repository is also responsible for maintaining version control when you change the database's design. When this book was written, Microsoft and Texas Instruments had joined forces to develop an object-oriented repository for 32-bit Windows database development.

- Database generation: After you've designed the database, the CASE tool creates the SQL Data Definition Language (DDL) statements necessary to create the database and its tables. You then send the statements to the RDBMS, which builds the database for you.

- Data flow diagramming: Some database CASE tools include the capability to create data flow diagrams that describe how data is added to tables and how tables are updated. However, data flow diagrams are application-related, not database-design-related. Thus, data flow diagramming capability is a prerequisite for qualification as a CASE database tool.

Mainframe database developers have a variety of CASE tools from which to choose. Several CASE tools serve the client-server market, such as Popkin Software's Data Architect. Developers using desktop DBMs haven't been so fortunate. No commercial CASE tools with the basic features in the preceding list were available for xBase and Paradox developers at the time this book was written.

Database modeling tools are a simplified version of CASE tools for information systems development. Modeling tools omit the business modeling aspects of CASE tools but implement at least the majority of the features described in the preceding list. An example of a database modeling tool designed specifically for Jet databases is Asymetrix Inc.'s InfoModeler. InfoModeler is a full-fledged database design system that you can use to create Jet databases from structured English statements that define entity and attribute classes. InfoModeler is described more fully in Chapter 22.

Rules for Relational Database Design

If you use a modeling tool to create your database structure, the modeling tool automatically creates tables that comply with the basic rules of relational database design. However, database developers often are faced with the task of importing or using existing data that isn't in a format suitable for a relational database. It's quite common for database developers to be faced with the task of transforming data contained in spreadsheet "databases" to tables of a relational database. Another scenario is the conversion of a poorly designed, dysfunctional database or a CODASYL network database that contains repeating groups into proper relational structure. (COBOL permits the use of the *GroupName* OCCURS *Several* TIMES statement to create repeating groups in network databases.)

The following sections describe the methods you use to transform nonrelational data to fully relational form.

Organizing Entity Classes

The section "Flat-File Databases" noted that the worksheet data model often contains inconsistent entities in rows. The stock prices example, shown in Figure 4.6, shows an Excel worksheet whose structure violates every rule applicable to relational database tables except attribute atomicity. STOCKS is a worksheet that lists the New York Stock Exchange's (NYSE) closing, high, and low price for shares and the sales volume of 25 stocks for a five-day period. Rows contain different entities, and columns B through F are repeating groups. The Stocks5.xls workbook in Excel 5.0/7.0 format, which is included on the CD-ROM that comes with this book, is used in the following examples. You'll find Stocks5.xls in the CHAPTR04 folder on the CD that comes with this book.

You need to separate the entity classes according to the object each entity class represents. The four entity classes of the STOCKS worksheet of the Stocks5.xls workbook are the closing price, the highest transaction price, the lowest transaction price, and the trading volume of a particular stock on a given day. To separate the entity classes, you need to add a column so that the stock is identified by its abbreviation in each row. You can identify the data entities by their classes—Close, High, Low, and Volume—plus the abbreviation for the stock, which is added to the new column with a simple recorded Excel VBA macro. Then, you sort the data with the

Entity and Key columns. The result of this process appears as shown for the Stocks1 worksheet, shown in Figure 4.7.

FIGURE 4.6.

A worksheet whose structure is the antithesis of proper database table design.

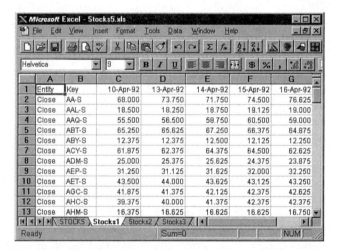

FIGURE 4.7.

The STOCKS worksheet with entities sorted by entity class.

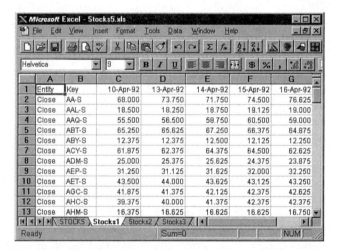

NOTE

The dates column represents a mixed entity type (three prices in dollars and the volume in shares), but each entity is now identified by its type. Thus, you can divide the entities into separate tables at any point in the transformation process.

Now you have a table that contains entities with consistent attribute values, because you moved the inconsistent stock name abbreviation to its own attribute class, Key, and replaced the stock abbreviation in the Entity column A to a value consistent with the Entity attribute class Close. However, the repeating-groups problem remains.

> **NOTE**
>
> This chapter uses manual worksheet methods of manipulating tabular data because worksheet techniques such as selecting, cutting, and pasting groups of cells represent the easiest and fastest way of changing the structure of tabular data. If you need to transform a large amount of worksheet data into relational tables, you should use Visual C++ OLE Automation methods to automate the transformation process.

Normalizing Table Data

The process of transforming existing data into relational form is called *normalization*. Normalization of data is based on the assumption that you've organized your data into a tabular structure wherein the tables contain only a single entity class. The objectives of normalization of data include the following:

- Eliminating duplicated information contained in tables
- Accommodating future changes to the structure of tables
- Minimizing the impact of changes to database structure on the front-end applications that process the data

The following sections describe the five steps that constitute full normalization of relational tables. In most cases, you can halt the normalization process at third normal form, or model. Many developers bypass fourth and fifth normal forms because these normalization rules appear arcane and inapplicable to everyday database design.

First Normal Form

First normal form requires that tables be flat and contain no repeating groups. A data cell of a flat table may contain only one atomic (indivisible) data value. If your imported data contains multiple data items in a single field, you need to add one or more new fields to contain each data item and then move the multiple data items into the new field.

The Northwind.mdb sample database included with Access 95 has a Customers table whose Address field contains data that violates first normal form—some cells contain a two-line address. Figure 4.8 shows the Customers table of Northwind.mdb (which was NWIND.MDB in earlier versions of Access) in datasheet mode. The multiline addresses for Hungry Coyote Import Store and Island Trading violate the atomicity rule. Thus, you need another field, such as Location, to contain the second line of two-line entries in the Address field. For parcel delivery services such as Federal Express, you need the physical address in the Location field for firms that use post office boxes to receive their mail.

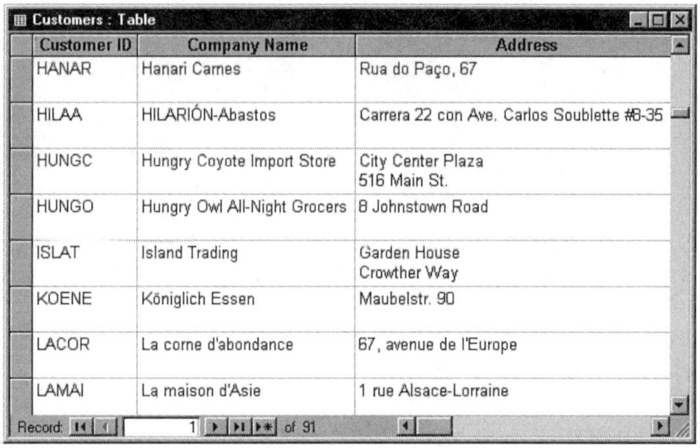

FIGURE 4.8.

First normal form violations in the Customers table of Access 95's Northwind.mdb sample database.

Customer ID	Company Name	Address
HANAR	Hanari Carnes	Rua do Paço, 67
HILAA	HILARIÓN-Abastos	Carrera 22 con Ave. Carlos Soublette #8-35
HUNGC	Hungry Coyote Import Store	City Center Plaza 516 Main St.
HUNGO	Hungry Owl All-Night Grocers	8 Johnstown Road
ISLAT	Island Trading	Garden House Crowther Way
KOENE	Königlich Essen	Maubelstr. 90
LACOR	La corne d'abondance	67, avenue de l'Europe
LAMAI	La maison d'Asie	1 rue Alsace-Lorraine

Record: 1 of 91

NOTE

If you're an xBase or Paradox developer, you might think that adding a field to contain the physical location portion of the address causes unwarranted expansion of the size of the Customers table. This isn't the case with Jet tables, because Jet databases use variable-length fields for the Text field data type. If an entry is missing in the Location field for a customer, the field contains only the Null value in databases that support Null values. The size issue is applicable to fixed-width xBase and Paradox table fields, because you must provide enough width to accommodate both lines of the address, whether one or two fields are used to contain the address data. Jet tables use variable-length fields for Text entries. An alternative to an additional Location field is to create a separate table for location data that has an optional one-to-one relation with the Customers table. This is a less efficient process than accepting Null or blank values in records that don't have Location values.

Eliminating repeating groups is often a tougher process when you're transforming worksheet data. Four of the five columns of stock price data shown in Figure 4.7 are repeating groups. The quick and dirty method of eliminating repeating groups is a series of copy, cut, paste, and fill operations. You add another column to specify the date for each entry. Then you cut and paste the cells for the four repeating groups into the column renamed from the beginning date of the series to PriceVolume. The final step is to sort the data on the Entity, Key, and Date fields. A portion of the resulting worksheet (Stocks2) appears in Figure 4.9. Instead of 101 rows for the 25 stocks, you now have 501 rows and what appears to be a large amount of duplicated data. However, your data is now in first normal form.

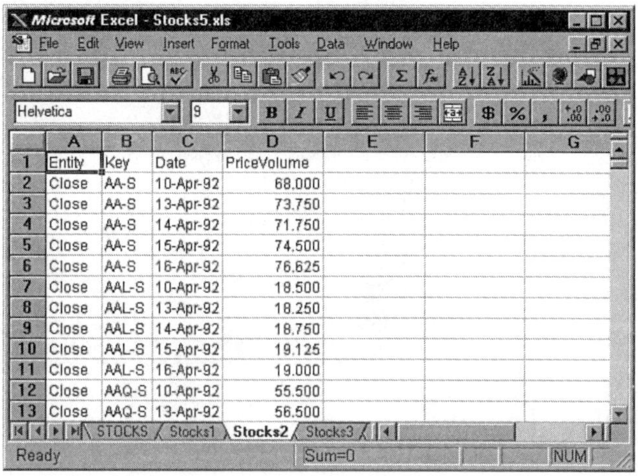

FIGURE 4.9.

The STOCKS worksheet transformed to first normal form in the Stocks2 worksheet.

Second Normal Form

Second normal form requires that all data in nonkey fields of a table be fully dependent on the primary key and on each element (field) of the primary key when the primary key is a composite primary key. "Fully dependent on" means the same thing as "uniquely identified by." It's clear from examining the data shown in Figure 4.9 that the only nonkey column of Stocks2 is PriceVolume. The Entity, Key, and Date fields are members of the composite primary key. The sorting process used in the preceding section proves this point.

There is a controversy among database designers as to whether objects that have a common attribute class, such as price, should be combined into a single table with an identifier to indicate the type of price, such as List, Distributor, or OEM for products—or in this case, Close, High, and Low transaction prices for the day. This process is called *subclassing* an entity. There's no argument, however, that the volume data deserves its own worksheet, at least for now, so you cut the volume data from Stocks2 and paste it to a new worksheet called Volume. You can delete the Entity column from the Volume sheet, because the name of the sheet now specifies the entity class.

The data in the volume sheet, with field names added, appears as shown in Figure 4.10. Each entity now is uniquely identified by the two-part composite primary key comprising the Key and Date fields. You can import the data from the Volume sheet into a table from any application that supports importing Excel 5.0/7.0 tables contained in a workbook, such as Access 95. Both the Stocks2 and Volume worksheets contain data in second normal form.

FIGURE 4.10.

The Volume worksheet in second normal form.

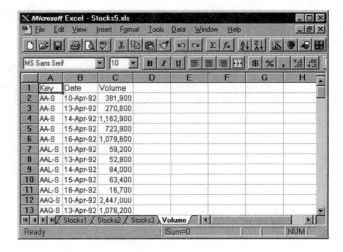

Third Normal Form

Third normal form requires that all nonkey fields of a table be dependent on the table's primary key and independent of one another. Thus, the data in a table must be normalized to second normal form in order to assure dependency on the primary key. The issue here is the dependencies of nonkey fields. A field is dependent on another field if a change in the value of one nonkey field forces a change in the value of another nonkey field.

At this point in the normalization process, you have the following choices for how to design the table(s) to hold the stock price data:

- Leave the data remaining in the Stocks2 worksheet as is and create one Prices table, using the Entity column to subclass the price entity. This method requires a three-field composite key.

- Create a Prices table with three columns, High, Low, and Close, using Key and Date as the composite primary key. You could even add the volume data to the Volume field and then have only one record per stock day.

- Create three separate prices tables, High, Low, and Close, and use Key and Date as the composite primary key. In this case, you don't subclass the entities.

Deciding on a table structure that meets third normal form is a judgment call based on the meaning of the term *independent*. Are stock prices and trading volumes truly independent of one another? Are the opening, high, and low prices dependent on the vagaries of the stock market and the whims of traders, and thus independent of one another? These questions mix the concepts of dependence and causality. Although it's likely that a higher opening price will result in a higher closing price, the causality is exogenous to the data itself. *Exogenous data* is determined by factors beyond the control of any of the users of the database. The values of the data in the table are determined by data published by the NYSE after the exchange closes for the day. Thus, the values of each of the attribute classes are independent of one another, and you can choose any of the three methods to structure your stock prices table(s).

Over-Normalizing Data and Performance Considerations

After you've determined that your data structure meets third normal form, the most important consideration is to avoid over-normalizing your data. Over-normalization is the result of applying too strict an interpretation of dependency at the third normal stage. Creating separate tables for high, low, and close prices, as well as share-trading volume, is overkill. You need to join three tables in a one-to-one relationship to display the four data values for a stock. This will be a very slow process unless you create indexes on the primary key of each table. You have four tables, so you need four indexes. Even after indexing, the performance of your stock prices database won't be as fast as a table that contains all the values. Plus, the four indexes will take up four times as much disk space as a single index on a table that contains fields for all four attributes.

The rule for third normal form should have two corollary rules:

1. Combine all entities of an object class that can be uniquely identified by the primary (composite) key and whose nonkey values either are independent of one another or are exogenous to the database and all related databases into a single table, unless the combination violates fourth normal form. Combining entities into a single table is called *integrating* data.

2. Decompose data into tables that require one-to-one relationships only when the relationship is optional or when you need to apply security measures to nonkey values and your RDBMS supports column-level permissions. *Decomposing* data means breaking a table into two or more tables without destroying the meaningfulness of the data.

Thus, you can find the answer to the question of which structure is best by considering the suggested corollary rules for third normal form. Create a new Stocks3 worksheet with fields for the high, low, and close prices, as well as for the trading volume. Then paste the appropriate cells to Stocks3 and add field names. Figure 4.11 shows the result of this process.

> **NOTE**
>
> A more elegant method of transforming worksheet data with repeating data groups to third normal form would use Excel's new Pivot feature, introduced with Excel 5.0, to perform some of the transformation operations for you. (The Pivot feature is related to the TRANSFORM and PIVOT statements of Jet SQL, which are discussed in Chapter 8.)

FIGURE 4.11.

The stock prices data in third normal form.

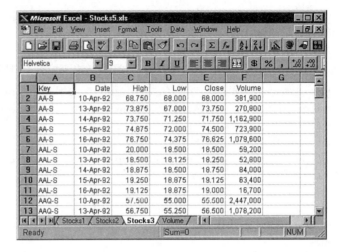

Fourth Normal Form

Fourth normal form requires that independent data entities not be stored in the same table when many-to-many relations exist between these entities. If many-to-many relations exist between data entities, the entities aren't truly independent, so such tables usually fail the third normal form test. Fourth normal form requires that you create a relation table that contains any data entities that have many-to-many relations with other tables. The stock prices data doesn't contain data in a many-to-many relation, so this data can't be used to demonstrate decomposition of tables to fourth normal form.

Fifth Normal Form

Fifth normal form requires that you be able to exactly reconstruct the original table from the new table(s) into which the original table was decomposed or transformed. Applying fifth normal form to your resulting table is a good test to make sure you didn't lose data in the process of decomposition or transformation. The Stocks3 worksheet contains every piece of data that is contained in the original STOCKS worksheet, so, with enough cutting, pasting, and sorting, you could restore it. It's often a tedious process to prove compliance with fifth normal form. Fortunately, compliance with the fifth normal form rule doesn't require that you be able to use ANSI SQL statements to reconstruct the original table.

Indexing Tables for Performance and Domain Integrity

The primary purpose of adding indexes to tables is to increase the speed of searches for specific data values. If you want to display all people named Smith in the LastName field of a table, creating an index on the LastName field results in a substantial improvement in the search performance. Without an index, the database manager must start at the beginning of the table and then test every record for the occurrence of "Smith" in the LastName field. If you create an index on the LastName field of the table, the searching operation uses the index, not the table itself, to find the first record where LastName = 'Smith'.

Joining two tables by the primary key fields of one table and the foreign key fields of another table is a special case of searching for records. When you join two tables, the search criterion becomes Table2.ForeignKey = Table1.PrimaryKey. The index must match every foreign key value to a primary key value. Without an index on both the primary key fields and the foreign key fields, joining large tables can take a very long time.

The following sections describe the indexing methods in common use with today's desktop DBMs and client-server RDBMSs, the structure of database tables and indexes, and how to choose which fields of tables to index so that you can achieve optimum application performance.

> **NOTE**
>
> An excellent discussion of indexing as it relates to the query optimizer in MS SQL Server 6.0 appears in the book *Microsoft SQL Server Unleashed* (Sams Publishing, 1996).

Table Indexing Methods

In simplified terms, an index consists of a table of pointers to records or groups of records. The records that contain pointer values, usually with an unsigned long integer data type, are organized in a binary hierarchy to reduce the number of tests that are required to find a record that matches the search criteria. Indexes traditionally refer to the three levels of the hierarchy as the root, branch, and leaf level. (Here again is the analogy to an inverted tree.) However, the number of levels in the branch hierarchy actually depends on the number of records in the indexed table. The root leads to one of two branches, and each branch leads to another branch until you reach the leaf level, which is indivisible. The leaf level of the index contains the pointers to the individual records or, in the case of Jet and most client-server databases, the pages that contain the records. The branches contain pointers to other branches in the index or to the leaves.

The exact method of indexing field values varies with the database manager you use. dBASE (.NDX and .MDX files), FoxPro (.IDX and .CDX), Clipper (.NTX), Paradox (.PX), Btrieve, and Jet indexes vary in structure. (Btrieve and Jet don't store indexes in separate files, so no file classifications are given for these two databases.) Regardless of the indexing method, indexing techniques reduce the number of records that must be searched to find the first record matching the search criteria. The most efficient indexes are those that find the first matching record with the fewest number of tests (passes) of the value of the indexed field.

Records and Data Pages

Traditional desktop DBMs store fixed-width records in individual files and store indexes on the fields of the file in one or more index files. FoxPro 2+ and dBASE IV let you store multiple indexes for a single table in a single .CDX or .MDX file, respectively. The table files used by these database managers have fixed-length records, so you can identify a record by its offset (its distance in bytes) from the beginning of the data in the file, immediately after the header portion of the file. Thus, pointers to records in these files consist of offset values.

Jet and the majority of client-server databases store indexes as special structures (not tables) within the database file. These database types support variable-length fields for Text (varchar), Memo (long varchar), OLE Object, and Binary field data types (varbinary and long varbinary). To prevent the tables from becoming full of holes when you delete records or extend the length of a variable-length field, Jet and SQL Server databases use pages to store data rather than records. Jet and SQL Server pages are 2K in length, corresponding to the standard size of a cluster on a fixed disk of moderate size formatted by Windows 95 or DOS. (As the size of fixed disk partitions grows, so does the size of the clusters. As an example, the cluster size of a 1G drive using DOS's and Windows 95's FAT file system is 32K.) Thus, if you increase the number of characters in a text field, the worst-case scenario is that the RDBMS must move 2K of data to make room for the data. If there isn't enough empty space (called slack) in the page to hold the lengthened data, the RDBMS creates a new page and moves the data in the record to the new page. Figure 4.12 illustrates the structure of the 2K data pages employed by Jet and SQL Server databases with about 1.7K of variable-length records and roughly 350 bytes of slack.

FIGURE 4.12.

A page in a Jet or SQL Server database with variable-length records.

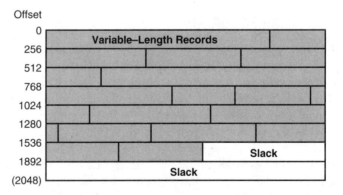

NOTE

The only drawback to the page-locking methodology is that you lock an entire page when updating a record in the page. If the record you're updating is very small, the lock can affect a number of records that you aren't editing. If you use the optimistic locking technique offered by Jet and SQL Server, the lock is likely to be transparent to other database users, especially if your front-end application is very fast. dBASE and Paradox tables use record locking, which affects only the single record being edited. Hopefully, future versions of Jet and Microsoft SQL server will support individual record locking.

Btrieve table files include data pages and index pages. Data pages consist of separate fixed-length and variable-length pages. The size of all pages within a Btrieve file must be equal. You can specify the size of the pages in the range of 512 to 4,096 bytes when you create the table. Choosing the correct page size for the type of data and the average length of records in the table can have a profound effect on the performance of Btrieve databases.

Balanced-Tree Indexes

The most common method of indexing tables is the balanced binary tree (B-tree) method, originally proposed by Russian mathematicians G. M. Adleson-Velski and E. M. Landis in 1963. Prior to the B-tree method, editing, inserting, and deleting indexed fields of records caused the index trees to become lopsided, increasing the number of passes required to find the record or page that had a matching value. The balanced B-tree method reorganizes the tree to ensure that each branch connects to two other branches or to a leaf. Thus, the B-tree index needs to be reorganized each time you add or delete a record. B-tree indexes speed decision-support queries at the expense of transaction-processing performance. In a B-tree index structure, the length of a search path to a leaf is never more than 145 percent of the optimum path.

Choosing Fields to Index

There is a truism in the database industry regarding the indexing of the fields of tables: Index only the fields you need to index in order to enhance the performance of your database front ends, and don't index any other fields. The more indexes you add to a table, the longer it takes to update entries that affect the values of indexed fields and to add a new record, which requires updating all indexes. The problem here is knowing which fields improve application performance. The first step is to determine what your options are. The following list discusses how the database types supported by the Jet database engine handle the indexing of primary key fields:

■ Jet tables for which you specify primary key fields in a `Tabledef` object have no-duplicates indexes that are automatically created by the Jet database engine on these fields. Most client-server databases that you connect with the ODBC API also have no-duplicates indexes on primary key fields, although the indexes usually aren't created automatically. A no-duplicates index prevents the addition of a record with duplicate values in the primary key fields. You can't remove the primary key index or specify "duplicates OK" without deleting the primary key designation.

■ Specify a clustered index for each table of client-server databases that support clustered indexes. (Microsoft and Sybase SQL Server offer clustered indexes.) Clustered indexes reorganize the pages of the database in the order of the clustered index. Chapter 20 discusses how to choose the field on which to add a clustered index.

■ Paradox tables also require no-duplicates indexes on the primary key fields. If FILENAME.PX index file isn't in the same directory as the corresponding FILENAME.DB file, your application can read the file but not update it. (If FILENAME.PX is missing, the Jet database engine creates a nonupdatable `Recordset` object of the `Snapshot` type, rather than the `Dynaset` type, from the table data.)

■ dBASE tables created by xBase applications don't support designating fields as primary key fields, and you can't create the equivalent of a no-duplicates index on dBASE tables. Even after you execute the xBase `SET UNIQUE ON` statement, xBase applications let you append as many records as you want with duplicate values in the indexed fields that you use in lieu of primary key fields. (The index ignores records with duplicate indexed field values.) Your application needs to test for duplicate values and prevent the addition of records that would cause duplicated indexed field values. (You need the index so that you can quickly find whether a duplicate value exists.) You can update data in dBASE table files with the Jet database engine, because no primary key can be specified.

■ Btrieve files support key fields, but they don't designate primary key fields. Btrieve doesn't provide a no-duplicates option. (You can create a no-duplicates key field by using Btrieve's auto-increment extended key field type to insert a consecutive long integer value to the records you add.) Unlike dBASE, Btrieve adds 8 bytes of data to the field to indicate the chronological order of the addition of fields with duplicate key values. Your application needs to test for existing key values to prevent duplication.

After you've determined whether you need to create a (primary) key fields index, you need to consider which other fields to index. The following list provides some suggestions that apply to all database types:

■ Use short codes to identify entities that don't have properties designed to identify the entity, such as part numbers for products. Creating indexes on long text fields, such as product names, unnecessarily increases the size of the index table, slows performance, and wastes disk space. The other side of the coin is that searches for text fields such as product names sometimes happen often.

■ Indexes based on numeric values usually have better performance than indexes on character fields. Using auto-incrementing fields (for example, Jet 3.0's AutoIncrement, formerly Counter, field data type) as a primary key field sometimes is feasible when you import existing data.

■ Index the foreign key fields that participate in joins with other tables.

■ Index the foreign key fields that your client will search most often.

■ Don't create a separate index for the indexed fields of the composite primary key. Almost all database management systems enable searches on partial key matches, so such an index would duplicate the existing primary key index.

■ Prior to Jet 2.0, you needed to use `Table` objects, not `Dynaset` or `Snapshot` objects, and the `Seek` method if you wanted to take advantage of indexes other than the primary key index in your Visual C++ 4.0 applications. When you use the `Find...` methods on Jet 2+ tables or queries, Jet uses the appropriate index (if it exists). Jet 2+ indexes use Rushmore technology (adopted from FoxPro), which provides a major improvement in indexed searches. 32-bit Jet 3.0 provides a major boost in the speed of indexing and indexed searches compared with Jet 2.0 and 2.5.

■ Avoid using the `Like "*Criteria"` statements in Jet SQL and `LIKE '%Criteria'` statements in ANSI SQL. Queries that contain these statements can't use indexes.

■ Don't try to create indexes on fields of the long data types, `long varchar` (Jet `Memo` fields) and `long varbinary` (Jet OLE object fields). Neither the Jet database engine nor client-server RDBMSs can create indexes on these field data types.

> **NOTE**
>
> The Jet database engine uses query optimization techniques to choose which indexes to use when your application processes an SQL query.

If you follow the rules in the preceding list, you probably won't go too far wrong in choosing which fields of your tables to index. If you're using Jet tables and have a copy of Microsoft Access, comparing the performance of queries with and without foreign key indexes is a simple process. Jet indexes as a whole are much smaller than dBASE and FoxPro 2+ indexes. Thus, you can relegate disk space issues to a lower priority when determining how many indexes to add to a Jet table. Chapter 15, "Designing Online Transaction-Processing Applications," compares index sizes of Jet and dBASE tables.

> **NOTE**
>
> You need at least several hundred records in order to test the effects of indexing foreign key fields on your application's performance. The more records, the better the test. If you or your client observes that the performance of your Visual C++ 4.0 front end deteriorates as the number of records in the database increases, you might have failed to add an index to an important foreign key. You won't need to change your application's code to utilize the new indexes, except where you use `Seek` operations on `Recordset` objects of the `Table` type, which you can now safely replace with `Find...`

methods on Recordset objects of the Dynaset and Snapshot types. The Jet database engine's query optimizer automatically uses the new index when the new index aids a query's performance.

Summary

This chapter introduced you to the methodology of designing efficient relational database structures, including modeling tools for Jet databases and normalizing tables that you create from existing data sources. Entire books are devoted to database design techniques, and at least one large book covers only Object Role Modeling design methods. If you're interested in the theoretical side of relational databases, including relational algebra, go to your local library and check out a copy of E. F. Codd's or Chris Date's book on the subject. Methods of indexing tables created by desktop DBMs and client-server RDBMSs received only cursory treatment here. Donald E. Knuth's *Searching and Sorting,* mentioned earlier in this chapter, provides an excellent introduction to indexing methods, despite the age of the book. The suggestions at the end of this chapter on how to optimize the indexing of tables are useful with any type of database.

The next chapter introduces you to structured query language (SQL), the third language you need to understand in order to fully utilize this book and Visual C++ 4.0 as a database front-end generator. If you're an Access developer, you're probably used to cutting and pasting SQL statements from the SQL window of query design mode into the RecordSource property of combo boxes or into your Access C++ code. Visual C++ 4.0 doesn't have a query design mode or an SQL window, so you really do need to learn SQL—specifically, the Jet dialect of ANSI SQL—to create commercial database applications with Visual C++ 4.0.

5

Learning Structured Query Language

Structured query language (SQL) is the *lingua franca* of relational database management systems. Visual C++ 4.0 and Microsoft Access both use SQL exclusively to process queries against desktop, client-server, and mainframe databases. Access includes a graphical query by example (QBE) tool—the query design mode window—to write Access SQL statements for you. You can develop quite sophisticated applications using Access without even looking at an SQL statement in Access's SQL window. Visual C++ 4.0 doesn't include a graphical QBE tool, so until some enterprising third-party developer creates a Query OLE Control, you'll need to learn Access SQL in order to create Visual C++ 4.0 applications that interact in any substantial way with databases.

NOTE

Microsoft Access without a version number refers to Access 2.0 and Access for Windows 95, version 7.0. There are no significant differences between Access SQL in these two versions of Access. Access 2.0 added a substantial number of reserved words to the SQL vocabulary of Access 1.x. SQL statements for adding tables to Access databases, plus adding fields and indexes to Access tables, are discussed in Chapter 8, "Running Crosstab and Action Queries." Microsoft calls the Visual C++ 4.0 dialect of SQL Microsoft Jet Database Engine SQL. This book uses the term Access SQL because the dialect originated in Access 1.0.

The first part of this chapter introduces you to the standardized version of SQL specified by the American National Standards Institute (ANSI), a standard known as X.3.135-1992 and called SQL-92 in this book. (When you see the terms SQL-89 and SQL-92, the reference is to ANSI SQL, not the Access variety.) ANSI SQL-92 has been accepted by the International Standards Organization (ISO), a branch of the United Nations headquartered in Geneva, and the International Electrotechnical Commission (IEC) as ISO/IEC 9075:1992, "Database Language SQL." A separate ANSI standard, X.3.168-1989, defines "Database Language Embedded SQL." Thus, SQL-92 is a thoroughly standardized language, much more so than xBase, for which no independent standards yet exist. Today's client-server RDBMSs support SQL-89 and many of SQL-92's new SQL reserved words; many RDBMSs also add their own reserved words to create proprietary SQL dialects. A knowledge of ANSI SQL is required to use SQL pass-through techniques with the Jet 3.0 database engine and to employ Remote Data Objects (RDO) and Remote Data Control (RDC). SQL pass-through is described in Chapter 20, "Creating Front Ends for Client-Server Databases."

The second part of this chapter, beginning with the section "Comparing the Access SQL Dialect and ODBC," discusses the differences between SQL-92 and Access SQL. If you're fluent in the ANSI versions of SQL, either SQL-89 or SQL-92, you'll probably want to skip to the latter part of this chapter, which deals with the flavor of SQL used by the Jet 3.0 database engine. Chapter 7, "Using the Open Database Connectivity API," describes how the Jet 3.0

database engine translates Access SQL into the format used by ODBC drivers. Although this chapter describes the general SQL syntax for queries that modify data (called *action queries* by Access and in this book) and the crosstab queries of Access SQL, examples of the use of these types of queries are described in Chapter 8.

Reviewing the Foundations of SQL

Dr. E. F. Codd's relational database model of 1970, discussed in the preceding chapter, was a theoretical description of how relational databases are designed, not how they're used. You need a database application language to create tables and specify the fields that the tables contain, establish relations between tables, and manipulate the data in the database. The first language that Dr. Codd and his associates at the IBM San Jose laboratory defined was Structured English Query Language (SEQUEL), which was designed for use with a prototype relational database that IBM called System R. The second version of SEQUEL was called SEQUEL/2. SEQUEL/2 was later renamed SQL. Technically, SQL is the name of an IBM data manipulation language, not an abbreviation for "structured query language." As you'll see later in this chapter, there are significant differences between IBM's SQL used for its DB2 mainframe and DB2/2 OS/2 databases, and ANSI SQL-92.

The sections that follow describe the differences between SQL and the procedural languages commonly used for computer programming, and how applications use SQL with desktop, client-server, and mainframe databases.

Elements of SQL Statements

This book has made extensive use of the term *query* without defining what it means. Because Visual C++ 4.0 uses SQL to process all queries, this book defines *query* as an expression in any dialect of SQL that defines an operation to be performed by a database management system. A query usually contains at least the following three elements:

- A *verb,* such as SELECT, that determines the type of operation
- A *predicate object* that specifies one or more field names of one or more table object(s), such as * to specify all of the fields of a table
- A *prepositional clause* that determines the object(s) in the database on which the verb acts, such as FROM *TableName*

The simplest SQL query that you can construct is SELECT * FROM *TableName,* which returns the entire contents of *TableName* as the query result set. Queries are classified in this book as select queries, which return data (query result sets), or action queries, which modify the data contained in a database without returning any data.

IBM's original version of SQL, implemented as SEQUEL, had relatively few reserved words and simple syntax. Over the years, new reserved words have been added to the language by publishers of database management software. Many of the reserved words in proprietary versions of SQL have found their way into the ANSI SQL standards. Vendors of SQL RDBMSs that claim adherence to the ANSI standards have the option of adding their own reserved words to the language, as long as the added reserved words don't conflict with the usage of the ANSI-specified reserved words. Transact-SQL, the language used by the Microsoft and Sybase versions of SQL Server (both of these products were originally developed from the same product), has many more reserved words than conventional ANSI SQL. Transact-SQL even includes reserved words that allow conditional execution and loops within SQL statements. (The CASE, NULLIF, and COALESCE reserved words of SQL-92 are rather primitive for conditional execution purposes.) Access SQL includes the TRANSFORM and PIVOT statements needed to create crosstab queries that, while missing from ANSI SQL, are a very useful construct. TRANSFORM and PIVOT can be accomplished using ANSI SQL, but the construction of such an ANSI SQL statement would be quite difficult.

A further discussion of the details of the syntax of SQL statements appears after the following sections, which describe the basic characteristics of the SQL language and tell you how to combine SQL and conventional 3GL source code statements.

Differences Between SQL and Procedural Computer Languages

All the dialects of SQL are fourth-generation languages (4GLs). The term *fourth-generation* derives from the following descriptions of the generations in the development of languages to control the operation of computers:

- ■ *First-generation* languages required that you program in the binary language of the computer's hardware, called *object* or *machine code*. (The computer is the object in this case.) As an example, in the early days of mini- and microcomputers, you started (booted) the computer by setting a series of switches that sent instructions directly to the computer's CPU. Once you booted the computer, you could load binary-coded instructions with a paper tape reader. 1GLs represent programming the hard way. The first computer operating systems (OS) were written directly in machine code and loaded from paper tape or punched cards.

- ■ *Second-generation* languages greatly improved the programming process by using assembly language to eliminate the necessity of setting individual bits of CPU instructions. Assembly language lets you use simple alphabetic codes—called *mnemonic* codes because they're easier to remember than binary instructions—and octal or hexadecimal values to substitute for one or more CPU instructions in the more arcane object code. Once you've written an assembly language program, you compile the assembly code into object code instructions that the CPU can execute. Microsoft's MASM is a popular assembly language compiler for Intel 80x86 CPUs. Assembly language remains widely used today when speed or direct access to the computer hardware is needed.

■ *Third-generation* languages, typified by the early versions of FORTRAN (Formula Translator) and BASIC (Beginners' All-purpose Symbolic Instruction Code), let programmers substitute simple statements, usually in a structured version of English, for assembly code. 3GLs are called *procedural* languages because the statements you write in a 3GL are procedures that the computer executes in the sequence you specify in your program's source code. Theoretically, procedural languages should be independent of the type of CPU for which you compile your source code. Few 3GL languages actually achieve the goal of being fully platform-independent; most, such as Microsoft Visual Basic and Visual C++, are designed for 80x86 CPUs. (You can, however, run Visual C++ applications on Digital Equipment's Alpha workstations and workstations that use the MIPS RISC (Reduced Instruction Set Computer) CPU using Windows NT as the operating system. In this case, the operating system, Windows NT, handles the translation of object code to differing CPUs.)

■ *Fourth-generation* languages are often called *nonprocedural* languages. The source code you write in 4GLs tells the computer the ultimate result you want, not how to achieve it. SQL is generally considered to be a 4GL language because, for example, your SQL query statements specify the data you want the database manager to send you, rather than instructions that tell the DBM how to accomplish this feat. Whether SQL is a true 4GL is subject to controversy, because the SQL statements you write are actually executed by a 3GL or, in some cases, a 2GL language that deals directly with the data stored in the database file(s) and is responsible for sending your application the data in a format that the application can understand.

Regardless of the controversy over whether generic SQL is a 4GL, you need to be aware of some other differences between SQL and conventional 3GLs. The most important of these differences are as follows:

■ SQL is a *set-oriented* language, whereas most 3GLs can be called *array-oriented* languages. SQL returns sets of data in a logical tabular format. The query-return sets are dependent on the data in the database, and you probably won't be able to predict the number of rows (data set members) that a query will return. The number of members of the data set may vary each time you execute a query and also may vary almost instantaneously in a multiuser environment. 3GLs can handle only a fixed number of tabular data elements at a time, specified by the dimensions that you assign to a two-dimensional array variable. Thus, the application needs to know how many columns and rows are contained in the result set of an SQL query so that the application can handle the data with row-by-row, column-by-column methods. Visual C++ 4.0's CRecordset object handles this transformation for you automatically.

■ SQL is a *weakly typed* language, whereas most 3GLs are *strongly typed*. You don't need to specify field data types in SQL statements; SQL queries return whatever data types have been assigned to the fields that constitute the columns of the query return set. Most compiled 3GL languages are strongly typed. COBOL, C, C++, Pascal,

Modula-2, and ADA are examples of strongly typed compiled programming languages. Strongly typed languages require that you declare the names and data types of all your variables before you assign values to the variables. If the data type of a query column doesn't correspond to the data type you defined for the receiving variable, an error (sometimes called an *impedance mismatch error*) occurs. Visual C++ is a compiled language and is strongly typed.

Consider yourself fortunate that you're using Visual C++ 4.0 to process SQL statements. You don't need to worry about how many rows a query will return or what data types occur in the query result set's columns. The CRecordset object receiving the data handles all of these details for you. With Visual C++ 4's incremental compile and incremental link, you don't need to recompile and link your entire Visual C++ application each time you change a query statement; just change the statement and rebuild your application. Visual C++ compiles and links only the functions that have been changed. The process is really quite fast.

Types of ANSI SQL

The current ANSI SQL standards recognize four different methods of executing SQL statements. The method you use depends on your application programming environment, as described in the following list:

- *Interactive SQL* lets you enter SQL statements at a command line prompt, similar to dBASE's dot prompt. As mentioned in Chapter 1, "Positioning Visual C++ in the Desktop Database Market," the use of the interactive dBASE command LIST is quite similar to the SELECT statement in interactive SQL. Mainframe and client-server RDBMSs also provide interactive SQL capability; Microsoft SQL Server provides the isql application for this purpose. Using interactive SQL is also called *direct invocation*. Interactive SQL is called a *bulk process;* if you enter a query at the SQL prompt, the result of your query appears on-screen. DBMs offer a variety of methods of providing a scrollable display of interactive query result sets.

- *Embedded SQL* lets you execute SQL statements by preceding the SQL statement with a keyword, such as EXEC SQL in C. Typically, you declare variables that you intend to use to receive data from an SQL query between EXEC SQL BEGIN DECLARE SECTION and EXEC SQL END DECLARE SECTION statements. You need a precompiler that is specific to the language and to the RDBMS to be used. The advantage of embedded SQL is that you assign attribute classes to a single variable in a one-step process. The disadvantage is that you have to deal with query-return sets on a row-by-row basis rather than the bulk process of interactive SQL.

- *Module SQL* lets you compile SQL statements separately from your 3GL source code and then link the compiled object modules into your executable program. SQL modules are similar to Visual C++ 4.0 code modules. The modules include declarations of variables and temporary tables to contain query result sets, and you can pass argument values from your 3GL to parameters of procedures declared in SQL modules. The stored procedures that execute precompiled queries on database servers have many characteristics in common with module SQL.

■ *Dynamic SQL* lets you create SQL statements whose contents you can't predict when you write the statement. (The preceding SQL types are classified as *static SQL*.) As an example of dynamic SQL, suppose you want to design a Visual C++ application that can process queries against a variety of databases. Dynamic SQL lets you send queries to the database in the form of strings. For example, you can send a query to the database and obtain detailed information from the database catalog that describes the tables and fields of tables in the database. Once you know the structure of the database, you or the user of your application can construct a custom query that adds the correct field names to the query. Visual C++'s implementation of Access SQL resembles a combination of dynamic and static SQL, although the Access database engine handles the details of reading the catalog information for you automatically when your application creates a CRecordset object from the database. Chapter 6, "The Microsoft Jet Database Engine," describes the methods you use to extract catalog information contained in Visual C++ collections.

Technically, static SQL and dynamic SQL are called methods of *binding* SQL statements to database application programs. Binding refers to how you combine or attach SQL statements to your source or object code, how you pass values to SQL statements, and how you process query result sets. A third method of binding SQL statements is the *call-level interface* (CLI). The Microsoft Open Database Connectivity (ODBC) API uses the CLI developed by the SQL Access Group (SAG), a consortium of RDBMS publishers and users. A CLI accepts SQL statements from your application in the form of strings and passes the statements directly to the server for execution. The server notifies the CLI when the data is available and then returns the data to your application. Details of the ODBC CLI are given in Chapter 7.

If you're a COBOL coder or a C/C++ programmer who is accustomed to writing embedded SQL statements, you'll need to adjust to Visual C++'s automatic creation of virtual tables when you execute a SELECT query, rather than executing CURSOR-related FETCH statements to obtain the query result rows one-by-one.

Writing ANSI SQL Statements

ANSI SQL statements have a very flexible format. Unlike all dialects of BASIC, which separate statements with newline pairs (a carriage return and a line feed), and C, C++, and Pascal, which use semicolons as statement terminators, SQL doesn't require you to separate the elements that constitute a complete SQL statement with newline pairs, semicolons, or even a space in most cases. (SQL ignores most white space, which comprises newline pairs, tabs, and extra spaces.) Thus, you can use white space to format your SQL statements to make them more readable. The examples of SQL statements in this book place groups of related identifiers and

SQL reserved words on separate lines and use indentation to identify continued lines. Here's an example of an Access SQL crosstab query statement that uses this formatting convention:

```
TRANSFORM Sum(CLng([Order Details].UnitPrice*Quantity*
    (1 - Discount)*100)/100) AS ProductAmount
    SELECT Products.ProductName, Orders.CustomerID
    FROM Orders, Products, [Order Details],
    Orders INNER JOIN [Order Details] ON Orders.OrderID =
        [Order Details].OrderID,
    Products INNER JOIN [Order Details] ON Products.ProductID =
        [Order Details].ProductID
    WHERE Year(OrderDate)=1994
    GROUP BY Products.ProductName, Orders.CustomerID
    ORDER BY Products.ProductName
    PIVOT "Qtr " & DatePart("q",OrderDate) In("Qtr 1",
        "Qtr 2","Qtr 3","Qtr 4")
```

NOTE

The square brackets surrounding the [Order Details] table name are specific to Access SQL and are used to group table or field names that contain spaces or other punctuation that is illegal in the naming rules for tables and fields of SQL RDBMSs. Access SQL also uses the double quotation mark (") to replace the single quotation mark (or apostrophe) ('), which acts as the string identifier character in most implementations of SQL. The preceding example of the SQL statement for a crosstab query is based on the tables in Access 95's Northwind.MDB sample database. Many field names in Access 2.0's NWIND.MDB contain spaces; spaces are removed from field names in NorthWind.MDB.

The sections that follow describe how you categorize SQL statements and how the formal grammar of SQL is represented. They also provide examples of writing a variety of select queries in ANSI SQL.

Categories of SQL Statements

ANSI SQL is divided into the following six basic categories of statements, presented here in the order of most frequent use:

- ■ *Data-query language* (DQL) statements, also called *data retrieval* statements, obtain data from tables and determine how that data is presented to your application. The SELECT reserved word is the most commonly used verb in DQL (and in all of SQL). Other commonly used DQL reserved words are WHERE, ORDER BY, GROUP BY, and HAVING; these DQL reserved words often are used in conjunction with other categories of SQL statements.

- ■ *Data-manipulation language* (DML) statements include the INSERT, UPDATE, and DELETE verbs, which append, modify, and delete rows in tables, respectively. DML verbs are used to construct action queries. Some books place DQL statements in the DML category.

■ *Transaction-processing language* (TPL) statements are used when you need to make sure that all the rows of tables affected by a DML statement are updated at once. TPL statements include BEGIN TRANSACTION, COMMIT, and ROLLBACK.

■ *Data-control language* (DCL) statements determine access of individual users and groups of users to objects in the database through permissions that you GRANT or REVOKE. Some RDBMSs let you GRANT permissions to or REVOKE permissions from individual columns of tables.

■ *Data-definition language* (DDL) statements let you create new tables in a database (CREATE TABLE), add indexes to tables (CREATE INDEX), establish constraints on field values (NOT NULL, CHECK, and CONSTRAINT), define relations between tables (PRIMARY KEY, FOREIGN KEY, and REFERENCES), and delete tables and indexes (DROP TABLE and DROP INDEX). DDL also includes many reserved words that relate to obtaining data from the database catalog. This book classifies DDL queries as action queries because DDL queries don't return records.

■ Cursor-control language (CCL) statements, such as DECLARE CURSOR, FETCHINTO, and UPDATE WHERE CURRENT, operate on individual rows of one or more tables.

It's not obligatory that a publisher of a DBM who claims to conform to ANSI SQL support all of the reserved words in the SQL-92 standard. In fact, it's probably safe to state that, at the time this book was written, no commercial RDBMS implemented all the SQL-92 keywords for interactive SQL. The Jet 3.0 database engine, for example, doesn't support any DCL reserved words. You use the Data Access Object's programmatic security objects with Visual C++ reserved words and keywords instead. The Jet 3.0 engine doesn't need to support CCL statements, because neither Visual C++ 4.0 nor Access manipulates cursors per se. Visual C++ 4.0's Data control creates the equivalent of a scrollable (bidirectionally movable) cursor. The Remote Data Object supports the scrollable cursors of Microsoft SQL Server 6.0.

This book uses the terminology defined by Appendix C of the Programmer's Reference for the Microsoft ODBC Software Development Kit (SDK) to define the following levels of SQL grammatical compliance:

■ *Minimum:* The statements (grammar) that barely qualify a DBM as an SQL DBM but not an RDBMS. A DBM that provides only the minimum grammar is not salable in today's market.

■ *Core:* Comprising minimum grammar plus basic DDL and DCL commands, additional DML functions, data types other than CHAR, SQL aggregate functions such as SUM() and AVG(), and a wider variety of allowable expressions to select records. Most desktop DBMs, to which SQL has been added, support core SQL grammar and little more.

■ *Extended:* Comprising minimum and core grammar, plus DML outer joins, more complex expressions in DML statements, all ANSI SQL data types (as well as `long varchar` and `long varbinary`), batch SQL statements, and procedure calls. Extended SQL grammar has two levels of conformance—1 and 2.

The Formal Grammar of SQL

The formal grammar of SQL is represented in the Backus Naur Form (BNF), which is used to specify the formal grammar of many computer programming languages. Here is the full BNF form of the verb that specifies the operation that a query is to perform on a database:

```
<action> ::=
SELECT
¦DELETE
¦INSERT [ <left paren> <privilege column list> <right paren>]
¦UPDATE [ <left paren> <privilege column list> <right paren>]
¦REFERENCES  [ <left paren> <privilege column list> <right paren>]
¦USAGE
...
<privilege column list> ::= <column name list>
...
<column name list> ::= <column name> [{<comma>, <column name>} ...]
```

To use BNF representation, you locate the class (`<action>` in the preceding example) where the reserved word is included. Members of the class are separated by the vertical bar (¦) character. Optional parameters of reserved words and elements are enclosed in square brackets ([ ]). Literal values, such as `<privilege column list>`, are enclosed in angle braces (<>), and elements that must be grouped, such as a comma preceding a second `<column name>`, are enclosed in French braces ({}). You then search the list of elements to find the allowable composition of an element. In this example, the `<privilege column list>` is composed of the `<column name list>`. Then check to see if `<column name list>` has a composition (in this case, one or more `<column name>` elements). This process is tedious, especially when the elements aren't arranged in alphabetical order.

Microsoft uses a simplified form of BNF to describe the grammar supported by the present version of the ODBC API. The Access SQL syntax rules eliminate the use of the ::= characters to indicate the allowable substitution of values for an element. Instead, they substitute a tabular format, as shown in Table 5.1. Ellipses (...) in the table indicate that you have to search for the element; the element is not contiguous with the preceding element of the table.

Table 5.1. The partial syntax of the Access SQL SELECT statement.

Element	Syntax
select-statement	SELECT[ALL¦DISTINCT¦DISTINCTROW]
	select-list table-expression
...	

Element	Syntax
select-list	*¦select-sublist[{, select-sublist}...]
select-sublist	table-name.*¦expression
	[AS column-alias]¦column-name
...	
table-expression	from-clause¦[where-clause]¦
	[group-by-clause]¦[having-clause]¦
	[order-by-clause]
...	
from-clause	FROM table-reference-list
table-reference-list	table-reference [{, table-reference}...]
table-reference	table-name [AS correlation-name¦joined-table]
...	
table-name	base-table-name¦querydef-name¦
	attached-table-name¦correlation-name

> **NOTE**
>
> The DISTINCTROW qualifier and the *querydef-name* element are specific to Access SQL. DISTINCTROW is discussed in the section "Theta Joins and the DISTINCTROW Keyword." Chapter 6 describes the Access QueryDef object.

After you've looked up all the allowable forms of the elements in the table, you might have forgotten the key word whose syntax you set out to determine. The modified Backus Naur form used by Microsoft is unquestionably easier to use than full BNF.

The Practical Grammar of a Simple SQL *SELECT* Statement

Here is a more practical representation of the syntax of a typical ANSI SQL statement, substituting underscores for hyphens:

```
SELECT [ALL¦DISTINCT] select_list
   FROM table_names
   [WHERE {search_criteria¦join_criteria}
   [{AND¦OR search_criteria}]
   [ORDER BY {field_list} [ASC¦DESC]]
```

The following list explains the use of each SQL reserved word in the preceding statement:

■ SELECT specifies that the query is to return data from the database rather than modify the data in the database. The *select_list* element contains the names of the fields of the table that are to appear in the query. Multiple fields appear in a comma-separated list. The asterisk (*) specifies that data from all fields of a table is returned. If more than one table is involved (joined) in the query, you use the `table_name.field_name` syntax, in which the period (.) separates the name of the table from the name of the field.

■ The `ALL` qualifier specifies that you want the query to return all rows, regardless of duplicate values; `DISTINCT` returns only nonduplicate rows. These qualifiers have significance only in queries that involve joins. The penalty for using `DISTINCT` is that the query will take longer to process.

■ `FROM` begins a clause that specifies the names of the tables that contain the fields you include in your `select_list`. If more than one table is involved in `select_list`, `table_list` consists of comma-separated table names.

■ `WHERE` begins a clause that serves two purposes in ANSI SQL: specifying the fields on which tables are joined, and limiting the records returned to records with field values that meet a particular criterion or set of criteria. The `WHERE` clause must include an operator and two operands, the first of which must be a field name. (The field name doesn't need to appear in the `select_list`, but the `table_name` that includes `field_name` must be included in the `table_names` list.)

■ SQL operators include `LIKE`, `IS {NULL¦NOT NULL}`, and `IN`, as well as the arithmetic operators—<, <=, =, =>, >, and <>. If you use the arithmetic equal operator (=) and specify `table_name.field_name` values for both operands, you create an *equi-join* (also called an *inner join*) between the two tables on the specified fields. You can create left and right joins by using the special operators `*=` and `=*`, respectively, if your DBM supports outer joins. (Both left and right joins are called *outer joins*.) Types of joins are discussed in the section "Joining Tables."

NOTE

If you use more than one table in your query, make sure that you create a join between the tables with a `WHERE Table1.field_name = Table2.field_name` clause. If you omit the statement that creates the join, your query will return the Cartesian product of the two tables. A Cartesian product is all the combinations of fields and rows in the two tables. This results in extremely large query-return set and, if the tables have a large number of records, it can cause your computer to run out of memory to hold the query result set. (The term *Cartesian* is derived from the name of a famous French mathematician, René Descartes.)

■ ORDER BY defines a clause that determines the sort order of the records returned by the SELECT statement. You specify the field(s) on which you want to sort the query result set by the *table_names* list. You can specify a descending sort with the DESC qualifier; ascending (ASC) is the default. As in other lists, if you have more than one *table_name*, you use a comma-separated list. You use the *table_name.field_name* specifier if you have joined tables.

Depending on the dialect of SQL your database uses and the method of transmitting the SQL statement to the DBM, you might need to terminate the SQL statement with a semicolon. (Access SQL no longer requires the semicolon; statements you send directly to the server through the ODBC driver don't use terminating semicolons.)

Using the MS Query Application to Explore Queries

The MS Query application that accompanies Visual C++ version 1.5 (\MSVC15\MSQUERY) is an excellent application that can be used to create SQL statements. Visual C++ 2.x and 4 don't include MS Query; however, because Visual C++ 1.5 is included with later versions of Visual C++, you can install that version from Visual C++ 1.5. Also, when you purchase Microsoft Office, you will receive a 32-bit version of Microsoft Query. It can be found on the Microsoft Office Pro CD in the \OS\MSAPPS\MSQUERY folder.

> **NOTE**
>
> MS Query as found on the Visual C++ 1.5x CD (a 16-bit application) works only with the Access 2 version of BIBLIO. It might not work correctly with the second version, called BIBLIO 95, which is an Access 7 version of the database. MSQRY32 (the 32-bit version of MS Query, which is on the Microsoft Office CD) will work with the Access 7 version of BIBLIO. The 32-bit version of MS Query is a little more reliable and should be used if possible.

MS Query falls into the category of *ad hoc* query generators. You can use MS Query to test some simple SQL statements by following these steps:

1. Start MS Query and choose File | New Query.

2. MS Query displays the Select Data Source dialog box. Select the BIBLIO datasource. If you haven't previously opened BIBLIO using MS Query, click the Other button to add BIBLIO to MS Query's list of datasources.

3. MS Query displays the Add Tables dialog box. Select the Authors table and click the Add button. Then click the Close button.

4. MS Query displays its Query 1 MDI child window. Click the SQL button on the toolbar.

5. Enter SELECT * FROM Authors in the SQL Statement window as a simple query to check whether MS Query works, as shown in Figure 5.1.

FIGURE 5.1.

An MS Query application with an SQL test query.

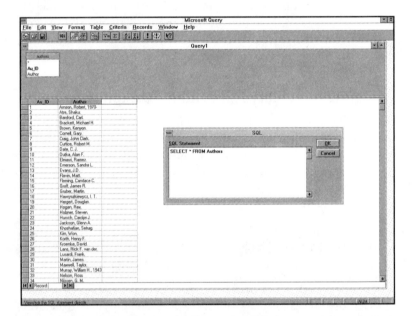

NOTE

Access SQL statements require a semicolon statement terminator. The MS Query application doesn't need a semicolon at the end of the SQL statement. Adding a semicolon will disable MS Query's graphical query representation, but the query will still work as expected.

---

6. Click the OK button in the SQL dialog box. The query result set appears in the child window.

7. Click the SQL toolbar button. The query, reformatted to fully qualify all names, appears in the SQL dialog box. The query now reads SELECT Authors.Au_ID, Authors.Author FROM Authors Authors. Figure 5.2 shows a portion of the query result set and the reformatted SQL query.

FIGURE 5.2.

The query result window and reformatted query in the MS Query application.

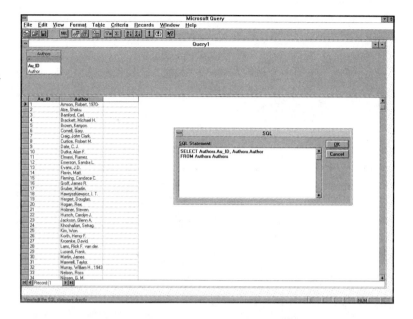

NOTE

A typical result of this type of query, which returns 46 rows in .0547 seconds, is approximately 840 rows/second. A 486DX2/66 with local bus video and 16M of RAM was used for these tests. These rates represent quite acceptable performance for a Windows database front end.

---

8. Reopen the SQL dialog box and clear the current SQL query edit box of the SQL Statement window. Enter SELECT * FROM Publishers WHERE State = 'NY' in the SQL Statement window and then click the OK button. The results of this query appear in Figure 5.3.

NOTE

In this case, the query-data return rate and the display rate are about 24 rows per second. The query-data return rate was reduced because there are more columns in the Publishers table (eight) than in the Authors table (two). However, if the query-data return rate is inversely proportional to the number of columns, the rate should be 840 * 2 / 8, or 210 rows per second. The extrapolated grid display rate, 170 * 2 / 8, is 42.5 rows per second, which is closer to the 24 rows per second rate of the prior example and can be accounted for by the greater average length of the data in the fields. Part of the difference between 24 and 210 rows per second for the query-data return rate is because the Access database engine must load the data from the table on the fixed disk into a temporary buffer. If you run the query again, you'll find that the rate increases to 8 / 0.0625, or 128 rows per second. The remainder of the difference in the query-data return rate is because the Access database engine must test each value of the State field for 'NY'.

FIGURE 5.3.

A query that returns records for publishers located in New York.

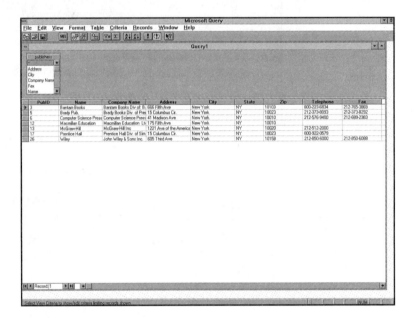

9. Open the SQL dialog box again and add ORDER BY Zip to the end of your SQL statement. Figure 5.4 shows the query and its result.

NOTE

The data return rate will now have dropped to about 68 rows per second. The decrease in speed can be attributed to the sort operation that you added to the query. The data-return rates and data-display rates you achieve will depend on the speed of the computer you use. As a rule, each clause you add to a query will decrease the data-return rate because of the additional data-manipulation operations that are required.

10. Replace the * in the SELECT statement, which returns all fields, with PubID, 'Company Name', City so that only three of the fields appear in the SnapShot window. The

result, shown in Figure 5.5, demonstrates that you don't have to include the fields that you use for the WHERE and ORDER BY clauses in the *field_names* list of your SELECT statement.

FIGURE 5.4.

The records for publishers in New York sorted by zip code.

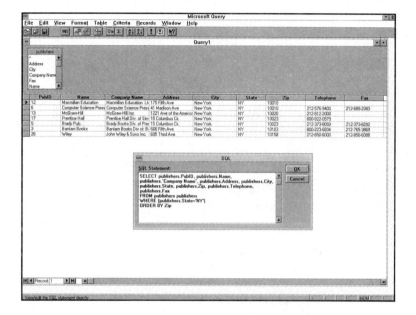

FIGURE 5.5.

The query return set displaying only three fields of the Publishers table.

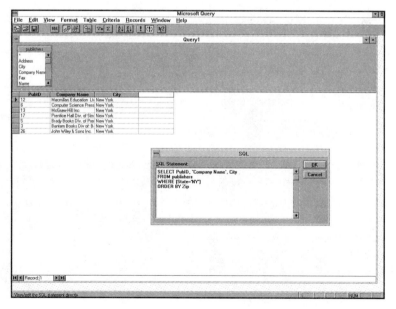

> **NOTE**
>
> The single quotes (') surrounding `Company Name` are necessary when a field name or table name contains a space. Only Access databases permit spaces and punctuation other than the underscore (_) in field names. Using spaces in field and table names, or in the names of any other database objects, is not considered good database-programming practice. Spaces in database field names and table names appear in this book only when such names are included in sample databases created by others.

> **NOTE**
>
> The MS Query toolbar provides a number of buttons that let you search for records in the table, filter the records so that only selected records appear, and sort the records on selected fields. A *filter* is the equivalent of adding a `WHERE` *field_name where_expression* clause to your SQL statement. The sort buttons add an `ORDER BY` *field_names* clause.

Microsoft designed the MS Query application to demonstrate the features of SQL and ODBC that pertain to manipulating and displaying data contained in the tables of databases. MS Query is a rich source of SQL examples. It also contains useful examples of user interface design techniques for database applications and MDI child forms.

SQL Operators and Expressions

As I mentioned earlier in this chapter, SQL provides the basic arithmetic operators (<, <=, =, =>, >, and <>). SQL also has a set of operators that are used in conjunction with values of fields of the text data type (`LIKE` and `IN`) and that deal with `NULL` values in fields (`IS NULL` and `IS NOT NULL`). The Access database engine also supports the use of many string and numeric functions in SQL statements to calculate column values of query return sets. (Few of these functions are included in ANSI SQL.)

> **NOTE**
>
> Access supports the use of user-defined functions (UDFs) in SQL statements to calculate column values in queries. Visual C++ and ODBC support only native functions that are reserved words, such as `Val()`. Functions other than SQL aggregate functions are called *implementation-specific* in ANSI SQL. Implementation-specific means that the supplier of the DBM is free to add functions to the supplier's implementation of ANSI SQL.

The majority of the operators you use in SQL statements are *dyadic*. Dyadic functions require two operands. (All arithmetic functions and BETWEEN are dyadic.) Operators such as LIKE, IN, IS NULL, and IS NOT NULL are *monadic*. Monadic operators require only one operand. All expressions that you create with comparison operators return True or False, not a value. The sections that follow describe the use of the common dyadic and monadic operators of ANSI SQL.

Dyadic Arithmetic Operators and Functions

The use of arithmetic operators with SQL doesn't differ greatly from their use in Visual C++ or other computer languages. The following is a list of the points you need to remember about arithmetic operators and functions used in SQL statements (especially in WHERE clauses):

■ The = and <> comparison operators are used for both text and numeric field data types. The angle-brace pair "not-equal" symbol (<>) is equivalent to the != combination used to represent "not equal" in ANSI SQL. (The equals sign isn't used as an assignment operator in SQL.)

■ The arithmetic comparison operators—<, <=, =>, and >—are intended primarily for use with operands that have numeric field data types. If you use the preceding comparison operators with values of the text field data type, the numeric ANSI values of each character of the two fields are compared in left-to-right sequence.

■ The remaining arithmetic operators—+, -, *, /, and ^ or ** (the implementation-specific exponentiation operator)—aren't comparison operators. These operators apply only to calculated columns of query result sets, the subject of the next section.

■ To compare the values of text fields that represent numbers, such as the zip code field of the Publishers table of BIBLIO.MDB, you can use the Val() function in a WHERE clause to process the text values as the numeric equivalent when you use the Access database engine. An example of this usage is SELECT * FROM Publishers WHERE Zip > 12000.

NOTE

If you attempt to execute the preceding SQL statement in MS Query (but not MSQRY32), you might receive an error message (usually with no text), or sometimes MS Query will simply GPF. The error is caused by Null values in the Zip Code data cells of several publishers in the table. Most expressions don't accept Null argument values. Thus, you need to add an IS NOT NULL criterion to your WHERE clause. If you use the form WHERE (Zip > '12000' AND (Zip IS NOT NULL), you get the same error message, because the order in which the criteria are processed is the sequence in which the criteria appear in your SQL statement. Using WHERE Zip IS NOT NULL AND Zip > '12000' solves the problem. The syntax of the NULL predicates is explained in the section "Monadic Text Operators, Null Value Predicates, and Functions."

■   The BETWEEN predicate in ANSI SQL and the Between operator in Access SQL are used with numeric or date-time field data types. The syntax is *field_name* BETWEEN *Value1* AND *Value2*. This syntax is equivalent to the expression *field_name* => *Value1* OR *field_name* <= *Value2*. Access SQL requires you to surround date-time values with number signs (#), as in *DateField* Between #1-1-93# And #12-31-93#. You can negate the BETWEEN predicate by preceding BETWEEN with NOT.

> **NOTE**
>
> Where Access SQL uses syntax that isn't specified by ANSI SQL, such as the use of number signs (#) to indicate date-time field data types, or where examples of complete statements are given in Access SQL, the SQL reserved words that are also keywords or reserved words appear in the upper-and-lowercase convention.

Calculated Query Columns

Using Access, you can create calculated columns in query return sets by defining fields that use SQL arithmetic operators and functions that are supported by the Access database engine or your client-server RDBMS. Ordinarily, calculated columns are derived from fields of numeric field data types. BIBLIO.MDB uses a numeric data type (the auto-incrementing long integer Counter field) for ID fields, so you can use the PubID field or Val(Zip) expression as the basis for the calculated field. Enter SELECT DISTINCTROW Publishers.Name, Val([Zip])*3 AS Zip_Times_3, Publishers.State FROM Publishers in Access's SQL query window. The query result set appears as shown in Figure 5.6.

FIGURE 5.6.

A calculated column added to the query against the publisher's table.

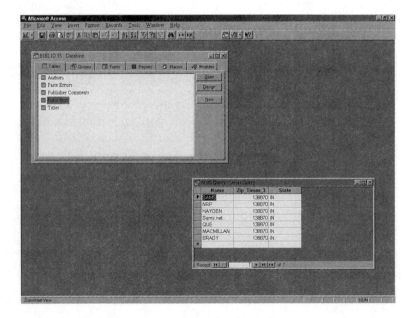

The AS qualifier designates an alias for the column name, `column_alias`. If you don't supply the AS `column_alias` qualifier, the column name is empty when you use the Access database engine. Access provides a default AS Expr1 column alias for calculated columns; the `column_alias` that appears when you use ODBC to connect to databases is implementation-specific. IBM's DB2 and DB2/2, for example, don't support aliasing of column names with the AS qualifier. ODBC drivers for DB2 and DB2/2 may assign the field name from which the calculated column value is derived, or apply an arbitrary name, such as Col_1.

> **NOTE**
>
> If you must include spaces in the `column_alias`, make sure that you enclose the `column_alias` in square brackets for the Access database engine and in single quotation marks for RDBMSs that support spaces in `column_alias` fields. (Although you might see column names such as Col_1 when you execute queries against DB2 or other mainframe databases in an emulated 3270 terminal session, these `column_alias` values are generated by the local query tool running on your PC, not by DB2.) If you use single or double quotation marks with the Access database engine, these quotation marks appear in the column headers.

Monadic Text Operators, Null Value Predicates, and Functions

One of the most useful operators for the WHERE criterion of fields of the text field data type is ANSI SQL's LIKE predicate, called the Like operator in Access SQL. (The terms *predicate* and *operator* are used interchangeably in this context.) The LIKE predicate lets you search for one or more characters you specify at any location in the text. Table 5.2 shows the syntax of the ANSI SQL LIKE predicate and the Access SQL Like operator used in the WHERE clause of an SQL statement.

Table 5.2. Forms of the ANSI SQL LIKE and Access SQL Like predicates.

ANSI SQL	*Access SQL*	*Description*	*What It Returns*
LIKE '%am%'	Like "*am*"	Matches any text that contains the characters.	ram, rams, damsel, amnesty
LIKE 'John%'	Like "John*"	Matches any text beginning with the characters.	Johnson, Johnsson
LIKE '%son'	Like "*son"	Matches any text ending with the characters.	Johnson, Anderson

continues

Table 5.2. continued

ANSI SQL	Access SQL	Description	What It Returns
LIKE 'Glen_'	Like "Glen?"	Matches the text and any single trailing character.	Glenn, Glens
LIKE '_am'	Like "?am"	Matches the text and any single preceding character.	dam, Pam, ram
LIKE '_am%'	Like "_am*"	Matches the text with one preceding character and any trailing characters.	dams, Pam, Ramses

The IS NULL and IS NOT NULL predicates (Is Null and Is Not Null operators in Access SQL) test whether a value has been entered in a field. IS NULL returns False and IS NOT NULL returns True if a value, including an empty string ("") or 0, is present in the field.

The SQL-92 POSITION() function returns the position of characters in a test field using the syntax POSITION(*characters* IN *field_name*). The equivalent Access SQL function is InStr(*field_name*, *characters*). If *characters* are not found in *field_name*, both functions return 0.

The SQL-92 SUBSTRING() function returns a set of characters with SUBSTRING(*field_name* FROM *start_position* FOR *number_of_characters*). This function is quite useful for selecting and parsing text fields.

Joining Tables

As I mentioned earlier in this chapter, you can join two tables by using *table_name.field_name* operands with a comparison operator in the WHERE clause of an SQL statement. You can join additional tables by combining two sets of join statements with the AND operator. SQL-86 and SQL-89 supported only WHERE joins. You can create equi-joins, natural equi-joins, left and right equi-joins, not-equal joins, and self-joins with the WHERE clause. Joins that are created with the equals (=) operator use the prefix *equi.*

SQL-92 added the JOIN reserved words, plus the CROSS, NATURAL, INNER, OUTER, FULL, LEFT, and RIGHT qualifiers, to describe a variety of JOINs. At the time this book was written, few RDBMSs supported the JOIN statement. (Microsoft SQL Server 4.2, for example, doesn't include the JOIN statement in Transact-SQL.) Access SQL supports INNER, LEFT, and RIGHT JOINs with SQL-92 syntax using the ON predicate. Access SQL doesn't support the USING clause or the CROSS, NATURAL, or FULL qualifiers for JOINs.

A CROSS JOIN returns the Cartesian product of two tables. The term CROSS is derived from *cross-product,* a synonym for Cartesian product. You can emulate a CROSS JOIN by leaving out the join components of the WHERE clause of a SELECT statement that includes a table name from more than one table. Figure 5.7 shows Access 95 displaying the first few rows of the 29-row Cartesian product created when you enter SELECT Publishers.Name, Authors.Author FROM Publishers, Authors in the SQL Statement window. There are seven Publishers records and 42 Authors records; thus, the query returns 294 rows (7 * 42 = 294). It is highly unlikely that you would want to create a CROSS JOIN in a commercial database application.

FIGURE 5.7.

The first few rows of the 29-row Cartesian product from the Publishers and Authors table.

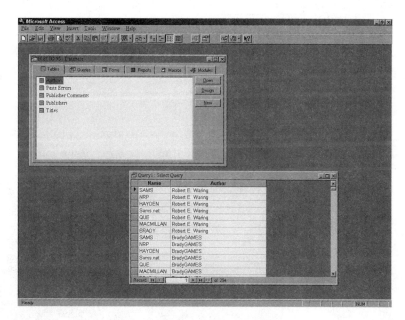

The common types of joins that you can create with SQL-89 and Access SQL are described in the following sections.

NOTE

All joins except the CROSS JOIN or Cartesian product require that the field data types of the two fields be identical or that you use a function (where supported by the RDBMS) to convert dissimilar field data types to a common type.

Conventional Inner or Equi-Joins

The most common type of join is the equi-join or INNER JOIN. You create an equi-join with a WHERE clause using the following generalized statement:

```
SELECT Table1.field_name, ... Table2.field_name ...
   FROM Table1, Table2
   WHERE Table1.field_name = Table2.field_name
```

The SQL-92 JOIN syntax to achieve the same result is as follows:

```
SELECT Table1.field_name, ... Table2.field_name ...
   FROM Table1 INNER JOIN Table2
   ON Table1.field_name = Table2.field_name
```

A single-column equi-join between the PubID field of the Publishers table and the PubID field of the Titles table of the BIBLIO.MAK table appears as follows:

```
SELECT Publishers.Name, Titles.ISBN, Titles.Title
   FROM Publishers INNER JOIN Titles
   ON Publishers.PubID = Titles.PubID;
```

When you execute this query with Access 95, the Publishers and Titles tables are joined by the PubID columns of both fields. Figure 5.8 shows the result of this join.

FIGURE 5.8.

Access displaying an equi-join on the Publishers and Titles tables.

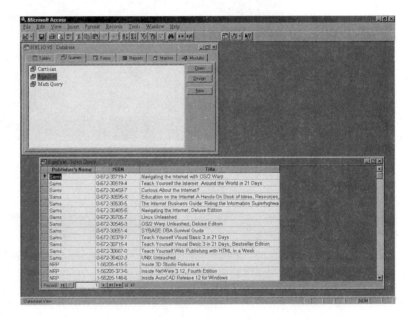

> **NOTE**
>
> The INNER qualifier is optional in SQL-92 but is required in Access SQL. If you omit the INNER qualifier when you use the Access database engine, you receive the message Syntax error in FROM clause when you attempt to execute the query.

> **NOTE**
>
> Natural equi-joins create joins automatically between identically named fields of two tables. Natural equi-joins eliminate the necessity of including the ON predicate in the JOIN statement. Access SQL doesn't support the NATURAL JOIN statement.

The Access SQL statements that you create in the graphical QBE design mode of Access generate an expanded JOIN syntax. Access separates the JOIN statement from a complete FROM clause with a comma and repeats the table names in a separate, fully defined join statement. Using the Access SQL syntax shown in the following example gives the same result as the preceding ANSI SQL-92 example:

```
SELECT DISTINCTROW Publishers.Name, Titles.ISBN, Titles.Title
   FROM Publishers, Titles,
   Publishers INNER JOIN Titles
   ON Publishers.PubID = Titles.PubID
```

The purpose of the DISTINCTROW statement in Access SQL is discussed in the section "Comparing the Access SQL Dialect and ODBC" later in this chapter.

Here is the equivalent of the two preceding syntax examples, using the WHERE clause to create the join:

```
SELECT Publishers.Name, Titles.ISBN, Titles.Title
   FROM Publishers, Titles
   WHERE Publishers.PubID = Titles.PubID
```

There is no difference between using the INNER JOIN and the WHERE clause to create an equi-join.

> **NOTE**
>
> Equi-joins return only rows in which the values of the joined fields match. Field values of records of either table, which don't have matching values in the other table, don't appear in the query result set returned by an equi-join. If there is no match between any of the records, no rows are returned. A query without rows is called a *null set*.

Multiple Equi-Joins

You can create multiple equi-joins to link several tables by pairs of fields with common data values. For example, you can link the Publishers, Titles, and Authors tables of BIBLIO.MAK with the following SQL-92 statement:

```
SELECT Publishers.Name, Titles.Title, Titles.Au_ID, Authors.Author
    FROM Publishers INNER JOIN Titles
    ON Publishers.PubID = Titles.PubID,
    INNER JOIN Authors
    ON Titles.Au_ID = Authors.Au_ID
```

You need to include the `Titles.Au_ID` field in the query because the second join is based on the result set returned by the first join.

Access SQL, however, requires that you explicitly define each `INNER JOIN` with the following syntax:

```
SELECT DISTINCTROW Publishers.Name, Titles.Title, Titles.Au_ID,
    Authors.Author
    FROM Publishers, Titles, Authors,
    Publishers INNER JOIN Titles
    ON Publishers.PubID = Titles.PubID,
    Titles INNER JOIN Authors
    ON Titles.Au_ID = Authors.Au_ID
```

The query result set from the preceding Access SQL query appears in Figure 5.9.

FIGURE 5.9.

*The query result set
with three tables joined.*

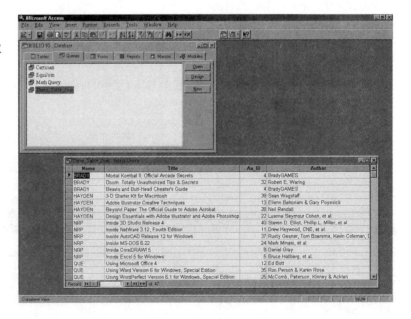

Here is the equivalent of the preceding example using the WHERE clause:

```
SELECT Publishers.Name, Titles.Title, Titles.Au_ID,
   Authors.Author
   FROM Publishers, Titles, Authors,
   WHERE Publishers.PubID = Titles.PubID AND
      Titles.Au_ID = Authors.Au_ID
```

> **NOTE**
>
> As a rule, using the WHERE clause to specify equi-joins results in simpler query statements than specifying INNER JOINs. When you need to create OUTER JOINs, the subject of the next section, you might want to use INNER JOIN statements to maintain consistency in Access SQL statements.

OUTER JOINs

INNER JOINs (equi-joins) return only rows with matching field values. OUTER JOINs return all the rows of one table and only those rows in the other table that have matching values. There are two types of OUTER JOINs:

- LEFT OUTER JOINs return all rows of the table or result set to the left of the LEFT OUTER JOIN statement and only the rows of the table to the right of the statement that have matching field values. In WHERE clauses, LEFT OUTER JOINs are specified with the *= operator.

- RIGHT OUTER JOINs return all rows of the table or result set to the right of the RIGHT OUTER JOIN statement and only the rows of the table to the left of the statement that have matching field values. WHERE clauses specify RIGHT OUTER JOINs with the =* operator.

It is a convention that joins are created in one-to-many form; that is, the primary table that represents the "one" side of the relation appears to the left of the JOIN expression, or the operator of the WHERE clause and the related table of the "many" side appears to the right of the expression or operator. You use LEFT OUTER JOINs to display all of the records of the primary table, regardless of matching records in the related table. RIGHT OUTER JOINs are useful for finding orphan records. *Orphan records* are records in related tables that have no related records in the primary tables. They are created when you violate referential integrity rules.

The SQL-92 syntax for a statement that returns all Publishers records, regardless of matching values in the Titles table, and all Titles records, whether authors for individual titles are identified, is as follows:

```
SELECT Publishers.Name, Titles.Title, Titles.Au_ID, Authors.Author
   FROM Publishers LEFT OUTER JOIN Titles
   ON Publishers.PubID = Titles.PubID,
   LEFT OUTER JOIN Authors
   ON Titles.Au_ID = Authors.Au_ID
```

The equivalent joins using the WHERE clause are created by the following query:

```
SELECT Publishers.Name, Titles.Title, Titles.Au_ID,
   Authors.Author
   FROM Publishers, Titles, Authors,
   WHERE Publishers.PubID *= Titles.PubID AND
      Titles.Au_ID *= Authors.Au_ID
```

Access SQL requires you to use the special syntax described in the preceding section, and it doesn't permit you to add the OUTER reserved word in the JOIN statement. Here is the Access SQL equivalent of the previous query example:

```
SELECT DISTINCTROW Publishers.Name, Titles.Title, Titles.Au_ID,
      Authors.Author
   FROM Publishers, Titles, Authors,
      Publishers LEFT JOIN Titles
   ON Publishers.PubID = Titles.PubID,
      Titles LEFT JOIN Authors
   ON Titles.Au_ID = Authors.Au_ID
```

Figure 5.10 shows the result of running the preceding query against the BIBLIO.MDB database.

FIGURE 5.10.

The result of substituting LEFT JOIN for INNER JOIN in a query against the BIBLIO.MDB database.

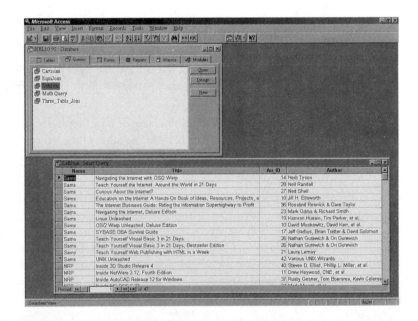

Access database engine. This restriction doesn't apply to SQL pass-through queries that you execute on servers that support *= and =* operators, such as Microsoft and Sybase SQL Server.

Theta Joins and the *DISTINCTROW* Keyword

You can create joins using comparison operators other than =, *=, and =*. Joins that are not equi-joins are called *theta joins*. The most common form of theta join is the not-equal (theta) join, which uses the WHERE `table_name.field_name` <> `table_name.field_name` syntax. The BIBLIO.MDB database doesn't contain tables with fields that lend themselves to demonstrating not-equal joins. However, if you have a copy of Access's NorthWind.MDB sample database, you can execute an Access SQL query to find records in the Orders table that have a Ship Address value that differs from the Address value in the Customers field by employing the following query:

```
SELECT  DISTINCTROW Customers.[Company Name], Customers.Address,
     Orders.[Ship Address]
  FROM Customers, Orders,
     Customers INNER JOIN Orders
  ON Customers.[Customer ID] = Orders.[Customer ID]
  WHERE ((Orders.[Ship Address]<>[Customers].[Address]))
```

The preceding query results in the query return set shown in Figure 5.11.

FIGURE 5.11.

A not-equal theta join to display customers whose shipping and billing addresses differ.

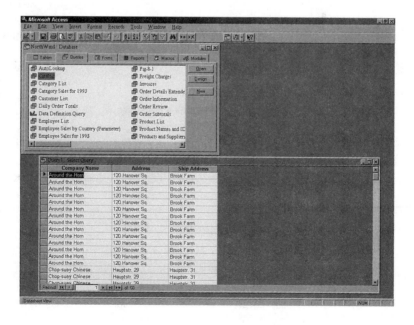

If you execute the same query without Access SQL's DISTINCTROW qualifier, you get the same result. However, if you substitute the ANSI SQL DISTINCT qualifier for Access SQL's DISTINCTROW, the result is distinctly different, as shown in Figure 5.12.

FIGURE 5.12.

The effect of applying the DISTINCT qualifier to the query shown in Figure 5.11.

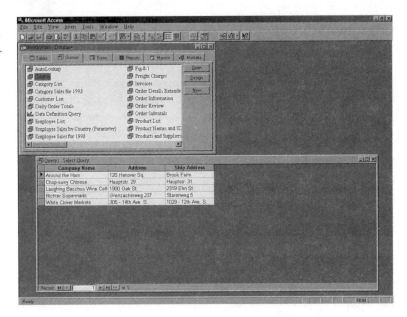

The query result set shown in Figure 5.12 is created by the following statement, which is the same in Access SQL and ANSI SQL, disregarding the unconventional table names enclosed in square brackets:

```
SELECT DISTINCT Customers.[Company Name], Customers.Address,
    Orders.[Ship Address]
  FROM Customers, Orders
  WHERE Customers.[Customer ID] = Orders.[Customer ID]
  AND Orders.[Ship Address] <> Customers.Address
```

The DISTINCT qualifier specifies that only rows that have differing values in the fields specified in the SELECT statement should be returned by the query. Access SQL's DISTINCTROW qualifier causes the return set to include each row in which any of the values of all of the fields in the two tables (not just the fields specified to be displayed by the SELECT statement) differ.

Self-Joins and Composite Columns

A *self-join* is a join created between two fields of the same table having similar field data types. The first field is usually the primary key field, and the second field of the join ordinarily is a foreign key field that relates to the primary key field, although this isn't a requirement for a self-join. (This may be a requirement to make the result of the self-join meaningful, however.)

When you create a self-join, the DBM creates a copy of the original table and then joins the copy to the original table. No tables in BIBLIO.MDB offer fields on which you can create a meaningful self-join. The Employees table of NorthWind.MDB, however, includes the Reports To field, which specifies the Employee ID of an employee's supervisor. Here is the Access SQL statement to create a self-join on the Employee table to display the name of an employee's supervisor:

```
SELECT Employees.[Employee ID] AS EmpID,
    Employees.[Last Name] & ", " & Employees.[First Name]
  AS Employee,
    Employees.[Reports To]
  AS SupID,
    EmpCopy.[Last Name] & ", " & EmpCopy.[First Name]
  AS Supervisor
  FROM Employees, Employees
AS EmpCopy,
    Employees INNER JOIN EmpCopy
  ON Employees.[Reports To] = EmpCopy.[Employee ID]
```

You create a temporary copy of the table, named EmpCopy, with the FROM... Employees AS EmpCopy clause. Each of the query's field names is aliased with an AS qualifier. The Employee and Supervisor columns are composite columns whose values are created by combining a last name, a comma, and a space with the first name. The query result set from the preceding SQL statement appears in Figure 5.13.

FIGURE 5.13.

The query result set of a self-join on the Employees table of NorthWind.MDB.

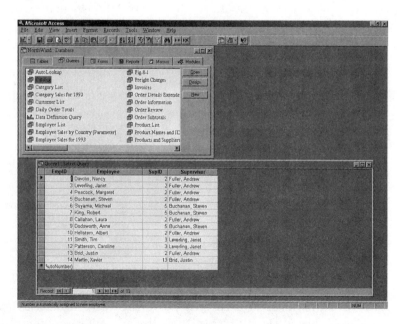

ANSI SQL doesn't provide a SELF INNER JOIN, but you can create the equivalent by using the ANSI version of the preceding statement. You can substitute a WHERE Employees.[Reports To] = EmpCopy.[Employee ID] clause for the INNER JOIN...ON statement.

> **NOTE**
>
> Self-joins are relatively uncommon, because a table that is normalized to fourth normal form wouldn't include an equivalent of the Reports To field. A separate table would relate the Employee ID values of employees and supervisors. However, creating a separate table to contain information that can be held in single table without ambiguity is generally considered over-normalization. This is the primary reason that most developers stop normalizing tables at the third normal form.

SQL Aggregate Functions and the *GROUP BY* and *HAVING* Clauses

ANSI SQL includes set functions (called *SQL aggregate functions* in this book), which act on sets of records. The standard SQL-92 aggregate functions are described in the following list. The *field_name* argument of the functions can be the name of a field (with a *table_name.* specifier, if required) or the all-fields specifier, the asterisk (*).

- COUNT(*field_name*) returns the number of rows that contain NOT NULL values of *field_name*. COUNT(*) returns the number of rows in the table or query without regard for NULL values in fields.

- MAX(*field_name*) returns the largest value of *field_name* in the set.

- MIN(*field_name*) returns the smallest value of *field_name* in the set.

- SUM(*field_name*) returns the total value of *field_name* in the set.

- AVG(*field_name*) returns the arithmetic average (mean) value of *field_name* in the set.

The SQL aggregate functions can act on persistent tables or virtual tables, such as query result sets. Here is the basic syntax of queries that use the SQL aggregate functions:

```
SELECT FUNCTION(field_name¦*) [AS column_alias]
```

This example returns a single record with the value of the SQL aggregate function you choose. You can test the SQL aggregate functions with BIBLIO.MDB using the following query:

```
SELECT COUNT(*) AS Count,
   SUM(PubID) AS Total,
   AVG(PubID) AS Average,
   MIN(PubID) AS Minimum,
   MAX(PubID) AS Maximum
   FROM Publishers
```

Figure 5.14 shows the result of the preceding aggregate query.

Databases with significant content usually have tables that contain fields representing the classification of objects. The BIBLIO.MDB database doesn't have such a classification, but the Products tables of NorthWind.MDB classifies an eclectic assortment of exotic foodstuffs into eight different categories. You use the GROUP BY clause when you want to obtain values of the SQL aggregate functions for each class of an object. The GROUP BY clause creates a virtual table called, not surprisingly, a grouped table.

FIGURE 5.14.

The five SQL aggregate functions for the Publishers table.

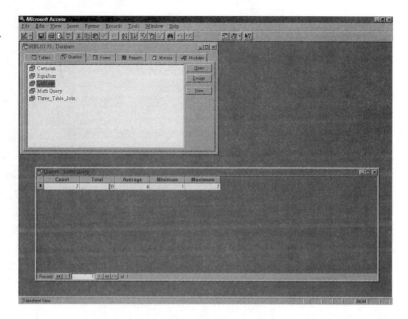

The following Access SQL query counts the number of items in each of the eight food categories included in the Category ID field and then calculates three total and average values for each of the categories:

```
SELECT [Category ID] AS Category,
    COUNT(*) AS Items,
    Format(AVG([Unit Price]), "$#,##0.00") AS Avg_UP,
    SUM([Units in Stock]) AS Sum_Stock,
    SUM([Units on Order]) AS Sum_Ordered
    FROM Products
    GROUP BY [Category ID]
```

NOTE

The preceding query uses the Access SQL Format() function to format the values returned for average unit price (Avg_UP) in conventional monetary format. This feature is not found in ANSI SQL.

The result of the preceding query appears in Figure 5.15.

FIGURE 5.15.

Using GROUP BY *with the SQL aggregate functions.*

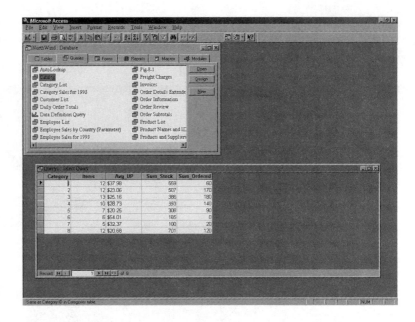

You might want to restrict group (category) membership using a particular criteria. You might think that you could use a WHERE clause to establish the criteria, but WHERE clauses apply to the entire table. The HAVING clause acts like a WHERE clause for groups. Therefore, if you want to limit the applicability of SQL aggregate functions to a particular set or group, you would add the HAVING clause and the IN() operator, as in the following Access SQL example, which returns only rows for the BEVR and COND categories:

```
SELECT [Category ID] AS Category,
    COUNT(*) AS Items,
    Format(AVG([Unit Price]), "$#,##0.00") AS Avg_UP,
    SUM([Units in Stock]) AS Sum_Stock,
    SUM([Units on Order]) AS Sum_Ordered
    FROM Products
    GROUP BY [Category ID]
    HAVING [Category ID] IN('BEVR', 'COND')
```

The result of the preceding query appears in Figure 5.16.

FIGURE 5.16.

Using GROUP BY with the SQL aggregate functions using the IN( ) operator.

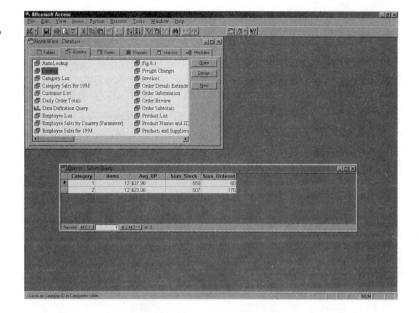

Comparing the Access SQL Dialect and ODBC

The preceding sections of this chapter have outlined many of the syntactical differences between Access SQL and ANSI SQL-92 (plus earlier versions of ANSI SQL, such as SQL-86 and SQL-89). Here are some of the more important differences between the present implementation of Access SQL (based on the Access definition of Access SQL) and SQL syntax supported by ODBC:

■ Access SQL doesn't support ANSI SQL Data Definition Language (DDL) statements. You modify the `Tables`, `Fields`, and `Indexes` collections with Visual C++ code to create or modify database objects. You can use the Microsoft ODBC Desktop Database Drivers kit to provide limited (ODBC Extended Level 1) DDL capability.

■ Access SQL doesn't support ANSI SQL Data Control Language (DCL), and Visual C++ doesn't offer an alternative method of granting and revoking user permissions for database objects. The Microsoft ODBC Desktop Database Drivers kit provides limited (ODBC Extended Level 1) DCL capability.

■ Access SQL doesn't support subqueries. To create the equivalent of a subquery, you need to execute a second query against a `Dynaset` object created by a query.

The following sections summarize the differences between the keywords of Access SQL and the reserved words of ANSI SQL, as well as how Access SQL deals with the data types defined by ANSI SQL.

ANSI SQL Reserved Words and Access SQL Keywords

ANSI SQL reserved words, by tradition, are set in uppercase type. Reserved words in ANSI SQL may not be used as names of objects, such as tables or fields, or as names of parameters or variables used in SQL statements. This book refers to elements of Access SQL syntax as keywords because, with the exception of some Access SQL functions, Access SQL keywords aren't reserved words in Visual C++. Table 5.3 lists the ANSI SQL reserved words.

Table 5.3. ANSI SQL reserved words that correspond to Access SQL keywords.

ALL	DELETE	HAVING	JOIN	SELECT
AND	DESC	IN	ON	SET
AS	DISTINCT	INNER	OPTION	UPDATE
ASC	FROM	INSERT	OR	WHERE
BY	GROUP	INTO	ORDER	WITH

This list shows the ANSI set functions that are identical to Access SQL aggregate functions:

```
COUNT()
SUM()
AVG()
MIN()
MAX()
```

Table 5.4 lists the commonly used ANSI SQL reserved words (including functions) and symbols that don't have a directly equivalent Access SQL reserved word or symbol. This table doesn't include many of the new reserved words added to SQL-89 by SQL-92, because these reserved words hadn't yet been implemented in the versions of client-server RDBMS that had been released as commercial products at the time this book was written.

Table 5.4. Common ANSI SQL reserved words that don't have a direct equivalent in Access SQL.

Reserved Word	Category	Substitute
ALL	DQL	Applies only to subqueries.
ALTER TABLE	DDL	Use Fields collection.
ANY	DQL	Applies only to subqueries.

Reserved Word	Category	Substitute
AUTHORIZATION	DCL	Access SQL doesn't support DCL.
BEGIN	TPL	Visual C++ MFC `BeginTrans()` member function.
CHECK	DDL	Access SQL doesn't support DDL.
CLOSE	DCL	Access SQL doesn't support DCL.
COMMIT	TPL	Visual C++ MFC `CommitTrans()` member function.
CREATE INDEX	DDL	Use `Indexes` collection.
CREATE TABLE	DDL	Use `Tables` collection.
CREATE VIEW	DDL	Equivalent to a `Snapshot` object.
CURRENT	CCL	Scrollable cursors are built into `Dynaset` and `Snapshot` objects.
CURSOR	CCL	Scrollable cursors are built into `Dynaset` and `Snapshot` objects.
DECLARE	CCL	Scrollable cursors are built into `Dynaset` and `Snapshot` objects.
DROP INDEX	DDL	Use `Indexes` collection.
DROP TABLE	DDL	Use `Tables` collection.
DROP VIEW	DDL	Use `Close` method on `Snapshot` object.
FETCH	CCL	Field name of a `Dynaset` or `Snapshot` object.
FOREIGN KEY	DDL	Access SQL doesn't support DDL.
GRANT	DCL	Access SQL doesn't support DCL.
IN *subquery*	DQL	Use a query against a query `Dynaset` instead of a subquery.
POSITION()	DQL	Use `InStr()`.
PRIMARY KEY	DDL	Access SQL doesn't support DDL.
PRIVILEGES	DCL	Access SQL doesn't support DCL.
REFERENCES	DDL	Access SQL doesn't support DDL.
REVOKE	DCL	Access SQL doesn't support DCL.
ROLLBACK	TPL	Visual C++ MFC `Rollback()` member function.
SUBSTRING()	DQL	Use `Mid()` functions.
UNION	DQL	UNIONs currently aren't supported by Access SQL.
UNIQUE	DDL	Access SQL doesn't support DDL.
WORK	TPL	Not required by Visual C++ `CDataBase` transaction functions.

continues

Table 5.4. continued

Reserved Word	Category	Substitute
*=	DQL	Use LEFT JOIN.
=*	DQL	Use RIGHT JOIN.
!= (not equal)	DQL	Use the <> for not equal.
: (variable prefix)	DQL	Use the PARAMETERS statement (if needed).

Table 5.5 lists Access SQL keywords that aren't reserved words in ANSI SQL. Many of the Access SQL keywords describe data types that you specify by using the DB_ constants. Data type conversion to and from ANSI SQL is discussed shortly.

Table 5.5. Access SQL keywords and symbols that aren't reserved words or symbols in ANSI SQL.

Access SQL	ANSI SQL	Category	Description
BINARY	No equivalent	DDL	Presently, not an official Access data type (used for SID field in SYSTEM.MDA).
BOOLEAN	No equivalent	DDL	Logical field data type (0 or -1 values only).
BYTE	No equivalent	DDL	Asc()/Chr() data type; 1-byte integer (tinyint of SQL Server).
CURRENCY	No equivalent	DDL	Currency data type.
DATETIME	No equivalent	DDL	Date/time field data type (Variant subtype 7).
DISTINCTROW	No equivalent	DQL	Creates an updatable Dynaset object.
DOUBLE	REAL	DDL	Double-precision floating-point number.
IN predicate with crosstab queries	No equivalent	DQL	Defines fixed-column headers or crosstab queries.
LONG	INT[EGER]	DDL	Long integer data type.
LONGBINARY	No equivalent	DDL	OLE Object field data type.
LONGTEXT	No equivalent	DDL	Memo field data type.
(WITH) OWNERACCESS	No equivalent	DQL	Runs queries with (OPTION) object owner's permissions.

Access SQL	ANSI SQL	Category	Description
PARAMETERS	No equivalent	DQL	User- or program-entered query parameters. Should be avoided in Visual C++ code.
PIVOT	No equivalent	DQL	Use in crosstab queries.
SHORT	SMALLINT	DDL	Integer data type; 2 bytes.
SINGLE	FLOAT	DDL	Single-precision real number.
TEXT	VARCHAR[ACTER]	DDL	Text data type.
TRANSFORM	No equivalent	DQL	Specifies a crosstab query.
? (LIKE wildcard)	_ (wildcard)	DQL	Single character with Like.
* (LIKE wildcard)	% (wildcard)	DQL	Zero or more characters.
# (LIKE wildcard)	No equivalent	DQL	Single digit, 0 through 9.
# (date specifier)	No equivalent	DQL	Encloses date/time values.
<> (not equal)	!=	DQL	Access uses ! as a separator.

Access SQL provides the four SQL statistical aggregate functions listed in Table 5.6 that are not included in ANSI SQL. These Access SQL statistical aggregate functions are set in upper- and lowercase type in the Microsoft documentation but are set in uppercase type in this book.

Table 5.6. Access SQL statistical aggregate functions.

Access Function	Description
STDDEV()	Standard deviation of a population sample.
STDDEVP()	Standard deviation of a population.
VAR()	Statistical variation of a population sample.
VARP()	Statistical variation of a population.

Table 5.7 lists the Access SQL keywords that often appear in upper- and lowercase rather than the all-uppercase SQL format of the Microsoft documentation.

Table 5.7. Typesetting conventions for Access SQL keywords and ANSI SQL reserved words.

Access SQL	ANSI SQL and This Book
And	AND
Avg()	AVG()

continues

Table 5.7. continued

Access SQL	ANSI SQL and This Book
Between	BETWEEN
Count()	COUNT()
Is	IS
Like	LIKE
Max()	MAX()
Min()	MIN()
Not	NOT
Null	NULL
Or	OR
Sum()	SUM()

Data Type Conversion Between ANSI SQL and Access SQL

Table 5.8 lists the data types specified by ANSI SQL-92 and the equivalent data types of Access SQL when equivalent data types exist. Categories of ANSI SQL data types precede the SQL-92 data type identifier.

Table 5.8. Data type conversion to and from ANSI SQL and Access SQL.

ANSI SQL-92	Access SQL	C Datatype	Comments
Exact Numeric	**Number**		
INTEGER	Long (integer)	long int	4 bytes
SMALLINT	Integer	short int	2 bytes
NUMERIC[(p[, s])]	Not supported		p = precision, s = scale
DECIMAL[(p[, s])]	Not supported		p = precision, s = scale
Approximate Numeric	**Number**		
REAL	Double (precision)	double	8 bytes
DOUBLE PRECISION	Not supported		16 bytes
FLOAT	Single (precision)	float	4 bytes

ANSI SQL-92	Access SQL	C Datatype	Comments
Character (Text)	**Text**		
CHARACTER[(n)]	String	char *	Text fields are variable-length.
CHARACTER VARYING	String	char *	
Bit Strings	**None supported**		
BIT[(n)]	Not supported		Binary fields are variable-length.
BIT VARYING	Not supported		Used by Microsoft.
Datetimes			
DATE	Not supported		10 bytes
TIME	Not supported		8 bytes (plus fraction)
TIMESTAMP	Date/Time	COleDateTime	19 bytes
TIME WITH TIME ZONE	Not supported		14 bytes
TIMESTAMP WITH TIME ZONE	Not supported		25 bytes
Intervals (Datetimes)	**None supported**		

Many of the data types described in the Access SQL column of Table 5.8 as not being supported are converted by ODBC drivers to standard ODBC data types that are compatible Access SQL data types. When you use attached database files, data types are converted by the Access database engine's ISAM driver for dBASE, FoxPro, Paradox, and Btrieve files. Data type conversion by ODBC and ISAM drivers is one of the subjects of the next chapter.

Summary

It's impossible to fully describe all the reserved words and syntax of Structured Query Language in a single chapter, especially when the chapter also must compare a particular dialect of SQL—Access SQL—to a "standard" version of the language. This is particularly true when the standard language is new, as is the case for SQL-92, and when no RDBMSs support more than a fraction of the reserved words added to SQL-89 by the new standard. For a full exposition of SQL-92, you need a reference guide, such as Jim Melton and Alan R. Simon's *Understanding the New SQL: A Complete Guide* (see the section "A Visual C++ and Database Bibliography" in this book's Introduction).

This chapter introduced newcomers to SQL—first to the ANSI variety, and then to the Access dialect. ANSI SQL (as implemented by the Microsoft ODBC API) must use the SQL pass-through technique, which lets you process queries on the back-end server of a client-server database. In order to use the Access database engine to process queries, you also need to know the Access dialect of SQL. There are many examples of both ANSI SQL and Access queries in this book, so you've just started down the path to fluency in using SQL with Visual C++ database applications. The next chapter delves into the innards of the Access database engine and its relationship to the ODBC API. Chapter 7 shows you how Visual C++ applications interface with ODBC drivers. The last chapter in Part II expands your SQL vocabulary to Access SQL's crosstab query syntax and shows you how to write SQL statements that modify the data in database tables.

6

The Microsoft Jet Database Engine

The Microsoft Jet Data Access Object (DAO) will become Visual C++ 4.0's primary method of connecting to and manipulating data that is stored in desktop and client-server databases. DAO is the term used by Microsoft and this book to describe the container (the base or master class) for all the data-related objects discussed in this chapter. The first part of this book gave you a brief introduction to the DAO and its member objects. This chapter describes the structure of the Jet DAO in detail, because the member objects of the DAO constitute the foundation on which the majority of your Visual C++ database applications are built. This chapter features examples that use the DAO's member objects to create instances of objects with C++ code and display the properties of the objects in list boxes. By the time you complete this rather lengthy chapter, it's very likely that you will have learned more than you ever wanted to know about data-related objects—or, more simply, data objects.

> **NOTE**
>
> There is not a one-to-one mapping between DAO objects and the MFC DAO classes. Wherever possible, I will show where a DAO object's functionality is found in an MFC DAO class member that is different.

Defining the Characteristics of Data Objects

In the object-oriented terminology of OLE, objects are *containers* for properties, methods, and other objects. Object *properties* are member function pairs of a programmable object; you can set or return information about the state of a programmable object, such as the value of a data item in the field of a table. One member function sets the data, and another member function returns the data—thus the term *pair*. An object *method* is a single member function of an object. Methods perform an action on the object, such as changing the object's color, size, or shape. All member functions are said to be *encapsulated* in an object. You don't need to know the internal operations of the object to create an instance of the object and to manipulate the object in C++ code. All you need is a description of the properties and methods exposed by the object.

> **NOTE**
>
> Technically, you should be able to alter any property of a programmable object by assigning an appropriate value to the Set member of the function pair. The ability to set property values under specific conditions depends on the type of object and the application in which the object is used. Access 1.x, for example, had many objects whose properties could be set only in design mode. Access 2.0 and Access 7.0 have far fewer of these "frozen" objects. Visual C++ 4.0 doesn't even have a design mode, as do Visual Basic and Access.

The Jet DAO is an OLE Automation in-process server that provides an object-oriented wrapper for the DLLs that comprise the Jet database engine. OLE Automation provides indirect access to properties and methods of programmable objects through a set of predefined interfaces. As a Visual C++ 4 programmer, you don't have to take any special steps to use the DAO features. Figure 6.1 shows AppWizard creating a DAO database project called DataDict.

FIGURE 6.1.

Visual C++ 4.0's AppWizard creating the DataDict project.

OLE Automation server applications are selective about which programmable objects and member functions are accessible to other applications. Making member functions of OLE Automation server applications accessible to OLE Automation container applications is called *exposing* the member function. OLE Automation servers have two classes of functions, `Public` and `Private`. Only `Public` functions are exposed to OLE Automation client applications, such as Visual C++. Once you create a reference to an OLE Automation server object, Visual C++'s Class Browser provides a convenient list of the collections and objects exposed by the server, plus the member functions of each object. Figure 6.2 shows the `CDaoRecordset` constructor in the Visual C++ 4 Browser. The syntax for the selected method or property appears to the right of the ? button, which opens the help topic for the property or method, as shown in Figure 6.3.

The Data Access Object classes in Visual C++ 4.0 are implemented by the seven main `CDao...` classes. (See Chapter 13, "Understanding MFC's DAO Classes," for more information on the MFC DAO classes.) These classes include all the objects that let you create, connect to, and manipulate the supported database types. This book uses the term *compound object* to describe an object that contains other objects to maintain consistency with OLE's compound document terminology. Like OLE's compound documents, compound objects have a hierarchical structure. Objects that are contained within other objects are called *member objects* of the container object. Visual C++ 4.0 treats member objects as properties of the container object.

Figure 6.4 illustrates the hierarchy of Visual C++ 4.0's DAO database classes. Access 2.0 and 7.0 have `Forms`, `Reports`, `Scripts` (macros), and `Modules Documents` collections that aren't supported in Visual C++ 4.0. In Visual C++ 4.0, `Container` objects and `Documents` collections are used to secure Jet databases in conjunction with System.mdw workgroup files that you create with Microsoft Access. (Visual C++ 4.0 can't create a workgroup file, previously called a system file.) Note that the `CDaoFieldExchange` class isn't derived from `CObject`.

FIGURE 6.2.

Visual C++ 4.0's Browser displaying the syntax for the `CDaoRecordset:: CDaoRecordset()` *constructor.*

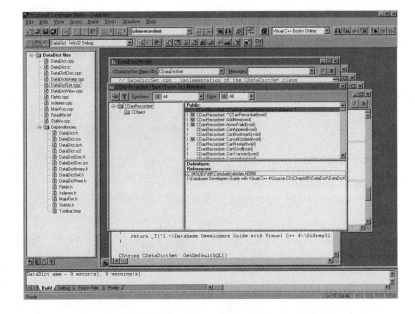

FIGURE 6.3.

The online help topic for the `CDaoRecordset:: CDaoRecordset()` *constructor.*

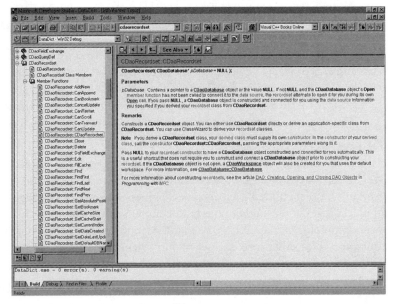

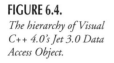

FIGURE 6.4.

The hierarchy of Visual C++ 4.0's Jet 3.0 Data Access Object.

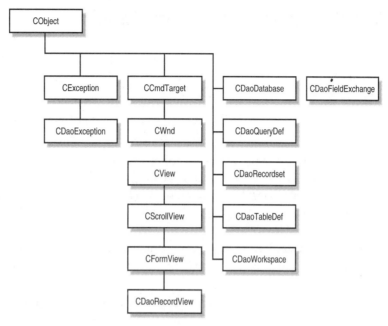

The following sections describe the version of the Jet DAO included with Visual C++ 4.0, how you create member objects of the data access object, and one method of classifying these member objects (by their persistency). As is the case for many other disciplines, the taxonomy of database objects isn't a settled issue. Detailed information on the properties and methods of the data objects discussed in the following sections appears later in this chapter.

CAUTION

You might find this chapter to be somewhat difficult. It has a grand mix of DAO terminology and MFC DAO terminology. For example, there is such a thing as a DAO Recordset, and there is also an MFC DAO CDaoRecordset class. Most of the methods and properties that are contained in the DAO Recordset are found as either member functions or member variables in the MFC DAO CDaoRecordset class object. However, that one-to-one relationship doesn't always carry through. Some of the native DAO methods and properties are simply not supported in the MFC DAO classes. I will tell you when a feature of DAO isn't directly supported.

For unsupported features, you can call directly to the DAO engine. See Books Online, MFC Technical Notes, Number 54 for more information about interacting directly with DAO. It will infrequently be necessary to interact directly with DAO.

Jet Data Access and Remote Data Objects

Visual Basic programmers will realize that there are actually three different versions of DAO. Visual C++ 4 is shipped only with DAO 3.0, a 32-bit version of DAO. MFC 4's DAO classes are only 32-bit. For programmers who are still developing 16-bit applications, DAO is just not available.

Here are the three versions of DAO (each of which can be found in your Windows 95 \Program Files\Common Files\Microsoft Shared\Dao folder):

■ The Microsoft DAO 3.0 Object Library is the standard 32-bit OLE Automation "wrapper" (Dao3032.dll) for the Jet 3.0 database engine (MSJT3032.DLL in \Windows\System). Dao3032.dll is included with Visual C++ 4.0 and can be used only with 32-bit applications. Microsoft Access 7.0 uses the DAO 3.0 Object Library and the Jet 3.0 database engine.

■ The Microsoft DAO 2.5/3.0 Compatibility Library is an alternative 32-bit OLE Automation type library (Dao2532.dll). Dao2532.dll isn't included with Visual C++ 4.0.

■ The Microsoft DAO 2.5 Object Library is a 16-bit OLE Automation wrapper (Dao2516.dll) for the Jet 2.0 database engine of Access 2.0 (Msajt200.dll). Dao2516.dll isn't included with Visual C++ 4.0 and is of no use to Visual C++ programmers because DAO isn't supported by the 16-bit version(s) of MFC.

Figure 6.5 shows the relationships between the Jet database engine used by Microsoft Access 1.1, 2.0, and 7.0 (Access 95), and Visual C++ 4.0.

With Visual C++ 4, the programmer is limited to using DAO 3.0. With DAO 3.0, you can create, open, or attach tables from 1.0, 1.1, 2.5, and 3.0 Jet databases. There's not too much in the way of limitations. Follow these guidelines:

■ Use the `CompactDatabase()` member function of the `CDaoWorkspace` class to convert Jet databases from one version to another for use with Visual C++ 4.0. The `CompactDatabase()` function doesn't convert Access-specific objects, such as forms, reports, macros, and modules, from one version to another.

■ Don't use the `CompactDatabase()` method to convert Jet 1.0, 1.1, or 2.5 .MDB files to version 3.0 if you plan to use the Jet 3.0 .MDB file with Access 7.0. Access 7.0 can't open an .MDB file that you convert from an earlier version to version 3.0 with Visual C++ 4.0's `CompactDatabase()` method.

■ Visual C++ 4.0 can't create workgroup (System.mdw) files that are necessary to secure .MDB databases. You need a copy of Access 7.0 to create a 32-bit workgroup file or a copy of Access 2.0 to create a 16-bit system file (SYSTEM.MDA). Workgroup or system files usually reside on a workgroup or file server, together with shared .MDB files.

■ Don't convert existing 16-bit Access system files (SYSTEM.MDA) to 32-bit work-group files (System.mdw) until all users of the system file have converted to Jet 3.0 databases. You can attach a 16-bit SYSTEM.MDA file to a Jet 3.0 database without difficulty.

FIGURE 6.5.

A simplified compara-tive diagram of the 16-bit and 32-bit implementations of the Jet database engine.

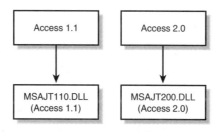

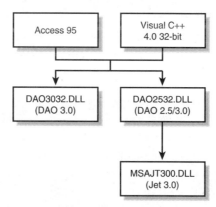

> **NOTE**
>
> Use Access's database conversion feature to upgrade versions of .MDB files that contain Access-specific objects. Converting Access 1.0 and 1.1 files is a two-way process. However, once you use Access to convert a version 1.0 or 1.1 .MDB file to Access 2.0 format, or convert a 1.0, 1.1, or 2.0 file to Access 7.0 format, the process isn't reversible. It's a safer practice to use the appropriate version of Access for all Jet database conversion operations.

Instances of Data Objects

You create an instance of the Data Access Object when you create an application that uses DAO and then reference that application's DAO object(s). Each time you add a reference (such as DataDict's dialog boxes, shown later), you add a reference to the object, not the object itself. With the data access object, a single CDaoDatabase object is created, and it is referenced throughout your application.

You create an instance of the DAO when you use an MFC DAO class that creates a DAO connection. Here's how you create an instance of the CDaoDatabase object data type (object class) for an existing database:

1. You declare an object variable with CDaoDatabase db.

2. You instantiate (create a pointer to) the new Database object with the CDaoDatabase::Open() member function.

NOTE

When you declare a class variable of one of the object data types, Visual C++ initially doesn't initialize any specific database parameters to this variable.

NOTE

It's a generally accepted programming practice (GAPP) to place variable declaration statements at the beginning of C++ procedures and to add inline comments that describe the use of the variable in your code. Unlike generally accepted accounting practices (GAAPs), which are promulgated by the AICPA (American Institute of Certified Public Accountants), GAPPs aren't certified by a standardizing body. GAPPs arise by tradition. Declaring variables at the beginning of your procedure keeps variable declarations in a single, known location. Typically, variables are declared in a header (.H) file if they're utilized in more than one source file and in the source file if that file is the only location where the variable is to be referenced.

Persistent Member Objects

Persistent member objects are objects whose properties are contained in a file. Persistent objects are often called *physical objects*. The properties of persistent member objects exist independently of your application. The following member objects of the Database object are persistent:

■ `TableDef`, `Field`, and `Index` objects are persistent table, field, and index definitions that are stored in one or more table(s) or files in the database. Jet databases store definitions in system tables of the .MDB file. If a database table isn't indexed, no `Index` objects exist for the specified `Table` object. (The `Indexes` collection of the `TableDef` object has a `Count` property value of `0`.) The FILE.DDF and FIELD.DDF files store table and index definitions for Btrieve databases. Without FILE.DDF and FIELD.DDF, you can't create a Visual C++ `Database` object for a Btrieve database.

■ `QueryDef` objects are persistent objects that are available only when you connect to a Jet database. `QueryDef` objects, which represent an SQL statement that is translated by the Access query optimizer, are stored in a system table of the Access .MDB file. `QueryDef` objects don't contain data from the tables that are involved in the query.

Changes your application makes to persistent member objects appear in each instance of a persistent data object in your application, as well as in instances of the same member object in other applications that are running in a multiuser environment. However, changes to persistent objects made by other applications may not appear until the object is reopened or refreshed. Concurrency and consistency of persistent objects are discussed in a forthcoming section.

Recordset Objects Created from Virtual Tables

Although the data in tables is persistent, the Jet representation of the data is impersistent. A `Recordset` is a virtual table that is a temporary image (copy) of all or a part of a table or the resulting set of columns and rows returned by running an SQL query against one or more tables. Instances of `Recordset` objects are referenced by an object variable of the `Recordset` type and don't have a `Name` property. `Recordset` objects are stored in RAM and have no physical manifestation; you can't copy a `Recordset` object directly to a disk file. If the image is larger than the amount of free RAM available to your application, portions of the virtual table are paged to a temporary file that usually is located in your \Windows\Temp folder (as pointed to by the TEMP = environment variable). The `Recordset` object exists only for the duration of the life of the variable of the `Recordset` data type that points to the virtual table. You can choose between creating the dynamic and static `Recordset` objects described in the following two sections.

Dynamic *Recordset* Objects

Dynamic `Recordset` objects, like persistent member objects, reflect changes made by others in a multiuser environment to the persistent objects of the database. Thus, your application sees the most current version of the physical tables that underlie your member objects. Your application can alter the data values of most, but not all, dynamic virtual tables; the exceptions are discussed later in this chapter. The following are the two types of dynamic `Recordset` objects that are based on virtual tables:

■ Recordset objects of the Table type represent the data contained in a single table and are the default Recordset type. Table-type Recordset objects use the Seek method to locate a specific record in an indexed field. You can't use the Find... methods with Table-type Recordset objects.

■ Recordset objects of the Dynaset type represent data contained in a single table or the result of executing an SQL SELECT query or a persistent QueryDef object against one or more tables. Dynaset-type Recordset objects are the most common type of Recordset object used by Visual C++ developers.

> **NOTE**
>
> The Recordset object replaces the Table, Dynaset, and Snapshot objects defined by Access 1.x.

The advantage of using Recordset objects of the Dynaset type is that the Recordset is populated initially with only a subset of the underlying records. For example, when you open a large Recordset object of the Dynaset type, only the first 100 rows are retrieved from the underlying table(s). Subsequent Move... operations on the record pointer of the Recordset retrieve additional groups of 100 rows as needed. Applying the MoveLast method to a Recordset retrieves all the rows, which might take a substantial amount of time if your Recordset contains thousands of rows.

Static *Recordset* Objects

A Recordset object of the Snapshot type is the Database object's sole static member. A Snapshot-type Recordset object captures a static image of a persistent member object or a Dynaset object. The data values contained in Snapshot-type Recordset objects are read-only at all times. You can apply any of the methods for Dynaset-type Recordset objects to conventional Snapshot objects, except methods that add, delete, or update data. You specify a Snapshot-type Recordset by substituting the intrinsic dbOpenSnapshot constant for the *nType* argument of the CDaoRecordset::Open() method.

> **NOTE**
>
> Intrinsic global database constants that begin with db are discussed in the section "Understanding Flags and Intrinsic Symbolic Constants."

Snapshot-type Recordset objects retrieve every row from underlying table or query, so opening a Snapshot-type Recordset object on a large table or query result set causes a performance hit. However, operations on Snapshot-type Recordsets with 100 or fewer rows usually are faster than those of the Dynaset type.

Consistency Issues with *Recordset* Objects

As noted in the two preceding sections, all instances of data objects based on persistent objects, and all instances of dynamic data objects based on virtual tables, reflect changes made to the object when any application changes the value of the data contained in a persistent object. Changes to the structure of a persistent object also are reflected in other instances of the object, but structural changes to database objects are drastic operations that should occur infrequently.

For example, if you change the Value property of a data item in the Field object of a Recordset object of the Table type in one instance of a Database object, the Value property of the corresponding data item changes in all other instances of the same Database object. However, the record pointers that determine the current record of each Recordset object of the Table or Dynaset type are independent of one another and of the record pointers of other instances of these objects. Thus, the new value would be apparent only to others in a multiuser environment whose open form coincidentally displays the changed data item. To ensure that the Recordset contains data that is consistent with underlying persistent objects, you apply the Refresh method. The Refresh method re-creates the Recordset object to which it is applied; if the Recordset is based on a QueryDef object, Refresh re-executes the query.

> **NOTE**
>
> You should apply the Refresh method to a Recordset object periodically to ensure that the Recordset object of instances of a Data control object sharing a multiuser Database object reflect current data. Applying the Refresh method to a Data control before and after updating or deleting records with transaction processing applications is good database programming practice. You must use the Refresh method with a Data control to open a database whose Connect and/or RecordSource properties you specify in run mode.

Understanding the Properties and Methods of the DAO *DBEngine* Object

The DBEngine object isn't directly exposed with the MFC DAO classes. Instead, it's accessed through a number of member functions that are in the CDaoWorkspace class. DBEngine has several properties and methods that are useful for advanced database applications. Table 6.1 lists the properties of the DBEngine object.

Table 6.1. Properties of the DBEngine object.

DAO Property	CDaoWorkspace *Member Property Function*	*Notes/Parameter Information*
DefaultUser	SetDefaultUser()	Takes a pointer to a string variable of 20 characters or less containing the default user ID (UID) to be used for all Workspace sessions if no user ID is provided. The default value is Access's default Admin user, "Admin."
DefaultPassword	SetDefaultPassword()	Takes a pointer to a string variable of 14 characters or less containing the default password (PWD) to be used for all Workspace sessions. The default value is an empty string (" ").
IniPath	SetIniPath() GetIniPath()	A pointer string containing the name of a Windows registry subkey that specifies the location of the System.mdw workgroup file (Jet 3.0) or System.mda system file (Jet1.x and 2.0) for secure Access applications.
LoginTimeout	GetLoginTimeout() SetLoginTimeout()	Gets or sets the number of seconds before an error is generated when you're attempting to log in to an ODBC data source. The default is 20 seconds.
Version	GetVersion()	Returns a CString object that will contain the version number of the Jet database engine.

You must set DBEngine property values before opening a CDaoWorkspace object that depends on the property values. Ordinarily, you place CDaoWorkspace.PropertyFunction() calls before you open the database.

Table 6.2 lists the methods applicable to the DBEngine object. Again, these methods are accessed using the CDaoWorkspace class object member functions. The most commonly used methods of the DBEngine object are Idle, CompactDatabase, and RepairDatabase.

Table 6.2. Methods for the DBEngine object.

Method	CDaoWorkspace *Member Method Function*	*Notes/Parameter Information*
Idle	Idle()	Allows the Jet database engine to catch up on background processing when there is substantial processing activity going on simultaneously in your multiuser application. The only valid parameter is dbFreeLocks.
CompactDatabase	CompactDatabase()	Compacts a Jet database that isn't open in any application to save file space or to convert a Jet database from one version to another. Don't use Jet's CompactDatabase method to change the version of .MDB files that are also used by Access applications.
RepairDatabase	RepairDatabase()	Repairs a damaged database (if possible). This function takes a single pointer to a string containing the name of the database to be repaired. It's recommended that you subsequently call the CompactDatabase() function after repairing the database.
CreateWorkspace	Create()	Creates a new named CDaoWorkspace object with a specified user ID and password.
RegisterDatabase	None	Creates an entry in the registry (32-bit) or in the ODBC.INI file (16-bit) for a named ODBC data source. This functionality isn't directly supported by the CDaoWorkspace object.

The RegisterDatabase() method isn't supported by the DAO MFC classes. If you need to use a DAO functionality that isn't supported by the DAO MFC classes, you can call the functionality directly. For more information, refer to Technical Note 54, "Calling DAO Directly While

Using MFC DAO Classes," which can be found on Books Online on the Visual C++ 4 distribution CD.

The full syntax of the CompactDatabase method is either this:

```
static void PASCAL CompactDatabase( LPCTSTR lpszSrcName,
LPCTSTR lpszDestName, LPCTSTR lpszLocale = dbLangGeneral,
int nOptions = 0 );
```

or, if you want to specify a password, this:

```
static void PASCAL CompactDatabase( LPCTSTR lpszSrcName,
LPCTSTR lpszDestName, LPCTSTR lpszLocale,
int nOptions, LPCTSTR lpszPassword );
```

Note that if you want to use a password, you must specify the locale string and options parameters.

If you specify the same path and filename for *lpszSrcName* and *lpszDestName*, the compacted file replaces the original file. The *lpszLocale* argument specifies the collating order of the file. The default value is dbLangGeneral (;LANGID=0x0409;CP=1252;COUNTRY=0). The *nOptions* argument lets you specify the type of the file and whether to encrypt or decrypt the file with the constants listed in Table 6.3.

Table 6.3. Constants (flags) for the *nOptions* argument of the CompactDatabase method.

Constant	Value	Purpose
dbVersion10	1	Compacts to a Microsoft Access 1.0 .MDB file.
dbVersion11	8	Compacts to a Microsoft Access 1.1 .MDB file.
dbVersion20	16	Compacts to a Jet 2.5 (Access 2.0) .MDB file.
dbVersion30	32	Compacts to a Jet 3.0 (Access 7.0) .MDB file.
dbEncrypt	2	Encrypts the compacted file.
dbDecrypt	4	Decrypts an encrypted file.

The syntax of the RepairDatabase() method function is

```
static void PASCAL RepairDatabase(LPCTSTR lpszName);
```

where *lpszName* is the well-formed path to and the filename of the Jet .MDB database file you want to repair.

In most cases, Jet databases are secured only in multiuser applications. Thus, use of the DefaultUser(), DefaultPassword(), and IniPath() property functions and the Idle() and CreateWorkspace() method functions is covered in Chapter 19, "Running Visual C++ Database Applications on a Network." The LoginTimeout property and the RegisterDatabase method are two of the subjects of Chapter 3, "Using Visual C++ Database Functions," and Chapter 20, "Creating Front Ends for Client-Server Databases."

Defining the *Workspace* and *Database* Objects

Most of the preceding sections of this chapter have been devoted to defining terms and classifying data objects by their behavior. This might have confused you, because both MFC DAO terms and "regular" DAO terms are spread throughout this chapter. Generally, if you're not sure whether a term is MFC or DAO, you can search in the Visual C++ Books Online to determine the usage of a particular term. The remainder of this chapter provides a detailed analysis of the properties of and the methods that apply to the CDaoWorkspace and CDaoDatabase objects and to member objects of the CDaoDatabase object. It also tells you how to use these properties and methods in your Visual C++ 4.0 database applications.

Before you can get or set the properties of a Database object or apply methods to a Database object, you need to create a variable of the CDaoDatabase type. You can create a class of type CDaoDatabase with the following two lines of Visual C++ code:

```
CDaoDatabase dbName;
dbName.Open(ConnectArguments);
```

Properties and Methods of the *Workspace* Object

The Workspace is defined as a *session* of the DBEngine object. A session is an instance of the DBEngine object for a single user, who is identified by a user ID and password, including the default Admin user ID and empty password. Technically, Open() and Create() are methods of the CDaoWorkspace object, because you can't apply a method, such as OpenDatabase, to an object for which a reference doesn't exist. Thus, the following syntax is better at keeping with the principles of object-oriented programming:

```
CDaoWorkspace wsName;

wsName.Create("database.mdb"); // Create default workspace
// Or call Append(...) to append to an existing workspace

CDaoDatabase dbName(wsName);
```

An additional benefit of creating the default CDaoWorkspace object variable is that you have a pointer for implementing security features and performing transactions for the session with desktop databases, such as Jet, that include security features and support transactions. Jet (Access) security features are one of the subjects of Chapter 19. The use of Jet transactions is covered in Chapter 15, "Designing Online Transaction-Processing Systems." The IsolateODBCTrans, Name, and UserName properties of the Workspace object, which are seldom used in Visual C++ database applications, are described in Chapters 19 and 20. For completeness, Table 6.4 lists the methods of the Workspace object.

Table 6.4. Methods applicable to the Workspace object.

Method	CDaoWorkspace *Member Function*	*Purpose/Parameters*
Open	Open()	Opens an existing Workspace object.
Create	Create()	Creates a new Workspace object.
CreateGroup	Not implemented	Creates a new Group object that you can append to the Groups collection or to a User object.
CreateUser	Not implemented	Creates a new User object that you can append to the Users collection or to a Group object.
BeginTrans	BeginTrans()	Specifies the beginning of a series of related operations that update data values in one or more persistent objects that underlie one or more Recordset objects.
CommitTrans	CommitTrans()	Specifies the end of persistent data object update operations that constitute a single transaction and causes the updates to be applied to the table object(s) underlying the Recordset(s).
Rollback	RollBack()	If the database type supports transactions (ws*Name*.Transactions = TRUE), cancels the updating of the table objects(s) underlying the Recordset(s) by a preceding CommitTrans statement.
Close	Close()	Closes the specified CDaoWorkspace and closes all Database objects opened in CDaoWorkspace.

Properties of the *Database* Object

The Database object has 11 properties whose values you can read to determine the characteristics of the database as a whole. The majority of these properties are read-only at all times. Table 6.5 lists the properties of the Database object in the approximate order of the frequency with which you're likely to use them. The last five properties listed aren't supported by MFC's implementation of DAO. You can access them by calling DAO directly, as noted in Visual C++ 4's Technical Note 54.

Table 6.5. Properties of the Database object.

Property	CDaoDatabase *Member Function*	*Purpose/Parameters*
Name	GetName()	Returns a CString pointer that contains a well-formed path to the open database and the name of the open database.
Connect	GetConnect()	Returns a CString pointer that contains the value of the string used to establish a connection to the database. The Connect property is an empty string for Access databases.
Updatable	CanUpdate()	Indicates if the database has been opened in read-write (TRUE) or read-only (FALSE) mode. The Updatable property itself is read-only. (See the section "Connecting to an Existing Jet Database.")
Transactions	CanTransact()	Indicates whether the database supports the Rollback transaction processing statement that lets you undo a group of changes to data values in the database's tables (TRUE). Access and most client-server databases support the rolling back of transactions.
QueryTimeout	GetQueryTimeout()	Specifies or indicates the length of time in seconds before a time-out error occurs when you execute a query against a client-server database via an ODBC driver. The default value is 60 seconds.

continues

Table 6.5. continued

Property	CDaoDatabase Member Function	Purpose/Parameters
Version	GetVersion()	Returns an Integer flag that indicates the version number of the Jet engine that created the database (see Table 6.4).
CollatingOrder	Not directly supported	An Integer flag that indicates the language whose rules are used by the database to sort text fields. The default value is 256 (for English and most Western European languages). The CollatingOrder property is read-only, except when you use the CreateDatabase() and CompactDatabase() methods. (These two methods expect the CollatingOrder flag to be a long integer.)
Replicable	Not directly supported	When set to TRUE, creates a replicable database from which you can create additional replicas for distribution to users. Once this is made replicable, you can't set the Replica property to FALSE. Returns TRUE for a replicable database.
DesignMasterID	Not directly supported	A globally unique ID (GUID) that identifies the replicable database from which user replicas are created.
ReplicaID	Not directly supported	A GUID that identifies each database replica.
V1xNullBehavior	Not directly supported	If set to TRUE, zero-length strings ("") in Jet (Access) 1.x fields of the Text and Memo type are converted to Null values.

> **NOTE**
>
> The replication properties in Table 6.5—`Replicable`, `DesignMasterID`, and `ReplicaID`—don't appear in the Properties list of the online help topic for the `Database` object. Replication is limited to Jet 3.0 (Access 7.0) databases. The `KeepLocal` property applies to objects contained in a replicable database, not to the `Database` object itself.

Methods Applicable to the *Database* Object

The `Database` object has many more methods than properties. Many of Visual C++ DAO's methods of the `Database` object are now methods of the `CDaoWorkspace`, `CDaoTableDef`, `CDaoRecordset`, and `CDaoQueryDef` objects. The `OpenRecordset` and `CreateQueryDef` methods are `Database` object methods, because data objects of these types can (and usually do) act on more than one table of the `Database` object. However, these two methods are attached to different DAO MFC objects (see Table 6.6). The methods that you can apply to `Database` objects are listed in Table 6.6. They are listed in groups of related methods rather than in alphabetical order. The DAO MRC class is also listed because it varies with each of these methods.

Table 6.6. Methods applicable to the `Database` object.

Method	DAO Class and Member Function	Purpose/Parameters
CreateTableDef	CDaoTableDef::Create()	Used in a `Set` statement to create a new persistent `TableDef` object that defines a newly created table in a database.
CreateRelation	CDaoDatabase::CreateRelation()	Used in a `Set` statement to establish a relationship between the primary key field of a base table and the foreign key field of a related table.
OpenRecordset	CDaoRecordset::Open()	Used in a `Set` statement to create a new `Recordset` object of the `Table`, `Dynaset`, or `Snapshot` type. `OpenRecordset` is the most commonly used method of the `Database` object.

continues

Table 6.6. continued

Method	DAO Class and Member Function	Purpose/Parameters
Refresh	CDaoRecordset::Requery()	Updates collections of persistent objects of the database, such as the QueryDefs and TableDefs collections, to reflect the current content of the collection.
CreateQueryDef	CDaoQueryDef::Create()	Used in a Set statement to create a new persistent QueryDef object based on an SQL statement.
Execute	CDaoQueryDef::Execute()	Executes a QueryDef or SQL statement that doesn't return records, such as an UPDATE, INSERT, or DELETE query. Access uses the term *action query* to indicate a query that doesn't return records.
CreateProperty	Not directly supported	Adds a user-defined property of a name you specify to the Database object and sets the data type and the initial value of the user-defined property.
MakeReplica	Not directly supported	Creates a user replica from the design-master replica of a replicable database. You specify the location and filename of the new replica and whether the replica is updatable or read-only with arguments of the MakeReplica method.
Synchronize	Not directly supported	Synchronizes the Database object with changes made to a replica of the database, which

Method	DAO Class and Member Function	Purpose/Parameters
		is specified by location and filename. You can receive changes, export changes, or perform bidirectional updates (the default), depending on the value of the argument.
Close	CDaoDatabase::Close()	Closes a Database object and frees resources consumed by the object.

All member objects of the CDaoDatabase object must be closed before you can close the CDaoDatabase object. If you've declared your CDaoDatabase object variable with local scope, you don't need to use the Close() function, because the CDaoDatabase object and its member object are closed by the destructor when the variables go out of scope at the termination of the procedure in which the variables were declared.

Connecting to an Existing Jet Database

Here is the full, generalized syntax of the Open() function that you use to connect to and create a named reference to an existing database:

```
CDaoDatabase::Open(
    LPCTSTR lpszName,
    BOOL bExclusive = FALSE,
    BOOL bReadOnly = FALSE,
    LPCTSTR lpszConnect = _T("") );
```

Table 6.7 lists the arguments used with the Open() function.

Table 6.7. The arguments of the Open() function.

Argument	Purpose
lpszName	Specifies the well-formed path (drive and directory) to the location of the database file(s), except for ODBC data sources. Only the path to the directory that contains the table and index files is required when you connect to dBASE, FoxPro, and Paradox databases. All the files of these databases must be located in the same directory. You can use the uniform naming convention

continues

Table 6.7. continued

Argument	Purpose
	(UNC) to specify database files that are located on a network server. For example, you can use \\\\Servername{\\Folder\\Sharename as the value. For databases connected through the ODBC API, use the data source name (DSN) of an ODBC data source that is registered in your registry or your \WINDOWS\ODBC.INI file. Alternatively, you can leave this argument empty for ODBC databases and provide the required connect string in the `lpszConnect` argument.
bExclusive	An Integer flag that determines if the database is to be opened in exclusive (TRUE) or shared (FALSE) mode. The default value is FALSE.
bReadonly	An Integer flag that determines if the database is to be opened in read-only (TRUE) or read-write (FALSE) mode. The default value is FALSE.
lpszConnect	A pointer to a character string whose content depends on the type of database you intend to open. The `lpszConnect` argument isn't used for Jet databases, but it's required for other desktop databases. The `lpszConnect` argument is necessary to prevent the Login dialog of ODBC databases from appearing when you specify an ODBC data source.

The following code fragment opens the Jet 2.5 Stdreg32.mdb sample database included with Visual C++ 4.0 for exclusive, read-only access:

```
CDaoDatabase  db;

    db.Open("Stdreg32.mdb",  TRUE, TRUE)
```

The following code creates a new Jet 2.5 (Access 2.0) database in the current directory:

```
CDaoDatabase  db;

    db.Create("new.mdb",_
        dbLangGeneral, dbVersion25)
```

To make a new Jet database useful, you must add tables to the database's TableDefs collection and then add fields and indexes to each table's Fields and Index collections. The following sections describe the process more fully.

Using the *TableDefs* Collection and *TableDef* Objects

The DAO `TableDefs` collection contains a member `TableDef` object for each table in the database. `TableDefs` are handled with the `CDaoTableDef` DAO MFC class. `TableDef` members qualify as objects because each `TableDef` has its own set of properties and has methods that are common to all members of the collection. The properties of the `TableDef` object describe each table in the database. Table 6.8 lists the properties of the `TableDef` object in the order in which the values might appear in a data dictionary.

Table 6.8. Properties of the `TableDef` object.

Property	Member Function	Description
Name	GetName()	Returns a CString object that contains the name of the table.
Connect	GetConnect()	Returns a CString object that contains the connect string used to attach tables to a Jet database. You can attach tables only to Jet .MDB databases.
SourceTableName	GetSourceTableName()	Returns a CString object that contains the name of an attached table. You can use the Name property to create an alias for an attached table.
ValidationRule	GetValidationRule()	Returns a CString object that contains a rule for maintaining table-level domain integrity, expressed as a string containing the WHERE criterion of a Jet SQL SELECT statement (without the WHERE SQL reserved word), such as InvoiceDate >= OrderDate. InvoiceDate and OrderDate are fields of the same table. Multiple validation rules must use the SQL AND conjunction. (Jet 2.5 and 3.0 databases only.)

continues

Table 6.8. continued

Property	Member Function	Description
ValidationText	GetValidationText()	Returns a CString object that contains the message that will appear if an attempted update to the table would violate the ValidationRule property. (Jet 2.5 and 3.0 databases only.)
ConflictTable	Not directly supported	The name of a "side table" that reports conflicts when an attempt is made to synchronize database replicas. Conflict tables are named TableName_conflict, where TableName is the value of the Name property of the TableDef. (Jet 3.0 databases only.)
DateCreated	GetDateCreated()	Returns a COleDateTime object that contains the date and time that the table was created.
LastUpdated	GetDateLastUpdated()	Returns a COleDateTime object that contains the date and time of the last modification to the data in the table.
Updatable	CanUpdate()	Returns TRUE if you have read-write access to the table and FALSE if you have read-only access.
Attributes	GetAttributes()	A long integer that contains the value of the option and status flags listed in Table 6.9.

The *Attributes* Property of *TableDef* Objects

The value of the Attributes property consists of the sum of the value of the flags listed in Table 6.9. A flag uses the individual bits of a long int (16 bits) to indicate if a particular attribute applies to the table. The values (bits set) of individual attributes can be represented by the decimal equivalent (value) of the position of the bit in the attribute flag or by the value of a symbolic constant. Table 6.9 shows the decimal and hexadecimal (hex, prefaced with 0x) values of each attribute value. Using hex values for the value of flags makes the concept of setting bits more evident. Always use the symbolic value when using these attributes, however.

Table 6.9. The flags used to indicate the attributes of table objects.

Attribute	Value	Description
dbSystemObject	-2147483646 0x80000002	Indicates that the table is a system table (read-only).
dbHiddenObject	1 0x1	Indicates that the table is a temp-orary hidden table that Jet uses for internal purposes (read-only).
dbAttachedTable	1073741824 0x40000000	Indicates that the table is a desktop database table (not an ODBC table) attached to an Access database. If the attached table is an Access table (a table from an Access database that is attached to the Access table of your Database object), the table has been opened in shared mode.
dbAttachedExclusive	65536 0x10000	Indicates that an attached Access table has been opened for exclusive use by your application.
dbAttachedODBC	536870912 0x20000000	Indicates that the table is an ODBC table attached to an Access database.
dbAttachSavePWD	131072 0x20000	Indicates that the user name and password for the database from which the table is attached are included in the value of the Connect property. This means that the user of your application doesn't need to enter the user name and password for a secure database each time your application attaches the table.

> **NOTE**
>
> The negative decimal value of `dbSystemObject` appears because the return value for `GetAttributes()` is in unsigned `long int` format. Thus, values of `0x80000000` and greater represent negative `long int` values, and values of `0x8000` represent negative `int` values.
>
> Had Microsoft defined `GetAttributes()` as returning a `DWORD` instead, these values would be correctly defined as nonnegative values.

Understanding Flags and Intrinsic Symbolic Constants

The values of flags in Windows applications are most commonly defined using `#define` statements. In DAO, these flags are actually defined as variables with the attribute of `const` in the file dbdaoint.h. In Visual C++, you ordinarily declare global constants in the header (.H) file, in the format of `#define symbol` *value*. In dbdaoint.h, these values are typically defined as

```
const long dbAttachSavePWD = 131072;
```

Usually symbols are in uppercase. (Notice, for example, that the identifiers in Table 6.9 are mixed case because they're not `#defined` values.) The symbolic constants for Visual C++'s data access object, each of which are prefaced by `db`, are *global constants* defined in dbdaoint.h. Figure 6.6 shows the definition of the variable `dbOpenDynaset` and shows where it's defined and used. You can use the Object Browser to determine the numeric value of any of the `db...` constants by double-clicking the constant name in the left pane or by double-clicking the listing under the Definitions heading in the right pane.

FIGURE 6.6.

A symbolic global database constant from the Microsoft DAO 3.0 Object Library.

If more than one attribute is applicable to the table, the attributes are combined with the logical or operator (¦), which performs an operation similar to decimal addition. (The difference between the ¦ and + operators is that the ¦ operator doesn't perform carry operations on bits involved in the addition.) Thus, if an attached Jet table includes the password for the database in the `Connect` property (`0x20000`) and is opened for exclusive use (`0x10000`), the value of the `Attributes` property is `0x30000`, or decimal `196608`. This value can be created by the statement

```
dbName.Attributes = dbAttachedSavePWD ¦ dbAttachExclusive;
```

Using masks to determine the value of flags is discussed in the next section.

TIP

It's good programming practice to always use symbolic constants to represent the values of flags, even when the decimal value of the flag is a small number. Although you might have to type more characters, using symbolic constants for flags makes your code more understandable, both to you and to others. In the unlikely event that a future version of an application will assign different values to attribute flags, you can substitute the new values for the constants in one location of your application. If an OLE Automation server defines new values for its symbolic constants, values are updated automatically when you create a reference to the server.

Mapping Database Member Objects with the *CDaoTableDef* Collection

You can use the members of the CDaoTableDef object to map the tables in the database. Mapping database tables is the first step in creating a data dictionary for a database. You can create the starting form of a simple data dictionary for any desktop database supported by Visual C++ 4.0. Use list boxes to display the properties of each TableDef object and add a few lines of Visual C++ code to populate (the object-oriented term for "fill") the list boxes.

For the most part, this book tries to use complete, self-contained sample database applications rather than code snippets to illustrate Visual C++ database application design and programming techniques. Some of the more complex sample applications are constructed in stages; the first stage is completed in one chapter, and other features are added to the application in successive chapters.

You start the first sample application, DataDict, in this section, and then add features that relate to QueryDef objects. Figure 6.7 shows the design of the TabelDefs dialog box of the DataDict application.

NOTE

All the source files for the DataDict application are included on the CD that comes with this book. If you installed the files that are on the CD, the DataDict files are located in your CHAPTR06 folder, unless you specified a different location during the installation process. Each Visual C++ sample application in this book is included in a separate subfolder named CHAPTR##, where ## is the chapter number. (Put a 0 before the number for Chapters 2 through 9.)

An identical structure of folders is also found on the CD itself, so that if you aren't rebuilding the sample programs, you won't need to take up valuable disk space for these projects.

FIGURE 6.7.
The design of Data-Dict's `TableDef` *form.*

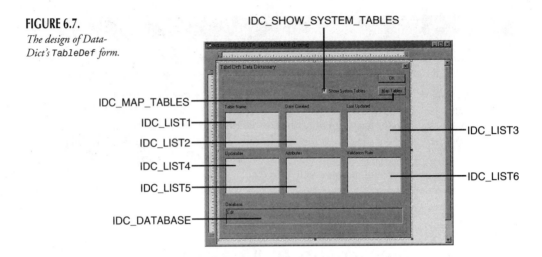

The `TableDefs` collection, like other `Database` object collections, has only one property, `Count`. You access this property using the `CDaoDatabase::GetTableDefCount()` member function. You use the `Count` property to index a `for()` loop to fill the list boxes with each table's attributes.

The list boxes in DataDict's dialog box are basically standard, but I've linked their current selections so that changing the current selection on any one of the list boxes will change the other five list boxes to match the new current selection made by the user, as shown in Listing 6.1. Each list box will scroll independently without affecting the current selection.

Listing 6.1. The code to populate the list boxes of the `IDD_DATA_DICTIONARY` dialog box.

```
// DataDictionary.cpp : implementation file
//

#include "stdafx.h"
#include "test.h"
#include "DataDictionary.h"

#ifdef _DEBUG
#define new DEBUG_NEW
#undef THIS_FILE
static char THIS_FILE[] = __FILE__;
#endif

/////////////////////////////////////////////////////////////////////////////
// DataDictionary dialog

DataDictionary::DataDictionary(CWnd* pParent /*=NULL*/)
    : CDialog(DataDictionary::IDD, pParent)
{
    //{{AFX_DATA_INIT(DataDictionary)
    m_Database = _T("");
    //}}AFX_DATA_INIT
```

```
        m_pDatabase = NULL;
        m_pTableDef = NULL;
}


void DataDictionary::DoDataExchange(CDataExchange* pDX)
{
        CDialog::DoDataExchange(pDX);
        //{{AFX_DATA_MAP(DataDictionary)
        DDX_Control(pDX, IDC_SHOW_SYSTEM_TABLES, m_SystemTables);
        DDX_Control(pDX, IDC_LIST6, m_List6);
        DDX_Control(pDX, IDC_LIST5, m_List5);
        DDX_Control(pDX, IDC_LIST4, m_List4);
        DDX_Control(pDX, IDC_LIST3, m_List3);
        DDX_Control(pDX, IDC_LIST2, m_List2);
        DDX_Control(pDX, IDC_LIST1, m_List1);
        DDX_Text(pDX, IDC_DATABASE, m_Database);
        //}}AFX_DATA_MAP
}


BEGIN_MESSAGE_MAP(DataDictionary, CDialog)
        //{{AFX_MSG_MAP(DataDictionary)
        ON_BN_CLICKED(IDC_MAP_TABLES, OnMapTables)
        ON_LBN_SELCHANGE(IDC_LIST1, OnSelchangeList1)
        ON_LBN_SELCHANGE(IDC_LIST2, OnSelchangeList2)
        ON_LBN_SELCHANGE(IDC_LIST3, OnSelchangeList3)
        ON_LBN_SELCHANGE(IDC_LIST4, OnSelchangeList4)
        ON_LBN_SELCHANGE(IDC_LIST5, OnSelchangeList5)
        ON_LBN_SELCHANGE(IDC_LIST6, OnSelchangeList6)
        //}}AFX_MSG_MAP
END_MESSAGE_MAP()

/////////////////////////////////////////////////////////////////////////////
// DataDictionary message handlers

BOOL DataDictionary::OnInitDialog()
{
        CDialog::OnInitDialog();

        // TODO: Add extra initialization here

        // Set up your CDaoTabledef object!

        m_Database = m_pDatabase->GetName();

        // Update the list boxes... Forces a refresh of dialog, too!
        OnMapTables();

        return TRUE;  // Return TRUE unless you set the focus to a control
                      // EXCEPTION: OCX Property Pages should return FALSE
}

void DataDictionary::OnMapTables()
{
        // TODO: Add your control notification handler code here
```

continues

Listing 6.1. continued

```cpp
    int nIndex = 0;
    CDaoTableDefInfo tabledefinfo;
    CString Formatted;

    m_List1.ResetContent();
    m_List2.ResetContent();
    m_List3.ResetContent();
    m_List4.ResetContent();
    m_List5.ResetContent();
    m_List6.ResetContent();

    for (nIndex = 0; nIndex < m_pDatabase->GetTableDefCount(); ++nIndex)
    {
        m_pDatabase->GetTableDefInfo(nIndex, tabledefinfo, AFX_DAO_ALL_INFO);

        if ((tabledefinfo.m_lAttributes & dbSystemObject) == 0 ||
            m_SystemTables.GetCheck() != 0)
        {
            m_List1.AddCString(tabledefinfo.m_strName);

            m_List2.AddCString(tabledefinfo.m_dateCreated.Format("%X %x"));

            m_List3.AddCString(tabledefinfo.m_dateLastUpdated.Format("%X %x"));

            m_List4.AddCString(tabledefinfo.m_bUpdatable ? "Updatable" :
                "NotUpdatable");

            Formatted.Format("0x%8.8X", tabledefinfo.m_lAttributes);

            m_List5.AddCString(Formatted);

            m_List6.AddCString(tabledefinfo.m_strValidationRule.IsEmpty() ?
                " - None defined " :
                "\"" + tabledefinfo.m_strValidationRule + "\"");
        }
    }

    m_List1.SetCurSel(1);
    m_List2.SetCurSel(1);
    m_List3.SetCurSel(1);
    m_List4.SetCurSel(1);
    m_List5.SetCurSel(1);
    m_List6.SetCurSel(1);

    // Force an update of the dialog box!
    UpdateData(FALSE);
}

// All of the OnSelchangedList?() functions cause each
// list box to follow the last selection in any other
// list box. An interesting concept...

void DataDictionary::OnSelchangeList1()
{
    // TODO: Add your control notification handler code here
    m_List2.SetCurSel(m_List1.GetCurSel());
    m_List3.SetCurSel(m_List1.GetCurSel());
```

```cpp
    m_List4.SetCurSel(m_List1.GetCurSel());
    m_List5.SetCurSel(m_List1.GetCurSel());
    m_List6.SetCurSel(m_List1.GetCurSel());
}

void DataDictionary::OnSelchangeList2()
{
    // TODO: Add your control notification handler code here
    m_List1.SetCurSel(m_List2.GetCurSel());
    m_List3.SetCurSel(m_List2.GetCurSel());
    m_List4.SetCurSel(m_List2.GetCurSel());
    m_List5.SetCurSel(m_List2.GetCurSel());
    m_List6.SetCurSel(m_List2.GetCurSel());
}

void DataDictionary::OnSelchangeList3()
{
    // TODO: Add your control notification handler code here
    m_List1.SetCurSel(m_List3.GetCurSel());
    m_List2.SetCurSel(m_List3.GetCurSel());
    m_List4.SetCurSel(m_List3.GetCurSel());
    m_List5.SetCurSel(m_List3.GetCurSel());
    m_List6.SetCurSel(m_List3.GetCurSel());

}

void DataDictionary::OnSelchangeList4()
{
    // TODO: Add your control notification handler code here

    m_List1.SetCurSel(m_List4.GetCurSel());
    m_List2.SetCurSel(m_List4.GetCurSel());
    m_List3.SetCurSel(m_List4.GetCurSel());
    m_List5.SetCurSel(m_List4.GetCurSel());
    m_List6.SetCurSel(m_List4.GetCurSel());
}

void DataDictionary::OnSelchangeList5()
{
    // TODO: Add your control notification handler code here

    m_List1.SetCurSel(m_List5.GetCurSel());
    m_List2.SetCurSel(m_List5.GetCurSel());
    m_List3.SetCurSel(m_List5.GetCurSel());
    m_List4.SetCurSel(m_List5.GetCurSel());
    m_List6.SetCurSel(m_List5.GetCurSel());
}

void DataDictionary::OnSelchangeList6()
{
    // TODO: Add your control notification handler code here

    m_List1.SetCurSel(m_List6.GetCurSel());
    m_List2.SetCurSel(m_List6.GetCurSel());
    m_List3.SetCurSel(m_List6.GetCurSel());
    m_List4.SetCurSel(m_List6.GetCurSel());
    m_List5.SetCurSel(m_List6.GetCurSel());
}
```

The DataDictionary dialog box is displayed using the code shown in the following code fragment. The only item of information passed to the DataDictionary dialog box is a pointer to the current `CDaoDatabase` object (in bold), which you can retrieve from the view class:

```
void CTestView::OnViewTabledefs()
{
    // TODO: Add your command handler code here
    DataDictionary    dd;

//    Pass the database object pointer:
    dd.m_pDatabase = m_pSet->m_pDatabase;

    dd.DoModal();
}
```

The Database text box at the bottom of the dialog box shows the currently open database. This program could have been written to prompt the user for a database to open, but for the purposes of this program, I didn't add this feature. Clicking on the Map Tables button will refresh the list boxes. This allows the Show System Tables check box to take effect when it's checked or unchecked.

When using the program, you can click a table name in any of the list boxes, and the corresponding selection in the other five list boxes will also change. Figure 6.8 shows the dialog box that displays the `TableDef` objects of Stdreg32.mdb. The Validation Rule list box, which displays the `Validation Rule` property, shows `- None defined` because none of the tables in Stdreg32.mdb includes a table-level validation rule.

FIGURE 6.8.

Displaying the
TableDefs collection
for Stdreg32.mdb with
system tables included.

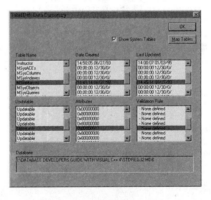

NOTE

Tables in Access databases whose names begin with MSys are system tables. For example, you would expect MSysMacros to have the Attributes value of 0x8000000 that most of the other MSys... tables share, not 0x00000002. MSysMacros is a system table that contains a definition of each macro object that you create with Microsoft Access;

thus, MSysMacros is useful only with Access applications. Using the value of the dbSystemObject constant, 0x80000002, includes MSysMacros and other Access-specific tables in the system table category. The following condition:

```
if ((tabledefinfo.m_lAttributes & dbSystemObject) == 0 ||
    m_SystemTables.GetCheck() != 0)
```

excludes system tables from the list boxes when the Show System Tables check box isn't checked.

Mapping the *Fields* and *Indexes* Collections

TableDef, QueryDef, Recordset, and Relation (CDaoTableDef, CDaoQueryDef, and CDaoRecordset) objects all contain Fields collections. In MFC's implementation of DAO, Fields collections are managed with a CDaoFieldInfo object, which is a structure. Table 6.10 lists the properties of the Field object and the CDaoFieldInfo object members. Some properties are valid for only one type of object or certain field data types.

Table 6.10. Properties of the Field object.

Property	*CDaoFieldInfo Member*	*Description*
AllowZeroLength	m_bAllowZeroLength	If TRUE, zero-length strings are allowed. Otherwise, at least one character must be entered. (Text or Memo fields only.)
Attributes	m_lAttributes	The sum of flags that determine the characteristics of the field (see Table 6.11).
CollatingOrder	m_lCollatingOrder	Specifies the sort order for text fields.
DataUpdatable	Not directly supported	TRUE if the field allows updates to data.
DefaultValue	m_strDefaultValue	The value automatically entered in a field when a new record is added.
ForeignName	m_strForeignName	The value of the Name property when the field is included in a relationship with another table.

continues

Table 6.10. continued

Property	CDaoFieldInfo *Member*	Description
Name	m_strName	The given name of the table. For attached tables and tables used in the execution of a QueryDef object, the value can be an alias (created by the AS SQL reserved word for QueryDef objects).
OrdinalPosition	m_nOrdinalPosition	The relative position of the field in the table, starting with 1 as the first field.
Required	m_bRequired	If TRUE, a non-Null entry is required. If AllowZeroLength is FALSE, a character must be entered in a Text field.
Size	m_lSize	The size in bytes of the field: fixed for numeric and logical fields, 0 for Memo and OLE Object (LongBinary) fields, and 1 to 255 characters for Text fields. (Unicode has no effect on the value.)
SourceField	m_strSourceField	The name of the field of an attached table or of a table used in executing a QueryDef object.
SourceTable	m_strSourceTable	The name of an attached table or a table used in executing a QueryDef object.
Type	m_nType	An Integer designating the field's data type (see Table 6.12).
ValidateOnSet	Not directly supported	If TRUE, tests the ValidationRule property immediately upon entry. Otherwise, the test occurs when the record pointer is moved from the current record. (Applies only to Recordset objects.)

Property	CDaoFieldInfo *Member*	Description
ValidationRule	m_strValidationRule	A field-level validation rule consisting of the WHERE clause of an SQL criterion, without the WHERE reserved word and the [Table.]Field identifier, as in <= Date.
ValidationText	m_strValidationText	The text that appears in a message box that is displayed when a field-level validation rule is broken.

Table 6.11. The value of flags for the Attributes property of a field.

Attributes *Flag*	Value	Description
dbFixedField	0x01	Indicates that the length of the field is fixed, not a Text, Date/Time, Memo, Binary, or long varbinary field.
dbVariableField	0x02	Indicates that the length of the field is variable, not a Number, Date/Time, or Boolean field.
dbAutoIncrField	0x10	Indicates that the field is of the AutoIncrement (formerly Counter) field data type, which is automatically incremented when you add new records to the table or recordset.
dbUpdatableField	0x20	Indicates that the data in the field or the structure of the field can be modified.

Table 6.12. Values of global symbolic constants for field data types.

Data Type Constant	Value	Field	Fundamental Data Type
dbBOOL	1	Boolean, Yes/No, Logical	int
dbByte	2	Number, Byte, tinyint	int

continues

Table 6.12. continued

Data Type Constant	Value	Field	Fundamental Data Type
dbInteger	3	Number, smallint	int
dbLong	4	Number, int	long
dbCurrency	5	Money, decimal, fixed-point	A COleCurrency object
dbSingle	6	Number, single-precision float	float
dbDouble	7	Number, double-precision float	double
dbDate	8	Date/Time, timestamp	A COleDateTime object
dbBinary	9	Binary, varbinary	Not implemented in Visual C++ 4
dbText	10	Text	CString
dbLongBinary	11	Binary, long varbinary, OLE object	OLE object
dbMemo	12	Text, long varchar	CString
dbGUID	15	A GUID value	A GUID object

Only the TableDef object contains an Indexes collection. In MFC's implementation of DAO, the Indexes collection is a struct called CDaoIndexInfo. Table 6.13 lists the properties of the Index object. Datatypes that are new to Jet 2.x and 3.0 are noted by an asterisk (*).

Table 6.13. The properties of the Index object.

Property	CDaoIndexInfo Member	Data Type	Description
Name	m_strName	CString	The name of the index, unique within a table.
Fields	m_pFieldInfos	CDaoIndexFieldInfo*	A pointer to a CDaoIndexFieldInfo object. The names of fields that comprise the index are preceded by a sign indicating the sort order (+ for ascending and - for descending). If the index has more than one field,

Property	CDaoIndexInfo Member	Data Type	Description
			the field names are separated by a semicolon.
Clustered	m_bClustered	BOOL	TRUE if the index represents a clustered index (except for ODBC databases). Jet 3.0 doesn't create clustered indexes.
Foreign	m_bForeign	BOOL	TRUE if the index is on a foreign key field. FALSE otherwise.
Required	m_bRequired	BOOL	TRUE if the index is on a required field. FALSE otherwise.
IgnoreNulls	m_bIgnoreNulls	BOOL	TRUE if the index is on a field that allows Null values. FALSE otherwise.
Primary	m_bPrimary	BOOL	TRUE if the index is the primary key index. FALSE otherwise.
Unique	m_bUnique	BOOL	TRUE if the index prohibits duplicate values. FALSE otherwise. The value of the Unique property is always TRUE for PrimaryKey indexes. Unique indexes don't permit Null values in the indexed field.

NOTE

xBase programmers probably will notice that there is no provision in Visual C++ 4.0 to create an index based on values returned by a function that uses a field value as an argument. Indexes on .DBF files created with expressions such as INDEX ON SUBSTR(*char_field*, 3,8) + DTOS(*date_field*) are common in xBase applications. Not only can you not create such an index with Visual C++, but you can't even open an index file of this type, much less maintain it.

Listing 6.2 shows the C++ code needed to add the capability to list in the DataDict application properties of the `Field` objects of a given `TableDef` of a Jet database. This is done as a second dialog box and is very similar to the one shown in Listing 6.1.

Listing 6.2. The added procedures needed by the DataDict application to list properties of the `Field` objects.

```cpp
// Fields.cpp : implementation file
//

#include "stdafx.h"
#include "test.h"
#include "Fields.h"

#ifdef _DEBUG
#define new DEBUG_NEW
#undef THIS_FILE
static char THIS_FILE[] = __FILE__;
#endif

/////////////////////////////////////////////////////////////////////////////
// Fields dialog


Fields::Fields(CWnd* pParent /*=NULL*/)
    : CDialog(Fields::IDD, pParent)
{
    //{{AFX_DATA_INIT(Fields)
    m_Database = _T("");
    //}}AFX_DATA_INIT
    m_pDatabase = NULL;
}


void Fields::DoDataExchange(CDataExchange* pDX)
{
    CDialog::DoDataExchange(pDX);
    //{{AFX_DATA_MAP(Fields)
    DDX_Control(pDX, IDC_LIST6, m_List6);
    DDX_Control(pDX, IDC_LIST5, m_List5);
    DDX_Control(pDX, IDC_LIST4, m_List4);
    DDX_Control(pDX, IDC_LIST2, m_List2);
    DDX_Control(pDX, IDC_LIST3, m_List3);
    DDX_Control(pDX, IDC_LIST1, m_List1);
    DDX_Text(pDX, IDC_DATABASE, m_Database);
    //}}AFX_DATA_MAP
}


BEGIN_MESSAGE_MAP(Fields, CDialog)
    //{{AFX_MSG_MAP(Fields)
    ON_LBN_SELCHANGE(IDC_LIST1, OnSelchangeList1)
    ON_LBN_SELCHANGE(IDC_LIST2, OnSelchangeList2)
    ON_LBN_SELCHANGE(IDC_LIST3, OnSelchangeList3)
    ON_LBN_SELCHANGE(IDC_LIST4, OnSelchangeList4)
    ON_LBN_SELCHANGE(IDC_LIST5, OnSelchangeList5)
```

```
    ON_LBN_SELCHANGE(IDC_LIST6, OnSelchangeList6)
    ON_BN_CLICKED(IDC_MAP_TABLES, OnMapTables)
    //}}AFX_MSG_MAP
END_MESSAGE_MAP()

/////////////////////////////////////////////////////////////////////////////
// Fields message handlers

BOOL Fields::OnInitDialog()
{
    CDialog::OnInitDialog();

    // TODO: Add extra initialization here

    // Set up your CDaoTabledef object!

    // Update the list boxes... Forces a refresh of dialog, too!
    OnMapTables();

    return TRUE;  // Return TRUE unless you set the focus to a control
                  // EXCEPTION: OCX Property Pages should return FALSE
}

void Fields::OnSelchangeList1()
{
    // TODO: Add your control notification handler code here
    m_List2.SetCurSel(m_List1.GetCurSel());
    m_List3.SetCurSel(m_List1.GetCurSel());
    m_List4.SetCurSel(m_List1.GetCurSel());
    m_List5.SetCurSel(m_List1.GetCurSel());
    m_List6.SetCurSel(m_List1.GetCurSel());
}

void Fields::OnSelchangeList2()
{
    // TODO: Add your control notification handler code here
    m_List1.SetCurSel(m_List2.GetCurSel());
    m_List3.SetCurSel(m_List2.GetCurSel());
    m_List4.SetCurSel(m_List2.GetCurSel());
    m_List5.SetCurSel(m_List2.GetCurSel());
    m_List6.SetCurSel(m_List2.GetCurSel());
}

void Fields::OnSelchangeList3()
{
    // TODO: Add your control notification handler code here
    m_List1.SetCurSel(m_List3.GetCurSel());
    m_List2.SetCurSel(m_List3.GetCurSel());
    m_List4.SetCurSel(m_List3.GetCurSel());
    m_List5.SetCurSel(m_List3.GetCurSel());
    m_List6.SetCurSel(m_List3.GetCurSel());

}

void Fields::OnSelchangeList4()
{
    // TODO: Add your control notification handler code here
```

continues

Listing 6.2. continued

```
        m_List1.SetCurSel(m_List4.GetCurSel());
        m_List2.SetCurSel(m_List4.GetCurSel());
        m_List3.SetCurSel(m_List4.GetCurSel());
        m_List5.SetCurSel(m_List4.GetCurSel());
        m_List6.SetCurSel(m_List4.GetCurSel());
}

void Fields::OnSelchangeList5()
{
        // TODO: Add your control notification handler code here

        m_List1.SetCurSel(m_List5.GetCurSel());
        m_List2.SetCurSel(m_List5.GetCurSel());
        m_List3.SetCurScl(m_List5.GetCurSel());
        m_List4.SetCurSel(m_List5.GetCurSel());
        m_List6.SetCurSel(m_List5.GetCurSel());
}

void Fields::OnSelchangeList6()
{
        // TODO: Add your control notification handler code here

        m_List1.SetCurSel(m_List6.GetCurSel());
        m_List2.SetCurSel(m_List6.GetCurSel());
        m_List3.SetCurSel(m_List6.GetCurSel());
        m_List4.SetCurSel(m_List6.GetCurSel());
        m_List5.SetCurSel(m_List6.GetCurSel());
}

void Fields::OnMapTables()
{
        // TODO: Add your control notification handler code here

        int nIndex = 0;
        CDaoFieldInfo    fieldinfo;

        CString Formatted;

        CDaoTableDef td(m_pDatabase);

        m_List1.ResetContent();
        m_List2.ResetContent();
        m_List3.ResetContent();
        m_List4.ResetContent();
        m_List5.ResetContent();
        m_List6.ResetContent();

        td.Open(_T("Student"));
        m_Database = td.GetName();

        for (nIndex = 0; nIndex < td.GetFieldCount(); ++nIndex)
        {
            // First, get the necessary information to work with!
            td.GetFieldInfo(nIndex, fieldinfo, AFX_DAO_ALL_INFO);

            // Process and format the data
```

```cpp
    m_List1.AddString(fieldinfo.m_strName);
    switch(fieldinfo.m_nType)
    {
        case dbBoolean:
            m_List2.AddString("Boolean");
            break;
        case      dbByte:
            m_List2.AddString("Byte");
            break;
        case      dbInteger:
            m_List2.AddString("Short");
            break;
        case      dbLong:
            m_List2.AddString("Long");
            break;
        case      dbCurrency:
            m_List2.AddString("Currency");
            break;
        case      dbSingle:
            m_List2.AddString("Single");
            break;
        case      dbDouble:
            m_List2.AddString("Double");
            break;
        case      dbDate:
            m_List2.AddString("Date/Time");
            break;
        case      dbText:
            m_List2.AddString("Text");
            break;
        case      dbLongBinary:
            m_List2.AddString("Long Binary (OLE Object)");
            break;
        case      dbMemo:
            m_List2.AddString("Memo");
            break;
        case      dbGUID:
            m_List2.AddString("A GUID");
            break;
        default:
            m_List2.AddString("Unknown field type");
            break;
    }

    Formatted.Format("%d", fieldinfo.m_lSize);
    m_List3.AddString(Formatted);

    Formatted.Format("0x%8.8X", fieldinfo.m_lCollatingOrder);
    m_List4.AddString(Formatted);

    Formatted.Format("0x%8.8X", fieldinfo.m_lAttributes);
    m_List5.AddString(Formatted);

    Formatted.Format("%d", (long)fieldinfo.m_nOrdinalPosition);
    m_List6.AddString(Formatted);
}
```

continues

Listing 6.2. continued

```
    m_List1.SetCurSel(0);
    m_List2.SetCurSel(0);
    m_List3.SetCurSel(0);
    m_List4.SetCurSel(0);
    m_List5.SetCurSel(0);
    m_List6.SetCurSel(0);

    // Force an update of the dialog box!
    UpdateData(FALSE);
}
```

When you double-click an item in the Field Name list box, the `Fields` class `CDialog` procedure displays the properties of members of the `Fields` collection for the predefined table, as shown in Figure 6.9.

FIGURE 6.9.

Properties of members of the `Fields` *collection of the Students table of Stdreg32.mdb.*

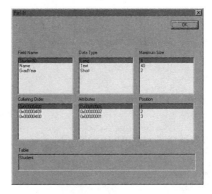

Listing 6.3 shows the C++ code needed to add the capability to list in the DataDict application properties of the `Index` objects of a given table of a Jet database. This is done as a third dialog box and is very similar to the one shown in Listing 6.2.

Listing 6.3. The added procedures needed by the DataDict application to list properties of `Index` objects.

```
// Indexes.cpp : implementation file
//

#include "stdafx.h"
#include "test.h"
#include "Indexes.h"

#ifdef _DEBUG
#define new DEBUG_NEW
#undef THIS_FILE
static char THIS_FILE[] = __FILE__;
#endif
```

```
///////////////////////////////////////////////////////////////////////
// Indexes dialog


Indexes::Indexes(CWnd* pParent /*=NULL*/)
    : CDialog(Indexes::IDD, pParent)
{
    //{{AFX_DATA_INIT(Indexes)
    m_Database = _T("");
    //}}AFX_DATA_INIT
    m_pDatabase = NULL;
}


void Indexes::DoDataExchange(CDataExchange* pDX)
{
    CDialog::DoDataExchange(pDX);
    //{{AFX_DATA_MAP(Indexes)
    DDX_Control(pDX, IDC_LIST6, m_List6);
    DDX_Control(pDX, IDC_LIST5, m_List5);
    DDX_Control(pDX, IDC_LIST4, m_List4);
    DDX_Control(pDX, IDC_LIST3, m_List3);
    DDX_Control(pDX, IDC_LIST2, m_List2);
    DDX_Control(pDX, IDC_LIST1, m_List1);
    DDX_Text(pDX, IDC_DATABASE, m_Database);
    //}}AFX_DATA_MAP
}


BEGIN_MESSAGE_MAP(Indexes, CDialog)
    //{{AFX_MSG_MAP(Indexes)
    ON_LBN_SELCHANGE(IDC_LIST1, OnSelchangeList1)
    ON_LBN_SELCHANGE(IDC_LIST2, OnSelchangeList2)
    ON_LBN_SELCHANGE(IDC_LIST3, OnSelchangeList3)
    ON_LBN_SELCHANGE(IDC_LIST4, OnSelchangeList4)
    ON_LBN_SELCHANGE(IDC_LIST5, OnSelchangeList5)
    ON_LBN_SELCHANGE(IDC_LIST6, OnSelchangeList6)
    //}}AFX_MSG_MAP
END_MESSAGE_MAP()

///////////////////////////////////////////////////////////////////////
// Indexes message handlers


BOOL Indexes::OnInitDialog()
{
    CDialog::OnInitDialog();

    // TODO: Add extra initialization here

    // Set up your CDaoTabledef object!

    // Update the list boxes... Forces a refresh of dialog, too!
    OnMapTables();

    return TRUE;  // Return TRUE unless you set the focus to a control
                  // EXCEPTION: OCX Property Pages should return FALSE
}
```

continues

Listing 6.3. continued

```cpp
void Indexes::OnSelchangeList1()
{
    // TODO: Add your control notification handler code here
    m_List2.SetCurSel(m_List1.GetCurSel());
    m_List3.SetCurSel(m_List1.GetCurSel());
    m_List4.SetCurSel(m_List1.GetCurSel());
    m_List5.SetCurSel(m_List1.GetCurSel());
    m_List6.SetCurSel(m_List1.GetCurSel());
}

void Indexes::OnSelchangeList2()
{
    // TODO: Add your control notification handler code here
    m_List1.SetCurSel(m_List2.GetCurSel());
    m_List3.SetCurSel(m_List2.GetCurSel());
    m_List4.SetCurSel(m_List2.GetCurSel());
    m_List5.SetCurSel(m_List2.GetCurSel());
    m_List6.SetCurSel(m_List2.GetCurSel());
}

void Indexes::OnSelchangeList3()
{
    // TODO: Add your control notification handler code here
    m_List1.SetCurSel(m_List3.GetCurSel());
    m_List2.SetCurSel(m_List3.GetCurSel());
    m_List4.SetCurSel(m_List3.GetCurSel());
    m_List5.SetCurSel(m_List3.GetCurSel());
    m_List6.SetCurSel(m_List3.GetCurSel());

}

void Indexes::OnSelchangeList4()
{
    // TODO: Add your control notification handler code here

    m_List1.SetCurSel(m_List4.GetCurSel());
    m_List2.SetCurSel(m_List4.GetCurSel());
    m_List3.SetCurSel(m_List4.GetCurSel());
    m_List5.SetCurSel(m_List4.GetCurSel());
    m_List6.SetCurSel(m_List4.GetCurSel());
}

void Indexes::OnSelchangeList5()
{
    // TODO: Add your control notification handler code here

    m_List1.SetCurSel(m_List5.GetCurSel());
    m_List2.SetCurSel(m_List5.GetCurSel());
    m_List3.SetCurSel(m_List5.GetCurSel());
    m_List4.SetCurSel(m_List5.GetCurSel());
    m_List6.SetCurSel(m_List5.GetCurSel());
}

void Indexes::OnSelchangeList6()
{
```

```
    // TODO: Add your control notification handler code here

    m_List1.SetCurSel(m_List6.GetCurSel());
    m_List2.SetCurSel(m_List6.GetCurSel());
    m_List3.SetCurSel(m_List6.GetCurSel());
    m_List4.SetCurSel(m_List6.GetCurSel());
    m_List5.SetCurSel(m_List6.GetCurSel());
}

void Indexes::OnMapTables()
{
    // TODO: Add your control notification handler code here

    int nIndex = 0;
    CDaoIndexInfo     indexinfo;

    CString Formatted;

    CDaoTableDef td(m_pDatabase);

    m_List1.ResetContent();
    m_List2.ResetContent();
    m_List3.ResetContent();
    m_List4.ResetContent();
    m_List5.ResetContent();
    m_List6.ResetContent();

    td.Open(_T("Student"));
    m_Database = td.GetName();

    for (nIndex = 0; nIndex < td.GetIndexCount(); ++nIndex)
    {
        // First, get the necessary information to work with!
        td.GetIndexInfo(nIndex, indexinfo, AFX_DAO_ALL_INFO);

        // Process and format the data

        m_List1.AddString(indexinfo.m_strName);

        Formatted.Format("%d", (long)indexinfo.m_nFields);
        m_List2.AddString(Formatted);

        m_List3.AddString(indexinfo.m_bPrimary ? "Primary" : "Not-primary");
        m_List4.AddString(indexinfo.m_bUnique ? "Unique" : "Not-unique");
        m_List5.AddString(indexinfo.m_bIgnoreNulls ?
            "Ignore Nulls" : "Nulls significant");
        m_List6.AddString(indexinfo.m_bForeign ? "Foreign" : "Not-foreign");
    }

    m_List1.SetCurSel(0);
    m_List2.SetCurSel(0);
    m_List3.SetCurSel(0);
    m_List4.SetCurSel(0);
    m_List5.SetCurSel(0);
    m_List6.SetCurSel(0);

    // Force an update of the dialog box!
    UpdateData(FALSE);
}
```

Figure 6.10 shows the properties of the members of the Indexes collection of Access 7's Stdreg32.mdb database file.

FIGURE 6.10.
*Properties of members
of the* Indexes *col-
lection of the Title
Author table of
Stdreg32.mdb.*

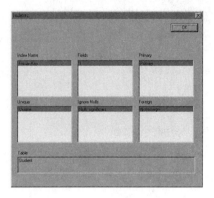

Using the *QueryDefs* Collection and *QueryDef* Objects

QueryDef objects are Jet's equivalent of the stored procedures offered by most client-server RDBMSs. Like stored procedures, QueryDef objects executed against Jet databases are optimized to achieve maximum performance. If you create a Recordset object by specifying an SQL statement as the value of the Source argument when applying the OpenRecordset method to the Database object, Jet must run the SQL statement through the query optimizer. MFC's implementation of QueryDef objects is done using the MFC class CDaoQueryDef.

QueryDef objects are the only method of executing an SQL pass-through query against a client-server RDBMS. An SQL pass-through query sends the SQL statement directly to the RDBMS for execution.

You use the following syntax to create a new CDaoQueryDef class object:

```
CDaoQueryDef( CDaoDatabase* pDatabase);
```

The parameter *pDatabase* is a pointer to an open CDaoDatabase object. The following example creates a QueryDef object named qryPubs that, when executed, returns all the records of the Students table of Stdreg32.mdb:

```
CDaoDatabase db;

    db.Open("Stdreg32.mdb");

    CDaoQueryDef qd(db);

    qd.Create(_T("Students"), _T("SELECT * FROM Students"))
```

QueryDef objects have many properties in common with TableDef objects. Table 6.14 lists the properties of the QueryDef object. The Name and SQL properties appear first in Table 6.14 because these are the two most commonly used properties when you create a QueryDef object. Chapter 5, "Learning Structured Query Language," describes the Jet and ANSI dialects of SQL. QueryDef objects have a Fields collection that is identical to the Fields collection of the TableDef object, except that the Name property of a Field object can use an alias created by the SQL AS reserved word. The SourceTable and SourceField property values of Fields of QueryDefs reflect the table name and field name, respectively, of the source tables for the query. Table 6.14 shows where the property is found in MFC's DAO implementation.

Table 6.14. Properties of the QueryDef object.

Property	MFC DAO Location	Description
Name	CDaoQueryDef::GetName()	The given name for a query. The default value is an empty string.
SQL	CDaoQueryDef::GetSQL()	The SQL statement to execute the query. Requires Jet SQL syntax unless the query is an SQL pass-through query, in which case the SQL syntax is that for the server RDBMS.
Connect	CDaoQueryDef::SetConnect()	Used only to create an SQL pass-through query. A connect string beginning with ODBC; is required.
DateCreated	CDaoQueryDef::GetDateCreated()	The date that the QueryDef was created with the CreateQueryDef method of the Database object, in MFC's DAO, CDaoQueryDef::Create().
LastUpdated	CDaoQueryDef::GetDateLastUpdated()	The date that the QueryDef was last updated by modifying the value of one or more of its properties.

continues

Table 6.14. continued

Property	MFC DAO Location	Description
LogMessages	Not supported directly	Set to TRUE to create a table in the database to which ODBC messages are added if the ODBC driver for your client server RDBMS supports logging messages. (You must use the CreateProperty method to add this property to a QueryDef object.)
ODBCTimeout	CDaoQueryDef::SetODBCTimeout()	Sets the number of seconds before Jet generates an error when attempting to execute a query against a client-server RDBMS. (Default value is 60 seconds.)
RecordsAffected	CDaoQueryDef::GetRecordsAffected()	The number of records affected by successful execution of an APPEND, UPDATE, or DELETE query.
ReturnsRecords	CDaoQueryDef::GetReturnsRecords()	For SQL pass-through queries (only). Returns TRUE if executing a SELECT query or a stored procedure that returns records. Otherwise, returns FALSE.
Type	CDaoQueryDef::GetType()	Specifies the type of query by the value of an Integer flag (see Table 6.15).
Updatable	CDaoQueryDef::CanUpdate()	TRUE if the properties of the QueryDef can be altered, which is usually the case.

Table 6.15. Values of the Type flag for the QueryDef object (from dbdaoint.h).

Constant	Value	Type of Query	SQL Reserved Words
dbQSelect	0	Select	SELECT
dbQCrosstab	16	Crosstab	TRANSFORM...PIVOT
dbQDelete	32	Delete	DELETE
dbQUpdate	48	Update	UPDATE
dbQAppend	64	Append	INSERT
dbQMakeTable	80	Make-table	INSERT INTO
dbQDDL	96	Data-definition	CREATE ...
dbQSQLPassThrough	112	SQL pass-through	
dbQSetOperation	128	Union	
dbQSPTBulk	144	Used with dbQSQLPassThrough to specify a query that doesn't return records (112 + 144 = 256)	
dbQAction	240	Action	DELETE, UPDATE, INSERT, INSERT INTO, CREATE ...

The Value column lists decimal, not hexadecimal, values because Type flags for QueryDef objects aren't used in combination (except for SQL pass-through queries that don't return records).

Table 6.16 lists, in the order of most frequent use, the methods of the QueryDef object. Since a CDaoQueryDef class object doesn't return records, you must create a CDaoRecordset object to retrieve records from the database when using a CDaoQueryDef object.

Table 6.16. Methods applicable to the QueryDef object.

Method	MFC's DAO Function	Purpose
OpenRecordset	Not directly supported	Opens a Recordset object over the result set of a SELECT query or an SQL pass-through query that returns records. Use CDaoRecordset::Open(CDaoQueryDef* *pQueryDef*, int *nOpenType* = dbOpenDynaset, int *nOptions* = 0);, which takes a pointer to a CDaoQueryDef object.

continues

Table 6.16. continued

Method	MFC's DAO Function	Purpose
Execute	Execute()	Executes a query that doesn't return records, such as an action or DDL query. (Replaces the ExecuteSQL method of Visual C++ 2.0 and 3.0.)
CreateProperty	Not directly supported	Lets you add the LogMessages property or a user-defined property to a QueryDef.

Applying the OpenRecordset method to a QueryDef object that returns records executes the query and creates a Recordset over the query result set. Here is the general syntax of the OpenRecordset method of the QueryDef object:

```
CDaoDatabase db;

CDaoRecordset rs;

    db.Open("Stdreg32.mdb");

    CDaoQueryDef qd(db);

    qd.Create(_T("Students"), _T("SELECT * FROM Students")

    rs.Open(qd, /*nOpenType*/ dbOpenDynaset, /*nOptions*/ 0 );
```

The value of the *nOpenType* argument can be either dbOpenDynaset (2) or dbOpenSnapshot (4); you can't open a Table-type Recordset over a QueryDef result set. Table 6.17 lists the values of flags for the *nOptions* argument. Constants marked with an X in the RS column apply to the OpenRecordset method.

The general syntax of the Execute method of the QueryDef object is

```
qdfName.Execute([nOptions]);
```

Table 6.17 also includes the values of flags for the *nOptions* argument of the Execute method. Only constants marked with an X in the EX column apply to the Execute method.

Table 6.17. Values of flags for the *nOptions* argument of the CDaoRecordset class object.

Constant	RS	EX	Value	Purpose
dbDenyWrite	X	X	0x1	Denies write permission to others while the query executes or while a Recordset is open.

Constant	RS	EX	Value	Purpose
dbDenyRead	X		0x2	Denies read permission to others while the query executes or while a Recordset is open.
dbReadOnly	X		0x4	Creates a read-only (nonupdatable) Recordset.
dbAppendOnly	X		0x8	Allows only INSERT queries (for data entry).
dbInconsistent	X	X	0x10	Permits *inconsistent updates,* the ability to change values in the primary key field of a query with a one-to-many relationship (default).
dbConsistent	X	X	0x20	Requires consistent updates. (Can't change values in the primary key field of a query with a one-to-many relationship.)
dbSQLPassThrough	X	X	0x40	Specifies an SQL pass-through operation.
dbFailOnError		X	0x80	Rolls back updates if an error occurs (creates a trappable error).
dbForwardOnly	X		0x100	Creates a forward-scrolling (only) Recordset of the Snapshot type. Forward scrolling provides very fast performance with the MoveNext method of the Recordset.
dbSeeChanges	X	X	0x200	Causes a trappable error if another user simultaneously changes the data to be updated by the query.

QueryDef objects also have a Parameters collection that defines user-replaceable criteria for the query. Parameter objects have Name, Type (field data type), and Value properties. With the exception of the Remote Data Object, use of replaceable parameters in queries is of limited utility in Visual C++ database applications. It's more straightforward to alter the SQL property of a QueryDef than to use members of the Parameters collection. The Parameters collection is intended primarily for use in interactive entry of parameter values in Access applications.

Creating Tables with C++ Code

You can add new tables to a Database object with Visual C++ code by using the TableDefs collection (CDaoTableDef) and adding a new TableDef object that describes the new table. You must add at least one Field object to a TableDef object before appending the new TableDef to the TableDefs collection. You also can append new Index objects to the Indexes collection of a TableDef object.

Table 6.18 lists the methods applicable to the TableDefs (the TDF column), QueryDefs (QDF), Fields (FLD), and Indexes (IDX) collections. Only Table objects contain the Indexes collection.

Table 6.18. Methods applicable to the TableDefs, QueryDefs, Fields, and Indexes collections.

Method	TDF	QDF	FLD	IDX	Purpose
Refresh	X	X	X	X	Requeries the structure of the underlying persistent objects to make the values of the members of the collection current.
Append	X	X	X	X	Adds a new member to the collection to create a new table, or adds a new field or index to an existing table of a database.
Delete	X	X		X	Deletes a TableDef object from a TableDefs collection (deletes the corresponding table from the database) or deletes an Index object from an Indexes collection (deletes the corresponding index in the database).

Using SQL's Data Definition Language, introduced in Jet 2.0, is a much more straightforward method of creating new tables, adding indexes, and establishing relationships between tables. Jet 2+ supports SQL's CREATE TABLE, CONSTRAINT, REFERENCES, CREATE INDEX, ALTER TABLE, DROP TABLE, and DROP INDEX reserved words, so you can use SQL statements to perform the same operations used by members of the TableDefs, Fields, Indexes, and Relations collections. Visual C++ 4.0's Books Online help provides examples of the use of each of these SQL reserved words.

Creating and Using *Recordset* Objects

As noted earlier in this chapter, the Recordset object comes in three different types: Table, Dynaset, and Snapshot. When you create a project with AppWizard, you get to choose from these three choices. Here is the general syntax for creating a Recordset object (CDaoRecordset) over a table in database:

```
CDaoDatabase db;

CDaoRecordset rs;

    db.Open("Stdreg32.mdb");

    CDaoTableDef td(db);

    td.Create(_T("Students"));

    rs.Open(td, /*nOpenType*/ dbOpenDynaset, /*nOptions*/ 0 );
```

If you don't specify the *nOpenType* argument, Jet opens a Table-type Recordset (*nOpenType* = dbOpenTable). The flags for the optional *nOptions* argument are listed in Table 6.17. To open a Recordset based on an SQL query, use the following syntax:

```
CDaoDatabase db;

    db.Open("Stdreg32.mdb");

    CDaoRecordset rs(db);

    rs.Open(AFX_DAO_USE_DEFAULT_TYPE, _T("SELECT * FROM Students")));
```

In this case, Jet opens a Dynaset-type Recordset unless you set the value of *nOpenType* to dbOpenSnapshot or set one of the *nOption* flags to create a Snapshot-type Recordset. The syntax for opening a Recordset over a QueryDef result set was provided in the section "Using the QueryDefs Collection and QueryDef Objects."

The following sections describe in detail the properties and methods that apply to Recordset objects of each of the three types.

Properties of *Recordset* Objects

Table 6.19 lists the properties that are applicable to the Table, Dynaset, and Snapshot types of Recordset objects. The entries in the TBL, DS, and SS columns in Table 6.19 indicate whether the property is applicable to Recordsets of the Table, Dynaset, or Snapshot type, respectively. Related properties listed in Table 6.19 are grouped by function, and properties that are new to Jet 2.x and 3.0 are noted by an asterisk (*).

Table 6.19. The properties of the Recordset object.

Property	CDaoRecordset Member	TBL	DS	SS	Description
Name	CDaoRecordset::GetName()	X	X	X	Name of the Recordset (read-only). Same as the Name property of the corresponding TableDef object for the Table type.
!Field.Value	CDaoRecordset::GetFieldValue()	X	X	X	The value (content) of the data in the Field of the current record.
Type	CDaoRecordset::GetType()	X	X	X	The type of Recordset object defined by the integer dbOpenTable, dbOpenDynaset, or dbOpenSnapshot constants.
DateCreated	CDaoRecordset::GetDateCreated()	X			The date and time that a Table object was originally created (read-only).
LastUpdated	CDaoRecordset::GetDateLastUpdated()	X			The date and time that the last change was made to the data in a Table object (read-only).
Updatable	CDaoRecordset::CanUpdate()	X	X		TRUE if access to the underlying data is read-write; FALSE if access is read-only. The Updatable property of Snapshot types is, by definition, FALSE. (If the Database object is opened read-only, all Table and Dynaset types in the database are read-only.)

Property			Method	Description
Restartable*	X	X	CDaoRecordset::CanRestart()	TRUE if the Requery method is supported; FALSE otherwise. (You must re-create the Recordset to refresh its content.)
Transactions	X		CDaoRecordset::CanTransact()	TRUE if the Table or Dynaset type supports rolling back of transactions; FALSE otherwise (read-only).
Bookmarkable	X	X	CDaoRecordset::CanBookmark()	TRUE if you can use the Bookmark property to specify a particular record in the Recordset; FALSE otherwise (read-only). Only Jet databases support Bookmarks.
Bookmark	X	X	CDaoRecordset::SetBookmark()	A binary value that indicates (points to) a specific record. A Bookmark's value is set and returned as a CString.
LastModified	X	X	CDaoRecordset::GetLastModifiedBookmark()	A Bookmark value that points to the record in the Table object that was updated most recently (read-only).
Index	X		CDaoRecordset::GetIndexInfo()	The name of the active index of the table that determines the order in which the records of the table appear. The value of the Index property can be a predetermined index name (such as PrimaryKey) or the name of a field on which the index was created.

continues

Table 6.19. continued

Property	CDaoRecordset Member	TBL	DS	SS	Description
Sort	CDaoRecordset::m_strSort		X	X	The names of one or more fields of a Dynaset or Snapshot object that determine the order in which the records of a Dynaset or Snapshot object that is created from the sorted Dynaset or Snapshot object appear. The sort statement consists of the ORDER BY clause of an SQL statement without the ORDER BY reserved words.
RecordCount	CDaoRecordset::GetRecordCount()	X	X	X	The number of records in a Recordset (read-only). In a multiuser environment, the value of RecordCount may be an approximate number, depending on the frequency with which the Recordset is updated. You can obtain an accurate, instantaneous value of the RecordCount property by applying the MoveLast method immediately before reading the value of the RecordCount property.
AbsolutePosition*	CDaoRecordset::GetAbsolutePosition() CDaoRecordset::SetAbsolutePosition()		X	X	A Long value that sets or gets the position of the record pointer (the first record is 0).

continues

Property	Functions				Description
PercentPosition*	CDaoRecordset::GetPercentPosition() CDaoRecordset::SetPercentPosition()		X	X	A Single value that sets or gets the position of the record pointer as a percentage of the total number of records (0.00 to 100.00).
BOF	CDaoRecordset::IsBOF()	X	X	X	TRUE when the record pointer is positioned before (above) the first record of a Recordset; FALSE otherwise (read-only).
EOF	CDaoRecordset::IsEOF()	X	X	X	TRUE when the record pointer is positioned after (below) the last record of a Recordset; FALSE otherwise (read-only). When both BOF and EOF return TRUE, there are no records in the Recordset (rsName.RecordCount = 0).
CacheSize*	CDaoRecordset::GetCacheSize() CDaoRecordset::SetCacheSize()		X		A Long value (between 5 and 1200) that sets or gets the number of records from an ODBC data source (only) that are stored in memory (cached). 100 is the typical setting.
CacheStart*	CDaoRecordset::GetCacheStart() CDaoRecordset::SetCacheStart()		X		A CString value that gets or sets the Bookmark value of the first record to be cached.
NoMatch	CDaoRecordset::Seek()	X	X	X	Seek() returns a nonzero value if a record meets the Seek method's criteria (Table objects only) or one of the Find... method's criteria (Dynaset and Snapshot types only). Zero otherwise.

Table 6.19. continued

Property	CDaoRecordset Member	TBL	DS	SS	Description
Filter	CDaoRecordset::m_strFilter		X	X	One or more criteria that determine which records appear in a Dynaset or Snapshot type. The Filter property is the WHERE clause of an SQL statement without the WHERE reserved word.
ValidationRule*	CDaoRecordset::GetValidationRule()	X	X	X	A table-level validation rule (read-only).
ValidationText*	CDaoRecordset::GetValidationText()	X	X	X	The text that appears in a message box when the validation rule is broken (read-only).
EditMode*	CDaoRecordset::GetEditMode() CDaoRecordset::SetEditMode()	X	X		int flags that indicate the editing status: dbEditNone (no editing in progress), dbEditInProgress (edited data are in the copy buffer), or dbEditAdd (AddNew method applied and tentative append record is in the copy buffer).
LockEdits	CDaoRecordset::GetLockingMode() CDaoRecordset::SetLockingMode()	X	X		A nonzero value when locking is pessimistic, or a zero when optimistic locking is used.

You can obtain the value of each of the properties listed in Table 6.19 that returns a value using the `CDaoRecordset::Get...()` form of the member function. Similarly, you can set the value of those properties (not indicated in the Description column as "read-only") using the `CDaoRecordset::Set...()` form of the member function. I've listed both the set and get forms where applicable in this table.

Values of `Recordset` and other data access member objects are always of an appropriate data type for the data that will be returned.

As mentioned earlier in this chapter, collections of `Database` objects, including the `Recordsets` collection, have only one property, `Count`.

Methods Applicable to *Recordset* Objects and Collections

Table 6.20 lists the methods applicable to `Recordset` objects in the same format as that used in Table 6.19 to list the properties of `Recordsets`. Properties that are new to Jet 2.x and 3.0 are noted by an asterisk (*).

Table 6.20. Methods applicable to `Recordset` objects.

Method	`CDaoRecordset` *Member*	*TBL*	*DS*	*SS*	*Purpose*
`Clone`	Not directly supported	X	X	X	Creates a duplicate `Recordset` object with an independent record pointer.
`OpenRecordset`*	`CDaoRecordset::Open()`	X	X	X	Opens a new `Recordset` based on the `Recordset` to which the method is applied.
`CopyQueryDef`*	Not directly supported		X	X	Returns a copy of the `QueryDef` used to create the `Recordset`. Returns `Null` if the `Recordset` isn't based on a `QueryDef`.
`Requery`	`CDaoRecordset::Requery()`		X	X	Re-creates the content of the `Recordset` by

continues

Table 6.20. continued

Method	CDaoRecordset *Member*	*TBL*	*DS*	*SS*	*Purpose*
					re-executing the underlying query.
Close	CDaoRecordset::Close()	X	X	X	Closes the Recordset.
Edit	CDaoRecordset::Edit()	X	X	X	Prepares a Field object of a current record for updating. (Places a lock on the record or page if the value of the LockEdits property is TRUE.)
AddNew	CDaoRecordset::AddNew()	X	X		Appends a new, empty record to a Table or Dynaset type. (Equivalent to xBase's APPEND BLANK.)
Delete	CDaoRecordset::Delete()	X	X		Deletes the current record from a Table or Dynaset type.
Update	CDaoRecordset::Update()	X	X		Causes pending updates to a Table or Dynaset type to be executed. (Removes the lock on the record or page.)
CancelUpdate*	CDaoRecordset::CancelUpdate()	X	X		Cancels pending updates if applied prior to the Update method.
Move*	CDaoRecordset::Move()	X	X	X	Moves the record pointer a specified number (Long) of rows.
MoveFirst	CDaoRecordset::MoveFirst()	X	X	X	Positions the record pointer at the

Method	CDaoRecordset *Member*	*TBL*	*DS*	*SS*	*Purpose*
					beginning of the Recordset.
MoveNext	CDaoRecordset::MoveNext()	X	X	X	Positions the record pointer to the next record in the index (for Table objects) or sort order (for sorted Dynaset or Snapshot types).
MovePrevious	CDaoRecordset::MovePrev()	X	X	X	Same as the MoveNext method, except in the opposite direction.
MoveLast	CDaoRecordset::MoveLast()	X	X	X	Positions the record pointer at the end of the Recordset.
Seek	CDaoRecordset::Seek()	X			Uses the current index of a Table object to position the record pointer to the first record that meets the criteria argument(s) of the method.
FindFirst	CDaoRecordset::FindFirst()		X	X	Tests each record, beginning with the first record, of a Dynaset or Snapshot type for conformity with the criteria argument(s) of the method.
FindNext	CDaoRecordset::FindNext()		X	X	Same as the FindFirst method, except that it tests records after the current matching record.

continues

Table 6.20. continued

Method	CDaoRecordset *Member*	TBL	DS	SS	Purpose
FindPrevious	CDaoRecordset::FindPrev()		X	X	Same as the FindFirst method, except that it tests records before the current matching record.
FindLast	CDaoRecordset::FindLast()		X	X	Same as the FindFirst method, except that it starts at the end of the first record and proceeds backward until a match is found.

Here is the generalized syntax of statements that apply methods to Recordset objects:

```
rsName.MethodName([Argument1 [, Argument2 [, Argument#]]]);
```

Some methods, such as Update, have no arguments. Other methods, like FindFirst, have several arguments, some of which are optional. The next chapter provides the syntax for most CDaoRecordset classes and uses many of the methods listed in Table 6.20.

Summary

You need a thorough understanding of the member objects that constitute Visual C++ 4.0's Data Access Object class to develop commercial-quality Visual C++ database applications. This chapter began by diagramming the hierarchy of the 32-bit Data Access Objects, and then it progressed to a detailed explanation of the member functions of each of the data-related member objects. The DataDict sample application introduced you to the code you use to address collections and member objects at each level of the hierarchy. This chapter also is intended to serve as a reference source for the properties and the methods of objects of the Jet 3.0 Data Access Object.

Chapter 13 discusses each of the major MFC DAO class. Chapter 14, "Using MFC's DAO Classes," contains examples of the MFC DAO classes in programs.

7

Using the Open Database Connectivity API

Microsoft's Open Database Connectivity API is one of the first members of the Windows Open Services API (WOSA) to be released as a commercial product. WOSA is a suite of application programming interfaces for Windows applications that are intended to simplify and standardize the programming of a variety of classes of Windows-based procedures. Other components of WOSA include the Open Data Services (ODS) API for connecting to mainframe and minicomputer databases, the Messaging API (MAPI) that is employed by Microsoft Mail, and the Telephony API (TAPI) for call routing and voice mail. (Microsoft had a variety of other WOSA member APIs in the development stage at the time this book was written.)

This chapter explains the structure of the ODBC API and how the Access database engine uses the ODBC API, and it gives examples of using the ODBC API with ODBC drivers for desktop databases. Chapter 20, "Creating Front Ends for Client-Server Databases," explains how to use the ODBC API and ODBC drivers for RDBMSs such as Microsoft SQL Server for OS/2 and Windows NT, IBM DB2 and DB2/2, and Watcom SQL.

Understanding the Structure of the ODBC API

The ODBC API consists of Windows DLLs that include sets of functions to provide the following two fundamental database services for all database types for which ODBC drivers are available:

■ Installing, setting up, and removing ODBC datasources. A *datasource* is a named connection to a database. You need an ODBC driver for each different type of database to which your applications connect. The ODBC API is designed primarily for use with client-server RDBMSs, but you also can use ODBC drivers to connect to desktop database files, worksheets, and flat text files. ODBC uses the ODBCCP32.DLL library to set up and remove datasources. ODBCAD32.EXE is a stand-alone, executable version of ODBCCP32.DLL that is supplied with Access and Visual C++.

■ Managing the communication of queries and other SQL statements from client front ends to database server back ends, and the transfer of query result sets or confirmations of the execution of action queries in the reverse direction. The ODBC driver manager, ODBC32.DLL, opens the ODBC driver for the datasource and then passes SQL statements to the driver. After a client-server RDBMS processes the query, the ODBC driver returns the rows through ODBC32.DLL to your application.

The ODBC API implements SQL as a call-level interface (CLI). A *call-level interface* employs a set of standard functions to perform specific duties, such as translating SQL queries from ANSI SQL to the dialect of SQL used by the RDBMS, representing the RDBMS's field data types by an extended set of SQL-92 field data types, and handling error conditions. The ODBC API conforms to the CLI standard (SQL CAE draft specification—1991) developed by the SQL Access Group (SAG), a consortium of client-server RDBMS software publishers and users who have a large stake in the success of client-server database technology.

Visual C++ database applications that use the ODBC API have a multitiered structure similar to the structure of the desktop databases supported by the Access database engine, shown in Figure 6.1 in the preceding chapter. The full structure of a Visual C++ database application that uses all the features of the ODBC API, including the Open Database Services (ODS) API to access mainframe and minicomputer databases, is shown in Figure 7.1.

FIGURE 7.1.

The full structure of the ODBC API as it is employed by Visual C++ database applications.

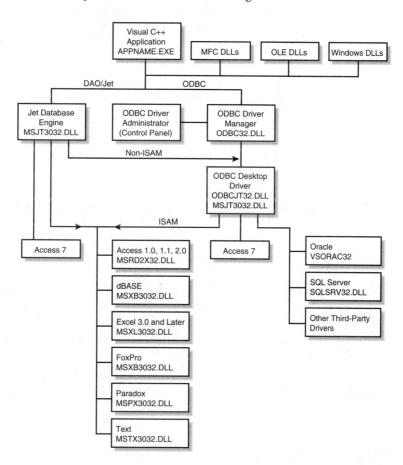

Microsoft supplies ODBC drivers for its versions of SQL Server for OS/2 and Windows NT, and Oracle databases with Visual C++. The Microsoft Query applet included with Excel and Word for Windows, as well as the Microsoft ODBC Desktop Database Drivers kit, incorporate each of the single-tier drivers shown in Figure 7.1 below the ISAM drivers path. Independent software vendors (ISVs) such as Q+E Software (Intersolv) supply suites of ODBC drivers for a variety of desktop DBMs and client-server RDBMSs. Sources of commercial ODBC drivers and mainframe/minicomputer gateways are listed in the section "Open Database Connectivity (ODBC) Drivers" in Appendix A, "Resources for Developing Visual C++ Database Applications."

> **NOTE**
>
> A group of Microsoft's competitors, including Borland International, Lotus Development Corporation, and IBM, have joined to promulgate an alternative database connectivity standard called Integrated Database Application Programming Interface (IDAPI). References to the IDAPI group in the computer trade press attribute its formation to a desire by these competitors to prevent Microsoft from creating a *de facto* industry standard database connectivity API. Being first in the market gives Microsoft's ODBC API the momentum to qualify as today's industry "standard" for database connectivity. It's likely that any competing standard, if such a product appears, will be compatible with or directly comparable to the ODBC API.

The following sections describe the basic features of the ODBC API and show how you can use the ODBC API with desktop DBMs and unconventional datasources such as worksheets and text files.

> **NOTE**
>
> Most of the information in the following sections is derived from Microsoft's *Programmer's Reference* for the ODBC SDK, and from a white paper called "Jet Database Engine ODBC Connectivity," written by Neil Black of Microsoft's Jet Program Management and Stephen Hecht of the Jet Development group. You can download the complete text of this white paper in Word for Windows .DOC format from Section 11 (ODBC Connectivity) of the MSACCESS forum on CompuServe as RJETWP.ZIP. The paper for Access 2 is in RJETV2.ZIP. This paper can also be found on the MSDN Level I CD.
>
> An additional document called *The Jet Database Engine 2.0: A User's Overview* by Paul Litwin can also be found on MSDN Level I.

Single-Tier and Multiple-Tier ODBC Drivers

ODBC drivers are classified as members of one of the two following categories:

■ *Single-tier* ODBC drivers are designed for use with DBMs that don't have the capability to process ANSI SQL statements. Single-tier drivers translate ANSI SQL statements into a long series of low-level instructions that operate directly on the files that constitute the database. At present, Microsoft and Q+E single-tier ODBC drivers connect to dBASE, FoxPro, Paradox, Btrieve, Excel, and text files. Microsoft is said to be currently working on a Lotus 1-2-3 spreadsheet driver, scheduled to be released in early 1996.

■ *Multiple-tier* ODBC drivers rely on the client-server RDBMS to process SQL statements. Using the back-end server to process queries is a more efficient process than the single-tier approach in a multiuser or networked environment. Network traffic is minimized because the server returns only the rows specified by the criteria of your SQL statement.

This chapter concentrates on the use of single-tier ODBC drivers.

ODBC API Conformance Levels

Three levels of conformance to the ODBC API are defined: core level, level 1, and level 2. Here are the general definitions for each of the three levels:

■ Core-level conformance provides for connecting to the database, preparing and executing SQL statements, receiving query result datasets, committing or rolling back transactions, and retrieving error information.

■ Level 1 conformance is similar to core-level conformance. It adds connectivity to datasources with dialogs designed specifically for the ODBC driver, get- and set-connection options, and obtain-catalog and driver/datasource capabilities.

■ Level 2 conformance is similar to level 1. It adds the capability to list and browse the connections to datasources available to the client, retrieve query result sets in array format, use scrollable cursors, and obtain additional catalog information, such as privileges, keys, and lists of stored procedures.

Core-level conformance meets the requirements of the SAG CLI specification. The majority of commercial ODBC drivers provide level 1 conformance, plus the scrollable cursor feature of level 2. Future versions of ODBC drivers probably will provide full level 2 conformance if the RDBMS that the driver is designed for supports level 2 features.

ODBC SQL Conformance Levels

The ODBC API specifies three levels of conformance to SQL grammar: minimum, core, and extended. The SQL conformance levels define the ANSI SQL reserved words that ODBC drivers and datasources must be able to process. Table 7.1 lists the Data Manipulation Language (DML), Data Definition Language (DDL), and Data Control Language (DCL) SQL reserved words required for each level of conformance. SQL data types and expressions also are listed. Successively higher levels of grammar include the grammar of the lower levels. The core SQL grammar conforms to the requirements of the SQL Access Group CAE SQL draft specification—1991; almost all commercial ODBC drivers conform to at least the core-level SQL grammar.

Table 7.1. SQL grammar, data type, and expression support for ODBC grammar conformance levels.

Level	DML Statements	DDL/DCL Statements	Data Types	Expressions
Minimum	SELECT, INSERT, UPDATED SEARCHED, DELETE SEARCHED, COMMIT TRANSACTION, ROLLBACK TRANSACTION	CREATE TABLE, DROP TABLE	SQL_CHAR	Simple arithmetic
Core	Full SELECT, positioned UPDATE, and positioned DELETE	ALTER TABLE, CREATE INDEX, DROP INDEX, CREATE VIEW, DROP VIEW, GRANT, REVOKE	SQL_VARCHAR, SQL_DECIMAL, SQL_NUMERIC, SQL_SMALLINT, SQL_INTEGER, SQL_REAL, SQL_FLOAT, SQL DOUBLEPRECISION	Subqueries and aggregate functions
Extended	LEFT OUTER JOIN, RIGHT OUTER JOIN	Batch SQL statements, stored procedures	SQL_LONGVARCHAR, SQL_BIT, SQL_TINYINT, SQL_BIGINT, SQL_BINARY, SQL_VARBINARY, SQL_LONGVARBINARY, SQL_DATE, SQL_TIME, SQL_TIMESTAMP	SUBSTRING, ABS

The extended-level SQL grammar category is a catch-all for extensions to ANSI SQL that were standardized in SQL-92, such as reserved words to enforce referential integrity and nonstandard reserved words that are found in many RDBMS implementations of SQL.

> **NOTE**
>
> At the time this book was written, no commercial ODBC drivers fully supported the equivalent of Access SQL's PIVOT and TRANSFORM keywords used to create crosstab queries. Crosstab queries, a subject of the next chapter, are one of the most useful forms of summary queries. In most cases, the Access database engine sends GROUP BY statements to the server and then transforms the results into crosstab form. It's likely that future versions of RDBMS and the ODBC drivers that accompany them will include PIVOT and TRANSFORM (or their equivalents) as SQL reserved words.

ODBC Data Types and the Access Database Engine

Table 5.8 in Chapter 5, "Learning Structured Query Language," provides a list of the field data types of SQL-92 and their Access SQL equivalents (where exact equivalents are supported). The names assigned to some ODBC data types that appear in Table 7.1 differ slightly from the formal SQL-92 naming conventions. You use the ODBC data type keywords in SQL statements unless you've specified the SQL pass-through option. Access converts most unsupported numeric data types to double-precision numbers. In most cases, a double-precision number is adequate to represent accurately any numeric value commonly found in database tables.

There is no provision in Access field data types to specify the precision and scale of a numeric data type. *Precision* is the number of digits that compose the number (including digits in the fractional portion of the number). *Scale* is the number of digits following the decimal point. In xBase, you specify the precision and scale of a field by specifying the width of the field (including a position for the decimal point) followed by the number of decimal places. Access converts numeric values to either single-precision or double-precision numbers based on the values of precision and scale of the ODBC numeric data type.

> **CAUTION**
>
> It's an uncommon practice to use a numeric field with decimal fraction values as the primary key field of a table. Doing so can cause the Access database engine to lose the bookmark values that specify the location of a record by its primary key value. If the precision or scale of a numeric value used as a primary key field on which a unique index is created exceeds the representational capability of Access's double-precision field, the message #Deleted appears in a text box bound to the field.

Access has a repertoire of field data types that is broader than that of any desktop database presently supported by commercial ODBC drivers.

Built-In ODBC Scalar Functions

The ODBC API contains a variety of built-in functions that you can use to make the ANSI SQL code that you send to the RDBMS's ODBC driver with the SQL pass-through option independent of the RDBMS in use. To implement the ODBC scalar functions, you use the ODBC escape shorthand syntax. *Escape shorthand syntax,* called simply *escape syntax* in this book, encloses the shorthand syntax in French braces ({}). The escape syntax for all ODBC functions is

```
{fn ODBCFunction([Argument(s)])}
```

Thus, if you want to return a person's first name and last name from values in the first_name and last_name fields of a table, you use the following statement:

```
{fn CONCAT(first_name, CONCAT(' ', last_name))}
```

You need an embedded CONCAT() function, because CONCAT() supports concatenation of only two strings. (This is unlike concatenation with Visual C++'s & symbol, which lets you concatenate any number of strings.) Note that the standard literal string identifier character is the single quote (') in ANSI SQL.

The following sections compare the ODBC scalar functions for string, numeric, and date/time values to the equivalent functions of Visual C++ (where equivalents exist). This information is derived from the *Programmer's Reference* for the Microsoft Open Database Connectivity Software Development Kit.

> **NOTE**
>
> In most cases, you can use Visual C++'s built-in functions in your application code to perform the same operations that are offered by the ODBC scalar functions. However, you might need to use the ODBC scalar functions to create joins between table fields of different data types.

String Manipulation Functions

Table 7.2 lists the ODBC string functions and their equivalent functions, where available, in Visual C++.

Table 7.2. The scalar string functions of ODBC version 1.0.

ODBC String Function	Purpose
ASCII(*string_exp*)	Returns the ASCII code value of the leftmost character of a string.
CHAR(*integer_exp*)	Returns the ASCII character whose code is *integer_exp*.

ODBC String Function	Purpose
CONCAT(*string1*, *string2*)	Concatenates *string1* and *string2*.
INSERT(*string1*, *start*, *length*, *string2*)	Replaces the *length* characters of *string1* beginning at *start* with *string2*.
LEFT(*string_exp*, *count*)	Returns the leftmost *count* characters.
LENGTH(*string_exp*)	Returns an integer representing the length of the string.
LOCATE(*string1*, *string2*[, *start*])	Returns an integer representing the position of *string2* in *string1*.
LCASE(*string_exp*)	Returns an all-lowercase string.
REPEAT(*string_exp*, *count*)	Returns a string consisting of *string_exp* repeated *count* times.
RIGHT(*string_exp*, *count*)	Returns the rightmost *count* characters.
RTRIM(*string_exp*)	Removes trailing blank spaces.
SUBSTRING(*string_exp*, *start*, *length*)	Returns *length* characters beginning at *start*.
UCASE(*string_exp*)	Returns an all-uppercase string.

Numeric Scalar Functions

Table 7.3 lists the ODBC numeric functions, except for trigonometric functions, and their equivalent functions, where available, in Visual C++.

Table 7.3. The numeric scalar functions available in ODBC version 1.0.

ODBC Numeric Function	Purpose
ABS(*numeric_exp*)	Returns the absolute value of the expression.
CEILING(*numeric_exp*)	Returns the next largest integer greater than the expression.
EXP(*numeric_exp*)	Returns the exponential value of the expression.
FLOOR(*numeric_exp*)	Returns the largest integer less than or equal to the expression.
LOG(*float_exp*)	Returns the natural (naperian) logarithm of the expression.
MOD(*integer_exp*)	Returns the remainder of integer division as an integer.
PI()	Returns the value of pi as a floating-point number.

continues

Table 7.3. continued

ODBC Numeric Function	Purpose
RAND([*integer_exp*])	Returns a random floating-point number with an optional seed value.
SIGN(*numeric_exp*)	Returns –1 for values less than 0, 0 for 0 values, and 1 for values greater than 0.
SQRT(*float_exp*)	Returns the square root of a floating-point value.

Date, Time, and Timestamp Functions

Table 7.4 lists the ODBC date, time, and timestamp functions and their equivalent functions, where available, in Visual C++.

Table 7.4. The date/time scalar functions of ODBC version 1.0.

ODBC Date/Time Function	Purpose
NOW()	Returns the date and time in TIMESTAMP format.
CURDATE()	Returns the current date.
CURTIME()	Returns the current time.
DAYOFMONTH(*date_exp*)	Returns the day of the month.
DAYOFWEEK(*date_exp*)	Returns the day of the week (Sunday = 1).
DAYOFYEAR(*date_exp*)	Returns the Julian date.
HOUR(*time_exp*)	Returns the hour (0 to 23).
MINUTE(*time_exp*)	Returns the minute (0 to 59).
MONTH(*date_exp*)	Returns the number of the month.
QUARTER(*date_exp*)	Returns the number of the calendar quarter.
SECOND(*time_exp*)	Returns the second (0 to 60).
WEEK(*date_exp*)	Returns the week number (1 to 52).
YEAR(*date_exp*)	Returns the four-digit year.

ODBC Initialization Files

The ODBC administrator applications, ODBCCP32.DLL and ODBCAD32.EXE, create or delete entries in the two ODBC initialization files in your \WINDOWS directory. The purpose of these two files and the relevance of the entries they contain are explained in the following sections.

ODBCINST.INI

After installing the ODBC driver manager and administrator files, the first step in providing SQL connectivity is to add ODBC drivers for the types of databases to which your applications connect. When you install an ODBC driver, the driver setup application adds an entry to the [ODBC Drivers] section of the installed drivers initialization file, ODBCINST.INI, and marks the driver as available with an Installed value. For the 32-bit drivers, the same technique is used, with the section named as [ODBC 32 bit Drivers]. It appears that 32-bit drivers use the ODBCINST.INI file for backwards compatibility.

The contents of the ODBCINST.INI file of the workstation computer used to write this book are as follows:

```
[ODBC Drivers]
Microsoft Excel Driver (*.xls)=Installed
Microsoft Text Driver (*.txt; *.csv)=Installed
SQL Server=Installed
Microsoft Access Driver (*.mdb)=Installed
Microsoft Dbase Driver (*.dbf)=Installed
Microsoft FoxPro Driver (*.dbf)=Installed
Access Data (*.mdb)=Installed

[ODBC Translators]
MS Code Page Translator=Installed

[Microsoft Access Driver (*.mdb) (32 bit)]
Driver=C:\WINDOWS\SYSTEM\odbcjt32.dll
Setup=C:\WINDOWS\SYSTEM\odbcjt32.dll
32Bit=1

[ODBC 32 bit Drivers]
Microsoft Access Driver (*.mdb) (32 bit)=Installed
Microsoft Dbase Driver (*.dbf) (32 bit)=Installed
Microsoft Excel Driver (*.xls) (32 bit)=Installed
Microsoft FoxPro Driver (*.dbf) (32 bit)=Installed
Microsoft Paradox Driver (*.db ) (32 bit)=Installed
Microsoft Text Driver (*.txt; *.csv) (32 bit)=Installed
SQL Server (32 bit)=Installed
Oracle (32 bit)=Installed
CR SQLBase (32 bit)=Installed
CR Oracle7 (32 bit)=Installed
CR Sybase System 10 (32 bit)=Installed

[Microsoft Dbase Driver (*.dbf) (32 bit)]
Driver=C:\WINDOWS\SYSTEM\odbcjt32.dll
Setup=C:\WINDOWS\SYSTEM\oddbse32.dll
32Bit=1

[Microsoft Excel Driver (*.xls) (32 bit)]
Driver=C:\WINDOWS\SYSTEM\odbcjt32.dll
```

```
Setup=C:\WINDOWS\SYSTEM\odexl32.dll
32Bit=1

[Microsoft FoxPro Driver (*.dbf) (32 bit)]
Driver=C:\WINDOWS\SYSTEM\odbcjt32.dll
Setup=C:\WINDOWS\SYSTEM\odfox32.dll
32Bit=1

[Microsoft Paradox Driver (*.db ) (32 bit)]
Driver=C:\WINDOWS\SYSTEM\odbcjt32.dll
Setup=C:\WINDOWS\SYSTEM\odpdx32.dll
32Bit=1

[Microsoft Text Driver (*.txt; *.csv) (32 bit)]
Driver=C:\WINDOWS\SYSTEM\odbcjt32.dll
Setup=C:\WINDOWS\SYSTEM\odtext32.dll
32Bit=1

[Microsoft Excel Driver (*.xls)]
Driver=C:\WINDOWS\SYSTEM\odbcjt16.dll
Setup=C:\WINDOWS\SYSTEM\odexl16.dll
SQLLevel=0
FileExtns=*.xls
FileUsage=1
DriverODBCVer=02.01
ConnectFunctions=YYN
APILevel=1

[Microsoft Text Driver (*.txt; *.csv)]
Driver=C:\WINDOWS\SYSTEM\odbcjt16.dll
Setup=C:\WINDOWS\SYSTEM\odtext16.dll
SQLLevel=0
FileExtns=*.,*.asc,*.csv,*.tab,*.txt
FileUsage=1
DriverODBCVer=02.01
ConnectFunctions=YYN
APILevel=1

[SQL Server]
Driver=C:\WINDOWS\SYSTEM\sqlsrvr.dll
Setup=C:\WINDOWS\SYSTEM\sqlsrvr.dll
APILevel=1
ConnectFunctions=YYY
DriverODBCVer=02.01
FileUsage=0
SQLLevel=1

[SQL Server (32 bit)]
Driver=C:\WINDOWS\SYSTEM\sqlsrv32.dll
Setup=C:\WINDOWS\SYSTEM\sqlsrv32.dll
32Bit=1

[Microsoft Access Driver (*.mdb)]
Driver=C:\WINDOWS\SYSTEM\odbcjt16.dll
Setup=C:\WINDOWS\SYSTEM\odbcjt16.dll
SQLLevel=0
FileExtns=*.mdb
FileUsage=2
```

```
DriverODBCVer=02.01
ConnectFunctions=YYN
APILevel=1

[Microsoft Dbase Driver (*.dbf)]
Driver=C:\WINDOWS\SYSTEM\odbcjt16.dll
Setup=C:\WINDOWS\SYSTEM\oddbse16.dll
SQLLevel=0
FileExtns=*.dbf,*.ndx,*.mdx
FileUsage=1
DriverODBCVer=02.01
ConnectFunctions=YYN
APILevel=1

[Microsoft FoxPro Driver (*.dbf)]
Driver=C:\WINDOWS\SYSTEM\odbcjt16.dll
Setup=C:\WINDOWS\SYSTEM\odfox16.dll
SQLLevel=0
FileExtns=*.dbf,*.cdx,*.idx,*.ftp
FileUsage=1
DriverODBCVer=02.01
ConnectFunctions=YYN
APILevel=1

[MS Code Page Translator]
Translator=C:\WINDOWS\SYSTEM\mscpxlt.dll
Setup=C:\WINDOWS\SYSTEM\mscpxlt.dll

[Access Data (*.mdb)]
Driver=C:\WINDOWS\SYSTEM\simba.dll
Setup=C:\WINDOWS\SYSTEM\simadmin.dll
"FileUsage"=2
"FileExtns"=*.mdb
"DirectConnect"=0

[Oracle (32 bit)]
Driver=C:\WINDOWS\SYSTEM\vsorac32.dll
Setup=C:\WINDOWS\SYSTEM\orstub32.dll
32Bit=1

[CR SQLBase (32 bit)]
Driver=C:\WINDOWS\SYSTEM\crgup07.dll
Setup=C:\WINDOWS\SYSTEM\crgup07.dll
32Bit=1

[CR Oracle7 (32 bit)]
Driver=C:\WINDOWS\SYSTEM\cror707.dll
Setup=C:\WINDOWS\SYSTEM\cror707.dll
32Bit=1

[CR Sybase System 10 (32 bit)]
Driver=C:\WINDOWS\SYSTEM\crsyb07.dll
Setup=C:\WINDOWS\SYSTEM\crsyb07.dll
32Bit=1
```

The preceding ODBCINST.INI file includes entries for the following 16-bit datasources, which can be used with legacy 16-bit applications:

- Six ODBC datasource types are provided by the Microsoft ODBC Desktop Database Drivers kit. They're included with 16-bit applications that come supplied with Microsoft ODBC:

    Microsoft Excel Driver (*.XLS)
    Microsoft Text Driver (*.TXT, *.CSV)
    SQL Server
    Microsoft Dbase Driver (*.DBF)
    Microsoft FoxPro Driver (*.DBF)
    Access Data (Simba version comes with ODBC driver pack)

- The Access 2.0 driver that is supplied with the Microsoft Office product:

    Microsoft Access Driver. (The Jet driver, which comes with Microsoft Office 2, can't be used with MFC applications.)

The preceding ODBCINST.INI file includes entries for the following 32-bit datasources, which can be used with newer 32-bit applications:

- Six ODBC datasource types are provided by the Microsoft ODBC Desktop Database Drivers kit. They're included with 32-bit applications that come supplied with Microsoft ODBC:

    Microsoft Access Driver (*.MDB) (32-bit)
    Microsoft Dbase Driver (*.DBF) (32-bit)
    Microsoft Excel Driver (*.XLS) (32-bit)
    Microsoft FoxPro Driver (*.DBF) (32-bit)
    Microsoft Paradox Driver (*.DB) (32-bit)
    Microsoft Text Driver (*.TXT, *.CSV) (32-bit)

- The ODBC SQL server provided by the Microsoft ODBC Desktop Database Drivers kit and included with 32-bit applications that come supplied with Microsoft ODBC:

    SQL Server (32-bit)

- The ODBC Oracle driver provided by the Microsoft ODBC Desktop Database Drivers kit and included with 32-bit applications that come supplied with Microsoft ODBC:

    Oracle (32-bit) installed

- Three ODBC drivers installed with the Crystal Reports generator, which is supplied with Crystal Reports. These are installed automatically when you install the Crystal Reports module, which is included with Visual C++ 4.0:

    CR SQLBase (32-bit)
    CR Oracle7 (32-bit)
    CR Sybase System 10 (32-bit)

The datasources appear in the Add Data Source dialog box, which appears when you launch the ODBC Administrator application (either from Control Panel or by executing ODBCAD32.EXE) and then click the Drivers button in the initial Data Sources dialog box. Figure 7.2 shows the drivers listed in the [ODBC Drivers] section of the system registry.

FIGURE 7.2.

The Add Data Source dialog box of the ODBC Administrator application.

With the Windows 3.1x 16-bit ODBC drivers, SIMBA.DLL is the master ODBC driver for all Microsoft single-tier database drivers. ("Simba" is the Swahili word for "lion.") With the exception of Excel worksheet and ASCII text files, the database file types supported by SIMBA.DLL are the same as those supported by the Access database engine: Access, dBASE, FoxPro, Paradox, and Btrieve.

Windows 95 (and Windows NT 3.5x) uses 32-bit ODBC drivers. ODBC no longer uses the original Simba driver model. Instead, all the ODBC drivers work at the same level, called directly by either ODBCJT32.DLL (for ODBC) or MSJT3032.DLL (for DAO). Examples of the use of Microsoft Query and the Access ODBC Desktop Database Drivers appear in the following sections.

ODBC.INI

Entries in the ODBC.INI initialization file designate the ODBC datasources that appear in the Data Sources dialog box of the ODBC Administrator application. As is the case for ODBCINST.INI, ODBC.INI has a two-tiered structure. A list of datasources appears in ODBC.INI's [ODBC Data Sources] section, followed by a section such as dbCMOLSC that provides additional information required by the ODBC driver for the datasource.

> **NOTE**
>
> Windows 95 (and Windows NT 3.5x) use the system registry rather than .INI files to store information used by applications and subsystems. Most ODBC information is contained in the registry keys (Windows 95) [HKEY_LOCAL_MACHINE\SOFTWARE\ODBC] and (usually) [HKEY_USERS\.Default\Software\ODBC]. The subkeys found under these keys are arranged in a manner similar to the 16-bit .INI files.

For 32-bit ODBC drivers, this information is contained in the system registration database. The 16-bit ODBC drivers save information in the ODBC.INI file. The ODBC.INI file that is used in conjunction with the ODBCINST.INI file described in the preceding section appears as follows:

```
[ODBC Data Sources]
MS Access 2.0 Databases=Microsoft Access Driver (*.mdb)
Text CSV=Microsoft Text Driver (*.txt; *.csv)
STARmanager=Microsoft dBASE Driver (*.dbf)
Student Registration=Microsoft Access Driver (*.mdb)
Nafta=Access Data (*.mdb)
NorthWind V2=Access Data (*.mdb)

[MS Access 2.0 Databases]
Driver=C:\WINDOWS\SYSTEM\odbcjt16.dll
FIL=MS Access;
DefaultDir=C:\ACCESS
JetIniPath=MSACC20.INI
UID=Admin
DriverID=25

[Text CSV]
Driver=C:\WINDOWS\SYSTEM\odbcjt16.dll
DefaultDir=E:\STARBETA
Description=Text CSV files
DriverId=27
FIL=text;
JetIniPath=odbcddp.ini

[STARmanager]
Driver=C:\WINDOWS\SYSTEM\odbcjt16.dll
DefaultDir=E:\STARBETA
Description=STARmanger
DriverId=21
FIL=dBASE III;
JetIniPath=odbcddp.ini

[Student Registration]
Driver=C:\WINDOWS\SYSTEM\odbcjt16.dll
DriverId=25
JetIniPath=odbcddp.ini
UID=admin
Driver32=C:\WINDOWS\SYSTEM\odbcjt32.dll

[ODBC 32 bit Data Sources]
dBASE Files=Microsoft dBASE Driver (*.dbf) (32 bit)
Excel Files=Microsoft Excel Driver (*.xls) (32 bit)
FoxPro Files=Microsoft FoxPro Driver (*.dbf) (32 bit)
Paradox Files=Microsoft Paradox Driver (*.db ) (32 bit)
CRSS=SQL Server (32 bit)
CRGUP=CR SQLBase (32 bit)
CROR7=CR Oracle7 (32 bit)
CRSYB=CR Sybase System 10 (32 bit)
Text Files=Microsoft Text Driver (*.txt; *.csv) (32 bit)
Student Registration=Microsoft Access Driver (*.mdb) (32 bit)

[dBASE Files]
Driver32=C:\WINDOWS\SYSTEM\odbcjt32.dll
```

```
[Excel Files]
Driver32=C:\WINDOWS\SYSTEM\odbcjt32.dll

[FoxPro Files]
Driver32=C:\WINDOWS\SYSTEM\odbcjt32.dll

[Paradox Files]
Driver32=C:\WINDOWS\SYSTEM\odbcjt32.dll

[Nafta]
Driver=C:\WINDOWS\SYSTEM\simba.dll
FileType=RedISAM
DataDirectory=T:\nafta.mdb
SingleUser=True
UseSystemDB=True
SystemDB=C:\MAPNGO\system.mda

[CRSS]
Driver32=C:\WINDOWS\SYSTEM\sqlsrv32.dll

[CRGUP]
Driver32=C:\WINDOWS\SYSTEM\crgup07.dll

[CROR7]
Driver32=C:\WINDOWS\SYSTEM\cror707.dll

[CRSYB]
Driver32=C:\WINDOWS\SYSTEM\crsyb07.dll

[NorthWind V2]
Driver=C:\WINDOWS\SYSTEM\simba.dll
Description=MS NorthWind Sample Database
FileType=RedISAM
DataDirectory=c:\access\sampapps\nwind.mdb
SingleUser=False
UseSystemDB=False

[Text Files]
Driver32=C:\WINDOWS\SYSTEM\odbcjt32.dll
```

Figure 7.3 shows the entries in the Data Sources dialog box of the ODBC Administrator that correspond to the entries in the preceding ODBC.INI file.

FIGURE 7.3.

ODBC datasources for dBASE datasources.

Figure 7.4 shows the registration database entries for the ODBC SQL Server 32-bit driver. The information in the registry typically matches the ODBC.INI file if both the 16-bit ODBC (which uses ODBC.INI) and the 32-bit ODBC (which is in the registry) are in sync.

FIGURE 7.4.

ODBC entries in the system registration database.

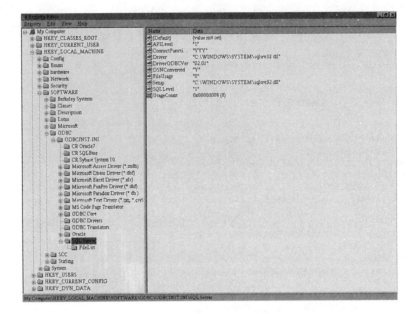

Using Desktop ODBC Datasources with Visual C++

If you have RED110.DLL, the Access ODBC driver that is supplied with the Microsoft ODBC Desktop Database Drivers kit and with Microsoft Query, you can compare the performance of queries executed against STDREG32.MDB directly by the Access database engine or by the single-tier ODBC driver for Access databases by adding an ODBC datasource created from STDREG32.MDB. The RED110.DLL file is a 16-bit driver. You could also compare the system's performance to a 32-bit driver/application combination.

The following sections show you how to create an ODBC datasource named Student Registration from the STDREG32.MDB Access database, run queries against the Student Registration datasource, and trace SQL statements and ODBC function calls.

Adding STDREG32.MDB as an ODBC Datasource

To create the Student Registration ODBC datasource, follow these steps:

1. Launch the ODBC Administrator application (called either "ODBC" or "32bit ODBC") from the Windows Control Panel. If you're using Windows 95, be sure to use the 32-bit version of ODBC.

2. Click the Add button in the Data Sources dialog box, shown in Figure 7.5, to display the Add Data Source dialog box.

FIGURE 7.5.

Choosing the Access database class for the ODBC datasource.

3. Double-click Microsoft Access Driver (*.mdb) in the Installed ODBC Drivers list box (see Figure 7.2) to display the ODBC Microsoft Access 7.0 Setup dialog box, shown in Figure 7.6. Click the Options button to display the additional choices that are available.

FIGURE 7.6.

The opening dialog box that is used to create a new Access ODBC datasource.

NOTE

If you don't have Microsoft Access Driver (*.mdb) displayed in your list of datasources, click the Add button and add the driver from there.

---

4. Enter Student Registration in the Data Source Name text box and a description of the STDREG32.MDB database in the Description text box (use Student Registration if you can't think of anything else). Click the Select button to open the Select Database dialog box.

5. If you're using Visual C++ 4.0, the STDREG32.MDB database is found in the directory V:\MSDEV\SAMPLES\MFC\DATABASE\STDREG, where V: is either the drive where you installed the sample applications or the Visual C++ 4.0 distribution CD. Users of other versions of Visual C++ should use the command dir /s for stdreg*.mdb to find the file. The non-Access 7 version of STDREG is usually called STDREG.MDB. Select the STDREG32.MDB database file as the datasource and close the Select Database dialog box.

6. Make sure that the None option button is selected, unless you have the correct version of Access installed and you want to use your SYSTEM.MDA library to demonstrate password-protected ODBC logon procedures. Your ODBC Microsoft Access 7.0 Setup dialog box appears as shown in Figure 7.7.

FIGURE 7.7.

The ODBC Microsoft Access 7.0 Setup dialog box that is used to create the Student Registration datasource.

7. Click the OK button to close the dialog box, and then click the Close button of the Data Sources dialog box to exit the ODBC Administrator application.

You now have an ODBC datasource, Student Registration, that you can use with any application that supports connections to ODBC datasources, such as Visual C++, Access, and Excel with Microsoft Query.

Using the Student Registration Datasource in a Visual C++ Program

To open the Student Registration datasource, follow these steps:

1. Open the Visual C++ sample application \MSDEV\SAMPLES\MFC\TUTORIAL\ ENROLL\STEP4 and build the program if necessary. Start the program to automatically open the Student Registration datasource.

> **NOTE**
>
> When you're building the examples supplied with Visual C++ 4, they must be located on a drive that you have the ability to write to. If you haven't copied the example from the CD to a hard drive, you must do so before you try to build it. You can't write to the Visual C++ 4 distribution CD.

2. Try using each of the functions available from the ENROLL program. If you have MS Query or Access, you can compare these two applications with the ENROLL program. Because MS Query uses ODBC to access datasources, MS Query won't exhibit much better performance than ENROLL.

Tracing the Execution of ODBC Function Calls and SQL Statements

To trace the behind-the-scenes activity that occurs when you execute a query from any application that uses ODBC to access a datasource, you need to enable ODBC's data logging option. You set this option using the ODBC Administrator (found in Control Panel). You must enable ODBC event logging by clicking the Options button in the ODBC Administrator Data Sources dialog box. The ODBC Options dialog box, shown in Figure 7.8, appears.

FIGURE 7.8.
The ODBC Administrator's ODBC Options dialog box.

In this dialog box, you can specify that all ODBC transactions be traced (that is, logged) to a file. You also can select the Stop Tracing Automatically check box to make the logging active for the current session.

> **WARNING**
>
> When ODBC tracing is enabled, ODBC's performance will be substantially affected. Enable tracing only when needed, and turn tracing off as soon as you're done using it.
>
> If you don't turn logging off, the resulting tracing files ultimately grow to mammoth proportions. Therefore, you must be careful not to fill all your disk's free space with the ODBC trace file, because any application that interacts with ODBC can write thousands of records to the file.

Using Microsoft Query and the Desktop Database Drivers

One of the many advantages of upgrading to (or acquiring) Excel 7, Word for Windows 7, or Microsoft Office 95 is that Microsoft Query and the suite of Microsoft Desktop Database Drivers are bundled with these three mega-apps. Microsoft Query is very useful for learning how to write ANSI SQL statements and how to use the Desktop Database drivers that accompany MS Query. MS Query uses ANSI SQL, with modifications to accommodate ODBC data types, not Access SQL to execute SELECT queries. (MS Query doesn't use the Access database engine to process queries.) Thus, you can use MS Query to validate SQL SELECT query statements you write in the form of string variables in your Visual C++ database applications that use the SQL pass-through option.

Microsoft Query also is part of Visual C++ 1.5x. Since Visual C++ 2.x includes Visual C++ 1.5x, you should always be able to find a copy of Microsoft Query there.

> **TIP**
>
> If nothing else, using MS Query is a way to avoid typing a lengthy query string. Do this by designing your query interactively, and then use the Clipboard to cut and paste the resulting SQL string.

The following sections describe how to create an ODBC datasource, MSQueryDBF, and how to use Microsoft Query as a stand-alone application to execute queries against the datasource.

Creating an ODBC Datasource from dBASE Files

Microsoft Query comes with a sample dBASE III database whose .DBF files are located, along with the Microsoft Query executable files, in your \WINDOWS\MSAPPS\MSQUERY directory. To create a dBASE III ODBC datasource called MSQueryDBF from these files, follow these steps:

1. Launch Microsoft Query (you probably will have an icon in either your Excel or Word folder). Choose File | New Query or click the New Query button to open the Select Data Source dialog box, shown in Figure 7.9. An empty Select Data Source dialog box appears if you haven't previously added an MS Query datasource.

> **NOTE**
>
> There are two versions of MS Query: a 16-bit version in MSQUERY.EXE and a 32-bit version in MSQRY32.EXE. You should use the 32-bit version if possible because it's compatible with the 32-bit ODBC drivers used with Windows NT and Windows 95.

FIGURE 7.9.

Microsoft Query's Select Data Source dialog box.

2. Click the Other button to open the ODBC Data Sources dialog box. ODBC datasources you have created previously, listed in ODBC.INI, appear in the ODBC Data Sources dialog box, shown in Figure 7.10.
3. Click the New button to display the Add Data Source dialog box, shown in Figure 7.11.

FIGURE 7.10.

*Microsoft Query's
ODBC Data Sources
dialog box.*

FIGURE 7.11.

*The ODBC Admin-
istrator's Add Data
Source dialog box.*

4. Double-click the Microsoft Dbase Driver (*.dbf) entry to open the ODBC dBASE Setup dialog box, shown in Figure 7.12.

FIGURE 7.12.

*The ODBC dBASE
Setup dialog box.*

5. Click the Options button to display the expanded version of the dialog box. Click the dBASE III option button and the Select Directory command button to display the Select Directory dialog box.

6. Choose the \WINDOWS\MSAPPS\MSQUERY directory, where six .DBF files appear, and then click the OK button to close the Select Directory dialog box.

7. Complete the entries in the ODBC dBASE Setup dialog box as shown in Figure 7.13. Click the OK button to close the dialog box and display the ODBC Data Source dialog box.

FIGURE 7.13.

*The ODBC dBASE
Setup dialog box for the
Microsoft Query sample
database.*

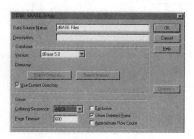

> **TIP**
>
> The collating sequence shown in Figure 7.13 is ASCII, which is the normal collating sequence for text fields of dBASE and FoxPro files created by DOS applications. The sample dBASE files supplied with Microsoft Query are exported from Access's North-Wind Traders sample database. These files use the ANSI (Windows) collating sequence. Choose the ANSI collating sequence for files that are created by Windows applications.

8. Double-click the MSQueryDBF entry in the ODBC Data Source dialog box to redisplay MS Query's Select Data Source dialog box with your new MS Query datasource added.

Microsoft Query maintains its own list of ODBC datasources in the MSQUERY.INI file that you'll find in your \WINDOWS directory. The typical contents of the MSQUERY.INI file are as follows:

```
[Table Options]
Tables=1
Views=1
Synonyms=1
SysTables=0

[Microsoft Query]
Tutorial=0
Maximized=0

[Data Sources]
MSQueryDBF=
```

Because MS Query maintains its own list of datasources, you need to create an explicit ODBC datasource for MS Query using the preceding procedure. Alternatively, you can use the ODBC Administrator application to create the ODBC datasource and then add the datasource to MSQUERY.INI's [Data Sources] section with a text editor or by choosing the ODBC datasource that you created in MS Query's ODBC Data Sources dialog box.

Like the Student Registration ODBC datasource you created earlier in this chapter, you can use the MSQueryDBF datasource with any ODBC-compliant application.

Using an ODBC Datasource with Microsoft Query

Microsoft Query offers a valuable resource to Visual C++ database programmers. It allows you to manipulate ODBC datasources, create SQL statements graphically, and view the results of a query easily and dynamically. That's the good news. The bad news is that Microsoft Query doesn't always work as well as it should, and it's not a proper Windows 95 application (it doesn't allow long filenames, for example).

Microsoft Query comes in two flavors, a 16-bit version and a 32-bit version. The 16-bit version works only with 16-bit ODBC drivers, and the 32-bit version works only with 32-bit ODBC drivers. The 32-bit version of Microsoft Query can be found on the Microsoft Office 95 distribution CD, in the directory U:\OFFICE95\OS\MSAPPS\MSQUERY, where U: is the drive containing the Microsoft Office 95 CD. The executable filename is MSQRY32.EXE. The 16-bit version of Microsoft Query isn't included with Office 95.

In setting up a dBASE data source, we'll assume that you created your Student Registration data source as outlined earlier and that you called it Student Registration. If by chance you didn't install the 32-bit version of the student registration database, you should do so before continuing with this part of the chapter.

1. Load your Student Registration database into Microsoft Query. Start Microsoft Query and click the New Query button (the first button on the left) or choose File | New Query. The Select Data Source dialog box appears.

2. If Student Registration doesn't appear in the list of available databases, add it using the same techniques discussed earlier, when you added the NorthWind Traders database to Microsoft Query.

3. Double-click the Student Registration datasource in the Available Data Sources list box. Microsoft Query will then display the Add Tables dialog box, shown in Figure 7.14.

FIGURE 7.14.

Microsoft Query's Add Tables dialog box.

4. Add the Course, Enrollment, Instructor, Section, and Student tables in sequence to the query by selecting the table name in the Table list box and then clicking the Add button. (You can ignore the table called Dynabind_Section.) Click the Close button when you've added the five tables. You'll see that the tables were added to the query design pane of Microsoft Query's main window.

5. Joins should already exist between each of these tables. There should be a join between CourseID and the Course, Enrollment, and Section tables. There should be a join between StudentID and the Enrollment and Student tables. There should be a join

between SectionNo and the Section and Enrollment tables. There should be a join between InstructorID and the Section and Instructor tables. If any of these joins are missing, either restore the original database from the Visual C++ CD or simply re-create the join.

6. Create joins between tables by clicking and dragging the column to be joined in the first table to the column to which it is to be joined in the second table. (Although the column names don't have to be identical, it makes sense to use the same name for columns that contain the same information when you design your database.) For example, to join the StudentID column in the Enrollment table with the StudentID column in the Student table, click and drag the StudentID column in the Enrollment table and drop it on the StudentID column in the Enrollment table.

7. To view your joins, select Table | Joins. You will see the dialog shown in Figure 7.15.

FIGURE 7.15.

The Microsoft Query Joins dialog box.

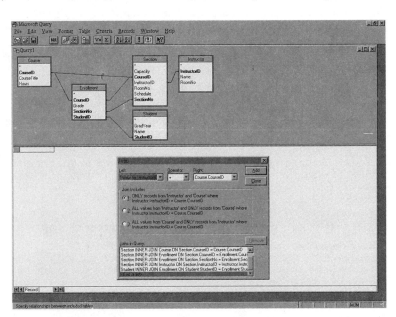

Once your database has been set up (it has been loaded, and the necessary joins have been created), you can the perform queries on it.

NOTE

After you've created your joins, they will continue as part of the database until they're removed. Joins are a feature of the database, not Microsoft Query.

8. An example of a simple query would be to display a group of records from a single table. For instance, you can show the records in the Student table by either selecting all columns (the * at the top of the lists of columns signifies all columns) or by selecting each desired column in the order you want it displayed. Figure 7.16 shows all the columns in the Student table in their default order.

FIGURE 7.16.

Student Registration's Student table with all columns displayed.

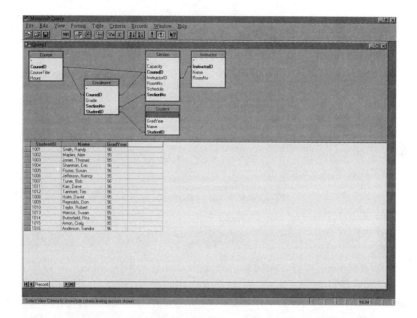

9. To create a more complex query, add all the fields from the Instructor and Course tables to your query. Reorder the fields so that the tables are displayed in this order: Course, Instructor, and Student. Leave the columns in their default order. See Figure 7.17.

FIGURE 7.17.

*Adding fields to the
Microsoft Query grid.*

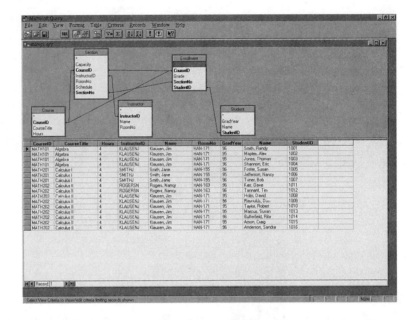

> **NOTE**
>
> You can also drag a field from a table into the open column (the rightmost column) to
> add a field to the query. If the Automatic Query button (the button with the ! and the
> semicircular arrows) is depressed, the column will be updated with the values for the
> new column.

10. To add a criterion to the query, select Criteria | Add Criteria. Choose the
    Student.GradYear field in the Field combo box and equals in the Operator combo
    box, and then enter 95 in the Value text box, as shown in Figure 7.18. Click the Add
    button to apply your criterion to the records in the grid.

11. Click the Close button to return to MS Query's main window. The Criteria pane
    appears. MS Query translates the peculiar date range syntax you typed in the Value
    list box of the Add Criteria dialog box to standard Access SQL date/time syntax.

12. Select the Name column by clicking the field name header cell. Then click the
    Ascending Sort button (AZ) to sort the students by name. Your data grid appears as
    shown in Figure 7.19.

13. You can click the SQL button on the toolbar to display the SQL statement that MS
    Query sends to the ODBC driver manager, ODBC32.DLL. The SQL statement that
    results from the preceding steps appears as shown in Figure 7.20.

FIGURE 7.18.

Microsoft Query's Add Criteria dialog box.

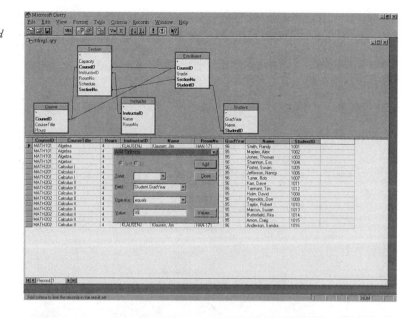

FIGURE 7.19.

The data grid of MS Query after you apply a criterion and a sort order.

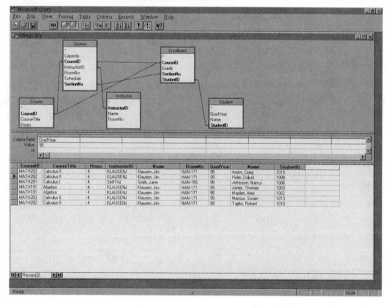

FIGURE 7.20.

The ANSI/ODBC SQL statement for the query shown in Figure 7.19.

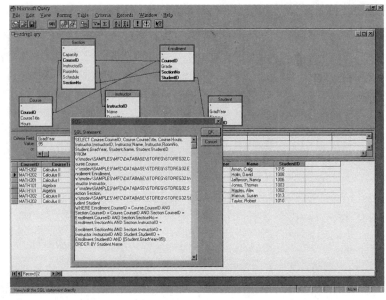

NOTE

Don't be surprised if your SQL window doesn't appear exactly like the one shown in Figure 7.20. Figure 7.20 is a composite image created from three bitmaps of the SQL window—one with the first part of the statement, and the others incorporating the last parts of the statement. This book has several composite images of this type.

Differences Between Access SQL and ANSI/ODBC SQL Statements

SQL statements generated by Microsoft Query, such as the ones shown in Figure 7.20, differ somewhat from Access SQL statements that you would send to the Access database engine in Visual C++ database applications. The following characteristics of SQL statements created by MS Query distinguish the statements from Access SQL:

■ ANSI/ODBC SQL doesn't support the DISTINCTROW qualifier to create updatable query result sets. You can, however, use the ANSI SELECT DISTINCT statement to eliminate duplicate rows.

■ ANSI/ODBC SQL employs the WHERE clause rather than the INNER JOIN reserved words to create equi-joins between tables. You use ODBC's special OUTER JOIN escape syntax {oj *table_name* {LEFT¦RIGHT} OUTER JOIN *table_name* ON join_condition} to create LEFT or RIGHT OUTER JOINs. The advantage of using ODBC escape syntax is that your SQL statement isn't specific to one RDBMS's dialect of SQL.

- ANSI/ODBC SQL uses the escape syntax to specify DATE, TIME, and TIMESTAMP data. For instance, a {d '1989-05-01'} entry is an example of the ODBC DATE escape syntax. Substitute t for d to specify TIME and ts for d to specify TIMESTAMP data.

- You use single quotation marks (') in ANSI/SQL to enclose string literals, including dates and times, instead of Access SQL's choice of single or double (") quotation-mark string identification characters.

- ANSI/ODBC SQL doesn't support Access SQL's WITHOWNERACCESS OPTION statement. You need explicit permissions for the tables that underlie your ANSI/ODBC queries.

- You don't end ANSI/ODBC SQL statements with a semicolon (;), as is done in Access SQL.

Summary

This chapter introduced you to version 2.5 of the Microsoft Open Database Connectivity API and provided the basic information you need to use Microsoft and third-party ODBC drivers with Visual C++ applications. I gave examples of creating ODBC datasources from Access files, from dBASE files, and from the Microsoft Query applet. I also covered the differences between Access SQL and ANSI/ODBC SQL statements and showed you when to implement the SQL pass-through option for your queries.

The next chapter deals with advanced SQL techniques that you use to transform time-series and similar data from row-column to column-row format. It also shows you how to write SQL statements in Visual C++ code to append, update, and delete records from database tables.

8

Running Crosstab and Action Queries

Up to this point in the book, you've been introduced to only the most basic SQL queries: SELECT queries. This chapter describes the five additional types of queries that you can execute with SQL's data manipulation language: crosstab, append, update, delete, and make-table queries. The crosstab query is a special form of SELECT query that summarizes data in spreadsheet style, most often in time-series format. You are likely to find that 75 percent or more of the decision-support applications you create for your firm or clients include crosstab queries. In many cases, the crosstab query result set serves as the datasource for graphs and charts.

The remaining four types of queries described in this chapter are called *action queries.* Microsoft Access introduced the action query category for manipulative (Data Manipulation Language or DML) queries, which update the data in existing tables and create new tables. Action queries can substitute for lengthy blocks of Visual C++ code when you need to modify the content of tables in your database or when you want to create a new database table.

Using Crosstab Queries to Present Summary Data

Even before the early days of the personal computer and the VisiCalc spreadsheet application, managers were accustomed to viewing summary data in the row-column format of accountants' worksheets. Worksheets that are used for comparative performance analysis fall into two basic categories:

■ Time-series format implies that column titles contain date intervals, such as months, quarters, or years, and that row titles designate the category of data being compared. The underlying detail data is grouped by both data category and time period. Time-series summary data often is used to prepare line graphs or bar charts with sales as the y-axis (vertical axis or *abscissa*) and time as the x-axis (horizontal axis or *ordinate*).

■ Classification format uses column titles with the names of individuals, regions, divisions, or other organizational categories and data categories for the row titles. This format is restricted to a single, predetermined time period. (Multiple time periods can be represented by "stacking" worksheets with an identical format that can be consolidated by adding the values of corresponding cells.) The most common graphical representation of data from classification worksheets is the pie chart.

Today's spreadsheet applications, such as Lotus 1-2-3 and Microsoft Excel, replace the drudgery of preparing handwritten worksheets with automated computer-based procedures. However, the majority of the detail information that is needed to prepare summary data for management is available only in the fields of tables of relational accounting databases. Chapter 4, "Optimizing the Design of Relational Databases," demonstrated that most spreadsheet data formats violate the "no repeating groups" rule of relational tables. Conventional ANSI SQL statements return data in relational format, not spreadsheet format. Thus, a substantial amount of data manipulation ordinarily is required to create a time-series or classification spreadsheet from relational data. In fact, the "denormalization" process is almost as complex as that described in Chapter 4 for normalizing spreadsheet data to relational form.

The following sections describe how summary data is returned by ANSI SQL and how you use Access SQL's TRANSFORM and PIVOT statements to automate the denormalization of relational data to spreadsheet format.

Summary Data Created by the *GROUP BY* Clause

Figure 8.1 illustrates the format of data returned by conventional SELECT queries that use the SQL aggregate function SUM() to prepare data from which you can create a time-series worksheet. The tables employed to create the query return set, shown in the Crosstab query window of Figure 8.1, are Categories, Products, Orders, and Order Details. These tables' values are derived from the Northwind Traders sample database that accompanies Access. The query return set totals orders that were received for each of eight categories of products for the four calendar quarters of 1996. Thus, the grid contains eight records with a Category Name field and four quarter fields.

FIGURE 8.1.

Using two GROUP BY criteria to sum the values of orders by category and date.

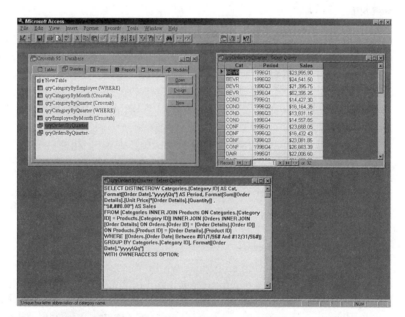

NOTE

The Access 95 CROSSTAB 95.MDB database (located in the CHAPTR08 subdirectory on the CD that comes with this book) is used for all the examples in this chapter. CROSSTAB 95.MDB contains records for the Categories, Products, and Employees tables that are the same as those in NorthWind.MDB (from Access), except that unnecessary fields have been deleted. The order dates have been updated. Records for years other than 1995 and 1996 have been deleted from the Orders and Order Details tables.

Access 95 was used to perform all the sample queries in this chapter.

The query that was used to create the data shown in Figure 8.1 is rather lengthy and deserves further explanation. The following list describes each element of the Access SQL statement that appears in Figure 8.1:

- The three AS predicates of the statement

```
SELECT Categories.[Category ID] AS Cat, Format([Order Date],"yyyy\Qq")
AS Period, Format(SUM([Order Details].[Unit Price]*[Order
Details].[Quantity]),
"$#,##0.00") AS Sales
```

  alias the Category ID field as Cat and the two formatted fields as Period and Sales, respectively.

- The first Format() function causes the order date to appear as the year (yyyy) followed by a literal Q (\Q) and the number of the quarter (q) that corresponds to the order date. A backslash (\) preceding a character in a format string designates the character that follows as a literal character rather than a format identifier character.

- The SUM() SQL aggregate function totals the product of the Unit Price and Quantity fields of the Order Details table, which is needed to compute the extended amount of each invoice line item.

- The Format() function embedded within the SUM() function adds the dollar sign ($), comma thousands separator (#,##0), and trailing cents columns (.00) to the values in the Sales column. This function isn't required in Access applications because Currency values are automatically formatted with "#,##0.00". Visual C++ bound controls and the grid control don't automatically format the Currency data type.

- FROM Categories, Products, Orders, [Order Details] identifies the tables in use. The trailing comma separates this statement from the three join statements that follow.

- Categories INNER JOIN Products ON Categories.[Category ID] = Products.[Category ID] creates the equi-join needed to identify products by category, because the Order Details table contains a Product ID field but not a Category ID field. (You could eliminate this join by substituting Products.[Category ID] for Categories.[Category

ID] in the SELECT statement. The join is included in the example because you might want to use the Category Name field rather than the Category ID field for the row titles.)

■ Products INNER JOIN [Order Details] ON Products.[Product ID] = [Order Details].[Product ID] creates the equi-join needed to join the Order Details table to the Products table so that the values in the Order Details table for each product category are associated with the Category ID value.

■ Orders INNER JOIN [Order Details] ON Orders.[Order ID] = [Order Details].[Order ID] creates a join so that you can use the following WHERE clause to limit to a range of dates the records of Order Details that are totaled for each category.

■ The WHERE Orders.[Order Date] Between #01/1/95# And #12/31/96# criterion limits the summation to records for the years 1995 and 1996. The WHERE clause in Figure 8.1 is enclosed in double parentheses, which are not necessary.

■ The GROUP BY Categories.[Category ID], Format([Order Date],"yyyy\Qq") clause results in data being grouped by product category and by the quarter of the year. The sequence of the grouping isn't significant in this query. It's customary to use the same Format() function in the GROUP BY clause as is used in the SELECT statement that displays the grouping value. The literal \Q, however, isn't necessary to achieve the proper grouping.

It's clear from the rows returned by the preceding query and illustrated in Figure 8.1 that a substantial rearrangement of worksheet cells is required if you import this data into a worksheet that is intended to display data in time-series format.

You can achieve a result that is similar to the preceding example with ANSI/ODBC SQL using Microsoft Query. The following ANSI/ODBC SQL statement returns sales for each of the eight categories by month in 96 rows and also illustrates the use of the scalar ODBC date function MONTH() in SQL statements that are processed by ODBC drivers:

```
SELECT Categories."Category ID" AS Cat,
    {fn MONTH(Orders."Order Date")} AS Month,
    Sum("Order Details"."Unit Price" * "Order Details".Quantity) AS Sales
    FROM Categories, "Order Details", Orders, Products
    WHERE Products."Category ID" = Categories."Category ID"
    AND "Order Details"."Order ID" = Orders."Order ID"
    AND "Order Details"."Product ID" = Products."Product ID"
    GROUP BY Categories."Category ID", {fn MONTH(Orders."Order Date")}
```

Figure 8.2 shows the SQL window of MS Query displaying the preceding SQL statement and 13 of the last records of the query result table created by executing the statement.

FIGURE 8.2.

An ANSI/ODBC SQL statement that summarizes category sales by month.

You can use MS Query's conventional SQL processing method, in which you write the SQL statement in MS Query's SQL window or choose File | Execute SQL from MS Query to send an SQL statement directly to the ODBC driver using SQL pass-through. Figure 8.3 shows MS Query's Execute SQL dialog box, ready to execute the SQL statement in Figure 8.2.

FIGURE 8.3.

MS Query's Execute SQL window, which is used to implement SQL pass-through.

The rows that return when you specify monthly data require even more rearrangement than the quarterly data returned from the Access query.

> **NOTE**
>
> MS Query can't represent the SQL statement graphically and therefore will give you an error message. The query will be successful regardless.

Using *TRANSFORM* and *PIVOT* to Create Crosstab Queries

Access SQL's crosstab query feature solves the data cell rearrangement problem. Two Access SQL keywords, TRANSFORM and PIVOT, handle the denormalization of the data. The elements of an Access SQL crosstab query are as follows:

■ The object of the TRANSFORM predicate specifies the values for the data cells and must contain one of the SQL aggregate functions, such as SUM() or AVG(). You use the Format() function to determine the data's appearance.

■ The SELECT statement designates the row titles. The field you specify with the SELECT statement must be the same as the GROUP BY field.

■ The FROM statement specifies each table involved in the query. The tables may be identified by the INNER JOIN statements, without the conventional comma-separated table_names list.

■ The GROUP BY clause aggregates row data. Only one field is permitted in the GROUP BY clause of a conventional crosstab query.

■ The optional ORDER BY clause sorts the rows by the value of the single field specified in the SELECT and GROUP BY statements. You don't need to add the ORDER BY clause if the field specified by the SELECT statement is a primary key field and you want the rows ordered by the primary key.

■ The PIVOT statement determines the column grouping and supplies the column titles. Column titles consist of the value of the grouping criterion. The object of the PIVOT predicate takes the place of the second GROUP BY field of the SQL statements of the two examples in the preceding section.

Figure 8.4 shows the initial syntax of the Access SQL statement that creates the crosstab query return set shown in Figure 8.5. The statement in the SQL window of Figure 8.4 consists of the SQL statement illustrated in Figure 8.1, plus the necessary modifications to make the statement conform to the rules of crosstab queries given in the preceding list.

FIGURE 8.4.

Executing a crosstab query with Access.

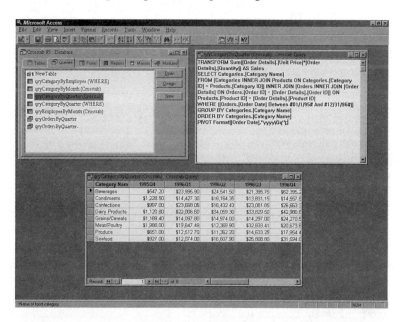

NOTE

Figure 8.4 is a composite. Access 95 won't show both a query SQL statement and the result of the query at the same time. You can toggle between the two views using the View menu when a query is open.

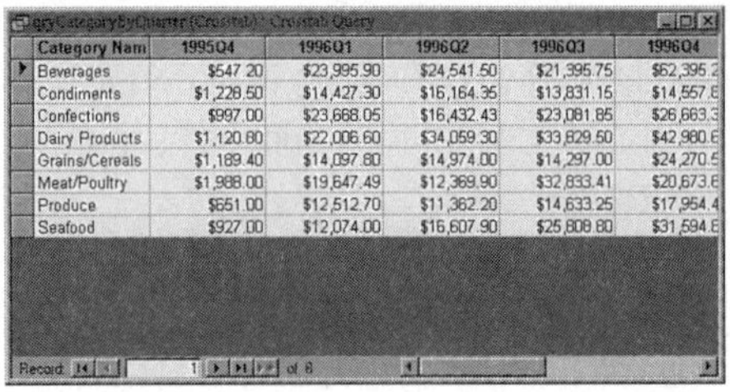

Category Nam	1995Q4	1996Q1	1996Q2	1996Q3	1996Q4
Beverages	$547.20	$23,995.90	$24,541.50	$21,395.75	$62,395.2
Condiments	$1,228.50	$14,427.30	$16,164.35	$13,831.15	$14,557.6
Confections	$997.00	$23,668.05	$16,432.43	$23,081.85	$26,663.3
Dairy Products	$1,120.80	$22,006.60	$34,059.30	$33,829.50	$42,980.6
Grains/Cereals	$1,189.40	$14,097.80	$14,974.00	$14,297.00	$24,270.5
Meat/Poultry	$1,988.00	$19,647.49	$12,369.90	$32,833.41	$20,673.6
Produce	$651.00	$12,512.70	$11,362.20	$14,633.25	$17,954.4
Seafood	$927.00	$12,074.00	$16,607.90	$25,808.80	$31,594.6

FIGURE 8.5.
The crosstab query result set from the SQL statement in Figure 8.4.

The CROSSTAB 95.MDB database includes a `QueryDef` object, `qryCategoryByMonth (Crosstab)`, that creates the query result set shown in Figure 8.5. Select the query tab in the Database window in Access. When a query is open, the query toolbar is displayed. The first three buttons let you change from the Design, SQL, and Datasheet view modes. You can then display the SQL statement. After that, click the Datasheet view toolbar button to execute the query. When you execute the crosstab query shown in Figure 8.4, the Access database engine's query optimizer modifies the `FROM` and `INNER JOIN` statements as follows:

```
TRANSFORM Format(Sum([Order Details].[Unit Price] *
    [Order Details].[Quantity]), "$#,##0") AS Sales
    SELECT Categories.[Category Name]
    FROM (Categories INNER JOIN Products ON Categories.[Category ID] =
    Products.[Category ID])
    INNER JOIN (Orders INNER JOIN [Order Details]
    ON Orders.[Order ID] = [Order Details].[Order ID])
    ON Products.[Product ID] = [Order Details].[Product ID]
    WHERE ((Orders.[Order Date] Between #01/1/95# And #12/31/96#))
    GROUP BY Categories.[Category Name]
    ORDER BY Categories.[Category Name]
    PIVOT Format([Order Date],"yyyy\Qq");
```

The preceding syntax example, which substitutes nested `INNER JOIN` syntax for individual `INNER JOIN` statements, more closely follows the SQL-92 syntax for `JOIN` statements. Each of the tables specified in the original `FROM` clause appears in the `INNER JOIN` statements, so it's not necessary to provide a separate *`table_names`* list. The first `INNER JOIN` of the `FROM` statement uses conventional `INNER JOIN` syntax. The succeeding nested `INNER JOIN` causes a join to be created between the result of the first `INNER JOIN` and the criterion of the last `ON` statement. The second and third `INNER JOIN`s use the second `ON` criterion. Nested `INNER JOIN` statements are quite difficult to interpret correctly and are even more difficult to write.

A simpler approach to specifying `INNER JOIN`s uses a compound `WHERE` clause. The following `WHERE` clause syntax achieves the same result as the `INNER JOIN` syntax of the preceding example:

```
TRANSFORM Format(Sum([Order Details].[Unit Price] *
    [Order Details].[Quantity]), "$#,##0") AS Sales
    SELECT Categories.[Category Name]
    FROM Categories, [Order Details], Orders, Products
    WHERE Products.[Category ID] = Categories.[Category ID]
    AND [Order Details].[Order ID] = Orders.[Order ID]
    AND [Order Details].[Product ID] = Products.[Product ID]
    AND Orders.[Order Date] Between #01/1/95# And #12/31/96#
```

```
GROUP BY Categories.[Category Name]
ORDER BY Categories.[Category Name]
PIVOT Format([Order Date],"yyyy\Qq");
```

> **TIP**
>
> If you use Access to create and test the text for SQL statements to generate crosstab queries, you'll find that Visual C++ executes Access crosstab query syntax without generating an error. However, your code will be simpler and more readable if you use the WHERE clause to create equi-joins.

Creating Fixed Column Headers with the *IN()* Predicate

If you change the PIVOT statement in the preceding example from PIVOT Format([Order Date],"yyyy\Qq") to PIVOT Format([Order Date],"mmm yy") to create a monthly rather than a quarterly crosstab query, the column titles appear in the strange sequence shown in Figure 8.6. The PIVOT statement automatically orders the columns alphabetically.

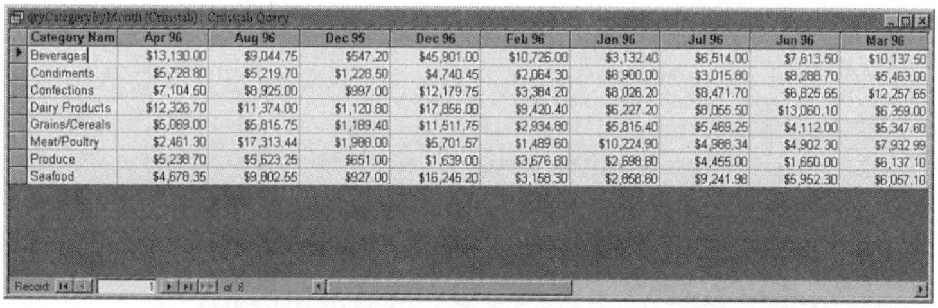

FIGURE 8.6.

Monthly column headings sorted alphabetically.

Category Nam	Apr 96	Aug 96	Dec 95	Dec 96	Feb 96	Jan 96	Jul 96	Jun 96	Mar 96
Beverages	$13,130.00	$9,044.75	$547.20	$45,901.00	$10,726.00	$3,132.40	$6,514.00	$7,613.50	$10,137.50
Condiments	$5,728.80	$5,219.70	$1,228.50	$4,740.45	$2,064.30	$6,900.00	$3,015.80	$8,288.70	$5,463.00
Confections	$7,104.50	$8,925.00	$997.00	$12,179.75	$3,384.20	$8,026.20	$8,471.70	$6,826.65	$12,257.65
Dairy Products	$12,326.70	$11,374.00	$1,120.80	$17,856.00	$9,420.40	$6,227.20	$8,055.50	$13,060.10	$6,359.00
Grains/Cereals	$5,069.00	$5,815.75	$1,189.40	$11,511.75	$2,934.80	$5,815.40	$5,469.25	$4,112.00	$5,347.60
Meat/Poultry	$2,461.30	$17,313.44	$1,988.00	$5,701.57	$1,489.60	$10,224.90	$4,988.34	$4,902.30	$7,932.99
Produce	$5,238.70	$5,623.26	$651.00	$1,639.00	$3,676.80	$2,698.80	$4,455.00	$1,650.00	$6,137.10
Seafood	$4,678.35	$9,802.55	$927.00	$16,245.20	$3,158.30	$2,858.60	$9,241.98	$5,952.30	$6,057.10

You could solve the column sequence problem by changing the PIVOT statement to PIVOT Format([Order Date],"mm/yy") to provide column titles 01/95 through 12/96, but many people prefer three-letter abbreviations for months. Access SQL lets you use the IN() predicate to create fixed column names that appear in any sequence you specify. The following example demonstrates a PIVOT...IN statement that creates monthly column titles for any year:

```
PIVOT Format([Order Date],"mmm")
    IN ("Jan", "Feb", "Mar", "Apr", "May", "Jun", "Jul", "Aug", "Sep",
    "Oct", "Nov", "Dec");
```

> **CAUTION**
>
> You can't use the IN() predicate with SQL statements that use the full INNER JOIN syntax of Access, as shown in Figure 8.4. If you attempt to execute such a query, you receive the error message Can't repeat field_name in FROM statement.

The preceding `PIVOT` statement gives the more satisfactory result shown in Figure 8.7.

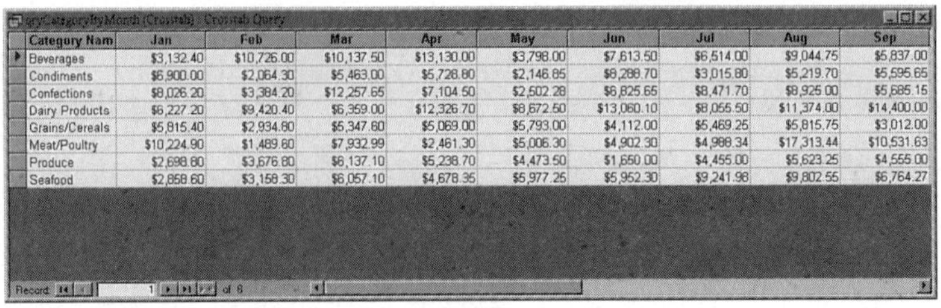

Category Nam	Jan	Feb	Mar	Apr	May	Jun	Jul	Aug	Sep
Beverages	$3,132.40	$10,726.00	$10,137.50	$13,130.00	$3,798.00	$7,613.50	$6,514.00	$9,044.75	$5,837.00
Condiments	$6,900.00	$2,064.30	$5,463.00	$5,728.80	$2,146.85	$8,288.70	$3,015.80	$5,219.70	$5,595.65
Confections	$8,026.20	$3,384.20	$12,257.65	$7,104.50	$2,502.28	$6,825.65	$8,471.70	$8,925.00	$5,685.15
Dairy Products	$6,227.20	$9,420.40	$6,359.00	$12,326.70	$8,672.50	$13,060.10	$8,055.50	$11,374.00	$14,400.00
Grains/Cereals	$5,815.40	$2,934.80	$5,347.60	$5,069.00	$5,793.00	$4,112.00	$5,469.25	$5,815.75	$3,012.00
Meat/Poultry	$10,224.90	$1,489.60	$7,932.99	$2,461.30	$5,006.30	$4,902.30	$4,988.34	$17,313.44	$10,531.63
Produce	$2,698.80	$3,676.80	$6,137.10	$5,238.70	$4,473.50	$1,650.00	$4,455.00	$5,623.25	$4,555.00
Seafood	$2,858.60	$3,158.30	$6,057.10	$4,678.35	$5,977.25	$5,952.30	$9,241.98	$9,802.55	$6,764.27

FIGURE 8.7.
The query from Figure 8.6 with fixed column heads.

The only restriction on the values of the `IN()` predicate's arguments is that, except for case, each value must exactly match the values returned by the formatted `PIVOT` statement. If you misspell an argument value, you will find that the data rows of the column with the mistaken header are empty.

NOTE

The Access documentation states that crosstab queries with fixed column heads execute faster than queries without the `IN()` predicate. In practice, the difference in execution speed is difficult to measure. Using the `IN()` predicate doesn't result in a demonstrable improvement in the performance of the preceding query when executed against the CROSSTAB 95.MDB or NorthWind.MDB database.

Creating a Classification Crosstab Query

With a few simple changes and additions to the preceding query, you can create a crosstab query in classification format to compare sales of product categories by employee during a specific period of time. The following SQL statement adds the Employees table to the query and displays the last name of each employee of Northwind Traders as column headings, with sales by category for 1996 as the data cell values:

```
TRANSFORM Format(Sum([Order Details].[Unit Price] *
    [Order Details].[Quantity]), "$#,##0") AS Sales
    SELECT Categories.[Category Name]
    FROM Categories, [Order Details], Orders, Products, Employees
    WHERE Products.[Category ID] = Categories.[Category ID]
    AND [Order Details].[Order ID] = Orders.[Order ID]
    AND [Order Details].[Product ID] = Products.[Product ID]
    AND Orders.[Employee ID] = Employees.[Employee ID]
    AND Orders.[Order Date] Between #01/1/95# And #12/31/96#
    GROUP BY Categories.[Category Name]
    ORDER BY Categories.[Category Name]
    PIVOT Employees.[Last Name];
```

Figure 8.8 shows the crosstab query result set returned by the preceding SQL statement that is executed in Access.

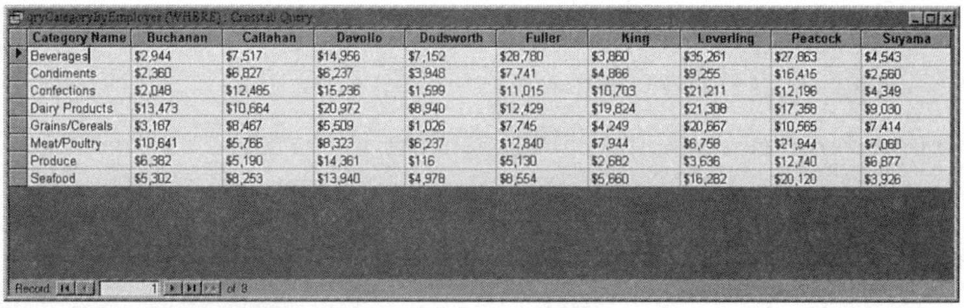

FIGURE 8.8.

A classification crosstab query executed in Access.

Category Name	Buchanan	Callahan	Davolio	Dodsworth	Fuller	King	Leverling	Peacock	Suyama
Beverages	$2,944	$7,517	$14,956	$7,152	$28,780	$3,860	$35,261	$27,863	$4,543
Condiments	$2,360	$6,827	$6,237	$3,948	$7,741	$4,866	$9,255	$16,415	$2,560
Confections	$2,048	$12,485	$15,236	$1,599	$11,015	$10,703	$21,211	$12,196	$4,349
Dairy Products	$13,473	$10,664	$20,972	$8,940	$12,429	$19,824	$21,308	$17,358	$9,030
Grains/Cereals	$3,167	$8,467	$5,509	$1,026	$7,745	$4,249	$20,867	$10,565	$7,414
Meat/Poultry	$10,641	$5,766	$8,323	$6,237	$12,840	$7,944	$6,758	$21,944	$7,060
Produce	$6,382	$5,190	$14,361	$116	$5,130	$2,682	$3,636	$12,740	$6,877
Seafood	$5,302	$8,253	$13,940	$4,978	$8,554	$5,860	$16,282	$20,120	$3,926

Record: 1 of 9

Defining Action Queries

Action queries provide a method of creating or modifying persistent database objects without the necessity of writing low-level Visual C++ code to manipulate table record pointers. Action queries are especially effective when you want to add, delete, or modify many records in a database with a single operation. (An operation that makes changes to multiple sets of records is called a *bulk update*.) The following list briefly describes the four types of action queries:

- Append queries use the INSERT INTO *table_name* predicate followed by a conventional SELECT statement to specify the fields and criteria used to determine the data to be appended to *table name*.

- Delete queries use the DELETE FROM *table_name* WHERE *criteria* syntax to delete records whose data meets the *criteria*.

- Update queries use the UPDATE *table_name* SET *field_name* = *expression* statement with a WHERE clause to establish which records are updated.

- Make-table queries use SELECT *field_names* INTO *dest_table* FROM *source_table* statements to create a new table, *dest_table*, with fields specified by the *field_names* list.

Using the SQL Action Queries

The following sections give examples of the use of each of the four types of action queries that Access SQL supports. All of the following examples use the CROSSTAB 95.MDB database opened in Access.

Creating New Tables with Make-Table Queries

To avoid modifying the existing tables in the CROSSTAB 95.MDB database, the first action query example creates a new table from the Orders table, tblOrders, that includes all orders that have order dates earlier than July 1, 1996. To test make-table action query syntax, enter the following in Access's Query SQL Statement window:

```
SELECT *, [Order Date]
    INTO tblOrders
    FROM Orders
    WHERE [Order Date]<#07/1/96#
```

You need to include the [Order Date] entry in the SELECT list because Access SQL doesn't let you specify a WHERE criterion on a field that isn't explicitly declared in the SELECT list.

> **NOTE**
>
> The NewOrders table doesn't appear in Access's Tables tab until you execute the query after saving it. After the query is executed (Access will warn you that a new table will be created), you can view the new table.

Use a make-table query to create a backup of a table before you test other SQL action statements on the table. If your append, update, or delete query gives an unexpected result, you can start fresh by deleting all the records in the original table and appending all the records from the backup table.

You can add an IN clause to your make-table query to create a table in another database. Here's the full syntax of an SQL make-table clause:

```
SELECT [ALL¦DISTINCT¦DISTINCTROW] select_list
    INTO dest_table [IN database_name[ connect_string]]
    FROM source_table
    WHERE criteria
```

Thus, you can create a tblOrders table in the C:\MSOffice\Access\Samples\NorthWind.MDB database (if you have the Northwind Traders database installed) with the following statement:

```
SELECT *, [Order Date]
    INTO tblOrders IN "c:\msoffice\access\samples\northwind.mdb"
    FROM Orders
    WHERE [Order Date]<#07/1/96#
```

Appending Records to Existing Tables

You can append the balance of the records for the year 1996 to the tblOrders table with the following append query statement:

```
INSERT INTO tblOrders ([Order ID], [Customer ID], [Employee ID],
    [Order Date], [Shipped Date], [Order Amount])
    SELECT [Order ID], [Customer ID], [Employee ID], [Order Date],
    [Shipped Date], [Order Amount]
    FROM Orders
    WHERE [Order Date] Between #07/1/96# And #12/31/96#
```

You need to explicitly declare the field list of both the destination table (tblOrders) and the source table (Orders) if you use a WHERE criterion. The field list of the destination table must be enclosed in parentheses. If you attempt to use the asterisk (*) to add all fields and then add the [Order Date] field to the SELECT statement, as in the make-table example, you receive a syntax error message.

Updating Data Values in Tables

To change values in data fields, you use the UPDATE predicate. The SET clause specifies the expression used to update one or more fields. The following update action query SQL statement reduces the dollar amount of each order received in April 1996 to 90 percent of its current value:

```
UPDATE tblOrders
    SET [Order Amount] = 0.9*[Order Amount]
    WHERE [Order Date] BETWEEN #4/1/96# AND #4/30/96#;
```

If you want to update the values of more than one field, add the field name, the equals sign (=), and an expression separated from the preceding SET expression by a comma (,).

Deleting Records from Tables

The simplest and most potentially destructive of the action queries is the delete query. If you execute a delete query and forget to add a WHERE criterion, all the records in your table can disappear in an instant. To delete the records for the last half of 1996 from the tblOrders table, use the following statement:

```
DELETE FROM tblOrders
    WHERE [Order Date] BETWEEN #7/1/96# AND #12/31/96#;
```

You now can safely verify that the DELETE FROM tblOrders statement without the WHERE clause does indeed delete all the records in the table.

Summary

This chapter demonstrated how to use the Access SQL TRANSFORM and PIVOT keywords to create crosstab queries and showed the syntax necessary to implement action queries with SQL statements. Crosstab queries are one of the most commonly used forms of SELECT queries in Visual C++ decision-support applications. The next chapter makes more extensive use of crosstab queries. Using action queries to create and update tables often can save you from writing a substantial amount of Visual C++ code.

This chapter ends Part II of this book. At this point, you have the background you need in database design and the use of both ANSI and Access SQL to develop meaningful database applications. Part III shows you how to design applications to display and print the information that you extract from databases with SQL SELECT queries.

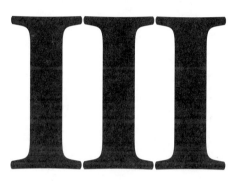

An Introduction to Database Front-End Design

9

Designing a Decision-Support Application

It's likely that your first production-database application that uses Visual C++ will be used for decision-support purposes. Industry sources estimate that decision-support applications constitute 75 percent or more of all of the database applications in use today. Also, decision-support applications are often easy to write and maintain. When you create a decision-support application for use with an existing relational database, you need not be concerned with database design, maintaining referential and domain integrity, or concurrency problems. (You do, however, need to take consistency issues into account if you're summarizing data.)

The purpose of a decision-support application is to transform raw data into useful information. Your primary task is to provide the users of your application with a simple, straightforward method of obtaining the data they need. This chapter begins by discussing how to organize the data you're converting to useful information with decision-support applications. It also discusses designing the user interface to make your application easy to understand and provides examples of forms that display information in graphical and tabular format. Finally, this chapter reviews examples of the Visual C++ code needed to create the graph, chart, and grid objects that display selected information to the user. Visual C++ doesn't support these display objects directly, so you will learn about a number of alternative add-in products that may be used for this purpose.

Organizing the Data Behind a Decision-Support Application

The objective of most of today's decision-support applications is to replace printed reports with on-screen presentations of information. A successful decision-support application supplies "Information at Your Fingertips" (a Microsoft-trademarked corporate slogan). For mid-level managers and below, the *video display unit* (VDU) of a PC is the most common presentation platform. At the vice-presidential and higher rungs of the corporate ladder, the information often is displayed on large-screen or projection video systems acting as a VDU for one PC in a conference setting.

Specifying the Datasources

Typical relationships of datasources and information systems for a typical manufacturing company appear in the hierarchical structure shown in Figure 9.1. Data-entry and transaction-processing activities primarily are confined to the lowest level of the hierarchy, operational databases. (The operational database level of the hierarchy often is called "the trenches.") The levels above the operational databases involve little or no data entry; these upper levels in the hierarchy are referred to as *information systems* (IS) or *management information systems* (MIS). Figure 9.1 divides the information systems category into functional information systems at the directorate and vice-presidential level and planning and forecasting information systems that are used by top management and corporate staff.

FIGURE 9.1.

The hierarchy of information systems and databases for a manufacturing firm.

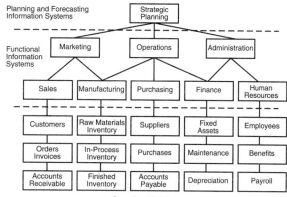

Depending on the size of the company and the type of computer hardware the firm uses, the operational databases may be located in a centralized mainframe system or distributed across several database servers in a client-server RDBMS environment. Combinations of mainframe and client-server environments are common for firms that are in the process of downsizing and distributing their operational databases. A small manufacturing firm might have all its operational databases in the form of multiple .DBF files that reside on a single file server.

If you're developing database applications for a firm with $10 million or more in annual sales, be prepared to deal with the connectivity issues raised by a wide variety of network operating systems and database management systems, including *legacy* (a synonym for "obsolete" among proponents of client-server RDBMSs) network and hierarchical DBMS. It's not uncommon for developers of database front ends to spend more time solving connectivity problems, both DBM- and network-related, than they spend designing, coding, and testing the entire front-end application.

You also might need to integrate data from online datasources into your database front-end application. Credit information from Dun and Bradstreet and TRW, stock prices from the Dow Jones News Service, and real estate transaction data from Damar are just a few of the uses for the data communication features of Visual C++. Another nontraditional datasource that you might need to incorporate in your applications is the CD-ROM. Virtually all the 1990 census data is available from the U.S. Bureau of the Census in .DBF format on CD-ROMs. Fortunately, ODBC lets developers work with .DBF format files.

Determining the Level of Detail Required

Before the advent of the RDBMS and client-server computing technology, the principal source of functional information, as well as planning and forecasting information, was a multitude of printed reports. Each report was the product of a batch operation that required a program, usually written in COBOL, to execute the Embedded SQL or other instructions that create a formatted report. In many cases, reports were created with more than the optimal level of detail because of a lack of programming resources to write, test, and deploy production programs to summarize the data. The capability of users of client applications to create their own ad hoc queries with whatever degree of detail they desire is the driving force behind the front-end application generator market. Generally, a management report that is more than two pages in length probably presents too much detail.

Unless you're dealing with data that has been *rolled up* (the subject of the next section), your decision-support front-end application will be accessing tables in operational databases. The level of detail you provide in a decision-support application usually varies inversely with the position of the users in the organizational hierarchy. As you progress upward in the corporate "food chain," tabular data gives way to graphs and charts for trend analysis, and the frequency of reporting slows from daily to monthly. Here are the three basic categories of decision-support applications:

- *Executive summaries* and planning information consist of graphs and charts that depict financial performance versus internal projections, versus prior fiscal periods, and often versus the results reported by competitors. This category of report is the most likely to require integration of data from online sources operated by data utilities, such as Dialog Information Services, or from firms that specialize in providing online econometric data.

- *Functional summaries*, such as reports of orders for the director of sales or daily cash-flow reports from the director of finance, are usually run weekly. At the directorate level, tabular data is the rule. The data from the directors' reports usually is consolidated into monthly reports issued at the vice-presidential level. Graphs compare current operating results with recent historical data, usually for a one-year period or shorter.

- *Operational data summaries* are required by supervisory personnel to evaluate day-to-day performance at the departmental or regional level. Credit managers need real-time access to the payment histories of customers placing new orders. Exception-reporting applications that are used on the shop floor, such as applications that identify parts shortages or quality control problems, may need to run on an hourly or shift basis. Tabular formats, rather than graphic presentations, are most common at the operational level.

Figure 9.2 shows the layers of information that constitute typical marketing decision-support applications corresponding to the three categories in the preceding list. The executive summary for the vice president of marketing consolidates sales of all products in all regions. The functional summary for the director of sales includes sales of a particular product line in all regions. The operational data viewed by the regional sales manager reports sales in one region for all products.

One of the principal objections of management personnel to MIS reports, whether displayed online or in the form of computer printouts, is excessive detail. If you use a 9-point MS Sans Serif font with a tightly spaced Visual C++ list box, you can display several times as much data on a VDU as is possible with a character-based DOS application. Running at higher resolutions (such as 1024×768) allows a large amount of data to be presented to the user. You have similar potential with today's laser printers. For management, it's the aggregate data that is important, together with exception highlighting. If you need to provide one or two levels of detail behind the summary data, first offer the detail behind the exceptions and then make additional detail information an option.

FIGURE 9.2.

Levels of information detail in summary and operational decision-support applications.

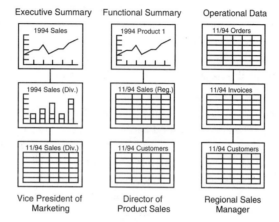

Maintaining Performance and Data Consistency with Rollups

Impatience is another personal trait that increases with the level of authority and responsibility in an organization. Operatives in the trenches might be satisfied with an application that takes a minute or more to present a screen of data, because a 3270 terminal on an overtaxed mainframe might take several minutes to update a session. If your summary queries (especially crosstab queries) need to traverse tens of thousands of records containing line items for a year's collection of invoices, you're certain to face an unsatisfied client when you deliver your production front end.

The traditional (and still the best) approach to maintaining adequate performance for time-series decision-support applications is to consolidate time-based detail data into new tables. This process is called *rolling up data,* a process that should be familiar to all mainframe CO-BOL programmers. Consolidating data, other than creating monthly and yearly rollups for accounting purposes, has been relatively uncommon in PC-based database applications. High-speed 66 to 100 MHz Intel 80486 and Pentium PCs now have become the most popular CPUs for database servers, and the cost of fixed disk storage has broken the $.20-per-megabyte barrier (no, that's not a misprint—20 cents a megabyte, and by the first quarter of 1996, it might be even lower!). Thus, the economic disincentive of replicating data is minimal.

Although rolling up data violates the no-duplicated-data rule for relational databases (because rolled up data is derived from existing tables), you'll probably want to aggregate data when your summary queries need to process more than a few thousand records. Here are some guidelines for how and when to roll up data:

- Avoid cascading rollups when possible. A *cascading rollup* is a rollup operation that summarizes data that has been rolled up at a greater detail level. If a retroactive change to the underlying detail occurs, you need to re-aggregate each level in the process.

- Roll up data at intervals that are likely to be the least subject to retroactive changes. An example is three-month rollups for corporations whose quarterly financial reports are subject to independent audit. Monthly rollups may be necessary to achieve acceptable application performance, but monthly rollups shouldn't be cascaded into quarterly aggregations because retroactive changes may be made in the underlying operational databases. Quarterly rollups are based on records in the operational databases.

- Never roll up data at the operational-database record level. An example of rolling up data at the operational level is the Order Amount field of the Orders table of the Northwind Traders database. The value in the Order Amount field is the sum of the product of the Order Quantity and Unit Price fields of the line item records in the Order Details table for a single order. Changes that occur in the Order Details table, including partial shipments, must be immediately rolled into records in the Orders table to maintain data consistency. Rollups should be executed on a real-time basis.

- Roll up data during periods of transaction-processing inactivity, such as nights or weekends. One of the advantages of rolling up data is the elimination of consistency errors that can occur when you aggregate detail information that is being updated simultaneously. You can write a stored procedure that runs unattended on the server to roll up data at predetermined intervals if your application uses Microsoft or Sybase SQL Server or another client-server RDBMS that supports stored procedures.

In the typical information-system hierarchy illustrated in Figure 9.1, rollups of sales, manufacturing, purchasing, finance, and human resources operational databases occur at the director level. Another rollup further consolidates data for the vice presidents of marketing, operations, and administration.

The performance improvement you can achieve by rolling up data lets you design Visual C++ decision-support applications that replace slide shows created with Microsoft PowerPoint or similar Windows presentation applications. Using a presentation application to export and re-create graphs and tables in the form of slides is an inefficient, time-consuming process. Many firms now prepare monthly or weekly presentations by transferring summary data to presentation slides. A well-designed Visual C++ decision-support application can return its development cost many times by eliminating the data import and conversion steps. Your Visual C++ presentation application needs to be totally bulletproof, and you'll probably want to store the rolled up data on a local fixed disk to avoid the embarrassment that accompanies the appearance of blank screens or messages that read Unable to connect to server during the presentation.

Query Strategies

After you've identified your datasources, you need to implement a *query strategy*. The following sections discuss some of the issues you need to resolve before you commit to a particular strategy to obtain the recordset objects on which to base your decision-support applications.

Persistent Versus Impersistent Queries

Decision-support applications that consist of a fixed feature set are likely candidates for the use of persistent QueryDef objects. You can store QueryDef objects in Access databases only, but if you're planning to roll up data from client-server or mainframe databases, an Access database is the most appropriate database type in which to store the rolled-up data, because you can attach foreign tables to an Access database if you want to.

You can pretest your SQL statements by using the MS Query application to create and store QueryDef objects for rollup or direct queries. MS Query's output windows give you a chance to preview the result of your query and to fine-tune the SQL statement that creates the QueryDef.

An alternative method of testing your SQL statements is to use Access. Like MS Query, Access can display the results of a given query for you in tabular format. Also, both MS Query and Access permit you to estimate how long a given query will take.

Alternatively, you can write the Access SQL statement for a query, then pass the value of the SQL statement as a char * variable to the szSqlStr argument of a call to the SQLPrepare() function in your code. The SQL statements of persistent QueryDef objects are stored after the Access database engine parses and optimizes them.

To optimize your application's performance, you need to test both persistent and impersistent versions of your queries. MS Query doesn't offer an exact method of timing different queries; however, manual timing techniques might suffice for large queries.

Designing Rollup Queries

Rollup queries are make-table queries that you execute from within a Visual C++ application. Rollup queries use the SQL aggregate SUM() function to total numeric values contained in tables of operational databases. Typically, a rollup query creates a new table with the following fields:

- Period: One or more fields that identify the range of dates for which the operational data is summed. You can use separate fields for the year and subperiod (quarter, month, or week). You also can combine these two fields with a coding system, such as 1994Q4 (the fourth quarter of 1994), 199412 (December 1994), or 1994W52 (the last week of 1994). As a rule, you'll find that using separate fields for the year and subperiod makes subsequent record selection simpler.

- Attribute: One or more optional fields that describe an object class or object. Attributes include categories of products, individual products, geographic regions, or persons (individual salespeople, for instance).

■ Value: One or more numeric fields that contain the result of the summation of the values of operational database records for the period. If you use more than one value field in the rollup table, the operational database table must contain each of the fields. For example, you can sum both the Quantity and [Unit Price]*Quantity values of a table containing invoice line items to obtain total units sold and total sales, and then divide total sales by total units sold to obtain average unit price.

The easiest method of developing rollup queries is to create a group of summary make-table SQL QueryDef objects in an Access database with Access. Then you write a simple Visual C++ application to execute the QueryDef objects that you created.

If necessary, your Visual C++ application can perform the data summarization. The program shown in Figure 9.3 does just that (this example is simple), summarizing data to create a bar chart of sales by month.

The DEC_SUPT.MDB sample database that is included on the CD and that provides the rolled-up data required by the sample decision-support forms in the section "Displaying Detail Data with the WinWidgets HGrid Control" contains several make-table QueryDef objects. An Access SQL statement of the qryMonthlySalesRollup QueryDef object is as follows:

```
SELECT Format(Orders.[Shipped Date],"yyyy") AS Year,
    Format(Orders.[Shipped Date],"mm") AS Month,
    SUM([Order Details].[Unit Price]*[Order Details].Quantity *
    (1-[Order Details].Discount)) AS Sales
    INTO tblSalesRollupMonth
    FROM Orders, [Order Details]
    WHERE Orders.[Order ID]=[Order Details].[Order ID]
    GROUP BY Format(Orders.[Shipped Date],"yyyy"),
    Format(Orders.[Shipped Date],"mm")
    HAVING Format([Orders].[Shipped Date],"yyyy"))="1991";
```

The Access SQL statement differs from ANSI SQL syntax in the use of the Access SQL Format() function to return parts of dates (in the Year and Month fields) and in the GROUP BY and HAVING clauses. If this query were executed with the SQL pass-through option, you would replace the Format() function with the appropriate ODBC SQL scalar function, YEAR() or MONTH(). The GROUP BY aggregations you use must correspond exactly to the corresponding SELECT descriptors in your SQL statement.

The SUM() SQL aggregate function totals the net sale amount, taking into account the discount, if any, offered to the customer on a particular product. The INTO statement identifies the name of the table that is created by the query. The initial GROUP BY criterion that groups orders by the year in which the order was shipped is included in the GROUP BY clause because you might want to specify more than one year in the HAVING clause with an AND operator.

If the tblSalesRollupMonth table doesn't exist, the query creates the table. If the tblSalesRollupMonth table exists, the existing table is deleted before the new table is created.

Most of the other make-table `QueryDef` objects in DEC_SUPT.MDB are more complex than the `qryMonthlySalesRollup` query. You can examine the syntax of each `QueryDef` object by opening the `QueryDef` object in the MS Query application.

Implementing Ad Hoc Queries

One of the incentives for purchasing database front-end application generators is that their users can generate their own ad hoc queries against large databases. The intensity of the desire to create ad hoc queries usually is inversely proportional to the individual's position in the corporate hierarchy. In the upper corporate echelons, executives want the click of a single button to deliver the summary information they need. At the operational level, managers and supervisors want the opportunity to choose from a multiplicity of record-selection options.

When an unhindered user executes a `SELECT *` query against large mainframe or client-server databases, it can bring even the highest performance RDBMS to its knees. Accidentally or intentionally returning all of the records in a monster table can cause severe network congestion, at least until the user's RAM and disk swapfile space are exhausted. The worst-case scenario is the accidental creation of a Cartesian product by the omission of a join condition when more than one table is involved in a query. This can create a very large result set. Some RDBMSs detect this condition and refuse to execute the query. Others, such as applications that use the Access database engine, attempt to return every combination of records in the tables.

Don't create decision-support applications that let users enter their own SQL `SELECT` statements against production databases. Use combo boxes or list boxes to restrict the fields to be displayed and to add required `WHERE` clause record-selection criteria.

This chapter concentrates on designing simple decision-support applications that use preprepared queries. Chapter 10, "Creating Your Own Data Access Controls," describes how to design queries that give users more freedom to define the data they want to summarize or display in detail. Chapter 15, "Designing Online Transaction-Processing Applications," shows you how to design a general-purpose query tool for generating user-defined queries that won't overtax your RDBMS or local area network.

Designing the User Interface

Microsoft Windows achieved its commercial success because Windows 3.x has a graphic interface that many users prefer to the DOS command-line prompt. Windows applications now dominate the PC software market because they use design elements that, at least in most cases, conform to the Common User Access (CUA) architecture developed by IBM in the 1980s. The CUA specification describes the design and operation of menus and other common control objects, such as check boxes, radio (now "option") buttons, and message dialog boxes.

Standards for the design of Windows applications appear in a Microsoft publication titled *The Windows Interface: An Application Design Guide* (1991), which is available in most large bookstores. The sample applications in this book employ the principles embodied in *The Windows Interface.*

Windows 95's new set of user interface standards must be followed if you wish to have the Windows 95 logo on a Windows 95 product that will be resold. Because the logo can be a valuable selling point, this fact must be taken into consideration when creating your applications.

The primary objective of the CUA specification is to create uniformity in the overall appearance and basic operational characteristics of computer applications. CUA principles apply to character-based DOS applications executed on PCs and to mainframe sessions running on 3270 terminals. The user interface of Windows 3.x and Windows 95, Windows NT and OS/2 for PCs, X Window and Motif for UNIX systems, and System 7.x for Macintosh computers conforms in most respects to IBM's basic CUA specification. Thus, if you're accustomed to Microsoft Word for the Macintosh, you can quickly adapt to using Microsoft Word for Windows on the PC.

The following sections describe some of the basic requirements of the user interface for database decision-support applications designed for use at the upper-management level. Subsequent chapters in this book provide similar guidance for more flexible decision-support applications and data-entry (transaction-processing) applications.

Optimizing Application Usability

The usability of mainstream Windows applications ultimately determines the products' success in the software market. Feature-list comparisons in product advertising and magazine reviews might influence the purchasing decisions of individual users, but the primary purchasers of Windows applications are large corporations. The objective of these corporate purchasers is to minimize the time and training expenses that are required for their personnel to learn to use the applications effectively. Thus, applications are rated by their usability, a wholly subjective attribute. An application that one user finds intuitive and easy to use might be totally incomprehensible to another.

Testing applications for usability is an art, not a science—and it's a primitive art at best. Commercial firms that conduct usability tests on major software products charge $100,000 or more for testing relatively simple Windows applications. Microsoft has invested millions of dollars in usability testing of its Windows applications. It's quite unlikely that the applications you create will undergo commercial usability tests. Instead, your client might simply inform you that he or she doesn't understand how to use your application without reading the manual. When that happens, your application has failed the ultimate usability test.

A simple method of determining an application's usability is to talk to your customer support staff. They will often be able to quickly point out shortcomings in the user interface and in other areas of the application.

The following sections describe characteristics of applications that achieve high usability ratings and show you how to implement these characteristics in the forms that constitute a simple executive-level decision-support application.

Striving for Simplicity

When you design decision-support applications, your watchword is *simplicity*. You achieve application simplicity by applying the following rules to your application design:

- Remember: You're writing the application for the client, not for yourself! Do what the client wants and needs, and put your desires to the side.

- Don't add features to an application that aren't needed to accomplish the client's fundamental objective. When in doubt, don't implement a feature that isn't in the minimum capabilities list. Wait for the client to request additional features. If you need special features to test the application, hide these features from other users.

- Don't attempt to display more than one type of information on a single form. For example, don't combine graphs and tabular information on the same form. Instead, hide the graph window and show the window with the tabular data.

These three rules are especially important for executive-summary decision-support applications because top executives are unlikely to be PC power users. A simple, intuitive user interface and a limited feature list are the two primary characteristics of professional-quality executive-summary applications.

Figure 9.3 illustrates the first form of a hypothetical executive-summary decision-support application that displays sales information for a one-year period. A toolbar is the application's primary navigation device. This toolbar lets the user make the following choices:

- Display total corporate sales by month using a line graph.

- Display total corporate sales by month using a bar chart.

- Display sales by product for the year to date or for a particular quarter or month in pie chart format.

- Attach the current object or parts of the object displayed by the form to an e-mail message that requests additional data about a particular element of an object. The graph, chart, or selected cells of a grid control in the window is copied to the clipboard and then pasted into an e-mail message.

- Create an e-mail message that requests information about, or that makes comments on, the object pasted into a message.

■ Save the current data, messages, and annotations in a file for future reference.

■ Exit the application when finished with the review of the current data.

FIGURE 9.3.

The opening form of an executive-summary decision-support application.

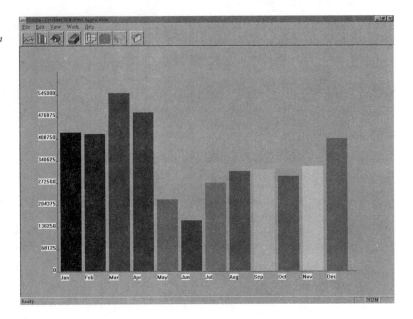

The datasource for the forms for Figure 9.3 is NorthWind.MDB, which is supplied with Access. Data for the year 1994 is shown in these examples because 1994 is the latest year for which 12 months of data is available in NorthWind.MDB. If you installed NorthWind in a location other than the default directory (usually \MSOffice\Access\Samples), you need to change the values in the code that point to the datasource (or be sure that your definition of the NorthWind datasource is the same as the one used here).

The following list describes the design principles embodied in the decision-support form shown in Figure 9.3.

■ The form uses a white background to present a contrast with colored objects. Large areas of white or vivid colors are distracting to the user of an application. Avoid dark-colored backgrounds. The preferred background is light gray.

■ There is no opening form or *splash screen*. A splash screen is a form or design element that identifies the application. (An example of a splash screen is the copyright message that appears when you first launch Word for Windows, Excel, or other mainstream Windows applications.) You might need an initial login window to obtain the password required to start the application and to log the user into a secure database.

NOTE

If your application is copyrighted, you might need to include a splash screen to display the program's copyright information. You should consult with your legal advisor for the requirements you must follow to protect your copyright.

■ The buttons present large targets for the mouse. Each button has an icon and an optional caption to explain the purpose of the button. In the status bar, a single line of help is provided for each of the toolbar buttons. Toolbars that substitute for common menu choices are common in today's Windows applications. The toolbar in Figure 9.3 is modeled on the Microsoft Mail application, which is an example of a Windows application with a simple and attractive user interface.

■ Three-dimensional group pushbuttons, provided by Visual C++, are used to indicate the user's current display choice or other operation. Disabled buttons are indicated by replacing colored bitmap elements with a grayscale image that, except for color, is identical to the icon when the button is enabled.

■ A menu is provided to let the user make choices that aren't implemented by buttons. In production applications, a menu choice duplicates the action of each button. Enabling and disabling menu choices follows the same pattern as that employed for the corresponding buttons.

■ The form is designed to occupy much of the display area in normal mode. If you're designing the application for presentation, set the size of the form to the entire display area.

■ The preferred user interface for decision-support applications is a *single document interface* (SDI) form that displays a single document (a graph, a chart, or a table) with common menus and toolbars. Showing and hiding objects on a single form is typical in this type of application.

The form shown in Figure 9.3 serves as the foundation of the form designs for the majority of the decision-support sample applications presented in this book.

I have created only bar charts for this chapter. If you want to, you can add line and pie charts yourself.

Maintaining Consistency

According to Ralph Waldo Emerson, "A foolish consistency is the hobgoblin of little minds." However, this doesn't apply to computer applications. Having both *internal* and *external consistency* of the user interface is a principal requirement of a properly designed Windows application.

■ *Internal (endogenous) consistency* implies that the appearance of all of the forms and the behavior of all of the controls on the forms that constitute your application are similar. If the behavior of a button or menu choice needs to differ under certain conditions, change the appearance of the icon (change a color, for example) or alter the caption for the menu choice.

■ *External (exogenous) consistency* means that the appearance and behavior of your application is similar to other mainstream Windows applications. If, for example, your client primarily uses Microsoft applications, the appearance and operational characteristics of your application should be modeled on the current version of Excel, Word for Windows, Microsoft Mail, or Microsoft Access.

You need to meet the following criteria to maintain internal consistency:

■ All the forms that constitute the application should have a similar appearance. Background colors, typeface families, and the size of display elements should remain constant throughout the application. It's easier to read serif fonts, such as Times New Roman and MS Serif, than fonts without serifs (sans serif), such as Arial and MS Sans Serif. Use the bold attribute for label captions, graph and chart labels and legends, and numerical values in grid controls. Use standard TrueType fonts that are supplied with Windows 95 or Windows NT; let users change the fonts to their own favorites if they want to.

■ The location and sequence of navigation devices should remain constant for all places. Buttons and menu choices that appear in more than one place always appear in the same sequence and in the same position (where feasible).

■ Icons that are used to identify objects or operations should have the same appearance in all places. If the images you use for icons adequately represent and distinguish the objects or operations, you can eliminate captions in second-level dialog boxes where you need more buttons than will fit in a single row if the buttons have captions.

Here are the rules for maintaining external application consistency:

■ Choose a mainstream Windows application as the model for your application's toolbar. Microsoft Word and Microsoft Mail are good choices as model for toolbar forms, and Excel's standard toolbar represents a good starting point for forms that need more than eight buttons.

■ Buttons with icons that are identical to or similar to icons found in other mainstream applications should perform the same or similar functions in your application. Using as much of Visual C++'s default toolbar buttons as possible will lead to a consistent application.

■ When creating 32-bit applications with Visual C++ 4 (and later versions), implement the toolbar tool tips features to allow the application's user to navigate the toolbar.

■ Use a consistent font for button captions if you create a toolbar with big, captioned buttons. Microsoft uses the 8.25-point MS Sans Serif Roman font for most button captions and as the default typeface for numeric values; your application should follow suit. *Roman* is the term for a font with no attributes—for example, not bold, not italic, and not underlined. MS Sans Serif is a bitmapped font that closely resembles Linotype Corp.'s Helvetica typeface family.

■ Use a common menu and toolbar on an MDI parent form and employ MDI child forms to present graphs, charts, and grid controls based on your application's queries.

■ Microsoft common dialog boxes (used for opening and saving files, as well as for other common operations) and message boxes usually have a sculpted appearance and a light gray background. You need to declare and use the functions contained in CTL3DV2.DLL to add the Microsoft style to your common dialog boxes and message boxes when you write applications for earlier versions of Windows, such as Windows 3.1x.

Borland International's products use stylized OK, Cancel, and Help buttons for message boxes. If you want to duplicate Borland's button style, you'll need to create your own custom bitmapped buttons. (Windows applications that were created with the Borland C++ compiler have stylized OK buttons with an adjacent shadowed check mark that Borland includes in its resources library.)

Identifying Toolbar Button Functions

Visual C++ supports the identification of toolbar buttons (and menu selections) in the status bar's output area. When you design the menu items, you need to provide only a prompt string, as shown in Figure 9.4. The part of the prompt string following the \n is the tooltip text.

It's difficult to create a collection of small icons (about 24×24 pixels) that unambiguously represents a variety of operations. Figure 9.5 illustrates the use of pop-up labels (usually called *tooltips*) that appear when the mouse pointer is positioned on the surface of the button. Tooltips are supported by Visual C++ 4's MFC 4.

Placing a pop-up label adjacent to the button with which it is associated is a better method of identifying the purpose of a button than displaying the same information in a status bar at the bottom of a form. No eye movement is necessary to read the adjacent label caption, whereas substantial eye movement is required to traverse the VDU from the top toolbar to the bottom status bar. Minimizing the eye movement required to accomplish each of the application's tasks is one of the principles of good user interface design, as shown in Figure 9.5.

FIGURE 9.4.

A prompt for a menu item that includes tooltip information.

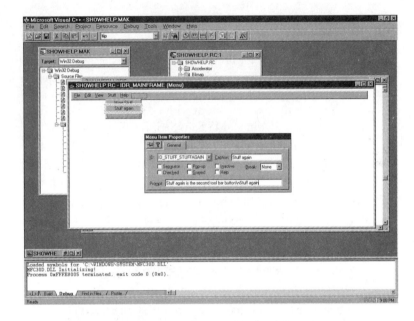

FIGURE 9.5.

Using a pop-up label to identify the purpose of a small toolbar button.

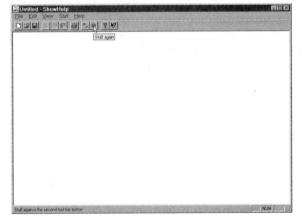

Creating and Using Toolbars

The documentation that accompanies Visual C++ describes how to use the graphics capabilities of Visual C++ but provides little or no practical advice for adding images to toolbar buttons and bitmap pushbutton controls. The following sections describe how to obtain the bitmapped images you need for your toolbar buttons, how to create Windows bitmap (.BMP) files with Windows Paint, and how to add the image contained in a .BMP file to a bitmap button.

Obtaining and Modifying Button Bitmaps

Visual C++ includes a plethora of icons and bitmaps, shown in Figure 9.6, that you can use to decorate conventional and 3-D command and group pushbuttons. Some of these bitmaps will seem familiar because they are found in Microsoft's word processors and other applications. You can find these files in the \MSVC20\SAMPLES\MFC\CLIPART directory on the Visual C++ 2 CD or the \MSDEV\SAMPLES\MFC\GENERAL\CLIPART folder on the Visual C++ 4 CD.

FIGURE 9.6.
The contents of the TOOLBAR_.BMP file.

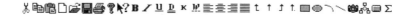

Each of the images in the TOOLBAR_.BMP file can be copied (using the clipboard) to an application's toolbar.

> **NOTE**
>
> These files aren't available with Visual C++ 4.0. If you have the subscription edition of Visual C++, you might want to retain your prior CDs.

Using the Image Editor Application to Create Button Bitmaps

Visual Basic 4.0 includes a bitmap editing tool called Image Editor, located on the Visual Basic CD in the \Tools\Imagedit folder. (You might need to manually copy this folder from the CD to your hard disk.) You need to transfer the data in icon (.ICO) files to Windows Paint using the Windows clipboard, because you can't open an .ICO file in Windows Paint. The Image Editor, however, does permit you to directly open and edit .ICO files. Figure 9.7 shows the sample Mail.bmp file being edited in the Image Editor application.

Select Edit | Copy in the Image Editor to copy the entire icon to the clipboard in .BMP format. Open Paint, add a light gray background with the paint roller tool, and choose Edit | Paste to add the icon to your Paint image. You can alter the button bitmap's appearance using either the Image Editor or Paint's toolkit. In general, you might find it easiest to use the Image Editor, which automatically magnifies the .BMP or .ICO image you're working with.

Generating Bitmaps with Desktop Publishing Packages

Many full-featured vector-based drawing packages are available. Most include a variety of clip-art images that you can use (or adapt for use) as button faces in your applications. Some desktop publishing applications have several thousand clip art images on their CDs. In addition, you can purchase CDs packed with nothing but various clip-art images.

FIGURE 9.7.

*The Image Editor
application displaying
the sample Mail.bmp
file.*

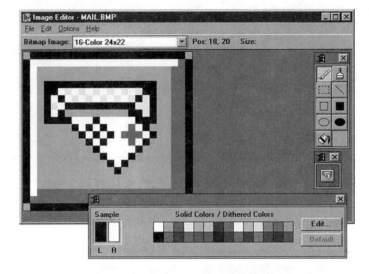

When you open an icon or clip-art image in a commercial publishing package, the image is typically much larger than you need or want for a button bitmap. Generally, you must reduce the image to create a bitmap that is approximately .25-inch high. Add a light gray background to the image so that the background matches the default background color of Visual Basic buttons. You'll probably have to export the image from its original clip-art format, which is usually some type of vector drawing format rather than a bitmap. Export the image to a 16-color Windows bitmap (.BMP) file.

> **NOTE**
>
> The CD that comes with this book has an application called Paint Shop Pro, a full-featured graphics editor. Paint Shop Pro can work as well as some of the higher-priced products for most Visual C++ programmers.

Displaying Detail Data with the WinWidgets HGrid Control

The WinWidgets HGrid control lets Visual C++ display tabular detail with a graphical presentation.

NOTE

It may well be easier to use the ListView Win32 Common Control to display tabular data. Another alternative is the grid OLE Custom Control, which is also shipped with Visual C++ 4. Each method presents advantages and disadvantages to the programmer.

The HGrid control can't be linked to a recordset object directly. However, you can write a simple Visual C++ routine to display data created by the qryMonthlyProductSalesParam query from the Products table and the qryMonthlyProductSalesCrosstab query of DEC_SUPT.MDB. The SQL statements used to create the two QueryDef objects that you use to generate a Dynaset object (which you manipulate to supply data to the grid) are as follows:

```
TRANSFORM Sum(tblProductRollupMonth.Sales) AS SumOfSales
    SELECT tblProductRollupMonth.[Product ID]
    FROM tblProductRollupMonth
    GROUP BY tblProductRollupMonth.[Product ID]
    PIVOT tblProductRollupMonth.Month
    IN ("01","02","03","04","05","06","07","08","09","10","11","12");

PARAMETERS CategID Text;
    SELECT Products.[Product ID], Products.[Product Name],
    [01], [02], [03], [04], [05], [06], [07], [08], [09], [10], [11], [12]
    FROM qryMonthlyProductSalesCrosstab, Products,
    qryMonthlyProductSalesCrosstab RIGHT JOIN Products ON
    qryMonthlyProductSalesCrosstab.[Product ID] =
    Products.[Product ID]
    WHERE Products.[Category ID]=CategID;
```

The TRANSFORM (crosstab) query creates a Dynaset object that consists of the Product ID column and 12 monthly columns labeled 01 through 12. One row is created for each product. The IN predicate is added to assure that the query returns 12 columns, even if no data is available for all of the months of the year. The SQL SELECT statement uses the Dynaset object created by the Access SQL TRANSFORM statement as if the Dynaset were a persistent table.

The purpose of the parameterized SELECT query is to assure that all rows for products within a category designated by the CategID parameter appear in the resulting dynaset, regardless of whether sales of the product occurred during the year, and to supply a column containing the name of the product. A RIGHT JOIN is needed to make all of the products in the category appear. You need to use Access SQL for the JOIN statement because the Access database engine doesn't recognize the ANSI SQL =* operator that designated a right join.

A detailed explanation of the WinWidgets package is beyond the scope of this book, but Table 9.1 lists some of the features that this package offers.

Table 9.1. Features of the WinWidgets package.

Feature	Description
DataEngine	A set of custom controls that format data, such as dates, time, and money, using supplied formatting.
HBUTT	Supports button controls, including multiline text support.
HCOMB	Support for a more powerful combo box control. Enhanced support for the programmer includes text attributes such as color and font.
HEDIT	An edit control that is designed to let data be displayed, edited, and validated.
HGRID	The grid control is a valuable tool that lets programmers display record data. Displayed data can be updated.
HLIST	The HLIST list box control offers many of the features of the HCOMB combo-box control.
HSPIN	The HSPIN control is an edit control with a pair of additional buttons that let the user increment or decrement the value displayed in the edit control. Often used with numeric data, the HSPIN control can be used with text-based data, as well (such as selecting from a list of colors).
HSTAT	The HSTAT control is used to display bitmaps, text, icons, and frames.
HTAB	The HTAB control lets you create a type of tabbed dialog box. Because Visual C++ already supports tabbed dialog boxes, this control isn't useful for Visual C++ programmers.
HTOOL	The HTOOL toolbar control offers improvements over Visual C++ 1.x's toolbar support. However, users of Visual C++ 2.x and later will most likely find that the Visual C++ MFC toolbar classes are the preferred implementation.
XTABLE	The XTABLE control provides the basic functionality of a spreadsheet. This control can be most useful when you're developing applications in which users must update records in a datasource or where any spreadsheet-type operations must be performed.

Summary

This chapter introduced you to an almost-commercial Visual C++ database application, the first such application to be presented in this book. The table rollup, query design, and user interface guidelines discussed in this chapter can start you on your way to creating production-decision support applications with Visual C++. The forms included in the UI_EXAMP application are the basis of the designs of all of the decision-support examples in the following chapters.

This chapter demonstrated that you can create an attractive and quite functional Visual C++ database decision-support application with relatively little code. The next chapter shows you how to add additional functionality to your decision-support applications with data-aware control objects and more sophisticated coding techniques.

10

Creating Your Own Data Access Controls

When OLE Custom Controls were first introduced, they were offered as a separate Software Development Kit (SDK). With current versions of Windows, and as of Visual C++ 2.0, Microsoft has added OLE Custom Controls to Windows and Visual C++. Visual C++ 4 offers built-in support for OLE controls and support for OLE control container applications. A custom OLE control AppWizard helps programmers develop OLE controls. Figure 10.1 shows Visual C++ 4's AppWizard, where the OLE ControlWizard is selected.

FIGURE 10.1.

Visual C++ 4's App-
Wizard creating an
OLE control using the
OLE ControlWizard.

This means that now there is one less development tool that you, the programmer, must integrate by hand. Using Visual C++ 4's OLE controls AppWizard lets you create an OLE control without using any external products or features.

NOTE

Versions of Visual C++ prior to version 4 don't offer integrated OLE control development. You must use the OLE control SDK (called the Control Development Kit, or CDK) with these earlier versions of Visual C++. Though developing OLE controls with versions of Visual C++ earlier than version 4 is possible, it will be easier if you upgrade to Visual C++ 4 if you intend to develop OLE controls. Also, Visual C++ 4 (and Visual Basic 4) lets you place OLE controls on the Resource Palette and, from there, place them on your forms. In previous versions, you had to hand-code the interface between the OLE control and your application. Another good reason to upgrade to Visual C++ 4!

When using the OLE control CDK to develop 16-bit controls, you must use Visual C++ 1.5.01 or later, which includes some fixes and changes to the Visual Workbench and ClassWizard to facilitate developing OLE Custom Controls.

Where has the "2" in "OLE 2" gone? Microsoft has announced its intention to change OLE's name from OLE 2 to just OLE. This change was made to allow Microsoft to expand OLE without changing the name, meaning that there will never be an OLE 3 or OLE 4.

This chapter covers the basics of OLE Custom Controls. The specifics of OLE Custom Controls and their use in database development will be discussed in later chapters.

The term *OLE Custom Controls* is a mouthful. Some publications use the term OCX for OLE Custom Controls (OCX is the accepted extension for an OLE control), but this book uses the term *OLE controls,* which is what Microsoft uses. The OLE Custom Controls Development Kit is referred to as the CDK when referring to Visual C++ 1.5x and 2.x. Visual C++ 4 doesn't have a separate CDK component.

WARNING

It's possible to have some rather nasty accidents when you're using applications that work with the registration database. On more than one occasion, I've destroyed the registration database, and the results are nothing short of awful. Some versions of Windows will refuse to run; others will run, but not well; and still others will never notice the loss of the registration database.

Make sure that you have a backup of your current registration database. Many versions of RegEdit, the utility that is used to make manual modifications to the registration database, also export the registration database. For Windows 3.x, the file is REG.DAT. For Windows 95, back up the SYSTEM.DA? and USER.DA? files. Some of these files might have the hidden attribute and therefore won't be visible unless you use the command DIR /AH. Windows NT has a similar set of database files to store the registry. You can look in \WINNT\SYSTEM32\CONFIG and back up all the files in this directory.

This information is also backed up when you create your emergency recovery disks for Windows 95 and Windows NT. But these disks will only cover the registry as it existed when you first installed your operating system. Any changes made by applications you installed later would be lost.

Remember: Back it up or lose it. Generally, losing the registration database means reinstalling Windows and many (if not all) of your Windows applications.

NOTE

Microsoft has included a utility called CFGBACK that can be used to back up the registry under Windows 95. Also, the utility ERU can be used to back up all critical files that are part of your Windows 95 system (CFGBACK backs up only the registry). The user would run these utilities before making changes, such as adding new software or hardware, or any time he wanted to make a backup copy of his configuration.

The CFGBACK utility can be found on the Windows 95 CD in the directory \OTHER\MISC\CFGBACK. It's also included as part of the Windows 95 Resource Kit. The ERU utility can be found in \OTHER\MISC\ERU, but it's not part of the Windows 95 Resource Kit. Both of these utilities are documented with .TXT files.

The backup created with the ERU utility is restored using the ERD utility—ERD.E_E. You must copy it to a directory on a writeable disk and rename it ERD.EXE in order to use it.

The Control Development Kit

The OLE Control Development Kit was a separate component of the Visual C++ 2.0 system. However, with Visual C++ 4, OLE control support is built-in and has no installable components. The following features moved from add-ons in version 2 to built-ins in version 4:

- ControlWizard: This is a new support wizard that works much like AppWizard. You can create a new control easily because the wizard writes the control's shell for you.
- ClassWizard: For Visual C++, the CDK installs a new ClassWizard that offers the necessary support for OLE controls.
- MFC: The CDK adds new classes to MFC to support OLE controls.
- Sample code: The CDK includes a number of sample controls that you can work with to learn some of the OLE control programming techniques.
- CDK Books Online: The CDK adds a new help file, CDK Books Online, that lets you easily look up information on OLE controls.
- Test Container: You can use this program to test your newly developed OLE controls. This program lets you test all of a new control's functionality.

Many of the new tools used to create OLE controls appear on the Visual Workbench Tools menu:

- ControlWizard is the equivalent of AppWizard for controls.
- Register Control lets you register your OLE control in the system registry.
- Unregister Control is used to remove your OLE control from the registry.
- Test Container lets you test your newly developed OLE control. It also offers the capability to test all of an OLE control's features.
- WPS (installed only under 16-bit environments) is a thread/process monitoring utility that lets you kill a thread or process if necessary. This utility isn't installed with Visual C++ 2.0 or later. However, Windows 95 users might find it useful because it performs many of the same tasks as the PStat (process status) and PView (process view) utilities, which don't run under Windows 95.

In Visual C++ 4, these functionalities are built into the IDE. This makes developing OLE controls simpler and alleviates the need to do many mundane tasks by hand. Visual C++ 4 has the following functionalities:

■ ClassWizard: With Visual C++ 4, ClassWizard includes extensive OLE support. Included are tabs for OLE Automation and OLE Events, as shown in Figure 10.2.

FIGURE 10.2.

Visual C++ 4's Class-Wizard, showing the OLE Automation tab.

■ AppWizard: A new project type, OLE ControlWizard, allows direct building of OLE controls.

■ MFC: MFC 4 gives you an excellent set of OLE supporting classes.

■ Sample code: Visual C++ 4 includes a number of sample controls that you can work with to learn some of the OLE control programming techniques. (See the list of OLE sample controls a little later in this chapter.)

■ Books Online: Books Online lets you easily look up information on OLE controls.

■ Test Container: You can use OLE Control Test Container to test your newly developed OLE controls. This program lets you test all of a new control's functionality.

Many of the new tools used to create OLE controls appear on the Visual Workbench Tools menu:

■ Register Control lets you register your OLE control in the system registry.

■ OLE Control Test Container lets you test your newly developed OLE control. It also offers the capability to test all of an OLE control's features.

■ OLE Object View, shown in Figure 10.3, is a utility that lets you gather information about installed OLE objects (including controls).

Chapter 16, "Creating OLE Controls with Visual C++ 4," describes each of these tools in detail.

For earlier versions of Visual C++ that use the CDK, the CDK is installed in a directory called either CDK32 (for Visual C++ 2.0) or CDK16 (for 16-bit versions of Visual C++) under Visual C++'s main directory (MSVC20 in most installations). Visual C++ 4 is installed in the directory MSDEV, and the OLE control components are integrated directly into the standard Visual C++ directory structure.

FIGURE 10.3.

OLE Object View, showing the OLE Grid Control.

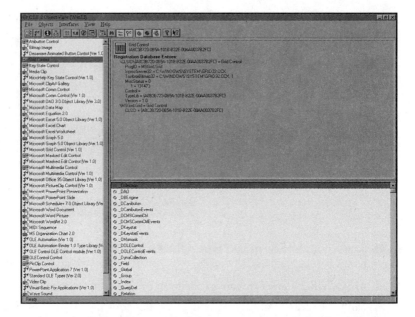

NOTE

Even though this book deals with the 32-bit compiler for Visual C++ 4.0, 16-bit products are mentioned because some programmers might have to maintain compatibility with existing versions of Windows for their applications.

There is a directory that contains sample source code for a number of OLE controls included with Visual C++ 4. The sample controls that are supplied with Visual C++ 4 (in the \MSDEV\SAMPLES\MFC\CONTROLS folder on the Visual C++ 4 CD) include the following:

- BUTTON: A simple pushbutton control.
- CIRC1: A control that implements a custom pushbutton.
- CIRC2: An advanced version of CIRC1.
- CIRC3: A more advanced version of CIRC1.
- DB: A database access control that uses simple ODBC and SQL...() functions to access a database.
- LICENSED: An example of a licensed control.
- LOCALIZE: A control showing localization techniques.
- PAL: A color palette control.
- PUSH: A custom pushbutton control.

■ REGSVR: A utility that can be used to register an OLE control.

■ SMILEY: A control that shows drawing icons in the control's client area.

■ SPINDIAL: An implementation of a spindial control.

■ TIME: A control that triggers an event at a timer interval.

■ XLIST: A custom list box control.

OLE controls are supported by a number of runtime DLL files when they're developed with either Visual C++ 1.5x or Visual C++ 2.x. OLE controls that are developed with Visual C++ 4 are supported directly by the system OLE DLL files. The Visual C++ 2.x and Visual C++ 1.5x DLL files include the following:

■ Visual C++ 1.5x: OC25.DLL contains the release (nondebug) version of the 16-bit OLE controls.

■ Visual C++ 1.5x: OC25D.DLL contains the debug version of the 16-bit OLE controls.

■ Visual C++ 2.x: OC30.DLL contains the release (nondebug) version of the 32-bit OLE controls. This 32-bit version of OLE controls supports ANSI/DBCS.

■ Visual C++ 2.x: OC30D.DLL contains the debug version of the 32-bit OLE controls. This 32-bit version of OLE controls supports ANSI/DBCS.

■ Visual C++ 2.x: OC30U.DLL contains the release (nondebug) version of the 32-bit OLE controls. This 32-bit version of OLE controls supports Unicode.

■ Visual C++ 2.x: OC30UD.DLL contains the debug version of the 32-bit OLE controls. This 32-bit version of OLE controls supports Unicode.

The appropriate DLL files are also installed in the WINDOWS\SYSTEM directory (or WINNT\SYSTEM32 for Windows NT) and are registered by the CDK setup program. If the registration database becomes corrupted and has to be replaced, you'll need to reinstall the CDK to use OLE controls when using Visual C++ 1.5x or Visual C++ 2.x. Of course, Visual C++ 4 eliminates this problem, because it doesn't have separate DLL files for OLE controls.

A Few OLE Definitions

This section defines a few of the more common terms used with OLE. We've included these definitions here because many of these terms aren't defined in a single location. Understanding each of them will greatly help you comprehend OLE and OLE controls.

OLE

OLE stands for Object Linking and Embedding. It was created as a wrapper for the original concept of Dynamic Data Exchange (DDE). OLE defines a set of standard interfaces to objects, such as IUnknown.

Objects

An *object* is an item that is placed in a document. Objects may be either linked, meaning that the object's data is external to the containing document, or embedded, meaning that the object's data is internal to the containing document. Objects may also be referred to as *servers*.

Containers

A *container* is a document into which objects may be embedded or linked. Generally, the term *container* refers to either a container application such as Word, Excel, or Access, or a container document such as a Word document, an Excel worksheet, or an Access report or form. Containers may also be referred to as *clients*.

Linked Objects

A *linked object* is an object whose basic data isn't part of the containing document. The information that is part of a linked object tells where the actual information is located and includes a view of the object.

When the user decides to change the object, the object's server uses the link information to retrieve the object's data. When a linked object is modified outside the container application, the container's representation of the object's data is also updated.

Embedded Objects

An *embedded object*'s data resides in the container document. Changes to the embedded object's original source data don't affect the embedded object or its data. An embedded object can be modified if necessary.

A document with embedded objects is larger than a document that has linked objects because the embedded objects' data must be included in the containing document.

Windows Objects

A *Windows object* is an OLE object that defines at least one interface, `IUnknown`.

Each object must provide a function table for each interface that the object supports. When you use ControlWizard to develop OLE controls, the details of the interface are managed for you.

Automation Servers

An OLE *automation server* is an application that exposes a programmable object (the server's functionality) to an OLE container application. This exposure is done using the `IDispatch` interface.

For example, a Geographical Information (GIS) program could expose its zip code validator to other applications for their own use. That way, a mail list program (perhaps part of an Access database) could verify that the street, city, state, and zip code portions of an address are correct before printing a mailing label.

Events

Events are simply things that happen (a crummy, but accurate, definition). A Windows event could be an action such as a mouse message (movement or clicking), a keyboard action, or perhaps a timer message (as in the digital clock OLE control).

Servers

A *server* is an application that is the source, or creator, of an object. Even if the preceding sentence says it all, it says nothing. It is simply jargon used to explain more jargon. No wonder Windows programming is getting so complex! The following section will clarify this definition.

The Relationship Between Servers, Documents, and Containers

Let's try to define a server again. Rather than using computer terms, let's try something else: a company picnic. I've planned the picnic because I want to butter up my boss (the chairman of the board) so that I can ask for a raise.

I set up a table, put on a tablecloth, silverware, and napkins, and ask each of my employees to bring something to eat.

The company, which is sponsoring the picnic, is the container application. The table is the document. Actually, the table is a compound document, because it has objects on it. (In OLE terminology, the objects would be embedded or linked; however, be careful how you embed a bowl of potato salad in the table. The results might be less than appealing if you embed the bowl too aggressively.)

You could place a bowl on the table with a picture of potato salad and a small card inside, telling those who want potato salad that "the potato salad is in the cooler." This would make the potato salad a linked object because its data (the actual salad) is stored externally to the main document (the picnic table).

However, in keeping with picnic tradition, you place an object full of potato salad on the table. Because you brought the potato salad, you are the server, the potato salad is an object, and the table is a compound document. (Please don't say I'm nuts—yet.)

When you brought your potato salad, you didn't bring it on a nice plate with the necessary garnishes. You transported it in a plastic Tupperware container. As president of the company, I ask you to present your potato salad, and you do so by putting it on an attractive plate with a little parsley on the side to make it look good. Now that the potato salad is presentable, I put it in the center of the table.

It just so happens that the company's chairman of the board (my boss, the person for whom we're having this picnic) has sampled your potato salad. He thinks he knows everything about salads, and he wants to change yours by adding some pepper. My boss (representing the user) tells me (the application) to get you (the server) to make the change. (He couldn't really tell the table; it's just a document.) You comply by adding the pepper, and you put the potato salad back on the table.

I figure that having you change your salad would satisfy my boss, but it doesn't. My boss (the user) tells me (the application) that he thinks the salad would look better at the end of the table, so I move it. Because I'm only moving the salad and not changing it, I can do this myself. Of course, each time I move the salad, you step in and adjust the plate so that it looks just right.

Now you can say I'm nuts, but basically, that's how OLE servers and containers work!

Just like the movies, let's give proper OLE credit to the players (cue the music):

> The Company: The application (the container).
> You: The object's server.
> My Boss: The user.
> The Potato Salad: The object to be embedded.
> The Table: The compound document.

What Are OLE Controls?

At this point you are well into the introduction to OLE Controls but you haven't learned about OLE Controls yet. You're probably wondering what an OLE Control is. Microsoft defines an OLE Control as being "implemented as an OLE compound document object with visual editing support. OLE Controls have additional capabilities beyond those of ordinary OLE objects, such as the ability to fire events."

An OLE control is a program that behaves like an object whose working interface with the user is through the OLE control's user area. An OLE control's format or layout generally is fixed, but its contents may vary. For example, a programmer can create an OLE control that looks similar to the standard list box found in many dialog boxes but that includes special properties such as multiple columns.

In Chapter 16 you will create an OLE control that is a digital clock. In this OLE control, you display the current time in a font and style that the end user can define. In fact, you could use the digital clock control in an Access 95 form or report to display the current time or embed it into a Word document. (However, Word and Excel don't fully support OLE controls in documents, so the actual performance of the OLE control in Word probably will be less than satisfactory.) When an OLE control is embedded into a Word or Excel document, it basically becomes an OLE automation server, which might not be the desired effect.

An automation server is an application that exposes a programmable object to another application. OLE controls become automation servers in Word and Excel documents because the current versions of Word and Excel don't support events. *Events* are responses by an OLE custom control to an outside action on the control, such as a mouse click.

One thing to keep in mind is that Microsoft has committed to supporting OLE controls in its database and development tools. Don't be surprised if Microsoft supports OLE controls in future versions of both Word and Excel.

Using OLE Controls in a Database Application

You can use OLE controls in many different applications. OLE controls let a developer interface with other applications such as Microsoft Access. Programmers also can add extensive flexibility using OLE controls in their applications. OLE controls can also add functionality to an existing application. A classic example is adding the OLE control digital clock, which you develop in Chapter 16, to the forms of an Access database program. Another possible OLE control is a calendar that displays the current month, perhaps with buttons to scroll forward and backward. There are many situations in which a person using an Access database might need to know a date or a date's day of the week.

Applications from Microsoft

As this book was being written in late 1995, the only application that fully supported OLE controls was Microsoft Access. This situation is rapidly changing. Visual C++ 4 applications can support OLE controls in dialog boxes. (See the sample programs OLE Container and OLE Control in the CHAPTR10 folder on the CD that comes with this book.) With this new flexibility, we can expect that there will be many, many OLE control-aware applications that will allow the embedding of OLE controls in dialog boxes or even documents. With Microsoft Access, you can place OLE controls in both forms and reports.

Access can work with OLE controls that you create, and also with the many aftermarket OLE controls that will be available for Access. Visual C++ 4 comes with a number of useful OLE controls that you can embed into your applications:

- ■ Anibutton: Uses icons, bitmaps, and metafiles.
- ■ Grid control: Displays a series of rows and columns.

■ Key state control: Returns information about the state of the Caps Lock, Num Lock, Scroll Lock, and Insert keys.

■ Microsoft comm control: Allows access to the serial ports.

■ Microsoft masked edit control: Allows the input and display of data based on a complex edit mask.

■ Microsoft multimedia control: Allows the display of multimedia.

■ PicClip Control: Allows the display of a portion of a bitmap.

Word for Windows and Excel both allow the insertion of OLE controls into documents. However, when an OLE control is subsequently copied to the clipboard, or when the container document is saved, the OLE control ceases to be an OLE control and becomes a standard OLE automation server—with a few minor differences.

Another excellent use of OLE controls created with Visual C++ 4 is with Visual Basic 4. Since Visual Basic 4 is also a 32-bit application, it can use all the OLE controls you create with Visual C++ 4.

It's still possible to create OLE controls that can be used in containers that don't support OLE controls. What must be taken into consideration is that the control won't receive event notifications (such as mouse actions or certain Windows messages) other than those necessary to manage the embedded control, such as resizing and movement.

Summary

This chapter introduced OLE controls, the CDK for Visual C++ 1.5x and 2.x, and the OLE concepts that make up OLE controls. The following topics were covered:

■ OLE controls, which are OLE compound objects with additional capabilities such as event support

■ CDK, the Control Development Kit

■ Definitions of some of the terms commonly used with OLE controls

In Chapter 16, you will develop an OLE control that can be embedded into any Visual C++ 4 application dialog box.

11

Using the New Win32 Common Controls

Windows 95 offers the programmer a new set of dialog controls that are available in Windows NT as of version 3.51. Throughout this chapter, these controls are referred to as the Win32 Common Controls. The sample program was created under Windows 95, but the details of an implementation under Windows NT are identical.

The Win32 Common Controls are supported with COMCTL32.DLL. When you use the Common Controls with Visual C++ 4, you need to include the AFXCMN.H header file. With Visual C++-created projects, Visual C++ should automatically include AFXCMN.H in the STDAFX.H file.

NOTE

Don't confuse COMCTL32.DLL, which supports Common Controls, with COMDLG32.DLL, which supports the common dialog boxes. The Common Controls are separate from the common dialog boxes.

Although you can write applications that are non-MFC-based that use the Common Controls, using MFC makes interacting with the Common Controls easier and cleaner. Microsoft has provided a sample program in the January 1996 release of the Microsoft Developer Library CD. Search for the keyword LISTVIEW and select ListView: Implements the List View Common Control in Windows 95. The program displays an application that shows the ListView Common Control without an MFC interface. You can compare the ListView example with the sample program in this chapter to see why you might want to use MFC to manage your ListView and other Common Control objects.

There are a number of Win32 Common Controls, which are documented in the next part of this chapter. In the final part of this chapter, you will develop a simple MFC application that demonstrates how to implement the ListView and TreeView controls. The other Win32 Common Controls are easy to use and should present no difficulties for the typical Visual C++ programmer.

Another source of information about the Win32 Common Controls is *Windows 95 Programming Unleashed* (Sams Publishing, 1995). This book covers all the controls and shows a non-MFC implementation of the RichText control.

CAUTION

Be careful, because the Win32 Common Controls will never be available for native Windows 3.x 16-bit programs. If backward compatibility is important to you, you might want to limit your usage of the Win32 Common Controls.

When you're creating new applications, you probably won't want backward compatibility with Windows 3.x, because there is a wide backward-compatibility gap between both Windows 3.x (16-bit) and the 32-bit versions of Windows—and also between Visual C++ 1.5x and Visual C++ 4.0.

The Win32 Common Controls

Ten Win32 Common Controls are available to the programmer. One of these controls—the Header control—is normally used by the ListView control and is seldom used by programmers directly.

Of the 10 controls, two (TreeView and ListView) could be very useful to database applications developers. These two controls let you display information in a logical manner. Of course, the other controls can also prove to be most valuable to database programmers.

In a moment, you'll take a quick look at the new Win32 Common Controls. The next part of this chapter offers a sample application that uses both the TreeView control and the ListView control to display data to the user.

This section also documents property sheets. The property sheet extensions to the Win32 interface are available to developers of 16-bit applications. Other (non-Win32 Common Control) MFC classes that provide simple toolbars and status bars also are available to developers of 16-bit applications.

All the examples in this chapter are implemented in a single source project called WIN32CC. The complete source for this project is found on the sample source CD that is supplied with this book.

The Status Bar Control

The Status Bar control lets an application provide visual and verbal feedback to the user. When AppWizard creates an application that includes status bar support, the CStatusBar class is used to manage the status bar. However, CStatusBar objects can be used only with frame windows, not with dialog windows.

In the sample program, a status bar has been added to a dialog box. This status bar could show virtually anything, but it's useful for extended help, debugging, and other messages that need to be communicated to the user unobtrusively. Both CStatusBar and CStatusBarCtrl controls include the capability to assign the status window's position to either the top or bottom of the application's window.

Most applications that are created by using AppWizard and that have a CStatusBar-implemented status bar will have a default set of attributes. These attributes include the following:

■ A status message area, which is the first area on the status bar's left. This output area is stretched to fill in the area that remains after the other status areas are created and sized.

■ A Caps Lock indicator, whose default text is CAP. This text is a string resource and may be changed by the developer.

■ A Num Lock indicator, whose default text is NUM. This text is a string resource and may be changed by the developer.

■ A Scroll Lock indicator, whose default text is SCRL. This text is a string resource and may be changed by the developer.

AppWizard also includes strings for the following indicators:

■ A recording indicator, normally implemented when the user is interactively recording a macro. Another use for this indicator would be to indicate that some form of multi-media recording is being performed. The default string for this indicator is REC.

■ The embedded selection indicator, whose default text is EXT.

■ The overwrite indicator, whose default text is OVR.

The MFC doesn't supply a default handler for these three indicators (REC, EXT, and OVR). If your application is going to use these three handlers, it must code its own handlers for each of them.

Figure 11.1 shows the main status bar in the sample application. This status bar has had all six of its panes activated, but no handler has been written for the three unsupported panes.

FIGURE 11.1.

The standard
CStatusBar in an
MFC application.

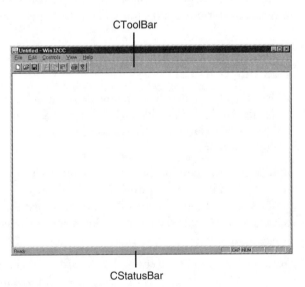

CToolBar

CStatusBar

With the sample application, I've added a simple status bar to a dialog box. I therefore needed to leave space for the status bar in the dialog box template (I could have resized the dialog box to make space if I wanted to). The status bar in the dialog box was implemented by using `CStatusBarCtrl` and has only one pane: an output area for simple status messages. Figure 11.2 shows the implementation of `CStatusBarCtrl`.

FIGURE 11.2.

A dialog box with a
`CStatusBarCtrl`
status bar.

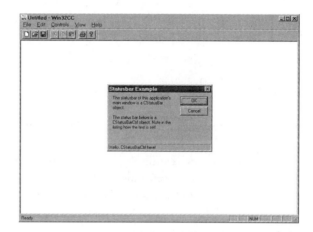

The code to implement the `CStatusBarCtrl` object is rather simple, as shown in Listing 11.1. In the header file for the dialog box (or in any other window), you must define a member variable of type `CStatusBarCtrl`. The line that shows this definition appears in bold.

Listing 11.1. Creating a `CStatusBarCtrl` object.

```
// statusba.h : header file
//


/////////////////////////////////////////////////////////////////////////
// StatusBar dialog

class StatusBar : public CDialog
{
// Construction
public:
    StatusBar(CWnd* pParent = NULL);    // Standard constructor

    CStatusBarCtrl      m_StatusBar;

// Dialog data
    //{{AFX_DATA(StatusBar)
    enum { IDD = IDD_STATUSBAR };
        // NOTE: ClassWizard will add data members here
    //}}AFX_DATA
```

continues

Listing 11.1. continued

```
// Overrides
    // ClassWizard-generated virtual function overrides
    //{{AFX_VIRTUAL(StatusBar)
    protected:
    virtual void DoDataExchange(CDataExchange* pDX);    // DDX/DDV support
    //}}AFX_VIRTUAL

// Implementation
protected:

    // Generated message map functions
    //{{AFX_MSG(StatusBar)
    virtual BOOL OnInitDialog();
    //}}AFX_MSG
    DECLARE_MESSAGE_MAP()
};
```

Listing 11.2 is the actual code that displays the status bar and places some text in the status bar's output area. Code that has been added to the AppWizard-generated application appears in bold. Most applications will place text in the status bar using a message handler.

Listing 11.2. The `CStatusBarCtrl` initialization code.

```
// statusba.cpp : implementation file
//

#include "stdafx.h"
#include "Win32CC.h"
#include "statusba.h"

#ifdef _DEBUG
#undef THIS_FILE
static char BASED_CODE THIS_FILE[] = __FILE__;
#endif

/////////////////////////////////////////////////////////////////////////////
// StatusBar dialog


StatusBar::StatusBar(CWnd* pParent /*=NULL*/)
    : CDialog(StatusBar::IDD, pParent)
{
    //{{AFX_DATA_INIT(StatusBar)
        // NOTE: ClassWizard will add member initialization here
    //}}AFX_DATA_INIT
}


void StatusBar::DoDataExchange(CDataExchange* pDX)
{
    CDialog::DoDataExchange(pDX);
    //{{AFX_DATA_MAP(StatusBar)
        // NOTE: ClassWizard will add DDX and DDV calls here
```

```
    //}}AFX_DATA_MAP
}


BEGIN_MESSAGE_MAP(StatusBar, CDialog)
    //{{AFX_MSG_MAP(StatusBar)
    //}}AFX_MSG_MAP
END_MESSAGE_MAP()


/////////////////////////////////////////////////////////////////////////
// StatusBar message handlers

BOOL StatusBar::OnInitDialog()
{
    CDialog::OnInitDialog();

    // TODO: Add extra initialization here

    RECT rect;  // Never really used! Default sizes used.
    rect.top = 0;
    rect.left = 0;
    rect.right = 100;
    rect.bottom = 20;


    m_StatusBar.Create(WS_CHILD | WS_VISIBLE | CCS_BOTTOM, rect, this, 0);

    m_StatusBar.SetWindowText("Hello, CStatusBarCtrl here!");

    return TRUE;   // Return TRUE unless you set the focus to a control
                   // EXCEPTION: OCX Property Pages should return FALSE
}
```

The `CStatusBarCtrl.Create()` function requires four parameters. The first parameter controls the style of the status bar. You can specify the style `SBARS_SIZEGRIP` to add a sizing grip to the right end of the status bar.

The `rect` parameter specifies the size of the Status Bar control, and the `this` keyword tells the status bar what the parent window is. The final parameter, `0`, is the control identifier (which isn't used in the sample program).

> **NOTE**
>
> Microsoft documentation states that the `SBARS_SIZEGRIP` sizing grip isn't functional when the status bar is aligned with the top of the window. Experiments I've performed have shown that this isn't true: Regardless of the placement of the status bar, the sizing grip is always active. However, it's difficult to use the sizing grip when the status bar isn't attached to the bottom of the parent window.

The RichText Control

The RichText control is based on the Microsoft rich text specification. Rich text could easily be used to store formatted text in a database. (All rich text documents use only the standard text character sets.)

Usually, your programs will use the `CRichEditCtrl` as an application's main window, probably using Visual C++ 4's AppWizard to create their applications. There are situations in which you might very well want to create an application that has a dialog with a rich text edit control that is located in a dialog box.

In the rich edit control section of the sample program, I've created the most basic implementation of a `CRichEditCtrl`: I create the control and fill it from a file that the user selects.

The RichText control offers a vast array of functionalities:

- Character formatting: The RichText control allows full character formatting, including typeface, size, color, and effects such as bold, italic, and protected.
- Paragraph formatting: The RichText control allows formatting of paragraphs, such as alignment, tabs, indentation, and numbering.
- Current selection: The RichText control allows for selection processing.
- Word breaks: The RichText control allows processing of word breaks to determine where it can optimally break a line.
- Clipboard operations: The RichText control supports both the clipboard and OLE.
- Stream operations: The RichText control can process its own input, both to files and to application buffers. This process uses callback functions that you, the programmer, write.
- Printing: The RichText control comes with an implementable printer interface.
- Bottomless rich edit controls: The RichText control can request that it be resized based on its contents. This resizing can be dynamic so that the control is resized as objects are added to the control.
- The RichText control supports notifications for a number of different events.

The example of a RichText control shown in Figure 11.3 creates a RichText control and serializes (from an existing .RTF file) some text into the control. You create this control by first providing a dummy frame control (so that you know the location and size when you create the RichText control) and then making a few modifications to the source files as created by ClassWizard.

Figure 11.3 shows the dialog box with its frame control to provide a place (both location and size) for the RichText control to be located. The attributes of this frame control aren't critical, because it will be completely covered with the RichText control when the dialog box is created.

FIGURE 11.3.

The dialog box that will have the RichEdit control example.

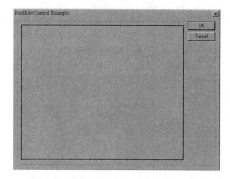

After the program executes (and a file has been loaded), your RichText control might look like that shown in Figure 11.4.

FIGURE 11.4.

The RichEdit control example in a dialog box.

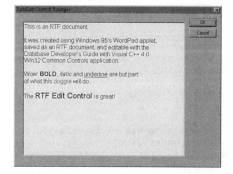

Listing 11.3 shows the header file RICHTEXT.H. In this file, a `CRichEditCtrl` member and prototypes for some functions that will be called have been added manually (and appear in bold). Remember that callback functions must be external to C++ classes, as Listing 11.3 shows.

Listing 11.3. The RICHTEXT.H file.

```
// RichText.h : header file
//

///////////////////////////////////////////////////////////////////////
// CRichEdit dialog

#define ID_RTFCTRL    12345

class CRichEdit : public CDialog
{
// Construction
public:
    CRichEdit(CWnd* pParent = NULL);   // Standard constructor
```

continues

Listing 11.3. continued

```
// Dialog data
    //{{AFX_DATA(CRichEdit)
    enum { IDD = IDD_RICHTEXT };
    CStatic     m_RichFrame;
    CRichEditCtrl     m_RichText;
    //}}AFX_DATA


// Overrides
    // ClassWizard generated virtual function overrides
    //{{AFX_VIRTUAL(CRichEdit)
    protected:
    virtual void DoDataExchange(CDataExchange* pDX);      // DDX/DDV support
    //}}AFX_VIRTUAL


    BOOL GetFileName(LPSTR szFileName, BOOL bOpen);

// Implementation
protected:

    // Generated message map functions
    //{{AFX_MSG(CRichEdit)
    virtual BOOL OnInitDialog();
    //}}AFX_MSG
    DECLARE_MESSAGE_MAP()
};

// Callbacks must be external to the class!
    DWORD CALLBACK OpenCallback
        (DWORD dwCookie, LPBYTE pbBuff, LONG cb, LONG *pcb);
```

In the source file, RICHTEXT.CPP, functions have been added to get the filename of the .RTF file and to serialize this file into the control. The WM_INITDIALOG handler has also been implemented where the CRichEditCtrl control has been created. Listing 11.4 shows the RICHTEXT.CPP file with edits marked in bold.

Listing 11.4. The RichText control implementation file, RICHTEXT.CPP.

```
// RichText.cpp : implementation file
//

#include "stdafx.h"
#include "win32cc.h"
#include "RichText.h"

#include "cderr.h" // For the common dialog error codes!

#ifdef _DEBUG
#define new DEBUG_NEW
#undef THIS_FILE
static char THIS_FILE[] = __FILE__;
#endif
```

```
////////////////////////////////////////////////////////////////////////////
// CRichEdit dialog


CRichEdit::CRichEdit(CWnd* pParent /*=NULL*/)
    : CDialog(CRichEdit::IDD, pParent)
{
    //{{AFX_DATA_INIT(CRichEdit)
    //}}AFX_DATA_INIT
}


void CRichEdit::DoDataExchange(CDataExchange* pDX)
{
    CDialog::DoDataExchange(pDX);
    //{{AFX_DATA_MAP(CRichEdit)
    DDX_Control(pDX, IDC_RICHFRAME, m_RichFrame);
    //}}AFX_DATA_MAP
}


BEGIN_MESSAGE_MAP(CRichEdit, CDialog)
    //{{AFX_MSG_MAP(CRichEdit)
    //}}AFX_MSG_MAP
END_MESSAGE_MAP()

////////////////////////////////////////////////////////////////////////////
// CRichEdit message handlers

BOOL CRichEdit::OnInitDialog()
{
    CDialog::OnInitDialog();

    WINDOWPLACEMENT lpwndpl;

//  We use the frame to locate our RTF control:

    m_RichFrame.GetWindowPlacement(&lpwndpl);

    m_RichText.Create(
        WS_CHILD | WS_VISIBLE | WS_BORDER |
        ES_NOHIDESEL | ES_AUTOHSCROLL | ES_AUTOVSCROLL |
        ES_MULTILINE | ES_WANTRETURN,
        lpwndpl.rcNormalPosition, this, ID_RTFCTRL);

    HFILE           hFile;          // File handle
    OFSTRUCT        OpenFileName;   // Open file strucuture
    EDITSTREAM      es;             // The EDITSTREAM structure
    char            szFileName[512]; // Filename buffer

    szFileName[0] = '\0';
    if(GetFileName(szFileName, TRUE))
    {
        // Open the file, read mode:

        hFile = OpenFile(szFileName, &OpenFileName, OF_READ);
```

continues

Listing 11.4. continued

```
        es.dwCookie    = 0;
        es.dwError     = 0;
        es.pfnCallback = (EDITSTREAMCALLBACK)NULL;

        if (hFile)
        {
            // Set up the EDITSTREAM structure
            es.dwCookie    = (DWORD)hFile; // Our file handle
            es.dwError     = 0;            // No errors
            es.pfnCallback = OpenCallback; // Use callback

            // Get the file using the callback:
            m_RichText.StreamIn(SF_RTF, es);

            // Close the file when done.
            _lclose(hFile);
        }
    }


    return TRUE;  // Return TRUE unless you set the focus to a control
                  // EXCEPTION: OCX Property Pages should return FALSE
}

BOOL CRichEdit::GetFileName(LPSTR szFileName, BOOL bOpen)
{
    BOOL nReturn = FALSE;

        OPENFILENAME OpenFileName;

        OpenFileName.lStructSize        = sizeof(OPENFILENAME);
        OpenFileName.hwndOwner          = (HWND)m_hWnd;
        OpenFileName.hInstance          = NULL;
        OpenFileName.lpstrFilter        = "RTF Files (*.RTF)\0*.RTF\0";
        OpenFileName.lpstrCustomFilter  = (LPSTR)NULL;
        OpenFileName.nMaxCustFilter     = 0L;
        OpenFileName.nFilterIndex       = 1L;
        OpenFileName.lpstrFile          = szFileName;
        OpenFileName.nMaxFile           = 512;
        OpenFileName.lpstrFileTitle     = NULL;
        OpenFileName.nMaxFileTitle      = 0;
        OpenFileName.lpstrInitialDir    = NULL;
        OpenFileName.lpstrTitle         = (LPSTR)NULL;
        OpenFileName.Flags              = OFN_HIDEREADONLY | OFN_PATHMUSTEXIST;
        OpenFileName.nFileOffset        = 0;
        OpenFileName.nFileExtension     = 0;
        OpenFileName.lpstrDefExt        = (LPSTR)"RTF";
        OpenFileName.lCustData          = 0L;
        OpenFileName.lpfnHook           = 0L;   // eliminate compiler warning
        OpenFileName.lpTemplateName     = (LPSTR)NULL;

        if (bOpen)
        {
            nReturn = GetOpenFileName (&OpenFileName);
        }
        else
```

```
{
    nReturn = GetSaveFileName(&OpenFileName);
}

if (!nReturn)
{
    // Process any errors here if desired!
    switch(CommDlgExtendedError())
    {// Generic common dialog box error handler:
        case CDERR_DIALOGFAILURE    :
            AfxMessageBox("The common dialog box procedure's call to "
                "the DialogBox function failed. ");
            break;
        case CDERR_FINDRESFAILURE    :
            AfxMessageBox("The common dialog box procedure failed to "
                "find a specified resource.");
            break;
        case CDERR_GENERALCODES        :
            AfxMessageBox("General error codes for common dialog "
                "boxes.");
            break;
        case CDERR_INITIALIZATION    :
            AfxMessageBox("The common dialog box procedure failed "
                "during initialization.");
            break;
        case CDERR_LOADRESFAILURE    :
            AfxMessageBox("The common dialog box procedure failed to "
                "load a specified resource.");
            break;
        case CDERR_LOADSTRFAILURE    :
            AfxMessageBox("The common dialog box procedure failed to "
                "load a specified string.");
            break;
        case CDERR_LOCKRESFAILURE    :
            AfxMessageBox("The common dialog box procedure failed to "
                "lock a specified resource.");
            break;
        case CDERR_MEMALLOCFAILURE    :
            AfxMessageBox("The common dialog box procedure was unable "
                "to allocate memory for internal ");
            break;
        case CDERR_MEMLOCKFAILURE    :
            AfxMessageBox("The common dialog box procedure was unable "
                "to lock the memory associated");
            break;
        case CDERR_NOHINSTANCE        :
            AfxMessageBox("The ENABLETEMPLATE flag was specified in "
                "the Flags member of a structure");
            break;
        case CDERR_NOHOOK            :
            AfxMessageBox("The ENABLEHOOK flag was specified in the "
                "Flags member of a structure");
            break;
        case CDERR_NOTEMPLATE        :
            AfxMessageBox("The ENABLETEMPLATE flag was specified in "
                "the Flags member of a structure ");
            break;
```

continues

Listing 11.4. continued

```
            case CDERR_REGISTERMSGFAIL    :
                AfxMessageBox("The RegisterWindowMessage function "
                    "returned an error code when it was called");
                break;
            case CDERR_STRUCTSIZE         :
                AfxMessageBox("The lStructSize member of a structure "
                    "for the corresponding common dialog box");
                break;
            case CFERR_CHOOSEFONTCODES    :
                AfxMessageBox("Error codes for the Font common dialog "
                    "box. These errors are in the range 0");
                break;
            case CFERR_MAXLESSTHANMIN     :
                AfxMessageBox("The size specified in the nSizeMax member "
                    "of the CHOOSEFONT structure is wrong");
                break;
            case CFERR_NOFONTS            :
                AfxMessageBox("No fonts exist.");
                break;
            case FNERR_BUFFERTOOSMALL     :
                AfxMessageBox("The buffer for a filename is too small.");
                break;
            case FNERR_FILENAMECODES      :
                AfxMessageBox("Error codes for the Open and Save As "
                    "common dialog boxes.");
                break;
            case FNERR_INVALIDFILENAME    :
                AfxMessageBox("A filename is invalid.");
                break;
            case FNERR_SUBCLASSFAILURE    :
                AfxMessageBox("An attempt to subclass a list box failed "
                    "because insufficient memory was available");
                break;
            case FRERR_BUFFERLENGTHZERO   :
                AfxMessageBox("A member in a structure for the "
                    "corresponding common dialog box points to a null buffer");
                break;
            case FRERR_FINDREPLACECODES   :
                AfxMessageBox("Error codes for the Find and Replace "
                    "common dialog boxes.  ");
                break;
            case PDERR_CREATEICFAILURE    :
                AfxMessageBox("The PrintDlg function failed when it "
                    "attempted to create an information context");
                break;
            case PDERR_DEFAULTDIFFERENT   :
                AfxMessageBox("An application called the PrintDlg "
                    "function with the DN_DEFAULTPRN flag specified");
                break;
            case PDERR_DNDMMISMATCH       :
                AfxMessageBox("The data in the DEVMODE and DEVNAMES "
                    "structures describes two different priters");
                break;
            case PDERR_GETDEVMODEFAIL     :
                AfxMessageBox("The printer driver failed to initialize "
                    "a DEVMODE structure. ");
                break;
```

```
                    case PDERR_INITFAILURE        :
                        AfxMessageBox("The PrintDlg function failed during "
                            "initialization");
                        break;
                    case PDERR_LOADDRVFAILURE      :
                        AfxMessageBox("The PrintDlg function failed to load "
                            "the device driver for the specified printer");
                        break;
                    case PDERR_NODEFAULTPRN        :
                        AfxMessageBox("A default printer does not exist.");
                        break;
                    case PDERR_NODEVICES           :
                        AfxMessageBox("No printer drivers were found.");
                        break;
                    case PDERR_PARSEFAILURE        :
                        AfxMessageBox("The PrintDlg function failed to parse "
                            "the strings in the [devices] section ");
                        break;
                    case PDERR_PRINTERCODES        :
                        AfxMessageBox("Error codes for the Print common dialog box. ");
                        break;
                    case PDERR_PRINTERNOTFOUND      :
                        AfxMessageBox("The [devices] section of the WIN.INI file "
                            "did not contain an entry...");
                        break;
                    case PDERR_RETDEFFAILURE       :
                        AfxMessageBox("The PD_RETURNDEFAULT flag was specified in "
                            "the Flags member of the PRINTDLG.");
                        break;
                    case PDERR_SETUPFAILURE        :
                        AfxMessageBox("The PrintDlg function failed to load the "
                            "required resources.");
                        break;
                    default :
                        AfxMessageBox("default: the call must have worked!");
                        break;
                }
            }
        return(nReturn);
}


DWORD CALLBACK OpenCallback
        (DWORD dwCookie, LPBYTE pbBuff, LONG cb, LONG *pcb)
{
// Read as much data as allowed in the cb variable

        *pcb = _lread((HFILE)dwCookie, pbBuff, cb);

        if(*pcb < cb)
        {// If done, say:
                return (0);     // All done!
        }

        return (unsigned long)*pcb;  // Otherwise, say: There is more to read!
}
```

Of course, this sample program doesn't do much. A full implementation of a RichText control requires a full user interface (how else can the user set how the text is to look?) and support for input, output, and printing as applicable.

A classic example of what a RichText control can really do is the Windows 95 WordPad application. WordPad was written as a shell around the RichText control and is actually a rather simple program. The source for WordPad can be found in a number of places, including the Visual C++ 4 directory \MSDEV\SAMPLES\MFC\OLE\WORDPAD.

> **NOTE**
>
> The WordPad sample program is an excellent example of the RichText control's implementation and of issues that must be addressed when you're creating an OLE application.

The Toolbar Control

When you create an AppWizard application, you can specify that a toolbar be included. This stock toolbar is implemented with the CToolBar class and will be located in the main frame window of the application.

You can add a toolbar to any other window (including the frame window) by using the CToolBarCtrl class. A toolbar created using CToolBarCtrl will offer some additional functionality (such as more configurability) that the CToolBar class toolbars don't offer. The standard CToolBar toolbar in the sample application's main frame window is shown in Figure 11.5.

FIGURE 11.5.

A CToolBar-*created toolbar in the application's main frame window.*

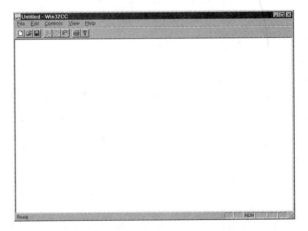

Figure 11.6 shows a dialog box that has a toolbar added to it. I gave this toolbar large buttons in order to show you how to implement a nonstandard-size toolbar button.

FIGURE 11.6.

A `CToolBarCtrl`-
*created toolbar in a
dialog box.*

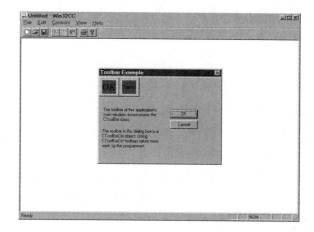

Creating a toolbar is simple. In the class header for the parent window, create a `CToolBarCtrl` object, as shown in Listing 11.5. Lines that were added to the original AppWizard shell appear in bold. Note that you must create an array of `TBBUTTON` objects to hold the toolbar button information. This array is then passed to your `CToolBarCtrl` object when the toolbar is created.

Listing 11.5. Creating a `CToolBarCtrl` object.

```
// toolbar.h : header file
//

/////////////////////////////////////////////////////////////////////////
// Toolbar dialog

class Toolbar : public CDialog
{
// Construction
public:
    Toolbar(CWnd* pParent = NULL);    // Standard constructor

    TBBUTTON        m_Buttons[5];
    CToolBarCtrl    m_ToolBar;

// Dialog data
    //{{AFX_DATA(Toolbar)
    enum { IDD = IDD_TOOLBAR };
        // NOTE: ClassWizard will add data members here
    //}}AFX_DATA


// Overrides
    // ClassWizard-generated virtual function overrides
    //{{AFX_VIRTUAL(Toolbar)
    protected:
    virtual void DoDataExchange(CDataExchange* pDX);    // DDX/DDV support
    //}}AFX_VIRTUAL
```

continues

Listing 11.5. continued

```
// Implementation
protected:

    // Generated message map functions
    //{{AFX_MSG(Toolbar)
    virtual BOOL OnInitDialog();
    //}}AFX_MSG
    DECLARE_MESSAGE_MAP()
};
```

Listing 11.6 shows the actual code that displays the status bar and places some text in the status bar's output area. Lines that were added to the original AppWizard shell appear in bold. In most applications, the placing of text in the status bar's output area will be done by using a message handler.

Listing 11.6. The `CStatusBarCtrl` initialization code.

```
// toolbar.cpp : implementation file
//

#include "stdafx.h"
#include "Win32CC.h"
#include "toolbar.h"

#ifdef _DEBUG
#undef THIS_FILE
static char BASED_CODE THIS_FILE[] = __FILE__;
#endif

/////////////////////////////////////////////////////////////////////
// Toolbar dialog


Toolbar::Toolbar(CWnd* pParent /*=NULL*/)
    : CDialog(Toolbar::IDD, pParent)
{
    //{{AFX_DATA_INIT(Toolbar)
        // NOTE: ClassWizard will add member initialization here
    //}}AFX_DATA_INIT
}


void Toolbar::DoDataExchange(CDataExchange* pDX)
{
    CDialog::DoDataExchange(pDX);
    //{{AFX_DATA_MAP(Toolbar)
        // NOTE: ClassWizard will add DDX and DDV calls here
    //}}AFX_DATA_MAP
}
```

```
BEGIN_MESSAGE_MAP(Toolbar, CDialog)
    //{{AFX_MSG_MAP(Toolbar)
    //}}AFX_MSG_MAP
END_MESSAGE_MAP()


/////////////////////////////////////////////////////////////////////////
// Toolbar message handlers

BOOL Toolbar::OnInitDialog()
{
    CDialog::OnInitDialog();

    // TODO: Add extra initialization here


    RECT rect;   // Never really used! Default sizes used.
    rect.top = 0;
    rect.left = 0;
    rect.right = 100;
    rect.bottom = 60;

    m_ToolBar.Create(WS_CHILD | WS_VISIBLE | CCS_TOP, rect, this, 0);

    m_Buttons[0].iBitmap = 0;
    m_Buttons[0].idCommand = IDOK;
    m_Buttons[0].fsState = TBSTATE_ENABLED;
    m_Buttons[0].fsStyle = TBSTYLE_BUTTON;
    m_Buttons[0].dwData = 0;
    m_Buttons[0].iString = IDS_FIRST_BUTTON;

    m_Buttons[1].iBitmap = 1;
    m_Buttons[1].idCommand = IDCANCEL;
    m_Buttons[1].fsState = TBSTATE_ENABLED;
    m_Buttons[1].fsStyle = TBSTYLE_BUTTON;
    m_Buttons[1].dwData = 0;
    m_Buttons[1].iString = IDS_SECOND_BUTTON;

    m_ToolBar.AddButtons(2, m_Buttons);

    m_ToolBar.AddBitmap(2, IDB_TOOLBAR);

    CSize sizeButton(55, 65);

    m_ToolBar.SetBitmapSize(sizeButton);

    CSize sizeBitmap(48, 45);

    m_ToolBar.SetBitmapSize(sizeBitmap);

    m_ToolBar.AutoSize();

    return TRUE;  // Return TRUE unless you set the focus to a control
                  // EXCEPTION: OCX Property Pages should return FALSE
}
```

Creating and implementing a toolbar by using CToolBarCtrl is more complex than creating and implementing a simple status bar. You must give the toolbar object information about each button, including the button's size and the bitmap size.

There are several steps to creating the toolbar. First, you must initialize your toolbar with a call to CToolBarCtrl::Create(). Then you must initialize the TBBUTTON array members as shown in Listing 11.6. After the TBBUTTON array has been initialized, it is then passed to CToolBarCtrl::AddButtons(). Finally, the bitmap for the buttons is given to the toolbar using a call to CToolBarCtrl::AddBitmap(). After the bitmap has been attached, the bitmap size and the button size are set, and a call is made to CToolBarCtrl::AutoSize() to resize the toolbar to fit the new sizes passed.

> **NOTE**
>
> You need to specify button and bitmap sizes only if your button bitmap isn't the same size as the default. For both CToolBar and CToolBarCtrl, the default size for a bitmap is 16×15 pixels. The default button size is 24×22 pixels. The button is larger than the bitmap to allow for three-dimensional borders on the button image.

The Up-Down (Spinbox) Control

The Up-Down control, usually called a *spinbox control* when combined with an edit control that displays the selected value, provides a handy way for users to enter or update a value when the normal action would be for the user to increment or decrement the value. The Up-Down control is implemented by using the CSpinButtonCtrl object.

Using the Up-Down control is simple. As with all the other Win32 Common Controls, you create a dialog box and place the Up-Down control somewhere on the dialog box. If you're creating a spinbox-type control, you also create an edit control and place the edit control next to the Up-Down control. Figure 11.7 shows the sample dialog box under development in the resource editor.

FIGURE 11.7.

The Up-Down control in the resource editor.

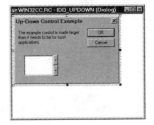

Figure 11.8 shows the Up-Down control in operation. This example shows the numeric value displayed in the edit control. Notice that when you use the standard font for the edit control (which is very large in this figure so that it will show up well), the number is too small to be seen well. If you're going to create a large edit control, you might want to use a larger typeface to make the displayed number more readable.

FIGURE 11.8.

The spin control, using an Up-Down control.

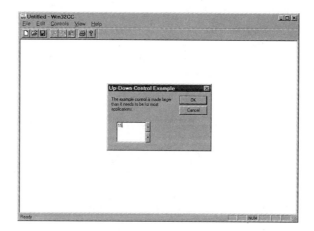

The edit control that is attached to the Up-Down control (logically, and usually physically) is referred to as the *buddy control*. This edit control is updated by the Up-Down control as the Up-Down control's value changes. Listing 11.7 shows the header file for the dialog box that contains the Up-Down control. This header file includes the definition of the Up-Down control, shown in bold. This code was added by using ClassWizard.

Listing 11.7. The `CSpinButtonCtrl` initialization code.

```
// updown.h : header file
//


/////////////////////////////////////////////////////////////////////////////
// UpDown dialog

class UpDown : public CDialog
{
// Construction
public:
    UpDown(CWnd* pParent = NULL);    // standard constructor

// Dialog data
    //{{AFX_DATA(UpDown)
    enum { IDD = IDD_UPDOWN };
    CEdit    m_EditWnd;
    CSpinButtonCtrl    m_UpDown;
```

continues

Listing 11.7. continued

```
    //}}AFX_DATA


// Overrides
    // ClassWizard-generated virtual function overrides
    //{{AFX_VIRTUAL(UpDown)
    protected:
    virtual void DoDataExchange(CDataExchange* pDX);    // DDX/DDV support
    //}}AFX_VIRTUAL

// Implementation
protected:

    // Generated message map functions
    //{{AFX_MSG(UpDown)
    virtual void OnOK();
    virtual BOOL OnInitDialog();
    //}}AFX_MSG
    DECLARE_MESSAGE_MAP()
};
```

The actual code to use the `UpDown` class is shown in Listing 11.8. This code shows how little programming is needed to create your spinbox control.

Listing 11.8. Creating a `CSpinButtonCtrl` object.

```
// updown.cpp : implementation file
//

#include "stdafx.h"
#include "Win32CC.h"
#include "updown.h"

#ifdef _DEBUG
#undef THIS_FILE
static char BASED_CODE THIS_FILE[] = __FILE__;
#endif


/////////////////////////////////////////////////////////////////////////////
// UpDown dialog


UpDown::UpDown(CWnd* pParent /*=NULL*/)
    : CDialog(UpDown::IDD, pParent)
{
    //{{AFX_DATA_INIT(UpDown)
    //}}AFX_DATA_INIT
}


void UpDown::DoDataExchange(CDataExchange* pDX)
{
```

```
        CDialog::DoDataExchange(pDX);
        //{{AFX_DATA_MAP(UpDown)
        DDX_Control(pDX, IDC_EDIT1, m_EditWnd);
        DDX_Control(pDX, IDC_UPDOWN, m_UpDown);
        //}}AFX_DATA_MAP
}


BEGIN_MESSAGE_MAP(UpDown, CDialog)
        //{{AFX_MSG_MAP(UpDown)
        //}}AFX_MSG_MAP
END_MESSAGE_MAP()


/////////////////////////////////////////////////////////////////////////////
// UpDown message handlers


void UpDown::OnOK()
{
        // TODO: Add extra validation here

        int        nPosition;
        char    szBuffer[255];
// OK, user is done. Get the Trackbar's current value:

        nPosition = m_UpDown.GetPos();
        sprintf(szBuffer, "Trackbar position = %d", nPosition);

        AfxMessageBox(szBuffer);


        CDialog::OnOK();
}

BOOL UpDown::OnInitDialog()
{
        CDialog::OnInitDialog();

        // TODO: Add extra initialization here

        m_UpDown.SetBuddy(&m_EditWnd);
        m_UpDown.SetRange(10, 100);
        m_UpDown.SetPos(10);


        return TRUE;  // Return TRUE unless you set the focus to a control
                      // EXCEPTION: OCX Property Pages should return FALSE
}
```

As Listing 11.8 shows (in bold), you assign the buddy control and then set the range of the Up-Down control as desired. Finally, you set the initial position. There are no defaults for the Up-Down control's range or desired position. It's good programming practice to initialize these values.

The Progress Indicator Control

The Progress Indicator control gives feedback to the user about the progress of a lengthy operation. For example, an install program that must copy and process files from disks or a CD-ROM might use the Progress Indicator control to tell the user how far the process has progressed. This is better than simply using a wait cursor because the user will know that something is happening! The Progress Indicator is implemented by using CProgressCtrl.

Using a Progress Indicator control is easy. You can set a few simple parameters and then utilize the control. First, you must define the control in a dialog box. Then, as with other controls, use ClassWizard to bind a control object (of type CProgressCtrl) to the Progress Indicator control. Figure 11.9 shows a Progress Indicator control in a simple dialog box. This indicator is being updated with a timer loop to simulate a lengthy process.

FIGURE 11.9.

The standard Progress Indicator control in an MFC application.

The code to implement the CProgressCtrl object is rather simple. In the header file for the dialog box (or any other window in which you place a Progress Indicator control), you must define a member variable of CProgressCtrl type. In most cases, you can use ClassWizard to link the CProgressCtrl object to the dialog box's control. The CProgressCtrl definition in Listing 11.9 appears in bold.

Listing 11.9. Creating a CProgressCtrl object.

```
// progress.h : header file
//

/////////////////////////////////////////////////////////////////////////
// Progress dialog

class Progress : public CDialog
{
// Construction
public:
    Progress(CWnd* pParent = NULL);    // Standard constructor

// Dialog data
    //{{AFX_DATA(Progress)
    enum { IDD = IDD_PROGRESS };
    CProgressCtrl    m_Progress;
    //}}AFX_DATA


// Overrides
    // ClassWizard-generated virtual function overrides
    //{{AFX_VIRTUAL(Progress)
    protected:
    virtual void DoDataExchange(CDataExchange* pDX);    // DDX/DDV support
    //}}AFX_VIRTUAL

// Implementation
protected:

    // Generated message map functions
    //{{AFX_MSG(Progress)
    virtual BOOL OnInitDialog();
    afx_msg void OnTimer(UINT nIDEvent);
    virtual void OnOK();
    virtual void OnCancel();
    //}}AFX_MSG
    DECLARE_MESSAGE_MAP()
};
```

Listing 11.10 shows the code used to initialize the CProgressCtrl control and to update the control. Lines that were added to the original AppWizard shell appear in bold. In this example, the CProgressCtrl is set to have a range of 0 to 100 and an increment of 1. A timer loop is then created, which increments the Progress Indicator control's display.

Listing 11.10. Creating a CProgressCtrl object.

```
// progress.cpp : implementation file
//

#include "stdafx.h"
#include "Win32CC.h"
```

continues

Listing 11.10. continued

```
#include "progress.h"

#ifdef _DEBUG
#undef THIS_FILE
static char BASED_CODE THIS_FILE[] = __FILE__;
#endif

/////////////////////////////////////////////////////////////////////////////
// Progress dialog


Progress::Progress(CWnd* pParent /*=NULL*/)
    : CDialog(Progress::IDD, pParent)
{
    //{{AFX_DATA_INIT(Progress)
        // NOTE: ClassWizard will add member initialization here
    //}}AFX_DATA_INIT
}


void Progress::DoDataExchange(CDataExchange* pDX)
{
    CDialog::DoDataExchange(pDX);
    //{{AFX_DATA_MAP(Progress)
    DDX_Control(pDX, IDC_PROGRESS, m_Progress);
    //}}AFX_DATA_MAP
}


BEGIN_MESSAGE_MAP(Progress, CDialog)
    //{{AFX_MSG_MAP(Progress)
    ON_WM_TIMER()
    //}}AFX_MSG_MAP
END_MESSAGE_MAP()


/////////////////////////////////////////////////////////////////////////////
// Progress message handlers

BOOL Progress::OnInitDialog()
{
    CDialog::OnInitDialog();

    // TODO: Add extra initialization here


    m_Progress.SetRange(0, 100);    // Default values!
    m_Progress.SetPos(0);           // Default value!
    m_Progress.SetStep(1);          // Default is 10


    SetTimer(999, 100, NULL);

    return TRUE;   // Return TRUE unless you set the focus to a control
```

```
                    // EXCEPTION: OCX Property Pages should return FALSE
}

void Progress::OnTimer(UINT nIDEvent)
{
    // TODO: Add your message handler code here and/or call default

//    Increment our progress. (When we exceed 100%,
//         CProgressCtrl will reset the indicator to 0!)
//         If this action is not desired, you must track
//         the current position and call CProgressCtrl::SetPos()
//         to set the Progress bar's position.

    m_Progress.StepIt();

    CDialog::OnTimer(nIDEvent);
}

void Progress::OnOK()
{
    // TODO: Add extra validation here

    KillTimer(999);

    CDialog::OnOK();
}

void Progress::OnCancel()
{
    // TODO: Add extra cleanup here

    KillTimer(999);

    CDialog::OnCancel();
}
```

The initialization process consists of this code:

```
m_Progress.SetRange(0, 100);    // Default values!
m_Progress.SetPos(0);           // Default value!
m_Progress.SetStep(1);          // Default is 10
```

The code to update the Progress Indicator control is a simple call to the member function StepIt(), which will increment the control's indicator by the step value defined when the control is initialized.

> **NOTE**
>
> The default range is 0 to 100, and the step value is 10. This can create a choppy-acting control. Generally, you will want to increment the control in about one-percent steps.

The Trackbar Control

A Trackbar control lets the user input an inexact value within a predefined range of values. Typical uses for Trackbar controls include multimedia volume and mixer controls and other pseudoanalog applications.

A Trackbar control is easy to implement. You first define the Trackbar control in a dialog box, and then you use ClassWizard to attach a `CSliderCtrl` object to the Trackbar control. The sample application in Figure 11.10 shows a simple Trackbar control. This control is a minimum implementation of the Trackbar control, with index marks (called *tick marks*) on the trackbar.

FIGURE 11.10.

The standard Trackbar control in an MFC application.

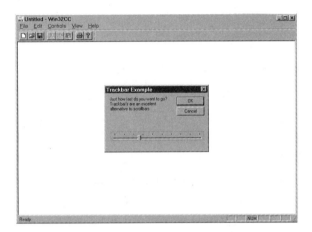

The code to implement a basic `CSliderCtrl` object is simple. In the header file for the dialog box (or in any other window), you must define a member variable of `CSliderCtrl` type, which is usually done by using ClassWizard. This line appears in bold.

Listing 11.11. Creating a `CSliderCtrl` object.

```
// trackbar.h : header file
//

/////////////////////////////////////////////////////////////////////////////
// TrackBar dialog

class TrackBar : public CDialog
{
// Construction
public:
    TrackBar(CWnd* pParent = NULL);    // Standard constructor

// Dialog data
    //{{AFX_DATA(TrackBar)
    enum { IDD = IDD_TRACKBAR };
```

```
    CSliderCtrl    m_Slider;
    //}}AFX_DATA


// Overrides
    // ClassWizard-generated virtual function overrides
    //{{AFX_VIRTUAL(TrackBar)
    protected:
    virtual void DoDataExchange(CDataExchange* pDX);    // DDX/DDV support
    //}}AFX_VIRTUAL

// Implementation
protected:

    // Generated message map functions
    //{{AFX_MSG(TrackBar)
    virtual BOOL OnInitDialog();
    virtual void OnOK();
    //}}AFX_MSG
    DECLARE_MESSAGE_MAP()
};
```

Listing 11.12 is the actual implementation of a `CSliderCtrl` object. This code implements the minimum programming needed to create a usable control. You could also modify the tick mark frequency and add numeric indicators at each end of the slider control to show minimum and maximum values.

The bold code in Listing 11.12 shows how you set both the range of the slider control and the display of tick marks that assist the user in determining just where the slider is positioned.

Listing 11.12. Creating a `CSliderCtrl` object.

```
// trackbar.cpp : implementation file
//

#include "stdafx.h"
#include "win32cc.h"
#include "trackbar.h"

#ifdef _DEBUG
#undef THIS_FILE
static char BASED_CODE THIS_FILE[] = __FILE__;
#endif

/////////////////////////////////////////////////////////////////////////////
// TrackBar dialog


TrackBar::TrackBar(CWnd* pParent /*=NULL*/)
    : CDialog(TrackBar::IDD, pParent)
{
    //{{AFX_DATA_INIT(TrackBar)
```

continues

Listing 11.12. continued

```
        // NOTE: ClassWizard will add member initialization here
    //}}AFX_DATA_INIT
}


void TrackBar::DoDataExchange(CDataExchange* pDX)
{
    CDialog::DoDataExchange(pDX);
    //{{AFX_DATA_MAP(TrackBar)
    DDX_Control(pDX, IDC_TRACKBAR, m_Slider);
    //}}AFX_DATA_MAP
}


BEGIN_MESSAGE_MAP(TrackBar, CDialog)
    //{{AFX_MSG_MAP(TrackBar)
    //}}AFX_MSG_MAP
END_MESSAGE_MAP()


/////////////////////////////////////////////////////////////////////////////
// TrackBar message handlers

BOOL TrackBar::OnInitDialog()
{
    CDialog::OnInitDialog();

    // TODO: Add extra initialization here

    // Set the slider's range from 10 to 100
    m_Slider.SetRange(10, 100);

    // Set the slider's ticks to every tenth point
    m_Slider.SetTicFreq(10);

    return TRUE;  // Return TRUE unless you set the focus to a control
                  // EXCEPTION: OCX Property Pages should return FALSE
}

void TrackBar::OnOK()
{
    // TODO: Add extra validation here

    int      nPosition;
    char     szBuffer[255];
// OK, user is done. Get the Trackbar's current value:

    nPosition = m_Slider.GetPos();
    sprintf(szBuffer, "Trackbar position = %d", nPosition);
```

```
        AfxMessageBox(szBuffer);

        CDialog::OnOK();
}
```

The Header Control

The Header control is used by the ListView control to display column headings when data is being displayed in the report view. There are bound to be other implementations for the Header control in the future, but currently there is only limited usage for the Header control as a stand-alone control in a dialog box. The Header control is automatically implemented by the ListView control.

The ListView Control

The ListView control is one of the most complex controls implemented by the Win32 Common Controls. This control supports four different views of the data:

■ Large Icon View displays the data as icons. These icons have multiline titles below them and are large and easy to select. Far fewer data objects can be represented in the Large Icon View than can be displayed by using the Small Icon View. The detail of the icon displayed in the Large Icon View is very detailed, however.

■ Small Icon View displays the data as small icons followed by a single line of title text. There can be multiple columns of small icons; the number of columns is determined by the size of the ListView control.

■ List View is a lot like the Small Icon View, except that only one column is presented, and the limitations on the title text length are not as severe.

■ Report View lets the user see multiple columns of data. Much like a spreadsheet view, the user can sort on any column (if you implement this capability). The program can set the width of the columns, and the user can resize a column at any time.

The sample program in Figure 11.11 shows the Report View mode of the ListView control. The Report View mode might be the most important mode that this control offers, and it's the most difficult mode to implement. Figure 11.11 also shows the ListView control displaying a set of columnar data. This data is from a simple table contained in the program; however, in database programs, the data can be retrieved from a datasource.

FIGURE 11.11.

The ListView control in Report View mode.

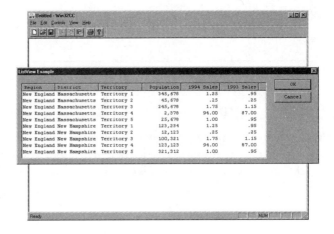

The code to implement the `CListCtrl` object (see Listing 11.13) is usually simple. In the header file for the dialog box (or any other window), you must define a member variable of `CListCtrl` type. You can use ClassWizard to do this. This line appears in bold.

Listing 11.13. Creating a `CListCtrl` object.

```
// listview.h : header file
//

/////////////////////////////////////////////////////////////////////////////
// ListView dialog

class ListView : public CDialog
{
// Construction
public:
    ListView(CWnd* pParent = NULL);    // Standard constructor

// Dialog data
    //{{AFX_DATA(ListView)
    enum { IDD = IDD_LISTVIEW };
    CListCtrl    m_ListView;
    //}}AFX_DATA


// Overrides
    // ClassWizard-generated virtual function overrides
    //{{AFX_VIRTUAL(ListView)
    protected:
    virtual void DoDataExchange(CDataExchange* pDX);    // DDX/DDV support
    //}}AFX_VIRTUAL

// Implementation
protected:

    // Generated message map functions
    //{{AFX_MSG(ListView)
```

```
    virtual BOOL OnInitDialog();
    //}}AFX_MSG
    DECLARE_MESSAGE_MAP()
};
```

The real work is done in the source file, where the ListView control must be initialized and have the data added. The code to do this is shown in Listing 11.14. Lines that were added to the original AppWizard shell appear in bold.

Listing 11.14. Creating a `CListCtrl` object.

```
// listview.cpp : implementation file
//

#include "stdafx.h"
#include "win32cc.h"
#include "listview.h"

#ifdef _DEBUG
#undef THIS_FILE
static char BASED_CODE THIS_FILE[] = __FILE__;
#endif

/////////////////////////////////////////////////////////////////////////////
// ListView dialog


ListView::ListView(CWnd* pParent /*=NULL*/)
    : CDialog(ListView::IDD, pParent)
{
    //{{AFX_DATA_INIT(ListView)
        // NOTE: ClassWizard will add member initialization here
    //}}AFX_DATA_INIT
}


void ListView::DoDataExchange(CDataExchange* pDX)
{
    CDialog::DoDataExchange(pDX);
    //{{AFX_DATA_MAP(ListView)
    DDX_Control(pDX, IDC_LISTVIEW, m_ListView);
    //}}AFX_DATA_MAP
}


BEGIN_MESSAGE_MAP(ListView, CDialog)
    //{{AFX_MSG_MAP(ListView)
    //}}AFX_MSG_MAP
END_MESSAGE_MAP()


/////////////////////////////////////////////////////////////////////////////
// ListView message handlers
```

continues

Listing 11.14. continued

```
BOOL ListView::OnInitDialog()
{
    CDialog::OnInitDialog();

    // TODO: Add extra initialization here

    char    *szColumn[6] = {"Region", "District", "Territory",
        "Population", "1994 Sales", "1993 Sales"};

    char    *szData[10][6] =
{{"New England", "Massachusetts", "Territory 1", "345,678", " 1.25", "  .95"},
 {"New England", "Massachusetts", "Territory 2", " 45,678", "  .25", "  .25"},
 {"New England", "Massachusetts", "Territory 3", "245,678", " 1.75", " 1.15"},
 {"New England", "Massachusetts", "Territory 4", "  2,378", "94.00", "87.00"},
 {"New England", "Massachusetts", "Territory 5", " 25,678", " 1.00", "  .95"},
 {"New England", "New Hampshire", "Territory 1", "123,234", " 1.25", "  .95"},
 {"New England", "New Hampshire", "Territory 2", " 12,123", "  .25", "  .25"},
 {"New England", "New Hampshire", "Territory 3", "100,321", " 1.75", " 1.15"},
 {"New England", "New Hampshire", "Territory 4", "123,123", "94.00", "87.00"},
 {"New England", "New Hampshire", "Territory 5", "321,312", " 1.00", "  .95"}};

    // Add the columns
    LV_COLUMN lvc;
    lvc.mask = LVCF_FMT | LVCF_WIDTH | LVCF_TEXT | LVCF_SUBITEM;
    lvc.fmt = LVCFMT_LEFT;

    for (int j = 0; j < 6; j++)
    {
        lvc.cx = m_ListView.GetStringWidth(szColumn[j]) + 25;
        lvc.pszText = szColumn[j];

        if (j > 2)
            lvc.fmt = LVCFMT_RIGHT;

        lvc.iSubItem = j;
        m_ListView.InsertColumn(j, &lvc);
    }

    // Need to add some items to the ListView control
    LV_ITEM lvi;
    lvi.mask = LVIF_TEXT | LVIF_IMAGE;
    lvi.iSubItem = 0;

    for (int i = 0; i < 10; i++)
    {
        lvi.iItem = i;
        lvi.pszText = szData[i][0];
        lvi.cchTextMax = 5;
        lvi.iImage = i;

        m_ListView.InsertItem(&lvi);

        for (int k = 1; k < 6; k++)
        {
//              m_ListView.SetItemText(i, k, TEXT("SubItem"));
            m_ListView.SetItemText(i, k, szData[i][k]);
```

```
        }
    }

    return TRUE;   // Return TRUE unless you set the focus to a control
                   // EXCEPTION: OCX Property Pages should return FALSE
}
```

Because of the complexity of the ListView control's initialization, take a closer look at the code presented in Listing 11.14. First, you need to create a dummy dataset. Rather than make this listing even more complex by calling an ODBC datasource, I have simply hard-coded some dummy data into the program.

```
char    *szColumn[6] = {"Region", "District", "Territory",
    "Population", "1994 Sales", "1993 Sales"};

    char    *szData[10][6] =
{{"New England", "Massachusetts", "Territory 1", "345,678", " 1.25", "  .95"},
{"New England", "Massachusetts", "Territory 2", " 45,678", "  .25", "  .25"},
{"New England", "Massachusetts", "Territory 3", "245,678", " 1.75", " 1.15"},
{"New England", "Massachusetts", "Territory 4", "  2,378", "94.00", "87.00"},
{"New England", "Massachusetts", "Territory 5", " 25,678", " 1.00", "  .95"},
{"New England", "New Hampshire", "Territory 1", "123,234", " 1.25", "  .95"},
{"New England", "New Hampshire", "Territory 2", " 12,123", "  .25", "  .25"},
{"New England", "New Hampshire", "Territory 3", "100,321", " 1.75", " 1.15"},
{"New England", "New Hampshire", "Territory 4", "123,123", "94.00", "87.00"},
{"New England", "New Hampshire", "Territory 5", "321,312", " 1.00", "  .95"}};
```

After you have some data to place in your ListView control, you can define the variables that are needed to fill the control. The LV_COLUMN structure is used to define the columns (whose names are stored in the szColumn[] array). You define the columns with certain attributes. The attributes that are being set are defined in the mask member variable, and in this example, the text attribute (the title for the column), the width (how wide the column will be), and the column's format are being defined.

```
// Add the columns
LV_COLUMN lvc;
lvc.mask = LVCF_FMT ¦ LVCF_WIDTH ¦ LVCF_TEXT ¦ LVCF_SUBITEM;
lvc.fmt = LVCFMT_LEFT;

for (int j = 0; j < 6; j++)
{
    lvc.cx = m_ListView.GetStringWidth(szColumn[j]) + 25;
    lvc.pszText = szColumn[j];

    if (j > 2)
        lvc.fmt = LVCFMT_RIGHT;

    lvc.iSubItem = j;
    m_ListView.InsertColumn(j, &lvc);
}
```

This fragment shows you how to use a loop to define each column. Notice how the final columns (columns four, five, and six) are right-justified to force the alignment of the columns.

Setting the width of the columns is important and can be difficult: Do you set the width based on the column's title, the column's data, or both? In this example, the width is set based on the width of the title string. The width is defined in pixels (not characters or dialog units). This could present a problem, so Microsoft has included a function called GetStringWidth(), which returns the width of a string in pixels. Knowing the string's width in pixels makes defining column widths easier.

The next step is to add items to the ListView control. You do this by first adding the main item (the first, extreme-left column) and then any following columns (which are called subitems).

```
// Need to add some items to the ListView control
LV_ITEM lvi;
lvi.mask = LVIF_TEXT | LVIF_IMAGE;
lvi.iSubItem = 0;

for (int i = 0; i < 10; i++)
{
    lvi.iItem = i;
    lvi.pszText = szData[i][0];
    lvi.cchTextMax = 5;
    lvi.iImage = i;

    m_ListView.InsertItem(&lvi);

    for (int k = 1; k < 6; k++)
    {
        m_ListView.SetItemText(i, k, szData[i][k]);
    }
}
```

Notice that Windows returns the index number for the item. You can assign an arbitrary 32-bit value to an item. This value is often the address or a pointer to a structure containing information about the item.

The TreeView Control

The TreeView control lets the user select items from a hierarchical structure. Directories and files are classic examples of this type of structure, where a directory tree (within the limits of the operating system) could be of any depth.

Using a TreeView to show hierarchical data lets the programmer present a visual representation of the data. One program that I developed is used for sales territories. Sales territories are often arranged in a hierarchy of regions, districts, and territories. Territories are areas that are actually serviced by an individual sales representative. A classic example of a sales territory definition is North East Region, New Hampshire District, Territory 1.

The example for the TreeView control shows a sales territory arrangement. Figure 11.12 shows the TreeView control, where the North East Region and the New Hampshire district branches have been expanded.

FIGURE 11.12.

*The TreeView control
in a dialog box.*

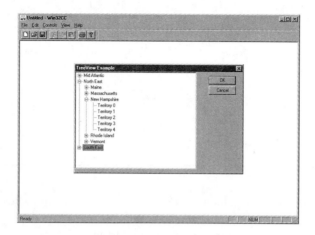

In the sample application, I didn't want to define icons for the items in the TreeView. No icons are defined (yet!) for sales territories.

The code to implement the `CTreeViewCtrl` object (see Listing 11.15) can be kept simple. In the header file for the dialog box (or any other window), you must define a member variable of `CTreeViewCtrl` type. You can use AppWizard to define this member variable. This line appears in bold.

Listing 11.15. Creating a `CTreeViewCtrl` object.

```
// treeview.h : header file
//

/////////////////////////////////////////////////////////////////////////////
// TreeView dialog

class TreeView : public CDialog
{
// Construction
public:
    TreeView(CWnd* pParent = NULL);   // Standard constructor

// Dialog data
    //{{AFX_DATA(TreeView)
    enum { IDD = IDD_TREEVIEW };
    CTreeCtrl    m_TreeView;
    //}}AFX_DATA


// Overrides
    // ClassWizard-generated virtual function overrides
    //{{AFX_VIRTUAL(TreeView)
    protected:
    virtual void DoDataExchange(CDataExchange* pDX);    // DDX/DDV support
```

continues

Listing 11.15. continued

```
    //}}AFX_VIRTUAL

// Implementation
protected:

    // Generated message map functions
    //{{AFX_MSG(TreeView)
    virtual BOOL OnInitDialog();
    //}}AFX_MSG
    DECLARE_MESSAGE_MAP()
};
```

The code to actually fill the TreeView control (see Listing 11.16) is a bit more complex. Your application must maintain the relationships of the items in the `CTreeViewCtrl` object. The code that creates the `CTreeViewCtrl` object appears in bold.

Listing 11.16. Creating a `CTreeViewCtrl` object.

```
// treeview.cpp : implementation file
//

#include "stdafx.h"
#include "Win32CC.h"
#include "treeview.h"

#ifdef _DEBUG
#undef THIS_FILE
static char BASED_CODE THIS_FILE[] = __FILE__;
#endif

/////////////////////////////////////////////////////////////////////
// TreeView dialog


TreeView::TreeView(CWnd* pParent /*=NULL*/)
    : CDialog(TreeView::IDD, pParent)
{
    //{{AFX_DATA_INIT(TreeView)
        // NOTE: ClassWizard will add member initialization here
    //}}AFX_DATA_INIT
}


void TreeView::DoDataExchange(CDataExchange* pDX)
{
    CDialog::DoDataExchange(pDX);
    //{{AFX_DATA_MAP(TreeView)
    DDX_Control(pDX, IDC_TREEVIEW, m_TreeView);
    //}}AFX_DATA_MAP
}


BEGIN_MESSAGE_MAP(TreeView, CDialog)
```

```
    //{{AFX_MSG_MAP(TreeView)
    //}}AFX_MSG_MAP
END_MESSAGE_MAP()


///////////////////////////////////////////////////////////////////////
// TreeView message handlers

BOOL TreeView::OnInitDialog()
{
    CDialog::OnInitDialog();

    // TODO: Add extra initialization here

// First the tree control: (WORKS!)
    int              nRegion;
    int              nDistrict;
    int              nTerritory;
    HTREEITEM        RegionParent;
    HTREEITEM        DistrictParent;
    HTREEITEM        TerritoryParent;
    TV_INSERTSTRUCT  InsertItem;

    char    szBuffer[255];
    char    *szRegion[3] = {"North East", "Mid Atlantic", "South East"};
    char    *szDistrict[3][5] =
        {{"New Hampshire", "Massachusetts", "Vermont", "Maine", "Rhode Island"},
         {"New York", "New Jersey", "Delaware", "DC", "Maryland"},
         {"Virginia", "North Carolina", "South Carolina", "Georgia", "Florida"}};

    for (nRegion = 0; nRegion < 3; ++nRegion)
    {
        InsertItem.item.mask = TVIF_TEXT;
        InsertItem.item.pszText = szRegion[nRegion];
        InsertItem.item.cchTextMax = 15;
        InsertItem.hParent = NULL;
        InsertItem.hInsertAfter = TVI_SORT;

        RegionParent = m_TreeView.InsertItem(&InsertItem);

        for (nDistrict = 0; nDistrict < 5; ++nDistrict)
        {
            InsertItem.item.pszText = szDistrict[nRegion][nDistrict];
            InsertItem.item.cchTextMax = 20;
            InsertItem.hParent = RegionParent;
            InsertItem.hInsertAfter = TVI_SORT;

            DistrictParent = m_TreeView.InsertItem(&InsertItem);

            for (nTerritory = 0; nTerritory < 5; ++nTerritory)
            {
                sprintf(szBuffer, "Territory %d", nTerritory);
                InsertItem.item.pszText = szBuffer;
                InsertItem.item.cchTextMax = 20;
                InsertItem.hParent = DistrictParent;
                InsertItem.hInsertAfter = TVI_SORT;
```

continues

Listing 11.16. continued

```
                TerritoryParent = m_TreeView.InsertItem(&InsertItem);
        }
    }
}


    return TRUE;   // Return TRUE unless you set the focus to a control
                   // EXCEPTION: OCX Property Pages should return FALSE
}
```

Take a closer look at the initialization of the TreeView control. First, you need to create some variables to assist you in filling your TreeView control:

```
//First the tree control: (WORKS!)
    int                nRegion;
    int                nDistrict;
    int                nTerritory;
    HTREEITEM          RegionParent;
    HTREEITEM          DistrictParent;
    HTREEITEM          TerritoryParent;
    TV_INSERTSTRUCT InsertItem;

    char    szBuffer[255];
    char    *szRegion[3] = {"North East", "Mid Atlantic", "South East"};
    char    *szDistrict[3][5] =
        {{"New Hampshire", "Massachusetts", "Vermont", "Maine", "Rhode Island"},
        {"New York", "New Jersey", "Delaware", "DC", "Maryland"},
        {"Virginia", "North Carolina", "South Carolina", "Georgia", "Florida"}};
```

In the preceding code fragment, you create a few integers that will be used to hold indexes. You also create the data for this example, as well as an HTREEITEM structure for each level in your tree. Finally, you create a TV_INSERTSTRUCT structure to be used to interface with the CTreeViewCtrl object.

```
for (nRegion = 0; nRegion < 3; ++nRegion)
{
    InsertItem.item.mask = TVIF_TEXT;
    InsertItem.item.pszText = szRegion[nRegion];
    InsertItem.item.cchTextMax = 15;
    InsertItem.hParent = NULL;
    InsertItem.hInsertAfter = TVI_SORT;

    RegionParent = m_TreeView.InsertItem(&InsertItem);

    for (nDistrict = 0; nDistrict < 5; ++nDistrict)
    {
        InsertItem.item.pszText = szDistrict[nRegion][nDistrict];
        InsertItem.item.cchTextMax = 20;
        InsertItem.hParent = RegionParent;
        InsertItem.hInsertAfter = TVI_SORT;

        DistrictParent = m_TreeView.InsertItem(&InsertItem);
```

```
for (nTerritory = 0; nTerritory < 5; ++nTerritory)
{
    sprintf(szBuffer, "Territory %d", nTerritory);
    InsertItem.item.pszText = szBuffer;
    InsertItem.item.cchTextMax = 20;
    InsertItem.hParent = DistrictParent;
    InsertItem.hInsertAfter = TVI_SORT;

    TerritoryParent = m_TreeView.InsertItem(&InsertItem);
}
    }
}
```

After the variables have been created, you use a loop to insert items into the `CTreeViewCtrl` class object. This is done in the object's hierarchies order: The regions are the first (called the root) level, then the districts, and finally the territories. That is, you add a region, then the first district, then the territories in the first district. You then add the second district, the territories in the second district, and so on.

The Tab Control

The Tab control lets you create property sheet dialog boxes. Visual C++ uses a property page dialog box for ClassWizard, in which there are property sheets for each of the functionalities that ClassWizard offers. This control is similar to the `CPropertySheet`/`CPropertyPage` class objects that are used to create property page dialog boxes.

I had to think for a few minutes about why someone would want to use `CTabCtrl` (which is more complex than `CPropertySheet`/`CPropertyPage`), but I did come up with a logical usage. Sometimes you just have to look under your own nose: Take a look at the Visual C++ Project Settings dialog box, shown in Figure 11.13. A dialog box such as this could be created only with the Tab Common Control and the `CTabCtrl` class object.

FIGURE 11.13.

Visual C++'s Project Settings dialog box.

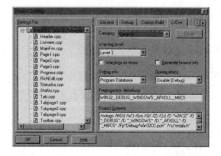

The Tab control is one of the most difficult Win32 Common Controls to implement. Locating a Tab control in a dialog box is easy, as is attaching the `CTabCtrl` object to the control. Even creating a set of tabs is not too difficult.

The fun begins when you want to place something in your Tab control. There is no direct support to do anything specific with the Tab control. However, it was possible to put together an example of a tabbed dialog box (or a property sheet, if that's what you want to call it). First, take a look at the final product. Figure 11.14 shows the Tab control in action.

FIGURE 11.14.

The Tab dialog control in action.

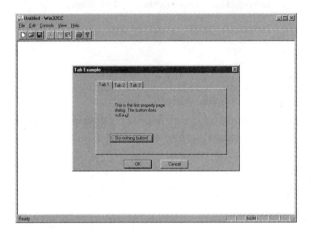

Next, take a look at the code used to produce the Tab dialog control and to make it work. Listing 11.17 shows the header file, where the main `CTabCtrl` object is defined. As in all the other Win32 Common Controls, you can use ClassWizard to create your control's class object. The `CTabCtrl` object's definition appears in bold.

Listing 11.17. Creating a `CTabCtrl` object.

```
// tab.h : header file
//

/////////////////////////////////////////////////////////////////////////////
// Tab dialog

class Tab : public CDialog
{
// Construction
public:
    Tab(CWnd* pParent = NULL);   // Standard constructor

// Dialog Data
    //{{AFX_DATA(Tab)
    enum { IDD = IDD_TAB };
    CTabCtrl     m_TabCtrl;
    //}}AFX_DATA


// Overrides
    // ClassWizard-generated virtual function overrides
    //{{AFX_VIRTUAL(Tab)
    protected:
```

```
    virtual void DoDataExchange(CDataExchange* pDX);    // DDX/DDV support
    //}}AFX_VIRTUAL

// Implementation
protected:

    // Generated message map functions
    //{{AFX_MSG(Tab)
    virtual BOOL OnInitDialog();
    afx_msg void OnSelchangingTab(NMHDR* pNMHDR, LRESULT* pResult);
    afx_msg void OnSelchangeTab(NMHDR* pNMHDR, LRESULT* pResult);
    afx_msg void OnDestroy();
    //}}AFX_MSG
    DECLARE_MESSAGE_MAP()
};
```

After you have created your CTabCtrl object, you can begin to create your tabs. Listing 11.18 contains TAB.CPP, which has the code to manage the Tab control.

> **NOTE**
>
> The three dialog boxes that are placed in the tabs in the Tab control example and in the following CPropertySheet/CPropertyPage example are simple dialog boxes with the child and thin border styles set.

Listing 11.18. The CStatusBarCtrl initialization code.

```
// tab.cpp : implementation file
//

#include "stdafx.h"
#include "Win32CC.h"
#include "tab.h"

#include "page1.h"
#include "page2.h"
#include "page3.h"

#ifdef _DEBUG
#undef THIS_FILE
static char BASED_CODE THIS_FILE[] = __FILE__;
#endif

/////////////////////////////////////////////////////////////////////////////
// Tab dialog


Tab::Tab(CWnd* pParent /*=NULL*/)
    : CDialog(Tab::IDD, pParent)
```

continues

Listing 11.18. continued

```
{
    //{{AFX_DATA_INIT(Tab)
        // NOTE: ClassWizard will add member initialization here
    //}}AFX_DATA_INIT
}


void Tab::DoDataExchange(CDataExchange* pDX)
{
    CDialog::DoDataExchange(pDX);
    //{{AFX_DATA_MAP(Tab)
    DDX_Control(pDX, IDC_TAB, m_TabCtrl);
    //}}AFX_DATA_MAP
}


BEGIN_MESSAGE_MAP(Tab, CDialog)
    //{{AFX_MSG_MAP(Tab)
    ON_NOTIFY(TCN_SELCHANGING, IDC_TAB, OnSelchangingTab)
    ON_NOTIFY(TCN_SELCHANGE, IDC_TAB, OnSelchangeTab)
    ON_WM_DESTROY()
    //}}AFX_MSG_MAP
END_MESSAGE_MAP()


/////////////////////////////////////////////////////////////////////////////
// Tab message handlers

BOOL Tab::OnInitDialog()
{
    CDialog::OnInitDialog();

    // TODO: Add extra initialization here

//    For the Tab control, we will add three tabs,
//    called 'Tab 1', 'Tab 2,' and 'Tab 3'

    TC_ITEM        TabItem;

    TabItem.mask = TCIF_TEXT;
    TabItem.pszText = "Tab 1";

    m_TabCtrl.InsertItem(0, &TabItem);

    TabItem.mask = TCIF_TEXT;
    TabItem.pszText = "Tab 2";

    m_TabCtrl.InsertItem(1, &TabItem);
    TabItem.mask = TCIF_TEXT;

    TabItem.pszText = "Tab 3";

    m_TabCtrl.InsertItem(2, &TabItem);

    Page1* pPage1;
    pPage1 = new Page1;
```

```
        TabItem.mask = TCIF_PARAM;
        TabItem.lParam = (LPARAM)pPage1;
        m_TabCtrl.SetItem(0, &TabItem);

        VERIFY(pPage1->Create(Page1::IDD, &m_TabCtrl));
        pPage1->SetWindowPos(NULL, 10, 30, 0, 0, SWP_NOSIZE | SWP_NOZORDER);
        pPage1->ShowWindow(SW_SHOW);



        Page2* pPage2;
        pPage2 = new Page2;

        TabItem.mask = TCIF_PARAM;
        TabItem.lParam = (LPARAM)pPage2;
        m_TabCtrl.SetItem(1, &TabItem);

        VERIFY(pPage2->Create(Page2::IDD, &m_TabCtrl));
        pPage2->SetWindowPos(NULL, 10, 30, 0, 0, SWP_NOSIZE | SWP_NOZORDER);
        pPage2->ShowWindow(SW_HIDE);


        Page3* pPage3;
        pPage3 = new Page3;

        TabItem.mask = TCIF_PARAM;
        TabItem.lParam = (LPARAM)pPage3;
        m_TabCtrl.SetItem(2, &TabItem);

        VERIFY(pPage3->Create(Page3::IDD, &m_TabCtrl));
        pPage3->SetWindowPos(NULL, 10, 30, 0, 0, SWP_NOSIZE | SWP_NOZORDER);
        pPage3->ShowWindow(SW_HIDE);

        return TRUE;  // Return TRUE unless you set the focus to a control
                      // EXCEPTION: OCX Property Pages should return FALSE
}

void Tab::OnSelchangingTab(NMHDR* pNMHDR, LRESULT* pResult)
{
        // TODO: Add your control notification handler code here

        int        iTab = m_TabCtrl.GetCurSel();
        TC_ITEM    tci;

        tci.mask = TCIF_PARAM;
        m_TabCtrl.GetItem(iTab, &tci);
        ASSERT(tci.lParam);

        CWnd* pWnd = (CWnd *)tci.lParam;
        pWnd->ShowWindow(SW_HIDE);

        *pResult = 0;
}

void Tab::OnSelchangeTab(NMHDR* pNMHDR, LRESULT* pResult)
{
```

continues

Listing 11.18. continued

```
    // TODO: Add your control notification handler code here
    int        iTab = m_TabCtrl.GetCurSel();
    TC_ITEM    tci;

    tci.mask = TCIF_PARAM;
    m_TabCtrl.GetItem(iTab, &tci);
    ASSERT(tci.lParam);

    CWnd* pWnd = (CWnd *)tci.lParam;
    pWnd->ShowWindow(SW_SHOW);

    *pResult = 0;
}

void Tab::OnDestroy()
{

    // TODO: Add your message handler code here


    int        iTab = 0;
    TC_ITEM    tci;
    CWnd* pWnd;
    tci.mask = TCIF_PARAM;

    m_TabCtrl.GetItem(0, &tci);
    ASSERT(tci.lParam);
    pWnd = (CWnd *)tci.lParam;
    pWnd->DestroyWindow();
    delete pWnd;

    m_TabCtrl.GetItem(1, &tci);
    ASSERT(tci.lParam);
    pWnd = (CWnd *)tci.lParam;
    pWnd->DestroyWindow();
    delete pWnd;

    m_TabCtrl.GetItem(2, &tci);
    ASSERT(tci.lParam);
    pWnd = (CWnd *)tci.lParam;
    pWnd->DestroyWindow();
    delete pWnd;


    CDialog::OnDestroy();
}
```

In your dialog box, you will need to create a handler for the WM_INITDIALOG message. This handler is common to most dialog box classes. The handler for your Tab control must first create the tabs (three tabs in this example) and then must create three dialog boxes that will be displayed in the Tab control. Which dialog box is displayed in the Tab control is controlled by which tab is currently active.

First, as the following code fragment shows, you create the tabs. A TC_ITEM structure is used to define the tabs, and a call to CTabCtrl::InsertItem() creates the tab.

```
//    For the Tab control, we will add three tabs,
//    called 'Tab 1', 'Tab 2,' and 'Tab 3'.

    TC_ITEM         TabItem;

    TabItem.mask = TCIF_TEXT;
    TabItem.pszText = "Tab 1";

    m_TabCtrl.InsertItem(0, &TabItem);

    TabItem.mask = TCIF_TEXT;
    TabItem.pszText = "Tab 2";

    m_TabCtrl.InsertItem(1, &TabItem);
    TabItem.mask = TCIF_TEXT;

    TabItem.pszText = "Tab 3";

    m_TabCtrl.InsertItem(2, &TabItem);
```

After you have created your tabs, you then need to create the dialog boxes. There must be one dialog box for each tab.

```
Page1* pPage1;
    pPage1 = new Page1;

    TabItem.mask = TCIF_PARAM;
    TabItem.lParam = (LPARAM)pPage1;
    m_TabCtrl.SetItem(0, &TabItem);

    VERIFY(pPage1->Create(Page1::IDD, &m_TabCtrl));
    pPage1->SetWindowPos(NULL, 10, 30, 0, 0, SWP_NOSIZE | SWP_NOZORDER);
    pPage1->ShowWindow(SW_SHOW);


    Page2* pPage2;
    pPage2 = new Page2;

    TabItem.mask = TCIF_PARAM;
    TabItem.lParam = (LPARAM)pPage2;
    m_TabCtrl.SetItem(1, &TabItem);


    VERIFY(pPage2->Create(Page2::IDD, &m_TabCtrl));
    pPage2->SetWindowPos(NULL, 10, 30, 0, 0, SWP_NOSIZE | SWP_NOZORDER);
    pPage2->ShowWindow(SW_HIDE);


    Page3* pPage3;
    pPage3 = new Page3;

    TabItem.mask = TCIF_PARAM;
    TabItem.lParam = (LPARAM)pPage3;
    m_TabCtrl.SetItem(2, &TabItem);
```

```
VERIFY(pPage3->Create(Page3::IDD, &m_TabCtrl));
pPage3->SetWindowPos(NULL, 10, 30, 0, 0, SWP_NOSIZE | SWP_NOZORDER);
pPage3->ShowWindow(SW_HIDE);
```

Page1, Page2, and Page3 are all simple dialog box classes. You can choose the controls in the dialog boxes that will be placed on the tabbed pages. The only requirement is that the dialog box must fit inside the Tab control; therefore, don't make the dialog boxes too large.

When the first tab is active, the first dialog box is displayed with a call to ShowWindow() using the parameter of SW_SHOW. The other two dialog boxes aren't active, so they're hidden using calls to ShowWindow() with the parameter of SW_HIDE. Note the call to m_TabCtrl.SetItem(), which saves the handle to the Tab dialog boxes by placing the handle in the TC_ITEM.lParam member.

The next thing you must program is the change from the current Tab dialog box to the new Tab dialog box when the user changes tabs. You do this in two steps. First, the current Tab dialog box is hidden. You accomplish this by using the CTabCtrl's TCN_SELCHANGING handler, which is called before the current tab changes. This handler is simple: Get the handle for the current Tab dialog box and call ShowWindow(SW_HIDE).

```
void Tab::OnSelchangingTab(NMHDR* pNMHDR, LRESULT* pResult)
{
    // TODO: Add your control notification handler code here

    int       iTab = m_TabCtrl.GetCurSel();
    TC_ITEM   tci;

    tci.mask = TCIF_PARAM;
    m_TabCtrl.GetItem(iTab, &tci);
    ASSERT(tci.lParam);

    CWnd* pWnd = (CWnd *)tci.lParam;
    pWnd->ShowWindow(SW_HIDE);

    *pResult = 0;
}
```

Next, the new Tab dialog box is shown. This is done with CTabCtrl's TCN_SELCHANGE handler, which is called after the current tab changes. This handler is simple: Get the handle for the current Tab dialog box and call ShowWindow(SW_SHOW).

```
void Tab::OnSelchangeTab(NMHDR* pNMHDR, LRESULT* pResult)
{
    // TODO: Add your control notification handler code here
    int       iTab = m_TabCtrl.GetCurSel();
    TC_ITEM   tci;

    tci.mask = TCIF_PARAM;
    m_TabCtrl.GetItem(iTab, &tci);
    ASSERT(tci.lParam);

    CWnd* pWnd = (CWnd *)tci.lParam;
    pWnd->ShowWindow(SW_SHOW);
```

```
    *pResult = 0;
}
```

That's all there is to changing the Tab dialog boxes. However, you must do a final bit of house-cleaning. When the main dialog box is destroyed, you must manually destroy the Tab dialog boxes. This is accomplished in the OnDestroy handler, which you can create by using ClassWizard. This handler is called when the main dialog window is destroyed. You then can destroy the Tab dialog boxes.

```
void Tab::OnDestroy()
{
    // TODO: Add your message handler code here

    int         iTab = 0;
    TC_ITEM     tci;
    CWnd* pWnd;
    tci.mask = TCIF_PARAM;

    m_TabCtrl.GetItem(0, &tci);
    ASSERT(tci.lParam);
    pWnd = (CWnd *)tci.lParam;
    pWnd->DestroyWindow();
    delete pWnd;

    m_TabCtrl.GetItem(1, &tci);
    ASSERT(tci.lParam);
    pWnd = (CWnd *)tci.lParam;
    pWnd->DestroyWindow();
    delete pWnd;

    m_TabCtrl.GetItem(2, &tci);
    ASSERT(tci.lParam);
    pWnd = (CWnd *)tci.lParam;
    pWnd->DestroyWindow();
    delete pWnd;

    CDialog::OnDestroy();
}
```

Finally, in a real program, you would code your OK and Cancel buttons. The OK button's handler would check each of the Tab dialog boxes to see what has changed and then would pass this information back to the caller, as appropriate.

Property Sheets

Property sheets aren't part of the Win32 Common Controls. However, property sheets are so closely related to the Tab Common Control that any discussion of the Tab Common Control would be incomplete without a mention of the Property Sheet dialog box.

Figure 11.15 shows a simple property sheet dialog box using the same set of Tab dialog boxes that you used with the Tab Common Control, as described earlier.

FIGURE 11.15.

A CPropertySheet/
CPropertyPage
dialog box.

Property sheet dialog boxes can contain only property sheets. If you need to have controls outside of the property sheets, you need to use a Tab Common Control, as described earlier.

The code to produce the property page shown in Figure 11.15 is contained in Listing 11.19.

Listing 11.19. Creating a CPropertyPage/CPropertySheet dialog box.

```
void CMainFrame::OnWin32commoncontrolsPropertypage()
{
    // TODO: Add your command handler code here

    Page1           OurPage1;
    Page2           OurPage2;
    Page3           OurPage3;

    CPropertySheet      PropertySheet(IDS_PROPERTY_SHEET_TITLE);

    PropertySheet.AddPage(&OurPage1);
    PropertySheet.AddPage(&OurPage2);
    PropertySheet.AddPage(&OurPage3);

//  A test to see if the user pressed cancel or OK should be
//  made on the call to DoModal()...

    PropertySheet.DoModal();

}
```

As you can see, it's not difficult to create property page dialog boxes in this manner. Simply create the property page dialog boxes and then add them to the property sheet. Finally, call `DoModal()` to create the dialog box. The text on each tab is extracted from the dialog box titles.

The Animation Control

The Animation control lets an application display certain types of animation (AVI) files (usually called AVI clips) in a window. The AVI file must meet certain criteria in order to be used with the Animation control:

■ The AVI file must be silent. No sound track is allowed.

■ The AVI file must be either uncompressed or compressed using the run-length encoded (RLE) compression technique. No other compression technique is supported.

■ The AVI must be either a file or an application resource.

At the time this book was written, Visual C++ 4 didn't enable direct creation of animation resources. To create an Animation resource, follow these steps:

1. Create a new type of resource called AVI.

2. Visual C++ will create an initial resource under AVI and open a binary edit window, as shown in Figure 11.16. You could use the keyboard to enter an AVI file's contents, but that would be rather time-consuming. Instead, go to step 3.

FIGURE 11.16.

An AVI resource in WIN32CC.RC.

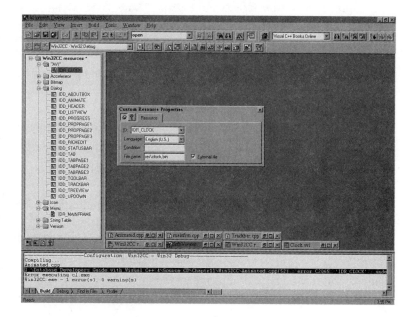

3. Rename the new resource with a logical name (I used IDR_CLOCK in my program).

4. Open the new AVI resource by double-clicking it.

5. Open the AVI file that you intend to use as your resource. In the sample program, the AVI file is called CLOCK.AVI. This file will be opened in binary mode, as shown in Figure 11.17.

FIGURE 11.17.

The CLOCK.AVI file opened in Visual C++.

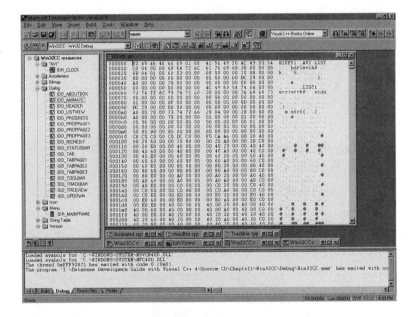

6. Select the entire contents of the AVI file by positioning the cursor at the first byte in the file and pressing Ctrl-Shift-End. Then copy the file's contents to the clipboard by pressing Ctrl-C.

7. In the AVI resource edit window, copy the clipboard's contents by pressing Ctrl-V.

8. The new AVI resource will now contain the contents of your AVI file. You can open the AVI resource with a call to CAnimateCtrl::Open():

   ```
   m_AnimateCtrl.Open(IDR_CLOCK);
   ```

Having your AVI clips as resources makes managing the application easier, because there won't be a separate AVI file for each animation effect. However, when AVI clips are resources, it's much more difficult to use a different AVI clip without more extensive programming. Generally, however, most applications will want to include their AVI clips as application resources.

Figure 11.18 shows a typical implementation of an Animation control in a dialog box. This example is from the sample program.

FIGURE 11.18.

An Animation control shown in a dialog box.

When your application uses a `CAnimateCtrl` class object, it won't need to manage the Animation control much. The application must open the AVI clip that will be displayed, and it may optionally start the playback of the AVI. An Animation control has a few special attributes, which are described in Table 11.1. In addition to these special attributes, the Animation control also supports the standard attributes for dialog box controls.

Table 11.1. The Animation control's special attributes.

Attribute	Description
Center	The actual window that is created will be centered in the window defined by either the dialog box template or the `rect` structure passed to the `Create()` function.
Transparent	The Animation control's background will be transparent instead of being the background color that was specified by the AVI file.
Autoplay	The AVI clip will automatically play once the Animation control has been created and is made visible. Once Autoplay has started, the AVI clip will repeat automatically until it is explicitly ended.

After you've added the Animation control to a dialog box, you can use ClassWizard to bind a `CAnimateCtrl` object to the Animation control. This `CAnimateCtrl` object is your interface with the Animation control.

Implementing a *CAnimateCtrl* Animation Control

If you're using an Animation control in a dialog box, you can use ClassWizard to bind a CAnimateCtrl object to the control. If you're implementing an Animation control in a window that isn't a dialog box, you need call the CAnimateCtrl::Create() function to create the Animation control. You might find a use for an Animation control in a normal window, or perhaps as part of a toolbar.

Figure 11.19 shows the dialog box (in Visual C++'s resource editor) with the properties for the Animate control. You can easily set these properties using the resource editor for Animation controls that are in dialog boxes. When the Animation control is in a window other than a dialog box, the properties are set when the Animation control is created.

FIGURE 11.19.

The Animation control and its properties in Visual C++'s resource editor.

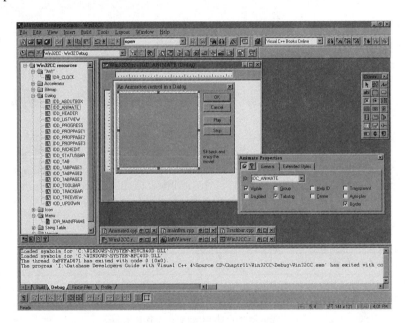

In Figure 11.19 you can see that I've added two new buttons, Play and Stop. The handlers for these two buttons simply call the CAnimateCtrl::Play() and CAnimateCtrl::Stop() functions.

Listing 11.20 is the code that manages the Animate sample dialog box. The basic code was developed using ClassWizard and then was modified to add the necessary features. The code that was added manually appears in bold.

Listing 11.20. The ANIMATED.CPP file.

```
// animated.cpp : implementation file
//

#include "stdafx.h"
```

```
#include "wpu32cc.h"
#include "animated.h"

#ifdef _DEBUG
#undef THIS_FILE
static char BASED_CODE THIS_FILE[] = __FILE__;
#endif

/////////////////////////////////////////////////////////////////////////////
// CAnimateDlg dialog


CAnimateDlg::CAnimateDlg(CWnd* pParent /*=NULL*/)
    : CDialog(CAnimateDlg::IDD, pParent)
{
    //{{AFX_DATA_INIT(CAnimateDlg)
    //}}AFX_DATA_INIT
}


void CAnimateDlg::DoDataExchange(CDataExchange* pDX)
{
    CDialog::DoDataExchange(pDX);
    //{{AFX_DATA_MAP(CAnimateDlg)
    DDX_Control(pDX, IDC_ANIMATE, m_AnimateCtrl);
    //}}AFX_DATA_MAP
}


BEGIN_MESSAGE_MAP(CAnimateDlg, CDialog)
    //{{AFX_MSG_MAP(CAnimateDlg)
    ON_BN_CLICKED(IDC_PLAY, OnPlay)
    ON_BN_CLICKED(IDC_STOP, OnStop)
    //}}AFX_MSG_MAP
END_MESSAGE_MAP()


/////////////////////////////////////////////////////////////////////////////
// CAnimateDlg message handlers

BOOL CAnimateDlg::OnInitDialog()
{
    CDialog::OnInitDialog();

    // TODO: Add extra initialization here

//  Use the filename to open a file, an identifier
//  to open a resource.

//  m_AnimateCtrl.Open("CLOCK.AVI");      // Use AVI file
    m_AnimateCtrl.Open(IDR_CLOCK);        // Use AVI resource


    return TRUE;  // Return TRUE unless you set the focus to a control
                  // EXCEPTION: OCX Property Pages should return FALSE
}
```

continues

Listing 11.20. continued

```
void CAnimateDlg::OnPlay()
{
    // TODO: Add your control notification handler code here

    m_AnimateCtrl.Play(0, (UINT)-1, 1);
}

void CAnimateDlg::OnStop()
{
    // TODO: Add your control notification handler code here

    m_AnimateCtrl.Stop();
}
```

Listing 11.21 is the ANIMATED.H header file that accompanies the ANIMATED.CPP file shown in Listing 11.20. ANIMATED.H was modified only by ClassWizard; no manual changes were necessary.

Listing 11.21. The ANIMATED.H file.

```
// animated.h : header file
//

/////////////////////////////////////////////////////////////////////
// CAnimateDlg dialog

class CAnimateDlg : public CDialog
{
// Construction
public:
    CAnimateDlg(CWnd* pParent = NULL);    // Standard constructor

// Dialog data
    //{{AFX_DATA(CAnimateDlg)
    enum { IDD = IDD_ANIMATE };
    CAnimateCtrl    m_AnimateCtrl;
    //}}AFX_DATA


// Overrides
    // ClassWizard generated virtual function overrides
    //{{AFX_VIRTUAL(CAnimateDlg)
    protected:
    virtual void DoDataExchange(CDataExchange* pDX);    // DDX/DDV support
    //}}AFX_VIRTUAL

// Implementation
protected:

    // Generated message map functions
    //{{AFX_MSG(CAnimateDlg)
```

```
    virtual BOOL OnInitDialog();
    afx_msg void OnPlay();
    afx_msg void OnStop();
    //}}AFX_MSG
    DECLARE_MESSAGE_MAP()
};
```

The *CAnimateCtrl* Class in a Dialog Box

As I mentioned earlier, you would usually bind your CAnimateCtrl object to an Animation control using ClassWizard. Once you have bound the CAnimateCtrl object, you can then initialize your Animation control in the OnInitDialog() function.

Generally, you will want to load an ANI clip (either from a resource or an ANI file). Often the animation will be started at this time. You can usually use the Autoplay attribute to start an animation at creation time.

The following code shows (in bold) the line that initializes the Animation control. I've also added the statement that would be used if you wanted to start the animation immediately when the animation window is created:

```
BOOL CAnimateDlg::OnInitDialog()
{
    CDialog::OnInitDialog();

    // TODO: Add extra initialization here

// The first example of Open() will open an AVI file:

//      m_AnimateCtrl.Open("CLOCK.AVI");

// The second example of Open() will open an AVI resource:

    m_AnimateCtrl.Open(IDR_CLOCK);

// Start playing the AVI clip, with frame zero,
// to the end of the clip. Play it one time only:

    m_AnimateCtrl.Play(0, (UINT)-1, 1);

    return TRUE;  // Return TRUE unless you set the focus to a control
                  // EXCEPTION: OCX Property Pages should return FALSE
}
```

Creating *CAnimateCtrl* Objects in Nondialog Windows

To create a CAnimateCtrl object in a window that isn't a dialog box, you can call CAnimateCtrl::Create(). This function takes four parameters: a style (only the standard dialog box control styles are supported by an Animation control), a rect structure specifying the Animation control's location and size, a pointer to the parent window, and the control ID.

```
CAnimateCtrl::Create(
    WS_CHILD ¦ WS_VISIBLE ¦ WS_BORDER ¦ WS_TABSTOP ¦ ACS_AUTOPLAY,
    rect, this, 0);
```

There are many situations in which you might want to create an Animation control in a nondialog window. Using `CAnimateCtrl::Create()` is an easy way to do so.

Table 11.2 lists the options for the window styles of an Animation control. None of these options are mandatory.

Table 11.2. `CAnimateCtrl::Create()` options.

Attribute	Description
ACS_CENTER	The actual window created will be centered in the window defined by either the dialog box template or the `rect` structure passed to the `Create()` function.
ACS_TRANSPARENT	The background of the Animation control will be transparent rather than the background color that was specified by the AVI file.
ACS_AUTOPLAY	The AVI clip will automatically play once the Animation control has been created and the control is visible. Once Autoplay has started, the AVI clip will repeat automatically until explicitly ended.

CAnimateCtrl Interaction

The `CAnimateCtrl` object lets you play, seek, and stop the animation. The Animation control doesn't have any facility to return the current frame, nor is there a method to determine the AVI file's size or number of frames.

> **NOTE**
>
> Once an Animation control has been stopped, you must restart it from a known point. There is no way to determine the currently stopped frame.

> **CAUTION**
>
> Animation controls only support AVI clips of 65,535 frames. At 20 frames per second, this limits your AVI clip to about 55 minutes in length. No full-length movies here!

Using the *CAnimateCtrl* Animate Object

The CAnimateCtrl Animate object takes no input from the user and can only provide output (the AVI clip). You can create start and stop buttons for the user, but the usefulness of such controls is questionable. For more advanced animation techniques, it would be best if you used the MCIWnd class window instead.

The *CAnimateCtrl* Animate Input

You can initialize the CAnimateCtrl Animation control using the CAnimateCtrl::Open() member function. This function takes either the filename for an AVI file or the resource identifier for an AVI resource. An example of how to create an AVI resource was provided earlier.

Summary

This chapter showed you how to use the Win32 Common Controls, which offer the programmer a new set of dialog box controls. Controls covered in this chapter include the following:

- The ListView control is used to display lists of data. The display in a CListViewCtrl control can be in a number of different formats.
- The TreeView control is used to display hierarchical data such as directory listings.
- The Trackbar control offers a way for the user to input an inexact value within a predefined range.
- The Progress Indicator control is used to provide visual feedback to the user on the status of a lengthy operation.
- The Up-Down control offers a way for the user to select an exact, sequential value from a predefined set of values.
- The Status Bar control supplements the MFC standard status bar control.
- The Toolbar control supplements the MFC standard toolbar control.
- The RichText edit control allows displaying of text formatted using the Microsoft rich text specifications.
- The Tab control is useful in creating property sheet dialog boxes.
- The Animation control is useful for creating animated displays for the users of your application.

12

Printing Reports with Report Generators

Previous versions of Visual C++ were oriented toward performing actions, not printing reports. C and C++ have never been noted for built-in printing prowess, so report generation has typically fallen on the programmer's shoulders. Prior to version 4, Visual C++ didn't have any report generator facilities or classes. Visual C++ 4 includes Crystal Reports, which programmers can redistribute with their applications. Also, several companies have produced products that let C/C++ programmers add report generation facilities to their Windows programs. This chapter highlights Crystal Reports and two add-on products, ReportEase and ReportSmith (a Borland product).

The first part of this chapter looks at what it takes to use the Crystal Reports package. Crystal Reports is the product of Seagate's Crystal division. Seagate acquired Crystal Services, Inc., in May of 1994. Crystal Reports packages are now included with Visual C++ 4 and a number of versions of Visual Basic. At the time this book was written, the most current version of Crystal Reports was 4.5. Visual Basic users are still using version 3, so we're ahead of the Visual Basic users for once!

Crystal Reports is an ODBC-based report generator (like ReportSmith) that doesn't directly interact with your application's data. The application must save the data in an ODBC-accessible database. Crystal Reports then generates the report from the database's contents and the report template.

In this chapter you will generate a project that uses the Crystal Reports AppWizard add-on that lets you quickly create Visual C++ applications with complete report-writing functionality. The Crystal AppWizard add-on looks very similar to the standard Visual C++ 4 AppWizard, but it includes additional options to include Crystal Reports functionality.

The final part of this chapter looks at ReportEase and ReportSmith. There are basic differences between these two products. ReportSmith is an ODBC application (like Crystal Reports) that can be called by a Visual C++ program (using DDE techniques) or a stand-alone application, and ReportEase is a non-ODBC application that must be incorporated into your application. ReportEase doesn't have a stand-alone report generator, so you must start your application in order to use ReportEase to print reports.

Using Crystal Reports in New Visual C++ Applications

The folks at Crystal have made it easy to create a new project with Crystal Reports support built in. They've taken advantage of Visual C++ 4's ability to create custom AppWizard projects. This allows the creation of a project with Crystal Reports support built in with little or no effort on the programmer's part!

To create a new project with Crystal Reports support, start AppWizard by selecting File | New. In the New dialog box, select Project Workspace and click OK. In the New Project Workspace dialog box, select Crystal Reports AppWizard, as shown in Figure 12.1. Usually this selection will be at or near the bottom of the list, following Custom AppWizard.

FIGURE 12.1.

The Crystal Reports selection of the New Project Workspace dialog box.

After you've selected Crystal Reports AppWizard and filled in the project's name and directory, click the Create button. The Crystal Reports AppWizard will be started, and you will see the first five Wizard dialogs that AppWizard displays for all MFC-type applications. The sixth Wizard dialog, shown in Figure 12.2, lets you configure the source of the reports that your application will allow the user to print. The two choices are to have a single, predefined report for the application or to allow the user to select reports using a dialog box.

FIGURE 12.2.

The sixth Crystal Reports AppWizard Wizard dialog: report source.

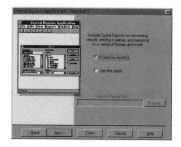

For most applications, you'll want to let the user select from a number of predefined reports. Some simpler applications might have only one report defined. You can predefine the report to give the user easier report printing capabilities.

As soon as AppWizard has completed its design of the Crystal Reports application, you see the New Project Information dialog box, shown in Figure 12.3. This dialog lets you see what files, classes, and features are selected for your new project.

FIGURE 12.3.

Crystal Reports' New Project Information dialog box.

> **NOTE**
>
> It's beyond the scope of this book to delve into the new custom AppWizard features that are part of Visual C++ 4. However, the Crystal Reports AppWizard is an excellent example of what can be done with the custom AppWizard features.

Click the OK button to have AppWizard create the project's files and then open the project in Visual C++ as the current project. You can choose to either initially build the project (a good idea) or immediately start customizing the project.

Let's take a look at what's really offered in the Crystal Reports application. Notice that the original File | Print selections are still included. Also notice that the Crystal Reports AppWizard has added a new menu called Report. Under the Report menu are the options of Open Report, Close Report, Close All, Print Preview, Printer, Export, and Mail.

As you can see in Figure 12.4, ClassWizard already has handlers for each of these menu selections.

FIGURE 12.4.

Visual C++'s ClassWizard showing handlers for the Crystal Reports menu items.

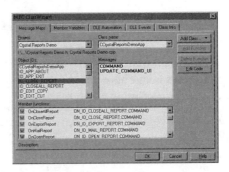

Each of these handlers is placed in the application's `CWinApp`-based class. For example, in our program, the handlers are in the `CCrystalReportsDemoApp` class. Handlers are already written for each menu selection. (You don't have to do any programming to complete the implementation of the Crystal Reports portion of your application.)

> **NOTE**
>
> Although you don't have to do major programming for most implementations of Crystal Reports in a Visual C++ MFC application, you do have to design all the reports that your application requires.

> **NOTE**
>
> The Crystal Reports report generator program can't be redistributed. You must either design the reports for your application or arrange for your application's users to obtain licensed copies of the Crystal Reports report generator.

Each report must be created by you, the programmer. Generally, end users of your product won't have regular access to the Crystal Reports report generator, shown in Figure 12.5, but it might be possible to have end users assist in the development of the application's reports. Because report specification files aren't part of your application, you can at any point upgrade or modify the reports and redistribute them to your users. Nothing in an application is dependent on a specific report unless you design the application to open a fixed report by name.

FIGURE 12.5.

The Crystal Reports report generator program.

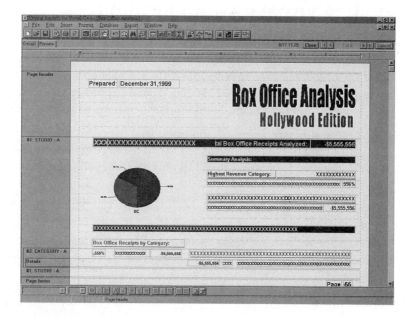

After designing a report (or several reports), you would usually include these reports in the same directory as the main application's executable file(s). Some applications have a separate folder for report specification files, especially when the application has a large number of reports. One way to avoid the problem of end users not having access to the report generator program is to give every conceivable report a separate folder (or a hierarchy of folders). This can greatly assist the users in managing their reports.

The next part of this chapter looks at what is necessary to add Crystal Reports to an existing 32-bit MFC Windows application.

NOTE

Crystal Reports is a 32-bit application. It can be used only with Visual C++ 4, but you might be able to make it work with Visual C++ 2.x by manually writing the interface calling code. You can't use Crystal Reports with any of the 16-bit versions of Visual C++.

Adding Crystal Reports to Existing Visual C++ Applications

Sometimes an exciting new feature or option comes along after you've started developing your application. Crystal Reports and Visual C++ 4 are an example of this. Converting an existing Visual C++ 2.x application to Visual C++ 4 is a simple task. You just open the project and resave it as a Visual C++ 4 project. Adding Crystal Reports to an existing application is a bit more complex. You must manually add several new items to your application:

■ A menu structure, either as a top-level menu item (this is how the Crystal Reports AppWizard does it) or perhaps as a nested menu option under the application's File | Print option. It's possible to call all the Crystal Reports functions from a dialog box, but I don't recommend it.

■ The Crystal Reports classes file, PEPLUS.CPP, and the Crystal Reports header file, PEPLUS.H.

■ Handlers for each applicable menu item. The following sections look at each function added to the application and the handler that Crystal Reports AppWizard would have created.

You also must generate any reports that the application will require.

Adding Crystal Reports to the Menu Bar

To add Crystal Reports to the application's menu bar, you must add a number of menu selections. The Crystal Reports AppWizard adds the following menu selections (in order) to the application's menu bar. Crystal Reports AppWizard adds a new top-level menu called Report, but there's no reason why you can't have this arranged as a submenu.

- ■ Open Report: This selection is present only if you design your application to allow the user to open (or use) multiple reports that won't be predefined in the application. If you don't use an Open Report menu option, you must have a menu option to allow the opening of a specific report. The default implementation of this menu option will open the report and display it in a print preview window.

- ■ Close Report: This menu selection allows the user to close a specific open report definition file.

- ■ Close All: This menu selection allows the user to close all currently open report definition files.

- ■ Print Preview: This menu selection opens an on-screen print preview that is very similar to Visual C++ MFC applications' print preview.

- ■ Printer: This menu selection allows an open report to be configured and printed.

- ■ Export: This menu selection lets the user export the report in a number of different formats, including Excel, DIFF, RTF, Word DOC, Lotus 1-2-3, and as a text file.

- ■ Mail: This menu selection lets the user send the report as a mail (MAPI) message. The Mail menu selection supports all the formats supported by the Export option.

After you've added menu selections to the menu and assigned them identifiers (you don't have to use the identifiers that I've listed, but it will make things easier if you do), you can add the handlers for each of these menu selections using ClassWizard.

Figure 12.6 shows the Crystal Reports menu structure added as a submenu under the application's File | Print menu option.

FIGURE 12.6.

Crystal Reports added as a submenu under File | Print.

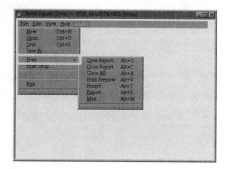

Adding Crystal Reports Classes to Your Application

To add the classes for Crystal Reports to your application's project, first copy PEPLUS.CPP and PEPLUS.H from the Crystal Reports main directory (C:\CRW if you installed Crystal Reports in the default installation directory). The PEPLUS files contain several classes that your Crystal Reports menu handles will use.

> **NOTE**
>
> You need to include the Crystal Reports .LIB file, CRPE32M.LIB, in your application's project. With Visual C++ 4, including PEPLUS.H and PEPLUS.CPP in your project is sufficient to force Visual C++ to include the correct library file. Crystal Reports includes a #pragma comment(lib, "crpe32m.lib") statement in CRPE.H, which is included into your project by PEPLUS.CPP.

To insert these new files into your project, select Insert | Files Into Project, and then select the file PEPLUS.CPP. (You don't need to include PEPLUS.H explicitly. It will be picked up when dependencies are scanned.) After you've added PEPLUS.CPP, your application's ClassView tab will look something like the one shown in Figure 12.7.

FIGURE 12.7.

Visual C++'s ClassView tab after PEPLUS.CPP has been added to the project.

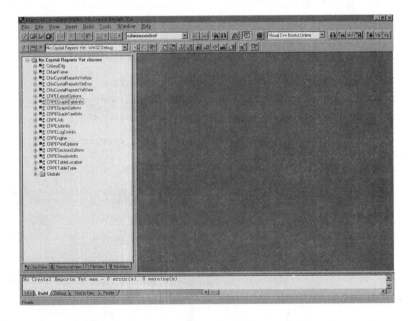

Figure 12.7 shows that PEPLUS.CPP adds a large number of classes. Actually, these aren't classes; they're structures. However, the distinction between a class and a structure (a class has a constructor and a destructor, and a structure doesn't) isn't significant for the purposes of this chapter.

Adding Handlers for Crystal Reports Menu Items

Earlier you added seven new menu items to an application. These menu items now need to have both a command handler and an update handler. The command handler is used to actually perform the work of the menu item, while the update handler performs the process of enabling and disabling the menu selections as appropriate. You will examine each of the menu items and learn about the command handler and the update handler. The default update handler generally has all the menu selections except Open Report disabled unless a report is open.

All the handlers are usually placed in the CWinApp-derived class. You must also add a number of supporting variables to this class, as shown in Listing 12.1. In addition, you must add #include PEPLUS.H to the CWinApp-derived class's include file list.

Listing 12.1. Crystal Reports support variables.

```
CRPEngine      m_printEng;
CRPEJob        *m_pPrintJob;
char           szFileTitle[256];
```

Open Report...

There are two possible ways to implement the Open Report menu selection. The first and most flexible is to present an open files dialog box listing the different report files available to the user. Because Windows 95 allows long filenames, the reports can have meaningful filenames. A second implementation would be to present a (fixed) list of reports for the user to select from.

> **TIP**
>
> In keeping with the philosophy of not doing more work than necessary, the easiest way to create the basic code for your Crystal Reports handlers is to first create a dummy Crystal Reports application using the Crystal Reports AppWizard (or the Crystal Reports sample application included on the CD that comes with this book) and then cut and paste from this dummy application into your main application. In fact, all the handlers shown next were actually created by the Crystal Reports AppWizard when it created a sample program.

The handler for Open Report is shown in Listing 12.2. This handler shows what Crystal Reports does when it opens a report file. This code first initializes the Crystal Reports report print engine (if it's not already initialized) and then displays the Open File common dialog box to allow the user to select a filename.

If the user enters a valid filename, the Crystal Reports report engine is run with the newly opened report by calling m_pPrintJob = m_printEng.OpenJob(), which opens the Crystal Reports report job; `m_pPrintJob->OutputToWindow()`, which displays the Print Preview window; and `m_pPrintJob->Start()`, which prints the report in the Print Preview window. As Listing 12.2 shows, each of these calls has error checking to ensure that the function is successful.

Listing 12.2. The Open Report command handler.

```
///////////////////////////////////////////////////////////////////////
// CCrystalReportsDemoApp commands
// Handler for Crystal Reports Open Report Command

void CCrystalReportsDemoApp::OnOpenReport()
{
    OPENFILENAME    ofn;
    char     szFile[256];
    UINT     i;
    CString csFilter, csDirName;
    char     chReplace, *szFilter, *szDirName;
    // char szFileTitle[] defined as data member

    // Open the Crystal Reports Print Engine if it hasn't been opened.
    if ( m_printEng.GetEngineStatus() != CRPEngine::engineOpen ) {
        // Verify the Print Engine is not missing.
        VERIFY( m_printEng.GetEngineStatus() != CRPEngine::engineMissing );
        // If Print Engine cannot be opened, display the error message
        // and the Print Engine error code.
        if ( !m_printEng.Open() ) {

            AfxMessageBox( m_printEng.GetErrorText() );
        }
    }

    // THE CODE BELOW IS ONLY A SAMPLE. YOU MAY MAKE ANY CHANGE OR WRITE
    // YOUR OWN CODE FOR YOUR SPECIFIC NEEDS.

    szFile[0] = '\0';
    // Load the CRW directory
    szDirName = csDirName.GetBuffer(256);
    if ( !csDirName.LoadString(IDS_CRWDIRECTORY) ) {
        TRACE0( "Cannot load String Table" );
    }
    // Load the File_Filter String
    szFilter = csFilter.GetBuffer(256);
    if ( !csFilter.LoadString(IDS_FILTERSTRING) ) {
        TRACE0("Can not load String Table");
    }

    chReplace = csFilter[csFilter.Find('\0') - 1]; // Retrieve wildcard
    for (i = 0; szFilter[i] != '\0'; i++) {
        if (szFilter[i] == chReplace)
            szFilter[i] = '\0';
    }

    memset(&ofn, 0, sizeof(OPENFILENAME)); // Set all structure members to zero
```

```
// Fill in struct OPENFILENAME
ofn.lStructSize = sizeof(OPENFILENAME);
ofn.hwndOwner = this -> m_pMainWnd->m_hWnd;
ofn.lpstrFilter = szFilter;
ofn.nFilterIndex = 1;
ofn.lpstrFile = szFile;
ofn.nMaxFile = sizeof(szFile);
ofn.lpstrFileTitle = szFileTitle;
ofn.nMaxFileTitle = sizeof(szFileTitle);
ofn.lpstrInitialDir = szDirName;
ofn.Flags = OFN_SHOWHELP | OFN_PATHMUSTEXIST |
    OFN_FILEMUSTEXIST | OFN_NOCHANGEDIR;

// Open a Crystal Reports Print Job.
if ( GetOpenFileName( &ofn ) ) {
    CRPEJob *pOldJob = m_pPrintJob;
    if ( ( m_pPrintJob=m_printEng.OpenJob( szFile ) ) == NULL) {
        AfxMessageBox( m_printEng.GetErrorText() );
        m_pPrintJob = pOldJob;
        return;
    }
    // YOU MAY CHANGE THE SIZE AND STYLE OF WINDOW FOR PREVIEW REPORT HERE
    if ( !m_pPrintJob->OutputToWindow(    szFileTitle, 50, 50, 550, 500,
        CW_USEDEFAULT | WS_SYSMENU | WS_THICKFRAME |
        WS_MAXIMIZEBOX | WS_MINIMIZEBOX,
        0) ) {
        AfxMessageBox( m_pPrintJob->GetErrorText() );
        m_pPrintJob = pOldJob;
        return;
    }
    if ( !m_pPrintJob->Start() ) {
        AfxMessageBox( m_pPrintJob->GetErrorText() );
        m_pPrintJob -> Close();
        m_pPrintJob = pOldJob;
    }
}
}
```

It wouldn't be difficult to create multiple open reports, because the m_pPrintJob member variable returned by the call to OpenJob() could easily be stored in a list.

Since the Open Report menu option is always active, the update handler isn't used. You can code an update handler that does nothing or code no handler at all.

Close Report

Closing a report is easier than opening one. It isn't necessary to ask the user which report to close; the current report is the one that gets closed. For example, the default Crystal Reports handler for Close Report, shown in Listing 12.3, simply closes the print window, closes the actual report, and sets the print job member variable m_pPrintJob to NULL (which the update handlers use to enable and disable the other menu selections).

Listing 12.3. The Close Report command handler.

```
void CCrystalReportsDemoApp::OnCloseReport()
{
    // Close a Crystal Reports print job.
    m_pPrintJob -> CloseWindow();
    m_pPrintJob -> Close();
    m_pPrintJob = NULL;
}
```

The update handler disables the Close Report menu selection based on whether there is a currently open Crystal Reports report. The variable m_pPrintJob is non-NULL if an existing Crystal Reports report is open. Listing 12.4 shows the update handler for this menu item.

Listing 12.4. The Close Report update handler.

```
void CCrystalReportsDemoApp::OnUpdateCloseReport( CCmdUI* pCmdUI )
{
    pCmdUI -> Enable( m_pPrintJob != NULL );
}
```

Close All

Closing all reports is easier than closing a specific report. It isn't necessary to ask the user which report to close; all reports are closed automatically. For example, the default Crystal Reports handler for Close Report, shown in Listing 12.5, simply sets the print job member variable m_pPrintJob to NULL (which the update handlers use to enable and disable the other menu selections) and then calls the print engine's Close() member function.

Listing 12.5. The Close All command handler.

```
void CCrystalReportsDemoApp::OnCloseAllReport()
{
    // Close the Print Engine, thereby closing all print jobs.
    m_pPrintJob = NULL;
    m_printEng.Close();
}
```

The update handler disables the Close All menu selection based on the value returned by the GetNPrintJobs() function. Listing 12.6 shows the update handler for this menu item.

Listing 12.6. The Close All update handler.

```
void CCrystalReportsDemoApp::OnUpdateCloseAllReport( CCmdUI* pCmdUI )
{
    pCmdUI -> Enable( m_printEng.GetNPrintJobs() );
}
```

Print Preview

Crystal Reports initially calls Print Preview when a report is first opened. The user can close the Print Preview window (without closing the actual report) and then later reopen it by selecting the Crystal Reports Print Preview menu option.

As you can see from Listing 12.7, the Print Preview handler calls the OutputToWindow() function exactly as it is called in the Open Report handler. It then calls the Start() function to do the actual printing in the Print Preview window. There is less error handling in the Print Preview handler, because the Open Report handler will have closed the report if Print Preview failed at that point. If you remove the automatic Print Preview from the Open Report handler, you should make sure that your Print Report and Print Preview handlers are sufficiently rugged to handle any problems that might arise.

Listing 12.7. The Print Preview command handler.

```
void CCrystalReportsDemoApp::OnPreviewReport()
{
    if ( !m_pPrintJob->OutputToWindow(    szFileTitle, 50, 50, 550, 500,
        CW_USEDEFAULT | WS_SYSMENU | WS_THICKFRAME |
        WS_MAXIMIZEBOX | WS_MINIMIZEBOX, 0) ) {
        AfxMessageBox( m_pPrintJob->GetErrorText() );
        return;
    }
    if ( !m_pPrintJob->Start() )
    {
        AfxMessageBox( m_pPrintJob->GetErrorText() );
    }
}
```

The update handler disables the Print Preview menu selection based on whether a Crystal Reports report is currently open. The variable m_pPrintJob is non-NULL if an existing Crystal Reports report is open. Listing 12.8 shows the update handler for this menu item.

Listing 12.8. The Print Preview update handler.

```
void CCrystalReportsDemoApp::OnUpdatePreviewReport( CCmdUI* pCmdUI )
{
    pCmdUI -> Enable(m_pPrintJob!= NULL );
}
```

Printer...

Printing reports entails displaying the Windows print dialog box (which lets the user select a printer, select which pages to print, and so on) and then printing the report.

When the report is printed, the user-entered information (such as starting and ending pages) is passed to the Crystal Reports print engine. Then the Crystal Reports printout is performed by calling OutputToPrinter() and then the Start() function, as shown in Listing 12.9. Do you notice something here? The Start() function is called regardless of whether the report is going to the screen (Print Preview) or the printer.

Listing 12.9. The Print command handler.

```
void CCrystalReportsDemoApp::OnPrinterReport()
{
    CRPEPrintOptions printOpt;
    CPrintDialog printDlg(FALSE, PD_ALLPAGES | PD_USEDEVMODECOPIES
                          | PD_HIDEPRINTTOFILE | PD_NOSELECTION,
                      this->m_pMainWnd);
    printDlg.m_pd.nMaxPage = 0xFFFF;
    printDlg.m_pd.nMinPage = 1;
    printDlg.m_pd.nFromPage = 1;
    printDlg.m_pd.nToPage = 0xFFFF;
    if(printDlg.DoModal() == IDCANCEL)
        return;

    if( printDlg.PrintRange() ) {
        printOpt.m_startPageN = (unsigned short)printDlg.GetFromPage();
        printOpt.m_stopPageN = (unsigned short)printDlg.GetToPage();
    }
    printOpt.m_nReportCopies = (unsigned short)printDlg.GetCopies();
    m_pPrintJob -> SetPrintOptions( &printOpt );
    m_pPrintJob -> OutputToPrinter( (short)printOpt.m_nReportCopies );
    if ( !m_pPrintJob->Start() )
    {
        AfxMessageBox( m_pPrintJob->GetErrorText() );
    }
}
```

The update handler disables the Print menu selection based on whether there is a currently open Crystal Reports report. The variable m_pPrintJob is non-NULL if an existing Crystal Reports report is open. Listing 12.10 shows the update handler for this menu item.

Listing 12.10. The Print update handler.

```
void CCrystalReportsDemoApp::OnUpdatePrinterReport( CCmdUI* pCmdUI )
{
    pCmdUI -> Enable( m_pPrintJob != NULL );
}
```

Export...

To export a report (which writes the report's output to a file), you need to set the output option to export and then call Start() to print the report, as shown in Listing 12.11. Generally, Export works much like both Print and Print Preview, because it calls a destination (ExportTo()) and then calls Start() to do the actual output.

Listing 12.11. The Export command handler.

```
void CCrystalReportsDemoApp::OnExportReport()
{
    CRPEExportOptions exportOpt;
    if( m_pPrintJob->GetExportOptions( &exportOpt ) ) {

        if( !m_pPrintJob->ExportTo( &exportOpt ) ) {
            AfxMessageBox( m_pPrintJob->GetErrorText() );
            return;
        }

        if( !m_pPrintJob->Start() ) {
            AfxMessageBox( m_pPrintJob->GetErrorText() );
        }
    }
}
```

The update handler disables the Export menu selection based on whether there is a currently open Crystal Reports report. The variable m_pPrintJob is non-NULL if an existing Crystal Reports report is open. Listing 12.12 shows the update handler for this menu item.

Listing 12.12. The Export update handler.

```
void CCrystalReportsDemoApp::OnUpdateExportReport( CCmdUI* pCmdUI )
{
    pCmdUI -> Enable( m_pPrintJob != NULL );
}
```

Mail...

To mail a report (which writes the report's output to a file and then uses MAPI to send the report to another user), you need to set the output option to export and then call Start() to print the report, as shown in Listing 12.13. Generally, Mail works much like both Print and Print Preview, because it calls a destination (ExportTo()) and then calls Start() to do the actual output.

In reality, the only difference between Export and Mail is that the user selects Mail in the Export destination rather than writing the report to a disk file. In fact, Export and Mail can be used interchangeably with Crystal Reports.

> **NOTE**
>
> Nothing limits you to using the same Export/Mail model that Crystal Reports uses. You could combine these two functions or write a different handler if you wanted to. For more information, look at the CRPEExportOptions structure shown in Listing 12.13.

Listing 12.13. The Mail command handler.

```
void CCrystalReportsDemoApp::OnMailReport()
{
    CRPEExportOptions mailOpt;
    if( m_pPrintJob->GetExportOptions( &mailOpt ) ) {

        if( !m_pPrintJob->ExportTo( &mailOpt ) ) {
            AfxMessageBox( m_pPrintJob->GetErrorText() );
            return;
        }

        if( !m_pPrintJob->Start() ) {
            AfxMessageBox( m_pPrintJob->GetErrorText() );
        }
    }
}
```

The update handler disables the Mail menu selection based on whether there is a currently open Crystal Reports report. The variable m_pPrintJob is non-NULL if an existing Crystal Reports report is open. Listing 12.14 shows the update handler for this menu item.

Listing 12.14. The Mail update handler.

```
void CCrystalReportsDemoApp::OnUpdateMailReport( CCmdUI* pCmdUI )
{
    pCmdUI -> Enable( m_pPrintJob != NULL );
}
```

Generating Reports for Crystal Reports

You must use the Crystal Reports report generator (CRW32.EXE) to create reports that will be printed with the Crystal Reports print engine that you are including with your application. You might find it expedient to either

- have someone who is talented at designing reports give your application's reports a finished look
- have the users of your application sit down with the Crystal Reports report generator and help you design the reports

Remember, the application is for the users, and if possible they should provide input into the report design phase.

Using Crystal Reports Pro

Even though Visual C++ 4 comes with Crystal Reports, the version shipped with Visual C++ isn't as full-featured as some applications might require. Crystal also has a product called Crystal Reports Pro. At the time this book was written, Crystal Reports Pro 4.5 was the only 32-bit report generator available for Visual C++ programmers.

> **NOTE**
>
> Unlike some producers of software, Crystal maintains and sells earlier versions of its products. This can be useful when a software project is on a restricted budget: Using earlier versions of Crystal Reports can be significantly less expensive.

> **NOTE**
>
> Things change rapidly in the Windows programming world. Other 32-bit report generators probably will be available by the time you read this book. If Crystal Reports Pro doesn't meet your needs, check suppliers of programming tools for other competitive products.

Table 12.1 shows the functionality that Crystal Reports Pro adds to Crystal Reports for Visual C++.

Table 12.1. Crystal Reports Pro functionality not present in Crystal Reports for Visual C++.

Functionality	Description
Adding new functions	Crystal Reports Pro lets you add new functions to the base product. These functions can be used to perform tasks specific to your application.

continues

Table 12.1. continued

Functionality	Description
Exporting reports using Crystal Reports Pro	Using Crystal Reports Pro, your applications can export reports in a number of word processor, spreadsheet, and popular data interchange formats.
Crystal custom controls bind to Visual Basic data controls	New features have been added to Crystal Reports Pro that let a Crystal custom control bind directly to a Visual Basic data control. Crystal Reports Pro is bundled with TrueGrid, a bound grid control by Apex Software Corporation that lets users generate reports using the grid layout.
PEDiscardSavedData	Discards data that was previously saved with the report.
PEGetGroupCondition	Determines the group condition information for a selected group section in the specified report.
PEGetLineHeight	Gets line height and ascent information for a specified line in a selected section of the report.
PEGetMargins	Retrieves the page margin settings for the specified report.
PEGetMinimumSectionHeight	Retrieves minimum section height information for selected sections in the specified report.
PEGetNDetailCopies	Returns the number of copies of each Details section in the report that are to be printed.
PEGetNLinesInSection	Determines the number of lines in a selected section of the specified report.
PEGetNParams	Retrieves the number of parameters needed by a stored procedure.
PEGetNthParam	Gets the *n*th parameter of a stored procedure.
PEGetPrintOptions	Retrieves the print options specified for the report (the options that are set in the Print common dialog box) and uses them to fill in the PEPrintOptions structure.
PEGetReportTitle	Returns the handle of the title string that is to appear on the title bar of the specified report when the report prints to a Preview window.

Functionality	Description
PEGetSectionFormat	Retrieves the section format settings for selected sections in the specified report and supplies them as member values for the PESectionOptions structure.
PEGetSelectedPrinter	Retrieves information about a nondefault printer if one is specified in the report.
PEGetSQLQuery	Retrieves the handle for the string containing the SQL query generated by the specified report.
PEHasSavedData	Queries a report to find if data is saved with it.
PEPrintControlsShowing	Checks whether the print controls are displayed in the Preview window.
PESetFont	Sets the font for field and/or text characters in the specified report section(s).
PESetGroupCondition	Changes the group condition for a group section.
PESetLineHeight	Sets the line height and ascent for a specified line in a selected section of the report.
PESetMargins	Sets the page margins for the specified report to the values you supply as parameters.
PESetMinimumSectionHeight	Sets the minimum height for specified report sections to the value supplied as a parameter.
PESetNDetailCopies	Prints multiple copies of the Details section of the report.
PESetNthParam	Sets the value of a parameter in a stored procedure.
PESetPrintOptions	Sets the print options for the report to the values supplied in the PEPrintOptions structure.
PESetReportTitle	Changes the Preview window title to the title string you supply as a parameter.
PESetSectionFormat	Sets the section format settings for selected sections in the specified report to the values in the PESectionOptions structure.
PESetSQLQuery	Changes the SQL query to the query string you supply as a parameter.

continues

Table 12.1. continued

Functionality	Description
PEShowNextPage	Displays the next page in the Preview window.
PEShowFirstPage	Displays the first page in the Preview window.
PEShowPreviousPage	Displays the previous page in the Preview window.
PEShowLastPage	Displays the last page in the Preview window.
PEShowPrintControls	Displays the print controls.

You can include Crystal Reports Pro in a Visual C++ project using the same techniques that you would use to include Crystal Reports for Visual C++. Many applications will do just fine using Crystal Reports for Visual C++, but mainstream applications will benefit from Crystal Reports Pro's increased functionality.

> **NOTE**
>
> Crystal maintains a flexible licensing policy for developers who need to include Crystal Reports' report generator module with their applications. Contact Crystal at (604) 681-3435 and talk to one of their OEM account managers.

Using ReportEase with Visual C++ Applications

The ReportEase program is installed as a DLL that can be called from your own applications. You also have the option of simply including the ReportEase source code with your application if you don't want to ship separate DLL files. One of the best features of ReportEase is that it's supplied with full source code, which lets developers make modifications to enhance the program's usability with the calling application. Also, you can fix those little annoying bugs that are often found in third-party applications.

As this book was being written, Sub Systems announced version 2.5 of ReportEase. This new version sports a number of new functionalities:

■ Support for multiple instances. The form designer and report generator may be executed at the same time.

■ Reports may now be saved to files in addition to being printed or sent to the screen.

- An improved print preview facility is included.
- Improvements to ReportEase's clipboard support.
- General improvements in ReportEase's performance.

Due to the fact that the new version of ReportEase wasn't available for review, this chapter discusses the earlier version.

This section of the chapter looks at the interface that ReportEase uses. You will also see examples of the code that is necessary to call ReportEase from a Windows application. The calling program in this instance is STARmanager, a sales territory GIS management system. STARmanager is a commercial Windows application available from

TTG Inc.
10 State Street
Woburn, MA 01801

ReportEase is designed to accept records from one or more logical files or sources. These records don't need to be kept in separate disk files, because when the report printer is run, your interface will supply the necessary data to the ReportEase report printer module.

Using ReportEase is a two-step process. First you must create a report (using the form editor), and then you can print it. You use the report printer to print either to the screen or to a printer. You must supply some common support routines. It's easy to actually incorporate ReportEase—the initial inclusion usually takes only a few hours.

> **NOTE**
>
> Because including ReportEase with a Visual C++ 4 project requires programming that is specific to each application, the source files in this part of the chapter are for example only. Your own implementation may vary significantly.

Creating Reports with ReportEase

When you use ReportEase, the first interface you need to create is the form editor interface. Listing 12.15 shows an example of the code that calls the form generator from a C++ application. All the examples in the ReportEase documentation are for C programs; however, ReportEase can be used with both C and C++ programs.

Listing 12.15. Calling the ReportEase form generator.

```c
/*  REPORTS.C */

#define  HAVEREPORT

#include "stdafx.h"
#include "STAR.H"

#include <time.h>
#include <stdio.h>
#include <stdlib.h>
#include <string.h>
#include <io.h>
#define REP_CPLUSPLUS extern "C"
#include "rep\rep.h"

#include "reportco.h"

/*****************************************************************************
**
**      TITLE: REPSYS.cpp
**
**   FUNCTION: Calls ReportEase PLUS's report generator to create
**             a new report or edit an existing report.
**
*****************************************************************************/

// LOCAL PROTOTYPES:
void InitDataField(void);
int FAR PASCAL _export UserFieldSelection(HWND hWnd,
    struct StrField huge * field, int SortFieldNo);

int FAR PASCAL _export VerifyField(struct StrField huge * field,
    int SortFieldNo);



// END LOCALS

// Externs
extern  HWND    hDlgPrint;
extern  BOOL    bUserAbort;
extern  int  nCurrentSelection;
// Extern  REPORT    Report;
extern  WORD    wReportType;

// End externs

// Defines
#define MAX_FILES    1  /* One file, the database...    */
#define MAX_FIELDS 65 /* Possible fields            */
int     nReportNumberFields = {0};

// End defines
```

```
#pragma pack(1)
struct StrDataField
{
        char    name[35];       // Field name
        int     width;          // Field width
        int     type;           // Field type
        int     DecPlaces;      // Decimal places
        int     FieldId;
} DataField[MAX_FILES][MAX_FIELDS];

#pragma pack()

#pragma pack(1)
StrForm FormParam;
#pragma pack()

void    ReportSystem(HWND       hWndParent)
{
//      First, initialize the DataField structure.
//      Initialize the report's columns
        InitDataField();

//      Got report filename. Now set up for the form generator.
        FormParam.x = CW_USEDEFAULT;
        FormParam.y = CW_USEDEFAULT;
        FormParam.width = CW_USEDEFAULT;
        FormParam.height = CW_USEDEFAULT;
        FormParam.UserSelection = UserFieldSelection;
        FormParam.VerifyField = VerifyField;
        strcpy(FormParam.file, ReportStuff.szFileName);
        strcpy(FormParam.DataSetName, "HUH");
        FormParam.ShowMenu = TRUE;
        FormParam.ShowHorBar = TRUE;
        FormParam.ShowVerBar = TRUE;
        FormParam.hInst = hInst;
        FormParam.hPrevInst = NULL;
        FormParam.hParentWnd = hWndParent;
        FormParam.hFrWnd = 0;
        FormParam.style=WS_OVERLAPPEDWINDOW;   // Editor window style
        FormParam.FontTypeFace[0] = '\0';
        FormParam.EndForm = NULL;
        FormParam.open = FALSE;
        FormParam.modified = FALSE;

//      It's set up. Now call the form generator:
        form(&FormParam);

//      Set up stuff to return, like the report's filename:

        strcpy(ReportStuff.szFileName, FormParam.file);
        return;
}
```

Figure 12.8 shows the ReportEase report generator being called using the code shown next.

FIGURE 12.8.

ReportEase's report generator in action.

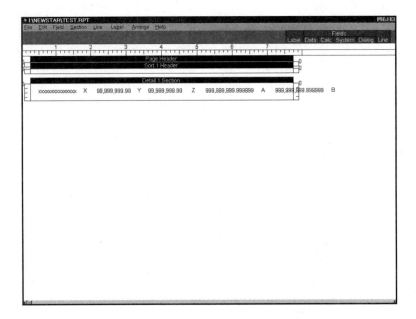

To incorporate ReportEase into your application, you must do the following. First, you must include an #include directive for the ReportEase include file, REP.H. This file contains the definitions that are needed to create the structures used by ReportEase. Next you must create the data structures that are used to hold information about the fields that will be available to the user when the report is being designed. The StrDataField structure is used for this purpose. It's configured as shown in this code fragment:

```
#define MAX_FILES    1    /* One file, the database... */
#define MAX_FIELDS  65    /* 65 possible fields */

struct StrDataField
{
    char     name[35];     // Field name
    int      width;        // Field width
    int      type;         // Field type
    int      DecPlaces;    // Decimal places
    int      FieldId;      // Identifier for each field
} DataField[MAX_FILES][MAX_FIELDS];
```

The DataField structure must contain certain information, but you can also include any additional information that might help your application process columns in the report. In my program, a field called `FieldId` has been added to hold an identifier for each field (otherwise, you would have to do string compares on the `name` field) to let a field be easily identified when the report is being processed.

The fields generally are self-explanatory, with the exception of the `type` field, which will contain values defined in REP.H. The valid values for the `type` field appear in Table 12.2.

Table 12.2. Values for the `type` field.

Value	*Description*
TYPE_TEXT	A text field. Text operations are allowed on this field.
TYPE_NUM	A fixed-point numeric field. Numeric operations are allowed on this field. The number of digits after the decimal point should be stored in the `DecPlaces` field. The user can alter the number of decimal places when the report form is generated.
TYPE_DBL	A double-precision floating-point numeric field. Numeric operations are allowed on this field. The number of digits after the decimal point should be stored in the `DecPlaces` field. The user can alter the number of decimal places when the report form is generated.
TYPE_DATE	A date field. Dates are stored in a long integer (32-bit) field in the format of either YYMMDD or YYYYMMDD.
TYPE_LOGICAL	A numeric field. Logical data is stored as either a long integer (32-bit) 1 or 0.

Next you must write a function to let the user select fields to place in the report. Here is the function prototype for this function:

```
int far PASCAL UserFieldSelection(HWND hWndParent,
            struct StrField,
    far * field, int SortFieldNumber);
```

This function can display a simple dialog box that contains a list box and an OK button. Figure 12.9 shows a typical field selection dialog box.

FIGURE 12.9.

A field selection dialog box.

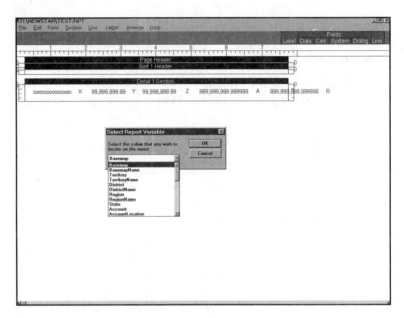

Listing 12.16 shows the code necessary to manage the field selection dialog box shown in Figure 12.9. Much of this code was actually generated using ClassWizard.

Listing 12.16. REPORTCO.CPP: Field selection dialog box code.

```cpp
// reportco.cpp : implementation file
//

#include "stdafx.h"
#include "starae.h"
#include "reportco.h"

#ifdef _DEBUG
#undef THIS_FILE
static char BASED_CODE THIS_FILE[] = __FILE__;
#endif

/////////////////////////////////////////////////////////////////////////////
// CReportColumns dialog


CReportColumns::CReportColumns(CWnd* pParent /*=NULL*/)
    : CDialog(CReportColumns::IDD, pParent)
{
    //{{AFX_DATA_INIT(CReportColumns)
    m_ColumnName = -1;
    //}}AFX_DATA_INIT
}
```

```
void CReportColumns::DoDataExchange(CDataExchange* pDX)
{
    CDialog::DoDataExchange(pDX);
    //{{AFX_DATA_MAP(CReportColumns)
    DDX_Control(pDX, IDC_REPORT_COLUMN, m_ColumnControl);
    DDX_CBIndex(pDX, IDC_REPORT_COLUMN, m_ColumnName);
    //}}AFX_DATA_MAP
}

BEGIN_MESSAGE_MAP(CReportColumns, CDialog)
    //{{AFX_MSG_MAP(CReportColumns)
    //}}AFX_MSG_MAP
END_MESSAGE_MAP()


/////////////////////////////////////////////////////////////////////////
// CReportColumns message handlers

// These defines are *also* in RepSys.CPP
//
#define MAX_FILES    1     /* One file, the database...    */
#define MAX_FIELDS  65     /* 65 possible fields           */

extern    int    nReportNumberFields;

// End defines

#pragma pack(1)
extern struct StrDataField
{
    char    name[35];       // Field name
    int         width;      // Field width
    int         type;       // Field type
    int         DecPlaces;  // Decimal places
    int         FieldId;    // Unique identifier for field
} DataField[MAX_FILES][MAX_FIELDS];

#pragma pack()

BOOL CReportColumns::OnInitDialog()
{
    CDialog::OnInitDialog();

    // TODO: Add extra initialization here
int      i = 0;

    while (DataField[0][i].name[0] && i <=  nReportNumberFields)
    {
        m_ColumnControl.AddString(DataField[0][i].name);
        ++i;
    }
    m_ColumnControl.SetCurSel(0);
    return TRUE;  // Return TRUE unless you set the focus to a control
}
```

The code to create the dialog box is shown next. This code works with a minimum amount of programming because the m_ColumnName is bound to the dialog box combo box control and is automatically updated each time the user makes a selection from the combo box. If m_ColumnName is less than zero, the user didn't have a column selected.

Here's a typical UserFieldSelection() function:

```
int FAR PASCAL _export UserFieldSelection(
HWND hWnd,
struct    StrField huge * field,
int       SortFieldNo)
{
// Display dialog box of field names and allow user to select one
// Return (TRUE) if selection was successful or !TRUE if unsuccessful
// Allow the user to select from a dialog box...
int       CurFile = 0;
int       CurField = -1;
int       nReturn = IDCANCEL;

    // CWnd used to tell dialog to return to report generator, not star
    CWnd cwForm;
    cwForm.Attach(FormParam.hFrWnd);
    CReportColumns reportcolumn(&cwForm);
    reportcolumn.m_ColumnName = 0;
    if (reportcolumn.DoModal() == IDOK &&
        reportcolumn.m_ColumnName >= 0)
    {
        CurField = reportcolumn.m_ColumnName;
        nReturn = IDOK;
    }

    cwForm.Detach();  // So we don't blow up in destructor

    if (nReturn != IDCANCEL)
    {//    User selected a column to use.
     //    Now save it...
        lstrcpy(field->name, DataField[CurFile][CurField].name);  // Field name
        field->type = DataField[CurFile][CurField].type;    // Alpha/num, etc.
        field->width = DataField[CurFile][CurField].width;  // Display width
        field->DecPlaces = DataField[CurFile][CurField].DecPlaces;  // Dec place
        field->FieldId = CurField;                 // Column ID (optional)
        field->FileId = 0;                         // File ID (optional)

        return (TRUE);
    }
    return (FALSE);
}
```

TIP

Notice how a CWnd object is used to set which window (the ReportEase window) will have focus during the field selection process. This was done to prevent focus from returning to the main application window.

Notice how each of the fields in the `StrField` structure is filled out based on the user's selection, and then `TRUE` is returned. If the user doesn't select a field (usually by clicking the Cancel button), `FALSE` is returned. Here are the fields that are required to be filled in:

- ■ `field->name`: This field contains the name of the field. This name must be alphanumeric, must start with a character (not a number), must not contain embedded spaces, and must not contain any of these characters: (,), *, /, +, #, <, =, \, ", ', or $. The first time I used ReportEase, I didn't follow this rule, and my reports didn't work very well.

- ■ `field->type`: The field's data type. Your selections are in the list of identifiers shown in Table 12.1.

- ■ `field->width`: The default width for this field.

- ■ `field->DecPlaces`: The number of digits to the right of the decimal point. This field is specified only for numeric or float data fields, not for character, date, or Boolean fields.

- ■ `field->ParaChar`: For word-wrapped character fields, this is the character that is used to designate a new paragraph. ReportEase recommends using 0x0D for this value.

Two optional, but useful, fields may be filled in as well. They let the field be more easily identified:

- ■ `field->FileId`: The identifier of the field's source. This data is used only by your program to locate the field.

- ■ `field->FieldId`: The identifier of the field's identifier. This data is used only by your program (not ReportEase) to identify the field.

Each of these fields is filled out using information stored in your `DataField` structure, so if you're filling out `field->FileId` or `field->FieldId`, you must add fields to your `DataField` structure for `field->FileId` or `field->FieldId`.

In addition to the field selection function, you must also provide a field verification function. This function is called by the form editor whenever a field must be verified as valid. This is necessary because a user who is creating a report might also directly enter a field name without using the field selection function that was described earlier.

The field verification function has the following prototype:

```
int far PASCAL VerifyField(struct StrField far * field,
    int SortFieldNo);
```

This function is called with the first parameter pointing to a field structure. The second parameter tells if the field is being sorted on. If `SortFieldNo` is zero, the field is not a sort field. If `SortFieldNo` is nonzero, this field is being sorted. This function should return `TRUE` if the field is valid and `FALSE` if the field isn't valid. Typically, the `VerifyField()` function will take the field name and attempt to look it up in a list of fields that are valid for this report.

The example shown next loops through the `DataField` structure's members. When a match is found, the field structure is reinitialized (which ReportEase requires) and TRUE is returned. If no match is found, the field isn't valid and the function returns FALSE. Because the program allows sorting on any field, the `SortFieldNo` parameter can be ignored. If the program doesn't allow sorting of certain fields, the `VerifyField()` function should return FALSE for those fields.

```
int FAR PASCAL export VerifyField(
struct    StrField huge * field,
int       SortFieldNo)
{
int       i;  // Loop counter
int       nReturnCode = FALSE;   // Not found yet
// Verify the field as correct
// Return (TRUE) if field is valid and !TRUE if invalid

//   First, if the DataField[] structure is not initialized,
//   initialize it (happens when an existing report is
//   reopened in subsequent runs):

    if (nReportNumberFields == 0)
        InitDataField();


    for (i = 0; i < nReportNumberFields && !nReturnCode; i++)
    {
        if (_stricmp(DataField[0][i].name, field[0].name) == 0)
        {// Found a match!
            field[SortFieldNo].FieldId   = DataField[0][i].FieldId;
            field[SortFieldNo].FileId     = 0;
            field[SortFieldNo].width      = DataField[0][i].width;
            field[SortFieldNo].type       = DataField[0][i].type;
            field[SortFieldNo].DecPlaces = DataField[0][i].DecPlaces;
            nReturnCode                   = TRUE;   // Found it. Go home.
        }
    }
    return(nReturnCode);
}
```

The call to `InitDataField()` is made to initialize the `DataField` structure. This function is shown in Listing 12.17. The `InitDataField()` function shown sets up a printed report for a GIS-type application. This report example has a substantial number of fields.

Listing 12.17. INITDF.C: The `InitDataField()` function.

```
void InitDataField()
{// Init data fields. Should read from resources in actual code.
int        i;
nReportNumberFields = 0;


    strcpy(DataField[0][nReportNumberFields].name, "Basemap");
    DataField[0][nReportNumberFields].width = 15;
    DataField[0][nReportNumberFields].type = TYPE_TEXT;
    DataField[0][nReportNumberFields].DecPlaces = 0;
```

```c
for (i = 1; i < 8; i++)
{//    Dup the name/description parameters...
    DataField[0][i] = DataField[0][i - 1];
}

for (i = 0; i < MAX_FIELDS; i++)
{// Init the field IDs:
    DataField[0][i].FieldId        = i;
}

strcpy(DataField[0][++nReportNumberFields].name,  "BasemapName");
strcpy(DataField[0][++nReportNumberFields].name,  "Territory");
strcpy(DataField[0][++nReportNumberFields].name,  "TerritoryName");
strcpy(DataField[0][++nReportNumberFields].name,  "District");
strcpy(DataField[0][++nReportNumberFields].name,  "DistrictName");
strcpy(DataField[0][++nReportNumberFields].name,  "Region");
strcpy(DataField[0][++nReportNumberFields].name,  "RegionName");

strcpy(DataField[0][++nReportNumberFields].name,  "State");
DataField[0][nReportNumberFields].width = 2;
DataField[0][nReportNumberFields].type = TYPE_TEXT;
DataField[0][nReportNumberFields].DecPlaces = 0;

strcpy(DataField[0][++nReportNumberFields].name,  "Account");
DataField[0][nReportNumberFields].width = 3;
DataField[0][nReportNumberFields].type = TYPE_LOGICAL;
DataField[0][nReportNumberFields].DecPlaces = 0;

strcpy(DataField[0][++nReportNumberFields].name,  "AccountLocation");
DataField[0][nReportNumberFields].width = 15;
DataField[0][nReportNumberFields].type = TYPE_TEXT;
DataField[0][nReportNumberFields].DecPlaces = 0;

strcpy(DataField[0][++nReportNumberFields].name,  "AccountType");
DataField[0][nReportNumberFields].width = 15;
DataField[0][nReportNumberFields].type = TYPE_TEXT;
DataField[0][nReportNumberFields].DecPlaces = 0;

strcpy(DataField[0][++nReportNumberFields].name,  "InView");
DataField[0][nReportNumberFields].width = 3;
DataField[0][nReportNumberFields].type = TYPE_LOGICAL;
DataField[0][nReportNumberFields].DecPlaces = 0;

for (i = 0; i <20; ++i)
{//    Create DataVariable 1 - 20:
    if (DataVariable[i].bValidData && !DataVariable[i].bIsAFormula)
    {
        ++nReportNumberFields;
        DataField[0][nReportNumberFields].FieldId = i + 100;
        // 100 is flag for a data field
        DataField[0][nReportNumberFields].width = 10;
        DataField[0][nReportNumberFields].type = TYPE_DBL;
        DataField[0][nReportNumberFields].DecPlaces = 2;
        sprintf(DataField[0][nReportNumberFields].name,
            DataVariable[i].szDescription);
    }
}
```

continues

Listing 12.17. continued

```
    for (i = 0; i <20; ++i)
    {//    Create DataVariable 1 - 20:
        ++nReportNumberFields;  // Increment to first data field...then loop
        DataField[0][nReportNumberFields].FieldId = i + 100;
        // 100 is flag for a data field
        DataField[0][nReportNumberFields].width = 10;
        DataField[0][nReportNumberFields].type = TYPE_DBL;
        DataField[0][nReportNumberFields].DecPlaces = 2;
        sprintf(DataField[0][nReportNumberFields].name,
            "DataVariable%d", i + 1);
    }

    return;
}
```

After you've set up your `DataField` structure and written your `VerifyField()` and `UserFieldSelection()` functions, you must then set up the `StrForm` structure that is passed to the form editor. Listing 12.18 shows the `StrForm` structure.

Listing 12.18. STRFORM.H.

```
typedef struct _StrForm {
        int     x;      // Initial x position of the editing window.
                        // You may specify CW_USEDEFAULT to use default values.
        int     y;      // Initial y position of the editing window.
        int     width;  // Initial width of the window in device units.
                        // You may specify CW_USEDEFAULT to use default values.
        int     height; // Initial height of the editing window. When you
                        // use CW_USEDEFAULT for width, the height parameter is
                        // ingnored.*/

        int (FAR PASCAL _export *UserSelection)
                            (HWND, struct StrField huge *,int);
                        /* A pointer to the function returning the user-
                        selected field through the structure pointer.
                        Your application returns the chosen field through
                        the first parameter. The second argument indicates
                        the sort field number. If it is equal to zero,
                        it means that the field being sought is not a sort
                        field. The function returns a TRUE value if
                        successful.

                        When using ReportEase as a DLL, this pointer must
                        be passed using the MakeProcInstance function. Your
                        application must define this function as
                        exportable and include it in the EXPORT section
                        of the definition file.
                        */
```

```
        int (FAR PASCAL _export *VerifyField)(struct StrField huge *,int);
                            /* A pointer to the user routine that validates a
                            field name. The field name is passed to the routine
                            by the 'name' variable in the StrField structure.
                            This routine should also fill the 'type' variable
                            in the structure. The second argument indicates the
                            sort field number. If it is equal to zero, it means
                            that the field to verify is not a sort field. The
                            function returns TRUE to indicate a valid field.

                            When using ReportEase as a DLL, this pointer must
                            be passed using the MakeProcInstance function. Your
                            application must define this function as
                            exportable and include it in the EXPORT section
                            of the definition file.
                            */

        char file[130];    // Form filename. If an existing file is specified,
                           // the following fields are ignored.

        char DataSetName[20];/* (Specify for a new file) Your application can
                            specify a data set name that can be used to
                            associate the application data to the form. This
                            is an optional field. */

        BOOL    ShowMenu;    // Show the menu bar?
        BOOL    ShowHorBar;  // Show the horizonatal scroll bar
        BOOL    ShowVerBar;  // Show the vertical scroll bar

        HANDLE hInst;        // Handle of the current instances.
        HANDLE hPrevInst;    // Handle of the previous instances.
        HWND   hParentWnd;   // Handle to the parent window
        HWND   hFrWnd;       // Form main window handle; will be filled by
                             // RE later
        DWORD  style;        //  Editor window style
        char   FontTypeFace[32]; // Default type face, example:
                             // TmwRmn Courier, etc.

        LPCATCHBUF EndForm;  // Error return location
        BOOL       open;     // TRUE indicates an open window
                             // (parameter block in use)
        BOOL       modified; // TRUE when the file modified
                             // and needs to be saved
        }StrForm;
```

The StrForm structure is used to pass information to the ReportEase report editor. Contained in this structure is information such as the window defaults, the routines that are used to select and verify report variables, fonts, and other information. An example of using the StrForm structure is shown in Listing 12.19.

Listing 12.19. Using `StrForm`.

```
void    ReportSystem(HWND    hWndParent)
{// Now using STARREPT (derived from ReportEase Plus)
//    First, initialize the DataField structure

//    Initialize the report's columns
    InitDataField();

//    Got report filename. Now set up for the form generator.
    FormParam.x = CW_USEDEFAULT;
    FormParam.y = CW_USEDEFAULT;
    FormParam.width = CW_USEDEFAULT;
    FormParam.height = CW_USEDEFAULT;
    FormParam.UserSelection = UserFieldSelection;
    FormParam.VerifyField = VerifyField;
    strcpy(FormParam.file, ReportStuff.szFileName);
    strcpy(FormParam.DataSetName, "HUH");
    FormParam.ShowMenu = TRUE;
    FormParam.ShowHorBar = TRUE;
    FormParam.ShowVerBar = TRUE;
    FormParam.hInst = hInst;
    FormParam.hPrevInst = NULL;
    FormParam.hParentWnd = hWndParent;
    FormParam.hFrWnd = 0;
    FormParam.style=WS_OVERLAPPEDWINDOW;   // Editor window style
    FormParam.FontTypeFace[0] = '\0';
    FormParam.EndForm = NULL;
    FormParam.open = FALSE;
    FormParam.modified = FALSE;
```

Finally, the following code fragment (the final part of the `ReportSystem()` function) calls the form editor that the user can use to create or modify the report:

```
// It's set up. Now call the form generator:
    form(&FormParam);

    return;
}
```

The call to `form()` returns immediately, and the report editor module starts. The report editor has focus, but the user may set focus to the calling application if desired.

Printing Reports with ReportEase

After the user has created a report with ReportEase, the next step is to print the report. When ReportEase exits, it prompts the user to save the generated report so that the calling application doesn't need to worry about the details of saving the report definition.

Listing 12.20 shows the code used to initialize the report printer, sort the data, pass the records to the report printer, and clean up after printing the report. Reports may be printed either to the screen (in a print preview mode) or to an actual printer. When the report is printed to the screen, the report printer maintains a buffer of all the records in the report to allow the user to scroll forward and backward in the report.

Figure 12.10 shows the ReportEase report previewer with a sample report.

FIGURE 12.10.

ReportEase's report generator in screen preview mode.

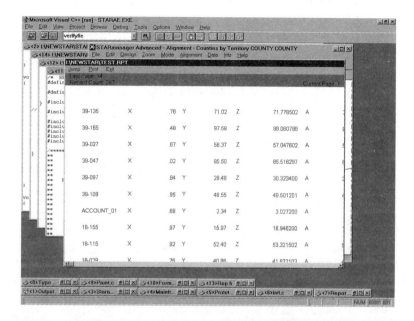

NOTE

When calling C code from a C++ application, you must "wrap" the C function prototypes in a C block, like this:

```
#ifdef   cplusplus
extern "C"
{
// C function prototypes
}
#endif  //  cplusplus
```

This tells the compiler and linker that the functions are C code and not C++.

Listing 12.20. REPPRINT.CPP: The report printer for ReportEase.

```
/*  REPPRINT.CPP */

#define  HAVEREPORT

#include "stdafx.h"
#include "STAR.H"

#include <time.h>
#include <stdio.h>
#include <stdlib.h>
```

continues

Listing 12.20. continued

```
#include <string.h>
#include <io.h>
#define REP_CPLUSPLUS extern "C"
#include "rep\rep.h"

#include "reportco.h"

/****************************************************************************
**
**        STAR: The Sales Territory Alignment Resource.
**
**        TITLE: REPPRINT.cpp
**
**    FUNCTION: Calls to ReportEase PLUS's report printer, to actually
**              print (to screen or printer) a report.
**
**      INPUTS: From the user
**
**     OUTPUTS: Report definition file
**
**     RETURNS: YES
**
**     WRITTEN: July 26, 1994
**
**       CALLS: ReportEase routines in STARREPT.DLL
**
**   CALLED BY: Star, from report, new/edit menu selection
**
**      AUTHOR: Peter D. Hipson
**
**       NOTES: For Windows 3.1+
**
**   COPYRIGHT 1990 - 1994 BY PETER D. HIPSON. All rights reserved.
**
****************************************************************************/

// LOCAL PROTOTYPES:

// END LOCALS

// Externs
extern  HWND    hDlgPrint;
extern  BOOL    bUserAbort;
extern  int  nCurrentSelection;
extern  WORD    wReportType;

int FAR PASCAL _export VerifyField(
    struct StrField huge * field, int SortFieldNo);

// End externs

// Defines
#define MAX_FILES   1   /* One file, the database...   */
#define MAX_FIELDS  30  /* 30 possible fields          */

// End defines
```

```
#pragma pack(1)

#ifdef __cplusplus
extern "C" { // De-mangle so that .C code can reference this variable:
#endif

StrRep  Report;

#ifdef __cplusplus
}
#endif

extern StrForm  FormParam;   // Defined in RepSys.CPP
#pragma pack()

void    ReportPrinter()
{// from ReportEase Plus
struct  StrField far *fld;
BOOL    bHaveRegions;
BOOL    bHaveDistricts;
BOOL    bHaveTerritories;
BOOL    bHaveGeocodes;
BOOL    bUseThisRecord;
DWORD   dwOldRegion;
DWORD   dwOldDistrict;
DWORD   dwOldTerritory;
DWORD   dwNextRecord;
int     i;
int     nErrorOccured = FALSE;

REPORTSORT  ReportSort;
char        szSortFileName[256];
CString     CState;

    HourGlass(TRUE);

    memset(&Report, '\0', sizeof(Report));

//  Save our filename and set a few other parameters:

    strcpy(Report.file, ReportStuff.szFileName);

    if (ReportStuff.nScreen == 0)  // Set the report destination
        Report.device='S';
    else
    {
        Report.device='P';
        HourGlass(TRUE);
    }

    if (FormParam.width == 0 && FormParam.height == 0)
    {// Specify the window coordinates for screen. New run, no default!
        RECT    rect;
        ::GetClientRect(hWndView, &rect);
        ::ClientToScreen(hWndView, (POINT *)&rect.left);
        ::ClientToScreen(hWndView, (POINT *)&rect.right);
        Report.x = rect.left;
        Report.y = rect.top;
```

continues

Listing 12.20. continued

```
        Report.width = rect.right - rect.left;
        Report.height = rect.bottom - rect.top;
    }
    else
    {// Report generator ran already; have defaults.
        Report.x=FormParam.x;
        Report.y=FormParam.y;
        Report.width=FormParam.width;      // Screen only (3/4)
        Report.height=FormParam.height;    // Screen only (4/4)
    }

    Report.hInst = hInst;
    Report.hParentWnd = hWnd;

    if (RepInit(&Report)!=0)  // Initialize ReportEase system...
    {// This is what happens if it fails:
        TRACE("RepInit()... failed!\n");
        return;
    }

//  For each record in VIEW, process:
    (void)GetTempFileName(0, "STR", 0, szSortFileName);

    CFile sortfile;
    TRY
    {
        sortfile.Open(szSortFileName,
            CFile::modeCreate | CFile::modeReadWrite);
    }
    CATCH( CFileException, e )
    {
        #ifdef _DEBUG
            afxDump << "File could not be opened " << e->m_cause << "\n";
        #endif
    }
    END_CATCH

// Figure out if it's a Region, District, Territory, or Geocode level report!
    bHaveRegions = FALSE;
    bHaveDistricts = FALSE;
    bHaveTerritories = FALSE;
    bHaveGeocodes = FALSE;

    fld = Report.field;

    for (i = 0; i < Report.TotalFields; i++)
    {
        if (fld[i].source == SRC_APPL)
        {
            switch(fld[i].FieldId)
            {// Need #defines here!
                case 0: // Basemap
                    bHaveRegions = TRUE;
                    bHaveDistricts = TRUE;
                    bHaveTerritories = TRUE;
```

```
                        bHaveGeocodes = TRUE;
                        break;
                case 1: // Basemap name
                        bHaveRegions = TRUE;
                        bHaveDistricts = TRUE;
                        bHaveTerritories = TRUE;
                        bHaveGeocodes = TRUE;
                        break;
                case 2: // Territory
                        bHaveRegions = TRUE;
                        bHaveDistricts = TRUE;
                        bHaveTerritories = TRUE;
                        break;
                case 3: // Territory name
                        bHaveRegions = TRUE;
                        bHaveDistricts = TRUE;
                        bHaveTerritories = TRUE;
                        break;
                case 4: // District
                        bHaveRegions = TRUE;
                        bHaveDistricts = TRUE;
                        break;
                case 5: // District name
                        bHaveRegions = TRUE;
                        bHaveDistricts = TRUE;
                        break;
                case 6: // Region
                        bHaveRegions = TRUE;
                        break;
                case 7: // Region name
                        bHaveRegions = TRUE;
                        break;
                default:
                        break;
            }
        }
    }

    if (!bHaveRegions && !bHaveDistricts &&
        !bHaveTerritories && !bHaveGeocodes)
    {// If none, give them all (a strange report, but then...)
        bHaveRegions = TRUE;
        bHaveDistricts = TRUE;
        bHaveTerritories = TRUE;
        bHaveGeocodes = TRUE;
    }
//===================
    dwOldRegion = 0;
    dwOldDistrict = 0;
    dwOldTerritory = 0;

    if (ReportStuff.bReportOnView)
    {// Force to in view for testing!
        dwNextRecord = GetFirstInProblem(&Info.ipSource);
    }
    else
    {
        dwNextRecord = GetFirstInDatabase(&Info.ipSource);
```

continues

Listing 12.20. continued

```
    }

    while(dwNextRecord)
    {// Now process this record:
        bUseThisRecord = TRUE;  // Always use this record, unless:

        if (bHaveTerritories && dwOldTerritory !=
            Info.ipSource.gcTerritory.dwSelf)
            bUseThisRecord = TRUE;

        if (bHaveTerritories && dwOldTerritory !=
            Info.ipSource.gcTerritory.dwSelf)
            bUseThisRecord = TRUE;

        if (bHaveDistricts && dwOldDistrict !=
            Info.ipSource.gcDistrict.dwSelf)
            bUseThisRecord = TRUE;

        if (bHaveRegions && dwOldRegion !=  Info.ipSource.gcRegion.dwSelf)
            bUseThisRecord = TRUE;

        if (Info.ipSource.gcGeocode.dwSelf == 0)  // Never use <none> records
            bUseThisRecord = FALSE;

        if (ReportStuff.bExcludeUnassigned &&
            Info.ipSource.gcTerritory.Polygon.bStateRecord)
        {
            bUseThisRecord = FALSE;
        }

        dwOldRegion = Info.ipSource.gcRegion.dwSelf;
        dwOldDistrict = Info.ipSource.gcDistrict.dwSelf;
        dwOldTerritory = Info.ipSource.gcTerritory.dwSelf;

        if (bUseThisRecord)
        {
            memset(&ReportSort, '\0', sizeof(ReportSort));
            ReportSort.gcGeocode = Info.ipSource.gcGeocode;
            strcpy(ReportSort.szTerritory,
                Info.ipSource.gcTerritory.Polygon.szGeocode);
            strcpy(ReportSort.szTerritoryName,
                Info.ipSource.gcTerritory.Polygon.szGeocodeName);
            strcpy(ReportSort.szDistrict,
                Info.ipSource.gcDistrict.Polygon.szGeocode);
            strcpy(ReportSort.szDistrictName,
                Info.ipSource.gcDistrict.Polygon.szGeocodeName);
            strcpy(ReportSort.szRegion,
                Info.ipSource.gcRegion.Polygon.szGeocode);
            strcpy(ReportSort.szRegionName,
                Info.ipSource.gcRegion.Polygon.szGeocodeName);
            Info.ipSource.gcGeocode.Polygon.bInCurrentProblem =
                Info.ipSource.gcTerritory.Polygon.bInCurrentProblem;
            if (Info.ipSource.gcGeocode.bAccount)
            {
                GetWorkFileRecord(Info.ipSource.gcGeocode.dwLocatedIn,
                    &Info.ipSource.gcAccount);
```

```
                strcpy(ReportSort.szAccountContainer,
                    Info.ipSource.gcAccount.Polygon.szGeocode);
            }

            TRY
            {
                sortfile.Write(&ReportSort, sizeof(ReportSort));
            }
            CATCH( CFileException, e )
            {
                #ifdef _DEBUG
                    afxDump << "Cannot write to file " << e->m_cause << "\n";
                #endif
            }
            END_CATCH
        }
        // Get next record (if any) in database/view:
        if (ReportStuff.bReportOnView)
        {
            dwNextRecord = GetNextInProblem(&Info.ipSource, FALSE);
        }
        else
        {
            dwNextRecord = GetNextInDatabase(&Info.ipSource);
        }
    }

//  Sort the workfile. Will have to close it, then reopen after sort:
//  Do actual sort, calling a file sort function:

    if (Report.TotalSortFields > 0)
    {// Then report must be sorted:
        sortfile.Close();

        SortReport(szSortFileName);

        TRY
        {
            sortfile.Open(szSortFileName, CFile::modeReadWrite);
        }
        CATCH( CFileException, e )
        {
            #ifdef _DEBUG
                afxDump << "File could not be opened " << e->m_cause << "\n";
            #endif
        }
        END_CATCH
    }

//  Done with sort. Now read each record in workfile, then do 'em:

    sortfile.SeekToBegin();

    fld = Report.field;

    HourGlass(FALSE);

    while (!nErrorOccured &&
```

continues

Listing 12.20. continued

```
            sortfile.Read(&ReportSort, sizeof(ReportSort)) == sizeof(ReportSort))
    {
        for (i = 0; i < Report.TotalFields; i++)
        {
            if (fld[i].source == SRC_APPL)
            {
                switch(fld[i].FieldId)
                {// Need #defines here!
                    case 0: // Basemap
                        strcpy(fld[i].CharData,
                            ReportSort.gcGeocode.Polygon.szGeocode);
                        break;
                    case 1: // Basemap name
                        strcpy(fld[i].CharData,
                            ReportSort.gcGeocode.Polygon.szGeocodeName);
                        break;
                    case 2: // Territory
                        strcpy(fld[i].CharData, ReportSort.szTerritory);
                        break;
                    case 3: // Territory name
                        strcpy(fld[i].CharData, ReportSort.szTerritoryName);
                        break;
                    case 4: // District
                        strcpy(fld[i].CharData, ReportSort.szDistrict);
                        break;
                    case 5: // District name
                        strcpy(fld[i].CharData, ReportSort.szDistrictName);
                        break;
                    case 6: // Region
                        strcpy(fld[i].CharData, ReportSort.szRegion);
                        break;
                    case 7: // Region name
                        strcpy(fld[i].CharData, ReportSort.szRegionName);
                        break;
                    case 8: // State
                        CState.LoadString(
                            ReportSort.gcGeocode.Polygon.wStateFIPS +
                            ID_SHORTNAME);
                        strcpy(fld[i].CharData, (const char *)CState);
                        break;
                    case 9:
                        if (ReportSort.gcGeocode.bAccount)
                            fld[i].NumData = 1;
                        else
                            fld[i].NumData = 0;
                        break;
                    case 10:
                        strcpy(fld[i].CharData, ReportSort.szAccountContainer);
                        break;
                    case 11:
                        strcpy(fld[i].CharData, (const char *)
                            GetAccountString(&ReportSort.gcGeocode));
                        break;
                    case 12: // Set true if in view!
                        if (ReportSort.gcGeocode.Polygon.bInCurrentProblem)
                            fld[i].NumData = 1;
```

```
                else
                    fld[i].NumData = 0;
                break;
            default: // Check for datafields (set to >= 100):
                if (fld[i].FieldId > 99)
                { // Finally, the datacolumns:
                    if (ReportSort.gcGeocode.fDataValue
                        [fld[i].FieldId - 100] >
                        Info.fMissingData)
                    {// Not missing data... Send true value
                        fld[i].DblData =
                            ReportSort.gcGeocode.fDataValue
                            [fld[i].FieldId - 100];
                    }
                    else
                    {// It's missing data. Force to zero...
                        fld[i].DblData = 0.0;
                    }
                }
                break;
            }
        }
    }

    if (RepRec() != 0)
    {// Something wrong!
        break;
    }
}

sortfile.Close();  // Close the workfile

// Delete the workfile, as it's not needed anymore:
unlink(szSortFileName);

RepExit();  // Print footers and exit
if (ReportStuff.nScreen != 0)  // Set the report destination
{
    HourGlass(FALSE);
}
return;
}
```

The process of printing the report consists of five steps, which are easy to implement.

First you must initialize the StrRep structure. This structure contains the initialization information that the report printer uses to initialize itself. This structure is much like the report editor's StrForm structure. Here is the StrRep structure initialization:

```
memset(&Report, '\0', sizeof(Report));

// Save our filename and set a few other parameters:

    strcpy(Report.file, ReportStuff.szFileName);

    if (ReportStuff.nScreen == 0) // Set the report destination
```

```
        Report.device='S';
    else
    {
        Report.device='P';
        HourGlass(TRUE);
    }

    if (FormParam.width == 0 && FormParam.height == 0)
    {// Specify the window coordinates for screen. New run; no default!
        RECT    rect;
        ::GetClientRect(hWndView, &rect);
        ::ClientToScreen(hWndView, (POINT *)&rect.left);
        ::ClientToScreen(hWndView, (POINT *)&rect.right);

        Report.x = rect.left;
        Report.y = rect.top;
        Report.width = rect.right - rect.left;
        Report.height = rect.bottom - rect.top;
    }
    else
    {// Report generator ran already; have defaults
        Report.x=FormParam.x;
        Report.y=FormParam.y;
        Report.width=FormParam.width;       // Screen only (3/4)
        Report.height=FormParam.height;  // Screen only (4/4)
    }

    Report.hInst = hInst;
    Report.hParentWnd = hWnd;
```

After the `StrRep` structure is filled, a call to the report printer initialization function, `RepInit()`, is made. The `RepInit()` function returns a Boolean value of `FALSE` if it's successful:

```
if (RepInit(&Report)!=0)  // Initialize ReportEase system...
    {// This is what happens if it fails: Give error message:
        TRACE("RepInit()... failed!\n");
        return;
    }
```

If `RepInit()` is successful, the next step is to prepare the data for the report. This preparation is a multistep process. First, the data must be arranged in records. The easiest way to do this is to create a temporary work file (either in memory or as a disk file), which we will call the "sort file," to hold the records that will be created. After the work file that contains the report's records has been created, the file can be sorted if there are sort fields. After the work file has been sorted, the records can be passed to the report printing routine one record at a time. The following code fragment shows the work file creation process. A `CFile` object is used for the sort file:

```
//  For each record in VIEW, process:
    (void)GetTempFileName(0, "STR", 0, szSortFileName);

    CFile sortfile;
    TRY
    {
        sortfile.Open(szSortFileName,
            CFile::modeCreate ¦ CFile::modeReadWrite);
    }
```

```
      CATCH( CFileException, e )
      {// No workfile, so end the report. Dump for the programmer!
          #ifdef _DEBUG
              afxDump << "File could not be opened " << e->m_cause << "\n";
          #endif
      }
      END_CATCH
```

After the sort file has been created, a record is added to the file for each line in the report. The following code fragment (edited to make it easier to read) shows this process. The functions GetFirstInDatabase() and GetNextInDatabase() get records from the application's master database; these records supply the necessary information for the report. The fld structure has a record for each field in the report. Your application needs to concern itself only with fields that have the SRC_APPL attribute. The SRC_APPL fields are the fields that your application will provide for the report. All other fields will be generated automatically by ReportEase.

```
      dwNextRecord = GetFirstInDatabase(&Info.ipSource);

      while(dwNextRecord)
      {// Now process this record:
          bUseThisRecord = TRUE; // Always use this record!
//        Add tests to see if the record may not be used here.
//        set bUseThisRecord to FALSE if the record is really
//        not usable:

          if (bUseThisRecord)
          {// This record is really wanted:
              memset(&ReportSort, '\0', sizeof(ReportSort));
              ReportSort.gcGeocode = Info.ipSource.gcGeocode;
              strcpy(ReportSort.szTerritory,
                  Info.ipSource.gcTerritory.Polygon.szGeocode);
              strcpy(ReportSort.szTerritoryName,
                  Info.ipSource.gcTerritory.Polygon.szGeocodeName);
              strcpy(ReportSort.szDistrict,
                  Info.ipSource.gcDistrict.Polygon.szGeocode);
              strcpy(ReportSort.szDistrictName,
                  Info.ipSource.gcDistrict.Polygon.szGeocodeName);
              strcpy(ReportSort.szRegion,
                  Info.ipSource.gcRegion.Polygon.szGeocode);
              strcpy(ReportSort.szRegionName,
                  Info.ipSource.gcRegion.Polygon.szGeocodeName);
              Info.ipSource.gcGeocode.Polygon.bInCurrentProblem =
                  Info.ipSource.gcTerritory.Polygon.bInCurrentProblem;

              TRY
              {
                  sortfile.Write(&ReportSort, sizeof(ReportSort));
              }
              CATCH( CFileException, e )
              {// Could not write the file... Disk full?
                  #ifdef _DEBUG
                      afxDump << "Sortfile Write Error " << e->m_cause << "\n";
                  #endif
              }
              END_CATCH
          }
```

```
        // Get next record (if any) in database/view:
        dwNextRecord = GetNextInDatabase(&Info.ipSource);
    }
```

In this code fragment, all possible field information is saved to the sort file and sorted. If the report were large, the program could have saved disk space by saving only the fields that were actually used in the report.

After the sort file has had all the records for the report written to it, it must be sorted. This is necessary only if there actually are sort fields in the report (not all reports are sorted). You can check for the presence of sort fields by using a piece of code such as the following. The StrRep member variable TotalSortFields indicates how many sort fields are present in the report.

```
if (Report.TotalSortFields > 0)
{
    sortfile.Close();

    SortReport(szSortFileName);

    TRY
    {// Try to reopen the sorted file:
        sortfile.Open(szSortFileName, CFile::modeReadWrite);
    }
    CATCH( CFileException, e )
    {// Could not reopen the sorted file:
        #ifdef _DEBUG
            afxDump << "File could not be opened " << e->m_cause << "\n";
        #endif
    }
    END_CATCH
}
```

After the records for the report have been sorted, they are then passed in order to the report printer routine. The function that accepts the records for the report is called RepRec(). Each variable in the report is contained in an array structure that is accessible through the StrRep structure. An array pointer called fld is created and is used to access this structure.

```
while (!nErrorOccured &&
    sortfile.Read(&ReportSort, sizeof(ReportSort)) == sizeof(ReportSort))
{
    for (i = 0; i < Report.TotalFields; i++)
    {
        if (fld[i].source == SRC_APPL)
        {
            switch(fld[i].FieldId)
            {// Need #defines here!
                case 0: // Basemap
                    strcpy(fld[i].CharData,
                        ReportSort.gcGeocode.Polygon.szGeocode);
                    break;
                case 1: // Basemap name
                    strcpy(fld[i].CharData,
                        ReportSort.gcGeocode.Polygon.szGeocodeName);
                    break;
                case 2: // Territory
```

```
        strcpy(fld[i].CharData, ReportSort.szTerritory);
        break;
case 3: // Territory name
        strcpy(fld[i].CharData, ReportSort.szTerritoryName);
        break;
case 4: // District
        strcpy(fld[i].CharData, ReportSort.szDistrict);
        break;
case 5: // District name
        strcpy(fld[i].CharData, ReportSort.szDistrictName);
        break;
case 6: // Region
        strcpy(fld[i].CharData, ReportSort.szRegion);
        break;
case 7: // Region name
        strcpy(fld[i].CharData, ReportSort.szRegionName);
        break;
case 8: // State
        CState.LoadString(
            ReportSort.gcGeocode.Polygon.wStateFIPS +
            ID_SHORTNAME);

        strcpy(fld[i].CharData, (const char *)Cstate);
        break;
case 9:
        if (ReportSort.gcGeocode.bAccount)
            fld[i].NumData = 1;
        else
            fld[i].NumData = 0;
        break;
case 10:
        strcpy(fld[i].CharData, ReportSort.szAccountContainer);
        break;
case 11:
        strcpy(fld[i].CharData, (const char *)
            GetAccountString(&ReportSort.gcGeocode));
        break;
case 12: // Set true if in view!
        if (ReportSort.gcGeocode.Polygon.bInCurrentProblem)
            fld[i].NumData = 1;
        else
            fld[i].NumData = 0;
        break;

default: // Check for datafields (set to >= 100):
        if (fld[i].FieldId > 99)
        { // Finally, the datacolumns:
            if (ReportSort.gcGeocode.fDataValue
                [fld[i].FieldId - 100] >
                Info.fMissingData)
            {// Not missing data... Send true value
                fld[i].DblData =
                    ReportSort.gcGeocode.fDataValue
                    [fld[i].FieldId - 100];
            }
            else
            {// It's missing data. Force to zero...
                fld[i].DblData = 0.0;
```

```
                    }
                }
                break;
            }
        }
    }

    if (RepRec() != 0)
    {// Something wrong! Could not add record to report!
        break;
    }
}
```

The process, for each record in the report, is to fill in each variable in the record (using the `fld` pointer, which points to an array of structures for each field in the record). After each record is built, it is passed to the `RepRec()` function.

As the following code shows, after each record is passed to the report printer, the report is finished by closing the sort file and calling the `RepExit()` function. `RepExit()` performs the final cleanup, such as printing final report totals. If the report is being sent to the printer, ReportEase is finished. However, if the report is being viewed in screen preview mode, ReportEase will be finished when the user closes the screen preview window.

```
    sortfile.Close();  // Close the workfile

//  Delete the workfile, as it's not needed anymore:
    unlink(szSortFileName);

    RepExit();   // Print footers and exit

    return;  // To caller
}
```

As the preceding code shows, ReportEase is designed to be integrated directly into your application. It can be used as a DLL file, or you can incorporate the ReportEase source directly into your project. One advantage of including ReportEase directly into your project is that you will have a program that is somewhat easier to debug. After you have fully debugged your program, you might want to consider placing ReportEase in a DLL. You might find that ReportEase doesn't always do things the way you want. The advantage of ReportEase's source is apparent here: You can modify the ReportEase source to make it more tightly integrated with your product. With ReportEase it's possible to create a reporting functionality in your program that is very professional and flexible, with a minimum of effort.

Using ReportSmith with Visual C++ Applications

ReportSmith works differently than ReportEase. For one thing, ReportSmith is primarily a stand-alone report generator, so it's more difficult to directly incorporate into an application.

ReportSmith uses ODBC to connect to data sources. If your database application uses ODBC to access a data source, ReportSmith can also access this data source and print reports on it.

Your application can use DDE to communicate with ReportSmith. ReportSmith will run as a DDE server and can respond to commands issued by your DDE client application.

Most of the documentation provided with ReportSmith deals with Visual Basic. Programmers using Visual C++ must try to convert the documentation and sample code provided by Borland to Visual C++-compatible code. Generally, your application must use WM_DDE_... messages to perform this communication.

At the time this book was written, the basic version of ReportSmith sold for about $100 but didn't include a runtime module. This isn't a limitation for in-house developers, but it does require your customers to own a copy of ReportSmith. The SQL version of ReportSmith, which sells for about $200 and is distributed with Borland's Delphi version 1.0, does include a distributable runtime module. This runtime module lets your users view and save a report but not edit it. The module has the same DDE links as the full version. ReportSmith is a powerful report generator whose cost isn't difficult to justify.

Figure 12.11 shows ReportSmith in report edit mode. ReportSmith doesn't have a screen print preview mode. Instead, the report edit mode lets you page through each page of the report and modify any page. This is very useful when the report is complex and the layout might not fit well on all pages. Figure 12.12 shows the second page of the report.

FIGURE 12.11.

ReportSmith editing the first page of a report.

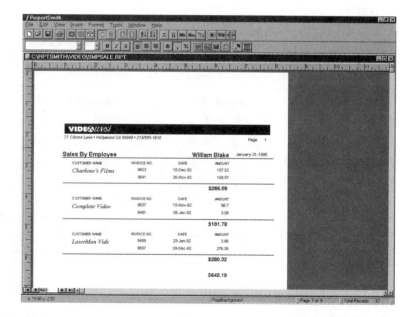

FIGURE 12.12.

ReportSmith editing the second page of a report.

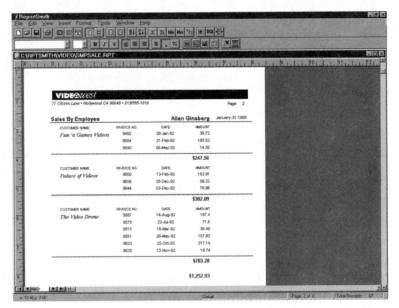

Summary

This chapter covered Crystal Reports, which is included with Visual C++ 4, and two other report generators, ReportEase (from Sub Systems, Inc.) and ReportSmith (from Borland). You saw examples of how to use both Crystal Reports and ReportEase.

This chapter also showed you how to add Crystal Reports to an existing Visual C++ project when using the Crystal Reports AppWizard isn't practical.

Visual C++ 4's inclusion of Crystal Reports has made the inclusion of professional-quality reporting facilities in applications much easier. However, Crystal Reports is an ODBC-based product that will accept input only from an ODBC data source.

This chapter completes Part III of this book. Up to this point, the subject matter of this book has been introductory in nature. The chapters in Part IV, "Advanced Programming with Visual C++," expand on the topics presented in Parts I, II, and III and introduce some of the more complex issues of database-application design with Visual C++, such as using OLE for interprocess communication.

IV

Advanced Programming with Visual C++

13

Understanding MFC's DAO Classes

Until Microsoft created Visual C++ 4, database programmers had some difficulty justifying Visual C++ as a mainstream database development platform. Visual C++'s sole support for database developers was ODBC. Visual C++ didn't support the more powerful (and useful) Microsoft Jet database engine. In fact, Visual C++ programmers often were told by Visual Basic programmers that they had a better database development platform. Today, with Visual C++ 4, Visual C++ programmers are no longer at such a disadvantage. They now have access to the Microsoft Jet database engine and DAO (Database Access Objects).

> **WARNING**
>
> The DAO database classes are meant for single-threaded operation only. Don't try to utilize these classes in more than one thread at one time.

With Visual C++ 4, the DAO database classes are considered distinct from the MFC ODBC database classes. All of the DAO database class names have a prefix of CDao. Usually the DAO classes are more powerful than the ODBC classes. DAO classes use the Microsoft Jet database engine to access data. In turn, the Microsoft Jet database engine uses ODBC drivers to access data that isn't supported directly. The DAO classes also support the Data Definition Language (DDL) operations—for example, operations for creating databases and adding tables and fields via the classes—all without having to call DAO directly.

This chapter documents the new MFC classes that support the DAO interface. These classes (seven main new classes and several more supporting classes and structures) are very similar to their ODBC database counterparts, such as CDatabase and CRecordset.

Generally, the majority of Visual C++ database applications will be written using AppWizard and will be expanded by the programmer to become complete, working database applications. It's possible to write a database application from scratch using the DAO database classes—and a few programmers do. However, neither Microsoft nor the authors recommend doing this. With this in mind, your database application will have a few of the classes included by AppWizard (these classes are described next). During the development cycle, you will probably add other classes.

The MFC classes for DAO are like all other MFC classes. They serve as wrappers, encapsulating DAO's basic functionality. For example:

- The CDaoWorkspace class encapsulates the functionality of the DAO Workspace object.
- The CDaoRecordset class encapsulates the functionality of the DAO Recordset object.
- The CDaoDatabase class encapsulates the functionality of the DAO Database object.

This process continues through the other DAO MFC classes.

Not all of the DAO functionality is encapsulated in the DAO MFC classes. You'll find that the major DAO objects are supported, but some objects, such as fields, indexes, parameters, and relations, aren't directly supported by the DAO MFC objects.

NOTE

There are three technical papers (called Technical Notes) specific to DAO:

TN053   Writing Custom DFX Routines for DAO Database Classes

TN054   Calling DAO Directly While Using MFC DAO Classes

TN055   Migrating MFC ODBC Database Class Applications to MFC DAO Classes

NOTE

Technical Note 54 (in the Visual C++ Books Online, see Visual C++ Books, MFC 4.0, MFC Technical Notes) has an example of using nonencapsulated DAO functionality in an MFC application.

Table 13.1 shows a mapping of DAO objects to MFC classes. The Comments and Related ODBC Classes column lists the corresponding ODBC class when applicable.

Table 13.1. The MFC-to-DAO object map.

MFC Class	DAO Object	Comments and Related ODBC Classes
CDaoWorkspace	Workspace	Manages the transaction space. Provides the Microsoft Jet database engine access.
CDaoDatabase	Database	Represents a connection to a specific database. Similar to CDatabase.
CDaoTableDef	Tabledef	Determines and manipulates the structure of a given table.
CDaoQueryDef	Querydef	Saves queries in a database.
CDaoRecordset	Recordset	Manages the result set, a set of records based on a table or selected by a query. Similar to CRecordset.
CDaoException	Error	MFC responds to all DAO errors by throwing exceptions of this type.
CDaoFieldExchange	None	Manages the exchange of data between a record in the database and the field data members of a recordset. Similar to CFieldExchange.

The DAO MFC Classes

The following sections document the DAO MFC classes by showing significant member functions and giving examples of usage.

As I mentioned earlier, some of the DAO MFC classes have ODBC analogues. This makes it easier to convert ODBC applications to use the DAO MFC classes. Generally, if you're unsure whether you should use DAO or ODBC, you should choose DAO to base your application on if the underlying database structure is either Access or one of the database structures that DAO supports directly (such as FoxPro).

> **NOTE**
>
> All DAO functions require the DAO header. Use the statement #include <afxdao.h>. When you use AppWizard to create an application, the #include is added automatically.

> **NOTE**
>
> See the DAO MFC documentation for more information about each of the DAO MFC classes. Simply search for the class name in the Books Online in Visual C++.

CDaoWorkspace

The CDaoWorkspace object is the highest object in the DAO hierarchy. It represents the DAO Workspace object. The DAO workspace defines the session for the user. It contains open databases and support for simultaneous transactions.

The CDaoWorkspace object manages named database sessions (from initial logon to logoff) for a single user. This database may be password protected. Generally, an application will use a single workspace. With AppWizard applications, it's unnecessary to create an explicit Workspace object. If your application needs multiple sessions, you can create additional Workspace objects. For each Workspace object, there may be more than one open database object at any given time. Under MFC's implementation, the workspace is basically a manager of transactions.

The CDaoWorkspace class provides the following functionality:

- It provides explicit access to a default workspace. This default workspace is created by initializing the database engine. Typically, you would use CDaoWorkspace's default workspace implicitly by creating DAO database and recordset objects.

■ It provides a transaction space where transactions will be applied to all databases that are open in the workspace. There are no restrictions in creating additional workspaces to manage separate transaction spaces.

■ It provides the interface to many of the properties of the Microsoft Jet database engine. The database engine can be initialized by opening or creating a workspace. The database engine can also be initialized by calling a static class member function before an open or create call.

■ It provides access to the Workspaces collection of the database engine. All active workspaces that have been appended to it will be stored in the Workspaces collection. It's also possible to create and work with workspaces without having to append a workspace to a Workspaces collection.

The DAO MFC classes don't implement the security control Users and Groups collections. When security is a concern, you will need to provide the necessary interface using direct calls to the underlying DAO interface.

NOTE

For information on accessing the underlying DAO interface, go to Books Online and search for the topic Technical Note 54.

The CDaoWorkspace call may be used to do the following things:

■ Open the default workspace explicitly. Typically, the opening of the default workspace is implicit—for example, when you open a new CDaoDatabase or CDaoRecordset object. However, a situation might arise where you have to access the default workspace explicitly—for example, to access database engine properties or the Workspaces collection.

■ Create a new workspace. If you want to add new workspaces, you would call Append.

■ Open an existing workspace that is in the Workspaces collection.

In order to use CDaoWorkspace to create a new workspace that doesn't exist in the Workspaces collection, use the CDaoWorkspace.Create() member function. With CDaoWorkspace, workspace objects won't persist between Microsoft Jet database engine sessions. If your application links MFC statically (that is, you link the MFC code using a static library rather than a DLL), when the application ends, the Microsoft Jet database engine will still be initialized. However, if the application uses MFC using the MFC DLL, the Microsoft Jet database engine will be uninitialized when the MFC DLL is unloaded.

Use the Open() member function to open an existing workspace. Use the Close() member function to close a workspace session. When Close() is called, all databases that haven't already been closed will be closed. Also, all uncommitted transactions will be rolled back (discarded).

DAO is used to manage transactions at the workspace level. As such, any transactions to workspaces with more than one open database will be applied to all open databases. For example, if there are two databases with uncommitted updates, and there is a call to CommitTrans(), all of the updates are committed, regardless of which database the changes are being applied to. When it's necessary to limit your transactions to one of a number of open databases, you must create a separate workspace object for the database to which you wish to limit your transactions.

Your application will use the DAO default workspace implicitly when the following events occur:

■ When a new CDaoDatabase object is created without using an existing CDaoWorkspace object, CDaoWorkspace will create a temporary workspace object for you. This temporary workspace will correspond to DAO's default workspace. This is true even when done with multiple databases—all the database objects will be associated with the default workspace. The database's workspace may then be accessed using the CDaoDatabase member.

■ If a CDaoRecordset is created that doesn't have a pointer to a CDaoDatabase object supplied to it, MFC will create a temporary CDaoDatabase DAO object. MFC will also create a temporary Workspace object. The database and its workspace may be accessed using the CDaoRecordset data member.

The CDaoWorkspace class provides a host of other database operations, such as repairing corrupted databases or compacting databases. Table 13.2 lists the members of the CDaoWorkspace class.

Table 13.2. The CDaoWorkspace class members.

Member	Description
Data Members	
m_pDAOWorkspace	A pointer to the basic underlying DAO workspace object.
Construction	
CDaoWorkspace()	A constructor for the CDaoWorkspace object. After creating the CDaoWorkspace object, you must call either Create() or Open().
Attributes	
GetIsolateODBCTrans()	Returns a value used to indicate whether multiple transactions that involve the same ODBC data source are isolated.
GetName()	Returns the user-defined name for the Workspace object.
GetUserName()	Returns the user name (workspace owner) specified when the workspace was created.
IsOpen()	Returns a nonzero value if the workspace is open.

Member	Description
SetIsolateODBCTrans()	Specifies whether multiple transactions that involve the same ODBC data source will be isolated.
	Operations
Append()	Appends a newly created workspace to the database engine's Workspaces collection.
BeginTrans()	Begins a new transaction. The new transaction will apply to all databases open in the workspace.
Close()	Closes the workspace and all of the objects it contains. If there are any pending transactions, they are rolled back (discarded).
CommitTrans()	Completes the current transaction and saves the specified changes.
CompactDatabase()	Compacts (or duplicates) the database.
Create()	Creates a new DAO Workspace object.
GetDatabaseCount()	Returns a value that indicates the number of DAO Database objects in the workspace's Databases collection.
GetDatabaseInfo()	Returns information about a specified DAO database defined in the workspace's Databases collection.
GetWorkspaceCount()	Returns the number of DAO Workspace objects in the database engine's Workspaces collection.
GetWorkspaceInfo()	Returns information about a specified DAO workspace defined in the database engine's Workspaces collection.
Open()	Explicitly opens a Workspace object associated with DAO's default workspace.
RepairDatabase()	Attempts to repair a damaged database.
Rollback()	Ends the current transaction. Any changes won't be saved.
Idle()	Allows the database engine to perform background tasks.
	Database Engine Properties
GetVersion()	Returns a string that contains the version of the database engine associated with the workspace.
GetIniPath()	Returns the location of the Microsoft Jet database engine's initialization settings in the Windows registry.
GetLoginTimeout()	Returns the number of seconds before an error occurs when the user attempts to log in to an ODBC database.

continues

Table 13.2. continued

Member	Description
	Database Engine Properties
SetDefaultPassword()	Sets the password that the database engine uses when a workspace object is created without a specific password.
SetDefaultUser()	Sets the user name that the database engine uses when a workspace object is created without a specific user name.
SetIniPath()	Sets the location of the Microsoft Jet database engine's initialization settings in the Windows registry.

CDaoDatabase

The CDaoDatabase object is used to represent the connection to a database (from the CDaoWorkspace object) through which you can operate on the database's data.

> **NOTE**
>
> For more information on which database formats are supported, refer to the CDaoWorkspace::GetName() member function in the Visual C++ Books Online.

More than one CDaoDatabase object may be active at a given time in a given CDaoWorkspace object. The workspace maintains a collection of open database objects called the Databases collection. For more information, see the section "CDaoWorkspace."

You can create CDaoDatabase database objects implicitly when you create Recordset objects. You also can create a CDaoDatabase object explicitly. If you want to use an existing database explicitly with CDaoDatabase, you can do one of the following:

- You can construct a CDaoDatabase object and pass it a pointer to an already open CDaoWorkspace object.
- You can create a CDaoDatabase object without specifying the workspace. In this situation, MFC will create a new, temporary CDaoWorkspace object.

> **NOTE**
>
> It's possible to create a new Microsoft Access (.MDB) database. First, construct a CDaoDatabase object, and then call the CDaoDatabase object's Create() member function. It's not proper to call Open() after Create() in this situation.

When using `CDaoDatabase`, you may open an existing database by creating the `CDaoDatabase` object and then calling the `Open()` member function.

Each of these techniques will append a `CDaoDatabase` object to your `CDaoWorkspace` object and then open a connection to the database's data. You then will create `CDaoRecordset`, `CDaoTableDef`, or `CDaoQueryDef` objects to utilize the database. When `CDaoRecordset`, `CDaoTableDef`, or `CDaoQueryDef` objects are created, you pass to the constructors for these objects a pointer to your `CDaoDatabase` object. When the application has finished working with the connection, a call to the `Close()` member function closes the connection. You then must close any recordsets that you haven't already closed and destroy the `CDaoDatabase` object.

> **NOTE**
>
> If you already know ODBC, things might be starting to look familiar since ODBC and DAO share a common model. The following paragraphs discuss transaction processing—which, except for class names, works like ODBC's transaction processing.

DAO provides transaction processing at the workspace level. See the `CDaoWorkspace::BeginTrans`, `CDaoWorkspace::CommitTrans`, and `CDaoWorkspace::Rollback` functions in the Visual C++ Books Online. For additional information about transactions, search for the article "DAO Workspace: Managing Transactions" in the *Programming with MFC* title in Books Online.

As I mentioned earlier, DAO can interface with ODBC data sources. Microsoft recommends that you attach your ODBC data sources to a Microsoft Access (.MDB) database as external tables. For further information about this technique, see the article "DAO External: Working with External Data Sources" in the *Programming with MFC* title in Books Online.

With DAO, each database will maintain its own collections of `Tabledef`, `Querydef`, `Recordset`, and `Relation` objects. The DAO `CDaoDatabase` class will supply the necessary member functions to allow your application to manipulate these objects. These objects are stored in DAO itself, not in the DAO MFC class objects. There are also MFC classes for `Tabledef`, `Querydef`, and `Recordset` objects. There is no MFC class for `Relation` objects at this time.

Table 13.3 lists the members of the `CDaoDatabase` class.

Table 13.3. The `CDaoDatabase` class members.

Member	Description
Data Members	
m_pWorkspace	A pointer to the `CDaoWorkspace` object that contains the database.
m_pDAODatabase	A pointer to the underlying DAO `CDaoDatabase` object.

continues

Table 13.3. continued

Member	Description
Construction	
CDaoDatabase	Constructs the CDaoDatabase object. After construction, you call Open() to connect the object to a database.
Attributes	
CanTransact()	Returns a nonzero value if the database supports transactions.
CanUpdate()	Returns a nonzero value if the CDaoDatabase object may be updated. If the Database object is read-only, this function returns a zero value.
GetConnect()	Returns the connect string that was used to connect the CDaoDatabase object to a database.
GetName()	Returns the name of the database currently in use.
GetQueryTimeout()	Returns the time-out period (in seconds) after which database query operations will time out.
GetRecordsAffected()	Returns a count of the number of records that were affected by the last update, edit, add operation, or call to Execute().
GetVersion()	Returns the version of the database engine associated with the database.
IsOpen()	Returns a nonzero value if the CDaoDatabase object is currently connected to a database.
SetQueryTimeout()	Sets in seconds the time-out period after which database query operations will fail. SetQueryTimeout() affects all subsequent open, add new, update, and delete operations.
Operations	
Close()	Closes the database connection.
Create()	Creates the underlying DAO database object and then initializes the CDaoDatabase object.
CreateRelation()	Defines a new relation among the tables in the database.
DeleteQueryDef()	Deletes a Querydef object saved in the database's QueryDefs collection.
DeleteRelation()	Deletes existing relations between tables in the database.
DeleteTableDef()	Deletes a table's definition in a database. When that table's definition is deleted, all the table's data is also deleted.
Execute()	Causes the action query to be executed. This query shouldn't return any results. If the executed query returns any results, an exception of type CDaoException is returned.

Member	Description
GetQueryDefCount()	Returns the number of queries defined for the database.
GetQueryDefInfo()	Returns information about a specified query defined in the database.
GetRelationCount()	Returns the number of relations defined between tables in the database.
GetRelationInfo()	Returns information about a specified relation defined between tables in the database.
GetTableDefCount()	Returns the number of tables defined in the database.
GetTableDefInfo()	Returns information about a specified table in the database.
Open()	Opens a database and establishes a connection to it.

CDaoTableDef

The DAO CDaoTableDef object is used to represent the stored definition of a base table or a table that is attached. Each DAO database object has a collection called TableDefs that contains all the saved DAO Tabledef objects.

You can manipulate a table definition with CDaoTableDef. Here are some things you can do using CDaoTableDef:

■ In databases, you can examine field and index structures of any local, attached, or external table.

■ You can call the SetConnect() and SetSourceTableName() member functions for attached tables. You also can use the RefreshLink() member function to update your connections to attached tables.

■ You can use the CanUpdate() member function to find out whether you can edit the field definitions in the table.

■ You can get and set validation rules and text using the GetValidationRule(), SetValidationRule(), GetValidationText(), and SetValidationText() member functions.

■ You can create a table-, dynaset-, or snapshot-type CDaoRecordset object by using the Open() member function.

To work with an existing table or create a new table, you will use Tabledef objects. First, construct a CDaoTableDef object. Next, give CDaoTableDef a pointer to a CDaoDatabase object to which the table belongs. Then you have to do one of the following things. What you do depends on what you want to do in your application:

■ Call the Tabledef object's Open() member function, supplying the name of the saved table to use an existing saved table.

- Call the `Tabledef` object's `Create()` member function, supplying the name of the table to create a new table. To add fields and indexes, call `CreateField()` and `CreateIndex()`.

- Call the `Tabledef` object's `Append()` member function to save the table you opened or created. You do this by appending the table to the database's `TableDefs` collection. Since `Create()` opens the `Tabledef`, it's not necessary to call `Open()`.

It's easy to create tables using Microsoft Access. Open the database in Access, create your tables, and save the database. Using Access for this type of manipulation is easier than trying to have your Visual C++ application perform these tasks. Of course, if your application must perform this functionality, and you're reasonably sure that all users of your application won't have Access available, you'll have to perform this task using your Visual C++ application instead of Access.

You specify a name for the `Tabledef` with a `dbOpenTable` value in the `nOpenType` parameter when opening a `CDaoRecordset`.

When using a `Tabledef` object to create a `CDaoRecordset` object, you might follow the steps just mentioned. After creating the object, construct your `Recordset` object using a pointer to your `Tabledef` object when you call `CDaoRecordset::Open()`. When you pass a `Tabledef`, it must be open.

As with other objects, when you're finished using the `Tabledef` object, call its `Close()` member function. After closing the `Tabledef` object, destroy it.

Table 13.4 lists the members of the `CDaoTableDef` class.

Table 13.4. The `CDaoTableDef` class members.

Member	Description
Data Members	
m_pDatabase	Contains a pointer to the source database for this table.
m_pDAOTableDef	Contains a pointer to the DAO interface underlying this `Tabledef` object.
Construction	
Append()	Adds a new table to the database.
CDaoTableDef()	Constructs a `CDaoTableDef` object.
Close()	Closes an open `Tabledef`.
Create()	Creates a table that can be added to the database using the `Append()` function.
Open()	Opens an existing `Tabledef` stored in the database's `TableDefs` collection.

Member	Description
Attributes	
CanUpdate()	Determines whether a table can be updated. If CanUpdate() returns a nonzero value, the table can be updated.
GetAttributes()	Determines the characteristics of a CDaoTableDef object.
GetConnect()	Gets information about the source of a table.
GetDateCreated()	Gets the creation date and time for the base table underlying a CDaoTableDef object.
GetDateLastUpdated()	Gets the date and time of the last change to the base table.
GetFieldCount()	Determines the number of fields in the table.
GetFieldInfo()	Obtains information about fields in the table.
GetIndexCount()	Determines the number of indexes to the table.
GetIndexInfo()	Obtains information about indexes to the table.
GetName()	Obtains the user-defined table name.
GetRecordCount()	Determines the number of records in the table.
GetSourceTableName()	Obtains the name of the attached table in the source database.
GetValidationRule()	Obtains the validation rule that is used to validate the data in a field as it is changed or added to a table.
GetValidationText()	Obtains a value that specifies the text of the message that your application displays if the value of a Field object doesn't satisfy the specified validation rule.
IsOpen()	Determines whether a table is open or not. Returns a zero value if the table isn't open.
SetAttributes()	Sets the value that is used to change one or more characteristics of a CDaoTableDef object.
SetConnect()	Sets values that are used in the connection to the table.
SetName()	Sets the name of the table.
SetSourceTableName()	Sets the source table's name.
SetValidationRule()	Sets a validation rule. The validation rule is used every time data in a field is changed (or added) to a table.
SetValidationText()	Sets the message that is to be displayed whenever data doesn't meet the specifications described by the validation rule.

continues

Table 13.4. continued

Member	Description
	Operations
CreateField()	Creates a field for a table.
CreateIndex()	Creates an index for a table.
DeleteField()	Deletes a field from a table.
DeleteIndex()	Deletes an index from a table.
RefreshLink()	Updates the connection information for an attached table.

CDaoQueryDef

A Querydef is a query definition that is usually (but doesn't have to be) stored or saved in a database. Access databases often have query definitions stored in them. Querydefs consist of SQL statements that describe a query, the query's properties (such as the date it was created), and the time-out value. Since Querydefs don't need to be stored in a database, they can also be temporary objects. It isn't unusual for a Visual C++ front-end application to create a temporary Querydef object.

> **NOTE**
>
> Querydefs are always more efficient if they're stored in the database. Any Querydef that is to be executed frequently should always be saved in the database.

The CDaoDatabase object will maintain a collection, the QueryDefs collection, containing the object's saved Querydefs.

You can use CDaoQueryDef to work with saved queries and to create a new saved or temporary query. You would use CDaoQueryDef in the following way. First, you would create and construct your CDaoQueryDef object. This object would be supplied with the pointer to your CDaoDatabase object to which the query will belong. Next, you must do one of the following:

- When using an existing, saved query, you would call CDaoQueryDef's Open() member function. In the call to Open(), you must provide the name of the saved query.

- When creating a new query that is to be saved, you would call CDaoQueryDef's Create() member function. In the call to Create(), you would provide the name of the query. You would then have to call the Append() member function to save the query. You save the query by appending it to the database's QueryDefs collection. Since the Create() function opens the query, it's not necessary to call the Open() function.

■ When creating a new, temporary query, you would call the `Create()` member function. Use an empty string as the name for the query, and don't call `Append()` to save the query.

After you've finished using the `Querydef` object, call the `Close()` member function to close it. As soon as the `Querydef` is closed, destroy the `CDaoQueryDef` object.

You can easily create `Querydef` objects using Microsoft Access. Open the database, design your query, and save it. Your Visual C++ database application can then use the query.

A `Querydef` object is used for either of the following:

■ You can use it to create a `CDaoRecordset` object.

■ You can call the object's `Execute()` member function to directly execute either an action query or an SQL pass-through query.

All types of queries can be used as `Querydef` objects. For example, queries can take the form of select, action, crosstab, delete, update, append, make-table, data definition, SQL pass-through, union, or bulk queries. The SQL statement that makes up the query determines the type of query.

See the `Execute()` and `GetType()` member functions in the Visual C++ Books Online for more information about queries. A query that would return a set of rows (as a recordset) is usually in the form of SELECT *rows* FROM *table types* of SQL statements.

When you use a `Querydef` to create a `CDaoRecordset` object, you create (or open) a `Querydef`. Then a `CDaoRecordset` object would be created and passed a pointer to your `Querydef` object. This pointer would be passed in the call to `CDaoRecordset::Open()`. The `Querydef` you pass must itself be open. If the `Querydef` isn't open, it can't be used to create a recordset.

You would use a `Querydef` object to gain access to the native SQL dialect for an external (non-Access) database. If you needed to create a Transact SQL query (Transact is the version of SQL used by Microsoft SQL Server), you would create the query and store it as a `Querydef` object.

Table 13.5 lists the members of the `CDaoQueryDef` class.

Table 13.5. The `CDaoQueryDef` class members.

Member	Description
Data Members	
`m_pDatabase`	Contains a pointer to the `CDaoDatabase` object to which the `Querydef` is associated, whether the `Querydef` is saved or not.
`m_pDAOQueryDef`	Contains a pointer to the OLE interface for the underlying DAO `Querydef` object.

continues

Table 13.5. continued

Member	Description
Construction	
CDaoQueryDef()	Constructs the CDaoQueryDef object. After the CDaoQueryDef object is created, you must call either Open() or Create().
Create()	Creates the underlying DAO Querydef object. The query can be either temporary or saved using a call to the Append() member function.
Append()	Appends the Querydef to the database's QueryDefs collection. This will make the Querydef a saved (not temporary) object.
Open()	Opens an existing Querydef stored in the database's QueryDefs collection.
Close()	Closes the Querydef object.
Attributes	
CanUpdate()	Returns a zero result if the database can't be updated.
GetConnect()	Obtains the connect string associated with the Querydef.
GetDateCreated()	Obtains the query's creation date.
GetDateLastUpdated()	Obtains the query's last update date.
GetName()	Returns the name of the Querydef.
GetODBCTimeout()	Obtains the ODBC time-out value.
GetRecordsAffected()	Determines the count of how many records have been affected by an action query.
GetReturnsRecords()	Returns zero if the query doesn't return any records.
GetSQL()	Returns the SQL string that specifies the query defined by the Querydef.
GetType()	Determines what the query type is. The query type could be delete, update, append, make-table, and so on.
IsOpen()	Returns zero if the Querydef isn't open or can't be executed.
SetConnect()	Sets the connect string for an SQL pass-through query on an ODBC data source.
SetName()	Sets the name of the saved query. This new name replaces the name that was in use when the Querydef was created.
SetODBCTimeout()	Sets the time-out period to be used by ODBC.
SetReturnsRecords()	Specifies that the Querydef will return records.
SetSQL()	Sets the SQL string that specifies the query defined by the Querydef.

Member	Description
Operations	
Execute()	Executes the query defined by the Querydef object.
GetFieldCount()	Determines the number of fields that this Querydef has defined.
GetFieldInfo()	Determines information about a field that is specified in the query.
GetParameterCount()	Determines the number of parameters defined for the query.
GetParameterInfo()	Obtains information about the specified parameter in the query.
GetParamValue()	Gets the value of a specified parameter to the query.
SetParamValue()	Sets the value of a specified parameter to the query.

CDaoRecordset

The DAO class CDaoRecordset is used to represent a set of records that have been selected from a datasource. CDaoRecordset corresponds directly to the CRecordset object that is used with ODBC.

The main difference between the DAO recordset and the ODBC recordset is that CDaoRecordset class objects access data through DAO, which is based on OLE, while the CRecordset classes access the database using ODBC.

A CDaoRecordset object is known as a recordset. A CDaoRecordset object can take one of three forms: a table-type recordset, a dynaset-type recordset, or a snapshot-type recordset:

◼ The table-type recordset represents a base table that you can use to examine records, change records, add records to, or delete records from a single database table.

◼ The dynaset-type recordset is the result of a query that can have records that are updatable. The dynaset-type recordset comprises a set of records that may be examined, added to, changed, or deleted from an underlying database table or tables. The dynaset-type recordset may contain fields from more than one table in a database if necessary.

◼ The snapshot-type recordset contains a static copy of a set of records returned from a query. This static set of records can be used to display information or create graphs or reports. Like a dynaset, a snapshot-type recordset may contain fields from one or more tables in a database.

The records contained in the recordset are fixed at the time the recordset is opened. Both the table-type recordset and dynaset-type recordset will reflect any changes made to data after the recordset was opened (by either the current process or perhaps by other users). In contrast, the snapshot recordset is static and isn't updated. Many applications use CDaoRecordset directly (usually using classes created using AppWizard). However, you can derive a class from CDaoRecordset if you wish. When you have a recordset object, you can do the following:

- Use a filter to limit the records selected from the recordset.
- Scroll through the records either forward or backward.
- With dynaset-type and snapshot-type recordsets, you can use comparison operations to find records. Typical operations include <, <=, =, >=, and >.
- With table-type recordsets, you can create an index and use the Seek() member function.
- With dynaset-type and table-type recordsets, you can update the records and specify a locking mode.
- Sort the recordset.
- At runtime, you can parameterize the recordset. This will serve to limit the records selected into the recordset.

To use the CDaoRecordset object, first you must open a database and construct your CDaoRecordset object. A pointer to your CDaoDatabase object must be passed to the constructor. Alternatively, it's possible to create a CDaoRecordset object and have MFC create a temporary CDaoDatabase object.

After you've created the CDaoRecordset, you must call the Open() member function. It takes a parameter that specifies whether the object is to be a table-type recordset, a dynaset-type recordset, or a snapshot-type recordset. Calling Open() selects data from the database and retrieves the first record.

After you've created your recordset object, you then can use the object's member functions and data members to scroll through the records and perform operations on them.

The CDaoRecordset class uses DAO record field exchange (DFX) to support the reading and updating of record fields through type-safe C++ members of your CDaoRecordset or CDaoRecordset-derived class. See the CDaoFieldExchange object in the Visual C++ Books Online for more information.

Table 13.6 lists the members of the CDaoRecordset class.

Table 13.6. The CDaoRecordset class members.

Member	Description
Data Members	
m_bCheckCacheForDirtyFields	Contains a flag indicating whether fields are automatically marked as changed or not.

Member	Description
m_pDAORecordset	A pointer to the DAO interface underlying the recordset object.
m_nParams	Has the number of parameter data members that will be found in the CDaoRecordset class.
m_pDatabase	Contains a pointer to the source database that the result set was created from. The pointer is of type CDaoDatabase.
m_strFilter	Contains a string that is used to construct an SQL WHERE statement.
m_strSort	Contains a string used to construct an SQL ORDER BY statement.

Construction

CDaoRecordset()	Constructs a CDaoRecordset object.
Close()	Closes a CDaoRecordset object.
Open()	Creates a new table, dynaset, or snapshot recordset.

Attributes

CanAppend()	Determines if new records may be added to a recordset using the AddNew() member function. This function returns zero if new records can't be added to the recordset.
CanBookmark()	If the recordset supports bookmarks, this function returns a nonzero value.
CanRestart()	If Requery() can be called to run the query again, this function returns a nonzero value.
CanScroll()	If you can scroll through the records, this function returns a nonzero value.
CanTransact()	If the datasource supports transactions, this function returns a nonzero value.
CanUpdate()	If the datasource supports updates, this member function returns a nonzero value.
GetCurrentIndex()	Used to obtain a CString that will contain the name of the index that was most recently used.
GetDateCreated()	Obtains the date and time that the base table underlying the CDaoRecordset object was created.

continues

Table 13.6. continued

Member	Description
	Attributes
GetDateLastUpdated()	Obtains the date and time of the most recent change made to the design of a base table underlying a CDaoRecordset object.
GetEditMode()	Returns a value that will indicate the editing state for the current record.
GetLastModifiedBookmark()	Determines the most recently added or updated record.
GetName()	Returns the name of the recordset as a CString.
GetParamValue()	Retrieves the current value of the specified parameter stored in the underlying DAOParameter object.
GetRecordCount()	Obtains the number of records accessed in a Recordset object.
GetSQL()	Gets the SQL string used to select records for the recordset.
GetType()	Determines the recordset's type: table, dynaset, or snapshot.
GetValidationRule()	Retrieves the validation rule for a field.
GetValidationText()	Retrieves the message text that is to be displayed when a validation rule isn't satisfied.
IsBOF()	Returns a nonzero value if the recordset has been positioned before the first record. There is no current record.
IsDeleted()	Returns a nonzero value if the recordset is currently positioned on a deleted record.
IsEOF()	Returns a nonzero value if the recordset has been positioned after the last record. There is no current record.
IsFieldDirty()	Returns a nonzero value if the specified field in the current record has been changed.
IsFieldNull()	Returns a nonzero value if the specified field in the current record is null. Remember that null is different from NULL.
IsFieldNullable()	Returns a nonzero value if the specified field in the current record can be set to null.

Member	Description
IsOpen()	Returns a nonzero value if Open() has been called previously.
SetCurrentIndex()	Sets an index on a table-type recordset.
SetParamValue()	Sets the current value of the specified parameter stored in the underlying DAOParameter object.
SetParamValueNull()	Sets the current value of the specified parameter to null.
	Recordset Update Operations
AddNew()	Sets up for adding new records. After the new records are prepared, a call to Update() will complete the record-adding process.
CancelUpdate()	Called when it's necessary to abort or cancel pending updates due to an Edit() or an AddNew() operation.
Delete()	Deletes the current record from the recordset. After the current record is deleted, it's necessary to explicitly scroll to another record.
Edit()	Prepares for edits in the current record. After completing the edits, you must call Update() to update the record or call CancelUpdate() to cancel the changes.
Update()	Completes an AddNew() or Edit() operation by saving the new or edited data on the data source.
	Recordset Navigation Operations
Find()	Finds the first, next, previous, or last location of a specified string in a recordset. The recordset must be a dynaset type that satisfies the specified criteria and makes that record the current record.
FindFirst()	Finds the first location of a specified string in a recordset. The recordset must be a dynaset type that satisfies the specified criteria and makes that record the current record.
FindLast()	Finds the last location of a specified string in a recordset. The recordset must be a dynaset type that satisfies the specified criteria and makes that record the current record.

continues

Table 13.6. continued

Member	Description
Recordset Navigation Operations	
FindNext()	Finds the next location of a specified string in a recordset. The recordset must be a dynaset type that satisfies the specified criteria and makes that record the current record.
FindPrev()	Finds the previous location of a specified string in a recordset. The recordset must be a dynaset type that satisfies the specified criteria and makes that record the current record.
GetAbsolutePosition()	Returns the record number of a recordset object's current record.
GetBookmark()	Returns a value that represents the bookmark on a record.
GetPercentPosition()	Returns the position of the current record as a percentage of the total number of records.
Move()	Repositions the recordset to a specified number of records relative to the current record. The move may be either forward or backward.
MoveFirst()	Positions the current record to the first record in the recordset.
MoveLast()	Positions the current record to the last record in the recordset.
MoveNext()	Positions the current record to the next record in the recordset.
MovePrev()	Positions the current record to the previous record in the recordset.
Seek()	Finds a record and makes that record the current record.
SetAbsolutePosition()	Sets the record number of a recordset object's current record.
SetBookmark()	Positions the recordset to a record that contains the specified bookmark.
SetPercentPosition()	Sets the position of the current record to a location that corresponds to a given percentage based on the total number of records in a recordset.

Member	Description
	Other Recordset Operations
FillCache()	Fills all (or a part) of the local cache for a recordset object.
GetCacheSize()	Returns the number of records in a dynaset-type recordset to be locally cached.
GetCacheStart()	Returns the bookmark value of the first record in the recordset to be cached.
GetFieldCount()	Returns the number of fields in the recordset.
GetFieldInfo()	Returns specific kinds of information about the fields in the recordset.
GetFieldValue()	Returns a field's value.
GetIndexCount()	Retrieves the number of indexes in a table.
GetIndexInfo()	Returns information on an index.
GetLockingMode()	Determines the type of locking that is in effect.
Requery()	Reruns the recordset's query to refresh the selected records.
SetCacheSize()	Sets the cache size.
SetCacheStart()	Sets the bookmark of the first record in the recordset to be cached.
SetFieldDirty()	Marks the specified field in the current record as changed.
SetFieldNull()	Specifies that the field is null.
SetFieldValue()	Specifies the value of a field in a recordset.
SetFieldValueNull()	Sets the value of a field to null.
SetLockingMode()	Sets the type of locking to put into effect during editing.
	Overridables
DoFieldExchange()	Performs the exchange of data between the field data members and the record set's current record.

CDaoException

The CDaoException object is used when handling exceptions when using the DAO MFC classes. The CDaoException class includes several public data members that may be used to analyze the error and assist you in determining the cause of the exception. `CDaoException` objects are constructed and thrown by member functions of the DAO database classes.

You can access exception objects within the scope of a `CATCH` expression. Your application also can throw a `CDaoException` object by using an `AfxThrowDaoException()` global function.

NOTE

The Microsoft documentation mentions the file DAOERR.H. This file is actually called DBDAOERR.H.

Table 13.7 lists error codes from DBDAOERR.H.

Table 13.7. DBDAOERR.H SCODE error code values.

Error Code	Description
E_DAO_InternalError	A reserved error, because there is no message for this error.
E_DAO_InvalidParameter	Invalid argument.
E_DAO_CantBegin	Couldn't start the session.
E_DAO_TransTooDeep	Couldn't start the transaction. Too many transactions were already nested.
E_DAO_DatabaseNotFound	Couldn't find the database.
E_DAO_DatabaseInvalidName	Name specified isn't a valid database name.
E_DAO_DatabaseLocked	Database is exclusively locked.
E_DAO_DatabaseOpenError	Can't open the library database.
E_DAO_TableLocked	Table is exclusively locked.
E_DAO_TableInUse	Couldn't lock table because it's currently in use.
E_DAO_TableDuplicate	Table already exists.
E_DAO_ObjectNotFound	Couldn't find object.
E_DAO_ObjectDuplicate	Object already exists.
E_DAO_CannotRename	Couldn't rename installable ISAM file.
E_DAO_TooManyOpenTables	Can't open any more tables.
E_DAO_IndexNotFound	The index specified isn't an index in this table.
E_DAO_ColumnDoesNotFit	Field won't fit in record.
E_DAO_ColumnTooBig	The size of a field is too long.

Error Code	Description
E_DAO_ColumnNotFound	Couldn't find the field.
E_DAO_NoCurrentIndex	Operation invalid without a current index.
E_DAO_RecordNoCopy	`Update` or `CancelUpdate` without `AddNew()` or `Edit()`.
E_DAO_NoCurrentRecord	No current record.
E_DAO_KeyDuplicate	Duplicate value in index, primary key, or relationship. Changes were unsuccessful.
E_DAO_AlreadyPrepared	`AddNew()` or `Edit()` already used.
E_DAO_FileNotFound	Couldn't find file.
E_DAO_TooManyOpenFiles	Can't open any more files.
E_DAO_DiskFull	Not enough space on the disk.
E_DAO_PermissionDenied	Can't update because the database or object is read-only.
E_DAO_CannotOpenSystemDb	Can't start the application. The system database is missing or opened exclusively by another user.
E_DAO_InvalidLogon	Not a valid account name or password.
E_DAO_InvalidAccountName	Not a valid account name.
E_DAO_InvalidPassword	Not a valid password.
E_DAO_InvalidOperation	Can't perform this operation.
E_DAO_AccessDenied	No permission for the operation has been granted.
E_DAO_NotInTransaction	`Commit` or `Rollback` without `BeginTrans`.
E_DAO_OutOfMemory	There is insufficient memory for the task.
E_DAO_CantAllocatePage	Database has reached maximum size.
E_DAO_NoMoreCursors	Can't open any more tables or queries.
E_DAO_OutOfBuffers	There are not enough buffers for the task.
E_DAO_TooManyIndexes	Couldn't create an index. Too many indexes are already defined.
E_DAO_ReadVerifyFailure	Disk I/O error during read.
E_DAO_FilesysVersion	Can't open a database created with a previous version of the application.
E_DAO_NoMoreFiles	Out of MS-DOS file handles.
E_DAO_DiskError	Disk or network error.

continues

Table 13.7. continued

Error Code	Description
E_DAO_InvalidPath	The path name specified isn't a valid path.
E_DAO_FileShareViolation	Couldn't use the specified database; file already in use.
E_DAO_FileLockViolation	Couldn't save the database; currently locked by another user.
E_DAO_RecordTooBig	Record is too large.
E_DAO_TooManyOpenDatabases	Can't open any more databases.
E_DAO_InvalidDatabase	Can't open the database. Your application might not recognize it, or the file might be corrupt.
E_DAO_FileLockingUnavailable	Couldn't lock file.
E_DAO_FileAccessDenied	Couldn't open file.
E_DAO_SharingBufferExceeded	MS-DOS file sharing lock count exceeded. You need to increase the number of locks installed with SHARE.EXE.
E_DAO_TaskLimitExceeded	Too many client tasks.
E_DAO_TooManyLongColumns	Too many Memo or OLE object fields.
E_DAO_InvalidFilename	Not a valid filename.
E_DAO_AbortSalvage	Couldn't repair this database.
E_DAO_LinkNotSupported	Operation isn't supported on attached (linked) tables.
E_DAO_NullKeyDisallowed	Index or primary key can't contain a null value.
E_DAO_OperationCanceled	The user canceled the operation.
E_DAO_QueryParmTypeMismatch	Wrong data type for the parameter.
E_DAO_QueryMissingParmsM	Too few parameters. Expected |.
E_DAO_QueryDuplicateAliasM	Duplicate output alias.
E_DAO_QueryDuplicateOutputM	Duplicate output destination.
E_DAO_QueryIsBulkOp	Can't open action query.
E_DAO_QueryIsNotBulkOp	Can't execute a nonaction query.
E_DAO_QueryNoOutputsM	Query or table must contain at least one output field.
E_DAO_QueryNoInputTablesM	Query input must contain at least one table or query.

Error Code	*Description*
E_DAO_QueryInvalidAlias	Not a valid alias name.
E_DAO_QueryInvalidBulkInputM	The action query can't be used as a row source.
E_DAO_QueryUnboundRef	Can't bind the name.
E_DAO_QueryExprEvaluation	Can't evaluate the expression.
E_DAO_EvalEBESErr	Error in the evaluation of the expression.
E_DAO_QueryNotUpdatable	Operation must use an updatable query.
E_DAO_TableRepeatInFromList	Can't repeat a table name in a FROM clause.
E_DAO_QueryExprSyntax	Syntax error in the expression.
E_DAO_QbeExprSyntax	Error in criteria expression.
E_DAO_FindExprSyntax	Find expression has a syntax error in the expression.
E_DAO_InputTableNotFound	Couldn't find the input table or query.
E_DAO_QueryAmbigRefM	Ambiguous field reference.
E_DAO_JoinTableNotInput	Joined table not listed in FROM clause.
E_DAO_UnaliasedSelfJoin	Can't join more than one table with the same name.
E_DAO_ColumnNotInJoinTable	JOIN operation refers to a nonjoined table.
E_DAO_QueryIsMGB	Can't use an internal report query.
E_DAO_QueryInsIntoBulkMGB	Can't insert data with an action query.
E_DAO_ExprUnknownFunctionM	Undefined function in the expression.
E_DAO_QueryCannotDelete	Couldn't delete from specified tables.
E_DAO_QueryTooManyGroupExprs	Too many expressions in a GROUP BY clause.
E_DAO_QueryTooManyOrderExprs	Too many expressions in an ORDER BY clause.
E_DAO_QueryTooManyDistExprs	Too many expressions in a DISTINCT output.
E_DAO_Column2ndSysMaint	Resultant table isn't allowed to have more than one Counter or Autonumber field.
E_DAO_HavingWOGrouping	HAVING clause without grouping or aggregation.
E_DAO_HavingOnTransform	Can't use the HAVING clause in a TRANSFORM statement.
E_DAO_OrderVsDistinct	ORDER BY clause conflicts with DISTINCT.
E_DAO_OrderVsGroup	ORDER BY clause conflicts with a GROUP BY clause.

continues

Table 13.7. continued

Error Code	Description
E_DAO_AggregateInArgument	Can't have an aggregate function in the expression.
E_DAO_AggregateInWhere	Can't have an aggregate function in a WHERE clause.
E_DAO_AggregateInOrderBy	Can't have an aggregate function in an ORDER BY clause.
E_DAO_AggregateInGroupBy	Can't have an aggregate function in a GROUP BY clause.
E_DAO_AggregateInJoin	Can't have an aggregate function in a JOIN operation.
E_DAO_NullInJoinKey	Can't set a field in a join key to null.
E_DAO_ValueBreaksJoin	There is no record in the table with key matching field(s).
E_DAO_QueryTreeCycle	Circular reference caused by the parameter supplied.
E_DAO_OutputAliasCycle	Circular reference caused by an alias in the query definition's SELECT list.
E_DAO_QryDuplicatedFixedSetM	Can't specify a fixed column heading in a crosstab query more than once.
E_DAO_NoSelectIntoColumnName	Missing a destination field name in a SELECT INTO statement.
E_DAO_NoUpdateColumnName	Missing a destination field name in an UPDATE statement.
E_DAO_QueryNoInsertPerm	Record(s) can't be added; no insert data permission is on.
E_DAO_QueryNoReplacePerm	Record(s) can't be edited; no update data permission is on.
E_DAO_QueryNoDeletePerm	Record(s) can't be deleted; no delete data permission is on.
E_DAO_QueryNoReadDefPerm	Couldn't read definitions; there's no read design permission for the table or query.
E_DAO_QueryNoTblCrtPerm	Couldn't create; there's no create permission for the table or query.
E_DAO_QueryNoReadPerm	Record(s) can't be read; no read data permission is on.

Error Code	Description
E_DAO_QueryColNotUpd	Can't update; the field isn't updatable.
E_DAO_QueryLVInDistinct	Can't include a Memo or OLE object when you select unique values.
E_DAO_QueryLVInAggregate	Can't have a Memo or OLE object in an aggregate argument.
E_DAO_QueryLVInHaving	Can't have a Memo or OLE object in a criteria for an aggregate function.
E_DAO_QueryLVInOrderBy	Can't sort on a Memo or OLE object.
E_DAO_QueryLVInJoin	Can't join on a Memo or OLE object.
E_DAO_QueryLVInGroupBy	Can't group on a Memo or OLE object.
E_DAO_DotStarWithGrouping	Can't group on fields selected with *.
E_DAO_StarWithGrouping	Can't group on fields selected with *.
E_DAO_IllegalDetailRef	Argument isn't part of the aggregate function or grouping.
E_DAO_StarNotAtLevel0	Can't use * in a crosstab query.
E_DAO_QueryInvalidMGBInput	Can't input from an internal report query.
E_DAO_InvalidName	Name supplied isn't a valid name.
E_DAO_QueryBadBracketing	Invalid bracketing of the name.
E_DAO_InsertIntoUnknownCol	INSERT INTO statement contains an unknown field name.
E_DAO_QueryNoDeleteTables	Must specify tables to delete from.
E_DAO_SQLSyntax	Invalid SQL statement; expected DELETE, INSERT, PROCEDURE, SELECT, or UPDATE.
E_DAO_SQLDeleteSyntax	Syntax error in a DELETE statement.
E_DAO_SQLFromSyntax	Syntax error in a FROM clause.
E_DAO_SQLGroupBySyntax	Syntax error in a GROUP BY clause.
E_DAO_SQLHavingSyntax	Syntax error in a HAVING clause.
E_DAO_SQLInsertSyntax	Syntax error in an INSERT statement.
E_DAO_SQLJoinSyntax	Syntax error in a JOIN operation.
E_DAO_SQLLevelSyntax	Syntax error in a LEVEL clause.
E_DAO_SQLMissingSemicolon	Missing semicolon (;) at end of an SQL statement.
E_DAO_SQLOrderBySyntax	Syntax error in an ORDER BY clause.

continues

Table 13.7. continued

Error Code	Description
E_DAO_SQLParameterSyntax	Syntax error in a PARAMETER clause.
E_DAO_SQLProcedureSyntax	Syntax error in a PROCEDURE clause.
E_DAO_SQLSelectSyntax	Syntax error in a SELECT statement.
E_DAO_SQLTooManyTokens	Characters found after the end of an SQL statement.
E_DAO_SQLTransformSyntax	Syntax error in a TRANSFORM statement.
E_DAO_SQLUpdateSyntax	Syntax error in an UPDATE statement.
E_DAO_SQLWhereSyntax	Syntax error in a WHERE clause.
E_DAO_RmtSQLCError	ODBC: Call failed.
E_DAO_RmtDataOverflow	Not documented by Microsoft.
E_DAO_RmtConnectFailed	Not documented by Microsoft.
E_DAO_RmtIncorrectSqlcDll	Not documented by Microsoft.
E_DAO_RmtMissingSqlcDll	Not documented by Microsoft.
E_DAO_RmtConnectFailedM	ODBC: Connection to the datasource failed.
E_DAO_RmtDrvrVer	Not documented by Microsoft.
E_DAO_RmtSrvrVer	Not documented by Microsoft.
E_DAO_RmtMissingOdbcDll	ODBC: Couldn't find the DLL.
E_DAO_RmtInsertFailedM	ODBC: Insert failed on an attached (linked) table.
E_DAO_RmtDeleteFailedM	ODBC: Delete failed on an attached (linked) table.
E_DAO_RmtUpdateFailedM	ODBC: Update failed on an attached (linked) table.
E_DAO_RecordLocked	Couldn't save record; currently locked by another user.
E_DAO_InvalidBookmark	Not a valid bookmark.
E_DAO_TableNotOpen	Table isn't open.
E_DAO_DecryptFail	Couldn't decrypt the file.
E_DAO_NullInvalid	Null is invalid.
E_DAO_InvalidBufferSize	Couldn't perform the operation; the data is too long for the field.
E_DAO_ColumnNotUpdatable	Field can't be updated.
E_DAO_CantMakeINFFile	Couldn't open the .INF file.

Error Code	Description
E_DAO_MissingMemoFile	Missing memo file.
E_DAO_RecordDeleted	Record is deleted.
E_DAO_INFFileError	Invalid .INF file.
E_DAO_ExprIllegalType	Illegal type in the expression.
E_DAO_InstalIsamNotFound	Couldn't find the installable ISAM.
E_DAO_NoConfigParameters	Couldn't find the net path or user name.
E_DAO_CantAccessPdoxNetDir	Couldn't open PARADOX.NET.
E_DAO_NoMSysAccounts	Couldn't open the table MSysAccounts in the system database file.
E_DAO_NoMSysGroups	Couldn't open the table MSysGroups in the system database file.
E_DAO_DateOutOfRange	Date is out of range or is in an invalid format.
E_DAO_ImexCantOpenFile	Couldn't open the file.
E_DAO_ImexBadTableName	Not a valid table name.
E_DAO_ImexOutOfMemory	Not documented by Microsoft.
E_DAO_ImexEndofFile	Encountered an unexpected end of file.
E_DAO_ImexCantWriteToFile	Couldn't write to the file.
E_DAO_ImexBadRange	Invalid range.
E_DAO_ImexBogusFile	Invalid file format.
E_DAO_TempDiskFull	Not enough space on the temporary disk.
E_DAO_RmtLinkNotFound	Couldn't execute the query; couldn't find the attached (linked) table.
E_DAO_RmtTooManyColumns	SELECT INTO remote database tried to produce too many fields.
E_DAO_ReadConflictM	Couldn't save; currently locked by another user on a different machine.
E_DAO_CommitConflictM	Couldn't read; currently locked by another user on a different machine.
E_DAO_SessionWriteConflict	Couldn't update; currently locked by another session on this machine.
E_DAO_JetSpecialTableLocked	Table is exclusively locked by another user.
E_DAO_TooManyColumns	Too many fields are defined.
E_DAO_ColumnDuplicate	Can't define a field more than once.

continues

Table 13.7. continued

Error Code	Description
E_DAO_OutputTableNotFound	Couldn't find the output table.
E_DAO_JetNoUserName	The user name is unknown.
E_DAO_JetNoMachineName	The machine name is unknown.
E_DAO_JetNoColumnName	The column name is unknown.
E_DAO_DatabaseInUse	Couldn't use the database; already in use.
E_DAO_DataHasChanged	Data has changed; operation was stopped.
E_DAO_TooManySessions	Couldn't start the session. Too many sessions are already active.
E_DAO_ReferenceNotFound	Couldn't find the reference.
E_DAO_IntegrityViolMasterM	Can't delete or change the record. Since related records exist in the table, referential integrity rules would be violated.
E_DAO_IntegrityViolSlaveM	Can't add or change the record. Referential integrity rules require a related record in the table.
E_DAO_ReadConflict	Couldn't save the database; currently locked by another user.
E_DAO_AggregatingHigherLevel	Can't specify a subquery in the expression.
E_DAO_DatabaseDuplicate	Database already exists.
E_DAO_QueryTooManyXvtColumn	Too many crosstab column headers.
E_DAO_SelfReference	Can't create a relationship between a field and itself.
E_DAO_CantUseUnkeyedTable	Operation isn't supported on a Paradox table with no primary key.
E_DAO_IllegalDeletedOption	Invalid deleted entry in the xBase section of the initialization setting.
E_DAO_IllegalStatsOption	Invalid stats entry in the xBase section of the initialization setting.
E_DAO_ConnStrTooLong	Connection string is too long.
E_DAO_TableInUseQM	Couldn't lock the table; currently in use.
E_DAO_JetSpecialTableInUse	Couldn't lock the specified table; currently in use by another user on a different machine.
E_DAO_IllegalDateOption	Invalid date entry in the xBase section of the initialization setting.

Error Code	Description
E_DAO_IllegalMarkOption	Invalid mark entry in the xBase section of the initialization setting.
E_DAO_BtrieveTooManyTasks	Too many Btrieve tasks.
E_DAO_QueryParmNotTableid	Parameter specified where a table name is required.
E_DAO_QueryParmNotDatabase	Parameter specified where a database name is required.
E_DAO_WriteConflict	Couldn't update; currently locked.
E_DAO_IllegalOperation	Invalid operation.
E_DAO_WrongCollatingSequence	Incorrect collating sequence.
E_DAO_BadConfigParameters	Invalid entries in the Btrieve section of the initialization setting.
E_DAO_QueryContainsDbParm	Query can't contain a database parameter.
E_DAO_QueryInvalidParmM	The parameter isn't a valid parameter name.
E_DAO_BtrieveDDCorrupted	Can't read the Btrieve data dictionary.
E_DAO_BtrieveDeadlock	Encountered record locking deadlock while performing a Btrieve operation.
E_DAO_BtrieveFailure	Errors encountered while using the Btrieve DLL.
E_DAO_IllegalCenturyOption	Invalid century entry in the xBase section of the initialization setting.
E_DAO_IllegalCollatingSeq	Invalid collating sequence.
E_DAO_NonModifiableKey	Btrieve: Can't change field.
E_DAO_ObsoleteLockFile	Out-of-date Paradox lock file.
E_DAO_RmtColDataTruncated	ODBC: Field would be too long; data truncated.
E_DAO_RmtCreateTableFailed	ODBC: Couldn't create the table.
E_DAO_RmtOdbcVer	Not documented by Microsoft.
E_DAO_RmtQueryTimeout	ODBC: Remote query time-out expired.
E_DAO_RmtTypeIncompat	ODBC: Data type isn't supported on the server.
E_DAO_RmtUnexpectedNull	Not documented by Microsoft.
E_DAO_RmtUnexpectedType	Not documented by Microsoft.
E_DAO_RmtValueOutOfRange	ODBC: Data is out of range.

continues

Table 13.7. continued

Error Code	Description
E_DAO_TooManyActiveUsers	Too many active users.
E_DAO_CantStartBtrieve	Btrieve: Missing the Btrieve engine.
E_DAO_OutOfBVResources	Btrieve: Out of resources.
E_DAO_QueryBadUpwardRefedM	Invalid reference in the SELECT statement.
E_DAO_ImexNoMatchingColumns	None of the import field names match fields in the appended table.
E_DAO_ImexPasswordProtected	Can't import a password-protected spreadsheet.
E_DAO_ImexUnparsableRecord	Couldn't parse field names from the first row of the import table.
E_DAO_InTransaction	Operation isn't supported in transactions.
E_DAO_RmtLinkOutOfSync	ODBC: Linked table definition has changed.
E_DAO_IllegalNetworkOption	Invalid NetworkAccess entry in the initialization setting.
E_DAO_IllegalTimeoutOption	Invalid PageTimeout entry in the initialization setting.
E_DAO_CantBuildKey	Couldn't build the key.
E_DAO_FeatureNotAvailable	Operation isn't supported for this type of object.
E_DAO_IllegalReentrancy	Can't open a form whose underlying query contains a user-defined function that attempts to set or get the form's RecordsetClone property.
E_DAO_UNUSED	Not documented by Microsoft.
E_DAO_RmtDenyWriteIsInvalid	ODBC: Can't lock all records.
E_DAO_ODBCParmsChanged	Not documented by Microsoft.
E_DAO_INFIndexNotFound	Index file isn't found.
E_DAO_SQLOwnerAccessSyntax	Syntax error in the WITH OWNERACCESS OPTION declaration.
E_DAO_QueryAmbiguousJoins	Query contains ambiguous outer joins.
E_DAO_InvalidColumnType	Invalid field data type.
E_DAO_WriteConflictM	Couldn't update; currently locked by another user on a different machine.

Error Code	Description
E_DAO_TableLockedM	Not documented by Microsoft.
E_DAO_TableInUseMUQM	Not documented by Microsoft.
E_DAO_InvalidTableId	Invalid database object.
E_DAO_VtoNoFields	No fields defined. Can't append Tabledef or Index.
E_DAO_VtoNameNotFound	Item isn't found in this collection.
E_DAO_VtoFieldInCollection	Can't append. The field is part of a TableDefs collection.
E_DAO_VtoNotARecordset	Property can be set only when the field is part of a Recordset object's Fields collection.
E_DAO_VtoNoSetObjInDb	Can't set this property once the object is part of a collection.
E_DAO_VtoIndexInCollection	Can't append. The index is part of a TableDefs collection.
E_DAO_VtoPropNotFound	Property isn't found.
E_DAO_VtoIllegalValue	Invalid property value.
E_DAO_VtoNotArray	Object isn't a collection.
E_DAO_VtoNoSuchMethod	Method isn't applicable for this object.
E_DAO_NotExternalFormat	External table isn't in the expected format.
E_DAO_UnexpectedEngineReturn	Unexpected error from the external database driver.
E_DAO_InvalidDatabaseId	Invalid database ID.
E_DAO_TooManyKeys	Can't have more than 10 fields in an index.
E_DAO_NotInitialized	Database engine hasn't been initialized.
E_DAO_AlreadyInitialized	Database engine has already been initialized.
E_DAO_ColumnInUse	Can't delete a field that is part of an index or is needed by the system.
E_DAO_IndexInUse	Can't delete this index. It's either the current index or is used in a relationship.
E_DAO_TableNotEmpty	Can't create the field or index in a table that is already defined.
E_DAO_IndexHasPrimary	Primary key already exists.
E_DAO_IndexDuplicate	Index already exists.

continues

Table 13.7. continued

Error Code	Description
E_DAO_IndexInvalidDef	Invalid index definition.
E_DAO_WrongMemoFileType	Format of the memo file doesn't match the specified external database format.
E_DAO_ColumnCannotIndex	Can't create an index on the given field.
E_DAO_IndexHasNoPrimary	Paradox index isn't primary.
E_DAO_DDLConstraintSyntax	Syntax error in a CONSTRAINT clause.
E_DAO_DDLCreateTableSyntax	Syntax error in a CREATE TABLE statement.
E_DAO_DDLCreateIndexSyntax	Syntax error in a CREATE INDEX statement.
E_DAO_DDLColumnDefSyntax	Syntax error in field definition.
E_DAO_DDLAlterTableSyntax	Syntax error in an ALTER TABLE statement.
E_DAO_DDLDropIndexSyntax	Syntax error in a DROP INDEX statement.
E_DAO_DDLDropSyntax	Syntax error in a DROP TABLE or DROP INDEX.
E_DAO_V11NotSupported	Join expression isn't supported.
E_DAO_ImexNothingToImport	Couldn't import the table or query. No records were found, or all records contain errors.
E_DAO_RmtTableAmbiguous	There are several tables with this name. Specify owner in the format *owner.table*.
E_DAO_JetODBCConformanceError	ODBC specification conformance error. This error should be reported to the ODBC driver vendor.
E_DAO_IllegalRelationship	Can't create a relationship.
E_DAO_DBVerFeatureNotAvailable	Can't perform this operation. Features in this version aren't available in databases with older formats.
E_DAO_RulesLoaded	Can't change a rule while the rules for this table are in use.
E_DAO_ColumnInRelationship	Can't delete this field. It's part of one or more relationships.
E_DAO_InvalidPin	You must enter a personal identifier (PID) consisting of at least four and no more than 20 characters and digits.
E_DAO_RmtBogusConnStr	Invalid connection string in pass-through query.

Error Code	Description
E_DAO_SingleColumnExpected	At most, one field can be returned from a subquery that doesn't use the EXISTS keyword.
E_DAO_ColumnCountMismatch	The number of columns in the two selected tables or queries of a union query don't match.
E_DAO_InvalidTopArgumentM	Invalid TOP argument in a select query.
E_DAO_PropertyTooLarge	Property setting can't be larger than 2K.
E_DAO_JPMInvalidForV1x	This property isn't supported for external data sources or for databases created in a previous version.
E_DAO_PropertyExists	Property specified already exists.
E_DAO_TLVNativeUserTablesOnly	Validation rules and default values can't be placed on system or attached (linked) tables.
E_DAO_TLVInvalidColumn	Can't place this validation expression on this field.
E_DAO_TLVNoNullM	Field can't contain a null value.
E_DAO_TLVNoBlankM	Field can't be a zero-length string.
E_DAO_TLVRuleViolationM	Not documented by Microsoft.
E_DAO_TLVRuleVioNoMessage	One or more values entered is prohibited by the validation rule set for the field.
E_DAO_QueryTopNotAllowedM	Top not allowed in delete queries.
E_DAO_SQLUnionSyntax	Syntax error in a union query.
E_DAO_TLVExprSyntaxM	Syntax error in a table-level validation expression.
E_DAO_NoDbInConnStr	No database is specified in the connection string or IN clause.
E_DAO_QueryBadValueListM	Crosstab query contains one or more invalid fixed column headings.
E_DAO_QueryIsNotRowReturning	Query can't be used as a row source.
E_DAO_QueryIsDDL	Query is a DDL query and can't be used as a row source.
E_DAO_SPTReturnedNoRecords	Pass-through query with ReturnsRecords property set to TRUE didn't return any records.

continues

Table 13.7. continued

Error Code	Description
E_DAO_QueryIsSnapshot	Recordset isn't updatable.
E_DAO_QueryExprOutput	Field is based on an expression and can't be edited.
E_DAO_QueryTableRO	Table is read-only.
E_DAO_QueryRowDeleted	Record in table was deleted by another user.
E_DAO_QueryRowLocked	Record in table is locked by another user.
E_DAO_QueryFixupChanged	To make changes to this field, first save the record.
E_DAO_QueryCantFillIn	Can't enter a value into a blank field on the "one" side of an outer join.
E_DAO_QueryWouldOrphan	Records in the table would have no record on the "one" side.
E_DAO_V10Format	Can be present only in version 1.0 format.
E_DAO_InvalidDelete	DeleteOnly called with a nonzero cbData.
E_DAO_IllegalIndexDDFOption	Btrieve: Invalid IndexDDF option in the initialization setting.
E_DAO_IllegalDataCodePage	Invalid DataCodePage option in the initialization setting.
E_DAO_XtrieveEnvironmentError	Btrieve: Xtrieve options aren't correct in the initialization setting.
E_DAO_IllegalIndexNumberOption	Btrieve: Invalid IndexDeleteRenumber option in the initialization setting.
E_DAO_QueryIsCorruptM	Query is corrupt.
E_DAO_IncorrectJoinKeyM	Current field must match the join key on the "one" side of the outer join because it has been updated.
E_DAO_QueryLVInSubqueryM	Invalid Memo or OLE object in the subquery.
E_DAO_InvalidDatabaseM	Unrecognized database format.
E_DAO_TLVCouldNotBindRef	Unknown or invalid reference in the validation expression or a default value in the table.
E_DAO_CouldNotBindRef	Unknown or invalid field reference.
E_DAO_QueryWrongNumDestCol	Number of query values and destination fields aren't the same.

Error Code	Description
E_DAO_QueryPKeyNotOutput	Can't add record(s); the primary key for the table isn't in the recordset.
E_DAO_QueryJKeyNotOutput	Can't add record(s); the join key of the table isn't in the recordset.
E_DAO_NumericFieldOverflow	Numeric field overflow.
E_DAO_InvalidObject	Object is invalid for the operation.
E_DAO_OrderVsUnion	ORDER BY expression uses nonoutput fields.
E_DAO_NoInsertColumnNameM	No destination field name in an INSERT INTO statement.
E_DAO_MissingDDFFile	Btrieve: Can't find the file FIELD.DDF.
E_DAO_SingleRecordExpected	At most, one record can be returned by this subquery.
E_DAO_DefaultExprSyntax	Syntax error in default value.
E_DAO_ExclusiveDBConflict	Database is opened by the user specified on the specified machine.
E_DAO_QueryIsNotDDL	Query isn't a properly formed data-definition query.
E_DAO_SysDatabaseOpenError	Can't open the Microsoft Jet engine system database.
E_DAO_SQLInvalidSPT	Pass-through query must contain at least one character.
E_DAO_QueryTooComplex	Query is too complex.
E_DAO_SetOpInvalidInSubquery	Unions aren't allowed in a subquery.
E_DAO_RmtMultiRowUpdate	Single-row update/delete affected more than one row of an attached (linked) table. The unique index contains duplicate values.
E_DAO_QueryNoJoinedRecord	Record(s) can't be added; there's no corresponding record on the "one" side.
E_DAO_QueryLVInSetOp	Can't use a Memo or OLE object field in a SELECT clause of a union query.
E_DAO_VtoInvalidOnRemote	Property value isn't valid for REMOTE objects.
E_DAO_VtoNoFieldsRel	Can't append a relation with no fields defined.
E_DAO_VtoObjectInCollection	Can't append. The object is already in the collection.

continues

Table 13.7. continued

Error Code	Description
E_DAO_DDLDiffNumRelCols	Relationship must be on the same number of fields with the same data types.
E_DAO_DDLIndexColNotFound	Can't find the field in the index definition.
E_DAO_DDLPermissionDenied	Can't modify the table's design. It's in a read-only database.
E_DAO_DDLObjectNotFound	Can't find the table or constraint.
E_DAO_DDLIndexNotFound	No such index on the table.
E_DAO_DDLNoPkeyOnRefdTable	Can't create the relationship. The referenced table doesn't have a primary key.
E_DAO_DDLColumnsNotUnique	Specified fields aren't uniquely indexed in the table.
E_DAO_DDLIndexDuplicate	Table already has an index with the same name.
E_DAO_DDLTableNotFound	Table doesn't exist.
E_DAO_DDLRelNotFound	No such relationship in the table.
E_DAO_DDLRelDuplicate	There is already a relationship named in the current database.
E_DAO_DDLIntegrityViolation	Can't create relationships to enforce referential integrity. Existing data in the table violates referential integrity rules with a related table.
E_DAO_DDLColumnDuplicate	Field already exists in the table.
E_DAO_DDLColumnNotFound	No field is named in the table.
E_DAO_DDLColumnTooBig	The size of the field is too long.
E_DAO_DDLColumnInRel	Can't delete the field. It's part of one or more relationships.
E_DAO_VtoCantDeleteBuiltIn	Can't delete a built-in property.
E_DAO_VtoUDPsDontSupportNull	User-defined properties don't support a Null value.
E_DAO_VtoMissingRequiredParm	Property must be set before using this method.
E_DAO_JetJetInitInvalidPath	Can't find the TEMP directory.
E_DAO_TLVExprUnknownFunctionM	Unknown function in the validation expression or default value.

Error Code	Description
E_DAO_QueryNotSupported	Query support unavailable.
E_DAO_AccountDuplicate	Account name already exists.
E_DAO_JetwrnPropCouldNotSave	An error has occurred. Properties weren't saved.
E_DAO_RelNoPrimaryIndexM	There is no primary key in the table.
E_DAO_QueryKeyTooBig	Can't perform a join, group, sort, or indexed restriction. A value being searched or sorted on is too long.
E_DAO_PropMustBeDDL	Can't save the property because it's a schema property.
E_DAO_IllegalRIConstraint	Invalid referential integrity constraint.
E_DAO_RIViolationMasterCM	Can't perform a cascading operation. Since related records exist in the table, referential integrity rules would be violated.
E_DAO_RIViolationSlaveCM	Can't perform a cascading operation. There must be a related record in the table.
E_DAO_RIKeyNullDisallowedCM	Can't perform a cascading operation. It would result in a null key in the table.
E_DAO_RIKeyDuplicateCM	Can't perform a cascading operation. It would result in a duplicate key in the table.
E_DAO_RIUpdateTwiceCM	Can't perform a cascading operation. It would result in two updates on fields in the table.
E_DAO_RITLVNoNullCM	Can't perform a cascading operation. It would cause a field to become null, which isn't allowed.
E_DAO_RITLVNoBlankCM	Can't perform a cascading operation. It would cause a field to become a zero-length string, which isn't allowed.
E_DAO_RITLVRuleViolationCM	Can't perform a cascading operation. Caused by the fact that there are related records in another table, and referential integrity rules would be violated.
E_DAO_RITLVRuleVioCNoMessage	Can't perform a cascading operation. The value entered is prohibited by the validation rule set.

continues

Table 13.7. continued

Error Code	Description
E_DAO_TLVRuleEvalEBESErr	Error in the validation rule.
E_DAO_TLVDefaultEvalEBESErr	Error in the default value.
E_DAO_BadMSysConf	The server's MSysConf table exists, but it's in an incorrect format. Contact your system administrator.
E_DAO_TooManyFindSessions	Too many FastFind sessions were invoked.
E_DAO_InvalidColumnM	Invalid field name in the definition of the index or relationship.
E_DAO_REPReadOnly	Not documented by Microsoft.
E_DAO_RIInvalidBufferSizeCM	Invalid entry. Can't perform the cascading operation specified in the table because the value entered is too big for the field.
E_DAO_RIWriteConflictCM	Not documented by Microsoft.
E_DAO_JetSpecialRIWriteConflictCM	Can't perform a cascading update on the table because it's currently in use by another user on a different machine.
E_DAO_RISessWriteConflictCM	Can't perform a cascading update on the table because it's currently in use.
E_DAO_NoBlank	Zero-length string is valid only in a text or Memo field.
E_DAO_FutureError	Not documented by Microsoft.
E_DAO_QueryInvalidBulkInput	An action query can't be used as a row source.
E_DAO_NetCtrlMismatch	Can't open the specified table. Another user has the table open using a different network control file or locking style.
E_DAO_4xTableWith3xLocking	Can't open this Paradox 4.x or 5.x table because ParadoxNetStyle is set to 3.x in the initialization setting.
E_DAO_VtoObjectNotSet	Object is invalid or not set.
E_DAO_VtoDataConvError	Data type conversion error.

All the error codes that appear in Table 13.8 are from DBDAOERR.H. You can edit this file and create an intelligent error handler if you want by creating a large select/case selection block.

Of course, you can elect not to handle the errors that aren't applicable to your application to keep your error handler's size within reason.

Table 13.8 lists the members of the CDaoException class.

Table 13.8. The CDaoException class members.

Member	Description
	Data Members
m_scode	The SCODE value associated with the error. See Table 13.7 for a list of the valid SCODE values.
m_nAfxDaoError	Contains the extended error code for errors that occur in the MFC DAO classes.
m_pErrorInfo	Contains a pointer to the CDaoErrorInfo object that will contain information about one DAO error object.
	Construction
CDaoException()	Constructs the CDaoException object.
	Operations
GetErrorCount()	Returns a count of how many errors are in the Microsoft Jet database engine's errors collection.
GetErrorInfo()	Returns error information about a particular error object, specified by the *nIndex* parameter, from the errors collection.

CDaoFieldExchange

The CDaoFieldExchange class is used to transfer data from fields in a result set to the CDaoRecordset member variables. You need to use this class only if you're going to write data exchange routines for custom data types. If you're only using standard data types, you won't need to use the CDaoFieldExchange object. This process, called DFX, manages the exchange in both directions from the result set and to the result set.

> **NOTE**
>
> Technical Note 53 (in Visual C++ Books Online, see Visual C++ Books, MFC 4.0, MFC Technical Notes) has an example of how to write DFX routines.

Like other features of DAO, the design and usage of the DAO record field exchange (DFX) is based on the same model as ODBC's record field exchange (RFX). If you're comfortable with ODBC's RFX, you'll find it easy to use DAO's DFX.

The CDaoFieldExchange object is used to provide the context information that DAO needs for the record field exchange. The CDaoFieldExchange object supports a number of operations, including binding parameters and field data members and setting various flags (null, dirty, and so on) on fields in the current record. The DFX operations are performed on CDaoRecordset data members defined by the enum FieldType in CDaoFieldExchange. Possible FieldType values are

- CDaoFieldExchange::outputColumn for field data members
- CDaoFieldExchange::param for parameter data members

You use the IsValidOperation() member when you're going to write your own (custom) DFX functions. You do this by using the SetFieldType() member function, which is often done in your CDaoRecordset::DoFieldExchange functions.

Table 13.9 lists the members of the CDaoFieldExchange class.

Table 13.9. The CDaoFieldExchange class members.

Member	Description
Data Members	
m_nOperation	Holds the current DFX operation being performed.
m_prs	Holds a pointer to the current CDaoRecordset on which the DFX operation is being performed.
Member Functions	
IsValidOperation()	Returns a zero if the current operation isn't appropriate for the type of field being updated.
SetFieldType()	Sets the type of CDaoRecordset data member that is to be represented until the next call to SetFieldType().

CDaoRecordView

The CDaoRecordView class is used to display database records using a dialog box template. This class, derived from CFormView (which is in turn derived from CScrollView, and so on), is virtually identical to ODBC's CRecordView.

The view presented by CDaoRecordView is connected directly to a CDaoRecordset object. As with CRecordView, you create a dialog box (usually with AppWizard) and locate appropriate dialog controls to display fields from the datasource. The CDaoRecordView object uses standard dialog data exchange (DDX) and DAO record field exchange (DFX) to actually move the record's data to and from the CDaoRecordView dialog box's controls. CDaoRecordView will also supply the default implementation for record navigation so that you can easily implement moves to the first, next, previous, or last record in the data source. CDaoRecordView also provides the interface for updating the record currently in view.

Most programmers (at least the nonmasochistic ones) will use AppWizard to create the shell for their DAO database application. If you don't use AppWizard, you'll find it rather difficult to create MFC Windows applications. The most common way to create your record view is with AppWizard. AppWizard creates both the record view class and its associated recordset class as part of your skeleton starter application.

You can use ClassWizard to add a CDaoRecordView later in the development process if necessary. However, before starting your application, you should decide what the application's user interface will look like.

When you use AppWizard to create your application's shell, you will be provided with toolbar buttons that the user will be able to use for record navigation. These AppWizard-supplied buttons let the user make the next, previous, first, or last record the current record.

The CDaoRecordView class maintains the current record's position in the recordset. The buttons for record navigation are enabled and disabled to prevent the user from making incorrect choices, such as attempting to select the previous record when the first record in the recordset is the current record.

Table 13.10 lists the members of the CDaoRecordView class.

Table 13.10. The CDaoRecordView class members.

Member	Description
Construction	
CDaoRecordView	Constructs the CDaoRecordView object.
Attributes	
OnGetRecordset()	Provides a pointer to an object derived from CDaoRecordset. When you're using ClassWizard, this function is automatically overridden, and a CDaoRecordset object is created automatically for you if necessary.
IsOnLastRecord()	Returns zero if the current record isn't the last record in the associated recordset.
IsOnFirstRecord()	Returns zero if the current record isn't the first record in the associated recordset.
Operations	
OnMove()	Moves to the specified record, first updating the current record with any changes that have been made. The specified record may be next, previous, first, or last.

Summary

DAO is new to Visual C++ programmers. Although Visual Basic has offered DAO support for some time, Visual C++ programmers have had to work with ODBC, which doesn't offer the same capabilities as DAO. Visual Basic programmers have had a substantial advantage when working with Access database files.

DAO is managed using a set of MFC classes. These classes are similar to the MFC ODBC classes, but there are some differences. The MFC DAO classes can either directly or indirectly access all of the functionality of the Microsoft DAO/Access Jet Database Engine. The MFC DAO database classes presented in this chapter include

```
CDaoDatabase
CDaoException
CDaoFieldExchange
CDaoQueryDef
CDaoRecordset
CDaoRecordView
CDaoTableDef
CDaoWorkspace
```

Each class was discussed, and the members of each class were described. This chapter also listed the errors that CDaoException handles.

14

Using MFC's DAO Classes

In Chapter 13, "Understanding MFC's DAO Classes," you looked at the new MFC 4 DAO data access classes. This chapter introduces you to these classes in actual working code. You'll create several examples of DAO applications using as many features of DAO as you can.

This chapter is divided into three parts. In the first part you'll create a standard DAO application using AppWizard. In the second part, you'll look at using each of the DAO MFC classes:

CDaoDatabase

CDaoException

CDaoFieldExchange

CDaoQueryDef

CDaoRecordset

CDaoRecordView

CDaoTableDef

CDaoWorkspace

In the final part of this chapter, you'll create a program that returns information about an Access database using calls to DAO. If possible, you should let AppWizard design the shell of your application. Generally, for simple front-end applications, AppWizard provides an excellent framework for your program and requires only minor filling out by you—usually only the user interface. For more complex applications, you probably will use AppWizard to create the application's shell and add the DAO support later by hand.

> **NOTE**
>
> This chapter uses two sample programs. The first part of this chapter uses the Addresses program, and the second part uses the DAO Direct program. Both of these programs use the Addresses Access database, found in the CHAPTR14 directory on the CD that comes with this book.

An AppWizard-Created DAO Application

In this, the first part of the chapter, you'll create an application using AppWizard, with support for DAO. Using DAO in this manner lets you create an application that looks (and feels) like an ODBC application, both from the programmer's viewpoint and from the user's viewpoint.

The main differences in a stock AppWizard DAO application and a stock AppWizard ODBC application are the names of the classes used. Generally, the functions and functionalities of DAO and ODBC are virtually identical. For example, there is a one-to-one correspondence between DAO classes and the ODBC classes, as shown in Table 14.1.

Table 14.1. Correspondence between MFC's DAO and ODBC classes.

DAO Class	ODBC Class	Functionality
CDaoDatabase	CDatabase	A CDaoDatabase (and CDatabase) class object represents a connection to a database through which you can operate on the data.
CDaoException	CDBException	The CDaoException class object represents an exception condition raised by one of the MFC DAO database classes.
CDaoFieldExchange	CFieldExchange	The CDaoFieldExchange (and CFieldExchange) class object supports record field exchange (DFX). Typically directly used when you're writing data exchange routines for custom data types. Otherwise, AppWizard and ClassWizard will manipulate this class for you. Technical Note 53, available under MFC in Books Online, contains the necessary information for writing your own custom DFX routines.
CDaoQueryDef	No ODBC equivalent	A CDaoQueryDef class object represents a query definition that is typically saved in a database.
CDaoRecordset	CRecordset	A CDaoRecordset (and CRecordset) class object represents a set of records selected from a data source.
CDaoRecordView	CRecordView	A CDaoRecordView (and CRecordView) class object is used to represent a view that displays database records in controls (such as in a CFormView-based application).
CDaoTableDef	No ODBC equivalent	A CDaoTableDef class object represents the stored definition of a base table or an attached table.
CDaoWorkspace	No ODBC equivalent	A CDaoWorkspace class object manages a named, password-protected database session from logon to logoff by a given user.

Since DAO is intended to work with Access databases (after all, DAO uses the Access Jet database engine), you need to have at least one Access database installed on your system prior to using AppWizard in order to generate a DAO MFC application. Finding an Access database isn't difficult. If nothing else is available, you can use one of the sample databases (such as Northwind.mdb, typically found in the \MSOffice\Access\Samples directory) to get started writing DAO applications.

> **NOTE**
>
> It's not necessary to register your Access database (using ODBC) when you're creating or using a DAO application. DAO doesn't use ODBC.

When creating your application, you will have to select the basic user interface. Select either MDI or SDI, but not dialog-based, because a dialog-based application can't have database access when generated using AppWizard. Once the user interface is configured, you must select the degree of database support. You have the standard levels regardless of whether your application will be ODBC or DAO. The levels that may be selected include header files only, database view without file support, and database view with file support. If your application won't be using a separately saved document file, selecting database view without file support will create the best application with the least amount of clutter. Selecting header files only will create an application that may have DAO or ODBC support added later.

> **NOTE**
>
> Which came first, the chicken or the egg? In creating your application, you face your first dilemma: You need an existing database in order for AppWizard to generate your DAO application, but the application will generate the database using File | New.
>
> The solution is relatively simple: You will create a template database using Access. This will allow you to design your database using Access's tools. Then later you can add code to the application to create new databases as needed.

Creating a Template Database

A template database is needed in order for Visual C++ 4's AppWizard to create a DAO project. I used Access 7 to create a new database using Access's Database Wizard. The Database Wizard's Address Book template was chosen as the type of database desired because it fit the needs of your sample application, a names database.

Access's Database Wizard lets you add and remove columns from a database and define the look and feel of the data entry forms. The columns can be customized to your application's needs. (Having the right mix of columns can be a sticky wicket: What's right for one user usually isn't adequate for another user.) You're not going to use the data entry forms, so the form style isn't relevant in this example. The database is called Address Book, and it contains two tables: Addresses and Switchboard. The Switchboard table is used to manage the forms in the Access version of this database and is of no use to a Visual C++ programmer. Ignore the Switchboard table, but don't remove it.

Once the database is created, it's a good idea to print a record of the Addresses table that is created using Access's Tools | Analyze | Documentor menu selection. This will provide you with a printed, permanent record of the Addresses table.

Using the Documentor utility, you will have a report that can be printed (or exported to a document). It will list each column's attributes, as shown in Listing 14.1.

Listing 14.1. Access's Documentor output for two columns in the Addresses table.

```
Columns

   Name                               Type               Size
   AddressID                          Number (Long)        4
        Allow Zero Length:   False
        Attributes:          Fixed Size, Auto-Increment
        Caption:             Address ID
        Collating Order:     General
        Column Hidden:       False
        Column Order:        Default
        Column Width:        Default
        Ordinal Position:    0
        Required:            False
        Source Field:        AddressID
        Source Table:        Addresses

   FirstName                          Text                50
        Allow Zero Length:   False
        Attributes:          Variable Length
        Caption:             First Name
        Collating Order:     General
        Column Hidden:       False
        Column Order:        Default
        Column Width:        Default
        Ordinal Position:    2
        Required:            False
        Source Field:        FirstName
        Source Table:        Addresses
```

The entire listing for the Addresses table is only six pages long, so it's easily printed. When exported as a Word document (in RTF format, readable by Windows 95's WordPad program), it's saved as doc_rptObjects.rtf in your My Documents directory. This report appears in the CHAPTR14 directory on the CD that comes with this book so that you can peruse it without having to run Access.

NOTE

Although the Access Database Wizard creates a complete database application (a basic application, however) when using DAO to create databases, you will create only the database, not an application. For example, DAO typically isn't used to create forms that may be part of an Access database.

Once you've created your application's database, you can use Visual C++'s AppWizard to create the database application itself.

Using AppWizard to Create a DAO Application

Once you've created an initial database for your application, you can use AppWizard to create the DAO application's shell. You should follow typical database application creation steps, making sure to select a data source in the AppWizard database support wizard dialog (Step 2 of 6), as shown in Figure 14.1.

FIGURE 14.1.

AppWizard's Step 2 of 6 database support wizard dialog.

Clicking the Data Source button will display the Database Options dialog box, shown in Figure 14.2, in which you should select DAO as the datasource. Click the ... button.

FIGURE 14.2.

The Database Options dialog box.

A select files dialog box appears, as shown in Figure 14.3, listing Access database files.

FIGURE 14.3.
The DAO Open dialog box.

After you select an Access database, you must select a table to use. After you close the Database Options dialog box, you will see the Select Database Tables dialog box, shown in Figure 14.4. It will have a list of all the tables that are contained within the database that was selected. For this example, there are two tables. You will be working with the Addresses table exclusively.

FIGURE 14.4.
Selecting the Addresses table in the Select Database Tables dialog box.

After you've selected your DAO Access database and table (variables will be bound for each column in the selected table), you can set whatever other options you would like your application to support. For most applications, you should include support for OLE controls, because several of the stock OLE controls are most useful for database applications.

After generating your application, you should do a test build to make sure that the creation was successful.

Binding Variables to Dialog Controls

The second step in a DAO program is to bind variables to the user interface dialog controls. A DAO program uses a CDaoRecordView class object for a user interface. The CDaoRecordView object works much like the standard ODBC CRecordView object: Design and lay out a dialog box with controls to match the database table's columns.

In this example (a simple address book application), you will affix a number of controls to the dialog box (you won't use every column in the database table) to create a basic functional program. Later, you can add dialog boxes for other, infrequently used controls if you want to.

NOTE

There are other alternatives to using a separate dialog box for infrequently used fields that would otherwise clutter up a good user interface. One alternative is to use an MDI model. One window would service the main columns, and other windows would hold other, infrequently used columns in the database. A second alternative would be a tab dialog (like Visual C++'s options dialog boxes).

Figure 14.5 shows the dialog box controls that are used to allow the user to enter (and retrieve) data in your database.

FIGURE 14.5.

A typical user interface for a DAO program.

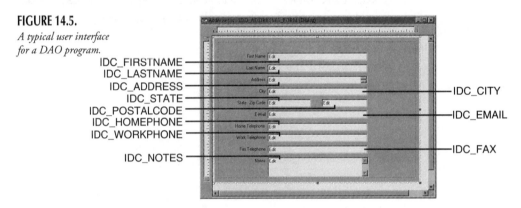

As soon as you've created your user interface, you can go on to the more advanced parts of your programming. Since this chapter is about using DAO, it doesn't cover topics such as printing, but you will need to add report generation facilities to virtually any application you create.

Implementing the File Menu

One primary functionality you need is to be able to handle the application's File menu. In a typical application, you would be able to open different files (or databases) and create a new file (database) for the user.

Opening and Closing a DAO Access Database

Opening (and closing for MDI applications, if applicable) a database file using DAO is a simple process. In the sample program, you close your database by adding a handler in your document class (`CAddressDoc` in the sample program) for the menu selections New and Open. Since the sample program is SDI, you don't implement a Close menu item. The Open selection will close an open database before you open a new one.

Since default DAO applications created using AppWizard have a "hardwired" default database name and SQL parameter, you must first change these constants to `CString` class variables. Here's an example of what AppWizard creates (the constants appear in bold):

```
CAddressesSet::CAddressesSet(CDaoDatabase* pdb)
    : CDaoRecordset(pdb)
{
    //{{AFX_FIELD_INIT(CAddressesSet)
    m_AddressID = 0;
    m_FirstName = _T("");
    m_LastName = _T("");
    m_SpouseName = _T("");
    m_Address = _T("");
    m_City = _T("");
    m_StateOrProvince = _T("");
    m_PostalCode = _T("");
    m_Country = _T("");
    m_EmailAddress = _T("");
    m_HomePhone = _T("");
    m_WorkPhone = _T("");
    m_WorkExtension = _T("");
    m_MobilePhone = _T("");
    m_FaxNumber = _T("");
    m_SendCard = FALSE;
    m_Nickname = _T("");
    m_Notes = _T("");
    m_Hobbies = _T("");
    m_nFields = 20;
    //}}AFX_FIELD_INIT
    m_nDefaultType = dbOpenDynaset;
}

CString CAddressesSet::GetDefaultDBName()
{
    return _T("I:\\Database Developers Guide with Visual C++ 4"
    "\\Source CD\\CHAPTR14\\Address Book.mdb");
}


CString CAddressesSet::GetDefaultSQL()
{
    return _T("[Addresses]");
}
```

You make your database and SQL strings modifiable by adding two CStrings to your document class and initializing them as shown in the following code fragment (changes appear in bold):

```
CAddressesSet::CAddressesSet(CDaoDatabase* pdb)
    : CDaoRecordset(pdb)
{
    //{{AFX_FIELD_INIT(CAddressesSet)
    m_AddressID = 0;
    m_FirstName = _T("");
    m_LastName = _T("");
    m_SpouseName = _T("");
    m_Address = _T("");
    m_City = _T("");
    m_StateOrProvince = _T("");
    m_PostalCode = _T("");
```

```
        m_Country = _T("");
        m_EmailAddress = _T("");
        m_HomePhone = _T("");
        m_WorkPhone = _T("");
        m_WorkExtension = _T("");
        m_MobilePhone = _T("");
        m_FaxNumber = _T("");
        m_SendCard = FALSE;
        m_Nickname = _T("");
        m_Notes = _T("");
        m_Hobbies = _T("");
        m_nFields = 20;
        //}}AFX_FIELD_INIT
        m_nDefaultType = dbOpenDynaset;
        m_DefaultDBName = _T("I:\\Database Developers Guide with Visual C++ 4"
        "\\Source CD\\CHAPTR14\\Address Book.mdb");
        m_DefaultSQL = _T("[Addresses]");
}

CString CAddressesSet::GetDefaultDBName()
{
    return m_DefaultDBName;
}


CString CAddressesSet::GetDefaultSQL()
{
    return m_DefaultSQL;
}
```

Don't forget to add `m_DefaultDBName` and `m_DefaultSQL` to your class definition's header file. This way, you can close the current database and then open a new one by modifying `DefaultDBName` and calling the `CDaoRecordset::Open()` function. First you create a handler for the File | Open menu selection in the `CAddressesDoc` class.

For example, in your document class, your handler for opening a new database is implemented as the following code fragment shows. To create this functionality, you must use ClassWizard to add a handler for the File | Open menu selection and then add code to that handler:

```
void CAddressesDoc::OnFileOpen()
{
    // TODO: Add your command handler code here

//  The m_addressSet member variable is a pointer to the CAddressSet class.

//  First, get a database file to be opened!

    CFileDialog dlg(TRUE,
        NULL,
        "*.mdb",
        OFN_OVERWRITEPROMPT,
        "Access Database Files (*.mdb) ¦ *.mdb ¦ "
        "All Files (*.*) ¦ *.* ¦¦");

    if (dlg.DoModal())
    {// User did not cancel the open file dialog:
```

```
    TRACE("File selected is '%s'\n", dlg.GetPathName());

    if (m_addressesSet.IsOpen())
    {// If open (avoid errors and crashes!), then close:
        m_addressesSet.Close();

        if (m_addressesSet.m_pDatabase != NULL)
        {// Close the DB too. If not closed, old DB is reopened!
            m_addressesSet.m_pDatabase->Close();
        }
    }

    //  Save the user's database filename and then (re)open:

    m_addressesSet.m_DefaultDBName = dlg.GetPathName();
    m_addressesSet.Open(AFX_DAO_USE_DEFAULT_TYPE);

    // Refresh the view to reflect the *new* database's data:

    CFrameWnd * pFrame = (CFrameWnd *)(AfxGetApp()->m_pMainWnd);
    CView * pView = pFrame->GetActiveView();

    if (pView)
    {
        pView->UpdateData(FALSE);
    }
}
else
{// User aborted. Do nothing, or clean up if appropriate.

}
}
```

This code is simple. First you get the name for the new database from the user. If the user cancels the dialog box, you simply do nothing. Otherwise, you close the currently open recordset and the database. Both must be closed to enable the opening of a new database. Next you take the user's new database name (the fully qualified path name) and stuff it into your m_addressesSet.m_DefaultDBName variable. You will use this name when you reopen your database.

Once you have a database name saved, you call your recordset's Open() function to do the actual open: m_addressesSet.Open(AFX_DAO_USE_DEFAULT_TYPE). Because you closed the original database, Open() will reopen the database using the database name returned by GetDefaultDBName(). If you had closed only your recordset and not the database, a call to Open() would simply have used the existing, still open, database.

Finally, after you've opened the new database, you must update the user interface. You do this by retrieving the current view (a simple process for any SDI application) and call the UpdateData() function with a parameter of FALSE to force an update of the application's data that is being presented to the user. The only thing special about this code is that it shows how to get a pointer to the application's view class from any point in an application:

```
        CFrameWnd * pFrame = (CFrameWnd *)(AfxGetApp()->m_pMainWnd);
        CView * pView = pFrame->GetActiveView();

        if (pView)
        {
        // pView is a valid pointer to the view class
        }
else
{
// pView is not valid: perhaps we have no view!
}
```

> **NOTE**
>
> You might have noticed that since this application's user interface is specific to the Address database, opening a database with a different table structure (NorthWind.MDB, for example) won't work. It's beyond the purpose of this example to add the complexity required to open and display any database. To test the database open functionality, I've included two versions of the Address database on the CD that comes with this book. These database files are located in the CHAPTR14 folder. The database called Address Book.mdb contains a standard set of five dummy records. The database called Special Address.mdb contains the same five records, but each first name is prefixed with the word SPECIAL.

Creating a New DAO Access Database

A necessary functionality in almost any application is to be able to create a new "document." In the case of a database program, a new document is actually a new database. You could simply not implement this functionality, or you could supply an empty database that the user (or your application) could copy to a new name. This isn't a very elegant solution. It looks kludgy and lacks professionalism. But with ODBC, this was often the way it was done.

> **NOTE**
>
> One trick of the trade was to take a new, empty database file and save it as a binary resource in the base application. When the user selected File | New, this binary resource was written out as a disk file and given the name that the user selected. When ODBC didn't provide a way for an application to create an Access database, it was a solution that was invisible to the user. DAO doesn't require you to use these tricks, because you can create an Access database directly.

> **NOTE**
>
> Several online documents are available that discuss using DAO to create Access databases. One topic that you can search for in Books Online is "Creating a Database with DAO."

To create a new database, follow these steps:

1. Create the basic database.
2. Create a table in your database.
3. Create columns in your table.
4. Create indexes as needed.
5. Repeat steps 2 through 4 as necessary.

You can add a new table to an existing database by following steps 2 through 5. You can add a new column to an existing table in a database by following steps 3 through 5. Here is your sample code:

```
void CAddressesDoc::OnFileNew()
{
    // TODO: Add your command handler code here

    // Create a new Access database, then open the doggie!

    // First, get a filename to use. Warn if we are overwriting an existing file:

    CFileDialog dlg(FALSE,
        NULL,
        "*.mdb",
        OFN_OVERWRITEPROMPT,
        "Access Database Files (*.mdb) ¦ *.mdb ¦ "
        "All Files (*.*) ¦ *.* ¦¦");

    if (dlg.DoModal())
    {// User did not cancel the open file dialog:

        TRACE("File selected is '%s'\n", dlg.GetPathName());

        // Close the existing database (if open):

        if (m_addressesSet.IsOpen())
        {// If open (avoid errors and crashes!), then close:
            m_addressesSet.Close();

            if (m_addressesSet.m_pDatabase != NULL)
            {// Close the DB too. If not closed, old DB is reopened!
                m_addressesSet.m_pDatabase->Close();
            }
        }
```

```
// Create, create, it's off to create we go!
// Notice: we are using CDaoDatabase's Create() function.

m_addressesSet.m_DefaultDBName = dlg.GetPathName();

if (m_addressesSet.m_pDatabase != NULL)
{// We are stuffed if m_pDatabase is NULL!
    m_addressesSet.m_pDatabase->Create(
        m_addressesSet.m_DefaultDBName,
        dbLangGeneral,
        dbVersion30);

    // Define the table (connected to our database)...

    CDaoTableDef TableDef(m_addressesSet.m_pDatabase);

    TableDef.Create(_T("Addresses"));

    // Define columns (hard-code them):

    TableDef.CreateField(_T("AddressID"),
        dbLong,      4, dbAutoIncrField);
    TableDef.CreateField(_T("FirstName"),
        dbText,     50, dbVariableField);
    TableDef.CreateField(_T("LastName"),
        dbText,     50, dbVariableField);
    TableDef.CreateField(_T("SpouseName"),
        dbText,     50, dbVariableField);
    TableDef.CreateField(_T("Address"),
        dbText,    255, dbVariableField);
    TableDef.CreateField(_T("City"),
        dbText,     50, dbVariableField);
    TableDef.CreateField(_T("StateOrProvince"),
        dbText,     20, dbVariableField);
    TableDef.CreateField(_T("PostalCode"),
        dbText,     20, dbVariableField);
    TableDef.CreateField(_T("Country"),
        dbText,     50, dbVariableField);
    TableDef.CreateField(_T("EmailAddress"),
        dbText,     50, dbVariableField);
    TableDef.CreateField(_T("HomePhone"),
        dbText,     30, dbVariableField);
    TableDef.CreateField(_T("WorkPhone"),
        dbText,     30, dbVariableField);
    TableDef.CreateField(_T("WorkExtension"),
        dbText,     20, dbVariableField);
    TableDef.CreateField(_T("MobilePhone"),
        dbText,     30, dbVariableField);
    TableDef.CreateField(_T("FaxNumber"),
        dbText,     30, dbVariableField);
    TableDef.CreateField(_T("Birthdate"),
        dbDate,      8, dbFixedField);
    TableDef.CreateField(_T("SendCard"),
        dbBoolean,   1, dbVariableField);
    TableDef.CreateField(_T("Nickname"),
        dbText,     30, dbVariableField);
    TableDef.CreateField(_T("Notes"),
        dbMemo,      0, dbVariableField);
```

```
            TableDef.CreateField(_T("Hobbies"),
                dbText,    255, dbVariableField);

            TableDef.Append();

            // Close the database, then reopen it using the CDaoRecordset class

            m_addressesSet.m_pDatabase->Close();

            m_addressesSet.Open(AFX_DAO_USE_DEFAULT_TYPE);

            // Refresh the view to reflect the *new* database's data:

            CFrameWnd * pFrame = (CFrameWnd *)(AfxGetApp()->m_pMainWnd);
             CView * pView = pFrame->GetActiveView();

            if (pView)
            {
                pView->UpdateData(FALSE);
            }
        }
    }
}
```

As in other listings, the code added manually appears in bold. Notice the sequence of events:

1. Create the database (you have already saved the database name in the `m_defaultDBName` member variable). An alternative to using `m_defaultDBName` would be to use a call to `GetDefaultDBName()` to return the correct name.

   ```
   m_addressesSet.m_pDatabase->Create(
       m_addressesSet.m_DefaultDBName,
       dbLangGeneral,
       dbVersion30);
   ```

2. Create the table (using a `CDaoTableDef` object):

   ```
   CDaoTableDef TableDef(m_addressesSet.m_pDatabase);
       TableDef.Create(_T("Addresses"));
   ```

   Create one table (and its fields) at a time.

3. Create the table's columns (fields):

   ```
   TableDef.CreateField(_T("AddressID"),
       dbLong,      4, dbAutoIncrField);
   TableDef.CreateField(_T("FirstName"),
       dbText,     50, dbVariableField);
   ```

   This code shows only two fields, but the sample program actually creates 19 columns (called fields) in the table.

4. Save the database's table definition:

   ```
   TableDef.Append();
   ```

   Each table must be saved using the `Append()` member function.

After you've created the database, tables, and table columns, you can close the database and reopen it. Although it's not strictly necessary to close a database after creating it, it makes sense to start off from a known state—freshly opened.

If you've been working along with this book, you now can create a database and open it. Here lies the wrinkle: Your application can open a database, but there is no provision to add new records! This shortcoming rather limits the program's usefulness. The next step is to create code to add records to the database.

Adding Indexes to a DAO Database

After you've created the database's tables and columns, you should also create any indexes your application will need. Although it's not strictly necessary to have indexes in a database, they can greatly enhance performance.

In the example, you will index the same columns that Microsoft did when Access's Database Wizard created your template database. Here are the indexes and the columns used by the indexes:

> PrimaryKey using the field `AddressID`, which will be the primary key
>
> EmailAddress using the field `EmailAddress`
>
> LastName using the field `LastName`
>
> PostalCode using the field `PostalCode`

> **NOTE**
>
> Indexes can have one or more fields. In the example, each index has only one field. Some database applications have indexes that comprise multiple fields. For a multiple-field index, you would define your `CDaoIndexFieldInfo` object as an array and indicate the number of fields used in the `CDaoIndexInfo::m_nFields` member.

To create an index, you must allocate a `CDaoIndexInfo` object and either a single `CDaoIndexFieldInfo` if your index will have only one field or an array of type `CDaoIndexFieldInfo` if your index will have more than one field. For example, your program uses this code:

```
// Finally, create the (optional) index fields. The example has
// four sets of indexes, each having only one field:

CDaoIndexInfo    idx;
CDaoIndexFieldInfo  fld; // Only one field per index in the example
```

After you've allocated your index and index field objects, you must fill them in. To create your primary key, use this code:

```
// Fill in your structure with revelant information, then build
// the index. CDaoTableDef::CreateIndex() calls Append
// automatically, unlike CDaoTableDef::CreateField(), which does not.

idx.m_strName = _T("PrimaryKey"); // Primary
idx.m_pFieldInfos = &fld;         // Primary
idx.m_nFields = 1;                // Primary
```

```
idx.m_bPrimary = TRUE;           // Secondary
idx.m_bUnique = TRUE;            // Secondary
idx.m_bClustered = FALSE;        // Secondary
idx.m_bIgnoreNulls = FALSE;      // Secondary
idx.m_bRequired = TRUE;          // Secondary
idx.m_bForeign = FALSE;          // Secondary
idx.m_lDistinctCount = 5;        // All - returned, not set!

fld.m_strName = _T("AddressID"); // Key field
fld.m_bDescending = FALSE;       // Ascending

TableDef.CreateIndex(idx);  // Create primary index
```

The comments //Primary, //Secondary, and //All refer to which fields are returned when you call the CDaoTableDef::GetIndexInfo() or CDaoRecordset::GetIndexInfo() functions. You must fill in all fields (except for CDaoIndexInfo::m_lDistinctCount, which is only used to return information about an existing index).

CAUTION

By design, a database can have one, and only one, primary key. The primary key is often used by the database engine to manage records in the table. A database table can have other, alternative keys if desired.

To create the secondary keys, use this code:

```
idx.m_strName = _T("EmailAddress"); // Primary
idx.m_pFieldInfos = &fld;        // Primary
idx.m_nFields = 1;               // Primary
idx.m_bPrimary = FALSE;          // Secondary
idx.m_bUnique = FALSE;           // Secondary
idx.m_bClustered = FALSE;        // Secondary
idx.m_bIgnoreNulls = FALSE;      // Secondary
idx.m_bRequired = FALSE;         // Secondary
idx.m_bForeign = FALSE;          // Secondary
idx.m_lDistinctCount = 5;        // All - returned, not set!

fld.m_strName = _T("EmailAddress"); // Key field
fld.m_bDescending = FALSE;       // Ascending

TableDef.CreateIndex(idx);  // Create secondary index

idx.m_strName = _T("LastName");  // Primary
idx.m_pFieldInfos = &fld;        // Primary
idx.m_nFields = 1;               // Primary
idx.m_bPrimary = FALSE;          // Secondary
idx.m_bUnique = FALSE;           // Secondary
idx.m_bClustered = FALSE;        // Secondary
idx.m_bIgnoreNulls = FALSE;      // Secondary
idx.m_bRequired = FALSE;         // Secondary
idx.m_bForeign = FALSE;          // Secondary
idx.m_lDistinctCount = 5;        // All - returned, not set!
```

```
fld.m_strName = _T("LastName");    // Key field
fld.m_bDescending = FALSE;         // Ascending

TableDef.CreateIndex(idx);  // Create secondary index


idx.m_strName = _T("PostalCode"); // Primary
idx.m_pFieldInfos = &fld;         // Primary
idx.m_nFields = 1;                // Primary
idx.m_bPrimary = FALSE;           // Secondary
idx.m_bUnique = FALSE;            // Secondary
idx.m_bClustered = FALSE;         // Secondary
idx.m_bIgnoreNulls = FALSE;       // Secondary
idx.m_bRequired = FALSE;          // Secondary
idx.m_bForeign = FALSE;           // Secondary
idx.m_lDistinctCount = 5;         // All - returned, not set!

fld.m_strName = _T("PostalCode"); // Key field
fld.m_bDescending = FALSE;         // Ascending

TableDef.CreateIndex(idx);  // Create secondary index

// Done creating the indexes...
```

There's no need to call Append(), because this is done automatically by MFC's DAO imple-mentation. Of course, in the preceding code, you should make sure that your parameters are set to reflect your database's design.

Adding Records to a DAO Database

To add records to a DAO database, you follow procedures that are very similar to those used with ODBC. To keep this functionality separate from your database creation, you add record addition, deletion, and refresh in the view class instead of in the recordset class. You could place this functionality in either class, but the view class is a better place for record addition, dele-tion, and refresh.

To add this functionality, I've added three new selections to the Record menu: Add, Delete, and Refresh. I also used ClassWizard to add a handler for OnMove(). To make the user interface easier, I also added three buttons to the toolbar to perform these functions. Visual C++ 4 makes adding toolbar buttons easy. It takes more time to design and draw the button bitmaps than it does to actually implement them!

After adding the new menu selections, handlers are generated using ClassWizard for each one. As noted earlier, the handlers are added to the view class, keeping them separate from other code used in this sample program. Listing 14.2 shows the view class implementation. Addi-tions and modifications appear in bold.

Listing 14.2. The view implementation class file.

```
// AddressesView.cpp : implementation of the CAddressesView class
//

#include "stdafx.h"
#include "Addresses.h"

#include "AddressesSet.h"
#include "AddressesDoc.h"
#include "AddressesView.h"

#ifdef _DEBUG
#define new DEBUG_NEW
#undef THIS_FILE
static char THIS_FILE[] = __FILE__;
#endif

/////////////////////////////////////////////////////////////////////////////
// CAddressesView

IMPLEMENT_DYNCREATE(CAddressesView, CDaoRecordView)

BEGIN_MESSAGE_MAP(CAddressesView, CDaoRecordView)
    //{{AFX_MSG_MAP(CAddressesView)
    ON_COMMAND(ID_RECORD_ADD, OnRecordAdd)
    ON_COMMAND(ID_RECORD_DELETE, OnRecordDelete)
    ON_COMMAND(ID_RECORD_REFRESH, OnRecordRefresh)
    //}}AFX_MSG_MAP
    // Standard printing commands
    ON_COMMAND(ID_FILE_PRINT, CDaoRecordView::OnFilePrint)
    ON_COMMAND(ID_FILE_PRINT_DIRECT, CDaoRecordView::OnFilePrint)
    ON_COMMAND(ID_FILE_PRINT_PREVIEW, CDaoRecordView::OnFilePrintPreview)
END_MESSAGE_MAP()

/////////////////////////////////////////////////////////////////////////////
// CAddressesView construction/destruction

CAddressesView::CAddressesView()
    : CDaoRecordView(CAddressesView::IDD)
{
    //{{AFX_DATA_INIT(CAddressesView)
    m_pSet = NULL;
    //}}AFX_DATA_INIT
    // TODO: add construction code here

    m_bAddMode = FALSE;
}

CAddressesView::~CAddressesView()
{
}

void CAddressesView::DoDataExchange(CDataExchange* pDX)
{
    CDaoRecordView::DoDataExchange(pDX);
    //{{AFX_DATA_MAP(CAddressesView)
```

continues

Listing 14.2. continued

```cpp
    DDX_FieldText(pDX, IDC_ADDRESS, m_pSet->m_Address, m_pSet);
    DDV_MaxChars(pDX, m_pSet->m_Address, 255);
    DDX_FieldText(pDX, IDC_CITY, m_pSet->m_City, m_pSet);
    DDV_MaxChars(pDX, m_pSet->m_City, 50);
    DDX_FieldText(pDX, IDC_EMAIL, m_pSet->m_EmailAddress, m_pSet);
    DDV_MaxChars(pDX, m_pSet->m_EmailAddress, 50);
    DDX_FieldText(pDX, IDC_FAX, m_pSet->m_FaxNumber, m_pSet);
    DDV_MaxChars(pDX, m_pSet->m_FaxNumber, 30);
    DDX_FieldText(pDX, IDC_FIRSTNAME, m_pSet->m_FirstName, m_pSet);
    DDV_MaxChars(pDX, m_pSet->m_FirstName, 50);
    DDX_FieldText(pDX, IDC_HOMEPHONE, m_pSet->m_HomePhone, m_pSet);
    DDV_MaxChars(pDX, m_pSet->m_HomePhone, 30);
    DDX_FieldText(pDX, IDC_LASTNAME, m_pSet->m_LastName, m_pSet);
    DDV_MaxChars(pDX, m_pSet->m_LastName, 50);
    DDX_FieldText(pDX, IDC_NOTES, m_pSet->m_Notes, m_pSet);
    DDX_FieldText(pDX, IDC_POSTALCODE, m_pSet->m_PostalCode, m_pSet);
    DDV_MaxChars(pDX, m_pSet->m_PostalCode, 20);
    DDX_FieldText(pDX, IDC_STATE, m_pSet->m_StateOrProvince, m_pSet);
    DDV_MaxChars(pDX, m_pSet->m_StateOrProvince, 20);
    DDX_FieldText(pDX, IDC_WORKPHONE, m_pSet->m_WorkPhone, m_pSet);
    DDV_MaxChars(pDX, m_pSet->m_WorkPhone, 30);
    //}}AFX_DATA_MAP
}

BOOL CAddressesView::PreCreateWindow(CREATESTRUCT& cs)
{
    // TODO: Modify the Window class or styles here by modifying
    // the CREATESTRUCT cs

    return CDaoRecordView::PreCreateWindow(cs);
}

void CAddressesView::OnInitialUpdate()
{
    m_pSet = &GetDocument()->m_addressesSet;
    CDaoRecordView::OnInitialUpdate();
}

/////////////////////////////////////////////////////////////////////////
// CAddressesView printing

BOOL CAddressesView::OnPreparePrinting(CPrintInfo* pInfo)
{
    // Default preparation
    return DoPreparePrinting(pInfo);
}

void CAddressesView::OnBeginPrinting(CDC* /*pDC*/, CPrintInfo* /*pInfo*/)
{
    // TODO: Add extra initialization before printing
}

void CAddressesView::OnEndPrinting(CDC* /*pDC*/, CPrintInfo* /*pInfo*/)
{
    // TODO: Add cleanup after printing
}
```

```
/////////////////////////////////////////////////////////////////////////////
// CAddressesView diagnostics

#ifdef _DEBUG
void CAddressesView::AssertValid() const
{
    CDaoRecordView::AssertValid();
}

void CAddressesView::Dump(CDumpContext& dc) const
{
    CDaoRecordView::Dump(dc);
}

CAddressesDoc* CAddressesView::GetDocument() // Non-debug version is inline
{
    ASSERT(m_pDocument->IsKindOf(RUNTIME_CLASS(CAddressesDoc)));
    return (CAddressesDoc*)m_pDocument;
}
#endif //_DEBUG

/////////////////////////////////////////////////////////////////////////////
// CAddressesView database support
CDaoRecordset* CAddressesView::OnGetRecordset()
{
    return m_pSet;
}


/////////////////////////////////////////////////////////////////////////////
// CAddressesView message handlers


BOOL CAddressesView::OnMove(UINT nIDMoveCommand)
{
    // TODO: Add your specialized code here and/or call the base class

    // Retrieve the current record set:

    CDaoRecordset* pRecordset = OnGetRecordset();

    if (m_bAddMode)
    {// Do special handling if you are adding records:

        if (!UpdateData())
        { // Could not get updated data from input dialog:
            return FALSE;
        }

        try
        {// Hope it works...
            pRecordset->Update();
        }
        catch (CDaoException* e)
        {// ...but if it doesn't...
            AfxMessageBox(e->m_pErrorInfo->m_strDescription);
            e->Delete();
            return FALSE;
        }
```

continues

Listing 14.2. continued

```
            pRecordset->Requery();
            UpdateData(FALSE);
            m_bAddMode = FALSE;
            return TRUE;
    }
    else
    {// If not adding records, just move around:
            return CDaoRecordView::OnMove(nIDMoveCommand);
    }
}

void CAddressesView::OnRecordAdd()
{
    // TODO: Add your command handler code here

    // If already in add mode, complete previous new record add:

    if (m_bAddMode)
    {// If adding, first add the current record:
        OnMove(ID_RECORD_FIRST);
    }

    // Switch into the Add mode (even if already adding):

    OnGetRecordset()->AddNew();
    m_bAddMode = TRUE;
    UpdateData(FALSE);

    return;
}

void CAddressesView::OnRecordDelete()
{
    // TODO: Add your command handler code here

    CDaoRecordset* pRecordset = OnGetRecordset();
    try
    {// It better work...
        pRecordset->Delete();
    }
    catch (CDaoException* e)
    {// ...but if it didn't...
        AfxMessageBox(e->m_pErrorInfo->m_strDescription);
        e->Delete();
        return;
    }

    // Move to the next record after the one just deleted
    pRecordset->MoveNext();

    // Ensure that the move is valid:
    if (pRecordset->IsEOF())
    {
        pRecordset->MoveLast();
    }
```

```
        if (pRecordset->IsBOF())
        {
            pRecordset->SetFieldNull(NULL);
        }

        UpdateData(FALSE);

        return;
    }

void CAddressesView::OnRecordRefresh()
{
    // TODO: Add your command handler code here

    if (m_bAddMode)
    {// Was the user adding a record? If so, exit add mode.
        try
        {// It better work...
            OnGetRecordset()->CancelUpdate();
            OnGetRecordset()->Move(0);
        }
        catch (CDaoException* e)
        {// ...but if it didn't...
            AfxMessageBox(e->m_pErrorInfo->m_strDescription);
            e->Delete();
            return;
        }
        m_bAddMode = FALSE;
    }

    // Restore the user's original values (as necessary):

    UpdateData(FALSE);

    return;
}
```

To manage the process of record addition, you must add a flag to your view class. I've used a Boolean variable called m_bAddMode, which is set to TRUE whenever the user is adding a new record to the database. This variable is initialized in the constructor to FALSE.

In addition to the code to manage the three new functions (add, delete, and refresh), you also must add code to manage the task of record navigation. This is necessary because if the user starts to add a new record and then selects one of the record navigation functions (next, previous, first, or last record), you must add the new record before you perform the navigation action requested by the user.

You do this using the add record flag m_bAddMode, which, if TRUE, tells you that a record is being added. When you're in add mode, you must save the record being added (if the database supports updating—that is, if it isn't read-only). The record is saved using the CDaoRecordset::Update() function (use exception handling to catch errors), which will add the current record to the database. Once the database has been updated, it is then requeried, the view is updated, and you return.

If the user isn't currently in the add record mode, you simply do the necessary move using the default `CDaoRecordView::OnMove(nIDMoveCommand)` handler:

```
CDaoRecordset* pRecordset = OnGetRecordset();

if (m_bAddMode)
{// Do special handling if you are adding records:

    if (!UpdateData())
    { // Could not get updated data from input dialog:
        return FALSE;
    }

    try
    {// Hope it works...
        pRecordset->Update();
    }
    catch (CDaoException* e)
    {// ...but if it doesn't...
        AfxMessageBox(e->m_pErrorInfo->m_strDescription);
        e->Delete();
        return FALSE;
    }

    pRecordset->Requery();
    UpdateData(FALSE);
    m_bAddMode = FALSE;
    return TRUE;
}
else
{// If not adding records, just move around:
    return CDaoRecordView::OnMove(nIDMoveCommand);
}
```

The add record handler checks the add flag. If the user is already in the add record mode, it adds the current record and then prepares for a new added record. A user who needs to add several records would simply select add prior to each record to be added:

```
if (m_bAddMode)
{// If adding, first add the current record:
    OnMove(ID_RECORD_FIRST);
}

// Switch into the Add mode (even if already adding):

OnGetRecordset()->AddNew();
m_bAddMode = TRUE;
UpdateData(FALSE);

return;
```

Deleting records is straightforward. You call the recordset's delete member function, which should delete the current record (if there is one). Next you must move to the next record (giving the user something to look at). Moving to the next record presents a problem, because the application must compute which record is next. The user could have deleted the last record (then the application must move back one record). Also, the application must handle the situation that arises when the user deletes all the records in the database:

```
CDaoRecordset* pRecordset = OnGetRecordset();
try
{// It better work...
    pRecordset->Delete();
}
catch (CDaoException* e)
{// ...but if it didn't...
    AfxMessageBox(e->m_pErrorInfo->m_strDescription);
    e->Delete();
    return;
}

// Move to the next record after the one just deleted
pRecordset->MoveNext();

// Ensure that the move is valid:
if (pRecordset->IsEOF())
{
    pRecordset->MoveLast();
}

if (pRecordset->IsBOF())
{
    pRecordset->SetFieldNull(NULL);
}

UpdateData(FALSE);

return;
```

Finally, when the user selects the refresh option, you must restore the current record's contents. This functionality is required to handle the situation in which the user has modified a record in error and realizes the error prior to updating the database by doing a record move. You must handle two situations with the refresh handler: the user is modifying an existing record, and the user has (in error) added a record that he doesn't want.

When aborting an add record situation, you must cancel the add using the CDaoRecordset::CancelUpdate() function. After you cancel the add, you move to the current record. You also turn off the add mode by setting m_bAddMode to FALSE. To cancel an update to an existing record, you simply retrieve the record's original contents and redisplay this information. You do this using the view class's UpdateData() member function:

```
if (m_bAddMode)
{// Was the user adding a record? If so, exit add mode.
    try
    {// It better work...
        OnGetRecordset()->CancelUpdate();
        OnGetRecordset()->Move(0);
    }
    catch (CDaoException* e)
    {// ...but if it didn't...
```

```
        AfxMessageBox(e->m_pErrorInfo->m_strDescription);
        e->Delete();
        return;
    }
    m_bAddMode = FALSE;
}

// Restore the user's original values (as necessary):

UpdateData(FALSE);

return;
```

Using *CDaoRecordset* Directly in a Dialog Box

To use the CDaoRecordset object directly, you must add a new class to your application using ClassWizard. Base your new class on CDaoRecordset. ClassWizard will prompt you for the DAO datasource and table to use. As in a typical CDaoRecordView application, all columns in the table(s) selected will be bound into your CDaoRecordset object. To display ClassWizard's Create New Class dialog, shown in Figure 14.6, select the Class Info tab in ClassWizard and then click the Add Class button.

FIGURE 14.6.

*Adding a
CDaoRecordset
object in a project.*

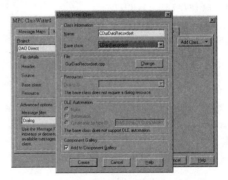

To use this new class (in the example, the new CDaoRecordset object is called COurDaoRecordset), simply add the header file to source file. For example, to include a COurDaoRecordset object in your dialog box, add the following to the #include statements in the dialog box's source file:

```
// DaoRecordsetDemo.h : header file
//

//////////////////////////////////////////////////////////////////////////
// CDaoRecordsetDemo dialog

#include "OurDaoRecordset.h"
```

Then add a member variable m_Set of type OurDaoRecordset in your DaoRecordsetDemo class definition.

You must have controls in your dialog box to bind to your database columns. In this example, two controls—IDC_FIRST_NAME and IDC_LAST_NAME—are used to display the first and last name columns from the database's Addresses table. When the CDaoRecordset object is created, it will have member variables for each of the columns in the table.

The following code fragment shows the binding of COurDaoRecordset's variables to the controls in the dialog box. Notice that you must write this code by hand: ClassWizard won't recognize the COurDaoRecordset member variables. Be careful to place these field exchange statements after the ClassWizard block:

```
void CDaoRecordsetDemo::DoDataExchange(CDataExchange* pDX)
{
    CDialog::DoDataExchange(pDX);
    //{{AFX_DATA_MAP(CDaoRecordsetDemo)
        // NOTE: ClassWizard will add DDX and DDV calls here
    //}}AFX_DATA_MAP
//  Add *after* the //AFX_DATA_MAP block!
    DDX_FieldText(pDX, IDC_FIRST_NAME, m_Set.m_FirstName, &m_Set);
    DDV_MaxChars(pDX, m_Set.m_FirstName, 50);
    DDX_FieldText(pDX, IDC_LAST_NAME, m_Set.m_LastName, &m_Set);
    DDV_MaxChars(pDX, m_Set.m_FirstName, 50);
}
```

The DDX_FieldText() macros (and all other DDX_Field...() macros) require a pointer to your CDaoRecordset object as the final parameter.

Next, the COurDaoRecordset object must be initialized. That is, the datasource must be opened. In a dialog box, you can do this in either the constructor or in the WM_INITDIALOG handler:

```
BOOL CDaoRecordsetDemo::OnInitDialog()
{
    CDialog::OnInitDialog();

    // TODO: Add extra initialization here

    m_Set.Open();
    UpdateData(FALSE);

    return TRUE;  // Return TRUE unless you set the focus to a control
                  // EXCEPTION: OCX Property Pages should return FALSE
}
```

When you do the COurDaoRecordset open in the OnInitDialog() handler, you must tell the dialog manager to update the controls with a call to UpdateData(FALSE). If you forget to do this, the controls that reflect records from the datasource will initially be blank.

At this stage, you have an open datasource. The first record in the datasource will be displayed in the dialog box's controls. You don't have any way to select another record, because there are no record navigation controls!

In the sample program, I've added four buttons to the dialog box: First, Next, Previous, and Last. These controls execute a set of simple functions when clicked, as you will see. The First button checks to see if any records in the datasource have been opened and then moves to the first record if there is one. In all the record navigation examples shown here, a call to MessageBeep() signals the user if the requested action can't be accomplished. Many applications might not need this type of notification. Disabling invalid navigation buttons might be a more elegant solution.

```
void CDaoRecordsetDemo::OnFirst()
{
    // TODO: Add your control notification handler code here

    if (!m_Set.IsEOF() || !m_Set.IsBOF())
    {// Ensure that it's not a null recordset!
        m_Set.MoveFirst();
        UpdateData(FALSE);
    }
    else
    {// For demo purposes...
        MessageBeep(MB_ICONEXCLAMATION);
    }
}
```

The Next record button's handler is similar to the First record button's handler, as the following code shows. In this case, it isn't necessary to check whether the recordset is empty. You only need to make sure that you aren't moving past the end of the recordset:

```
void CDaoRecordsetDemo::OnNext()
{
    // TODO: Add your control notification handler code here

    if (!m_Set.IsEOF())
    {// Ensure that it's not a null recordset!
        m_Set.MoveNext();

        if (m_Set.IsEOF())
        {// Off the end of the world?
            m_Set.MovePrev();
        }

        UpdateData(FALSE);
    }
    else
    {// For demo purposes...
        MessageBeep(MB_ICONEXCLAMATION);
    }
}
```

After you've moved to the next record, you then check to make sure you haven't moved past the end of the recordset (this would cause the user to see a blank record). If you *have* moved past the end of the recordset, you move back one record. When you're done moving, you tell the dialog manager to update the dialog box's controls. As in the other record navigation examples, you sound a beep if the user's requested move can't be performed.

For programs that need to access a datasource and that aren't presenting records to the user (such as a program that rolls up data for reports or graphs), the techniques are virtually identical: Create your CDaoRecordset object, open it, and navigate through each record in turn until you've reached the end of the records. Use the `CDaoRecordset` member variables to access the column's data.

Using DAO Dynamically

Sometimes you will need to use DAO to open a database on-the-fly. The application usually won't know which columns or tables are present in the database at design time, so they'll have to query the database for this information.

For example, your application would create a `CDaoDatabase` object and then open this database. You would have to either query the user for the datasource (typical) or obtain the datasource name from another location that your application knows about. A typical example of this is the inclusion of the database information in either the registry or an .INI file.

The sample program's dynamic DAO dialog box prompts the user for a datasource name and then queries the datasource for the name and other information about each table in the datasource. Each table is in turn queried about columns (fields) that are contained within the table. For each table that has records, the first record is retrieved. If the column type is character, you present the contents of the first record. This process is actually rather simple, as Listing 14.3 shows. In this listing, the major change is the addition of code in the handler for the Open button in the dialog box.

Listing 14.3. DAO using direct calls: DaoDatabaseDlg.cpp.

```
// DaoDatabaseDlg.cpp : implementation file
//

#include "stdafx.h"
#include "dao direct.h"
#include "DaoDatabaseDlg.h"

#ifdef _DEBUG
#define new DEBUG_NEW
#undef THIS_FILE
static char THIS_FILE[] = __FILE__;
#endif


/////////////////////////////////////////////////////////////////////////////
// CDaoDatabaseDlg dialog


CDaoDatabaseDlg::CDaoDatabaseDlg(CWnd* pParent /*=NULL*/)
    : CDialog(CDaoDatabaseDlg::IDD, pParent)
{
    //{{AFX_DATA_INIT(CDaoDatabaseDlg)
        // NOTE: ClassWizard will add member initialization here
    //}}AFX_DATA_INIT
}
```

continues

Listing 14.3. continued

```
void CDaoDatabaseDlg::DoDataExchange(CDataExchange* pDX)
{
    CDialog::DoDataExchange(pDX);
    //{{AFX_DATA_MAP(CDaoDatabaseDlg)
        // NOTE: ClassWizard will add DDX and DDV calls here
    //}}AFX_DATA_MAP
}


BEGIN_MESSAGE_MAP(CDaoDatabaseDlg, CDialog)
    //{{AFX_MSG_MAP(CDaoDatabaseDlg)
    ON_BN_CLICKED(IDC_OPEN_DATABASE, OnOpenDatabase)
    //}}AFX_MSG_MAP
END_MESSAGE_MAP()

/////////////////////////////////////////////////////////////////////////////
// CDaoDatabaseDlg message handlers

void CDaoDatabaseDlg::OnOpenDatabase()
{
    // TODO: Add your control notification handler code here

    // Create a CDaoDatabase object first:

    CDaoDatabase cdb;
    CDaoTableDef TableDef(&cdb);
    CDaoRecordset    Recordset(&cdb);
    CDaoTableDefInfo tabledefinfo;
    CDaoFieldInfo fieldinfo;
    COleVariant OleVariant;
    CString     output;

    int nCount = 0;
    int nFieldCount = 0;


    CFileDialog dlg(TRUE,
        NULL,
        "*.mdb",
        OFN_OVERWRITEPROMPT,
        "Access Database Files (*.mdb) ¦ *.mdb ¦ "
        "All Files (*.*) ¦ *.* ¦¦");

    if (dlg.DoModal())
    {// User did not cancel the open file dialog:

        TRACE("File selected is '%s'\n", dlg.GetPathName());

        // As applicable, check to see if the database is already open

        if (cdb.IsOpen())
        {// If open (avoid errors and crashes!), then close:
            cdb.Close();
        }
```

```
// Save the user's database filename if necessary

// Open the database
cdb.Open(dlg.GetPathName());

nCount = cdb.GetTableDefCount();

for (int i = 0; i < nCount; i++)
{
    cdb.GetTableDefInfo(i, tabledefinfo, AFX_DAO_ALL_INFO);

    TRACE("Table %d m_strName '%s' m_lRecordCount '%d'\n",
        i,
        tabledefinfo.m_strName,
        tabledefinfo.m_lRecordCount);

    // Open the current table (for column names)
    TableDef.Open(tabledefinfo.m_strName);

    // Get number of columns in table:
    nFieldCount = TableDef.GetFieldCount();

    for (int j = 0; j < nFieldCount; j++)
    {
        try
        { // This should work...
            TableDef.GetFieldInfo(j, fieldinfo, AFX_DAO_ALL_INFO);
        }
        catch (CDaoException* e)
        {// ...but if it doesn't...
            AfxMessageBox(e->m_pErrorInfo->m_strDescription);
            e->Delete();
        }

        if (tabledefinfo.m_lRecordCount > 0)
        {
            Recordset.Open(&TableDef, dbOpenTable);

            OleVariant = Recordset.GetFieldValue(fieldinfo.m_strName);

            if (fieldinfo.m_nType == 10) //CString type...
            {// Character data. Convert to CString:
                output = VARIANT(OleVariant).pbVal;

                TRACE("    Column %d: m_strName '%s' "
                    "First Record Data '%s'\n",
                    j,
                    fieldinfo.m_strName ,
                    output);
            }
            else
            {// A datatype we don't handle in this example!
                TRACE("    Column %d: m_strName '%s' Type '%d'\n",
                    j,
                    fieldinfo.m_strName,
                    fieldinfo.m_nType);
            }
            Recordset.Close();
```

continues

Listing 14.3. continued

```
                    }
                    else
                    {
                        TRACE("    Column %d: m_strName '%s' Type '%d'\n",
                            j,
                            fieldinfo.m_strName,
                            fieldinfo.m_nType);
                    }
                }

            TableDef.Close();
        }

        // When done, close up to be nice to the world:

        cdb.Close();
    }
    else
    {// User aborted. Do nothing, or clean up if appropriate.
    }
}
```

The process is a simple set of steps:

1. Obtain the name of the datasource.
2. Open the CDaoDatabase database object.
3. Get a count of the number of tables in the database.
4. Loop through the tables in the database and determine which table the user wants. Typically, a list box or combo box is used to allow the user to select the table, although you could also use a lookup table.
5. Get a count of fields (columns) in the desired table.
6. Loop through the fields in the table and determine which fields are needed.
7. For each field in the table desired, get the current row's data.
8. Repeat step 7 for each row in the table.

Typically, the table's data will be retrieved row by row. Applications normally wouldn't store or otherwise save a row's data specifically, except to place the data into a control such as a grid control. Rather, the application would retrieve a row's data as needed.

The preceding program might, for the Addresses database, return the information in Visual C++ 4.0's debug window (note the TRACE functions). A sample output is shown in Listing 14.4. When you run this sample program, you might receive slightly different results, but the basic output will be the same as that shown in the listing.

Listing 14.4. The output of a direct DAO database access.

```
File selected is 'I:\Database Developers Guide with Visual C++ 4
        ➥\Source CD\CHAPTR14\Address Book.mdb'
Table 0 m_strName 'Addresses' m_lRecordCount '5'
    Column 0: m_strName 'AddressID' Type '4'
    Column 1: m_strName 'FirstName' First Record Data 'Nancy'
    Column 2: m_strName 'LastName' First Record Data 'Davolio'
    Column 3: m_strName 'SpouseName' First Record Data 'Paul'
    Column 4: m_strName 'Address' First Record Data '507-20th Ave. E. Apt. 2A'
    Column 5: m_strName 'City' First Record Data 'Seattle'
    Column 6: m_strName 'StateOrProvince' First Record Data 'WA'
    Column 7: m_strName 'PostalCode' First Record Data '98122'
    Column 8: m_strName 'Country' First Record Data 'USA'
    Column 9: m_strName 'EmailAddress' First Record Data 'nancyd@anywhere.com'
    Column 10: m_strName 'HomePhone' First Record Data '(504) 555-9857'
    Column 11: m_strName 'WorkPhone' First Record Data '(504) 555-9922'
    Column 12: m_strName 'WorkExtension' First Record Data ''
    Column 13: m_strName 'MobilePhone' First Record Data '(504) 555-8822'
    Column 14: m_strName 'FaxNumber' First Record Data '(504) 555-7722'
    Column 15: m_strName 'Birthdate' Type '8'
    Column 16: m_strName 'SendCard' Type '1'
    Column 17: m_strName 'Nickname' First Record Data ''
    Column 18: m_strName 'Notes' Type '12'
    Column 19: m_strName 'Hobbies' First Record Data
        ➥'Drinking white wine while composing music'
Table 1 m_strName 'MSysACEs' m_lRecordCount '81'
Table 2 m_strName 'MSysIMEXColumns' m_lRecordCount '0'
    Column 0: m_strName 'DataType' Type '3'
    Column 1: m_strName 'FieldName' Type '10'
    Column 2: m_strName 'IndexType' Type '2'
    Column 3: m_strName 'SkipColumn' Type '1'
    Column 4: m_strName 'SpecID' Type '4'
    Column 5: m_strName 'Start' Type '3'
    Column 6: m_strName 'Width' Type '3'
Table 3 m_strName 'MSysIMEXSpecs' m_lRecordCount '0'
    Column 0: m_strName 'DateDelim' Type '10'
    Column 1: m_strName 'DateFourDigitYear' Type '1'
    Column 2: m_strName 'DateLeadingZeros' Type '1'
    Column 3: m_strName 'DateOrder' Type '3'
    Column 4: m_strName 'DecimalPoint' Type '10'
    Column 5: m_strName 'FieldSeparator' Type '10'
    Column 6: m_strName 'FileType' Type '3'
    Column 7: m_strName 'SpecID' Type '4'
    Column 8: m_strName 'SpecName' Type '10'
    Column 9: m_strName 'SpecType' Type '2'
    Column 10: m_strName 'StartRow' Type '4'
    Column 11: m_strName 'TextDelim' Type '10'
    Column 12: m_strName 'TimeDelim' Type '10'
Table 4 m_strName 'MSysModules' m_lRecordCount '8'
    Column 0: m_strName 'Flags' Type '4'
    Column 1: m_strName 'Form' Type '11'
    Column 2: m_strName 'Module' Type '11'
    Column 3: m_strName 'Name' First Record Data 'Lock'
    Column 4: m_strName 'ReplicationVersion' Type '4'
    Column 5: m_strName 'Type' Type '4'
    Column 6: m_strName 'TypeInfo' Type '11'
    Column 7: m_strName 'Version' Type '4'
```

continues

Listing 14.4. continued

```
Table 5 m_strName 'MSysObjects' m_lRecordCount '28'
Table 6 m_strName 'MSysQueries' m_lRecordCount '0'
Table 7 m_strName 'MSysRelationships' m_lRecordCount '0'
Table 8 m_strName 'MSysToolbars' m_lRecordCount '0'
    Column 0: m_strName 'Grptbcd' Type '11'
    Column 1: m_strName 'TbName' Type '10'
Table 9 m_strName 'Switchboard Items' m_lRecordCount '11'
    Column 0: m_strName 'SwitchboardID' Type '4'
    Column 1: m_strName 'ItemNumber' Type '3'
    Column 2: m_strName 'ItemText' First Record Data 'Main Switchboard'
    Column 3: m_strName 'Command' Type '3'
    Column 4: m_strName 'Argument' First Record Data 'Default'
```

Summary

In this chapter you developed two programs. The first used DAO to manipulate an Access database, and the second returned information about an Access database, including table and column information. These two programs showed you how to use the DAO MFC class objects, including

       CDaoDatabase

       CDaoException

       CDaoFieldExchange

       CDaoQueryDef

       CDaoRecordset

       CDaoRecordView

       CDaoTableDef

       CDaoWorkspace

You saw several sample programs and routines, as well as a typical session with AppWizard creating a DAO project. You also saw how to use DAO directly, without using AppWizard- or ClassWizard-created code.

15

Designing Online Transaction-Processing Applications

Transaction-processing (TP) applications are classified in this book as database applications that update data contained in tables. An update to a table occurs when the application changes the value of data in existing records, adds new records, or deletes records from the database.

You update data with Visual C++ applications that are easily developed using AppWizard. Updating is done with SQL statements that Microsoft calls *action queries*. Semantically, the term *query* isn't an appropriate description of an SQL statement that doesn't return rows. For consistency with the Microsoft documentation for Access, this book uses the term *action query* to include SQL update, append, and make-table queries. You also can use the `CDatabase::BeginTrans()` and `CDatabase::CommitTrans()` member functions to make changes to recordset objects.

Online transaction processing (OLTP) is a category of TP in which the updates occur on a real-time basis. The alternative to OLTP is batch processing, in which updates to database tables are accumulated as rows of temporary tables. A separate database application processes the data in the temporary tables. The second application deletes the temporary tables when the batch update process is complete. Batch processing often is used in accounting applications. This chapter deals primarily with OLTP, but most of the techniques you will learn here are also applicable to batch processing methods.

Categorizing Transaction-Processing Applications

All database applications fall into either the decision-support or transaction-processing class. Decision-support applications need only (and always should be restricted to) read-only access to the database tables. By definition, transaction-processing applications require read-write access to the tables being updated. This section defines some of the terms used in this book, as well as by the industry, to describe transaction-processing applications.

The majority of transaction-processing applications fall into one of these three categories or subclasses:

■ Interactive transaction-processing applications combine decision-support and transaction-processing methods. Interactive applications let the user review and edit existing information. Most allow new records to be added to tables. Personal information management (PIM), live (telephone) order entry, and airline reservations systems are typical interactive OLTP applications. Concurrency (page- or record-locking) issues arise in multiuser interactive TP applications. Chapter 19, "Running Visual C++ Database Applications on a Network," discusses page- and record-locking methods to resolve concurrency issues in multiuser applications.

■ Input-only TP applications add records to database tables. The majority of input-only applications only let the user append new records; they don't provide the capability to review data other than the data currently being entered—although lookup tables often are used to speed the data-entry process. Many input-only applications fall into the "heads-down" data-entry class, in which data-entry operators process information found on paper forms. OLTP applications for heads-down data entry emphasize use of the keyboard rather than the mouse to perform every data-entry function. Concurrency problems seldom arise in multiuser input-only applications, because the data-entry operator "owns" the new record until the record is added to the table.

■ Data-validation applications are used to test update data for errors before making final updates to primary database tables. The most common use of data-validation applications is in batch processing systems. In a multiuser environment, data-validation applications need to take into account pending changes to the same record in a primary table initiated by more than one user. The problem of resolving conflicts that arise as a result of multiple changes to a single primary record is one of the reasons that OLTP is favored over batch processing in today's transaction-processing environment. Consistency is the primary issue in data-validation applications.

Another category of transaction-processing application that is becoming more widely used in conjunction with downsizing projects involves distributed databases. Transaction-processing applications that make almost-simultaneous updates to tables in more than one database are called *distributed OLTP* (DOLTP) applications. Transaction processing in a distributed database environment, where the databases involved are located on different servers that may be geographically dispersed, is one of the subjects of Chapter 19.

Transaction monitors (TMs or OLTMs) are a class of transaction-processing applications that were originally designed to manage very large numbers of simultaneous transactions against mainframe database management systems. TMs are more robust and handle more simultaneous transactions than conventional client-server RDBMSs. IBM's Customer Information Control System (CICS) transaction-monitor application is undoubtedly the most widely used mainframe TM in North America. IBM has released client-server version 2.0.1 of CICS for OS/2. CICS For OS/2 version 2.0.1 lets you use the CICS TM to update data in a three-tiered structure (such as a PC client running OS/2 or Windows, a PC server running IBM's LAN Server application, and an IBM mainframe running CICS-MVS) to distribute transaction-processing applications over a LAN instead of using 3270-style terminals. However, you also can run CICS for OS/2 version 2.0.1 in an IBM LAN Server-only environment in which the server holds the database and the applications reside on the client PCs.

Using SQL Statements and Recordsets for Transaction Processing

As mentioned earlier, you can use either SQL action queries or Visual C++ code generated using AppWizard in transaction-processing applications. Traditional character-based desktop database applications such as dBASE, Clipper, and FoxPro use GET statements to assign entered data to a variable and REPLACE statements to update a table field with the variable's value.

Visual C++ is more flexible than DOS desktop database applications, because it offers the three methods of updating database tables that are discussed in the following sections.

Determining When You Can Update Joined Tables

Action queries that involve joined tables, using either the SQL-92 or Access SQL JOIN syntax or the equals operator in the WHERE clause, must operate against updatable recordsets. Although action queries don't return recordsets, the rules for updating records of joined tables apply just as if action queries created "invisible" recordsets (which, in fact, they do). Access provides a visual clue that identifies a query as nonupdatable by omitting the tentative append record (the blank record with an asterisk in the record selector button) as the last record in the datasheet view of a recordset or by omitting an empty record as the last record of a continuous form or subform.

SQL and Set-Oriented Transactions

SQL is a set-oriented language. The SELECT queries you write define a set of records (rows) that Visual C++ and the Microsoft Jet database engine or an ODBC driver return to your application as a recordset object. Similarly, SQL action queries define a set of records that are to be updated, appended, or deleted. (Appending a new record to a table creates a set of one new record.) You can create SQL action queries with Visual C++ code or employ parameterized QueryDef objects to specify the set of records to which the action query applies. Using SQL action queries that act on multiple records is similar in concept to the batch-processing method described earlier in this chapter. SQL action queries attempt to update all records that meet the criteria of the SQL statement's WHERE clause.

A Review of SQL Action Query Syntax

Chapter 5, "Learning Structured Query Language," briefly discussed the SQL syntax for action queries. The following list describes the Access SQL and ANSI SQL reserved words that you use to create action queries.

■ The INSERT, UPDATE, and DELETE verbs append, modify, and delete rows in tables, respectively. These verbs are part of ANSI and Access SQL's data manipulation language (DML). The Microsoft Jet database engine and all ODBC drivers support these three verbs. If the engine can't execute the action query in its entirety, the query fails and you receive an error. (No changes are made to any records.)

■ All client-server RDBMSs support the COMMIT and ROLLBACK statements of SQL's transaction-processing language (TPL) to ensure that all the rows of tables affected by a DML statement are updated at once. A full discussion of the COMMIT and ROLLBACK statements appears later in this chapter. Some RDBMSs, such as IBM's DB2, use the term *unit of work* to define a transaction and use COMMIT WORK and ROLLBACK WORK to commit or roll back a unit of work. A *unit of work* is defined as all statements since the last COMMIT or point of known consistency of the table's data. The majority of client-server RDBMSs use the BEGIN TRANS[ACTION] statement to explicitly specify the beginning of a transaction. Access SQL employs the unit of work approach and doesn't support TPL statements. If the database to which the Microsoft Jet database engine is connected supports transactions, the engine automatically rolls back an action query that encounters errors during its execution.

■ The SELECT...INTO structure lets you create new tables in a database with the Microsoft Jet database engine and most ODBC drivers. (DB2 uses the SELECT...INTO structure to assign variables in a single row to a host program variable.) Using SELECT...INTO to create a new table is much simpler than writing Visual C++ code to add a new TableDef object to the TableDefs collection. The majority of single- and multiple-tier ODBC drivers also support the SQL data definition language (DDL) statements to create new tables (CREATE TABLE), add indexes to tables (CREATE INDEX), and prevent empty field values (NOT NULL). Some ODBC drivers let you delete tables and/or indexes (DROP TABLE and DROP INDEX). Access SQL doesn't support ANSI SQL DDL statements.

■ Few ODBC drivers currently support the SQL-92 domain integrity enforcement (CHECK and CONSTRAINT) or referential integrity enforcement (PRIMARY KEY, FOREIGN KEY, and REFERENCES). Client-server RDBMSs such as Sybase SQL Server use triggers (a form of stored procedure) to detect domain or referential integrity violations. Access action queries enforce referential integrity when you create your database with the retail version of Access. You specify default relationships and check the Maintain Referential Integrity check box of the Relationships dialog box to emulate the effect of the PRIMARY KEY, FOREIGN KEY, and REFERENCES clauses. Although you can apply domain integrity rules (using the ValidationRule property) to fields of tables you create with Access, Visual C++ doesn't recognize these rules. You need to create your own data validation procedures with Visual C++ code.

When you use the Microsoft Jet database engine and an Access .MDB database with Visual C++, an action query is an "all-or-nothing" proposition—either all the records in the set are updated, appended, or deleted, or the query fails and you receive an error message. When you use the ODBC API and a multiple-tier ODBC driver with a client-server RDBMS, your ANSI SQL statement and the RDBMS are responsible for determining whether the action query can succeed. Some single-tier ODBC drivers—such as Intersolv Software's ODBC Driver Pack drivers for dBASE, Paradox, and FoxPro databases—support the three ANSI TPL reserved words. Version 1.0 of the Microsoft ODBC Desktop Database Drivers kit supports TPL only when you use the Access ODBC driver or the Btrieve ODBC driver. Support for TPL should be a major determinant in your choice of desktop database drivers if you're using Visual C++ with dBASE, FoxPro, or Paradox files.

> **NOTE**
>
> Both ANSI and Access SQL statements need the source recordset objects of all queries to be persistent, and the source recordsets must be Table objects. You can't execute an SQL statement with virtual tables as source recordsets. Although you can include user-defined functions (UDFs) in Access's version of Access SQL, UDFs aren't permitted in SQL queries you execute with Visual C++.

Executing SQL Action Queries with Visual C++ Code

You execute action queries by using one of two Visual C++ methods:

■ The SQLExecDirect() function lets you execute an SQL statement that has been previously prepared using the SQLPrepare() function. In most cases, you pass the operands of the criteria statements in the WHERE clause as parameters. Alternatively, you can substitute an SQL statement as a string variable and use the SQLExecDirect() function.

■ The CDatabase member function ExecuteSQL() is applicable only to databases connected by the ODBC API and uses SQL pass-through exclusively. ExecuteSQL() doesn't return records. Therefore, to execute an SQL command that returns records, you must create and use a CRecordset object. You can't specify options when you use the ExecuteSQL() member function; the sole argument of ExecuteSQL() is the SQL statement.

The Visual C++ syntax for the preceding SQLExecDirect() and ExecuteSQL() functions appears in Chapter 2, "Understanding MFC's ODBC Database Classes," and Chapter 3, "Using Visual C++ Database Functions." The MS Query application lets you execute SQL statements on a database directly. After the SQL statement has been built and tested using MS Query, it can be pasted into a Visual C++ application.

> **TIP**
>
> When you use the ExecuteSQL() method when running action queries against client-server databases, your action query might involve updates to more than one record.

Recordset Transactions with Bound Controls

You can use edit boxes or other controls to display data and to update fields of an updatable CRecordset class object that aren't calculated fields. Using edit boxes is the most common (but not necessarily the best) method of updating table data in Visual C++ and Access applications. You also can use third-party grid custom controls with Visual C++ transaction-processing applications. The following sections describe the benefits and drawbacks of using these two types of controls for data entry.

Using Edit Boxes for Data Entry

The simplest way to create a data-entry form for transaction processing is to add an edit box to the form for each field of the table or column of the datasource that your CRecordset is accessing. You bind the edit box to the application variable (using ClassWizard).

Using Visual C++ Code for Transaction Processing

Bound controls minimize the code you need to write to create data-entry applications. Here are a few of the principal issues involved in using bound edit controls in conjunction with Visual C++ AppWizard-created database applications for transaction processing:

- The data-entry operator can make changes to the content of the edit controls at will without affecting the status of the database tables until he or she is satisfied that the edit is correct. Although edit changes to tables don't occur until the record pointer is moved and you call the CRecordset::Update() member function in your code (CRecordset won't automatically call Update() when the pointer is moved), a new record is added to the table when any field of the tentative append record is filled.

- You can validate all the entries at once when the user clicks the OK button (or presses an Alt-*key* accelerator key combination) to accept the edited values instead of validating each entry individually. All-at-once validation is particularly useful when entries are interdependent, as in the case of city, state, and zip code entries.

- When you use bound controls to update existing records, the application places a lock on the current page (Access, Btrieve, and SQL Server databases) or record (dBASE, FoxPro, and Paradox databases) for the duration of the editing process. If the person who is editing the record goes to lunch without completing the edit, no one else can edit the record (or any record in the same 2K page) for the duration.

The following sections describe the use of edit boxes in conjunction with an AppWizard-created database application. The methods used here are for the sake of simplicity; production-grade applications use command buttons to commit or cancel edits and to manipulate record-pointers.

Emulating an Access Continuous Subform in Visual C++

If you're converting an Access database application to Visual C++, you often need to emulate the continuous subform controls that are commonly employed in Access applications. There are several ways to do this. This chapter looks at two methods. The first method to emulate an Access continuous subform is to use a dialog box that has individual edit boxes for each displayed record (row) and field. A second method is to use Visual C++ 4's OLE Grid control. A third method (not discussed in this chapter) is to use a ListView control.

> **NOTE**
>
> Both of the sample programs in this chapter use the Access 95 version of the North-wind Traders database (typically installed as \MSOffice\Access\Samples \Northwind.MDB), accessed using ODBC with the ODBC name of Access 95 Northwind. If you've installed the Northwind Traders database using a different name, you can modify the source dataset name to reflect the name you used for your Northwind sample database as necessary. This name is found in the `GetDefaultConnect` function in the `CRecordset` class implementation, as this example shows:
>
> ```
> CString CContinusingGridControlSet::GetDefaultConnect()
> {
>     return _T("ODBC;DSN=Access 95 Northwind");
> }
> ```

Figure 15.1 shows an Access continuous subform. Figure 15.2 shows the Visual C++ version of this subform. Figure 15.3 shows a Visual C++ 4 OLE Grid control version of the program shown in Figure 15.2.

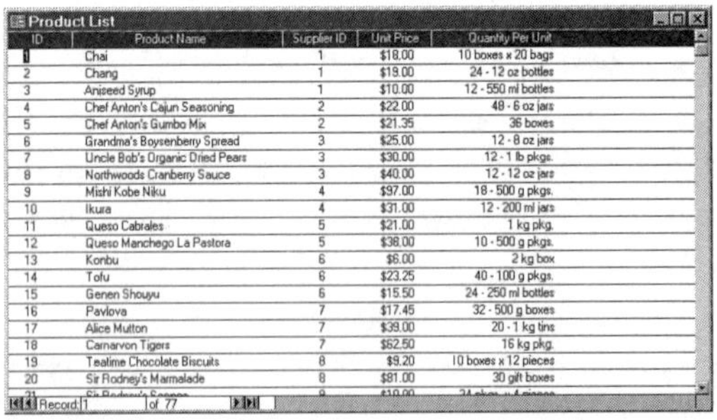

FIGURE 15.1.

An Access continuous subform.

In Figure 15.2, the form's Product Name, English Name, Unit Price, Units in stock, and Units on Order are text-box controls. The Visual C++ code you write to fill the control arrays is similar to the C++ code needed to fill in a single control.

FIGURE 15.2.

A Visual C++ form that emulates an Access continuous subform.

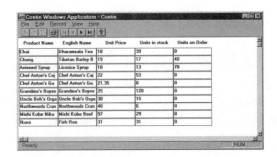

In Figure 15.3, all the form's fields are contained in a single Visual C++ 4 OLE Grid control. This OCX control could be supplemented with edit boxes to let the user modify the values displayed. Unlike the examples shown in Figures 15.1 and 15.2, in-place editing isn't supported using an OLE Grid control.

FIGURE 15.3.

A Visual C++ 4 OLE Grid control that emulates an Access continuous subform.

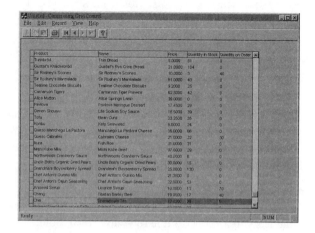

The most important thing to remember about a continuous form-type view is that more than one record from the recordset must be accessed at any one time. In Figure 15.2, this is done by simulation. Ten rows are displayed, and 10 rows in the recordset are accessed sequentially to fill in the 10 rows in the display.

The OLE Grid example in Figure 15.3 displays more than 10 rows. When I created this sample program, it was impossible to determine exactly how many rows would be visible to the user.

NOTE

The OLE Grid control has some limitations. The maximum number of rows is 16,352, and the maximum number of columns is 5,450. It's unlikely that your application will exceed the column limitation, but it's possible to generate a query that can return more than 16,352 rows of data. You must check for this situation and warn the user that not all records returned are displayed.

NOTE

Contin, the sample application shown in Figure 15.2, is located by default in the CHAPTR15 directory on the CD that comes with this book. The project called Contin using Grid Control is also found in this directory.

NOTE

There are several versions of the Northwind database. The version used with this chapter's sample programs is the one that is supplied with Access 95. Some other versions of Northwind have an additional column in the Products table called EnglishName. All the code in this chapter supports the EnglishName column, which has been commented out. If your version of Northwind has the EnglishName column, you can remove the comments from these lines to include the EnglishName column's data in the program.

Listing 15.1 shows the code you need to write in order to fill a simulated continuous subform with data from the table or query specified when the application was created. You need to explicitly handle null values, because the Microsoft versions of text boxes and edit controls don't convert null values to empty strings.

All the necessary changes are made in two files: the view class source file (in this program, CONTINVW.CPP) and the header file for the view class (CONTINVW.H). In Listing 15.1, the code that lets you access multiple rows appears in bold.

Listing 15.1. Code to emulate an Access subform using edit boxes.

```
// contivw.cpp : implementation of the CContinView class
//

#include "stdafx.h"
#include "contin.h"

#include "contiset.h"
#include "contidoc.h"
#include "contivw.h"

#ifdef _DEBUG
#undef THIS_FILE
static char BASED_CODE THIS_FILE[] = __FILE__;
#endif

/////////////////////////////////////////////////////////////////////////////
// CContinView

IMPLEMENT_DYNCREATE(CContinView, CRecordView)

BEGIN_MESSAGE_MAP(CContinView, CRecordView)
    //{{AFX_MSG_MAP(CContinView)
        // NOTE - the ClassWizard will add and remove mapping macros here.
        //    DO NOT EDIT what you see in these blocks of generated code!
    //}}AFX_MSG_MAP
    // Standard printing commands
    ON_COMMAND(ID_FILE_PRINT, CRecordView::OnFilePrint)
    ON_COMMAND(ID_FILE_PRINT_PREVIEW, CRecordView::OnFilePrintPreview)
END_MESSAGE_MAP()
```

```
//////////////////////////////////////////////////////////////////////////
// CContinView construction/destruction

CContinView::CContinView()
    : CRecordView(CContinView::IDD)
{
    //{{AFX_DATA_INIT(CContinView)
    m_pSet = NULL;
    //}}AFX_DATA_INIT
    // TODO: add construction code here
    for (int i = 0; i < 10; i++)
    {
//        m_EnglishName[i] = "";
        m_ProductName[i] = "";
        m_UnitPrice[i] = "";
        m_UnitsInStock[i] = 0;
        m_UnitsOnOrder[i] = 0;
    }

    m_ArraySet = FALSE;
}

CContinView::~CContinView()
{
}


BOOL    CContinView::OnMove(UINT nIDMoveCommand)
{
int     i;
int     nStepBack;
//--------START OF DBVIEW.CPP OnMove()...

    if (CDatabase::InWaitForDataSource())
    {
#ifdef _DEBUG
        if (afxTraceFlags & 0x20)
            TRACE0("Warning: ignored move request\n");
#endif // _DEBUG
        return TRUE;
    }

//    CRecordset* pSet = OnGetRecordset();

    if (m_pSet->CanUpdate())
    {
        if (!UpdateData())
            return TRUE;

        nStepBack = 0;
        for (i = 0; i < 10; i++)
        {// Save the current record, then get next one!
            m_pSet->Edit();

//            m_pSet->m_EnglishName = m_EnglishName[i];
            m_pSet->m_ProductName = m_ProductName[i];
            m_pSet->m_UnitPrice = m_UnitPrice[i];
            m_pSet->m_UnitsInStock = m_UnitsInStock[i];
```

continues

Listing 15.1. continued

```
                m_pSet->m_UnitsOnOrder = m_UnitsOnOrder[i];

                m_pSet->Update();

                if (!m_pSet->IsEOF())
                {
                    TRY
                    {// Use old-style exceptions for Visual C++ 1.5x
                        m_pSet->MoveNext();
                        --nStepBack;
                    }
                    CATCH(CDBException, e)
                    {// Died, should use message box to user!
                        TRACE("MoveNext() fail Ret = %d Error '%s', cause '%s'\n",
                            e->m_nRetCode,
                            (const char *)e->m_strError,
                            (const char *)e->m_strStateNativeOrigin);
                    }
                    END_CATCH
                }
                else
                {
                    break;
                }
            }

//      Restore the record pointer! Take nStepBack giant steps back!

        TRY
        {// Use old-style exceptions for Visual C++ 1.5x
            m_pSet->Move(nStepBack);  // Back to original record...
        }
        CATCH(CDBException, e)
        {// Died, should use message box to user!
            TRACE("Move(nStepBack) failed Ret = %d Error '%s', cause '%s'\n",
                e->m_nRetCode,
                (const char *)e->m_strError,
                (const char *)e->m_strStateNativeOrigin);
        }
        END_CATCH
    }

    switch (nIDMoveCommand)
    {
        case ID_RECORD_PREV:
            m_pSet->MovePrev();
            if (!m_pSet->IsBOF())
                break;

        case ID_RECORD_FIRST:
            m_pSet->MoveFirst();
            break;

        case ID_RECORD_NEXT:
            m_pSet->MoveNext();
            if (!m_pSet->IsEOF())
```

```
                break;
            if (!m_pSet->CanScroll())
            {
                // Clear out screen since we're sitting on EOF
                m_pSet->SetFieldNull(NULL);
                break;
            }

        case ID_RECORD_LAST:
            m_pSet->MoveLast();
            break;

        default:
            // Unexpected case value
            ASSERT(FALSE);
    }

//--------END OF DBVIEW.CPP OnMove()...

    SetArray();

    // Show results of move operation
    UpdateData(FALSE);

    return(TRUE);
}

void    CContinView::SetArray()
{
int     i;
int     nStepBack;

    nStepBack = 0;
    for (i = 0; i < 10; i++)
    {// Save the current record, then get next one!
//       m_EnglishName[i] = m_pSet->m_English_Name;
        m_ProductName[i] = m_pSet->m_ProductName;
        m_UnitPrice[i] = m_pSet->m_UnitPrice;
        m_UnitsInStock[i] = m_pSet->m_UnitsInStock;
        m_UnitsOnOrder[i] = m_pSet->m_UnitsOnOrder;

        if (!m_pSet->IsEOF())
        {
            TRY
            {// Use old-style exceptions for Visual C++ 1.5x
                m_pSet->MoveNext();
                --nStepBack;
            }
            CATCH(CDBException, e)
            {// Died, should use message box to user!
                    TRACE("MoveNext() failed Ret = %d Error '%s', cause '%s'\n",
                        e->m_nRetCode,
                        (const char *)e->m_strError,
                        (const char *)e->m_strStateNativeOrigin);
            }
            END_CATCH
        }
        else
```

continues

Listing 15.1. continued

```
            {
                m_pSet->SetFieldNull(NULL);
            }
        }

//      Restore the record pointer! Take nStepBack giant steps back!
        TRY
        {// Use old-style exceptions for Visual C++ 1.5x
            m_pSet->Move(nStepBack);
        }
        CATCH(CDBException, e)
        {// Died, should use message box to user!
            TRACE("Move(nStepBack) failed Ret = %d Error '%s', cause '%s'\n",
                e->m_nRetCode,
              (const char *)e->m_strError,
                (const char *)e->m_strStateNativeOrigin);
        }
        END_CATCH

        m_ArraySet = TRUE;
    }

    void CContinView::DoDataExchange(CDataExchange* pDX)
    {
        if (!m_ArraySet)
            SetArray();

        CRecordView::DoDataExchange(pDX);
        //{{AFX_DATA_MAP(CContinView)
        //}}AFX_DATA_MAP
//      DDX_Text(pDX,    IDC_ENGLISH_NAME1,    m_EnglishName[0]);
        DDX_Text(pDX,    IDC_PRODUCT_NAME1,    m_ProductName[0]);
        DDX_Text(pDX,      IDC_UNIT_PRICE1,      m_UnitPrice[0]);
        DDX_Text(pDX, IDC_UNITS_IN_STOCK1, m_UnitsInStock[0]);
        DDX_Text(pDX, IDC_UNITS_ON_ORDER1, m_UnitsOnOrder[0]);
//      DDX_Text(pDX,    IDC_ENGLISH_NAME2,    m_EnglishName[1]);
        DDX_Text(pDX,    IDC_PRODUCT_NAME2,    m_ProductName[1]);
        DDX_Text(pDX,      IDC_UNIT_PRICE2,      m_UnitPrice[1]);
        DDX_Text(pDX, IDC_UNITS_IN_STOCK2, m_UnitsInStock[1]);
        DDX_Text(pDX, IDC_UNITS_ON_ORDER2, m_UnitsOnOrder[1]);
//      DDX_Text(pDX,    IDC_ENGLISH_NAME3,    m_EnglishName[2]);
        DDX_Text(pDX,    IDC_PRODUCT_NAME3,    m_ProductName[2]);
        DDX_Text(pDX,      IDC_UNIT_PRICE3,      m_UnitPrice[2]);
        DDX_Text(pDX, IDC_UNITS_IN_STOCK3, m_UnitsInStock[2]);
        DDX_Text(pDX, IDC_UNITS_ON_ORDER3, m_UnitsOnOrder[2]);
//      DDX_Text(pDX,    IDC_ENGLISH_NAME4,    m_EnglishName[3]);
        DDX_Text(pDX,    IDC_PRODUCT_NAME4,    m_ProductName[3]);
        DDX_Text(pDX,      IDC_UNIT_PRICE4,      m_UnitPrice[3]);
        DDX_Text(pDX, IDC_UNITS_IN_STOCK4, m_UnitsInStock[3]);
        DDX_Text(pDX, IDC_UNITS_ON_ORDER4, m_UnitsOnOrder[3]);
//      DDX_Text(pDX,    IDC_ENGLISH_NAME5,    m_EnglishName[4]);
        DDX_Text(pDX,    IDC_PRODUCT_NAME5,    m_ProductName[4]);
        DDX_Text(pDX,      IDC_UNIT_PRICE5,      m_UnitPrice[4]);
        DDX_Text(pDX, IDC_UNITS_IN_STOCK5, m_UnitsInStock[4]);
        DDX_Text(pDX, IDC_UNITS_ON_ORDER5, m_UnitsOnOrder[4]);
//      DDX_Text(pDX,    IDC_ENGLISH_NAME6,    m_EnglishName[5]);
        DDX_Text(pDX,    IDC_PRODUCT_NAME6,    m_ProductName[5]);
```

```
       DDX_Text(pDX,       IDC_UNIT_PRICE6,      m_UnitPrice[5]);
       DDX_Text(pDX, IDC_UNITS_IN_STOCK6,  m_UnitsInStock[5]);
       DDX_Text(pDX, IDC_UNITS_ON_ORDER6,  m_UnitsOnOrder[5]);
//     DDX_Text(pDX,    IDC_ENGLISH_NAME7,    m_EnglishName[6]);
       DDX_Text(pDX,     IDC_PRODUCT_NAME7,    m_ProductName[6]);
       DDX_Text(pDX,       IDC_UNIT_PRICE7,      m_UnitPrice[6]);
       DDX_Text(pDX, IDC_UNITS_IN_STOCK7,  m_UnitsInStock[6]);
       DDX_Text(pDX, IDC_UNITS_ON_ORDER7,  m_UnitsOnOrder[6]);
//     DDX_Text(pDX,    IDC_ENGLISH_NAME8,    m_EnglishName[7]);
       DDX_Text(pDX,     IDC_PRODUCT_NAME8,    m_ProductName[7]);
       DDX_Text(pDX,       IDC_UNIT_PRICE8,      m_UnitPrice[7]);
       DDX_Text(pDX, IDC_UNITS_IN_STOCK8,  m_UnitsInStock[7]);
       DDX_Text(pDX, IDC_UNITS_ON_ORDER8,  m_UnitsOnOrder[7]);
//     DDX_Text(pDX,    IDC_ENGLISH_NAME9,    m_EnglishName[8]);
       DDX_Text(pDX,     IDC_PRODUCT_NAME9,    m_ProductName[8]);
       DDX_Text(pDX,       IDC_UNIT_PRICE9,      m_UnitPrice[8]);
       DDX_Text(pDX, IDC_UNITS_IN_STOCK9,  m_UnitsInStock[8]);
       DDX_Text(pDX, IDC_UNITS_ON_ORDER9,  m_UnitsOnOrder[8]);
//     DDX_Text(pDX,   IDC_ENGLISH_NAME10,   m_EnglishName[9]);
       DDX_Text(pDX,    IDC_PRODUCT_NAME10,   m_ProductName[9]);
       DDX_Text(pDX,      IDC_UNIT_PRICE10,     m_UnitPrice[9]);
       DDX_Text(pDX, IDC_UNITS_IN_STOCK10, m_UnitsInStock[9]);
       DDX_Text(pDX, IDC_UNITS_ON_ORDER10, m_UnitsOnOrder[9]);
}

void CContinView::OnInitialUpdate()
{
    m_pSet = &GetDocument()->m_continSet;
    CRecordView::OnInitialUpdate();

}

/////////////////////////////////////////////////////////////////////////////
// CContinView printing

BOOL CContinView::OnPreparePrinting(CPrintInfo* pInfo)
{
    // Default preparation
    return DoPreparePrinting(pInfo);
}

void CContinView::OnBeginPrinting(CDC* /*pDC*/, CPrintInfo* /*pInfo*/)
{
    // TODO: add extra initialization before printing
}

void CContinView::OnEndPrinting(CDC* /*pDC*/, CPrintInfo* /*pInfo*/)
{
    // TODO: add cleanup after printing
}

/////////////////////////////////////////////////////////////////////////////
// CContinView diagnostics

#ifdef _DEBUG
void CContinView::AssertValid() const
{
```

continues

Listing 15.1. continued

```
    CRecordView::AssertValid();
}

void CContinView::Dump(CDumpContext& dc) const
{
    CRecordView::Dump(dc);
}

CContinDoc* CContinView::GetDocument() // Nondebug version is inline
{
    ASSERT(m_pDocument->IsKindOf(RUNTIME_CLASS(CContinDoc)));
    return (CContinDoc*)m_pDocument;
}
#endif //_DEBUG

/////////////////////////////////////////////////////////////////////////////
// CContinView database support

CRecordset* CContinView::OnGetRecordset()
{
    return m_pSet;
}


/////////////////////////////////////////////////////////////////////////////
// CContinView message handlers
```

CAUTION

If you want to use more than one record at a time from the CRecordView class object (which has a CRecordset object contained in it), you must override the default OnMove() CRecordView member function. This function normally isn't overridden, so there is no documentation from Microsoft on how the OnMove() member function actually works.

You can easily overcome this shortcoming in documentation by simply taking a peek at the MFC source code for the OnMove() member function, which is found in the source file DBVIEW.CPP (on the Visual C++ 4 distribution CD in the MSDEV\MFC\SRC folder).

To fully emulate Access's continuous subform, you need to add a vertical scroll bar to position the data control's record pointer. Because AppWizard-generated applications have record navigation buttons in their toolbars, it's usually not necessary to have a scroll bar as well. When your database access is part of a dialog box (dialog boxes don't have AppWizard-generated toolbars), you might want to code a scroll bar to let the user easily navigate through the database's records.

The problem you encounter when using scroll bars to position the record pointer is that scroll bars use numeric values, but recordsets don't have corresponding record number properties. As mentioned in Chapter 1, "Positioning Visual C++ in the Desktop Database Market," neither Access nor Visual C++ offers the equivalent of xBase's RECNO() function to return a record number.

You can choose from several approaches in order to create the equivalent of record numbers for recordset objects:

■ Create an array of the data in the recordset object and use the array elements instead of the data in the recordset object to populate the emulated subform. The element number of the array substitutes for the record number. However, you need to update the array each time you edit or add a new record to the recordset object. Conventional 16-bit Visual C++ arrays are limited to 64K (for all practical purposes), so this approach works best with small tables. You can create an array larger than 64K, but you need to have the length of the array elements be a power of 2, which might waste substantial storage space.

With Visual C++ 2.x (or any other version of Visual C++ that creates 32-bit programs, including Visual C++ 4.x), an array isn't limited to 64K, and elements in the array don't need to be a power of 2.

■ Create an array of bookmarks for the recordset. This is a faster process than creating an array of the recordset data, but you still have a 64K limit on the size of the array when you're writing 16-bit legacy applications. An SQL_C_BOOKMARK object is an unsigned long int (4 bytes long), so you could have up to 16,385 bookmark objects in a 64K block of memory. You can easily define a huge array of SQL_C_BOOKMARK objects because sizeof(unsigned long int) is a power of 2.

With Visual C++ 2.x (or any other version of Visual C++ that creates 32-bit programs, including Visual C++ 4.x), an array isn't limited to 64K, and you don't have to take this limitation into consideration.

■ Save the last value of the vertical scroll bar's position and use the MoveNext or MovePrevious methods to position the record pointer incrementally. Set the Min value of the scroll bar to 1 and the Max value to CRecordset::GetRecordCount(). (You must read all records in the recordset to ensure that CRecordset::GetRecordCount() returns the actual number of records in the recordset.) The range of scroll bars is limited to the range of integer variables (+32,767 to −32,768). If you expect your recordset to contain more than 32,000 records, you need to use math to move the record pointer more than one record for each scroll bar Value increment or decrement.

This last approach usually is the simplest and is used in the emulated subform application. Listing 15.3 shows the code for the function that overrides the CRecordView::OnMove() member function. This function started as a direct cut-and-paste of the original CRecordView::OnMove() code that is shown in Listing 15.2.

Listing 15.2 has some comments that explain the steps that OnMove() performs when moving from one record to another. These comments appear in bold.

Listing 15.2. CRecordView::OnMove() original handler.

```
// This is a part of the Microsoft Foundation Classes C++ library.
// Copyright (c) 1993 Microsoft Corporation
// All rights reserved.
//
// This source code is intended only as a supplement to the
// Microsoft Foundation Classes Reference and Microsoft
// QuickHelp and/or WinHelp documentation provided with the library.
// See these sources for detailed information regarding the
// Microsoft Foundation Classes product.


#include "stdafx.h"

#ifdef AFX_DB_SEG
#pragma code_seg(AFX_DB_SEG)
#endif

#ifdef _DEBUG
#undef THIS_FILE
static char BASED_CODE THIS_FILE[] = __FILE__;
#endif

#define new DEBUG_NEW

/////////////////////////////////////////////////////////////////////////////

// Lines deleted ...

BOOL CRecordView::OnMove(UINT nIDMoveCommand)
{

// First, there are checks to make sure that we are not waiting for
// the datasource:

    if (CDatabase::InWaitForDataSource())
    {
#ifdef _DEBUG
        if (afxTraceFlags & 0x20)
            TRACE0("Warning: ignored move request\n");
#endif // _DEBUG
        return TRUE;
    }

// If we're not waiting for the datasource, we get the recordset.
// Then we check to see if we can update the current database. We
// then tell the recordset that we're going to edit (using Edit())
// the current record. We get the user's edits (if any) and then
// update (using Update()) the record in the recordset.

    CRecordset* pSet = OnGetRecordset();
    if (pSet->CanUpdate())
```

```
    {
        pSet->Edit();
        if (!UpdateData())
            return TRUE;

        pSet->Update();
    }

// The next step depends on what the move is. There are four
// choices: next record, previous record, first record, and
// last record. The switch() block manages these four choices.

    switch (nIDMoveCommand)
    {
        case ID_RECORD_PREV:
            pSet->MovePrev();
            if (!pSet->IsBOF())
                break;

        case ID_RECORD_FIRST:
            pSet->MoveFirst();
            break;

        case ID_RECORD_NEXT:
            pSet->MoveNext();
            if (!pSet->IsEOF())
                break;
            if (!pSet->CanScroll())
            {
                // Clear out screen since we're sitting on EOF
                pSet->SetFieldNull(NULL);
                break;
            }

        case ID_RECORD_LAST:
            pSet->MoveLast();
            break;

        default:
            // Unexpected case value
            ASSERT(FALSE);
    }

// Once the specified move has been made, we simply update
// the view's display of the record (for the user) and return.

    // Show results of move operation
    UpdateData(FALSE);
    return TRUE;
}
```

Listing 15.2, the `CRecordView::OnMove()` handler, shows what the default action for `OnMove()` is. In the original handler, the current record (if there is one) is updated, and then the new record (if there is one) is loaded. At `OnMove()`'s completion, the view is updated to reflect the changes.

Listing 15.3 shows the new OnMove() handler. Much like the default OnMove(), this version updates the current records (all 10 of them) and then loads 10 "new" records. The facility can handle only single moves at a time, so nine of the 10 reads aren't necessary and could be replaced with assignments to move the currently loaded data to the new locations.

Listing 15.3 differs from Listing 15.1 in that the OnMove() handler doesn't call other functions that have been written. (In other words, it can run on its own.)

Listing 15.3. The OnMove() handler.

```
BOOL     CContinView::OnMove(UINT nIDMoveCommand)
{
int       i;
int       nStepBack;
//--------START OF DBVIEW.CPP OnMove()...

    if (CDatabase::InWaitForDataSource())
    {
#ifdef _DEBUG
        if (afxTraceFlags & 0x20)
            TRACE0("Warning: ignored move request\n");
#endif // _DEBUG
        return TRUE;
    }

//     CRecordset* pSet = OnGetRecordset();

    if (m_pSet->CanUpdate())
    {
        if (!UpdateData())
            return TRUE;

        nStepBack = 0;
        for (i = 0; i < 10; i++)
        {// Save the current record, then get next one!
            m_pSet->Edit();

//            m_pSet->m_EnglishName = m_EnglishName[i];
            m_pSet->m_ProductName = m_ProductName[i];
            m_pSet->m_UnitPrice = m_UnitPrice[i];
            m_pSet->m_UnitsInStock = m_UnitsInStock[i];
            m_pSet->m_UnitsOnOrder = m_UnitsOnOrder[i];

            m_pSet->Update();

            if (!m_pSet->IsEOF())
            {
                TRY
                {// Use old-style exceptions for Visual C++ 1.5x
                    m_pSet->MoveNext();
                    --nStepBack;
                }
                CATCH(CDBException, e)
                {// Died, should use message box to user!
                    TRACE("MoveNext() fail Ret = %d Error '%s', cause '%s'\n",
                        e->m_nRetCode,
```

```
                                 (const char *)e->m_strError,
                                 (const char *)e->m_strStateNativeOrigin);
                }
                END_CATCH
            }
            else
            {
                break;
            }
        }

//        Restore the record pointer! Take nStepBack giant steps back!

        TRY
        {// Use old-style exceptions for Visual C++ 1.5x
            m_pSet->Move(nStepBack);  // Back to original record...
        }
        CATCH(CDBException, e)
        {// Died, should use message box to user!
                TRACE("Move(nStepBack) failed Ret = %d Error '%s', cause '%s'\n",
                    e->m_nRetCode,
                    (const char *)e->m_strError,
                    (const char *)e->m_strStateNativeOrigin);
        }
        END_CATCH
    }

    switch (nIDMoveCommand)
    {
        case ID_RECORD_PREV:
            m_pSet->MovePrev();
            if (!m_pSet->IsBOF())
                break;

        case ID_RECORD_FIRST:
            m_pSet->MoveFirst();
            break;

        case ID_RECORD_NEXT:
            m_pSet->MoveNext();
            if (!m_pSet->IsEOF())
                break;
            if (!m_pSet->CanScroll())
            {
                // Clear out screen since we're sitting on EOF
                m_pSet->SetFieldNull(NULL);
                break;
            }

        case ID_RECORD_LAST:
            m_pSet->MoveLast();
            break;

        default:
            // Unexpected case value
            ASSERT(FALSE);
    }
```

continues

Listing 15.3. continued

```
//--------END OF DBVIEW.CPP OnMove()...

    SetArray();

    // Show results of move operation
    UpdateData(FALSE);

    return(TRUE);
}
```

Adding Update Capability

The code in Listings 15.1, 15.2, and 15.3 not only displays data but also updates any records the user has modified. The code in Listing 15.4 shows the process of updating.

This process is straightforward: Move to the correct record (the record that is to be updated), get the "new" values for the record, put the new values in the recordset's column variables, and update the record. In the sample program, this is accomplished 10 times (because 10 records can be displayed at once). This lets the user update 10 records at a time, eliminating the inconvenience of being able to edit only the current record.

Listing 15.4. The update code.

```
    if (m_pSet->CanUpdate())
    {
        if (!UpdateData())
            return TRUE;

        nStepBack = 0;
        for (i = 0; i < 10; i++)
        {// Save the current record, then get next one!
            m_pSet->Edit();

//          m_pSet->m_EnglishName = m_EnglishName[i];
            m_pSet->m_ProductName = m_ProductName[i];
            m_pSet->m_UnitPrice = m_UnitPrice[i];
            m_pSet->m_UnitsInStock = m_UnitsInStock[i];
            m_pSet->m_UnitsOnOrder = m_UnitsOnOrder[i];

            m_pSet->Update();

            if (!m_pSet->IsEOF())
            {
                TRY
                {// Use old-style exceptions for Visual C++ 1.5x
                    m_pSet->MoveNext();
                    --nStepBack;
                }
```

```
        CATCH(CDBException, e)
        {// Died, should use message box to user!
            TRACE("MoveNext() fail Ret = %d Error '%s', cause '%s'\n",
                e->m_nRetCode,
                (const char *)e->m_strError,
                (const char *)e->m_strStateNativeOrigin);
        }
        END_CATCH
    }
    else
    {
        break;
    }
}

//      Restore the record pointer! Take nStepBack giant steps back!

    TRY
    {// Use old-style exceptions for Visual C++ 1.5x
        m_pSet->Move(nStepBack);  // Back to original record...
    }
    CATCH(CDBException, e)
    {// Died, should use message box to user!
        TRACE("Move(nStepBack) failed Ret = %d Error '%s', cause '%s'\n",
            e->m_nRetCode,
            (const char *)e->m_strError,
            (const char *)e->m_strStateNativeOrigin);
    }
    END_CATCH
}
```

NOTE

You can add code to the OnMove() handler that tests the validity of the updates you make to any of the fields before the changes are processed.

Using an OLE Grid Control

The OLE Grid control sample program (called Contin using Grid Control) is simpler than the example just shown. The OLE Grid control sample program doesn't implement user editing of database data, as shown in Listing 15.5, but you can easily add this functionality. This listing shows the view class, which is the only modification needed to implement this program. As with other listings, the lines in bold provide the increased functionality.

Listing 15.5. Contin using Grid ControlView.cpp.

```cpp
// Contin using Grid ControlView.cpp : implementation of
// the CContinusingGridControlView class

#include "stdafx.h"
#include "Contin using Grid Control.h"

#include "Contin using Grid ControlSet.h"
#include "Contin using Grid ControlDoc.h"
#include "Contin using Grid ControlView.h"
#include "gridctrl.h"

#ifdef _DEBUG
#define new DEBUG_NEW
#undef THIS_FILE
static char THIS_FILE[] = __FILE__;
#endif

/////////////////////////////////////////////////////////////////////////////
// CContinusingGridControlView

IMPLEMENT_DYNCREATE(CContinusingGridControlView, CRecordView)

BEGIN_MESSAGE_MAP(CContinusingGridControlView, CRecordView)
    //{{AFX_MSG_MAP(CContinusingGridControlView)
    ON_WM_DESTROY()
    //}}AFX_MSG_MAP
    // Standard printing commands
    ON_COMMAND(ID_FILE_PRINT, CRecordView::OnFilePrint)
    ON_COMMAND(ID_FILE_PRINT_DIRECT, CRecordView::OnFilePrint)
    ON_COMMAND(ID_FILE_PRINT_PREVIEW, CRecordView::OnFilePrintPreview)
END_MESSAGE_MAP()

/////////////////////////////////////////////////////////////////////////////
// CContinusingGridControlView construction/destruction

CContinusingGridControlView::CContinusingGridControlView()
    : CRecordView(CContinusingGridControlView::IDD)
{
    //{{AFX_DATA_INIT(CContinusingGridControlView)
        // NOTE: the ClassWizard will add member initialization here
    m_pSet = NULL;
    //}}AFX_DATA_INIT
    // TODO: add construction code here

}

CContinusingGridControlView::~CContinusingGridControlView()
{
}
```

```
void CContinusingGridControlView::DoDataExchange(CDataExchange* pDX)
{
    static bFirstTime = TRUE;

    CRecordView::DoDataExchange(pDX);
    //{{AFX_DATA_MAP(CContinusingGridControlView)
    DDX_Control(pDX, IDC_GRID1, m_GridControl);
    //}}AFX_DATA_MAP

    int Column = 0;
    int Row = 0;
    CString    Formatted;
    VARIANT    item;

    // Go to and get first record
    m_pSet->MoveFirst();

    while (!m_pSet->IsEOF())
    {// First, process the current record
        item.lVal = ++Row;

        m_GridControl.SetRow(Row);

        m_GridControl.SetSelStartRow(Row);
        m_GridControl.SetSelEndRow(Row);

        // The grid control allows filling multiple columns in a
        // record by separating each column with a tab. You can
        // also fill multiple rows by separating each row with a
        // CR (\x0D) (do not use a /n, however...).
        Formatted.Format(_T(" \t%s\t%s\t%s\t%d\t%d"),
            m_pSet->m_ProductName,
//            m_pSet->m_EnglishName,
            "", // Some versions of NorthWind don't have an EnglishName column
            m_pSet->m_UnitPrice,
            m_pSet->m_UnitsInStock,
            m_pSet->m_UnitsOnOrder);

        m_GridControl.AddItem(Formatted, item);

        m_pSet->MoveNext();
    }

    // Swap first and last entry to create a fixed first (title) row:
    for (Column = 0; Column <= 5; Column++)
    {// Do each column in the first and last rows:
        m_GridControl.SetRow(0);
        m_GridControl.SetCol(Column);
        Formatted = m_GridControl.GetText();
        m_GridControl.SetRow(Row);
        m_GridControl.SetText(Formatted);
    }
```

continues

Listing 15.5. continued

```
// Set title row's text:
m_GridControl.SetRow(0);
m_GridControl.SetCol(0);
m_GridControl.SetText(_T(""));
m_GridControl.SetCol(1);
m_GridControl.SetText(_T("Product"));
m_GridControl.SetCol(2);
m_GridControl.SetText(_T("Name"));
m_GridControl.SetCol(3);
m_GridControl.SetText(_T("Price"));
m_GridControl.SetCol(4);
m_GridControl.SetText(_T("Quantity in Stock"));
m_GridControl.SetCol(5);
m_GridControl.SetText(_T("Quantity on Order"));

// And fix the first row as a title row
m_GridControl.SetFixedRows(1);

if (bFirstTime)
{// Set column widths the first time only. Do not reset on redraw!
    bFirstTime = FALSE;

    // Our default widths are just guesses based on the title's
    // width. For the first two columns, the data is really wide,
    // and the titles are narrow, so we add a bit more for a
    // better view.

    m_GridControl.SetColWidth(0,
        AfxGetApp()->GetProfileInt(_T("GridStuff"), _T("ColWidth1"), 50));

    m_GridControl.SetColWidth(1,
        AfxGetApp()->GetProfileInt(_T("GridStuff"), _T("ColWidth2"),
            strlen(_T("Product")) * 100 + 1000));

    m_GridControl.SetColWidth(2,
        AfxGetApp()->GetProfileInt(_T("GridStuff"), _T("ColWidth3"),
            strlen(_T("Name")) * 100 + 1000));

    m_GridControl.SetColWidth(3,
        AfxGetApp()->GetProfileInt(_T("GridStuff"), _T("ColWidth4"),
            strlen(_T("Price")) * 100));

    m_GridControl.SetColWidth(4,
        AfxGetApp()->GetProfileInt(_T("GridStuff"), _T("ColWidth5"),
            strlen(_T("Quantity in Stock")) * 100));

    m_GridControl.SetColWidth(5,
        AfxGetApp()->GetProfileInt(_T("GridStuff"), _T("ColWidth6"),
            strlen(_T("Quantity on Order")) * 100));
}
}
```

```
BOOL CContinusingGridControlView::PreCreateWindow(CREATESTRUCT& cs)
{
    // TODO: Modify the Window class or styles here by modifying
    // the CREATESTRUCT cs

    return CRecordView::PreCreateWindow(cs);
}

void CContinusingGridControlView::OnInitialUpdate()
{
    m_pSet = &GetDocument()->m_continusingGridControlSet;
    CRecordView::OnInitialUpdate();
}

/////////////////////////////////////////////////////////////////////////////
// CContinusingGridControlView printing

BOOL CContinusingGridControlView::OnPreparePrinting(CPrintInfo* pInfo)
{
    // Default preparation
    return DoPreparePrinting(pInfo);
}

void CContinusingGridControlView::OnBeginPrinting(CDC* /*pDC*/,
    CPrintInfo* /*pInfo*/)
{
    // TODO: add extra initialization before printing
}

void CContinusingGridControlView::OnEndPrinting(CDC* /*pDC*/,
    CPrintInfo* /*pInfo*/)
{
    // TODO: add cleanup after printing
}

/////////////////////////////////////////////////////////////////////////////
// CContinusingGridControlView diagnostics

#ifdef _DEBUG
void CContinusingGridControlView::AssertValid() const
{
    CRecordView::AssertValid();
}

void CContinusingGridControlView::Dump(CDumpContext& dc) const
{
    CRecordView::Dump(dc);
}

CContinusingGridControlDoc* CContinusingGridControlView::GetDocument()
// Nondebug version is inline
{
    ASSERT(m_pDocument->IsKindOf(RUNTIME_CLASS(CContinusingGridControlDoc)));
    return (CContinusingGridControlDoc*)m_pDocument;
}
```

continues

Listing 15.5. continued

```
#endif //_DEBUG

/////////////////////////////////////////////////////////////////////////
// CContinusingGridControlView database support
CRecordset* CContinusingGridControlView::OnGetRecordset()
{
    return m_pSet;
}


/////////////////////////////////////////////////////////////////////////
// CContinusingGridControlView message handlers

BEGIN_EVENTSINK_MAP(CContinusingGridControlView, CRecordView)
    //{{AFX_EVENTSINK_MAP(CContinusingGridControlView)
    ON_EVENT(CContinusingGridControlView, IDC_GRID1, -600 /* Click */,
        OnClickGrid1, VTS_NONE)
    //}}AFX_EVENTSINK_MAP
END_EVENTSINK_MAP()

void CContinusingGridControlView::OnClickGrid1()
{
    // TODO: Add your control notification handler code here

    // When the user clicks on an item in our grid control, we
    // get this message. You could pop the item into an edit box
    // for further modifications by the user.

    //    m_GridControl.GetSelStartCol()
    //    m_GridControl.GetSelEndCol()
    //    m_GridControl.GetSelStartRow()
    //    m_GridControl.GetSelEndRow()
    //
    // Functions to determine the current selection. Be sure
    // to correctly handle a range selection when doing this.
}

void CContinusingGridControlView::OnDestroy()
{
    CRecordView::OnDestroy();

    m_GridControl.SetRow(0);

    AfxGetApp()->WriteProfileInt(_T("GridStuff"), _T("ColWidth1"),
        m_GridControl.GetColWidth(0));

    AfxGetApp()->WriteProfileInt(_T("GridStuff"), _T("ColWidth2"),
        m_GridControl.GetColWidth(1));
```

```
    AfxGetApp()->WriteProfileInt(_T("GridStuff"), _T("ColWidth3"),
        m_GridControl.GetColWidth(2));

    AfxGetApp()->WriteProfileInt(_T("GridStuff"), _T("ColWidth4"),
        m_GridControl.GetColWidth(3));

    AfxGetApp()->WriteProfileInt(_T("GridStuff"), _T("ColWidth5"),
        m_GridControl.GetColWidth(4));

    AfxGetApp()->WriteProfileInt(_T("GridStuff"), _T("ColWidth6"),
        m_GridControl.GetColWidth(5));
}
```

In Listing 15.5, you can see how the OLE Grid control is filled in. The OLE Grid control is initially created with two rows. It is then expanded as needed (using the `AddItem()` function). Because `AddItem()` doesn't work when your OLE Grid control has fixed columns (this shortcoming might be fixed in the next release of Visual C++), the column titles must be added to the control last and moved to the top and fixed after the control has been populated.

When you create an OLE Grid control using the dialog box editor, you can't specify column widths. This means that you must either accept the default width of 600 twips or modify the column widths at execution time. The user can modify column widths (and row heights) at runtime, so it's a good idea to save the column widths when your program exits. In the sample program, you simply write these values to an .INI file.

> **NOTE**
>
> Chapter 16, "Creating OLE Controls with Visual C++ 4," documents all the OLE controls supplied with Visual C++ 4.

Processing Multitable Transactions

In everyday English, the term *transaction* implies a business deal, such as trading cash for a new CD player or a tank car of acrylonitrile. The dictionary defines *transact* as "to drive through" or "to complete." Database transactions can involve changes to or additions of one or more records in a single table or in several tables. When more than one record or table is involved in a transaction, it's vital that all the records be updated simultaneously or as close to simultaneously as possible. The database is said to be in an inconsistent state until the records of each of the tables involved in the transaction have been updated successfully.

If hardware or software errors occur, if a domain or referential integrity violation is detected, or if the application can't alter or add a record because another user in a multiuser environment has placed locks on one or more of the records involved, the updates to all tables must be canceled. Any changes made to tables before the transaction operation terminates must be undone. An example is an automatic teller transaction. Your bank credits its cash account and debits your checking account whenever you make a cash withdrawal at an ATM. Obviously, your bank doesn't want a one-sided transaction to occur wherein you receive the cash but your account isn't debited. Canceling or undoing a transaction is called *rolling back* the transaction.

The following sections describe how and when Visual C++ supports the rolling back of aborted transactions.

Maintaining Transactional Consistency with Visual C++ Code

Visual C++'s MFC provides the CDatabase::BeginTrans(), CDatabase::CommitTrans(), and CDatabase::Rollback() functions to maintain database consistency in transaction-processing applications. Also, the SQLTransact() function is a (more) direct method of managing transactions for applications that aren't based on MFC. This section covers the MFC methods, because SQLTransact() differs from the MFC functions only in that a single call to one function with a parameter specifying the different actions is made.

These three functions actually are methods that apply an invisible recordset (a buffer) that contains the pending update(s) to the database tables. Another invisible recordset, the transaction log, stores a copy of the data contained in the affected rows of the recordset before the updates occur. You can use CDatabase's three TPL instructions to ensure that all updates to database tables proceed to completion and that the database returns to a consistent state when the transaction completes or when the updates are rolled back. The following two sections describe the structure of code that employs Visual C++'s transaction-processing instructions and the limited applicability of the ROLLBACK instruction to supported database types.

The Structure of the Transaction Instructions

The general structure of the Visual C++ transaction-processing commands, expressed in metacode, is as follows:

```
Name()
{
    ...
    TRY
    {
        CDatabase.BeginTrans()
        while(Whatever Condition)
        {
            [CDatabase.Edit()¦AddNew()]
            [Field update code...]
            CDatabase.{Update()¦Delete()}
        }
```

```
        CDatabase.CommitTrans()
    }

    CATCH_ALL(e)
    {
        CDatabase.Rollback()
        AFXMsgBox()
    }

    return()
}
```

The following is the metacode for an alternative structure that incorporates error processing within a loop structure:

```
Name()
{
    ...
    CDatabase.BeginTrans
    While (Whatever Condition  && !fError)
    {
        TRY
        {
            [CDatabase.Edit¦AddNew]
            [Field update code...]
            CDatabase.{Update¦Delete}
        }
        CATCH_ALL(e)
        {
            fError = TRUE
        }
    }

    If (fError)
    {
        Error = FALSE
        CDatabase.Rollback()
    }
    else
    {
        CDatabase.CommitTrans()
    }
}
```

The CDatabase.BeginTrans() and CDatabase.CommitTrans() statements always are used in pairs. If you use CDatabase.BeginTrans() and forget CDatabase.CommitTrans(), the transaction log fills with all the pre-update recordset values that occur after the CDatabase.BeginTrans() statement is encountered. The accumulated data ultimately consumes all of your computer's memory, and all hell breaks loose. Code within the CDatabase.BeginTrans()...CDatabase.CommitTrans() structure can be indented to identify the elements that constitute the transaction. You can nest transactions applied to Access databases up to five levels deep. When you nest transactions, you need to write code that rolls back each set of transactions, beginning with the innermost nested transaction. For example, you can use the fError flag set in the preceding metacode example to cause ROLLBACK instructions to be executed at each transaction level.

When the CDatabase.BeginTrans() statement is executed, the following operations occur (with Access databases):

1. Visual C++ instructs the Microsoft Jet database engine to open a temporary update buffer and a temporary transaction log. Both the update buffer and the transaction log are virtual tables that are stored in memory.

2. All records for transactions that occur before the execution of the CDatabase.CommitTrans() statement are stored in the update buffer.

3. When the CDatabase.CommitTrans() statement is reached, the Microsoft Jet database engine commences the execution of the transactions stored in the update buffer.

4. Before records are replaced or deleted, the record that is to be updated or deleted is saved in the transaction log.

5. The Microsoft Jet database engine attempts to update, delete, or add new records to the table. If no errors occur, an SQL COMMIT statement is executed, the changes are made permanent in the tables, and the temporary transaction log is cleared.

6. If an error is generated during the transaction process, the update buffer is cleared, program execution jumps to the error-handling routine, and an SQL ROLLBACK instruction is executed.

7. The SQL ROLLBACK instruction replaces records that were updated or deleted with records from the transaction log file. Any records added to tables using the AddNew method are deleted.

8. When the SQL ROLLBACK operation is completed, the temporary transaction log file is cleared.

One of the advantages of using Visual C++'s transaction-processing instructions is that bulk updates to tables occur much faster than when you apply the Update or Delete methods to a single record. Each time you apply the Update or Delete methods singly, the Microsoft Jet database engine opens an instance of the table; adds, modifies, or deletes parts of the physical table file; and then closes the instance, flushing all disk write buffers in the process. When you use the transaction-processing instructions, all the operations are conducted in buffers (in memory), with a single write-buffer flush operation at the end of the process.

Listing 15.6 shows an actual transaction-processing function. This example updates more than one dataset.

Listing 15.6. A function to perform transaction processing.

```
BOOL CFoodDoc::RemoveIngredient(CString strIngredient)
{
    // Remove Ingredient from all the recipies that the Ingredient is used in
    CRecipiesSet  rsRecipiesSet(m_dbIngredientReg);
    rsRecipiesSet.m_strFilter = "IngredientID = " + strIngredient;
    rsRecipiesSet.Open(CRecordset::dynaset);
    CIngredientSet  rsIngredientSet(m_dbIngredientReg);
    rsIngredientSet.m_strFilter = "IngredientID = " + strIngredient;
    rsIngredientSet.Open(CRecordset::dynaset);
    if (!m_dbIngredientReg.BeginTrans())
        return FALSE;
    TRY
    {
        while (!rsRecipiesSet.IsEOF())
        {
            rsRecipiesSet.Delete();
            rsRecipiesSet.MoveNext();
        }

        // Delete the Ingredient record
        rsIngredientSet.Delete();

        m_dbIngredientReg.CommitTrans();
    }
    CATCH_ALL(e)
    {
        m_dbIngredientReg.Rollback();
        return FALSE;
    }
    return TRUE;
}
```

The Applicability of Visual C++ Transaction Instructions

Only Access databases fully support transaction-processing instructions when you connect these databases with the Microsoft Jet database engine. Transaction-processing support is inherent in Access databases, but Btrieve databases require the special network transactions file BTRIEVE.TRN. FoxPro, dBASE, and Paradox databases don't support the rolling back of transactions. You can test whether a Table or a Dynaset object supports transactions by testing the value of the object's Transactions property. You can roll back changes to most tables if the value of the Transactions property is TRUE.

TIP

The Microsoft Jet database engine doesn't support rolling back transactions on Access tables that are attached to the Access database that underlies the active database object. If you need to provide rollback capability for transactions that span multiple Access databases, don't attach Access tables to your primary database. Instead, open each of the databases that contain the native tables required by your `Dynaset` object.

The Microsoft Jet database engine doesn't support the rolling back of transactions on client-server databases attached by the ODBC API if the attached client-server database ODBC driver doesn't support transactions. (Access SQL doesn't recognize the ANSI SQL TPL reserved words.) To take advantage of the transaction-processing capabilities of client-server databases, you need to apply the `ExecuteSQL()` method or apply the `Execute` method with the SQL pass-through option. Instead of using the `CDatabase.BeginTrans()...CDatabase.CommitTrans()` code structure, you use the ANSI SQL `BEGIN TRANS[ACTION] COMMIT TRANS[ACTION]` structure (or its equivalent) to enclose the action query statements. The method of detecting the failure of `COMMIT` in order to execute the `ROLLBACK TRANS[ACTION]` statement varies with the RDBMS you use.

The SQL statement you pass to the server RDBMS must correspond to the transaction syntax requirements of the particular RDBMS in use. Some client-server RDBMSs, such as SQL Server, require that you identify the beginning of a transaction with a `BEGIN TRANS[ACTION]` statement. DB2, on the other hand, uses intrinsic transactions. A DB2 unit of work commences with the first change you make to a database that is in a consistent condition and terminates with a `COMMIT` statement. If the `COMMIT` is unsuccessful, the `ROLLBACK [WORK]` statement undoes the unit of work.

Regardless of whether you can roll back changes you make to tables, using the `CDatabase.BeginTrans()...CDatabase.CommitTrans()` structure for bulk changes to tables almost always improves your application's performance. However, substantial risk is inherent in using `CDatabase.BeginTrans()...CDatabase.CommitTrans()` when you can't roll back changes. If your transaction fails, there's no way to determine at what point the failure occurred.

WARNING

A failure in the middle of a bulk update can make it unlikely that you will ever bring the database back to a consistent state. Thus, the safe approach when you can't roll back transactions is to write code to duplicate the action of the update buffer and transaction log and then execute each transaction individually. If an error occurs, your error-processing routine can undo the related changes that were made before the error was encountered.

Summary

This chapter covered the basic principles of the design of Visual C++ transaction-processing applications using either SQL action queries or Visual C++ code to perform updates on database tables. A sample application, Contin (and Contin using Grid Control), showed you how to write code to aggregate multiple updates into a single set of transactions. This chapter concluded with a discussion of the Visual C++ transaction-processing instructions `CDatabase.BeginTrans()`, `CDatabase.CommitTrans()`, and `CDatabase.Rollback()`, which you can use in conjunction with updates to tables in Access databases.

The next two chapters deal primarily with interprocess communication (IPC) between Visual C++ database applications that act as OLE 1.0, OLE 2.0, and DDE clients.

16

Creating OLE Controls
with Visual C++ 4

This chapter describes the development of OLE controls and is divided into two parts. The first part covers the OLE control development tools that Visual C++ offers the database programmer, and the second part takes you through the process of creating your own OLE control.

This book isn't about writing OLE controls. One or two chapters can't cover everything you need to know about writing (or using) OLE controls. If you're thinking about developing OLE controls, you should consider a book oriented toward OLE controls. (The next chapter teaches you how to use OLE controls, something that most database programmers will find useful.)

This chapter doesn't take into consideration who you're developing an OLE control for. You could be developing OLE controls for your own internal use, for others in your company or organization, or for sale to other programmers. There will be a large market for OLE controls in the future. This could be a field that smart programmers could exploit to their advantage.

OLE Control Development Tools

Supplied with Visual C++ 1.5x and Visual C++ 2.x is a separate development kit called the OLE Controls Development Kit (CDK). This facility is integrated into Visual C++ 4, making Visual C++ 4 an easier-to-use system. Since it can be assumed that some developers will have to develop 16-bit OLE controls using Visual C++ 1.5x (which is included with Visual C++ 4), I've included some information about the CDK and other related tools in this chapter.

This section describes the development tools that are supplied with the OLE control CDK and are built into Visual C++ 4. These tools make the process of developing OLE controls easy and (hopefully) painless, and they vary depending on the platform under which you're developing. For instance, the Make TypeLib (MKTYPLIB) utility isn't called by the programmer directly, except when you're using 16-bit versions of Visual C++. Visual C++ 2's WPS (Windows Process Status) utility, used to view process threads (specifically, to see what DLLs are loaded), isn't used under Windows NT because the PStat and PView utilities are part of the Visual C++ 2.0 package. With Visual C++ 4, the Windows NT system has both PView and PStat, neither of which can be used under Windows 95. The PView95 program is available for Windows 95 users of Visual C++ 4. It can be found on the Visual C++ 4 CD in the directory \MSDEV\BIN\WIN95.

CAUTION

When you're converting OLE controls created with the CDK supplied with Visual C++ 1.5x and 2.x, you should read the topic *OLE Controls: Converting a CDK Project to a Visual C++ Project* in the *Programming with MFC Encyclopedia,* which is part of the Visual C++ Books Online documentation.

Unless otherwise noted, the descriptions of the tools in this chapter are for how they run under Visual C++ 4. When a tool works significantly differently under other versions of Visual C++ (including the 16-bit version, 1.5x), the differences are noted.

ControlWizard

This section introduces you to ControlWizard. You use ControlWizard to develop the shell for your OLE controls. Its user interface looks and feels very much like that of AppWizard in Visual C++, because it's an integrated AppWizard in Visual C++ 4. This is a major improvement to earlier versions of Visual C++, in which ControlWizard was a separate application, external to Visual C++'s Developer Studio.

To create a new OLE control, you first start AppWizard and select an OLE control project type, as shown in Figure 16.1. This figure shows that an OLE control is being created; the name for the control has been entered. After it's started, AppWizard's ControlWizard displays the main dialog box, shown in Figure 16.2.

FIGURE 16.1.

AppWizard showing the OLE control project type.

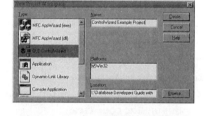

FIGURE 16.2.

ControlWizard's Step 1 of 2 dialog box.

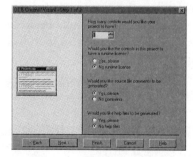

Before you name the new OLE control, you must select the directory in which the new control will be created. When you specify the control's name, that name is used to create the control's subdirectory. If you like, either before or after specifying the control's name, you can change the path to the project's directory.

After you name your new control and specify its location, you can specify its options and configuration. These options and configurations are grouped using two Wizard dialogs. The first is shown in Figure 16.2, and the second is shown in Figure 16.3. These Wizard dialogs are described in the following sections.

FIGURE 16.3.

ControlWizard's Step 2 of 2 dialog box.

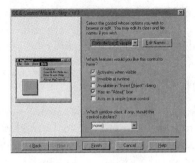

OLE ControlWizard's Step 1 of 2 Dialog Box

The following options are available in OLE ControlWizard's first step:

■ You can set the number of controls that you will have in this project at development time. You can modify this number later if you want. However, if you know that your project will have more than one control, you should specify the number of OLE controls at this time. The default is to have one control in a project.

■ The runtime license validation option, which normally isn't selected, tells Control-Wizard to add calls to enforce licensing and to create a .LIC license file for your control. You can later modify both the validation code and the .LIC file as desired.

■ The generation of source comments can be specified. Usually selected, this option tells ControlWizard to create comments in the source and header files to assist you in adding and modifying the code created.

■ Help files can be created automatically for your OLE control project. Generally, a control that you will distribute should be documented, while a control that will be used only by you can be documented in the control's code. The default is to not create a help file for the control.

As soon as you've set the desired options for the first step in ControlWizard, you can move to the second step.

NOTE

Remember when using ControlWizard that you can go back and change settings made in previous steps. You aren't locked into any choice until you actually create your project. You can even back up to the initial selection of the project's name and location if you want to.

OLE ControlWizard's Step 2 of 2 Dialog Box

The following options are available in OLE ControlWizard's second and final step. Each control in the project may have different options that can be set in the second step. Also, the second step is where you can modify the names for your project's controls.

> **NOTE**
>
> Regardless of the number of controls in a project, you can rename the controls at the second step. A control's name doesn't have to be the project's name, for example.

Each of the options in the second step is associated with a specific control. That way, you can have controls with different attributes in the same project. The following options may be set for each control.

- The Activate when visible option specifies that when the control is visible, it's active. You would check this box if you wanted to tell the container that the control prefers to be automatically activated when it's visible. Even if you select this option, container applications aren't required to support it.

- The Invisible at runtime option specifies that the control is visible only when it's in design mode. When in run mode, the control is invisible. (In other words, the user can't see the control when the application is running.) Even if this option is selected, container applications aren't required to support it.

- The Available in 'Insert Object' dialog option specifies that the control will be listed in the container application's Insert Object dialog box.

- The Has an 'About' box option specifies that ControlWizard will create a standard About dialog box and `AboutBox` method for the currently selected control. The About dialog is displayed when the container invokes your control's `AboutBox` method. You can later customize the About box as desired.

- The Acts as a simple frame control option specifies that the currently selected control support will be the `ISimpleFrameSite` protocol. When the control and the container both support this protocol, the container uses simple frame controls as parents for other controls in the container. The result is that the simple frame control will operate as an OLE compound document container, but the frame control's container will do virtually all the work.

- The Which window class, if any, should this control subclass? option specifies that the control will subclass a common Windows control, such as a button, toolbar, or edit box. Table 16.1 lists the possibilities for this selection.

Table 16.1. Windows controls that an OLE control may subclass.

Control	Description
BUTTON	The standard button control.
COMBOBOX	The standard combo-box control.
EDIT	The standard edit control (not the RTF edit control).
LISTBOX	The standard list box control.
mscrls_hotkey32	The Win32 hot key control.
mscrls_progress32	The Win32 progress bar control.
mscrls_status32	The Win32 status control.
mscrls_trackbar32	The Win32 track bar control.
mscrls_updown32	The Win32 up-down control.
SCROLLBAR	The standard scrollbar control.
STATIC	The standard static control.
SysAnimate32	The Win32 animation control.
SysHeader32	The Win32 header control.
SysListView32	The Win32 list view control.
SysTabControl32	The Win32 tab control.
SysTreeView32	The Win32 tree view control.

The Edit Names Dialog Box

To access the Edit Names dialog box, shown in Figure 16.4, click the Edit Names button in ControlWizard's Step 2 of 2 dialog box. It lets you define a number of names associated with each of the controls in your project.

FIGURE 16.4.
ControlWizard's Edit Names dialog box.

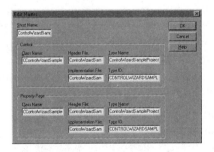

The following names and attributes may be changed:

- ■ Short Name: The short name for this control, which is usually the same as the control's project name. If your control's project name doesn't make a clear name for the control, you should specify a new short name.

For the control itself, the following names may be specified:

- ■ Class Name: The name of the control's main class.
- ■ Header File: The filename of the main header file.
- ■ Type Name: The name that will appear in the Insert Object dialog box in the container application at design time.
- ■ Implementation File: The name of the main source file.
- ■ Type ID: The string that an OLE control registers in the registry when it's applied to a project. This string is then used by container applications to create instances of the OLE control.

For the control's property page, the following may be specified:

- ■ Class Name: The name of the control's property page class.
- ■ Header File: The filename of the property page header file.
- ■ Type Name: The name that will appear in the Insert Object dialog box in the container application at design time. Rarely used by anyone.
- ■ Implementation File: The name of the property page source file.
- ■ Type ID: The string that an OLE control registers in the registry when it's applied to a project. This string is then used by container applications to create instances of the OLE control's property page.

Generating Your OLE Control

After you've defined your new OLE control, you can click the Finish button in ControlWizard's Step 2 of 2 dialog box. When you click Finish, the New Product Information dialog box, shown in Figure 16.5, appears. This dialog shows the various options, names, and configurations that you selected in the OLE control creation stage.

Review this dialog box and, if all is in order, click OK. Visual C++ 4 will then open the new control in Developer Studio.

Sometimes you'll want to create both 16-bit and 32-bit versions of your OLE control. To create a 16-bit version of your control, you must use Visual C++ 1.5x and its 16-bit OLE Control Development Kit. This might prove to be difficult, and I don't recommend it unless you have no alternative and must create 16-bit versions of your OLE controls. If you try to use Visual C++ 4 to create a 16-bit control, you must make sure that the control's project name is no more than four characters long, because the project's filenames must be short under Visual C++ 1.5x. You also need to create a new .MAK file for the control, a nontrivial task.

FIGURE 16.5.
ControlWizard's New Product Information dialog box.

Register/Unregister Control

Register Control and Unregister Control are two separate menu options on the Tools menu in versions of Visual C++ prior to 4. (If you don't have an Unregister Control option, you can add it to your Tools menu using the Customize option and the REGSVR32 program.) However, both options call the registration program (REGSVR.EXE for Windows 3.x and REGSVR32.EXE for Windows NT and Windows 95) that is found in Visual C++'s \MSDEV\BIN directory. Visual C++ 4's controls automatically register themselves when created (as part of the project build process), but you can have a Register Control menu option on your Visual C++ 4 Tools menu too.

The REGSVR32 program takes as an argument the name of the control to be registered or unregistered. This name generally is the OLE control's DLL filename with the file extension. REGSVR32 also takes the following optional parameters, which aren't case-specific:

- The /s option tells REGSVR32 not to generate normal output. This option is similar to the Linker's /NOLOGO option.
- The /c option tells REGSVR32 to run in console mode.
- The /v option tells REGSVR32 that it's running under Visual C++.
- The /u option tells REGSVR to unregister the control rather than register it.

REGSVR32 is both small and efficient. It has no features or options other than those just described. REGSVR32 can't be redistributed. Other developers who are using your controls must use their own tools to register and install controls. The source for REGSVR32 is available on the Visual C++ CD in the directory \MSDEV\SAMPLES\MFC\CONTROLS\REGSVR.

Test Container

Test Container (TSTCON16 or TSTCON32, depending on the version of Windows to which you're targeting your OLE controls) is a very useful utility that lets you embed OLE controls and test their functionality. Test Container doesn't have all the usability of a full-fledged application, but it does let you test most of the aspects of your control. However, you still must test your control in its final environment, such as in an Access form.

Test Container runs externally to Visual C++ and therefore doesn't come in a debugging version. Generally, when you debug your control, you load it into Visual C++ and then start OLE Control Test Container from Visual C++'s Tools menu.

When Test Container is loaded and running, the first thing you'll do is insert an OLE control. After you insert a control into Test Container's document space, you can work with the control's interface. (You'll need to test both the user interface and the OLE control's interface with the container.)

Test Container's user interface is both a menu bar and a toolbar. The menu bar offers the options described in Table 16.2.

Table 16.2. Test Container's menu options.

Menu	Option	Description
File	Save to Stream	Saves the currently selected OLE control to a stream. A stream can hold one or more OLE controls, and an OLE control can be saved to the stream more than once. After an OLE control has been saved to a stream, the Save to Substorage selection is disabled until the stream has been cleared.
	Save to Substorage	Saves the currently selected OLE control to substorage. Substorage can hold one or more OLE controls, and an OLE control can be saved to substorage more than once. After an OLE control has been saved to substorage, the Save to Stream selection is disabled until substorage has been cleared.
	Load	Loads the currently saved stream or substorage.
	Save Property Set	Saves the properties of the currently selected OLE control to a document file.
	Load Property Set	Creates a new OLE control and initializes it from the previously saved document file.

continues

Table 16.2. continued

Menu	Option	Description
	Register Controls	Registers a new OLE control. Performs the same function as Visual C++'s Tools | Register Control menu option.
	Exit	Ends the Test Container program.
Edit	Insert OLE Control...	Opens the Insert OLE control dialog box and lets you select a new control to be added to Test Container's document space.
	Delete	Deletes the currently selected OLE control.
	Delete All	Deletes all the OLE controls that are in Test Container's document.
	Set Ambient Properties	The Ambient Properties dialog box sets the container properties that affect all OLE controls. Properties such as UserMode, BackColor, Font, and so on can be set in this dialog box.
	View Event List	Lets you specify the logging of events, such as the clicking of the mouse button.
	Invoke Methods	Lets you test the OLE control's methods. All OLE controls that are created using ControlWizard at least have an About method, which displays the control's About box.
	Draw Metafile	Draws the control's metafile so that you can see the effects of metafile drawing of your control's client area.
	Embedded Object Functions	Provides a submenu of choices: Hide: Hides the control and puts it in the Loaded state. Calls `COleClientItem::Activate(OLEIVERB _HIDE, ...)`.

Menu	Option	Description
		Primary Verb: Invokes the control's primary verb.
		Activate: Activates the control and puts it in the Loaded state. Calls `COleClientItem::Activate (OLEIVERB_PRIMARY, ...)`.
		UI Activate: Puts the control in the UI Active state.
		Close: Closes the control and puts it in the Loaded state. Calls `COleClientItem::Close()`.
		Deactivate: Deactivates the control and puts it in the Loaded state. Calls `COleClientItem::Deactivate()`. Also discards the contents of the Undo buffer.
		Deactivate UI Only: Restores Test Container's user interface to its original state. Calls `COleClientItem::DeactivateUI()`.
		Open: Opens the control in stand-alone mode and puts it in the Open state. Calls `COleClientItem::Activate(OLEIVERB_OPEN, ...)`.
		Reactivate and Undo: Reactivates a control and puts it in the Loaded state. Calls `COleClientItem::ReactivateAndUndo()`.
		Run: Runs the control and puts it in the Loaded state. Calls `COleClientItem::Run()`.

continues

Table 16.2. continued

Menu	Option	Description
		Show: Activates the control and puts it in the UI Active state. Calls `COleClientItem::Activate(OLEIVERB_SHOW, ...)`.
	Properties	Shows the currently active OLE control's property sheet.
View	Toolbar	Shows or hides the toolbar.
	Status Bar	Shows or hides the status bar.
	Event Log	Displays the event log.
	Notification Log	Displays the notification log.
	Saved Control Stream	Displays a dump of the currently saved stream. This dump is divided into sections, one per saved control.
	Properties	Shows or hides the Properties dialog box for the selected control.
Options	Passive Container Mode	Tells the container not to automatically change the control's state. Selecting Passive Container Mode automatically deselects Simulated Design Mode.
	Simulated Design Mode	Tells the container to automatically change the control's state. Selecting Simulated Design Mode automatically deselects Passive Container Mode.
	Freeze Events	Freezes or releases the on-event firing for all controls.
	Honor `ACTIVATEWHENVISIBLE`	Turns support on or off for the `OLEMISC_ACTIVATEWHENVISIBLE` flag.
	Honor `INVISIBLEATRUNTIME`	Turns support on or off for the `OLEMISC_INVISIBLEATRUNTIME` flag. This option is supported only by TSTCON16.
Help	Contents	Provides help on Test Container by displaying the Contents help page.
	About Test Container	Displays Test Container's About box.

Test Container also has a customized status bar that provides information about the currently selected control and Test Container. The following is a list of the panes in the status bar from left to right:

■ Test Container's Status: Provides menu prompts and Test Container's general status.

■ OLE Control Name: The name of the currently selected control is displayed in the second pane. If there is no currently selected control, this pane is blank.

■ OLE Control Count: Test Container keeps a count of how many instances of each control type are currently loaded. This pane displays the count for the currently selected control. For example, if you load three copies of the digital clock control, the Count pane will be either 01, 02, or 03, depending on which copy of the digital clock control is currently selected. If no control is currently selected, this pane is blank.

■ OLE Control UI Status: The pane on the far right provides the status of the currently selected control. To change the control's UI status, select Edit | Embedded Object Functions. If no control is currently selected, this pane is blank.

Figure 16.6 shows Test Container's main window and its client area with the calendar custom control. Notice how the calendar looks in Test Container. This is almost exactly how it would appear when embedded into an application.

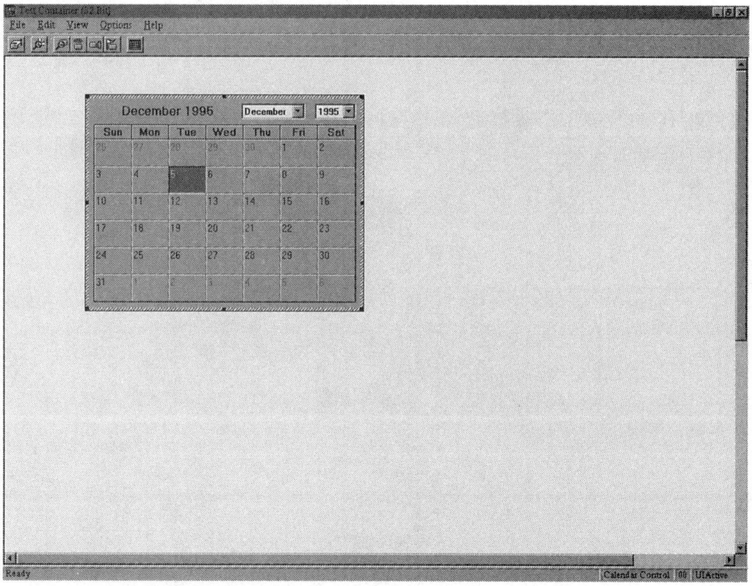

FIGURE 16.6.

Test Container's main window, with Access 7's calendar control loaded.

Test Container also provides a dialog box to configure the logging of events, as shown in Figure 16.7. You can tell Test Container which events you want to log (see the description of the Event Log that follows). You can select each event and choose to have it logged or not logged.

Also, there are buttons to turn event logging on or off for all events. Compare the events shown in Figure 16.7 with the Event Log window shown in Figure 16.8 (Test Container's logging windows).

FIGURE 16.7.

Test Container's Events for... dialog box.

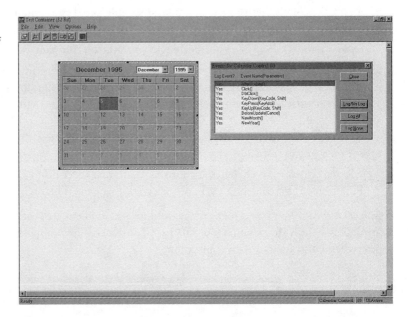

FIGURE 16.8.

Test Container's logging windows.

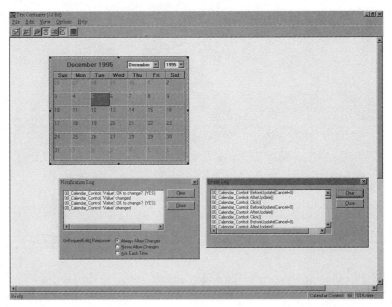

With Test Container's status windows, you can see the OLE control's Event Log and Notification Log. Both the Event Log and the Notification Log dialog boxes are modeless and can be left displayed for the entire Test Container session.

The Event Log window shows the events for the currently active control. For example, the Circ3 control posts events for mouse clicks, both inside and outside the circle. For mouse clicks inside the circle, the event routines are configured to show the relative coordinates of the mouse cursor.

The Notification Log window notifies you of changes in the controls' properties. Figure 16.9 shows the notifications received when the Calendar control has had its Today property changed.

FIGURE 16.9.

Test Container's Notification Log with changes to Calendar.

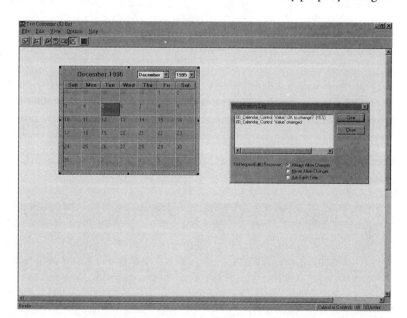

Also part of the Notification Log dialog box are radio buttons to configure the response to the OnRequestEdit() call. Choices include the following:

■ Always Allow Changes: The response to the OnRequestEdit() call will be yes.

■ Never Allow Changes: The response to the OnRequestEdit() call will be no.

■ Ask Each Time: The user is shown a confirmation dialog box that lets him decide whether it's OK to change the property. If he selects Yes, the property is changed. If he selects No, the property isn't changed.

WPS

WPS is a utility—part of the 16-bit version of the CDK (supplied with Visual C++ 1.5x and found on the MSDN Level I CD)—that lets you view both running tasks and loaded modules. You can perform a number of functions with WPS, such as freeing a task or a module, saving the list of currently running tasks and loaded modules in a file, or forcing the loading of a module. Although this utility is intended for use with Windows 3.x, it will run under Windows 95.

> **NOTE**
>
> Programmers using Windows 95 should use the PView95 utility instead of WPS. PView95 works in the same manner as Windows NT's PView program.

Programmers who are developing OLE controls can use WPS in several ways. First, when a container program (such as Access) uses an OLE control, the container program won't unload the control when the control terminates. You can't make changes to a DLL file while it's loaded, so you must force Windows to unload the DLL before rebuilding it with Visual C++.

As a side benefit, WPS is useful as both a general process viewer and as a method to delete an undesirable process.

> **WARNING**
>
> As with any system-level utility, WPS can bring Windows to a screeching halt. If you free a module or task that Windows needs to run, the world as Windows knows it will come to an end. Processes and tasks to steer clear of include those that have the names *kernel* and *KRNL,* as well as other names that you can associate with the Windows system components.

WPS presents itself as a window split horizontally into two unequal parts. Processes appear in the top third of the window, and loaded modules appear in the lower two-thirds. One small flaw is that you can't change the size of the two parts of the window.

WPS offers several menus, which are listed in Table 16.3.

Table 16.3. WPS menu options.

Menu	Option	Description
File	Load Module...	Lets you force the loading of a module (an .EXE or a .DLL file).
	Dump	Lets you save the main window's contents in a standard text file format. The saved file's contents can then be reviewed later.
	About WPS	Displays the About dialog box, giving the authors' names and their company.
	Exit	Ends the current WPS session.
Options	Free Module	Frees the module that is currently selected.
	Free Task	Frees the task that is currently selected.
	Font	Lets you change the font that WPS uses. Selecting a smaller font lets you display more lines of information.
Edit	Copy	Copies the contents of the WPS window to the clipboard.
Update!		Tells WPS to update its display.

Figure 16.10 shows WPS running on a system. Notice that there are more tasks running than will fit into the Tasks part of the window (the top part), and many more modules loaded than will fit into the Modules part (the bottom part). However, because both of these lists are sorted by name, it isn't difficult to find a specific task or module.

When you look at Figure 16.10 you can see several columns. Table 16.4 describes the columns and how they're used.

Table 16.4. Columns in WPS.

Column	Description
	Tasks Section
Name	The name of the running task. Generally, this is the eight-character program name. Often it's the same as the task's eight-character filename.
hTask	The handle for the task (see hParent).
hParent	The hTask for the parent task of this task. If the parent task is zero, the task is a 32-bit task owned by Windows.

continues

Table 16.4. continued

Column	Description
	Tasks Section
nEvents	The count of the hardware resources (such as communications ports) for the task.
hInst	The instance handle for the task.
Version	The version number from the task's version resource (if the task has a version resource). If there is no version resource, this field is blank.
Exe	The fully qualified filename for the task. Some versions of Windows use UNC names for files that are on shared, nonlocal network drives.
	Modules Section
Name	The name of the loaded module. This name may be the same as the module's filename.
hModule	The handle for the module.
Usage	The usage count (lock count) that indicates the number of references to this module. Most nonsystem modules have a usage count of 1 or 2. System modules may have usage counts of 50 or more.
Version	The version number from the task's version resource (if the task has a version resource). If there is no version resource, this field is blank.
Exe	The fully qualified filename for the task. Some versions of Windows use UIC names for files that are on shared, nonlocal network drives.

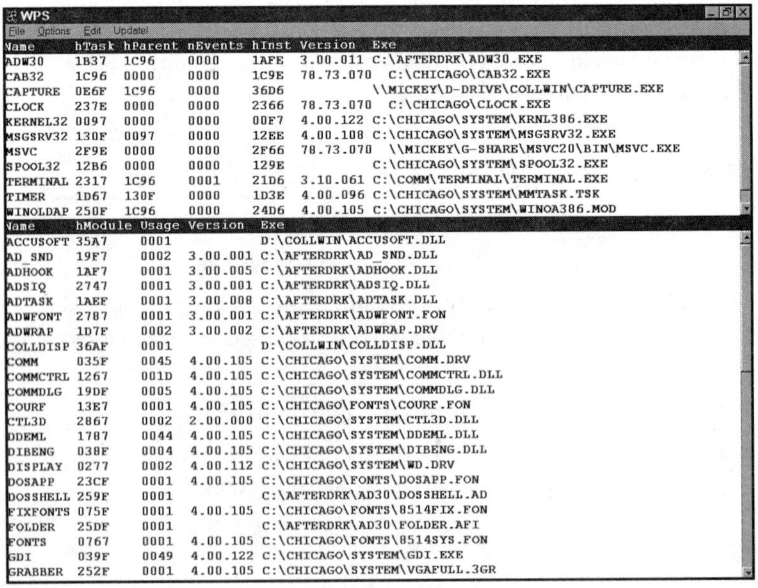

FIGURE 16.10.

WPS's main window.

```
WPS
File  Options  Edit  Update!
Name      hTask  hParent  nEvents  hInst  Version    Exe
ADW30     1B37   1C96     0000     1AFE   3.00.011  C:\AFTERDRK\ADW30.EXE
CAB32     1C96   0000     0000     1C9E   78.73.070 C:\CHICAGO\CAB32.EXE
CAPTURE   0E6F   1C96     0000     36D6             \\MICKEY\D-DRIVE\COLLWIN\CAPTURE.EXE
CLOCK     237E   0000     0000     2366   78.73.070 C:\CHICAGO\CLOCK.EXE
KERNEL32  0097   0000     0000     00F7   4.00.122  C:\CHICAGO\SYSTEM\KRNL386.EXE
MSGSRV32  130F   0097     0000     12EE   4.00.108  C:\CHICAGO\SYSTEM\MSGSRV32.EXE
MSVC      2F9E   0000     0000     2F66   78.73.070 \\MICKEY\G-SHARE\MSVC20\BIN\MSVC.EXE
SPOOL32   12B6   0000     0000     129E             C:\CHICAGO\SYSTEM\SPOOL32.EXE
TERMINAL  2317   1C96     0001     21D6   3.10.061  C:\COMM\TERMINAL\TERMINAL.EXE
TIMER     1D67   130F     0000     1D3E   4.00.096  C:\CHICAGO\SYSTEM\MMTASK.TSK
WINOLDAP  250F   1C96     0000     24D6   4.00.105  C:\CHICAGO\SYSTEM\WINOA386.MOD
Name       hModule  Usage  Version   Exe
ACCUSOFT   35A7     0001             D:\COLLWIN\ACCUSOFT.DLL
AD_SND     19F7     0002   3.00.001  C:\AFTERDRK\AD_SND.DLL
ADHOOK     1AF7     0001   3.00.005  C:\AFTERDRK\ADHOOK.DLL
ADSIQ      2747     0001   3.00.001  C:\AFTERDRK\ADSIQ.DLL
ADTASK     1AEF     0001   3.00.008  C:\AFTERDRK\ADTASK.DLL
ADWFONT    2787     0001   3.00.001  C:\AFTERDRK\ADWFONT.FON
ADWRAP     1D7F     0002   3.00.002  C:\AFTERDRK\ADWRAP.DRV
COLLDISP   36AF     0001             D:\COLLWIN\COLLDISP.DLL
COMM       035F     0045   4.00.105  C:\CHICAGO\SYSTEM\COMM.DRV
COMMCTRL   1267     001D   4.00.105  C:\CHICAGO\SYSTEM\COMMCTRL.DLL
COMMDLG    19DF     0005   4.00.105  C:\CHICAGO\SYSTEM\COMMDLG.DLL
COURF      13E7     0001   4.00.105  C:\CHICAGO\FONTS\COURF.FON
CTL3D      2867     0002   2.00.000  C:\CHICAGO\SYSTEM\CTL3D.DLL
DDEML      1787     0044   4.00.105  C:\CHICAGO\SYSTEM\DDEML.DLL
DIBENG     038E     0004   4.00.105  C:\CHICAGO\SYSTEM\DIBENG.DLL
DISPLAY    0277     0002   4.00.112  C:\CHICAGO\SYSTEM\WD.DRV
DOSAPP     23CF     0001   4.00.105  C:\CHICAGO\FONTS\DOSAPP.FON
DOSSHELL   259F     0001             C:\AFTERDRK\AD30\DOSSHELL.AD
FIXFONTS   075F     0001   4.00.105  C:\CHICAGO\FONTS\8514FIX.FON
FOLDER     25DF     0001             C:\AFTERDRK\AD30\FOLDER.AFI
FONTS      0767     0001   4.00.105  C:\CHICAGO\FONTS\8514SYS.FON
GDI        039F     0049   4.00.122  C:\CHICAGO\SYSTEM\GDI.EXE
GRABBER    252F     0001   4.00.105  C:\CHICAGO\SYSTEM\VGAFULL.3GR
```

All in all, I've found WPS to be a very useful tool for looking at what's loaded and running under Windows. I find it amazing how much is going on in Windows that I wouldn't be aware of otherwise.

PView95

The PView95 program is used to view processes while running under Windows 95. This program was developed to complement the Windows NT program PView. Using PView95 is easy, because it has a simple user interface that includes the menus listed in Table 16.5.

Table 16.5. PView95 menu options.

Menu	Option	Description
File	Exit	Ends the current PView95 session.
Process	Refresh	Updates the list of current tasks.
	Kill	Kills the selected task.
Help	About	Displays the PView95 About box.

Figure 16.11 shows PView95 running on a system. Notice that there are both 16-bit and 32-bit applications running under Windows 95. Both of these lists are sorted by name, so it isn't difficult to find a specific task or module.

FIGURE 16.11.

PView95's main window.

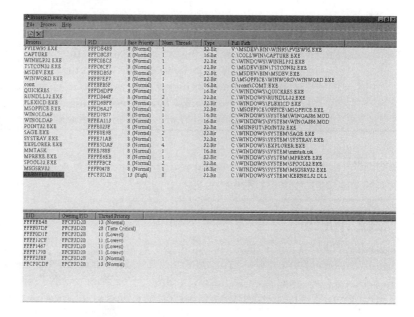

Figure 16.11 has several columns. Table 16.6 lists these columns and describes how they're used.

Table 16.6. Columns in PView95.

Column	Description
	Process (Top) Section
Process	The name of the running process. Generally, this is the eight-character program name, often with an extension of .EXE or .DLL.
PID	The process identifier, a 32-bit value assigned to identify this process.
Base Priority	A priority value, typically 8 for most processes (KERNEL32 has a base priority of 13). Threads of a process can have a lower or higher priority as needed. A value of 28 usually indicates a critical thread or process.
Num. Threads	The number of threads owned by this process.
Type	The program's type: 16-bit or 32-bit. Windows 95 is a mixed-type operating system that has both 16-bit and 32-bit components.
Full Path	The full path to the executable file (either .EXE or .DLL) for this process.
	Threads (Bottom) Section
TID	The thread identifier.
Owning PID	The process identifier for this thread's owner.
Thread Priority	The priority for this thread, relative to the owning process's priority. The priority value is based on the process priority and can be either lower or higher than the process's priority. Each of a process's threads may have a lower or higher priority as needed. A value of 28 usually indicates a critical thread or process.

All in all, I've found PView95 to be a useful tool for looking at what processes and threads are loaded and running under Windows 95.

Make TypeLib

Make TypeLib is a utility that is run only as a separate step (by you, the programmer) under 16-bit versions of Visual C++. You don't use it when you're developing OLE controls using Visual C++ 2 or Visual C++ 4 under Windows 95 or Windows NT. Instead, the 32-bit versions of Visual C++ create the typelib as part of the project's build process by calling MKTYPLIB directly as part of the project's make process. The Make TypeLib command is found on Developer Studio's Tools menu when you're using Visual C++ 1.5. Make TypeLib invokes the MKTYPLIB program.

A *typelib* lets other applications determine which properties, methods, and events your OLE control will support. MKTYPLIB's input files have a file type of ODL, whereas output typelib files have a file type of TLB.

When you use ControlWizard to create an OLE control, an initial ODL file is created for you. ClassWizard updates this file as you add new properties, methods, or events to your OLE control. When you're developing under Visual C++ 1.5, you must use Tools | Make TypeLib to update the typelib file.

The MKTYPLIB program has a number of options, which are described in Table 16.7. These options are specified when you start MKTYPLIB from the Visual C++ 1.5 Tools menu. MKTYPLIB can also be started from a DOS prompt. These options may then be specified in the command line. The current version of MKTYPLIB is 2.01.

Table 16.7. MKTYPLIB options.

Option	Description
/help or /?	Displays a message specifying the options for MKTYPLIB.
/tlb <filename>	Specifies the name of the output type library file. If it's not specified, the output file defaults to the same name as the input file, with a file type of TLB.
/h [filename]	Specifies the output .H filename.
/<system>	Available in both versions of MKTYPLIB. Use this option to specify which type of TLB is produced. Valid types of typelibs include WIN16, WIN32, MAC, MIPS, ALPHA, PPC, and PPC32. Defaults to WIN32 for the 32-bit version of MKTYPLIB and to WIN16 for the 16-bit version.
/align <#>	Available in the 32-bit version of MKTYPLIB only. Use this option to override the default alignment setting.
/o filename	Tells MKTYPLIB to redirect its output to the specified file. Normally, MKTYPLIB sends the output to the stdout device.
/nologo	Tells MKTYPLIB not to display the startup logo or copyright message.
/w0	Tells MKTYPLIB to disable all warnings.
/nocpp	Tells MKTYPLIB not to spawn the C preprocessor.

continues

Table 16.7. continued

Option	Description
/cpp_cmd *<path>*	Specifies the path for the C preprocessor, which is part of the C/C++ compiler. Defaults to CL.EXE. If MKTYPLIB is to be used with compilers other than Visual C++, this option might have to be changed to reflect the actual name of the preprocessor.
/cpp_opt "*<opt>*"	Specifies the C/C++ preprocessor's options. The default options are /C /E /D__MKTYPLIB. The actions taken with the default options are as follows:

	c	Doesn't strip any comments from the preprocessor output.
	/E	Performs a preprocessor pass only, writing the output to stdout.
	/D__MKTYPLIB	Defines the identifier MKTYPLIB that is referenced in OLECTL.H.

Option	Description
/D*define*[=*value*]	Defines additional C/C++ preprocessor identifiers. This option is used in addition to the /cpp_opt "*<opt>*" option.
/I includepath	Specifies paths for any include files.

The default installation for Visual C++ 1.5 (as completed by the CDK setup program) uses the following option list. Comments have been added.

```
/cpp_cmd D:\MSVC15\BIN\cl   // Defines the preprocessor command
/W0                         // Disables all warnings
/I D:\MSVC15\CDK16\INCLUDE  // Sets the include path
/nologo                     // Disables the startup logo
$Proj.odl                   // The input filename
/tlb tlb16\$Proj.tlb        // The output filename (and directory)
```

You could modify these options, but you probably won't need to.

The following code fragment shows the default commands for MKTYPLIB for Visual C++ 4. Notice that there are four different calls to MKTYPLIB—ANSI debug and release and Unicode debug and release. This code fragment is set up to create a 32-bit ANSI Windows release version.

```
SOURCE=.\clock.odl

!IF  "$(CFG)" == "clock - Win32 Release"


"$(OUTDIR)\clock.tlb" : $(SOURCE) "$(OUTDIR)"
   $(MTL) /nologo /D "NDEBUG" /tlb "$(OUTDIR)/clock.tlb" /win32 $(SOURCE)


!ELSEIF  "$(CFG)" == "clock - Win32 Debug"
```

```
"$(OUTDIR)\clock.tlb" : $(SOURCE) "$(OUTDIR)"
   $(MTL) /nologo /D "_DEBUG" /tlb "$(OUTDIR)/clock.tlb" /win32 $(SOURCE)


!ELSEIF  "$(CFG)" == "clock - Win32 Unicode Debug"


"$(OUTDIR)\clock.tlb" : $(SOURCE) "$(OUTDIR)"
   $(MTL) /nologo /D "_DEBUG" /tlb "$(OUTDIR)/clock.tlb" /win32 $(SOURCE)


!ELSEIF  "$(CFG)" == "clock - Win32 Unicode Release"


"$(OUTDIR)\clock.tlb" : $(SOURCE) "$(OUTDIR)"
   $(MTL) /nologo /D "NDEBUG" /tlb "$(OUTDIR)/clock.tlb" /win32 $(SOURCE)


!ENDIF
```

With Visual C++ 4, you set the typelib options by accessing the Project Settings dialog box. In this dialog, select the .ODL file in the Settings For list box. You see two tabs, General and OLE Types. Under the General tab, you can choose to exclude the typelib from the build. If you do so, you must build the typelib manually if you make any changes to the control's properties, methods, or events.

Figure 16.12 shows the General tab of Visual C++ 4's Project Settings for CLOCK's typelib generation.

FIGURE 16.12

The General tab of CLOCK.ODL's project settings.

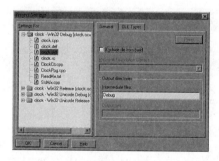

Under the OLE Types tab, shown in Figure 16.13, you can specify the output TBL filename, output header filenames, additional include directories, and preprocessor definitions. You also can specify whether MKTYPLIB's startup banner is displayed. In addition, there is a Reset button so that you can reset the typelib options to their default values.

FIGURE 16.13.
The OLE Types tab of
CLOCK.ODL's project
settings.

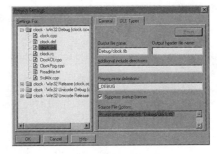

Creating an OLE Control

In this chapter you will create an OLE Custom Control and learn how an OLE control handles events, properties, and methods. The control created in this chapter can be embedded in an Access 7 form or report or in any other container that supports OLE controls, including a Visual C++ 4 MFC 4 program dialog box.

There is little reason to create an OLE control without using ControlWizard. If you create an OLE control manually, you can't use ClassWizard to manage the control's classes, and you'll have difficulty creating a project file that is compatible with Visual C++. If you convert an existing VBX control to an OLE control, ControlWizard offers an option to assist you in automating the conversion process.

> **NOTE**
>
> Remember, Windows NT and OLE are Unicode-compatible. You should always code string literals using the _T() macro. For example, the string "Peter D. Hipson" should be written as _T("Peter D. Hipson"). The _T() macro takes care of the conversions to Unicode when necessary.

If you're using Visual C++ 2, you must have the OLE control CDK installed before you create an OLE control. Versions of Visual C++ earlier than 1.50.01 (including 1.5) must be upgraded before you install the CDK. Visual C++ 4 has OLE control development support built in, not as a separate component.

Creating an OLE Control Shell

To create your new OLE control, which you'll call Clock, first you must start AppWizard's ControlWizard by choosing File | New from Visual C++. Then follow these steps:

1. Select the directory under which the new OLE control's project directory will be created. Make sure that this directory doesn't already have a subdirectory with the same name.

2. Name your new project in the Project Name edit box. For your sample Clock OLE control, use the name *clock*. In earlier versions of ControlWizard, you were restricted to lowercase letters. This restriction doesn't apply to Visual C++ 4's ControlWizard.

3. Select OLE Control Wizard as the type of project.

4. Click the Create button to display ControlWizard's first dialog box. Make sure that the all the default options are selected (one control, no runtime license, comments, and no help files).

5. Click Next to move to the Step 2 of 2 dialog box, shown in Figure 16.14.

FIGURE 16.14.

ControlWizard's Step 2 of 2 dialog for the clock project.

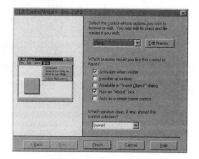

6. Accept the default control name (Clock), and again accept the default options (Activate when visible and Has an "About" box). Don't select any Windows control to subclass.

7. Click the Edit Names button.

8. In the Edit Names dialog box, shown in Figure 16.15, make sure that the Short Name is Clock and that the class is CClockCtrl. Change the Type Name to Digital Clock Control. Accept the default names for the Header File, Implementation File, and Type ID.

FIGURE 16.15.

ControlWizard's Edit Names dialog box for Clock.

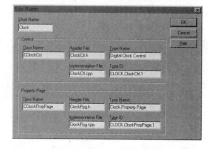

9. Click OK in the Edit Names dialog box.

10. Click OK in the OLE ControlWizard - Step 2 of 2 dialog box.

11. The New Project Information dialog box appears. Compare the results in your session with those shown in Figure 16.16. The only difference should be the Install Directory field (located at the bottom of the dialog box), because you won't be using the same directory structure as I am.

FIGURE 16.16.

The New Project Information dialog box.

12. Click OK.

In 12 simple steps, you've created your OLE control. You didn't have to know a single thing about OLE, controls, containers, embedding, or linking to create the control.

After you've created your OLE control, you should perform a full build. If you're building a Windows 95 control, you need to select the Win32 Debug version. If you're building a Windows NT control, use the default, the Win32 Unicode Debug version. Building a new project ensures you that the project will build before you've made any changes. When the build completes successfully, your control will be registered by Visual C++ 4, and you can test it using Test Container. Because your control has no real functionality, it simply shows up in Test Container as an ellipse inside the control's user area. Your clock control should look like the one shown in Figure 16.17, which shows Clock running in Test Container.

Now that you have a basic OLE control that you can use, the next step in the development process is to add some properties.

> **NOTE**
>
> In this chapter, properties, events, and methods are added—in that order. You don't need to follow a certain order when you add features to your OLE control. I followed the order described simply because it made this chapter easier to write!

FIGURE 16.17.

Clock, fresh from ControlWizard, in Test Container.

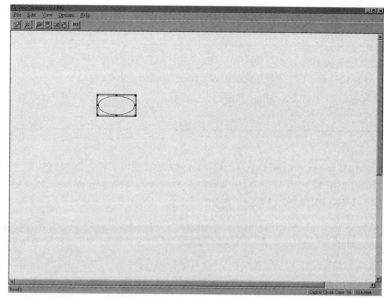

Adding Properties to an OLE Control

Properties are divided into two categories: stock (which are part of the OLE control system) and custom (which are specific to a given OLE control). You will learn about stock properties first. After you create your stock properties, you will add a custom property to your clock.

Stock Properties: Colors

The OLE Custom Control system lets you rely on a set of stock properties for your control. With stock properties, you don't have to design a dialog box to set the property, because the stock property dialog boxes are already included in the OLE control support DLL file. OLE supports the stock properties shown in Table 16.8.

Table 16.8. Stock properties supported by OLE.

Property	Description
Appearance	The control's appearance.
BackColor	The control's background color. The default is white.
BorderStyle	The style of the border around the control.
Caption	The control's caption.
Enabled	The control's enabled state.

continues

Table 16.8. continued

Property	Description
Font	The font used for text in the control.
ForeColor	The control's foreground color.
hWnd	The control's hWnd.
Text	The control's text.

The first properties that you add are for foreground and background colors. These properties are supported with a stock color selection dialog box. The process of adding a stock property in an OLE control isn't very difficult.

NOTE

In Visual C++ 1.5 you must manually call the Make TypeLib utility (MKTYPLIB) to build the type library before you rebuild your project. In the 32-bit versions of Visual C++, Developer Studio takes care of building the type library. When you build OLE controls in Visual C++ 1.5, you should always select Tools | Make TypeLib after you've changed properties, events, or methods and before you rebuild the OLE control.

The following is the process to add a stock property:

1. Start ClassWizard by pressing Ctrl-W. Select the OLE Automation tab, shown in Figure 16.18. Make sure that the class listed in the Class name combo box is the OLE control class (CClockCtrl for the clock control).

FIGURE 16.18.

The OLE Automation tab in ClassWizard.

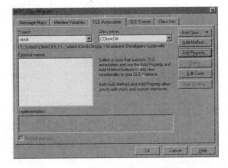

2. Click the Add Property button to display the Add Property dialog box, shown in Figure 16.19. You must provide the property's external name in the External name combo box. You can select one of the stock property names (see Table 16.8), or you

can enter the name of a custom property (see the section "Custom Properties" later in this chapter).

The first stock property you will add in your Clock OLE control is `BackColor` (which can be found in the External name combo box). After you've selected the name of a stock property, you must make sure that the Stock radio button in the Implementation group is selected. You can override a stock property by changing the Implementation.

3. When you're finished with the Add Property dialog box, click OK. You're returned to the OLE Automation tab, where in the External names list box you see the new property that you've added (`BackColor`), with an S preceding it to indicate that `BackColor` is a stock property.

4. The changes that you've made with ClassWizard have added an interface that lets you change the background color. However, there still is no code in the control's drawing function to actually implement this.

At this stage, you must make whatever changes are necessary to implement your stock property. For example, the `BackColor` property is the background for the control (most Windows applications' controls are a light gray color). To fill the OLE control's background, you must add a few lines to the OLE control's `OnDraw()` function. This function exists as a basic shell that you modify to draw whatever the control must display for the user. The original `OnDraw()` function (in CLOCKCTL.CPP) supplied by ControlWizard is as follows:

```
/////////////////////////////////////////////////////////////
// CClockCtrl::OnDraw - Drawing function

void CClockCtrl::OnDraw(
    CDC* pdc, const CRect& rcBounds, const CRect& rcInvalid)
{
// TODO: Replace the following code with your own drawing code.
    pdc->FillRect(rcBounds, CBrush::FromHandle(
        (HBRUSH)GetStockObject(WHITE_BRUSH)));
    pdc->Ellipse(rcBounds);
}
```

You must modify this function because it has been hard-coded to fill the OLE control's background using the stock WHITE_BRUSH. This raises a question: ClassWizard added the interface to set the background color, but how does the program find out what color the user selected? Easy enough: There is a set of functions you can call to obtain the necessary attributes for a given property.

To obtain the color of the background, you use the GetBackColor() function, which retrieves the current background color. The format that GetBackColor() returns must then be processed by the TranslateColor() function, after which the value from TranslateColor() can be used to create a new brush. The following code shows in bold the changes necessary to implement a background color property:

```
/////////////////////////////////////////////////////////////////
// CClockCtrl::OnDraw - Drawing function

void CClockCtrl::OnDraw(
    CDC* pdc, const CRect& rcBounds, const CRect& rcInvalid)
{
// TODO: Replace the following code with your own drawing code.
//  pdc->FillRect(rcBounds, CBrush::FromHandle(
//      (HBRUSH)GetStockObject(WHITE_BRUSH)));

    CBrush bkBrush(TranslateColor(GetBackColor()));
    pdc->FillRect(rcBounds, &bkBrush);

    pdc->Ellipse(rcBounds);
}
```

You must also add the necessary property page information to the BEGIN_PROPPAGEIDS() section. This change tells OLE which dialog boxes to display. Property pages are displayed when the user selects properties for the control. Originally, the BEGIN_PROPPAGEIDS() section looked like the following:

```
/////////////////////////////////////////////////////////////////
// Property pages

// TODO: Add more property pages as needed.
// Remember to increase the count!
BEGIN_PROPPAGEIDS(CClockCtrl, 1)
    PROPPAGEID(CClockPropPage::guid)
END_PROPPAGEIDS(CClockCtrl)
```

You must add a new property page to the list. To do this, you must make two changes. First, the number of property page sheets will change from 1 (the default page for the clock control) to 2 (the default page and a color page). The page count is in the opening macro:

```
BEGIN_PROPPAGEIDS(CClockCtrl, 1)
```

In the BEGIN_PROPPAGEIDS() macro, the second parameter specifies the count and must be changed from 1 to 2:

```
BEGIN_PROPPAGEIDS(CClockCtrl, 2)
```

Second, you must add a new `PROPPAGEID()` macro to the list, changing the `BEGIN_PROPPAGEIDS()` block as follows:

```
//////////////////////////////////////////////////////////////

// Property pages

// TODO: Add more property pages as needed.
// Remember to increase the count!
BEGIN_PROPPAGEIDS(CClockCtrl, 2)
    PROPPAGEID(CClockPropPage::guid)
    PROPPAGEID(CLSID_CColorPropPage)
END_PROPPAGEIDS(CClockCtrl)
```

5. After making these changes, you must rebuild the OLE control.

6. After successfully rebuilding your control, try it out in the Test Container application. You should be able to select the control's property sheets, and there should be two tabs: General and Colors. If you select the Colors tab, you'll see a dialog box similar to the one shown in Figure 16.20.

FIGURE 16.20.

The Colors tab of the Digital Clock Control Properties dialog box.

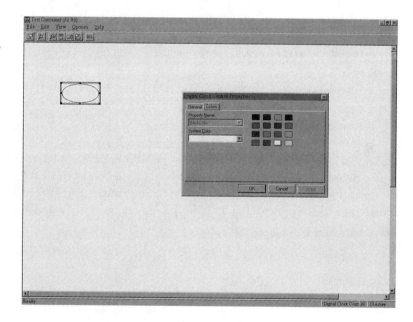

Adding Functionality to the Clock Control

Now that you've added a stock property, it's time to add some functionality to your clock control. You need to do the following:

1. Set up a timer loop with a one-second resolution.

2. Add code in your `OnDraw()` function to display the time.

3. Add code to kill the timer when the control ceases to run.

Setting up the timer isn't very difficult. You need to add code to the OnCreate() function (which you will create with ClassWizard) to start the timer. To create your timer, follow these steps:

1. Start ClassWizard and go to the Message Maps tab. Select the CClockCtrl class and CClockCtrl in the Object Ids list. You will see the Messages list box filled with the various WM_ messages. Select WM_CREATE and then click the Add Function button.

2. The Member Functions list box shows a new member, OnCreate. It will have the handler ON_WM_CREATE.

3. Click the Edit Code button, which ends ClassWizard and places the cursor in the OnCreate() member function in CLOCKCTL.CPP.

You must add some code to OnCreate() to set up the timer. The following code fragment shows in bold the changes that are needed in the OnCreate() function:

```
int CClockCtrl::OnCreate(LPCREATESTRUCT lpCreateStruct)
{
    TRACE(_T("OnCreate() called\n"));

    if (COleControl::OnCreate(lpCreateStruct) == -1)
        return -1;

    m_IDTimer = SetTimer(999, 1000, NULL);
    if (m_IDTimer == 0)
    {
        AfxMessageBox(_T("Couldn't set the timer in OnCreate()\n"));
    }

    return 0;
}
```

Notice that in OnCreate() you reference a new member variable, m_IDTimer. This member variable is used to hold the timer's ID, which SetTimer() returns. The timer ID is needed later to kill the timer, and it should be checked whenever a timer interrupt occurs so that you know which timer's interval has expired. In CLOCKCTL.H, you must add a declaration for m_IDTimer:

```
class CClockCtrl : public COleControl
{
        DECLARE_DYNCREATE(CClockCtrl)

// Constructor
public:
        CClockCtrl();

// Overrides

        // Drawing function
        virtual void OnDraw(
            CDC* pdc, const CRect& rcBounds, const CRect& rcInvalid)

        // Persistence
        virtual void DoPropExchange(CPropExchange* pPX);

        // Reset control state
        virtual void OnResetState();
```

```
// Implementation
protected:
        ~CClockCtrl();

        UINT   m_IDTimer;
```

As with any member function, in the constructor for the CClockCtl object you must initialize your member variable m_IDTimer:

```
CClockCtrl::CClockCtrl()
{
        InitializeIIDs(&IID_DClock, &IID_DClockEvents);

        // TODO: Initialize your control's instance data here
        m_IDTimer = 0;
}
```

Now you have the code to create a timer. You also need code to kill the timer when the OLE control ends execution. This is important, because timers are a limited system resource (especially under 16-bit versions of Windows). You get rid of your timer in the WM_DESTROY message handler. You need to create this handler in the same manner that you did when you created the WM_CREATE handler. Start ClassWizard, select WM_DESTROY, and then click the Add Function button to create the function handler. When creation is complete, click the Edit Code button to end ClassWizard and begin editing your function.

The following is the changed OnDestroy() function. The changes to kill the timer are in bold:

```
void CClockCtrl::OnDestroy()
{
    COleControl::OnDestroy();

    // TODO: Add your message handler code here

    if (m_IDTimer > 0)
    {// We have allocated a timer, so let's kill it:
        KillTimer(m_IDTimer);
        m_IDTimer = 0;
    }
}
```

Take a moment to take stock of what you've done. You now have a timer that is started when the OLE control starts and that ends when the OLE control ends. It's up to you to make use of this timer. To do so, you must make two more changes.

First, you need a handler for the WM_TIMER messages that will be sent to the application whenever the timer's interval expires. Again, with ClassWizard you need to create a handler, this time for WM_TIMER. In your OnTimer() function, you need to tell the control to update its display:

```
void CClockCtrl::OnTimer(UINT nIDEvent)
{
    // TODO: Add your message handler code here and/or call default

    if (nIDEvent == m_IDTimer)
```

```
{// It is our timer, so we'll handle it now!
    InvalidateControl();
}

COleControl::OnTimer(nIDEvent);
}
```

The process of telling a control to update itself is very similar to the process of telling a window to update itself. A window is updated whenever a call is made to `InvalidateRect()`, and a control is updated whenever a call is made to `InvalidateControl()`. Check to see whether the timer message is the correct one so that you don't do more updates than you need to. Once a second is sufficient for a displayed clock.

Second, you must update the control's display of the time. Until now, your Clock OLE control has simply displayed the default ellipse. You now need to delete the ellipse drawing code and add whatever functionality is needed to display the time.

With the advent of `strftime()`, it has become easy to format a time value. However, because an OLE control is in a DLL, you can't call the `strftime()` function. You must manually format the time for display. Fortunately, this isn't too difficult. First, you add an `#include` to the CLOCKCTL.CPP file to include the TIME.H file.

After you have the header file for the standard time functions, you can add the time display code to the `OnDraw()` function:

```
void CClockCtrl::OnDraw(
                  CDC* pdc, const CRect& rcBounds, const CRect& rcInvalid)
{
    // TODO: Replace the following code with your own drawing code
//  pdc>FillRect(rcBounds,
//         CBrush::FromHandle((HBRUSH)GetStockObject(WHITE_BRUSH)));
    CBrush  bkBrush(TranslateColor(GetBackColor()));
    pdc->FillRect(rcBounds, &bkBrush);

//  pdc->Ellipse(rcBounds);

    struct  tm *newtime;
    char    am_pm[] = _T("AM");
    time_t long_time;
    char    szBuffer[80];

    time(&long_time);
    newtime = localtime(&long_time);

    if (newtime->tm_hour > 12)
    {
        strcpy(am_pm, _T("PM"));
        newtime->tm_hour -= 12;
    }

    sprintf(szBuffer, _T("%2.2d:%2.2d:%2.2d %s"),
        newtime->tm_hour,
        newtime->tm_min,
        newtime->tm_sec,
        am_pm);
```

```
    pdc->SetTextAlign(TA_LEFT | TA_TOP);

    pdc->ExtTextOut(rcBounds.left, rcBounds.top,
        ETO_CLIPPED, rcBounds,
        szBuffer, strlen(szBuffer), NULL);

}
```

After you have made these changes, you should rebuild your control and test it. If all goes well, you'll get a display like the one shown in Figure 16.21. It's not fancy, but it does display the time.

FIGURE 16.21.

Test Container with Clock showing the time.

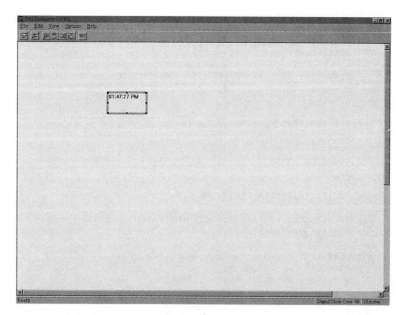

You still need one more stock color property. You can set the background color; wouldn't it be nice if you could set the color of the text? No sooner said than done. Again, you must follow a process very similar to the one you followed to add the BackColor property. The main difference is that you don't need to add a stock dialog page because you have one already, created for the BackColor property.

In ClassWizard, select the OLE Automation tab. Click the Add Property button and, in the External Name combo box, select ForeColor. Make sure that Stock Implementation is selected, and then click OK. Close ClassWizard by clicking OK in the main ClassWizard dialog box.

Next, you must modify the OnDraw() function to utilize the new color. You will use the ForeColor property for the text that will display the time:

```
void CClockCtrl::OnDraw(
                CDC* pdc, const CRect& rcBounds, const CRect& rcInvalid)
{
```

```
    // TODO: Replace the following code with your own drawing code
//  pdc>FillRect(rcBounds,
//        CBrush::FromHandle((HBRUSH)GetStockObject(WHITE_BRUSH)));
    CBrush  bkBrush(TranslateColor(GetBackColor()));
    pdc->FillRect(rcBounds, &bkBrush);

//  pdc->Ellipse(rcBounds);

    struct  tm *newtime;
    char    am_pm[] = _T("AM");
    time_t long_time;
    char    szBuffer[80];

    time(&long_time);
    newtime = localtime(&long_time);

    if (newtime->tm_hour > 12)
    {
        strcpy(am_pm, _T("PM"));
        newtime->tm_hour -= 12;
    }

    sprintf(szBuffer, _T("%2.2d:%2.2d:%2.2d %s"),
        newtime->tm_hour,
        newtime->tm_min,
        newtime->tm_sec,
        am_pm);

    pdc->SetTextAlign(TA_LEFT ¦ TA_TOP);

    pdc->SetTextColor(TranslateColor(GetForeColor()));
    pdc->SetBkMode(TRANSPARENT);

    pdc->ExtTextOut(rcBounds.left, rcBounds.top,
        ETO_CLIPPED, rcBounds,
        szBuffer, strlen(szBuffer), NULL);

}
```

You added only two new lines to set the text color. Now rebuild your clock control and try it. When you do so, you see that the colors' property page now has two selections: BackColor and ForeColor. When you change the ForeColor property, the color of the displayed time changes to match.

More Stock Properties: Fonts

The OLE Custom Control system lets you rely on a set of stock properties for your control. With stock properties, you don't have to design a dialog box to set the property, because the stock property dialog boxes are already included in the OLE control support DLL file.

Now that your clock has color, the next logical addition is the ability to change the font of the time display. Many digital clock users will appreciate the ability to change the font. Nothing beats having a digital clock in a font that looks digital.

To add a font property, first start ClassWizard. Select the OLE Automation tab and then click the Add Property button. The Add Property dialog box appears. In the External name combo box, select Font. Make sure that Stock Implementation is also selected, and then click OK to close the Add Property dialog box. Click OK again to close ClassWizard.

You haven't yet installed a stock property dialog box for fonts. You can fix this by making an addition to the BEGIN_PROPPAGEIDS() block:

```
// TODO: Add more property pages as needed. Remember to increase the count!
BEGIN_PROPPAGEIDS(CClockCtrl, 3)
    PROPPAGEID(CClockPropPage::guid)
    PROPPAGEID(CLSID_CColorPropPage)
    PROPPAGEID(CLSID_CFontPropPage)
END_PROPPAGEIDS(CClockCtrl)
```

Don't forget to change the number of property page IDs from 2 to 3 (BEGIN_PROPPAGEIDS (CClockCtrl, 3)).

Next, you must again make a change to the OnDraw() function to utilize the correct font. In the previous version, you simply used the default font that was already selected. This time you want to use the font that the user selects, draw the text, and then restore the original default font:

```
void CClockCtrl::OnDraw(
                CDC* pdc, const CRect& rcBounds, const CRect& rcInvalid)
{
    // TODO: Replace the following code with your own drawing code
//  pdc>FillRect(rcBounds,
//        CBrush::FromHandle((HBRUSH)GetStockObject(WHITE_BRUSH)));
    CBrush  bkBrush(TranslateColor(GetBackColor()));
    pdc->FillRect(rcBounds, &bkBrush);

//  pdc->Ellipse(rcBounds);

    struct  tm *newtime;
    char    am_pm[] = _T("AM");
    time_t long_time;
    char    szBuffer[80];

    time(&long_time);
    newtime = localtime(&long_time);

    if (newtime->tm_hour > 12)
    {
        strcpy(am_pm, _T("PM"));
        newtime->tm_hour -= 12;
    }

    sprintf(szBuffer, _T("%2.2d:%2.2d:%2.2d %s"),
        newtime->tm_hour,
        newtime->tm_min,
        newtime->tm_sec,
        am_pm);

    pdc->SetTextAlign(TA_LEFT | TA_TOP);
```

```
pdc->SetTextColor(TranslateColor(GetForeColor()));
pdc->SetBkMode(TRANSPARENT);

CFont* pOldFont;
pOldFont = SelectStockFont(pdc);

pdc->ExtTextOut(rcBounds.left, rcBounds.top,
    ETO_CLIPPED, rcBounds,
    szBuffer, strlen(szBuffer), NULL);

pdc->SelectObject(pOldFont);

}
```

Notice that a call to `SelectStockFont()` has been added, a function that inserts into the specified device context the font that the user selects. The `SelectStockFont()` function returns a `CFont` pointer to the previous font that was selected. After drawing your text, you can restore the original font by calling `SelectObject()` with the pointer that was returned by `SelectStockFont()`.

Figure 16.22 shows the stock Fonts property tab. This dialog box lets you select any installed font available on the system. The Effects group box offers strikeout and underline fonts. You also can select bold, italic, or both.

FIGURE 16.22.

The Fonts tab of the Digital Clock Control Properties dialog box.

Again, rebuild the clock control. When the rebuild is done (without errors), try the clock control again. You'll notice an immediate change—the default font is now different. This is caused by the call to `SelectStockFont()`, which returns a different font than was originally selected into the device context. Using the clock's properties sheet, change to a new font. To see the effect of the change, look at your clock control, shown in Figure 16.23, for an example of the clock with a different font.

You should keep several things in mind when you're working with stock properties. First, whenever a new stock property page is selected, the changes made on the previous property page are implemented. When the stock property pages exit (when you click OK or a different tab), an `InvalidateControl()` call is made.

As you can see, it's very easy to add stock properties to an OLE control. Next you will add a few customized properties.

FIGURE 16.23.

A new font in Clock.

Custom Properties

Not everything in an OLE control can be configured with the stock properties. Some things (sometimes many things) can only be set using a custom properties sheet.

Fortunately, Microsoft decided to make custom properties easy. First, the ControlWizard applet creates a default properties dialog box for you, to which you can add dialog controls that you can use to customize the operation of your OLE control.

For the clock control, the first change you want is the ability to configure the time display format. In your original format for Clock, the time was formatted with the string `"%2.2d:%2.2d:%2.2d %s"`. There is always a leading zero when the time is earlier than 10:00. Also, you might want to display the hours, minutes, and seconds separated by dashes rather than colons.

You need to have an edit control in your default properties page with which you can edit the display format. This could be a difficult change, but ClassWizard does most of the work for you.

Here are the steps for creating a custom property:

1. Start ClassWizard and click the OLE Automation tab.
2. Click the Add Property button to display the Add Property dialog box, shown in Figure 16.24.

FIGURE 16.24.

*TimeFormat in the
Add Property dialog
box.*

3. In the External Name combo box, enter the name TimeFormat. The Implementation should be member variable. In the Variable name field, the default name of m_timeFormat is displayed. In the Notification function field, the default name of OnTimeFormatChanged is displayed. The Type box should have a CString selected. When you're satisfied with the names for the name, variable, and function, click OK.

4. Figure 16.25 shows ClassWizard's main dialog box and the implementation of the TimeFormat property. Notice that the TimeFormat property is prefixed with a C. This indicates that TimeFormat is a custom property. When you've finished reviewing the TimeFormat property, click OK to end ClassWizard.

FIGURE 16.25.

*ClassWizard showing
the TimeFormat
property.*

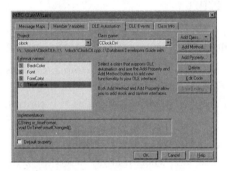

5. After you end ClassWizard, you must implement whatever code is necessary to make the TimeFormat property work. ClassWizard has created a member variable in CClockCtrl called m_timeFormat. This variable must be initialized and used where necessary. To initialize m_timeFormat, you must change the CClockCtrl() constructor, adding an assignment for the m_timeFormat variable:

```
CClockCtrl::CClockCtrl()
{
        InitializeIIDs(&IID_DClock, &IID_DClockEvents);

        // TODO: Initialize your control's instance data here
        m_IDTimer = -1;

        m_timeFormat = _T("%2.2d:%2.2d:%2.2d %s");
}
```

Now that you have your default format in the m_timeFormat variable, you must use it. This means changing your OnDraw() function so that the sprintf() function that you use to format the time uses m_timeFormat rather than a character constant. Notice the cast on m_timeFormat. This casting is necessary because sprintf() expects a pointer to a character string, and just passing m_timeFormat would pass a CString object, making sprintf() very confused:

```
if (newtime->tm_hour > 12)
{
        strcpy(am_pm, _T("PM"));
        newtime->tm_hour -= 12;
}

sprintf(szBuffer, (const char *)m_timeFormat,
        newtime->tm_hour,
        newtime->tm_min,
        newtime->tm_sec,
        am_pm);

pdc->SetTextAlign(TA_LEFT | TA_TOP);
```

At this point you've done everything except allow the user to actually change the time format. You still need to add an edit control to the default property page dialog box and connect this edit control to the m_timeFormat variable in CClockCtrl.

6. To add an edit control to your default property page dialog box, you must edit the dialog box by selecting the IDD_PROPPAGE_CLOCK dialog box into an edit window. Next, locate a group box at the left side of the property page dialog box and label it Display Format. Inside this group box, add an edit control named IDC_TIME_FORMAT (or something equally meaningful). When you have finished, the IDD_PROPPAGE_CLOCK dialog box will look like the one shown in Figure 16.26.

FIGURE 16.26.
IDD_PROPPAGE_CLOCK
with
IDC_TIME_FORMAT.

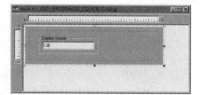

7. When you've added the IDC_TIME_FORMAT control to the default property page dialog (and saved the dialog box), you must link the control to the m_timeFormat variable that's in CClockCtrl.

8. Again, start ClassWizard. Click the Member Variables tab, and then select the IDC_TIME_FORMAT line in the Controls IDs list box. Click the Add Variable button. The Add Member Variable dialog box, shown in Figure 16.27, appears.

FIGURE 16.27.

ClassWizard's Add Member Variable dialog box.

9. You must supply a variable name. You can reuse the name m_timeFormat, because this class (CClockPropPage) can't see the m_timeFormat variable in CClockCtrl. In the Category combo box, select Value. In the Variable type combo box, select CString. To link this control in the property page dialog box with the m_timeFormat variable in CClockCtrl, you must provide the Optional OLE property name. This is the name you entered in the External name field when you created the custom property in step 3. With this information, ClassWizard can create all the necessary links to manage the time display format. Click OK.

There is no need in your clock control to have length validation for your format string. In a more finished project, you would want to make sure that the results from using the format string would fit in the buffers. However, in your clock control, you will omit this error-checking for clarity.

10. After closing ClassWizard's main dialog box, you must rebuild your clock control. Visual C++ should build the control for you with no errors (if you have errors, find and correct them). Next, try the control in the Test Container application. After you embed the clock control, access the control's properties dialog. Your dialog box should look like the one shown in Figure 16.28, in which a new format string has already been set and the Apply Now button has been clicked, thereby updating the control's appearance.

You will make one final change to your clock control before you move on to other things (such as events). To make your clock have a 24-hour format in which 6 p.m. is displayed as 18:00, you will add a set of radio buttons to change the format of the displayed time.

To make this change, you first must add a set of radio buttons to your properties dialog box. I chose radio buttons because they seem to convey more information about the exclusive nature of the a.m./p.m. versus 24-hour display format than a check box could.

> **NOTE**
>
> Remember to use the Group property to allow MFC to properly manage the radio buttons. If you don't see your radio buttons in ClassWizard, you've probably forgotten to set the Group property. Remember: A group box is only a cosmetic object in a dialog box. The Group property is invisible but affects the operation of controls in a dialog box. Be careful not to confuse the two.

FIGURE 16.28.

Test Container showing custom properties for Clock.

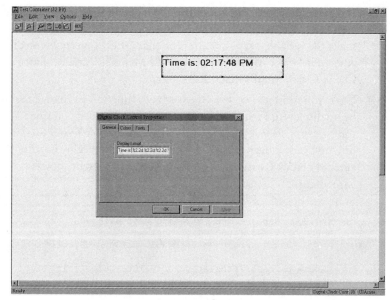

To enclose the radio buttons, you can use the group box that you created when you added the TimeFormat property. Follow these steps to make changes to the clock control:

1. In ClassWizard, create a new custom property called Display24Hour, which is created as a type short. In the constructor, initialize the new variable (m_display24Hour) to 0:

```
CClockCtrl::CClockCtrl()
{
    InitializeIIDs(&IID_DClock, &IID_DClockEvents);

    // TODO: Initialize your control's instance data here.
    m_IDTimer = 0;
    m_display24Hour = 0;
    m_timeFormat = "%2.2d:%2.2d:%2.2d %s";
}
```

2. Add two radio buttons, IDC_AM_PM and IDC_24_HOUR, to the IDD_PROPPAGE_CLOCK dialog box. Figure 16.29 shows these two new dialog controls. When you're finished with the IDD_PROPPAGE_CLOCK dialog box, save it using File | Save.

FIGURE 16.29.

IDD_PROPPAGE_CLOCK with AM/PM and 24 Hour radio buttons.

3. Invoke ClassWizard and select the Member Variables tab. Select the IDD_AM_PM control and select Add Member Variable. Use the name m_display24Hour for the variable, and make the variable's type int. In Optional OLE Property Name, use the name you entered in step 1. Click OK in the Add Member Variable dialog box, and then click OK in ClassWizard's main dialog box.

4. Next, you must add code to the OnDraw() function to change the format of the time being displayed. First, in the CClockCtrl constructor, you must add an initializer for the m_display24Hour variable. Initialize this variable to 0. Next, modify the OnDraw() function to test the m_display24Hour variable. Replacing an if() block with a switch() block is easy, as the following code fragment shows:

```
void CClockCtrl::OnDraw(
            CDC* pdc, const CRect& rcBounds, const CRect& rcInvalid)
{
    // TODO: Replace the following code with your own drawing code.
//    pdc->FillRect(rcBounds,
//        CBrush::FromHandle((HBRUSH)GetStockObject(WHITE_BRUSH)));

    CBrush bkBrush(TranslateColor(GetBackColor()));
    pdc->FillRect(rcBounds, &bkBrush);

    struct  tm *newtime;
    char    am_pm[] = _T("AM");
    time_t long_time;
    char    szBuffer[80];

    time(&long_time);
    newtime = localtime(&long_time);

//  I replaced if (newtime) with a switch() block

//      if (newtime->tm_hour > 12)
//      {
//          strcpy(am_pm, _T("PM"));
//          newtime->tm_hour -= 12;
//      }

    switch(m_display24Hour)
    {
        case(0): // First radio button; AM/PM format used!

            strcpy(am_pm, _T("PM"));
            newtime->tm_hour -= 12;
            break;

        case(1): // Second radio button; 24 Hour format used!

            strcpy(am_pm, _T(""));
            break;

        default:

            TRACE("ERROR: An unhandled radio button selected!\n");
            break;
    }
```

```
        sprintf(szBuffer, (const char *)m_timeFormat,
        newtime->tm_hour,
        newtime->tm_min,
        newtime->tm_sec,
        am_pm);

        pdc->SetTextAlign(TA_LEFT | TA_TOP);

        pdc->SetTextColor(TranslateColor(GetForeColor()));
        pdc->SetBkMode(TRANSPARENT);

        CFont* pOldFont;
        pOldFont = SelectStockFont(pdc);

        pdc->ExtTextOut(rcBounds.left, rcBounds.top,
            ETO_CLIPPED, rcBounds,
            szBuffer, strlen(szBuffer), NULL);

        pdc->SelectObject(pOldFont);

//      pdc->Ellipse(rcBounds);
    }
```

Now your clock has all the properties you need. You can add more properties (such as an alarm function) later by simply following the preceding steps as a guideline.

Next you will add some events to your clock control.

Adding Events to an OLE Control

Your birthday, my birthday, the day the cow jumped over the moon—all are examples of events, but not the events that OLE controls are interested in. The term *events,* when used with OLE controls, refers to the process in which the control notifies the container that an event of some significance has occurred. This event might be as simple as the user clicking in the control's user area or (using your clock control as an example) as complex as the expiration of a time period.

When a container is notified that an event has occurred, the event has been *fired.* All event functions are called *firing functions* and usually are prefixed with the word Fire, as in FireClick().

Like properties, events come in two flavors: stock and custom. You will learn about stock events first, and then you will add a custom event to your clock.

Stock Events

Table 16.9 lists the stock events that are available to an OLE control. You can add these events by simply clicking the Add Event button in ClassWizard's OLE Events tab. The stock events have default functions defined for them. Each function has zero or more parameters and never has a return value.

Table 16.9. OLE control stock events.

Event	Firing Function	When It Gets Fired
Click	void FireClick(), which has no parameters	The mouse has been captured by the control, and a button-up message (WM_LBUTTONUP, WM_RBUTTONUP, or WM_MBUTTONUP) is received when the mouse is located over the control's user area. Before this event, the stock MouseDown and MouseUp events are fired (if defined).
DblClick	void FileDblClick(), which has no parameters	The mouse has been captured by the control, and any button has been double-clicked. A WM_LDBLCLICK, WM_RDBLCLICK, or WM_MDBLCLICK message is received when the mouse is located over the control's user area. Before this event, the stock Click, MouseDown, and MouseUp events are fired (if defined).
Error	void FireError(SCODE *scode*, LPCSTR *lpszErrorDescription*, UINT *nHelpID* = 0)	This event is fired whenever an error condition occurs in the control. The FireError() function has parameters to describe the actual error.
KeyDown	void FireKeyDown(USHORT *pnChar*, short *nShiftState*)	This event is fired whenever a key (either WM_SYSKEYDOWN or WM_KEYDOWN) is pressed and the control has input focus. The FireKeyDown() function has parameters to tell which key was pressed and the state of the Shift keys.
KeyPress	void FireKeyPress(USHORT * *pnChar*)	This event is fired whenever a WM_CHAR message has been received. The FireKeyPress() function has a parameter that points to the character for the key that was pressed.

Event	Firing Function	When It Gets Fired
KeyUp	void FireKeyUp(USHORT *pnChar, short nShiftState)	This event is fired whenever a key (either WM_SYSKEYUP or WM_KEYUP) is pressed and the control has input focus. The FireKeyUp() function has parameters to tell which key was pressed and the state of the Shift keys.
MouseDown	void FireMouseDown(short nButton, short nShiftState, OLE_XPOS_PIXELS x, OLE_YPOS_PIXELS y)	This event is fired when a WM_LBUTTONDOWN, WM_RBUTTONDOWN, or WM_MBUTTONDOWN message is received. The mouse is captured just before the MouseDown event is fired. The FireMouseDown() function has parameters to indicate which mouse button was pressed, the state of the Shift keys, and the mouse's x- and y-coordinates.
MouseMove	void FireMouseMove(short nButton, short nShiftState, OLE_XPOS_PIXELS x, OLE_YPOS_PIXELS y)	This event is fired when a WM_MOUSEMOVE message is received. The FireMouseDown() function has parameters to indicate which mouse button was pressed, the state of the Shift keys, and the mouse's x- and y-coordinates.
MouseUp	void FireMouseUp (short nButton, short nShiftState, OLE_XPOS_PIXELS x, OLE_YPOS_PIXELS y)	This event is fired when a WM_LBUTTONUP, WM_RBUTTONUP, or WM_MBUTTONUP message is received. The mouse is released from capture just before the MouseUp event is fired. The FireMouseUp() function has parameters to indicate which mouse button was pressed, the state of the Shift keys, and the mouse's x- and y-coordinates.

Your control can't offer a great deal of functionality in implementing a stock event. You'll add the stock event DblClick to your clock control as an exercise in adding stock events.

To add a stock event, start ClassWizard and then click the OLE Events tab. You will see a dialog box in which you can view currently defined events and add new events. To add an event, click the Add Event button. ClassWizard displays the Add Event dialog box, shown in Figure 16.30, which lets you select the event's external name. The External name combo box lets you select stock events from the drop-down list box or create a custom event by entering the event name.

FIGURE 16.30.

The Add Event dialog box.

In the External name list box, select DblClick. Stock implementation should be selected. The Internal name field changes to FireDblClick and becomes read-only so that the name of the event-firing function can't be changed. If you're defining the DblClick event as a Custom implementation, you can edit the function's name if you want to.

The Parameter list box also is disabled because the stock DblClick event doesn't take any parameters.

After you've defined the DblClick event, click OK in the Add Event dialog box. You're returned to the OLE Events tab in ClassWizard. You should see a single event defined—DblClick, which is prefixed with an S symbol. This indicates that DblClick is a stock event. See Figure 16.31.

FIGURE 16.31

The OLE Events tab in ClassWizard with the DblClick event displayed.

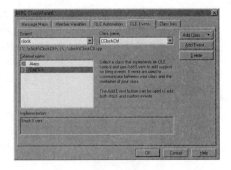

After you've reviewed your stock event, close ClassWizard by clicking OK, and rebuild the control. When you've successfully rebuilt the control, you can test it using Test Container, in which you can view the event log by selecting View | Event Log. Double-clicking the clock control causes an event notification to be logged in the Event Log dialog box.

Custom Events

Stock events are defined for you, but a custom event is totally up to your imagination. Take a trip back to the days of the first digital watches. Almost as soon as digital watches appeared, some smart engineer designed one with an alarm. Hey, what a concept—a digital alarm clock!

If you added a field to your clock's property page for the alarm time (a simple edit field, for example), which you could then parse out to an alarm time, you could compare this alarm time with the current time whenever you received a WM_TIMER message.

First, add a set alarm section to your property page. Adding a set alarm time field presents a minor problem: You really could use a custom time control that would validate your alarm time. However, to keep your clock custom control simple, you will use a set of simple combo box fields with the hours, minutes, and seconds entered in three separate combo boxes. You can use combo boxes to force the user to enter a valid time value.

> **NOTE**
>
> The MFC implementation of IDispatch lets you use a maximum of 15 parameters (the alarm function uses three). Be careful not to exceed this limitation.

The process of defining the alarm property is exactly the same as adding the properties that you added earlier. First, using ClassWizard, add three new properties: AlarmHours, AlarmMinutes, and AlarmSeconds. After adding these properties, you will have three new property variables: m_alarmHours, m_alarmMinutes, and m_alarmSeconds. When the clock control starts, you need to initialize the alarm to the current time:

```
CClockCtrl::CClockCtrl()
{
        InitializeIIDs(&IID_DClock, &IID_DClockEvents);

        // TODO: Initialize your control's instance data here
        m_IDTimer = -1;

        m_timeFormat = _T("%2d:%2.2d:%2.2d %s");

        m_display24Hour = 0;


        struct  tm *newtime;
        time_t long_time;
```

```
        time(&long_time);
        newtime = localtime(&long_time);

        m_alarmHours   = newtime->tm_hour;
        m_alarmMinutes = newtime->tm_min;
        m_alarmSeconds = newtime->tm_sec;
}
```

Next you must add to the stock property page a set of controls to allow the user to set the alarm time. In the sample OLE control, you do this using a set of combo boxes that are initialized to the desired values. Each of these combo boxes is a DropList style with the sort attribute set to off. If you don't specify DropList, you can't bind an integer variable to the combo box.

Figure 16.32 shows the properties dialog box with the new controls installed. Each of these controls has a fixed set of data. The hours control is 0 to 23, and the minutes and seconds controls have values of 0 to 59. I've used the dialog control editor to initialize the controls. (See the sample program in the CHAPTR16\clock folder on the CD that comes with this book.)

FIGURE 16.32.

*IDD_PROPPAGE_CLOCK
with an alarm feature
added.*

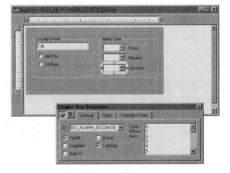

You also need a way to disable the alarm feature. To do this, you will add a property called Alarmed using ClassWizard.

> **NOTE**
>
> Throughout this chapter you've bound variables to the property page dialog box that were identical to the property variable names in the clock project. Why? To keep the names consistent. The critical name is the optional OLE property name, which OLE uses to communicate your changes in the property dialog to the control itself.

After the clock control has started, each time the WM_TIMER message is received in the OnTimer() function, the time must be compared with the alarm time. If the clock time and the alarm time match, your alarm event is fired.

The container application determines what happens when the alarm event fires. If the clock control is embedded in an Access form, the alarm might be used to remind the user to perform a task, such as backing up or saving data.

Next, you must add the alarm event handler. To add a custom event handler, you use ClassWizard's OLE Events tab. Select CClockCtrl in the Class Name combo box. Click the Add Event button to display the Add Event dialog box, shown in Figure 16.33.

FIGURE 16.33.

The Add Event dialog box.

Specify an external name of Alarm. The internal name (which Visual C++ will generate for you) should be FireAlarm (you couldn't have picked a better name if you tried). In the Parameter list combo box, double-click the left side of the top (current) line. An edit field appears, in which you can enter a variable name. Enter the first variable as nHour. Next, either tab forward or double-click the right side of the current line. You're presented with a drop-down list from which you can select nHour's variable type. Use short. After creating nHour, create nMinute (double-click the line under nHour) and nSecond (double-click the line under nMinute).

When the FireAlarm event is fired, it will pass the time (using the nHour, nMinute, and nSecond parameters) that the alarm occurred. Since Windows is a multitasking operating system, it's likely that the container will receive the FireAlarm event long after (in computer time) the actual event occurred. Click OK.

The final step in adding your alarm event is adding the actual alarm code. You must take into consideration several factors when you're comparing the alarm time with the current time. First and foremost is that there is no guarantee that there will be a WM_TIMER message every second. If Windows is busy, there might be one (or more) skipped WM_TIMER messages. This presents a problem, because you're testing for an exact time. Probably the best thing to do is to find out whether the alarm time has passed. If it has and an alarm hasn't yet been sounded, fire the alarm. You do this by setting a flag that signals that an alarm is set and hasn't been sounded. Of course, if the user sets an alarm time that is earlier than the current time, this generates an immediate alarm, which is a minor problem in this sample program.

First, take a look at the final OnDraw() function. You've added code to OnDraw() to find out whether the alarm has been set (if m_alarmed is TRUE) and whether the current time is later than the alarm time. If both tests are true, an alarm event is triggered.

```
void CClockCtrl::OnDraw(
         CDC* pdc, const CRect& rcBounds, const CRect& rcInvalid)
{
   // TODO: Replace the following code with your own drawing code
   CBrush  bkBrush(TranslateColor(GetBackColor()));
   pdc->FillRect(rcBounds, &bkBrush);

   struct    tm *newtime;
   char      am_pm[] = _T("AM");
   time_t long_time;
   char      szBuffer[80];

   time(&long_time);
   newtime = localtime(&long_time);

//    Check for alarms. If past alarm time, sound it!

   if (m_alarmed &&
       m_alarmHours    <= newtime->tm_hour &&
       m_alarmMinutes <= newtime->tm_min &&
       m_alarmSeconds <= newtime->tm_sec)
   {//    It's an alarming event!
       m_alarmed = FALSE;
       FireAlarm(m_alarmHours, m_alarmMinutes, m_alarmSeconds);
   }

//    Format time for display

   switch (m_display24Hour)
   {  // Shows how to handle radio buttons:
      case 0:  // First radio button, AM/PM format, being used
         if (newtime->tm_hour > 12)
         {
             strcpy(am_pm, _T("PM"));
             newtime->tm_hour -= 12;
         }
         break;
      case 1:  // Second radio button, 24 Hour format
         am_pm[0] = '\0';
         break;
      default:  // ERROR: An unhandled radio button selected!
         break;
   }

   sprintf(szBuffer, (const char *)m_timeFormat,
      newtime->tm_hour,
      newtime->tm_min,
      newtime->tm_sec,
      am_pm);

//    Set up display of time

   pdc->SetTextAlign(TA_LEFT ¦ TA_TOP);

   pdc->SetTextColor(TranslateColor(GetForeColor()));
   pdc->SetBkMode(TRANSPARENT);

   CFont* pOldFont;
```

```
    pOldFont = SelectStockFont(pdc);

    pdc->ExtTextOut(rcBounds.left, rcBounds.top,
        ETO_CLIPPED, rcBounds,
        szBuffer, strlen(szBuffer), NULL);

//    Restore device context

    pdc->SelectObject(pOldFont);
}
```

When the alarm time has passed, a call is made to `FireAlarm()` with the alarm time. The `FireAlarm()` function is created by ClassWizard in the CLOCKCTL.H file as a single-line function that calls the OLE controls function `FireEvent()` with the correct parameters:

```
// Event maps
    //{{AFX_EVENT(CClockCtrl)
    void FireAlarm(short nHour, short nMinute, short nSecond)
        {FireEvent(eventidAlarm,EVENT_PARAM(VTS_I2  VTS_I2  VTS_I2),
            nHour, nMinute, nSecond);}
    //}}AFX_EVENT
    DECLARE_EVENT_MAP()
```

The `m_alarmed` variable is tied to a property that is, in turn, mapped to a check box in Clock's property page dialog box. This lets the user turn the alarm function on or off. Also, whenever an alarm occurs, the alarm function is turned off.

Adding this alarm functionality was a bit complex. Let's recap in a step-by-step manner:

1. Add four properties—`AlarmHours`, `AlarmMinutes`, `AlarmSeconds`, and `Alarmed`—to your clock.

2. Add an event called `Alarm` to your clock. It should have the parameters `nHour`, `nMinute`, and `nSecond`.

3. Add to the properties dialog box a group box (cosmetic), three `DropList` combo boxes, and a single check box. Bind the variables (for simplicity, you can use the same variable names created in step 1) and the properties created in step 1 to these controls.

4. Add code to the control's constructor to initialize the alarm time (set it to the current time) and set the alarm function to off. You set the alarm function to off because there would be a risk of having an immediate alarm as soon as the control were initialized.

5. Add code to the `OnDraw()` function (or, if you wish, the `OnTimer()` function, but this would take more code) to compare the current time with the alarm time and to check to see if the alarm function is turned on. If the times match and the alarm function is on, fire the event using the `FireAlarm()` function.

There, in five easy steps, is what is necessary to add alarm functionality to the digital clock OLE control. The actual process of adding an event is simple: Use ClassWizard's OLE Events tab to design the event and add whatever data the event requires.

Adding Methods to an OLE Control

Along with properties, methods are another way that a control's container can communicate with the control. As with properties, there are both stock methods and custom methods. Methods fall within the realm of OLE Automation, allowing the container application to communicate with the OLE control.

A method can do everything that a property can do, plus the following:

- Simulate user-interface actions such as mouse clicks
- Send commands such as Refresh to the control
- Send control-specific commands to the control

In the next two sections, you will add both a stock method and a custom method to your clock control. First you will add the stock method Refresh, which tells the control to update its user area. Because a stock method is implemented by the OLE control's base class, most of the work is performed using ClassWizard.

Adding a Stock Method

To add a method to an OLE control, you must start ClassWizard, choose the OLE Automation tab, and click the Add Method button. You will see the Add Method dialog box, shown in Figure 16.34, in which you define the method's external name. For a stock method, you must select one of the names available in the External name combo box: DoClick or Refresh. For your stock method, choose Refresh. Note that the implementation must be Stock and that all other data entry controls in the Add Method dialog box are disabled.

FIGURE 16.34.

The Add Method dialog box in ClassWizard.

Click OK to add the new method. You are returned to ClassWizard's main dialog box, which should look like Figure 16.35. The new method, Refresh (which is highlighted), is preceded by an M, indicating that it is a method.

Next, rebuild the clock control. After the control has been built, you can test your new method. Start the Test Container program and load the clock control into it. In Test Container, select Edit | Invoke Methods to display the Invoke Control Method dialog box, shown in Figure 16.36. Your clock control actually has two methods: your new stock Refresh method and the preexisting AboutBox method that ControlWizard created.

FIGURE 16.35.

ClassWizard showing the Refresh *method.*

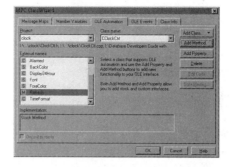

FIGURE 16.36.

Test Container's Invoke Control Method dialog box.

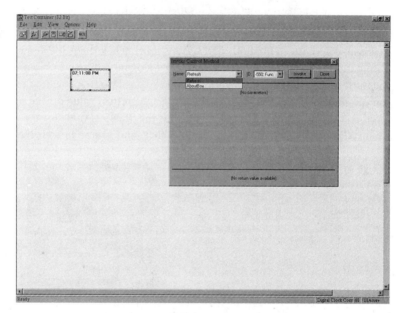

With Refresh selected, you can click the Invoke button to update the clock's display. The effects of the Refresh method probably will be a bit difficult to see, because the clock is updated automatically. However, if you set the timer interrupt interval from one second to one minute, the effect of the Refresh method is much more visible.

Next you will create a custom method for your clock control.

Adding a Custom Method

Besides stock methods, there are custom methods, which let your control be manipulated in ways that are unique to it. For example, you'll create a method to let the container set the alarm.

First, make a minor modification to your alarm function. Until now, the alarm function simply fired an event. Next, tell the user that the alarm is ringing. To do this, you simply add a call to MessageBeep() in your alarm handler:

```
//    Check for alarms. If past alarm time, sound it!

   if (m_alarmed &&
       m_alarmHours    <= newtime->tm_hour &&
       m_alarmMinutes <= newtime->tm_min &&
       m_alarmSeconds <= newtime->tm_sec)
   {//    It's an alarming event!
       m_alarmed = FALSE;
       FireAlarm(m_alarmHours, m_alarmMinutes, m_alarmSeconds);
       MessageBeep(MB_ICONEXCLAMATION);
   }
```

With this audible alarm, the user will know when a container initiates an alarm.

Now design your custom method. This method (call it SetAlarm) takes four parameters: hours, minutes, seconds, and a flag called alarmed that specifies whether the alarm is on or off.

To create your custom method, start ClassWizard. Click the Add Methods button in the OLE Automation tab to display the Add Method dialog box, shown in Figure 16.37. In this dialog, you must specify the external name (SetAlarm). ClassWizard provides the internal name, which you can modify if you like. You also can specify a return value for the method. In SetAlarm, I specified the return value as a short, which is the previous value for the alarm on/off flag. You also need to specify the hours, minutes, seconds, and alarmed parameters for your method.

FIGURE 16.37.
The Add Method dialog box with the SetAlarm *method shown.*

When you're finished with the Add Method dialog box, click OK to add the new method, and then click OK to end ClassWizard. ClassWizard then adds a member to the DISPATCH_MAP, describing the new method, and also creates an empty function that you, the programmer, can fill with whatever code is necessary to perform the method's function.

In Clock, you must set the alarm's time and the flag that specifies whether the alarm is on or off. The following code fragment shows how this might be done. The changes appear in bold:

```
short CClockCtrl::SetAlarm(short Hours, short Minutes, short Seconds,
    short Alarmed)
{
    // TODO: Add your dispatch handler code here

    short nReturnCode = m_alarmed;

    m_alarmHours = Hours;
```

```
    m_alarmMinutes = Minutes;
    m_alarmSeconds = Seconds;
    m_alarmed = Alarmed;

    return (nReturnCode);

//    return 0;
}
```

You need only to save the new alarm time and the state of the alarm on/off flag. After you've added the SetAlarm method and the preceding changes to your SetAlarm() function, rebuild the clock control.

Figure 16.38 shows Test Container with the clock control installed. The Invoke Control Method dialog box lets the user set the alarm time and turn the alarm on or off.

FIGURE 16.38.

Test Container's Invoke Control Method dialog box with SetAlarm.

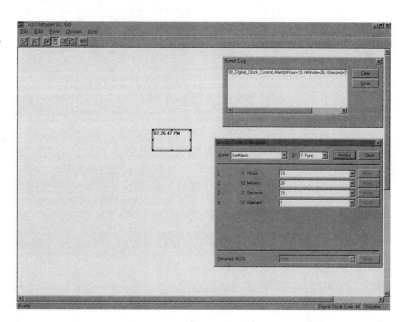

A custom method lets the container application set virtually any possible attribute or control almost any aspect of an OLE control's operation. Don't be limited by the examples shown here. Let your imagination run wild.

Interfacing with the Clock OLE Control from a Visual C++ 4 Application

Prior to Visual C++ 4, there were few opportunities to actually use the Clock OLE control. You could include it in an Access form, but that was of little use to the typical Visual C++ programmer. Visual C++ programmers want to write their applications using Visual C++, not Access!

With Visual C++ 4, you can add OLE controls to dialog boxes. This support is independent of the actual control's design. (You don't need the source for the control. Visual C++ 4 determines what functionality is needed to interface with the control and creates a wrapper class to create this interface.)

For example, Figure 16.39 shows the Clock OLE control inserted into a dialog box (the application Clock Container's About box). It also shows the properties page for the Clock OLE control that Visual C++ 4 displays. Also, notice that the toolbox has a button for inserting the Clock OLE control.

FIGURE 16.39.
The Clock OLE control in an application.

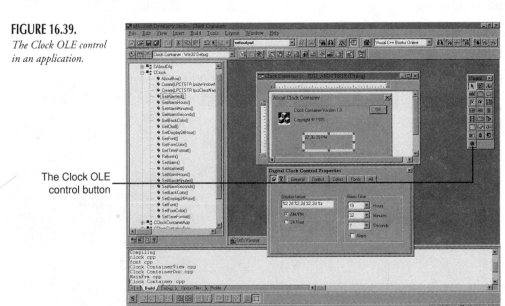

The Clock OLE control button

When an OLE control is inserted into a project (and each OLE control must be explicitly inserted into each project that it will be used in), Visual C++ creates a wrapper class. (Some OLE controls use more than one class, but the Clock OLE control uses both the basic class and a class for the font.) The wrapper class source is generated automatically. You shouldn't modify it, because Visual C++ might need to regenerate the wrapper occasionally. (If you must modify the OLE control, you can reinsert it into the project and update the wrapper class.) Listing 16.1 shows the Clock OLE control's wrapper class.

Listing 16.1. The CClock wrapper class (CLOCK.CPP) created by Visual C++ 4.

```
//Machine-generated IDispatch wrapper class(es) created by Microsoft Visual C++

//NOTE: Do not modify the contents of this file. If this class is regenerated by
//  Microsoft Visual C++, your modifications will be overwritten.
```

```
#include "stdafx.h"
#include "clock.h"

// Dispatch interfaces referenced by this interface
#include "font.h"

/////////////////////////////////////////////////////////////////////////////
// CClock

IMPLEMENT_DYNCREATE(CClock, CWnd)

/////////////////////////////////////////////////////////////////////////////
// CClock properties

OLE_COLOR CClock::GetBackColor()
{
    OLE_COLOR result;
    GetProperty(DISPID_BACKCOLOR, VT_I4, (void*)&result);
    return result;
}

void CClock::SetBackColor(OLE_COLOR propVal)
{
    SetProperty(DISPID_BACKCOLOR, VT_I4, propVal);
}

OLE_COLOR CClock::GetForeColor()
{
    OLE_COLOR result;
    GetProperty(DISPID_FORECOLOR, VT_I4, (void*)&result);
    return result;
}

void CClock::SetForeColor(OLE_COLOR propVal)
{
    SetProperty(DISPID_FORECOLOR, VT_I4, propVal);
}

COleFont CClock::GetFont()
{
    LPDISPATCH pDispatch;
    GetProperty(DISPID_FONT, VT_DISPATCH, (void*)&pDispatch);
    return COleFont(pDispatch);
}

void CClock::SetFont(LPDISPATCH propVal)
{
    SetProperty(DISPID_FONT, VT_DISPATCH, propVal);
}

CString CClock::GetTimeFormat()
{
    CString result;
    GetProperty(0x1, VT_BSTR, (void*)&result);
    return result;
}
```

continues

Listing 16.1. continued

```
void CClock::SetTimeFormat(LPCTSTR propVal)
{
    SetProperty(0x1, VT_BSTR, propVal);
}

short CClock::GetDisplay24Hour()
{
    short result;
    GetProperty(0x2, VT_I2, (void*)&result);
    return result;
}

void CClock::SetDisplay24Hour(short propVal)
{
    SetProperty(0x2, VT_I2, propVal);
}

short CClock::GetAlarmHours()
{
    short result;
    GetProperty(0x3, VT_I2, (void*)&result);
    return result;
}

void CClock::SetAlarmHours(short propVal)
{
    SetProperty(0x3, VT_I2, propVal);
}

short CClock::GetAlarmMinutes()
{
    short result;
    GetProperty(0x4, VT_I2, (void*)&result);
    return result;
}

void CClock::SetAlarmMinutes(short propVal)
{
    SetProperty(0x4, VT_I2, propVal);
}

short CClock::GetAlarmSeconds()
{
    short result;
    GetProperty(0x5, VT_I2, (void*)&result);
    return result;
}

void CClock::SetAlarmSeconds(short propVal)
{
    SetProperty(0x5, VT_I2, propVal);
}

short CClock::GetAlarmed()
{
    short result;
```

```
    GetProperty(0x6, VT_I2, (void*)&result);
    return result;
}

void CClock::SetAlarmed(short propVal)
{
    SetProperty(0x6, VT_I2, propVal);
}

/////////////////////////////////////////////////////////////////////////////
// CClock operations

void CClock::Refresh()
{
    InvokeHelper(DISPID_REFRESH, DISPATCH_METHOD, VT_EMPTY, NULL, NULL);
}

BOOL CClock::SetAlarm(short Hours, short Minutes, short Seconds, short Alarmed)
{
    BOOL result;
    static BYTE parms[] =
        VTS_I2 VTS_I2 VTS_I2 VTS_I2;
    InvokeHelper(0x7, DISPATCH_METHOD, VT_BOOL, (void*)&result, parms,
        Hours, Minutes, Seconds, Alarmed);
    return result;
}

void CClock::AboutBox()
{
    InvokeHelper(0xfffffdd8, DISPATCH_METHOD, VT_EMPTY, NULL, NULL);
}
```

For example, your application could call the `CClock::SetAlarm()` function to set an alarm time. This function maps the `SetAlarm` custom method that you created earlier. In fact, all of the Clock OLE control's methods, events, and properties can be accessed using the `CClock` class!

A Few More Bells and Whistles

What else could your Clock OLE control have? One enhancement is to expand what the user sees when the clock is running: You could display both the current time and the alarm time. It also might be a good idea to have some visual indicator that there is an active alarm.

Perhaps a digital clock isn't the best display. After all, this is a graphical environment. You could make the time display an analog format.

Most digital clocks offer some kind of date display. Your clock control might benefit from having a date display along with the time. Perhaps the date display could be optional, or the time could change to the date whenever the user clicks on the control.

A dynamic calendar display, in which previous and future months could be viewed, would enhance the clock control. Perhaps the date could be displayed when the left mouse button is pressed and the calendar could be displayed when the right mouse button is pressed.

Enhancements to the clock control are almost limitless. Adding a simple reminder system (to remind the user to perform a certain task, such as backing up or saving data) isn't difficult. Of course, you would want multiple reminders and multiple alarms. If you have reminders and multiple alarms, why not add an address book feature as well? The possibilities are endless, and all within a single OLE control. How endless? Take a look at the Calendar OLE control that is supplied with Access 7 to see what you can do with an OLE control. (The Calendar OLE control is discussed in Chapter 17, "Using OLE Controls and Automation with Visual C++ Applications.")

License Validation

The OLE control system includes a feature called license validation, which lets you determine who can distribute or use your OLE control at design time. To use license validation, you ship your control with the .LIC license file to other developers. These other developers then ship the control embedded in their application but don't ship the .LIC file. This prevents the users of the application in which your control is embedded from reusing the control on their own, because the OLE control can't be used in design mode without the license file. However, you must make sure that the people you've licensed to use your control and to whom you've given the .LIC file never distribute the .LIC file.

> **WARNING**
>
> You shouldn't rely on the default implementation of the licensing validation routines, because it can easily be defeated. You should write your own validation routines, keeping security in mind. Simple comparisons with text files probably won't prove sufficiently secure.

Adding License Validation to a New Control

To add license validation to a new OLE control, you simply check the License validation check box in ControlWizard. This adds the necessary code to check license validation.

With license validation, Windows looks for a specific string in the .LIC file. For example, if you had generated the Clock OLE control with license validation, the Clock OLE control's license file would resemble Listing 16.2.

Listing 16.2. CLOCK.LIC: The license file for Clock.

```
Copyright (c) 1995

Warning:  This product is licensed to you pursuant to the terms of the
license agreement included with the original software, and is
protected by copyright law and international treaties.  Unauthorized
```

```
reproduction or distribution may result in severe civil and criminal
penalties, and will be prosecuted to the maximum extent possible under
the law.
```

To actually verify the license file, Windows looks at the first line in the file. This line is compared to the license string that is contained in the program.

Adding License Validation to Clock

To add licensing to an existing control, you need to make several changes to the control. First, you must have a .LIC file. If you can't come up with your own, you can copy the file shown in Listing 16.2 and change its name to the name you're using.

Next, in the control's ?????CTL.H file, you must change the class factory and guid macro to include license checking. The following code fragment shows the necessary changes:

```
// DECLARE_OLECREATE_EX(CClockCtrl)  // Class factory and guid

BEGIN_OLEFACTORY(CClockCtrl)             // Class factory and guid
    virtual BOOL VerifyUserLicense();
    virtual BOOL GetLicenseKey(DWORD, BSTR FAR*);
END_OLEFACTORY(CClockCtrl)
```

First you must comment out the original class factory line:

```
// DECLARE_OLECREATE_EX(CClockCtrl)    // Class factory and guid
```

Then you must add a new class factory macro:

```
BEGIN_OLEFACTORY(CClockCtrl)             // Class factory and guid
    virtual BOOL VerifyUserLicense();
    virtual BOOL GetLicenseKey(DWORD, BSTR FAR*);
END_OLEFACTORY(CClockCtrl)
```

The final change is to add a single parameter to the control's .ODL file. This file contains the control's typelib information.

The change is simply the addition of the keyword licensed to the help file line. In the following code fragment, I've used the Clock OLE control's name and uuid. In other controls, the control's name and uuid will be different than the values shown in these fields. The keyword you must add appears in bold:

```
[ uuid(D0CA5D3C-2F3C-11CF-A0CB-444553540000), licensed,
        helpstring("Digital Clock Control"), control ]
    coclass Clock
    {
            [default] dispinterface _DClock;
            [default, source] dispinterface _DClockEvents;
    };
```

NOTE

Gotcha! When Visual C++ 2.0 and 4 compile a project, they create subdirectories for the output. Creating subdirectories lets you have both debugging and release versions of the same project at the same time. In Visual C++ 1.5 and earlier versions, creating a release version when a debugging version exists and vice versa overwrites the debugging version. Visual C++ 2.0 and 4 create a separate subdirectory for each executable type. (An OLE control has four types: Unicode release, Unicode debug, ANSI release, and ANSI debug.)

The .LIC file must be in the same directory as the executable for the control. This means that you must manually copy the .LIC file to the directory that the control's .OCX file is in. If you don't have the .LIC file in the same directory as the control's executable file, the license verification will fail.

Time lost finding this problem: two hours.

How does licensing work? The call to `AfxVerifyLicFile()` opens the specified license file and reads the first line. If the first line in the license file matches the provided license string, the license verification is deemed a success.

Now that you know this, there are a few issues that you need to keep in mind:

■ For each new control that you develop, you should modify the license check line in both the .LIC file and the application's `_szLicString[]` variable so that each control's licensing is unique. If you don't do this, all controls that you develop will have the same license string, and an unscrupulous user or developer could misuse your controls.

■ You must resist the urge to peek at the license string in a licensed control and not create a new (bogus) license validation file. Be honest, and don't misappropriate someone else's OLE controls. Of course, if the developers of an OLE control retained Microsoft's simplistic license checking scheme, they could expect their OLE control's security to be rather weak.

■ If you don't need to license your controls, don't add license validation. For controls that are distributed using shareware distribution techniques, license validation has no real use.

WARNING

Microsoft really expects you to write your own validation function and not rely on the Visual C++ supplied function, which simply compares the first line in the license file with a constant found in the program. Your license validation routine should be a bit more sophisticated than this.

Overall, the default license validation provides a weak method of ensuring that a user or developer has actually licensed your control. It's easily defeated by anyone who is reasonably skilled, so don't depend on it for absolute security. If you rewrite the validation routine, you can enhance the OLE control's security substantially.

Using Your OLE Control Outside Visual C++ Programs

It's relatively easy to use your OLE control. Earlier you saw how to use an OLE control in a Visual C++ program. However, OLE controls have value in other applications as well, such as Visual Basic and Access, for example.

First, you must have an application that can use an OLE control. At the time this book was written, the most common nonprogramming platform application that could use OLE controls was Access. Access has been able to use OLE controls since version 2.

Inserting an OLE control into an Access form or report is simple. When you're designing the form, decide where you want to insert the OLE control. Then, from Access, select Insert | Object.

Figure 16.40 shows your clock control installed in an Access form. An appropriate font has been set, the digits are colored dark blue, and the background is set to match the form's background. Notice how well the custom control blends in with the form.

FIGURE 16.40.

Your clock control in an Access form.

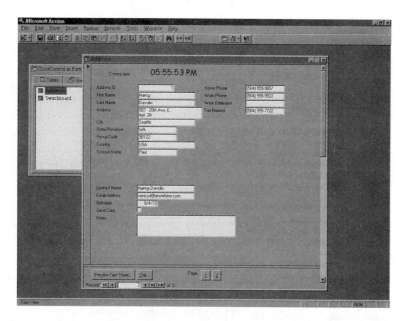

Shipping Your OLE Control

After you've developed your new OLE control, you must distribute it to your users. The installation process can be either a separate step (in which your product is only the OLE control) or part of another application's installation process.

For the 16-bit versions of your OLE controls, you should change the extension of the control's file from .DLL to .OCX. This will cause all the OLE controls to have the same file extension. Make this change to the DLL's name before you register the control, because the system won't find a control that is renamed after registration. OLE controls that are created using one of the 32-bit versions of Visual C++ are already named with the .OCX extension.

Microsoft recommends that you install your OLE controls in the Windows system directory on the user's machine. Your OLE control installation program can obtain the name of the system directory by using the GetSystemDirectory() function. Make sure that you don't install your OLE controls in the main Windows directory.

A number of redistributable DLL files might be needed with your OLE control. These files should be placed on the target system if either of the following is true:

■ No DLL file with this name exists on the target system.

■ An existing DLL of the same name has an earlier version number.

Using a proper installation program such as InstallShield can make version checking much easier. You don't have to distribute the entire OLE set of DLL files. Your OLE control will be used only in an OLE container application that will already have installed the necessary OLE DLL files.

Before a user can use your OLE control, the control must be registered. This is done by having the container application call the CCtrlFactory::UpdateRegistry(BOOL *bRegister*) function. This function takes one parameter, *bRegister*, which, if TRUE, registers the control, and if FALSE, unregisters the control. In order to let all developers use your control (and insert the control into a program), there must be a method to register the control. For example, Visual C++ users can use the REGSVR32.EXE program to register a control if necessary.

Although some OLE control container applications have a way to register an OLE control, you shouldn't depend on the availability of such a feature. A developer could register a control by calling either REGSVR.EXE or REGSVR32.EXE (as appropriate for the target version of Windows).

If your control is licensed, you must make sure that the license control file (the .LIC file) is available to any developer who will use your control, and that the license file is installed in the same directory that the control has been installed in. You and the developers using your control should take care not to inadvertently distribute the .LIC file to end users if you intend to enforce licensing!

Summary

This chapter introduced the OLE control development tools, which let the developer create OLE controls with a minimum of effort. The following topics were covered:

- ControlWizard: A part of AppWizard that is used to create an OLE control program shell. The programmer can define a number of the control's attributes.

- Register/Unregister: You can register or unregister controls using REGSVR or REGSVR32.

- Test Container: A program that lets the developer test the OLE control that is being developed.

- PView95: A utility that shows the processes and threads that are currently loaded. PView95 lets you kill a process if necessary.

- Make TypeLib: The MKTYPLIB utility is used in the 16-bit environment to create type libraries.

You also learned that it isn't difficult to develop OLE controls. Even if you haven't had any experience in using OLE, you can develop OLE controls using the ControlWizard and ClassWizard applets that are supplied with Visual C++ 4.0.

You also developed the Clock OLE control, which can be embedded into any container application that supports OLE controls. It also can be embedded into an OLE container application, where it will function as an OLE Automation Server.

The following topics also were covered:

- Events: OLE control events are the method by which the OLE control can communicate events and information to the container application.

- Properties: OLE control properties let the container application communicate information to the control.

- Methods: OLE control methods are a way for the container application to communicate with the control.

- Licensing: OLE controls can be protected with a simple form of license validation. This validation lets the programmer control who can embed the control into applications.

- Using the ControlWizard applet.

- Customizing your OLE control.

- Packaging and shipping your OLE control.

17

Using OLE Controls and Automation with Visual C++ Applications

Three different groups are involved with an OLE control: the OLE control developer, the application's developer, and the end user. Each has different objectives, wants, and needs. You were an OLE control developer when you developed the clock control in Chapter 16, "Creating OLE Controls with Visual C++ 4." An OLE control developer creates a control that he or she might (or might not) use in an application. This person knows how the OLE control works but might have only incidental information about how the application's developer will actually use the OLE control.

The application's developer is the person who develops applications, perhaps using a system such as Microsoft Access. If this person is using Access, he or she will develop data entry forms, tables, reports, and so on. The forms and reports probably will need OLE controls to perform special functions. Just look at your clock control, which can be embedded in an Access data entry form. The application's developer might have some understanding of how the OLE control works internally but doesn't need to fully understand its inner workings in order to use it.

Finally, the end user has his own needs and wants. Often developers try to guess what the user will want and like. However, successful developers listen to the user and provide the features that he needs. If the user says he needs a clock in the data entry form, it's needed. The user is rarely interested in the mechanics of the OLE control as long as it works as intended.

The Application User

The application user wants an application that is easy to use and that works well. Microsoft can't provide all the types of controls that a typical application might need. Typical custom controls might include

- Clocks and timer controls
- Spreadsheet-type controls for data display
- Data access controls that show the data from a data source
- Specialty pushbutton controls (which typically have bitmap images)

The Application Developer

The application developer creates applications for the application user. This person might also be the OLE control developer, but that isn't always the case.

If the application developer is restricted to using just the controls that are supplied with Windows, many applications won't present a user interface with the needed functionality. When the application developer must use an OLE control, the control must be easy to use and have an attractive appearance. The control's look and feel must match both Windows and the application being created.

OLE controls for application developers typically are more complex than those used by application users. Controls such as calendars, database grid controls, and graphing controls are all possible objects that application developers would use.

The OLE Control Developer

The OLE control developer is responsible for creating OLE controls that can be used by both the application developer and the application user. The OLE control developer must work with the application developer to create controls that can perform the needed tasks.

Access and OLE Controls

At the time this book was written, Access was the most common end-user application that offered support for OLE controls. With Access, you can create an application that has OLE controls in forms and reports. As shown in Chapter 16, a control can easily be integrated into an Access form.

> **NOTE**
>
> Because this isn't an Access book, I've skipped a number of minor details about custom controls in the following sections that use your Clock OLE control in an Access form. The skipped details will become self-evident when you add an OLE control to an Access form.

Now, see what you can do with your OLE control in an Access form. First, as Chapter 16 showed, your Clock OLE control is included in an Access form. Figure 17.1 reminds you what this form looks like.

Figure 17.1 shows the clock control in an Access form that is currently in user mode. There are two modes: user mode, in which the user interacts with the form, and design mode, in which the form is designed or modified. Notice that the time is displayed on the form.

You might remember that when you designed the clock control you added a few bells and whistles. One of these additions was an alarm function. Now your Access user wants to implement the alarm function to display a message box on-screen at a certain time. To do this, you must have two things:

■ A way to display the message when the clock control sends an Alarm event
■ A way to set the alarm attributes, such as the time for the alarm to go off

FIGURE 17.1.
The Clock OLE control in an Access form.

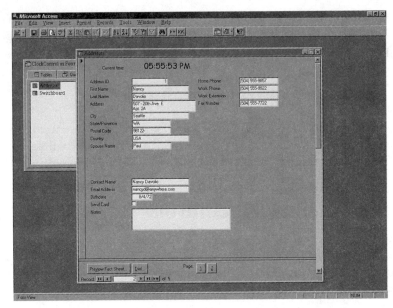

To display a message or take any other action when an OLE control fires an event, you must add an event handler for the OLE control. As the application developer, you should open the form in design mode and then follow these steps to add an event handler for the OLE control:

1. Right-click the OLE control. You see a pop-up menu that has a Build Event selection. When you select Build Event, you're presented with an event handler shell, shown in Figure 17.2.

FIGURE 17.2.
Clock's event handler for the alarm event.

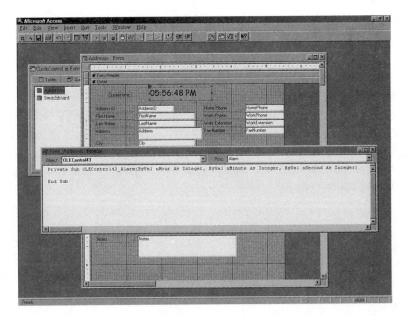

2. The Events window has an empty implementation of the OLE control's registered events. You can scroll through each of the event handlers using the Page Up and Page Down keys. Figure 17.2 shows the alarm event handler.

   Notice that the alarm event handler already has the three parameters (nHour, nMinute, and nSecond) that you defined when you created the clock control. Your function will be able to determine which alarm occurred if you decide to allow for multiple alarms in your handler.

   For your handler, you want a simple message box that displays a message saying that the alarm has occurred. To display a message box in Access Basic, you can use the MsgBox() function, as shown in Figure 17.3.

FIGURE 17.3.

Clock's alarm function showing the MsgBox() *call.*

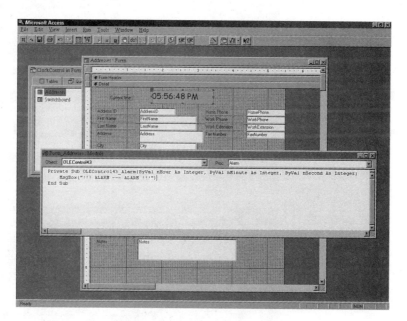

After you've written your handler for the OLE control event, you can compile it by selecting Run | Compile Loaded Modules from Access. When it's compiled, save the code and test the clock's alarm function.

To test the alarm function, you must become the user and then set the clock's alarm time and enable the alarm. First, close the Design Form window to save the changes you've made to the form. Next, to set the alarm time and enable the alarm, use the control's property page. You included the necessary controls in the property sheet dialog box for just such an occasion. In order to access the clock's property page dialog box, the user must do the following:

1. Make the clock control the current, active control by clicking one of the clock's digits. The Clock OLE control doesn't provide any feedback to tell the user that it has input focus, but Access knows which control has focus.

2. From Access, the user must select Edit | Digital Clock Control Object | Properties, as shown in Figure 17.4. This displays the clock's property page dialog box, shown in Figure 17.5.

FIGURE 17.4.

Menu selections to activate the clock's property page dialog box.

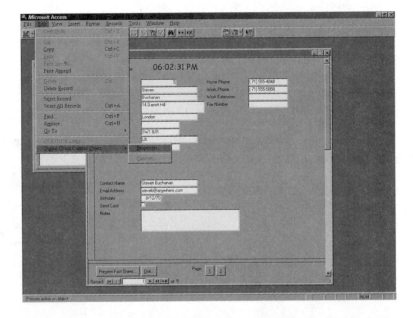

FIGURE 17.5.

The clock's property page dialog box in Access.

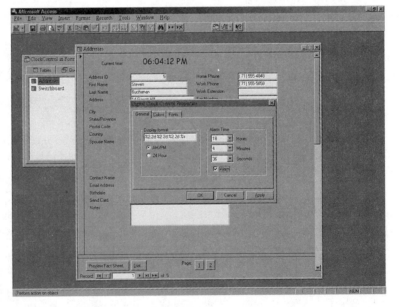

When the alarm time has been set and the alarm has been enabled, simply wait for the alarm to occur. When this happens, the alarm message box is displayed, as shown in Figure 17.6. Needless to say, it's an alarming experience!

FIGURE 17.6.

The clock control: It's alarming!

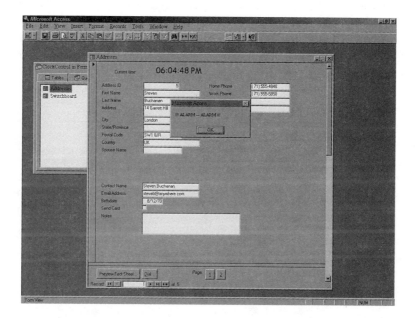

With an OLE control, you can emulate many of the functions that are provided with other Access forms' objects. For example, you could have a custom button that supports animation (actually, the clock control is just such a control) or an OLE control button that displays information in a format that isn't possible using a standard control. An example of an OLE control that provides a unique display of information might be a "gas gauge" type of control that could be used to show the quantity of an item in stock for an inventory database system. Many cars have a "low fuel" light, so perhaps this control should have a "low inventory level" light.

Using *VARIANT* Types

What is a VARIANT and why do I need one? These are often two of the first questions that new Visual C++ OLE programmers have. It's bad enough that we have to deal with short, long, int, float, and so on without adding another type to our list of variable types. Well, it gets even worse: the VARIANT type can actually be of virtually any type!

VARIANT types are used to mask the type of variable that will be passed to an OLE object so that the variable's type doesn't need to be known in advance. The VARIANT type object contains information (placed there at runtime, not design time) about the type of object that is contained in the VARIANT variable.

Table 17.1 lists the types of variables that can be placed in a VARIANT type. The TYPEDESC column describes the array's dimensions and the type of the array's elements. Perhaps you're wondering what property sets are. According to the original OLE 2.0 *Programmer's Reference* (Appendix B, page 636), "property sets are tagged collections of values whose meaning (schema) is known to the code that manipulates them; that is, as much as that code needs to know the meaning." When arrays are passed by IDispatch::Invoke within VARIANTARGs, they are called *safe arrays*. Safe arrays contain information about the number of dimensions and bounds within them.

Table 17.1. VARIANT types.

Type	VARIANT	TYPEDESC	OLE Property Set	Safe Array	Description
VT_EMPTY	X		X		Nothing
VT_NULL	X				SQL-style null
VT_I2	X	X	X	X	2-byte signed int
VT_I4	X	X	X	X	4-byte signed int
VT_R4	X	X	X	X	4-byte real (float)
VT_R8	X	X	X	X	8-byte real (double)
VT_CY	X	X	X	X	Currency
VT_DATE	X	X	X	X	Date
VT_BSTR	X	X	X	X	OLE Automation string
VT_DISPATCH	X	X		X	IDispatch FAR*
VT_ERROR	X	X		X	SCODE
VT_BOOL	X	X		X	TRUE = -1; FALSE = 0
VT_VARIANT	X	X		X	VARIANT FAR*
VT_UNKNOWN	X	X		X	IUnknown FAR*
VT_I1		X			signed char
VT_UI1	X	X			unsigned char
VT_UI2		X			unsigned short
VT_UI4		X			unsigned short

Type	VARIANT	TYPEDESC	OLE Property Set	Safe Array	Description
VT_I8	X		X		signed 64-bit int
VT_UI8	X				unsigned 64-bit int
VT_INT	X				signed machine int
VT_UINT	X				unsigned machine int
VT_VOID	X				C-style void
VT_HRESULT	X				HRESULT type
VT_PTR	X				Pointer type
VT_SAFEARRAY	X				Use VT_ARRAY in VARIANT
VT_CARRAY	X				C-style array
VT_USERDEFINED	X				User-defined type
VT_LPSTR	X		X		Null-terminated string
VT_LPWSTR	X		X		Wide null-terminated string
VT_FILETIME			X		FILETIME type
VT_BLOB			X		Length-prefixed bytes
VT_STREAM			X		Name of the stream follows
VT_STORAGE			X		Name of the storage follows
VT_STREAMED_OBJECT			X		Stream contains an object
VT_STORED_OBJECT			X		Storage contains an object
VT_BLOB_OBJECT			X		Blob contains an object

continues

Table 17.1. continued

Type	VARIANT TYPEDESC	OLE *Property Set*	*Safe Array*	Description
VT_CF		X		Clipboard format
VT_CLSID		X		Class ID
VT_VECTOR		X		Simple counted array
VT_ARRAY	X			SAFEARRAY*
VT_BYREF	X			The object is a pointer

The VARIANT type works by stuffing all these types into a single union object, as shown in Listing 17.1.

Listing 17.1. The VARIANT type.

```
struct tagVARIANT{
    VARTYPE vt;
    WORD wReserved1;
    WORD wReserved2;
    WORD wReserved3;
    union
    {
        long          lVal;      /* VT_I4                 */
        unsigned char bVal;      /* VT_UI1                */
        short         iVal;      /* VT_I2                 */
        float         fltVal;    /* VT_R4                 */
        double        dblVal;    /* VT_R8                 */
        VARIANT_BOOL  bool;      /* VT_BOOL               */
        SCODE         scode;     /* VT_ERROR              */
        CY            cyVal;     /* VT_CY                 */
        DATE          date;      /* VT_DATE               */
        BSTR          bstrVal;   /* VT_BSTR               */
        IUnknown      *punkVal;  /* VT_UNKNOWN            */
        IDispatch     *pdispVal; /* VT_DISPATCH           */
        SAFEARRAY     *parray;   /* VT_ARRAY|*            */
        unsigned char *pbVal;    /* VT_BYREF|VT_UI1       */
        short         *piVal;    /* VT_BYREF|VT_I2        */
        long          *plVal;    /* VT_BYREF|VT_I4        */
        float         *pfltVal;  /* VT_BYREF|VT_R4        */
        double        *pdblVal;  /* VT_BYREF|VT_R8        */
        VARIANT_BOOL  *pbool;    /* VT_BYREF|VT_BOOL      */
        SCODE         *pscode;   /* VT_BYREF|VT_ERROR     */
        CY            *pcyVal;   /* VT_BYREF|VT_CY        */
        DATE          *pdate;    /* VT_BYREF|VT_DATE      */
```

```
         BSTR          *pbstrVal;      /* VT_BYREF¦VT_BSTR     */
         IUnknown      **ppunkVal;     /* VT_BYREF¦VT_UNKNOWN  */
         IDispatch     **ppdispVal;    /* VT_BYREF¦VT_DISPATCH */
         SAFEARRAY     **pparray;      /* VT_BYREF¦VT_ARRAY¦*  */
         VARIANT       *pvarVal;       /* VT_BYREF¦VT_VARIANT  */
         void          * byref;        /* Generic ByRef        */
    }
#if(defined(NONAMELESSUNION))
    u
#endif
    ;
};
```

Perhaps you're thinking that there must be an easier way. A VARIANT has things you've never seen before, such as DATE and BSTR. Well, there is help. The MFC class COleVariant comes to the rescue, making management of the VARIANT type easier. The COleVariant class has the following members and operations:

■ COleVariant, which constructs a COleVariant object

■ ChangeType(), which changes the variant type of this COleVariant object

■ Clear(), which clears the COleVariant object

■ Detach(), which detaches a VARIANT object from the COleVariant class and returns the VARIANT

■ The LPCVARIANT operator, which converts a COleVariant value into an LPCVARIANT

■ The LPVARIANT operator, which converts a COleVariant object into an LPVARIANT

■ The = operator, which copies a COleVariant value

■ The == operator, which compares two COleVariant values

■ The << operator, which outputs a COleVariant value to CArchive or CDumpContext

■ The >> operator, which inputs a COleVariant object from CArchive

For an example of how to use the COleVariant class object, refer to the Microsoft Communications OLE control example later in this chapter. The Microsoft Communications OLE control uses a bstr VARIANT object to pass characters to be written out of the communications port.

Generally, you will want to use COleVariant in your MFC applications. It's easier to use, and it provides a more programmer-friendly application.

Using OLE Controls in a Visual C++ 4 Project

This part of the chapter discusses the issues in using OLE controls in a Visual C++ application, describes the OLE controls supplied with Visual C++ 4, and describes using the Clock OLE control.

First, let's revel in the fact that Visual C++ 4 is the first release of Visual C++ that actually lets you use an OLE control. You've been able to develop OLE controls for some time, but a Visual C++ program hasn't been able to use OLE controls itself. You could make them, but you couldn't use them.

Now, with Visual C++ 4, you can include OLE controls on dialog boxes. When you create an MFC application's project, the OLE page has a check box that you would check if you planned to use OLE controls in your project, as shown in Figure 17.7. If by chance you forgot to check this box, or you're importing an existing project from an earlier version of Visual C++, you can add this capability by selecting Insert | Component. The dialog box shown in Figure 17.8 appears.

FIGURE 17.7.
An MFC project's OLE properties wizard page.

FIGURE 17.8.
Adding OLE control support to existing projects.

You can easily use OLE controls in Visual C++ dialog boxes and in other locations as well—typically anywhere where you might create a window. There is no hard and fast rule that says an OLE control must have a window. Later in this chapter you'll see two controls from Microsoft that don't create any window when used in execute mode.

Microsoft-Supplied OLE Controls

Microsoft supplies with Visual C++ 4 a set of OLE controls. You will create a simple example of each of these controls using the sample program for this chapter. The supplied OLE controls include the following:

- The Anibutton is used to display simple animation. You design bitmaps to display when various events occur.
- The Grid control looks much like a spreadsheet, with addressable locations arranged in a grid. You can have title columns and rows.
- The Keystate control provides feedback to the user on the state of a number of keys, such as the Caps Lock key.
- The Microsoft Communications control is used to manipulate communications ports. Ports can be configured and I/O can be performed using this control. This control is an example of an OLE control that isn't visible in run mode.
- The Microsoft Masked Edit control lets you accept and display formatted input in your application. A typical example is the obtaining of a telephone number.
- The Microsoft Multimedia control lets your application display and manipulate multimedia clips, such as .AVI files.
- The PicClip control lets your application obtain a portion of a bitmap easily. This control is an example of an OLE control that isn't visible in run mode.

In addition to these fully supported OLE controls, Visual C++ 4 also includes as sample applications a number of OLE controls. These controls aren't supported by Microsoft (and might not work as expected), but because they're available in source format, they can be quite valuable:

- BUTTON: A simple button control.
- CIRC1: Part one of the OLE control tutorial project.
- CIRC2: Part two of the OLE control tutorial project.
- CIRC3: Part three of the OLE control tutorial project.
- DB: A database access control. Lets you access a single column in a table.
- LICENSED: An example of using licensing of OLE controls.
- LOCALIZE: An example of a localized control.
- PAL: An example of a color palette manipulation control.
- PUSH: An example of a customized pushbutton control.
- SMILEY: A smiley-face pushbutton.
- SPINDIAL: A spindial example.
- TIME: A timer-based control. Basically, an alarm function.
- XLIST: An OLE control that subclasses a Windows list box.

In this chapter you will create a project to illustrate each of the Visual C++ 4 supplied OLE controls. However, none of the sample controls is displayed in the sample program. This chapter uses a single project with seven dialog boxes (one for each of the seven OLE controls) to demonstrate the use of these OLE controls.

To include an OLE control in your project (assuming that your project supports OLE controls), choose Insert | Component. Doing so will display a dialog box that has a tab for OLE controls (usually the second tab), as shown in Figure 17.9. You will notice a few additional controls, including the digital clock control from Chapter 16, the Db sample control, and Access 7's Calendar control.

FIGURE 17.9.

Visual C++ 4's Component Gallery dialog with OLE controls displayed.

NOTE

Perhaps you're wondering why you can't see all those controls in your copy of Visual C++ at one time. Actually, Figure 17.9 is a composite of all the controls available. I can see only six at a time, too!

Here is one of the fantastic things that Visual C++ 4 does: Each time you add (register) a control to your system, Visual C++ sees it and adds the control to the Component Gallery for you. Yes, you can even add that nifty Access 7 Calendar control to a Visual C++ project!

NOTE

All controls are generally available in Visual C++ 4's Component Gallery. This doesn't mean that you can legally use all controls, however. You must abide by the licensing agreement that came with the control. This applies to the Access 7 Calendar control, for example.

A future set of imaging OLE controls from Wang looks interesting. The Wang Image Controls are free for both runtime and development. They are supposed to be included in future releases of Windows and Windows NT. The end user will get the controls in a package oriented around the Windows Fax Viewer application.

In the Component Gallery dialog box, select the OLE control that you want to include in your project and click the Insert button. You need to insert a control into a project only one time, even if you'll need to use the control in multiple locations. For example, if you wanted to include a Grid control in your project, you would select the Grid Control icon in the Component Gallery and click the Insert button. Then, whenever the dialog box editor were displayed, the toolbox would include a button for the Grid control. Figure 17.10 shows the dialog editor toolbox after you insert all the OLE controls for the sample program.

FIGURE 17.10.
The dialog editor's toolbox with buttons for each OLE control.

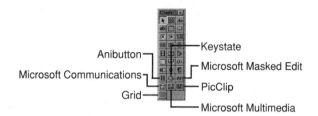

Anibutton
Microsoft Communications
Grid
Keystate
Microsoft Masked Edit
PicClip
Microsoft Multimedia

You can either add all the OLE controls that your project will use at one time or add them as needed. There's no advantage in adding all of them at the same time, other than convenience.

The Anibutton OLE Control

The Anibutton is used to display simple animation. You design bitmaps to display when various events occur.

The Anibutton OLE control is a rather useful button type control that uses an icon, bitmap, or metafile to define the appearance of a custom button control. Typical applications of the Anibutton OLE control include animated buttons, multistate buttons, and animated check boxes. The sample program creates a multistate button.

Each of your Anibutton OLE controls may have zero or more images. The Anibutton may also have an optional text caption. In most circumstances, the Anibutton OLE control may be considered to be simply a group of frames (defined with bitmaps, icons, or metafiles) that may be displayed in a given sequence.

The programmer uses the CCanibuton::SetPicture() property function to load images into the Anibutton OLE control. The CCanibuton::GetFrame() property indicates which picture is currently accessible through the CCanibuton::SetPicture() property. In other words, the CCanibuton::GetFrame() property is an index of the array of images in the control. You could use CCanibuton::SetFrame() to set the frame to be displayed if you want.

The images are displayed within the control's border. The default is to display the images in the center of the control, but you can use the CCanibuton::SetPictureXpos() and CCanibuton::SetPictureYpos() properties to position the image within the control. You can also use the CCanibuton::SetPictDrawMode() property to scale the image to the exact size of the control or to adjust the control to the size of your image.

The Anibutton's text can be displayed next to the images or on the images, depending on the CCanibuton::SetTextPosition() property.

There are a number of Anibutton OLE control types. The type of control is set either at design time by setting the Button type property or at runtime by calling the CCanibuton::SetCycle() property. The values listed in Table 17.2 are the valid styles for the Anibutton OLE control.

Table 17.2. Anibutton OLE control cycle types.

Button Type	Cycle	Description
Animated (1/2 and 1/2)	0	Each time the left mouse button is clicked, the first half of the frames are displayed in order. When the left button is released, the remaining frames are displayed in order. After the frames are displayed, the Anibutton OLE control returns to the first frame. If the Anibutton OLE control has only two frames defined, this type is referred to as an Enhanced button style.
Multistate	1	Each frame is used to specify a given state. There will be as many states as there are frames in the Anibutton OLE control. Each time the left button is clicked, the Anibutton OLE control automatically switches to the next state and displays the appropriate frame. If the Anibutton OLE control has only two frames defined, this type is referred to as an Enhanced check box style.
2-state animated (two state 1/2 and 1/2)	2	The first time the left mouse button is clicked, the first half of the frames are displayed in order. The Anibutton OLE control's state changes to the second state. When the left button is clicked for the second time, the remaining frames are displayed in order. The state is then returned to the first state. After the frames are displayed, the Anibutton OLE control returns to the first frame.

There are no real limits to the size of the Anibutton OLE control. Usually it's sized to be comparable to other dialog button type controls. However, you can use large bitmaps in the Anibutton OLE control if you want. The bitmaps and icons used by the Anibutton OLE control don't use many Windows resources. This data is stored in global memory using a private format. The Anibutton OLE control won't use Windows bitmap or icon resource handles. Microsoft has even suggested that the Anibutton can be used as a method of storing or archiving bitmaps or icons.

To use the Anibutton OLE control, first install it into your project. Once it's installed, your dialog editor tool palette (or toolbox) will have a new button for the Anibutton OLE control; it will have a picture of a small piece of film. (See Figure 17.10.) Next, open the dialog box that will receive the Anibutton OLE control and locate your control. After you've located, sized, and named the control, you should set whatever properties you want (including defining the frame bitmaps) for this control.

Figure 17.11 shows the sample Anibutton OLE control, along with the Control Properties page. Notice that I've chosen to use the multistate type for this control.

FIGURE 17.11.

The Anibutton OLE control located in a dialog, along with the property sheet.

After you've created your control in the dialog editor, start ClassWizard (while the dialog has focus, press Ctrl-W) and bind a CCanibuton class variable to the control. The example uses a variable name of m_Anibutton for this variable, as shown in Figure 17.12. Once the CCanibuton class variable is bound to the control, you can work with the control in the dialog handler class, as shown in Listing 17.2. The added lines appear in bold.

FIGURE 17.12.

The Anibutton OLE control bound CCanibuton variable in ClassWizard.

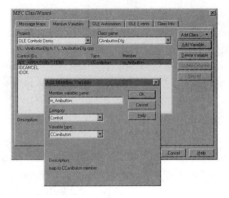

Listing 17.2. The AnibuttonDlg.CPP dialog box handler file.

```cpp
// AnibuttonDlg.cpp : implementation file
//

#include "stdafx.h"
#include "OLE Controls Demo.h"
#include "AnibuttonDlg.h"

#ifdef _DEBUG
#define new DEBUG_NEW
#undef THIS_FILE
static char THIS_FILE[] = __FILE__;
#endif


/////////////////////////////////////////////////////////////////////////////
// CAnibuttonDlg dialog


CAnibuttonDlg::CAnibuttonDlg(CWnd* pParent /*=NULL*/)
    : CDialog(CAnibuttonDlg::IDD, pParent)
{
    //{{AFX_DATA_INIT(CAnibuttonDlg)
        // NOTE: the ClassWizard will add member initialization here
    //}}AFX_DATA_INIT
}


void CAnibuttonDlg::DoDataExchange(CDataExchange* pDX)
{
    CDialog::DoDataExchange(pDX);
    //{{AFX_DATA_MAP(CAnibuttonDlg)
    DDX_Control(pDX, IDC_ANIPUSHBUTTON1, m_Anibutton);
    //}}AFX_DATA_MAP
}


BEGIN_MESSAGE_MAP(CAnibuttonDlg, CDialog)
    //{{AFX_MSG_MAP(CAnibuttonDlg)
        // NOTE: the ClassWizard will add message map macros here
    //}}AFX_MSG_MAP
```

```
END_MESSAGE_MAP()

//////////////////////////////////////////////////////////////////////////
// CAnibuttonDlg message handlers

BEGIN_EVENTSINK_MAP(CAnibuttonDlg, CDialog)
    //{{AFX_EVENTSINK_MAP(CAnibuttonDlg)
    ON_EVENT(CAnibuttonDlg, IDC_ANIPUSHBUTTON1, 1
        /* Click */, OnClickAnipushbutton1, VTS_NONE)
    //}}AFX_EVENTSINK_MAP
END_EVENTSINK_MAP()

void CAnibuttonDlg::OnClickAnipushbutton1()
{
    // TODO: Add your control notification handler code here

    // This function is called each time the button is clicked
    // by the user. You can use this function to determine the
    // button's state:

    switch(m_Anibutton.Get_Value())
    {
        case 0:
            MessageBox("Value is zero");
            break;
        case 1:
            MessageBox("Value is one");
            break;
        case 2:
            MessageBox("Value is two");
            break;
        case 3:
            MessageBox("Value is three");
            break;
        case 4:
            MessageBox("Value is four");
            break;
        default:
            MessageBox("Value is undefined!");
            break;
    }
}
```

You only needed to add code to receive the Anibutton OLE control's clicks and report the state to the user. A typical application probably would set a member variable to reflect the Anibutton OLE control's state and process this information as appropriate.

The Grid OLE Control

The Grid OLE control looks much like a spreadsheet. It has addressable locations arranged in a grid. You can have title columns and rows.

With the Grid OLE control, you can put either text or a picture in any cell. You need to use the Row and Col properties to specify the current cell in a grid. The two Visual C++ functions that do this are `CGridCtrl::SetRow()` and `CGridCtrl::SetCol()`. However, a large number of functions are available in the `CGridCtrl` class to manipulate your Grid OLE control. When you initialize your Grid OLE control, you may specify the current Row and Col. At runtime, the user can change the current Row and Col using either the keyboard or the mouse. Your application can obtain the contents of the current cell using the `CGridCtrl::GetText()` property function.

The Grid OLE control uses text wrapping if a cell's text won't fit within the currently defined columns. If a column isn't sufficiently wide, the Grid OLE control won't extend it automatically like Excel does. When text is wrapped, the cell must be made wider or taller to let the user read all the text. At runtime, the user can modify cells' height and width. If you want, your application can query the cells' width and save these values to be used the next time the control is used. (To see a grid control saving column widths, refer to the application called Contin using Grid Control in Chapter 15, "Designing Online Transaction-Processing Applications.")

You can set the number of Cols and Rows in your Grid OLE control at design time, or you can use the `CGridCtrl::SetCols()` and `CGridCtrl::SetRows()` properties to set the number of columns and rows in a Grid control at runtime. The Grid OLE control can't have more than 16,352 rows and 5,450 columns.

To use the Grid OLE control, first install it into your project. Once it's installed, your dialog editor tool palette (or toolbox) will have a new button for the Grid OLE control; it will have a picture of a small grid. (See Figure 17.10.) Next, open the dialog box that will receive the Grid OLE control and locate your control. After you've located, sized, and named the control, you should set whatever properties you want for this control.

Figure 17.13 shows the sample Grid OLE control, along with the Control Properties page.

FIGURE 17.13.

The Grid OLE control located in a dialog, along with the property sheet.

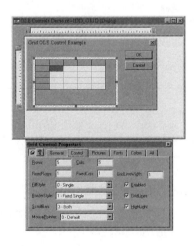

After you've created your control in the dialog editor, start ClassWizard (while the dialog has focus, press Ctrl-W) and bind a `CGridCtrl` class variable to the control. The example uses a variable name of `m_GridCtrl` for this variable, as shown in Figure 17.14. Once the `CGridCtrl` class variable is bound to the control, you can work with the control in the dialog handler class, as shown in Listing 17.3.

FIGURE 17.14.

The Grid OLE control bound CGridCtrl variable in Class-Wizard.

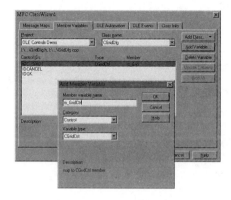

Listing 17.3. The GridDlg.CPP dialog box handler file.

```cpp
// GridDlg.cpp : implementation file
//

#include "stdafx.h"
#include "OLE Controls Demo.h"
#include "GridDlg.h"

#ifdef _DEBUG
#define new DEBUG_NEW
#undef THIS_FILE
static char THIS_FILE[] = __FILE__;
#endif

/////////////////////////////////////////////////////////////////////////////
// CGridDlg dialog


CGridDlg::CGridDlg(CWnd* pParent /*=NULL*/)
    : CDialog(CGridDlg::IDD, pParent)
{
    //{{AFX_DATA_INIT(CGridDlg)
        // NOTE: the ClassWizard will add member initialization here
    //}}AFX_DATA_INIT
}


void CGridDlg::DoDataExchange(CDataExchange* pDX)
{
    CDialog::DoDataExchange(pDX);
    //{{AFX_DATA_MAP(CGridDlg)
```

continues

Listing 17.3. continued

```
    DDX_Control(pDX, IDC_GRID1, m_Grid);
    //}}AFX_DATA_MAP
}


BEGIN_MESSAGE_MAP(CGridDlg, CDialog)
    //{{AFX_MSG_MAP(CGridDlg)
    //}}AFX_MSG_MAP
END_MESSAGE_MAP()

/////////////////////////////////////////////////////////////////////////////
// CGridDlg message handlers

BOOL CGridDlg::OnInitDialog()
{
    CDialog::OnInitDialog();

    // TODO: Add extra initialization here

    int Column = 0;
    int Row = 0;
    CString Formatted;

    // Fill in the Grid control's column titles:

    m_Grid.SetRow(0);
    for (Column = 1; Column < m_Grid.GetCols(); ++Column)
    {// Fill only the predetermined number of columns...
        m_Grid.SetCol(Column);
        Formatted.Format(_T("Col %d"), Column);
        m_Grid.SetText(Formatted);
    }

    // Fill in the Grid control's row titles:

    m_Grid.SetCol(0);
    for (Row = 1; Row < m_Grid.GetRows(); ++Row)
    {// Fill only the predetermined number of columns...
        m_Grid.SetRow(Row);
        Formatted.Format(_T("Row %d"), Row);
        m_Grid.SetText(Formatted);
    }

    // Fill in the Grid control's data area.
    // See Chapter 15 for an expanded example of how to
    // use the Grid control in an application.

    for (Row = 1; Row < m_Grid.GetRows(); ++Row)
    {// Fill only the predetermined number of rows...
        m_Grid.SetRow(Row);
        for (Column = 1; Column < m_Grid.GetCols(); ++Column)
        {// Fill only the predetermined number of columns...
            m_Grid.SetCol(Column);
            Formatted.Format(_T("R%dC%d"), Row, Column);
```

```
        m_Grid.SetText(Formatted);
    }
}

return TRUE;  // Return TRUE unless you set the focus to a control
              // EXCEPTION: OCX Property Pages should return FALSE
}
```

You needed to add code to initialize the Grid OLE control's cells. This control was created with fixed top and left side columns, used for column and row titles. You fill the title column and row first and then fill in the data area.

The Keystate OLE Control

The Keystate control provides user feedback on the state of a number of keys, including Caps Lock, Num Lock, Insert, and Scroll Lock. Your application also can query the state of these keys using the Keystate OLE control. You use one Keystate OLE control for each key whose state is to be monitored.

> **NOTE**
>
> Although Microsoft doesn't mention this, having two Keystate controls can lead to interesting results. Once I had the sample program running and the Keystate OLE control open in design mode at the same time. Whenever I pressed the Caps Lock key, the light would constantly flash at me. Interesting, but not quite the desired effect!

The Style property determines which key the control affects. A control can affect only one key at a time. At runtime, you turn a key on and off by setting the CKeystate::Value() property to TRUE and FALSE, respectively. The user can also change the state of a key at runtime by clicking a Keystate control or pressing the key itself.

The first 16 Keystate OLE controls automatically update their appearance when the user presses the corresponding key. If more than 16 Keystate OLE controls are defined, the subsequent controls will be visible, but their display won't be updated when the key is pressed.

To use the Keystate OLE control, first install it into your project. Once it's installed, your dialog editor tool palette (or toolbox) will have a new button for the Keystate OLE control; it will have a picture of a small key from a keyboard. (See Figure 17.10.) Next, open the dialog box that will receive the Keystate OLE control and locate your control. After you've located, sized, and named the control, you should set whatever properties you want (including defining the frame bitmaps) for the Keystate OLE control.

Figure 17.15 shows the sample Keystate OLE control, along with the Control Properties page. Notice that I've chosen to use the multistate type for this control.

FIGURE 17.15.

The Keystate OLE control located in a dialog, along with the property sheet.

After you've created your control in the dialog editor, start ClassWizard (while the dialog has focus, press Ctrl-W) and bind a `CKeystate` class variable to the control. The example uses a variable name of `m_Keystate` for this variable, as shown in Figure 17.16. Once the `CKeystate` class variable is bound to the control, you can work with the control in the dialog handler class, as shown in Listing 17.4.

FIGURE 17.16.

The Keystate OLE control bound `CKeystate` *variable in ClassWizard.*

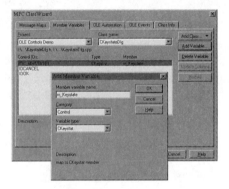

Listing 17.4. The KeystateDlg.CPP dialog box handler file.

```
// KeystateDlg.cpp : implementation file
//

#include "stdafx.h"
#include "OLE Controls Demo.h"
#include "KeystateDlg.h"

#ifdef _DEBUG
#define new DEBUG_NEW
#undef THIS_FILE
static char THIS_FILE[] = __FILE__;
#endif
```

```
/////////////////////////////////////////////////////////////////////////
// CKeystateDlg dialog


CKeystateDlg::CKeystateDlg(CWnd* pParent /*=NULL*/)
    : CDialog(CKeystateDlg::IDD, pParent)
{
    //{{AFX_DATA_INIT(CKeystateDlg)
        // NOTE: the ClassWizard will add member initialization here
    //}}AFX_DATA_INIT
}


void CKeystateDlg::DoDataExchange(CDataExchange* pDX)
{
    CDialog::DoDataExchange(pDX);
    //{{AFX_DATA_MAP(CKeystateDlg)
    DDX_Control(pDX, IDC_MHSTATE1, m_Keystate);
    //}}AFX_DATA_MAP
}


BEGIN_MESSAGE_MAP(CKeystateDlg, CDialog)
    //{{AFX_MSG_MAP(CKeystateDlg)
        // NOTE: the ClassWizard will add message map macros here
    //}}AFX_MSG_MAP
END_MESSAGE_MAP()

/////////////////////////////////////////////////////////////////////////
// CKeystateDlg message handlers

BEGIN_EVENTSINK_MAP(CKeystateDlg, CDialog)
    //{{AFX_EVENTSINK_MAP(CKeystateDlg)
    ON_EVENT(CKeystateDlg, IDC_MHSTATE1, 1 /*Change*/, OnChangeMhstate1, VTS_NONE)
    //}}AFX_EVENTSINK_MAP
END_EVENTSINK_MAP()

void CKeystateDlg::OnChangeMhstate1()
{
    // TODO: Add your control notification handler code here

    switch(m_Keystate.Get_Value())
    {
        case 0:
            MessageBox("Keystate is zero");
            break;
        case 1:
            MessageBox("Keystate is one");
            break;
        default:
            MessageBox("Keystate is undetermined!");
            break;
    }
}
```

You only needed to add code to receive the Keystate OLE control's change in state and report the state to the user. A typical application probably would set a member variable to reflect the Keystate OLE control's state and process this information as appropriate.

The Microsoft Communications OLE Control

The Microsoft Communications control is used to manipulate communications ports. Ports can be configured and I/O can be performed using this control. This control is an example of an OLE control that isn't visible in run mode.

The Microsoft Communications OLE control offers two methods of managing communications—event-driven and polling methods.

Event-driven communication allows the application to be notified directly when an event occurs. This technique is more efficient, because until an event occurs, the application isn't required to devote resources to communications. Typical events include reception of characters and changing the Carrier Detect (CD) or Request To Send (RTS) lines. To use event-driven communications, you would use event handlers. In such cases, you would use the communications control's OnComm event message to trap and handle these communications events. The OnComm event message can also be used to detect and handle communications errors. Figure 17.17 shows ClassWizard being used to include this handler.

FIGURE 17.17.
ClassWizard with the OnComm *event handled.*

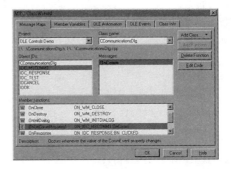

Your application also can manage the Microsoft Communications OLE control by polling for events. Using this technique, your application would at regular intervals check for received characters, errors, and changes in the state of the communications port status lines. Your application can also check for various events, errors, and changes in status after all critical functions. Microsoft suggests using polling when designing simple applications such as telephone dialers, because this method usually is less complex than using event handlers.

There is a one-to-one correlation between a Microsoft Communications OLE control and a communications port. For applications that need to access more than one port, you must have more than one Microsoft Communications OLE control. Also, each communications port can be reconfigured from Windows as necessary.

To use the Microsoft Communications OLE control, first install it into your project. Once it's installed, your dialog editor tool palette (or toolbox) will have a new button for the Microsoft Communications OLE control; it will have a picture of a small telephone. (See Figure 17.10.) Next, open the dialog box that will receive the Microsoft Communications OLE control and locate your control. After you've located, sized, and named the control, you should set whatever properties you want (including defining the frame bitmaps) for this control.

Figure 17.18 shows the sample Microsoft Communications OLE control, along with the Control Properties page. Notice that I've chosen to use the multistate type for this control.

FIGURE 17.18.

The Microsoft Communications OLE control located in a dialog, along with the property sheet.

After you've created your control in the dialog editor, start ClassWizard (while the dialog has focus, press Ctrl-W) and bind a `CCMSCommCtrl` class variable to the control. The example uses a variable name of `m_Communications` for this variable, as shown in Figure 17.19. Once the `CCMSCommCtrl` class variable is bound to the control, you can work with the control in the dialog handler class, as shown in Listing 17.5.

FIGURE 17.19.

The Microsoft Communications OLE control bound `CCMSCommCtrl` variable in ClassWizard.

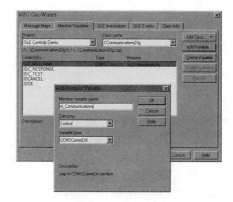

Listing 17.5. The CommunicationsDlg.CPP dialog box handler file.

```cpp
// CommunicationsDlg.cpp : implementation file
//

#include "stdafx.h"
#include "OLE Controls Demo.h"
#include "CommunicationsDlg.h"

#ifdef _DEBUG
#define new DEBUG_NEW
#undef THIS_FILE
static char THIS_FILE[] = __FILE__;
#endif

/////////////////////////////////////////////////////////////////////////////
// CCommunicationsDlg dialog


CCommunicationsDlg::CCommunicationsDlg(CWnd* pParent /*=NULL*/)
    : CDialog(CCommunicationsDlg::IDD, pParent)
{
    //{{AFX_DATA_INIT(CCommunicationsDlg)
    //}}AFX_DATA_INIT
}


void CCommunicationsDlg::DoDataExchange(CDataExchange* pDX)
{
    CDialog::DoDataExchange(pDX);
    //{{AFX_DATA_MAP(CCommunicationsDlg)
    DDX_Control(pDX, IDC_MSCOMM1, m_Communications);
    //}}AFX_DATA_MAP
}


BEGIN_MESSAGE_MAP(CCommunicationsDlg, CDialog)
    //{{AFX_MSG_MAP(CCommunicationsDlg)
    ON_BN_CLICKED(IDC_TEST, OnTest)
    ON_WM_CLOSE()
    ON_BN_CLICKED(IDC_RESPONSE, OnResponse)
    ON_WM_DESTROY()
    //}}AFX_MSG_MAP
END_MESSAGE_MAP()

/////////////////////////////////////////////////////////////////////////////
// CCommunicationsDlg message handlers

void CCommunicationsDlg::OnTest()
{
    // TODO: Add your control notification handler code here

    COleVariant    propVal;

    MessageBox(m_Communications.GetSettings());

    propVal = OLESTR("ATZ\r");
    m_Communications.SetOutput(propVal);
```

```
    propVal = OLESTR("ATDT 1 800 555 1212 \r");
    m_Communications.SetOutput(propVal);

TRACE("AT returned: '%s'\n", m_Communications.GetInput());
}

void CCommunicationsDlg::OnClose()
{
    // TODO: Add your message handler code here and/or call default

    TRACE("Closing the port...\n");
    m_Communications.SetPortOpen(FALSE);

    CDialog::OnClose();
}

BOOL CCommunicationsDlg::OnInitDialog()
{
    CDialog::OnInitDialog();

    // TODO: Add extra initialization here

    TRACE("Opening the port...\n");
    m_Communications.SetPortOpen(TRUE);

    return TRUE;  // Return TRUE unless you set the focus to a control
                  // EXCEPTION: OCX Property Pages should return FALSE
}

void CCommunicationsDlg::OnResponse()
{
    // TODO: Add your control notification handler code here

    MessageBox(m_Communications.GetInput());

}

void CCommunicationsDlg::OnDestroy()
{
    CDialog::OnDestroy();

    // TODO: Add your message handler code here

    TRACE("Closing the port in DESTROY...\n");
    m_Communications.SetPortOpen(FALSE);
}
```

The following code fragment shows the default OnComm event handler as created by ClassWizard for the sample Microsoft Communications OLE control. You would have to fill in code to determine which event occurred and to handle the event.

```
void CCommunicationsDlg::OnOnCommMscomm1()
{
    // TODO: Add your control notification handler code here

}
```

You need to add code to open the communications port when the control is made active and to close the communications port when the control is to be destroyed. This is easy to do. You use the `OnInitDialog()` and `OnDestroy()` handlers for this purpose. ClassWizard makes adding these handlers easy. Then you add two buttons that are basically used for testing—one called test, which resets the modem (sending the ATZ modem reset command) and then tells the modem to dial the telephone number 1-800-555-1212, and another button that will receive whatever characters are received from the modem and display them in a message box. A typical application probably would do more than simply dial directory information. This is work for the application designer.

The Microsoft Masked Edit OLE Control

The Microsoft Masked Edit OLE control lets you accept and display formatted input in your application. A typical example is the obtaining of a telephone number.

Typically, the Microsoft Masked Edit OLE control behaves much like a standard Windows text box control, with added enhancements for the optional masked input and formatted output. When you don't specify an input mask, the Microsoft Masked Edit OLE control is like a standard text box with the addition of dynamic data exchange (DDE) capabilities.

Masks, which are either defined at design stage or inserted at runtime, may have either placeholders or literal characters. For example, the mask (###) ###-####, used for telephone numbers, consists of literal characters (the characters (,), space, and -) and the placeholder character (#), which signifies a numeric value (the user would be unable to enter a character in this field). The Microsoft Masked Edit OLE control signals a `ValidationError` event message whenever the user tries to enter an invalid character.

To clear a Microsoft Masked Edit OLE control's `Text` property when you have a mask defined, you must set the mask to be an empty string and then set the `Text` property to an empty string, as the following code fragment shows:

```
m_MaskedEdit.SetMask("");
M_MaskedEdit.SetText("");
```

Typically, when a Microsoft Masked Edit OLE control's selection is copied to the Windows clipboard, the entire selection, including the mask's literals, is transferred to the clipboard (just like the `GetText()` function returns). You can use the `SetClipMode()` property to modify the transfer of data to the clipboard.

To use the Microsoft Masked Edit OLE control, first install it into your project. Once it's installed, your dialog editor tool palette (or toolbox) will have a new button for the Microsoft Masked Edit OLE control; it will have a picture of an edit mask (##¦). (See Figure 17.10.) Next, open the dialog box that will receive the Microsoft Masked Edit OLE control and locate your control. After you've located, sized, and named the control, you should set whatever properties you want (including defining the frame bitmaps) for this control.

Figure 17.20 shows the sample Microsoft Masked Edit OLE control, along with the Control Properties page. Notice that I've set the mask (for a telephone number) for this control.

FIGURE 17.20.

The Microsoft Masked Edit OLE control located in a dialog, along with the property sheet.

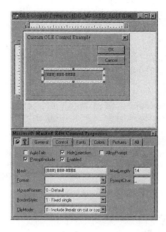

After you've created your control in the dialog editor, start ClassWizard (while the dialog has focus, press Ctrl-W) and bind a CMSmask class variable to the control. The example uses a variable name of m_MaskedEdit for this variable, as shown in Figure 17.21. Once the CMSmask class variable is bound to the control, you can work with the control in the dialog handler class, as shown in Listing 17.6.

FIGURE 17.21.

The Microsoft Masked Edit OLE control bound CMSmask variable in ClassWizard.

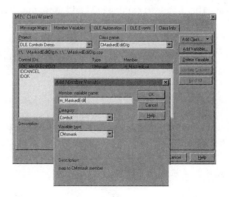

Listing 17.6. The MaskedEditDlg.CPP dialog box handler file.

```
// MaskedEditDlg.cpp : implementation file
//

#include "stdafx.h"
#include "OLE Controls Demo.h"
#include "MaskedEditDlg.h"
```

continues

Listing 17.6. continued

```
#ifdef _DEBUG
#define new DEBUG_NEW
#undef THIS_FILE
static char THIS_FILE[] = __FILE__;
#endif

/////////////////////////////////////////////////////////////////////////
// CMaskedEditDlg dialog


CMaskedEditDlg::CMaskedEditDlg(CWnd* pParent /*=NULL*/)
    : CDialog(CMaskedEditDlg::IDD, pParent)
{
    //{{AFX_DATA_INIT(CMaskedEditDlg)
        // NOTE: the ClassWizard will add member initialization here
    //}}AFX_DATA_INIT
}


void CMaskedEditDlg::DoDataExchange(CDataExchange* pDX)
{
    CDialog::DoDataExchange(pDX);
    //{{AFX_DATA_MAP(CMaskedEditDlg)
    DDX_Control(pDX, IDC_MASKEDBOX1, m_MaskedEdit);
    //}}AFX_DATA_MAP
}


BEGIN_MESSAGE_MAP(CMaskedEditDlg, CDialog)
    //{{AFX_MSG_MAP(CMaskedEditDlg)
        // NOTE: the ClassWizard will add message map macros here
    //}}AFX_MSG_MAP
END_MESSAGE_MAP()

/////////////////////////////////////////////////////////////////////////
// CMaskedEditDlg message handlers

BEGIN_EVENTSINK_MAP(CMaskedEditDlg, CDialog)
    //{{AFX_EVENTSINK_MAP(CMaskedEditDlg)
    ON_EVENT(CMaskedEditDlg, IDC_MASKEDBOX1, 1
        /* Change */, OnChangeMaskedbox1, VTS_NONE)
    //}}AFX_EVENTSINK_MAP
END_EVENTSINK_MAP()

void CMaskedEditDlg::OnChangeMaskedbox1()
{
    // TODO: Add your control notification handler code here

    TRACE("Masked Edit returned '%s'\n", m_MaskedEdit.GetText());
    TRACE("Masked Edit returned '%s' cliped\n", m_MaskedEdit.GetClipText());
}
```

In the Microsoft Masked Edit OLE control, you only added code to receive the Microsoft Masked Edit OLE control's OnChange event and report the control's current string to the user.

A typical application probably would set a member variable to reflect the Microsoft Masked Edit OLE control's contents and process this information as appropriate.

In the sample code, two strings are retrieved from the control. The first string, retrieved using `GetText()`, returns the string, including the mask characters. For example, if the user entered `8005551212`, `GetText()` would return (800)555-1212. However, `GetClipText()` would return just the user-entered data, 8005551212, exactly as the user entered it.

The Multimedia OLE Control

The Microsoft Multimedia OLE control lets your application display and manipulate multimedia clips, such as .AVI files.

The Microsoft Multimedia OLE control can be used to play back and record. This makes this control a very powerful tool for database programmers. Imagine a real estate database with tours through each property, all contained within a single, shared database.

To use the Microsoft Multimedia OLE control, first install it into your project. After it's installed, your dialog editor tool palette (or toolbox) will have a new button for the Microsoft Multimedia OLE control; it will have a picture of a clapper. (See Figure 17.10.) Next, open the dialog box that will receive the Microsoft Multimedia OLE control and locate your control. After you've located, sized, and named the control, you should set whatever properties you want (including defining the frame bitmaps) for this control.

Figure 17.22 shows the sample Microsoft Multimedia OLE control, along with the Control Properties page. Notice that I haven't specified a multimedia clip (I'll let the user choose what will be played, as shown in Listing 17.7), nor have I specified the control's type.

FIGURE 17.22.

The Microsoft Multimedia OLE control located in a dialog, along with the property sheet.

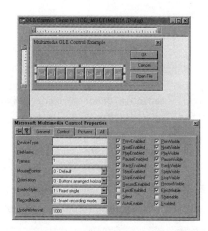

After you've created your control in the dialog editor, start ClassWizard (while the dialog has focus, press Ctrl-W) and bind a `CMciCtrl` class variable to the control. In the example, you use a variable name of m_Multimedia for this variable, as shown in Figure 17.23. Once the CMciCtrl class variable is bound to the control, you can work with the control in the dialog handler class, as shown in Listing 17.7.

FIGURE 17.23.

The Microsoft Multimedia OLE control bound CMciCtrl variable in ClassWizard.

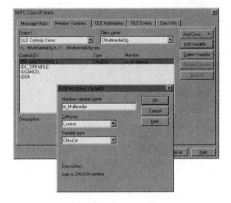

Listing 17.7. The MultimediaDlg.CPP dialog box handler file.

```cpp
// MultimediaDlg.cpp : implementation file
//

#include "stdafx.h"
#include "OLE Controls Demo.h"
#include "MultimediaDlg.h"

#ifdef _DEBUG
#define new DEBUG_NEW
#undef THIS_FILE
static char THIS_FILE[] = __FILE__;
#endif

/////////////////////////////////////////////////////////////////////////////
// CMultimediaDlg dialog


CMultimediaDlg::CMultimediaDlg(CWnd* pParent /*=NULL*/)
    : CDialog(CMultimediaDlg::IDD, pParent)
{
    //{{AFX_DATA_INIT(CMultimediaDlg)
        // NOTE: the ClassWizard will add member initialization here
    //}}AFX_DATA_INIT
}


void CMultimediaDlg::DoDataExchange(CDataExchange* pDX)
{
    CDialog::DoDataExchange(pDX);
    //{{AFX_DATA_MAP(CMultimediaDlg)
    DDX_Control(pDX, IDC_MMCONTROL1, m_Multimedia);
    //}}AFX_DATA_MAP
}
```

```
BEGIN_MESSAGE_MAP(CMultimediaDlg, CDialog)
    //{{AFX_MSG_MAP(CMultimediaDlg)
    ON_WM_DESTROY()
    ON_BN_CLICKED(IDC_OPENFILE, OnOpenfile)
    //}}AFX_MSG_MAP
END_MESSAGE_MAP()

/////////////////////////////////////////////////////////////////////////////
// CMultimediaDlg message handlers

BOOL CMultimediaDlg::OnInitDialog()
{
    CDialog::OnInitDialog();

    // TODO: Add extra initialization here

// If you hard code an MCI clip, you can open the control in
// the dialog's initializer by calling Set_Command("Open"); -
// m_Multimedia.Set_Command("Open");

    return TRUE;  // Return TRUE unless you set the focus to a control
                  // EXCEPTION: OCX Property Pages should return FALSE
}


void CMultimediaDlg::OnDestroy()
{
    CDialog::OnDestroy();

    // TODO: Add your message handler code here

    if (m_Multimedia.GetMode() != 524 /* mciModeOpen */)
    {// Close Multimedia control if it's open...
        m_Multimedia.Set_Command("Close");
    }
}

void CMultimediaDlg::OnOpenfile()
{
    // TODO: Add your control notification handler code here

    // You can support the following types of MCI sources:
    // AVIVideo, CDAudio, DAT, DigitalVideo, MMMovie,
    // Other, Overlay, Scanner, Sequencer, VCR, Videodisc,
    // and WaveAudio.

    CFileDialog dlg(TRUE,
        NULL,
        "*.avi",
        OFN_OVERWRITEPROMPT,
        "AVI Files (*.avi) | *.avi | "
        "WAV Files (*.wav) | *.wav | "
        "All Files (*.*) | *.* ||");

    if (dlg.DoModal())
```

continues

Listing 17.7. continued

```
    {
        TRACE("File selected is '%s'\n", dlg.GetFileName());

        if (m_Multimedia.GetMode() != 524 /* mciModeOpen */)
        {// Close Multimedia control if it's already opened...
            m_Multimedia.Set_Command("Close");
        }

        m_Multimedia.SetFileName(dlg.GetFileName());
        m_Multimedia.Set_Command("Open");
    }
}
```

You needed to add code to allow the user to open a multimedia clip. (We chose a default file type of .AVI, but the user can actually open any supported type.) If you had set the Microsoft Multimedia OLE control's clip at design time, you would have had to open the control only when it was being initialized. The comments in Listing 17.7 show how this might be done.

In this listing, a `CFileDialog` class object is used to get the file name of a multimedia file. In the past, programmers had to write hundreds of lines of code to display a simple dialog to let the user select a file to be opened. Now, with MFC 4, you can display an advanced dialog box with only two lines of code—the allocator/constructor and `DoModal()`.

The PicClip OLE Control

The PicClip control (actually called the Picture Clip control) lets your application obtain a portion of a bitmap easily. This control is an example of an OLE control that isn't visible in run mode.

The Picture Clip OLE control is an efficient method of storing multiple picture (bitmap or icon) resources. Rather than using several bitmaps or icons, you can create a bitmap that will contain all the images (in a tiled arrangement) needed by the application. To access an individual image, you would use the Picture Clip OLE control to select the region in the source bitmap that contains the desired image. Typical applications might be toolbox images, for example.

To use the Picture Clip OLE control, first install it into your project. Once it's installed, your dialog editor tool palette (or toolbox) will have a new button for the Picture Clip OLE control; it will have a picture mapped to a grid. (See Figure 17.10.) Next, open the dialog box that will receive the Picture Clip OLE control and locate your control. After you've located, sized, and named the control, you should set whatever properties you wish (including defining the frame bitmaps) for this control.

Figure 17.24 shows the sample Picture Clip OLE control, along with the Rows/Cols Control Properties page.

FIGURE 17.24.

The Picture Clip OLE control located in a dialog, along with the property sheet.

After you've created your control in the dialog editor, start ClassWizard (while the dialog has focus, press Ctrl-W) and bind a `CPicClipCtrl` class variable to the control. In the example, you use a variable name of `m_PicClip` for this variable, as shown in Figure 17.25. Once the `CPicClipCtrl` class variable is bound to the control, you can work with the control in the dialog handler class, as shown in Listing 17.8.

FIGURE 17.25.

The Picture Clip OLE control bound CPicClipCtrl variable in ClassWizard.

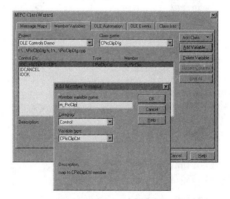

Listing 17.8. The PicClipDlg.CPP dialog box handler file.

```
// PicClipDlg.cpp : implementation file
//

#include "stdafx.h"
#include "OLE Controls Demo.h"
#include "PicClipDlg.h"

#ifdef _DEBUG
#define new DEBUG_NEW
#undef THIS_FILE
static char THIS_FILE[] = __FILE__;
#endif
```

continues

Listing 17.8. continued

```
/////////////////////////////////////////////////////////////////////////
// CPicClipDlg dialog


CPicClipDlg::CPicClipDlg(CWnd* pParent /*=NULL*/)
    : CDialog(CPicClipDlg::IDD, pParent)
{
    //{{AFX_DATA_INIT(CPicClipDlg)
        // NOTE: the ClassWizard will add member initialization here
    //}}AFX_DATA_INIT
}


void CPicClipDlg::DoDataExchange(CDataExchange* pDX)
{
    CDialog::DoDataExchange(pDX);
    //{{AFX_DATA_MAP(CPicClipDlg)
    DDX_Control(pDX, IDC_PICTURECLIP1, m_PicClip);
    //}}AFX_DATA_MAP
}


BEGIN_MESSAGE_MAP(CPicClipDlg, CDialog)
    //{{AFX_MSG_MAP(CPicClipDlg)
    //}}AFX_MSG_MAP
END_MESSAGE_MAP()

/////////////////////////////////////////////////////////////////////////
// CPicClipDlg message handlers

BOOL CPicClipDlg::OnInitDialog()
{
    CDialog::OnInitDialog();

    // TODO: Add extra initialization here

    m_PicClip.SetClipX(10);
    m_PicClip.SetClipY(10);

    m_PicClip.SetClipHeight(20);
    m_PicClip.SetClipWidth(20);

//  The PicClip control doesn't do much by itself. The output must
//  be retrieved using the GetPicture() member function and then
//  be displayed or manipulated as desired.

    return TRUE;  // Return TRUE unless you set the focus to a control
                  // EXCEPTION: OCX Property Pages should return FALSE
}
```

You only added code to specify the area of the bitmap that was to be used. A typical application would retrieve the bitmap from the Picture Clip OLE control and use it.

Summary

This chapter described the usage of OLE controls. Topics included the steps involved in adding OLE controls to applications, such as an Access database form. You also saw how to add controls to Visual C++ 4 projects by selecting Insert | Component. This chapter also showed you how to install an OLE control into Windows.

You also learned about the standard Microsoft OLE controls supplied with Visual C++ 4. These controls include the Anibutton, the Grid control, the Keystate control, the Microsoft Communications control, the Microsoft Masked Edit control, the Microsoft Multimedia control, and the PicClip control.

18

Translating Visual Basic for Applications Code to Visual C++

Until the advent of Visual C++ 4, the premier database front-end generator was Visual Basic. Visual Basic offered programmers the necessary database access tools. Although earlier versions of Visual C++ did offer ODBC (both with MFC and call-level interfaces), access to the very powerful Microsoft Jet database engine was missing from Visual C++ until version 4 was released. This resulted in many database front-end applications being written in Visual Basic.

Some database developers will want to convert from Visual Basic to the more advanced object-oriented programming language that Visual C++ offers. Not all Visual Basic programmers will convert (which is why the book *Database Developer's Guide with Visual Basic 4* exists), but for database developers who need to convert applications from Visual Basic for Applications or Visual Basic to Visual C++, this chapter might help.

If I don't sound too positive about converting database applications that are written using Visual Basic, it's because there are major differences between Basic and C/C++ programming. There is no simple, easy way to do a conversion. No set of global changes, no magic incantations, no secret words exist to make the conversion easier. Hard work and a thorough understanding of Basic programming are the tools that will make for a successful conversion. Generally, this chapter concentrates on Visual Basic for Applications. If you're writing Visual Basic applications (using either Visual Basic 3 or 4), you'll see differences, but nothing too extensive. Generally, this chapter uses the terms *Visual Basic* and *Visual Basic for Applications* interchangeably. For most conversions, the flavor of Visual Basic isn't a crucial issue.

Fortunately, Visual C++ 4 offers some interesting tools to help you do the conversions. First, you can convert a Visual Basic form into a dialog box by using the Resource Editor and importing the Visual Basic form as a dialog box. Generally, many of the controls that are part of the Visual Basic form will also be imported, but there are some notable exceptions. You can't convert VBX controls in a form if the VBX control wasn't installed with the project. (Because VBX controls are 16-bit, they won't work in a 32-bit Visual C++ 4 application.) Also, some controls that are native to Visual Basic are noted for causing problems when forms are converted. Don't expect Visual Basic nested controls to be converted or to perform correctly, either. You will end up with a dialog box that has many of the standard controls correctly placed, but you will need to add or simulate any specialized controls.

The following is a list of some Visual Basic controls that won't be fully converted when a Visual Basic form is imported into Visual C++ 4.0:

■ Drive and directory list boxes. These controls will be converted to standard Windows list boxes that your code can then fill as needed. You probably will want to use the file open common dialog boxes for most filename management.

■ MDI forms will be imported as normal dialog boxes. The menu will be ignored, but you can have a menu in a dialog box if you implement it yourself. (For an example of a menu in a dialog box, refer to page 677 of *Programming Windows 95 Unleashed* (Sams Publishing, 1995).)

■ Data controls aren't supported.

■ Line and shape controls aren't supported.

■ Horizontal and vertical scroll bars. You can use standard scroll bars if needed.

■ Timers aren't supported. Use a custom implementation or an OLE custom control.

■ Printers aren't supported.

■ Screens aren't supported.

■ Clipboards aren't supported.

■ Queries aren't supported.

■ Applications aren't supported.

It's also possible to convert a Visual Basic VBX control into an OLE Custom Control using the VBX Template Tool, which is part of Visual C++ 1.5x and Visual C++ 2.x. In the long run, it would probably be easier to simply fully rewrite the VBX as an OLE control.

NOTE

The VBX Template Tool is no longer part of Visual C++ as of version 4.0. If you need to convert a VBX control, you must either use Visual C++ 2.x or perform the conversion by hand. Thanks to Microsoft's subscription program, many Visual C++ 4.x programmers still have old copies of Visual C++ 2.x on hand.

There are a variety of reasons for migrating (also called *porting*) an Access database application written in Visual Basic for Applications to Visual C++—reasons that are discussed in earlier chapters of this book. Whatever the motive for migrating the application, you need to convert Access macro actions to Visual C++ event-handling functions and deal with reserved words, such as DoCmd, that are recognized by Access's interpreter but not Visual C++.

The most common method of responding to events in Access applications is to use one or more of Access's 40-plus macro commands. Macros, rather than Visual Basic for Applications functions, are the default event handlers of Access. Microsoft added an application-specific macro language to Access at the same time that the company's programmers were working hard to supplant specialized macro languages in Microsoft's other mainstream applications with dialects of Object Basic. The final result of this process is Visual Basic for Applications, which is part of most Microsoft Office applications (Access, Word, and Excel all have Visual Basic for Applications). Access also has its own specialized macro language. The goal of adding macros to Access was to create a desktop relational database development environment for Windows that didn't require writing code. Microsoft almost achieved its goal, at least if you don't consider complex macros with conditional execution and looping statements to be "code." The missing element is the IsLoaded("FormName") Visual Basic for Applications function that almost every Access application needs.

This chapter begins by showing you how to convert a Visual Basic form to a Visual C++ dialog box. This is followed by an explanation of how to convert applications written with Access's Visual Basic for Applications that are based primarily on macros as event handlers. Most Access applications use macros to control the execution of Access applications in response to user- or application-generated events. All of the code used in this chapter is from Access 7's NorthWind database example. The NorthWind database application is basically written using Access macros, with supporting routines written in Visual Basic for Applications.

Converting Visual Basic Forms to Visual C++ Dialog Boxes

Wow, you mean we can really do that? Short answer: Yes. For Visual Basic code, however, Access's Visual Basic for Applications is a different story. Forms are stored in the database and generally aren't accessible by external applications such as Visual C++ 4. Long answer: You will have problems with Visual Basic, and you will have to do substantial work by hand for any but the most trivial form. With Visual Basic for Applications, you might as well start from scratch: You will have to lay out a dialog box by hand, probably using a screen print of the original Access Visual Basic for Applications form. Because only Visual Basic forms (not Visual Basic for Applications forms) can be converted, this section applies only to Visual Basic.

Follow these steps to convert a Visual Basic form to a Visual C++ dialog box:

1. In Visual C++, select Insert | Resource. You see the Insert Resource dialog box, shown in Figure 18.1.

FIGURE 18.1.

Visual C++'s Insert Resource dialog box.

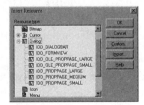

2. Click the Import button on the right side of the Insert Resource dialog. Visual C++ will display the Import Resource dialog box, shown in Figure 18.2.
3. Select the Visual Basic Forms (*.frm) file type in the list box. Then select the Visual Basic form to be imported.

You will usually get a series of messages from Visual C++ when you import Visual Basic controls. Typically, these messages will include the following:

■ `The OLE control "control" is not installed in the project.`

■ `Syntax error in VB form description.`

■ The form's binary data file "*data*.FRX" cannot be opened.

For the first two errors, you will be given the opportunity to edit the VBX source. Be aware that it will take a substantial amount of work to convert the form when you receive these errors.

FIGURE 18.2.

Visual C++'s Import Resource dialog box.

NOTE

What is a Visual Basic .FRM file? Basically (pun intended), a .FRM file is the equivalent of both a dialog box definition and the handlers for the controls in the dialog box. You could look at it as a mixture of a dialog resource and the CDialog object implementation.

Deciding on the Structure of Your Converted Visual C++ Application

Before you begin converting Visual Basic for Applications code to Visual C++, you need to determine how to structure your application. Although this chapter is devoted primarily to importing Visual Basic for Applications code into C and C++ modules and Visual C++ functions that serve as event handlers, your migration strategy can affect how you go through the importation process. The following sections explain the use of Visual C++ MDI forms and dialog boxes to duplicate the windowing environment of Access and how to duplicate Access menus and forms.

Emulating Access Forms with Visual C++ MDI Windows

Access database applications use MDI child windows to display

■ Data tables

■ All Access forms

■ Other visible objects, such as the Database window and datasheet views of Table objects

■ The query result sets returned by QueryDef or *ad hoc* queries

■ The design views of all Access database objects

You open the MDI parent window by executing Access and opening a database. Many modern Windows applications with any degree of complexity use an MDI parent window together with as many MDI child windows as are necessary to accomplish the objectives of the application and the user.

NOTE

With the more document-centric model of Windows 95, Microsoft recommends not using the MDI interface for applications. For applications that simply provide multiple views of a single object, the MDI interface is acceptable. Microsoft recommends that a single instance of an application not open more than one document at a time.

You don't need to use MDI forms for a simple data-entry application. MDI is overkill for single-purpose, transaction-processing applications that might employ a dialog view, a form view (CFormView), or a few modal dialog boxes for input prompting or list selection. However, unless you have a compelling reason not to do so, you can use Visual C++'s MDI form for multiform Access applications. Create an MDI parent form and then add MDI child windows that correspond to each of the forms of your Access application. Using form views and MDI in the same application is an accepted practice. Microsoft includes several examples of this, including the CheckBook program in the \MSDEV\SAMPLES\MFC\ADVANCED\CHKBOOK folder on the Visual C++ 4 CD.

NOTE

A second method of creating a form-based application that has more than one view of the data is to use an SDI CFormView class and use simple dialog boxes to emulate the other forms in the application. You can have multiple dialog boxes open at a time by making the dialog boxes modeless. A number of applications use modeless dialog boxes as status windows. Visual C++'s properties boxes are one example.

You can use the Database Documentor add-in tool supplied with Access to create a table that lists the forms in your Access application, together with supplemental tables that list the control objects contained in each of the forms. Figure 18.3 shows a page from Access's Database Documentor for the Categories form. The full report is included on the CD that comes with this book in the CHAPTR18 folder as CATFORM.TXT. Typically, this approach will quickly lead to a severe case of information overload. This report contains a massive amount of information, as a quick perusal of CATFORM.TXT will show.

FIGURE 18.3.

Access's Database Documentor showing the Categories form.

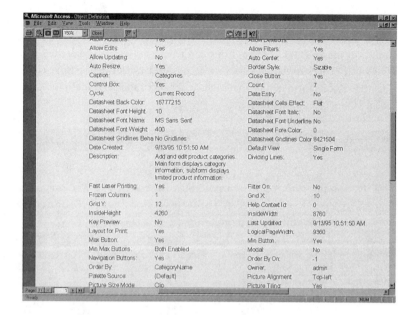

Another approach is to use FMS Inc.'s Total Access documenting application to create printed listings of all the database objects of your Access application. Total Access is described in Chapter 22, "Documenting Your Database Applications."

TIP

Whether you choose to use Database Documentor, acquire Total Access, create and print screen shots, or use a yellow pad and pencil, you need to create a written inventory of the objects of the Access application, especially objects that won't be accessible with Visual C++'s data-access classes. You can't open Access forms, reports, macros, or modules in Visual C++ applications.

Handling Access Object Names in Visual C++

Visual C++ uses dialog boxes to emulate Access forms. You can identify a dialog box with either an identifier (which is actually an integer) or a string. The best choice is to use an identifier (which is the Visual C++ default); it offers slightly better performance and better conforms to the Visual C++ standards for dialog box names. The documentation that accompanies Access encourages the use of spaces in form and report names, as well as in the names of other Access database objects. Visual C++ programmers usually use mixed-case names (such as StockReportDialog), because spaces aren't allowed in C and C++ names. Some programmers use underscores (such as stock_report_dialog) or a mixture of underscores and mixed case. Names with spaces or illegal punctuation can be referenced as literal strings enclosed in double quotation marks ("Table Name") but can't be used to name a Visual C++ object. Visual C++ can handle spaces in database object names, but not in dialog box template names. You need to change Access form names that include spaces or special punctuation symbols to create proper Visual C++ object variable names.

> **NOTE**
>
> If you or the author of the application have complied with the Leszinsky-Reddick (L-R) naming conventions proposed for Access variable and object names, you might want to rename your forms. With few exceptions, the L-R naming convention for Access variable and object names doesn't correspond to the Microsoft object-naming conventions for Visual C++ objects (commonly referred to as *Hungarian Notation*). Naming conventions for Access objects, based on the L-R conventions, appear in Chapter 3 of the *Visual Basic Programmer's Guide.* Naming conventions for Visual C++ objects appear in Appendix B, "Naming and Formatting Conventions for Visual C++ Objects and Variables."

Converting Menu Macros

Menu macros are the easiest of all Access macros to convert to Visual C++. Because you can't execute the AddMenu action with the Visual Basic for Applications DoCmd statement, converting Access menu macros to Visual C++ menus is discussed in this section of the chapter rather than in the next section, which deals directly with code conversion. To make the conversion, just duplicate the menu structure defined by the hierarchy of macros that employ the AddMenu action with entries in Visual C++'s menu resource editor window for each of the menu items of your Access application that you have reconstructed as Visual C++ forms. You then can use ClassWizard to add event handlers for the menu items.

With Visual C++, you typically have a single menu structure for the entire application rather than a menu for each form or MDI child window. If the Access application doesn't use its own set of macros, you can add a minimal menu structure to the MDI parent form. A minimal menu structure consists of the following elements, all of which are generated automatically when you use AppWizard to create your application shell:

- A File menu with a single option, Exit. You can tell AppWizard to add print support; however, a form view application doesn't directly support printing, so you will have to create the print routines yourself.
- An Edit menu with Undo, Cut, Copy, and Paste selections. If your application can't implement these actions (and that isn't good programming practice), you should

delete whichever menu items in the Edit menu can't be implemented. If none can be implemented, eliminate the entire Edit menu.

■ A Record menu that lets the user navigate between records in the dataset. Virtually all database applications need record selection menu and toolbar support.

■ A View menu that lets the user display or hide the toolbar and status bar. If you don't include toolbars and status bars in the application, this menu selection won't be present.

■ A Window menu that provides a submenu with the MDI window arrangement commands (Tile, Cascade, and Arrange Icons), plus the Window List option, which is separated from the arrangement commands with a horizontal bar. You need to display the Window menu only if you want to let the user choose between viewing more than one MDI child window at a time or to be able to select the active window from a menu rather than from a button bar. MFC does most of the work in creating and managing the MDI windows, so you will usually be able to rely on MFC's implementation of the Window menu.

■ A Help menu with at least one submenu choice, About, which displays the application's name, version number, and copyright information. For a professional application, you should include context-sensitive help using AppWizard's "include context-sensitive help" option.

TIP

If a help file is available for your Access application and you duplicate the structure of the Access application with your Visual C++ derivative, you can use the same help file, making only minor edits to account for the somewhat different structure of the Visual C++ version. Like Access forms, each Visual C++ dialog box and control has its own `HelpContextID` property. Access lets you assign different values to the `HelpFile` property of each form.

If your Access application uses multiple help files, you can call the `WinHelp()` API function in your Visual C++ code to display the specific help file for a dialog or situation. It's usually easier to call the `WinHelp()` function than to re-create a single help file from a collection. You might find that `HelpContextID` values are duplicated in the combined files if you combine a collection of help files.

Converting Macro Actions to Visual C++

Access applications that rely primarily on macros for event handling require more effort to convert to Visual C++ than applications that use Visual Basic for Applications code for event handling. You need to translate macros into Visual C++ event-handling code. Most Visual Basic for Applications functions import into Visual C++ modules but must be rewritten to C/C++ code. It's possible to do a line-by-line conversion of Visual Basic for Applications (or, for that matter, Visual Basic) code. The following sections provide a cross-reference between Access and Visual C++ events and list the Visual C++ methods and properties that correspond to Access macro actions.

Events That Trigger Macro Actions

Visual C++ has a much broader repertoire of general-purpose events than Access, but Access offers finer granularity in events that are related to forms and controls bound to database objects. *Granularity* is a term used by programmers to define the degree of precision of control (sometimes called *resolution*) that you can achieve with a language's code. (Granularity is similar to the term *graininess*, which is used in photography to describe the size of the grains of silver halide that form the image. The grain size determines the potential sharpness or acuity of an image.) In the documentation that accompanies Access, Microsoft refers to Access events as *properties*, presumably because events are included in Access's Properties window list for forms and controls. This book uses the term *event* rather than *property*.

An example of the fine granularity of Access events triggered by bound controls is the sequence of OnEnter, BeforeUpdate, AfterUpdate, and OnExit events that occur when you update the value of a field of the current record. Table 18.1 lists Access events and their equivalent Visual C++ events (where an equivalent exists). Table 18.1 shows that Visual C++ offers the WM_INITDIALOG, CRecordset::Update(), and WM_CLOSE (or WM_EXIT) events, which correspond to Access's OnEnter, BeforeUpdate, and OnExit events, respectively. However, there is no Visual C++ event that directly corresponds to Access's AfterUpdate event, and the CRecordSet::Update() function performs a number of functions. The OnCurrent event also isn't available in Visual C++. There is no direct substitute or universal workaround for the OnCurrent event.

Table 18.1. Visual Basic for Applications events and corresponding Visual C++ events.

Event	Object It Applies To	Occurrence in Access	Visual C++ Event
AfterDelConfirm	Forms	After the user confirms a deletion and the record is actually deleted or the deletion is canceled.	Use CRecordset member functions to manage this event.
AfterInsert	Forms	After a new record is added.	Use CRecordset member functions to manage this event.

Event	Object It Applies To	Occurrence in Access	Visual C++ Event
AfterUpdate	Forms and controls	After a change to a record is made permanent.	Use CRecordset::Update() to manage updating.
BeforeDelConfirm	Forms	After the user deletes one or more records, and before Access displays a confirmation dialog box.	Write a custom handler for CRecordset.
BeforeInsert	Forms	When the user types the first character in a new record.	Write a custom handler for CRecordset.
BeforeUpdate	Forms and controls	Before a change to a record is made permanent.	Use CRecordset::Update() to manage updating.
OnActivate	Forms and reports	When a form or report receives focus and becomes the active window.	Write and use the WM_INITDIALOG handler.
OnApplyFilter	Forms	When the user chooses Records | Filter | Apply Filter/Sort or clicks the Apply Filter button on the toolbar.	No equivalent.
OnChange	Controls (combo box, text box) on a form	When the contents of a text box or the text portion of a combo box change.	Use a CComboBox or CListBox object and an ON_LBN_SELCHANGE handler.
OnClick	Forms and controls	When the user presses and then releases the mouse button over an object.	Use the appropriate control object.

continues

Table 18.1. continued

Event	Object It Applies To	Occurrence in Access	Visual C++ Event
OnClose	Forms and reports	When a form is closed, but before it disappears.	Create and code a handler for the WM_CLOSE message.
OnCurrent	Forms	Before a record becomes the current record.	Use the CRecordset::OnMove() function.
OnDblClick*	Forms and controls	When the user double-clicks an object.	Use the appropriate control object.
OnDeactivate	Forms and reports	When a form or report loses focus.	Write a WM_CLOSE handler for the dialog box.
OnDelete	Forms	Before deleting a record.	Use CRecordset::Delete() to perform this functionality.
OnEnter	Controls	When a control receives focus.	No equivalent.
OnError	Forms and reports	When a runtime error is produced in Access.	No equivalent.
OnExit	Controls	When focus is lost.	Handle the BN_CLICKED message.
OnFilter	Forms	When the user chooses Records | Filter | Filter By Form.	No equivalent.
OnFormat	Report sections	When Access determines which data belongs in a report section.	No equivalent.
OnGotFocus	Forms and controls	When a form or control receives focus.	Use the appropriate control object.

Event	Object It Applies To	Occurrence in Access	Visual C++ Event
OnKeyDown	Forms and controls	When the user presses a key while a form or control has focus.	Use the appropriate control object.
OnKeyPress	Forms and controls	When the user presses and releases a key or key combination.	Use the appropriate control object.
OnKeyUp	Forms and controls	When the user releases a key while a form or control has focus.	Use the appropriate control object.
OnLoad	Forms	When a form is opened and its records are displayed.	Use the WM_INITDIALOG handler.
OnLostFocus	Forms and controls	When a form or control loses focus.	No equivalent. Dialogs generally can call GetFocus() to determine which window has focus.
OnMouseDown	Forms and controls	When the user presses the mouse button.	Use the appropriate control object.
OnMouseMove	Forms and controls	When the user moves the mouse.	Use the appropriate control object.
OnMouseUp	Forms and controls	When the user releases the mouse button.	Use the appropriate control object.
OnNoData	Reports	After a report is formatted and has no data.	No equivalent.

continues

Table 18.1. continued

Event	Object It Applies To	Occurrence in Access	Visual C++ Event
OnNotInList	Controls	When the user enters a value in the text box portion of a combo box that isn't in the combo box list.	No equivalent.
OnOpen	Forms and reports	On opening a form before the first record is displayed.	Add a handler for the WM_INITDIALOG message.
OnPage	Reports	After a page of a report is formatted for printing, but before the page is printed.	No equivalent.
OnPrint	Report sections	When data in a report section is formatted for printing, but before the section is printed.	No equivalent.
OnResize	Forms	When a form is opened and whenever the size of a form changes.	Write a handler for the WM_SIZE message. Most dialog boxes don't allow for resizing. Database applications using the CFormView class should probably monitor resizing requests.
OnRetreat	Report sections	Occurs when Access returns to a previous report section during report formatting.	No equivalent.

Event	Object It Applies To	Occurrence in Access	Visual C++ Event
OnTimer	Forms	When the interval specified by the form's TimerInterval property elapses.	Create a timer with the desired interval.
OnUnload	Forms	When a form is closed but not yet removed.	Handle the WM_CLOSE message.
OnUpdated	Controls	When an OLE object's data has been modified.	No direct equivalent.

Actions That Manipulate Forms, Reports, and Controls

Many of the Access macro actions that manipulate forms and controls have corresponding Visual C++ functionality. Creating reports using the ReportEase, ReportSmith, or Crystal Reports products in Visual C++ applications differs greatly from using Access's integrated report generator, as discussed in Chapter 12, "Printing Reports with Report Generators." Thus, Access macro actions that pertain to reports don't have Visual C++ counterparts. See Table 18.2 for a few examples of macro actions and possible Visual C++ workarounds.

Table 18.2. Visual C++ counterparts of Access form and control actions.

Access Action	Purpose	Visual C++ Substitute
Close (form or report)	Closes a form or report object.	Use CWnd::OnClose().
GoToControl	Sets the focus to a control on a form.	Use CWnd::SetFocus().
Maximize, Minimize, Restore	Sets the window style of a form.	Use SetWindowPlacement().
MoveSize	Determines the size and position of a form.	Use either SetWindowPos() or SetWindowPlacement().
OpenForm	Opens and displays a form.	Use CDialog::DoModal().

continues

Table 18.2. continued

Access Action	Purpose	Visual C++ Substitute
OpenReport	Opens a report for print preview or printing.	No equivalent.
Print	Prints the active object (forms only).	No equivalent.
RepaintObject	Redraws the selected object.	Use CWnd::Invalidate().
Requery	Updates a specified control.	Use CDatabase::Close(), and then modify m_strFilter to reflect the new WHERE parameters. Then reopen the datasource with CDatabase::Open().
SetValue	Sets the value of a property (macros only).	No equivalent.

Generally it's not difficult to add reporting on Access databases using Crystal Reports, because it's included with Visual C++ 4. If you need to distribute the Crystal Reports report designer, it's possible to license the report designer for redistribution.

You can create reports using the more traditional method of simply writing the code. However, using a report generator package will provide a much more professional product with much less effort. Visual C++ and MFC don't have any built-in report generation facilities. You will have to create your own reporting system if you don't use a report generator such as Crystal Reports. Generally, most programmers find that it isn't cost effective to design and code the report generation portions of their applications.

Actions That Manipulate Database Objects

The Access macro actions listed in Table 18.3 manipulate Access's equivalent of a Visual C++ data-access object. It's important to bear in mind the distinctions between the Access Table and QueryDef objects that underlie Access forms and reports and the same database objects opened in Visual C++. Using Access, you can manipulate only the record pointer of a Table or QueryDef object to which an Access form or report is bound with Access macro actions. Visual C++ lets you manipulate the record pointer of a data control directly with the Move...() functions. The only Access macro action you can't imitate directly in Visual C++ is an OpenQuery action that specifies a search parameter. Visual C++ CDatabase objects must be closed and then reopened with a new m_strFilter string.

Table 18.3. Visual C++ counterparts of Access database object manipulation actions.

Access Action	Purpose	Visual C++ CRecordSet Substitute
Close (Table or QueryDef object)	Closes a database object.	Use CRecordSet::Close().
FindNext	Finds the next record that meets specified criteria.	Use CRecordSet::MoveNext().
FindRecord	Finds the first record that meets specified criteria.	Use CRecordSet::MoveFirst().
GoToRecord	Goes to the record specified by an argument value (previous, next, first, last, record number, new record).	Use CRecordSet::Move().
OpenQuery	Opens a QueryDef object in datasheet, design, or print preview views, or executes an action query.	Close the current query using CRecordSet::Close(), modify the m_strFilter to specify the WHERE clause, and then use CRecordSet::Open()to reopen the recordset with the new query value.
OpenTable	Opens a specified Table object in datasheet, design, or print preview views.	Use CRecordSet::Open().

Actions That Translate Directly to Visual C++ or Windows Functions

Many of Access's general-purpose macro actions have exact counterparts in Visual C++ and Windows. Table 18.4 lists Access macro actions that are duplicated in Visual C++ and Windows.

Table 18.4. Access macro actions that have exact Visual C++ counterparts.

Access Action	Purpose	Visual C++ Substitute
Hourglass	Turns the mouse pointer into the hourglass shape.	Use the `CCmdTarget::BeginWaitCursor()` function.
MsgBox	Displays a message box with an optional title.	Use either `AFXMessageBox()` or `::MessageBox()`.
Quit	Exits the Access application.	Send a message to the application to quit. Typical AFX programs send a `WM_COMMAND` message with the `ID_APP_EXIT` parameter to simulate the selection of eXit from the main menu.
RunApp	Runs another Windows application.	Use `LoadModule()` to do this.
SendKeys	Sends keystrokes to the application that has the focus.	Send a `WM_CHAR` message.
Beep	Sounds the standard Windows message beep.	Use `::MessageBeep()`.

Actions with No Direct Counterpart in Visual C++

Table 18.5 lists the Access macro actions that have no direct equivalents in Visual C++. Some of the actions listed, such as RunMacro, StopMacro, and StopAllMacros, aren't applicable to Visual C++ because you convert all Access macros to Visual C++ functions. Menus you create in Visual C++'s resource edit menu windows substitute for Access menus created by the AddMenu action. There is no need to use the Echo False and Echo True actions in Visual C++ applications, because you don't need to inhibit screen repainting.

In cases where a macro action listed in Table 18.5 is applicable to Visual C++ programming methodology, a workaround usually exists or can be created with Visual C++ code. Some workarounds are simpler than others. You can use flags to selectively execute event-handling code to duplicate the effect of the CancelEvent action. On the other hand, a substantial amount of code and programming expertise is required to write a workaround for Visual C++'s lack of Access's TransferSpreadsheet action. However, you can use OLE Automation to export data to an Excel worksheet object and then save the worksheet.

Table 18.5. Access macro actions with no direct Visual C++ counterparts.

Access Action	Purpose	Visual C++ Workaround
AddMenu	Adds a menu or submenu choice to a form and specifies the macro or function to execute.	Use the CMenu member functions such as InsertMenu().
ApplyFilter	Applies a WHERE clause filter to a Table or QueryDef object.	Use CRecordSet::Close(), modify m_strFilter to specify the WHERE clause, and then use CRecordSet::Open() to reopen the recordset with the new query value.
CancelEvent	Cancels the event that initiated the macro execution.	End the function.
DoMenuItem	Executes a menu choice.	Call the OnItem() menu Item handler.
Echo	Halts repainting of most visible objects.	Not applicable. Ignore Echo actions.
GoToPage	Sets the focus to the first control of the specified page of a multipage form.	Not applicable. Multi-page forms aren't supported.
Print (except forms)	Prints the specified datasheet.	Not applicable. Create your own printing code or use a report generator.
RunCode	Runs a specified Visual Basic for Applications function from a macro.	Not applicable. The closest equivalent is to call a function.
RunMacro	Runs a designated macro.	Not applicable. Macros aren't supported.

continues

Table 18.5. continued

Access Action	Purpose	Visual C++ Workaround
SelectObject, CopyObject, Rename	Selects, copies, or renames database objects.	Not applicable to Visual Basic database objects.
SetWarnings	Enables or disables Access warning messages primarily related to manipulating database objects.	Not applicable. Access warning messages don't appear.
ShowAllRecords	Removes filters applied to a Table or QueryDef object.	Use CRecordSet::Close(), modify m_strFilter to specify the WHERE clause, and then use CRecordSet::Open() to reopen the recordset with the new query value.
StopMacro, StopAllMacros	Stops execution of the current macro or all macros.	Not applicable. Macros aren't supported.
Transfer Database, Transfer Spreadsheet, TransferText	Imports data from or exports data to database tables, worksheets, or text files.	Must be accomplished with code. Use Visual C++'s file I/O instructions or OLE Automation.

Importing Visual Basic for Applications Code into Visual C++ Modules

Access's Visual Basic for Applications, the successor to Access Basic originally called Embedded Basic, is a direct descendant of Visual Basic. Visual Basic inherited most of its data-access functions from Access 1.0 (although much has been added since then), along with Access's Jet database engine. Visual C++, however, shares nothing significant with either Visual Basic for Applications or Visual Basic. The not-so-close relationship of the two languages makes importing Visual Basic for Applications code into Visual C++ modules a rather difficult task that often involves a significant amount of time and energy. The following sections describe the alterations to Visual Basic for Applications code that are necessary when you import Access functions into Visual C++ modules.

> **NOTE**
>
> I don't want to imply by the preceding statements that it isn't feasible to convert Access's Visual Basic for Applications to Visual C++ code. I only want to point out that you should also consider the feasibility of rewriting the entire application from scratch.

User-Defined Access Functions

User-defined functions written in Visual Basic for Applications that simply return calculated values or modified strings are usually imported into Visual C++ with rewriting to adapt them to the C/C++ syntax. You need to make changes for the differences in the arithmetic and comparison operators (as well as the string and datatype conversion functions) of Visual Basic for Applications and Visual C++, which differ significantly. The widely used Visual Basic for Applications IsLoaded() function, however, must be translated to Visual C++ when you need it. The IsLoaded() function returns True or False, depending on whether a form named in the function's argument is loaded. (The IsLoaded() function is used primarily in Access macros.) Listing 18.1 shows the Visual Basic for Applications version of IsLoaded() as it appears in the Introduction to Programming module of NorthWind.MDB.

Listing 18.1. The Visual Basic for Applications version of the IsLoaded() function.

```
Function IsLoaded(ByVal strFormName As String) As Integer
' Returns True if the specified form is open in Form view or Datasheet view.

    Const conObjStateClosed = 0
    Const conDesignView = 0

    If SysCmd(acSysCmdGetObjectState, acForm, strFormName) <> conObjStateClosed
        Then
        If Forms(strFormName).CurrentView <> conDesignView Then
            IsLoaded = True
        End If
    End If

End Function
```

If you copy the preceding code for the IsLoaded() function to a Visual C++ source file and then attempt to do a line-for-line conversion, you will find that there is no direct counterpart to the concept of whether a form is loaded or not (the functions SysCmd() and Forms() have no counterpart in Visual C++). In Visual C++, forms are actually dialog boxes, and as such, their presence in memory (in Access terminology, *being loaded*) isn't meaningful unless they are modeless. With Visual C++ you simply create a dialog box, use it, and then, when the dialog box is no longer needed, destroy it. Some dialog boxes might need to be displayed for longer periods of time and should perhaps be created as modeless dialog boxes. You need to track these dialog boxes: You wouldn't want to create multiple copies of a modeless dialog box that serves a single purpose. The user would soon become confused or convinced that the programmer never tested the final program (or both). A simple modeless dialog box manager with a list of currently displayed modeless dialog boxes would suffice in this situation.

You also can keep a record of which modeless dialog boxes your application currently has displayed by simply making the modeless dialog box classes members of one of the application's main MFC classes (such as the `CMainFrame` class). You can then query the dialog box's status to determine if it exists.

Access Event-Handling Functions

Visual Basic for Applications event-handling functions can be called by either of two methods:

- Enter the function name preceded by an equals sign (=) in the property text boxes of Access events (direct execution).

- Assign the function name as the argument of the `RunCode` action in Access macros (indirect execution).

Whether a Visual Basic for Applications function is called directly or from a macro has no effect on the alterations you need to make to conform the code to Visual C++ standards.

> **TIP**
>
> If the Visual Basic for Applications function is called by a complex macro, you need to make a decision: Should any additional code that is required to duplicate other actions in the calling macro be incorporated within the function? The best answer usually is "Not initially." Preserving the original structure of the Access application until you have the Visual C++ version running makes debugging easier, because both applications have parallel execution paths.

The following sections provide specific advice on the major issues that face developers porting Visual Basic for Applications applications that include substantial amounts of Visual Basic for Applications code to Visual C++ applications.

Importing Visual Basic for Applications Code to Visual C++ Modules

You can import Visual Basic for Applications code to Visual C++ modules using either of the following methods:

■ Copy or cut each Visual Basic for Applications function or subprocedure to the Clipboard and then paste the code into the Visual C++ module. Cutting the code from a copy of the application's .MDB file is a better approach, because cutting prevents accidental duplication of procedures in the Visual C++ module.

■ Generate a text file of the code in each Visual Basic for Applications module by opening the module and then choosing File | Save Text from Access. You can make preliminary changes to the text file by using Notebook or another Windows or DOS text editor, but using Visual C++'s code editor usually is a better approach.

Using text files to import Visual Basic for Applications module code *en masse* to Visual C++ applications is the better approach when there are more than about 100 lines of code or more than a few procedures in the module. Although you won't actually use the Visual Basic for Applications code, it becomes very useful as a frame of reference while you develop your C/C++ code. Typically you would comment out the original Access Visual Basic for Applications code and intersperse your Visual C++ code in it.

Replacing Access *DoCmd* Statements

Visual Basic for Applications' DoCmd statement is used to execute macro actions in Visual Basic for Applications code. Only macro actions can manipulate Access database objects such as forms, reports, and the recordset objects to which forms, reports, and controls are bound. Therefore, you're likely to encounter a substantial number of DoCmd statements in the Visual Basic for Applications code that you need to convert to Visual C++. In most cases, the code you substitute for DoCmd ActionName Arguments... statements is identical to the code you write to substitute for the ActionName macro action. The tables of Visual C++ code counterparts for Access macro actions given earlier in this chapter apply equally to actions executed by DoCmd statements.

Generally, DoCmd statements will be converted to calls to native C/C++ functions, or perhaps to the MFC database classes. Sometimes, however, a programmer will find it more expedient to simply code the functionality inline.

DoCmd statements that employ global symbolic constants to represent the values of arguments are quicker and easier to convert than statements that use literal arguments. Using symbolic constants instead of literal values for arguments makes the objective of the DoCmd statement readily understandable.

> **NOTE**
>
> Because Visual C++ relies so heavily on symbolic constants (using the `#define` statement), it's considered poor programming practice to use literal values. You should also look into the use of the `const` keyword as a method of preserving the integrity of a value.

An alternative method of translating argument values to meaningful terms is to open a new macrosheet in Access and choose the macro action you're replacing from the drop-down combo box list in the Action column. Macro action arguments in the Action pane of the macro design window that require integer values have drop-down combo boxes, as shown in Figure 18.4. Open the drop-down combo box and count list items from the first entry (0) to the value assigned to the argument. The list entry provides the required translation. For example, if you encounter a `DoCmd DoMenuItem 1, 2, 0` statement in the Visual Basic for Applications code, add a `DoMenuItem` macro action to the new macrosheet. Open the list box for Menu Bar and count down to the second item to identify the object to which the menu is applicable—the Database window. Then open Menu Name and count down to the third item to identify the View menu. Finally, open the Command list box to identify the first menu choice—Tables.

FIGURE 18.4.

Using the macro design window to translate integer action arguments.

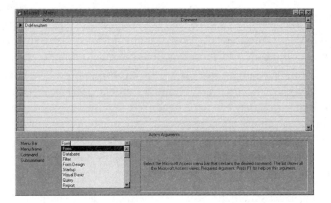

Handling Visual Basic for Applications Keywords That Are Missing from or Differ in Visual C++

A number of Visual Basic for Applications reserved words and keywords aren't duplicated exactly in Visual C++. *Domain aggregate functions* are examples of Visual Basic for Applications keywords that Visual C++ lacks. Domain aggregate functions return values that represent the count, average, and a number of other characteristics of a specified *domain* (a set of records). To duplicate a domain aggregate function in Visual C++, you need to create a recordset object that corresponds to the domain and then perform a record-by-record arithmetic operation on the recordset object.

Visual Basic for Applications DDE... instructions and functions differ greatly from the methods you apply in Visual C++. Generally, you will only be using OLE to manage interapplication interfaces, because OLE has superseded DDE in Windows programs.

Summary

Similarities between Visual Basic for Applications and Visual C++ make it appear that converting Access applications to Visual C++ database applications is a simple, straightforward process. Most Access applications, however, use macro actions rather than Visual Basic for Applications code to respond to events. Replacing macros with Visual C++ code requires ingenuity on the part of the Visual C++ programmer. This chapter began by providing an outline of the approach to use and the basic steps involved in converting a macro-based Access application to Visual C++. Suggestions for translating Access macro actions to code that sets the value of Visual C++ object properties or applies Visual C++ methods to objects were provided in tabular form. A detailed example of converting a code-intensive Access DDE client application to Visual C++ completed this chapter.

This chapter completes Part IV, "Advanced Programming with Visual C++." The next section of this book deals with creating multiuser Visual C++ database applications designed for use in a workgroup, department, or enterprise-wide network environment.

V

Multiuser Database Applications

19

Running Visual C++
Database Applications
on a Network

The majority of Visual C++ databases that you create are likely to be used in a multiuser environment. By definition—at least in the world of PCs running DOS, Windows, or Windows NT, and Macs running System 7+—a multiuser environment requires that all users of a database application be connected by a network in order to share one or more common files. Several surveys conducted in 1993 indicate that about 75 percent of all Windows database applications, excluding terminal-emulation applications for Windows, are installed on networked computers. In 1996, it can be expected that except for home systems and very small business systems, all computers will be networked in the business or commercial environment. Windows terminal-emulation applications, such as Wall Data's Rumba, let you communicate with mainframe computers by simulating a terminal, such as IBM's ubiquitous 3270, in conjunction with a terminal-emulation adapter card, such as DCA's IRMA product line.

Developers who are migrating DOS database applications to Visual C++ applications running under Windows (both Windows 95 and Windows NT) need to understand how Windows fits into the network picture. Visual C++ developers whose applications have been limited to single-user products also need a grasp of networking methods and terminology. Access is designed specifically for creating multiuser database applications, but Visual C++ isn't "network-ready" when it comes to such issues as maintaining the security of Access or other desktop database files. Therefore, this chapter begins with a general discussion of network structures, network operating systems and applications, communication protocols, adapter cards, cabling, and other issues that face developers who need to get database applications up and running on a variety of networks. The remainder of this chapter is devoted to network security issues, primarily for desktop database file types.

Understanding Network Topology and Operations

In the world of computers, the term *topology* describes how computers are connected in a network. Users can be connected to the network by a variety of network interface cards (NICs), network operating protocols, and cables. A local-area network (LAN) consists of computers in a single facility that are connected by some form of cabling. You're not restricted to a copper (wire) or glass (fiber-optic) connection to the network; you also can connect using remote dial-up access through a conventional or cellular telephone equipped with a modem, a leased telephone line, a low-power wireless (radio-frequency or RF) connection, or even a satellite link. LANs in different locations can be connected into wide-area networks (WANs) by high-speed telephone lines using T1, ISDN, or ATM hardware and communication protocols. The concentrators, routers, bridges, gateways, and protocols that are used to create WANs are discussed later in this chapter. Both Windows 95 and Windows NT support dial-in network connections, which can provide usable performance when high-speed (28K or greater) modems are used.

> **NOTE**
>
> In late 1995, AT&T Paradyne introduced a new technology that makes it possible to transfer 6Mbps of data through ordinary copper phone lines. Dubbed GlobeSpan, this AT&T system uses an asymmetric digital subscriber line modem to achieve these speeds without requiring telephone companies to install a new infrastructure of fiber-optic and coaxial cable. If everything works as AT&T plans, all this high-speed band-width will be made accessible inexpensively by the end of 1996. AT&T says Globe-Span could be available in most parts of the country at rates that are comparable to standard phone service.

The following sections describe the topology of workgroup and client-server networks, the inner workings of a newly upgraded network operating system (Windows NT Server 3.5), and Transmission Control Protocol/Internet Protocol (TCP/IP), which has become a *de facto* industry standard for implementing wide-area PC networks.

The Scope of PC Networks

The primary classification of networks is by scope. The *scope* of a network is determined by the number and proximity of the computers connected to the network. The basic network scope classifications—workgroup, departmental, and enterprise-wide—are described in the following sections.

Workgroup Networks

Workgroup networks connect a limited number of users (usually 25 or less) who share files, printers, and other computer resources. Microsoft's Windows 95 and Windows NT Workstation, Novell's NetWare Lite, and Artisoft's LANtastic networks are typical network operating systems (NOSs). Workgroup networks are usually self-administered; in other words, the members of the workgroup control *permissions* (also called *authority*) to share workgroup resources.

Workgroup computers usually are connected by peer-to-peer networks and use a single network protocol. Any computer in a peer-to-peer network may share its resources, such as files and printers, with other computers in the workgroup. Access is designed specifically for workgroup computing. Figure 19.1 shows a five-member workgroup network using Ethernet adapter cards and cabling. One of the workgroup computers shares a fax modem and a printer with other members of the workgroup.

FIGURE 19.1.

A five-member workgroup network with a shared fax modem and laser printer.

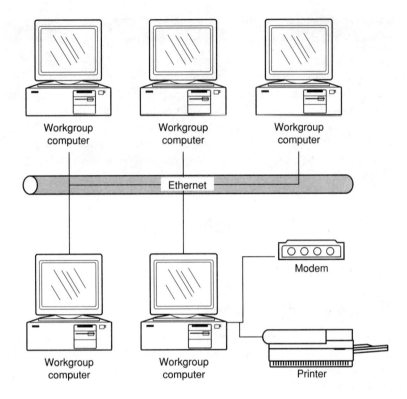

Departmental Networks

Departmental networks use dedicated server computers that provide resources to client workstations, usually within a single facility. Novell NetWare 3.x and 4.x, Microsoft LAN Manager and Windows NT Server 3.51, IBM's LAN Server, and Banyan VINES are examples of client-server NOSs. Departmental networks often include remote access services (RAS) that let users, such as field salespeople, connect to the server with a modem-equipped computer. Servers fall into the following three classes:

■ File servers let many users share files that contain data required by a common application. Typically, these files contain word-processing documents, worksheets, or desktop database tables. The applications that access the files are responsible for page or record locking to prevent two users from modifying the same record in a database. Word-processing and spreadsheet applications usually lock the entire file while a user has the file open.

■ Application servers let users run applications from the server instead of a local fixed disk drive. Running the .EXE files and opening the DLLs of today's Windows mega apps from the network can cause severe network congestion. The advantage of using an application server is that all users work with the same version of the application, and updates and upgrades to applications are much easier to administer. A single server can provide both file- and application-sharing services.

■ Database servers are computers that usually are devoted to running the back end of a client-server RDBMS. The performance of the RDBMS is degraded if the server computer also is used for file or application sharing. The database administrator (DBA) usually administers the RDBMS from a workstation. Database servers often run as NOS applications. For example, the Sybase version of SQL Server and Raima's Database Server are available as NetWare-loadable modules (NLMs) that run under NetWare 3.11 or higher. Microsoft SQL Server for Windows NT 6.0 (NTSQLS) runs under Windows NT 3.51, which is considered a NOS (as well as a general-purpose operating system) in this book.

A variety of computer types (PCs, Macs, and UNIX workstations, for example), each of which uses a different network protocol (such as NetBEUI, IPX, and TCP/IP), may be connected as clients in a departmental network. Departmental networks use gateways to connect to mainframe computers. One or more full-time network administrators (NAs or NWAs) usually are assigned to manage departmental networks. Independent, self-administered workgroups may exist within the departmental network. Figure 19.2 shows a simple departmental network with a single file and/or application server. The server is equipped with a modem to provide remote access service.

FIGURE 19.2.

A simple departmental network with a shared printer and a RAS modem.

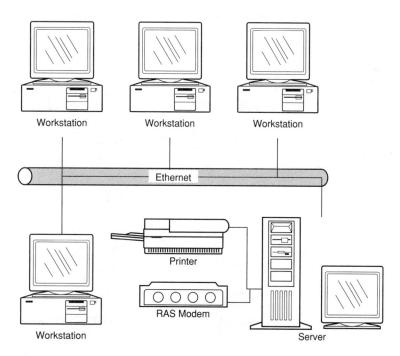

> **NOTE**
>
> Technically, of the examples of NOSs just listed, only NetWare 3.11 and Banyan VINES are true network operating systems. NOSs use proprietary operating systems rather than DOS, UNIX, OS/2, or Windows NT. LAN Manager, Windows NT Server, and LAN server are network applications (layers) that run under (or on top of, depending on your point of view) an operating system. LAN Manager 2.2 runs under Microsoft OS/2 version 1.3, Windows NT Server runs under Windows NT 3.51, and LAN Server runs under IBM OS/2 2+. After Windows 95 has started, most of the DOS components are no longer accessed except under special—exceptional—circumstances. For the sake of simplicity, this book uses the term *NOS* to describe any software product that lets computers share files.

Enterprise-Wide Networks

Enterprise-wide networks connect departmental LANs, often across large distances. Figure 19.3 shows one of the departmental or headquarters LANs that makes up an enterprise-wide network. Most enterprise-wide networks use a variety of communication methods to link LANs into a WAN; the type of interconnection depends on the distance between the individual LANs. Concentrators, bridges, and routers are hardware devices that transfer packets of data between the LANs.

FIGURE 19.3.

A headquarters LAN that acts as the hub of a wide-area network.

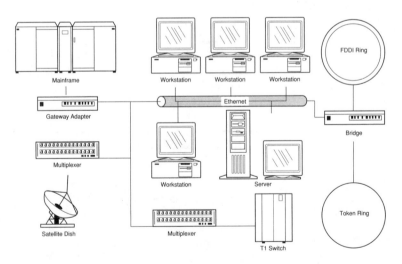

The LAN in Figure 19.3 uses Ethernet running the TCP/IP protocol and includes a connection to a mainframe computer through a gateway, as well as a bridge to a fiber-optic (FDDI) and copper token-ring network. Connections to North American LANs in the WAN are made through a T1 switch that provides access to high-speed telephone lines. Overseas subsidiaries communicate through a satellite link. Because of the complexity of WANs, most firms that operate enterprise-wide networks have a staff that manages the communications aspects of the WAN.

Domains, Workgroups, Servers, and Workstations

Early in the history of PC-based networks, the most common configuration was the departmental LAN (shown in Figure 19.2), a single server sharing its resources with a group of workstations. As the number of users in a LAN grows, additional servers are added to accommodate more shared files and applications, as well as expanding database files. When users number in the thousands and WANs span continents, the simple client-server model no longer suffices for network administration. Therefore, an additional tier, the *domain,* was added to the client-server hierarchy.

Figure 19.4 shows the relationships between two domains (represented by the two domain controllers), servers, and workstations. The interconnection between the Ethernet backbone of each of the domains, represented by a lightning bolt in Figure 19.4, could be twisted-pair (10baseT) wire, coaxial cable (10base2), a fiber-optic link (FDDI), or a T1 data line. Only two workstations per domain are shown in this figure, but a single domain commonly supports 100 or more workstations. Domains are named, and users in one domain can share files that are stored on another domain's servers.

The advantage of assigning servers and workstations to domains is that a workstation user can gain access to any server in the domain with a single logon operation. Network administrators don't need to create new user accounts for each server in a domain, because each user account is validated by the domain controller, not by the server(s) in the domain. The domain controller maintains the user account records for each person who is authorized to use a workstation in the domain. Domain controllers also can act as conventional file, application, and/or database servers.

NOTE

Windows NT Server carries the single-logon process one step further by authenticating user accounts across trusting domains. If the domain that is responsible for the user's account data is trusted by the other domains to which the domain with the user account is connected, the user automatically has an account in each of the other domains. A full discussion of trust relationships between domains is beyond the scope of this book. The *Concepts and Planning Guide* that accompanies Windows NT Server provides a complete explanation of domain topology.

FIGURE 19.4.
*Two interconnected
network domains.*

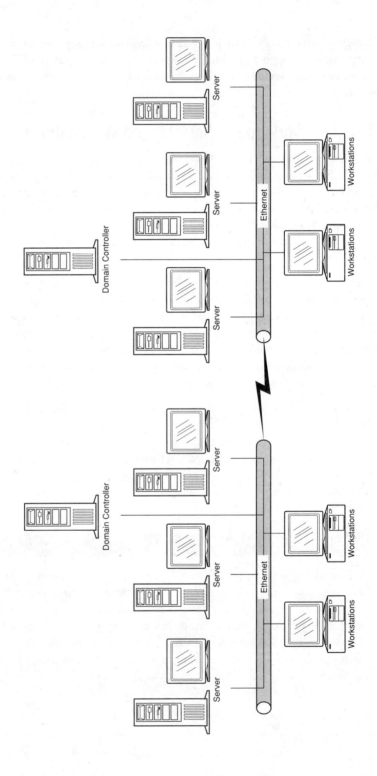

If you have more than one server in a Windows NT Server domain, every five minutes or so the domain controller replicates the user-account data on each of the servers in the domain. To minimize replication overhead, only changes to the user-account records are reflected in the servers' user-account tables. Replicating user-account data provides a backup in case the domain controller fails. If a domain controller failed and then was restored online, it would be automatically demoted to a domain server. This is done to prevent the failed domain controller's possibly out-of-date user account data from being used.

The domain administrator can promote any server to domain controller status. Promoting a server to domain controller demotes the current domain controller to server status.

The Topology and Protocols Used in This Chapter's Examples

The examples in this chapter use Windows 95 as the peer-to-peer NOS, Windows NT Server 3.51 as the client-server NOS, and both Windows NT Workstation 3.51 and Windows 95 as client workstation environments. Windows NT Server 3.51 is a superset of Windows NT Workstation 3.51 that provides a number of additional features that aren't included in Windows NT's built-in peer-to-peer (workgroup) networking capability. One of the additional features offered by Windows NT Server is trust relationships between domains (as discussed earlier). Other added features, such as fixed-disk fault tolerance and directory replication, are discussed in a section later in this chapter. SQL Server for Windows NT 6.0, used in Chapter 20, "Creating Front Ends for Client-Server Databases," runs as a service of Windows NT Server.

In order to understand many of the examples shown in this and the next chapter, you need to know the configuration of the computers and the topology of the network used to create the examples. Otherwise, you might not know why drives with letters such as G: and H: appear in the examples. Each of the computers uses generic NE-2000-compatible Ethernet cards connected by thin Ethernet (10base2) cabling. Following are the specifications and configurations of the disk drives of the server and workstation computers:

■ The domain (Darkstar) controller and file server (GayDeceiver) is a Pentium-90 MHz PCI/ISA-bus PC with 32M of RAM and a 2G (2 gigabyte) PCI SCSI (Small Computer Systems Interface), 8-ms disk drive running Windows NT Server 3.51 and Windows 95 in a dual-boot configuration. The drive is configured as a 1.6G C: FAT drive, a Windows 95 DRVSPACE drive of 500M (I:), and a 300M NTFS partition (D:). A second 1G SCSI drive serves for temporary storage. The Windows NT file system (NTFS, which is accessible only by Windows NT Server), provides faster file access and additional security features.

The V: drive is a simple Panasonic CD drive connected to a SoundBlaster sound card. The U: drive is a Sony CDU-33A double-speed CD-ROM drive connected to an IBM Audiovation mWave Sound System. A Panasonic IDE/ATPI quad-speed CD drive provides fast access to CDs when needed. There is also a Toshiba CD drive connected to the SCSI bus. The SCSI adapter is an Adaptec 2940 PCI interface adapter that uses Windows 95's protected-mode drivers when running under Windows 95. The file server also acts as a database server for Microsoft SQL Server for Windows NT (SQLNT), which is located on the NTFS D: drive. The remaining 250M partition was doubled using DRVSPACE to allow for efficient storage of many thousands of sample files. Darkstar supports NetBIOS Extended User Interface (NetBEUI), IPX/SPX, and TCP/IP protocols, both for Ethernet and for dialup connections. Connections to the Internet are made through a 28K BPS dialup PPP connection. The Internet node name is darkstar.mv.com.

■ One client workstation (Pixel) is an 80486DX2/50 ISA-bus PC with 16M of RAM running Windows 95. A 2G IDE drive is divided into two partitions on this system. The first partition, C:, is about 1G and contains the operating system and system files. The remaining space (1G) then becomes the D: partition, which is used for temporary storage. Drive S: is a Mitsumi CD-ROM drive connected to a Mitsumi card, and drive Z: is a Panasonic IDE/ATPI quad-speed CD drive that provides an additional CD drive. Server shares (shared server directories) appear as drives H: and higher on Pixel. Pixel uses both NetBEUI and IPX/SPX protocols. Pixel accesses the Internet using Windows 95's TCP/IP protocol and dialup networking.

Pixel also hosts a digital voice mail and fax system that is connected to a special telephone line. You can call in to this system and have it read any pending e-mail. In the future, maybe you'll be able to call in from a telephone and create outgoing e-mail!

■ Another client workstation (Long) is an 80386DX-33 ISA-bus PC with 8M of RAM and an 850M IDE fixed disk drive (C:) that runs Windows 95. The Long workstation is used primarily for testing and developing Windows applications and as a Fax/e-mail server. If you send me a fax, Long gets it. The Server shares appear as drive D: and higher on Long. This workstation uses only the NetBEUI protocol.

Windows NT Server 3.51 is used as the client-server NOS in this chapter because Windows NT Server 3.51 and SQL Server for Windows NT (NTSQLS) replace LAN Manager 2.2 and Microsoft SQL Server 4.2 for OS/2 in Microsoft's new enterprise networking strategy. With the release of Windows NT 3.51, the success of Windows NT is expected to hinge on the acceptance of Windows NT Server as an enterprise-wide NOS for both large and small organizations. Acceptance of NTSQLS also will influence the adoption of Windows NT Server, because the two products are designed to work best when they are combined. Oracle Corporation has announced the availability of a Windows NT implementation of its Oracle 7 RDBMS. Oracle also has been experimenting with distributing software using the Internet.

> **NOTE**
>
> Oracle Corporation has been experimenting with several methods of software distribution, including low-cost CDs using shareware techniques and online distribution using the Internet. In late 1995 you could download a fully functional version of Oracle's

product from the Internet and try it for free for 30 days. Whether Oracle continues to support these new policies is yet to be seen, but the techniques have garnered Oracle substantial press coverage. Check the www.oracle.com World Wide Web page for more information and pricing.

Although the GayDeceiver workstation is configured to boot either Windows NT 3.51 or Windows 95, this chapter doesn't include examples of using Windows NT 3.51 as a network client, except for remote domain administration. Virtually all Windows 95 applications run quite effectively under Windows NT 3.51. The resources required to run Windows NT effectively (an 80486DX PC with at least 16M of RAM) and the lack of mainstream client-side applications that take advantage of Windows NT's 32-bit multithreaded, multitasking capabilities preclude Windows NT from replacing a substantial portion of the 30 million or so registered copies of Windows 3.1 and Windows 95 running on today's PCs. In late 1995, Microsoft released 32-bit versions of Excel and Word for Windows, which will help make Windows NT Workstation 3.51 more accepted than its predecessor. This book was written using the Windows 95 version of Word for Windows, which runs under both Windows NT and Windows 95.

NOTE

At the time this book was written, there were indications that Windows NT was becoming more popular in the business environment. When Microsoft introduces a version of Windows NT with the Windows 95 user interface, Windows NT might become a serious contender for the majority of the business (but not home) users of PCs.

Windows NT Workstation is bound to become more popular; however, it will have difficulty competing with Windows 95. Windows NT Workstation will probably be desirable only in instances in which Windows NT's enhanced robustness and security are essential.

Independent software vendors appear more optimistic than Microsoft about the future of Windows NT as a client OS. Performance of compilers and complex mega-apps can benefit greatly from 32-bit multithreaded operation. Frame Technology has announced that its FrameMaker 3.0 publishing application will be available for Windows NT. Micro Focus has introduced a COBOL compiler for Windows NT. AGE Logic supplies XoftWave/32 for Windows NT so that you can run UNIX applications in an X server environment on your PC. Welcom Software Technologies' Texim Project is a high-end project management application for Windows NT. AutoDesk, Inc., has released a version of AutoCAD for Windows NT.

The performance improvement of these types of products under Windows NT is likely to induce power users to install dual-boot Windows NT on their Windows 3.1+ workstations. Of course, the release of Windows 95 will help bring new 32-bit applications to Windows NT Workstation, because Microsoft has stated that it wants all Windows 95 applications to also run under Windows NT.

At the time this book was written, the combination of Windows NT Server 3.51 and NTSQLS had the lowest entry cost of any product combination that implements a full-featured, networked client-server computing environment. (Depending on the number of users, the cost of a Windows NT Server/NTSQLS installation is likely to be less than 25 percent of the cost of a comparable UNIX-based client-server database system.) Windows NT Server is much easier to install, administer, and maintain than any other currently available client-server NOS for enterprise-wide networks, such as Novell NetWare 4.x and Banyan VINES. NTSQLS is equally easy to install and includes server administrative tools and utilities that run under Windows on Windows NT, Windows 95, and WfWg (Windows for Workgroups) workstations. The capability to run Windows NT Server and NTSQLS on RISC-based computers using either the MIPS 4000/4400 or the Digital Alpha chipsets provides an alternative to using PCs based on Intel 80x86 MPUs (multiprocessor units). Substantial improvements in price-performance ratings of both Windows NT Server and NTSQLS are in store when the production volume of RISC-based computers speeds up in 1996 and beyond.

> **NOTE**
>
> Windows NT Workstation 3.51 and Windows NT Server 3.51 also offer scalability. *Scalability* means that you can add more microprocessor (MPU) chips to a Windows NT Server (or workstation) to achieve improved performance. Windows NT Workstation and Windows NT Server can divide processing chores between up to four 80x86 MPUs. However, increasing the number of MPUs doesn't always lead to improved server performance. Many server operations, such as file replication, import, and export, are I/O bound. Adding more memory (beyond 32M) to increase the size of the disk cache often is more effective in increasing server throughput than adding more MPU chips. Other options for improving I/O include dedicated caching HD controllers and high-speed fast-wide SCSI controllers and drives. You should also consider using mirroring and/or duplexing.
>
> Workstations that run high-performance graphics packages (such as photo editing) also show a considerable performance improvement when the standard video card is replaced with a high-performance 32- or 64-bit video card.

Logging on to Servers and Joining Workgroups

When you log on to a Windows NT Server network from a Windows NT workstation, you specify the domain you want to join in the From combo box of the Logon to Windows NT dialog box. If you're using a Windows for Workgroups 3.11 workstation or a Windows 95 workstation, you can join a workgroup and simultaneously log on to Windows NT Server when you run Windows for Workgroups by following these steps (for WfWg 3.11):

1. Create an account for yourself in your Windows NT Server domain. You need to have an account with the same name and password in the Windows NT Server domain and the workgroup in order for simultaneous logon to work.

2. Open the Microsoft Windows Network dialog box by double-clicking the Network icon in Control Panel's application group window.

3. In the Workgroup text box, type the name of the workgroup you want to join, as shown in Figure 19.5.

FIGURE 19.5.

Entries in WfWg 3.11's Control Panel Network dialog box to log on to the Darkstar domain.

4. Click the Startup button to display the Startup Settings dialog box, shown in Figure 19.6. Check the Log On at Startup and Log On to Windows NT or LAN Manager Domain check boxes.

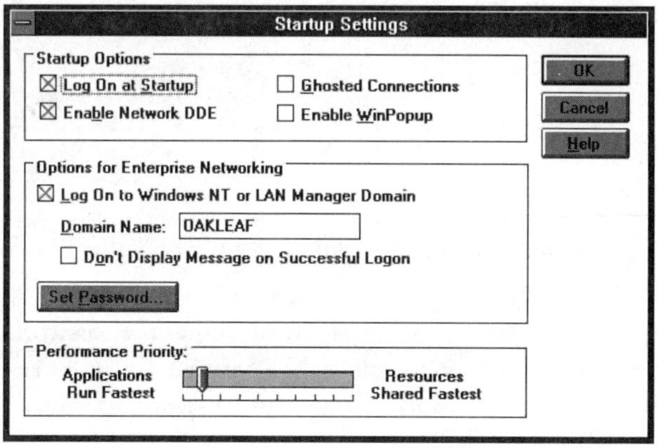

FIGURE 19.6.

The Startup Settings dialog box for automatic logon to a Windows NT Server domain.

5. Type your domain name in the Domain Name text box.

6. If you need to change your password so that the password used by WfWg is the same as that for your Windows NT Server account, click the Set Password button and change your password.

7. Click the OK button to close the Startup Settings dialog box, click the OK button in the Microsoft Windows Network dialog box to close it, and then close Control Panel. If you changed the workgroup name, the Network dialog box advises you that you need to reboot your computer in order for the change to become effective. (You don't need to reboot if you changed only the Domain Name entry in the Startup Settings dialog box.)

For Windows 95, you should follow these steps:

1. Create an account for yourself in your Windows NT Server domain. You need to have an account with the same name and password in the Windows NT Server domain and the workgroup in order for simultaneous logon to work.

2. Open the Microsoft Windows network dialog box by double-clicking the Network icon in Control Panel's application group window.

3. Click the Identification tab in the Network dialog box, shown in Figure 19.7. Type the name of the workgroup you want to join in the Workgroup edit box.

FIGURE 19.7.

Entries in Windows 95's Control Panel Network dialog box to log on to the Darkstar domain.

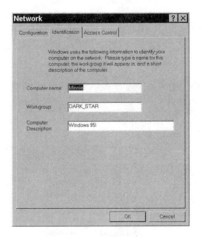

4. Click the Access Control tab in the Network dialog box to display the Access Control settings dialog box. Choose the option you want to use.

5. If you need to change your password so that the password used by Windows 95 is the same as that for your Windows NT Server account, open the Passwords dialog box from Control Panel and change your password, as shown in Figure 19.8. The Passwords dialog box lets you activate remote administration and support for user profiles.

FIGURE 19.8.

*The Properties for
Passwords dialog box
in Windows 95.*

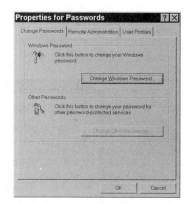

6. Click the OK button to close the Network dialog box, and then close Control Panel. If you changed the workgroup name, the Network dialog box advises you that you need to reboot your computer in order for the change to become effective.

The next time you run Windows 95, the Welcome to Windows for Workgroups dialog box appears, as shown in Figure 19.9. When you enter your password and click the OK button, the Windows for Workgroup message box shown in Figure 19.10 indicates that you were successfully logged on to the domain name you chose. (\\DORA is the unified naming convention (UNC) name of the server that acts as the domain controller for the Darkstar domain.) You can skip the logon confirmation by clicking the Don't Display Message on Successful Logon check box in the Startup Settings dialog box.

FIGURE 19.9.

*The initial logon dialog
box that appears when
you start Windows for
Workgroups 3.11 as a
Windows NT Server
client.*

FIGURE 19.10.

*The message box that
confirms successful
logon to the domain.*

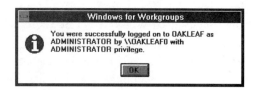

If the domain controller is down or you have a network connection problem, a message box such as that shown in Figure 19.11 appears to inform you that the Windows NT Server shares you specified in File Manager to reconnect at logon weren't reconnected. Using File Manager to connect to shared files and directories is discussed later in this chapter. (Click the Yes button to preserve the reconnect at logon status of shares.) After any other failure-to-connect messages, the message box shown in Figure 19.12 appears. When you click the OK button, you are logged on to the workgroup. Any workgroup shares you specified to reconnect at startup are available to your computer, but you can't access shares on Windows NT Server(s).

FIGURE 19.11.

The message box that indicates that a server share connection failed.

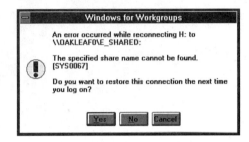

FIGURE 19.12.

The message box that indicates a failure of the domain controller or your network connection.

Server Redundancy and Backup Systems

Windows NT Server provides fault tolerance for the fixed disks of network servers by employing Redundant Array of Inexpensive Disks (RAID) methodology. The following five levels (strategies) for providing fault tolerance with RAID hardware are available:

■ RAID level 1, disk mirroring, uses a disk mirror set to provide an exact duplicate of data on two fixed disk drives. Disk writes to one member of the mirror set are duplicated on the other member. If one disk of the mirror set fails, Windows NT Server automatically transfers disk operations to the remaining operable disk. The advantage of disk mirroring is that only two disk drives are required; other methods of providing fault tolerance require three or more disks. Only one mirror set disk drive can have a boot sector, so you need to boot from the Windows NT recovery disk that you created when you installed Windows NT Server if the disk with the boot sector fails.

■ RAID level 2 writes blocks of data across multiple disks (a process called *disk striping*) and uses an error-correcting code to regenerate good data from the data blocks on a failed drive. RAID level 2 requires at least two data disks and usually more than one disk to store the error-correction data. RAID level 2 provides a faster read data rate than level 1, but it's no longer in common use because of its inefficient method of storing data.

■ RAID level 3 is a disk-striping method similar to RAID level 2, but it offers better price-performance ratings because the size of the error-correcting code is smaller. (Only one disk drive is required to store the parity information for data on the other disk drives.) RAID level 3 often is used for applications such as client-server RDBMSs that use relatively few large files.

■ RAID level 4 is the same as RAID level 3, except that the blocks of striped data are larger.

■ RAID level 5 uses a technique called *striping with parity*. RAID level 5 uses the large-block striping method of RAID level 4 but also stripes the parity data across all disks. Logic in the software and RAID disk controller assures that the parity information for a data block and the data block itself never reside on the same disk drive. Read performance is better than with RAID level 1, but write performance is slower because of the time required to calculate and write the parity values.

NOTE

RAID level 0 (disk striping only) provides improved fixed-disk read performance by sequentially placing blocks of data on multiple disks. RAID level 0 isn't included in the preceding list because RAID level 0 disk striping by itself doesn't provide fault tolerance.

Windows NT Server lets you choose either RAID level 1 or RAID level 5 redundancy to keep the network operating despite the failure of a single disk drive. Unless you have a particular reason for choosing RAID level 1, RAID level 5 is currently the favored method of providing disk drive fault tolerance. If more than one disk drive at a time fails, you're out of luck, because you can't reconstruct the missing data with either RAID level 1 or level 2 strategies. Low-cost fixed-disk drives ($200 per gigabyte and still falling) with an advertised MTBF (mean time between failures) of 800,000 to 1,000,000 hours were available at the time this book was written, so multiple-drive failure is unlikely unless the server experiences a power surge that your power-line conditioning system can't take in stride.

WARNING

No form of RAID is effective when drives are killed. Natural disasters, especially lightning, can easily destroy all the drives in a RAID system at one time.

CAUTION

If you believe advertised MTBF figures, the probability of two disk drives failing simultaneously because of mechanical or on-board electronic component malfunction is extremely small. On the other hand, the first disk drive installed in the Darkstar domain controller experienced an unexplained catastrophic failure within the first few days of operation. The replacement drive then failed less than 60 days after it was installed. MTTF (mean time to failure) is a more useful measure of the reliability of fixed disk drives, but manufacturers rarely report MTTF values. Fault-tolerance strategies are never a substitute for regular backups of server data.

Windows NT Server doesn't expand on Windows NT 3.51's tape backup system. Windows NT supports a variety of SCSI and QIC tape drives, including drives that use the 4-mm DAT (digital audio tape) format. Many suppliers of backup tape drives that aren't supported by the drivers included with Windows NT Server provide their own drivers for Windows NT 3.51. Windows 95 supports QIC drives connected to floppy controllers and some limited QIC drives connected either to parallel or dedicated controllers. At the time this book was written, Windows 95 didn't support SCSI or DAT tape drives. Aftermarket backup programs for SCSI and DAT tape drives are available to Windows 95 users.

NOTE

Hardware products that have been tested and found to perform satisfactorily with Windows NT 3.51 and the hardware drivers that are included with the retail versions of Windows NT Server 3.51 and Windows NT Workstation 3.51 are listed in the *Hardware Compatibility List* that accompanies Windows NT. Periodic additions to the list of tested hardware products appear in updated versions of the list and are available for downloading from Library 1 of the WINNT forum on CompuServe. Microsoft also maintains a WWW server at `www.microsoft.com`, where there are links to a vast array of information about Microsoft, including the extensive Knowledge Base. Virtually any files that are available from Microsoft may be found on `ftp.microsoft.com`.

Network Adapter Cards and Operating Protocols

Windows 95, Windows NT Workstation, and Windows NT Server support a variety of network adapter cards (also called *NICs,* Network Interface Cards) and operating protocols. Both Windows NT 3.51 and Windows 95 use the Open Systems Interconnection (OSI) Reference Model, which divides the flow of data in a connection between an application running under a computer operating system and the network hardware into the seven layers shown in Figure 19.13. This layered configuration results in the various protocols used to communicate between networked computers as a stack. Each of the layers in the workstation's stack communicates with the same layer in the server's stack.

FIGURE 19.13.
OSI Reference Model protocol stacks for a workstation and a server.

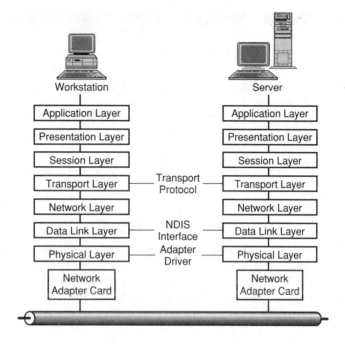

The OSI Reference Model has been adopted by the United Nations' International Standards Organization (ISO) and is accepted on a worldwide basis as the standard methodology for network software implementation. The following sections provide the details of Microsoft's implementation of the OSI Reference Model.

The Network Driver Interface Specification and Network Adapter Card Drivers

The protocol stack (also called protocol, transport protocol, or protocol driver) for WfWg 3.11, Windows 95, Windows NT Workstation 3.51, and Windows NT Server 3.51 includes the transport and network layers. The application, presentation, and session layers are attached to the operating system kernel (Windows 95, Windows NT Workstation, and Windows NT Server) or the environment (WfWg 3.11). The data-link layer of each of the three products is based on Microsoft's Network Driver Interface Specification (NDIS) standard for Windows. When you install WfWg 3.11, Windows 95, Windows NT Workstation 3.51, or Windows NT Server 3.51, you choose the NDIS driver supplied by Microsoft for the adapter card in your computer. The process of connecting the driver to the data-link layer and the adapter card is called *binding*.

NOTE

Some network protocols include the transport, network, data link, and physical layer in a single monolithic protocol. The advantage of Microsoft's NDIS approach is that you can use more than one protocol with a single adapter card. In this case, the multiple protocols share the transport and network layers of the protocol stack. The computer first transmits data in the primary protocol and then in the other protocols (if multiple protocols are used). Windows automatically assigns a new number (LANA number) to the adapter card for each protocol in use. Novell's Open Datalink Interface (ODI) is similar in concept to NDIS and also allows multiple protocol stacks.

Network Protocol Stacks Included with Windows NT Server

Windows NT 3.51 and Windows 95 include a number of protocol stacks: NetBEUI, TCP/IP, IPX/SPX, Novell IPX/ODI, DEC Pathworks, Banyan Vines, SunSelect PC-NFS protocol, and DLC. Windows NT Server also includes a protocol stack for the AppleTalk networking system built into all Macintosh computers. (Macintosh connectivity was an extra-cost option for LAN Manager 2.2.) The following list briefly describes the purpose and capabilities of each of the most commonly used protocols supplied with Windows NT Server:

■ NetBEUI (NetBIOS Extended User Interface) is a protocol developed by IBM that has been used in both IBM and Microsoft products since the mid-1980s. (IBM LAN Server and Microsoft LAN Manager both derive from the original 3-Com NOS that Microsoft licensed for incorporation in OS/2.) NetBEUI is a very fast protocol within a single LAN, but it's not a routable protocol. WANs require routable protocols, which include a hierarchical addressing method to specify the destination of data packets. Therefore, NetBEUI is best suited for use on a single LAN.

■ TCP/IP (Transmission Control Protocol/Internet Protocol) is a routable protocol that was developed by the ARPA (later DARPA, the U.S. Defense Advanced Research Projects Agency) for communication among government agencies and contractors (especially university research institutes) participating in defense-related research activities. The wide-area network created by ARPA was called the Internet. Admission to the Internet later was granted to corporations, to individuals able to afford a direct connection, and to Internet service providers who provided dial-up access to the Internet. At the time this book was written, about 50 percent of the Internet host sites were commercial. The Internet is now the ultimate in wide-area networks and links several million computers around the world. TCP/IP is discussed in two later sections.

■ IPX/SPX (Internetwork Packet Exchange) is the Novell protocol for NetWare networks. Windows NT and Windows NT Server implement IPX through an NDIS-compliant data-link layer called NWLink, which supports the STREAMS interface. NWLink currently isn't a complete solution to accessing files on NetWare servers.

You need to install and run NetWare workstation software on PCs that share files on NetWare servers. This two-vendor approach to a protocol stack has been the subject of much consternation among NetWare users. (Roughly 60 percent of the networked PCs in North America used NetWare in 1993, but the percentage of non-NetWare networks is increasing.)

■ Services for Macintosh includes the ability to share files and printers between PCs and Macs. Windows NT Server can act as the sole file server for all Macs connected to the network. Windows NT Server's Services for Macintosh also lets you create an Apple-Talk "internet" that connects two or more separate AppleTalk networks. Services for Macintosh supports AppleTalk Phase 2, which supports routing and network protocols other than the AppleTalk protocol. (The current version of Services for Macintosh doesn't support AppleTalk Phase 1.)

■ DLC (IBM data-link control) protocol can be (but seldom is) used to connect Windows NT clients to IBM mainframe computers. DLC also lets you use printers that are connected directly to the network rather than connected to a network server or WfWg workstation. (The Hewlett-Packard LaserJet IIIsi printer, for example, supports DLC using the JetDirect interface card.) Microsoft's SNA Server for Windows NT, which costs about $400, is a more satisfactory approach to IBM mainframe connectivity. Windows 95 supports the Microsoft DLC protocol.

Windows 95 includes five categories of network protocols arranged by manufacturers. Figure 19.14 shows the Select Network Protocol dialog box for Windows 95.

FIGURE 19.14.

Windows 95 network protocols.

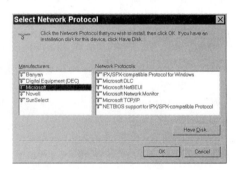

The five manufacturer protocols include Banyan, Digital Equipment (DEC), Microsoft, Novell, and SunSelect. The following list briefly describes the purpose and capabilities of each of the protocols supplied with Windows 95:

■ Banyan Vines Protocol was developed by Banyan for their networks. It's not as common as the Microsoft and Novell protocols.

■ DEC protocols are included so that Windows 95 can communicate directly with DEC VAX servers. There are four supported protocols under DEC: PATHWORKS

V4.1 Ethernet, PATHWORKS 4.1 Token Ring, Pathworks V5.0A Ethernet, and Pathworks V5.0A Token Ring.

■ Microsoft NetBEUI is a protocol developed by IBM that has been used in both IBM and Microsoft products since the mid-1980s. (IBM LAN Server and Microsoft LAN Manager both derive from the original 3-Com NOS that Microsoft licensed for incorporation in OS/2.) NetBEUI is a very fast protocol within a single LAN, but it's not a routable protocol. WANs require routable protocols, which include a hierarchical addressing method to specify the destination of data packets. Therefore, NetBEUI is best suited for use on a single LAN.

■ Microsoft TCP/IP is a routable protocol that was developed by ARPA for communication among government agencies and contractors (especially university research institutes) participating in defense-related research activities. The wide-area network created by ARPA was called the Internet. Admission to the Internet later was granted to corporations, to individuals able to afford a direct connection, and to Internet service providers who provided dial-up access to the Internet. At the time this book was written, about 50 percent of the Internet host sites were commercial. The Internet is now the ultimate in wide-area networks and links several million computers around the world. TCP/IP is discussed in two later sections.

■ Microsoft IPX/SPX is the Novell protocol for NetWare networks. Windows NT and Windows NT Server implement IPX through an NDIS-compliant data-link layer called NWLink, which supports the STREAMS interface. NWLink currently isn't a complete solution to accessing files on NetWare servers. You need to install and run NetWare workstation software on PCs that share files on NetWare servers. This two-vendor approach to a protocol stack has been the subject of much consternation among NetWare users. (Roughly 60 percent of the networked PCs in North America used NetWare in 1993; however, the percentage of non-NetWare networks is increasing.)

■ Microsoft Network Monitor is a protocol used for network monitoring and is useful for debugging network problems.

■ Microsoft DLC (IBM data-link control) protocol can be (but seldom is) used to connect Windows NT clients to IBM mainframe computers. DLC also lets you use printers that are connected directly to the network rather than connected to a network server or to a WfWg workstation. (The Hewlett-Packard LaserJet IIIsi printer, for example, supports DLC using the JetDirect interface card.) Microsoft's SNA Server for Windows NT, which costs about $400, is a more satisfactory approach to IBM mainframe connectivity. Windows 95 supports the Microsoft DLC protocol.

■ Novell's IPX ODI protocol is also supported. This protocol lets a Windows 95 user access Novell networks using two protocols—Novell's IPX ODI or Microsoft's IPX/SPX protocol.

■ SunSoft's SunSelect PC-NFS protocol is also supported, allowing you to connect to SunSoft servers. Currently, the SunSelect network isn't commonly used.

Although Windows NT Server supports the TCP/IP protocol that is used primarily by UNIX applications, there is no provision in Windows NT Server for connecting to Network File System (NFS) servers that let UNIX and DOS/Windows applications share a common set of files. NFS was developed by Sun Microsystems, Inc., in 1983 for use with Sun UNIX workstations. Sun offers PC-NFS, an add-in application for Windows 3.1 and WfWg clients that provides NFS connectivity in Ethernet environments.

TCP/IP in Windows NT Server 3.51 and Windows NT Workstation 3.51

TCP/IP is rapidly attaining the status of a *de facto* protocol standard for wide-area communication between local-area networks. Most firms that have heterogeneous LANs (LANs that support a variety of workstation types or transport protocols) also use TCP/IP as their primary LAN transport protocol. Virtually all mainframes, minicomputers, RISC workstations, and PC operating systems support TCP/IP, at least over Ethernet cabling. Thus, if you're developing Visual C++ database applications for large organizations, it's likely that you'll need to deal with TCP/IP.

> **NOTE**
>
> Included with Windows NT Server is the Microsoft Windows NT Server TCP/IP manual. This document describes Windows NT's implementation of TCP/IP.

TCP/IP is a connection-oriented protocol that is made up of two protocols—TCP and IP. The IP protocol establishes a connection between two devices on a network, based on 4-byte (32-bit) addresses; inclusion of the IP address makes TCP/IP a routable protocol. The IP address is represented by the decimal values of each of the four bytes of the address, separated by periods, as in 115.27.88.33, which corresponds to 0x731B5821 in Visual C++ hexadecimal notation. The IP address consists of the following two components:

■ A system network ID that identifies groups of devices (hosts) that are located on the same network

■ A system host ID that identifies a particular device on the network, such as a workstation or a server, with the specified network ID

A second 4-byte value, called the *subnet mask,* specifies which bytes of the IP address are to be interpreted as the network ID and which are host ID values. You create a subnet mask by creating a 32-bit binary value that has bits that are set to 1 in positions corresponding to the network ID byte(s) and to 0 in positions representing the host ID byte(s). Thus, a subnet mask with a value of 255.255.0.0 (0xFFFF0000) applied to the IP address used in the preceding example specifies that the network ID is 115.27 and the host ID is 88.33.

NOTE

An address with a 2-byte network ID and a 2-byte host ID is called a class B network address. A 1-byte network ID and 3-byte host ID is a class A address. A 3-byte network ID and 1-byte host ID is a class C address. Using different address classes lets you determine how many individual networks can be addressed. As you assign more bytes to network addresses, the number of devices allowed on each network decreases. All computers connected on a single network must use the same network ID and subnet mask.

After the connection is created between the two network devices specified by the IP address and subnet mask, TCP creates individual IP packets from the data to be transmitted. Each packet has a header that includes the following information:

■ A port ID that identifies the application running on the transmitting device.

■ A checksum that is used to verify that the packet was transmitted without error. If an error occurs, the packet is retransmitted.

■ A sequence number that lets the receiving device reassemble the packets into a stream of received data that is identical to the original transmitted data.

■ Other control information related to the type of data and the transmitting application.

Windows NT Server provides the following 17 basic utility services that are associated with the TCP/IP network protocol.

NOTE

To obtain help on one of the TCP/IP utilities, enter the command with the help option (-?). For example, arp -? gives you help information about the options for the arp utility.

WARNING

Utilities such as ftp, ftpsvc, rexec, and telnet require the use of passwords. The password is sent to the host system in an unencrypted (plain-text) form. I strongly recommend that you make sure these passwords are unique and different from the passwords used on the local Windows NT network for users, domains, and workgroups.

■ The arp utility is used to display and modify the IP-to-Ethernet of token-ring physical address translation tables that are used by the Address Resolution Protocol (ARP). You can choose to display the current entries (all entries or those based on a specific interface), delete an entry, or add an entry.

■ The finger utility is a connectivity command that is used to display information about a user who is on a specific system that is running the finger service. The output of the finger utility varies depending on the remote systems responses.

■ The ftp utility uses the file transfer protocols to let you send and receive files over TCP/IP networks with File Transfer Protocol (FTP) and Trivial File Transfer Protocol (TFTP). Both of these protocols use the Windows NT command line. The ftp utility can take its input either directly from the command line or from an ASCII text file. Anonymous FTP, one mode of which lets you use Anonymous as the user name and usually your e-mail address as the password, is the most common method of transferring text and binary files over the Internet.

■ The hostname command is used to display the name of the current TCP/IP host. This command has no options.

■ The ipconfig utility is used for diagnostics. It displays information about the configuration of the current machine. This utility is most useful on systems that are running Dynamic Host Configuration Protocol (DHCP) servers.

■ The lpq utility is used to obtain the status of a specific printer queue on a specific server. An option lets you obtain detailed status information.

■ The lpr utility lets you print a file to a host system that is running as an LPD server.

■ The nbtstat command is used to display statistics about the protocol and the current TCP/IP connection. You use this command when you're using NetBIOS over TCP/IP.

■ The ping utility can be used to verify the connections to one or more remote hosts. The connection is verified by having the host send one or more ECHO packets to the client. The ping utility returns information that can be used to estimate the performance of the connection to the host.

■ The rcp command can be used to copy files between the Windows NT system and a remote system running rshd (remote shell server). You can also copy files between two other systems running rshd when you issue the rcp command from the Windows NT system.

■ The rexec command lets a user run a command on a remote host that is running the rexecd service. This command will authenticate the user's name on the remote system (by using a password) before executing the command.

■ The route utility is used to manage and modify the network routing tables. With the route utility you can print, add, delete, or change routing.

■ The rsh command is used to run commands on hosts that are running the RSH (Remote Process Execution) service. This command is similar to the rexec command.

■ The snmp (Simple Network Management Protocol) utility reports the current status of a server or workstation on a network. Using snmp, you can specify the communities and host(s) from which the server or workstation will accept requests for network status information and send an authentication trap (request for identification) when an unspecified community or host makes a request from the server or workstation. Communities are called user groups in a TCP/IP network environment.

■ The telnet command provides character-based terminal emulation that lets you operate TCP/IP hosts that support Telnet. You can start Telnet from Control Panel's Services option. After Telnet services start, Windows NT's Terminal applet launches with the Telnet port open. Under Windows 95, you can start Telnet from either the Explorer or from a DOS session command prompt.

■ The tftp command is used to transfer files to and from a remote computer that is running the TFTP. The tftp command is very similar to the ftp command; however, TFTP doesn't provide for user authentication.

■ The tracert utility is used to determine the route that is taken to a specified destination. It does this by sending ECHO packets that have varying Time-To-Live values. Because each router is required to decrement the Time-To-Live value, the Time-To-Live value can be used to determine the number of routers in the ECHO packet's path. When Time-To-Live becomes zero, the ECHO packet should be returned to the sender. Not all routers actually return the packet. Those that don't won't be discovered by the tracert utility.

NOTE

Microsoft's implementation of TCP/IP does not, in itself, provide file-sharing services between PC clients and UNIX client-server network systems. TCP/IP originally was designed for communication and file transfer instead of sharing files in a multiuser environment. Suppliers of UNIX-based RDBMSs license connectivity products to let DOS/Windows, DOS/WfWg, and Windows NT act as RDBMS clients. You currently need an NFS server (described briefly in the preceding section) and an NFS add-on application to share other types of files, such as desktop database table files, with UNIX workstations. (Microsoft didn't adapt its LAN Manager/X product, developed in the late 1980s to share files between computers using the UNIX and OS/2 operating systems, to Windows NT or Windows NT Server.) NFS software licenses currently cost approximately $200 to $400 per client (although these prices might have changed).

Windows NT Workstation and Windows NT Server also offer a variety of other command-line utilities, principally for testing network connections and interacting with UNIX systems that were described earlier. A full description is found in Chapter 11, "Utilities Reference," of the TCP/IP booklet that accompanies Windows NT Workstation and Windows NT Server. A complete technical description of TCP/IP, UNIX utilities, and sharing files between computers running UNIX, DOS/WfWg, and Windows NT is beyond the scope of this book. A variety of books are devoted to the subject of UNIX networking. If you're developing a Visual C++ database application that uses a UNIX-based RDBMS such as Sybase SQL Server or that needs to share database files with UNIX workstations, your investment in a good UNIX networking book will quickly be repaid.

NetBIOS Over TCP/IP and the Windows Sockets API

TCP/IP for Windows is implemented with both NBT (NetBIOS over TCP/IP) and the Windows Sockets API. The two implementations share the same levels in the protocol stack. NBT provides naming services so that NetBIOS applications can locate NetBIOS workstations and servers on the TCP/IP network by a valid NetBIOS name rather than a numeric IP network ID. NetBIOS names are the computer names, such as Pixel, that you assign to PC servers and workstations; NetBIOS names derive from the original PC peer-to-peer networking application developed by IBM and PC-LAN, and they must comply with DOS filenaming conventions. You use the LMHOSTS (LAN Manager hosts) file to associate NetBIOS names with IP addresses. The format of the LMHOSTS file is identical to that used for the HOSTS file associated with implementations of TCP/IP for DOS, such as FTP Software's PC/TCP, which also includes NFS services. Here is a typical entry in the LMHOSTS file:

```
199.125.78.23    Darkstar
```

When you specify a computer name or an IP address, the corresponding entry in LMHOSTS provides the required name resolution.

Windows Sockets is modeled after the Berkeley Sockets included in the BSD (Berkeley Software Distribution) version 4.3 of UNIX developed by people at the University of California at Berkeley. In UNIX terminology, a *socket* is a bidirectional connector to an application. Two sockets, each identified by an address, participate in a two-way network conversation. If you intend to create a Visual C++ application that needs to connect directly to another application with TCP/IP, using the Windows Sockets API is the most straightforward approach.

NetManage, Inc., publishes NEWT-SDK, a collection of DLLs that let you add TCP/IP networking capability to Windows applications. NEWT-SDK is compatible with the Windows Sockets API and provides APIs for FTP, SNMP, SMTP (Simple Mail Transmission Protocol), SLIP (Serial Link Interface Protocol), and PPP (Point to Point Protocol). Windows NT Server doesn't provide SMTP (Microsoft Mail provides e-mail service). SLIP is used for the RAS service to allow interoperability with other third-party remote access software. SLIP lets you redirect TCP/IP transmission from the network adapter card to a serial port, allowing remote dial-up connections to a network with a server that implements SLIP. NEWT-SDK includes API function prototype declarations for Visual C++. You need a fundamental understanding of TCP/IP, UNIX, and C programming in order to use the NEWT-SDK APIs effectively.

NOTE

Other than the support included with Windows NT 3.51 (RAS supports CSLIP/SLIP and PPP), at the time this book was written, no commercial products were available to add SLIP services to Windows NT Server. Thus, you're currently limited to using SLIP to access UNIX RDBMSs remotely. It's likely that one or more enterprising ISVs (independent software vendors) will provide add-in products to implement SLIP as Windows NT Server gains market share.

Windows 95 includes built-in PPP support, and an add-in SLIP protocol handler is part of the Plus! Package.

NetManage also publishes Chameleon, a set of stand-alone Windows TCP/IP applications. Chameleon lets you use FTP, TFTP, SNMP, SMTP, and SLIP services with Windows 3.1 and WfWg clients. Chameleon also includes Telnet with IBM 3270 terminal emulation and a newsreader application, NEWTNews, for the Internet. Chameleon's application group is shown in Figure 19.15. TCP/IP for Visual C++ is designed to simplify the incorporation of TCP/IP and the five basic services to Visual C++ applications with custom controls and source code examples.

FIGURE 19.15.

The application group for NetManage's Chameleon TCP/IP applications.

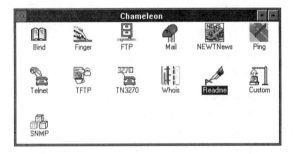

For World Wide Web browsers, a number of very interesting products are available, including NetScape (shareware with a low registration price), which has truly outstanding performance. Also available is a product called Mosaic, which is freeware. Windows 95's Plus! Package includes Internet Explorer, which is based on Mosaic.

Hubs, Bridges, Routers, and Gateways

The following four types of hardware devices commonly are employed in LANs and WANs and to connect to mainframe computers:

■ Hubs are used to connect groups of computers to LANs that use topologies that are more complex than Ethernet's simple inline connections. For example, you need a hub to connect one or more computers to a network that uses unshielded twisted pair (UTP, 10baseT) cabling or to token-ring networks.

> **NOTE**
>
> It's possible to connect two computers using twisted pair without using a hub and thereby create a very simple two-node network. If you need to add a third computer to the network, however, you must install a hub.

- Bridges provide connectivity between dissimilar LANs. You use a bridge, for example, to connect an Ethernet LAN to a token-ring LAN.

- Routers are used in WANs to direct network data packets to the appropriate transmission device. If you have a T1 switch and a satellite link that serve remote computers, the router connects the LAN to the switch and link hardware. Routers are similar to multiplexers that are used to combine multiple voice conversations and data transmission on a single telephone line. Smart routers maintain a list of addresses and handle the switching chores without the need for intervention by computers on the network.

- Gateways provide connectivity between PC LANs and mini- or mainframe computers. IBM provides a token-ring gateway for its AS/400 minicomputer and all of its current mainframe computers. Gateways often consist solely of software that you add to the mainframe's operating system or a specific application, such as an IBM DB2 server, and to the client application. In this case, the client connects to an IBM I/O controller. Information Builders, Inc.'s EDA/SQL combined with EDA/Link for Windows is an example of a gateway from Windows front-end applications to a DB2 back end running under MVS on IBM mainframes.

> **NOTE**
>
> Terminal-emulation cards, such as DCA's IRMA card, which let PCs run mainframe terminal (IBM 3270 or 5250) sessions in conjunction with terminal-emulation software, aren't LAN components. Terminal-emulation cards connect to a mainframe I/O controller by a coaxial cable; however, that connection isn't properly a LAN connection.

Maintaining Database Security in a Network Environment

This book has mentioned several times that Visual C++ database applications don't have the capability to manage database security features. You can't implement or alter the security features of Access databases, nor can you change passwords or alter password protection of Paradox 3+ table files. In a multiuser environment, however, you can control access to database files by individual users or groups of users through the security features of the network.

The majority of Visual C++ applications can achieve results that are similar or equivalent to the security features built into Access if you implement a well-planned network security system. Even when you use Access, the first line of defense against unauthorized viewing or modification of database files is network security. The following sections describe how network security works in a Windows NT Server environment and how to design Visual C++ database applications to take maximum advantage of network security. If you're an Access developer, much of the terminology in the sections devoted to network security will be familiar to you. Access databases use the network security model.

Network Authority, Permissions, and Accounts

Network operations are divided into the following two basic categories:

- Administration of the network, which includes adding and deleting user accounts; assigning accounts to particular groups of users; granting users the ability to read from, write to, copy, or delete specific files or a collection of files in a specific directory; and backing up server files. The administrator's authority determines what administrative activities he or she can perform. Windows NT Server defines authority as a combination of rights and abilities that are inherent in a user's group. Firms with large client-server networks usually employ one or more full-time network administrators to manage the LAN.

- Use of network resources, which encompasses file transfer and file sharing, access to database servers on the network, printing on network printers, using network modems to send faxes or to communicate with remote computers, and the like. A user's permissions determine which network resources he or she can use and how the resources can be used.

The basic element of network security in client-server networks is the user account. Administrators and users each must have a user account that lets them log on to the network. The user account record, at the minimum, includes fields to hold the user's logon ID and password and to indicate the group(s) to which the user belongs. Regular network users must belong to at least one group, most commonly called Users, but there is no limit to the number of groups to which users can be assigned. Most NOSs create a unique, encrypted system ID (SID) to identify the user. A system ID prevents confusion between users who might accidentally use the same logon ID. Duplicate logon IDs can easily be intercepted and prevented on a LAN. However, a user on a WAN in San Francisco might unknowingly use the same logon ID as a WAN user in Sydney, Australia. Maintaining user accounts is one of the principal duties of network administrators.

Security Limitations of Workgroup Networks

There is little distinction between network administrators and users in workgroup environments. Workgroup networks are self-administered; any user can share files located in directories on his or her computer with other members of a workgroup. Workgroups don't maintain user accounts. Therefore, files in any directory that are shared by a user are, by default, "up for grabs" by anyone else who is connected to the network. The user sharing files can restrict other users from modifying the files by sharing the files in read-only mode and can require that workgroup members enter a password to gain access to files in the shared directory. The limited security offered by conventional workgroup networking environments has limited their acceptance by IS departments of large firms. Using the Access database security system with Visual C++ applications (the subject of the next section) can overcome the security limitations of WfWg 3.1+ and Windows 95.

The peer-to-peer networking features of Windows NT 3.51 provide an increased level of security compared to that offered by WfWg 3.11 and Windows 95. Windows NT requires that you log on to Windows NT with a user ID and password, whereas logon IDs and passwords are optional for WfWg. If you have administrative authority, you can assign users of individual computers to groups and then grant group authority to share your directories. The normal practice is to create a user group with the same name as the workgroup. If you use the Windows NT file system (NTFS) instead of the DOS file allocation table (FAT) system, you can grant users permissions on a file-by-file basis. The FAT file system, required by dual-boot installations, restricts you to granting permissions to share entire directories. Using predefined groups and creating new groups, as well as granting directory and file permissions to members of groups, are subjects of later sections in this chapter.

Windows NT overcomes many of the objections of MIS managers to the lack of security within self-administered networks, but peer-to-peer networking remains a threat to the centralized authority (and in many organizations, the perceived status) of IS departments. The likelihood of a large number of corporate PC clients running Windows NT instead of Windows 95 or WfWg 3.11 (at least in the economic climate that prevailed at the time this book was written) is quite small because of the expense of upgrading PCs to meet the resource requirements of Windows NT.

Supplementing Workgroup Security with Access Database Security Features

One of the advantages of using Access databases with Visual C++ applications is that you can use the retail version of Access to implement database security with SYSTEM.MDW in addition to restricting access to the DATABASE.MDB file through network security. Access uses the SYSTEM.MDW file to store group names, user IDs, passwords, and SIDs. When you add a new user to an Access security group, you enter the user ID and a four-digit PIN (personal identification number). (The PIN distinguishes between users with the same user ID.) Access combines the user ID and PIN to create an encrypted binary SID (system ID) value that is used by Access .MDB files to identify each user who has permissions for files that exceed the scope of default permissions (also called *implicit permissions*) granted to the group(s) to which the user belongs.

> **NOTE**
>
> Access 2 uses SYSTEM.MDA, and Access 7 uses SYSTEM.MDW. Access 7 will use an Access 2 .MDA file, or you can convert the Access 2 .MDA file to an Access 7 .MDW file. Using an Access 2 .MDA file with Access 7 uses more memory than using an .MDW file.

Using Access database security features means that at least one individual must be appointed as a database administrator (DBA) to manage the user accounts in the SYSTEM.MDW file that is shared by members of one or more workgroups. You can use a single SYSTEM.MDW file that is shared by all members of all workgroups, or multiple SYSTEM.MDW files, each of which is located in the directory that contains the .MDB file(s) that the workgroup members share. Workgroup members must have read-write access to SYSTEM.MDW so that users can change their password periodically to enhance database security. Thus, if you want to use network security to provide one group of users read-only permissions and to grant another group of users read-write permissions, you should use the single SYSTEM.MDW approach and place SYSTEM.MDW in a directory to which all members of all workgroups have read-write network permissions.

Access lets you grant read-only or read-write permissions to groups and individual users for tables in the database; however, members of the User group, by default, have read-write permissions (read data and modify data) on all database tables. You need to explicitly remove write (modify data) permissions for the Users group and then assign write permissions to authorized users.

SYSTEM.MDW is the default name for the security library database of Access databases. You can specify a name other than SYSTEM.MDW for the security database, but doing so requires that you use the Change Workgroups application supplied with Access or that you manually edit the `SystemDB=d:\path\library.mdw` entry in the `[Options]` section of the MSACCESS.INI file. This line specifies the security library that the retail version of Access attaches to the currently open database.

Access database security is modeled on the security system of LAN Manager 2.2 and Windows NT Server, so describing network security before discussing Access database security methodology makes Access's labyrinthine security features a bit more comprehensible.

Network Administrators, Operators, and Users

Windows NT Server has an extraordinary number of predefined groups of administrators and users. Table 19.1 lists the predefined groups that are created when you install Windows NT Server, the groups predefined by Windows NT 3.51 workstations, and the groups of database users defined by Access. The rows in Table 19.1 are ordered by descending level of authority-to-administer and permission-to-use domain resources. The Domain Admins and Domain Users groups are global groups; the remainder of the groups are local to a specific server computer. An N/A entry indicates that the group isn't available in the particular environment.

Table 19.1. The authority and permissions of predefined groups.

Windows NT Server Domains	Windows NT Workstations	Access
Domain Admins	Administrators	Admins
Administrators	Administrators	Admins
Backup Operators	Backup Operators	N/A
Server Operators	N/A	N/A
Account Operators	N/A	N/A
Print Operators	N/A	N/A
Replicators	N/A	N/A
N/A	Power Users	N/A
Everyone	Everyone	N/A
Domain Users	Users	Users
Users	Users	Users
(Guests)	Guests	Guests

The following list briefly describes the basic categories of predefined groups for Windows NT Server, Windows NT Workgroup, and Access:

■ Administrators: A person with an administrator account on a domain controller is given domain administrator authority as a member of the Domain Admins group. The trust relationship between Windows NT Server domains also lets a domain administrator who has an account with the same authority in another domain administer that domain. This lets a domain administrator in North America administer a domain located in Europe or Asia. Members of the Domain Admins and Administrators groups have the rights and abilities to do *anything* within the domains and on the servers that are within the scope of their authority. When you install Windows NT Server, you're automatically granted domain administrator authority. Similarly, an administrator of a Windows NT workstation exercises full authority over that workstation. Members of the Access Admins group in a particular SYSTEM.MDW file have full permissions for all objects that were created *with the specific SYSTEM.MDW file in use.* (The emphasis is added because this is a very important point that is discussed at the end of this chapter.) Admins members can't revoke the permissions of the *creator* of an object in an Access database, nor is it possible to prevent a user from *creating* objects in an Access database.

■ Operators: Windows NT Server administrators can delegate some of their responsibilities to members of the Backup, Server, Account, and Print Operators groups. The names assigned to Operators groups imply the scope of authority of members of these groups. There is no equivalent to Operators groups in Windows NT or Access. The Replicators group is used only in conjunction with file replication services.

■ Users: The term *users* encompasses any group that is not an administrative or operative group. "Everyone" is a *special entity* that refers to all users, but not to Administrators or Operators. (Operators don't have user privileges.) Special entities also include SYSTEM, NETWORK, INTERACTIVE, and CREATOR OWNER. The CREATOR OWNER entity is equivalent to the Access Creator (object owner) entity. People who simply use the network to get their work done usually are made members of the Users group. Windows NT Workstation's Power Users group has limited administrative authority; this group is designed primarily for establishing and maintaining secure workgroups. Access requires that anyone who opens a secure Access database be a member of the Users group. (Being a member of the Admins group isn't sufficient to open a secure Access database. Members of the Admins group, however, are the only people who can directly modify the SYSTEM.MDW file.)

■ Guests: Guests aren't permitted to do anything at a Windows NT Server computer, including log on to the server (thus the parentheses surrounding Windows NT Server Guests in Table 19.1). Guests are allowed to log on to Windows NT workstations, but they can't participate in any network activities. Access gives Guests read-only permissions for database tables. The Guest user of the Guests group (neither of which you can delete) is used for transitory access to a Windows NT workstation or to Access database applications. The best approach with secure Access databases is to assign a password to the mandatory Guest account and then forget the password.

Chapter 3, "How Network Security Works," in the *Concepts and Planning Guide for Windows NT Server* provides a complete description of the rights and abilities of each predefined group and special entity of Windows NT Server and Windows NT.

File Permissions Using Windows NT File System Partitions

Windows NT Server and Windows NT Workstation directories that are located on fixed-disk partitions formatted as FAT (DOS) partitions can be shared on the network, but you can't control network access to individual files or subdirectories of a shared FAT directory. In order for you to control access to individual files, the files must be located in a directory of an NTFS partition. Only the most courageous early adopters of Windows NT Server are likely to run Windows NT Server itself, which must boot from the C: drive, in an NTFS partition. Most installations are likely to be Windows NT/DOS dual-boot types that use a FAT partition to hold both the DOS and Windows NT operating systems. You can gain the benefits of NTFS for file-sharing operations and NTSQLS databases by establishing one or more logical drives in extended partitions that you format with NTFS. This method was used to create the NTFS

E: logical drive on the extended partition of the Darkstar server used in this chapter's examples. You might want to create a separate NTFS logical drive in an extended partition to install NTSQLS.

> **NOTE**
>
> After you've gained experience with Windows NT Server and are fully confident of its capabilities, you can reformat the FAT partition to NTFS without losing the data that the partition contains by running the CONVERT.EXE application. Make sure you back up the FAT partition before running CONVERT.EXE. You can't change an NTFS partition to a FAT (or HPFS) partition. Instead, you delete the partition, along with all the data on the partition, and then re-create the partition and format it as a FAT (or HPFS) partition. If Windows NT Workstation or Windows NT Server is located on the NTFS partition you want to reformat, you need to run the Windows NT setup application to delete the partition.

After you've added the NTFS logical drive (volume), you create the directory structure for the files to be shared by the server. Files in directories and subdirectories on NTFS drives can be assigned one or more of the permissions listed in Table 19.2 for individual users or groups of users.

Table 19.2. NTFS file and subdirectory permissions.

Permission	Abbreviation
Read	R
Write	W
Delete	D
Execute	X
Change permission	P
Take ownership	O

Table 19.3 lists the standard Windows NT permissions for shared NTFS directories. The Directory column lists the abbreviations of the permissions that apply to the directory itself, and the New Files column lists the abbreviations of the permissions for files that are added to the shared directory after directory-level permissions are granted. Permissions you assign to file and subdirectory shares apply to users who log on to the server itself, as well as to users of workstations. Only members of the Administrators and Operators groups are allowed to log on to the server with Windows NT Server's default security settings.

Table 19.3. Standard permissions for shared directories and their files in NTFS partitions.

Permissions	Directory	New Files	Description
No access	None	None	The user can't obtain access to the directory or its subdirectories.
List	RX	N/S	The user can list the files and subdirectories but not read the files.
Read	RX	RX	The user can read and execute files in the directory (basic read-only access).
Add	WX	N/S	The user can add and execute files but can't read or change existing files.
Add and read	RWX	RX	The user can read and execute files in the directory but can't modify files.
Change	RWXD	RWXD	The user can read, write, and delete files in the directory.
Full control	All	All	In addition to having change permissions, the user can set permissions for and take ownership of any file in the directory.

Table 19.4 lists the standard Windows NT permissions and the Access database file permissions applicable to Access `Table` and `QueryDef` objects that correspond to the Windows NT file permissions. Permissions that apply to Access forms, reports, macros, and modules aren't applicable to Visual C++ database applications, because they can't access these objects.

Table 19.4. Standard permissions for shared files in NTFS partitions and Access database files.

Permissions	Files	Description	Microsoft Access
No access	None	The user can't obtain access to the file.	No permissions
Read	RX	The user can read or execute the file.	Read definitions, read data
Change	RWXD	The user can read, write, or delete the file.	Read definitions, read data, modify data

Permissions	Files	Description	Microsoft Access
Full control	All	The user can read, write, delete, set permissions for, or take ownership of the file.	Full permissions (includes modify definitions)

The Windows NT File Manager is similar to that of WfWg 3.11, except an additional toolbar button with a key icon lets you set file permissions for individual files on NTFS volumes. To assign permissions for a file or a group of files, select the file(s) in File Manager's window and then click the File Permissions button to display the File Permissions dialog box. Click the Add button to display the Add Users and Groups dialog box. Figure 19.16 shows the Add Users and Groups dialog box for file permissions. Double-click the names of the existing groups for which you want to assign permissions to add the name of the group to a semicolon-separated list in the Add Names text box. If you want to add an individual user to the list, select the group to which the user belongs and click the Show Users button to display a list of users in the group.

FIGURE 19.16.

The Add Users and Groups dialog box of Windows NT Server.

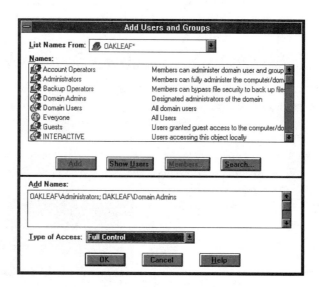

A full description of Windows NT Workstation and Windows NT Server share security for both FAT and NTFS partitions is provided in Chapter 5, "Managing Network Files," of the *Windows NT Server Concepts and Planning Guide.*

Fathoming the Access Security System

The Access database security system has been called labyrinthine, Byzantine, and even Machiavellian. As noted earlier in this chapter, Access's security methodology is derived from a mixture of LAN Manager, SQL Server, and Windows NT security techniques. If you decide to implement Access security in conjunction with Visual C++ database applications, or your Visual C++ database applications share secure .MDB files with Access applications, you need to have a fundamental understanding of how Access implements security for Table and QueryDef objects. You don't need to worry about security issued for other Access objects, forms, reports, macros, and modules, because Visual C++ applications don't recognize these objects.

> **WARNING**
>
> Before you use any Access security features that are discussed in the following sections, make a backup copy of the SYSTEM.MDW file in the \ACCESS directory and back up any .MDB files that have permissions you plan to modify. If you haven't made any changes to the default values in the SYSTEM.MDW file that was installed when you set up Access, make a copy of the SYSTEM.MDW file on a disk and save it for future use as the base SYSTEM.MDW file for creating new applications.

Assigning Access User Accounts and Securing Access Databases

When you first launch Access, you're assigned a default user ID of Admin, a member of Access's Admins group, with an empty password. This combination of user ID and empty password prevents Access's Logon dialog box, shown in Figure 19.17, from appearing when you launch Access. If the Logon dialog box appears when you launch Access, you have the beginnings of a secure database system. (This statement assumes that unauthorized users don't know the valid user ID and password combinations contained in SYSTEM.MDW.)

FIGURE 19.17.
*Access's Logon
dialog box.*

To initiate database security with Access, you need to add a new user ID and assign the new user account membership in the Admins group. After you add the new member of the Admins group and take ownership of the objects in the database(s) you intend to secure, you can delete the default Admin user account (if other Access .MDB files don't depend on the presence of the Admin user). Follow these steps to secure Access so that only DBAs can launch Access:

1. Launch Access and open any .MDB file (NorthWind.MDB is a good choice) so that the Security menu bar appears. (You can't enter Access's security subsystem without opening a database.)
2. Choose Security | Users to display the Users dialog box.
3. Click the Add button to display the New User/Group dialog box.
4. Type the new Admins user ID in the Name text box and add a four-digit PIN (personal identification number) in the Personal ID Number text box, as shown in Figure 19.18. (Access user IDs aren't case-sensitive.)

FIGURE 19.18.

The Users and New User/Group dialog boxes of Access's security system.

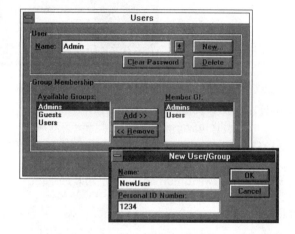

5. Click the OK button of the New User/Group dialog box to close it. Access automatically makes the new user a member of the Users group.
6. Select Admins in the Available Groups list box and click the Add button to add the new user to the Admins group. The Users dialog box appears, as shown in Figure 19.19. (This is the first critical step in the process. The new user must be a member of both the Admins and Users groups.) Click the Close button to complete the record for the new user's account and close the Users dialog box.

FIGURE 19.19.

The Users dialog box after you add a new Admins user.

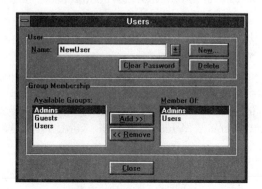

7. Choose Security | Change Password to display the Change Password dialog box, shown in Figure 19.20. You need to add a password for the Admin user so that the Logon dialog box appears when you next launch Access. (This is the second critical step.) Note that you are still logged on to Access as Admin. Tab past the Old Password text box (to indicate an empty password for the Admin user). Type a password for the Admin user in the New Password text box and type the password again for confirmation in the Verify text box. (Access passwords are case-sensitive.)

FIGURE 19.20.

Access's Change Password dialog box.

8. Click the OK button to close the Change Password dialog box and exit Access.

9. Relaunch Access. If you followed the instructions in step 7, the Logon dialog box will appear. Enter your new user ID in the Name text box and click the OK button. (You haven't yet assigned a password to the new user account.) Open a database file.

10. Choose Security | Change Password and repeat steps 7 and 8. The password you choose for your new Admins account should contain at least eight characters and should have a combination of letters and numbers. Using a combination of upper- and lowercase letters provides even better password security.

11. Relaunch Access and enter your new user ID and the new password.

You can inspect the contents of the SYSTEM.MDW file at this point by following these steps:

1. Use File Manager to create a copy of SYSTEM.MDW as SYSTEM.MDB. (You can't open SYSTEM.MDW because it's attached as a library database to the currently open database.)

2. Choose View | Options to display the Options dialog box. Change the value of the Show System Objects property in the default General options category to Yes and click the OK button to close the Options dialog box.

3. The system tables that begin with the prefix "MSys" now appear in the Table list box of the Database window. Double-click the MSysAccounts table to display its contents, as shown in Figure 19.21.

Records in MSysAccounts with a value of –1 (TRUE) in the FGroup field are group accounts. The Engine and Creator accounts are entity accounts corresponding to Windows NT Server's SYSTEM and CREATOR OWNER entities, respectively. You can't delete the Engine, Creator, or guest account. Values in the Password and SID fields are encrypted for security purposes.

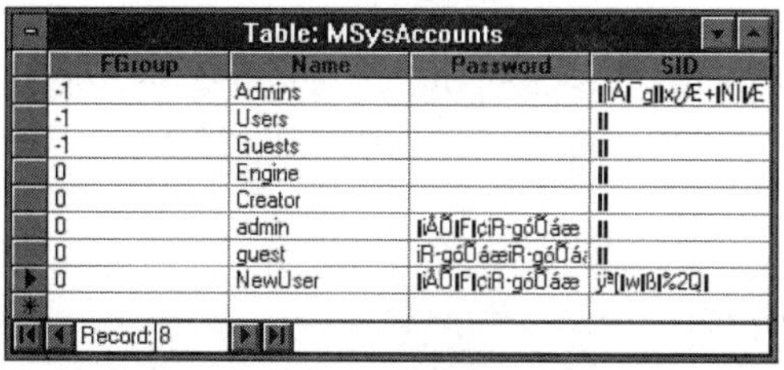

FIGURE 19.21.

The contents of the MSysAccounts table with a single new user added.

FGroup	Name	Password	SID
-1	Admins		‖Ã˾́ȯᵢⱯ+‖Ñ‖Æ
-1	Users		‖
-1	Guests		‖
0	Engine		‖
0	Creator		‖
0	admin	‖Ã˾́Ƒ‖ȼᵢȒ·ɡȯˮᵉˊ	‖
0	guest	ȓ·ɡȯˮᵉˊᵢȓ·ɡȯˮᵉˊᵢ	‖
0	NewUser	‖Ã˾́Ƒ‖ȼᵢȓ·ɡȯˮᵉˊ	ÿᵃ‖ɯ‖ß‖%2Q‖

Record: 8

WARNING

You might be tempted at this point to delete the Admin account. The Access documentation recommends that you delete the Admin user at this point. *Don't do it.* The next section explains why you shouldn't delete the default Admin user now.

Securing Existing Database Files

At this point, Access is secure, and any new Access databases you create also will be secure. Henceforth, your new user ID is the owner of any new database objects you create. However, no Access database objects that you and others created with the Admin account (using the blank password) are secure. The reasons are as follows:

■ The Admin user is the owner (the "creator" in Access) of all objects in every database you or others created using the Admin account, as well as the sample databases supplied with Access.

■ No user, including the Admin user, has the authority to revoke the object owner's permissions. By default, the owner of an object has full permissions for the object.

■ The SID (system ID) of the default Admin user is created by combining the user name and company name (if any) you entered when you installed Access and then encrypting the combination. SETUP.EXE imprints setup disk 1 with your user name and company name. (Both names are encrypted on the disk.)

■ Anyone who gains possession of your Access setup disks can install a bootleg copy of Access that creates a SYSTEM.MDW file with the same SID that you (and possibly others) used to create database objects until you (and others) logged on with new user IDs and passwords.

■ The user with the bootleg copy of Access has full permissions for every database object in every unsecure database.

■ You *do not* delete the Admin user at this point because it's possible that something could be wrong with your new account in the Admins group. If this is the case, you wouldn't be able to secure the database with the process described in the following steps. (To solve this problem, relaunch Access and log on as the Admin user and make sure that the Admins group has full permissions for all objects in the database. Delete the newly added account and create another new user ID with membership in the Admins group.)

To secure database objects that have a creation date that precedes the time when you secured Access, you need to take ownership of the database objects by importing the objects into a new database file. To assume ownership of objects in existing Access databases, follow these steps:

1. Launch Access with your new user ID and password and choose File | New Database to open the New Database Wizard. Select Blank Database in the General tab and click OK.

2. Type a name for the new database in the File Name text box and click the Create button to create the new database.

3. Choose File | Get External Data | Import to display the Import dialog box. Search for the database in which you're going to take ownership of objects, and click the Import button. For this example, you will use the NorthWind.MDB database.

4. Select one or more `Tables`, and any other object that you want to import, from the Objects dialog box, as shown in Figure 19.22, and then click the OK button to import the table into your new database. (Make sure that the default Definition and Data option button is selected before you click the Import button.)

FIGURE 19.22.

The Import Objects dialog box for Table objects in NorthWind.MDB.

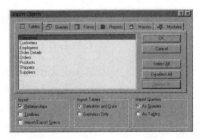

5. Access confirms that the tables (and other selected objects) have been imported by listing them in the NewDatabase window, as shown in Figure 19.23.

FIGURE 19.23.

Successful importation of an Access object.

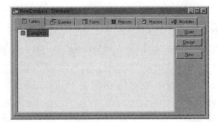

6. After you've imported all the objects into the new database, inspect the Table, QueryDef, and any other imported Access objects to make sure that the objects imported properly.

7. Make a backup copy of the original database and then delete the original database and rename the new database to that of the original.

You now have a secure database in which you are the undisputed owner of all the database objects. If Microsoft had made the take ownership (O) permission of Windows NT applicable to Access database objects, the transfer of title would be a much simpler process.

Granting and Revoking Access Permissions for Groups and Users

By default, Access grants full permissions on all Table and QueryDef objects to members of the Users group. Granting full permissions by default to the Users group has been the subject of many complaints from Access developers. It's unlikely that you want everyone who can open the database to have read-write access to all or even any of the tables in the database. This is especially true of databases that are the source of data for decision-support applications. (One of the Canons of Database Administration is this: *I shall grant no one with a title other than Data Entry Operator or Data Entry Supervisor read-write privileges in my databases.*)

Because all except the Guest user of Access databases must be a member of the Users group, you need to revoke modify data privileges from the Users group and create a new group, DataEntry, that has both read data and modify data privileges. (Everyone with access to the database should be granted read definitions privileges.)

Revoking Permissions from the User Group

To revoke modify definitions and modify data permissions from the Users group for objects in your databases, follow these steps:

1. Open the database that has permissions you want to modify and choose Security | Permissions to open the Permissions dialog box. The first Table object in the database is the default object.

2. Click the Groups option button in the List group to display groups instead of users in the Name combo box. Select Users from the Name combo box.

3. Click the Modify Definitions and Modify Data check boxes to clear the check marks, as shown in Figure 19.24.

4. Click the Assign button to make the revocation of modify definitions and modify data permissions permanent.

5. Choose the remaining objects in the database and repeat steps 3 and 4 to revoke the write permissions for each object.

6. When you've completed this tedious operation, click the Close button to return to Access's main window.

FIGURE 19.24.

Revoking modify definitions and modify data permissions from the Users group for a database object.

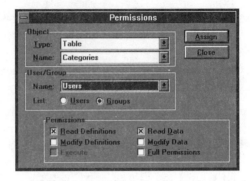

Members of the Users group no longer have default (implicit) permissions to modify the design of tables or queries, or to update tables in this database. You can give specific members of the Users group modify data permission by listing users instead of groups, selecting the user from the combo box, and clicking the Modify Data check box. Implicit permissions of users inherited from group membership don't appear in the check boxes when you display individual user permissions. (This is a peculiarity of the Access security system.)

Creating a New Access Group and Assigning Group Permissions

Follow these steps to create a new DataEntry user group and set up the correct permissions for the new group:

1. Open one of the databases that you want to make available for updating by members of the DataEntry user group. Choose Security | Groups to open the Groups dialog box.

2. Click the New button to open the New User/Group dialog box, shown in Figure 19.25. Type the name of the new group (DataEntry) in the Name text box and type a PIN for the group in the Personal ID Number text box.

FIGURE 19.25.

Creating a new Access group.

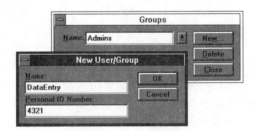

3. Click the OK button to close the New User/Group dialog box. Click the OK button of the Groups dialog box to close it.

4. Perform steps 2 through 6 of the preceding section, with the following exceptions: Select the DataEntry group in step 2 and remove only the check mark in the Modify Definitions check box in step 3 so that members of the DataEntry group can update tables in the database.

Summary

This chapter covered a great deal of territory, from an elementary description of PC networking systems to the intricacies of security management with Windows NT Server to creating Access databases that have both network and internal security. Although this chapter could have been divided into two chapters that separately discussed networking and Access security topics, the relationships described between network and Access security methodology are an aid to a better understanding of Access's security features.

The next chapter delves into the issues you face when you create front ends for client-server RDBMSs instead of desktop databases. The Microsoft ODBC API and SQL Server 4.21 for Windows NT running under Windows NT Server are used for the sample applications in Chapter 20.

20

Creating Front Ends for Client-Server Databases

Up to this point, this book has used desktop database files in all the examples of Visual C++ database applications. Sample applications that use Access database files predominated in the preceding chapters because the .MDB file format is Microsoft's (and the authors') preferred database file structure for applications that don't need to maintain interoperability with existing DOS applications that share dBASE, FoxPro, or Paradox 3+ table files. Another reason for using the .MDB database file structure is that .MDB files resemble the file structures used by client-server databases.

This chapter introduces you to the principles employed to create Visual C++ database applications that serve as front ends for client-server RDBMS back ends. The RDBMS used for the majority of the examples in this chapter is Microsoft SQL Server for Windows NT 6.0 (SQL Server) running as a service of Windows NT Server 3.51 (NTS). Therefore, this chapter begins with a description of SQL Server and the use of the new Enterprise Manager database tools provided with SQL Server 6.0.

The examples in this chapter use the Microsoft ODBC API (version 2.0) and use either the MFC database classes or the `SQL...()` functions. The examples are equally applicable to most client-server RDBMSs for which ODBC drivers that support core-level SQL grammar and offer level-1 ODBC compliance are available. For example, a program that interacts with an Access .MDB file could easily interact with an xBase file as well. Chapter 7, "Using the Open Database Connectivity API," describes Visual C++'s interface to the ODBC API in detail and explains how to use single-tier ODBC drivers. Therefore, this chapter discusses only those elements of the ODBC API, such as creating client-server ODBC datasources, that are specific to multiple-tier ODBC drivers and Visual C++ front ends for client-server RDBMSs. This chapter includes an example of exporting data from Access databases to client-server tables because Visual C++ developers often are called on to upgrade Visual C++ (and Access) applications from desktop RDBMSs to client-server database front ends.

Designing Visual C++ front ends for client-server databases follows the same methodology as designing applications that manipulate tables of conventional desktop databases, as described in earlier chapters. If you have an RDBMS table structure that duplicates the structure of the tables that compose your desktop database, you can simply change the open statements to open tables in the ODBC datasource instead of those in the desktop database. In most cases, however, using the `SQLExecDirect()` function instead of the `SQLExecute()` method greatly improves the performance of client-server front ends when the query is a one-time execution. Thus, this chapter ends with a discussion of how to use SQL pass-through with client-server RDBMSs.

Using Microsoft SQL Server for Windows NT 6.0

Microsoft SQL Server for Windows NT is a major upgrade from Microsoft SQL Server version 4.21. In this chapter, the term *SQL Server* refers to SQL Server for Windows NT version 6.0; references to the Sybase version for UNIX computers are preceded by the word "Sybase."

You can run SQL Server for Windows NT 6.0 either under Windows NT Workstation 3.5 or Windows NT Server 3.5. The SQL Server Setup program can install client software on SQL Server, MS-DOS, Windows, and Windows NT operating environments.

> **NOTE**
>
> Prices and configurations of products such as SQL Server change frequently. You should think of the prices and configurations described next as a quick reference only. Before you make any decisions about these products, contact your favorite reseller.

SQL Server is available in the following license versions (the prices are based on MSRP and were verified in early 1995):

- Any number of clients may be used with the server, but each client must also be licensed.
- Single users (16 or fewer) are licensed at a per-user fee, typically less than $200. Microsoft defines the break point as 20 users; however, one 20-user license costs less than 16 single-user licenses.
- A 20-user license pack costs about $2,000.
- Licenses for more than 50 users are negotiated on a case-by-case basis.
- SQL Workstation is a single-user version that allows up to 15 simultaneous connections. This version contains the ODBC SDK and programming files for the DB-Library. SQL Workstation is intended as a development platform.

> **NOTE**
>
> In mid-1995, Oracle began giving away its product to anyone who wanted to pay shipping and handling or was willing to spend the time downloading the product from Oracle's Internet site for a 30-day evaluation. Only time will tell whether this approach will be successful. However, it's difficult to compete against a free product, especially when that product is as high-quality as Oracle's.

Networking Features and Server Performance

The networking features of Windows NT Server 3.5 and SQL Server are designed for maximum user convenience. For example, you can set up SQL Server so that users are automatically logged on to it when they log on to Windows NT Server 3.5. Automatic logon to the SQL Server server also is provided across remote servers in Windows NT Server 3.5 domains that share a trust relationship.

SQL Server supports simultaneous NetBEUI, IPX/SPX, and TCP/IP connections.

Connections, Threads, and Symmetric Multiprocessing

A conversation between an application and SQL Server takes place through one or more connections established by the named-pipes service that originated in OS/2. A connection is similar in concept to that of the Windows Sockets for TCP/IP communication described in the preceding chapter. The default named-pipes protocol for communicating with SQL Server is provided by the DBNMP3.DLL library, which must be present in your \WINDOWS\SYSTEM or WINNT\SYSTEM directory or the current directory for the application. Named-pipes protocols for the other network operating systems are included on the SQL Server disks.

> **NOTE**
>
> The following information relating to the Access database engine's use of SQL Server connections is based on Microsoft's "Jet Database Engine ODBC Connectivity" white paper, dated July 19, 1993, and written by Neil Black of Microsoft's Jet Program Management group and Stephen Hecht of the Jet Development group. You can download this white paper in Word for Windows format as RJETWP.ZIP from the ODBC Library 11 of the MSACCESS forum on CompuServe. If you use or intend to use ODBC with Visual C++ database applications, you need a copy of this white paper to understand how the Access database engine interacts with the ODBC drivers for client-server databases.

When you use the Access database engine to connect to a server back end with the ODBC API and create a Dynaset object from a query, the operation usually requires at least two connections. (One connection obtains information about the query from the server, and the other passes the data to your application.) If your query is based on a complex SQL statement that involves multiple JOINs or GROUP BYs or creates a crosstab query, it's likely that your application will open several connections at once. Although the Access database engine attempts to share connections when it can, there are many situations in which your application might need several simultaneous connections.

> **TIP**
>
> In a multiuser environment, it's possible to run out of connections with substantially fewer simultaneous users than you've specified as the maximum number of users for SQL Server. It's a common practice to set the number of users as low as practical to conserve memory resources, which are required for each user, for data caching. If you run out of connections, as indicated by an error message returned when your Visual C++ application attempts to run a query, your only solution is to increase the number of users. To do this, you might need to upgrade your SQL Server user license.

With today's trend toward more and more memory in servers, the practice of limiting connection counts to conserve memory might not be meaningful. Also, in regard to licensing, SQL Server will count each workstation as a single connection regardless of how many actual connections there are between the workstation and the server.

OS/2, Windows 95, and Windows NT are multithreaded operating systems. A *thread* is a single task that is executed by an application or the operating system. Multithreaded operating systems let multiple tasks appear to run simultaneously; the operating system determines the priority of the task and lets tasks with the highest priority execute first and most often. Tasks with higher priorities can suspend the processing of lower-priority tasks. Operating systems that let task priorities govern tasks' flow of execution are called *preemptive multitasking* operating systems.

Windows NT provides a thread for each connection from a worker pool of threads whose population is set by the sp_configure stored procedure of SQL Server. When a client workstation makes a request from SQL Server, one of the threads from the worker pool is assigned to the workstation's connection. When the request is fulfilled and the connection is terminated, the connection thread is returned to the pool. If a client workstation requests a thread and none is available in the pool, the first thread released by another connection is assigned to the request. When a fault occurs during the execution of a thread, only the connection associated with the thread is affected. Thus, a page fault on a single connection doesn't bring down the server.

The advantages of a multithreaded operation are particularly evident when you add more than one microprocessor unit to the server. SQL Server supports thread-level multiprocessing, usually called *symmetric multiprocessing* (SMP), and is referred to as a *scalable operating system*. These terms mean that multiple processors that share the same memory region can execute any thread. This process is also called *symmetric load balancing*. If a thread is executing on a processor that is running near capacity, the thread can be transferred so that it executes on another processor. Windows NT Server, and thus SQL Server, supports up to eight 80x86 processors. Multithreaded SMP operation and the capability to run on a variety of microprocessors, not just members of the Intel 80x86 series, are the two most distinguishing features of Windows NT.

NOTE

Finding an eight-CPU computer to run Windows NT Server might be an interesting task. When this book was written, four CPUs was the practical limit.

An Overview of SQL Server 6.0 Features

SQL Server 6.0 has new features that simplify installation and aid in the administration of SQL Server servers and clients. Here are the most important new SQL Server features:

■ The capability to address up to 2GB of RAM. Increasing the amount of RAM to create large data caches greatly improves SQL Server's performance. 32M is the smallest amount of RAM you should consider for an SQL Server server. Installations with more than 10 users should use servers with 48M to 64M of RAM. SMP servers should start with 128M of RAM.

> **NOTE**
>
> In addition to having sufficient RAM, it's important to have a very fast data path to the system's hard disks. Pentium systems with the PCI bus structure, using the Adaptec 2940w PCI SCSI controller, offer an incredible rate of transfer between the hard disks and the system.

■ Graphical database management tools. SQL Server includes 16-bit Windows and 32-bit Windows NT versions of the SQL Security Manager, SQL Enterprise Manager, SQL Transfer Manager, and the ISQL command-line SQL processor that you can execute from Windows for Workgroups, Windows 95, or Windows NT workstations. Figure 20.1 shows the SQL Server for Windows NT application group that appears in the server computer's Program Manager window. Windows NT provides additional Setup, Service Manager, Tape Utility, Security Manager, and Performance monitoring tools. These management tools are discussed in the following sections.

FIGURE 20.1.

The SQL Server application group on an SQL Server.

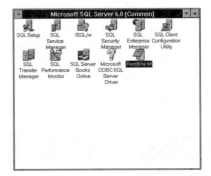

■ Extended stored procedures. Extended stored procedures that carry the prefix xp_ instead of sp_ let you call functions in Windows DLLs or execute Windows NT command-line instructions directly from SQL Server rather than from your front-end application. As an example, you can use the command-line instruction execute master..xp_cmdshell "net send *groupname 'Message'*" to transmit a message to members of a group based on a conditional expression in a Transact SQL trigger. (Transact SQL is the dialect of SQL used by both the Microsoft and Sybase flavors of ANSI SQL. SQL Server triggers are explained later in this chapter.)

■ Simplified installation and setup. As with Windows NT Server 3.5, installing SQL is a simple process. You can perform a basic installation of Windows NT Server 3.5 from a CD-ROM, add SQL Server (from its own CD-ROM or the distribution disks) as a Windows NT Server 3.5 process, and get one or two WfWg or Windows 95 workstations running in an hour or less. Installation time doesn't include the time required to fully configure SQL Server or Windows NT Server 3.5.

■ The capability to store the tempdb database in RAM. SQL Server uses the temporary database, tempdb, for workspace and temporary tables that are needed for some sorting and JOIN operations. If you have sufficient RAM for tempdb and the data cache, you can specify that the tempdb database be stored in memory. Storing tempdb in RAM speeds operations that use temporary tables when SQL Server needs to use tempdb.

■ Tape-backup procedures. Automatic timed backup of the database and transaction log is provided as a function of the Enterprise Manager application. You can perform a dump of more than one object to a single tape. This is an important consideration when you use certified tapes for DAT back-up drives. These tapes are expensive.

The following two sections demonstrate how to use the Microsoft Enterprise Manager to create a new database object, nwind, in the MASTER.DAT device, and how to add a sample table, test, to the nwind database.

Using the Microsoft Enterprise Manager to Create a New Database

The Microsoft Enterprise Manager lets you create and manage the following types of objects:

■ Devices, such as new database (.DAT) files and data dump devices that save data to fixed disk and diskette files as well as to tape drives. When you install SQL Server, default master database file (MASTER.DAT), diskdump, diskettedumpa (drive A), and diskettedumpb (drive B) devices are created for you.

■ Databases that exist within database file devices. You can add new databases or drop databases from .DAT files. During installation, SQL Server creates the master, model, pubs, and tempdb databases within the MASTER.DAT device.

■ Segments that constitute a portion of one or more databases. You use segmented databases to spread a database over more than one disk drive. Segmentation improves the performance of large databases stored on RAID 0 or RAID 5 disk arrays. (Segments actually are pointers to the location of the segment.)

The advantage of the Microsoft Enterprise Manager is that you don't need to type Transact SQL statements at the ISQL command prompt or in the ISQL/w application's query pane to create or modify devices. The following example shows you how to use Enterprise Server Manager to create an nwind database in the MASTER.DAT device:

1. Launch the Microsoft Enterprise Manager from the SQL Server application group.

2. The Register Server dialog box, shown in Figure 20.2, appears. If you have more than one server in your domain, go to the Server combo box and select the server to which you want to connect.

FIGURE 20.2.

The Register Server dialog box in the Microsoft Enterprise Manager.

3. Type your server user ID and password in the Login ID and Password text boxes. If you haven't established an account for yourself, type sa (for "system administrator") in the Login ID text box and leave the Password text box empty.

4. Click the Close button to activate Enterprise Server Manager's main window.

5. Click the DB button on the toolbar or choose Manage | Database to display the Manage Databases MDI child window, shown in Figure 20.3.

6. Click the New Database icon to display the New Database dialog box, shown in Figure 20.4.

FIGURE 20.3.

The default databases in MASTER.DAT.

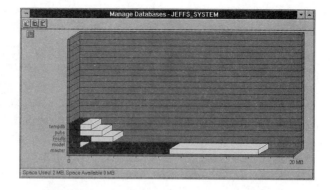

FIGURE 20.4.

The New Database dialog box for adding a new database and log to the MASTER.DAT device.

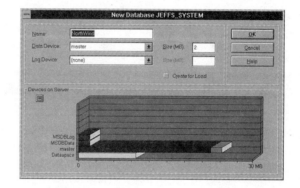

7. Type NorthWind in the Name text box and accept the default master as the Data Device and (none) as the Log Device. Type 2 in the Size (MB) text box to create a database object with a maximum size of 2M. Then click the OK button. (NorthWind.MDB is more than 1M in size, and you can specify database sizes only in 1M increments.)

NOTE

Most client-server RDBMSs require that you specify a maximum size for a database and its corresponding transaction log file. This is a sample database, so you don't need a transaction log file to restore the database in case of hardware failure. (In order to store the log file, you need to create a new device located on a disk drive other than the one on which the database file device is located.) The default size of an SQL Server database is the remaining space in the database file device.

---

8. After a few seconds, the New Database dialog disappears and the Manage Databases dialog appears, showing the new database, NorthWind (see Figure 20.5).

FIGURE 20.5.

The Manage Databases dialog box, confirming the creation of a new database in the MASTER.DAT device.

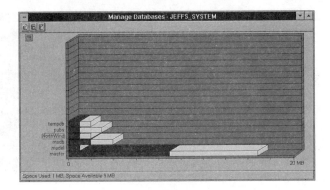

9. Close Enterprise Manager by double-clicking the application control menu box or by choosing File | Exit. Closing Enterprise Server Manager also closes the connection to the server.

NOTE

RDBMSs that have their roots in UNIX conventionally use lowercase letters to identify all database devices and objects, just as it is the norm (actually, a requirement) to use uppercase letters to identify database objects in mainframe databases such as IBM DB2.

Using the Object Management Section of Enterprise Manager to Add a Test Table to NorthWind

You can use Enterprise Manager to create or modify objects in database containers. Using Enterprise Manager isn't much different from creating a new table in Access's table-design mode or using the table-design function of the MS Query sample application.

To add a sample table called "test" to the NorthWind database and define some sample fields, follow these steps:

1. Using the procedure described in steps 2, 3, and 4 in the preceding section, launch Enterprise Manager and connect to the server to display the Enterprise Server Manager window, shown in Figure 20.6.

2. Select the desired server and expand its outline. From the expanded outline, choose the NorthWind database.

3. Choose Manage | Tables to open the Manage Tables window, shown in Figure 20.7. The default name for a new database table is, not surprisingly, <New>.

FIGURE 20.6.

The Enterprise Server Manager window.

FIGURE 20.7.

Adding fields to a new table definition with SQL Enterprise Manager.

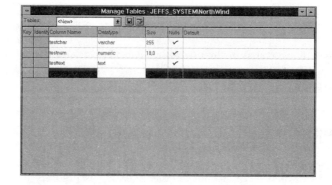

4. Add some fields to the table by entering a field name in the Column Name cell, and then choose a data type for the field by selecting the Datatype cell. Figure 20.7 shows typical field names and Transact SQL data types for the test table.

5. After you've added a representative collection of fields to the test table, click the Save icon. The Specify Table Name dialog, shown in Figure 20.8, appears.

FIGURE 20.8.

The Specify Table Name dialog box, in which you name a new table.

6. Type `test` in the New table name text box and click the OK button to add the fields to the table. Notice that the outline under the NorthWind database has changed to include the new table (see Figure 20.9). Other database objects, Rules, Stored Procedures, and Views, can be manipulated in a similar way.

FIGURE 20.9.

The Server Manager window after you complete the design of the test table.

7. Close the Enterprise Manager application.

The test table created in the preceding steps is used later in this chapter to demonstrate the correspondence between Transact SQL data types and the data types supported by the Access database engine.

Creating ODBC Datasources from Client-Server Databases

Examples in Chapter 7 explain the procedure for creating ODBC datasources from desktop databases using the ODBC database drivers included with Microsoft Office, Excel, and the Microsoft ODBC Desktop Database Drivers kit. The procedure described in the following section for adding the NorthWind database as an ODBC datasource is typical of the method of adding a datasource from the majority of popular client-server RDBMSs for which ODBC drivers are available. Each supplier has a slightly different approach to the design and collection of control objects in the dialog boxes used to set RDBMS-specific options for the datasource.

The following two sections describe how to add the NorthWind database as an SQL datasource and how to test the validity of your new ODBC datasource with the MS Query application.

Adding the nwind Database as an ODBC Datasource

To use the SQL Server ODBC database driver to add the NorthWind database as an ODBC, follow these steps:

1. Launch the ODBC Administrator application. If you installed the ODBC Desktop Database Drivers kit, Microsoft Office, or Microsoft Excel (or almost any ODBC application, such as ReportSmith), the ODBC Administrator's icon is located in Control Panel's window to display the Data Sources dialog box.

2. Click the Add button to display the Add Data Source dialog box, shown in Figure 20.10.

FIGURE 20.10.

The ODBC Administrator application's Add Data Source dialog box.

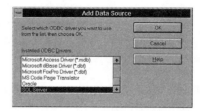

3. Choose SQL Server from the Installed ODBC Drivers list box and click the OK button to display the ODBC SQL Server Setup dialog box, shown in Figure 20.11.

FIGURE 20.11.

Creating a NorthWind ODBC datasource.

4. Click the Options button to expand the ODBC SQL Server Setup dialog box and type NorthWind in the Data Source Name text box. Add an optional description in the Description text box.

5. Go to the Server combo box and select the server for the NorthWind database. If no entries appear, type in the server name. Accept the (Default) entries for the Network Address and Network Library if you're using NetBEUI (the default) as your network protocol.

6. Type NorthWind in the Database Name text box and select (Default) in the Language Name combo box.

7. Click the OK button to close the ODBC SQL Server Setup dialog box. Your new datasource appears in the Data Sources dialog box, as shown in Figure 20.12.

FIGURE 20.12.

The Data Sources dialog box with the new NorthWind datasource added.

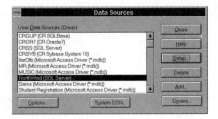

8. Click the Close button to close the Data Sources dialog box.

Testing the ODBC Datasource with the MS Query Application

The ODBC Administrator application doesn't test the validity of your ODBC datasource when you create the datasource within the ODBC Server Setup dialog box. Therefore, you need to verify that the entries created by the ODBC Administrator application in your ODBC.INI file are correct. The entries in the [ODBC Data Sources] and [NorthWind] sections of ODBC.INI in your \WINDOWS directory (assuming that you're using WfWg or Windows 95 and not Windows NT) are as follows. A more thorough discussion of ODBC and the Windows 95 registry is found in Chapter 7.

```
[ODBC Data Sources]
Northwind=Access Data (*.mdb)
Bibliography=Access Data (*.mdb)
MSQueryDBF=dBase Files (*.dbf)
AccessCrosstab=Access Data (*.mdb)
nwind=SQL Server

[NorthWind]
Driver=D:\WINDOWS\SYSTEM\sqlsrvr.dll
Description=Northwind Traders on SQL Server
Server=oakleaf0
Database=nwind
OemToAnsi=No
LastUser=sa
34Cancel=
```

> **NOTE**
>
> The first four entries in the [ODBC Data Sources] section of ODBC.INI result from the examples of using the desktop database drivers that are described in Chapter 9, "Designing a Decision-Support Application." All the entries in the [NorthWind] section result from the entries in the ODBC SQL Server Setup dialog box described in the preceding section.

To test your SQL Server ODBC datasource, follow these steps:

1. Launch MS Query using the MS Query icon or the Microsoft Office Toolbar button for MS Query.

2. From MS Query, choose File | New Query.

3. Choose NorthWind from the Select Data Source dialog box, shown in Figure 20.13. In the resulting dialog box, entries in the [NorthWind] section of ODBC.INI fill in the Database and User ID text boxes for you. Leave the password blank and click the OK button to create a connection to the NorthWind database. (Enter your user ID and password for SQL Server if you're using an account other than the default system administrator account.)

FIGURE 20.13.

MS Query's Select Data Source dialog box for ODBC datasources.

4. A list of all the tables in the NorthWind database appears in MS Query's Add Tables dialog box.

5. Getting this far validates your connection to the NorthWind database. To display and modify the structure of the test table, click the Close button. Select File | Table Structure, choose the NorthWind database, and click the View button. The View Table Definition dialog box appears, as shown in Figure 20.14.

> **NOTE**
>
> The Access database engine doesn't convert some of the Transact SQL field data types to the expected Access field data types. The primary problem is that the longbinary field, specified as Transact SQL's image data type, which is not supported by Access, converts to a binary field of 0 length instead of the expected longbinary field of variable length. Access also doesn't support fixed-length binary fields. These problems are expected to be resolved by future versions of the SQL Server ODBC driver and the Access database engine.
>
> For more information on type conversions, refer to the following topics found in the ODBC 2.0 *Programmer's Reference:*
>
> Converting Data from SQL to C Data Types
>
> Core C Data Types
>
> Extended C Data Types

FIGURE 20.14.

The View Table
Definition dialog box.

6. Click the Cancel button in the View Table Definition dialog box to return to MS Query's main window, and then close MS Query.

Regardless of the problems relating to conversion between Transact SQL and Access data types, you have verified the operability of your SQL Server ODBC datasource.

Using Visual C++'s *SQLConfigDataSource()* Function

The `SQLConfigDataSource()` function lets you perform the same functionality as making entries in an ODBC setup dialog box (such as the ODBC SQL Server Setup dialog box, shown in Figure 20.11). You can use the `SQLConfigDataSource()` function to create, delete, or modify ODBC datasource entries in ODBC.INI, identical to those you create with the ODBC Administrator's setup procedure. Your code needs to execute the `SQLConfigDataSource()` function before executing the `OpenDatabase()` function that refers to the ODBC datasource that has been modified by the `SQLConfigDataSource()` function.

The syntax of the `SQLConfigDataSource()` instruction is as follows:

```
//      Add the datasource to ODBC for the user:

    sprintf(szBuffer,
        "DESCRIPTION=STARmanager saved DB.¦"
        "DSN=StarDatabase files¦"
        "FileType=RedISAM¦"
        "SingleUser=True¦"
        "UseSystemDB=FALSE¦"
        "DataDirectory=%s¦"
        "DATABASE=%s¦¦", szOutFileName, szOutFileName);

    nLength = (int)strlen(szBuffer);

    for (i = 0; i < nLength; i++)
    {
        if (szBuffer[i] == '¦')
        {
            szBuffer[i] = '\0';
        }
```

```
    }

    SQLConfigDataSource(NULL, ODBC_ADD_DSN, "Access Data (*.mdb)",
        szBuffer);
```

`SQLConfigDataSource()`'s prototype is

`SQLConfigDataSource(`*hwndParent, fRequest, lpszDriver, lpszAttributes*`);`

The *hWndParent* argument is the parent window's handle. The *fRequest* argument is one of the following manifest constants: `ODBC_ADD_DSN`, `ODBC_CONFIG_DSN`, or `ODBC_REMOVE_DSN`. The *lpszDriver* argument points to a string that contains the driver description (typically the name of the associated DBMS) that is presented to the user in lieu of the physical driver's name. The *lpszAttributes* argument points to a string containing a list of keyword-value pairs. A typical *lpszAttributes* string might contain this:

`DSN=Personel Data\0OUID=Jones\0OPWD=Password\0DATABASE=Personel\0`

This code fragment shows the keyword-value pairs for an Access database. These keyword-value pairs are described further in the `SQLDriverConnect()` function's description and in the documentation for each specific ODBC driver.

When an `ODBC_CONFIG_DSN` request is made, any of the values in the *lpszAttributes* argument that don't match current entries in the ODBC.INI topic for the datasource are updated. Attribute values aren't case-sensitive.

Creating Tables in ODBC Datasources

You can create new tables in an ODBC database by exporting the structure and data of Access tables to the ODBC datasource using the retail version of Access. The most common situation in which you need to export tables is when you upgrade a Visual C++ database application that uses the Access .MDB file structure to a client-server RDBMS front end. Exporting Access tables is often a more convenient method of creating RDBMS tables than using Enterprise Manager or writing SQL `CREATE TABLE` statements to define the table's structure. Exporting table data is simpler but slower than using SQL Server's bulk copy program, BCP, or equivalent applications of other RDBMSs to add records to the table. The following sections describe how to use Access to export tables from NorthWind.MDB to the NorthWind database on SQL Server.

Exporting Tables in NorthWind.MDB to the NorthWind Database on SQL Server

The NorthWind Traders sample database supplied with Access provides a variety of tables that you can use to test the capabilities of both Access and the ODBC API to create tables in client-server RDBMSs. However, using Access's export feature with the ODBC API and the latest version of the SQL Server ODBC driver isn't a rapid process when it involves tables that contain a large number of records. Be prepared for a very long wait if you export NorthWind.MDB's Order Details table to SQL Server. If you have less than 8M of RAM on the workstation running Access, don't even think about trying the following example; the wait becomes interminable.

To export an Access table to SQL Server, follow these steps:

1. Open Access and NorthWind.MDB.

2. From Access, choose File | Save As to display the Save As dialog box. Select To an external File or Database and click the OK button. The Save Table...In... dialog box, shown in Figure 20.15, appears.

FIGURE 20.15.

Access 7's Save Table...In... dialog box.

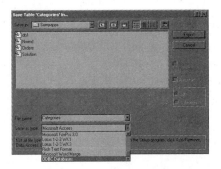

3. Select ODBC Databases from the Save as type list box and click the Export button to display the Export dialog box, shown in Figure 20.16. This dialog box confirms the table that will be exported. Click OK to display the SQL Data Sources dialog box, shown in Figure 20.17.

FIGURE 20.16.

Selecting the Customers table to export to an ODBC database.

FIGURE 20.17.

Access's SQL Data Sources dialog box for ODBC datasources.

4. Select the SQL Server datasource. If you don't have an SQL Server datasource configured, click the New button to add one.

5. Click the OK button to display the SQL Server Login dialog box, shown in Figure 20.18. Your own login user ID automatically appears in the Login ID text box, but you can change it if you want to. Enter your password if you aren't using the default system administrator user ID.

FIGURE 20.18.

The SQL Server driver's SQL Server Login dialog box.

6. Click the OK button to begin the export process. Access's status bar displays the completion percentage of the process, so you can estimate how long it takes to export all of the records.

Displaying the Result of the Export Operation with the Object Management Section of Enterprise Manager

You can use the MS Query application to display the structure of the table you exported in the preceding section. MS Query, however, creates a Snapshot object of the entire contents of the table when you open your query. This can take an appreciable amount of time for a table with many records. Using Enterprise Manager to display the table structure is a faster approach.

Follow these steps to display the structure of the SQL Server version of one of NorthWind.MDB's tables you exported to the temp database and run a simple query to verify that its records are present:

1. Launch Enterprise Manager and connect to the server.

2. Select NorthWind in the Server Manager window and select the Objects folder under the NorthWind database. Open the Tables folder to display the exported tables, as shown in Figure 20.19.

3. Double-click one of the new tables you exported to display the structure of the table, as shown in Figure 20.20.

NOTE

SQL Server, as well as other client-server RDBMSs, doesn't allow spaces in table or field names. The SQL Server ODBC driver substitutes underscores (_) for spaces and any other illegal punctuation in the names of Access tables or fields. Although field names in SQL Server databases traditionally use lowercase letters, capitalization of Access field names is preserved in the export operation.

FIGURE 20.19.

The Server Manager window showing all the objects, including the tables in the North Wind database.

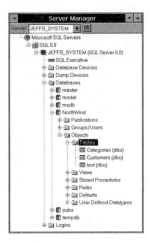

FIGURE 20.20.

Displaying the structure of an exported Access table in the Manage Tables dialog.

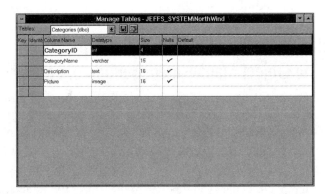

4. Select Tools | Query Analyzer to display the Query window. Enter a simple query, such as the one shown in Figure 20.21.

FIGURE 20.21.

Entering a simple SELECT query in Enterprise Server Manager's Query window.

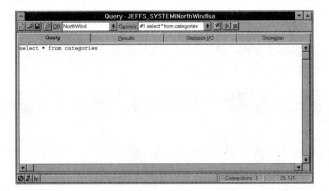

NOTE

Table and field names are case-sensitive in SQL Server. Therefore, you need to type them exactly as they appear in the Column Name column of the Manage Tables window.

5. Click the Execute button or choose Query | Execute to display the query result in the Results window for query #1, as shown in Figure 20.22.

FIGURE 20.22.

The result of the SELECT query shown in Figure 20.21.

The Execute button

TIP

Use the SQL Server's BCP utilities to speed the import of data from large Access tables to SQL Server databases. Create copies of the Access tables using the clipboard and then delete all but a few records in the cloned tables. Export the table structure and the few records to the SQL Server database to create the new table structure and then delete the records in the SQL Server tables. Export the data from the Access tables to a comma-delimited text file. Then use Enterprise Manager's BCP utility to run a bulk copy operation to each SQL Server table. Michael J. Smith, a software engineer and DBA, reported in the article "SQL Server for Windows NT: A Case Study" in the May/June 1993 issue of *SQL Forum* that he was able to achieve a bulk copy rate of 530 records per second over a busy network running the BCP utility from a workstation. (Running BCP from the server reduces the bulk copy rate by about 50 percent.)

Adding an Index to an SQL Server Table with the Object Management Section of Enterprise Manager

When you export an Access table to a client-server database, Access doesn't create indexes on the client-server table. You need to use the SQL CREATE INDEX statement or Enterprise Manager to manually add indexes to the client-server table. You can add one clustered or as many nonclustered indexes as you want to a table with Enterprise Manager. Clustered indexes, which physically place the pages of the table in the index order, greatly improve the performance of SQL Server databases. However, you gain a performance improvement with a clustered index only if you specify that the index must be unique. (Clustered indexes are not unique by default.)

To use Enterprise Manager to create a clustered primary key index on an imported table or any other table in an SQL Server database, follow these steps, which assume that the table you chose for the preceding example is open:

1. Choose Manage | Indexes to display the Manage Indexes dialog box for a new index, as shown in Figure 20.23. Choose the table you want to index from the Table combo box.

FIGURE 20.23.

The dialog box to create a new index on an SQL Server table.

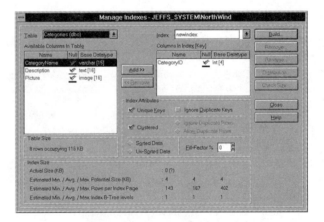

2. Enter a name for the index in the Index field.
3. If you're creating an index on the primary key, click the Clustered and Unique check boxes. Then choose the field(s) you want to index in order to create the primary key in the cells corresponding to the field names.
4. Click the Build button to create the new index. You will then be asked if you want to schedule the build for later or execute it now.
5. When indexing is complete (the Build Button will change to Rebuild), close the Enterprise Manager application.

You can verify that the index is present and is recognized by the SQL Server ODBC driver by attaching the table to Access and then opening the table in design mode. Access assumes that a unique clustered index is the primary key index of an SQL Server table and indicates the key field(s) with the key symbol in the field selector button(s).

Using ODBCTEST to Display the Capabilities of an ODBC Driver

ODBCTEST is an application included with the Microsoft ODBC SDK that lets you inspect and use the low-level functions of the ODBC API. ODBCTEST is used primarily by developers of ODBC database drivers to debug and test the drivers' performance. If you intend to use different types of ODBC datasources or evaluate different drivers for a single data type, ODBCTEST lets you inspect and test each of the drivers' functions.

> **NOTE**
>
> ODBCTEST replaces the GATOR.EXE program that was part of the ODBC version 1.x SDK. There are only minor differences between ODBCTEST and GATOR.

Figure 20.24 shows the ODBC Test window of ODBCTEST after you connect to the NorthWind database and then choose Connect I GetInfo All. The hdbc and hstmt combo boxes let you select the handle to the connected datasource(s) and statement(s) you execute either in the upper pane of the ODBC Test window or by choosing options from a menu.

FIGURE 20.24.

The first few items returned by ODBCTEST's GetInfo All menu option.

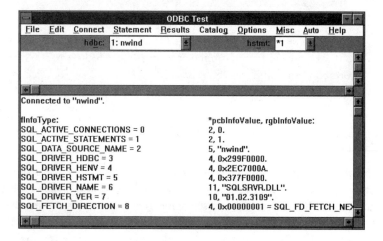

The GetInfo All menu choice returns more than you might want to know about the ODBC driver used to create the connection to the ODBC datasource. One of the most important features of the display provided by the GetInfo All command is the capability to determine the functions and data type conversions that the driver supports. You can use only those functions in your SQL statements that the ODBC driver translates into the appropriate syntax for the RDBMS in use. The documentation for supported functions that is supplied with ODBC drivers often doesn't include this information, and other times the information provided is incomplete. Figure 20.25 shows a few of the functions supported by version 1.02.3109 of the SQL Server ODBC driver.

FIGURE 20.25.

ODBCTEST's list of some of the functions supported by the Microsoft ODBC driver for SQL Server.

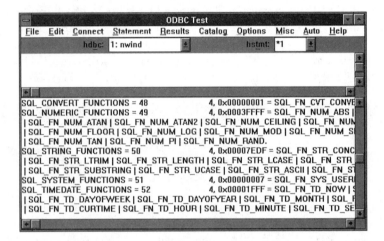

TIP

ODBCTEST's File menu has a Print option, but it's always disabled. You can copy the information in the lower pane of the ODBCTEST's info window to the clipboard. If you want, you can then paste the data into Notepad in order to format and print the information so that it's easier to read.

Summary

This chapter emphasized that creating Visual C++ front-end client-server applications doesn't differ substantially from designing similar applications that connect to conventional desktop databases with the Access database engine. The principal issues for the Visual C++ database developer are setting up the server database and the ODBC datasource(s) for the client-server back end. Thus, this chapter was devoted primarily to discussing the characteristics of a new, fast, and powerful client-server RDBMS, Microsoft SQL Server for Windows NT, and the Microsoft ODBC API.

The next chapter describes how to create mail-enabled Visual C++ applications that use the MAPI interface.

21

Interacting with Microsoft Mail, MAPI, and TAPI

Microsoft Mail is one of the leading contenders in the e-mail application market. With Windows 95, Exchange is the new e-mail client that is gaining popularity with users. When Windows NT is given the Windows 95 user interface, it too will offer an Exchange client. According to BIS Strategic Decisions, a consulting firm in Massachusetts, there were about 2.5 million Microsoft Mail users at the time this book was written. Many Windows 95 users also are connected to some form of e-mail, including internal systems, Microsoft Network (MSN), Internet connections, and other services such as CompuServe, Prodigy, and America Online. Windows NT includes a workgroup version of Microsoft Mail, and future versions of Windows NT will include Exchange. Windows 95's Exchange client supports a wide array of mail types, including the Internet, fax, and MSN. Windows NT's new Exchange Server will be most useful in implementing custom interuser communications.

> **NOTE**
>
> Microsoft has announced its Exchange Server product. This system, which will run under Windows NT Server, lets larger organizations manage mail, Schedule+, Internet mail, and other information-based services. This product should be released in early 1996.

> **NOTE**
>
> It can be expected that eventually Microsoft Mail will be totally replaced with the Microsoft Exchange products. However, at this time it's still as common to see Microsoft Exchange as it is to see Microsoft Mail. Actually, the Microsoft Exchange Server replaces the Microsoft Mail Server.

Applications such as Excel, Word for Windows, and Project, which provide Send and Add Routing Slip menu choices on the File menu, are called *mail-aware applications*. A mail-aware application (MAA) lets you send an object created by the application to one or more users as an attachment to a Microsoft Mail message.

Schedule+ is a simple appointment scheduling and to-do list application that is closely coupled with Microsoft Mail. Schedule+ 7 is included with Microsoft Office 95. Schedule+ is a workgroup scheduling tool that lets you or your designee set up appointments and schedule meetings with other members of your workgroup. Schedule+ checks the appointment calendar of prospective attendees and notifies you of conflicts. You can let Schedule+ find a date and time when all attendees have an open schedule. This can save a substantial amount of time when your meeting involves a large number of people.

Developers who are migrating their consulting practice from DOS to Windows are likely to find that clients are interested in database applications that interact with Microsoft Mail and Microsoft Exchange. This chapter describes how you might create mail-aware Visual C++ database applications. It also shows you how to obtain and use the Schedule+ Libraries (version 1.0a2), which lets you duplicate the functions contained in the Schedule+ application within a 16-bit Visual C++ application. A brief description of the Windows Telephony API (TAPI), which is part of the Windows Telephony SDK, appears near the end of this chapter.

> **NOTE**
>
> The Schedule+ Libraries are available only in a 16-bit version (as of January 1996). The 32-bit version of these libraries is currently not available from Microsoft. Schedule+ 7 is a 32-bit application.

Creating mail-aware database applications with Visual C++ 4 is as simple as selecting the correct option when creating your project using Visual C++ 4's AppWizard. Making an existing application mail-aware is a much more complex topic, one that is beyond the scope of this book. It would probably be easier to create a new mail-aware application shell, grafting on the working parts of an existing application, than to try to add mail-awareness to an existing application. This book's space limitations restrict the discussion of mail-aware Visual C++ applications to an overview of how MFC 4 implements the transfer of documents using Mail and Microsoft Exchange. Sources of additional background information for mail-aware applications, as well as sample applications, are also included in this chapter.

Understanding Microsoft Mail

Microsoft Mail 3.5 for PC Networks was the current version of the full implementation of Microsoft Mail at the time this book was written. The competitive upgrade retail version of Microsoft Mail 3.5 includes one server license and licenses for 10 client workstations. Microsoft Mail 3.5 is designed for enterprise-wide e-mail applications using client-server methodology. Microsoft Mail 3.5 isn't a Windows application. It runs under DOS on a network-connected system.

A variety of mail gateways to networks other than Windows NT Server (NTS) and LAN Manager are available. Novell Corporation has an upgrade to NetWare's *Global Message Handling Service (MHS)* that lets Microsoft Mail 3.5 users connect directly to MHS. Direct connection to NetWare's directory management system eliminates the need for a NetWare gateway to read the NetWare bindery that provides user mail addresses. An optional application, *Microsoft Mail Remote* for Windows (also known as *Remote*), lets modem-equipped computers dial in to the Microsoft Mail 3.5 server. Remote also includes gateways for online e-mail services, such as

CompuServe and AT&T's EasyLink. Windows 95 includes Microsoft Exchange, a comprehensive mail system that lets users use Microsoft AtWork Fax, Microsoft Mail, and Internet E-Mail. Microsoft Exchange also may be used to access other services such as CompuServe. Both Windows 95 and Windows NT allow dial-in/dial-out connections, using Microsoft's RAS (remote access server) technology.

MAPI also supports X.400, an international messaging standard developed by the Consultative Committee for International Telephone and Telegraph (CCITT). The X.400 standard is used for wide-area messaging systems and is the standard messaging protocol in most countries outside North America. X.400 deals with messages that are transmitted by the switched telephone network, as well as dedicated telephone lines, satellite links, and other communication services provided by public and private carriers. X.400 compatibility isn't included in Mail.

The following sections provide a brief introduction to Microsoft Exchange, which is included with Windows 95, and a discussion of the Microsoft Messaging API (MAPI) on which Microsoft Mail 3.5 and Microsoft Exchange are based.

Workgroup Mailboxes, Postoffices, and Administration

Windows for Workgroups, Windows 95, Windows NT Workstation (NTW), and Windows NT Server (NTS) include a workgroup version of Microsoft Mail (also known as Mail). Windows 95 includes Microsoft Exchange, a comprehensive mail system that will be moved to Windows NT with the next release of Windows NT. Microsoft Exchange (called Exchange hereafter) lets the user interface with Microsoft Mail, Internet mail, the Microsoft Network, AtWork Fax, and other mail systems including CompuServe. Exchange is a flexible, powerful system.

User e-mail accounts (called *mailboxes*) are maintained in a group of files that are collectively called a *postoffice*. Mail uses the \WGPO0000 folder and a collection of folders in the \WGPO0000 folder to store postoffice files. (There are more than 100 items in an initial set of postoffice folders and files.)

Windows 95's and Windows NT's Mail are limited to communication with users whose e-mail accounts are maintained in a single workgroup postoffice. This postoffice can reside on either a Windows NT Server or a Windows 95 machine. If you're using NTS and all Windows 95 and Windows NT users log on to one Windows NT Server domain, you can maintain a single Mail postoffice for the entire domain. You can create additional postoffices for individual workgroups, but you need to duplicate the e-mail accounts in each workgroup postoffice manually. This could be an administrative nightmare if your system has many users. The examples in this chapter use the Windows 95 version of Mail. Figure 21.1 shows the information that is contained in an individual e-mail account record.

FIGURE 21.1.

An account record for a workgroup postoffice.

The person who creates a workgroup postoffice directory structure is the administrator of the postoffice. Only the postoffice administrator can add, delete, or edit e-mail accounts. Figure 21.2 shows an example of the Postoffice Manager window with a three-member workgroup. The administrator of the postoffice usually maintains a separate account for administrative messages. In this case, the account sa is for system messages.

FIGURE 21.2.

The Postoffice Manager window.

Information pertaining to the administrator's and/or user's mailbox is stored in MSMAIL32.INI and in Windows' registration database. The private profile file in the \WINDOWS directory contains only a few entries. Most of the information is stored in the registry. Following is an example of the MSMAIL32.INI file for the postoffice administrator shown in Figure 21.2:

```
[Microsoft Mail]
ServerPath=E:\wgpo0000
Login=GayDeciev
```

Microsoft designed Mail to be extensible with add-in applications such as AtWork Fax and Microsoft Electronic Forms (MEF), Microsoft Voice (a voice mail system for Windows 95), and applications provided by independent software vendors (ISVs). The registration database is used to notify Mail of the presence of add-in applications and to provide menu choices to launch the add-ins.

Sending Faxes with AtWork Fax

Windows 95 provides the capability to send faxes from within Microsoft Exchange; this capability isn't included with the Windows NT version of Mail that was current when this book was written. The fax subsystem of Windows 95 is called AtWork Fax, a reference to the Microsoft AtWork API designed to manage compatible office equipment, such as a stand-alone fax machine, over a network. Windows 95 also lets you share a fax modem with other members of your workgroup. If you send the fax with a Class 1 fax modem (Class 1 modems have high-speed data-transmission capability) to another Microsoft Exchange user with a Class 1 fax modem, the fax is transmitted as an e-mail message rather than as a .TIF (bitmap) file. AtWork Fax uses the .DCX format, a modification of the .TIF format that provides multiple fax pages in a single file.

All messages, regardless of their type, are stored in the same mail database. For example, users of Microsoft Voice have their voice mail messages stored in the same postoffice as e-mail documents and faxes.

The Microsoft Messaging API (MAPI)

Microsoft Mail is based on the *Microsoft Messaging API (MAPI)*, one of the components of *Microsoft Windows Open Services Architecture (WOSA)*. MAPI consists of the following three categories of functions:

■ *Simple MAPI* is a set of 12 basic functions that you can use to create simple mail-aware applications. Simple MAPI was the first API used to implement Microsoft Mail. Visual C++'s MAPI custom controls, MEF, and Schedule+ Libraries use Simple MAPI. Simple MAPI is limited to receiving, transmitting, and forwarding messages. Complex message-routing features aren't included in Simple MAPI. Table 21.1 lists the 12 basic MAPI functions, sometimes referred to as the Simple MAPI functions.

Table 21.1. The 12 basic MAPI functions.

Function	Description
MAPIAddress	Creates and modifies address lists.
MAPIDeleteMail	Deletes mail messages.
MAPIDetails	Provides details on a specific address.
MAPIFindNext	Enumerates messages of a given type.
MAPIFreeBuffer	Frees memory allocated for the messaging system.
MAPILogoff	Ends the session with the messaging system.
MAPILogon	Initiates a session with the messaging system.
MAPIReadMail	Reads mail messages.

Function	Description
MAPIResolveName	Resolves a recipient's name (as entered by the user) to a unique mail address.
MAPISaveMail	Saves mail messages.
MAPISendDocuments	Sends a standard mail message attachment.
MAPISendMail	Sends a standard mail message.

■ *Common mail call (CMC)* functions implement Simple MAPI in a standardized format that provides an interface to mail APIs of other software publishers. CMC is the preferred format for creating new mail-aware applications because you can also access messages from other e-mail systems that provide an interface to CMC.

■ *Extended MAPI* is a set of object-oriented functions that let you create *mail-enabled applications (MEAs)*. Extended MAPI lets Visual C++ applications manage creating and manipulating large numbers of complex messages, as well as structured addressing and routing information. Extended MAPI is particularly well suited to developing workflow applications, the subject of the following section.

NOTE

You can download the current version (which was 1.08 at the time this book was written) of the entire MAPI specification in the form of a PostScript file (MAPIPS.ZIP) or a Windows help file (MAPIHL.ZIP) from Microsoft's Internet FTP site at `ftp://ftp.microsoft.com/bussys/mail/pcmail-docs`. You need a PostScript or TrueImage printer to use the expanded version of MAPIPS.ZIP. Another file in the same library, MAPIWP.ZIP, provides detailed information on the client side of MAPI 1.0 in the form of multiple Word for Windows 2.0 .DOC files.

Microsoft also is documenting MAPI in the Win32 SDK. Another source to check is the MSDN CDs, both Level I and Level II. Another source of MAPI documentation is the Visual C++ 4 CD. Look in Books Online, SDKs | WIN32 Extensions | MAPI.

A variety of e-mail applications compete with Microsoft Mail, such as Lotus cc:Mail, DaVinci Mail, and the e-mail component of Corel's Perfect Office. Lotus cc:Mail, for example, includes both the e-mail function and a scheduling application similar to Schedule+. Lotus has proposed another industry standard, *Vendor-Independent Messaging (VIM)*, for e-mail applications. Lotus Notes, the most successful of the workgroup productivity tools to date, uses VIM as its messaging protocol. Oracle Corp. also has introduced an e-mail system, Oracle Mail, that uses the Oracle RDBMS to maintain user accounts on an enterprise-wide scale.

> **NOTE**
>
> Most e-mail applications for Windows include bridges or "glue" that enable the interchange of messages with Microsoft Mail. Conversely, it's likely that future versions of Microsoft products will provide some form of connectivity to the Lotus Notes database. If and when the capability to manipulate the Notes database with a future version of Visual C++ becomes a reality, a variety of new opportunities will be opened to Visual C++ database developers.
>
> Lotus has developed a Notes ODBC driver, which is available from Lotus's forum on CompuServe. This driver might be available from other sources as well. Check `http://www.lotus.com/` for information if you have Internet access.

A practical example of using MAPI to exchange information between users is that of a local software company. Each employee has a computer connected to a Microsoft Windows NT Server, and Microsoft Mail is configured on each machine.

The receptionist fields incoming calls and attempts to connect the caller with the recipient. However, sometimes a caller can't be connected. In this case, the receptionist uses a custom Visual C++ application to create a special mail message that has specific information about the call.

The message is then sent to the recipient, who also is running this application. The application receives the mail and takes the message's contents and places the information about the call in a dialog box for the user. This user may then respond to the message when he or she returns. Although the recipient will probably call back the person who called originally, the message could be edited and forwarded to another person.

Creating Workflow Applications with Visual C++

The primary use of mail-enabled Visual C++ database applications is to create workflow products. Workflow applications substitute e-mail routing methods for the conventional interoffice mail envelope to fill in forms and process documents. The objective of workflow applications is to eliminate the handling of paper documents. The database contains a primary record that identifies each document, plus related records that are used to route the document and to record the events that occur during the processing of the document.

Workflow products fall into three major classifications:

■ *Electronic document interchange (EDI),* which negates shuffling paper purchase orders, shipping notices, bills of lading, invoices, packing slips, and other documents involving the sale and shipment of tangible products. EDI originally was developed to automate transactions between auto makers and their suppliers. EDI forms are based on standard templates for a specific industry. Texas Instruments, Inc. is one of the few firms that provide standard EDI applications for Windows.

■ *Document-management systems (DMS)* that rely primarily on scanned images of incoming and intracompany paper documents. The primary users of document-management systems are insurance companies and financial services firms whose principal activities involve processing paper. Storing bitmapped images, even when they are compressed, occupies very large amounts of disk space, so image files often are stored on high-capacity multiple *write-once-read-many (WORM)* CD-ROM drives called *carousels*. WORM drives can contain from 640M to several gigabytes. The database maintains a record of the filename, the CD-ROM volume, and the CD-ROM drive on which the document is located for retrieval and archiving purposes. Keyfile Corp. and Reach Software Corp. are two of the major suppliers of large-scale, enterprise-wide document-management systems.

■ *Workgroup productivity applications* (groupware), such as Lotus Notes, are database-oriented products that apply to conventional text, word-processing, and worksheet files that are shared among members of workgroups or an entire firm. Lotus Notes also supports faxes and other bitmapped or vector images. The database is used to route the files and to record changes to the documents by members of the workgroup. One of the primary duties of the database is to maintain version control for the original document. Lotus currently relies on independent software vendors to provide enhancements to Notes, such as workflow and document-imaging capabilities, as well as integration with client-server RDBMSs.

You can use Visual C++ to create specialized workflow applications that fall into any of these three categories. Only commercial workgroup productivity applications currently rely on e-mail systems for managing document routing. There is no fundamental reason, however, why customized EDI and DMS applications can't use e-mail methodology for document transmittal. The question is which e-mail methodology to use.

Looking to the Future of Workflow Applications

Ordinarily in this book, discussions of the future of applications and programming tools follow the text that describes today's products. In this case, however, I reversed the order to provide perspective on the development of database-related MAAs and MEAs. The future of mail-aware and mail-enabled applications in the Microsoft environment has been projected in a number of review articles in the computer press. Forewarned is forearmed when it comes to profiting from the development of MAAs and MEAs based on Microsoft Mail, because Microsoft Mail currently is a moving target.

Microsoft's approach to competing with the highly successful Lotus Notes groupware application is to provide toolkits that let developers create their own MAAs. Windows 95 is extensively tuned to the concept of MAPI. Windows NT also is becoming MAPI-enabled. The next section discusses the (limited) applicability of the MAPI to Visual C++ database applications.

Windows 95 and the Win32 SDK offer a powerful punch in the MAPI arsenal. This toolkit will work both with Windows NT and with Windows 95, and it represents Microsoft's attempts to combine the Windows development platforms.

Enterprise Messaging Server (EMS) is a 32-bit Windows NT application that Microsoft demonstrated at the Microsoft Mail Users Conference in mid-1993. EMS is now called Exchange Server and is targeted for an early 1996 release. The server is an add-on to Windows NT Server, in the same vein as SNA Server and SQL Server for Windows NT Server. Exchange Server takes advantage of the international X.400 messaging standard instead of the Microsoft Mail protocol, and it also supports other standard network and messaging protocols such as TCP/IP, Simple and Extended MAPI, X.25, and X.500 directory-naming services. Exchange Server provides the Multipurpose Internet Mail Extensions (MIME) being developed by the Internet Management Group. The backbone of Exchange Server is an RDBMS for storing messages. Using an RDBMS rather than Microsoft Mail 3.5 or Notes' flat file structure lets users create joins and run queries against the database in order to manage messages and attached OLE objects.

Microsoft's challenge is to integrate these officially and unofficially announced products into a cohesive workflow-management development strategy to gain market share from Lotus Notes. The challenge facing Visual C++ database developers is to decide whether to wait for Exchange Server before investing the time required to learn the intricacies of Simple and Extended MAPI. Of course, Microsoft Exchange and Windows 95 became available to users in mid-1995, and a version of Windows NT with Exchange might be released in 1996.

Considering MAPI for Database Applications

You can use the MAPI functions, MAPI Session, and MAPI Messages to create mail-enabled Visual C++ database applications.

■ MAPI Session provides logon services to establish a MAPI session and to close (log off) the session when the messaging operation is complete. Each MAPI session has an individual session handle that is similar in concept to the connection handle for an ODBC datasource (discussed in the preceding chapter). You can establish multiple MAPI sessions within a single application. The important thing to remember is to explicitly close each MAPI session your application opens.

■ MAPI Messages provides all message-handling services for a MAPI session. An instance of MAPI Messages creates two buffers, *compose* and *read*, that contain the text and objects of messages you transmit and receive, respectively. The *compose buffer* contains only one message at a time. The *read buffer* contains an indexed array of messages, starting with an index of 0 for the first message.

> **NOTE**
>
> Generally, if you retain MFC's document-oriented structure, enabling MAPI support when you create your application will provide most of the mail support that most database decision tool applications will require.

> **NOTE**
>
> The MSDN CDs also include additional articles on MAPI, including "Using Mail and MAPI—the Possibilities," an overview of the use of Mail in Executive Information Systems (EISs), and "Creating Workgroup Solutions Using Microsoft Word, Microsoft Mail, and MAPI," which was presented by Michel Girard and Eric Wells at Tech*Ed. Both of these articles provide additional assistance in learning how to use the Mail APIs. "Using Mail and MAPI" makes a vague reference to combining MAPI and ODBC in EISs.

Mail-aware and mail-enabled database applications rely on a fill-in-the-blanks approach to obtaining information to add to specified fields of database tables. You can develop a mail-aware Visual C++ application that generates messages based on choices made from combo boxes and text entered from text boxes, but you can't easily create applications that let the recipient modify the message with control objects. Parsing a completed message to update the database also is a complex process. The Microsoft Electronic Forms Designer add-in for Visual C++, discussed in the following section, provides a solution to these problems.

> **TIP**
>
> To add MAPI to an existing MFC 4 application, follow these steps:
>
> 1. Using the Visual C++ resource editor, modify the application's File menu by adding a new command called Send Mail. Use the command identifier `ID_FILE_SEND_MAIL`. This identifier is defined in the AFXRES.H file.
>
> 2. Add the following bold lines to your application's document message map. Be sure to add these lines outside of the `AFX_MSG_MAP` block:
>
> ```
> BEGIN_MESSAGE_MAP(CMailAwareDoc, CDocument)
>     //{{AFX_MSG_MAP(CMailAwareDoc)
>         // NOTE: ClassWizard will add and remove mapping macros here.
>         // DO NOT EDIT what you see in these blocks of generated code!
> ```

```
        //}}AFX_MSG_MAP
        ON_COMMAND(ID_FILE_SEND_MAIL, OnFileSendMail)
        ON_UPDATE_COMMAND_UI(ID_FILE_SEND_MAIL, OnUpdateFileSendMail)
END_MESSAGE_MAP()
```

This technique works for both CDocument- and COleDocument-based applications.

3. After making these changes, rebuild the project.

Creating a New MAPI-Compliant Application

This section describes the Visual C++ AppWizard steps used to create a new application that supports MAPI. The changes that AppWizard makes to the application are slight; it follows the same steps described in the preceding section.

To create a MAPI-compatible application, start AppWizard. In the Step 4 of 6 dialog, select the MAPI (Messaging API) option, as shown in Figure 21.3.

FIGURE 21.3.

Adding MAPI support in AppWizard's Step 4 of 6 dialog.

After you've created your new project, it will have the necessary support for MAPI. The CD that comes with this book has an example of a Visual C++ 4 AppWizard-created MAPI program. Look in the CHAPTR21\Mail Aware folder.

Obtaining and Using the Schedule+ Libraries

Schedule+ is a mini-PIM (personal information management) system that is included with Microsoft Mail 3+, Windows for Workgroups, and Windows NT. Schedule+ 7, included with Microsoft Office 95, incorporates an appointment calendar, a workgroup appointment management system, and a prioritized to-do (project and task) list. Figure 21.4 shows the to-do list window with three projects and a few prioritized tasks for each project. You can assign scheduled completion dates for each task and block time in your appointment calendar to complete the tasks. Figure 21.5 shows the planning window of Schedule+ with time blocked to complete some of the writing tasks for this book.

FIGURE 21.4.

Schedule+'s project and task manager window.

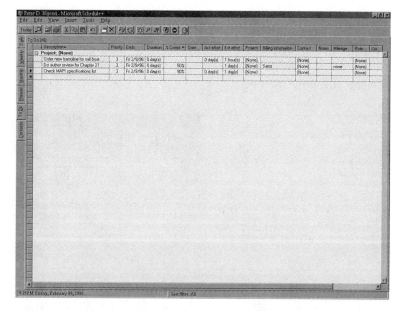

FIGURE 21.5.

Schedule+'s Planner window with time blocked for task completion.

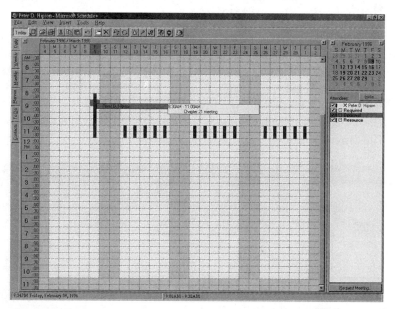

The appointment management system uses Mail to arrange meetings with other members of a workgroup by comparing the participants' free and busy times. When you request a meeting for a specific date and time, Schedule+ creates a graphic overlay of all of the participants' schedules, including your own. If the time you choose conflicts with a participant's schedule, you can select another time or date. Schedule+ also lets you set up postoffice accounts for resources, such as meeting rooms and equipment. Thus, you also can take into account the availability of the resources you need for the meeting. Figure 21.6 shows the dialog box that you use to request a meeting with other members of your workgroup. Users can respond that they will, won't, or might attend the meeting.

FIGURE 21.6.

The dialog box that is used to set up a workgroup meeting.

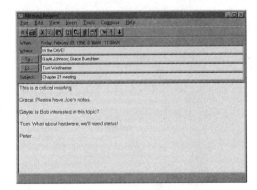

The Schedule+ Libraries for C

The Schedule+ Libraries for C consist of SPLUS.DLL, which contains the functions to manipulate Schedule+ data, documentation for declaring and calling the functions in both Visual C++ and C, and a sample Visual C++ and C application with source code. The Schedule+ Libraries are available for downloading as SAL.ZIP from Library 15, MS Schedule+, of the MSWRKGRP forum on CompuServe and are also included on the MSDN Level I CDs. The Visual C++ documentation is contained in SPLUS-C.DOC, a Word for Windows file. The current version of the Schedule Libraries is 1.0a2.

> **WARNING**
>
> The Schedule+ Libraries are available only in a 16-bit version. At the time this book was written, Microsoft hadn't announced a 32-bit version.

The functions contained in SPLUS.DLL fall into the following two categories:

- *Meeting message functions,* which let you manipulate request-for-meeting messages and responses to request messages
- *Calendar functions,* which let you manipulate the dates, times, and durations of tasks and appointments

In addition to declaring SAL function prototypes and global constants, you also need to declare several user-defined data types (structures).

The SALAPP Sample Application

The demonstration project, SALAPP.MAK, includes a program to create tasks and appointments, to specify user information, and to review replies to meeting request messages. The SALAPP form, which probably wouldn't win a prize in a Visual C++ application beauty contest, is shown in Figure 21.7.

FIGURE 21.7.

The SALAPP form used to create a new appointment.

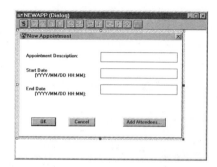

> **NOTE**
>
> Because SALAPP is a 16-bit application, it shouldn't be compiled with Visual C++ 4. Use Visual C++ 1.52, which is included with Visual C++ 4.

SALAPP.MAK also includes the following modules:

- DLGDALLS.C, which manages the dialog boxes in the sample application.
- SALCALLS.C, which receives the input and output from dialog boxes. Other utility functions can be found in this file as well.
- SALMAIN.C, which has the main functions for SAL.
- STRUCTS.C, which has support functions.

Although SALAPP.MAK doesn't perform any functions that you can't handle better with the Schedule+ application itself, the declarations and functions contained in the .C modules can save you a substantial amount of time when it comes to writing your own Visual C++ application that uses SAL.

Visual C++ Database Applications and Schedule+

There are only a few Visual C++ database applications in which you might want to incorporate SAL functions compared to mail-aware and telephony-aware or telephony-enabled applications, the subject of the next section. One application provides a connection between the built-in database of Microsoft Project 4.0 and Schedule+ to create tasks, assign completion dates, and block task times in the schedule of each member of the project team. An automated task assignment system can save a substantial amount of time and prevent errors associated with each member having to manually enter the data.

To create a task database, you can export Microsoft Project's task list to an ASCII file or an Excel worksheet and then use Access to import the ASCII file or worksheet into an Access database table. With Project 4.0, which supports OLE Automation and includes VBA, you could bypass the Access importation step and create a table with Visual C++. Alternatively, you can write VBA code to read the task data into an array and then process tasks for each member of the team without the intervening database.

The Windows Telephony API (TAPI) and Visual C++

Microsoft's new *Telephony API (TAPI)* is the latest addition to the Windows Open Services Architecture. TAPI was developed jointly by Microsoft and Intel Corp. and is a member of Microsoft's "AtWork" series of APIs and applications that are designed to use network connections to interrogate and control devices other than computers. When Microsoft adds the final touches to the other AtWork products, you'll be able to attach and control stand-alone fax machines, copiers, and perhaps even document-filing and transport systems over your network. One of the reasons for including this section in the same chapter as MAPI is that TAPI and MAPI (together with TSPI and MSPI, the service-provider interfaces) share a common model and perform similar functions.

The version of TAPI that was available at the time this book was written (and as supported by Visual C++ 4) is in the process of being finalized. Once TAPI is finalized, the necessary hardware is produced, and the software is written to provide access to telephony devices, you can expect PC vendors to supply computers with built-in telephone handsets or headsets. A phone built into a PC is a natural extension of the audio capabilities now being added to motherboards of PCs, eliminating the need to install an audio adapter card. Plus, a PC with a phone frees the desktop real estate you'll need in order to stack the documentation for these new APIs. The following sections provide a brief introduction to TAPI and show how TAPI fits into the Visual C++ database application picture.

> **NOTE**
>
> There is no MFC wrapper for the TAPI functionality with MFC 4.

NOTE

Microsoft has indicated that, unlike Windows for Workgroups 3.1x, Windows 95 won't have built-in support for ISDN. Microsoft expects others to provide this support. There have been indications that Microsoft will be working on improving Windows 95's ISDN support, probably as part of a Service Pack.

NOTE

Much of the information that follows is based on "The Windows Telephony Approach," a Microsoft white paper that provides a general description of TAPI, and the Microsoft Telephony API and Telephony SPI Specifications that were published in MSDN CD4. The 16-bit version of the TAPI SDK was available on the January 1996 MSDN Level II CDs. For Win32, TAPI support is built in and doesn't use a separate SDK. You can download the preliminary TAPI specification as AP0503.EXE (a self-extracting .ZIP file) from Library 1 of the WINEXT forum or as TAPI.EXE from Library 7 of the Windows User's Group forum (WUGNET) on CompuServe.

You also can search for information about TAPI on Microsoft's Internet site. The Microsoft World Wide Web page (`www.microsoft.com`) provides linkages to help you find this information. The TAPI SDK is available at `ftp://ftp.microsoft.com./Softlib/MSLFILES/TAPISDK.EXE`.

Additional information may be found in the WIN32SDK directory of the Windows SDK.

NOTE

To get a list of all the files available from Microsoft on its FTP site, fetch and unzip the file ls-lr.zip. This file is updated daily with the complete listing of the FTP server. Be careful: The resulting text file is more than 160,000 lines long and more than 7M in size—a big chunk for most text editors!

TAPI Devices

TAPI is designed to provide a computer-based connection between line devices and phone devices. TAPI defines these two device classes as follows:

■ A member of the line-device class is the abstract equivalent of one or more telephone lines. A line device can be one of the following:

A single, conventional telephone company (telco) trunk line

A line that provides both voice and signaling capability (used to connect extensions to a telephone control cabinet). Devices such as the popular digital key systems fit into this category.

Multiple lines, such as those provided by Centrex service

Voice store and forward services (voice mail) provided by a voice server

A .WAV digital sound file on your computer

Each line represents a channel of the line-device class. All channels in a line-device class must be identical.

■ A member of the phone-device class emulates a telephone handset. Phone devices can be conventional handsets, multiline telephone (key) sets, or an audio adapter card that has a microphone and drives headphones or small speakers. PicturePhones and other teleconferencing devices also are included in the phone device class. Video services are provided by Windows 3.1's media control interface (MCI), part of the multimedia extensions to Windows, and multimedia video device drivers.

> **NOTE**
>
> Microsoft recently released Microsoft Voice. This product, available to OEMs of voice-compatible modems, adds a complete voice mail and audio messaging system to a PC. Two modem vendors who are planning or producing products incorporating Microsoft Voice are Diamond MultiMedia (TeleCommander 2500 and TeleCommander 3500 voice modem/sound cards) and Creative Labs (the Phone Blaster voice modem/sound card). Other voice-compatible modem producers will certainly offer either Microsoft Voice or a similar product. Microsoft Voice is fully integrated with both TAPI and MAPI.

The purpose of TAPI is to provide connection methodology between devices of the line and phone classes that is transparent to the physical implementation of the devices. Figure 21.8 represents a configuration in which a telephone connected to an adapter card in a workstation serves as a phone device. A voice server that is connected to a public telephone switch through conventional telco line pairs and to the workstation by an Ethernet LAN serves as the line device. Both the workstation and the server require adapter cards or built-in hardware interfaces to the devices, plus a TSPI-compliant driver for the hardware interface. TSPI is discussed in the following section.

FIGURE 21.8.

Devices connected to a TAPI-compliant workstation and voice server.

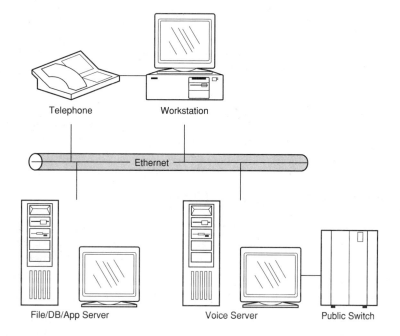

Telephone   Workstation

Ethernet

File/DB/App Server   Voice Server   Public Switch

Windows Telephony Interfaces

Like MAPI, TAPI actually consists of two categories of interfaces. One interface is used to connect external devices to a computer or a LAN, and the other provides the services required by computer applications that use the external telephony devices. The two interfaces defined for Windows telephony are described as follows:

■ The Telephony *Service Provider* (SP) *Interface* (TSPI) that independent suppliers of line and phone devices use to conform their products to TAPI. In most cases, the service provider supplies a plug-in card or (preferably) network adapter to connect the device to a conventional Ethernet, token-ring, or other type of LAN, together with a TSPI-compliant driver. A standard TSPI overcomes the problems created by the current set of widely differing interfaces to services such as the analog Public Service Telephone Network (PSTN), proprietary PBXs, key telephone systems, cellular networks, and the Integrated Service Digital Network (ISDN) that the regional telcos and independent carriers are creating. Examples of SP interfaces include the TeleCommander and Phone Blaster cards mentioned earlier.

■ The Telephony *Application Programming Interface* (the actual TAPI component) lets applications control telephony functions. These functions include the basic telephony activities, such as establishing, answering, and terminating a telephone call. TAPI also provides supplementary functions, such as holding and transferring calls, setting up conference calls, and call parking. TAPI is extensible so as to let service providers define additional custom functions for their particular hardware or communication services. TAPI is designed to isolate the application from the underlying line and phone devices, much as Print Manager isolates Windows applications from the various printer devices attached to computers or directly to the network. An example of an application that fully uses TAPI is Microsoft Voice.

Both TAPI and TSPI are designed for compiling into 16-bit Windows 3.1 applications and 32-bit applications for 32-bit versions of Windows (Windows NT and Windows 95). Both interfaces use 32-bit (double word, 4-byte) unsigned integers for handles.

Simple TAPI and Extended TAPI

TAPI, again like MAPI, provides two levels of sophistication of telephony services within Windows applications. The differences between Simple TAPI and Extended TAPI, which roughly correspond to the differences between Simple MAPI and Extended MAPI, are as follows:

■ *Simple TAPI* lets telephony-aware applications incorporate outbound calling functions from within the application. For example, you might double-click a telephone number or a toolbar button with a telephone icon in a word-processing, spreadsheet, database, or PIM application to make an outbound call. Assuming that you have a built-in PC phone, the TSPI driver places the line device off-hook and then uses dual-tone multifrequency (DTMF) or Touch-Tone dialing to call the number. The process is identical to printing to a fax and then sending it through a local or network fax modem card, except that you don't need the modem.

■ *Extended TAPI* (also called *Full TAPI*) provides telephony-enabled applications with full control of all operations associated with a telephone call. Most telephone-enabled applications run in first-party mode, where the phone device is an end point (originator or recipient) of the call. Telephony-enabled applications can place calls, receive notification of inbound calls, answer inbound calls, activate call-switching features (such as hold, transfer, conference, pickup, and park), and detect and generate DTMF signals that control remote devices. Extended TAPI also enables third-party control of calls. Third-party mode is similar to the operation of a private branch exchange (PBX); the PBX operator is the third party to the conversation, not an end-point of the call.

NOTE

Microsoft Voice is an example of an Extended TAPI application. It can be configured to work as an automated customer support system, can have multiple mailboxes, and can handle distinctive ringing and Caller ID signals.

Simple TAPI and MAPI are sufficient to handle most of the basic messaging requirements of an e-mail system. The proof of this is that, at the time this book was written, Microsoft Mail had reached version 3.5 and had obtained about 30 percent of the mail market. (Lotus's cc:Mail is estimated to have about 50 percent of the market.) Simple TAPI is quite limited in its capabilities. Therefore, you can expect that most applications will implement Extended TAPI and MAPI support.

Visual C++ Database Applications and TAPI

MAPI uses flat-file databases, created when you install Microsoft Mail 3.5, Windows NT, or Windows 95, to store the data required for workgroup and enterprise-wide postoffices, as well as messages. Microsoft's forthcoming Exchange Server replaces the flat file with an RDBMS that serves the same purpose. The file MAILBOX.PST (typically) holds the messages, while the file MAILBOX.PAB (typically, although the user may select other names for these files) holds the user's address book. TAPI, on the other hand, doesn't include a database element; it stores no user information. The lack of a built-in database gives independent software vendors and Visual C++ database developers a new opportunity to expand their product lines and the scope of their consulting activities.

> **NOTE**
>
> .PST files aren't in Microsoft Access format. This format is proprietary and unpublished.

Microsoft and the ISVs are expected to make existing Windows applications telephony-aware in the first upgrade that follows the widespread availability of line and phone devices and the TSPI drivers to support these products. This should start happening in mid-1996, because TAPI-compatible hardware devices are now available. The initial hardware and TSPI drivers are expected to come from existing telephone switch manufacturers, such as Northern Telecom and Rolm Corp., and vendors of PC-based telephone adapter cards and call-management applications. Both Diamond MultiMedia and Creative Labs have hardware on the market, and other manufacturers are quickly adding voice-compatible products to their communications lines. There are a variety of opportunities for designing and writing large-scale telephony-enabled Visual C++ database applications, such as applications to manage telemarketing "boiler rooms," as well as for add-in products that telephony-enable existing Visual C++ database applications with Extended TAPI, rather than making applications only telephony-aware with Simple TAPI.

NOTE

The authors of this book had the pleasure of testing some of the Microsoft Voice products (including Diamond's TeleCommander). The capabilities of these products offer great potential for database developers. Adding a telephone to the test computer required no new hardware. The TeleCommander (which is also a sound card) speakers and microphone formed a working speaker phone. Replacing the speakers with a headset offered an additional degree of flexibility.

Database Applications That Use Inbound Caller ID Services

It is likely that forthcoming Visual C++ database applications will take advantage of the Caller ID services that are provided by local telco exchanges under Signaling System No. 7 (SS7). The Caller ID (Individual Calling Line Identification (ICLID)) service provides the date and time of an inbound call, the calling line number, and a message. The message can be the name of the calling party as it appears in the telephone directory, "Private" (indicating that the caller has invoked ICLID's Block feature to prevent the calling line number from being transmitted), or "Out of Area" (indicating that ICLID services aren't available at the caller's location).

NOTE

At the time this book was written, Caller ID was available in all states except California. The value of Caller ID can't be downplayed. Telephone users can screen calls, let answering machines answer incoming calls, and obtain a number to call back when they receive calls that they can't answer. Caller ID is proving to be quite useful in minimizing harassing, nuisance, and other undesirable phone calls—not the least of which are phone solicitors!

ICLID data is transmitted by FSK (frequency-shift keying, a method similar to that used by 1,200-bps modems) during the silent period between the first and the second rings. A related service, Automatic Number Identification (ANI), is provided by local telcos for 1-800 inbound WATS (wide-area telephone service) lines and ISDN lines. ANI data is transmitted in the form of DTMF signals before the first ring. Generally, TAPI-compatible hardware will respond to or monitor both ICLID and ANI signals.

You can use ICLID or ANI data to perform a Seek operation on a table that contains an indexed field with the telephone numbers of clients, customers, or subscribers. An application can display the inbound caller's record before the first or second ring. TV shopping channels can use reverse telephone directories stored on CD-ROMs to acquire name and address information on the calling buyer.

> **NOTE**
>
> Most large companies now use Centrex systems (or an equivalent) so that each employee with a telephone has a direct line for inbound and outbound calling. Thus, you can create database records for individuals within large firms. Reverse directories, however, don't include entries for individual Centrex lines.

Integrated Messaging Systems

Another application for TAPI is integrating voice-mail messages with e-mail messages in your in-box. Using MAPI, ICLID, TAPI, and a database similar to that described in the preceding section, you can create applications that make voice-mail messages appear in a format similar to that of Mail messages. Double-clicking a voice-mail message header brings up the caller's record (if one exists) or a blank record for an unidentified caller, and simultaneously plays the voice-mail message through your handset or a set of PC speakers.

Microsoft Voice can be programmed to read your e-mail to you over the phone. This feature can be very useful for people who aren't in their offices and receive important e-mail that must be responded to.

MSComm Services

Visual C++ 4 offers a new set of functionality: the Microsoft Comm Control. This OLE control allows an application to interface with a serial port directly. Don't confuse interfacing with a serial port directly with the task of interfacing with a modem. You should interface with modems using TAPI. There are situations in which you've dedicated hardware that is connected to a serial port (perhaps a bar code scanner) that the application must interface with.

You can use the communications control to provide serial communications between your application and a selected serial port. These controls are managed with the MSComm class, which is inserted into your application's project using Insert | Component.

The application can use event-driven communications, a very powerful method of handling serial ports, or use polling to check for events and errors.

Often your application will want to be notified when an event takes place, such as when a character arrives or a change occurs in a comm port status line. The MSComm class permits this type of notification.

The application also can poll for events and errors. This is done by checking the value of an MSComm property (usually after each critical function in your application). Polling is often preferable when the application is small and self-contained. An example is a simple phone dialer.

> **NOTE**
>
> The Microsoft Communications control is covered more fully in Chapter 17, "Using OLE Controls and Automation with Visual C++ Applications."

Summary

This chapter covered MAPI, TAPI, and Microsoft Exchange. It discussed mail-aware applications and interfacing with Schedule+. You also saw how to add MAPI support to a Visual C++ 4 application.

Relatively few commercial Visual C++ database applications use the Messaging API. Fewer yet use the Schedule+ Libraries, and none currently use the Telephony APIs. As the use of e-mail becomes more pervasive and service providers create the hardware and drivers required to implement TAPI, the demand for applications that integrate MAPI, TAPI, and perhaps even Schedule+ will increase dramatically. This chapter demonstrated that employing MAPI MFC 4 support is currently the best approach to creating mail-aware Visual C++ database front-end applications.

This chapter completes Part V of this book. The three chapters in Part VI, "Distributing Production Database Applications," describe the process of upgrading a completed Visual C++ database application to full-fledged production status.

VI

Distributing Production Database Applications

22

Documenting Your Database Applications

A database application isn't complete until you've prepared professional-grade documentation for each element of the application. The "Visual C++" qualifier is missing from the preceding truism of professional database developers because this statement applies to all database applications created with any front-end development tool or programming language. Visual C++ doesn't provide any documentation tools specific to database applications, and what *is* provided (help file shells and source comments) is rather basic.

This chapter describes the following three basic documentation elements for all database applications:

■ Data dictionaries that fully describe the tables of the database(s) used by the application and each field of the tables that the application reads or updates. Data dictionaries also specify primary and foreign key fields and relations between tables, as well as security restrictions that apply to the tables. (Some RDBMSs let you enforce security provisions at the field level.) Referential and domain integrity rules that are enforced at the database and table levels, respectively, or that must be incorporated into every application that updates the tables, are also included in the data dictionary.

■ Code and form printouts that include sufficient commentary to make the source code comprehensible to others who need to maintain the application by revising the code and/or the form design. A programmer should be able to totally reconstruct the original application from this documentation element. Code and form printouts also contain version control information that identifies modifications made to the original code, who made the revisions, the purpose of the revision, and when the revision was made (including the version number to which the revision applies). A flow diagram of the application also aids others who need to understand the concept and construction of your database front end.

■ User manuals that provide instructions for installing and using the application the way you intended. Regardless of how intuitive your application is or how complete its built-in help system is, a printed user manual should be provided as a distributable item of any database application. Although users seldom refer to printed manuals (except as a last resort), your online help system can be created from the user manual if you have WexTech Systems' Doc-To-Help application, which is described near the end of this chapter. Using Doc-To-Help to create Windows help files is covered in Chapter 23, "Creating Help Files for Database Applications."

The major sections of this chapter deal sequentially with each of the documentation elements in the preceding list.

Preparing a Data Dictionary

Data dictionaries are the most important element of database documentation. If you use a product such as Asymetrix's InfoModeler, the process of documenting the database will be a bit easier. InfoModeler provides a vast array of printed reports, tables, and charts to document your database. This chapter describes some of InfoModeler's capabilities, as well as other database documentation techniques.

At the very least, data dictionaries should include the following components:

■ A narrative description of the purpose and overall structure of the database.

■ A detailed description of each table in the database, usually in tabular format.

■ The name of each field of the tables in the database, together with the field data type and field size (if not determined by the field data type).

■ Entries that identify primary and foreign key fields in each table.

■ A list of constraints (validation rules) for field values that are used to maintain domain integrity and an indication of whether these constraints are enforced at the table level by the RDBMS or must be maintained by application code.

■ A graphical or tabular description of the relations between the key fields of the tables and an indication of whether the relational integrity is enforced by the RDBMS or by applications.

■ A list of stored procedures and triggers, including the source code for the stored procedures and triggers, if the RDBMS supports these features.

The following sections describe writing your own Visual C++ application to create a data dictionary, using a CASE tool to create an Access database (including a data dictionary for the database), obtaining table data from Access's Database Documentor (described later), and using a commercial Access documentation tool such as InfoModeler to create data dictionaries for Access databases. The emphasis of this chapter is on the .MDB database format, because the Access database structure is the most likely to be used in the majority of new Visual C++ applications.

Writing a Visual C++ Application to Create a Data Dictionary

It's relatively easy to write a Visual C++ database application to create a fully formatted data dictionary as a text file that you can import into Word for Windows or any other word processing or spreadsheet application. It's an even simpler process if you've created (or have access to the source code for) a data dictionary generator for Access databases that relies primarily on C or C++ code.

DOCDB, the sample data dictionary application that is described in the following sections, is based on the ODBC access routines described in Chapter 7, "Using the Open Database Connectivity API."

DOCDB is a simple form-view Visual C++ program. It was originally developed with Visual C++ 1.5 and was then recompiled as a 32-bit application using Visual C++ 4. It's not uncommon to have to convert 16-bit applications to 32-bit when you're converting to either Visual C++ 2.x or 4. The 32-bit version of DOCDB is available on the CD-ROM that comes with this book.

DOCDB performs a simple task: It provides all the information that ODBC can provide about the columns in a specified table. This information is presented in a form. It would be easy to add report printing capabilities to DOCDB, and even to add the capability to report on all tables in a given database when you create a printed report. However, printed reports would be secondary to adding additional functionality to DOCDB to enhance DOCDB's retrieval of information about a database.

DOCDB is a simple program. It was created using AppWizard, with only two changes to the default "stock" program: It is a Single Document Interface (SDI) program with a `CFormView` view class. Neither database nor OLE support has been added to DOCDB, because these features weren't needed.

After DOCDB has been created, the first step is to incorporate the ODBC routines. Adding this support is detailed in Chapter 3, "Using Visual C++ Database Functions," and it consists of these steps:

1. Copy the ODBC helper routines (ODBC1.C, ODBCMISC.H, ODBC2.CPP, ODBCTABL.CPP, and ODBCINFO.CPP) to the \DOCDB directory.

2. Edit the DOCDB project and add the ODBC helper source files (the .CPP and .C files from step 1) to the project.

3. Edit the ODBC C/C++ source files and add this DOCDB header file `#include` statement:

   `#include "odbcmisc.h"`

4. Copy the dialog box templates from ODBC.RC to the DOCDB resources.

5. Add the ODBC library to the ODCDB library list.

You can refer to Chapter 3 for more-detailed steps if you need to.

After you've followed the preceding steps, you can do a test compile of the ODCDB project. If the compilation succeeds without errors, you can continue to create the DOCDB program.

The next step is to use the resource editor to add the controls to the DOCDB main dialog box. Figure 22.1 shows this dialog box, including the dialog control IDs.

NOTE

All unmarked controls in Figure 22.1 are `IDC_STATIC`.

Each control in DOCDB must be bound to a variable, with the exception of the New Database button, which has an attached function, and the Column Name combo box, which calls a function whenever the current selection (the column in the table) has changed. The dialog is managed by the `CDocdbView` class (found in DOCDBVW.CPP).

FIGURE 22.1.

DOCDB's main window dialog box.

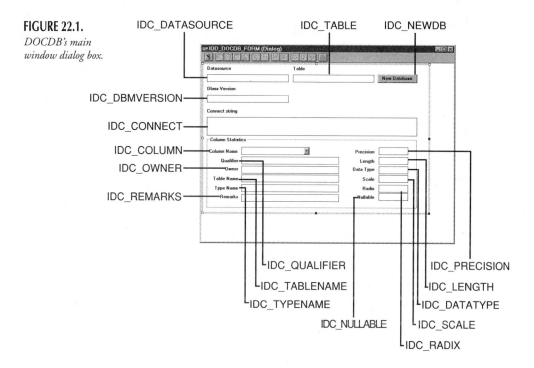

After the dialog box has been created, in Visual C++ use ClassWizard to bind variables to the controls, as shown in Table 22.1.

Table 22.1. Variable names for DOCDB's controls.

Control	Variable Name	Variable Type	Description
IDC_COLUMN	m_ColumnList	CComboBox	The list of all the columns in the selected table is stored here. This is both an input and an output control.
IDC_CONNECT	m_Connect	CString	This output control shows the current connect string.
IDC_DATASOURCE	m_DataSource	CString	This output control shows the datasource name.

continues

Table 22.1. continued

Control	Variable Name	Variable Type	Description
IDC_DATATYPE	m_DataType	int	This output control shows the column's data type.
IDC_NULLABLE	m_Nullable	int	This output control indicates whether the column supports nulls.
IDC_OWNER	m_Owner	CString	This output control shows the table's owner.
IDC_QUALIFIER	m_Qualifier	CString	This output control shows the table's qualifier.
IDC_RADIX	m_Radix	int	This output control shows the column's radix, if applicable.
IDC_REMARKS	m_Remarks	CString	This output control shows remarks on this column, if any.
IDC_SCALE	m_Scale	int	This output control shows the scale of the column, if applicable.
IDC_TABLENAME	m_TableName	CString	This output control shows the name of the table.
IDC_TYPENAME	m_TypeName	CString	This output control shows the column's data type, in character format.
IDC_PRECISION	m_Precision	int	This output control shows the precision of the column.
IDC_LENGTH	m_Length	int	This output control shows the length of the column.
IDC_TABLE	m_Table	CString	This output control shows the name of the current table.

Although DOCDB can show information about columns in a table in a database, it's important to realize that not all ODBC drivers can return all the information. For example, in a text datasource (such as a CSV file), it isn't reasonable to have remarks, scale, or precision information. In fact, most ODBC drivers don't return all the information that DOCDB tries to display. Any information that is unavailable will be displayed as either a blank or a zero, depending on the variable's data type.

When Visual C++'s ClassWizard binds a variable to a control, it creates the code to initialize the variable and to actually transfer the variable's contents to the control. When there must be conversions (such as the conversion of integer variables to text for edit controls), the DDX_Text() macros take care of this conversion automatically.

In addition to binding variables to the controls (as described earlier), it's necessary to also have functions for the IDC_NEWDB button and the IDC_COLUMN combo box. Using ClassWizard (see Figure 22.2), create two functions. For the IDC_NEWDB button, create a function for the message BN_CLICKED. This function will be called each time the user clicks the New Database button. For the IDC_COLUMN button, create a function for the message CBN_SELCHANGE. This function will be called each time the user changes the current column in the table.

FIGURE 22.2.

Functions bound to controls in DOCDB.

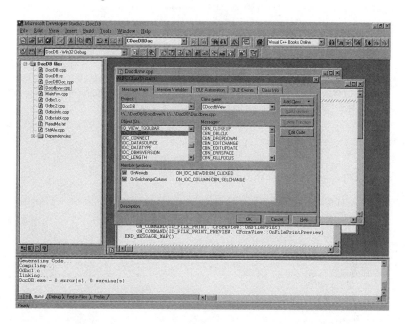

The only changes you need to make to the code created by AppWizard are in DOCDBVW.CPP. You must add the functionality of the two functions created by ClassWizard. Listing 22.1 shows DOCDBVW.CPP. All the code that must be added appears in bold.

Listing 22.1. DOCDBWV.CPP with added code.

```cpp
// docdbvw.cpp : implementation of the CDocdbView class
//

#include "stdafx.h"
#include "docdb.h"

#include "docdbdoc.h"
#include "docdbvw.h"

#include "odbcmisc.h"


#ifdef _DEBUG
#undef THIS_FILE
static char BASED_CODE THIS_FILE[] = __FILE__;
#endif

/////////////////////////////////////////////////////////////////////////////
// CDocdbView

IMPLEMENT_DYNCREATE(CDocdbView, CFormView)

BEGIN_MESSAGE_MAP(CDocdbView, CFormView)
    //{{AFX_MSG_MAP(CDocdbView)
    ON_BN_CLICKED(IDC_NEWDB, OnNewdb)
    ON_CBN_SELCHANGE(IDC_COLUMN, OnSelchangeColumn)
    //}}AFX_MSG_MAP
    // Standard printing commands
    ON_COMMAND(ID_FILE_PRINT, CFormView::OnFilePrint)
    ON_COMMAND(ID_FILE_PRINT_PREVIEW, CFormView::OnFilePrintPreview)
END_MESSAGE_MAP()

/////////////////////////////////////////////////////////////////////////////
// CDocdbView construction/destruction

CDocdbView::CDocdbView()
    : CFormView(CDocdbView::IDD)
{
    //{{AFX_DATA_INIT(CDocdbView)
    m_Connect = "";
    m_DataSource = "";
    m_DataType = 0;
    m_Nullable = 0;
    m_Owner = "";
    m_Qualifier = "";
    m_Radix = 0;
    m_Remarks = "";
    m_Scale = 0;
    m_TableName = "";
    m_TypeName = "";
    m_Precision = 0;
    m_Length = 0;
    m_Table = "";
    m_DbmsVersion = "";
    //}}AFX_DATA_INIT
    // TODO: Add construction code here
}
```

```
CDocdbView::~CDocdbView()
{
}

void CDocdbView::DoDataExchange(CDataExchange* pDX)
{
    CFormView::DoDataExchange(pDX);
    //{{AFX_DATA_MAP(CDocdbView)
    DDX_Control(pDX, IDC_COLUMN, m_ColumnList);
    DDX_Text(pDX, IDC_CONNECT, m_Connect);
    DDX_Text(pDX, IDC_DATASOURCE, m_DataSource);
    DDX_Text(pDX, IDC_DATATYPE, m_DataType);
    DDX_Text(pDX, IDC_NULLABLE, m_Nullable);
    DDX_Text(pDX, IDC_OWNER, m_Owner);
    DDX_Text(pDX, IDC_QUALIFIER, m_Qualifier);
    DDX_Text(pDX, IDC_RADIX, m_Radix);
    DDX_Text(pDX, IDC_REMARKS, m_Remarks);
    DDX_Text(pDX, IDC_SCALE, m_Scale);
    DDX_Text(pDX, IDC_TABLENAME, m_TableName);
    DDX_Text(pDX, IDC_TYPENAME, m_TypeName);
    DDX_Text(pDX, IDC_PRECISION, m_Precision);
    DDX_Text(pDX, IDC_LENGTH, m_Length);
    DDX_Text(pDX, IDC_TABLE, m_Table);
    DDX_Text(pDX, IDC_DBMSVERSION, m_DbmsVersion);
    //}}AFX_DATA_MAP
}

/////////////////////////////////////////////////////////////////////////////
// CDocdbView printing

BOOL CDocdbView::OnPreparePrinting(CPrintInfo* pInfo)
{
    // Default preparation
    return DoPreparePrinting(pInfo);
}

void CDocdbView::OnBeginPrinting(CDC* /*pDC*/, CPrintInfo* /*pInfo*/)
{
    // TODO: Add extra initialization before printing
}

void CDocdbView::OnEndPrinting(CDC* /*pDC*/, CPrintInfo* /*pInfo*/)
{
    // TODO: Add cleanup after printing
}

void CDocdbView::OnPrint(CDC* pDC, CPrintInfo*)
{
    // TODO: Add code to print the controls
}

/////////////////////////////////////////////////////////////////////////////
// CDocdbView diagnostics

#ifdef _DEBUG
void CDocdbView::AssertValid() const
```

continues

Listing 22.1. continued

```
{
    CFormView::AssertValid();
}

void CDocdbView::Dump(CDumpContext& dc) const
{
    CFormView::Dump(dc);
}

CDocdbDoc* CDocdbView::GetDocument() // Non-debug version is inline
{
    ASSERT(m_pDocument->IsKindOf(RUNTIME_CLASS(CDocdbDoc)));
    return (CDocdbDoc*)m_pDocument;
}
#endif   //_DEBUG

/////////////////////////////////////////////////////////////////////////////
// CDocdbView message handlers


typedef struct {
    UCHAR   szQualifier[STR_LEN];
    UCHAR   szOwner[STR_LEN];
    UCHAR   szTableName[STR_LEN];
    UCHAR   szColName[STR_LEN];
    UCHAR   szTypeName[STR_LEN];
    UCHAR   szRemarks[REM_LEN];
    SDWORD  Precision;
    SDWORD  Length;
    SWORD   DataType;
    SWORD   Scale;
    SWORD   Radix;
    SWORD   Nullable;
} COLUMN_ATTRIBUTES;

COLUMN_ATTRIBUTES Columns[70];

void CDocdbView::OnNewdb()
{
// Declare storage locations for result set data

UCHAR   szQualifier[STR_LEN];
UCHAR   szOwner[STR_LEN];
UCHAR   szTableName[STR_LEN];
UCHAR   szColName[STR_LEN];
UCHAR   szTypeName[STR_LEN];
UCHAR   szRemarks[REM_LEN];

SDWORD Precision = 0;
SDWORD Length = 0;
SWORD   DataType = 0;
SWORD   Scale = 0;
SWORD   Radix = 0;
SWORD   Nullable = 0;

// Storage locations for returned bytes stored
```

```
SDWORD   cbQualifier;
SDWORD   cbOwner;
SDWORD   cbTableName;
SDWORD   cbColName;
SDWORD   cbRemarks;
SDWORD   cbDataType;
SDWORD   cbTypeName;
SDWORD   cbPrecision;
SDWORD   cbLength;
SDWORD   cbScale;
SDWORD   cbRadix;
SDWORD   cbNullable;

// Declare miscellaneous variables

char     szSource[60];
char     szDirectory[132];
char     szTable[60];
char     szDSN[256];
char     szConStrOut[256];
char     szDbmsVersion[256];
char     szBuffer[513];
int      i;
int      j;
HENV     henv;
HDBC     hdbc;
HSTMT    hstmt = SQL_NULL_HSTMT;
RETCODE  RC;
int      nConStrOut;
SWORD    swReturn;


    szSource[0] = '\0';
    szTable[0] = '\0';
    szDirectory[0] = '\0';

    GetODBC(
        szSource, sizeof(szSource),
        szTable, sizeof(szTable),
        szDirectory, sizeof(szDirectory));

    m_DataSource = szSource;
    m_Table = szTable;

    SQLAllocEnv(&henv);
    SQLAllocConnect(henv, &hdbc);

    sprintf(szBuffer, "DSN=%s", szSource);
    strcpy(szDSN, szBuffer);

//    To display ConnectDlg(), set the DSN to a null-length string:
//    szDSN[0] = '\0';

    RC = SQLDriverConnect(hdbc, m_hWnd,
        (unsigned char far *)szDSN, SQL_NTS,  // strlen(szDSN),
        (unsigned char far *)szConStrOut, sizeof(szConStrOut),
        (short far *)&nConStrOut,
```

continues

Listing 22.1. continued

```
            SQL_DRIVER_COMPLETE);

    if (RC != SQL_SUCCESS && RC != SQL_SUCCESS_WITH_INFO)
    {
        SQLPrintError(henv, hdbc, hstmt);
    }
    else
    {// Display the connect string returned:
        for (i = 0, j = 0; i < (int)strlen(szConStrOut); i++)
        {// Copy and format. Add space after each ';' in string:
            szBuffer[j++] = szConStrOut[i];

            if (szConStrOut[i] == ';')
                szBuffer[j++] = ' ';
        }
        szBuffer[j++] = '\0';

        m_Connect = szBuffer;
    }

    RC = SQLAllocStmt(hdbc, &hstmt);
    if (RC != SQL_SUCCESS && RC != SQL_SUCCESS_WITH_INFO)
    {
        SQLPrintError(henv, hdbc, hstmt);
    }


//    Get the columns in the specified table:
    RC = SQLColumns(hstmt,
        NULL, 0,     // All qualifiers
        NULL, 0,     // All owners
        (unsigned char __far *)szTable, SQL_NTS,  // The table!
        NULL, 0);    // All columns

    if (RC != SQL_SUCCESS && RC != SQL_SUCCESS_WITH_INFO)
    {
        SQLPrintError(henv, hdbc, hstmt);
    }

// Get and display the DBMS version number:

    SQLGetInfo(hdbc, SQL_DBMS_VER, szDbmsVersion,
        sizeof(szDbmsVersion), &swReturn);

    m_DbmsVersion = szDbmsVersion;

//    Now bind variables to columns!

    RC = SQLBindCol(hstmt, 1,  SQL_C_CHAR, szQualifier, STR_LEN,&cbQualifier);
    RC = SQLBindCol(hstmt, 2,  SQL_C_CHAR, szOwner, STR_LEN, &cbOwner);
    RC = SQLBindCol(hstmt, 3,  SQL_C_CHAR, szTableName, STR_LEN,&cbTableName);
    RC = SQLBindCol(hstmt, 4,  SQL_C_CHAR, szColName, STR_LEN, &cbColName);
    RC = SQLBindCol(hstmt, 5,  SQL_C_SSHORT,
        &DataType, sizeof(DataType), &cbDataType);
    RC = SQLBindCol(hstmt, 6,  SQL_C_CHAR, szTypeName, STR_LEN, &cbTypeName);
    RC = SQLBindCol(hstmt, 7,  SQL_C_SLONG,
        &Precision, sizeof(Precision), &cbPrecision);
```

```
RC = SQLBindCol(hstmt, 8,  SQL_C_SLONG, &Length, sizeof(Length), &cbLength);
RC = SQLBindCol(hstmt, 9,  SQL_C_SSHORT, &Scale, sizeof(Scale), &cbScale);
RC = SQLBindCol(hstmt, 10, SQL_C_SSHORT, &Radix, sizeof(Radix), &cbRadix);
RC = SQLBindCol(hstmt, 11, SQL_C_SSHORT,
    &Nullable, sizeof(Nullable), &cbNullable);
RC = SQLBindCol(hstmt, 12, SQL_C_CHAR, szRemarks, REM_LEN, &cbRemarks);


// Then get the column names (clear list and fill array)

m_ColumnList.ResetContent();
i = 0;
j = 0;
while(i < 70)  // Maximum number of columns we allow!
{
    RC = SQLFetch(hstmt);
    if (RC == SQL_ERROR || RC == SQL_SUCCESS_WITH_INFO)
    {
        SQLPrintError(henv, hdbc, hstmt);
    }
    if (RC == SQL_SUCCESS || RC == SQL_SUCCESS_WITH_INFO)
    {
        // Save this column for the future!
        strcpy((LPSTR)Columns[i].szQualifier, (LPCSTR)szQualifier);
        strcpy((LPSTR)Columns[i].szOwner, (LPCSTR)szOwner);
        strcpy((LPSTR)Columns[i].szTableName, (LPCSTR)szTableName);
        strcpy((LPSTR)Columns[i].szColName, (LPCSTR)szColName);
        strcpy((LPSTR)Columns[i].szTypeName, (LPCSTR)szTypeName);
        strcpy((LPSTR)Columns[i].szRemarks, (LPCSTR)szRemarks);
        Columns[i].Precision = Precision;
        Columns[i].Length = Length;
        Columns[i].DataType = DataType;
        Columns[i].Scale = Scale;
        Columns[i].Radix = Radix;
        Columns[i].Nullable = Nullable;


        j = m_ColumnList.AddString((LPCSTR)szColName);
        m_ColumnList.SetItemData(j, i++);
    }
    else
    {// That's all, folks...
        break;
    }
}

m_ColumnList.SetCurSel(0);

OnSelchangeColumn();

 SQLFreeStmt(hstmt, SQL_CLOSE);
SQLFreeStmt(hstmt, SQL_UNBIND);

//    END: Got the columns in the specified table:

SQLDisconnect(hdbc);
SQLFreeConnect(hdbc);
```

continues

Listing 22.1. continued

```
    SQLFreeEnv(henv);
}

void CDocdbView::OnSelchangeColumn()
{

int    nCurSel = (int)m_ColumnList.GetItemData(m_ColumnList.GetCurSel());

    m_Qualifier = (LPSTR)Columns[nCurSel].szQualifier;
    m_Owner = (LPSTR)Columns[nCurSel].szOwner;
    m_TableName = (LPSTR)Columns[nCurSel].szTableName;
    m_TypeName = (LPSTR)Columns[nCurSel].szTypeName;
    m_Remarks = (LPSTR)Columns[nCurSel].szRemarks;

    m_Precision = Columns[nCurSel].Precision;
    m_Length = Columns[nCurSel].Length;
    m_DataType = Columns[nCurSel].DataType;
    m_Scale = Columns[nCurSel].Scale;
    m_Radix = Columns[nCurSel].Radix;
    m_Nullable = Columns[nCurSel].Nullable;

    UpdateData(FALSE);
}
```

In this listing you see how the ODBC helper routine `GetODBC()` has been called, which prompts the user for database, table, and (if applicable) directory names. The names will be stored in the locations specified in the call:

```
szSource[0] = '\0';
szTable[0] = '\0';
szDirectory[0] = '\0';

GetODBC(
    szSource, sizeof(szSource),
    szTable, sizeof(szTable),
    szDirectory, sizeof(szDirectory));
```

After you have the name of the database and table, you can open the database and determine attributes. This is done using the `SQL...()` functions, which are described more fully in Chapter 3.

The process of using a database consists of the following steps:

1. Allocate the environment using `SQLAllocEnv()`. This function takes only one parameter, a pointer to an unused environment handle.

2. Allocate the connection using `SQLAllocConnect()`. This function takes two parameters: the environment handle (returned by the `SQLAllocEnv()` function) and a pointer to a database connection handle. The connection handle is then used by virtually all the other `SQL...()` functions.

3. Connect to the database using `SQLConnect()` (or `SQLDriverConnect()`) and the connection handle that was returned by the `SQLAllocConnect()` function, as well as the database connection information such as the database name, user name, and password.

4. After connecting to the database, you must allocate a statement. You do this with the `SQLAllocStmt()` function.

5. After the statement has been allocated, you can issue an SQL command. For example, you could issue a `SELECT * FROM` statement to get records from each column in the database. The actual fetching of the data from the columns would be done in a loop that has an `SQLFetch()` call.

6. When the application is done with the database, you must free the statement handle, disconnect from the database, free the connect handle, and free the environment handle. You perform these steps in the opposite order of steps 1 through 4.

The following code fragment shows the function that gets information about the columns in a given table. All the lines that aren't directly related to the database process have been eliminated:

```
SQLAllocEnv(&henv);
SQLAllocConnect(henv, &hdbc);

RC = SQLDriverConnect(hdbc, m_hWnd,
    (unsigned char far *)szDSN, SQL_NTS,  // strlen(szDSN),
    (unsigned char far *)szConStrOut, sizeof(szConStrOut),
    (short far *)&nConStrOut,
    SQL_DRIVER_COMPLETE);


RC = SQLAllocStmt(hdbc, &hstmt);

RC = SQLColumns(hstmt,
    NULL, 0,    // All Qualifiers
    NULL, 0,    // All owners
    (unsigned char __far *)szTable, SQL_NTS,  // The table!
    NULL, 0);   // All columns

//    Now bind variables to columns!

RC = SQLBindCol(hstmt, 1,  SQL_C_CHAR, szQualifier, STR_LEN,&cbQualifier);
RC = SQLBindCol(hstmt, 2,  SQL_C_CHAR, szOwner, STR_LEN, &cbOwner);
RC = SQLBindCol(hstmt, 3,  SQL_C_CHAR, szTableName, STR_LEN,&cbTableName);
RC = SQLBindCol(hstmt, 4,  SQL_C_CHAR, szColName, STR_LEN, &cbColName);
RC = SQLBindCol(hstmt, 5,  SQL_C_SSHORT,
    &DataType, sizeof(DataType), &cbDataType);
RC = SQLBindCol(hstmt, 6,  SQL_C_CHAR, szTypeName, STR_LEN, &cbTypeName);
RC = SQLBindCol(hstmt, 7,  SQL_C_SLONG,
    &Precision, sizeof(Precision), &cbPrecision);
RC = SQLBindCol(hstmt, 8,  SQL_C_SLONG, &Length, sizeof(Length), &cbLength);
RC = SQLBindCol(hstmt, 9,  SQL_C_SSHORT, &Scale, sizeof(Scale), &cbScale);
RC = SQLBindCol(hstmt, 10, SQL_C_SSHORT, &Radix, sizeof(Radix), &cbRadix);
RC = SQLBindCol(hstmt, 11, SQL_C_SSHORT,
    &Nullable, sizeof(Nullable), &cbNullable);
RC = SQLBindCol(hstmt, 12, SQL_C_CHAR, szRemarks, REM_LEN, &cbRemarks);
```

```
while()
{
    RC = SQLFetch(hstmt);
    // Save this column for the future!
}

SQLFreeStmt(hstmt, SQL_CLOSE);
SQLFreeStmt(hstmt, SQL_UNBIND);

SQLDisconnect(hdbc);
SQLFreeConnect(hdbc);
SQLFreeEnv(henv);
```

Adding CTL3DV2V2.DLL to Create Three-Dimensional, Shaded Dialog Boxes

No accoutrements, such as progress-metering gauges, are added to DOCDB, because one of the purposes of this sample application is to demonstrate the ease with which databases created with Access can be accessed by Visual C++ applications. However, the CTL3DV2.DLL library is used to add a gray background and a 3-D effect to dialog boxes and message boxes under some versions of Windows.

> **NOTE**
>
> At this stage in the life of Windows, only Windows 3.x and Windows NT really need to use CTL32V2.DLL. Windows 95 has this functionality built in. However, there is a version of CTL32V2.DLL for Windows 95 for applications that need it.

CTL3DV2.DLL is a small (about 25K) library that is included with Visual C++, Microsoft Office, and several other Microsoft applications. CTL3DV2 can be found in the \REDIST directory, where the ODBC and SQL redistributable components reside.

Because CTL3DV2.DLL is included as part of ODBC's installation, you can generally assume that most users of Windows database applications have a copy of CTL3DV2.DLL in their \WINDOWS\SYSTEMS directory. Excel 5, Word 6, and other Microsoft products released in late 1993 use CTL3DV2.DLL rather than CTL3D.DLL because of problems caused by incompatible versions of CTL3D. Some software suppliers modified CTL3D for their applications without renaming the files. There are also several versions of CTL3DV2.DLL, some of which might not be compatible with Visual C++ and the current releases of other Microsoft applications. The version used in DOCDB is dated 9/16/95, has a file size of 27,136 bytes, and is for Windows NT. For Windows 95, this file is 26,624 bytes long and is dated 9/16/95. CTL3DV2.DLL files with dates later than mid-1995 (when Windows 95 was released) that have approximately the same file size should work as well, because Microsoft often redates files using the release date of the product that the file is distributed with.

TIP

You can obtain a copy of CTL3DV2.DLL by copying it from the \MSDEV\REDIST directory from your Visual C++ CD. For applications that will be created to run solely under Windows 95, you don't need to include CTL3DV2, because this functionality is built into Windows 95. Windows NT users should use the file CTL3D32.DLL (or copy it and rename it CTL32NT.DLL), which is in the \MSDEV\REDIST directory on the Visual C++ 4 CD.

NOTE

The CTL3DV2.DLL and CTL3D32.DLL libraries are copyrighted by Microsoft, and the license to distribute Microsoft's copyrighted files in conjunction with your Visual C++ applications does include the right to distribute CTL3DV2.DLL as part of the OLE and ODBC distribution kit you include with your applications. You need to determine whether prospective users of your applications currently have access to CTL3DV2.DLL from \WINDOWS\SYSTEM on their local computers. If it isn't installed, you must install it. If it's already installed, and it's an older version than the one your application is supplying, you should replace it.

Running DOCDB

To run DOCDB, follow these steps:

1. Create and compile the DOCDB project. The source is on the source code disk. Alternatively, you can create your own project using the listings from this chapter. If you're not comfortable using Visual C++, practice by creating your own version of DOCDB.

2. Start the DOCDB program, shown in Figure 22.3. You can run DOCDB either from the Visual C++ workbench or from Windows.

3. Select from the list the database you want to open. If your database hasn't been installed in the ODBC system, install it and rerun DOCDB. Click the New Database button to display the SQL Data Sources dialog, shown in Figure 22.4. Figure 22.5 shows the NorthWind example opened in DOCDB.

FIGURE 22.3.

DOCDB's dialog box to open the source database file.

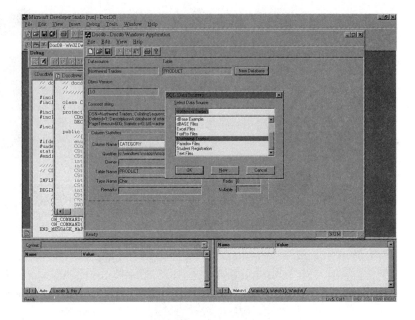

FIGURE 22.4.

DOCDB and the dialog allowing a database file to be opened.

FIGURE 22.5.

The DOCDB program with the NorthWind sample database open.

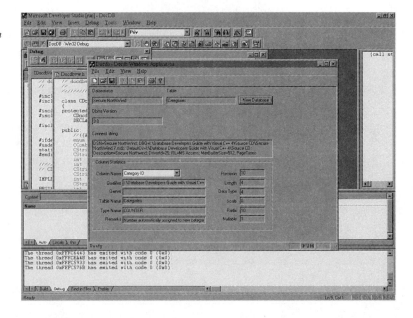

NOTE

If you receive an `Error Opening File` message, or if the Column Name combo box is blank, open the database in Access and make sure that the Admin user (or your user ID) has read permissions on all system tables in the database.

TIP

You can compare the speed of operation of Access and Visual C++ database applications on your computer by timing the execution of both a Visual C++ application and an equivalent application that runs under Access.

Also, if you're competent with Visual C++ 4's DAO, you might want to compare DAO with both ODBC and Access. The results might be enlightening!

Altering the Visual C++ Code in DOCDB

You have the capability to print reports that contain the information that DOCDB displays in its main window. A `CFormView` application doesn't have printing enabled by default, and there is no code to print the window's contents. However, it's not difficult to take the information contained in the `Columns[]` array and format a simple report for your records. The `SQLGetInfo()` function will return a vast amount of information about drivers, SQL, and datasources.

Exporting Access's Database Documentor Output

Access 2's Database Documentor lets you export a database document report; however, it won't export the subreports. This makes the exporting of database documents virtually useless. There is a solution, however, that requires only a minimal amount of work. You must install a generic, text-only printer in Windows, and then assign this printer to a file instead of a printer port. When the Database Documentor report is printed, it will be printed to a standard ASCII file. You can then import this file into Excel as desired. This problem has been fixed in Access 7, which exports in text formats and as an Excel spreadsheet.

NOTE

Access 7 allows you to directly save your documentation in an Excel, RTF, or DOS text format. If you will be using this documentation in Excel, you should export it directly in the Excel format rather than trying to load the text-formatted file into Excel.

Listing 22.2 shows the NorthWind database documentation saved using the technique just described. This file can be saved directly in an Excel or Word (RTF) format or in a DOS text file format. Of course, any formatting that the report originally contained will be lost if exported in a DOS text file, but the report's information will be complete. In Listing 22.2, I've included only one table for the sake of brevity. The full report as produced by Access is over 50 pages long. (You can find this listing on the CD that comes with this book. It's called rptObjects.txt.)

Listing 22.2. NorthWind documented by Access's Database Documentor.

```
                                          Thursday, January 18, 1996
Table: Categories                                         Page: 1




Properties
Date Created:      3/17/94 3:01:37 PM      Def. Updatable:    True
Last Updated:      3/17/94 3:02:46 PM      Record Count:      8




Columns

         Name                              Type             Size

         Category ID                       Number (Long)       4
             Allow Zero Length:    False
             Attributes:           Fixed Size, Auto-Increment
             Collating Order:      General

             Column Hidden:        False
             Column Order:         Default
             Column Width:         1110
             Description:          Number automatically assigned
                                             to new category.

             Ordinal Position:     0

             Required:             False
             Source Field:         Category ID
             Source Table:         Categories

         Category Name                     Text               15
             Allow Zero Length:    False
             Attributes:           Variable Length
             Collating Order:      General

             Column Hidden:        False
             Column Order:         Default
             Column Width:         1395
             Description:          Name of food category.

             Ordinal Position:     1
             Required:             True
             Source Field:         Category Name
```

```
            Source Table:              Categories


Description                               Memo
            Allow Zero Length:         False
            Attributes:                Variable Length

            Collating Order:           General
            Column Hidden:             False
            Column Order:              Default
            Column Width:              4380

            Ordinal Position:          2
            Required:                  False
            Source Field:              Description
            Source Table:              Categories


    Picture                               OLE Object
            Allow Zero Length:         False
            Attributes:                Variable Length
            Collating Order:           General

            Column Hidden:             False
            Column Order:              Default
```

```
                                    Thursday, January 18, 1996
Table: Categories                              Page: 2


            Column Width:              1470
            Description:               A picture representing
                                              the food category.

            Ordinal Position:          3
            Required:                  False
            Source Field:              Picture
            Source Table:              Categories
```

```
Relationships

    Reference1_Products

                Categories                        Products

            Category ID            1        Category ID


            Attributes:                Enforced
            Attributes:                One-To-Many
```

continues

Listing 22.2. continued

```
Table Indexes

        Name                                Number of Fields
        Category Name                       1

                Clustered:          False
                Distinct Count:     8
                Foreign:            False

                Ignore Nulls:       False
                Name:               Category Name
                Primary:            False

                Required:           False
                Unique:             True
                Fields:             Category Name, Ascending

        PrimaryKey                          1
                Clustered:          False
                Distinct Count:     8

                Foreign:            False
                Ignore Nulls:       False
                Name:               PrimaryKey

                Primary:            True
                Required:           True
                Unique:             True

                Fields:             Category ID, Ascending



                                        Thursday, January 18, 1996
Database: I:\Database Developers Guide with Visual C++ 4\Source      Page: 3
CD\NorthWind 7.mdb



Properties
AccessVersion:          06.68               Build:                  4
Collating Order:        General             Def. Updatable:      True

Query Timeout:          60                  Records Affected:       0
Transactions:           True                Version:              3.0

User Permissions

        admin

        User
        User1
```

Group Permissions

    Admins

    Users

Relationships: All

Relationships

    Reference

             Customers   Orders

        Customer ID   1   Customer ID

             Attributes: Enforced, Cascade Updates
             Permissions: One-To-Many

    Reference1

             Suppliers   Products

        Supplier ID   1   Supplier ID

             Attributes: Enforced
             Attributes: One-To-Many

    Reference1_Products

             Categories   Products

        Category ID   1   Category ID

             Attributes: Enforced
             Attributes: One-To-Many

    Reference2

             Products   Order Details

continues

Listing 22.2. continued

```
                    Product ID              1       Product ID



            Attributes:                 Enforced
            Attributes:                 One-To-Many


                                            Thursday, January 18, 1996
Relationships: All                                        Page: 5


    Reference3


                    Shippers                            Orders
                                        1
                Shipper ID                          Ship Via


            Attributes:                 Enforced
            Attributes:                 One-To-Many



    Reference4


                    Orders                          Order Details
                                        1
                Order ID                            Order ID


            Attributes:                 Enforced, Cascade Deletes

            Attributes:                 One-To-Many



    Reference5

                    Employees                           Orders

                Employee ID             1           Employee ID


            Attributes:                 Enforced

            Attributes:                 One-To-Many
```

Of course, you can simply print the report generated by the Database Documentor using a high-quality printer. Figure 22.6 shows the first page of the report in Access. The actual print-out is identical to the screen image.

FIGURE 22.6.

The first page from Database Documentor.

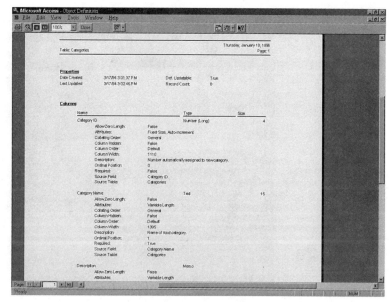

Using Access's Database Documentor to Document Databases

Access 2's Database Documentor lets you create tables you can use to develop a data-dictionary application. The Database Documentor is located under Tools | Analyze | Documentor in Access 7.

To use the Database Documentor to create information from which you can build a data dictionary, follow these steps:

1. Launch Access's Database Documentor by selecting Tools | Analyze | Documentor. You will see the Database Documentor dialog, shown in Figure 22.7. If you want to, you can use this dialog to display a list of all the objects in the currently open database by changing the Object Type selection.

2. Click the Select All button to select all the tables, and then click the OK button to display the results of Database Documentor. You can add the tables to any Access database file, including the database that you're analyzing. In this case, select NorthWind.MDB and click the OK button to start the analysis.

3. After a period of intense disk activity, you will see the results of Database Documentor. When you have finished viewing the results (and printing, if desired), you can simply close the Database Documentor window.

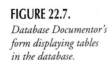

FIGURE 22.7.

Database Documentor's form displaying tables in the database.

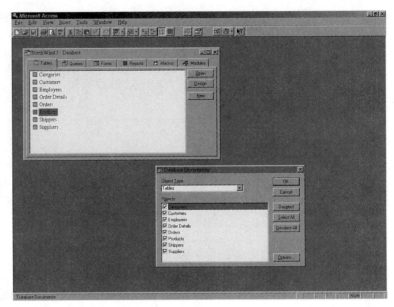

Documenting Databases Created with CASE Tools

If you create your Access or client-server databases with a computer-aided software engineering (CASE) tool, such as Asymetrix's InfoModeler, you can expand the contents of your data dictionary to include descriptions of the underlying object types, fact types, and constraints from which the design of the database is created. Using InfoModeler to create Access databases is one of the subjects of Chapter 4, "Optimizing the Design of Relational Databases." Figure 22.8 shows part of one page (Advertising) of the database diagram of the MailOrder tutorial application that accompanies InfoModeler version 1.5.

All the information about object types, fact types, and constraints is stored in a repository, a database that contains information about databases. Using InfoModeler's reporting features, you can create a report that you can integrate with a data dictionary for the database that InfoModeler creates for you. A part of the report that InfoModeler creates for the Advertising element of the MailOrder application is shown in Figure 22.9. (The entire report is eight pages long.)

After you've completed your database design, InfoModeler creates the database for you. If you have the retail version of Access, you can create an Access database. Otherwise, InfoModeler creates the ANSI (generic) SQL statements required to build the database. Figure 22.10 shows Access's design-mode view of the CoopAd table. InfoModeler creates the CoopAd table from the information stored in the repository that underlies the database diagram shown in Figure 22.8 and that is described in the report file, part of which appears in Figure 22.9.

FIGURE 22.8.

A part of the Advertising element of InfoModeler 1.5's MailOrder tutorial application.

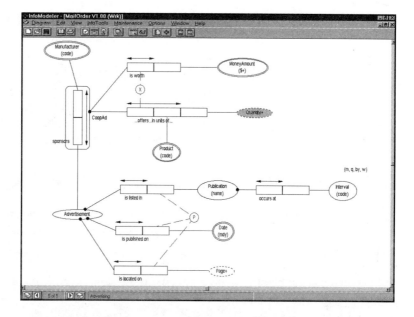

FIGURE 22.9.

Part of an InfoModeler report in print preview mode.

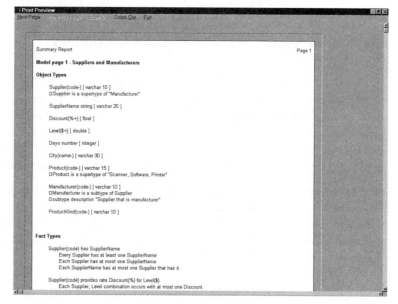

FIGURE 22.10.

An Access table in the MAIL_ORD.MDB database created by InfoModeler.

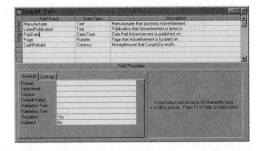

> **NOTE**
>
> One of the advantages of using a CASE tool such as InfoModeler is that you can include the table and field descriptions in your data dictionary. The table and field descriptions originate in InfoModeler, not in Access, so the values of the Description property of the Table and Field objects that InfoModeler creates are available to your data dictionary application. You'll need to dig a bit, however, to obtain the data from Raima's Vista database, which is used as InfoModeler's repository.

Using Total Access to Create a Data Dictionary

Financial Modeling Specialists (FMS), Inc.'s Total Access is an Access 2 library database that you attach to the retail version of Access using a setup program supplied by FMS. FMS's Total Access provides comprehensive documentation and analysis of Access databases, not just the simple listing of some table and field properties that Access's Database Documentor generates. Total Access includes a large number of built-in reports that you can use to print a complete description of the database, including a detailed data dictionary for Table and Field objects. You also can modify Total Access's reports to suit your own requirements.

Total Access generates thorough documentation for all Access database objects. Figure 22.11 shows Total Access's Document Form, which corresponds to the Database Analyzer, with NorthWind.MDB as the active database. If you're using Access databases only with Visual C++ applications, you'll only be able to take advantage of Total Access's Table and Queries documentation features.

Start Total Access by selecting File | Add-ins | Total Access Analyzer. After you've selected the objects you want to document, click the Next button and wait while Total Access does its job. A progress monitor shows you how much of the documentation process has been completed. Preparing the documentation for the 125 objects of NorthWind.MDB (everything in the NorthWind.MDB database) took about 10 minutes on a Pentium server and a Pentium 90 computer with 32M of RAM and a total of 6 gigabytes of high-speed SCSI fixed-disk space. If you limit your documentation to tables and queries, for example, this processing time will be less.

FIGURE 22.11.

Total Access's main analysis window.

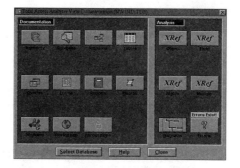

Figure 22.11 shows all objects contained in NorthWind.MDB following an analysis.

After Total Access builds the required tables, creating and printing reports such as the Table Dictionary shown in Figure 22.12 is a fast process.

FIGURE 22.12.

Total Access's Table Dictionary report in print preview mode.

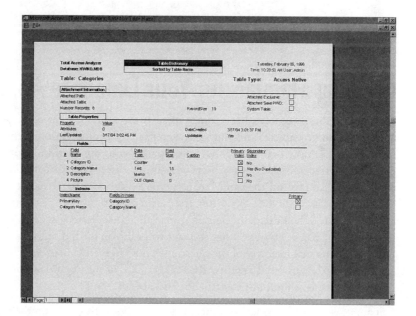

One of the principal benefits of using Total Access for creating data dictionaries is that you can open TA2DOC_C.MDA as a database in your Visual C++ data dictionary generator. Total Access creates one or more internal tables with a TA2_ prefix for each class of Access database object. Figure 22.13 shows part of the TA2_OutputFields table for the NorthWind.MDB database. Total Access includes the Description properties of Table and Field objects in its tables and reports. FMS obtains this information by opening each Table object in design mode and reading the value of the property.

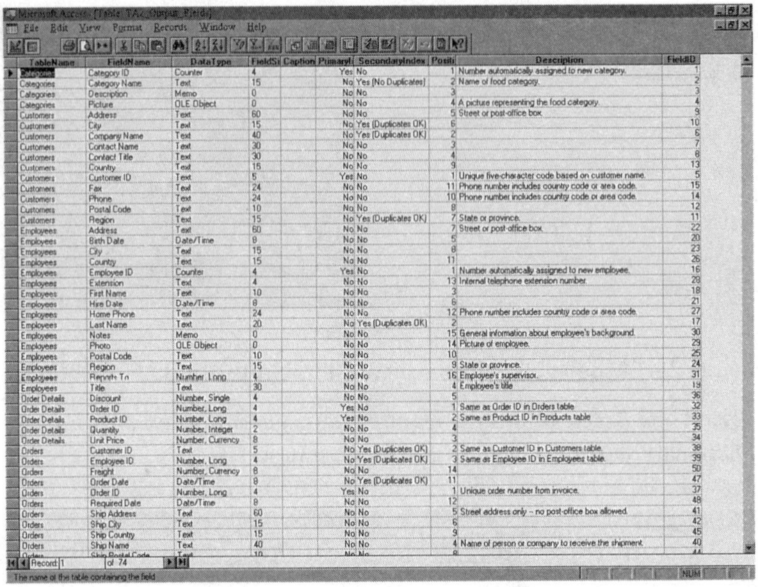

FIGURE 22.13.

One of the tables created by Total Access to document Access Table objects.

Creating Manuals for Your Database Applications

Despite the almost universal reluctance of software users to refer to printed manuals, your application isn't complete until you've written its user documentation. Relying on users to read or print the README.TXT file that accompanies your application before installing it is seldom an effective approach. Most users will simply insert your distribution disk 1 in a drive, choose File | Run from Program Manager, type a:\setup or b:\setup in the Command Line text box, and then click the OK button. If this entry doesn't work, the user next tries a:\install or b:\install. When this fails, he might read the "Installation" section of your documentation. It's more likely, however, that the user will call you to find out what's wrong. Microsoft reports that the vast majority of the questions posed to members of the Product Support Staff for Access can be answered in either README.TXT or the documentation that accompanies Access. The same is undoubtedly true for Visual C++.

Of course, you could be smart and include installation instructions on the label of the first disk of your application. If the installation instructions don't fit on the label, the installation is probably too complex and should be reworked.

Remember that Windows 95 has specific installation requirements, many of which are discussed in Chapter 24, "Creating Distribution Disks for Visual C++ Applications." You should also refer to the Windows 95 documentation for more information about the Windows 95 logo requirements.

The Structure of User Manuals

The structure of user manuals for Visual C++ is similar to that of a book, even if the manual contains only a few pages. The following three sections describe the basic structure of a conventional software user manual.

> **NOTE**
>
> Much of the material in the following sections is based on information contained in *Graphic Design for the Electronic Age* by Jan V. White, a Xerox Press book published by Watson-Guptill Publications of New York. The book's subtitle, *The Manual for Traditional and Desktop Publishing,* aptly describes its content. *Graphic Design for the Electronic Age* provides background and pointers on type selection, page design, and publication construction.

Front Matter

Front matter for user manuals usually is more extensive than that for a conventional textbook and follows the general structure of the front matter for computer software tutorial and reference works, such as this book. The following are the elements of front matter for a typical user manual:

- Title page, which includes the name of the application, the version number(s) of the application to which the manual applies, the publication date, the copyright information, the name of the author and the sponsoring organization (if applicable), and similar information.

- Introduction and acknowledgments, both of which are optional in application manuals. The introduction might include a brief description of the application and its objectives, as well as the objective of the manual.

- Typographic conventions, which describe how the text is formatted to distinguish information you read on-screen or type on the keyboard from the rest of the text. Conventions used to describe multikey operations, such as Alt-*key* or Ctrl-*key,* also are included in the front matter. The typographic conventions section should precede the first use of the conventions in the manual.

■ Equipment requirements, which list the minimum PC configuration required to run the application. This section should include descriptions of any special hardware (such as a mouse), network connections, or software that is required to make full use of the application. In addition to minimum RAM requirements, you should specify the amount of free disk space required to install the application, separated into space required in the application's home directory and in the \WINDOWS and \WINDOWS\SYSTEM directories.

■ Installation instructions, which describe the procedure required to set up the application. If the application makes changes to the user's CONFIG.SYS, AUTOEXEC.BAT, WIN.INI, or SYSTEM.INI files, these changes should be described in this section. A list of files that the installation requires and the location of those files also should be included here or in an appendix.

■ Uninstall instructions, which describe the process of removing the application from the user's disk drive. This includes undoing changes made to WIN.INI, SYSTEM.INI, and any other private initialization files, such as MSMAIL.INI. Alternatively, uninstall instructions can be located in an appendix.

■ Other front matter that won't be incorporated into the online help file. An example is a bibliography, which lists other publications needed to use the application effectively or that describe how the application is integrated into a suite or collection of applications.

■ Table of contents, which diagrams the book's structure. The table of contents (TOC) should include the titles and page numbers of each of the chapters or the principal elements of the book. The Contents choice of the help file is based on your manual's TOC.

Except for the table of contents, front matter normally isn't included in the online help file for your application. You can move the installation instructions to the text section of the book if you want, but the preferred location is close to the front of the manual. Users are more likely to refer to the instructions if they appear in the first few pages of the manual.

Text

The text of manuals usually is broken into chapters and sections. If the manual consists of more than about 10 chapters, you might want to break the text into collections of related chapters, called parts. If your manual contains a tutorial and a reference guide for the application, separate parts should be assigned to contain the chapters in each category. The text component of the manual is used to create the online help file. Separate help files often are used for the tutorial and reference parts.

Back Matter

Material that is supplemental to the text or that assists readers in understanding the text is included in the back matter. Back matter may contain the following elements:

■ A glossary, which explains terms that might be unfamiliar to readers. A good practice is to explain unfamiliar terms when they're first used and to include the explanation in the glossary. This lets the reader look up the meaning of the term if he or she missed the initial definition.

■ An appendix, which might include "Most-Frequently-Asked Questions," a list of error messages (and explanations of why the errors occur and what to do when the user encounters them), a general troubleshooting guide, and, if necessary, an abbreviated data dictionary for the database(s) used by the application.

■ An index, with references to the page number(s) for all significant topics covered in the text. The index serves as the list of search terms for your online help file. Reviewers of software documentation consistently pan user manuals that don't include complete and accurate indexes.

Adding the glossary to the online help system is optional but recommended. Appendixes don't usually appear in help files, and the index serves as the backbone of the search topics in the help system.

Using Doc-To-Help to Create Convertible Manuals

WexTech Systems, Inc.'s Doc-To-Help application consists of a set of templates for Word for Windows that are specifically designed for writing software user manuals, plus other files that are associated with converting the manuals into Windows WinHelp (.HLP) files. Chapter 23 describes how to use Doc-To-Help to convert the user manuals you write into .HLP files. Standard templates are included for conventional 8 1/2- by 11-inch manuals with conventional section headings, like those used in this book (D2H_NORM.DOT), or a side-head style, in which the headings appear in the left margin (D2H_SIDE.DOT). Doc-To-Help also supports the standard 7- by 9-inch manual format (D2H_SMAL.DOT). Figure 22.14 shows a WexTech sample file, D2HINTRO.DOC, that uses D2H_NORM.DOT opened in Word for Windows.

> **NOTE**
>
> Doc-to-Help comes in two versions. Version 1.7 supports both Word 2 and Word 6. Version 2 supports Word 7. There is an upgrade path to let Doc-To-Help 1.6 users upgrade to either version 1.7 or 2 as needed.

FIGURE 22.14.

A Doc-To-Help sample file with an embedded illustration in metafile format.

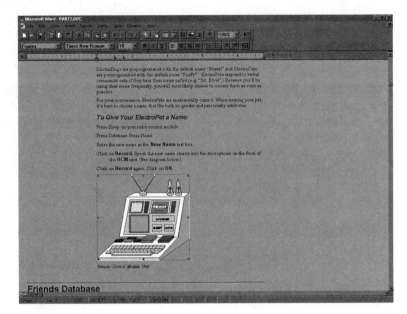

Although you can write manuals that you can convert to WinHelp .HLP files with any word processing application that supports footnotes and can export text and images as Microsoft rich text format (.RTF) files, using Word for Windows together with Doc-To-Help saves considerable time in creating the printed version of your manual. Doc-To-Help's standard templates provide the foundation for attractively formatted manuals, but you can alter the styles employed by the standard templates if you need to conform to company-wide publication standards. Figure 22.15 illustrates Doc-To-Help's standard 8 1/2- by 11-inch manual style. The major time-saving feature of Doc-To-Help—and thus the principal justification for acquiring Doc-To-Help—is the ease with which you can compile your manuals into WinHelp .HLP files that provide access to almost every feature offered by the Windows 3.1 version of WINHELP.EXE.

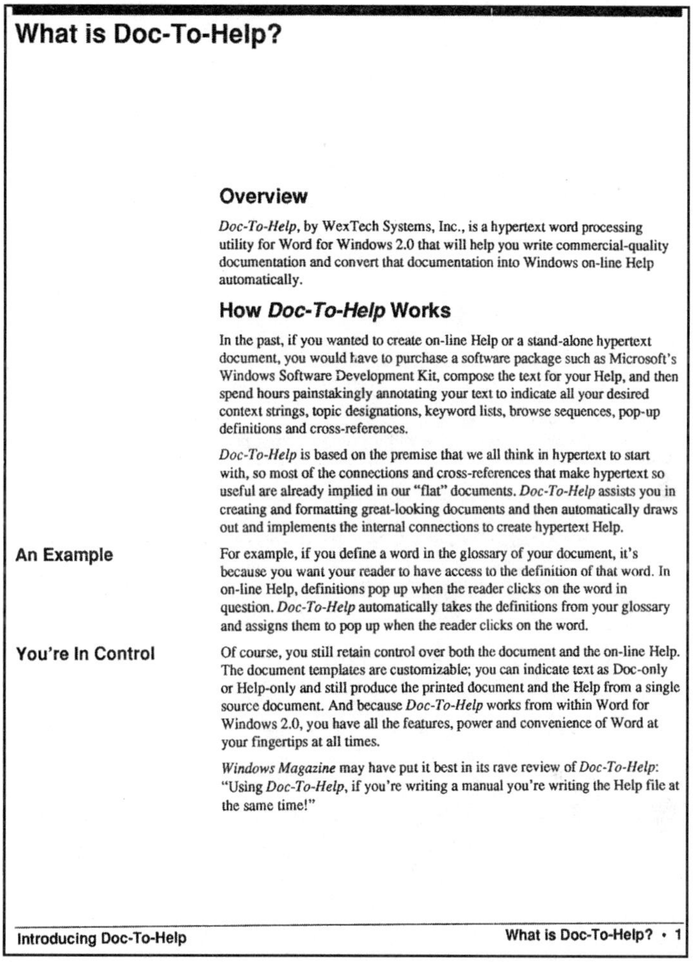

FIGURE 22.15.

A page that illustrates Doc-To-Help's standard manual style.

What is Doc-To-Help?

Overview

Doc-To-Help, by WexTech Systems, Inc., is a hypertext word processing utility for Word for Windows 2.0 that will help you write commercial-quality documentation and convert that documentation into Windows on-line Help automatically.

How *Doc-To-Help* Works

In the past, if you wanted to create on-line Help or a stand-alone hypertext document, you would have to purchase a software package such as Microsoft's Windows Software Development Kit, compose the text for your Help, and then spend hours painstakingly annotating your text to indicate all your desired context strings, topic designations, keyword lists, browse sequences, pop-up definitions and cross-references.

Doc-To-Help is based on the premise that we all think in hypertext to start with, so most of the connections and cross-references that make hypertext so useful are already implied in our "flat" documents. *Doc-To-Help* assists you in creating and formatting great-looking documents and then automatically draws out and implements the internal connections to create hypertext Help.

An Example

For example, if you define a word in the glossary of your document, it's because you want your reader to have access to the definition of that word. In on-line Help, definitions pop up when the reader clicks on the word in question. *Doc-To-Help* automatically takes the definitions from your glossary and assigns them to pop up when the reader clicks on the word.

You're In Control

Of course, you still retain control over both the document and the on-line Help. The document templates are customizable; you can indicate text as Doc-only or Help-only and still produce the printed document and the Help from a single source document. And because *Doc-To-Help* works from within Word for Windows 2.0, you have all the features, power and convenience of Word at your fingertips at all times.

Windows Magazine may have put it best in its rave review of *Doc-To-Help*: "Using *Doc-To-Help*, if you're writing a manual you're writing the Help file at the same time!"

Introducing Doc-To-Help | What is Doc-To-Help? • 1

Summary

This chapter described several methods of creating data dictionaries for your Visual C++ database applications, how to use a commercial cross-referencing application to document your Visual C++ code, and the basic structure of the printed manual that should accompany every production database application.

The next chapter shows you how to use WexTech's Doc-To-Help to convert user manuals to Windows WinHelp files.

23

Creating Help Files for Database Applications

Users of Windows expect and deserve context-sensitive online help for all their Windows applications. All but the simplest Visual C++ applications need a custom Windows help file that lets users press F1 to obtain context-sensitive help for field entries, click a toolbar button to obtain help for a specific button, or choose Help | Contents to select a topic from the help system's opening window.

No matter how much or how little written documentation you supply with your database application, few users will take the time to read the documentation before they begin to use the application. This is especially true for decision-support applications that you design for supervisory and management personnel.

Your Visual C++ applications should be sufficiently intuitive in their operation such that all but the Windows neophyte can take full advantage of their features without employing online help. In reality, however, few Windows applications of any significance are fully comprehensible to the first-time user. Therefore, you need to create Windows help files to make sure that users employ all the features of your application and use the features in the way you intended. If you develop a database application to a written specification, the contract undoubtedly stipulates that comprehensive printed documentation is to accompany the production version of the application. Therefore, this chapter is oriented toward converting the text and graphics of your printed documentation to a help file for the application. Making your documentation do "double duty" as a help file saves time and expense.

This chapter is designed to supplement, not replace, the "Creating Help Files: Help Compiler" chapter in the *Programming Tools for Windows* manual that comes with Visual C++ 1.5x, the *Help Compiler Guide* included with Visual C++ 2.x, or the *Help Author's Guide* included with Visual C++ 4's Help Workshop program. In addition, programmers who have access to the Office Developer's Kit can refer to the Help Compiler Guide supplied with that product. Chapter 22, "Documenting Your Database Applications," taught you how to document the objects in your database application and prepare a data dictionary. This chapter shows you how to use several commercial software products. The non-Microsoft products described are Blue Sky Software's WinHelp Office 95, which is a number of useful products packaged together, and WexTech Systems, Inc.'s Doc-To-Help, which is used to convert your Word for Windows documentation files into a full-fledged, professional Windows help system.

Often help files are developed by people other than the programmer. This usually means that the programmer will be required to set up a system to assist the help file writers in creating the final help file. Visual C++ 4 automatically generates shell help files. This is fine if the programmer is the person who is developing the help files. If not, you might need to set up a system such as the one discussed in the following sections.

NOTE

It's usually better that someone other than the programmer write the documentation for an application. For example, I have a major Windows GIS application on the market for which I didn't write the documentation. Often the programmer isn't the best person to write the manuals and online help. Programmers often make too many assumptions about the user's ability. Furthermore, good programmers aren't always good writers.

In some organizations, the responsibility for documentation is assigned to the customer support department. They work with the product and the customers and often know which areas are the weakest and need improvement.

Understanding How Visual C++ and WinHelp Interact

The help file display features of Windows are commonly referred to as the *WinHelp engine*. The Windows 95 help engine is quite powerful.

NOTE

Windows 95 has a very powerful and flexible help engine. This help engine has been migrated to other Windows platforms (Windows NT, for example) and will continue to be expanded upon in the future.

WINHELP.EXE is the Windows application in your \WINDOWS directory that implements the help system. Under the 32-bit versions of Windows (Windows 95 and Windows NT), the file is named WINHLP32.EXE. Under Windows 95, WINHELP.EXE is a stub program that calls WINHLP32.EXE.

Visual C++ includes features that let you assign individual help windows to forms and controls to create context-sensitive help. The interface between your Visual C++ application and your WinHelp .HLP file(s) is comprised of the following two basic elements:

■ The *APPNAME*.HLP file is the master WinHelp file for your application. Most applications use a single help file, but you can specify different help files if necessary by calling the WinHelp engine directly.

■ The context ID number (long) corresponds to a help context string embedded in your WinHelp file. You add entries to the [MAP] section of your help project (.HPJ) file to assign context ID numbers to the help context strings. Context ID numbers are the key to creating context-sensitive help. You assign context ID numbers as the `HelpContextID` property of forms and controls. You also can set the current context ID value with a `[FormName]![ControlName].HelpContextID = lngContextID` statement.

The following sections describe how to create WinHelp files and how to assign context IDs to topics in order to create context-sensitive help.

> **NOTE**
>
> Making use of all the features that the WinHelp engine offers is beyond the scope of this book. Microsoft's *Help Authoring Guide* is available for downloading as HAG.ZIP in .HLP format from the Windows Users Group forum (GO WUGNET). The *Help Authoring Guide* also is included on the Microsoft Developer Network (MSDN) CD-ROMs.

Using AppWizard's Automatic Help Facility

Programmers who use AppWizard to create their applications have the option of including basic context-sensitive help. Figure 23.1 shows AppWizard's graphical programmer interface, which shows that when you add context-sensitive help, the Help menu is added automatically.

FIGURE 23.1.

Visual C++ 4's
AppWizard, including
context-sensitive help.

> **NOTE**
>
> Figure 23.1 shows Visual C++ 4's AppWizard, which is virtually identical to the one in Visual C++ 2.x. The programmer interface of Visual C++ 1.5x is different from the one in Visual C++ 2.x, but the help files that AppWizard creates are virtually identical to those created using later versions of Visual C++.

NOTE

It's easy to convert an application's help file that was created with the 16-bit versions of Visual C++ (1.5x in particular) to 32-bit versions of Visual C++ (2.x and 4.x in particular). The final help file is actually created as a separate step outside of Visual Workbench using a batch file supplied with Visual C++ when using versions prior to Visual C++ 4.0. With Visual C++ 4's Developer Studio, when a help file is added to the project, Developer Studio correctly calls the help compiler and creates the desired help file.

When Visual C++ creates the shell for your application's help file, this shell resides in a subdirectory located in the project's directory. This subdirectory is called HLP and contains one or two .RTF files and a number of bitmap files (usually about 20 to 25) for such objects as toolbar buttons. Figure 23.2 shows a typical HLP directory.

FIGURE 23.2.

The files created by AppWizard in the HLP subdirectory.

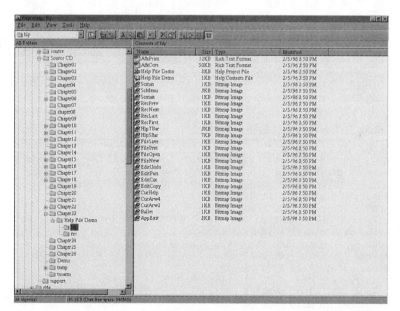

NOTE

Visual C++ 4 automatically creates help files (by executing the MakeHelp.Bat file) as part of the project build. You don't need to manually execute MakeHelp.Bat if you're using Visual C++ 4 and have used AppWizard to create your application with help features. Of course, if you want to manually compile the help files using MakeHelp.Bat, you can do so.

The two .RTF files are

■ AfxCore.rtf, which contains the main help for the application. This file is always present and is the main file from which the application's .HLP file will be created.

■ AfxPrint.rtf, which contains help that is specific to printing. If you don't include printing support (see Figure 23.1), AppWizard doesn't create this file.

PROJECT.HPJ is the help project file. .HPJ files are discussed later in this chapter.

Not all the help support is located in the HLP subdirectory. The project's main directory contains the batch file used to generate WinHelp files. MakeHelp.Bat, shown in Listing 23.1, actually calls the help compiler and generates the help file. This batch file is usually executed from a command-line prompt (in a DOS window), but you can create an icon or a menu shortcut from Visual C++'s Tools menu for MakeHelp.Bat. This filename never changes, so making a shortcut for Visual C++'s Tools menu would be effective for all AppWizard-created projects.

> **NOTE**
>
> Generally, if you delegate the help file authoring, whoever was doing the help file development would use the MakeHelp.Bat file to create the help files rather than Visual C++'s Developer Studio.

Listing 23.1. A typical MakeHelp.Bat file.

```
@echo off
REM -- First make map file from Microsoft Visual C++ generated resource.h
echo // MakeHelp.Bat generated Help Map file.
    ➥Used by HELP FILE DEMO.HPJ. >"hlp\Help File Demo.hm"
echo. >>"hlp\Help File Demo.hm"
echo // Commands (ID_* and IDM_*) >>"hlp\Help File Demo.hm"
makehm ID_,HID_,0x10000 IDM_,HIDM_,0x10000 resource.h >>"hlp\Help File Demo.hm"
echo. >>"hlp\Help File Demo.hm"
echo // Prompts (IDP_*) >>"hlp\Help File Demo.hm"
makehm IDP_,HIDP_,0x30000 resource.h >>"hlp\Help File Demo.hm"
echo. >>"hlp\Help File Demo.hm"
echo // Resources (IDR_*) >>"hlp\Help File Demo.hm"
makehm IDR_,HIDR_,0x20000 resource.h >>"hlp\Help File Demo.hm"
echo. >>"hlp\Help File Demo.hm"
echo // Dialogs (IDD_*) >>"hlp\Help File Demo.hm"
makehm IDD_,HIDD_,0x20000 resource.h >>"hlp\Help File Demo.hm"
echo. >>"hlp\Help File Demo.hm"
echo // Frame Controls (IDW_*) >>"hlp\Help File Demo.hm"
makehm IDW_,HIDW_,0x50000 resource.h >>"hlp\Help File Demo.hm"
REM -- Make help for Project HELP FILE DEMO


echo Building Win32 Help files
start /wait hcrtf -x "hlp\Help File Demo.hpj"
echo.
```

```
if exist Debug\nul copy "hlp\Help File Demo.hlp" Debug
if exist Debug\nul copy "hlp\Help File Demo.cnt" Debug
if exist Release\nul copy "hlp\Help File Demo.hlp" Release
if exist Release\nul copy "hlp\Help File Demo.cnt" Release
echo.
```

NOTE

Visual C++ 2.x's AppWizard might add an `EndLocal` statement to the end of the MakeHelp.Bat file. This command should cause no problems (even though it isn't currently supported by DOS). Oddly, AppWizard doesn't include an opening `SetLocal` statement.

Visual C++ 4 doesn't add the erroneous `EndLocal` statement. Instead, it adds an `echo` command to the end of MakeHelp.Bat, as Listing 23.1 shows.

After you've created your project, you will compile the initial help files when you first build your project. You don't need to make any changes in these files; however, you will find that as supplied by AppWizard, the help files don't provide much help!

The AfxCore.rtf file has a number of place markers. These are marked with the characters << and >>. For example, you will need to substitute the application's name wherever the phrase <<*AppName*>> is found. To do this, simply use a global substitution command in Word for Windows or whichever RTF editor you're using.

Any place markers that aren't listed in the help source file are verbose enough that you will readily understand what information needs to be substituted.

WARNING

The WordPad editor that is part of Windows 95 can't be used to create help files. This is because help file topics are linked to footnotes, and WordPad doesn't support footnotes. You must use a fully functional RTF-enabled editor, such as Word for Windows, to create or modify a help .RTF file.

Creating Rich Text Format Files for Help Systems

A WinHelp .HLP file is a compiled version of a word processing document file saved in Microsoft rich text format (RTF). *Rich text format* is a page description language used to exchange formatted text between document processing applications. For example, you use .RTF files to transfer Word for Windows files to the Macintosh version of Word. Most Windows word processing applications can save documents as .RTF files. Rich text format is similar in concept to Adobe's PostScript page description language, but .RTF isn't used to print documents. Figure 23.3 shows part of the .RTF version of AfxCore.rtf (the CHAPTR23\Help File Demo\hlp\AfxCore.rtf file) displayed in Notepad's window. Figure 23.4 shows the same file loaded into Word for Windows.

FIGURE 23.3.

Part of the AfxCore.rtf WinHelp file in Notepad.

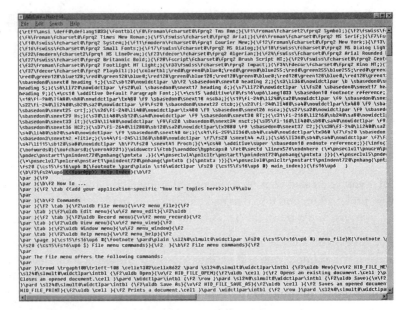

FIGURE 23.4.

The same part of the AfxCore.rtf WinHelp file in Word for Windows.

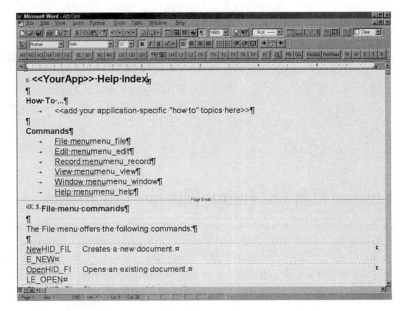

The .RTF files that you create include a header that describes the page format, fonts, and styles in use. PostScript files contain a header that serves a similar purpose. An escape character (\) precedes page and character formatting data in .RTF files, and French braces ({}) enclose groups of formatting data and text to which the formatting applies. Most of the header information in Word .RTF files is derived from the template (.DOT file) in use when you write the document. Only a small part of the .RTF file header appears in Figure 23.3; the first few words of the text are highlighted to identify the point where the paragraph starts.

Adding Instructions to the WinHelp Engine

Instructions to the WinHelp engine are embedded in the .RTF file in the form of footnotes designated by footnote symbols, such as $ and #, rather than conventional footnote numbers. Topic titles are designated by $ footnotes. The context strings that uniquely identify a topic to the WinHelp engine use the # symbol. A topic is a help window that is devoted to a single subject. Topics are separated from one another in your word processing document by hard page breaks (usually created using the Ctrl-Enter key combination). Figure 23.5 shows part of a simple help topic from the HELPEX example included with the *Windows Help Authoring Guide* on the Microsoft Developer's Network CD-ROM.

FIGURE 23.5.

*Part of the second topic
of the HELPEX.RTF
file used to create
HELPEX.HLP.*

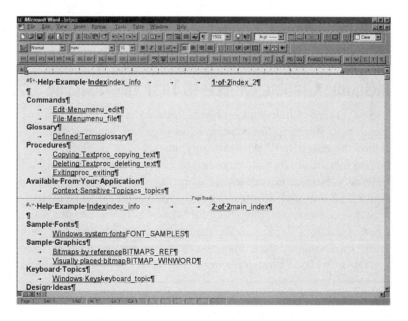

In Figure 23.5, `Help Example Index` is the topic title and `ctxContents` is the help context string for the topic. *Hotspots* are individual words or blocks of text that are formatted with the double-underline or strikethrough attribute and are followed by a help context string formatted as hidden text. When you click a hotspot, WinHelp jumps to the topic identified by the context string that follows the hotspot text. Figure 23.6 shows the first two help topic windows of HELPEX.HLP. Hotspots appear in green in help windows, so you should avoid using the green color attribute in your help text.

FIGURE 23.6.

The first two help topic windows of HELPEX.HLP.

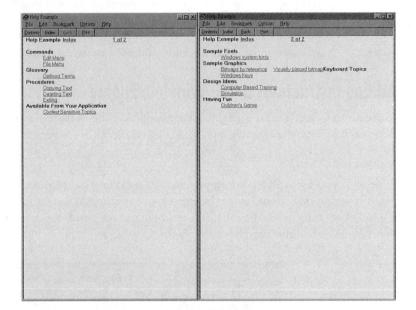

Including Graphic Objects in Your WinHelp File

You can embed or link graphic objects contained in bitmap (.BMP) or vector image (.WMF) files in your WinHelp files. The easiest way to add bitmapped images to your help files is to embed the image in .BMP format in your .DOC or .RTF file using Word. However, large bitmap files usually are handled more efficiently by linking the graphic file to the WinHelp file by using its filename as a reference. Figure 23.7 shows Microsoft's logo as an embedded bitmap. Figure 23.8 shows Microsoft's logo as it appears in the final help file. To embed the bitmap (a bitmap image captured from Word for Windows' toolbar) in the .RTF document, you choose Insert | Picture in Word to display the Picture dialog box and then double-click cmdialog.bmp in the File Name list box. The {bmc cmdialog.bmp} entry below the line of text causes the CMDIALOG.BMP bitmap file to be inserted at the position of the { character.

FIGURE 23.7.

A help topic with an embedded bitmap.

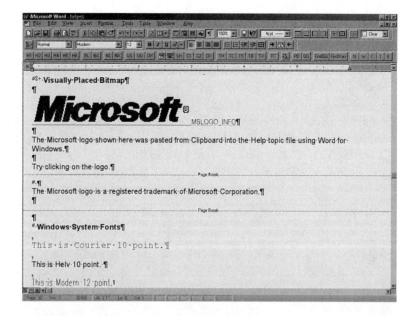

FIGURE 23.8.

An embedded bitmap of Microsoft's logo in WinHelp.

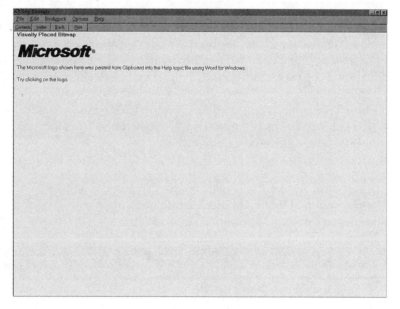

> **NOTE**
>
> When you use bitmapped graphics, you might need to include a version of the bitmap file for each type of display resolution that might be employed by users of the help system. The Microsoft multiple-resolution bitmap compiler, MRBC.EXE, lets you create a single bitmap file that supports VGA, SVGA, and 8514 resolutions. It's unlikely that any users of Visual C++ database applications will be using resolutions less than standard VGA, but MRBC.EXE is useful to provide scaleable bitmaps for 640×480 (VGA), 800×600 (SVGA), and 1,024×768 (8514, XGA, or UVGA) display resolutions. It won't be long before 1280×1024 resolutions become common. Your help files should take into account the trend toward higher resolution and more colors. Many Windows database applications still run on "plain vanilla" 16-color VGA systems, but more and more users are converting to 256-color or better systems. When you convert a .BMP file with MRBC.EXE, you substitute .MRB for the .BMP extension when you refer to the file. One of the advantages of using .WMF vector image files in help files is that the Windows metafiles are device-independent.

> **NOTE**
>
> The term *link* is used in this chapter to differentiate between embedding a graphics file in the .RTF file and creating a reference to a separate graphics file with {bm? *filename.ext*} entries in your .RTF file. The ? placeholder determines whether the graphic is placed as a character (bmc), at the left margin (bml), or at the right margin (bmr). When you compile the help file with the WinHelp compiler, the graphic that you link is embedded into the .HLP file you create. (You don't need to supply the .BMP file along with your .HLP file.)

You can create hotspots in graphic images that you link to your WinHelp file by using the Hotspot Editor, SHED.EXE, which is included with Visual C++. (You can't add hotspots to bitmaps you embed in WinHelp .RTF files.)

> **NOTE**
>
> If there is no link to SHED in the Visual C++ 4 folder, you can add one. An alternative is to start SHED from a DOS command prompt window, but this really isn't efficient unless you frequently use a DOS window.

The Hotspot Editor creates an .SHG (system hypergraphic) file from .BMP, .DIB (device-independent bitmap), or .WMF files. To add hotspots to a .BMP, .DIB, or .WMF file, follow the next steps.

> **NOTE**
>
> The bitmap file used in this example is setup.bmp, found in Windows 95's directory. It was copied to the help project folder and saved in SHED as setup.shg.

1. Launch SHED.EXE and choose File | Open from the editor to display the File Open dialog box (which isn't a Windows 95 common dialog box).

> **NOTE**
>
> Because SHED isn't long-filename-compliant, you will have to select files using their short filenames.

2. Select the directory and filename of the bitmap in the Directories and Files list boxes, and then click the OK button to close the File Open dialog box and display the image.
3. Position the mouse pointer in the upper-left corner of the area that you want to make active as a hotspot. Click and hold the left mouse button, drag the enclosing rectangle to define the hotspot area, and then release the mouse button.
4. With the frame for your hotspot selected (the one with the eight sizing handles), choose Edit | Attributes to display the Attributes dialog box. Alternatively, you can select Attributes by right-clicking in the hotspot area. Enter the context string corresponding to the topic for the hotspot item in the Context String text box. Select Pop-up to create a pop-up window or select Jump to jump to a new topic. Accept the default value, Visible, in the Attribute combo box and the Hotspot ID text box. You can manipulate the position of the enclosing rectangle by changing the entries in the text boxes within the Bounding Box frame. Figure 23.9 shows the typical entries that define the attributes of a hotspot.

FIGURE 23.9.

Defining the boundaries and attributes of a hotspot in a hypergraphic (.SHG) file.

> **NOTE**
>
> All the hotspots in this example were defined as pop-ups. You can also define hotspots as either jumps (which would jump to a certain topic) or as a WinHelp macro that would be run when the hotspot was selected.

5. Click the OK button to assign the attributes to the hotspot. Add more hotspots as needed by repeating steps 3 and 4.

6. When you've completed the definitions of the hotspots you want, choose File | Save As and save your file with the same name as the original bitmap but with an .SHG extension to indicate that the bitmap file is now a hypergraphic file. Close SHED.EXE.

7. If you've used the .BMP extension to refer to the bitmap in your .RTF file, change the file extension to .SHG. (You also might need to change the reference in the [BITMAPS] section of the project file if the bitmaps are in folders other than the help file's project directory. This is discussed in the next section.)

8. Add new topics to your WinHelp file for the pop-up or conventional help windows that appear when you click the hotspots. Each topic has a context string that corresponds to the context string you added during the editing process. Figure 23.10 shows entries for the pop-up window that opens when you click the mouse hotspot on the bitmap.

FIGURE 23.10.

Pop-up help window topics for hotspots of the set-up bitmap image.

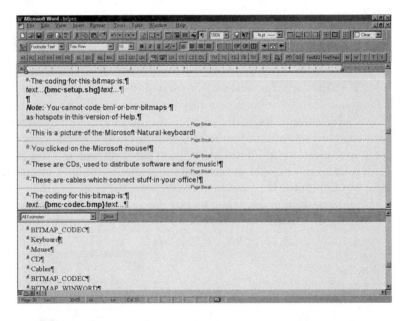

9. After you compile your WinHelp .RTF file to a .HLP file, clicking the hotspot displays the pop-up window that has a context string that corresponds to the context string you assigned as the hotspot's attribute. (Compiling .RTF to .HLP files is the subject of the next section.) Figure 23.11 shows the pop-up window that appears when you click the area within the dashed lines surrounding the image of the Microsoft mouse. The dashed lines appear because Visible was selected as the attribute for the hotspot regions. (Normally you choose Invisible, so the dashed lines don't appear.)

FIGURE 23.11.

The pop-up window displayed when you click the picture of the mouse in the image.

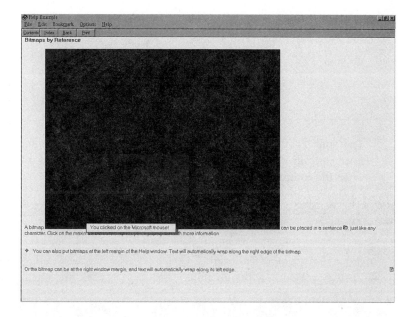

> **NOTE**
>
> One of the advantages of using SHED.EXE is that the Hotspot Editor compresses .BMP files. For example, setup.bmp requires 38,462 bytes of storage, whereas setup.shg occupies only 36,959 bytes and has four jumps defined.

Compiling .RTF Files to Create WinHelp .HLP Files

Creating the final WinHelp .HLP file from your .RTF file and any graphics that are referenced in the .RTF file is a three-step process.

1. Create a project file that provides information to the help compiler on the files that constitute your help file and assigns help context ID values to the help context string. If your help file was originally created with Visual C++, this file has already been created for you.

2. Use the Microsoft Help Workshop program (there should be an icon for it in the Visual C++ program folder) and load the help project's .HPJ file. Click the compile button on the toolbar or select File | Compile to compile your help menu. Prior to the compilation process, the dialog box shown in Figure 23.12 is displayed to allow you to select options for the help file.

FIGURE 23.12.

*Microsoft Help
Workshop's compile
options dialog box.*

3. Test your .HLP file to make sure it conforms to your expectations. If you select the Automatically display Help file option, your help file will be loaded into WinHelp when the compilation is complete.

> **NOTE**
>
> Even though the HELPEX sample help file that is supplied on the MSDN CD is intended to be compiled with the DOS-based help compilers, using Microsoft Help Workshop will work, with only minor warnings about improper labels. It will create a valid help file.

The following three sections describe the preceding steps in detail.

Creating a Project File

Help project files, which are usually named *APPNAME*.HPJ, are similar in concept to Visual C++ makefiles or project files. Listing 23.2 shows the contents of the project file for the Help Example help file, HELPEX.HPJ.

Listing 23.2. Sections and entries in the HELPEX.HPJ help project file (after loading into Microsoft Help Workshop).

```
; This file is maintained by HCW.  Do not modify this file directly.

[OPTIONS]
HCW=0
; error message:
;
;    R1023: Keyword(s) defined without title in page 59
;           of file helpex.rtf
;
; This message indicates that a topic will be listed in
; the Search Topics Found box as ">>Untitled Topic<<"
COMPRESS=60 Hall Zeck
LCID=0x409 0x0 0x0 ;English (United States)
REPORT=Yes
TITLE=Help Example
HLP=.\helpex.hlp
```

```
[FILES]
helpex.rtf  ; main topics

[MAP]
#include <helpids.h>
```

> **CAUTION**
>
> Once you've loaded an .HPJ file into Microsoft Help Workshop, you shouldn't edit the file by hand. Instead, use Microsoft Help Workshop to make changes to the help project file.

Help project files are text files that are organized into sections and are similar in structure to Windows .INI files. Table 23.1 lists the most commonly used sections of a help project file, states whether the section is required in the file, and briefly describes the section's purpose. Keywords for entries in the [OPTIONS] section also appear.

Table 23.1. The sections of a help project (.HPJ) file.

Section of .HPJ File	Section Required?	Description	
[OPTIONS]	No (but usually present)	Defines the options that control the WinHelp compilation process. Some of the more common option entries include the following:	
		ROOT=*d:\path*	Defines the path to your help source files.
		CONTENTS= *ContextString*	Sets the context string for the index topic with the Windows 3.1 Help compiler, HC31.EXE.
		TITLE= *AppName Help*	Sets the title for the WinHelp file, which appears in the help window's title bar.

continues

Table 23.1. continued

Section of .HPJ File	Section Required?	Description
		`ICON=` `IconFile.ICO`	Sets the icon that is displayed when the help window is minimized.
		`COMPRESS=0¦FALSE`	Controls file compression. 0, or `FALSE`, means "do not compress files." 1, or `TRUE`, compresses the file. Compressing .HLP files saves disk space at the expense of speed in displaying help windows (due to the time required to decompress the file). HC31.EXE supports varying degrees of compression.
		`WARNING=3`	Determines what errors are reported. 0 through 3 control the level of error reporting. 0 = no error reports, 1 = most-severe warnings, 2 = intermediate warning level, and 3 = report all warnings.
		`REPORT=1¦ON`	Determines whether progress reports of the compilation are provided. 1, or `ON`, = report progress of compile. 0, or `OFF`, = no report.

Section of .HPJ File	Section Required?	Description
[FILES]	Yes	Specifies the help source files included in the compilation.
[BUILD]	No	Specifies topics to include in or exclude from the compiled file.
[BUILDTAGS]	No (yes if [BUILD] is specified)	Names valid build tags, allowing the selection of topics to be compiled within a file.
[CONFIG]	Only if DLL functions are called	Registers custom DLLs that have functions that are called by WinHelp RegisterRoutine macros.
[BITMAPS]	No	Specifies bitmap or .WMF files that are used in the compilation and not embedded in your WinHelp document. This section isn't required if you used the ROOT= entry in the [OPTIONS] section to specify the path to the referenced bitmap files.
[MAP]	No	Associates context strings with context ID numbers. You need a map section to use the Context ID property of Access forms and control objects.
[ALIAS]	No	Lets you assign more than one context string to a subject.
[WINDOWS]	No	Describes the main WinHelp window and any secondary window types in the help file.
[BAGGAGE]	No	Names any additional data files that are to be incorporated within the WinHelp file.

Using Microsoft Help Workshop to Compile Your WinHelp .RTF File

Microsoft Help Workshop is a DOS application that converts .RTF files to the format required by WinHelp .HLP files, incorporates graphics files, and creates the required look-up tables for help context strings and context IDs. Select the Windows 95 Help icon (or whatever icon is assigned to the help compiler) to start Microsoft Help Workshop. Load the help project file either by selecting File | Open or by selecting it from the MRU file list if the project help file was previously opened.

Figure 23.13 shows the results of compiling the HELPEX.hpj file using Microsoft Help Workshop. A number of errors were flagged in the compilation stage, but the help file was generally usable for testing purposes. (However, you wouldn't want to distribute a help file with these errors.)

FIGURE 23.13.

Compiling HELPEX.HPJ in Microsoft Help Workshop.

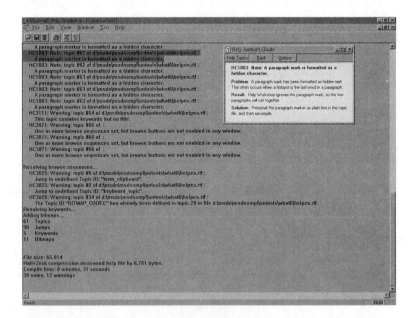

TIP

You can find the cause of an error (and suggested fixes) by searching the Microsoft Help Workshop help file for the error number. In Figure 23.13, the help error message HC1003 is highlighted, and the appropriate *Help Authoring Guide* topic is displayed.

Microsoft Help Workshop can run in a noninteractive mode. This mode isn't documented by Microsoft, and programmers shouldn't need it directly. Microsoft Help Workshop is called in noninteractive mode by Visual C++ 4 when a project's help file is being rebuilt.

Using WinHelp Office 95 and RoboHELP 95

One of the newest and most extensive products to assist programmers in developing help files is from Blue Sky Software. This section looks at this suite of products, which form a comprehensive tool for Windows software developers who are documenting their products. WinHelp Office 95 is available at an introductory price of $599. The core of WinHelp Office 95 is the RoboHELP help development engine. WinHelp Office 95 includes the following tools:

- RoboHELP 95, a product to help you develop help files
- SmartHelp OLE control, an OLE control to add help facilities to application dialog boxes
- WinHelp Video Kit, which provides facilities to add video to help files
- The Moving to WinHelp '95 Kit, a set of applications that eases the migration to WinHelp Office 95
- WinHelp HyperViewer, a utility that gives your Windows 3.x files the look and feel of Windows 95 help files
- WinHelp Tool Kit, a set of helper utilities
- Mastering WinHelp, a videotape that helps you learn the basics of creating help files

The following sections take a quick look at each of these tools.

RoboHELP 95

RoboHELP 95 turns Microsoft Word 7 for Windows 95 and 32-bit Word 6.0 and 7.0 for Windows NT into hypertext authoring tools. RoboHELP 95 includes both 32-bit and 16-bit versions of RoboHELP, thereby providing support for all versions of Microsoft Word. RoboHELP includes an Enhanced Hotspot Editor, a screen capture utility, and much more.

RoboHELP 95 is a 32-bit version of RoboHELP that turns Microsoft Word 7 for Windows 95 and Word 6 for Windows NT into high-performance hypertext authoring tools. A 16-bit version of RoboHELP is included with RoboHELP 95 to provide support for Microsoft Word 6 and Word 2 for Windows 3.x.

RoboHELP guides you through the entire process of creating help systems and electronic Hypertext documents, from standard help features such as jumps, topics, and pop-ups to advanced features such as macros, secondary windows, and colors. RoboHELP 95 supports all the new Windows 95 help features.

RoboHELP automatically converts existing documentation into a help system or vice versa. You also can import existing help systems, graphics, and documents.

RoboHELP 95 includes a variety of new and improved features specifically designed to stream-line the process of creating help systems for Windows 95 and Windows NT:

An enhanced tool palette
New Windows 95 templates
A Contents tab composer
Easy creation of a-links and k-links
New help macro support
More support for Visual Basic
Multimedia support
Advanced graphic support
Authorable button support: shortcuts and see also buttons
Easy creation of What's This? context-sensitive help
SmartHelp OLE control

SmartHelp OLE Control

The new SmartHelp OLE control included in RoboHELP 95 eliminates the need to program context-sensitive help into any application developed with Visual Basic 4.0, Visual C++ 4.0, Access 95, Visual FoxPro 3.0, or other environments that support the OLE control standard.

WinHelp Video Kit

The WinHelp Video Kit provides everything you need to integrate video and sound into Windows help systems and to create "live" video product tutorials. The WinHelp Video Kit includes a Software Video Camera, a Video Wizard, a Video Tester, a Video Player, and Video for Windows Runtime.

Moving to WinHelp '95 Kit

The Moving to WinHelp '95 Kit provides you with the tools to quickly convert Windows 3.x help systems to Windows 95 help systems. It also comes with the first book solely dedicated to Windows 95 help. This kit is intended to make the transition to Windows 95 help fast and easy.

WinHelp HyperViewer

WinHelp HyperViewer lets you give Windows 3.x help systems the look and feel of Windows 95. WinHelp HyperViewer features a powerful full-text search, multiple-topic printing, and an expandable, collapsible hypertext view of the entire help system.

WinHelp Tool Kit

The WinHelp Tool Kit is a collection of powerful tools. It includes Help-To-Word, Help-To-Source, WinHelp Inspector, WinHelp BugHunter, WinHelp Graphics Locator, WinHelp Graphics Library, and WinHelp Internet Access. The following list describes some of these tools.

> **WARNING**
>
> The WinHelp Tool Kit includes tools that "decompile" Windows help files into Word for Windows .DOC and .RTF files. This functionality is quite valuable when you no longer have access to the original source files, for example. However, you should be careful not to violate copyright laws by decompiling help files for products for which you have no right to do so.

- Help-To-Word decompiles Windows 3.1x help files into Word for Windows .DOC files. The resulting files are formatted using the styles that WinHelp uses. All jumps and pop-ups are marked in green so that they can be found easily. Help-To-Word doesn't convert Windows 95 or Windows NT help files; use Help-To-Source to convert these types of files. This process is useful when you need to create printed manuals from your help files using the formatting that WinHelp uses.

- Help-To-Source decompiles .HLP format help files (all versions of Windows, including Windows 95 and Windows NT) into .RTF and .HPJ files. The resulting files will contain all topics, jumps, pop-ups, graphics, hypertext links, and other characteristics that the original file had.

- WinHelp Inspector lets you quickly inspect any help system. Most of the information provided by the WinHelp Inspector normally isn't available without the source files. WinHelp Inspector displays information such as the startup macros, fonts, and DLLs used, the compression, the copyright notice, topic titles, search keywords, and the name, date, and size of the help system.

- WinHelp BugHunter is used to display all calls made by running applications to any Windows help system (either Windows 95 or Windows 3.x). WinHelp BugHunter is valuable in resolving any broken or incorrect context-sensitive help links between the application and its help system.

- WinHelp Graphics Locator assists you in searching for graphics (.SHG, .WMF, .MRB, .BMP, .ICO, and .CUR files) and other files in a specific directory, drive, or even across multiple drives. You can also preview these graphics and copy them to their help project directory. The WinHelp Graphics Locator displays information such as the number of colors in the selected graphic, the width and height of the graphic, and so on.

■ WinHelp Graphics Library lets you select graphics such as bullets, buttons, and pictures from the WinHelp Graphics Library and easily integrate them into your help file.

■ WinHelp Internet Access includes tools to integrate your help files with Internet access. Blue Sky Software is a Netscape development partner, and with the new WinHelp Internet Access, you can add Internet access to any Windows help system via Netscape, Mosaic, and Microsoft Internet Explorer.

WinHelp Internet Access opens the door to interactive Windows help by integrating Windows help with the World Wide Web (WWW). Help users can jump from Windows help to any World Wide Web site via the Web browser (Netscape, Mosaic, and Microsoft Internet Explorer) installed on their desktop. With a click of the mouse, help users can also download any file from the Internet or send e-mail.

WinHelp Internet Access includes the following:

Internet Access Wizard, which automatically adds the WinHelp Internet Access functionality to any Windows help project.

The WinHelp Internet Access sample help file, which includes full source code for Internet access commands to many Internet locations and macro commands for downloading files from the Internet. These sample macro commands are available to help you add Internet access to your Windows help systems.

Mastering WinHelp

With the Mastering WinHelp video, you can become productive immediately and create professional help systems with a minimum amount of effort. Mastering WinHelp also includes advanced tips for experienced users and a WinHelp sample disk for Windows 95.

Creating Help Files from Your Application Manual

The process of manually creating help files for Visual C++ applications is thoroughly documented in Microsoft's *Help Compiler User's Guide* and the *Help Author's Guide*. Today, few help-file authors write help files in the manner described in the *Help Compiler User's Guide*. Third-party help-file authoring applications, such as Doc-To-Help by WexTech Systems Inc. (New York) and RoboHELP 95 by Blue Sky Software (San Diego), speed the organization and writing of help files. This book assumes that most database developers possess the writing skills that are needed to prepare a better-than-adequate manual for the application. Developers who aren't authors by nature usually employ technical writers to prepare the required written documentation. Therefore, this chapter is oriented toward the design and use of text from the application manual as the basis for your application's help file(s). Almost without exception,

Word for Windows is the preferred application for creating the rich text format (.RTF) files needed by the help compiler that you use to create the final WinHelp (.HLP) file. All commercial help-file generation applications are based on Word for Windows.

Using Doc-To-Help to Create Help Files for Database Applications

Doc-To-Help 2.0, which works with Word for Windows 95, allows users to create and distribute commercial-quality printed documentation and sophisticated Windows 95, 3.1, and 3.0 help files from a single source without compromise in either medium or any platform. Doc-To-Help 2.0 includes the following:

■ 32-bit architecture with long filename and UNC support

■ Automatic and nearly instantaneous generation of contents (.CNT) files

■ Authorable buttons

■ Easy inclusion of multimedia elements in Help files

Users will also find updated versions of the Doc-To-Help Hyperformance Tools, providing Doc-To-Help Navigator, video support, and watermark support for 32-bit WinHelp. The Microsoft Windows 95, 3.1, and 3.0 help compilers are included in this package.

New to Doc-To-Help 2.0 are Topic Types. Using this feature, help authors can mark topics as conceptual, procedural, or context-sensitive. Doc-To-Help makes sure that the topics appear automatically in the correct Help window and with proper formatting. Doc-To-Help 2.0 also offers a "smart" contents tab feature, which allows the help author to place the Doc-To-Help Navigator in the Help topics contents tab. This gives help authors greater flexibility in creating and controlling the contents tab's hierarchical outline.

Doc-To-Help consists of the following components:

■ A collection of Word for Windows template (.DOT) files for producing manuals that will be copied to 8 1/2- by 11-inch or 7- by 9-inch paper, as well as a special template (D2H_HELP.DOT) that you use when you produce WinHelp files from the text of your manual. The templates make extensive use of Word Basic code to provide supplemental features, such as semiautomatic indexing.

■ A DLL that is used to convert large bitmap files for incorporation into help files.

■ Licensed copies of the Microsoft Help Compiler, HCP.EXE, the protected-mode version of HC31.EXE, which lets you compile larger help files than are possible with HC31.EXE. Generally, you will want to use the Microsoft Help Workshop program that was described earlier.

■ A set of tutorial and sample files, from which many of the figures in this section are derived.

■ A 300-page application manual created with Doc-To-Help.

Doc-To-Help has a preset collection of styles that are likely to meet your needs if your client or firm hasn't already established a set of graphic-design standards. You can alter these basic styles to suit others' requirements or your own taste in layout and typography.

Organizing Your Manual to Optimize Help File Conversion

One of the advantages that authors of application manuals have over authors of developers' guides for software is that the application itself provides the organizational framework for your work. The structure of your application's manual is dictated by the relationship between the forms that constitute the user interface of your application. Thus, a database application manual consists of the following major sections or topics:

- A table of contents (TOC), which lays the groundwork for the window that appears when the user chooses Help | Contents. The level-1 heading, called the supertitle, appears as the heading of the Contents window.

- An overview of the application as a whole, including a brief description of the purpose of the application and the underlying database(s). The overview corresponds to the main switchboard form or the start-up form of your application. This window or series of windows appears when the user presses the F1 key or clicks the Help button of a toolbar with the opening form displayed. The overview is a level-2 heading.

- Instructions on installing the application from the distribution disks. You don't include this topic in the help file, because the user can't read the help file until he or she completes the installation.

- One chapter for each main form of your application. For example, an accounting package would have individual chapters for the General Ledger, Accounts Receivable, Accounts Payable, Payroll, Inventory, and Job Cost Accounting modules, each of which is likely to have its own main form. This help window appears when the user presses F1 or clicks the Help button when the control with the focus doesn't have a corresponding subtopic. Chapter headings are level 2 and appear in the Help Contents window.

- Topics within each chapter that explain the next layer down in the hierarchy of forms. Using the Accounts Receivable module of the accounting system as an example, topics might include Invoice Creation, Printing Invoices, Receiving Payments, and Aging the Accounts Receivable. Topic names appear in green with underscores and usually are identified by larger, bold typefaces. Topics use level-3 headings.

- Subtopics within each chapter that explain how to enter data in text boxes and how to use any subsidiary forms that are at the next level of the hierarchy. You open subtopic help windows from the main topic (chapter) help windows or by pressing F1 when a control object is assigned a subtopic window. Subtopic names have the same format as topic names but use a font that is one or two points smaller than that used for topic names. Subtopic headings are level 4.

■ A glossary of potentially unfamiliar terms or familiar terms that are used in an unusual context or have an uncommon meaning in the manual. Doc-To-Help converts glossary entries into pop-up windows that you open by clicking highlighted text with dashed underscores.

■ Index entries that create the entries that users see in the list box when they choose Help | Search.

Figure 23.14 shows a sample Doc-To-Help document, D2HSETUP.DOC, in Word for Windows' outline mode. This help document has three heading levels; thus, D2HSETUP.DOC typifies the structure of help files for Windows applications. Writing your manual with one of Doc-To-Help's standard templates attached simplifies the help-file conversion process. Alternatively, you can convert existing manuals to Doc-To-Help's format by importing the styles contained in the standard Doc-To-Help template. The graphics shown in D2HSETUP.DOC import directly into your help file.

FIGURE 23.14.

A Doc-To-Help manual shown in Word for Windows' outline mode.

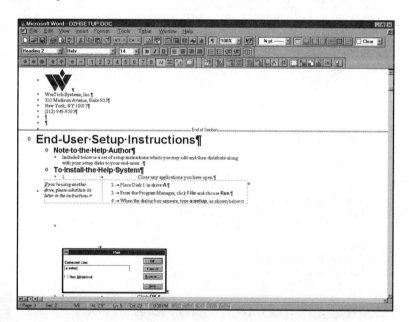

NOTE

Don't forget that Doc-To-Help has a toolbar that may be used in Word for Windows when you're creating or modifying a help file. A programmer can save a great deal of time and effort by using toolbars.

Creating the Help File from the Source Document

After you've completed and printed proof copies of your application manual, you convert the manual to a Microsoft rich text format (.RTF) file. Rich text format files are text files that include embedded page-, line-, and character-formatting instructions. Doc-To-Help adds several menu choices to Word for Windows' Tools and Format menus that display special-purpose dialog boxes in which you select options for converting your manual to the required .RTF file and compiling the .RTF file to a help file.

Help Project Files and the Compilation Process

The help project file (.HPJ) tells the compiler the names and locations of the .RTF and bitmap (.BMP) files to be included in the .HLP file. The structure of .HPJ files is similar to a Windows initialization file such as MSACCESS.INI and is related to the structure of the .MAK files used by Visual Basic and C compilers. Headings are enclosed in square brackets and are followed by related entries. Here is a truncated version of the D2HSETUP.HPJ file that is automatically generated by Doc-To-Help and that creates D2HSETUP.HLP:

```
[OPTIONS]
INDEX=HelpContents1
ROOT=C:\DOC2HELP
COMPRESS=FALSE
TITLE=Doc-To-Help Introduction

[FILES]
C:\DOC2HELP\D2HSETUP.RTF

[MAP]
HelpContents1          1    ; Help Contents
Overview.2             2    ; Overview
HowDoc.To.HelpWorks.3  3    ; How Doc-To-Help Works
AnExample.4            4    ; An Example
You.reInControl.5      5    ; You're In Control

[BITMAPS]
C:\DOC2HELP\HELP0003.BMP
C:\DOC2HELP\HELP0001.BMP
```

> **NOTE**
>
> Unless you specify otherwise, the names of the .RTF, .HPJ, and .HLP files are the same as the names of the source .DOC file. The extensions change to designate the type of file.

The preceding example of a help project file includes only sections and entries that are required to compile a simple help file with five help topics and two bitmaps. The .HPJ files for complex .HLP files become quite lengthy. Compiling a large help file can take several minutes on a slow computer, especially one that doesn't have enough RAM. After compilation, the Contents window of D2HSETUP.HLP appears, as shown in Figure 23.15.

FIGURE 23.15.

The Contents window of D2HSETUP.HLP.

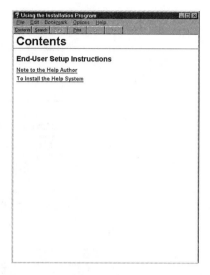

Including Graphic Images in Help Files

You can include large bitmap files, such as images captured from the forms of your application, in both your manual and the help file. The Hotspot Editor (SHED.EXE) included with Visual C++ lets you assign help context strings to control objects on your form. When the user clicks a control object, the window that explains the purpose of the control object appears. Figure 23.16 shows how to create a pop-up window that displays information about the Command Line edit control in the sample dialog box. This sample dialog box was captured and saved as a bitmap image.

If you use SHED.EXE to assign help context strings to the buttons and other dialog box controls of the Run dialog box that is shown in the help file, you can cause a jump to the window that deals with each of these subjects when the user clicks the control in the Run dialog box. Figure 23.17 shows the bitmap illustration of the dialog box from Figure 23.16 opened in SHED.EXE. You drag the mouse pointer to define a rectangular area that serves as the hotspot. Then you assign the help context string of the help topic you want to jump to. When the user double-clicks the area defined as the hotspot, the command line's help topic appears.

FIGURE 23.16.

Creating a pop-up window.

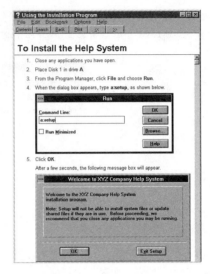

FIGURE 23.17.

Adding a help context string to a bitmap with the Hotspot Editor.

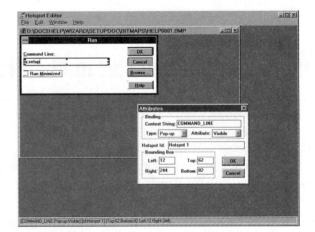

Assigning Help File and Context ID Numbers to Objects

Each topic window requires a help context string that the WinHelp engine (WINHELP.EXE) uses to create a jump from the Contents window to the topic window. Help context strings are footnotes that are identified by the pound symbol (#).

If you want a specific help topic to appear when the user presses the F1 key, a feature called *context-sensitive help,* you need to assign a unique help context ID number to each of the topic and subtopic windows of your help file. You add help entries that contain the context string and the associated help context ID number as entries in the [MAP] section of your .HPJ file.

After you create the final version of your help file, you enter the context ID number of the topic that corresponds to the form or control object in your application as the HelpContextID property of the object. To test your help, run your application under Windows.

> **NOTE**
>
> If you assign values to the HelpContextID property of control objects on your form, the help topic window corresponding to the HelpContextID value of the control object with the focus appears when the user presses the F1 key. If you assign a value to the HelpContextID property of the control object that receives the focus when you open the form (the first object in the tab order), F1 doesn't open the help topic window assigned to the form itself. If you want F1 to open a help topic window for the form, make sure that you assign the form's help topic ContextID value to the ContextID value of the first control object in the tab order.

Calling the *WinHelp()* Function with Visual C++ Code

With C Windows programs, you can call the WinHelp() function to display the application's help file. If you're using Windows applications designed with AppWizard, you're better off calling the MFC CWinApp::WinHelp() function. With this function, you need to specify only the command and any additional data that might be necessary.

To control the action of the WinHelp engine with Visual C++ code, you call the CWinApp::WinHelp() function when you need to change a context ID value. The syntax of the CWinApp::WinHelp() function call, which calls ::WinHelp() (the sole help function contained in the USER.EXE DLL), is as follows:

```
virtual void CWinApp::WinHelp(DWORD dwData, UINT fuCommand);
```

Here is the Windows WinHelp() function's prototype:

```
BOOL WinHelp(HWND hWnd, LPCSTR lpszHelpFile, UINT fuCommand, DWORD dwData);
```

The Windows WinHelp() function returns a BOOL value which, if nonzero, indicates that the function was successful. The arguments of the WinHelp() function are explained in the following list:

- *hWnd* is a Windows handle (code number or integer) to the window that is active when the WinHelp() function is called with the F1 key. The *hWnd* property of a form or control provides this 16-bit handle.
- *lpszHelpFile* is the name of the WinHelp file, including the .HLP extension.
- *fuCommand* is an integer value that specifies the action that the function is to perform. Table 23.2 describes the *fuCommand* constant values.
- *dwData* is a long integer argument.

Table 23.2 describes how the data of the *dwData* argument changes with the value of *fuCommand*.

Table 23.2. WinHelp *fuCommand* constant values and corresponding actions.

fuCommand Constant	*Value*	*Description*
HELP_CONTEXT	1	Causes a specific help topic, identified by a long integer specified as the *dwData* argument, to be displayed.
HELP_QUIT	2	Notifies WinHelp that the specified help file is no longer in use and can be closed. The *dwData* argument is ignored.
HELP_INDEX	3	Displays the index of the specified WinHelp file, as designated by the author. The *dwData* argument is ignored.
HELP_HELPONHELP	4	Displays help for using the WinHelp application itself. The *dwData* argument is ignored.
HELP_SETINDEX	5	Sets the context number specified by the *dwData* argument, a long integer, as the current index for the specified WinHelp file.
HELP_KEY	257	Displays the first corresponding topic found in a search for the keyword specified by the *dwData* argument—in this case, a string variable.
HELP_MULTIKEY	513	Displays help for a keyword found in an alternative keyword table. The *dwData* argument is a data structure (user-defined data type) containing the size of the string, the letter of the alternative table, and the keyword string.

Listing 23.3 shows the additions that you make to the Declarations section of your module to take advantage of all the features that WinHelp() offers.

Listing 23.3. Declarations needed to use the WinHelp() function.

```
// Call CWinApp::WinHelp()

// Define global constants for fuCommand
#define HELP_CONTEXT      0x1     /* Display a specified topic */
#define HELP_QUIT         0x2     /* Terminate WinHelp for application */
#define HELP_INDEX        0x3     /* Display the Help index */
#define HELP_HELPONHELP   0x4     /* Display Help on using Help */
#define HELP_SETINDEX     0x5     /* Set the current Help index */
#define HELP_KEY          0x101   /* Display a topic for keyword */
#define HELP_MULTIKEY     0x201   /* Use the alternative keyword table */
#define KEY_F1            0x70    /* Key code for Help key */
```

You don't need to add the constants to your source file if you want to substitute the integer values shown in Table 23.2 as the *fuCommand* argument when you use the WinHelp() function.

Summary

Online help is a critical component of all but the most rudimentary database applications. This statement applies not only to Visual C++ Windows database applications, but also to database front ends you create in any language. This chapter isn't meant to be a substitute for the *Help Compiler Guide,* nor does it cover as much information as books that are devoted to authoring WinHelp files, such as Microsoft's *Help Authoring Guide.* If this chapter's examples of using the commercial help-authoring tools accomplished their purpose, you'll want to acquire one of these tools to accelerate the development of online WinHelp for your Visual C++ database applications.

The next chapter, the last in this book, describes how you organize the Setup application for your Visual C++ database front ends and how to manage the distribution of your applications on disks.

24

Creating Distribution Disks for Visual C++ Applications

Some Visual C++ database applications might call for a one-time-only installation by you, the developer. If that's the case, you can copy the applications' .EXE, .HLP, and .VBX files, together with any database and ancillary files that might be required, onto a set of disks that you will copy to the appropriate directories of the client's computer. If your Visual C++ database front end will be used by a large number of people, or if you want to impress your clients with a sophisticated setup application similar to those used to install mainstream Windows applications, you need to create "official" distribution disks.

This chapter is intended primarily for developers who are creating applications that will be used with Windows 95 and later versions of Windows. The techniques shown here are very useful for versions of Windows earlier than Windows 95; however, it's unlikely that readers of this book will be creating many applications for earlier versions of Windows. In the future, expect Windows NT to offer facilities that are comparable to those offered by Windows 95.

Most of the setup tools are part of the WIN32SDK. The AutoPlay facility is entirely part of Windows, and the developer's portion of AutoPlay consists of a five-page Word for Windows document. The InstallSHIELD Professional toolkit expands on the InstallSHIELD SDK product included with Visual C++ 4 and that is part of the WIN32SDK. It's available from InstallShield Corporation. (InstallShield Corporation used to be called Stirling Technologies, Inc. They changed their name to reflect their most successful product.)

The WIN32SDK, which is part of the MSDN Level II product, includes Microsoft Setup, the "standard" setup program that has been used extensively by Microsoft and other application vendors. One problem with Microsoft Setup is that it requires the setup program to be created as an application (you edit C source code and then build your own SETUP.EXE program). With InstallSHIELD SDK, you need to modify only a single script file—a much simpler process.

The Sax Setup Wizard product from Sax Software is entirely Windows-based. It uses no scripting at all, because all user input is accomplished through wizard dialog boxes.

All three installation generator programs described in this chapter create professional installations that will help assure the user that your product is professional and of high quality—an important factor in today's competitive software market.

Using Microsoft Setup, the Microsoft Installation Program

The Microsoft Setup program (which is also referred to as MS Setup or MSSETUP) is based on the design of the wizards included with Access 1.0, which predated the release of Visual C++. The Microsoft Setup program resembles the SetupWizard of the Access 1.1 Distribution

Kit (ADK), but the C version uses a different approach to create the distribution files and execute the setup application. The primary differences between the methods used by Visual C++ and the ADK wizards to create the distribution disks are explained in the following sections.

> **NOTE**
>
> Microsoft no longer supports the Microsoft Setup program. It's still included with Visual C++, but it hasn't changed for some time, and Microsoft won't update it in the future. Unless you're already using Microsoft Setup, you shouldn't consider it for new projects.

Configuring Microsoft Setup

When you use Microsoft Setup, you don't get the same effects as with the other, newer setup programs such as Sax Setup Wizard and InstallSHIELD. For example, the Microsoft Setup program doesn't support the uninstall process automatically. If you use Microsoft Setup, you must write your uninstall code completely on your own, something that both InstallSHIELD and Sax Setup Wizard do for you.

Using Microsoft Setup is a multistep process. Follow these steps to create your own setup application:

1. Create your SETUP.EXE program using the sample code provided in the WIN32SDK CD's \WIN32SDK\MSTOOLS\MSSETUP\SAMPLE folder as a starting point. You can customize this sample program from Microsoft for your own purposes.

   In your version of Setup, you can specify the background bitmap, title, and billboards (messages that tell the user to register the product, and so on).

2. Lay out the files on the distribution media (usually disks, but now more commonly CD-ROMs). To lay out your application, use the DSKLAYT program, shown in Figure 24.1.

FIGURE 24.1.

The DSKLAYT program in action.

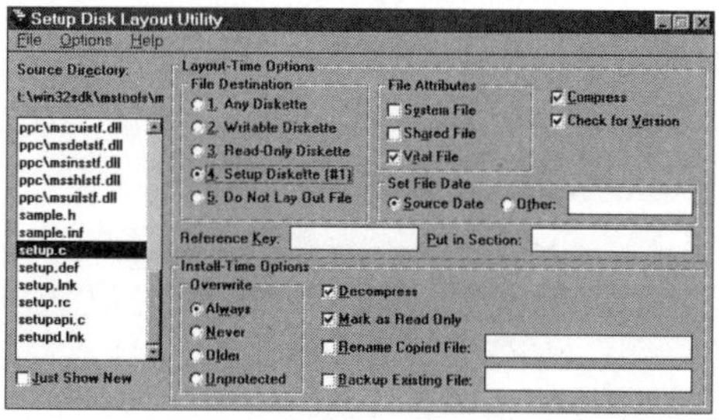

3. Create the SETUP.INF file and distribution disks. Your setup program uses the SETUP.INF file to control the application installation. The SETUP.INF file contains at least three sections, as shown in Listing 24.1. The DSKLAYT2.EXE program takes the layout file created by DSKLAYT.EXE, as well as the files included with your application, and creates the SETUP.INF file for you. The DSKLAYT2.EXE program also creates distribution media images, each in their own directory.

Listing 24.1. A sample SETUP.INF file.

```
[Source Media Descriptions]
    "1", "Disk 1", "", ""

[Minimum Files]
        1, setupapi.c,,,COPY,1992-01-30,,,,,,,,,,52174,,999,,,

[Extra Files]
        1, sample.inf,,,!COPY,1992-01-30,,,,,,,,,,10,,999,,,

[Default File Settings]
"STF_BACKUP"    = ""
"STF_COPY"      = "YES"
"STF_DECOMPRESS" = "YES"
"STF_OVERWRITE"  = "ALWAYS"
"STF_READONLY"   = "YES"
"STF_ROOT"      = ""
"STF_SETTIME"   = "YES"
"STF_TIME"      = "1"
"STF_VITAL"     = "YES"
```

Figure 24.2 shows the process of developing your application's distribution disks. Note that the DSKLAYT2.EXE program is a DOS-based application that runs in a DOS window under Windows 95 and Windows NT. This application won't run under Windows 3.x or native-mode DOS because it's an NT console mode application.

FIGURE 24.2.
The Microsoft Setup process.

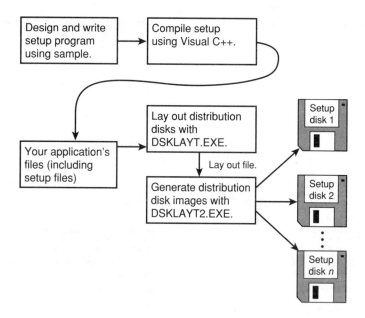

NOTES:
1. DSKLAYT2 creates a directory for each distribution diskette.
2. DSKLAYT2 compresses files as necessary.

Using the Sax Setup Wizard

Sax Software markets an application installation system called the Sax Setup Wizard. This product was initially developed for Windows 3.x; it now fully supports Windows 95. The Sax Setup Wizard is a powerful yet easy-to-use setup generator, excellent for many types of projects.

Using Sax Setup Wizard is much simpler than using the Microsoft Setup program. Sax Setup Wizard is a totally Windows-based installation program that offers extensive user feedback to assist in creating installation disks. Sax Setup Wizard can create not only disk-based installations but also installations for CD-ROM-based products. This is very helpful, because the AutoRun facility (described later) can call the Sax Setup Wizard-created setup program if needed.

Sax Setup Wizard is a single program that requires no additional scripts or other manual input from the user. This differs from Microsoft Setup and InstallSHIELD, both of which are multistep processes that require some form of script from the user.

Figure 24.3 shows Sax Setup Wizard's main window before a project has been opened.

FIGURE 24.3.

Sax Setup Wizard's main window.

After a project has been opened, the values defined by the programmer are displayed in Sax Setup Wizard's main window, as shown in Figure 24.4.

FIGURE 24.4.

Sax Setup Wizard's main window with a project opened.

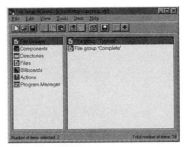

The main thing the user sees when installing applications is the installation program's background. All installation programs let you set the background when the setup program is being developed, and Sax Setup Wizard is no different. With Sax Setup Wizard, you can configure the shading (the trend for a gradient color in installation programs has almost become the standard). Also, your application's title can be text. You specify this in the General tab of the Project Options dialog box, shown in Figure 24.5.

FIGURE 24.5.

Sax Setup Wizard's Project Options dialog with the Background tab open.

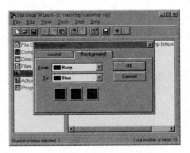

Building a distribution disk set is a simple process with Sax Setup Wizard. You can specify the destination (most of the time you will build to a directory on a hard disk) and the disk size (you can choose from all of the common sizes, including CD-ROM distribution media, which offers a virtually unlimited size), or e-mail distribution.

After you have configured the distribution of your application and generated the disk images, you can copy these images to disks and distribute your application. If I were writing a review, I'd certainly rate the Sax Setup Wizard as the easiest setup generator currently on the market.

Using the InstallSHIELD SDK Version

The documentation from InstallShield Corporation refers to the InstallSHIELD SDK version as InstallSHIELD SE. This chapter uses the same designation. InstallSHIELD SE is a basic application installation system that is very compatible with Windows 95. Applications that are installed using InstallSHIELD SE can be easily removed later using the Add/Remove Programs option under the Windows 95 Control Panel applet.

The InstallSHIELD SE program works like this:

1. Either write or modify an existing script file to be used with your application.

2. Process the script file using the InstallSHIELD SE "compiler" to create the installation script that the InstallSHIELD SE Setup program will use for input.

3. Process all temporary resource files (such as bitmaps, DLLs, and dialog boxes) using the ICOMP.EXE program to create the _SETUP.LIB file that the Setup program uses.

4. Use the ICOMP.EXE program to process your application's file(s) and create a single (compressed) output (.Z) file that is used by Setup.

5. For larger applications that will require more than one disk, use the SPLIT.EXE program to split the .Z file that you created in step 4. If your entire application with the InstallSHIELD SE files will fit on a single disk, you don't need to use SPLIT.EXE.

Figure 24.6 shows the process of creating a distribution disk set for a Windows 95 application.

Take a look at each of the files you must create in order to use InstallSHIELD SE. This example uses the files from InstallShield Corporation's sample program because they represent an excellent starting point and can be easily modified to work with different applications.

The first file you need is the rules file. This file, which is a standard text file created using any editor you want (such as Notepad), is shown in Listing 24.2. The rules file is processed using the InstallSHIELD SE Compile program. The Compile program converts the rules file into an .INS file, which must be named SETUP.INS and be placed on the first disk of your product's distribution disk set, where the InstallSHIELD SE program will look for it.

> **NOTE**
>
> The files shown in the listings for InstallSHIELD SE are all found in the Install-SHIELD SE directory of the WIN32SDK. They are not found on this book's CD-ROM.

FIGURE 24.6.

The InstallSHIELD SE process.

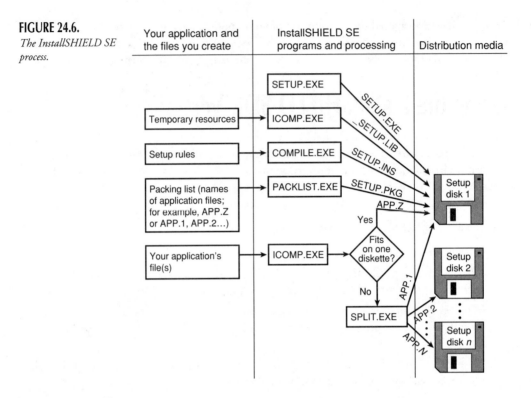

Listing 24.2. SETUP.RUL: The rules file.

```
/*-------------------------------------------------------------------------\

    IIIIIIII SSSSSSSS
       II    SS                   InstallSHIELD SDK Edition (R)
       II    SSSSSSSS        (c) 1995, Stirling Technologies, Inc.
       II          SS              All Rights Reserved.
    IIIIIIII SSSSSSSS


    This source code is intended as a supplement to Stirling Technologies,
    Inc., product documentation.  Refer to your Stirling Technologies, Inc.,
    product documentation for more detailed information.

\-------------------------------------------------------------------------/


/*-------------------------------------------------------------------------\

        Filename:   SETUP.RUL

     Description:   InstallSHIELD SDK Edition Template One template script.


         Author:   Stirling Technologies, Inc.   Date: 2-4-95
```

```
        External
          Files:

        Comments:    This template script performs a basic installation to a
                     Windows 95 or Windows NT platform.  The installation
                     includes components: Application Program Files, Sample and
                     Template Files, Online Help Files, and Multimedia Tutorial
                     Files.  With minor modifications, this template can be
                     adapted to create new, customized installations.

   Modifications:    (Precede each entry with "+" sign. Include name and date.)

                 +                              Date:

\-------------------------------------------------------------------*/


        // Size of components
#define SIZE_REQ_SAMPLES         1400000
#define SIZE_REQ_TEMPLATES         10000
#define SIZE_REQ_PROGRAM          200000


#define APP_NAME                 "Sample App"
#define PROGRAM_GROUP_NAME       "Sample App Group"
#define APPBASE_PATH             "Company\\SampleApp\\"
#define COMPANY_NAME             "SampleCompany"
#define PRODUCT_NAME             "SampleApp"
#define PRODUCT_VERSION          "3.0"
#define PRODUCT_KEY              "designer.exe"
#define UNINSTALL_KEY            "SampleAppV3"
#define APPBASE_DIR95            "Program Files"
#define BASE_REGISTRYNT \
    "Software\\Microsoft\\Windows NT\\CurrentVersion\\App Paths\\"
#define BASE_REGISTRY95 \
    "Software\\Microsoft\\Windows\\CurrentVersion\\App Paths\\"

#define SYS_BOOTMACHINE          3

#define STR_COMPLETE95 \
    "by selecting the program icon in the Programs menu.\n\n"
#define STR_COMPLETENT \
    "by selecting the program icon in the program group.\n\n"

declare

        //--- Global variable definition ---
        STRING  svGrp, szMsg, szFileSet, szTitle, szAppPath, szAppSharedDir;
        STRING  szProgram, szTemp, svUninstLogFile, szRegKey;
        STRING  svMainDirectory[ _MAX_STRING ];
        BOOL    bSpaceOk, bReshowSetupType;
        NUMBER  nResult, nStatusId, nType;

        BOOL    bIncludeProgram, bIncludeSamples, bIncludeHelp, bIncludeTut;
        BOOL    bWinNT;

        // --- Function definition ---
        prototype SetupScreen();
```

continues

Listing 24.2. continued

```
        prototype CheckRequirements();
        prototype CheckSpaceRequirements( number, number, number, string );
        prototype CreateRegDBEntries();

program

StartHere:
        Disable( BACKGROUND );

        // Setup installation screen
        SetupScreen();

        // Set installation info that is required for other functions.
    InstallationInfo( COMPANY_NAME, PRODUCT_NAME, PRODUCT_VERSION, PRODUCT_KEY );

        // Create a Welcome dialog.
WelcomeDlg:
        Disable( BACKBUTTON );
        Welcome( "Welcome", 0 );
        Enable( BACKBUTTON );

        // --- System test for proper configuration ---
        CheckRequirements();

        // --- Ask user for the path to place installed application ---
GetTargetDirectory:

        svMainDirectory = TARGETDISK ^ APPBASE_DIR95 ^ APPBASE_PATH;

        if ( AskDestPath( "Choose Destination Location", szMsg,
                        svMainDirectory, 0 ) = BACK ) then
           goto WelcomeDlg;
        endif;

        szAppSharedDir = svMainDirectory ^ "System";

DetermineUserSelection:

        nType = SetupType( "Setup Type", "", svMainDirectory, TYPICAL, 0 );
        if ( nType = BACK ) then goto GetTargetDirectory; endif;

        bReshowSetupType = FALSE;

        switch (nType)
        case TYPICAL:
            bIncludeSamples  = TRUE;
            bIncludeProgram  = TRUE;
            bIncludeHelp = TRUE;
        case COMPACT:
            bIncludeProgram  = TRUE;
        case CUSTOM:
            SetDialogTitle( DLG_ASK_OPTIONS, "Select Components" );
            bIncludeSamples  = TRUE;
            bIncludeProgram  = TRUE;
            bIncludeHelp = TRUE;
            szMsg = "Select the components that you wish to install.\n"+
```

```
                        "If the check box is unchecked, that component will not be "+
                        "installed. Click Next to continue with the installation.";

            nResult = AskOptions( NONEXCLUSIVE, szMsg,
                                "Application Program Files", bIncludeProgram,
                                "Sample and Template Files", bIncludeSamples,
                                    "On-Line Help Files", bIncludeHelp,
                                    "Multimedia Tutorial", bIncludeTut );

            if ( nResult = BACK ) then goto DetermineUserSelection; endif;
            // Handle exiting of setup
            if (nResult = CANCEL) then
                if (AskYesNo( "Are you sure you would like to exit setup?", NO)
                    = YES) then
                    abort;
                else
                    bReshowSetupType = TRUE;
                endif;
            endif;
        endswitch;

        if (bReshowSetupType = TRUE) goto DetermineUserSelection;

        // Check space requirements
        bSpaceOk = CheckSpaceRequirements( bIncludeSamples,
                                           bIncludeProgram,
                                           bIncludeHelp,
                                           svMainDirectory );

        if (bSpaceOk = FALSE) goto DetermineUserSelection;
                                    // Ask user to try again

FolderSelection:
        if ( bWinNT ) then
            svGrp = PROGRAM_GROUP_NAME;

            // Allow user to modify folder name
            if ( SelectFolder( "Folder Selection", svGrp, svGrp ) = BACK ) then
                goto DetermineUserSelection;
            endif;
        endif;

FileTransferSetup:

        // Set the deinstallation information
        DeinstallStart( svMainDirectory, svUninstLogFile, UNINSTALL_KEY, 0 );
        RegDBSetItem( REGDB_UNINSTALL_NAME, APP_NAME );

        // Set APPPATH for the main application
        szAppPath = svMainDirectory ^ "PROGRAM" + ";" + szAppSharedDir;
        RegDBSetItem( REGDB_APPPATH, szAppPath );
        szProgram = svMainDirectory ^ "PROGRAM\\designer.exe";
        RegDBSetItem( REGDB_APPPATH_DEFAULT, szProgram );

        // Set APPINFO for auxiliary application
        if (bWinNT) then
            szRegKey = BASE_REGISTRYNT ^ "demo.exe";
        else
```

continues

Listing 24.2. continued

```
        szRegKey = BASE_REGISTRY95 ^ "demo.exe";
    endif;
    RegDBSetDefaultRoot( REGKEY_LOCAL_MACHINE );
    RegDBSetKeyValueEx( szRegKey, "Path", REGDB_STRING,  szAppPath, -1 );
    szProgram = svMainDirectory ^ "PROGRAM\\demo.exe";
    RegDBSetKeyValueEx( szRegKey, "", REGDB_STRING,  szProgram, -1 );

    // --- Define the file to be copied to the user's machine ---
    szFileSet = "General";
    TARGETDIR = svMainDirectory;

    FileSetBeginDefine( szFileSet );

      SetStatusWindow( -1, "Copying program files..." );

      // Always copy readme and related
      CompressGet( "data.z", "*.*", COMP_NORMAL );

      if (bIncludeProgram) then
          TARGETDIR = svMainDirectory ^ "PROGRAM";
          CompressGet( "data.z", "program\\*.*", INCLUDE_SUBDIR );
          CompressGet( "data.z", "shared\\*.*", COMP_NORMAL );
          TARGETDIR = szAppSharedDir;
          CompressGet( "data.z", "shared\\*.*", SHAREDFILE | COMP_NORMAL );
      endif;

      if (bIncludeSamples) then
          TARGETDIR = svMainDirectory ^ "SAMPLES";
          CompressGet( "data.z", "samples\\*.*", INCLUDE_SUBDIR );
      endif;

      if (bIncludeHelp) then
          TARGETDIR = svMainDirectory ^ "TEMPLATE";
          CompressGet( "data.z", "template\\*.*", INCLUDE_SUBDIR );
      endif;

    FileSetEndDefine( szFileSet );

DoFileTransfer:
        // --- Set up status bar/file info and perform file transfer ---
        Enable( EXIT );
        Enable( STATUS );
        Enable( FEEDBACK_FULL );
        StatusUpdate( ON, 90 );

        // --- Copy all files on all disks ---
        nResult = FileSetPerformEz( szFileSet, 0 );

        switch (nResult)

        case FS_DONE: // --- Successful completion ---

        case FS_CREATEDIR: // --- Create Directory Error ---
            MessageBox( "Unable to create a directory under " + TARGETDIR + "."+
              "Please check write access to this directory.", SEVERE );
            abort;
```

```
        default: // --- Group all other errors under default label ---
            NumToStr( szTemp, nResult );
            MessageBox( "General file transfer error."+
                        "Please check your target location and try again."+
                        "\n\n Error Number:"+szTemp, SEVERE );

            abort;
        endswitch;

SetRegistryEntries:
//      RegDBSetAppInfo( "Template", REGDB_STRING, "good.tpl", -1 );
//      RegDBSetAppInfo( "TemplatePath", REGDB_STRING,
//          svMainDirectory ^ "TEMPLATE", -1 );

        Disable( FEEDBACK_FULL );
        CreateRegDBEntries( );

        // --- Create program groups and icons ---

CreateFolderIcons:
        SetStatusWindow( 95, "Creating Folder and Icons...." );

        if ( bWinNT ) then
            CreateProgramFolder( svGrp );
            ShowProgramFolder( svGrp, 0 );
            LongPathToShortPath( svMainDirectory );
            Delay(1);
        endif;

        TARGETDIR = svMainDirectory;

        if (bIncludeProgram) then
            szProgram = TARGETDIR ^ "PROGRAM\\DESIGNER.EXE";
            if ( bWinNT ) then
                AddFolderIcon( svGrp, APP_NAME, szProgram,
                            TARGETDIR ^ "PROGRAM",
                            "", 0, "", REPLACE );
            else
                LongPathToQuote( szProgram, TRUE );
                AddFolderIcon( "", APP_NAME, szProgram,
                            TARGETDIR ^ "PROGRAM",
                            "", 0, "", REPLACE );
            endif;
            Delay( 1 );
        endif;

        if ( bWinNT ) then
            if (bIncludeSamples) then
                szProgram = TARGETDIR ^ "PROGRAM\\DEMO.EXE ";
                AddFolderIcon( svGrp, "Example1",
                            szProgram + TARGETDIR ^ "PROGRAM\\MULTI.DBD",
                            TARGETDIR ^ "PROGRAM",
                            "", 0, "", REPLACE );
                Delay( 1 );
            endif;
```

continues

Listing 24.2. continued

```
            if (bIncludeSamples) then
                AddFolderIcon( svGrp, "Example2",
                               szProgram + TARGETDIR ^ "SAMPLES\\LAUNCHER.DBD",
                               TARGETDIR ^ "SAMPLES",
                               "", 0, "", REPLACE );
                Delay( 1 );
            endif;

            AddFolderIcon( svGrp, "ReadmeFile",
                           "NOTEPAD.EXE " + TARGETDIR ^ "README.TXT",
                           TARGETDIR,
                           "", 0, "", REPLACE );
            Delay( 1 );

            szProgram = WINDIR ^ "UNINST.EXE";
            LongPathToShortPath( szProgram );
            LongPathToShortPath( svUninstLogFile );
            AddFolderIcon( svGrp, "Uninstaller",
                           szProgram + " -f" + svUninstLogFile,
                           WINDIR,
                           "", 0, "", REPLACE );
            Delay( 1 );
        endif;

        // Setup complete and readme file

        SetStatusWindow( 100, "Installation complete." );

// If shared files could not be installed, users must restart system
        if (BATCH_INSTALL = TRUE) then
            szMsg = "Some files could not be installed because they are "+
            "currently in use by other programs in the system.  "+
            "To allow for proper operation of the new program you should restart"+
            "your system at this time.";
        if (RebootDialog( "Restart Windows", szMsg, SYS_BOOTMACHINE ) = 0) then
            // Still must ensure proper installation
            CommitSharedFiles(0);
        endif;
    else

            szMsg = "Setup is complete.  You may run the installed program ";
            if ( bWinNT ) then
                szMsg = szMsg + STR_COMPLETENT;
            else
                szMsg = szMsg + STR_COMPLETE95;
            endif;

            MessageBeep( 0 );
            MessageBox( szMsg, INFORMATION );
        endif;

        exit;
```

```
/*------------------------------------------------------------------

    Name    : SetupScreen

    Purpose : This function will set up the screen look.  This includes
              colors, fonts, text to be displayed, etc.

------------------------------------------------------------------*/
function SetupScreen()
      begin

        Enable( DEFWINDOWMODE );
        Enable( INDVFILESTATUS );

        SetTitle( APP_NAME + " Setup", 36, WHITE );

        SetTitle( "Setup", 0, BACKGROUNDCAPTION );  // Caption bar text

        Enable( BACKGROUND );

      end;


//------------------------------------------------------------------
//
//    Name    : CheckRequirements
//
//    Purpose : This function will check all minimum requirements for the
//              application being installed.  If any fail, the user
//              is informed and the installation is terminated.
//
//------------------------------------------------------------------
function CheckRequirements()
        number  nvDx, nvDy;
        number nvResult;
        STRING szResult;
      begin

        // --- Determine if NT or Windows 95 not ---
        GetSystemInfo( WINMAJOR, nvResult, szResult );
        bWinNT = TRUE;
        if (nvResult = 4) then
           bWinNT = FALSE;  // Running Windows 95
        endif;

        // --- Check screen resolution ---
        GetExtents( nvDx, nvDy );
        if (nvDy < 480) then
   MessageBox( "This program requires VGA or better resolution.", WARNING );
          exit;
        endif;

      end;

//------------------------------------------------------------------
//
//    Name    : CheckSpaceRequirements
```

continues

Listing 24.2. continued

```
//
//    Purpose : This function will check space requirements based on the
//              elements being installed.
//
//------------------------------------------------------------------
function CheckSpaceRequirements( bIncludeSamples,
                                 bIncludeProgram,
                                 bIncludeHelp,
                                 szDir )
        number  nSizeRequired;
    begin

        nSizeRequired = 0;

        // Determine total size
        if (bIncludeSamples) then
          nSizeRequired = nSizeRequired + SIZE_REQ_SAMPLES;
        endif;

        if (bIncludeHelp) then
          nSizeRequired = nSizeRequired + SIZE_REQ_TEMPLATES;
        endif;

        if (bIncludeProgram) then
          nSizeRequired = nSizeRequired + SIZE_REQ_PROGRAM;
        endif;

        // Space check of target drive
        bSpaceOk = TRUE;
        if (GetDiskSpace( szDir ) < nSizeRequired) then
        szMsg = "There is not enough space available on the disk\n" +
                "'" + svMainDirectory + "' \n" +
                "Please free up some space or change the target location\n" +
                "to a different disk";
          MessageBeep(0);
          MessageBox( szMsg, WARNING );
          bSpaceOk = FALSE;
        endif;

        return bSpaceOk;
    end;


//------------------------------------------------------------------
//
//    Name    : CreateRegDBEntries
//
//    Purpose : This function will create necessary keys and values for
//              the sample program.
//
//------------------------------------------------------------------
function CreateRegDBEntries()
        string szKey[255], szValue, szDemo, szProgram;
    begin
        // Create PRODUCT_KEY key
        szKey = "SOFTWARE\\" + COMPANY_NAME + "\\" + PRODUCT_NAME + "\\" +
```

```
            PRODUCT_VERSION + "\\" + "DESIGNER";
RegDBCreateKeyEx( szKey, "" );

RegDBSetKeyValueEx( szKey, "Template", REGDB_STRING, "good.tpl", -1 );
RegDBSetKeyValueEx( szKey, "TemplatePath", REGDB_STRING,
                szMainDirectory ^ "TEMPLATE", -1 );

if (bIncludeSamples) then
    // Create "DEMOS" key
    szKey = "SOFTWARE\\" + COMPANY_NAME + "\\" + PRODUCT_NAME + "\\" +
            PRODUCT_VERSION + "\\" + "DEMOS";
    RegDBCreateKeyEx( szKey, "" );

    szDemo    = svMainDirectory ^ "PROGRAM\\MULTI.DBD";
    szProgram = svMainDirectory ^ "PROGRAM\\DEMO.EXE";
    RegDBSetKeyValueEx( szKey, "path0", REGDB_STRING, szDemo, -1 );
    RegDBSetKeyValueEx( szKey, "exe0", REGDB_STRING, szProgram, -1 );
    RegDBSetKeyValueEx( szKey, "active0", REGDB_STRING, "Play", -1 );

    szDemo    = svMainDirectory ^ "SAMPLES\\LAUNCHER.DBD";
    szProgram = svMainDirectory ^ "PROGRAM\\DEMO.EXE";
    RegDBSetKeyValueEx( szKey, "path1", REGDB_STRING, szDemo, -1 );
    RegDBSetKeyValueEx( szKey, "exe1", REGDB_STRING, szProgram, -1 );
    RegDBSetKeyValueEx( szKey, "active1", REGDB_STRING, "Play", -1 );

    RegDBSetKeyValueEx( szKey, "exe2", REGDB_STRING, szProgram, -1 );
    RegDBSetKeyValueEx( szKey, "active2", REGDB_STRING, "Play", -1 );

    RegDBSetKeyValueEx( szKey, "exe3", REGDB_STRING, szProgram, -1 );
    RegDBSetKeyValueEx( szKey, "active3", REGDB_STRING, "Play", -1 );

    RegDBSetKeyValueEx( szKey, "exe4", REGDB_STRING, szProgram, -1 );
    RegDBSetKeyValueEx( szKey, "active4", REGDB_STRING, "Play", -1 );

    RegDBSetKeyValueEx( szKey, "exe5", REGDB_STRING, szProgram, -1 );
    RegDBSetKeyValueEx( szKey, "active5", REGDB_STRING, "Play", -1 );

    RegDBSetKeyValueEx( szKey, "exe6", REGDB_STRING, szProgram, -1 );
    RegDBSetKeyValueEx( szKey, "active6", REGDB_STRING, "Play", -1 );

    RegDBSetKeyValueEx( szKey, "exe7", REGDB_STRING, szProgram, -1 );
    RegDBSetKeyValueEx( szKey, "active7", REGDB_STRING, "Play", -1 );

    RegDBSetKeyValueEx( szKey, "exe8", REGDB_STRING, szProgram, -1 );
    RegDBSetKeyValueEx( szKey, "active8", REGDB_STRING, "Play", -1 );

    RegDBSetKeyValueEx( szKey, "exe9", REGDB_STRING, szProgram, -1 );
    RegDBSetKeyValueEx( szKey, "active9", REGDB_STRING, "Play", -1 );

endif;

// Create "HELPMENU" key
szKey = "SOFTWARE\\" + COMPANY_NAME + "\\" + PRODUCT_NAME + "\\" +
        PRODUCT_VERSION + "\\" + "HELPMENU";
RegDBCreateKeyEx( szKey, "" );

RegDBSetKeyValueEx( szKey, "MaxNum", REGDB_NUMBER, "1", -1 );
```

continues

Listing 24.2. continued

```
        RegDBSetKeyValueEx( szKey, "path0", REGDB_STRING, svMainDirectory ^
                                   "README.TXT", -1 );
        RegDBSetKeyValueEx( szKey, "exe0", REGDB_STRING, "NOTEPAD.EXE", -1 );
        RegDBSetKeyValueEx( szKey, "active0", REGDB_STRING, "Read Me", -1 );

end;
```

Even though SETUP.RUL is a long file (more than 500 lines), it's well-documented and logical. You should have little difficulty modifying this file to suit your purposes.

The packing list file, shown in Listing 24.3, is much shorter. Like the SETUP.INS file, the packing list file must be processed (using the PACKLIST.EXE program) and placed on the first disk of your product's distribution disk set.

Listing 24.3. PACK.LST: The packing list input file.

```
1;
..\disk1\data.z
```

In this example, the application's files will fit on a single disk, so there is only one source file for Setup to process.

Using InstallSHIELD Professional

The documentation from InstallShield Corporation refers to the InstallSHIELD Professional version as InstallSHIELD PE. This chapter uses the same designation. InstallSHIELD PE is very much an expanded version of InstallSHIELD SE. The Professional version covers more operating systems, including Windows 3.x, Windows 95, Windows NT, and OS/2.

InstallSHIELD PE offers the following features:

■ The capability to create a single installation system that includes Windows 3.1, Windows 32s, 32-bit Windows 95, and 32-bit Windows NT 3.5

■ A complete set of installation templates

■ More than 50 built-in user interface objects and complete customization of all objects in InstallSHIELD PE

■ The ability to integrate your own custom dialog boxes

■ The InstallSHIELD Visual Debugger, a Windows hosted debugger designed specifically for installation building and testing

■ The ability to use your company logo, corporate look, animated bitmaps, and billboards during installation

- The ability to selectively install components of a multicomponent application
- The capability for your installation program to launch help files, readme files, and other applications at any time during or after the installation process
- The capability to intelligently update or modify system files, AUTOEXEC.BAT and CONFIG.SYS, private and system .INI files, and the Windows Registry
- The capability to call any function in any DLL—including any Windows API—directly from the script

If after using InstallSHIELD SE you find that you need a more powerful and flexible installation program, you can migrate to InstallSHIELD PE. The InstallSHIELD PE product is compatible with InstallSHIELD SE. This means that you can create a simple installation using InstallSHIELD SE, and, as your needs expand, you can easily migrate to InstallSHIELD PE.

Modifying the CONFIG.SYS and AUTOEXEC.BAT Files

You can incorporate Visual C++ binary file instructions and functions in your setup application to read the AUTOEXEC.BAT and CONFIG.SYS files on the recipient's fixed disk to determine whether you need to make modifications to these files so that your application will execute properly. If the user isn't running Windows for Workgroups, you must load SHARE.EXE in order for OLE 2.0, OLE Automation, and data access to operate properly. Thus, you might need to add a SHARE.EXE /L:500 entry to the AUTOEXEC.BAT file. (The parameter reserves DOS environment space for 500 locks, which is sufficient for most applications.)

Your setup program must open and manipulate the AUTOEXEC.BAT and CONFIG.SYS files by reading and parsing them. It's important to realize that it's unacceptable to simply add more lines to the ends of these files. Your application must test to see whether the desired command or string is present and then add the string only if it's missing. This addition usually can be done at the end (or beginning) of the AUTOEXEC.BAT and CONFIG.SYS files, but not always.

There are few cases with Windows 95 in which you need to work with either the CONFIG.SYS or AUTOEXEC.BAT files. With Windows 95, neither of these files needs to exist, and with Windows NT, neither of these files does exist.

> **TIP**
>
> Polite setup applications use a message box to advise the user that the CONFIG.SYS and AUTOEXEC.BAT files might need to be altered. Before making any changes to these files, save a copy of the original versions with the FileCopy instruction and advise

the user of the names of the backup files. An even more polite approach is to offer the user the option of modifying the existing AUOTEXEC.BAT and CONFIG.SYS files or creating a new set of files that the user can inspect before copying over AUTOEXEC.BAT and CONFIG.SYS.

The CD-ROM AutoPlay Facility

Microsoft has added a new feature to Windows 95—the capability to have a program run whenever an AutoPlay-enabled CD is inserted into the CD-ROM drive. This enables software developers who distribute by (or execute from) CD-ROMs to have either the program or an installation routine start whenever the CD-ROM is inserted into the drive. The AutoPlay facility enables "Plug-n-Play" to extend into the software arena.

Users benefit from a product that is easy to use. Using CDs under Windows 95 is easy. You can select the property page for a given CD-ROM by right-clicking on the CD in Explorer, as shown later in Figure 24.7.

Many users (and developers) have decried the poor interface between CD-ROM-based applications and Windows. With applications created before AutoPlay, the user had to insert a CD-ROM into the drive and enter a command (often, but not always, called setup) to install the product. Many setup programs ran well, but the concept behind CD-ROM-based applications is that the application (and much of its static data) doesn't need to be copied to the computer's local hard disk; instead, it may remain on the CD-ROM. This permits the user to have a large library of CD-ROM-based applications without having to dedicate substantial portions of the hard disk to these CD-ROM applications.

With AutoPlay, the following things happen when you insert a CD:

■ AutoPlay-enabled CD-ROMs execute the designated program. This program typically either is a setup program (less optimal) or actually executes the CD-ROM's main program (more optimal).

■ Audio CDs automatically play using the CD Player applet, which is a standard part of Windows 95. CD Player works very much like your home CD player and offers many of the options and features of a typical CD player.

■ All other CD-ROMs behave as they do under Windows 3.x—that is, they do nothing special.

Sometimes users won't want to activate a program (or play an audio CD) automatically. In this case, they can hold down the Shift key when the CD-ROM (or CD) is inserted to disable AutoPlay. This enables the user to perhaps simply do a directory of the CD-ROM, run a different program from the CD-ROM, or otherwise use the CD-ROM.

NOTE

People tend to believe that if they stick a CD into their computer, it won't have a virus, trojan horse, or other nasty surprise in store. However, it would be wise to treat most CDs with the same care you would give a diskette or a file downloaded from a BBS: Do a virus scan!

NOTE

One alternative would be for AutoPlay to display a dialog that gives the user one button to continue the AutoPlay process and another button to kill the process and continue with the task that had focus. With this technique, the user doesn't need to remember to press the Shift key. Microsoft also recommends this technique: a quick-loading splash screen that lets the user abort.

Using the AUTORUN.INF Files

To make AutoRun work, Windows 95 looks at the CD or CD-ROM that the user inserts. If it's an audio CD, the CD Player applet is launched and the CD is played. If the CD-ROM has an AUTORUN.INF file, this file is examined, and the actions specified in the AUTORUN.INF file are followed. (The AUTORUN.INF file is stored in the CD-ROM's root directory.)

The minimum necessary AUTORUN.INF file is shown in Listing 24.4.

Listing 24.4. The minimal AUTORUN.INF file for AutoRun compliance.

```
[autorun]
open=filename.exe
icon=filename.ico
```

Even this minimal AUTORUN.INF file, with only three lines of information, can be expanded. Take a look at each of the options available and what you can use in your AUTORUN.INF files:

■ open=: This line specifies which program is to be executed whenever the user inserts the CD. This program can reside in the same directory as AUTORUN.INF (the CD's root directory) or in any other directory. To specify a subdirectory, use the format
`open=subdir1\subdir2\filename.exe`

In this example, Windows 95 will search the CD's directory structure and insert the correct drive letter as necessary. When the program specified in the `open=` line is executed, the current directory isn't changed. Microsoft recommends that a "teaser" application be launched using the `open=` line. This teaser application might give the user an opportunity to execute the program or do an installation. A more complex teaser program might check to see whether the application has been installed and, if it has, launch the application rather than the installation program.

■ `icon=`: The icon for the CD is contained in either an .ICO, .BMP, .EXE, or .DLL file. If the file contains more than one icon (the STARmanager application has a number of different icons), you could specify the icon using the following syntax:

```
icon=filename.exe,2
```

In this example, you have specified that the third icon (the icons are zero-based) will be used. Unlike the `open=` expression, the `icon=` line doesn't let you use a path. To use a path, you should use the `defaulticon=` expression, which is discussed next.

■ `defaulticon=`: The `defaulticon=` line specifies an icon path. This path is relative to the CD-ROM drive if no drive specification is provided. I strongly recommend that you not use a drive specification. You can't depend on finding any drive at a known location, nor can an application require drives to be at specific places.

> **WARNING**
>
> Don't code your programs to expect a C: drive to be present or writeable. There is no guarantee that a computer will have a C: drive, or that it will be accessible to applications. Diskless workstations might have drives that are found at different locations each time the system is started. You must take this into consideration when you're writing your application.

When an AutoPlay-enabled CD is inserted into the CD-ROM drive, the user can right-click the CD's icon and get a menu of choices. If your AUTORUN.INF file has an `open=` line, the menu that Explorer displays includes the commands shown in Figure 24.7.

The AutoRun facility added the AutoPlay selection to the list of actions in the pop-up menu. If you add the following lines to your AUTORUN.INF file, a new menu item will be added to the menu with the text `Item For Menu`. When this menu item is selected, the program specified in the command line will be executed.

```
shell\verb\command=filename.exe
shell\verb=Item For Menu
```

For example, to have the user check out a README file, you could add the following to the AUTORUN.INF file:

```
shell\readme\command=notepad readme.txt
shell\readme=Read &Me
```

FIGURE 24.7.

An AutoPlay-enabled CD-ROM in Explorer.

In this example, the user's menu will include a Read Me selection. When selected, it will execute the Notepad program, loading and displaying the README.TXT file. Normally, the default menu selection for an AutoPlay-enabled CD is AutoPlay (as shown in Figure 24.7). You can change this default by adding

```
shell=verb
```

The shell= line specifies the action that will take place when the user selects the AutoPlay menu option. For example, to activate the readme selection, you could include the following lines in your AUTORUN.INF file:

```
shell=readme
shell\readme\command=notepad readme.txt
shell\readme=Read &Me
```

In this example, if the user selects AutoPlay from the menu, the README.TXT file will be loaded in Notepad.

Suggestions for Creating AutoPlay CDs

Microsoft has several suggestions for developers who are creating AutoPlay CDs. The most important is that the application that is launched automatically be small. For performance reasons, Microsoft recommends that you not try to load a large application whenever the CD is inserted. Instead, load the smaller teaser application, which will then let the user load the larger application.

For CD-ROMs that contain only data and no executable program, the teaser program could simply display a README file. This lets the user quickly determine the CD-ROM's contents.

For data CD-ROMs, be sure to date the data using a date format that is easily understood. Don't use summer/winter/spring/fall designators: these seasons mean different things to people in different parts of the world. Also, don't use "1Q" designators, because these terms aren't always meaningful to all users. Instead, use months and years, such as January 1995, to date data. Your README file should also indicate how often the data on the CD-ROM is updated. For example, for a database of company information that is updated on a quarterly basis, you will want to inform the user when the data has become "stale" so that he or she can get an update to the CD-ROM. Here is the potential for marketing upgrades to products that are prone to become obsolete.

With applications in which the teaser or introduction program includes a button to let the user launch the full application, you can take advantage of Windows 95's multithreaded processes to begin the loading process. That way, if the user decides to start the application, you're one step ahead of the game and will be able to start the application (hopefully) without having to incur a long delay while the main program loads.

Try to create applications that run well from CD-ROMs when possible. This lets the user better manage his or her hard disk. If you must install programs or other files on the hard disk, use a recognized installation program (such as the InstallSHIELD SDK program, mentioned earlier) to let the user easily uninstall the program from his or her hard disk. There's nothing worse than having a CD-ROM-based application create a directory that contains virtually everything that is on the CD-ROM.

Demos and Shows

It's always nice to be able to send a demo (either a working version or a canned demo, usually called a *show*) to a prospective purchaser. It's now possible to publish demos of your products using traditional techniques (such as either by itself or as part of a CD-ROM compilation) or using online publication techniques, including the Internet.

Using DemoSHIELD

There are a number of packages for creating demo programs. One such product is Demo-SHIELD. It lets the developer create a professional demonstration of the product's capabilities without having to resort to low-level programming.

Using DemoSHIELD is easy. The WIN32SDK has a working demo model of DemoSHIELD that you can use. This version of the product is limited to three panels, but even with this limitation, you can still examine the product and see its capabilities.

Working Demos

Many programmers distribute their applications using the "working demo" technique. This enables the potential user to use the application, get a feel for its weaknesses and strengths, and see how well the application fills his or her projected needs.

There is a difference between a working demo and using shareware to distribute your application. A working demo is almost always a copy of a product and has some limitation, such as a disabled save function. There is no way for most working demo programs to be upgraded without the user being sent a new copy of the program, whereas shareware programs typically either are fully functional or can be upgraded to full functionality by the user when the application is registered.

Distributing working demos and shareware applications is no different from distributing any other application. A smooth installation of the demo version goes a long way toward convincing a potential user to buy your product. A poor installation will convince users that your product is substandard, regardless of how well the application has been written.

Summary

Creating distribution disks is the final step in developing a Visual C++ database application, so it's fitting that this chapter closes this book. The objective of this book was to give DOS database developers and Visual C++ programmers who are new to database applications the background needed to create professional-grade database front ends with Visual C++. We hope this objective was accomplished.

Visual C++ is reportedly Microsoft's most successful and profitable language product. Therefore, you can expect Microsoft to release a continuing series of upgrades to Visual C++. Fortunately for Visual C++ developers, Microsoft has given its highest development priority to ensuring the compatibility of new versions of Visual C++ with code written for prior versions.

The remainder of this book consists of appendixes. Appendix A lists sources of add-on products and provides additional information for Visual C++ programmers. Appendix B lists the standard naming conventions for Visual C++ objects and variables. Appendix C gives you instructions for using the CD that comes with this book.

VII

Appendixes

Resources for Developing Visual C++ Database Applications

A wide variety of supplemental and add-in products to assist database developers are available for character-based RDBMS applications such as xBase and Paradox. Fewer products in this category are available to Visual C++ and Access database application developers. This appendix lists products and information sources for Visual C++ developers that expand the capability of Visual C++ and improve database development efficiency. Generally, there are not (yet) as many OLE custom controls as there are VBX controls. This will change. There will probably be a wide variety of OLE custom controls by mid-1996 (if not sooner).

This appendix is divided into the following sections:

- Data-aware custom controls
- Open database connectivity (ODBC) drivers
- Special-purpose database tools and add-ins
- Add-in and auxiliary applications for Visual C++
- Windows help-file authoring and Visual C++ documentation applications
- Third-party OLE servers for Visual C++
- Visual C++ and Access periodicals
- Periodicals devoted to general database and Windows topics
- Using the Internet for support
- Books for database developers
- Online sources for database technical support and sample applications
- Other tools for Visual C++ developers

Within each category, products are listed in alphabetical order by product name.

Data-Aware Custom Controls

A number of publishers have plans to introduce data-aware OLE controls. Also, Visual C++ includes a sample data-aware OLE control that could be modified to meet a programmer's needs. Data-aware OLE controls are controls that use Visual C++'s MFC database classes to provide connectivity to recordset objects. You can expect a wider range of data-aware custom controls to become available as the number of Visual C++ database developers increases. The following sections describe the data-aware custom controls that are used in the sample applications in this book.

The one product listed in this category doesn't offer a data-aware OLE control. However, the controls offered by WinWidgets can be useful to programmers of database applications.

WinWidgets

WinWidgets is a collection of controls that the Visual C++ programmer can use when developing database applications. There are a number of different products in the WinWidgets family, including WinWidgets XGrid OCX and WinWidgets XTable OCX. WinWidgets controls include a set of data-related controls (such as date, time, currency, string, and mask), as well as a grid and a spreadsheet control.

> Lifeboat Publishing
> 1163 Shrewsbury Avenue
> Shrewsbury, NJ 07702-9949
> Telephone orders: (908) 389-0037
> Fax: (908) 389-9227
> BBS: (908) 389-9783

Open Database Connectivity (ODBC) Drivers

Microsoft supplies ODBC drivers for Microsoft and Oracle client-server databases with Visual C++ 4. Many other client-server database publishers and third-party software developers currently supply or were in the process of developing multiple-tier and single-tier ODBC drivers at the time this book was published. The following sections describe some of the ODBC drivers that were available for commercial applications in 1995 and early 1996 and that were tested during the writing of this book.

Information Builders, Inc.'s EDA/SQL

Enterprise Data Access/SQL, or EDA/SQL, was introduced in 1991 and has since become the industry standard in data access middleware. EDA/SQL provides SQL and stored procedure-based access to more than 60 relational and nonrelational data structures across all major operating platforms and networks. This middleware technology lets customers build departmental and enterprise-wide client/server systems that integrate heterogeneous data, application tools, and operating environments seamlessly and transparently.

Through comprehensive support of all major application programming interfaces, such as ODBC, DB-Library, DDCS/2, OCI, and X/Open, EDA/SQL simplifies the challenge of operating in environments comprised of multiple standards. EDA/SQL's marketplace leadership has caused it to be adopted by IBM, Microsoft, Hewlett-Packard, Digital, Informix, and Oracle into their information warehouse and DBMS products.

> Information Builders, Inc.
> EDA Division
> 1250 Broadway
> New York, NY 10001-3782

Telephone: (800) 969-INFO, (212) 736-4433
Fax: (212) 629-3612
http://www.idi.com

Microsoft ODBC Desktop Database Drivers

The Microsoft ODBC Desktop Database Drivers kit consists of single-tier drivers for Access (.MDB), dBASE III, IV, and V (.DBF), FoxPro (.DBF), and Paradox (.PX) databases, as well as drivers for Excel worksheet files (.XLS) and text files (.CSV, .TXT, and .ASC). All these drivers are supplied with Visual C++ 4 in the MSDEV\REDIST folder on the Visual C++ distribution CD.

Microsoft Corp.
One Microsoft Way
Redmond, WA 98052-6399
Telephone: (800) 227-4679, (206) 882-8080
http://www.microsoft.com

Intersolv ODBC Driver Pack

Intersolv, Inc. supplies an ODBC DataDirect driver pack, a collection of ODBC drivers for a variety of desktop and client-server databases. In addition to supplying the ODBC Driver Pack, Intersolv develops ODBC drivers on a contract basis for publishers of client-server RDBMSs. Intersolv's drivers are possibly the most extensive available to the database programmer.

One of the advantages of Intersolv's single-tier drivers is that the dBASE and Paradox drivers support transaction processing. The Intersolv DataDirect ODBC pack supports ALLBASE, Btrieve, CA-Ingres, Clipper, DB2, DB2/2, DB2/6000, dBASE, Excel, FoxBase, FoxPro, Gupta SQLBase, IMAGE/SQL, INFORMIX, InterBase, Microsoft SQL Server, Oracle, Paradox, PROGRESS, Scalable SQL (formerly Netware SQL), SQL/400, SQL/DS, SYBASE System 10, SYBASE SQL Server 4, Teradata, text files, and XDB.

Intersolv
1800 Perimeter Park Drive, Suite 210
Morrisville, NC 27560
Telephone: (800) 876-3101
Fax: (919) 461-4526
http://www.intersolv.com

Special-Purpose Database Tools and Add-Ins

This section includes products that are designed specifically to aid in the development of Visual C++ database applications. Some of the products listed in this section are specifically designed for use with Access database files and require the retail version of Access.

Btrieve for Windows

Novell, Inc. was supplying Btrieve for Windows as a component of many of its NetWare products. In 1994, Btrieve Technologies (founded by a group of former Novell employees) purchased Novell's database products.

Btrieve Technologies USA
8834 Capital of Texas Highway North, Suite 300
Austin, TX 78759
Telephone: (800) BTRIEVE, (512) 794-1719
Fax: (512) 794-1778
CompuServe: GO BTRIEVE
E-mail: info@btrvtech.com, salessupport@btrvtech.com, techsupport@btrvtech.com

DDF Builder for Windows

DDF Builder lets you design and create your own data definition files (FIELD.DDF and INDEX.DDF) for Novell Btrieve tables. DDF Builder also can create new Btrieve tables. If you plan to import or attach to Access Btrieve tables created by other applications, you'll probably need DDF Builder to reconstruct the data-definition files to meet the requirements of the Btrieve driver of the Access database engine.

Smithware, Inc.
2416 Hillsboro Road, Suite 201
Nashville, TN 37212
Telephone: (800) 828-7438, (615) 386-3100
Fax: (615) 386-3135
E-mail: info@smithware.com

InfoModeler

InfoModeler is an application that lets you quickly and accurately build databases for the leading desktop, client-server, and mainframe database systems. This product lets you produce graphical documentation of the database and produces documentation for record-keeping.

The InfoModeler product uses Formal Object Role Modeling (FORML) to assist the developer in designing the database.

Asymetrix, Inc.
110 110th Avenue N.E., Suite 700
Bellevue, WA 98004-5840
Sales telephone: (800) 448-6543
Support telephone: (206) 637-1600
Fax: (206) 637-1504
http://www.asymetrix.com

MTX Accounting Software Development Kit

The MTX Accounting Software Development Kit (SDK) is a full-featured accounting application created in Access. General Ledger, Accounts Receivable, Accounts Payable, and Payroll modules are included. MTX ported the Access application from its DOS accounting application. The advantage of the MTX Accounting SDK for Visual C++ programmers who are developing accounting applications is that the database file structure for a complete accounting package is ready-made.

> MTX International, Inc.
> 98 Inverness Dr. East, Suite 110
> Englewood, CO 80112
> Telephone: (800) 888-MTXI, (303) 790-1400
> Fax: (303) 888-6894
> CIS: 71201,1714

Total Access

Total Access is a comprehensive documentation, analysis, and reporting tool for Access databases. Using Total Access is one of the subjects of Chapter 22, "Documenting Your Database Applications." All of the data that Total Access uses to create its 30 built-in reports is stored in tables that you can read with Visual C++ database applications. You also can customize Total Access's reports or create your own reports. Although Total Access was designed for Access database developers, it's equally useful for Visual C++ database applications that use the .MDB database structure.

> Financial Modeling Specialists, Inc.
> 8027 Leesburg Pike, Suite 410
> Vienna, VA 22182
> Telephone: (703) 356-4700
> Fax: (703) 448-3861

WINGate

WINGate is a unique programming toolkit that provides interprocess communication between DOS and Windows applications. WINGate's initial applications are designed to let Clipper, dBASE, and FoxPro applications running under DOS interchange data with Windows applications. The heart of WINGate is a Windows enhanced-mode virtual device driver (VxD), VWINGD.386, which lets applications running in virtual machines (VMs) communicate. WINGate uses client-server terminology in the same manner as DDE and OLE.

> WINGate Technologies (a division of MITech, Inc.)
> High Street Court, Suite 303
> Morristown, NJ 07960

Telephone: (201) 539-2727
Fax: (201) 539-2838
`http://www.wingate.com`

Add-In and Auxiliary Applications for Visual C++

This section describes add-in products and custom controls that aid in the creation of Visual C++ applications but are not specifically oriented to database applications.

Quicture

Quicture is an application that can be used by documentation developers (and other users of Microsoft Word for Windows) to enhance graphics included in documents. This product enhances the performance of Word for Windows by using placeholders for graphic objects.

WexTech Systems, Inc.
310 Madison Avenue, Suite 905
New York, NY 10071
Telephone: (800) 939-8324, (212) 949-9595

WinFax PRO 7.0

WinFax PRO 7.0 is a fax-management application that you can use in conjunction with a Visual C++ database application to create a fully automated fax transmission system integrated with other Windows applications, such as Word for Windows or Excel. You can use WinFax as a DDE fax server by executing Visual C++'s `LinkPoke` statement; the data argument consists of WinFax PRO's `Recipient()` function, which specifies the fax number and the other arguments needed to send a fax. Alternatively, you can manipulate WinFax PRO's dBASE IV-format phone book files as a Visual C++ `Database` object. The product includes a sample macro for Word for Windows that you can translate to Visual C++. WinFax PRO also includes an optical character recognition (OCR) feature that lets you convert the text of incoming or outgoing faxes to rich text format (.RTF) or ASCII text (.TXT) files.

Delrina (US) Corporation, San Jose—USA Sales and Operations
6320 San Ignacio Avenue
San Jose, CA 95119-1209
Telephone: (408) 363-2345
Sales telephone: (800) 268-6082
Fax: (408) 363-2340

Windows Help-File Authoring and Visual C++ Documentation Applications

Developers who include online help in their Access applications can choose from a variety of commercial Windows help-file authoring applications. Two of the leading products, each of which takes a different approach to help-file creation, are described in the sections that follow.

Doc-To-Help

WexTech Systems' Doc-To-Help application is a collection of Word for Windows document templates (.DOT files) combined with a single Windows dynamic link library (DLL). Doc-To-Help lets you create electronic help files for an application from its formatted documentation. Although you can convert existing application manuals to Doc-To-Help's format, the most efficient use of the application requires that you first create the manuals yourself using Doc-To-Help's templates. When you complete your document, Doc-To-Help converts the document to an .RTF file and compiles the .RTF file to a Windows .HLP file. Using Doc-To-Help is one of the subjects of Chapter 22 and Chapter 23, "Creating Help Files for Database Applications."

Doc-To-Help 2.0 is available now, and Doc-To-Help 1.7 was supposed to be available in January of 1996. Doc-To-Help 1.7 is for Word for Windows 2.0 and 6.0 users who work in Windows 95 or Windows 3.1. Version 2.0 is for Word for Windows 7. Features new to version 1.7 include automatic generation of contents files (.CNT files); Doc-To-Help Navigator, video, and Watermark support for 32-bit WinHelp; Doc-To-Help Navigator support in author mode; and support for Windows 95 Help second-level indexes.

> WexTech Systems, Inc.
> 310 Madison Avenue, Suite 905
> New York, NY 10017
> Telephone: (212) 949-9595
> Fax: (212) 949-4007

RoboHelp

Blue Sky Software's RoboHelp application, and its WinHelp Office product, are oriented to creating help files directly rather than from a preexisting application manual. Like Doc-To-Help, RoboHelp consists of Word for Windows templates and Windows DLLs. RoboHelp is less automatic in operation than Doc-To-Help, but RoboHelp lets you exercise more control over the individual elements of your help system, such as assigning special values to help context strings and ID numbers. RoboHelp is discussed in Chapter 23.

Blue Sky Software Corporation
7486 La Jolla Blvd., Suite 3
La Jolla, CA 92037-9582
Telephone: (800) 677-4946, (619) 459-6365
Fax: (619) 459-6366
http://www.blue-sky.com

SpellPro

SpellPro is a DLL that lets you include spell checking in your applications. A thesaurus is also available. This product works either as a DLL or as a VBX custom control.

MicroHelp, Inc.
4359 Shallowford Industrial Parkway
Marietta, GA 30066
Telephone: (404) 526-0898

Third-Party OLE Servers for Visual C++

Visual C++'s OLE controls let you display graphics or play sound and music from files. Although you can use Windows OLE server applets such as Paintbrush and Microsoft Draw to create graphics, professional-quality graphic applications created by such companies as Micrografx and Corel Systems provide a host of features that aren't included in the applets that accompany Windows and its mainstream applications. The multimedia OLE server applets, Sound Recorder and Media Player, are adequate for simple multimedia databases, but you need commercial multimedia toolkits when you want to control VCRs or laserdisc players from your Visual C++ application. The following sections describe representative commercial OLE server applications that you can use with Visual C++.

CorelDRAW!

CorelDRAW! is the fifth iteration of a highly successful vector drawing application that is a favorite of graphic artists. CorelDRAW! 3.0 was the first of Corel Systems' products to bundle a suite of graphics applications, including a bitmapped image editor (Corel PhotoPaint), a presentation application (CorelSHOW!), and an image database (Corel Mosaic). CorelDRAW! 4.0 added CorelMOVE!, an application that you can use to animate and add sound to CorelDRAW! images. CorelDRAW! can import images in a variety of vector formats. The CD-ROM version of CorelDRAW! includes more than 250 TrueType fonts and several thousand clip-art objects. CorelDRAW! 6 might well hold the record for the largest distribution set. It comes on many CD-ROMs!

Corel Systems Corporation
1600 Carling Avenue
Ottawa, Ontario, Canada K1Z 8R7
Telephone: (613) 728-8200
Fax: (613) 761-9176

Micrografx Designer and Windows DRAW! with OLE

Micrografx Designer is a vector image drawing application that is oriented toward technical illustration. This venerable Windows drawing product includes an updated user interface, improved color-separation capabilities, and a 32-bit graphics engine to speed the redrawing of images. Micrografx Windows DRAW! with OLE offers a subset of designer's capabilities at a substantially lower price. Both products can import and export vector image files in a variety of common formats.

Micrografx, Inc.
1303 Arapaho Road
Richardson, TX 75081
Telephone: (214) 234-1769
Sales telephone: (800) 671-0144
Fax: (214) 994-6475
http://www.micrografx.com

MEDIADEVELOPER 2.0

MEDIADEVELOPER 2.0 provides the tools to quickly build multimedia applications. With virtually any Windows development environment and MEDIADEVELOPER, you can write interactive multimedia programs that play video, animation, graphics, and audio. You can even build applications that interface with camcorders, laserdisc players, and VCRs. MEDIADEVELOPER supports thumbnails and "hot spots," unique media segmenting, and continuous-play universal media format. VBX, OLE 2.0 Automation Server, C++ libraries, and DLL packages are available.

Lenel Systems International, Inc.
290 Woodcliff Office Park
Fairport, NY 14450-4212
Telephone: (716) 248-9720
Fax: (716) 248-9185

Picture Publisher 3.1

Micrografx's Picture Publisher 3.1 is a full-featured, OLE 1.0-compliant image-editing application for full-color (16-bit) and high-color (24-bit) bitmapped image files. Picture Publisher is one of the few image editing applications that is directly compatible with images stored in Kodak's PhotoCD file format (.PCD). You can use Picture Publisher 3.0 to embed or link images stored in a variety of compression formats, such as JPEG (Joint Photographic Experts Group—.JPG—format).

Micrografx, Inc.
1303 Arapaho Road
Richardson, TX 75081
Telephone: (214) 234-1769
Sales telephone: (800) 671-0144
Fax: (214) 994-6475
http://www.micrografx.com

Visio

Visio is an OLE-compliant, stencil-based drawing application that uses drag-and-drop techniques to simplify the creation of the most common types of drawings and illustrations required for business communication. Visio 2.0, introduced in October 1993, was the first retail software product to fully implement OLE 2.0 and OLE Automation.

Visio Corporation
520 Pike Street, Suite 1800
Seattle, WA 98101
Telephone: (206) 521-4500
Fax: (206) 521-4501
Customer service telephone: (800) 24-VISIO, (716) 586-0030
Customer service fax: (716) 586-0820
Customer service e-mail: csdirect@visio.com
Technical support telephone: (206) 521-4600
Technical support fax: (206) 521-4601
Fax information system: (206) 521-4550
Pre-sales technical information: (206) 521-4750
http://www.visio.com

Watermark Imaging Software

As the first company to ship document-imaging solutions based on Microsoft Windows NT, Watermark has the largest installed base of imaging users for this platform. The company's Enterprise Edition software for Microsoft Windows NT Server was named "Outstanding New Product" at the 1995 Association for Information and Image Management (AIIM) show. FileNet supports UNIX, Windows, Windows NT, OS/2, and NetWare. The Windows NT Server version of FileNet's WorkFlo Business System software, which began shipping in early 1996, is compatible with all other versions of the company's software.

Watermark Software, Inc.
129 Middlesex Turnpike
Burlington, MA 01803
Telephone: (617) 229-2600
Fax: (617) 229-2989

Visual C++ and Access Periodicals

One of the measures of the success of a PC application is the number of periodicals that cover the use of the application exclusively or that devote a substantial portion of their editorial content to it. The following sections describe periodicals that are of special interest to users of either Visual C++ or Access.

Access Advisor Magazine

Access/Visual Basic Advisor is written by developers for developers. It helps you understand and use the best designs, tools, techniques, add-ons, and management and business practices to implement strong solutions. This publication is very useful for Visual C++ programmers who aren't fluent in various Access techniques. Even though this publication is oriented toward Visual Basic, the Visual C++ programmer can gather useful information from it.

The practical "how-to" information in each issue will save you hours, days, even weeks of programming time. It's essential reading for developers who use Access, Visual Basic, Office (Excel, Word, PowerPoint, and Schedule+), BackOffice (SQL Server), Project, Exchange, OLE Controls, OLE Automation, Visual Basic for Applications, and the many third-party products that integrate with Microsoft's products.

An optional companion resource disk is available with every issue. It contains source code, support files, databases, program objects, samples, utilities, and more, all in ready-to-use electronic format.

Other Advisor publications include the following:

Data Based Advisor: The authority on all areas of database and client-server Windows application development and management. Relied on by professional developers since 1983. Companion resource disks and complete CD-ROMs are available.

Internet Advisor: The technical magazine for designing and building online integrated applications of all types, including those for the World Wide Web, commercial services, private and internal "intranet" networks, multimedia, and CDs. Companion resource disks are available.

Access/Visual Basic Advisor: The only technical magazine devoted to building solutions with the full range of Microsoft's business development software: Access, Visual Basic, Office (Excel, Word, PowerPoint, and Schedule+), BackOffice (SQL Server), Project, Exchange, OLE Automation, OLE Controls, and Visual Basic for Applications. Companion resource disks and complete CD-ROMs are available.

Lotus Notes Advisor: The only magazine serving Lotus Notes application developers, managers, and users worldwide, with "how to" technical guidance, design and deployment advice, reviews of Notes-related products, and management insights. Companion resource disks and complete CD-ROMs are available.

PowerBuilder Advisor: The comprehensive technical guide to building client-server database applications with PowerBuilder and related products and technologies. Companion resource disks are available.

FoxPro Advisor: Exclusively for developing database applications with Microsoft Visual FoxPro and FoxPro 2.x. *Advisor* has been the source of FoxPro technical guidance since 1984. Companion resource disks and complete CD-ROMs are available.

Visual Objects Advisor: The only magazine dedicated to creating superior client-server business applications with Computer Associates' CA-Visual Objects. Companion resource disks are available.

> Advisor Communications International, Inc.
> 4010 Morena Blvd., Suite 200
> San Diego, CA 92117
> Telephone: (800) 336-6060, (619) 483-6400
> Fax: (619) 483-9851
> E-mail: `70007.1614@compuserve.com`, `advisor@advisor.com`

Smart Access Newsletter

Smart Access is a monthly newsletter directed at Access developers and power users. Articles cover a variety of advanced topics, ranging from relational database design to using the Windows API functions in Access Basic. Because *Smart Access* is aimed at independent and in-house developers, many of its articles are devoted to runtime Access and the Access Distribution Kit. A diskette that includes sample databases, Access libraries, and related files accompanies each issue. *Smart Access* also offers a variety of tips and techniques for writing more effective macros and Access Basic code. You can import many of the code examples into Visual C++ forms and modules. The magazine's parent company, Pinnacle Publishing, Inc., publishes a variety of journals on other database applications. This publication is useful to Visual C++ programmers who are planning to develop Access-based applications or who want to improve their Access skills.

Pinnacle Publishing
18000 72nd Avenue South, Suite 217
Kent, WA 98032
Telephone: (800) 788-1900, (206) 251-1900
Fax: (206) 251-5057

Visual C++ Professional Magazine

Visual C++ Professional is a monthly journal for professional Visual C++ users. It provides information about MFC, C++, and Win32 application development.

Oakley Publishing Company
P. O. Box 70087
Eugene, OR 97401-0143
Telephone: (800) 234-0368
Fax: (503) 746-0071

Periodicals Devoted to General Database and Windows Topics

The magazines listed in this section are devoted to the general topic of client-server and desktop database design, performance, and front-end applications. Also included in this section are descriptions of two newsletters that provide valuable background on and forecasts for Windows and its applications.

Database Programming and Design Magazine

Database Programming and Design magazine is directed toward users of mainframe database products, as well as users of client-server RDBMSs running on minicomputers, RISC workstations, and 80x86-based PCs in enterprise-wide computing environments. This publication is useful for Visual C++ programmers who are working on client-server database systems.

Database Programming and Design
Miller-Freeman, Inc.
600 Harrison Street
San Francisco, CA 94107
Telephone: (800) 269-0169, (303) 447-9330

DBMS Magazine

DBMS, another Miller-Freeman publication, primarily covers the field of PC and workstation client-server computing, although it also covers stand-alone desktop database applications such as dBASE, Paradox, and FoxPro. DBMS is published 13 times per year. (A DBMS Buyer's Guide issue is published each June.) This publication is useful for Visual C++ programmers who are working on PC-based desktop database systems.

> DBMS Magazine
> Miller-Freeman, Inc.
> 411 Borel Ave., Suite 100
> San Mateo, CA 94402
> Telephone: (800) 456-1859, (303) 447-9330
> Fax: (415) 905-2233

Microsoft Directions Newsletter

Microsoft Directions is a monthly newsletter published by former Microsoft executives who claim to have "extensive organizational contacts" within Microsoft. Each month, *Microsoft Directions* features in-depth articles focusing on one or two aspects of Microsoft's product strategy.

> Redmond Communications, Inc.
> 15127 N.E. 24th Street, Suite 293
> Redmond, WA 98052
> Telephone: (206) 882-3396
> Fax: (206) 644-7670

SQL Forum Magazine

SQL Forum magazine's subhead reads "The Journal for the International SQL Server Community." *SQL Forum* is a bimonthly journal that has Microsoft and Sybase as corporate sponsors. *SQL Forum* features in-depth analysis of the technical aspects of SQL Server. For example, the May/June 1993 issue was devoted entirely to analyses and performance reviews of SQL Server for Windows NT.

> SQL Forum
> P.O. Box 240
> Lynnwood, WA 98046-0240
> Telephone: (206) 382-6607

Windows Watcher Newsletter

Jesse Berst's (now Ziff-Davis's) *Windows Watcher* was the first monthly newsletter devoted to analyzing and forecasting trends in the Windows "industry." A subscription to *Windows Watcher* is indispensable if you want to keep up-to-date on the peregrinations of Microsoft's development programs for future versions of Windows and Windows applications. *Windows Watcher* provides lists of important Windows applications in the development stage ("Product Watch"), as well as popularity charts of Windows products that are based on North American and European sales by major software distributors ("Sales Watch").

Windows Watcher
15127 N.E. 24th State, Suite 344
Redmond, WA 98052
Telephone: (800) 553-4386, (206) 881-7354
Fax: (206) 883-1452

Using the Internet for Support

Many programmers and software developers who have access to the Internet can use the World Wide Web (WWW) to access information and support. Many companies offer Internet support, including (but not limited to) the following:

Macmillan Computer Publishing (`www.mcp.com`)
Microsoft Corporation (`www.microsoft.com`)
IBM Corporation (`www.ibm.com`)

Generally, to find the WWW page for a company, you should first try `www.company.com`, where *company* is the company name. For example, `www.lotus.com` is the home page for Lotus Development Corporation.

The Internet is growing and maturing at a fantastic rate. There are many excellent books on the Internet. Checking Macmillan's home page will show you which titles are available. Searching for a product or company is another way to locate products and companies. Searches are usually done using one of the popular search engines, such as Yahoo, Excite, Infoseek, Lycos, or Magellan. If you're using Microsoft's Internet Explorer, simply click the search button on the toolbar to go to the `http://www.msn.com/access/allinone.hv1` search page.

A typical search would be to look for a company name, a product name, or some other word that you think is relatively unique to that company. A poorly designed search will return hundreds of possible matches, indicating that your search criteria is too broad. For example, searching for the word "Microsoft" wouldn't be wise. There are literally hundreds of thousands of matches for "Microsoft." On the other hand, a search for "Lifeboat Publishing" would find a reasonable number of matches, the first of which probably would be the one you were searching for.

NOTE

Searches are based on databases of information contained in pages on the Web. Most search engines routinely search the Web, finding new and changed pages and building keyword indexes.

NOTE

How good are search engines? When I searched for my name, "Hipson," the search engine found not only my Web pages, but also all the pages that had links to me—as well as a real estate company in Dublin, Ireland. Not bad—even I didn't know about the real estate company!

Books for Database Developers

Microsoft Jet Database Engine Programmer's Guide (Microsoft Press, 1996), by Dan Haught and Jim Ferguson, takes the programmer through the basics of the Microsoft Jet database engine and on to advanced topics. This book includes a CD-ROM that contains an online version of the book, code samples, and other valuable materials.

Online Sources for Database Technical Support and Sample Applications

The primary sources of technical support for Visual C++ database developers are the Microsoft-sponsored forums on CompuServe. Microsoft product support specialists (PSSs) answer developers' and end users' questions about Visual C++ and related Microsoft products. Developers and independent software vendors (ISVs) are regular participants in these forums. *Data Based Advisor* and *DBMS* magazines sponsor forums that cover a wide range of database-related topics. If you don't have a CompuServe account, call CompuServe at (800) 848-8199 for a sign-up package.

In addition to a membership in CompuServe, you'll need a modem, a CompuServe access program (such as WinCIM), and the current version of PKWare's PKUNZIP.EXE application (or WinZip) to expand the files you download that are archived (compressed). Most archived files have an extension of .ZIP, although some archived files are available as self-extracting archive files with the extension .EXE. When you execute a self-extracting archive file, the file expands the individual files that it contains. Most archive files include one or more text files that document the contents of the archive and tell how to use the application contained in the archive.

The current version of the PKZIP utilities is available in Library 15 of the MSACCESS forum in the form of a self-extracting file, PK204G.EXE. The PKZIP utilities are shareware; if you use the PKZIP utilities you download, you're obligated to pay the registration and license fee specified by PKWare. The WinCIM program is available from CompuServe and other sources. It's sometimes distributed as an attachment to magazines and may be mailed free to CompuServe customers. You can reach CompuServe using a terminal program, but CompuServe is phasing out this support in an attempt to improve its system's efficiency. The Visual C++ 4 distribution CD has a copy of WinCIM. However, at the time this book was written, this version was out of date.

The Client-Server Computing Forum

Microsoft's Client-Server Computing forum (GO MSNET) is directed toward users of Microsoft LAN Manager and its extensions. This forum incorporates support for Windows NT Server.

The Data Based Advisor Forum

Advisor Communications International, Inc. sponsors the Data Based Advisor forum (GO DBA), a forum devoted to database topics. Library 14 of the DBA forum is devoted to Microsoft Access. Many of the applications described in *Access Advisor* magazine are available for downloading from the DBA forum.

The DBMS Forum

DBMS magazine operates the DBMS forum (GO DBMS), which covers topics of general interest to database developers. Client-server database systems and SQL topics receive the emphasis in this forum.

The EMS C/C++ Utilities

The EMS C/C++ Utility Library is a collection of all freely distributable (public domain, freeware, shareware, contribution requested, demo code, and so on) source code, utilities, and applications for PC C/C++ developers. A directory database accompanying the library is a dBASE-compatible .DBF file with a DOS search program. The database also lists all existing commercial products for one-stop shopping for all existing C/C++ tools. The directory database and library are updated at least every two months. *C/C++ Users Journal* (February 1995) called it "a comprehensive collection for one-stop shopping." In the May 1991 issue of *PC World,* Tom Swan said he was "impressed with this one's quality" and that "the EMS library is a bargain hunter's dream." He went on to include extracts from the library to accompany his book *Learning C++.*

> EMS Professional Shareware Libraries
> 4505 Buckhurst Court
> Olney, MD 20832
> Telephone: (301) 924-3594
> Fax: (301) 963-2708

Independent Software Vendors

Independent software vendors (ISVs) have their own sections of the Windows Vendors forums, coordinated by Microsoft. At the time this book was written, there were several ISV forums. Intersolv Software, for example, supports its ODBC drivers in the WINVEN D forum. Type GO WINVEN and then select the number corresponding to the forum you want to explore.

> **NOTE**
>
> Forums on CompuServe change frequently. As a vendor becomes larger and more successful, the increased traffic warrants the creation of a new forum. If information for a vendor isn't where you expected it, check to see if the vendor has moved to a private forum.

The Macmillan Computer Publishing Forum

Macmillan Computer Publishing, the parent organization of Sams Publishing, sponsors a CompuServe forum (GO MACMILLAN or GO PHCP). This forum provides information on books published by MCP subsidiaries under the imprints of Sams Publishing, Sams.net, Que, New Riders, Hayden, BradyGAMES, and Ziff-Davis Press. The libraries include lists of books available from MCP, tables of contents, sample chapters, sample files, sample programs, and other material extracted from MCP books. The message sections and libraries of the MCP forum are organized as shown in Table A.1.

Table A.1. MCP libraries.

Library Number	Library Name	Subject Matter
1	General Library	Files of general interest
2	What's New	New stuff for this forum
3	Graphics & DTP	Files related to graphics and desktop publishing
4	Database	Files related to databases
5	Spreadsheets	Files related to spreadsheets
6	Operating Systems	File related to operating systems
7	Networking & Comms	Files related to networking and communications
8	CAD	Files related to computer-aided design

continues

Table A.1. continued

Library Number	Library Name	Subject Matter
9	Programming	Files related to programming
10	Games	Files related to games
11	Utilities	General utility files
12	Macintosh	Apple Macintosh files
13	Multimedia	Files related to multimedia
14	Windows & Utilities	Various Windows and Windows utility files
15	News Releases	Various MCP news releases
16	Que Software	Software from Que Software
17	The Internet	Internet-related topics
18	Sample Chapt./TOCs	Sample chapters and tables of contents
19	Word Processing	Files related to word processing
20	Windows 95	Items related to Windows 95

The Microsoft Access Forum

The Microsoft Access forum (GO MSACCESS) is one of the most active product-support forums on CompuServe. The files that you can download include sample databases and Access libraries created by Microsoft and independent Access developers and consultants, as well as end users of Access applications. You can import much of the code contained in Access modules into Visual C++ database applications using the techniques described in Chapter 18, "Translating Visual Basic for Applications Code to Visual C++." You can download current versions of the Access-specific Windows dynamic link libraries (DLLs) that are described in this book from one of the 15 libraries of the MSACCESS forum.

The Microsoft Developer Network Forum and Access Developer Program

Microsoft sponsors the Microsoft Developer Network forum on CompuServe (GO MSDNLIB) and at the WWW URL http://198.105.232.6/devonly/. It contains more than 300 technical articles and sample applications, primarily related to Microsoft Windows and Windows NT. The MSDNLIB forum is part of the Microsoft Developer Network for Windows that is now the company's primary means of distributing support for developers of Windows applications.

Membership in the Microsoft Developer Network includes a quarterly CD-ROM containing documentation and code examples for Windows and Win32s applications, plus Microsoft's mainstream Windows applications.

To obtain more information about the Microsoft Developer Network and the Microsoft Access Developer Program, call Microsoft Developer Services at (800) 227-4679. Membership in the Level I program costs $295. Levels II and III are more expensive.

The Microsoft Knowledge Base and Download Services

The Microsoft Knowledge Base (GO MSKB) is a database of technical publications, bug reports, workarounds, and press releases on Microsoft products. You can search for the latest tips on making better use of Visual C++ by specifying Visual C++ as the product name and searching with the keywords that specify the topic you're interested in. You can download sample applications that MSKB articles refer to from the Microsoft Software Library (GO MSL).

The Microsoft MFC Forum

The Microsoft MFC forum (GO MSMFC) is the main forum that supports the Microsoft Foundation Classes. This forum is the first place to go when you have questions or problems that are directly related to using MFC.

Substantial peer group support is generated in this and many other Microsoft forums. Posting a question often results in a quick response from other users.

The Microsoft SNA Server Forum

The Microsoft SNA Server forum (GO MSSNA) provides support for IBM mainframe and AS/400 connectivity using protocols supported by SNA Server.

The Microsoft SQL Server Forum

The Microsoft SQL Server forum (GO MSSQL) is devoted to Microsoft SQL Server for Windows NT.

The Microsoft Workgroup Applications Forum

The Microsoft Workgroup Applications forum (GO MSWGA) covers Microsoft Mail, Schedule+, gateways for connecting to MS Mail and other e-mail systems, and Microsoft Electronic Forms Designer for creating transportable e-forms. You can download the current version of the Microsoft Workgroup Templates from this forum.

The ODBC Section of the WINEXT Forum

Section 10 of the Windows Extensions forum (GO WINEXT) provides technical support for the Microsoft Open Database Connectivity (ODBC) API. As Microsoft adds its own certified drivers to extend ODBC connectivity to new database applications, the drivers often are posted to Library 10 of the WINEXT forum. Microsoft supports third-party ODBC driver developers in this forum; read the messages in Section 10 to keep abreast of the new ODBC drivers under development by Microsoft, RDBMS publishers, and other independent software vendors.

The Visual C++ Forum

The Visual C++ forum (GO MSLANG) is the main forum that supports Visual C++. This forum is the first place to go when you have questions or problems that are directly related to the Visual C++ product.

Substantial peer group support is generated in this and many other Microsoft forums. Posting a question often results in a quick response from other users.

The Windows SDK Forum

The Windows SDK forum (GO WINSDK) is designed to support developers writing 16-bit Windows applications in C, C++, and Visual C++. The Microsoft Win32 SDK for NT forum (GO MSWIN32) supports developers who are developing 32-bit applications using Visual C++.

The Windows for Workgroups Forum

The Windows for Workgroups forum (GO MSWRKG) has a variety of sections that cover peer-to-peer networking and the applets that accompany Windows for Workgroups, such as Schedule+ and Microsoft Mail. Support for the API functions that you can use to create an interface between Access applications, Schedule+ (SP), and Microsoft Mail (MAPI) now appears in this forum.

The 32-Bit Windows Forums

Microsoft provides support for users of Windows NT and its 32-bit Win 32s applications in the Windows NT forum (GO WINNT). The WINNT forum also includes updated information on the features of other applications for Windows NT (such as the SNA Server for Windows NT), bug fixes, and tools. The majority of the documentation files in this forum are in Word for Windows format.

Developers of 32-bit Win32s applications for use under Windows 3.1 with the 32-bit extensions and Windows NT receive technical support in this forum.

Other Microsoft CompuServe Developers' Forums

Table A.2 lists CompuServe's most popular forums for developers.

Table A.2. CompuServe developers' forums.

Forum Name	GO *Command*
Microsoft Developer Knowledge Base	GO MDKB
Microsoft Software Library (search for support by product)	GO MSL
Microsoft Developer Network Forum	GO MSDN
Microsoft Basic Forum	GO MSBASIC
Microsoft Access Forum	GO MSACCESS
Microsoft Languages Forum	GO MSLANG
Microsoft Foundation Classes Forum	GO MSMFC
Microsoft FoxPro Forum	GO FOXFORUM
Microsoft Fox Users Forum	GO FOXUSER
Microsoft Visual FoxPro Forum	GO VFOX
Microsoft Windows SDK Forum	GO WINSDK
Microsoft Win32 SDK for NT Forum	GO MSWIN32
Microsoft Windows International Developer's Forum	GO WINTLDEV
Microsoft Windows Extensions Forum	GO WINEXT
Microsoft Windows Objects Forum	GO WINOBJECTS
Microsoft OLE Industry Solutions Forum	GO OLESOLNS
Microsoft Programming Applications Forum	GO PROGMSA
Microsoft Windows Multimedia Developer Forum	GO WINMM
Windows Components A Forum	GO COMPA
Windows Components B Forum	GO COMPB
Windows Connectivity Forum	GO WINCON
Windows Networking A Forum	GO WINETA

Other Online Support for Windows Developers

Microsoft offers the Developer's Connection on the Internet at WWW URL `http://198.105.232.6/devonly/`. This WWW page offers links to various areas where developers can obtain support, query the Microsoft Knowledge Base, and obtain information from Microsoft.

Microsoft also maintains the MSN (Microsoft Network) on the Internet at `http://www.msn.com`. This is primarily a user-oriented system, but a number of useful features are available to developers at this site.

Other Tools for Visual C++ Developers

This category includes tools that are used in the development or debugging cycle but aren't actually incorporated into your products.

Bounds Checker

Bounds Checker is an automated tool that helps developers check for a wide number of possible error conditions. Bounds Checker checks problems such as array overwrites, memory leaks, and parameter errors to Windows functions. Bounds Checker has very tight integration with Visual C++ 4. Microsoft used it to help debug Visual C++.

> Nu-Mega Technologies, Inc.
> P.O. Box 7790
> Nashua, NH 03060-7780
> Telephone: (603) 889-2386
> Fax: (603) 889-1135
> `http://www.numega.com`

WinMaker Pro 6.0

WinMaker Pro 6.0 is a prototyper and C/C++ code generator for both Windows 95 and Windows NT. You can create full-featured MFC, OWL, and ANSI C 32-bit Windows applications by using an easy-to-use interface. This product can be most helpful for programmers who (for various reasons) must create non-C++ applications and who don't want to write their applications from scratch.

> Blue Sky Software Corporation
> 7486 La Jolla Blvd., Suite 3
> La Jolla, CA 92037-9582
> Telephone: (800) 677-4946, (619) 459-6365
> Fax: (619) 459-6366

B

Naming and Formatting Conventions for Visual C++ Objects and Variables

This book's Introduction lists the Hungarian Notation prefixes that are most commonly used. This appendix expands on prefixes and covers the formatting of code, which can help you write better applications.

These naming conventions use a modified form of Hungarian Notation that commonly is used in C and C++ programming. The term *Hungarian* comes from the nationality of the conventions' inventor, Charles Simonyi, who worked on the development of Access 1.0 at Microsoft. The prefix sz, which defines a zero-terminated string variable in C, is a common letter combination in the Hungarian language.

You might wonder why you should follow these rules when naming your variables. The long and short of it is that when we all follow the same set of rules, it's much easier to interact with each other. Of course, no variable name, no matter how well formed, will make poorly written code good. But well-written and well-formatted code, with variable names that follow standards, is much easier to debug and maintain.

> **NOTE**
>
> It's a good idea to learn and use as many of the established standards as you can. When you're thinking about making a career change, the ability to show well-written code that conforms to standards will generally be a positive influence on prospective employers.

Hungarian Notation for Variables and Objects

There are a number of simple rules that you should follow when naming your variables and objects. The following is a set of rules that will assist you in making your code as readable as possible.

> **NOTE**
>
> Microsoft doesn't always follow these guidelines. The file DBDAOERR.H has #defined variables that are mixed case, and other Windows header files demonstrate the same use of mixed case.

■ For defined identifiers created using the #define directive, use all capital letters. Use underscores to break the name into logical words as necessary. For example, the NULL symbol is defined as follows:

```
#define NULL    ((void *)0)
```

Notice that the name NULL is in capitals. Also notice that NULL is defined as an address, not a scalar variable.

> **NOTE**
>
> Remember that NULL (as used in C/C++) is different from null as used by databases. NULL in C/C++ is used to indicate an address that is undefined. The database null indicates a field that has no value, which is different from a field that contains a string of zero characters. A character field of zero characters isn't a null field.

- For all other identifiers, use mixed-case names. Don't use underscores as part of a regular name. For example:

Correct	**Incorrect**
FirstName	FIRSTNAME
	firstname
	Firstname
	first_name

- For class definitions, use a preceding capital C, as in COurClass. This helps identify the item as a class definition.

- For member variables in a class, precede the name with an m_. For example, use m_szFirstName as the name of a variable that holds a first name. The m_ prefix tells you (and anyone else reading your code) that this is a member variable.

- Use Hungarian Notation for all simple variables. For variables that are classes, structures, or unions, don't use a prefix.

- It's permissible to use single-character variables for short loop counters, but for no other purpose. If a loop is more than a few lines long, use a significant name for the loop counter. Most loop counters are the characters i, j, and k, used in that order.

Table B.1 lists the more commonly used prefixes of Hungarian Notation. Nothing in the concept of using prefixes prevents you from creating your own prefixes for types that don't already have a prefix defined. However, resist the urge to change a prefix of a data type that already has a prefix defined.

Table B.1. Hungarian Notation prefixes.

Prefix	*Description*
b	BOOL (int)
by	BYTE (unsigned char)
c	char
cx, cy	short (used as x or y length; the c stands for "count")
dw	DWORD (unsigned long)

continues

Table B.1. continued

Prefix	Description
fn	Function (not used often)
h	Handle (generic)
i	int
l	LONG (long)
n	short or int
p	Pointer
s	String
sz	A string terminated by the 0 byte
w	UINT (unsigned int) or WORD (unsigned word)
x, y	short (used as an x-coordinate or y-coordinate)

Formatting Your C/C++ Source Code

When writing C or C++ code, you should try to make your source as attractive as possible.

■ Don't comment the obvious. The comment in the following statement is meaningless, because the statement's action is clear without it:

```
++i;  // Increment i
```

■ Align your code so that opening and closing French braces are in the same column and on lines by themselves. Don't place an opening brace at the end of a statement that begins a block. The following example shows how you can easily see the beginning of the block, even if the indentation isn't always correct. When braces are on lines by themselves (with comments, if necessary), they're easier to see:

```
    for (i = 0; i < 5; I++)
    {// Document the loop's purpose!
        j = nIndexArray[i];
//      Other statements....
    }
```

■ Place variable declarations at the beginning of a module whenever possible. Don't put more than one declaration on a line, and always initialize variables:

```
#define ARRAY_SIZE    5

double function(double * dParameter)
{
double    dOurTotal[ARRAY_SIZE] = {0.0, 0.0, 0.0, 0.0, 0.0};
double    dTotal = 0.0;
double    dAverage = 0.0;
int       i = 0;
```

```
int      nIndex = 0;
WORD     wWord = 0;
char *   pString = NULL;
```

...declarations by one tab stop

...++)

...; (such as =, +, -, *, and /), constants, variable
...ng and trailing spaces:

...ers, this is most of the time), use parentheses in
...show how hard it can be to quickly see the order
...e no parentheses:

...e programmer didn't want the default order of

...ve more than one executable statement per line
...ifficult to follow the flow of the program and
...here other than at the first executable statement

■ Indent, indent, indent. Never skip indentations. Whenever you do, you will usually induce a program logic error (this is Murphy's Law).

C

Using the CD-ROM

The CD-ROM that comes with this book contains a collection of Visual C++ database applications and the databases that are used in conjunction with the applications. Most of the databases are in Access 95 .MDB format, although examples of database files in Access 2, dBASE, Paradox, and Btrieve formats are provided so that you can experiment with Visual C++ applications that use these database file formats.

CAUTION

The authors' sample programs utilize long filenames. In order to maintain these long filenames, the sample programs and databases have been compressed and will need to be installed to your hard disk. The CD-ROM browser will easily allow you to install these files with a simple click of the install button found in the Author's Sample Programs section.

After you install the code to your hard disk, you will find the code organized by chapters under the \DDGVC4 directory. Not every chapter has a sample application. Therefore, the numbering of the subdirectories isn't consecutive in all cases. Each chapter that has a sample application mentions which files are included in the ...\CHAPTR## directory for that chapter.

Index

Add to Your Sams Library Today with the Best Books for Programming, Operating Systems, and New Technologies

The easiest way to order is to pick up the phone and call
1-800-428-5331
between 9:00 a.m. and 5:00 p.m. EST.
For faster service please have your credit card available.

ISBN	Quantity	Description of Item	Unit Cost	Total Cost
0-672-30874-6		Visual C++ 4 Unleashed (book/CD-ROM)	$49.99	
0-672-30762-6		32-Bit Windows Programming (book/CD-ROM)	$39.99	
0-672-30903-3		Microsoft SQL Server 6 Unleashed (book/CD-ROM)	$55.00	
0-672-30849-5		Microsoft BackOffice Administrator's Survival Guide (book/CD-ROM)	$59.99	
0-672-30758-8		Visual FoxPro 3 Unleashed, Second Edition (book/CD-ROM)	$45.00	
0-672-30739-1		Excel for Windows 95 Unleashed (book/CD-ROM)	$39.99	
0-672-30474-0		Windows 95 Unleashed (book/CD-ROM)	$39.99	
0-672-30902-5		Windows NT 3.51 Unleashed, Third Edition (book/CD-ROM)	$49.99	
0-672-30860-6		Windows NT Server Survival Guide (book/CD-ROM)	$55.00	
0-57521-041-X		The Internet Unleashed 1996 (book/CD-ROM)	$49.99	
0-57521-040-1		The World Wide Web 1996 Unleashed (book/CD-ROM)	$49.99	
		Shipping and Handling: See information below.		
		TOTAL		

❏ 3 ½" Disk

❏ 5 ¼" Disk

Shipping and Handling: $4.00 for the first book, and $1.75 for each additional book. Floppy disk: add $1.75 for shipping and handling. If you need to have it NOW, we can ship product to you in 24 hours for an additional charge of approximately $18.00, and you will receive your item overnight or in two days. Overseas shipping and handling adds $2.00 per book and $8.00 for up to three disks. Prices subject to change. Call for availability and pricing information on latest editions.

201 W. 103rd Street, Indianapolis, Indiana 46290

1-800-428-5331 — Orders   1-800-835-3202 — FAX   1-800-858-7674 — Customer Service

Book ISBN 0-672-30913-0

ProtoView DataTable
The Fastest Grid Component Anywhere

DataTable is an industrial grid control. DataTable strength lies in its ability to handle massive amounts of data in an efficient manner. With a compact size, only 90K of memory, virtual memory and advanced data cache scheme, DataTable is clearly designed for industrial, real world applications.

Set colors, fonts and picture formatting for cells. Has built-in column sorting. It's visual and easy. Supports the clipboard, hidden columns, row and column selection and resizing. Cells may have drop-down combo boxes or check boxes. Full message and property set. MFC classes and message based programming interface. 16 and 32 bit DLL version, VBX and OCX available. Source code is available.

New features include bitmaps in cells, horizontal and vertical splitter window, numeric column totaling, column searching, cell overwriting, improved keyboard handling, auto row insert, region selection, European formatting for date, time, and numbers, and 3D effects. Windows 95-compatible look.

ProtoView Interactive Diagramming Object
The Visual Way to Add Diagramming To Your Application

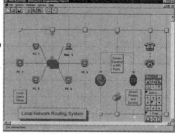

The Interactive Diagramming Object gives you advanced capabilities for creating easy to read diagrams. Choose from a wide assortment of shapes, pictures, lines and arrows to design pleasing presentation visuals, outlines, process flows, hierarchy charts, floor plans and much more.

With it you can: load and save diagrams, set colors, fonts and 3D effects, create custom design palettes, respond to notifications and events for complete program control. It supports diagrams of any size with scrolling, zooming, printing and the clipboard.

Simply drop the IDO on a form and it's ready to go. It's easy to use and easy to program. Whether you want to explain a process or present a plan, the IDO helps you effectively communicate ideas and create applications that are more powerful, yet easier to use. Available as OCX, or DLL. Source code is available.

ProtoView Interface Component Set
Polished User Interface Components

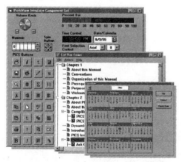

PICS offers sophisticated controls for calendar, date, time and numeric input using your choice of odometer, LED readout and normal display. Add to these a slick looking percent/gauge control, multi-directional spin button, a stereo volume control and fancy icon buttons. You also get a font and point size selection control for your toolbars or dialogs. Also included are 21 PICS button controls with bitmap images.

You also get a powerful hierarchical list box that includes: setting unlimited number of bitmaps per list, lines between bitmaps and names, over 100 functions for complete control of subtrees, selection, display, search and item manipulation.

Complete on-line help, MFC classes and message based programming interface. 16 and 32 bit DLL, VBX and OCX available. Source code is available. Windows 95 compatible look. With PICS you can create the sharpest looking applications in no time at all.

ProtoView Visual Help Builder
The Fastest Way To Build Help Systems!

The ProtoView Visual Help Builder is the fastest way to author help systems. Developers can document an application, whether they have that application's "source" programs or not. With a few clicks of the mouse, ProtoView Visual Help Builder captures every dialog box, menu and control field of an application and creates a full blown help system. Only ProtoView Visual Help Builder brings you these innovative features.

Add multimedia support for video, sound and high-res graphics. It provides the advanced features you need to create help systems, including macros, secondary windows, multiple hotspot graphics, help topics, hypertext links, jumps, browse sequences and more. Integrates into version control software. Includes help compiler. Requires

PROTOVIEW™
The Visual Development Edge™

Installing Your CD-ROM

Installing the CD-ROM

The companion CD-ROM contains author source code, plus an assortment of third-party tools and product demos. The disc is designed to be explored using a browser program. Using Sams' Guide to the CD-ROM browser, you can view information about products and companies and install programs with a single click of the mouse. To install the browser, follow the next instructions.

Windows NT Installation Instructions

1. Insert the CD-ROM into your CD-ROM drive.
2. From File Manager or Program Manager, choose File | Run.
3. Type <*drive*>\setup and press Enter. <*drive*> corresponds to the drive letter of your CD-ROM. For example, if your CD-ROM is drive D:, type D:\SETUP and press Enter.
4. Installation creates a Program Manager group named DDG with Visual C++4. To browse the CD-ROM, double-click the Guide to the CD-ROM icon inside this Program Manager group.

Windows 95 Installation Instructions

1. Insert the CD-ROM into your CD-ROM drive. If the AutoPlay feature of your Windows 95 system is enabled, the setup program will start automatically.
2. If the setup program doesn't start automatically, double-click the My Computer icon.
3. Double-click the icon representing your CD-ROM drive.
4. Double-click the icon called Setup.exe to run the installation program. Follow the on-screen instructions that appear. When setup ends, double-click the Guide to the CD-ROM icon to begin browsing the disc.

Following the installation, you can restart the Guide to the CD-ROM program by pressing the Start button and selecting Programs, DDG with Visual C++4, and Guide to the CD-ROM.

NOTE

The Guide to the CD-ROM program requires at least 256 colors. For best results, set your monitor to display between 256 and 64,000 colors. A screen resolution of 640 × 480 pixels is also recommended. If necessary, adjust your monitor settings before using the CD-ROM.